CANADA

MINNESOTA

WISCONSIN

MICHIGAN

IOWA

MISSOURI

ILLINOIS

INDIANA

OHIO

KENTUCKY

TENNESSEE

ARKANSAS

MISSISSIPPI

ALABAMA

GEORGIA

LOUISIANA

FLORIDA

MAINE

VT.

N.H.

MASS.

CONN.

R.I.

NEW YORK

PENNSYLVANIA

NEW JERSEY

DELAWARE

MARYLAND

WEST VIRGINIA

VIRGINIA

NORTH CAROLINA

SOUTH CAROLINA

Lake Superior

Lake Michigan

Lake Huron

Lake Ontario

Lake Erie

Mississippi River

Missouri River

Illinois River

Ohio River

Tennessee River

Mississippi River

Alabama River

Red River

St. Lawrence River

Hudson River

Susquehanna River

Delaware River

James River

Potomac River

Knoxville River

ADIRONDACK MTS

APPALACHIAN MOUNTAINS

ALLEGHENY MTS

BLUE RIDGE MTS

OZARK PLATEAU

CENTRAL PLAINS

PIEDMONT

ATLANTIC COASTAL PLAIN

COASTAL PLAIN

DELMARVA PENINSULA

FLORIDA PENINSULA

Chesapeake Bay

ATLANTIC OCEAN

Gulf of Mexico

Mt. Mitchell 6,684 ft. (2,030 m)

and Forks

Fargo

Duluth

St. Paul

Minneapolis

oux Falls

Madison

Milwaukee

Green Bay

Grand Rapids

Lansing

Detroit

Toledo

Cleveland

Buffalo

Rochester

Albany

Burlington

Montpelier

Concord

Manchester

Boston

Worcester

Providence

Hartford

Bridgeport

Augusta

Lewiston

Portland

Cape Cod

New York City

Newark

LONG ISLAND

Jersey City

Trenton

Harrisburg

Philadelphia

Wilmington

Dover

Baltimore

Annapolis

WASHINGTON D.C.

Pittsburgh

Wheeling

Columbus

Cincinnati

Frankfort

Lexington

Louisville

Indianapolis

Springfield

Peoria

Rockford

Chicago

Gary

Ft. Wayne

Des Moines

Omaha

ncoln

Cedar Rapids

Davenport

Kansas City

Topeka

Kansas City

St. Louis

Jefferson City

Tulsa

Fort Smith

Little Rock

Pine Bluff

Memphis

Nashville

Knoxville

Huntington

Charleston

Richmond

Newport News

Norfolk

Greensboro

Raleigh

Charlotte

Greenville

Columbia

Cape Fear

Cape Hatteras

Atlanta

Birmingham

Jackson

Meridian

Montgomery

Columbus

Shreveport

Baton Rouge

Biloxi

Mobile

New Orleans

ouston

as

Tallahassee

Jacksonville

Savannah

Charleston

Cape Canaveral

Tampa

Lake Okeechobee

Miami

Mississippi Delta

PLAIN

COASTAL

95°W

90°W

85°W

80°W

75°W

40°N

35°North Latitude

70°West Longitude

20°N

90°W

85°W

65°W

Tropic of Cancer

Florida Keys

Straits of Florida

CUBA

Bay of Fundy

International boundaries

State boundaries

⊛ *National capital*

★ *State capitals*

• *Other cities*

▲ *Mountain peaks*

ATLANTIC OCEAN

PUERTO RICO (U.S.)

San Juan

0   100 Miles

0   100 Kilometers

0   100   200 Miles

0   100   200 Kilometers

America

PAST
AND PRESENT

Scott, Foresman and Company

Glenview, Illinois
Dallas, Texas
Oakland, New Jersey
Palo Alto, California
Tucker, Georgia
London, England

America
PAST
AND PRESENT

Robert A. Divine
University of Texas

T. H. Breen
Northwestern University

George M. Fredrickson
Northwestern University

R. Hal Williams
Southern Methodist University

Covers (detail) and Title Page: *Salem Common on Training Day*, by George Ropes, 1808. Courtesy of The Essex Institute, Salem, Massachusetts. (Photo by Mark Sexton.)

Map, p. xxv: Map of America, 1646, from *Le Theatre du Monde*, Jean Blaeu, cartographer. Courtesy of the Edward E. Ayer Collection, The Newberry Library, Chicago.

Acknowledgments for the copyrighted materials not credited on the page where they appear are listed in the "Credits" section beginning on page A-30. This section is to be considered an extension of the copyright page.

Library of Congress Cataloging in Publication Data
Main entry under title:
America, past and present.
   Includes bibliographies and index.
   1. United States—History. I. Divine, Robert A.
E178.1.A4894 1984   973   83-19146

ISBN 0-673-15420-3
ISBN 0-673-15882-9 (soft : v. 1)
ISBN 0-673-15883-7 (soft : v. 2)

About the Authors

Robert A. Divine

Robert A. Divine, the George W. Littlefield Professor in American History at the University of Texas at Austin, received his Ph.D. degree from Yale University in 1954. A specialist in American diplomatic history, he has taught at the University of Texas since 1954, where he has been honored by the Student Association for teaching excellence. His extensive published work includes *The Illusion of Neutrality, · Second Chance: The Triumph of Internationalism in America During World War II* (1968) and *Blowing on the Wind* (1978). His most recent book is *Eisenhower and the Cold War* (1981). In 1962–1963, he was a fellow at the Center for Advanced Study in the Behavioral Sciences and in 1968 he gave the Albert Shaw Lectures in Diplomatic History at Johns Hopkins University.

T. H. Breen

T. H. Breen received his Ph.D. from Yale University in 1968. Since 1975 he has been a Professor of History and American Culture at Northwestern University. Breen's major books include *The Character of the Good Rule: A Study of Puritan Political Ideas in New England* (1974), *Puritans and Adventurers: Change and Persistence in Early America* (1980), and with S. Innes of the University of Virginia, *"Myne Owne Ground": Race and Freedom on Virginia's Eastern Shore* (1980). In addition to receiving an award for outstanding teaching at Northwestern, Breen has been the recipient of research grants from the American Council of Learned Societies, the Guggenheim Foundation, the Institute for Advanced Study (Princeton), and the National Humanities Center. He is currently preparing a volume for the Oxford University Press *History of the United States in Early America.*

George M. Fredrickson

George M. Fredrickson is William Smith Mason Professor of American History at Northwestern University. He is the author or editor of several books, including *The Inner Civil War* (1968), *The Black Image in the White Mind* (1971), and *A Nation Divided* (1975). His latest work, *White Supremacy: A Comparative Study in American and South African History* (1982) won both the Ralph Waldo Emerson Award from Phi Beta Kappa and the Merle Curti Award from the Organization of American Historians. He received both the A.B. and Ph.D. degrees from Harvard and has been the recipient of a Guggenheim Fellowship, a National Endowment for the Humanities Senior Fellowship, and a Fellowship from the Center for Advanced Studies in the Behavioral Sciences. While teaching at Northwestern, he has also served as Fulbright lecturer in American History at Moscow University and as a Mellon visiting professor at Rice University.

R. Hal Williams

R. Hal Williams has been Dean of Dedman College at Southern Methodist University since 1980. He received his A.B. degree from Princeton University (1963) and his Ph.D. degree from Yale University (1968). His books include *The Democratic Party and California Politics, 1880–1896* (1973) and *Years of Decision: American Politics in the 1890s* (1978). He taught at Yale University from 1968 to 1975 and came to SMU in 1975 as Chair of the Department of History. He has received outstanding teaching awards at both Yale and SMU. Williams has received grants from the American Philosophical Society and the National Endowment for the Humanities, and he serves on the Texas Committee for the Humanities.

Preface

America: Past and Present is a history of the United States that tells the unfolding story of national development from the days of the earliest inhabitants to the present. We emphasize *telling the story* because we strongly believe in the value of historical narrative to provide a vivid sense of the past. Weaving the various strands of the American experience, we have sought in each chapter to blend the excitement and drama of that experience with insights into the underlying social, economic, and cultural forces that brought about change.

In a clear chronological organization, we have used significant incidents and episodes to reflect the dilemmas, the choices, and the decisions made by the people as well as by their leaders. After the colonial period, most of the chapters deal in short time periods, usually about a decade, that permit us to view major political and public events as points of reference and orientation around which social themes are integrated. This approach gives unity and direction to the text.

As the title suggests, our book is a blend of the traditional and the new. The strong narrative emphasis and chronological organization are traditional; the incorporation of the many fresh insights that historians have gained from the social sciences in the past two decades is new. In recounting the story of the American past we see a nation in flux. The early Africans and Europeans developed complex agrarian folkways that departed greatly from their experiences in the Old World—an evolution that established new cultural identities and finally led the settlers to accept the idea of political independence. People who had been subjects of the British Crown created a system of government that challenged later Americans to work out the full implications of social and economic equality. As we move to the growing sectional rift between North and South, the focus shifts to divergent modes of labor utilization and disparate social values that culminated in civil war. The westward movement and the accompanying industrial revolution severely tested the values of an agrarian society, while leading to an incredibly productive economic system. In the early twentieth century, progressive reformers sought to infuse the industrial order with social justice, and the First World War demonstrated the extent of American power in the world. The resiliency of the maturing American nation was tested by the Great Depression and World War II but despite setbacks, the United States overcame these challenges. The Cold War ushered in an era of crises, foreign and domestic, that revealed both the strengths and weaknesses of modern America.

The impact of change on human lives adds a vital dimension to historical understanding. We need to comprehend how the Revolution affected the lives of ordinary citizens; what it was like for both blacks and whites to live in a plantation society; how men and women fared in the shift from an agrarian to an industrial economy; and what impact technology, in the form of the automobile and the computer, has had on patterns of life in the twentieth century.

Our primary goal has been to write a clear, relevant, and balanced history of the United States. Our commitment is not to any particular ideology or point of view; rather, we hope to challenge our readers to rediscover the fascination of the American past and reach their own conclusions. At the same time, we have not tried to avoid controversial issues and have sought to offer reasoned judgments on such morally charged subjects as the nature of slavery and the advent of nuclear weapons. We believe that what happened in the entire nation, not just New England and the Northeast, deserves retelling, and thus we have given special emphasis to developments in the South and West. (Kenneth

Bain helped prepare the picture essay on the Mexican-American Experience in the Southwest.)

The structure and features of the book are intended to stimulate student interest and reinforce learning. Chapters begin with a **vignette** or incident that relates to the chapter themes stated in the introductory section, which also serves as an overview of the topics covered. Each chapter has a **chronology, recommended readings, bibliography,** and a two-page **special feature** on a topic that combines high interest and instructional value. In addition, the very extensive full-color map program, the many charts and graphs, and the full-color illustrations throughout are directly related to the narrative. They serve to advance and expand the themes, provide elaboration and contrast, tell more of the story, and generally add another dimension of learning. The illustrations also serve as a mini-survey of American painting styles. Eight **picture essays** explore facets of American life, and a six-page **map series** at the front of the text highlights the sweep of American history. The **Appendix** contains the vital documents, a ten-column chart on choosing the president and other political information, the cabinet members in every administration, and the Supreme Court justices.

Although this book is a joint effort, each author took primary responsibility for writing one section. T. H. Breen contributed the first eight chapters from the Native American period to the second decade of the nineteenth century; George M. Fredrickson wrote chapters 9 through 16, carrying the narrative through the Reconstruction era. R. Hal Williams is responsible for chapters 17 through 24, focusing on the industrial transformation and urbanization, and the events culminating in World War I; and Robert A. Divine wrote chapters 25 through 32, bringing the story through the Depression, World War II, and the Cold War to the present. Each contributor reviewed and revised the work of his colleagues and helped shape the material into its final form.

THE AUTHORS

Acknowledgments

This book owes much to the conscientious historians who reviewed chapters and sections, and offered valuable suggestions that led to many important improvements in the text. We are grateful to the following:

Frank W. Abbott
University of Houston

Kenneth G. Alfers
Mountain View College
Dallas

Thomas Archdeacon
University of Wisconsin-Madison

Kenneth R. Bain
Pan American University
Edinburg, Texas

Lois W. Banner
Hamilton College
Clinton, New York

Thomas Camfield
Sam Houston State University
Huntsville, Texas

Clayborne Carson
Stanford University

Jerald Combs
San Francisco State University

John Cooper
University of Wisconsin-Madison

Nancy F. Cott
Yale University

Eric Foner
Columbia University

Stephen Foster
Northern Illinois University

Sondra Herman
DeAnza Community College
Cupertino, California

John R. Howe
University of Minnesota

Nathan I. Huggins
Harvard University

John Kelley
Shawnee State Community College
Portsmouth, Ohio

Richard S. Kirkendall
Iowa State University

Harbert F. Margulies
University of Hawaii

Myron Marty
National Endowment for the Humanities
Washington, D.C.

John M. Murrin
Princeton University

John K. Nelson
University of North Carolina at Chapel Hill

Nora Ramirez
San Antonio Community College

Ronald Walters
Johns Hopkins University

Frank Wetta
Galveston Community College

We are also indebted to many people at Scott, Foresman, our publisher. Bruce Borland was instrumental in initiating the project and taking it from a gleam in the eyes of the authors to a final manuscript. His successor as history editor, Christine Silvestri, carried it through to its full development as an American history text. Developmental editor Charlotte Iglarsh did a marvelous job of keeping the authors faithful to their commitment to clear writing and compelling prose, as well as to their deadlines. Betty Slack expertly copyedited the manuscript and deftly guided it into production. Other members of the Scott, Foresman staff who gave valuable assistance include the photo research department, especially Nina Page and Leslie Cohn; designer Barbara Schneider, who is responsible for the visual clarity and elegance of the book design; cartographer Paul Yatabe, who conceived many of the maps, Cathy Wacaser, who served as editorial liaison to production, and Victoria Moon, the production coordinator.

Finally, each author received aid and encouragement from many colleagues, friends, and family members over the four years to research, reflection, drafting, and revising that went into this book.

Robert A. Divine wishes to thank Lisa Divine for typing and retyping his chapters, Barbara Renick Divine for superb editorial advice, Ricardo Romo for several helpful suggestions, and Brian Duchin and Louis Gomolak for preparing many of the special features in the last eight chapters of the book.

T. H. Breen wishes to thank John Williams, Robyn Muncy Champagne, E. Faber, James Axtell, George Breen, Sarah Breen, and Bant Breen. Special appreciation goes to Chester Pach, Professor of History at Texas Tech, for assistance at all stages of the project.

George M. Fredrickson wishes to thank Keith Schlesinger and Barbara McElroy for help with map research and special features, and Hélène Fredrickson and Joan Stahl for typing drafts of his chapters.

R. Hal Williams wishes to thank Lewis L. Gould, Kathleen Triplett, Edith Duncan, Alice McCaulley, Dorothy Friedlander, N. Coulter, Pat Hurst, Ann Nurre, Linda, Lise, and Scott Williams. Special thanks go to Jane Yoder and John Nicholson, who participated in every stage, and to Henry L. Gray and Michael R. Best, who lightened the administrative burden and allowed a Dean to research and write.

Contents

Maps

Charts and Graphs

Maps

Map 1   Major Indian Tribes and Culture Areas in North America, 1500

ARCTIC OCEAN

Eskimo

Koyukon

Eskimo
Ingalik
Tanaina
Kutchin
Aleut
Tanana
Eskimo

Eyak
Hare

Tuchone
Kaska

Tlingit
Tahltan
Slave

NORTHWEST
Sekani
Chipewyan

Tsimshian
Haida   Bella
Coola
COAST
Beaver
SUB-ARCTIC

Bella Bella
Carrier   Sarsi
Kwakiutl
Shuswap
Chilcotin
Cree

Nootka
Salish
Makah
Okanagan
Kutenai
Blackfeet
Quinault
PLATEAU
Colville
Chehalis
Spokane
Blackfeet
Gros Ventre
Chinook
Yakima
Tillamook
Klikitat
Nez
Percé
Flathead
Crow
Rogue
River
Cayese
Bannock
Umpqua
Klamath
Yurok
Modoc
Northern
Paiute
Shasta
Pomo
Maidu
GREAT BASIN
Shoshoni
Goshute
Miwok
Costanoan
Yokuts
Southern
Paiute
Ute
CALIFORNIA
Chumash
Serrano
Yavapi
Navajo
Hopi
Pueblo
Zuñi
Jicarilla
Apache
Cahuilla
Digueño
Yuma
Pima
SOUTHWEST
Papago
Maricopa
Mescalero
Apache
Western
Apache
Opata
Lipan
Apache
Cochimi
Seri
Concho
Canita
NORTHERN
MEXICO
Karankawa
Yaqui
Waiguri
Acaxee
Pericu
Tepehuan
Coahuiltec
Tamaulipec
Guachichil
Totonac
Otomi
Tarascan
Toltec
MIDDLE AMERICA
Maya
Aztec
Mixtec
Olmec
Zapotec
Maya
Mosquito
Lenca
Cuna
Guaymí

Mackenzie R.
Athabasca R.
Missouri R.
Colorado R.

ARCTIC
Eskimo
Eskimo
Eskimo

Hudson Bay
Eskimo

Cree
Naskapi
Montagnais

Beothuk

Chippewa
(Ojibwa)
Micmac
Malecite
Algonquin
Abnaki
Mahican
Chippewa
(Ojibwa)
Huron
Ottawa
Pennacook
Menominee
Iroquois
Mohawk
Oneida
Onondaga
Cayuga
Seneca
Massachusetts
Wampanoag
Narragansett
Sauk
Fox
Potawatomi
Winnebago
Kickapoo
EASTERN
Erie
Susquehanna
Delaware
Miami
WOODLAND
Oglala
Sioux
Omaha
Iowa
Illinois
Powhatan
Arapaho
Pawnee
Tutelo
Southern
Cheyenne
Kansa
Missouri
GREAT PLAINS
Shawnee
Tuscarora
Kiowa
Osage
Cherokee
Catawba
Quapaw
Chickasaw
SOUTHEAST
Wichita
Creek
Yamasee
Comanche
Caddo
Choctaw
Timucua
Tonkawa
Biloxi
Apalachee
Atakapa
Seminole

Teton Sioux
Santee
Sioux
Hidatsa
Mandan
Arikara
Ponca
Northern
Cheyenne

Rio Grande
Mississippi R.
Ohio R.
Great Lakes
St. Lawrence R.

PACIFIC
OCEAN

ATLANTIC OCEAN

Gulf of Mexico
Lucayo
Ciboney
Subtaino
Carib
Taino
CARIBBEAN
Caribbean Sea

Tropic of Cancer
Arctic Circle
Assiniboin

| 0 | 300 | 600 Miles |
| 0 | 300 | 600 Kilometers |

Map 2 Thirteen Colonies: Distribution of Major Immigrant Groups and Extent of Settlement

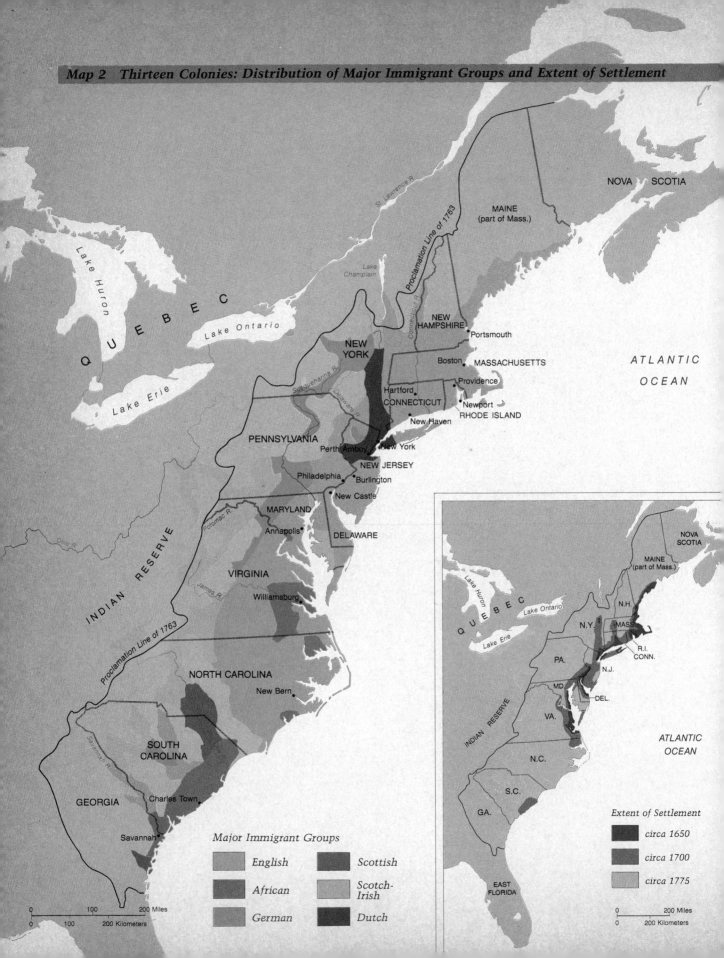

QUEBEC

Lake Huron

Lake Ontario

Lake Erie

St. Lawrence R.

Lake Champlain

NOVA SCOTIA

MAINE (part of Mass.)

Connecticut R.

NEW HAMPSHIRE

• Portsmouth

NEW YORK

Boston • MASSACHUSETTS

Susquehanna R. *Delaware R.*

Hartford •   • Providence

CONNECTICUT   • Newport

New Haven •   RHODE ISLAND

ATLANTIC OCEAN

PENNSYLVANIA

Perth Amboy •   • New York

NEW JERSEY

Philadelphia •   • Burlington

• New Castle

MARYLAND

Annapolis •

DELAWARE

Ohio R.

INDIAN RESERVE

Potomac R.

VIRGINIA

James R.

Williamsburg •

Proclamation Line of 1763

NORTH CAROLINA

New Bern •

SOUTH CAROLINA

GEORGIA

Savannah R.

Charles Town •

Savannah •

Major Immigrant Groups

- English
- African
- German
- Scottish
- Scotch-Irish
- Dutch

0   100   200 Miles

0   100   200 Kilometers

Inset map

QUEBEC

Lake Huron

Lake Ontario

Lake Erie

NOVA SCOTIA

MAINE (part of Mass.)

N.H.

N.Y.

MASS.

R.I.

CONN.

PA.

N.J.

MD.

DEL.

INDIAN RESERVE

VA.

N.C.

S.C.

GA.

EAST FLORIDA

ATLANTIC OCEAN

Extent of Settlement

- circa 1650
- circa 1700
- circa 1775

0   200 Miles

0   200 Kilometers

Map 3 The Advancing Frontier: America at Mid-nineteenth Century

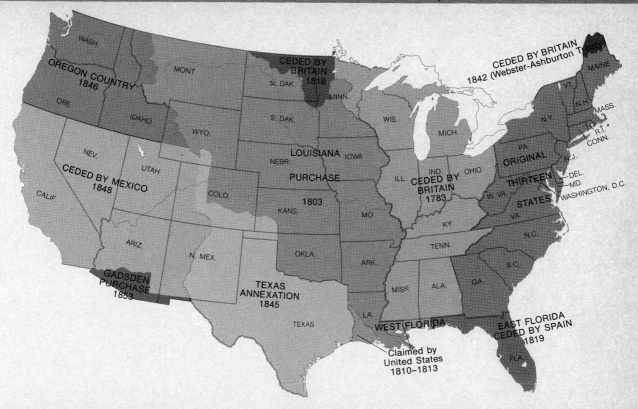

CEDED BY BRITAIN 1842 (Webster-Ashburton Treaty)

OREGON COUNTRY 1846

CEDED BY BRITAIN 1818

WASH.

MONT.

N. DAK.

MINN.

ORE.

IDAHO

S. DAK.

WIS.

MICH.

WYO.

LOUISIANA

IOWA

NEV.

UTAH

NEBR.

PURCHASE

ILL.

IND

OHIO

CEDED BY MEXICO 1848

CALIF.

COLO.

1803

KANS.

MO.

KY.

CEDED BY BRITAIN 1783

W. VA.

VA.

ORIGINAL

THIRTEEN

STATES

PA.

N.Y.

VT.

N.H.

MASS.

R.I.

CONN.

N.J.

DEL.

MD.

WASHINGTON, D.C.

ARIZ.

N. MEX.

OKLA.

ARK.

TENN.

N.C.

S.C.

GADSDEN PURCHASE 1853

TEXAS ANNEXATION 1845

MISS.

ALA.

GA.

LA.

WEST FLORIDA

EAST FLORIDA CEDED BY SPAIN 1819

TEXAS

Claimed by United States 1810–1813

FLA.

Map 4 Secession: A Nation Divided

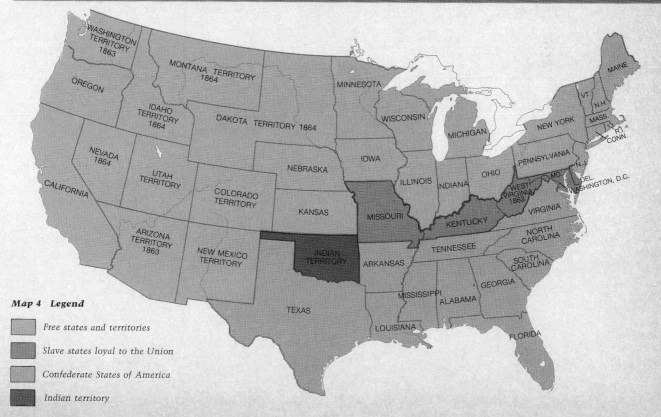

WASHINGTON TERRITORY 1863

MONTANA TERRITORY 1864

MINNESOTA

MAINE

OREGON

IDAHO TERRITORY 1864

DAKOTA TERRITORY 1864

WISCONSIN

MICHIGAN

NEW YORK

VT.

N.H.

MASS.

R.I.

CONN.

NEVADA 1864

UTAH TERRITORY

NEBRASKA

IOWA

ILLINOIS

INDIANA

OHIO

PENNSYLVANIA

N.J.

MD.

DEL.

WASHINGTON, D.C.

CALIFORNIA

COLORADO TERRITORY

KANSAS

MISSOURI

KENTUCKY

WEST VIRGINIA 1863

VIRGINIA

ARIZONA TERRITORY 1863

NEW MEXICO TERRITORY

INDIAN TERRITORY

ARKANSAS

TENNESSEE

NORTH CAROLINA

SOUTH CAROLINA

TEXAS

MISSISSIPPI

ALABAMA

GEORGIA

LOUISIANA

FLORIDA

Map 4 Legend

- Free states and territories
- Slave states loyal to the Union
- Confederate States of America
- Indian territory

Map 5   Major Armed Interventions of the United States (excluding declared wars)

NORTH AMERICA

UNITED STATES

Iceland 1941
Greenland 1941
U.S. troops land

Tunis
Algiers
MOROCCO
Wars Against
the Barbary States
1801–1805

Dominican Republic
1916–1924
U.S. occupation
1965
U.S. troops land

Vera Cruz 1914
Seized by U.S. Navy

Haiti
1915–1934
U.S. occupation

Grenada 1983
U.S. troops land

Nicaragua
1912–1925, 1927–1933
Marines enforce
U.S. position

ATLANTIC
OCEAN

Equator

SOUTH
AMERICA

PACIFIC
OCEAN

Map shows present-day boundaries

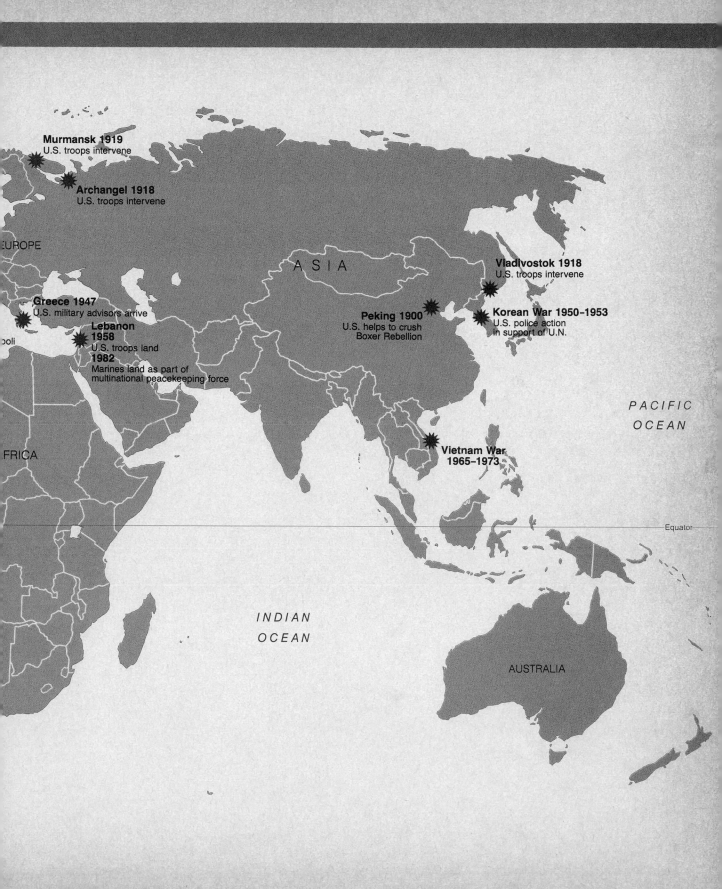

Murmansk 1919
U.S. troops intervene

Archangel 1918
U.S. troops intervene

EUROPE

A S I A

Vladivostok 1918
U.S. troops intervene

Greece 1947
U.S. military advisors arrive

**Lebanon
1958**
U.S. troops land
1982
Marines land as part of
multinational peacekeeping force

Peking 1900
U.S. helps to crush
Boxer Rebellion

Korean War 1950–1953
U.S. police action
in support of U.N.

oli

FRICA

PACIFIC

OCEAN

**Vietnam War
1965–1973**

Equator

INDIAN

OCEAN

AUSTRALIA

PAST
AND PRESENT

Prom.Lupi.

chapter 1

PATTERNS
OF DISCOVERY

One day in 1926, George McJunkin, a black cowboy, was riding along a dry creek known as Dead Horse Gulch, near Folsom, New Mexico. Suddenly he noticed some unusual bones protruding from the mud. Probing these remains with his knife, the cowboy uncovered several flint points. Although they somewhat resembled Apache arrowheads, they were strikingly different from anything McJunkin had ever found in the area. News of the discovery excited the curiosity of archaeologists, who concluded that McJunkin had stumbled across the skeleton of an ancient bison and tips from the spears of early Native American hunters. These "Folsom Men" lived at least ten thousand years ago, far earlier than anyone had previously dated even the oldest Native American civilizations. And as later discoveries revealed, their ancestors were Stone Age hunters from Siberia who had migrated to North America some twenty thousand years earlier.

Native Americans had inhabited the continent for millenia when European explorers crossed the Atlantic Ocean in the fifteenth century and proclaimed the discovery of a New World. These navigators were justly proud of their achievement. They did not, however, fully comprehend exactly what they had accomplished. As J. H. Parry, a historian of Spain's American empire, observed, "Columbus did not discover a new world; he established contact between two worlds, both already old."

Once Europeans learned of a land they imagined was filled with incalculable treasure, they flocked to its shores. The experiences of these people in the New World varied widely. Indeed, there was no typical European pattern of settlement. Emigrants from England, France, and Spain attempted as best they could to transfer familiar, local institutions to America. They wanted to reproduce the particular societies that they had known in the Old World.

The success of these colonial experiments depended upon complex elements over which the colonists often exercised little control. The support of the mother countries and the availability of investment capital, for example, profoundly affected the character of colonial settlements. The land itself played an important role. The St. Lawrence River valley clearly did not afford the same economic opportunities as did the fertile farmlands of the Chesapeake Bay area or the mineral-rich Valley of Mexico. The abundance of game and timber, the quality of the soil, the harshness of the weather, and the characteristics and density of the local Native American population all shaped the course of empire in the New World. Hence, it is not surprising that colonies established by English, French, and Spanish settlers developed in substantially different ways, adding to the rich variety of cultures that had long existed in the Americas.

Native American Cultures

The peopling of America began some thirty thousand years ago. At that time the earth's climate was considerable colder than it is today, and huge glaciers, often more than a mile thick, pushed their way as far south as the present states of Illinois and Ohio. Much of the world's moisture was transformed into ice, and the oceans dropped several hundred feet below their current level. The receding waters created a land bridge between Asia and America, an area now submerged beneath the Bering Sea.

This reclaimed land was free of glacial ice, and small bands of spear-throwing Siberian hunters chased giant mammals, woolly mammoths and mastodons—now all extinct species—across the open tundra. These hunters had no idea that they were the first people to set foot on a vast, uninhabited continent. They pursued big game wherever it led them. The migration of these nomadic groups took place over thousands of years. By 8000 B.C. men and women had reached the tip of South America.

The people who participated in this great trek were unaware of earlier nomads who had preceded them, and they did not know that many thousands would follow. They concentrated mainly on surviving in a harsh environment. The haphazard nature of this migration helps explain why Native Americans did not think of themselves as representatives of a single people or race.

Over the centuries relatively isolated tribal groups developed distinct cultures, patterns of kinship, and spoken languages. They seldom shared military or economic goals. Anthropologists estimate that Native Americans who settled north of Mexico had evolved between 300 and 350 separate languages by the time that Europeans first arrived. The concept of an homogeneous Native American culture was invented in a much later period by persons largely ignorant of the complexity of the history of these early people.

The discovery of agriculture revolutionized the life of Native Americans. No one knows exactly when people first cultivated plants for food in North America, but archaeologists working in the Southwest have uncovered evidence suggesting that some groups were farming as early as 2000 B.C. These primitive cultivators depended upon maize (corn), beans, and squash. Knowledge of their domestication of plants spread slowly north and east. By the year 800 B.C. for example, cultivation of squash had reached present-day Michigan.

Farming had an immense impact upon the societies of Native Americans. It freed men and women from the insecurity of an existence based solely upon hunting and gathering. The harvest made it possible to establish permanent villages. As the supply of food increased, the Native American population expanded, and the more advanced cultures turned their attention to art and architecture. As one authority on Native Americans observed, "Although cultivated plants alone are not sufficient to produce an advanced civilization, their history in both the Old World and the New World shows that they are a necessary part of such a development." The Agricultural Revolution also helps explain obvious differences among the North American tribes. Groups who knew nothing of the domestication of plants or who learned of it relatively late relied more heavily upon hunting and gathering than did the farming peoples of Mexico or the Southwest.

Development of Civilizations

The most advanced Native American cultures appeared in Mexico and Central America. The Maya and Toltec peoples built vast cities, formed

An interesting division of labor between the sexes is depicted in this sixteenth-century engraving by Jacques Le Moyne of American Indians sowing beans and maize. The men prepare the soil with hoes made of fishbones attached to wooden handles; then the women dig holes, neatly spaced, and drop seeds into them. Le Moyne visted Florida in 1564–1565.

sophisticated government bureaucracies that dominated large sedentary populations, and developed an accurate calendar and a complex form of writing. Their cities were especially impressive. Some were as large as Paris or London, housing several hundred thousand inhabitants. When the Spanish conquerors first saw them, they compared these American cities to Venice, one of Italy's most stunning artistic and engineering achievements. Indeed, so spectacular were the temples and towers of one Mexican city that an explorer proclaimed it "the most beautiful . . . in the world."

Even before the arrival of Europeans, Native American civilizations rose and fell, and not long before Columbus set out on his first voyage across the Atlantic, an aggressive, militant people, the Aztec, swept through the Valley of Mexico, conquering the great cities that their enemies had constructed. The Aztecs ruled by the sword and carried out human sacrifice on a scale previously unknown in Mexico.

The people who inhabited the present-day territories of the United States and Canada were less technologically accomplished than their Mexican neighbors. The tribes of the Southwest and the Mississippi Valley practiced intensive agriculture. Some even built elaborate irrigation systems. To the east, however, Native Americans generally mixed farming with hunting and gathering. Small bands formed villages during the warm summer months and cultivated corn. In the winter, the difficulties connected with feeding so many people forced these villages to disperse, each family living off the land to the best of its ability. The dangers were great; survival could never be taken for granted. The many Algonquian bands who occupied the Atlantic coast from North Carolina to Maine observed this seasonal cycle. Included in this large tribal group were the Powhatan who dominated the lower Chesapeake region, the Narragansett of southern New England, and the Abnakis who controlled the coast of Maine.

Despite common linguistic roots, the members of different Algonquian groups could have communicated only with the greatest difficulty. In their isolated environments, they had developed distinct dialects, and a sixteenth-century Narragansett would have found it as difficult to understand a Powhatan as a modern Rumanian would a Portuguese. Although these rather poor Algonquians failed to provide English and French explorers with gold, they did produce a fortune in furs and taught the inexperienced newcomers how to contend with an inhospitable wilderness.

Native American cultures were never static. In the "precontact" period, before Europeans arrived in the New World, major tribal groups frequently migrated. While the reasons for these migrations remain obscure, the distances involved were sometimes considerable. The tribes of the famed Iroquois League, for example, seem to have originated in the Southwest. They began to move northward as early as 1000 A.D., perhaps driven by aggressive enemies or in pursuit of better hunting grounds. By the sixteenth century, when European explorers first landed, the Iroquois were well established in what is now upper New York State. Other tribes such as the Ojibwa migrated west from the Saint Lawrence Valley to their current homes in the Lake Superior region. (See the map of the Indian tribes in the front pages of the book.)

European Contact

There is no question that the arrival of white men and women on this continent radically altered the lives of the native inhabitants. European colonizers regarded their own cultures as superior to those of the Indians, and whether the newcomers came from England or Spain, it seemed imperative to introduce civilization as quickly as possible to those they regarded as savages. The attempt was a universal failure.

Some Indians paid lip service to Christianity, but neither Catholic nor Protestant theology deeply affected their inner convictions. One Huron confessed to a French priest, "It would be useless for me to repent having sinned, seeing that I never have sinned." Another Huron was even more disarming. "We have no such apprehensions [about punishments after death] as you have," the Indian announced, "of a good and bad Mansion after this life, provided for the good and bad Souls; for we cannot tell whether everything that appears faulty to Men, is so in the Eyes of God." The white settlers' educational system proved no more successful in winning converts to European culture. Young Indian scholars deserted stuffy classrooms at the first opportunity. In 1753 Benjamin Franklin offered to enroll several talented Indian boys in the local college. The tribe's leaders rejected the idea, however, noting that boys who had been educated there in the past "were absolutely good for nothing being neither acquainted with the true methods of killing deer, catching Beaver or surprising an enemy."

Nor did the Native Americans show enthusiasm for European clothes, diet, or houses. Even matrimony seldom eroded the Indians' attachment to their own customs and habits. When Native Americans and whites married—unions which the English found less desirable than did the French or Spanish—the European partner usually elected to live among the Indians. Impatient settlers sometimes adopted more coercive methods, such as enslavement, to achieve cultural conversion. Again, from the white perspective, the results were discouraging. Indian slaves ran away or died. But they refused to become Europeans.

Although Native Americans rejected white values and customs, they coveted the products of European manufacturing. Arrows tipped with metal rather than flint possessed obvious advantages. Hunting became more efficient, and with the introduction of firearms Indian warfare became more deadly than it had ever been in the pre-contact period. The tribes located closest to the white settlements obtained firearms more quickly than did those that lived further west. The Iroquois, for example, carried guns into battle long before the tribes of the Great Lakes region did. Differences in weapons technology put the interior tribes at a great disadvantage, and it is not surprising that the tribes that traded directly with the whites, whether French, English, or Dutch, dominated other Native Americans armed only with bows and arrows.

Effects of Disease

Disease ultimately destroyed the cultural integrity of many North American tribes. European explorers exposed Native Americans to germs against which they possessed no natural immunities. Smallpox, measles, and typhus decimated the Indian population. Within a generation of contact, the Carib Indians, for whom the Caribbean was named, were extinct. The Algonquians of New England experienced appalling rates of death. One Massachusetts colonist reported in 1630 that the Indians of New England "above twelve yeares since were swept away by a great & grievous Plague . . . so that there are verie few left to inhabite the Country." Settlers who possessed no knowledge of germ theory speculated that God had providentially cleared the wilderness of heathens.

Modern historians believe that some tribes suffered a 90 to 95 percent population loss within the first century of European contact. The death of so many Indians deprived the conquerors, especially the Spanish, of indigenous workers needed to operate new mines and plantations. Throughout the New World, the disastrous loss of native populations may have caused colonists of all nationalities to seek a substitute labor force in Africa.

Indians who survived the epidemics found themselves in an extremely difficult situation. The enormity of the death toll and the agony that accompanied it called into question traditional religious beliefs and practices. In one curious case, members of a Canadian tribe, the Micmac, seem to have reacted to the demographic disaster by slaughtering wild animals. In the precontact period, these furbearing animals had possessed sacred meaning for the Micmac, but as the death toll mounted, the Indians concluded that the game had betrayed them. The animals had lost their magic, and in their anger and confusion, the Micmac retaliated by killing as many animals as they could. The destruction of an important element of their economy—however rational it may have appeared to the Micmac—only added to the Indians' suffering. The psychological impact of these events upon tribes located in other regions is not known, but wherever they may have lived, this catastrophic mortality weakened the fabric of traditional Native American cultures.

Some tribes certainly withstood the threat of disease better than did others. The Iroquois, for example, remained a formidable military force until the American Revolution. On the whole, however, the disaster reinforced racial stereo-

The Columbian Exchange

Sudden and sweeping disruptions of the environment are now almost commonplace, but an even greater ecological revolution than that witnessed following the end of World War II occurred in the century after Columbus' voyages. European explorers brought together two remarkably different worlds, physically separated for millenia, and the exchange of plants, animals, and diseases transformed the social history of the Old World as well as the New.

Differences in the forms of life in the two hemispheres astonished the first explorers. They had expected America to be an extension of Europe, a place inhabited by familiar plants and animals. They were in for a surprise. The exotic flora of the New World, sketched here from sixteenth-century drawings, included the food staple, maize, and the succulent pineapple. Equally strange to European eyes were buffalo, rattlesnakes, catfish, and the peculiar absence of horses and cattle. No domestic animal was common to both sides of the Atlantic except the dog. And perhaps the most striking difference was between the people themselves. Both Native Americans and Europeans found each other the most exotic people they had ever encountered.

The most immediate biological consequence of contact between the people of these two startlingly dissimilar continents was the transfer of disease. Within a year of Columbus' return from the Caribbean, syphilis appeared in Europe for the first time and was known as the "American" disease. By 1505, it had spread all the way to China.

The effect of European illnesses in the Americas was catastrophic. Native Americans had little natural immunity to common Old World diseases. The reasons for this are not clear, but when they were exposed to influenza, typhus, measles, and especially to smallpox, they died by the millions. Indeed, European exploration of America set off the worst demographic disaster in world history. Within fifty years of the first contact, epidemics virtually exterminated the native population of Santo Domingo and devastated the densely populated Valley of Mexico. So horrible was the toll that one Mayan cried in despair, "We were born to die!"

Also unsettling, but by no means as destructive, was the transfer of plants and animals from the Old World to the New. Spanish colonizers carried sugar and bananas across the Atlantic, and in time, these crops transformed the economies of Latin America. Even more spectacular was the success of European animals in America. During the sixteenth century, pigs, sheep, and cattle arrived as passengers on European ships, and in the lush New World environment, they multiplied more rapidly than they had in Europe. Some animals survived shipwrecks. On Sable Island, a small desolate island off the coast of Nova Scotia, one can still see small, long-haired cattle, the ancestors of the earliest cattle transported to America. Other animals escaped from the ranches of New Spain, generating new wild breeds, like the fabled Texas longhorn.

No European animal more profoundly affected Native American life than the horse. Once common in North America, the horse mysteriously disappeared from the continent sometime during the last Ice Age. The early Spanish explorers reintroduced the horse to North America, and the sight of this large, powerful animal at first terrified the Indians. Mounted conquistadores discovered that if they could not frighten Indian foes into submission, they could simply outmaneuver them. The Native Americans of the Southwest quickly adopted the horse to their own use. Sedentary farmers acquired new hunting skills, and soon the Indians were riding across the Great Plains in pursuit of the buffalo. The Commanche, Apache, Sioux, and Blackfoot tribes —just to name a few—became dependent on the horse. Mounted Indian warriors galloped into battle, unaware that their enemies had brought the horse to America.

Equally dramatic was the effect of American crops on European society. On his first trip to the New World, Columbus brought back a plant that revolutionized the diets of both humans and livestock—maize. During the next century, American beans, squash, and sweet potatoes appeared on European tables. The pepper and tomato, other New World discoveries, added a distinctive flavor to Mediterranean cooking. Despite strong prohibitions on its use (in Russia a user might have his nose amputated), European demand for American tobacco grew astronomically during the seventeenth century. The potato caught on more slowly in Europe, because of a widespread fear that root-crops caused disease. The most rapid acceptance of the white potato came in Ireland, where it became a diet staple in the 1600s. Indeed, Irish immigrants—unaware of the genealogy of this native American crop— reintroduced the potato into Massachusetts Bay in 1718.

These sweeping changes in agriculture and diet helped reshape the European economy. Partly because of the rich new sources of nutrition from America, the population of Europe, which had long been relatively stable, nearly doubled in the eighteenth century. Even as cities swelled and industries flourished, European farmers were able to feed the growing population. In many ways, the seeds and plants of the New World were far more valuable in Western development than all the silver of Mexico.

types in the white mind. Europeans already regarded Native Americans as an uncivilized people. The Indians whom the colonists encountered after the first wave of exploration were often sick and dispirited, and Europeans may have described American Indians in derogatory terms precisely because they only saw men and women whose lives had been shattered.

European Background of Exploration

In ancient times the West possessed a mythical appeal to people living along the shores of the Mediterranean Sea. Classical writers speculated about the fate of Atlantis, a great civilization that had mysteriously sunk beneath the ocean. Fallen Greek heroes allegedly spent eternity in an uncharted western paradise. But because the ships of Greece and Rome were ill-designed to sail the open waters, the lands to the west remained the stuff of legend and fantasy. In the fifth century an intrepid Irish monk, Saint Brendan, reported finding enchanted islands far out in the Atlantic. He even claimed to have met a talking whale named Jasconius, who allowed the famished voyager to cook a meal on his back. Such stories aroused mild curiosity, but as one might expect, they proved difficult to verify.

In the tenth century, Scandinavian seafarers known as Norsemen or Vikings actually established settlements in the New World, but almost a thousand years passed before they received credit for their accomplishment. In the year 984 a band of Vikings led by Eric the Red sailed west from Iceland to a large island in the North Atlantic. Eric, who possessed a fine sense of public relations, named the island Greenland, reasoning that others would more willingly colonize this icebound region "if the country had a good name." A few years later, Eric's son Leif founded a small settlement he named Vinland at a location in northern Newfoundland now called L'Anse aux Meadows. The hostility of Native Americans, poor lines of communication, and political upheavals in Scandinavia soon made maintenance of these distant outposts impossible. The Norse voyages went unnoticed at the

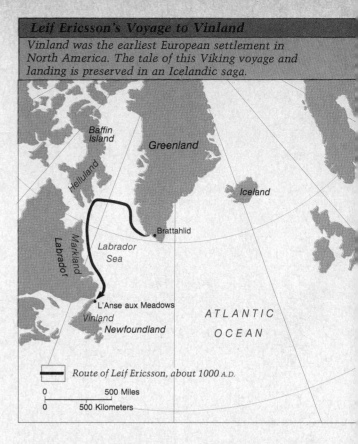

Leif Ericsson's Voyage to Vinland

Vinland was the earliest European settlement in North America. The tale of this Viking voyage and landing is preserved in an Icelandic saga.

Route of Leif Ericsson, about 1000 A.D.

time, largely because printing presses, which could have carried the news, had not yet been invented. When Columbus set out on his great adventure in 1492, he seemed to have been unaware of these earlier exploits.

Rise of Nation-States

The Viking achievement went unnoticed because other Europeans were unprepared to sponsor trans-Atlantic exploration and settlement. Medieval kingdoms were loosely organized, and for several centuries fierce provincial loyalties, widespread ignorance of classical learning, and dreadful plagues such as the Black Death discouraged people from thinking imaginatively about the world beyond their immediate villages.

In the fifteenth century, however, these conditions began to change. Europe became more prosperous, its people more expansive in their outlook. A central element in this shift was the slow but steady growth of population. Historians are uncertain about the cause of this increase—after all, neither the quality of medicine nor sanitation improved much—but the result was a substantial rise in the price of land, since there were more people to feed. Landlords, of course, profited from these trends, and as their income expanded, they demanded more of the luxury items, spices and jewels, that came from distant ports. Economic prosperity created a powerful new incentive for exploration and trade.

This period also witnessed the centralization of political authority under a group of rulers known collectively as the "new monarchs." Before the mid-fifteenth century, feudal nobles dominated small districts throughout Europe. Conceding only nominal allegiance to larger territorial leaders, these local barons taxed the peasants and waged war pretty much as they pleased. They dispensed what passed for justice. The new monarchs challenged the nobles' autonomy. The changes came slowly, and in many areas violently, but wherever they occurred, the results altered traditional political relationships between the nobility and the crown, between the citizen and the state. The new monarchs of Europe recruited national armies and supported these expensive organizations with revenues from national taxes. They created effective national courts. While these new rulers were often despotic, they personified the emergent nation-states of Europe and brought a measure of peace to local communities tired of chronic feudal war.

The story was the same throughout most of western Europe. The Tudors of England, represented by Henry VII (1485–1509), ended a long civil war known as the War of the Roses. Loùis XI, the French monarch (1461–1483), strengthened royal authority by reorganizing state finances. The political unification of Spain began in 1469 with the marriage of Ferdinand of Aragon and Isabella of Castile. These strong-willed monarchs forged a nation out of a group of independent kingdoms. If these political changes had not occurred, the major European countries could not possibly have generated the financial and military resources necessary for worldwide exploration. Indeed, the formation of aggressive nation-states prepared the way for the later wars of empire.

Technology and Knowledge

While the New Monarchs reorganized European politics, seafarers—many of them anonymous individuals—worked a revolution in naval technology. Before the fifteenth century, the ships that plied the Mediterranean were clumsy and slow. These galleys could maneuver into the wind only with the greatest difficulty, and without scores of oarsmen, they often could not move at all. But by the time Columbus sailed from Spain, naval innovators had developed a fast, highly maneuverable class of ships called caravels. These vessels did not require large crews of oarsmen and thus were far less expensive to operate. Moreover, European navigators adopted a new type of rigging (the lateen sail) first developed by the Arabs that allowed large ships to sail into the wind. Without this important advance, explorers could not possibly have crossed the

■ *This facsimile of a small caravel appears on a maritime publication dated 1502. It shows the type of ship used by Columbus.*

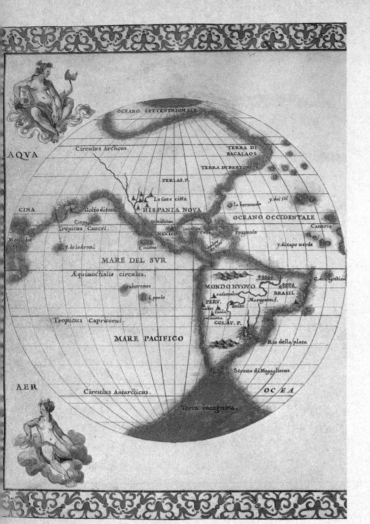

■ *An early sixteenth-century map of the Western Hemisphere. Note the inclusion of sites in New Spain for the legendary Seven Cities of Cibola. Note also that China appears to be connected to North America.*

was round. During the Middle Ages, however, this learning was lost. European scholars' rediscovery of the classical texts in the fifteenth century helped stimulate fresh investigation of the globe. The invention of printing from movable type sometime in the 1430s greatly facilitated the spread of this geographical knowledge. Sea captains published their findings as quickly as they could engage a printer, and by the beginning of the sixteenth century a growing body of educated readers throughout Europe were well informed about the exploration of the New World. The printing press opened the European mind to exciting possibilities that had only been dimly perceived when the Vikings sailed the North Atlantic.

Spain and the New World

In Spain, centralization of authority and advances in maritime technology and geographic knowledge brought the country to a remarkable rise to world power. In the early fifteenth century Spain consisted of several autonomous kingdoms. Its population was poor. It lacked rich natural resources and possessed few first-rate deep-water ports. In fact, there was little about this land that suggested that its people would take the lead in conquering and colonizing the New World.

At the beginning of the sixteenth century, however, Spain suddenly came alive with creative activities. The union of Ferdinand and Isabella sparked a drive for political consolidation which, because of the monarchs' fanatic Catholicism, took on the characteristics of a religious crusade. Spurred by the militant faith of its monarchs, the armies of Castile and Aragon waged holy war upon the independent states in southern Spain that were still under Moslem control. In 1492 the Moorish (Moslem) kingdom of Granada fell, and for the first time in centuries the entire nation was united under Christian rulers. Spanish authorities showed no tolerance for people who rejected the Catholic faith. Thousands of Jews and Moors were driven from the country; many more were convicted as heretics by the Inquisition and then executed, usually by burning. From this volatile social and political environment came the *conquistadores*, men eager for personal

Atlantic Ocean nor worked their way along the rocky, uncharted coasts of North America. Coupled with the discovery of more accurate ways to read latitude, these technological innovations meant that sailors could set out on long voyages with a new sense of confidence. Not only could they assume that they would reach remote destinations, but also that they would return home alive.

A final prerequisite to exploration was knowledge. Ptolemy (second century A.D.) and other ancient geographers had mapped the known world and had even demonstrated that the world

glory and material gain, uncompromising in matters of religion, and unswerving in their loyalty to the Crown. They were prepared to employ fire and sword in any cause sanctioned by God and king, and it was the misfortune of the American Indians that these particularly militant adventurers carried European culture to the most populous regions of the New World.

Admiral of the Ocean Sea

If it had not been for Christopher Columbus (Cristoforo Colombo), of course, Spain might never have gained an American empire. Little is known about the early life of this brilliant though misunderstood adventurer. Born in Genoa in 1451 of humble parentage, Columbus devoured the classical learning that had so recently been rediscovered. He mastered geography and at some point in his career became obsessed with the idea of sailing west across the Atlantic Ocean to reach Cathay, as China was then known.

In 1484, Columbus presented his plan to the king of Portugal. His choice of patrons was a good one, at least in theory. The Portuguese were recognized as the most advanced navigators in the world. Their great patron of exploration, Prince Henry the Navigator, who died in 1460, had sponsored important technological innovations in sailing. While the Portuguese were just as interested as Columbus in reaching Cathay, they elected to voyage around the continent of Africa rather than across an ocean of unknown dimensions. The strategy paid off handsomely, for in 1498 a Portuguese captain, Vasco da Gama, returned from the coast of India where he had loaded his ships with spices and other luxury goods. Columbus received a polite audience, but the Portuguese crown offered the eager Italian no support. A final report issued by the Portuguese described Columbus' scheme "as vain, simply founded on imagination, or things like that . . ."

Undaunted by rejection, Columbus petitioned Isabella and Ferdinand for financial backing. They were initially no more interested in his grand

■ *This sixteenth-century engraving by Théodore De Bry depicts a broadly romanticized version of the departure of Columbus from the port of Palos, Spain, in August 1492. Queen Isabella and King Ferdinand bid him a stiffly formal farewell as he begins his first voyage to find Cathay.*

The routes of the major voyages in the Age of Exploration. The great explorers and navigators established land claims for the European nations.

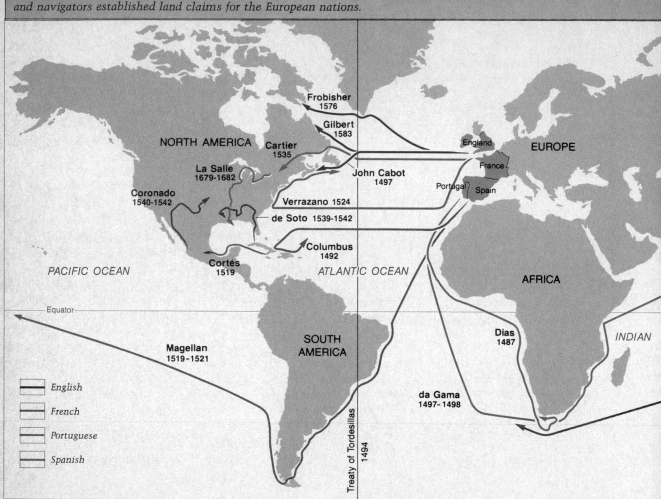

design than the Portuguese had been. But time was on Columbus' side. Spain's aggressive New Monarchs were becoming increasingly uneasy about the successes of their neighbor, Portugal. Columbus boldly played on upon this rivalry; he talked of wealth and empire. Indeed, for a person in his circumstances, he was supremely confident. One contemporary reported that when Columbus "made up his mind, he was as sure he would discover what he did discover, and find what he did find, as if he held it in a chamber under lock and key." Columbus' stubborn lobbying on behalf of the Enterprise for the Indies gradually wore down opposition in the Spanish court, and the two sovereigns provided him with a small fleet that contained two of the most famous caravels ever constructed, the *Niña* and *Pinta*, as well as the square-rigged *Santa Maria*. The indomitable admiral set sail for Cathay in August 1492, the year of Spain's unification.

Educated Europeans of the fifteenth century knew that the world was round. No one seriously believed that Columbus and his crew would tumble off the edge of the earth. The problem was size, not shape. Columbus estimated the distance to the mainland of Asia to be about 3000 nautical miles, a voyage that his small ships would have no difficulty in completing. The actual distance is 10,600 nautical miles, however, and had the New World not been in his way, his crew would have

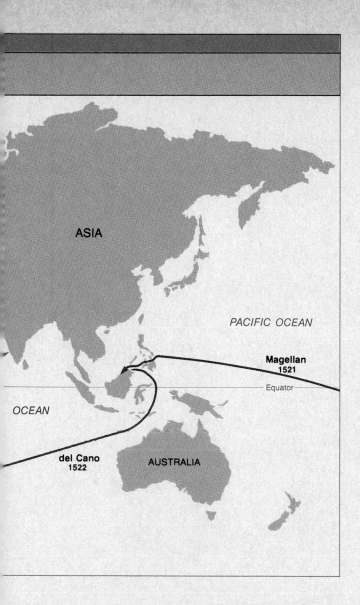

ASIA

PACIFIC OCEAN

Magellan
1521

Equator

OCEAN

del Cano
1522

AUSTRALIA

Columbus met friendly, though startled, Native Americans, whom he called Indians. These people wanted to please the explorer but could not comprehend his quest for gold and spices.

After his first voyage of discovery, Columbus returned to the New World three more times. But despite his considerable courage and ingenuity, he could never find the wealth that his financial supporters in Spain angrily demanded. Columbus died in 1506 a frustrated, impoverished dreamer, unaware that he had reached a previously unknown continent separating Asia from Europe. The final disgrace came in December 1500 when an ambitious falsifier Amérigo Vespucci, published a sensational account of his travels across the Atlantic that convinced German mapmakers that he had beaten Columbus to the New World. Before the error could be corrected, the name "America" gained general acceptance throughout Europe.

Only two years after Columbus' first voyage, Spain and Portugal divided the entire New World into two spheres of influence. Negotiated with the assistance of Pope Alexander VI, the Treaty of Tordesillas (1494) kept the two countries from going to war over America. More important, the treaty helped prevent other European powers from sharing in the wealth of the new continent for more than a century. Portugal gained Brazil, and Spain laid claim to all the remaining territories of the New World. The agreement was a bold stroke that quickly transformed Spain into Europe's richest state.

The Rise of the Conquistadores

Spain's good fortune unleashed a horde of conquistadores on the Caribbean. These independent adventurers carved out small settlements on Cuba, Hispaniola, Jamaica, and Puerto Rico in the 1490s and early 1500s. They were not interested in creating a permanent society in New World. Rather, they came for instant wealth, preferably in gold, and they were not squeamish about the means they used to obtain it. Bernal Díaz, one of the first Spainiards to migrate to this region, explained that he had traveled to America "to serve God and His Majesty, to give light to those who were in darkness, and to grow rich, as all men desire to do." In less than two decades the

run out of food and water long before they had reached China.

After stopping in the Canary Islands to refit the ships, Columbus continued his westward voyage in early September. When the tiny Spanish fleet sighted an island in the Bahamas after only thirty-three days at sea, the admiral concluded that he had reached Asia. Since his mathematical calculations had obviously been correct, he assumed that he would soon encounter the Chinese. It never occurred to Columbus that he had stumbled upon a large land mass completely unknown in Europe. He searched for the fabled cities of Asia, certain that one must be located around the next point of land or on the next island. Instead,

Indians who had inhabited the Caribbean islands had been exterminated, victims of exploitation and disease.

For a quarter century the conquistadores concentrated their energies on the major islands that Columbus had found. Rumors of fabulous wealth in Mexico, however, aroused the interest of many Spaniards, including Hernán Cortés, a minor government functionary in Cuba. Like so many members of his class, he dreamed of glory, of military adventure, of riches that would transform an ambitious drifter into an honored nobleman. On November 18, 1518, Cortés and a small army left Cuba to verify the stories of Mexico's treasure. He had lived in the New World for fourteen years, and while his personal daring, bordering on audacity, won him local acclaim, Cortés had shown no signs of the talents of a great empire builder. Events in Mexico soon demonstrated that Cortés was a leader of extraordinary ability, a person of intellect and vision who managed to rise above the goals of his avaricious followers.

His adversary was the legendary Aztec emperor, Montezuma. The conflict between these two powerful personalities is one of the most exciting sagas of early American history. To cut off his army from possible retreat, Cortes burned the ships that had carried his men to Mexico. Convinced that rival conquistadores would try to destroy his expedition, yet intent on conquering an Indian empire of millions of people, he led his band of six hundred followers across difficult mountain trails. Through courage, bluff, persistence, and a good measure of luck, Cortés subdued the Aztec warriors.

Cortés possessed obvious technological superiority in waging war. The sound of gunfire frightened the Indians. Moreover, Aztec troops had never seen horses, much less ones armored and carrying sword-wielding Spaniards. But these elements would have counted for little had Cortés not also gained a psychological advantage over his opponents. At first Montezuma thought that the Spaniards were gods, representatives of the fearful plumed serpent, Quetzalcoatl. Instead of resisting immediately, the emperor hesitated. When Montezuma's resolve hardened, it was too late. Cortés' victory in Mexico, coupled with other Spanish conquests in South America, transformed the mother country into the wealthiest state in Europe.

The Spanish Colonial System

Following the conquest of Mexico, renamed New Spain, the Spanish crown found itself confronted with a difficult problem. The conquistadores had to be brought under royal authority, a task easier said than done. Adventurers like Cortés were stubbornly independent, quick to take offense, and thousands of miles away from the seat of government. The crown found a partial solution in the *encomíenda* system. The monarch rewarded the leaders of the conquest with Indian villages. The people who lived in these settlements provided the *encomenderos* with labor tribute in exchange for legal protection and religious guidance. The system, of course, cruelly exploited Indian laborers. One historian concluded, "The first encomenderos, without known exception, understood Spanish authority as provision for unlimited personal opportunism." Cortés alone was granted the services of over 23,000 Indian workers. The *encomíenda* system did bring the colonizers into greater dependence upon the king, for it was he who legitimized their title. In the words of one scholar, the new economic structure helped to transform "a frontier of plunder into a frontier of settlement."

Bureaucrats dispatched directly from Spain soon replaced the aging conquistadores. After 1535 a viceroy, a nobleman appointed to oversee the king's colonial interests, ruled the people of New Spain. The crown also formed in 1538 a judicial body independent of the viceroy called an *audiencia*. This appellate court located in Mexico City not only brought a measure of justice to the Indians and Spaniards, but also made certain that the viceroys did not slight their responsibilities to the king. In Spain, the Council of the Indies handled colonial business.

The contrast between this governing system and the one that evolved later in England's mainland American colonies is striking. Spain's rulers maintained tight control over their American possessions. The volume of correspondence between the two continents, much of it concerning mundane matters, was staggering. All documents were duplicated several times by hand, and the trip to Madrid often took months. Sometimes a year passed before receipt of an answer to a simple request. But somehow the cumbersome system worked. In Mexico, Spanish officials established a rigid hierarchical order, directing the affairs of the countryside from urban centers. Persons born in the New World, even those of Spanish parentage (*criollos*), were regarded as socially inferior to natives of the mother country (*peninsulares*).

The Spanish also brought Catholicism to the New World. The Dominicans and Franciscans, the two largest religious orders, established Indian missions throughout New Spain, and some barefoot friars protected the Native Americans

■ *A Spanish friar baptizes a Mexican Indian.*

from the worst forms of exploitation. One courageous Dominican, Fra Bartolomé de Las Casas, published an eloquent defense of Indian rights, *Historia de las Indias*, which among other things questioned the European conquest of the New World. Las Casas' work provoked heated debate in Spain, and while the king had no intention of repudiating his vast American empire, he did initiate certain reforms designed to bring greater "love and moderation" to Spanish-Indian relations. It is impossible to ascertain how many converts these friars made. In 1531, however, a newly converted Christian reported a vision of the Virgin, a dark-skinned woman of obvious Indian ancestry, who became known throughout the region as the Virgin of Guadalupe. This figure served as a powerful symbol of Mexican nationalism in the Wars for Independence fought against Spain almost three centuries later. Parish priests served the spiritual needs of the colonists. During the colonial period, the Catholics of New Spain constructed more than twelve thousand churches.

About 750,000 people migrated to the New World from Spain. Most of the colonists were impoverished, single males in their late twenties in search of economic opportunities. They generally came from the poorest agricultural regions of southern Spain, almost 40 percent migrating from Andalusia. One weaver living in Mexico City, for example, told his Spanish cousin in 1576, "Therefore you would make me happy getting away from the misery over there by coming here." Since so few Spanish women migrated, especially in the sixteenth century, the men often married Indians and blacks, unions which produced "mestizos" and "mulattos." The frequency of interracial marriage affected the character of race relations in New Spain. Racial categories were much less rigidly defined there than they were in the English colonies, where the sex ratio of the settlers was more balanced and the racially mixed population comparatively small.

The Spanish Borderlands

Eager to duplicate Cortés' feat, several lesser-known conquistadores explored the lands to the north of Mexico. Between 1539 and 1541, Hernando de Soto trekked across the Southeast from

■ *The ruthless de Soto was well-known for his cruelty. But his atrocities, such as the mutilation shown here, could not lead him to gold or other treasure.*

Florida to the Mississippi River looking for gold and glory. At roughly the same time, Francisco Vasquez de Coronado set out from New Spain in search of the fabled "Seven Cities of Cibola," centers of wealth that upon closer inspection turned out to be Zuni pueblos. Coronado's fruitless journey took him to the present states of Texas, Kansas, New Mexico, and Arizona. Not until the early decades of the seventeenth century did Spanish settlers, led by Juan de Oñate, establish outposts in the Southwest. The Indians of this region constantly harassed the colonists, and in a major uprising in 1680 they drove the whites completely out of the territory. The viceroys of New Spain subsequently decided to maintain only a token presence in present-day Texas and New Mexico in order to discourage French encroachment upon Spanish lands. A similar concern over the French presence in the Southeast led to the establishment of a Spanish colony in Saint Augustine, Florida, in 1565.

California never figured prominently in Spain's plans for the New World. Early explorers found poor Indians but little else in the region. They saw no natural resources worth mentioning, and since the area was difficult to reach from Mexico City, California was ignored until 1769. Permanent settlements were established along the Pacific coast under the guidance of two remarkably energetic persons, Fra Junípero Serra and Don Gaspar de Portolá. Serra, a man in his fifties when he set out on this adventure, founded missions and presidios (forts) at San Diego, Monterey, San Francisco, and Santa Barbara.

Spain claimed far more of the New World than it could possibly manage. After the era of the conquistadores, Spain's rulers regarded the American colonies primarily as a source of precious metal, and between 1500 and 1650 an estimated two hundred tons of gold and sixteen thousand tons of silver were shipped back to the Spanish treasury in Madrid. This great wealth, however, proved a mixed blessing. The sudden acquisition of so much money stimulated a horrendous inflation that hurt the common people of Spain. Moreover, American gold and silver funded long, debilitating wars. Instead of developing its own industry, Spain became dependent upon the annual shipment of bullion from America, and in 1603 one insightful Spaniard declared, "the New World conquered by you, has conquered you in its turn." Poor leadership during the seventeenth century hastened Spain's decline. Despite its weakness, however, Spain managed to hold on to most of its colonial empire longer than England and France did theirs. And Spain made a cultural contribution to the American people that is still very much alive today.

French Exploration and Settlement

French interest in the New World developed more slowly. More than three decades after Columbus' discovery, King Francis I sponsored the unsuccessful efforts of Giovanni da Verrazano to find a short water route to China, a northwest passage around or through North America. In 1534, the king sent Jacques Cartier on a similar quest. The rocky, barren coast of Newfoundland depressed the explorer. He grumbled, "I am rather inclined to believe that this is the land God gave to Cain."

Discovery of a large, promising waterway soon raised Cartier's spirits. He reconnoitered the Gulf of the Saint Lawrence, traveling up this magnificent river as far as Montreal. Despite his high expectations, however, Cartier got no closer to China. In later voyages to Canada, Cartier searched for the mythical kingdom of Saguenay, a land supposedly even richer in precious metals than New Spain. Cartier soon realized that Canada would not produce the gold and silver of Mexico, and discouraged by the harsh winters, he headed home in 1542. Not until seventy-five years later did the brilliant navigator Samuel de Champlain rediscover this region for France. He founded Quebec in 1608.

In Canada the French developed an economy based primarily on the fur trade, a commerce that required close cooperation with the Native Americans. Brave, solitary individuals called *coureurs de bois* ("voyagers of the woods") paddled deep into the heart of the continent. In 1673 Père Jacques Marquette journeyed down the Mississippi River, and nine years later Sieur de La Salle traveled all the way to the Gulf of Mexico. In the early eighteenth century, the French established small settlements in Louisiana, the most important being New Orleans. These successes worried English colonists living along the Atlantic coast, for it appeared as if the French were intent upon encircling the English and cutting them off from the development of the trans-Appalachian west.

The French dream of a vast American empire, however, suffered from several serious flaws. The king remained largely indifferent to colonial affairs. Royal officers stationed in New France received limited and sporadic support from the mother country. An even greater problem was the French decision to settle the inhospitable northern country. This harsh environment offered little incentive to rural peasants or urban artisans, and throughout the colonial period, New France was underpopulated. Several minor noblemen attempted to transfer the French feudal system to the Saint Lawrence Valley, but highly individualistic settlers undermined these schemes. In a colony where land was abundant, feudal obligations made no sense, and they proved unenforceable.

While the population of New France continued to grow—more rapidly in Louisiana than in other areas—the French colonies never prospered. By the first quarter of the eighteenth century, the English settlements had outstripped their French

■ *In the dead of winter the streams of New France were frozen solid. The French voyageurs built sledges, placed their canoes and their supplies on them, and proceeded down the frozen course into the heart of the continent.*

neighbors in population as well as in volume of trade. According to one historian, "as future struggles with the English were to show, it [New France] was an inadequate base for long-term colonial expansion."

Background of English Exploration

The first English visit to North America remains something of a mystery. Fishermen working out of Bristol and other western English ports may have landed in Nova Scotia and Newfoundland as early as the 1480s. The codfish of the Grand Banks drew vessels of all nations, and during the summer months some sailors probably dried and salted their catches on Canada's convenient shores. John Cabot (Giovanni Caboto), a Venetian sea captain, completed the first recorded trans-Atlantic voyage by an English vessel in 1497. Henry VII had rejected Columbus' Enterprise for the Indies, but the Tudor monarch apparently experienced a change of heart after hearing of Spain's success. He commissioned Cabot "to sail to all parts, regions, and coasts of the eastern, western and northern sea . . . to find, discover and investigate whatsoever islands . . . which before this time were unknown to all Christians."

Like other explorers of the time, Cabot believed that he could find a northwest passage to Asia. After making the first landfall on the North American continent since the Norsemen, Cabot doggedly searched the northern waters for a likely opening, but a direct route to Cathay eluded him. Cabot died during a second attempt in 1498. Although Sebastian Cabot continued his father's explorations in the Hudson Bay region in 1508–1509, England's interest in the New World waned. For the next three quarters of a century, the English people were preoccupied with more pressing domestic and religious concerns. When curiosity in the New World revived, however, Cabot's voyages established England's belated claim to American territory.

The English Reformation

At the time of Cabot's death, England was not prepared to compete with Spain and Portugal for the riches of the Orient. Although Henry VII brought peace to England after a bitter civil war, the country still contained too many "over-mighty subjects," powerful local magnates who maintained armed retainers and often paid little attention to royal authority. Henry possessed no standing army; his small navy intimidated no one. Nor was he a fervent Catholic like Ferdinand and Isabella of Spain. To be sure, the Tudors gave nominal allegiance to the pope in Rome, but they were not crusaders for the faith.

By the end of the sixteenth century, however, conditions within England had changed dramatically. Tudor monarchs, especially Henry VIII (1509–1547) and his daughter Elizabeth I (1558–1603), developed a strong central government and transformed England into a Protestant nation. These changes affected all aspects of public life. They propelled England into a central role in European affairs and were crucial to the creation of England's North American empire.

The Protestantism that eventually provided impetus to colonization was definitely not of English origin. In 1517 a relatively obscure German monk, Martin Luther, publicly challenged the central tenets of Roman Catholicism, and within a few years the religious unity of Europe was forever shattered. The Reformation divided kingdoms, sparked bloody wars, and unleashed an extraordinary flood of scholarly writings. Luther's message was straightforward, one that the common people could easily comprehend. God spoke through the Bible, Luther maintained, not through the pope or priests. Scripture taught that people were saved by faith alone. Pilgrimages, fasts, alms, indulgences, none of these traditional acts could assure salvation. Luther's ideas spread rapidly across northern Germany and Scandinavia.

Other Protestant reformers soon spoke out against Catholicism. The most important of these was John Calvin, a lawyer turned theologian, who lived in the Swiss city of Geneva. Calvin stressed God's omnipotence over human affairs. The Lord, he maintained, chose some persons for "election," the gift of salvation, while

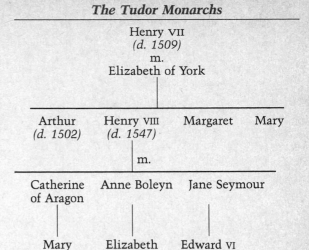

The Tudor Monarchs

Henry VII
(d. 1509)
m.
Elizabeth of York

Arthur (d. 1502) — Henry VIII (d. 1547) — Margaret — Mary

m.

Catherine of Aragon — Anne Boleyn — Jane Seymour

Mary (d. 1558) — Elizabeth (d. 1603) — Edward VI (d. 1553)

condemning others to eternal damnation. There was nothing that a man or woman could do to alter this decision. Human beings were helpless, mere doomed worms on the face of the earth, unless they had received election.

Common sense suggests that such a bleak doctrine might lead to fatalism or hedonism. After all, why not enjoy the world's pleasures to the fullest, if such actions have no effect on God's judgment? But common sense would be wrong. Indeed, Calvinists were constantly up and doing, searching for signs that they had received God's gift of grace. The uncertainty of their eternal state proved a powerful psychological spur, for as long as people did not know whether they were scheduled for heaven or hell, they worked diligently to demonstrate that they possessed at least the seeds of grace. The doctrine of "predestination" became the distinguishing mark of this form of Protestantism. Calvin's *Institutes of the Christian Religion* (1536) was a powerful statement of the new faith, and it spawned religious movements in most northern European countries. In France the Calvinists were known as Huguenots. In seventeenth-century England and America, those who carried Calvin's teachings to an extreme were called Puritans.

Popular anticlericalism was the foundation of the Reformation in England. The English people had long resented paying monies to the Catholic church. Early in the sixteenth century, opposition to and criticism of the clergy grew increasingly vocal. Cardinal Thomas Wolsey, the most powerful prelate in England, flaunted his immense wealth and unwittingly became a symbol of spiritual corruption. Parish priests were objects of ridicule. Poorly educated men for the most part, they seemed theologically ignorant and perpetually grasping. Anticlericalism did not run as deep in England as it had in Germany, but without question, by the late 1520s the Catholic church had lost the allegiance of the great mass of the population. The people's pent-up anger is central to an understanding of the English Reformation. Put simply, if common men and women throughout the kingdom had not supported separation from Rome, then Henry VIII could not have forced them to leave the church.

The catalyst for Reformation in England was the king's desire to rid himself of his wife, Catherine of Aragon, daughter of the king of Spain. Their marriage in 1509 had produced a daughter, Mary, but, as the years passed, no son. The need for a male heir obsessed Henry. He and his counselors assumed that a female ruler could not maintain domestic peace and England would fall once again into civil war. The answer seemed to be remarriage. Henry, who anticipated no serious problems, petitioned Pope Clement VII for a divorce (technically, an annulment), but the Spanish had other ideas. Unwilling to tolerate the public humiliation of Catherine, they forced the pope to procrastinate. In 1527 time ran out. The passionate Henry fell in love with beautiful Anne Boleyn, who later bore him a daughter, Elizabeth. The king decided to divorce Catherine with or without papal consent.

The final break with Rome came swiftly. Between 1529 and 1536 the king, acting through Parliament, severed all ties with the pope, seized church lands, and dissolved many of the monasteries. In March 1534 the Act of Supremacy boldly announced, "The King's Majesty justly and rightfully is supreme head of the Church of England." The entire process, which one historian termed a "state reformation," was conducted with impressive unanimity. Land formerly owned by the Catholic church passed quickly into private hands, and within a short period, property holders throughout England had acquired a vested interest in Protestantism. Beyond breaking with the papacy, Henry showed little enthusiasm for theological change. Many Catholic ceremonies survived.

The split with Rome, however, could not be contained. In 1539 William Tyndale and Miles Coverdale issued an English edition of the Bible. For the first time in English history, the bulk of the common people could read the word of God in their own language. It was a liberating experience that caused some men and women to question whether Henry's reformation had gone far enough.

With Henry's death in 1547, England entered a period of acute instability. Edward VI, Henry's young son by his third wife, Jane Seymour, came to the throne, but he was still a child and sickly besides. Militant protestants took advantage of the political uncertainty to introduce Calvinism into England and insist that the Church of England remove every trace of its Catholic origins. With the death of young Edward in 1553, these ambitious efforts came to a sudden halt. Henry's eldest daughter, Mary, next ascended the throne. Fiercely loyal to the Catholic faith of her mother, Catherine of Aragon, Mary I vowed to return England to the pope.

However misguided were the queen's plans, she demonstrated her father's iron will. Hundreds of Protestants were executed; others scurried off to the safety of Geneva and Frankfurt where they absorbed the most radical Calvinist doctrines of the day. When Mary died in 1558 and was succeeded by Elizabeth, these "Marian exiles" flocked back to England, more eager than ever to purify the Tudor church of Catholicism. Mary had inadvertently advanced the cause of Calvinism by creating so many Protestant martyrs, reformers burnt for their faith and now celebrated in the woodcuts of the most popular book of the period, John Foxe's *Acts and Monuments* (1563). The Marian exiles served as the leaders of the Elizabethan church, an institution that remained fundamentally Calvinist until the end of the sixteenth century.

Elizabeth Settles the Question

Elizabeth demonstrated that Henry and his advisers had been mistaken about the capabilities of female rulers. She was a woman of such talent

■ Foxe's Book of Martyrs *provided powerful propaganda for the ever growing Protestant religion in England.*

that even modern biographers find little to criticize in her decisions. She governed the English people from 1558 to 1603, an intellectually exciting period during which some of her subjects took the first halting steps toward colonizing the New World.

Elizabeth recognized that her most urgent duty as queen was to end the religious turmoil that had divided the country for a generation. Following Henry VIII's break with the Catholic church in 1529, each new Tudor sovereign had introduced a different theology—Catholicism, Anglo-Catholicism, Calvinism, something in between—until, in the words of one confused Englishman, people's consciences were *"tost up and Down (even like Tenis-bals)."* Elizabeth had no desire to restore Catholicism. After all, the pope openly referred to her as a woman of illegitimate birth. Nor did she want to recreate the church exactly as it had been in the final years of her father's reign. Rather, Elizabeth established a unique and heterogeneous institution, Catholic in much of its ceremony and government but clearly Protestant in doctrine. Under her so-called Elizabethan settlement, the queen assumed the title "Supreme Head of the Church." Some churchmen who had studied with Calvin in Geneva urged her

to drop immediately all Catholic rituals, but she ignored these strident reformers. The young queen understood that she could not rule effectively without the full support of her people, and as the examples of Edward and Mary demonstrated, neither radical change nor widespread persecution gained a monarch lasting popularity.

The state of England's religion was not simply a domestic concern. One scholar aptly termed this period of European history "the Age of Religious Wars." Catholicism and Protestantism influenced the way that average men and women across the continent interpreted the experiences of everyday life. Religion shaped political and economic activities. Protestant leaders, for example, purged the English calendar of many saint's days that had punctuated the agricultural year in Catholic countries. The Reformation certainly had a profound impact upon the economic development of Calvinist countries. Max Weber, a brilliant German sociologist of the early twentieth century, argued in his *Protestant Ethic and the Spirit of Capitalism* (1930) that a gnawing sense of self-doubt created by the doctrine of "predestination" drove Calvinists to extraordinary diligence. They generated large profits not because they wanted to become rich, but because they wanted to be doing the Lord's work, to demonstrate that they might really be among God's "elect."

Indeed, it is helpful to view these two warring faiths as ideologies, bundles of deeply held beliefs that divided countries and families much as communism and capitalism do today. The confrontation between Protestantism and Catholicism affected Elizabeth's entire reign. Soon after she became queen, Pope Pius V excommunicated her, and in his papal bull *Regnans in Exelsis* (1570), he stripped Elizabeth of her "pretended title to the kingdom." Spain, the most fervently Catholic state in Europe, vowed to restore England to the "true" faith, and Catholic terrorists constantly plotted to overthrow the Tudor monarchy.

Religion, War, and Nationalism

Slowly, yet steadily, English Protestantism and English nationalism merged. A loyal English subject in the late sixteenth century loved the queen, supported the Church of England, and hated Catholics, especially those who happened to live

■ *An allegory of the Tudor succession shows Bloody Mary with Philip of Spain and the god Mars at left, Henry the Eighth seated, his son and successor Edward the Sixth kneeling, and Elizabeth, the last of the line, at right ushering in the personified goddesses Peace and Plenty.*

in Spain. Elizabeth herself came to symbolize this militant new chauvinism. Her subjects adored the Virgin Queen, and they applauded when her famed "Sea Dogs"—dashing figures such as Sir Francis Drake and Sir John Hawkins—seized Spanish treasure ships in American waters. The English sailors' raids were little more than piracy, but in this undeclared state of war, such harassment passed for grand victories. There certainly seemed to be no reason why patriotic Elizabethans should not share in the wealth of the New World. With each engagement, each threat, each plot, English nationalism took deeper root. By the 1570s it had become obvious that the English people were driven by powerful ideological forces similar to those that had moved the subjects of Isabella and Ferdinand almost a century earlier.

In the mid-1580s, Philip II, who had united the empire of Spain and Portugal in 1580, decided that England's arrogantly Protestant queen could be tolerated no longer. He ordered the construction of a mighty fleet, hundreds of transport vessels designed to carry Spain's finest infantry across the English channel. When one of Philip's lieutenants viewed the Armada at Lisbon in May 1588, he described it as "La felicissima armada," the invincible fleet. The king believed that with the support of England's oppressed Catholics, Spanish troops would sweep Elizabeth from power.

It was a grand scheme; it was even a grander failure. In 1588 a smaller, more maneuverable English navy dispersed Philip's Armada, and soon his hopes for a Catholic England lay wrecked along the rocky shores of Scotland and Ireland. According to English legend, a Protestant storm helped defeat the Catholic enemy: "God breathed and they were scattered." Elizabeth's subjects remained loyal throughout the crisis. This dramatic victory altered the course of New World development. The defeat of the Armada revealed the vulnerability of England's archenemy. Inspired by success in the channel, bolder personalities dreamed of acquiring riches and planting colonies across the North Atlantic. Spain's American monopoly had been broken.

Irish Rehearsal for American Colonization

England's laboratory for the colonization of the New World was Ireland. It was on this island that enterprising Englishmen first learned to subdue a foreign population and seize its lands. When Elizabeth assumed the throne, Ireland's one million inhabitants were scattered across the countryside. There were few villages, and they were located mainly along the coast. To the English eye, the Irish people seemed wild and barbaric. They were also fiercely independent and difficult to control. The English dominated a small region around Dublin by force of arms, but much of Ireland's territory remained in the hands of Gaelic-speaking Catholics who presumably lived beyond the reach of civilization.

English Colonization in Ireland

During the 1560s and 1570s various enterprising English people decided that considerable fortunes could be made in Ireland. There were substantial risks, of course, not the least of which was the hostility of the Irish. Nevertheless, private "projectors" sponsored English settlements, and in turn, these colonists forced the Irish either into tenancy or off the land altogether. It was during this period that semimilitary colonies were planted in Ulster and Munster. According to one historian, the leading English figure in Irish colonization, Sir Henry Sidney, regarded the small English garrisons "as oases of civility in a desert of barbarism."

As one might expect, colonization produced severe cultural strains. The English settlers, however humble their own origins, felt superior to the Irish. After all, the English people had championed the Protestant religion. They had constructed a complex market economy and created a powerful nation state. To the English settlers, the Irish appeared to be lazy, licentious, superstitious, even stupid. English settlers ridiculed unfamiliar local customs, and it is not surprising that even educated representatives of the two cultures found communication almost impossible. En-glish colonists, for example, criticized the pastoral farming methods prevalent in sixteenth-century Ireland. It seemed perversely wasteful for the Irish to be forever moving about, since as any English person could see, such practices retarded the development of towns. Sir John Davies, a leading English colonizer, declared that if the Irish were left to themselves, they would "never (to the end of the world) build houses, make townships or villages or manure or improve the land *as it ought to be.*" Such stubborn inefficiency—surely (the English reasoned) the Irish must have known better—became the standard English justification for the seizure of large tracts of land. No matter what the Irish did, they could never be sufficiently English to please their new masters.

English Brutality

English ethnocentrism was relatively benign so long as the Irish accepted the subservient roles that the colonizers assigned them. But when they rebelled against the invaders, something they did with great frequency, English condescension turned quickly to violence. Resistance smacked of disrespect, and for the good of the Irish and the safety of the English, it had to be crushed. The brutality of Sir Humphrey Gilbert in Ireland would have made even the most insensitive Spanish conquistadore uneasy. Gilbert was a talented man who wrote treatises on geography, explored the coast of North America, and entertained Queen Elizabeth with witty conversation. But as a colonizer in a strange land, he tolerated no opposition.

In 1569 he was appointed military governor of Munster, and when the Irish in his district rose up, he executed everyone he could catch, "mane, woman and childe." Gilbert's excesses would never have been permitted in England no matter how serious the rebellion. He cut off the heads of many enemy soldiers killed in battle, and in the words of one contemporary, Gilbert laid his macabre trophies "on the ground by each side of the way leading into his tent, so that none should come into his tent for any cause but commonly he must pass through a lane of heads." Such behavior was not only unprecedented, it was also calamitous. Instead of bringing peace and security, it generated a hatred so deep that Ireland remains divided to this day.

The Irish experiments served as models for later English colonies in the New World. Indeed, one modern Irish scholar argues that "English colonization in Virginia was a logical continuation of the Elizabethan conquest of Ireland." The attitudes that prominent "projectors" such as Sir Humphrey Gilbert, Sir Walter Raleigh, and Sir Richard Grenville had formed in Ireland, shaped their views of America and its people. It was common for English adventurers in the New World to compare Native Americans with the "wild" Irish, a kind of ethnocentric shorthand that equated all alien races. This mental process was a central element in the transfer of English culture to America. The English, like the Spanish and the French, did not perceive America in objective terms. Instead they saw an America that they had already constructed in their imaginations, and the people and objects that greeted them on the other side of the Atlantic were forced into Old World categories, some of them Irish.

England Turns to America

By the 1570s, English interest in the New World had revived. An increasing number of gentlefolk were in an expansive mood, ready to challenge Spain and reap the profits of Asia and America. Yet the adventurers who directed Elizabethan expeditions were only dimly aware of Cabot's voyages, and their sole experience in settling distant outposts was in Ireland. Over the last three decades of the sixteenth century, English adventurers made almost every mistake that one could possibly imagine. They did, however, acquire valuable information about winds and currents, supplies and finance. While neither Gilbert nor Raleigh established permanent American colonies, they prepared the way for later, more successful ventures. Samuel Eliot Morison, an authority on New World exploration, observed, "the English record of northern voyaging between 1575–1600 is a series of glorious failures which left experiences as a foundation for the English colonies of the seventeenth century."

Sir Humphrey Gilbert's Adventure

The pioneer of English colonization in the New World was Sir Humphrey Gilbert. He was drawn to America in the 1560s by complex, often contradictory aims. This militantly anti-Spanish promoter who had experimented with colonization in Ireland originally set out to discover the northwest passage to Cathay. Gilbert never doubted the existence of this elusive strait. He published an entire book on the subject, which showed exactly where the passage might be found. He even tantalized his readers—persons he hoped would become investors—with stories of the "Gold, silver, precious stones, cloth of gold, silks" that awaited those who first seized control of the short route to Asia. Gilbert also envisioned the creation of vast New World estates, much like those he and his associates had carved out in Ireland. Unfortunately, Gilbert could never resist get-rich-quick schemes that inevitably undermined successful exploration and colonization.

Gilbert's enterprise got off to a bizarre start. In 1576, he sent Martin Frobisher, a sea captain noted for his strength and courage though not for his intellect, to find the passage. Frobisher missed the route to Cathay, but he returned with tons of American "gold." His discovery set off a flurry of activity. In three separate voyages to one of the most desolate locations in North America, Hall's Island, Frobisher mined an incredible amount of sparkling dirt that turned out upon closer analysis to be worthless chunks of iron pyrite (fool's gold).

In 1578 Gilbert tried a different approach. He persuaded Elizabeth to grant him a charter for "remote heathen and barbarous landes." It is not clear what he had in mind. After one abortive attempt and against the advice of the queen, who bluntly noted that he was a mediocre navigator, in 1583 Gilbert sailed to Newfoundland and before an amazed audience of fishermen from many countries, claimed the territory as his very own. On the return voyage Gilbert's ship was lost without a trace. The tough old adventurer was last seen sitting on the open deck during a storm, reading from the works of Sir Thomas More. His final advice was "We are as neere to heaven by sea as by land."

The Roanoke Tragedy

Sir Walter Raleigh shared Gilbert's dreams. The men were half-brothers, and after Gilbert's death, Raleigh announced his own intention of establishing a colony in America. A man of boundless optimism, he consistently underestimated the cost of creating and supplying a New World settlement. In 1585 he dispatched two captains to the coast of the present-day North Carolina to claim land granted to him by Elizabeth. The men returned with glowing reports, no doubt aimed in part at potential financial backers. "The soile," declared Captain Arthur Barlow, "is the most plentifull, sweete, fruitfull, and wholesome of all the world."

Raleigh diplomatically renamed this marvelous region Virginia, in honor of his patron, the Virgin Queen. Elizabeth encouraged her favorite in private conversation but turned down his persistent requests for money. With rumors of war in the air, she did not want to alienate Philip II unnecessarily by sponsoring a colony on land long ago claimed by Spain.

Raleigh's enterprise seemed ill-fated from the start. Despite careful planning, everything went wrong. In 1585 Sir Richard Grenville transported a group of men, most of them fresh from the Irish settlements, to Roanoke Island. Grenville, however, wasted valuable time on the way to America chasing Spanish treasure ships in the Caribbean, and the colonists did not arrive in Virginia until nearby autumn. Their settlement also was poorly situated. Located inside the Outer Banks— perhaps to avoid detection by the Spanish—the Roanoke colony proved extremely difficult to reach. Even experienced navigators feared the treacherous currents and storms off Cape Hatteras. Grenville added to the colonists' troubles by destroying an entire Indian village in retaliation for the theft of a silver cup. Needless to say, a group of Englishmen living three thousand miles from home were foolish to alienate the local Native American population.

Grenville hurried back to England in the autumn of 1585, leaving the colonists to fend for themselves. They performed quite well. The men explored their region; they built shelters. But just when there was reason for optimism, a peculiar series of accidents transformed Raleigh's settle-

Chronology

30,000–25,000 B.C. Indians cross the Bering Strait into North America

2000–1500 B.C. Agricultural revolution transforms Native American life

1001 A.D. Norsemen establish a small settlement in Vinland (Newfoundland)

1438 (Ca.) Invention of printing method using movable type

1469 Marriage of Isabella and Ferdinand leads to the unification of Spain

1492 Columbus lands at San Salvador

1497 Cabot leads first English exploration of North America

1498 Vasco Da Gama of Portugal reaches India by sailing around Africa

1502 Montezuma becomes emperor of the Aztecs

1506 Columbus dies in Spain after four voyages to America

1517 Martin Luther's protest sets off Reformation in Germany

1521 Cortés achieves victory over the Aztecs at Tenechtitlan

1529–1536 Henry VIII provokes English Reformation

1534 Cartier claims Canada for France

1536 Calvin's *Institutes* published

1540 Coronado explores the Southwest for Spain

1558 Elizabeth becomes queen of England

1583 Sir Humphrey Gilbert dies

1585 First Roanoke settlement established on coast of North Carolina

1588 Spanish Armada defeated by the English

1603 Elizabeth I dies

1608 Champlain founds Quebec

1682 La Salle travels the length of the Mississippi River

1769 Junípero Serra directs Spanish occupation of California

ment into a ghost town. In the spring of 1586 Sir Francis Drake was returning from a Caribbean voyage and for reasons known only to himself, decided to put in at Roanoke. Since an anticipated shipment of supplies was overdue, the colonists climbed aboard Drake's ships and went home. They were apparently relieved to escape an island that contained neither gold nor silver. Whatever their thinking, their irresponsible behavior nearly destroyed the entire experiment.

In 1587 Raleigh launched a second colony. This time he placed in charge John White, a capable administrator and talented artist, who left a magnificent sketchbook of the Algonquian Indians who lived near Roanoke. The new settlement contained women, children, and even two infants who were born within weeks after the colonists crossed the Atlantic. The settlers feasted upon Roanoke's fish and game and bountiful harvests of corn and pumpkin. Yet within weeks after arriving, White returned to England at the colonists' urging to obtain additional food and clothing and to recruit new immigrants.

■ *The wife and daughter of an Algonquin chief, drawn by John White. The child is holding an English doll.*

Once again, Raleigh's luck turned sour. The Spanish Armada severed communication between England and America. Every available English vessel was pressed into military service, and between 1587 and 1590 no ship visited the Roanoke colonists. When rescuers eventually reached the island, they found the village deserted. White, who lost several members of his own family, sadly reported, "We let fall our Grapnel neere the shore, & sounded with a trumpet a Call, & afterwardes many familiar English tunes or Songs; and called to them friendly, but we had no answere." The fate of the "lost" colonists remains a mystery. The best guess is that they paid for Grenville's attack upon the Indians with their lives.

The Roanoke debacle discouraged others from emulating Raleigh. He had squandered a fortune and had nothing to show for it. During the 1590s smart investors turned to privateering or other less exhausting ventures. Had it not been for Richard Hakluyt, who publicized the explorers' accounts of the New World, the dream of American colonization might have died in England.

Keeping the Dream of America Alive

Hakluyt, a supremely industrious man, never saw America. Nevertheless, his vision of the New World powerfully shaped English public opinion. He interviewed captains and sailors upon their return from distant voyages and carefully collected their stories in a massive book entitled *The Principall Navigations, Voyages, and Discoveries of the English Nation* (1589). The work appeared to be a straightforward description of what these sailors had seen across the sea. That was its strength. In reality, Hakluyt edited each piece so that it would drive home the book's central point: England needed American colonies. Indeed, they were essential to the nation's prosperity and independence. English settlers, he argued, would provide the mother country with critical natural resources, and in the process they would grow rich themselves. In Hakluyt's America, there were no losers. "The earth bringeth fourth all things in abundance, as in the first creation, without toil or labour," he wrote of Virginia. His blend of piety, patriotism, and self-interest proved immensely popular, and his *Voyages* went through many editions.

As a salesman for the New World, Hakluyt was as misleading as he was successful. He failed to appreciate or purposely ignored the rich cultural diversity of the Native Americans and the varieties of experience of European colonists. Instead, he led many common men and women who traveled to America to expect nothing less than a paradise on earth. As the history of Jamestown was soon to demonstrate, the harsh realities of America bore little relation to those golden dreams.

Recommended Reading

The events surrounding the exploration of the New World have been the subject of a rich historical literature. These titles have been recommended because they provide readers who do not have a background in early modern history with a fine introduction to the major events of this period. A particularly well-written account of the background of European expansion is J. H. Parry, *The Age of Reconnaissance* (1963). Two books of narrower focus are Samuel E. Morison, *The European Discovery of America: The Southern Voyages, 1492–1616* (1971) and John Bartlet Brebner, *The Explorers of North America 1492–1806* (1933). Charles Gibson provides an excellent introduction to the history of New Spain in *Spain in America* (1966). There are many fine studies of sixteenth-century England, but one might start with G. R. Elton, *England Under the Tudors* (1974) and J. E. Neale, *Queen Elizabeth I* (1934). Two sensitive books on Native American cultures that draw upon the insights of anthropology as well as history are Bruce Trigger, *The Children of Aataentsic: A History of the Huron People to 1660* (1976) and Cornelius Jaenen, *Friend and Foe: Aspects of French-Amerindian Cultural Contact in the Sixteenth and Seventeenth Centuries* (1976).

Additional Bibliography

The historical and anthropological literature on Native American cultures includes Harold E. Driver, *Indians of North America* (1961) as well as a full bibliography of recent articles and monographs in Robert F. Spencer and Jesse D. Jennings et al., *The Native Americans: Ethnology and Backgrounds of the North American Indians* (1977).

Of more limited regional scope, but extremely well presented is Michael D. Coe's *Mexico* (1967). Sherburne F. Cook and Woodrow Borah provide a comprehensive analysis of the demographic crisis in *The Aboriginal Population of Central Mexico on the Eve of the Spanish*

Conquest (1963). See Frank Raymond Secoy, *Changing Military Patterns on the Great Plains* (1953) and Calvin Martin, *Keepers of the Game: Indian-Animal Relationships and the Fur Trade* (1978) on the Indians' responses to white culture. Also of interest are Shepard Krech, ed., *Indians, Animals, and the Fur Trade: A Critique of Keepers of the Game* (1981); James Axtell, *The European and the Indian* (1981); Francis Jennings, *The Invasion of America: Indians, Colonialism, and the Cant of Conquest* (1975); and Neal Salisbury, *Manitou and Providence: Indians, Europeans, and the Making of New England* (1982).

The transformation of early modern Europe, especially economic shifts, is discussed in Ralph Davis' brilliant synthesis, *The Rise of Atlantic Economies* (1973). Three studies explore the European response to the discovery of the New World: Edmundo O'Gorman, *The Invention of America* (1961); Fredi Chiappelli, ed., *First Images of America* (1976); and Hugh Honour, *New Golden Land* (1975). Alfred Crosby provides insights into the unintended results of exploration in *Columbian Exchange: Biological and Cultural Consequences of 1492* (1972).

Spain's rise to a world power can be traced in J. H. Elliott, *Imperial Spain, 1469–1716* (1963), and J. H. Parry, *The Spanish Seaborne Empire* (1966). A fine study of the leading personalities in the expansion of Spain is S. E. Morison, *Admiral of the Ocean Sea, A Life of Christopher Columbus* (1942).

The historical literature on Spain's American possessions includes Michael C. Mayer and William Sherman, *The Course of Mexican History* (1979); Charles Gibson, *The Aztecs under Spanish Rule* (1964); and William B. Taylor, *Drinking, Homicide and Rebellion in Colonial Mexican Villages* (1979).

Two books by W. J. Eccles, *Canada Under Louis XIV, 1663–1701* (1964) and *The Canadian Frontier, 1534–1760* (1969), provide considerable insight into the development of New France. And for the excitement of early French exploration see S. E. Morison, *Samuel de Champlain, Father of New France* (1972).

A. G. Dickens examines England's religious transformation in *The English Reformation* (1964). One should also look at J. Bossy, "The Counter-Reformation and the People of Catholic Europe, "*Past and Present*, no. 47 (1970) as well as Patrick Collinson, *The Religion of Protestants, The Church in English Society 1559–1625* (1982).

The two best studies of Ireland in this period are Nicholas P. Canny, *The Elizabethan Conquest of Ireland* (1976) and David B. Quinn, *The Elizabethans and the Irish* (1966).

An indispensible work on English exploration remains S. E. Morison, *The European Discovery of America: The Northern Voyages, A. D. 500–1600* (1974). See also two works by D. B. Quinn, *England and the Discovery of America, 1481–1620* (1974) and *North America from Earliest Discovery to First Settlements* (1977). To understand Hakluyt's impact, read a good edition of his *Principal Navigations, Voyages, Traffiques & Discoveries* (1907).

chapter 2

THE
SPECTRUM
OF SETTLEMENT

Fearful that Rhode Island and its neighbors might go to war over a border dispute, in 1665 a group of royal commissioners surveyed the land and recommended a compromise settlement. The disputed land concerned the territory around Narragansett Bay, an area claimed by Connecticut, Massachusetts Bay, Plymouth, and Rhode Island. Each colony possessed documents signed by the king of England confirming its title. In addition, in 1663 Rhode Island had received a royal charter which contained a detailed but nearly unintelligible description of the colony's borders. Even this document failed to settle the question, nor did the 1665 report of the royal commissioners resolve the controversy. No sooner had the commissioners returned to England than the dispute flared up again. In fact, almost a century passed before Massachusetts and Rhode Island finally agreed upon a common boundary.

This dispute, almost impossible to resolve, revealed how English colonization transformed maps of North America into a crazy quilt of territorial claims and counterclaims. English monarchs assumed that the area across the Atlantic Ocean was theirs to distribute as they pleased. Often without possessing the slightest knowledge of local geography, they awarded large tracts of land to merchant adventurers or court favorites. Each royal decision generated new boundaries, some of which were so vague or conflicting that they set off disputes, like the one between Rhode Island and its neighbors, that lasted well into the eighteenth century.

Such a haphazard method of granting land also suggests the extraordinary lack of unity in England's American colonies. English colonization did not spring from a desire to build a centralized empire, like that of Spain or France. Instead the Crown awarded colonial charters to a wide variety of merchants, religious idealists, and aristocratic adventurers who established separate and profoundly different colonies. Not only did New Englanders have little in common with the earliest Virginians and Carolinians, but they often divided among themselves. By the end of the seventeenth century, the spectrum of English settlements existing in America was remarkable for the diversity of its religious practices, political institutions, and economic arrangements.

Motives for Migration

Changes occurring throughout the period of settlement help explain the diversity of English colonization. Seventeenth-century England was a complex society undergoing far-reaching economic, political, and religious transformation. Even though many people remained rooted in tiny rural villages, many others took to the road in search of fresh opportunities. In fact, even by modern standards, the English population was quite mobile. Thousands of men and women moved each year from the countryside to London, already a city of several hundred thousand inhabitants.

Other, more exotic destinations also beckoned. A large number of English settlers migrated to Ireland, while lucrative employment and religious freedom attracted people to Holland. For the most adventurous individuals, however, there was always the New World. Even after making that choice, one that involved a long and difficult voyage across the Atlantic Ocean, English emigrants enjoyed a range of possibilities. They could select a Caribbean island such as Barbados, just as easily as New England or Virginia.

English colonists crossed the Atlantic for many different reasons. Some, of course, wanted to institute a purer form of worship, more closely based on Scripture. Others dreamed of owning land and perhaps, of bettering their social position. And a few came to escape bad marriages, jail terms, and the dreary prospect of life-long poverty. Seldom is it possible to isolate a single cause that explains emigration. Often colonists who were poor also insisted upon reforming religion; well-to-do Puritans were also attracted to the "fat, black earth" of New England.

Whatever their reasons for crossing the ocean, English men and women who emigrated to America in the seventeenth century left a mother country wracked by recurrent, often violent political and religious controversy. During the 1620s, the Stuart monarchs—James I (1603–1625) and his son Charles I (1625–1649)—who succeeded Queen Elizabeth on the English throne fought constantly with the elected members of Parliament. Tensions grew so severe that in 1629 Charles decided to rule England without their assistance. The strategy backfired. When Charles was finally forced to recall Parliament in 1640, it demanded extreme reforms. The king took up arms against the supporters of Parliament and his stubbornness sparked a bloody civil war. In 1649 the victorious parliamentarians beheaded Charles, and for almost a decade Oliver Cromwell, a brilliant general and religious reformer, governed the English people.

In 1660, following the death of Cromwell, the Stuarts were restored to the throne. During a period known as the Restoration, neither Charles II (1660–1685) nor James II (1685–1688)—both sons of Charles I—could quell political unrest. When the authoritarian James openly patronized his fellow Catholics, the nation rose up in what was called the "Glorious Revolution" (1688) and sent him into permanent exile.

Such political events coupled with periodic economic recession determined in large measure the direction and flow of emigration to America. During times of political turmoil, religious persecution, and economic insecurity men and women thought more seriously about living in the New World than they did during periods of peace and prosperity. Obviously, people who moved to America at different times came from different social environments. A person who emigrated to Pennsylvania in the 1680s, for example, left an England unlike the one that a Virginian in 1607 or a Bay Colonist in 1630 had known. Political and religious changes in seventeenth-century English society help explain the diversity of American settlement.

Regardless of the exact timing of departure, however, American settlers brought with them a bundle of ideas, beliefs, assumptions that helped them make sense of their everyday experiences in an unfamiliar environment. Their values were tested and sometimes transformed in the New World, but they were never destroyed. Settlement involved a complex process of adjustment. The colonists developed several different subcultures in America, and in each of these, one can trace the interaction between the settlers' values and the physical elements such as the climate, crops, and soil of their new surroundings. The Chesapeake, the New England colonies, the Middle Colonies, and the Carolinas formed distinct regional identities that persisted long after the first settlers had passed from the scene.

The Stuart Monarchs

James I
(d. 1625)

Charles I
(executed 1649)

Charles II   James II
(d. 1685)   (deposed 1688,
                      d. 1701)

Mary m.   William III,   Anne
            Prince of Orange   (d. 1714)
(d. 1695)   (d. 1702)

The Chesapeake

After the Roanoke debacle (see chapter 1), interest in American settlement declined, and only a few aging visionaries like Richard Hakluyt kept alive the dream of English colonies in the New World. These advocates argued that the North American mainland contained resources of incalculable value. An innovative group, they insisted, might reap great profits and at the same time, supply the mother country with items that it would otherwise be forced to purchase from European rivals, Holland, France, and Spain. Moreover, any enterprise that annoyed Catholic Spain or revealed its weakness in America seemed a desirable end in itself to patriotic English citizens. Soon after James I ascended to the throne, the settlers were given an opportunity to put their theories into practice in the colonies of Virginia and Maryland, an area known as the Chesapeake.

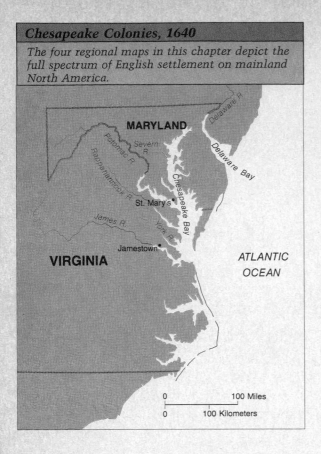

MARYLAND

Delaware R.

Potomac R.

Severn R.

Rappahannock R.

Chesapeake Bay

Delaware Bay

St. Mary's

James R.

York R.

Jamestown

VIRGINIA

ATLANTIC OCEAN

0   100 Miles
0   100 Kilometers

Tragic Adventure at Jamestown

Earlier, during Elizabeth's reign, the major obstacle to successful colonization had been money. No single person, no matter how rich or well connected, could underwrite the vast expenses that a New World settlement required. The solution to this financial problem was the "joint-stock company," a business organization in which scores of people could invest without fear of bankruptcy. A merchant or landowner could purchase a share of stock at a stated price, and at the end of several years, could anticipate recovering the initial investment plus a portion of whatever profits the company had made. Joint-stock ventures sprang up like mushrooms. English citizens of means, and even some of more modest fortunes, rushed to invest in these companies, and as a result, some enterprises were able to amass large amounts of capital, enough certainly to finance a new colony in Virginia.

On April 10, 1606, James issued the first Virginia charter. This document authorized the London Company to establish plantations in Virginia. The London Company was a dynamic business venture. Its leader, Sir Thomas Smith, was reputed to have been London's wealthiest merchant. Smith and his partners gained possession of the territory lying between Cape Fear and the Hudson River. These were vague, overlapping boundaries, to be sure, but the Virginia Company—as the London Company soon called itself—set out immediately to find the treasure that Hakluyt had promised.

In December 1606 the *Susan Constant*, the *Godspeed*, and the *Discovery* sailed for America. The ships carried 104 men and boys who had been instructed to establish a fortified outpost some hundred miles up a large navigable river. The natural beauty and economic potential of the region was apparent to everyone. A voyager on this expedition reported seeing "faire meaddowes and goodly tall trees, with such fresh waters running through the woods, as almost ravished [us] at first sight."

The leaders of the colony selected what they considered a promising location more than thirty miles from the mouth of the James River. A marshy peninsula jutting out into the river became the site for one of America's most ill-fated villages, Jamestown. Modern historians have criticized this choice. The low-lying ground proved to be a disease-ridden death trap; even the drinking water was contaminated with salt. But the first Virginians were neither stupid nor suicidal. Jamestown seemed the ideal place to build a fort, since surprise attack rather than sickness appeared the more serious threat in the early months of settlement.

Almost instantly the colonists began quarreling. The adventurers were simply not prepared for the difficult challenge that confronted them in America. They had traveled to the New World in search of instant wealth. Tales of rubies and diamonds lying on the beach inflamed their greed. While these people may seem exceptionally gullible, they behaved in Virginia as if they fully expected to become rich. Instead of cooperating for the common good—guarding the palisade or farming, for example—each individual pursued personal interests. They searched for gold when they might have planted corn. No one was willing to take orders, and those who were

■ *Because it was surrounded by water on three sides, the marshy peninsula on the James River seemed an easy-to-defend and thus ideal location for the Jamestown fort. By 1614 there were "two faire rowes of howses" protected by a palisade.*

supposed to govern the colony looked after their private welfare while disease, Indians, and starvation ravaged the hapless settlers.

The Amazing Captain John Smith

Virginia might have gone the way of Roanoke had it not been for Captain John Smith. By any standard, he was a remarkable man. Before coming to Jamestown, he had traveled throughout Europe, fought with the Hungarian army against the Turks, and if Smith is to be believed, was saved from certain death by various beautiful women. Because of his reputation for boasting, historians have tended to discount Smith's account of life in early Virginia. Recent scholarship, however, has reaffirmed the truthfulness of his story. In Virginia, Smith brought order out of anarchy. While members of the council in James-

town debated petty topics, he traded with the local Indians for food, mapped the Chesapeake Bay, and was even rescued from execution by a precocious Indian princess, Pocahontas. In the fall of 1608 he seized control of the ruling council and instituted a tough military discipline. Under Smith, no one enjoyed special privilege. Lazy individuals whom he forced to work came to hate him. But he managed to keep them alive, no small achievement in this deadly environment.

Leaders of the Virginia Company in London recognized the need to reform the entire enterprise. After all, they had spent considerable sums and had received nothing in return. In 1609, the company directors obtained a new charter from the king, which completely reorganized the Virginia government. Henceforth all commercial and political decisions affecting the colonists rested with the company, a fact that had not been made sufficiently clear in the 1606 charter. More-

■ This etching depicts the Indian maiden Pocahontas pleading with her father, chief Powhatan, to spare John Smith from the flames.

■ The title page of a 1609 brochure promoting the colony of Virginia.

over, in an effort to obtain scarce capital, the original partners opened the "joint-stock" to the general public. For a little more than £12—approximately ten month's wages for an unskilled English laborer—a person or group of persons could purchase a stake in Virginia. It was agreed that in 1616 the profits from the colony would be distributed among the shareholders. The company sponsored a publicity campaign; pamphlets and sermons extolled the colony's potential and exhorted patriotic English citizens to invest in the enterprise.

This burst of energy came to nothing. Bad luck and poor planning plagued the Virginia Company. A vessel carrying settlers and supplies went aground in the Caribbean, and while this misadventure did little to help the people at Jamestown, the incident provided Shakespeare with the idea for *The Tempest*. The governor, Lord De La Warr, added to the confusion by postponing his departure for America. Even the indomitable Captain Smith suffered a debilitating accident and was forced to return to England.

Between 1609 and 1611 the remaining Virginia settlers lacked capable leadership, and perhaps as a result, they lacked food. The terrible winter of 1609–1610 was termed the "starving time." A few desperate colonists were driven to cannibalism. Smith wrote that one colonist killed his wife, powdered (salted) her, and "had eaten part of her before it was known; for which he was executed." The captain, who possessed a curious sense of humor, observed: "Now, whether she was better roasted, broiled, or carbonadoed, I know not, but such a dish as powdered wife I never heard of." Other people simply lost the will to live.

In June 1610 the survivors actually abandoned Virginia, but through a stroke of luck, they encountered De La Warr just as they commenced their voyage down the James River. The governor and the deputy governors who succeeded him, Sir Thomas Gates and Sir Thomas Dale, ruled by martial law. The new colonists, many of them male and female servants employed by the company, were marched to work by the beat of the drum. Such methods saved the colony but could not make it flourish. The people in Virginia sent furs and timber to England and experimented with other crops, but nothing they produced even came close to covering the company's expenditures. In 1616 there were no profits for the share-holders, only a vast expanse of unsurveyed land three thousand miles from London.

A "Stinking Weed" Saves the Colony

The solution to Virginia's problems grew in the vacant lots of Jamestown. Only Indians bothered to cultivate tobacco until John Rolfe, a settler who achieved notoriety by marrying Pocohantas, realized that this local weed might be a valuable export. Rolfe experimented with the crop, eventually growing in Virginia a milder variety which had been developed in the West Indies and which was more appealing to European smokers.

Virginians suddenly possessed a means to make money. Tobacco proved relatively easy to grow, and settlers who had avoided work now threw themselves into its production with single-minded diligence. In 1617 one observer found that Jamestown's "streets and all other spare places [are] planted with tobacco . . . the Colony dispersed all about planting tobacco." Although King James I first considered smoking immoral and unhealthy, he changed his mind when the duties he collected on tobacco imports began to mount. He was neither the first nor the last ruler who decided that a vice that generates revenue is not really a vice.

The company launched one last effort to transform Virginia into a profitable enterprise. In 1618 Sir Edwin Sandys (pronounced Sands) led a faction of stockholders that began to pump life into the dying organization by instituting a series of sweeping reforms and eventually ousting Sir Thomas Smith and his friends. Sandys wanted private investors to develop their own estates in Virginia. Before 1618 there had been little incentive to do so, but by relaxing Dale's martial law and promising a representative assembly called the House of Burgesses, Sandys thought the colony might be more attractive to wealthy speculators. Even more important was his method for distributing land. Colonists who covered their own transportation cost to America were guaranteed a "headright," a fifty-acre lot for which they paid only a small annual rent. Adventurers were granted additional headrights for each servant that they brought to the colony. This procedure

Ætatis suæ 21. A. 1616.

Matoaks als Rebecka daughter to the mighty Prince Powhatan Emperour of Attanoughkomouck als Virginia converted and baptized in the Christian faith, and Wife to the Wor.[ll] *M.* [r] *Tho. Rolff.*

■ *Pocahontas later married John Rolfe, a settler who pioneered the cultivation of tobacco as a cash crop. She converted to Christianity, taking the name Rebecka. This portrait, painted during a 1616 visit to London, shows her in her court dress.*

allowed prosperous planters to build up huge estates at the same time that they acquired dependent laborers. This land system persisted long after the company's collapse.

Sandys had only just begun. He also urged the settlers to diversify their economy. Tobacco alone, he argued, was not a sufficient base. He envisioned colonists busily producing iron and tar, silk and glass, sugar and cotton. There was no end to his suggestions. He scoured Europe for skilled artisans and exotic plant cuttings. His ambitious blueprint, no doubt, owed much to the writings of Richard Hakluyt. To finance such a huge project, Sandys relied upon a lottery, a game of chance that promised a continuous flow of capital into the company's treasury. The final element in the grand scheme was people. Sandys sent new settlers by the thousand to Jamestown, men and women swept up by the same hopes that had carried the colonists of 1607 to the New World. In both cases, the harsh realities of American life shattered the settlers' ill-conceived dreams.

Life and Death in Virginia

Between 1619 and 1622 colonists arrived in Virginia in record number. Company records reveal that during this short period 3570 individuals were sent to the colony. These people seldom moved to Virginia in families. Although the first women arrived in Jamestown in 1608, most emigrants were single males in their teens or early twenties who came to the New World as indentured servants. In exchange for transportation across the Atlantic, they agreed to serve a master for a stated number of years. The length of service depended in part upon the age of the servant. The younger the servant, the longer he or she served. In return, the master promised to give the laborers proper care and, at the conclusion of their contracts, to provide them with tools and clothes according to "the custom of the country."

■ *Beginning with the first shipment from Virginia, smoking tobacco soon became a popular and fashionable activity, as shown in this etching of a British smoking house.*

Whenever possible, planters in Virginia purchased able-bodied workers, in other words, persons (preferably male) capable of performing hard agricultural labor. This preference dramatically skewed the colony's sex ratio. In the early decades, men outnumbered women by as much as six to one. As one historian, Edmund S. Morgan, explained, "Women were scarcer than corn or liquor in Virginia and fetched a higher price." Such sexual imbalance meant that even if a male servant lived to the end of his indenture, he could not realistically expect to start a family of his own. Moreover, despite apparent legal safeguards, masters could treat dependent workers as they pleased. Servants were sold, traded, even gambled away in a hand of cards. It does not require much imagination to see that a society that tolerated such an exploitative labor system might later embrace slavery.

Most Virginians did not live long enough to worry about marriage. Death was omnipresent in this society. Indeed, extraordinarily high mortality was a major reason why the Chesapeake colonies developed so differently than did those of New England. On the eve of the 1618 reforms, Virginia's population stood at approximately 700. The company sent at least three thousand more people, but by 1622 only 1240 were still alive. "It Consequentilie followes," declared one angry shareholder, "that wee had then lost 3000 persons within those 3 yeares." The major killers were contagious diseases. Salt poisoning also took a toll. And on Good Friday, March 22, 1622, the local Indians slew 347 settlers in a well-coordinated surprise attack. No one knows for certain what effect such a horrendous mortality rate had upon the men and women who survived. At the very least, it must have created a sense of impermanence, a desire to escape Virginia with a little money before sickness or Indians ended the adventure. The settlers who drank to excess aboard the tavern ships anchored in the James River described the colony "not as a place of Habitacion but only of a short sojourninge."

The King Takes Charge

On both sides of the Atlantic people wondered who should be blamed. Why had so many colonists died in a land so rich in potential? The burden of responsibility lay in large measure with the Virginia Company. Sandys and his supporters were in too great a hurry to make a profit. At every stage, their planning proved inadequate, their funds insufficient. Settlers were shipped to America, but neither housing nor food awaited them in Jamestown. Weakened by the long sea voyage, they quickly succumbed to contagious disease.

Company officials in Virginia also bore a share of guilt. They were so eager to line their own pockets that they consistently failed to provide for the common good. Various governors and their councillors grabbed up the indentured servants, sent them to their own private plantations to cultivate tobacco and as the 1622 tragedy demonstrated, ignored the colony's crumbling defenses. Jamestown took on the characteristics of a "boomtown." There was no shared sense of purpose, no common ideology, except perhaps unrestrained self-advancement, to keep the society from splintering into highly individualistic, competitive fragments.

The company's scandalous mismanagement embarrassed the king, and in 1624 he dissolved the bankrupt enterprise and transformed Virginia into a royal colony. The Crown appointed a governor and a council. No provision was made, however, for a representative assembly, an institution that the Stuarts heartily opposed. The House of Burgesses had first convened in 1619. While elections to the Burgesses were hardly democratic, the assembly did provide wealthy planters with a voice in government. Even without the king's authorization, the representatives gathered annually after 1629, and in 1639 Charles recognized the body's existence.

He had no choice. The colonists who served on the council or in the assembly were strong-willed, ambitious men. They had no intention of surrendering their control over local affairs. When in 1635 Governor John Harvey ignored the wishes of several members of the council, they sent him back to England, warning that if he ever returned he would be shot. Since Charles was having troubles of his own and lived three thousand miles from Jamestown, he usually allowed the Virginians to have their own way. In 1634 the assembly divided the colony into eight counties. In each one a group of appointed justices of the peace—the wealthy planters of the area—sat as a

Heavy iron siege helmet of the Spanish style, and a hilted rapier made in Germany, c. 1600. Both items were unearthed in an excavation near Jamestown in the 1950s.

court of law and executive board. The "county court" was the most important institution of local government in Virginia, and long after the American Revolution, it served as a center for social, political, and commercial activities.

The changes in government had little impact upon the character of daily life in Virginia. The planters continued to grow tobacco, and as the Indians were pushed west, Virginians took up large tracts of land along the colony's many navigable rivers. The focus of their lives was the isolated plantation, a small cluster of buildings housing the planter's family and dependent workers. These were modest wooden structures. Not until the next century did the Virginia gentry build the great Georgian mansions that still attract tourists. The dispersed pattern of settlement retarded the development of institutions such as schools and churches. Besides Jamestown there were no population centers, and as late as 1704 Robert Beverley, a leading planter, reported that Virginia did not have a single place "that may reasonably bear the Name of a Town."

What Happened at Roanoke?

People have always been fascinated by unexpected disappearances, and after four centuries, the mystery of the "Lost Colony" of Roanoke still arouses considerable curiosity. What happened to the 120 English settlers abandoned in 1587 on the shore of Albemarle Sound? Were they massacred by local Indians, or did they migrate to some other location where they dropped from the pages of history? The absence of evidence has not discouraged the advancement of various theories, some of them bizarre, about the colony's strange end.

John White, the settlement's original leader, returned to the North Carolina coast in 1590 and found the Roanoke site deserted. He saw no signs of violence. White's investigation did reveal that before their departure, the colonists (eighty-four men, seventeen women, and eleven children) had carefully buried their personal belongings, including their armor. The only clue that they gave to their current whereabouts was the word *Croatoan* carved on a post and the letters *CRO* on a tree trunk. White and the settlers had arranged that in an emergency they would leave a sign of a cross to alert a rescue party to danger or foul play. But nowhere was such a cross to be seen. White desperately wanted to conduct a more thorough search—after all his own daughter was among the missing colonists—but stormy weather forced his

fleet to put out before the mystery could be solved.

The fate of the lost colonists immediately aroused public curiosity in England. Some people assumed that the settlers were living a life of leisure among the Indians. The authors of a play first produced in London in 1605 declared that the Roanoke colonists "have married with the Indians, and make 'hem bring forth as beautifull faces as any we have in England: and therefore the Indians are so in love with 'hem, thal all the treasure they have they lay at their feete." While such romantic fiction kept the story alive, other English citizens concluded that the lost colonists had probably perished. But no one possessed convincing evidence.

Numerous expeditions searched for survivors. Even the hard-nosed Captain John Smith tried to locate the lost colonists. Serious efforts to make contact with these people continued into the 1620s. The results were always the same, tantalizing rumors but no colonists. Instead of putting the matter to rest, persistent failure stimulated ever more fantastic conjecture. Soon the history of the Roanoke settlement was transformed into legend.

A good guess about the colonists' fate is that, discouraged by lack of news from England, they went to live among the local Indians. White supported this theory. He believed that the settlers moved to Croatoan, an area not far from Roanoke. White's watercolor drawing (opposite page) shows the type of Algonquian village to which the ill-fated colonists may have been removed. The houses were constructed of poles and matting, surrounded by a palisade for defense. Some theorists have speculated that the settlers later migrated northward, perhaps even to Chesapeake Bay, in hope of contacting an English ship. According to this hypothesis, the powerful chief, Powhatan, killed the colonists just before Captain John Smith arrived in 1607. A variation on this story insists that survivors of this massacre were adopted by friendly Indians living on the Chowan River in what is now North Carolina.

The theory that the colonists joined the Croatoan Indians receives strong support from the Lumbee, a group of Indians currently living in Robeson County, North Carolina. According to local tradition, the Lumbee were described in official documents as "Croatoan" as recently as the nineteenth century. The Lumbee contend that the lost colonists intermarried with their ancestors, forming a community that was part white, part Indian. Samuel Eliot Morison, a respected historian, observed that "the existence of blue-eyed and fair-haired types among them, as well as the incorporation of Elizabethan words in their language and their using surnames from John White's lost colonists, bears this out." Other scholars are skeptical of the legend of Lumbee origin. To be sure, the members of the tribe reflect a racial mix, but their ties with the Roanoke colonists of the sixteenth century have not been persuasively demonstrated.

A curious story involving the lost colonists came to light in 1937. In that year someone presented a professor at Emory University with a carved stone containing a message from Eleanor Dare, mother of Virginia Dare, to her father John White. The stone, it was said, had been discovered near the Chowan River. It allegedly told White where his daughter and the other settlers had gone. The professor made the mistake of offering a reward for additional stones. By the end of 1940, forty-eight stones had been found, most by a local stonemason.

The carved rocks narrated the story of the colonists' long, difficult journey from Roanoke along the Chattahoochee River to the site of present-day Atlanta. To the embarrassment of the expert scholars, a local newspaper reporter exposed the hoax. He demonstrated that several words found on the stones had been used in ways that no Elizabethan settler would have understood.

A stonecutter fooled the professors, and the fate of the colonists still remains a mystery. Other "genuine" evidence no doubt, will appear from time to time. After all, lack of data has not discouraged the search for the lost continent of Atlantis or the Loch Ness monster.

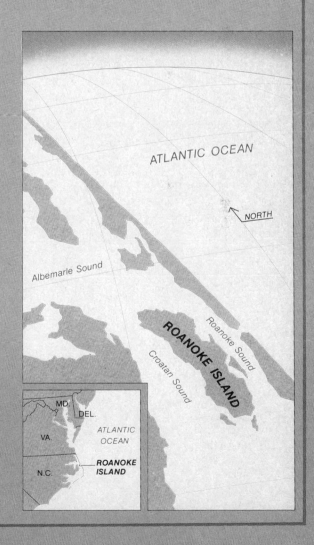

A Refuge for Catholics: The Founding of Maryland

By the end of the seventeenth century, Maryland society looked remarkably like that of its neighbor, Virginia. At the time of Maryland's founding, however, no one could have predicted this similarity. Maryland's roots lay not in a wild scramble for wealth, but in a nobleman's desire to create a sanctuary for England's persecuted Catholics.

The driving force behind the settlement of Maryland was Sir George Calvert, later Lord Baltimore. Calvert came from an excellent English family. He was well educated, and by 1620 his charm and ambition had made him a favorite at the Stuart court. James appointed him to the Privy Council and designated him secretary of state. Whether Calvert was a Catholic at the time is not known as he kept his religious opinions to himself. He did show great interest in various joint-stock companies, including the Virginia Company and the New England Company. In 1621 he even sponsored a small American settlement of his own in Newfoundland. Charles could not change the climate or the environment, however. In 1629 Baltimore gave up on this "remote wilde part of the Worlde," and turned his attention to the south.

On June 30, 1632, Charles granted George Calvert's son, Cecilius, a charter for a colony to be located on the Chesapeake Bay north of Virginia. Cecilius' father, George, died while the negotiations were in progress, but his vision unquestionably shaped the character of the new settlement. The second Lord Baltimore named the territory "Mariland in memory and honor of the Queene." For his part, Charles wanted to halt the southward spread of Dutch influence from New Netherland and regarded Baltimore's project as a cheap and convenient way to do so.

The charter itself was an odd document, a mixture of medievel custom and daring innovation. It transformed Baltimore into a "palatine lord," a proprietor with almost royal powers. Settlers swore an oath of allegiance not to the king of England, but to Lord Baltimore. In the mother country such practices had passed into obsolescence, but for reasons not entirely clear, the Calverts obtained the right to create a vast feudal estate in America. As proprietor, Lord Baltimore owned the land outright; he possessed

■ *Cecilius Calvert, second Lord Baltimore, is shown with his grandson.*

absolute authority over anyone living in his domain. On paper at least, everyone was assigned a place in an elaborate social hierarchy. Members of a ruling class, persons who purchased 6000 acres, were called lords of the manor. These landed aristocrats were permitted to establish their own local courts of law. People with less acreage enjoyed fewer privileges, particularly in government. Lord Baltimore thought that land sales would adequately finance his venture. He also adopted Virginia's headright system, requiring only that colonists pay him a small annual fee known as a "quitrent."

Embedded in this feudal scheme was a concept that broke boldly with the past. At a time when European rulers regularly persecuted people for their religious beliefs, Baltimore championed liberty of conscience—with certain qualifications. The colony's famous "Act concerning Religion" drafted by Cecilius in 1648 extended toleration only to individuals who accepted the divinity of Christ. While this statute did not ensure complete religious liberty to all people or separation of church and state, the proprietor promoted the idea that men and women ought not harass each other because of religion. Even though Maryland's early settlers—Catholics as well as Protestants—revived the persecuting spirit, Baltimore's commitment to toleration never flagged.

Actual settlement commenced in 1634 when several hundred emigrants—men and women—under the direction of Cecilius' brother, Leonard Calvert, landed at St. Mary's. Maryland attracted both Catholics and Protestants, and for a brief period, the two groups seemed capable of living in peace. Unlike the Virginia settlers, these early colonists were not threatened with starvation. They maintained friendly relations with the local Indians.

Baltimore's feudal system never took root in Chesapeake soil. People simply refused to play the social roles that he had assigned. These tensions affected the operation of Maryland's government. Baltimore assumed that his brother, acting as deputy proprietor in America, and a small appointed council would pass necessary laws and carry out routine administration. When an elected assembly first met in 1635, the proprietor allowed the representatives to discuss only those acts that he had prepared. The members of the assembly bridled at such restrictions and insisted upon exercising traditional parliamentary privileges that eventually undermined Baltimore's authority. Neither side gained a clear victory. With each passing year, however, the proprietor's absolute control over the men and women of Maryland progressively weakened.

Despite Baltimore's efforts to establish liberty of conscience, Maryland's gravest problems were caused by the colonists' religious intolerance. Overly aggressive Jesuits frightened Protestant settlers. Even more disturbing were Puritans who accepted Baltimore's offer to acquire land and then attempted to unseat the proprietor because he and his chief advisers were Catholic. For almost two decades, vigilantes roamed the countryside, and during the "Plundering Time" (1644–1646), one faction temporarily drove Leonard Calvert out of Maryland. In 1655 civil war flared again. At the battle of Severn River, the Puritans swept the proprietary forces from the field and briefly gained control of the government. No other American colony, with the possible exception of Rhode Island, experienced such extreme political instability in its founding generation.

In this troubled sanctuary, planters cultivated tobacco on dispersed riverfront plantations. No towns developed. In 1678 Baltimore complained that he could not find fifty houses in a space of thirty miles. Indeed, tobacco affected almost every aspect of daily life. "In Virginia and Maryland," one Calvert explained, "Tobacco, as our Staple, is our all, and indeed leaves no room for anything Else." A steady stream of indentured servants supplied the plantations with dependent laborers, that is, of course, until they were replaced at the end of the seventeenth century by slaves. Regarding the two Chesapeake colonies as a single cultural unit, historian Wesley Frank Craven declared, "the most noticeable feature of their life is the absence of common purpose and goal except as was dictated principally by the requirements of individual interests."

The Colonies of New England

The Pilgrims enjoy almost mythic status in American history. These brave refugees crossed the cold Atlantic in search of religious liberty, signed a democratic compact aboard the *Mayflower*, landed at Plymouth Rock, and gave us our Thanksgiving Day. As with most legends, this one contains only a core of truth.

The Pilgrims were not crusaders who set out to change the world. Rather, they were humble English farmers. Their story began in the early 1600s in Scrooby Manor, a small community located approximately one hundred and fifty miles north of London. Many people living in this area believed that the Church of England retained too many traces of its Catholic origin. To support such a corrupt institution was like winking at the devil. Its very rituals compromised God's true believers, and so, in the early years of the reign of James I, the Scrooby congregation formally left the state church. Like others who followed this logic, they were called "Separatists." The most famous spokesman for this point of view was Robert Browne, a minister who wrote *Reformation without Tarrying for Any* (1583). Since English statute required citizens to attend Anglican

■ *This is the cradle of Peregrine White, the first English child born in New England, who lived to the ripe age of eighty-four years.*

service, the Scrooby Separatists moved to Holland in 1608–1609 rather than compromise their souls.

The Netherlands provided the Separatists with a good home—too good. The members of the little church feared that they were losing their distinct identity; their children were becoming Dutch. In 1617, therefore, a portion of the original Scrooby congregation vowed to sail to America. Included in this group was William Bradford, a wonderfully literate man who wrote *Of Plymouth Plantation*, one of the first and certainly most moving accounts of an early American settlement. Poverty presented the major obstacle to their plans. They petitioned for a land patent from the Virginia Company of London. At the same time, they looked for someone willing to underwrite the staggering costs of colonization. These negotiations went well, or so it seemed. After stopping in England to take on supplies and laborers, the Pilgrims set off for America in 1620 aboard the *Mayflower*, armed with a patent to settle in Virginia and indebted to a group of English investors who were only marginally interested in Separatism.

Hardship soon shattered the voyagers' optimism. Because of an error in navigation, the Pilgrims landed not in Virginia, but in New England. The patent for which they had worked so diligently had no validity in this region. In fact, the Crown had granted New England to another company. Without a patent, the colonists possessed no authorization to form a civil government, a serious matter since some sailors who were not Pilgrims threatened mutiny. To preserve the struggling community from anarchy, forty-one men agreed on November 11 to "covenant and combine our selves together into a civill body politick." In other words, a contract voluntarily drawn up by the settlers themselves became the foundation of government in early Plymouth.

Unfortunately, the Mayflower Compact could not ward off disease and hunger. During the first months in Plymouth, death claimed approximately half of the 102 people who had initially set out from England. Moreover, debts contracted in the mother country severely burdened the new colony. To their credit, the Pilgrims honored their financial obligations, but it took almost twenty years to satisfy the English investors. Without Bradford, whom they elected as governor, the settlers might have allowed adversity to overwhelm them. Through strength of will and self-sacrifice, Bradford persuaded frightened men and women that they could survive in America.

In time, the Pilgrims replicated the humble little farm communities that they had once known in England. They formed Separatists congregations to their liking; the population slowly increased. The settlers experimented with commercial fishing and the fur trade, but these efforts never generated substantial income. Most families relied upon mixed husbandry, grain and livestock. Because Plymouth offered relatively few economic opportunities, it attracted only a trickle of new settlers. In 1691 the colony was absorbed into its larger and more prosperous neighbor, Massachusetts Bay.

The Power of Puritanism

In the early decades of the seventeenth century, an extraordinary spirit of religious reform burst forth in England, and before it had burnt itself out, Puritanism had transformed the face of England and America. Modern historians have difficulty comprehending this powerful force. Some consider the Puritans rather neurotic individuals who condemned liquor and sex, dressed in drab clothes, and minded their neighbors' business.

This crude caricature is based on a fundamental misunderstanding of the actual nature of this broad popular movement. The seventeenth-century Puritans were more like today's radical political reformers, men and women committed to far-reaching institutional change, than Victorian do-gooders. To their enemies, of course, the Puritans were a bother, always pointing out civil and ecclesiastical imperfections. A great many people, however, shared their vision, and not only did they found several American colonies, but also they sparked the English civil war, an event that generated bold new thinking about republican government and popular sovereignty.

The Puritans were products of the Protestant Reformation. They accepted the notion that an omnipotent God predestined some people to salvation and damned others throughout eternity (see chapter 1). But instead of waiting passively for Judgment Day, the Puritans monitored themselves for signs of grace, hints that God had in fact placed them among his "elect." A member of this select group, they argued, would try to live according to Scripture, to battle sin and eradicate corruption. Indeed, this particular theology became the driving engine for reform on this earth.

For the Puritans the logic of everyday life was clear. If the Church of England contained unscriptural elements—clerical vestments, for example —then they must be eliminated. If the pope in Rome was in league with the Antichrist, then Protestant kings had better not form alliances with Catholic states. If God condemned licentiousness and intoxication, then local officials should punish drunks and whores. There was nothing improper about an occasional beer or physical love within marriage, but when sex and drink became ends in themselves, the Puritans thought England's ministers and magistrates should speak out. Persons of this temperament were more combative than the Pilgrims had been. They wanted to purify the Church of England from within, and before the 1630s at least, separatism held little appeal for them.

From the Puritan perspective, the early Stuarts, James I and Charles I, seemed unconcerned about the spiritual state of the nation. James tolerated corruption within his own court; he condoned gross public extravagance. His foreign policy appeased European Catholic powers. At one time, he even tried to marry his son to a Spanish princess. Neither king showed interest in purifying the Anglican church. In fact, Charles assisted the rapid advance of William Laud, a cleric who represented everything the Puritans detested. Laud defended church ceremonies that they found obnoxious. He persecuted Puritan ministers, forcing them either to conform to his theol-

This satire of William Laud and the court bishops who were allowed by the king to rule the Anglican church reflects the Puritans' dissatisfaction with people and practices they wished to cast out of the church. Unlike the Pilgrims, who were willing to leave the church, the Puritans wanted to restore the church to its original, pure form.

Matth. 15.13. Every plant which mine heavenly Father hath not planted should be rooted up.

Of God,   Of Man,   Of the Divell.

Loe, here are three men, standing in degree, The least of these, the greatest ought to be.

The other two, of men and of the Devill, Ought to be rooted out for ere as evill.

ogy or lose their licenses to preach. As long as Parliament met, Puritan voters in the various boroughs and counties throughout the nation elected men sympathetic to their point of view. These outspoken representatives criticized royal policies and hounded Laud. And because of their defiance, Charles decided in 1629 to rule England without Parliament and four years later named Laud archbishop of Canterbury. The last doors of reform slammed shut. The corruption remained.

John Winthrop, the future governor of Massachusetts Bay, was caught up in these events. Little about his background suggested such an auspicious future. He owned a small manor in Suffolk, one that never produced sufficient income to support his growing family. He dabbled in law. But the core of Winthrop's life was his faith in God, a faith so intense that his contemporaries immediately identified him as a Puritan. The Lord, he concluded, was displeased with England. Time for reform was running out. In May 1629 he wrote to his wife, "I am verily perswaded God will bringe some heavye Affliction upon this lande, and that speedylye." He

■ *John Winthrop was a friendly and outgoing person by nature, but he deliberately trained himself from youth to show reserve and sobriety.*

was, however, confident that the Lord would "provide a shelter and a hidinge place for us."

Other Puritans, some of them wealthier and better connected than Winthrop, reached similar conclusions about England's future. They turned their attention to the possibility of establishing a colony in America, and on March 4, 1629, their Massachusetts Bay Company obtained a charter directly from the king. He and his advisors apparently thought the Massachusetts Bay Company was a commercial venture no different from the dozens of other joint-stock companies that had recently sprung into existence.

Winthrop and his associates knew better. On August 26, 1629, twelve of them met secretly and signed the Cambridge Agreement. They pledged to be "ready in our persons and with such of our severall familyes as are to go with us . . . to embark for the said plantation by the first of March next." There was one hitch. The charters of most joint-stock companies designated a specific place where business meetings were to be held. For reasons not entirely clear—a timely bribe is a good guess—the charter of the Massachusetts Bay Company did not contain this standard clause. It could hold meetings anywhere the stockholders, called "freemen," desired, even America, and if they were in America, the king could not easily interfere in their affairs.

"A City on a Hill"

The Winthrop fleet departed England in March 1630. By the end of the first year, almost two thousand people had arrived in Massachusetts Bay, and before the "Great Migration" concluded in the early 1640s, over sixteen thousand men and women had arrived in the new Puritan colony.

A great deal is known about the background of these particular settlers. A large percentage of them originated in an area northeast of London called East Anglia, a region in which Puritan ideas had taken deep root. London, Kent, and the West Country also contributed to the stream of emigrants. In some instances, entire villages were reestablished across the Atlantic. Many Bay Colonists had worked as farmers in the mother country, but a surprisingly large number came from

English industrial centers, like Norwich, where cloth was manufactured for the export trade.

Whatever their backgrounds, they moved to Massachusetts as nuclear families, fathers, mothers, and their dependent children, a form of migration strikingly different from the one that peopled Virginia and Maryland. Moreover, because the settlers had already formed families in England, the colony's sex ratio was more balanced than that found in the Chesapeake colonies. Finally, and perhaps more significantly, once they had arrived in Massachusetts, these men and women survived. Indeed, their life expectancy compares favorably to that of modern Americans. Many factors help explain this phenomenon—clean drinking water and a healthy climate, for example. While the Puritans could not have planned to live longer than did colonists in other parts of the New World, this remarkable accident reduced the emotional shock of long-distance migration.

The first settlers possessed another source of strength and stability. They were bound together by a common sense of purpose. God, they insisted, had formed a special covenant with the people of Massachusetts Bay. On his part, the Lord expected them to live according to Scripture, to reform the church, in other words, to create a "city on a hill" that would stand as a beacon of righteousness for the rest of the Christian world. If they fulfilled their side of the bargain, the settlers could anticipate peace and prosperity. No one, not even the lowliest servant, was excused from this divine covenant, for as Winthrop stated, "Wee must be knitt together in this worke as one man." Even as the first ships were leaving England, John Cotton, a popular Puritan minister, urged the emigrants to go forth "with a publicke spirit, looking not on your owne things onely, but also on the things of others." Many people throughout the ages have espoused such communal rhetoric, but these particular men and women went about the business of forming a new colony as if they truly intended to transform a religious vision into social reality.

In ecclesiastical affairs the colonists proceeded by what one of the founders called "experimental foot-steps." They arrived in Massachusetts Bay without a precise plan for their church. They refused to separate formally from the Church of England. After all, what was the point of reforming an institution if the reformers were no longer part of it. The rituals and ceremonies enforced by Laud had no place in Massachusetts. The colonists gradually came to accept a form of church government known as Congregationalism. Under this system, each congregation was independent of outside interference. The people (the "saints") *were* the church. They pledged as a body to uphold God's law. In the Salem Church, for example, the members covenanted "with the Lord and with one another and do bind ourselves in the presence of God to walk together in all his ways." In Congregational churches, full members —men and women who testified that they were among the Lord's "elect"—selected a minister, punished errant members, and determined matters of theology. There were limits on Congregational autonomy, to be sure, and colonial magistrates sometimes ferreted out heretical beliefs. But perhaps because of the homogeneity of the colony's population, this loose structure held together for more than a century.

In creating a civil government, the Bay Colonists faced a particularly difficult challenge. Their charter allowed the investors in a joint-stock company to set up a business organization. When the settlers arrived in America, however, company leaders—men like Winthrop—moved quickly to transform the commercial structure into a colonial government. An early step in this direction took place on May 18, 1631, when the category of "freeman" was extended to all adult males who had become members of a Congregational church. This decision greatly expanded the franchise of Massachusetts Bay, and historians estimate that during the 1630s at least 40 percent of the colony's adult males could vote in elections. While this percentage may seem low by modern or even Jacksonian standards, it was higher than anything the emigrants would have known in the mother country. The freemen voted annually for a governor, a group of magistrates called the Court of Assistants, and after 1634, deputies who represented the interests of the individual towns. Even military officers were elected in Massachusetts Bay.

Two popular misconceptions about this government should be dispelled. It was neither a democracy nor a theocracy. The magistrates elected in Massachusetts did not believe that they represented the voters, much less the whole populace. They ruled in the name of the electorate; but their responsibility as rulers was to God. In 1638 Winthrop warned against overly democratic forms, since "the best part [of the people] is always the least and of the best part [,] the wiser is always the least." And second, the Congregational ministers possessed no formal political authority in Massachusetts Bay. They could not even hold civil office, and it was not unusual for the voters to ignore the recommendations of a respected minister like John Cotton.

In this colony the town, rather than the county, became the center of public life. Groups of men and women voluntarily covenanted together to live by certain rules. The community constructed a meetinghouse where church services and town meetings were held, formed a village government, passed bylaws regulating agricultural practices, and "warned out" those individuals who refused to accept local ordinances. Each townsman received land sufficient to build a house and to support a family. The house lots were clustered around the meetinghouse; the fields were located on the village perimeter. The land was given free.

No one was expected to pay quitrents or other feudal dues. Villagers were obliged, however, to contribute to the minister's salary, pay local and colony taxes, and serve in the town militia.

Dealing with Dissent

The settlers of Massachusetts Bay managed to live in peace. This was a remarkable achievement considering the chronic instability that plagued other colonies at this time. The Bay Colonists disagreed over many issues, sometimes vociferously; whole towns disputed with neighboring villages over common boundaries. But the people inevitably relied upon the courts to mediate differences. They believed in a rule of law, and in 1648 the colonial legislature, called the General Court, drew up the *Lawes and Liberties*, the first alphabetized code of law printed in English. This is a document of fundamental importance in American constitutional history. In clear prose, it explained to the colonists their rights and responsibilities as citizens of the commonwealth. The code engendered public trust in government and discouraged magistrates from the arbitrary exercise of authority.

■ *In this 1630 view of Plymouth we see that the meetinghouse (center left) was the focus of community life. Around the meetinghouse, house lots were set aside for each townsman. The fields were located on the outside perimeter of the village.*

The most serious challenges to Puritan orthodoxy in Massachusetts Bay came from two remarkable individuals. The first, Roger Williams, arrived in 1631 and immediately attracted a body of loyal followers. Indeed, everyone seems to have liked Williams as a person.

It was Williams' ideas that created controversy. He preached extreme separatism. The Bay Colonists, he exclaimed, were impure in the sight of the Lord so long as they remained even nominal members of the Church of England. Moreover, he questioned the validity of the colony's charter since the king had not first purchased the land from the Indians, a view that threatened the integrity of the entire colonial experiment. Williams also insisted that the civil rulers of Massachusetts had no business punishing settlers for their religious beliefs. It was God's responsibility, not man's, to monitor people's consciences. The Bay magistrates were prepared neither to tolerate heresy nor to accede to Williams' other demands, and in 1636, after attempts to reach a compromise had failed, they banished him from the colony. Williams worked out the logic of his ideas in Providence, a village he founded in what would become Rhode Island.

The magistrates of Massachusetts Bay believed that Anne Hutchinson posed an even graver threat to the peace of the commonwealth. This extremely intelligent woman followed John Cotton to the New World in 1634. Even contemporaries found her religious ideas, usually termed Antinomianism, somewhat confusing. Whatever her thoughts, Hutchinson shared them with other Bostonians, many of them women. Her outspoken views scandalized orthodox leaders of church and state. She suggested that some respected ministers in the colony had lost touch with the "Holy Spirit" and were preaching a doctrine in the Congregational churches that was little better than that of Archbishop Laud. When authorities demanded that she explain her unusual opinions, she announced that she experienced divine inspiration independently of either the Bible or the clergy. In other words, Hutchinson's teachings could not be tested by Scripture, a position that seemed dangerously subjective. Indeed, Hutchinson's theology called the very foundation of Massachusetts Bay into question. Without clear, external standards, one person's truth was as valid as that of anyone else, and from Winthrop's

Puritans often persecuted Quakers. Here an unfortunate Quaker has been tied to a cart and whipped out of town.

perspective, Hutchinson's teachings invited civil and religious anarchy.

When she described Congregational ministers —some of them the leading divines of Boston—as unconverted men, the General Court intervened. For two days in 1637 the ministers and magistrates of Massachusetts Bay cross-examined Hutchinson, but in this intense theological debate, she more than held her own. She knew as much about the Bible as her inquisitors did. She defied them to demonstrate the heresy of her ideas. Just when it appeared that Hutchinson had outmaneuvered—indeed, thoroughly embarrassed—her adversaries, she made a slip that led to her undoing. She stated that what she knew of God came "by an immediate revelation." She had heard a voice. This heretical declaration challenged the authority of the Bay rulers, and they were relieved to exile Hutchinson and her followers to Rhode Island.

Breaking Away

Massachusetts Bay spawned four new colonies, three of which survived to the American Revolution. New Hampshire became a separate colony

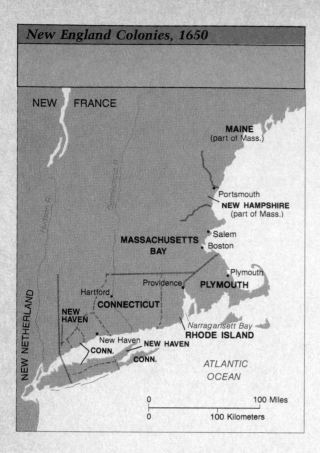

New England Colonies, 1650

NEW FRANCE

MAINE (part of Mass.)

Portsmouth
NEW HAMPSHIRE (part of Mass.)

MASSACHUSETTS BAY

Salem
Boston

Plymouth

Providence
PLYMOUTH

Hartford

CONNECTICUT

NEW HAVEN

Narragansett Bay
RHODE ISLAND

New Haven
NEW HAVEN
CONN.
CONN.

ATLANTIC OCEAN

NEW NETHERLAND

Connecticut R.

Hudson R.

0   100 Miles
0   100 Kilometers

Island Sound. These emigrants, many of whom had come from London, lived briefly in Massachusetts Bay, but they insisted upon forming a Puritan commonwealth of their own, one that established a closer relationship between church and state than the Bay colonists had allowed. The New Haven colony never prospered, and in 1662 it was absorbed into Connecticut.

Rhode Island experienced a wholly different history. From the beginning, it was populated by exiles and troublemakers, and according to one Dutch visitor, Rhode Island was "the receptacle of all sorts of riff-raff people . . . All the cranks of New-England retire thither." This description, of course, was an exaggeration. Roger Williams founded Providence in 1636; two years later Anne Hutchinson took her followers to Portsmouth. Other groups settled around Narragansett Bay. Not surprisingly, these men and women appreciated the need for toleration. No one was persecuted in Rhode Island for his or her religious beliefs.

One might have thought that these separate Rhode Island communities would cooperate for the common good. That did not occur. Villagers fought over land and schemed with outside speculators to divide the tiny colony into even smaller pieces. In 1644 Parliament issued a patent for the "Providence Plantations," and in 1663 the Rhode Islanders obtained a royal charter. These successes did not calm political turmoil. For most of the seventeenth century, colonywide government existed in name only. Despite their constant bickering, however, the settlers of Rhode Island built up a profitable commerce in agricultural goods. By the end of the century, almost half of the colony's people were Quakers.

in 1677. Its population grew very slowly, and for much of the colonial period, New Hampshire remained economically dependent upon Massachusetts, its neighbor to the south.

Far more people were drawn to the fertile lands of the Connecticut River Valley. In 1636 settlers founded the villages of Hartford, Windsor, and Wethersfield. No one forced these men and women to leave Massachusetts, and in their new surroundings, they created a society that looked much like the one they had known in the Bay Colony. Through his writings, Thomas Hooker, Connecticut's most prominent minister, helped all New Englanders define Congregational church polity. Puritans on both sides of the Atlantic read Hooker's beautifully crafted works. In 1639 representatives from the Connecticut towns passed the Fundamental Orders, a blueprint for civil government, and in 1662 Charles II awarded the colony a charter of its own.

In 1638 another group, led by Theophilus Eaton and the Reverend John Davenport, settled New Haven and several adjoining towns along Long

Diversity in the Middle Colonies

New York, New Jersey, Pennsylvania, and Delaware were settled for quite different reasons. William Penn, for example, envisioned a Quaker sanctuary; the Duke of York worried chiefly about his own income. Despite the founders' intentions, however, some common characteristics emerged. Each colony developed a strikingly heterogeneous population, men and women of different ethnic and religious backgrounds. This cultural diversity became a major influence upon the economic, political, and ecclesiastical institutions of the Middle Colonies. The raucous, partisan public life of the Middle Colonies foreshadowed later American society.

English Conquer a Dutch Colony

By the early decades of the seventeenth century, the Dutch had established themselves as Europe's most aggressive traders. Holland—a small, loosely federated nation—possessed the world's largest merchant fleet. Its ships vied for the commerce of Asia, Africa, and America. Dutch rivalry with Spain, a fading though still formidable power, was in large measure responsible for the settlement of New Netherland. While searching for the elusive Northwest Passage, Henry Hudson, an English explorer employed by a Dutch company, sailed up the river that bears his name in 1609. Further voyages led to the establishment of trading posts in New Netherland, although permanent settlement did not occur until 1624. The area also seemed an excellent base from which to attack Spain's colonies in the New World.

The directors of the Dutch West Indies Company sponsored two small outposts, Fort Orange (Albany) located well up the Hudson River and New Amsterdam (New York City) on Manhattan Island. The first Dutch settlers were not actually colonists. Rather, they were salaried employees, and their superiors in Holland expected them to spend most of their time gathering animal furs. They did not receive land for their troubles. Needless to say, this arrangement attracted relatively few Dutch immigrants.

The colony's population may have been small, only 270 in 1628, but it contained an extraordinary ethnic mix. One visitor to New Amsterdam in 1644 maintained that he had heard "eighteen different languages" spoken in the city. Even if this report was exaggerated, there is no doubt that the Dutch colony drew Finns, Germans, and Swedes. By the 1640s a sizable community of free blacks (probably former slaves who had gained their freedom through self-purchase) had developed in New Amsterdam, adding African tongues to the hodgepodge of languages. The colony's culture was further fragmented by New England Puritans who left Massachusetts and Connecticut to stake out farms on Long Island.

New Netherland lacked capable leadership. The company sent a number of director-generals to oversee judicial and political affairs. Without exception, these men were temperamentally unsuited to govern an American colony. They adopted autocratic procedures, lined their own pockets, and in one case (William Kieft, 1638–1647), blundered into a war that needlessly killed scores of Indians and settlers. The company made no provision for an elected assembly. As much as they were able, the scattered inhabitants living along the Hudson River ignored company directives. They felt no loyalty to the trading company that had treated them so shabbily. Long Island

■ *New Amsterdam as it appeared about 1640. This colony, which was founded as a trading outpost by the Dutch West Indies Company, was to be characterized by a diverse ethnic mix and a succession of inept governors.*

NIEUW AMSTERDAM
op t Eylant Manhattans.

A. Het Fort B. de Kerck C. de Wintmolen D. defe Vlagge wert op gehaelt als daer Schepen in de Haven komen. E. t goevangen huys F. de N. Generaels huys G. t Gerecht H. de Kaeck I. Compagnies Pachuys K. Stadts Herberch

Puritans complained bitterly about the absence of representative institutions. The Dutch system has aptly been described as "unstable pluralism."

In August 1664 the Dutch lost their tenuous hold on New Netherland. The English Crown, eager to score an easy victory over a commercial rival, dispatched a fleet of warships to New Amsterdam. The commander of this force, Colonel Richard Nicolls, ordered the colonists to surrender. The last director-general, a colorful character named Peter Stuyvesant (1647–1664), rushed wildly about the city urging the settlers to resist the English. But no one obeyed. Even the Dutch remained deaf to Stuyvesant's appeals. They accepted the Articles of Capitulation, a generous agreement that allowed Dutch nationals to remain in the province and to retain their property.

Charles II had already granted his brother, James, the Duke of York a charter for the newly captured territory and much else besides. The duke became absolute proprietor over Maine, Martha's Vineyard, Nantucket, Long Island, and the rest of the New York all the way to Delaware Bay. The king perhaps wanted to encircle New England's potentially disloyal Puritan population, but whatever his aims may have been, he created a bureaucrat's nightmare.

During the English civil war, the duke acquired a thorough aversion to representative assemblies. After all, Parliament had executed the duke's father, Charles I, and raised up Oliver Cromwell. The new proprietor had no intention of letting participatory government take root in New York. "I cannot *but* suspect," the duke announced, that an assembly "would be of dangerous consequence." The Long Islanders felt betrayed. In part to appease these outspoken critics, Nicolls—now the colony's governor—drew up a legal code known as the Duke's Laws. It guaranteed religious toleration and created local governments.

There was no provision, however, for an elected assembly. When the duke's officers attempted to collect taxes on Long Island, the people protested that "they are inslav'd under an Arbitrary Power." The Dutch kept silent. For several decades they remained a large, unassimilated ethnic group. They continued to speak their own language, worship in their own churches (Dutch Reformed Calvinist), and eye their English neighbors with suspicion. In fact, the colony seemed little different from what it had been under the Dutch West India Company, a loose collection of independent communities ruled by an ineffectual central government.

Divisions in New Jersey

Only three months after receiving a charter for New York, the duke made a terrible blunder—something this stubborn, humorless man was quite prone to do. He awarded the land lying between the Hudson and Delaware Rivers to two courtiers, John, Lord Berkeley and Sir George Carteret. This colony was named New Jersey in honor of Carteret's birthplace, the Isle of Jersey in the English Channel. When Nicolls heard what the duke had done, he exploded. In his estimation this region contained the "most improveable" land in all New York, and to give it away so casually seemed the height of folly.

The duke's impulsive act bred confusion. Soon it was not clear who owned what in New Jersey. Before Nicolls had learned of James' decision, the governor allowed migrants from New England to take up farms west of the Hudson River. He promised these settlers an opportunity to establish an elected assembly, a headright system, and liberty of conscience. In exchange for these privileges, Nicolls asked only that they pay a small annual quitrent to the duke. The proprietors, Berkeley and Carteret, recruited colonists on similar terms. They assumed, of course, that they would receive the rent money.

The result was chaos. Some colonists insisted that Nicolls had authorized their assembly. Others, equally insistent, claimed that Berkeley and Carteret had done so. Both sides were wrong. Neither the proprietors nor Nicolls possessed any legal right whatsoever to set up a colonial government. James could transfer land to favorite courtiers, but no matter how many times the land changed hands, the government remained his personal responsibility. Knowledge of the law failed to quiet the controversy. Through it all, the duke showed not the slightest interest in the peace and welfare of the people of New Jersey.

Berkeley grew tired of the venture. It generated headaches rather than quitrents, and in 1674 he sold his proprietary rights to a group of surprisingly quarrelsome Quakers. The sale necessitated the division of the colony into two separate

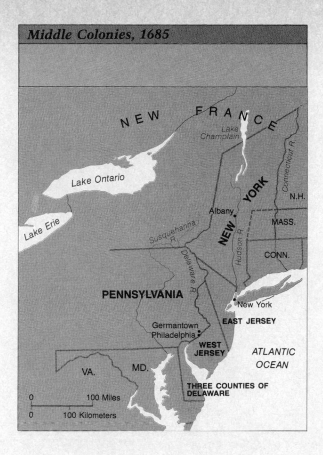

Middle Colonies, 1685

governments known as East and West Jersey. Neither half prospered. Carteret and his heirs tried unsuccessfully to turn a profit in East Jersey. In 1677 the Quaker proprietors of West Jersey issued a remarkable democratic plan of government, the Laws, Concessions, and Agreements. But they fought among themselves with such intensity that not even William Penn could bring tranquillity to their affairs. Penn wisely turned his attention to the unclaimed territory across the Delaware River. The West Jersey proprietors went bankrupt, and in 1702 the Crown mercifully reunited the two Jerseys into a single royal colony.

In 1700 the population of New Jersey stood at approximately fourteen thousand. Largely because it lacked a good deep-water harbor, the colony never developed a commercial center to rival New York City or Philadelphia. Its residents lived on scattered, often isolated farms; villages of more than a few hundred people were rare. Visitors commented upon the diversity of the settlers. There were colonists from almost every European nation. Congregationalists, Presbyterians, Quakers, Baptists, Anabaptists, and Anglicans somehow managed to live together peacefully in New Jersey.

Quaker Colony

The founding of Pennsylvania occurred because of the efforts of the Quakers. Believers in an extreme form of Antinomianism, the Quakers saw no need for a learned ministry since one person's interpretation of Scripture was as valid as anyone else's. Led first by James Nayler, this radical religious group gained its name from the derogatory term that English civil authorities used to describe those who "tremble at the word of the Lord." The name persisted even though the Quakers preferred being called Professors of the Light or Children of the Light.

By the time the Stuarts were restored to the throne in 1660, the Quakers had developed strong popular support throughout England. One reason for their success was George Fox (1624–1691), a tireless spokesman for his faith. Fox told common men and women that Christ was "present in the soul of every man." In fact, if they would only look, they would discover that they possessed a powerful, consoling "Inner Light." This was a wonderfully liberating message, especially for persons of lower-class origin. With the Lord's personal assistance, they could attain greater spiritual perfection on this earth. Gone was the stigma of original sin; discarded was the notion of eternal predestination. Everyone could be saved.

Quakers practiced humility. They wore simple clothes and employed old-fashioned forms of address that set them apart from their neighbors. Quakers (or Friends as they were sometimes called) refused to honor worldly position and accomplishment or to swear oaths in courts of law. They were also pacifists. According to Fox, all persons were equal in the sight of the Lord, a belief that annoyed people of rank and achievement. Moreover, the Quakers never kept their thoughts to themselves. They preached conversion constantly, spreading the light throughout England, Ireland, and America. In many places the "publishers of Truth" wore out their welcome. English authorities harassed the Quakers. Thousands were jailed. The persecution reached

One of the liberating aspects of the Quaker religion was the idea that the "Inner Light" of Christ was present in everyone. By implication, all men and women were equal before the lord and required no intermediaries. This belief was reflected in the Quaker meeting, in which individuals rose to speak as the spirit moved them, without the formal guidance of a minister conducting a service.

into several American colonies. In Massachusetts Bay, for example, Puritan magistrates ordered several Friends put to death. Such measures proved counterproductive, for persecution only inspired the Quakers to redouble their efforts.

Penn's "Holy Experiment"

William Penn lived according to the Inner Light, a commitment that led eventually to the founding of Pennsylvania. Penn possessed a curiously complex personality. He was an athletic person who threw himself into intellectual pursuits. He was a bold visionary capable of making pragmatic decisions. He came from an aristocratic family and yet spent his entire adult life involved with a religious movement associated with the lower class.

Penn's father had served with some distinction in the English navy. Through luck and skill, he acquired a considerable estate in Ireland, and as a wealthy landowner, he naturally hoped his son would be a favorite at the Stuart court. He befriended the king, the Duke of York, and several other powerful Restoration figures. But William disappointed his father. He was expelled from

Oxford University for holding unorthodox religious views. Not even a grand tour through Europe could dissuade the young man from joining the Society of Friends. His political connections and driving intellect quickly propelled him to a position of prominence within the struggling sect. Penn wrote at least forty-two books testifying to his deep attachment to Quaker principles. Even two years in an English jail could not weaken his faith.

Precisely when Penn's thoughts turned to America is not known. He was briefly involved with the West Jersey proprietorship. This venture may have suggested the possibility of an even larger enterprise. In any case, Penn negotiated in 1681 one of the more impressive land deals in the history of American real estate. Charles II awarded Penn a charter making him the sole proprietor of a vast area called Pennsylvania (literally, Penn's woods). The name embarrassed the modest Penn, but he knew better than to look the royal gift horse in the mouth.

Why the king bestowed such generosity upon a leading Quaker who had recently been released from prison remains a mystery. Perhaps Charles wanted to repay an old debt to Penn's father. The monarch may have regarded the colony as a means of ridding England of its troublesome Quaker population, or quite simply, he may have liked Penn. In 1682 the new proprietor purchased from the Duke of York the so-called Three Lower Counties that eventually became Delaware. This astute move guaranteed that Pennsylvania would have open access to the Atlantic and determined even before Philadelphia had been established that it would become a great commercial center.

Penn lost no time in launching his "Holy Experiment." In 1682 he set forth his ideas in an unusual document known as the Frame of Government. The charter gave Penn the right to create any form of government he desired, and his imagination ran wild. His plan blended traditional notions about the privileges of a landed aristocracy with quite daring concepts of personal liberty. Penn guaranteed that settlers would enjoy among other things liberty of conscience, freedom from persecution, no taxation without representation, and due process of law.

In designing his government, Penn drew heavily upon the writings of James Harrington (1611–1677). This English political philosopher argued that no government could ever be stable unless it reflected the actual distribution of landed property within society. Both the rich and poor had to have a voice in political affairs; neither should be able to overrule the legitimate interests of the other class. The Frame of Government envisioned a governor appointed by the proprietor, a seventy-two-member Provincial Council responsible for initiating legislation, and a two hundred-person Assembly that could accept or reject the bills presented to it. Penn apparently thought that the Council would be filled by the colony's richest landholders, or in the words of the Frame, "persons of most note for their wisdom, virtue and ability." The governor and Council were charged with the routine administration of justice. The smaller landowners spoke through the Assembly. It was a fanciful, clumsy structure, and in America the entire edifice crumbled under its own weight.

Penn promoted his colony aggressively throughout England, Ireland, and Germany. He had no choice. His only source of revenue was the sale of land and the collection of quitrents. Penn commissioned pamphlets in several languages extolling the quality of Pennsylvania's rich farmland. The response was overwhelming. People

■ *William Penn brought great verve and determination to the movement when he became a Quaker.*

poured into Philadelphia and the surrounding area. In 1685 alone eight thousand emigrants arrived. Most of these settlers were Irish, Welsh, and English Quakers, and they generally moved to America as families. But Penn opened the door to men and women of all nations. He asserted that the people of Pennsylvania "are a collection of divers nations in Europe, as French, Dutch, Germans, Swedes, Danes, Finns, Scotch, Irish, and English."

The settlers were by no means all Quakers. The founder of Germantown, Francis Daniel Pastorius, called the vessel that brought him to the New World a "Noah's Ark" of religions, and within his own household, there were servants who subscribed "to the Roman [Catholic], to the Lutheran, to the Calvinistic, to the Anabaptist, and to the Anglican church, and only one Quaker." Ethnic and religious diversity were crucial in the development of Pennsylvania's public institutions, and its politics took on a quarrelsome quality absent in more homogeneous colonies such as Virginia and Massachusetts.

Penn himself emigrated to America in 1682. His stay, however, was unexpectedly short and unhappy. The Council and Assembly—reduced now to more manageable size—fought over the right to initiate legislation. Wealthy Quaker merchants, most of them residents of Philadelphia, dominated the Council. By contrast, the Assembly included men from rural settlements and the Three Lower Counties who showed no concern for the "Holy Experiment." They demanded traditional parliamentary privileges, for which Penn accused them of being too "governmentish." The colonists generally refused to pay quitrents. Some popular political leaders even suggested that the proprietor played favorites in the distribution of land. The Baltimore family added to Penn's problems when it announced in an English court of law that much of Pennsylvania actually lay in Maryland. In 1684, to defend his charter against Baltimore's attack, Penn returned to London, leaving colonial affairs in the hands of men who had little incentive to preserve proprietary authority.

Penn did not see his colony again until 1699. During his enforced absence much had changed. The settlement had prospered. Its agricultural products, especially its excellent wheat, were in demand throughout the Atlantic world. Despite this economic success, however, the population remained deeply divided. Even the Quakers had briefly split into hostile factions. Penn's hand-picked governors had failed to win general support for the proprietor's policies, and one of them exclaimed in anger that each Quaker "*prays* for his neighbor on First Days and then *preys* on him the other six." As the seventeenth century closed, few colonists still shared the founder's desire to create a godly, paternalistic society.

In 1701 legal challenges in England again forced Penn to depart for the mother country. Just before he sailed, Penn signed the Charter of Liberties, a new frame of government that established a unicameral or one-house legislature (the only one in colonial America) and gave the representatives the right to initiate bills. Penn also allowed the Assembly to conduct its business without proprietary interference. The charter also provided for the political separation of the Three Lower Counties (Delaware) from Pennsylvania, something people living in this area had demanded for years. This hastily drafted document served as Pennsylvania's constitution until the American Revolution.

His experience in America must have depressed Penn, now both old and sick. In England Penn was imprisoned for debts incurred by dishonest colonial agents, and in 1718 Pennsylvania's founder died a broken man.

Settling the Carolinas

In some ways Carolina society looked very much like the one that had developed in Virginia and Maryland. In both areas white planters forced unfree laborers to produce staple crops for a world market. But such superficial similarities masked substantial regional differences. In fact, "the South"—certainly the fabled solid South of the early nineteenth century—did not exist during the colonial period. The Carolinas, joined at a much later date by Georgia (see chapter 4), stood apart from their northern neighbors. As a historian of colonial Carolina explained, "the southern colonies were never a cohesive section in the same way that New England was. The great diversity of population groups . . . discouraged southern sectionalism."

Proprietors of the Carolinas

Carolina was a product of the Restoration of the Stuarts to the English throne. Court favorites who had followed the Stuarts into exile during the civil war demanded tangible rewards for their loyalty. New York and New Jersey were obvious plums. So too was Carolina. Sir John Colleton, a successful planter recently returned to England from Barbados, organized a group of eight powerful courtiers who styled themselves the True and Absolute Lords Proprietors of Carolina. On March 24, 1663, the king granted these proprietors a charter to the vast territory between Virginia and Florida and running west as far as the "South Seas."

Like so many Englishmen before them, the eight proprietors thought of America in terms of instant wealth. They never intended to put their own funds at risk in order to generate profits. They reasoned that with the proper incentives—a generous land policy, for example—they could attract men and women from established American colonies and thus avoid the great expense of transporting settlers across the Atlantic. The proprietors promised settlers a representative assembly, liberty of conscience, and a liberal headright system. In exchange for these privileges, they demanded only a small annual quitrent.

The Carolina proprietors divided their grant into three distinct jurisdictions, anticipating no doubt that these areas would become the centers of settlement. Albemarle abutted upon Virginia. As the earlier, ill-fated Roanoke colonists had discovered, the region lacked a good deep-water port, but it attracted a number of dissatisfied Virginians who drifted south in search of fresh land. Further south, the mouth of the Cape Fear River seemed a likely site for development. And third, within the present state of South Carolina, the Port Royal region contained a maze of fertile islands and meandering tidal streams.

Colleton and his associates waited for the money to roll in, but to their dismay, no one seemed particularly interested in moving to the Carolina frontier. A tiny settlement at Port Royal failed. One group of New Englanders briefly considered taking up land in the Cape Fear area, but these people were so disappointed by what they saw that they departed, leaving behind only a sign that "tended not only to the disparagement of the Land . . . but also to the great discouragement of all those that should hereafter come into these parts to settle." By this time a majority of the surviving proprietors had given up on Carolina.

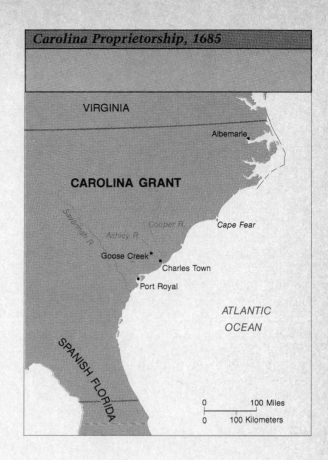

Carolina Proprietorship, 1685

The Barbadian Connection

Anthony Ashley Cooper, later earl of Shaftesbury, was the exception. In 1669 he persuaded the remaining proprietors to invest their own capital in the colony. Without such financial support, Ashley recognized, the project would surely fail. Once he received sufficient funds, this energetic organizer dispatched three hundred English colonists to Port Royal under the command of Joseph West. The fleet put in briefly at Barbados to pick up additional recruits, and in March 1670, after being punished by Atlantic gales that destroyed one ship, the expedition arrived at its destination. Only one hundred people were still alive. The earliest settlers clustered along the Ashley River. Later the colony's administrative center, Charles Town (it did not become Charleston until 1783), was established at the junction of the Ashley and Cooper rivers.

Ashley also wanted to bring order to the new society. With assistance from John Locke, the famous English philosopher (1632–1704), Ashley devised the Fundamental Constitutions of Carolina. Like Penn, Ashley had been influenced by the writings of Harrington. The constitutions created a local aristocracy consisting of proprietors and lesser nobles called landgraves and cassiques, terms as inappropriate to the realities of the New World as was the idea of creating an hereditary landed elite. Persons who purchased vast tracts of land automatically received a title and the right to sit in the Council of Nobles, a body designed to administer justice, oversee civil affairs, and initiate legislation. A parliament in which smaller landowners had a voice could accept or reject bills drafted by the council. The very poor were excluded from political life altogether. Ashley thought his scheme mainintained the proper "Balance of Government" between aristocracy and democracy, a concept central to Harrington's philosophy. Not surprisingly, the Constitutions had little impact upon the actual structure of government. It reaffirmed religious toleration,

Chronology

1607 First English settlers arrive at Jamestown

1608–1609 Scrooby Congregation (Pilgrims) leaves England for Holland

1609–1611 "Starving time" in Virginia threatens survival of the colonists

1619 Virginia assembly, called House of Burgesses, meets for the first time

1620 Pilgrims sign the Mayflower Compact

1622 Surprise attack by local Indians devastates Virginia

1624 Dutch investors create permanent settlements along Hudson River
James I, king of England, dissolves Virginia Company

1625 Charles I ascends English throne

1630 John Winthrop transfers Massachusetts Bay charter to New England

1634 Colony of Maryland is founded

1636 Harvard College established

1638 Anne Hutchinson exiled to Rhode Island
Theophilus Eaton and John Davenport lead settlers to New Haven Colony

1639 Connecticut towns accept Fundamental Orders

1649 Charles I executed during English civil war

1660 Stuarts are restored to the English throne

1663 Rhode Island obtains royal charter
Proprietors receive charter for Carolina

1664 English force conquers New Netherland

1677 New Hampshire becomes a royal colony

1681 William Penn granted patent for his "Holy Experiment"

---

their sons and daughters with sufficient land to maintain social status, and as the crisis intensified, Barbadians looked to Carolina for relief.

These migrants, many of whom were quite rich, traveled to Carolina both as individuals and family groups. Some even brought gangs of slaves with them to the American mainland. The Barbadians carved out plantations on the tributaries of the Cooper River and established themselves immediately as the colony's most powerful political faction. "So it was," writes historian Richard Dunn, "that these Caribbean pioneers helped to create on the North American coast a slave-based plantation society closer in temper to the islands they fled from than to any other mainland English settlement."

Much of the planters' time was taken up with the search for a profitable crop. The early settlers experimented with a number of plants: tobacco, cotton, silk, and grapes. The most successful items turned out to be beef, furs, and naval stores (especially tar used to maintain ocean vessels). By the 1680s some Carolinians had built up great herds of cattle, seven or eight hundred head in some cases. Indian traders brought back thousands of deerskins from the interior—often the traders returned with Indian slaves as well—which together with tar and turpentine enjoyed a good market. It was not until the 1690s that the planters came to appreciate fully the value of rice, but once they had done so, it quickly became the colony's main staple.

Proprietary Carolina was in a constant political uproar. Factions vied for special privilege. The Barbadian settlers, known locally as the "Goose Creek Men," resisted the proprietors' policies at every turn. A large community of French Huguenots located in Craven County distrusted the Barbadians. The proprietors—an ineffectual group following the death of Shaftesbury—appointed a series of utterly incompetent governors who only made things worse. One visitor observed that "the Inhabitants of Carolina should be as free from Oppression as any [people] in the Universe . . . if their own Differences amongst themselves do not occasion the contrary." By the end of the century, the Commons House of Assembly had assumed the right to initiate legislation. In 1719 the colonists overthrew the last proprietary governor, and in 1729 the king created separate royal governments for North and South Carolina.

but since so few men bought manors, the Council of Nobles remained a paper dream.

Before 1680 almost half the men and women who settled in the Port Royal area came from Barbados. This small Caribbean island, which produced an annual fortune in sugar, depended upon slave labor. By the third quarter of the seventeenth century, Barbados had become overpopulated. Wealthy families could not provide

Seventeenth-Century Legacy

The seventeenth-century English colonies had little in common beyond their allegiance to the king. A contemporary visitor could find along the Atlantic coast a spectrum of settlements, one that ranged from the quasi-feudal hierarchy of Carolina to the visionary paternalism of Pennsylvania to the Puritan commonwealth of Massachusetts Bay. The diversity of English colonization needs to be emphasized precisely because it is so easy to overlook. Even though the colonists eventually banded together and fought for independence and established a federal government, persistent differences separated New Englanders from Virginians, Pennsylvanians from Carolinians. Indeed, even on the eve of the American Revolution, John Adams expressed amazement at how little the members of the Continental Congress had in common. "Fifty gentlemen," Adams reported, "meeting together all strangers [who] are not acquainted with each other's languages, ideas, views, [or] designs." Such differences had their roots in the first decades of settlement.

Recommended Reading

The most detailed investigation of the founding of the early American colonies remains Charles M. Andrews, *The Colonial Period of American History*, 4 vols. (1934–1938). The best analysis of the early settlement of Virginia is Edmund S. Morgan, *American Slavery, American Freedom* (1975). There are many excellent studies of early New England, but Kenneth A. Lockridge, *A New England Town: The First Hundred Years* (1970) and E. S. Morgan, *Puritan Dilemma: The Story of John Winthrop* (1958), provide fine introductions to this complex and fascinating topic. Perhaps the best single book on the political history of early Pennsylvania is Gary B. Nash, *Quakers and Politics: Pennsylvania, 1681–1726* (1968). A comprehensive general description of the early Carolina settlements can be found in Wesley F. Craven, *The Southern Colonies in the Seventeenth Century, 1607–1689* (1949).

Additional Bibliography

Some books that contribute to an understanding of the English background of colonization are J. Thirsk, ed., *The Agrarian History of England and Wales: IV 1500–1640* (1967); Carl Bridenbaugh, *Vexed and Troubled Englishmen, 1590–1642* (1968); Peter Clark and Paul Slack, *English Towns in Transition 1500–1700* (1976);

and David Ogg, *England in the Reign of Charles II* (1956). T. H. Breen, *Puritans and Adventurers: Change and Persistence in Early America* (1980), specifically explores the problem of cultural transfer. Also helpful is David Grayson Allen, *In English Ways: The Movement of Societies and the Transferal of English Local Law and Custom* (1981).

On the founding of England's mainland colonies, see J. Franklin Jameson, ed., *Original Narratives of Early American History*. Two collections of interpretative essays provide valuable insights: James Morton Smith, ed., *Seventeenth-Century America, Essays in Colonial History* (1959) and Ray Allen Billington, ed., *The Reinterpretation of Early American History* (1966).

The most exciting account of the founding of Jamestown is John Smith, *Travels and Works*, edited by Edward Arber (2 vols., 1910). On Roanoke, see D. B. Quinn, ed., *The Roanoke Voyages, 1584–1590* (1967). For a masterful analysis of current research see Thad W. Tate and David L. Ammerman, eds., *The Chesapeake in the Seventeenth Century* (1979). New insights are offered in David B. Quinn, ed., *Early Maryland in a Wider World* (1982) and in Gloria L. Main, *Tobacco Colony, Life in Early Maryland, 1650–1720* (1982).

Two of colonial New England's most capable historians were William Bradford and John Winthrop. See especially Bradford's *Of Plymouth Plantation*, edited by Samuel E. Morison (1952) and Winthrop's "History of New England," edited by James Kendall Hosmer (2 vols., 1908). On Puritan ideas, see Perry Miller, *New England Mind: From Colony to Province* (1953) and *Errand into the Wilderness* (1956). See also Stephen Foster, *Their Solitary Way* (1971); George D. Langdon, Jr., *Pilgrim Colony* (1966); T. H. Breen, *Character of the Good Ruler* (1970); David T. Konig, *Law and Society in Puritan Massachusetts* (1979); John Demos, *A Little Commonwealth: Family Life in Plymouth Colony* (1970); Philip Greven Jr., *Four Generations: Population, Land, and Family in Colonial Andover* (1970); and Darrett Rutman, *Winthrop's Boston: A Portrait of a Puritan Town, 1630–1649* (1965). On Rhode Island, see Sydney V. James, *Colonial Rhode Island* (1975) and Carl Bridenbaugh, *Fat Mutton and Liberty of Conscience* (1974).

The best accounts of New York and the transition from Dutch to English rule are Michael Kammen, *Colonial New York* (1975) and Robert C. Ritchie, *The Duke's Province* (1977). To understand the Quaker movement, read Frederick B. Tolles, *Quakers and the Atlantic Culture* (1960). William Penn's life and political thought are the subject of Mary M. Dunn, *William Penn, Politics and Conscience* (1967) and Edwin B. Bronner, *William Penn's "Holy Experiment"* (1962). Also see Stephanie G. Wolf's excellent *Urban Village: Population, Community, and Family Structure in Germantown, Pennsylvania* (1977).

Anyone curious about the founding of Carolina should examine M. Eugene Sirmans, *Colonial South Carolina: A Political History, 1663–1763* (1966) and Clarence L. Ver Steeg, *Origins of a Southern Mosaic* (1975).

chapter 3

COLONISTS
IN AN EMPIRE:
REGIONAL PATTERNS

During the 1640s, Governor John Winthrop of the Massachusetts Bay Colony recorded in his diary the story of a master who could not afford to pay his servant's wages. To meet this obligation, the master sold a pair of oxen, but that transaction barely covered the cost of keeping the servant. In desperation, the master asked the employee, a man of lower social status, "how shall I do. . . when all my cattle are gone?" The servant replied, "you shall then serve me, so you may have your cattle again." In the margin of his diary next to this account, Winthrop scribbled "insolent."

The servant's presumptiousness appalled Winthrop because it violated the governor's concept of social order. From Winthrop's perspective, the idea of improving one's social status was unthinkable. "God Almightie . . . ," he observed, "hath soe disposed of the Condition of mankinde, as in all times some must be rich, some poore, some highe and eminent in power and dignitie; others meane and in subjeccion." Every person had an assigned place in God's hierarchy.

Conditions in the New World, however, eroded this conception of the structure of society. Some individuals rose, others fell. People refused to stay in their assigned places. To Winthrop's dismay, the social order that developed in the American colonies did not conform to some divine plan. Instead, it was the product of several critical elements: shortage of labor, abundance of land, unusual demographic patterns, and commercial ties with European markets.

These factors varied from place to place. In the Chesapeake, for example, the staple economy based on tobacco created an almost insatiable demand for the controlled labor of slaves and servants. In Massachusetts Bay, the extraordinary longevity of the early settlers generated a level of social and political stability that Virginians and Marylanders did not attain until the end of the seventeenth century. In short, regional differences appeared during the earliest decades of settlement. Like Winthrop's concept of social order, the ideas and assumptions transported from Europe and Africa were recast to meet the demands of these particular colonial environments. Unfortunately, historians know little about the details of family life in other seventeenth-century colonies such as New York, Pennsylvania, and South Carolina, so this discussion focuses upon New England and the Chesapeake, England's wealthiest and most populous possessions.

Stable Societies: The New England Colonies in the Seventeenth Century

The family was central to the development of social stability in early New England. This observation may seem commonplace, but the modern reader must remember that in the seventeenth century many activities now performed by the state were the responsibility of the family. It was within the family unit that men and women earned a livelihood, educated their children, maintained religious traditions, nursed each other in sickness; in short, established a societal and cultural identity. The healthy environment of New England allowed the family to thrive. Indeed, New Englanders expected social institutions—church and state, in particular—to complement and support rather than to take over family functions. The character of the family life cycle, therefore, was of fundamental importance in shaping the stable economic and political patterns of early New England.

Immigrant Families and Social Order

Early New Englanders believed that God ordained the family for human benefit. It was essential to the maintenance of social order, since outside the family, men and women succumbed to carnal temptation. Such people had no one to sustain them, no one to remind them of Scripture. "Without *Family care*," declared the Reverend Benjamin Wadsworth, "the labour of Magistrates and

Ministers for Reformation and Propagating Religion, is likely to be in great measure unsuccessful.''

The godly family, at least in theory, was ruled by a patriarch, father to his children, husband to his wife, the source of authority and object of unquestioned obedience. The wife shared responsibility for the raising of children, but in decisions of importance, especially those related to property, she was expected to defer to her spouse.

The New Englanders' concern about the character of the godly family is not surprising. This institution played a central role in shaping their society, for in contrast to those who migrated to the colonies of Virginia and Maryland, New Englanders crossed the Atlantic within *nuclear* families. That is, they moved within established units consisting of a father, mother, and their dependent children, rather than as single youths and adults.

This familial experience exercised a powerful influence upon early New England life. People who migrated to America within families, mature adults in their twenties and thirties, preserved local English customs more fully than did the youths who traveled to other parts of the continent as single men and women. The comforting presence of immediate family members reduced the shock of adjusting to a strange environment three thousand miles from home. Even in the 1630s, the ratio of men to women in New England was fairly well balanced, about three males for every two females. Persons who had not already married in England could expect to form nuclear families of their own.

The great migration of the 1630s and '40s brought approximately 20,000 persons to New England. After 1642, the English Civil War reduced the flood of people moving to Massachusetts Bay to a trickle. Nevertheless, by the end of the century, the population of New England had reached almost 150,000, an amazing increase considering the small number of original immigrants. Historians have been hard pressed to explain this striking rate of growth. Some have suggested that New Englanders married very young, thus giving couples extra years in which to produce large families. Other scholars have maintained that New England women must have been more fertile than were their Old World counterparts.

■ *An anonymous painter commemorates the one-hundredth birthday of Anne Pollard (1721). Her life span exemplified the striking longevity of New England settlers.*

Neither theory adequately explains how so few migrants produced such a large population. Early New England marriage patterns, for example, did not differ substantially from those recorded in seventeenth-century England. The average age for men at first marriage was the mid-twenties. Wives were slightly younger than their husbands, the average age being about twenty-two. There is no evidence that New Englanders favored child brides. Nor, for that matter, were Puritan families unusually large by the standards of the period.

The explanation for the region's extraordinary growth turned out to be longevity, rather than fertility. Put simply, people who, under normal conditions, would have died in contemporary Europe survived in New England. Indeed, the life expectancy of seventeenth-century settlers was not very different from our own. Males who survived infancy might have expected to see their seventieth birthday. Twenty percent of the men of the first generation reached the age of eighty. The figures for women were only slightly lower. Why the early settlers lived so long is not entirely clear. No doubt, pure drinking water, a cool climate that retarded the spread of fatal contagious disease, and a dispersed population promoted general good health.

Longer life altered family relations. New England males lived not only to see their own children reach adulthood, but also to witness the birth of grandchildren. One historian, John Murrin, observed that New Englanders "invented" grandparents. In other words, this may have been one of the first societies in recorded history in which a person could reasonably anticipate knowing his or her grandchildren, a demographic surprise that contributed to social stability. The traditions of particular families and communities literally remained alive in the memories of the colony's oldest citizens.

Family Life Cycle

The life cycle of the family in New England began with marriage. Young men and women generally selected their own partners, and if parents had a voice in such matters, it was only to veto an objectionable choice. New Englanders usually managed to fall in love with a neighbor, and most marriages took place between persons living less than thirteen miles apart. Prospective brides were expected to possess a dowry worth approximately one half what the bridegroom brought to the union. Women often contributed money or household goods, while men provided farmland. The overwhelming majority of the region's population married, for in New England, the single life was not only physically difficult, but also morally suspect.

The household was primarily a place of work—very demanding work. One historical geographer estimates that a Pennsylvania family of five needed seventy-five acres of cleared land just to feed itself. Additional cultivation allowed the farmer to produce a surplus that could then be sold, and since agrarian families required items that could not be manufactured at home—metal tools, for example—they usually grew more than they consumed. Early American farmers were not self-sufficient; the belief that they were is a popular misconception.

During the seventeenth century, men and women generally lived in the communities of their parents and grandparents. Moving to a more fertile region might, of course, have increased their earnings, but such thoughts seldom occurred to early New Englanders. Religious values, a sense of common purpose, and the importance of family reinforced traditional communal ties.

Towns, in fact, were collections of families, not individuals. Over time, these families intermarried, so that the community became an elaborate kinship network. Social historians have discovered that in many New England towns the original founders dominated local politics and economic affairs for several generations. Not surprisingly, newcomers who were not absorbed into this family system tended to move away from the village with greater frequency than did the sons and daughters of the established lineage groups.

Congregational churches were also built upon a family foundation. During the earliest years of settlement, the churches accepted persons who could demonstrate that they were among God's "elect." Members were drawn from a broad social spectrum. Once the excitement of creating a new society had passed, however, New Englanders began to focus their attention upon the spiritual welfare of the members of their own families. Because many of their sons and daughters failed to experience saving grace, a synod in 1662 adopted the so-called Half-Way Covenant. This compromise allowed the grandchildren of persons in full communion to be baptized even though *their* parents could not demonstrate conversion. Congregational ministers assumed that "God cast the line of election in the loins of godly parents." Obsession with family—termed "tribalism" by some historians—meant that by the end of the century, Congregational churches failed to meet the religious needs of New Englanders who were not members of the select families.

Colonists regarded education as primarily a family responsibility. Parents were suppose to instruct children in the principles of Christianity; and so it was necessary to teach boys and girls how to read. In 1642 the Massachusetts General Court reminded the Bay Colonists of their obliga-

THE IMAGE
OF THE
AMERICAN INDIAN:
≈1500-1850≈

*T*he discovery of the New World presented European artists with an unusual challenge. A curious public demanded visual representations of the Native Americans, but since few talented painters or engravers ever ventured across the Atlantic, much of their knowledge of the Indians' appearance was drawn from oral and written reports, both notoriously unreliable. Many sketches of Native Americans were simply products of the artists' rich imagination. Not surprisingly, in the early prints the Indians looked like Europeans who had taken off their clothes; some Native Americans even acquired beards and mustaches.

In the sixteenth century, two well-established, though conflicting, preconceptions about the character of the New World held sway. First, many European scholars assumed that America swarmed with fearful monsters, headless people, and other freaks of nature. And second, many perceived the New World as a sort of Garden of Eden, an idyllic place where men and women enjoyed a carefree life amid great abundance.

The earliest explorers were apprehensive about meeting the inhabitants of the New World. Christopher Columbus reported, almost apologetically, "I have not found the human monstrosities which many people expected." What European adventurers encountered were often described as a gentle, hospitable race of men and women who seemed to live in a kind of childlike innocence. Contemporaries claimed the Indians were part of a "golden world" celebrated by the writers of antiquity.

A German artist drew this Indian, brought from Mexico by Cortés to the Spanish court of Emperor Charles V.

A less flattering image of the Indian also flourished. Armed clashes between Europeans and Native Americans led explorers to the conviction that the inhabitants of the New World were actually bloodthirsty savages, heathens who obstructed the spread of civilization. Most shocking to Europeans were reports of cannibalism. While the practice was in fact rare, artists seized upon this barbaric trait, creating woodcuts that depicted Indians preparing dismembered captives for dinner.

A few skilled artists traveled to the New World. John White produced a splendid sketchbook of watercolors showing the Indians of the North Carolina coast fishing, dancing, and praying. These drawings provide modern anthropologists with invaluable insight into the culture of these Algonquian people. Even a careful observer like White, however, succumbed to ethnocentrism, for in some ways his Indians looked remarkably like sixteenth-century Englishmen.

Jacques Le Moyne was the first European artist to visit what is now mainland USA. This watercolor (1560) depicts a Florida Indian chief showing a French explorer an object of worship—a column erected by an earlier explorer!

◄Europeans were looking for the East Indies when they bumped into the Western Hemisphere. This seventeenth-century allegorical painting is typical of their confusion about Native Americans. The woman and child dancing through the doorway resemble the inhabitants of India, and the armor in the corner appears to be Asian. The New World is represented by the dark-skinned figure in feathers surrounded by gold and pearls, treasure that Cortés brought back from Mexico in the 1520s.

Cultivated Europeans did not appreciate White's artistic achievement. They preferred complex allegorical motifs to represent America. Engravers depicted the New World as a comely Indian woman, usually adorned with a plumed headdress surrounded by exotic plants and animals. "America" often rode on the back of an armadillo or alligator, and while it is impossible to tell whether Europeans mistook this iconography for reality, these images enjoyed great popularity.

Not until the middle of the eighteenth century did Europeans develop the concept of the "noble savage." Paintings of this period stressed the Indians' lofty spirit. This romantic image, however, was no more accurate than were the earlier representations. Philosophers invented the "noble savage" as a foil against which to criticize the alleged decadence of European society. While these paintings won praise from urbane Londoners and Parisians, frontiersmen in America continued to view the Indian as a treacherous foe.

Supporters of the American Revolution adopted the Indian as the pictorial symbol for independence and liberty. Political cartoonists portrayed poor, beleaguered "America" as an Indian princess, and after the war, she came to symbolize the new nation. Looking like a Greek goddess bedecked with ostrich feathers, this Indian princess appeared in popular prints alongside Washington and Franklin. During the nineteenth century, the image of the princess lost out to more masculine symbols of nationalism, such as Uncle Sam. Of the earlier iconographic tradition, only the "cigar-store" Indian survived.

The question of the Indians' color compounded the problem of artistic representation. During the earliest years of settlement, Native Americans were perceived as olive, tawny, or even white. Not until the mid-eighteenth century were Indians viewed as significantly different in color from Europeans, and not until the nineteenth century did "red" become the universally accepted color label for American Indians.

Meissen porcelain figures of 1745 portray America symbolically with a voluptuous Indian maiden in feathered costume, exotic creatures such as the alligator and parrot, and the cornucopia of abundance.

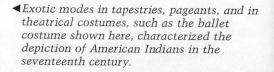

◄*Exotic modes in tapestries, pageants, and in theatrical costumes, such as the ballet costume shown here, characterized the depiction of American Indians in the seventeenth century.*

A painting of the early 1800s in the heroic style depicting a young woman about to be scalped.

Chief Black Hawk and his son, noble and proud, painted from observation in 1833, after they had been defeated. Portrayals of Indians became more realistic as artists traveled the frontier.

The cigar-store Indian originated in English carvings during the seventeenth century. By the mid-nineteenth century, its use in America was widespread.

This charming Shoshoni girl was observed by artist Alfred Jacob Miller on a trip to the Green River Valley in Wyoming in 1837.

tion to catechize their families. Five years later the legislature ordered towns containing at least fifty families to open an elementary school supported by local taxes. Villages of one hundred or more families had to maintain more advanced grammar schools, which taught a basic Latin curriculum. At least eleven schools were operating in 1647, and despite their expense, new schools were established throughout the century.

This family-based education system worked. A majority of the region's adult males could read and write, an accomplishment not achieved in the Chesapeake colonies for another century. The literacy rate for women was somewhat lower, but by the standards of the period, it was still impressive. A printing press operated in Cambridge as early as 1639. *The New-England Primer*, first published in Boston by Benjamin Harris, taught children the alphabet as well as the Lord's Prayer. This primer announced, "He who ne'er learns his ABC, forever will a blockhead be. But he who to his book's inclined, will soon a golden treasure find."

But the best-seller of seventeenth-century New England was Michael Wigglesworth's *The Day of Doom* (1662), a poem of 224 stanzas describing in terrifying detail the fate of sinners on Judgment Day. In words that even young readers could comprehend, Wigglesworth wrote of these unfortunate souls:

> They cry, no, no: Alas! and wo!
>   Our Courage all is gone:
> Our hardiness (fool hardiness)
>   Hath us undone, undone.

Many New Englanders memorized the entire poem. After 1638 young men could attend Harvard College, the first institution of higher learning founded in England's mainland colonies. Yale College followed, admitting its first students in 1702.

Women's Work and Women's Rights

The role of women in the agrarian society north of the Chesapeake is a controversial subject among colonial historians. Some scholars point out that common law as well as English custom treated women as inferior to men. Other histori-

■ *New England parents took seriously their responsibility for the spiritual welfare of their children. To seek the word of God, young people had to learn to read. The* New-England Primer, *shown here, was their primary vehicle.*

ans, however, depict the colonial period as a "golden age" for women. According to this interpretation, wives worked alongside their husbands. They were not divorced from meaningful, productive labor. They certainly were not transformed into those frail, dependent beings much admired by middle-class males of the nineteenth century. Both views provide insights into the lives of early American women, but neither fully recaptures their experiences as members of communities.

Spinning wool and linen fibers into yarn and thread was a skill that women had to master in New England households. Clothes making was a task assigned to females in the family.

curtailed the rights of colonial women. According to common law practice, a wife exercised no control over property. She could not, for example, sell land, although if her husband decided to dispose of their holdings, he was free to do so without her permission. Divorce was extremely difficult to obtain in any colony before the American Revolution. Indeed, a person married to a cruel or irresponsible spouse had little recourse but to run away or accept the unhappy situation.

Yet most women were neither prosperous entrepreneurs nor abject slaves. Surviving letters indicate that men and women generally accepted the roles that they thought God had ordained. One of early America's most creative poets, Anne Bradstreet, wrote movingly of the fulfillment she had found with her husband. In a piece entitled "To my Dear and loving Husband," Bradstreet declared:

If ever two were one, then surely we.
If ever man were lov'd by wife, then thee;
If ever wife was happy in a man,
Compare with me the women if you can.

Although Puritan couples worried that the affection they felt for a husband or a wife might turn their thoughts away from God's perfect love, this was a danger they were willing to risk.

Rank and Status

During the seventeenth century, the New England colonies attracted neither noblemen nor paupers. The absence of these social groups meant that the American social structure seemed incomplete by contemporary European standards. The settlers were not displeased that the poor remained in the Old World. The lack of very rich persons—and in this period great wealth frequently accompanied noble title—was quite another matter. According to the prevailing hierarchical view of the structure of society, well-placed individuals were *natural rulers*, people intended by God to exercise political authority over the rank and file. Migration forced the colonists, however, to choose their rulers from men of more modest status. One minister told a Plymouth congregation that since its members were "not furnished with any persons of *special emi-*

To be sure, women worked on family farms. They did not, however, necessarily do the same jobs that men performed. Women usually handled separate tasks, including cooking, washing, clothes-making, dairying, and gardening. Their production of food was absolutely essential to the survival of most households. Sometimes wives raised poultry, and by selling surplus birds achieved some economic independence. When people in one New England community chided a man for allowing his wife to peddle her fowl, he responded, "I meddle not with the geese nor turkeys for they are hers." Women also joined churches in greater numbers than did men, and it is possible that their involvement in these institutions encouraged them to express their ideas. From this perspective, the Anne Hutchinson affair (see chapter 2) takes on new meaning, since Hutchinson implicitly challenged the commonly imposed constraints on the public role of women.

In political and legal matters, society sharply

nency above the rest, to be chosen by you into office of government," they would have to make due with neighbors, "not beholding in them the *ordinariness of their persons.*"

The colonists gradually sorted themselves out into distinct social groupings. Persons who would never have been "natural rulers" in England became provincial gentry in the various northern colonies. It helped, of course, if an individual possessed wealth and education, but these attributes alone could not guarantee that a newcomer would be accepted into the local ruling elite, at least not during the early decades of settlement. In Massachusetts and Connecticut, Puritan voters expected their leaders to join Congregational churches and defend orthodox religion.

The Winthrops, Dudleys, and Pynchons—just to cite a few of the more prominent families—fulfilled these expectations, and in public affairs they assumed dominant roles. They took their responsibilities quite seriously and certainly did not look kindly upon anyone who spoke of their "ordinariness." A colonist who jokingly called a Puritan magistrate a "just ass" found himself in deep trouble with civil authorities.

The problem was that while most New Englanders accepted a hierarchical view of society, they disagreed over their assigned places. Both Massachusetts Bay and Connecticut passed sumptuary laws—statues that limited the wearing of fine apparel to the wealthy and prominent —to curb the pretentions of those of lower status. Yet such restraints could not prevent some people from rising and others from falling within the social order. Indeed, by the end of the century, the character of the ruling class in New England had changed, and personal piety figured less importantly in social ranking than did family background and large estate.

Most northern colonists were yeomen (independent farmers) who worked their own land. While few became rich in America, even fewer fell hopelessly into debt. Their daily lives, especially for those who settled New England, centered upon scattered little communities where they participated in village meetings, church-related matters, and militia training. Possession of land gave agrarian families a sense of independence from external authority, but during the seventeenth century, this independence was balanced by an equally strong feeling of local identi-

■ *The matchlock musket used by the colonists was so heavy it had to be propped on a forked stick when it was fired.*

ty. Not until the late eighteenth century, when many New Englanders left their familial villages in search of new land, did many northern yeoman place personal material ambition above traditional community bonds.

It was not unusual for northern colonists to work as servants at some point in their lives. This system of labor differed greatly from the servitude that developed in seventeenth-century Virginia and Maryland. New Englanders seldom recruited servants from the Old World. The forms of agriculture practiced in this region, mixed cereal and dairy farming, made employment of large gangs of dependent workers uneconomic. Rather, New England families placed their adolescent children in nearby homes. These young persons contracted for four or five years and seemed more like apprentices than servants. Servitude was not simply a means by which one group exploited another. It was an almost vocational training program in which the children of the rich as well as the poor participated.

Roots of Southern Plantation Societies

An entirely different regional society developed in England's Chesapeake colonies. This contrast with New England seems puzzling. After all, the two areas were founded at roughly the same time by men and women from the same mother country. In both regions, settlers spoke English, accepted Protestantism, and gave allegiance to one crown. And yet, to cite an obvious example, seventeenth-century Virginia looked nothing like Massachusetts Bay. In an effort to explain the difference, colonial historians have studied environmental conditions, labor systems, and agrarian economies. The most important reason for the distinctiveness of these early southern plantation societies, however, turned out to be the Chesapeake's death rate, a frighteningly high mortality that tore at the very fabric of family life.

Family Life in a Perilous Environment

Unlike New England's settlers, the men and women who emigrated to the Chesapeake region did not move in family units. They traveled to the New World as young, unmarried servants, youths cut off from the security of traditional kin relations. Although these immigrants came from a cross section of English society, most had been poor to middling farmers in the mother country. It is now estimated that 70 to 85 percent of the white colonists who went to Virginia and Maryland during the seventeenth century were not free, that is, they owed four or five years' labor in exchange for the cost of passage to America. If the servant was under fifteen, he or she had to serve a full seven years. The overwhelming majority of these laborers were males between the ages of eighteen and twenty-two. In fact, before 1640 the ratio of males to females stood at 6 to 1. This figure dropped to about 2 1/2 to 1 by the end of the century, but the sexual balance in the Chesapeake was never as favorable as it had been in early Massachusetts.

Most immigrants to the Chesapeake region died soon after arriving. It is difficult to ascertain the exact cause of death in most cases, but malaria and other diseases took a frightful toll. Recent studies also indicate that drinking water contaminated with salt killed many colonists living in low-lying areas. Throughout the entire seventeenth century, high mortality rates had a profound effect upon this society. Life expectancy for Chesapeake males was about forty-three, some ten to twenty years less than for men born in New England! For women, life was even shorter. A full 25 percent of all children died in infancy; another 25 percent did not see their twentieth birthday. The survivors were often weak or ill, unable to perform hard physical labor.

These demographic conditions retarded normal population increase. Young women who might have become wives and mothers could not do so until they had completed their terms of servitude. They thus lost several reproductive years, and in a society in which so many children died in infancy, late marriage greatly restricted family size. Moreover, because of the unbalanced sex ratio, many adult males simply could not find wives. Migration not only cut them off from their English families, but also deprived them of an opportunity to form new ones. Without a constant flow of immigrants, the population of Virginia and Maryland would have actually declined.

■ Gravestones from churchyards in Virginia and Maryland illustrate the shorter life span in these colonies, when compared to New England.

High mortality compressed the family life cycle into a few short years. Marriages, for example, were extremely fragile, and one partner usually died within seven years. Only one in three Chesapeake marriages survived as long as a decade. Not only did children not meet grandparents, they often did not even know their own parents. Widows and widowers quickly remarried, bringing children by former unions into their new homes, and it was not uncommon for a child to grow up with persons to whom he or she bore no blood relation. The psychological effects of such experiences on Chesapeake settlers cannot be measured. People probably learned to cope with a high degree of personal insecurity. However they adjusted, it is clear that family life in this region was vastly more impermanent than it was in the New England colonies during the same period.

Women were obviously in great demand in the early southern colonies. Some historians have argued that scarcity heightened the woman's bargaining power in the marriage market. If she was an immigrant, she did not have to worry about obtaining parental consent. She was on her own in the New World and free to select whomever she pleased. If a woman lacked beauty or strength, if she were a person of low moral standards, she could still be confident of finding an American husband. Such negotiations may have provided Chesapeake women with a means of improving their social status. Nevertheless, liberation from some traditional restraints upon seventeenth-century women must not be exaggerated. As servants, women were vulnerable to sexual exploitation by their masters. Moreover, childbearing was extremely dangerous, and women in the Chesapeake usually died twenty years earlier than did their New England counterparts.

Rank and Status in Plantation Society

Colonists who managed somehow to survive grew tobacco, as much tobacco as they possibly could. This crop became the Chesapeake staple, and since it was relatively easy to cultivate, anyone with a few acres of cleared land could produce leaves for export. Cultivation of tobacco did not, however, produce a society roughly similar in wealth and status. To the contrary, tobacco generated inequality. Some planters amassed large fortunes; others barely subsisted. The difference was labor, for to succeed in this staple economy, one had to control the labor of other men and women. More workers in the fields meant larger harvests, and, of course, larger profits. Since free persons showed no interest in growing another man's tobacco, not even for wages, wealthy planters relied upon laborers who were not free, as well as on slaves. The social structure that developed in the seventeenth-century Chesapeake reflected a wild, often unscrupulous scramble to bring men and women of three races—black, white, and Indian—into various degrees of dependence.

Great planters dominated Chesapeake society. The group was small, only a trifling percent of the population of Virginia and Maryland. During the early decades of the seventeenth century, the composition of Chesapeake gentry was continually in flux. Some gentlemen died before they could establish a secure claim to high social status; others returned to England, thankful to have survived. Not until the 1650s did the family names of those who would become famous eighteenth-century gentry appear in the records. The first gentlemen were not—as genealogists sometimes discover to their dismay—dashing Cavaliers who had fought in the English civil war for King Charles I. Rather, such Chesapeake gentry as the Burwells, Byrds, Carters, and Masons consisted originally of the younger sons of English merchants and artisans.

These ambitious men arrived in America with capital. They invested immediately in laborers, and one way or another, they obtained huge tracts of the best tobacco-growing land. The members of this gentry were not technically aristocrats, for they did not possess titles that could be passed from generation to generation. They gave themselves military titles, sat as justices of the peace on the county courts, and directed local (Anglican) church affairs as members of the vestry. Over time, these gentry families intermarried so frequently that they created a vast network of cousins. During the eighteenth century it was not uncommon to find a half dozen men with the same surname sitting simultaneously in the Virginia House of Burgesses.

Freemen formed the largest class in this society. Their origins were strikingly different from those of the gentry, or for that matter, from those of New England's yeomen farmers. Chesapeake freemen traveled to the New World as indentured servants and by sheer good fortune, managed to remain alive to the end of their contracts. If they had dreamed of becoming great planters, they were gravely disappointed. Most seventeenth-century freemen lived on the edge of poverty. Some freemen, of course, did better in America than they would have done in contemporary England, but in both Virginia and Maryland, historians have found a sharp economic division separating the gentry from the rest of white society.

Below the freemen came indentured servants. Membership in this group was not demeaning; after all, servitude was a temporary status. But servitude in the Chesapeake colonies was not the benign institution that it was in New England. Great planters purchased servants to grow tobacco. No one worried whether these laborers received decent food and clothes, much less whether they acquired trades. These young people, thousands of them, cut off from family ties, sick often to the point of death, unable to obtain normal sexual release, regarded their servitude as a form of "slavery." Not surprisingly, the gentry worried that unhappy servants and impoverished freemen, what the planters called the "giddy multitude," would rebel at the slightest provocation, a fear that turned out to be fully justified.

The character of social mobility—and this observation applies only to the whites—changed considerably during the seventeenth century. Until the 1680s, it was relatively easy for a newcomer who possessed capital to become a member of the planter elite. No one paid much attention to the reputation or social standing of one's English family. After the 1680s, however, life expectancy rates in the Chesapeake improved, and the sons of the great planters replaced their fathers in powerful government positions. They carved out large estates of their own. New arrivals, even those with funds to invest, found it increasingly difficult to enter a ruling class tightly knit by blood and marriage.

Opportunities for advancement also decreased for the region's freemen. Studies of mid-seventeenth-century Maryland reveal that some servants managed to become moderately prosperous farmers and small officeholders. But as the gentry consolidated its hold on political and economic institutions, ordinary people discovered that it was much harder to rise in Chesapeake society. Those men and women with more ambitious dreams headed for Pennsylvania, North Carolina, or western Virginia.

Social institutions that figured importantly in the daily experience of New Englanders were either weak or nonexistent in the Chesapeake colonies. In part this sluggish development resulted from the continuation of high infant mortality rates. There was little incentive to build elementary schools, for example, if half the children would die before reaching adulthood. The great planters sent their sons to England or Scotland for their education, and even after the founding of the College of William and Mary in Virginia in 1693, the gentry continued to patronize English schools. As a result of this practice, higher education in the South languished for much of the colonial period.

Tobacco also influenced the spread of other institutions in this region. Planters were scattered along the rivers, often separated from their nearest neighbors by miles of poor roads. Since the major tobacco growers traded directly with English merchants, they had no need for towns. Whatever items they required were either made on the plantation or imported from Europe. Other than the centers of colonial government, Jamestown (and later Williamsburg) and St. Mary's (and later Annapolis), there were no villages capable of sustaining a rich community life before the late eighteenth century. Seventeenth-century Virginia did not even possess a printing press. In fact, Governor Sir William Berkeley bragged in 1671, "there are no free schools, nor printing in Virginia, for learning has brought disobedience, and heresy . . . into the world, and printing had divulged them . . . God keep us from both!"

The Black Experience in English America

Many people who landed in the colonies had no desire to come to the New World. They were taken as slaves to cultivate rice, sugar, and tobacco, and as the Native Americans were exterminated and the supply of white indentured servants dried up, European planters demanded ever more African laborers.

Roots of Slavery

A great deal is known about the transfer of African peoples across the Atlantic. During the entire history of this human commerce, between the sixteenth and nineteenth centuries, slave traders carried between eight and eleven million blacks to the Americas. Most of these men and women were sold in Brazil or in the Caribbean. Only a small number of Africans ever reached British North America, and of this group, the majority arrived after 1700. Because slaves performed hard physical labor, planters preferred purchasing young males. In many early slave communities, black men outnumbered women by a ratio of two to one.

English colonists did not hesitate to enslave black people. While the institution of slavery had long ago died out in the mother country, New World settlers quickly discovered how well this particular labor system operated in the Spanish and Portuguese colonies. The decision to bring African slaves to the British colonies, therefore, was based primarily upon economic considerations.

English masters, however, never justified the practice purely in terms of planter profits. Indeed, they adopted a quite different pattern of rhetoric. English writers associated blacks in Africa with heathen religion, barbarous behavior, sexual promiscuity; in fact, with evil itself. From such a perspective, the enslavement of African men and women seemed unobjectionable. The planters maintained that if black slaves converted to Christianity, and so abandoned their supposedly savage ways, they would actually benefit from their loss of freedom.

Africans first landed in Virginia in 1619. For the next fifty years, the status of the colony's black people remained unclear. English settlers classified some black laborers as slaves for life, as

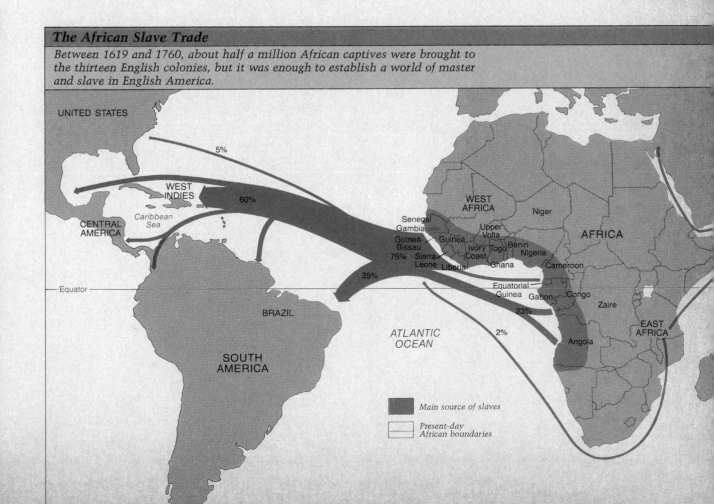

The African Slave Trade

Between 1619 and 1760, about half a million African captives were brought to the thirteen English colonies, but it was enough to establish a world of master and slave in English America.

Anthony Johnson:
Black Patriarch of Pungoteague Creek

During the first decades of settlement, a larger proportion of Virginia's black population achieved freedom than at any time until the Civil War ended slavery. Despite considerable obstacles, these free black men and women—their number in these early years was quite small—formed families, acquired property, earned community respect, and helped establish a distinctive Afro-American culture. One member of this group was Anthony Johnson, an immigrant who rose from slavery to prominence on Virginia's Eastern Shore.

Johnson came to Virginia aboard the English vessel *James* in 1621, just two years after the first blacks had arrived in the colony. As a slave known simply as "Antonio a Negro," Johnson found life a constant struggle for survival. Working in the tobacco fields of the Bennett plantation located on the south side of the James River, he endured long hours, poor rations, fearful epidemics, and haunting loneliness which, more often than not, brought an early death to slaves as well as indentured servants. Johnson, however, was a tough, intelligent, and lucky man.

Exactly how Johnson achieved freedom is not known. Early records reveal that while still living at the Bennett plantation, he took a wife, "Mary a Negro woman." Anthony was fortunate to find her. Because of an exceedingly unequal sex ratio in early Virginia, few males—regardless of color—had an opportunity to form a family. Anthony and Mary reared at least four children. Even more remarkable, in a society in which most unions were broken by death within a decade, their marriage lasted over forty years.

Sometime during the 1630s, Anthony and Mary gained their freedom, perhaps with the help of someone named Johnson. Their bondage probably ended through self-purchase, an arrangement that allowed enterprising slaves to buy their liberty through labor. Later, again under unknown circumstances, the Johnsons migrated to Northampton County on the Eastern Shore of Virginia. During the 1640s, they acquired an estate of 250 acres on Pungoteague Creek, where they raised cattle, horses, and hogs and cultivated tobacco. To work these holdings, Anthony Johnson apparently relied upon the labor of indentured servants and at least one black slave named Casor.

As the "patriarch on Pungoteague Creek," Johnson participated as fully as most whites in

Northampton society. He traded with wealthy white landowners and apparently shared their assumptions about the sanctity of property and the legitimacy of slavery. When two white neighbors attempted to steal Casor, Johnson hauled them into court and forced them to return his laborer. On another occasion, Johnson appealed to the court for tax relief after an "unfortunate fire" destroyed much of his plantation.

The Johnsons also maintained close ties with other free blacks, such as Anthony Payne and Emanuel Driggus who had similarly attained freedom and prosperity through their own efforts. Johnson's strongest links were with his family. Although his children lived in separate homes after reaching adulthood, his two sons laid out holdings in the 1650s adjacent to their father's plantation, and in times of crisis, parents and children participated in family conferences. These close bonds persisted even after the Johnson clan moved to Somerset County, Maryland, in the 1660s, and Anthony Johnson's subsequent death. When he purchased land in Somerset in 1677, Johnson's grandson, a third-generation free black colonist, named his plantation "Angola," perhaps in memory of his grandfather's African homeland.

Interpreting Johnson's remarkable life has proved surprisingly difficult. An earlier generation of historians considered Johnson a curiosity, a sort of black Englishman who did not fit neatly into familiar racial categories. Even some recent writers, concerned about tracing the roots of slavery and prejudice in the United States, have paid scant attention to Johnson and the other free blacks on the Eastern Shore.

Most historians would now agree that Johnson's life illustrated the complexity of race relations in early Virginia. His surprising progression from slave to slaveholder, his easy participation in the world of the white gentry and in a network of black friendships and family ties demonstrated that relations among blacks and whites conformed to no single pattern in the fluid society of mid-seventeenth-century Virginia. Rather, they took a variety of forms—conflict, cooperation, exploitation, accommodation—depending on the goals, status, experience, and environment of the participants. Race was only one—and by no means the decisive—factor shaping relations among colonists.

The opportunities that had been available to Anthony Johnson and other Virginia blacks, however, disappeared during the last quarter of the seventeenth century. A growing reliance on slave labor rather than indentured servitude brought about a rapid increase in the black population of Virginia and an accompanying curtailment of civil liberties on racial grounds. The rise of a group of great planters who dominated the colonial economy soon drove free black farmers into poverty. No longer did they enjoy the security, as had one black farmer in the 1640s of having "myne owne ground and I will work when I please and play when I please." It is not surprising that after 1706, a time when Virginia's experiment in a genuinely multiracial free society was all but over, the Johnson family disappeared from the colonial records. When modern Americans discuss the history of race relations in the United States, they might remember that some of the first blacks to settle America achieved a high level of economic and social success.

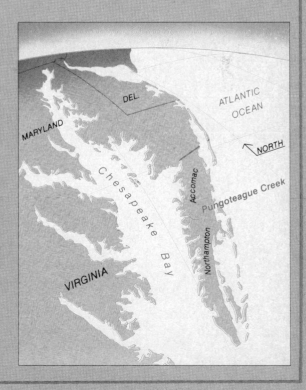

73

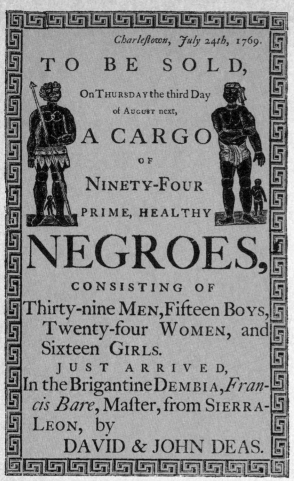

■ *This notice publicizes a slave auction to be held at the Charlestown wharf (1769).*

chattel to be bought and sold at the master's will. But other Africans became servants, presumably for stated periods of time, and before 1660, it was even possible for a few blacks to purchase their freedom. Several seventeenth-century Africans became successful Virginia planters (see pp. 72–73).

One reason that Virginia lawmakers tolerated such confusion was that the black population remained very small. By 1660 only about fifteen hundred people of African origin lived in the entire colony (compared to a white population of approximately twenty-six thousand), and it hardly seemed necessary to draw up an elaborate slave code to control so few men and women. If the planters could have obtained more black laborers, they certainly would have done so. There is no

evidence that the great planters preferred white indentured servants to black slaves. The problem was supply. During this period, slave traders sold their cargoes on Barbados or the other sugar islands of the West Indies, where they fetched a higher price than Virginians could afford. In fact, before 1680 most blacks who reached England's colonies on the North American mainland came from Barbados or through New Netherland rather than directly from Africa.

By the end of the seventeenth century, the status of Virginia's black people was no longer in doubt. They were slaves for life, and so were their children after them. This transformation reflected changes in the supply of Africans to British North America. After 1672 the Royal African Company was chartered to meet the colonial planters' demands for black laborers. Historian K. G. Davies terms this organization "the strongest and most effective of all European companies formed exclusively for the African trade." Between 1695 and 1709 over eleven thousand Africans were sold in Virginia alone; many others went to Maryland and the Carolinas. During the eighteenth century, American merchants entered the trade, and Rhode Island sent more ships to the African coast than did any other colony.

The expanding black population apparently frightened white colonists, for as the number of Africans increased, lawmakers drew up ever stricter slave codes. It was during this period that racism, always a latent element in New World societies, was fully revealed. By 1700 slavery was unequivocally based on the color of a person's skin. Blacks fell into this status simply because they were black. A vicious pattern of discrimination had been set in motion. Even conversion to Christianity did not free the African from bondage. The white planter could deal with his black property as he alone saw fit, and one extraordinary Virginia statute excused a master who killed a slave on the grounds that no rational person would purposely "destroy his own estate." Children born to a slave woman became slaves regardless of the father's race. Unlike the Spanish colonies where persons of lighter color enjoyed greater privileges in society, the English colonies officially tolerated no mixing of the races. Mulattoes received the same treatment as did pure Africans.

An eighteenth-century diagram demonstrates British regulations for stowing human cargo aboard the slave ships. Because it was expected that many slaves would die en route, ship captains sometimes attempted to increase their profits by crowding even more slaves into the hold than these regulations allowed.

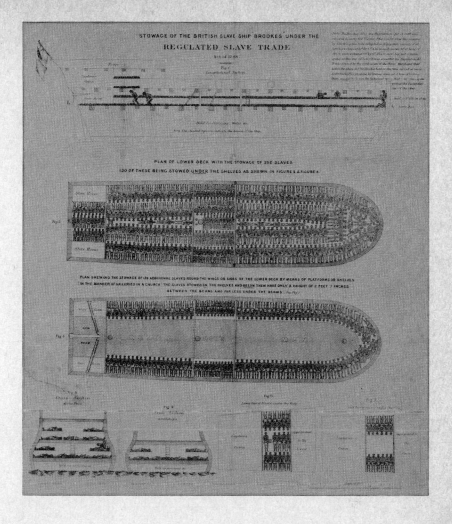

Afro-American Cultures

The slave experience varied substantially from colony to colony. The daily life of a black person in South Carolina, for example, was quite different from that of an Afro-American who happened to live in Pennsylvania or Massachusetts Bay. The size and density of the slave population determined in large measure how successfully blacks could maintain a separate cultural identity. In the lowlands of South Carolina during the eighteenth century, 60 percent of the population was black. These men and women were placed on large, isolated rice plantations, and their contact with whites was limited. In these areas blacks developed creole languages, which mixed the basic vocabulary of English with words borrowed from various African tongues. Until the end of the nineteenth century, one creole language, Gullah, was spoken on some of the Sea Islands along the Georgia-South Carolina coast. Slaves on these large rice plantations were also able to establish elaborate and enduring kinship networks that may have helped reduce the more dehumanizing aspects of bondage.

In the New England and Middle Colonies, and even in Virginia, the blacks made up a smaller percentage of the population: 40 percent in Virginia, 8 percent in Pennsylvania, 3 percent in Massachusetts. In such social environments contact between blacks and whites was more frequent than in South Carolina and Georgia. These population patterns had a profound effect upon northern and Chesapeake blacks, for while they escaped the physical drudgery of rice cultivation,

■ *In the northern colonies most slaves worked as house and body servants, as shown in this eighteenth-century overmantel (oil on wood) depicting the Potter family and their slave.*

they found the preservation of an independent African identity more difficult. In northern cities slaves usually worked as domestics and lived in the houses of their masters. While they saw other blacks, they had less opportunity to develop creole languages or reaffirm a common African past.

In eighteenth-century Virginia, native-born blacks, people who had learned to cope with whites on a daily basis, looked with contempt upon slaves who had just arrived from Africa. These "outlandish" Negroes, as they were called, were forced by blacks as well as whites to accept elements of English culture. It was especially important for newcomers to speak English. Consider, for example, the pain of young Olaudah Equiano, an African sold in Virginia in 1757. This twelve-year-old slave declared, "I was now exceedingly miserable, and thought myself worse off than any . . . of my companions; for they could talk to each other [in English], but I had no person to speak to that I could understand. In this state I was constantly grieving and pining, and wishing for death."

Despite such wrenching experiences, black slaves creatively preserved elements of an African heritage. The process of establishing Afro-American traditions involved an imaginative re-shaping of African and European customs into something that was neither African nor European. It was Afro-American. The slaves accepted Christianity, but they did so on their own terms —terms that their masters seldom fully understood. Blacks transformed Christianity into an expression of religious feeling in which an African element remained vibrant. In music and folk art they gave voice to a cultural identity that even the most degrading conditions could not eradicate.

A major turning point in the history of Afro-American people occurred during the early decades of the eighteenth century. At this time blacks living in England's mainland colonies began to reproduce themselves successfully. In other words, the number of live births exceeded deaths, and from that date, the expansion of the Afro-American population owed more to natural increase than to the importation of new slaves. This demographic shift did not take place in the Caribbean or South American colonies until a much later date. Historians believe that North American blacks enjoyed a healthier climate and better diet than did other New World slaves.

Even if mainland blacks had known that they lived longer than did the blacks of Jamaica or

■ *"Old Plantation"; watercolor by an unknown artist (about 1800), shows that some African identity and customs survived plantation life. The man and women in the center dance (possibly to celebrate a wedding), to the music of drum and banjo. Instruments, turbans, and scarves have African elements.*

Barbados, they would not have been impressed. After all, they were still slaves. They protested their debasement in many ways, some in individual acts of violence, others in organized revolt. The most serious slave rebellion of the colonial period was the Stono Uprising which took place in September 1739. One hundred and fifty South Carolina blacks rose up and murdered several white planters. "With Colours displayed, and two Drums beating," they marched toward Spanish Florida where they had been promised freedom. The local militia soon overtook the rebellious slaves and killed most of them. Although the uprising was shortlived, such incidents helped persuade whites everywhere that their own blacks might secretly be planning bloody revolt. Fear bred paranoia. When an unstable white servant woman in New York City announced in 1741 that blacks intended to burn the town, frightened authorities executed 32 suspected arsonists and dispatched 175 others to the West Indies. While the level of interracial violence in colonial society was quite low, fear of slave rebellions often prompted whites to take defensive measures. Everyone recognized that the blacks—in the words of one Virginia governor—longed "to Shake off the fetters of Slavery."

Blueprint for Empire

Until the middle of the seventeenth century, English political leaders largely ignored the American colonists. Private companies and aristocratic proprietors had created these societies, some for profit, others for religious sanctuary, but in no case did the Crown provide financial or military assistance. After the Restoration of Charles II in 1660, intervention replaced indifference. Englishmen of various sorts—courtiers, merchants, parliamentarians—concluded that the colonists should be brought more tightly under the control of the mother country. The regulatory policies evolved during this period formed a framework for empire that survived with only minor adjustment until 1765.

Fitting the Colonies into a Mercantilist System

The famous eighteenth-century Scottish economist, Adam Smith, coined the term *mercantilist system* to describe Great Britain's commercial regulations, and ever since, his phrase has appeared in history books. Smith's term, however, is misleading. It suggests that English policymakers during the reign of Charles II had developed a well-integrated set of ideas about the nature of international commerce and a carefully planned set of government policies to implement them.

They did nothing of the sort. Administrators responded to particular problems, usually on an individual basis. In 1668 Charles informed his sister, "The thing which is nearest the heart of the nation is trade and all that belongs to it." National interest alone, however, did not shape mercantilist policy. Instead, the needs of several powerful interest groups led to the rise of English commercial regulation.

Each group looked to colonial commerce to solve a different problem. For his part, the king wanted money. Charles had incurred huge debts, and his closest advisers reasoned that by collecting customs duties on American goods imported into England or transshipped through English ports, they could enrich the king without having to raise new domestic taxes. For their part, English merchants were eager to exclude Dutch rivals from lucrative American markets, but without government assistance, English merchants could not compete successfully with the Dutch, not even in Virginia or Massachusetts Bay. From the perspective of the landed gentry who sat in Parliament, England needed a stronger navy and that in turn meant expansion of the domestic shipbuilding industry. And almost everyone agreed that the mother country should establish a more favorable balance of trade, that is, increase exports, decrease imports, and grow richer at the expense of other European states. None of these ideas was particularly innovative— Oliver Cromwell's government had passed some commercial regulations during his short reign— but taken together they provided a blueprint for England's first empire.

Navigation Acts Transform Colonial Trade

After some legislation in that direction during the Commonwealth, Parliament passed a Navigation Act in 1660. This statute was the most important piece of imperial legislation drafted before the American Revolution. It stated (1) that no ship could trade in the colonies unless it had been constructed in either England or America and carried a crew that was at least 75 percent English (for these purposes colonists counted as Englishmen), and (2) that certain *enumerated* goods of great value that were not produced in England— tobacco, sugar, cotton indigo, dye wood, ginger— could be transported from the colonies *only* to an English or another colonial port. In 1704 Parliament added rice and molasses to the enumerated list; in 1705 wood rosins, tars, and turpentines needed for shipbuilding were included.

The act of 1660 was masterfully conceived. It encouraged the development of domestic shipbuilding and prohibited European rivals from obtaining enumerated goods anywhere except in England. Since the Americans had to pay customs fees (for this purpose colonists did not count as Englishmen) on such items as sugar and tobacco, the legislation also provided the Crown with another source of income.

In 1663 Parliament supplemented this legislation with a second Navigation Act known as the *Staple Act*, which stated that, with a few noted exceptions, nothing could be imported into America unless it had first been transshipped through the mother country, a process that greatly added to the price ultimately paid by colonial consumers.

The Navigation Acts attempted to eliminate the Dutch, against whom the English fought three wars in this period (1652–1654, 1664–1667, and 1672–1674), as the middlemen of American commerce. Just as English merchants were celebrating their victory, however, an unanticipated rival appeared on the scene. New England Merchantmen sailed out of Boston, Salem, and Newport to become formidable world competitors in maritime commerce.

During the 1660s Americans showed little enthusiasm for the new imperial system. Virginians bitterly protested the Navigation Acts. The collection of English customs on tobacco greatly reduced the colonial planters' profits. Moreover, the exclusion of the Dutch from the trade meant that growers often had to sell their crops at artificially low prices. The Navigation Acts hit the small planters especially hard, for they were least able to absorb increased production costs. Even though the governor of Virginia lobbied on

■ *Trade rivalry between England and Holland became intense in the 1660s, culminating in open warfare. This painting depicts the Dutch fleet destroying the Royal Navy. The Dutch burnt four ships and towed away a battleship.*

the planters' behalf, the Crown turned a deaf ear. By 1670, import duties on tobacco accounted for almost £100,000, a sum the king could scarcely do without.

New Englanders simply ignored the commercial regulations. Indeed, one Massachusetts merchant reported in 1664 that Boston entertained "near one hundred sail of ships, this year, of ours and strangers." The strangers, of course, were the Dutch, who had no intention of obeying the Navigation Acts so long as they could reach colonial ports. Some New England merchants found clever ways to circumvent the Navigation Acts. These crafty traders picked up cargoes of enumerated goods such as sugar or tobacco, sailed to another colonial port (thereby technically fulfilling the letter of the law), and then made directly for Holland or France. Along the way they paid no customs.

To plug this loophole, Parliament passed the Navigation Act of 1673. This statute established a *plantation duty*, a sum of money equal to normal English customs duties to be collected at the various colonial ports. New Englanders could now sail wherever they pleased within the empire, but they could not escape paying customs. Parliament also extended the jurisdiction of the London Customs Commissioners to America. And in 1675, as part of this new imperial firmness, the Privy Council formed a powerful subcommittee, the Lords of Trade, whose members monitored colonial affairs.

Despite these legal reforms, serious obstacles impeded the execution of imperial policy. The customs service did not have enough effective agents in American ports to enforce the Navigation Acts fully, and some men sent from the mother country did more harm than good. Edward Randolph was such a person. He was dispatched to Boston in 1676 to gather information about the conduct of colonial trade. New England Puritans did not look kindly upon intervention into their affairs, but even considering their irritability, Randolph seems to have been extraordinarily inept. His behavior was so obnoxious, his reports about New Englanders so condescending, that he became the most hated man in late seventeenth-century Massachusetts.

There were difficulties in England as well. Put simply, the imperial kitchen contained too many cooks. The customs office maintained an interest in America, but so too did the Treasury, the Admiralty, and the Privy Council. Often these independent bodies worked at cross-purposes. For example, some Stuart officials considered establishing "garrison governments" throughout English America. Under this short-sighted scheme, the colonies would have been transformed into military outposts, and army officers would have exercised civil authority. To people accustomed to representative assemblies such ideas sounded outrageous, but the military pressed ahead. Unaccountably, just as these plans were about to be put into effect (they were actually tried for brief periods in Jamaica and Virginia) the king awarded William Penn one of the most liberal charters ever granted (see chapter 2). Since Penn had no interest whatsoever in creating a garrison government, it appeared that the monarch had forgotten to consult with the army or vice versa.

Parliament passed the last major piece of imperial legislation in 1696. First, the statute ordered all colonial governors to swear oaths promising to uphold the Navigation Acts; governors who failed to carry out their responsibilities were threatened with loss of office. Second, Parliament established a regular, greatly expanded American customs service with collectors stationed in every colony. They were granted broad powers to search suspicious vessels and to prosecute suspected smugglers. Third, the 1696 act called for the creation of American vice-admiralty courts. Established to settle disputes that occurred at sea, vice-admiralty courts required neither juries nor oral cross-examination. At the time, because the number of new courts was small, extension of admiralty jurisdiction did not create serious friction between the colonists and the mother country. On the eve of the American Revolution, however, a sudden expansion of the admiralty system became a major colonial grievance.

The members of Parliament believed that these reforms would belatedly compel the colonists to accept the Navigation Acts, and in large measure, they were correct. By 1700 American goods transshipped through the mother country accounted for a quarter of *all* English exports, an indication that the colonists found it profitable to obey the commercial regulations. In fact, during the eighteenth century, smuggling from Europe to America dried up almost completely.

In 1696 the king also made administrative changes in the imperial system. William III replaced the ineffective Lords of Trade with a body called the Lords Commissioners of Trade and Plantations. Most people simply called it the Board of Trade. Half of the members of this Board were politicians, the rest were civil servants, allegedly well informed about American affairs. Although they possessed no direct authority over the formulation of imperial policy, the Crown and Parliament usually listened to their recommendations. Eventually during the eighteenth century, the Board of Trade became a refuge for political hacks, but in its first two decades, it aggressively addressed imperial problems.

Political Unrest, 1676–1691: Colonial Gentry in Revolt

The Navigation Acts created an illusion of unity. English administrators superimposed a system of commercial regulation upon a number of different, often unstable American colonies and called it an empire. But these statutes did not remove long-standing differences. Within each society men and women struggled to bring order out of disorder, to establish stable ruling elites, to diffuse ethnic and racial tensions, and to cope with population pressures that imperial planners only dimly understood. During the final decades of the seventeenth century, these efforts sometimes sparked revolt.

First, the Virginians rebelled, and then a few years later, political violence swept through Maryland, New York, and Massachusetts Bay, England's most populous mainland colonies. Historians once interpreted these events as rehearsals for the American Revolution, or even for Jacksonian Democracy. They perceived these rebels as frontier democrats, rising in protest against an entrenched aristocracy.

Recent research suggests, however, that this view seriously misconstrued the character of these late seventeenth-century rebellions. These uprisings certainly did not involve confrontations between the common people and their rulers. Indeed, these events were not in any modern sense of the word ideological. In each colony, the local gentry split into factions, usually the "outs" versus the "ins," and each side proclaimed its political legitimacy.

Bacon's Rebellion Sweeps Virginia

After 1660, the Virginia economy steadily declined. Returns from tobacco had not been good for some time, and the Navigation Acts reduced profits even further. Into this unhappy environment came thousands of indentured servants, people drawn to Virginia, as the governor explained, "in hope of bettering their condition in a Growing Country."

The reality bore little relation to their dreams. A hurricane destroyed one entire tobacco crop, and in 1667 Dutch warships added to the general misery by capturing the tobacco fleet just as it was about to sail for England. Servants complained about lack of food and clothing. Those who managed to win their freedom found little opportunity to better their lives. No wonder that Virginia's governor, Sir William Berkeley, despaired of ruling "a People where six parts of seven at least are Poor, Endebted, Discontented and Armed." In 1670 he and the House of Burgesses disfranchised all landless freemen, persons they regarded as troublemakers, but the threat of social violence remained.

Nathanial Bacon arrived in Virginia in 1674. Nothing about this ambitious young man suggested that he was a potential rebel. He came from a respectable English family and brought enough money to America to set himself up immediately as a substantial planter. Berkeley even appointed Bacon to the Virginia Council. Such honors did not satisfy Bacon, however, for as yet he was excluded from the "Green Spring" faction, a group of Berkeley's cronies who enjoyed special access to government patronage. When Bacon attempted to obtain a license to trade furs with the local Indians, he was rebuffed. This commerce was Berkeley's monopoly. If Bacon had been willing to wait, he would probably have been accepted into the "Green Spring" group, but Bacon was not known for his patience.

Sir William Berkeley was governor of Virginia between 1660 and 1676. He faced much political unrest during his term.

Events beyond Bacon's control thrust him suddenly into the center of Virginia politics. In 1675 Indians attacked several outlying plantations, killing a few colonists, and Virginians expected the governor to send an army to retaliate. Instead, early in 1676 Berkeley called for the construction of a line of defensive forts, a plan which seemed to the settlers both expensive and ineffective. Indeed, this strategy raised embarrassing questions. Was Berkeley protecting his own fur monopoly? Was he planning to reward his friends with contracts to build useless forts?

While people speculated about such matters, Bacon stepped forward. He boldly offered to lead a volunteer army against the Indians at no cost to the hard-pressed Virginia taxpayers. All he demanded was an official commission from Berkeley giving him military command, and that the governor steadfastly refused. With some justification, Berkeley regarded his upstart rival as a fanatic on the subject of Indians. The governor saw no reason to exterminate peaceful tribes simply to avenge the death of a few white settlers.

What followed would have been comic had not so many people died. Bacon thundered against the governor's treachery; Berkeley labeled Bacon a traitor. Both men appealed to the populace for support. On several occasions Bacon marched his followers to the frontier, but they either failed to find the enemy, or worse, massacred friendly Indians. At one point, Bacon burned Jamestown to the ground, forcing the governor to flee to the colony's Eastern Shore. Bacon's bumbling lieutenants chased Berkeley across Chesapeake Bay only to be captured themselves. Thereupon, the governor mounted a new campaign.

As the civil war dragged on, it soon became apparent that Bacon and his followers had only the vaguest notion of what they were trying to achieve. When Charles II heard of the fighting in Virginia, he dispatched a thousand regular soldiers to Jamestown. By the time they arrived, Berkeley had regained full control of the colony's government. In October 1676, Bacon died after a brief illness, and his band of rebel followers dispersed within a few months.

Berkeley, now an old and embittered man, was recalled to England in 1677. His successors, especially Lord Culpeper (1680–1683) and Lord Howard of Effingham (1683–1689) seemed interested primarily in enriching themselves at the expense of the Virginia planters. Their self-serving policies, coupled with the memory of near anarchy, helped heal divisions within the Virginia ruling class. For almost a century, in fact, the local gentry formed a united front against greedy royal appointees. Summing up Bacon's Rebellion, historian Edmund S. Morgan concludes, "It was a rebellion with abundant causes but without a cause: it produced no real program of reform, no revolutionary manifesto, not even any revolutionary slogans." Unlike later revolutionary heroes in America, Bacon quickly faded from popular memory.

The Glorious Revolution in the Bay Colony

During John Winthrop's lifetime, Massachusetts settlers developed an inflated sense of their independence from the mother country. After 1660, however, it became difficult even to pretend that the Puritan colony was a separate state. Royal officials like Edward Randolph demanded full compliance with the Navigation Acts. Moreover, the growth of commerce attracted new merchants to the Bay Colony, men who were Anglicans rather than Congregationalists and who maintained close business contacts in London. These persons complained loudly of Puritan intolerance. The Anglican faction was never large, but its presence, coupled with Randolph's unceasing demands, divided Bay leaders. A few Puritan ministers and magistrates regarded compromise with England as treason, a breaking of the Lord's covenant. Other spokesmen, recognizing the changing political realities within the empire, urged a more moderate course.

In 1675 the Indians dealt the New Englanders a terrible setback. Metacomet, a Wampanoag chief whom the whites called King Philip, declared war against the colonists. The powerful Narragansetts, whose lands the settlers had long coveted, joined Metacomet, and in little more than a year of fighting, the Indians destroyed scores of frontier villages, killed hundreds of colonists, and

■ *The Wampanoag chief, King Philip, in an early nineteenth-century portrait.*

■ *William and Mary, joint monarchs of England after the Glorious Revolution of 1688. Mary ascended the throne when her father, James II, was deposed. Her husband William ruled Holland before ascending the English throne.*

disrupted the entire regional economy. Douglas Leach, a military historian, explains that "In proportion to population, King Philip's War inflicted greater casualties upon the people than any other war in our history." At least a thousand New Englanders died in the conflict. The war left the people of Massachusetts deeply in debt and more than ever uncertain of their future.

In 1684 the debate over the colony's relation to the mother country ended abruptly. The Court of Chancery, sitting in London and acting upon a petition from the king, annulled the charter of the Massachusetts Bay Company. In one stroke of a pen, the patent that Winthrop had so lovingly carried to America in 1630, the foundation for a "city on a hill," was gone. The decision forced the most stubborn Puritans to recognize that they were part of an empire run by people who did not share their particular religious vision.

James II, a monarch who disliked representative institutions—after all Parliament, a representative assembly, had executed his father, Charles I—decided to restructure the government of the entire region in the Dominion of New England. In various stages from 1686 to 1689, it incorporated Massachusetts, Connecticut, Rhode Island, Plymouth, New York, New Jersey, and New Hampshire under a single appointed royal governor. For this demanding position, James selected Sir Edmund Andros (pronounced Andrews), a military veteran of tyrannical temperament. Andros arrived in Boston in 1686, and within a matter of months he had alienated everyone, Puritans, moderates, even Anglican merchants. Not only did Andros abolish elective assemblies, but also he enforced the Navigation Acts with such rigor that he brought about commercial depression. Andros declared normal town meetings illegal, collected taxes that the people never approved, and packed the courts with strangers who detested the local population. The great eighteenth-century historian and governor, Thomas Hutchinson, compared Andros unfavorably with the Roman tyrant, Nero.

Early in 1689 news of the Glorious Revolution reached Boston. The people had deposed James II, an admitted Catholic, and placed his daughter Mary and her husband, William of Orange, on the throne as joint monarchs (see the chart of the Stuart monarchs on p. 33). As part of the settlement, William and Mary accepted a Bill of Rights, a document stipulating the constitutional rights of all Englishmen. Almost immediately the Bay Colonists overthrew the hated Andros regime. The New England version of the Glorious Revolution (April 18, 1689) was so popular that no one came to the governor's defense. Andros was jailed without a single shot having been fired. According to Cotton Mather, a leading Congregational minister, the colonists were united by the "most *Unanimous Resolution* perhaps that was ever known to have Inspir'd any people."

However united as they may have been, the Bay Colonists could not take the Crown's support for granted. William III could have declared the New Englanders rebels and summarily reinstated Andros. But thanks largely to the tireless efforts of Increase Mather, Cotton's father, who pleaded the colonists' case in London, William abandoned the Dominion of New England, and in 1691 Massachusetts received a new royal charter. This document differed substantially from the company patent of 1629. The freemen no longer selected their governor. The choice now belonged to the king. Membership in the General Court was determined by annual election, and these representatives in turn chose the men who sat in the council or upper house, subject always to the governor's veto. Moreover, the franchise was determined on the basis of personal property rather than church membership, a change that brought Massachusetts into conformity with general English practice. On the local level, town government remained much as it had been in Winthrop's time.

Trouble with Witches

The instability of the Massachusetts government following Andros' arrest—what Reverend Samuel Willard described as "the short *Anarchy* accompanying our late Revolution"—allowed what under normal political conditions would have been an isolated, though ugly, local incident to expand into a major colonial crisis. Hysterical men and women living in Salem Village, a small, unprosperous farming community, nearly overwhelmed the new rulers of Massachusetts Bay. Accusations of witchcraft were not uncommon in

seventeenth-century New England. Puritans believed that an individual might make a compact with the devil, but during the first decades of settlement, authorities executed only about fifteen alleged witches. Sometimes villagers simply left suspected witches alone. Never before had fears of witchcraft plunged an entire community into panic.

The terror in Salem Village began in late 1691, when several adolescent girls began to behave in strange ways. They cried out for no apparent reason; they twitched on the ground. When concerned neighbors asked what caused their suffering, the girls announced that they were victims of witches, seemingly innocent persons who lived in the community. The arrest of several alleged witches did not relieve the girls "fits," nor did prayers solve the problem. Additional accusations were made, and at least one person confessed, providing a frightening description of the devil as "a thing all over hairy, all the face hairy, and a long nose." In June 1692, a special court convened and began to send men and women to the gallows. By the end of the summer, the court had hanged nineteen people; another was pressed to death. Many more suspects awaited trial.

Then suddenly, the storm was over. Led by Increase Mather, a group of prominent Congregational ministers urged leniency and restraint. Especially troubling to the clergymen was the court's decision to accept "spectral evidence," that is, reports of dreams and visions in which the accused appeared as the devil's agent. Worried about convicting people on such dubious testimony, Mather declared, "It were better that ten suspected witches should escape, than that one innocent person should be condemned." The colonial government accepted the ministers' advice and convened a new court, which promptly acquitted, pardoned, or released the remaining suspects. After the Salem nightmare, witchcraft ceased to be a capital offense.

No one knows exactly what sparked the terror in Salem Village. The community had a history of discord, and during the 1680s, the people split into angry factions over the choice of a minister. Jealousy and bitterness apparently festered to the point that adolescent girls who normally would have been disciplined were allowed to incite judicial murder. As often happens in incidents

Frontispiece of The Discovery of Witches *by Matthew Hopkins, published in 1647. Most Puritans believed in the existence of black magic. Books by such luminaries as Increase and Cotton Mather described how people behaved when they were bewitched.*

like this one—the McCarthy hearings of the 1950s, for example—the accusers later came to their senses and apologized for the needless suffering that they had caused.

Leisler's Rebellion Shakes New York

The Glorious Revolution in New York was more violent than it had been in Masschusetts Bay. Divisions within New York's ruling class ran deep and involved ethnic as well as religious differences. English newcomers and powerful Anglo-Dutch families who had recently risen to commercial prominence in New York City opposed the older Dutch elite.

Much like Nathaniel Bacon, Jacob Leisler was a man entangled in events beyond his control.

Leisler, the son of a German minister, emigrated to New York in 1660, and through marriage aligned himself with the Dutch elite. While he achieved moderate prosperity as a merchant, Leisler resented the success of the Anglo-Dutch.

When news of the Glorious Revolution reached New York City in May 1689, Leisler raised a group of militiamen and seized the local fort in the name of William and Mary. He apparently expected an outpouring of popular support, but it was not forthcoming. His rivals waited, watching while Leisler desperately attempted to legitimize his actions. Through bluff and badgering, Leisler managed to hold the colony together, especially after French forces burned Schenectady (February 1690), but he never established a secure political base.

In March 1691 a new royal governor, Henry Sloughter, reached New York. He ordered Leisler

Coode's Rebellion Divides Maryland

During the last third of the seventeenth century, the colony of Maryland stumbled from one political crisis to another. Protestants in the colony's lower house resisted Lord Baltimore's Catholic friends in the upper house or council. When news of James' overthrow reached Maryland early in 1689, pent-up anti-proprietary and anti-Catholic sentiment exploded. John Coode, a member of the assembly and an outspoken Protestant, formed a group called the Protestant Association, which in August forced Baltimore's governor, William Joseph, to resign.

Coode avoided Leisler's fatal mistakes. The Protestant Association, citing many wrongs suffered at the hands of local Catholics, petitioned the Crown to transform Maryland into a royal colony. After reviewing the case, William accepted Coode's explanation, and in 1691 the king dispatched a royal governor to Maryland. A new assembly dominated by Protestants declared Anglicanism the established religion. Catholics were excluded from public office on the grounds that they might be in league with French Catholics in Canada. Lord Baltimore lost control of the colony's government, but he and his family did retain title to Maryland's undistributed lands. In 1715, the Crown restored to full proprietorship the fourth Lord Baltimore, who had been raised a member of the Church of England, and Maryland remained in the hands of the Calvert family until 1776.

Common Experiences, Separate Cultures

"It is no little Blessing of God," Cotton Mather announced proudly in 1700, "that we are part of the *English* nation." A half century earlier John Winthrop would not have spoken these words, at least not with such enthusiasm. Mather's world was different from his. Colonial Americans had become more, not less, English. They had been drawn into an imperial system, Carolinians, Virginians, New Englanders, all regulated now by the same commercial statutes.

But profound sectional differences remained,

to surrender his authority, but when Sloughter refused to prove that he had been sent by William rather than by the deposed James, Leisler hesitated. The pause cost Leisler his life. Sloughter declared Leisler a rebel, and in a hasty trial, a court sentenced him and his chief lieutenant, Jacob Milbourne, to be hanged "by the Neck and being Alive their bodyes be Cutt downe to Earth and Their Bowells to be taken out and they being Alive, burnt before their faces . . . " In 1695 Parliament officially pardoned Leisler, but he not being "Alive," the decision arrived a bit late. Long after his death, political factions calling themselves Leislerians and Anti-Leislerians struggled to dominate New York government. Indeed, in no other eighteenth-century colony was the level of bitter political rivalry so high.

indeed had grown stronger, so that during the eighteenth century, the colonists felt increasingly torn between the culture of the mother country and the culture of their own region.

Recommended Reading

The best account of seventeenth-century New Englanders' views on the family remains Edmund S. Morgan, *The Puritan Family* (1966). Morgan has also produced a masterful analysis of a southern colony. His *American Slavery, American Freedom: The Ordeal of Colonial Virginia* (1975) examines the impact of an extraordinarily high death rate upon an evolving tri-racial plantation society. Anyone interested in the history of slavery should start with David B. Davis, *The Problem of Slavery in Western Culture* (1966) and Winthrop D. Jordan, *White Over Black: American Attitudes Toward the Negro, 1550–1812* (1968). A complete discussion of the drafting of the Navigation Acts and England's efforts to enforce them can be found in C. M. Andrews, *The Colonial Period of American History*, vol. 4 (1938). David S. Lovejoy provides a comprehensive survey of the various late seventeenth-century rebellions in *The Glorious Revolution in America* (1972).

Additional Bibliography

The historical literature dealing with early New England is immense. A good starting place is Stephen Foster, *Their Solitary Way* (1971), a highly readable analysis of the ways in which Puritans perceived their society. Two books that examine the relationship between the life cycle and social structure are John Demos, *A Little Commonwealth* (1970) and Philip J. Greven, *Four Generations* (1969). The best introduction to the demographic writings is John Murrin's brilliant "Review Essay," *History and Theory* 11 (1972): 226–275. There is no completely satisfactory examination of daily life in the northern colonies, but James T. Lemon's *The Best Poor Man's Country* (1972) is a fine investigation of rural culture in Pennsylvania. The role of women in this society is the subject of Roger Thompson, *Women in Stuart England and America* (1974); Lyle Koehler, *A Search for Power: "The Weaker Sex" in Seventeenth-Century New England* (1980); and Laurel T. Ulrich, *Good Wives: Image and Reality in the Lives of Women in Northern New England 1650–1750* (1982).

Readers interested in women or the family should see *William and Mary Quarterly, Maryland Historical Magazine, Journal of Interdisciplinary History,* and *Journal of Social History.* Education and literacy are treated from different perspectives in S. E. Morison, *Harvard College in the Seventeenth Century,* 2 vols. (1936); James Axtell, *The School Upon a Hill* (1974); and Kenneth Lockridge, *Literacy in Colonial New England* (1974).

The development of colonial society in the South is explored in two excellent essay collections: T. W. Tate and D. L. Ammerman, eds., *The Chesapeake in the Seventeenth Century* (1979) and A. C. Land et al., eds., *Law, Society, and Politics in Early Maryland* (1977). Wesley Frank Craven provides a useful introduction to the social history of the Chesapeake colonies in *White, Red, and Black* (1971), but anyone interested should read Bernard Bailyn, "Politics and Social Structure in Virginia," in J. M. Smith, ed., *Seventeenth-Century America* (1959). In *Colonists in America* (1947), A. E. Smith discusses indentured servitude, but see also David W. Galenson, *White Servitude in Colonial America: An Economic Analysis* (1981). Julia Cherry Spruill, *Women's Life and Work in the Southern Colonies* (1938) contains some interesting seventeenth-century material, although the book focuses on the eighteenth century. T. H. Breen speculates on the cultural values of early Virginians in *Puritans and Adventurers* (1980).

The black experience in colonial America has been the topic of several recent interdisciplinary studies: Philip D. Curtin, *The Atlantic Slave Trade: A Census* (1969); Peter Wood, *Black Majority* (1974); G. W. Mullin, *Flight and Rebellion* (1972); T. H. Breen and Stephen Innes, *"Myne Owne Ground," Race and Freedom on Virginia's Eastern Shore* (1980); Allan Kulikoff, "Origins of Afro-American Society in Maryland and Virginia," *William and Mary Quarterly,* 3d ser. 35 (1978); and Ira Berlin, "Time, Space, and the Evolution of Afro-American Society in British Mainland North America," *American Historical Review* 85 (1980): 44–78.

The development of the British imperial system has been exhaustively analyzed by historians L. W. Labaree, O. M. Dickerson, G. L. Beer, and L. A. Harper. A recent book that discusses the intellectual origins of Stuart economic policy is Joyce O. Appleby, *Economic Thought and Ideology in Seventeenth-Century England* (1978). A more controversial reassessment of imperial planning is S. S. Webb, *The Governors-General: The English Army and the Definition of Empire* (1979). On the impact of the Navigation Acts on seventeenth-century colonial society, see Bernard Bailyn, *The New England Merchants* (1965) and M. G. Hall, *Edward Randolph and the American Colonies* (1960).

There are several good studies of rebellions in specific colonies: W. Washburn, *The Governor and the Rebel* (1957) on Bacon's Rebellion; Thomas J. Archdeacon, *New York City, 1664–1710* (1976) on Leisler's Rebellion; and Lois Carr and D. W. Jordan, *Maryland's Revolution of Government* (1974) on Coode's Uprising. On King Philip's War, the best study is Douglas Leach, *Flintlock and Tomahawk* (1958). Of the many studies of Salem Village witchcraft, the most imaginative are Paul Boyer and Stephen Nissenbaum, *Salem Possessed* (1974) and John Demos, *Entertaining Satan: Witchcraft and the Culture of Early New England* (1982).

chapter 4

EXPANDING HORIZONS: EIGHTEENTH-CENTURY AMERICA

In the 1970s a group of archaeologists using sophisticated computer technology excavated two sites in the northwest corner of Massachusetts. It was in this area that more than two hundred years earlier the royal governor of Massachusetts had ordered construction of a "line of forts" to protect the colonists from marauding French and Indian troops. What the archaeologists found provided startling new insights into eighteenth-century American culture.

Artifacts taken from the sites indicated that the colonial farmers who defended the line of forts were linked in a score of ways to the cosmopolitan culture of Great Britain (following the union of England and Scotland in 1707, the mother country was called Great Britain, or more commonly, Britain). The provincial militiamen were not crude frontiersmen dressed in homespun garments; they wore clothes made from textiles manufactured in Britain. They drank rum from imported glasses, tea from delicate Staffordshire ceramics. They smoked pipes produced in London. Even their weapons had come from the mother country. One archaeologist concluded that the artifacts gathered in western Massachusetts were little different than those one might expect to find in the ruins of one of London's eighteenth-century "bawdy houses."

Life in the colonies during the eighteenth century was certainly different than it had been in the time of Captain John Smith and John Winthrop. After 1690, men and women were gradually drawn into a larger Anglo-American world. Colonists whose parents or grandparents had tamed a "howling wilderness" relied increasingly upon imported goods, read London journals, traveled to the mother country, fought Britain's enemies, and sought favors from a growing number of royal officials who now resided in the New World. Colonial women modeled themselves on the ideal of the English "genteel lady." As these changes occurred, people shed the purely local identities that had been so apparent during the seventeenth century. As their cultural horizons expanded to include not only the mother country but also other colonies, Americans gained a greater awareness of what it meant to be American.

The process produced severe strains. It was not unusual for colonists who adopted the latest London fashions to condemn the corrupting influence of British life. The same Americans who read the *Tatler* or *Spectator*—two popular British journals—often bragged about the superior virtue and simplicity of provincial society. Like the Scots and Irish of this period, they were simultaneously attracted to and repelled by the mother country, ambivalent about their own cultural identities.

Various colonists dealt with tensions in different ways. Benjamin Franklin, one of the most cosmopolitan figures of the age, championed American liberties. William Byrd, a Virginia planter who spent most of his adult life in Great Britain chasing celebrities, insisted that the air of America was purer than that of the mother country. Like inhabitants of the Garden of Eden, Byrd told a British correspondent, "we sit securely under our vines and our fig-trees." When British administrators treated these sensitive colonists as inferiors or country bumpkins, they forced Americans to choose between two cultural worlds, between European sophistication and provincial simplicity—or put another way, between reliance on the mother country and colonial independence.

People and Trade in an Expanding Empire

America's phenomenal growth during the eighteenth century amazed Benjamin Franklin. The population doubled approximately every twenty-five years, and according to calculations Franklin made in 1751, if the expansion continued as such a high level for another century or so, "the greatest Number of Englishmen will be on this Side [of] the water." Not only was the total population increasing at a very rapid rate, it also was becoming more dispersed and heterogeneous. Each year witnessed the arrival of thousands of non-English Europeans, most of whom were soon scattered along the colonial frontier. (See the maps of colonial settlement in the front pages of the text.)

Population Explosion

Accurate population data from the colonial period are extremely difficult to find. The first national census occurred in 1790. Still, various sources that have survived from prerevolutionary times indicate quite clearly that the total white population of Britain's mainland colonies rose from about 250,000 in 1700 to 2,150,000 in 1770, an annual growth rate of 3 percent. Few societies in recorded history have expanded so rapidly, and if the growth rate had not dropped substantially during the nineteenth and twentieth centuries, the current population of the United States would stand at well over a billion people. Natural reproduction was responsible for most of the growth. More families bore children who in turn lived long enough to have children of their own. Be-

cause of this extraordinary expansion, the population of the late colonial period was strikingly young; approximately one half of the populace at any given time was under the age of sixteen.

Immigration further swelled the colonial population. Non-English colonists poured into American ports throughout the eighteenth century, creating rich ethnic diversity in areas originally settled by Anglo-Saxons. The largest group of newcomers consisted of Scotch-Irish. The experiences of these people in Great Britain influenced not only their decision to move to the New World but also their behavior once they arrived.

During the seventeenth century, English rulers thought that they could bring order to Catholic Ireland by transporting thousands of lowland Scottish Presbyterians to the northern region of that war-torn country. The plan failed. English officials who were members of the Anglican church discriminated against the Presbyterians. They passed laws that placed the Scotch-Irish at a severe disadvantage when they traded in England; they taxed them at exorbitant rates. After several poor harvests, many of the Scotch-Irish elected to emigrate to America where they hoped to find the freedom and prosperity that had been denied in Ireland. "I have seen some of their letters to their friends here [Ireland]," one British agent reported in 1729, " . . . in which after they set forth and recommend the fruitfulness and commodities of the country [America], they tell them, that if they will but carry over a little money with them, they may for a small sum purchase considerable tracts of land." It is estimated that about 250,000 Scotch-Irish migrated to the colonies before the Revolution.

Most Scotch-Irish immigrants landed initially in Philadelphia, but instead of remaining in that city, they carved out farms on Pennsylvania's western frontier. The colony's proprietors welcomed the influx of new settlers, for it seemed as if they would form an ideal barrier between the Indians and the older, coastal communities. The Penn family soon had second thoughts, however. The Scotch-Irish squatted on whatever land looked best, and when colony officials pointed out that large tracts had already been reserved, the immigrants retorted "it was against the laws of God and nature that so much land should be idle when so many Christians wanted it to labour

Estimated Population, 1720–1760

		New England Colonies	Middle Colonies	Southern Colonies
1720	White	166,937	92,259	138,110
	Black	3,956	10,825	54,098
1730	White	211,233	135,298	191,893
	Black	6,118	11,683	73,220
1740	White	281,163	204,093	270,283
	Black	8,541	16,452	125,031
1750	White	349,029	275,723	309,588
	Black	10,982	20,736	204,702
1760	White	436,917	398,855	432,047
	Black	12,717	29,049	284,040

New England Colonies *New Hampshire, Massachusetts, Rhode Island, and Connecticut*

Middle Colonies *New York, New Jersey, Pennsylvania, and Delaware*

Southern Colonies *Maryland, Virginia, North Carolina, South Carolina, and (after 1740) Georgia*

Source: Adapted from R. C. Simmons, The American Colonies: From Settlement to Independence. ©1976 by R. C. Simmons. Reprinted by permission of the Harold Matson Company, Inc.

on and to raise their bread." Wherever they located, the Scotch-Irish challenged established authority.

A second large body of non-English settlers, more than 100,000 people, came from the upper Rhine Valley, the German Palatinate. Some of these people belonged to small, pietist Protestant sects whose views were somewhat similar to those of the Quakers; they came to America in hope of finding religious toleration. The Mennonites and Moravians—just to cite two such groups—achieved both peace and prosperity in the New World. The majority of the German immigrants, however, crossed the Atlantic for the same reasons as the Scotch-Irish. Lutherans and Calvinists fled from a region torn by war and hunger. These people—mistakenly called Pennsylvania Dutch—began reaching Philadelphia in large numbers after 1717, and by 1766 persons of German stock accounted for more than one third of Pennsylvania's total population. Even their detractors admitted that the Germans were the best farmers in the colony.

Ethnic differences in Pennsylvania bred disputes. The Scotch-Irish as well as the Germans preferred to live with people of their own background, and they sometimes fought to keep members of the other nationality out of their neighborhoods. The English were suspicious of both groups. They could not comprehend why the Germans insisted on speaking German in America. In 1753, for example, Franklin described these settlers as "the most stupid of their nation." He warned that "unless the stream of [German] importation could be turned from this to other colonies . . . they will soon outnumber us, [and] . . . all the advantages we have, will in my opinion, be not able to preserve our language, and even our government will become precarious."

Such open prejudice may have persuaded members of both groups to search for new homes. After 1730 Germans and Scotch-Irish pushed south from western Pennsylvania into the Shenandoah Valley. Thousands of men and women settled in the backcountry of Virginia and the Carolinas. The Germans usually remained wherever they found unclaimed fertile land. By contrast, the Scotch-Irish moved two or three times and acquired a reputation as a rootless people.

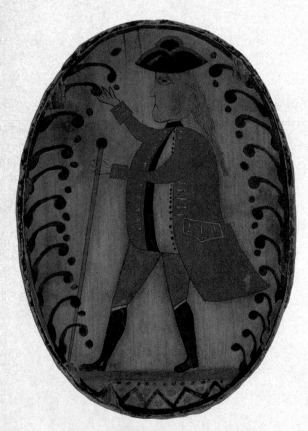

■ *This folk-art painting, from the cover of an old clothes box, shows a typical eighteenth-century German immigrant farmer, pigtail and all.*

Culture of the Cities

Considering the rate of population growth, it is surprising to discover how few eighteenth-century Americans lived in cities. Boston, Newport, New York, Philadelphia, and Charleston—the five largest cities—contained only about 5 percent of the colonial population. In 1775, none had more than forty thousand persons. The explanation for the relatively slow development of colonial American cities lies in their highly specialized commercial character. Colonial port towns served as entrepôts, intermediary trade and shipping centers where bulk cargoes were broken up for inland distribution and where agricultural products were gathered for export. They did not support large-scale manufacturing. Indeed, the pool of free urban laborers was quite small, since the type of person who was forced to work for wages in Europe usually became a farmer in America.

	Boston	%	Newport	%	New York	%	Philadelphia	%	Charleston	%
1720	12,000	—	3,800	—	7,000	—	10,000	—	3,500	—
1730	13,000	8	4,640	22	8,622	23	11,500	15	4,500	29
1740	15,601	20	5,840	26	10,451	21	12,654	10	6,269	39
1750	——	—	6,670	14	14,225	36	18,202	44	7,134	14
1760	15,631	—	7,500	12	18,000	27	23,750	30	8,000	12
1770	15,877	2	9,833	31	22,667	26	34,583	46	10,667	33

Source: R. C. Simmons, The American Colonies: From Settlement to Independence. *©1976 by R. C. Simmons. Reprinted by permission of the Harold Matson Company, Inc.*

Yet despite the limited urban population, cities profoundly influenced colonial culture. It was in the cities that Americans were exposed to and welcomed the latest English ideas. Wealthy colonists—merchants and lawyers—tried to emulate the culture of the mother country. They sponsored concerts and plays; they learned to dance. Women as well as men picked up the new fashions quickly, and even though most of them had never been outside the colony of their birth, they sometimes appeared to be the products of London's best families. One Englishman who thoroughly hated Americans confessed, "There are throughout these colonies, very lovely women, who have never passed the bounds of their respective provinces, and yet, I am persuaded, might appear to great advantage in the most brilliant circles of gaiety and fashion."

It was in the cities, also, that wealthy merchants transformed commercial profits into architectural splendor, for in their desire to outdo one another, they built grand homes of enduring beauty. Most of these buildings are descibed as Georgian because they were constructed during the reign of Britain's early Hanoverian kings, who all happened to be named George. Actually these homes were provincial copies of British country houses. They drew their inspiration from the great Italian Renaissance architect, Andrea Palladio (1518–1580), who had incorporated classical themes into a rigidly symmetrical form. Palladio's ideas were popularized in the colonies by James Gibbs, an Englishman whose *Book of Architecture* (1728) provided blueprints for the most spectacular homes of mid-eighteenth-century America.

■ *Merchants involved in the flourishing shipping trade required a corps of record clerks and bookkeepers.*

■ *John Singleton Copley's portraits convey a powerful sense of the subject's physical presence—a real person, as he or she really is—as in* Boy with the Squirrel.

could not find the training they required in the colonies; America seemed devoid of kind of subject matter that inspired the great European masters. Benjamin West left Philadelphia for London in 1759. John Singleton Copley, perhaps colonial America's finest painter, built up an enthusiastic following among the affluent merchants of Boston. He always wondered, however, whether the English would respect his work. After he had sent Sir Joshua Reynolds, the most famous painter of the age, a copy of his *The Boy with the Squirrel*, Copley received this advice. "If you are capable of producing such a piece by the mere efforts of your own genius," Reynolds explained, "with the advantages of example and instruction you would have in Europe you would be valuable acquisition to the art and one of the finest painters in the world." In 1774 Copley joined West and other Americans in London.

Economic Expansion

The colonial economy kept pace with the stunning growth in population. During the first three quarters of the eighteenth century, the population increased at least tenfold, and yet even with so many additional people to feed and clothe, the *per capita* income did not decline. Indeed, with the exception of poor urban dwellers, such as sailors whose employment varied with the season, white Americans did quite well. An abundance of land and the extensive growth of agriculture accounted for their economic success. New farmers were not only able to provide for their families' well-being but to sell their crops in European and West Indian markets as well. Each year more Americans produced more tobacco, wheat, or rice—just to cite the major export crops—and by this means, they maintained a high level of individual prosperity without developing an industrial base.

At mid-century colonial exports flowed along well-established routes. Over half of American goods produced for export went to Great Britain. The Navigation Acts (see chapter 3) were still in effect and "enumerated" items such as tobacco had to be landed first at a British port. Furs were added to the restricted list in 1722. The White Pines Acts passed in 1711, '22, and '29 forbade Americans from cutting white pine trees without a license. The purpose of this legislation was to

Their owners filled these houses with fine furniture. Each city patronized certain skilled craftsmen, but the artisans of Philadelphia were known for producing magnificent copies of the works of Thomas Chippendale, Great Britain's most famous furniture designer. These developments gave American cities an elegance that they had not possessed in the previous century. One foreign visitor noted of Philadelphia in 1748, " . . . its natural advantages, trade, riches and power, are by no means inferior to any, even of the most ancient towns of Europe." As this traveler understood, the cultural impact of the cities went far beyond the number of people who actually lived there.

For some American artists colonial society became an increasing frustration. As they learned more and more about the culture of the mother country, especially about its painting and sculpture, the more depressed they became. They

reserve the best trees for the use of the Royal Navy. The Sugar Act of 1733—also called the Molasses Act—placed a heavy duty on molasses imported from foreign ports, while the Hat and Felt Act of 1732 and the Iron Act of 1750 attempted to limit the production of colonial goods that competed with British exports.

These statutes might have created tensions between the colonists and the mother country had they been rigorously enforced. Crown officials, however, generally ignored the new laws. New England merchants imported molasses from French Caribbean islands without paying the full customs; ironmasters in the Middle Colonies continued to produce iron. But even without the Navigation Acts, a majority of colonial exports would have been sold on the English market. The emerging Industrial Revolution in Great Britain was beginning to create a new generation of consumers who possessed enough income to purchase American goods, especially sugar and tobacco. This rising demand was the major market force shaping the colonial economy.

Colonial merchants operating out of Boston, Newport, and Philadelphia also carried substantial tonnage to the West Indies. In 1768 this market accounted for 27 percent of all American exports. If there was a triangular trade that included the west coast of Africa, it does not seem to have been economically significant. Colonial ships carrying food sailed for the Caribbean and returned immediately to the Middle Colonies or New England with cargoes of molasses, sugar, and rum. In fact, recent research indicates that during the eighteenth century, trade with Africa involved less than 1 percent of all American exports. Slaves were transported directly to colonial ports where they were sold for cash or credit.

The West Indies played a vital role in preserving American credit. Without this source of income, colonists would not have been able to pay for the manufactured items that they purchased in the mother country. To be sure, they exported American products in great quantity to Great Britain, but the value of these exports seldom equaled the cost of British goods shipped back to the colonists. To cover this small but recurrent deficit, colonial merchants relied upon profits made in the West Indies.

After mid-century, however, the balance of trade turned dramatically against the colonists.

■ *Luxury items, such as George Washington's Chinese porcelain punch bowl, were ordered and shipped through agents in London.*

The reasons for this change were complex, but in simplest terms, Americans began buying more English goods than their parents or grandparents had done. Between 1740 and 1770 English exports to the American colonies increased by an astounding 360 percent.

In part, this shift reflected a fundamental transformation in the British economy. The mother country had entered the Industrial Revolution—a full half-century before the Americans—and British factories produced certain goods more efficiently and more cheaply than the colonists could. The availability of these products altered the lives of most Americans, even those with modest incomes. Staffordshire china replaced crude earthenware; imported cloth replaced homespun. Franklin noted in his *Autobiography* how changing consumer habits affected his life. For years he had eaten his breakfast in an earthenware bowl with a pewter spoon, but on one morning it was served "in a china bowl, with a spoon of silver." Franklin observed that "this was the first appearance of plate and china in our house which afterwards in the course of years, as our wealth increased, augmented gradually to several hundred pounds in value." In this manner, British industrialization undercut Americn handicraft and folk art.

To help Americans purchase manufactured goods, British merchants offered generous credit. Colonists deferred settlement by agreeing to pay interest on their debts. For many people, the temptation to acquire English finery blinded them to hard economic realities. They gambled on the future, hoping that bumper farm crops would reduce their dependence upon the large merchant houses of London and Glasgow. Some persons obviously lived within their means, but the aggregate American debt continued to grow. By 1760 total indebtedness had reached £2 million. Colonial leaders tried various expedients to remain solvent—issuing paper money, for example—and while these efforts delayed a crisis, the balance of payments problem was clearly very serious.

The eighteenth century also saw a substantial increase in intercoastal trade. Southern planters sent tobacco and rice to New England and the Middle Colonies where these staples were exchanged for meat and wheat as well as goods imported from Great Britain. By 1760 approximately 30 percent of the colonists' total tonnage capacity was involved in this extensive "coastwise" commerce. In addition, backcountry farmers in western Pennsylvania and the Shenandoah Valley carried their grain to market along an old Iroquois trail that became known as the "Great Wagon Road," a rough, hilly highway that by the time of the Revolution stretched 735 miles along the Blue Ridge Mountains to Camden, South Carolina. Most of their produce was carried in long, gracefully designed Conestoga wagons. These vehicles—sometimes called the "wagons of empire"—had been invented by German immigrants living in the Conestoga River Valley in Lancaster County, Pennsylvania.

These shifting patterns of trade had an immense effect on the development of an American culture. First, the flood of British imports eroded local and regional identities. Or, put another way, commerce helped to "anglicize" American culture by exposing colonial consumers to a common range of British manufactured goods. Deep sectional differences remained, of course, but Americans from New Hampshire to Georgia were increasingly drawn into a sophisticated economic network centered in London.

Second, the expanding coastwise and overland trade brought colonists of different backgrounds into more frequent contact. Ships that sailed between New England and South Carolina, between Virginia and Pennsylvania provided dispersed Americans with a means to exchange ideas and experiences on a more regular basis. Mid-eighteenth-century printers, for example, established several dozen new journals; these were weekly newspapers that carried information not

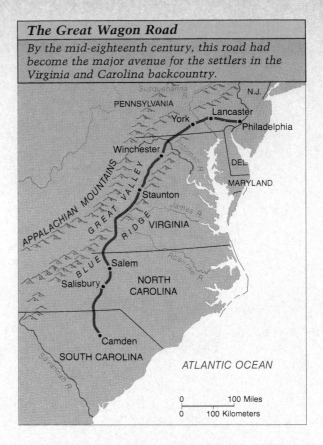

The Great Wagon Road

By the mid-eighteenth century, this road had become the major avenue for the settlers in the Virginia and Carolina backcountry.

only about the mother country and world commerce but also about events in other colonies. As the editor of the *New Hampshire Gazette* announced in his first issue (October 7, 1756), ". . . every lover of Mankind must feel a strong desire to know what passes in the world, as well as within his own private sphere; and particularly to be acquainted with the affairs of his own nation and Country." Americans were expanding their horizons.

Religious Revival in an Age of Reason

Two great forces—one intellectual, the other religious—transformed the character of eighteenth-century American life. Although both movements originated in Europe, they were redefined in a New World context and soon reflected the peculiarities of the colonial experience. The

Enlightenment changed the way that educated, urbane colonists looked at their world; the *Great Awakening* brought the "new birth" to thousands of men and women scattered along the Atlantic coast. Both movements made Americans aware of other persons, often complete strangers, who shared their beliefs. These voluntary networks undercut traditional community ties and helped the colonists forge new cultural identities.

American Enlightenment

European historians often refer to the eighteenth century as an Age of Reason. During this period, a body of new, often radical, ideas swept through the salons and universities, altering the way that educated Europeans thought about God, nature, and society. This intellectual revolution, called the Enlightenment, involved the work of Europe's greatest minds, men like Newton and Locke, Voltaire and Hume. The writings of such thinkers eventually reached the colonies, where they received a mixed reception. On the whole, the American Enlightenment was a rather tame affair compared to its European counterpart, for while the colonists welcomed experimental science, they defended the tenets of traditional Christianity.

Enlightenment thinkers shared basic assumptions. Philosophers of the Enlightenment replaced the concept of original sin with a much more optimisic view of human nature. A benevolent God, having set the universe in motion, gave human beings the power of reason to enable them to comprehend the orderly workings of his creation. Everything, even human society, operated according to these mechanical rules. The responsibility of right-thinking men and women, therefore, was to make certain that institutions such as church and state conformed to self-evident natural laws. It was possible—or so some of the *philosophes* claimed—to achieve perfection in this world. In fact, human suffering had come about only because people had lost touch with the fundamental insights of reason.

For many Americans, the appeal of the Enlightenment was its focus on a search for useful knowledge, ideas, and inventions that would improve the quality of human life. What mattered was practical experimentation. A speech delivered in 1767 before the members of the American Society in Philadelphia reflected the new utilitarian spirit: "Knowledge is of little Use when confined to mere Speculation," the colonist explained, "But when speculative Truths are reduced to Practice, when Theories grounded upon Experiments . . . and the Arts of Living made more easy and comfortable . . . Knowledge then becomes really useful." The Enlightenment spawned scores of earnest scientific tinkerers, people who dutifully recorded changes in temperature, the appearance of strange plants and animals, and the details of astronomic phenomena. While these eighteenth-century Americans made few earth-shattering discoveries, they did encourage their countrymen, especially those who attended college, to apply reason to the solution of social and political problems.

Benjamin Franklin (1706–1790) epitomized the Enlightenment in colonial America. European thinkers regarded him as a genuine *philosophe*, a role that he self-consciously cultivated when he visited England and France in later life. Franklin did not receive a college education, but as a young man working in his brother's printshop, he managed to keep up with the latest intellectual currents. In his *Autobiography*, Franklin described the excitement of discovering a new British journal. It was like a breath of fresh air to a boy growing up in Puritan New England. "I met with an odd volume of *The Spectator*," Franklin recounted, " . . . I had never before seen any of them. I bought it, read it over and over, and was much delighted with it. I thought the writing excellent, and wished if possible to imitate it."

Franklin's opportunity came in August 1721 when he and his brother founded *The New-England Courant*, a weekly newspaper that satirized Boston's political and religious leaders in the manner of the contemporary British press. Writing under the name "Silence Dogood," young Franklin asked his readers "Whether a Commonwealth suffers more by hypocritical Pretenders to Religion, or by the openly Profane?" Proper Bostonians were not prepared for a journal that one minister described as "full freighted with Nonesense, Unmannerliness, Railery, Prophaneness, Immorality, Arrogance, Calumnies, Lyes, Contradictions, and what not, all tending to Quarrels and Divisions and to Debauch and Corrupt the Minds and Manners of New England."

■ *Benjamin Franklin (left) exemplified the Enlightenment's scientific curiosity and search for practical knowledge. Franklin's experiments on electricity became world famous and inspired many others to study the effects of this strange force. These people are rubbing rods to produce static electricity.*

Franklin got the point; he left Massachusetts in 1723 in search of a less hostile intellectual environment.

After he had moved to Philadelphia, leaving behind his brother as well as New England Puritanism, Franklin devoted himself to the pursuit of useful knowledge, ideas that would increase the happiness of his fellow Americans. Franklin never denied the existence of God. Rather, he pushed the Lord aside, making room for the free exercise of human reason. Franklin tinkered, experimented, and reformed. Almost everything that he encountered in his daily life aroused his curiosity. His investigation of electricity brought him world fame, but Franklin was never satisfied with his work in this field until it yielded practical application. In 1756 he invented the lightning rod. He also designed a marvelously efficient stove that is still used today. In modern America, Franklin has become exactly what he would have wanted to be, a symbol of material progress through human ingenuity.

Franklin energetically promoted the spread of Enlightenment ideas. In Philadelphia, he con-

stantly organized groups that discussed the latest European literature, philosophy, and science. In 1727, for example, he "form'd most of my ingenious Acquaintances into a Club for mutual Improvement, which we call'd the Junto." Four years later Franklin took a leading part in the formation of the Library Company, a voluntary association that for the first time allowed people like himself to pursue "useful knowledge." The members of these societies communicated with Americans living in other colonies, providing them not only with new information but also with models for their own clubs and associations. Such efforts broadened the intellectual horizons of many colonists, especially those who lived in cities.

Great Awakening

The Great Awakening had a far greater impact on the lives of the common people than did the Enlightenment. This unprecedented evangelical outpouring altered the course of American history. In our own time, of course, we have witnessed the force of religious revival in different regions throughout the world. It is no exaggeration to claim that a similar revolution took place in mid-eighteenth-century America, for it caused men and women to rethink basic assumptions about church and state, institutions and society.

Only with hindsight does the Great Awakening seem a unified religious movement. Revivals occurred in different places at different times; the intensity of the event varied from region to region. The first signs of a spiritual awakening appeared in New England during the 1740s, but within a decade the revivals in this area had burnt themselves out. It was not until the 1750s and '60s that the Awakening made more than a superficial impact upon the people of Virginia. The revivals were most important in Massachusetts, Connecticut, Rhode Island, Pennsylvania, New Jersey, and Virginia. Their effect upon religion in New York, Delaware, and the Carolinas was marginal. No single religious denomination or sect monopolized the Awakening. In New England revivals shattered Congregational churches, but in the South, especially in Virginia, they involved Presbyterians, Methodists, and Baptists. Moreover, there was nothing peculiarly American about the Great Awakening. Mid-eighteenth-century Europe experienced a similar burst of religious emotionalism.

Whatever their origins, the seeds of revival were generally sown on fertile ground. In the early decades of the century, many Americans—but especially New Englanders—complained that organized religion had lost vitality. They looked back at Winthrop's generation with nostalgia, assuming that common people at that time must have possessed greater piety than did later, more worldly colonists. Congregational ministers seemed obsessed with dull, scholastic matters; they no longer touched the heart. And in the southern colonies, there were simply not enough ordained ministers to tend to the religious needs of the population. The problem was so acute that in 1701 an English Anglican, Thomas Bray (1656–1730), launched a missionary endeavor called the Society for the Propagation of the Gospel in Foreign Parts. The "Foreign Parts" were places like South Carolina and Connecticut. While Bray and his missionaries worked diligently, they did not command sufficient resources to meet the challenge.

The Great Awakening began unexpectedly in Northampton, a small farm community in western Massachusetts, sparked by Jonathan Edwards, the local Congregational minister. Edwards accepted the traditional teachings of Calvinism (see chapter 1), reminding his parishioners that their eternal fate had been determined by an omnipotent God, that there was nothing they could do to save themselves, and that they were totally dependent upon the Lord's will. He thought his fellow ministers had grown soft. They left men and women with the mistaken impression that sinners might somehow avoid eternal damnation simply by performing good works. "How dismal will it be," Edwards told his complaisant congregation, "when you are under these racking torments, to know assuredly that you never, never shall be delivered from them." Edwards was not exaggerating his message in an attempt to be dramatic. He spoke of God's omnipotence with such calm self-assurance that even people who had not thought deeply about religious matters were shaken by his words.

Why this uncompromising message set off several religious revivals during the late 1730s is not known. Whatever the explanation for the sudden popular response to Edwards' preaching, young people began flocking to the church. They experienced a searing conversion, a sense of "new birth" and utter dependence upon God. "Surely," Edwards pronounced, "this is the Lord's doing, and it is marvelous in our eyes." The excitement spread, and evangelical ministers concluded that God must be preparing Americans, his chosen people, for the millennium. "What is now seen in America and especially in New England," Edwards explained, "may prove the dawn of that glorious day."

Edwards was a brilliant theologian, but he did not possess the dynamic personality required to sustain the revival. That responsibility fell to George Whitefield, a young, inspiring preacher from England who toured the colonies from New Hampshire to Georgia. While Whitefield was not an original thinker, he was an extraordinarily effective public speaker. According to Edwards' wife, it was wonderful to witness what a spell Whitefield " . . . casts over an audience . . . I have seen upwards of a thousand people hang on his words with breathless silence, broken only by an occasional half-suppressed sob."

Religious Revival in an Age of Reason

■ *The fervor of the Great Awakening was intensified by the eloquence of touring preachers like George Whitefield, who enthralled his audiences.*

Whitefield's audiences came from all groups of American society, rich and poor, young and old, rural and urban. One obscure Connecticut farmer, Nathan Cole, left a moving account of a sermon Whitefield delivered in Middleton in 1741. Rushing with his wife along the dirt roads, Cole encountered "a stedy streem of horses & their riders scarcely a horse more than his length behind another all of a lather and fome with swet ther breath rooling out of their noistrels in the cloud of dust every jump every hors seemed to go with all his might to carry his rider to hear the news from heaven for the saving of their Souls." When Cole heard the great preacher, the farmer experienced what he called "a heart wound." While Whitefield described himself as a Calvinist, he welcomed all Protestants. He spoke from any pulpit that was available. "Don't tell me you are a Baptist, an Independent, a Presbyterian, a dissenter," he thundered, "tell me you are a Christian, that is all I want."

Other, American-born itinerant preachers followed Whitefield's example. The most famous was Gilbert Tennent, a Presbyterian of Scotch-Irish background who had been educated in the Middle Colonies. His sermon, "On the Danger of an Unconverted Ministry," printed in 1742 set off a storm of protest from established ministers who were understandably insulted. Lesser known revivalists traveled from town to town, colony to colony challenging local clergymen who seemed hostile to evangelical religion. Men and women who thronged to hear the itinerants were called "New Lights," and during the 1740s and '50s, many congregations split between defenders of the new emotional preaching and those who regarded the entire movement as dangerous nonsense.

Despite Whitefield's successes, many ministers remained suspicious of the itinerants and their methods. Some complaints may have amounted to little more than sour grapes. One "Old Light" spokesman labeled Tennent "a monster! impudent and noisy." He claimed that Tennent told anxious Christians that "they were *damned! damned! damned!* This charmed them; and, in the most dreadful winter I ever saw, people wallowed in snow, night and day, for the benefit of his beastly brayings; and many ended their days under these fatigues." Charles Chauncy, minister of the prestigious First Church of Boston, raised much more troubling issues. How could the revivalists be certain that God had sparked the Great Awakening? Perhaps the itinerants had relied too much upon emotion? "Let us esteem those as friends of religion," Chauncy warned, " . . . who warn us of the danger of enthusiasm, and would put us on our guard, that we may not be led aside by it."

While Tennent did not condone the excesses of the Great Awakening, his attacks on formal learning invited the crude anti-intellectualism of such fanatics as James Davenport. This deranged revivalist traveled along the Connecticut coast in 1742 playing upon popular emotion. At night, under the light of smoky torches, he danced and stripped, shrieked and laughed. He also urged people to burn books written by authors who had not experienced the new light as defined by Davenport. Like so many fanatics throughout history who have claimed a special knowledge of the "truth," Davenport later recanted and begged pardon for his unfortunate behavior.

To concentrate upon the bizarre activities of Davenport—as many critics of the Great Awakening have done—is to obscure the positive ways in which this vast revival changed American society. First, despite occasional anti-intellectual outbursts, the New Lights founded several important centers of higher learning. They wanted to train young men who would carry on the good works of Edwards, Whitefield, and Tennent. In 1747 New Light Presbyterians established the College of New Jersey, which later became Princeton University. Just before his death, Edwards was appointed its president. The evangelical minister, Eleazar Wheelock, launched Dartmouth (1769), while other revivalists founded Brown (1764) and Rutgers (1766).

The Great Awakening also encouraged men and women who had been taught to remain silent before traditional figures of authority to speak up, to take an active role in their salvation. They could no longer rely upon ministers or institutions. The individual alone stood before God. Knowing this, New Lights made religious choices that shattered the old harmony among Protestant sects, and in its place, they introduced a noisy, often bitterly fought competition. As one New Jersey Presbyterian explained, "There are so many particular *sects* and *Parties* among professed Christians . . . that we know not . . . in which of these different *paths*, to steer our course for *Heaven*."

With religious contention, however, came an awareness of a larger community, a union of fellow believers that extended beyond the boundaries of town and colony. In fact, evangelical religion was one of several forces at work during the mid-eighteenth century that brought scattered colonists into contact with one another for the first time. In this sense, the Great Awakening was a "national" event long before a nation actually existed.

People who had been touched by the Great Awakening shared an optimism about the future of America. With God's help, social and political progress was possible, and from this perspective, of course, the New Lights did not sound much different than the mildly rationalist American spokesmen of the Enlightenment. Both groups prepared the way for the development of a revolutionary mentality in colonial America.

Anglo-American Politics: Theory and Practice

The balanced constitution of Great Britain was an object of nearly universal admiration during the eighteenth century. According to its defenders, it protected life, liberty, and property better than did any other contemporary government. The English constitution contained three distinct parts. The monarch was at the top, advised by a Cabinet Council of handpicked court favorites. Next came the House of Lords, a body of 180 aristocrats who served with 26 Anglican bishops as the upper house of Parliament. And third was the House of Commons, composed of 558 members elected by various constituencies scattered throughout the realm.

Political theorists waxed eloquent on why the British constitution worked so well. Each of the three parts of government, it seemed, represented a separate socioeconomic interest: king, nobility,

■ *An early eighteenth-century painting by Peter Tillemans of the House of Commons in session.*

and common people. Acting alone each body would run to excess, even tyranny, but operating within a mixed system, they automatically checked each other's ambitions for the common good. Unlike the delegates who wrote the Constitution of the United States, eighteenth-century Englishmen did not perceive the constitution as a balance of executive, legislative, and judicial branches.

The Reality of British Politics

The reality of daily political life, however, bore little relation to theory. The three elements of the constitution did not, in fact, represent distinct socioeconomic groups. Men elected to the House of Commons often came from the same social background as did those who served in the House of Lords. All represented the interests of Britain's landed elite. Moreover, there was no attempt to maintain strict constitutional separation. The king, for example, organized parliamentary associations, loose groups of political followers who sat in the House of Commons and who openly supported the monarch's policies in exchange for patronage or pension.

The claim that the members of the House of Commons represented all the people of England also seemed farfetched. As of 1715 roughly no more than 20 percent of Britain's adult males had the right to vote. Property qualifications or other restrictions often greatly reduced the number of eligible voters. In addition, the size of the electoral districts varied throughout the kingdom. In some boroughs representatives to Parliament were chosen by several thousand voters. In many districts, however, a handful of electors controlled the result. These tiny or "rotten" boroughs were an embarrassment. The Methodist leader, John Wesley, complained that Old Sarum, an almost uninhabited borough, "in spite of common sense, without house or inhabitant, still sends two members to the parliament." Since these districts were so small, a wealthy lord or ambitious politician could easily bribe or otherwise "influence" the entire constituency, something they did regularly throughout the century.

Before 1760 few people in England spoke out against these constitutional abuses. The main exception was a group of radical publicists whom historians have labeled the "Commonwealthmen." These writers decried the corruption of political life, noting that a nation that compromised civic virtue, that failed to stand vigilant against fawning courtiers and would-be despots, deserved to lose its liberty and property. The most famous Commonwealthmen were John Trenchard and Thomas Gordon, who penned a series of essays entitled *Cato's Letters* between 1720 and 1723. If England's rulers were corrupt, they warned, then the people could not expect the balanced constitution to save them from tyranny. In one typical article, Trenchard and Gordon observed "The Appitites . . . of Men, especially of Great Men, are carefully to be observed and stayed, or else they will never stay themselves. The Experience of every Age convinces us, that we must not judge of Men by what they ought to do, but by what they will do." Another much more famous and allegedly more conservative political theorist, the Tory Lord Bolingbroke, shared this morally charged perspective on the constitution.

But however shrilly these writers protested, however many newspaper articles they published, these figures won little support for their political reforms. Most eighteenth-century Englishmen admitted that there was more than a grain of truth in the commonwealth critique, but they were not willing to tamper with a system of government that had so recently survived a civil war and a Glorious Revolution. Americans, however, took Trenchard and Gordon to heart.

American Political Culture at Mid-Century

The colonists assumed—perhaps naively—that their own governments were modeled upon the balanced constitution of Great Britain. They argued that within their political systems, the governor corresponded to the king, and the governor's council to the House of Lords. The colonial assemblies were perceived as American reproductions of the House of Commons and were expected to preserve the interests of the people against those of the monarch and aristocracy. As the colonists discovered, however, English theories about the mixed constitution were no more

The Election *by William Hogarth illustrates just one aspect of electoral corruption in England—voters were openly willing to sell their votes to either (or both) sides in an election. The proceeding was by no means remarkable.*

relevant in America than they were in the mother country.

By mid-century royal governors appointed by the Crown ruled a majority of the mainland colonies. Many of the appointees were career army officers who through luck, charm, or family connection had gained the ear of someone close to the king. These patronage posts did not generate income sufficient to interest the most powerful or talented personalities of the period, but they did draw middle-level bureaucrats who were ambitious, desperate, or both.

George Clinton, who served as New York's governor from 1743 to 1753, was probably typical of the men who received appointment. Before coming to the colonies, Clinton had compiled an extraordinary record of ineptitude as a naval officer. He gained the governorship more as a means to get him out of England than as a sign of trust or respect. When he arrived in New York City, Clinton ignored the colonists. "In a province given to hospitality," wrote one critic, "he [Clinton] erred by immuring himself in the fort, or retiring to a grotto in the country, where his time was spent with his bottle and a little trifling circle."

Before departing for the New World, royal governors received an elaborate set of instructions drafted by the Board of Trade. This document dealt with almost every aspect of colonial life, political, economic, and religious, and it would have been an exceptional man who could have carried out even a small number of these instructions. Horace Walpole, a respected man of letters in the mother country, described the instructions prepared for Governor Osborn of New York in 1753 as "better calculated for the latitude of Mexico and for a Spanish tribunal than for a free rich British settlement." No one knew for certain whether these orders even possessed the force of law.

About the governor's powers, however, there was no doubt. They were enormous. In fact, royal governors could do certain things in America that a king could not do in eighteenth-century Britain. Among these were the right to veto legislation and dismiss judges. The governors also served as commanders in chief in each province.

Royal governors were advised by a council, usually a body of about twelve wealthy colonists selected by the Board of Trade in London upon the recommendation of the governor. During the seventeenth century, the council had played an important role in colonial government, but its ability to exercise independent authority declined steadily over the course of the eighteenth centu-

The Challenge of Travel in Eighteenth-Century America

Travel in eighteenth-century America required stamina and courage. Roads were unpaved and unlit and even a light rain could transform a dusty surface into impassable mud. Taverns of questionable quality appeared at unpredictable intervals. Despite these problems, adventurous men and women accepted the challenge of travel, and a few even described their experiences in published reports.

Colonial authorities paid little attention to the way roads were laid out. Local farmers usually petitioned a colonial assembly or county court for permission to build a new road, but these bodies neither funded nor supervised the projects. Villagers cleared and maintained their own highways. They repaired only the roads that were most important to the life of the community, allowing others to return to forest or pasture.

Even roads well maintained by eighteenth-century standards were difficult to travel. Colonial roads often divided into unmarked branches, and if no local residents were available to give directions, the traveler might spend hours following the wrong path. While returning from a campaign during the French and Indian War, a company of Massachusetts troops marched thirty miles out of the way before discovering the mistake. Most regiments employed surveyors and engineers just to determine whether the roads and bridges that appeared on their maps were in fact passable.

The width of the eighteenth-century roads varied immensely. Some were described as more than sixty feet wide. Other rural roads were so narrow that colonists feared that wild beasts would leap out of the underbrush and devour them. In 1775, a Scotwoman riding along such a road exclaimed, "All I had ever heard of lions, bears, tigers and wolves now rushed to my memory, and I secretly wished I had been made a feast to the fishes rather than to those monsters of the woods." One man living in Massachusetts refused to visit Maryland because he thought he might be attacked by wild animals.

River crossings were a colonial traveler's nightmare. Since bridges were difficult to build and expensive to maintain, people generally crossed the rivers via ferries. Licensed by colonial authorities, ferries were privately owned and varied in dependability. A single boat usually served each crossing, and travelers summoned ferry operators from the opposite bank by yelling, ringing bells, or lighting fires. If the boatman was working in his fields or if he just did not feel like responding to the call, he ignored the traveler, and it was not unusual for persons to wait hours to cross even a small river. One terrified woman had to hire a canoe to take her over a stream, but it was so poorly balanced that she dared not "so much as to lodge my tongue a hair's breadth more on one side of my mouth than t'other."

Inns, often called "ordinaries" in colonial America, offered the weary traveler a good meal, stalls for horses, a place to sleep, and recreational facilities (see scene below). They advertised with brightly colored signs, often depicting magnificent animals. One imaginative innkeeper in Frankford, Pennsylvania, lured customers with this rhyme:

> Here in this hive we're all alive,
> Good liquor makes us funny.
> If you are dry, step in and try
> The flavor of our honey.

The owner of "the Yellow House" in New Jersey hung out a sign depicting a horse, a fish, a bird, and this doggerel verse:

> This is the Horse that never ran,
> This is the Fish that never swam,
> This is the Bird that never flew
> Here's good fare for your horse and you.

A good many inns were apparently guilty of false advertising. The food they served to travelers was so revolting that hungry men and women went to bed without supper rather than risk a public meal. Once they had been assigned a bedroom, the travelers often found strangers, some of them drunk, sleeping on the floor in their room or even climbing into bed with them. Madam Knight, a woman who was traveling alone, reported that two men whom she did not know slept in her room. A visitor to New Haven was given a room in which three beds accommodated six men.

Colonists, especially members of the gentry, complained that many ordinaries catered to a particularly unsavory clientele. Luke Dean of Georgia, for example, was arrested "for keeping a disorderly house, and entertaining horse-stealers, and other persons of ill-fame; and also for entertaining and harbouring slaves." Travelers protested the drinking and gambling that continued well into the morning. Perhaps the most unusual complaint came from a wealthy Marylander who confronted some "rabble" at an inn in Saybrook, Connecticut. These local farmers had clearly been converted by an evangelical preacher, and they lectured the stranger about "regeneration, repentance, free grace, reprobation, original sign, and a thousand other such pretty chimerical knick-knacks, as if they had done nothing but studied divinity all their life-time."

By mid-century the quality of roads and ferries had gradually improved. The creation of stagecoach lines and the development of more reliable "post" roads on which mail was carried reflected

the growing desire to travel and communicate over longer distances. In 1736, the first stage line opened between Boston and Newport, Rhode Island. By 1751 coaches ran regularly between New York and Philadelphia. Ferry operators scheduled more boats. In 1760, some Connecticut residents petitioned to enlarge the road between Torrington and Winchester, explaining in words that were becoming common throughout colonial America that their old road would "never accommodate one half the people that want to travel."

ry. Its members certainly did not represent a distinct social class within American society.

If royal governors did not look like kings, nor councils like the House of Lords, colonial assemblies bore but a faint resemblance to the eighteenth-century House of Commons. The major difference was the extent of the American franchise. In most colonies adult white males who owned a small amount of land could vote in colony-wide elections. One historian estimates that 95 percent of this group in Massachusetts were eligible to participate in elections. The number in Virginia was about 85 percent. These high figures—much larger than those of contemporary England—have led some scholars to view the colonies as "middle-class democracies," societies run by moderately prosperous yeomen farmers who—in politics at least—exercised independent judgment. There were too many of them to bribe, no "rotten" boroughs, and when these people moved west, colonial assemblies usually created new electoral districts.

One should not leap to the conclusion that colonial governments were democracies in the modern sense of that term. Possessing the right to vote was one thing, exercising it quite another. Americans participated in elections when major issues were at stake—the formation of banks in mid-eighteenth-century Massachusetts, for example—but most of the time they were content to let members of the rural and urban gentry represent them in the assemblies. The point to remember, however, is that the potential to expel legislative rascals was always present in America, and it was this political reality that kept aristocratic gentlemen from straying too far from the will of the people.

Rise of the Colonial Assemblies

Members of the assemblies were convinced that they had a special obligation to preserve colonial liberties. Any attack upon the legislature was perceived as an assault upon the rights of Americans. The elected representatives brooked no criticism, and several colonial printers landed in jail because they foolishly published demeaning statements about the actions of the lower house.

So aggressive were these bodies in seizing privileges, determining procedures, and controlling

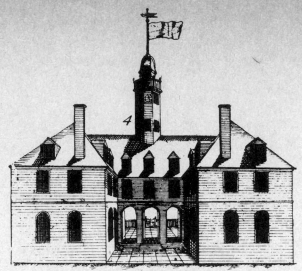

■ *This copperplate engraving by an unknown artist (c. 1740) is a rendering of the north elevation of the first Capitol at Williamsburg.*

money bills that some historians have described the political development of eighteenth-century America as "the rise of the assemblies." No doubt, this is an exaggeration, but the long series of imperial wars against the French, each of which demanded high levels of public expenditure, transformed the small, amateurish assemblies of the seventeenth century into the more professional, vigilant legislatures of the eighteenth.

This political system seemed designed to generate hostility. There was simply no reason for the colonial legislators to cooperate with appointed royal governors. Alexander Spotswood, Virginia's governor 1710 to 1723, attempted to institute a bold new land program backed by the Crown. He tried persuasion and gifts, and when these failed, chicanery. But the members of the House of Burgesses refused to support a plan that did not suit their own interests. To underscore their displeasure, they cut off funds for a war against the Indians. In utter frustration, Spotswood reported to British superiors that the obstinate assemblymen tried "to recommend themselves to the populace upon a received opinion among them, that he is the best Patriot that most violently opposes all Overtures for raising money." Before he left office, Spotswood gave up trying to carry out royal policy in America. Instead, he allied himself with the plantation gentry who controlled the House as well as the Council, and in the process, became a wealthy man.

A few governors managed briefly to recreate in America the political culture of patronage, the system that eighteenth-century Englishmen took for granted. Most successful in this endeavor was William Shirley, who held office in Massachusetts from 1741 to 1757. The secret was connections to people who held high office in Great Britain. But Shirley's practices—and those of men like him—clashed with the colonists' perception of politics. They *really* believed in the purity of the balanced constitution. They insisted upon complete separation of executive and legislative authority. And therefore, when Americans suspected a governor, or even some of their own representatives, of employing patronage to influence government decisions, they protested in words that seem to have been lifted directly from the pages of *Cato's Letters*.

A major source of shared political information was the weekly journal, a new and vigorous institution in American life. In New York and Massachusetts especially, weekly newspapers urged readers to preserve civic virtue, to exercise extreme vigilance against the spread of privileged power. In the first issue of the *Independent Reflector* published in New York (November 30, 1752), the editor announced defiantly that no discouragement shall " . . . deter me from vindicating the *civil* and *religious RIGHTS* of my Fellow-Creatures: From exposing the peculiar Deformity of publick *Vice*, and *Corruption*; and displaying the amiable Charms of *Liberty*, with the detestable Nature of *Slavery* and *Oppression*." Through such journals, a pattern of political rhetoric that in Britain had gained only marginal respectability, became after 1765 America's normal form of political discourse.

The rise of the assemblies shaped American culture in other, subtler ways. Over the course of the century, the language of the law became increasingly anglicized. The Board of Trade, the Privy Council, and Parliament scrutinized court decisions and legislative actions from all thirteen mainland colonies. As a result, varying local legal practices that had been widespread during the seventeenth century became standardized. Indeed, according to one historian, the colonial legal system by 1750 "was substantially that of the mother country." Not surprisingly, many men who served in colonial assemblies were either lawyers or persons who had received legal training. When Americans from different regions met—as they frequently did in the years before the Revolution—they discovered that they shared a commitment to the preservation of the English common law.

But if eighteenth-century political developments drew the colonists closer to the mother country, they also brought Americans a greater awareness of each other. As their horizons widened, they learned that they operated within the same general imperial system, and the problems confronting the Massachusetts House of Representatives were not too different from those facing Virginia's House of Burgesses or South Carolina's Commons House. Like the revivalists and merchants—people who crossed old boundaries—colonial legislators laid the foundation for a larger cultural identity.

Century of Imperial War

The scope and character of warfare in the colonies changed radically during the eighteenth century. The founders of England's mainland colonies had engaged in intense local conflicts with the Indians, such as King Philip's War (1675–1676) in New England. But after 1690, the colonists were increasingly involved in hostilities that originated on the other side of the Atlantic, in rivalries between Great Britain and France over political and commercial ambitions. The external threat to security forced people in different colonies to devise unprecedented measures of military and political cooperation.

On paper at least, the British settlements enjoyed military superiority over the settlements of New France. Louis XIV (1643–1715) possessed an impressive army of 100,000 well-armed troops, but he dispatched few of them to the New World. He left the defense of Canada and the Mississippi Valley to the companies engaged in the fur trade. Meeting this challenge seemed almost impossible for the French outposts strung out along the Saint Lawrence River and the Great Lakes. In 1754 New France contained only 75,000 inhabitants as compared to 1,200,000 people living in Britain's mainland colonies.

French Claims in North America, 1750

By 1750 the French had established a chain of settlements southward through the heart of the continent from Quebec to New Orleans. The English saw this as a menace to their seaboard colonies, which were expanding westward.

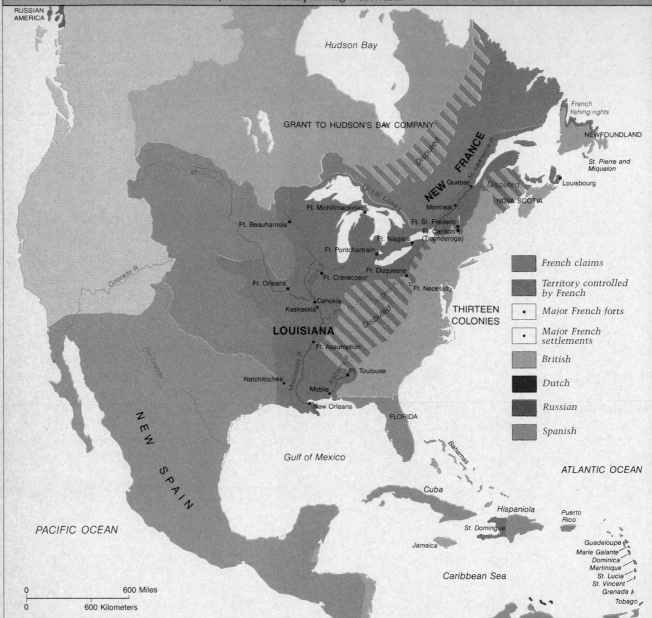

RUSSIAN AMERICA

Hudson Bay

GRANT TO HUDSON'S BAY COMPANY

French fishing rights

NEWFOUNDLAND

St. Pierre and Miquelon

NEW FRANCE

Disputed

St. Lawrence R.

Quebec

Disputed

Louisbourg

Montreal

NOVA SCOTIA

Missouri R.

Ft. Michilimackinac

Great Lakes

Ft. Beauharnois

Ft. St. Frédéric

Ft. Carillon (Ticonderoga)

Ft. Niagara

Colorado R.

Ft. Pontchartrain

Ft. Duquesne

Ft. Crevecoeur

Ft. Necessity

Ft. Orleans

Disputed

Cahokia

Kaskaskia

THIRTEEN COLONIES

LOUISIANA

Ft. Assumption

Rio Grande

Mississippi R.

Alabama R.

Ft. Toulouse

Natchitoches

Mobile

New Orleans

FLORIDA

N E W   S P A I N

Gulf of Mexico

Bahamas

Cuba

ATLANTIC OCEAN

Hispaniola

Puerto Rico

St. Domingue

PACIFIC OCEAN

Jamaica

Guadeloupe
Marie Galante
Dominica
Martinique
St. Lucia
St. Vincent
Grenada
Tobago

Caribbean Sea

0   600 Miles

0   600 Kilometers

Legend:
- French claims
- Territory controlled by French
- Major French forts
- Major French settlements
- British
- Dutch
- Russian
- Spanish

For most of the century, the English advantage proved more apparent than real. While the British settlements possessed a larger and more prosperous population, they were divided into separate governments that sometimes seemed more suspicious of each other than of the French. When war came, French officers and Indian allies exploited these jealousies with considerable skill. Moreover, although the population of New France was comparatively small, it was concentrated along the Saint Lawrence, so that while the French found it difficult to mount effective offensive operations against the English, they could easily mass the forces needed to defend Montreal and Quebec.

King William's and Queen Anne's Wars

Colonial involvement in imperial war began in 1689, when England's new king, William III, declared war on Louis XIV. Europeans called this struggle the War of the League of Augsburg, but to the Americans, it was simply King William's War. Canadians commanded by the Comte de Frontenac raided the northern frontiers of New York and New England, and while they made no territorial gains, they caused considerable suffering among the civilian population of Massachusetts and New York.

The war ended with the Treaty of Ryswick (1697), but the colonists were drawn almost immediately into a new conflict. Queen Anne's War, known in Europe as the War of Spanish Succession (1702-1713), was fought across a large geographic area. Colonists in South Carolina as well as New England battled against the French and Indians. The bloody combat along the American frontier was formally terminated in 1713 when Great Britain and France signed the Treaty of Utrecht. European negotiators showed little interest in the military situation in the New World. Their major concern was preserving a balance of power among the European states. More than two decades of intense fighting had taken a fearful toll in North America, but neither French nor English colonists had much to show for their sacrifice.

After George I, the first Hanoverian king of Great Britain, replaced Anne on the throne in 1714, parliamentary leaders determined to preserve peace—mainly because of the rising cost of war. Yet on the American frontier, the hostilities continued with raids and reprisals. As people on both sides of this conflict now realized, the stakes of war were very high: control over the entire West, including the Mississippi Valley.

Both sides viewed this great contest in conspiratorial terms. From South Carolina to Massachusetts Bay, colonists believed that the French planned to "encircle" the English settlements, to confine the English to a narrow strip of land along the Atlantic coast. The English noted that in 1682

La Salle had claimed for the king of France, a territory—Louisiana—that included all the people and resources located on "streams and Rivers" flowing into the Mississippi River. To make good on their claim, the French constructed forts on the Chicago and Illinois rivers. In 1717 they established a military post two hundred miles up the Alabama River, well within striking distance of the Carolina frontier, and in 1718 they settled New Orleans. One New Yorker declared in 1715 that " . . . it is impossible that we and the French can both inhabit this Continent in peace but that one nation must at last give way to the other, so 'tis very necessary that without sleeping away our time, all precautions imaginable should be taken to prevent its falling to our lotts to remove."

On their part, the French suspected that their rivals intended to seize all of North America. Land speculators and Indian traders pushed aggressively into territory claimed by the French. In 1716 one Frenchmen urged his government to hasten the development of Louisiana, since "it is not difficult to guess that their [the British] purpose is to drive us entirely out. . . of North America." To their great sorrow and eventual destruction, the original inhabitants of the frontier, the Native Americans, became pawns in this undeclared war. The Iroquois favored the British, while the Algonquian peoples generally supported the French. But regardless of the tribes to which they belonged, Indian warriors unwittingly carried out imperial policies set by distant European kings.

Founding of Georgia

In these wars for empire, Spain often acted as France's ally against Great Britain, and in the event of formal hostilities, Spanish bases in Florida could be used to harass English settlements in the South. In part, this struggle led to the founding of the last of the mainland colonies, Georgia.

The colony owed its existence primarily to James Oglethorpe, a British general and member of Parliament who believed that he could thwart Spanish designs on the area south of Charleston while at the same time providing a fresh start for London's debtors. Although Oglethorpe envisioned Georgia as an asylum as well as a garrison,

■ *The French, led by Sieur d'Iberville, founded a colony at Biloxi (shown here) in 1699. They moved on to Mobile in 1702 and then to the mouth of the Mississippi River at New Orleans in 1718.*

the military aspects of his proposal were especially appealing to the leaders of the British government. In 1732 the king granted Oglethorpe and a board of trustees a charter for a new colony to be located between the Savannah and Altamaha rivers and from "sea to sea." The trustees living in the mother country were given complete control over Georgia politics, a condition that the settlers soon found intolerable.

During the first years of colonization, Georgia fared no better than had earlier utopian experiments. Few English debtors showed any desire to move to an inclement frontier, and the trustees, in their turn, provided little incentive for emigration. Each colonist received only fifty acres. Fifty additional acres could be added for each servant transported to Georgia, but in no case could a settler amass more than five hundred acres. Moreover, land could be passed only to an eldest son, and if a planter had no sons at the time of his death, the holding reverted to Oglethorpe and the trustees. Slavery was prohibited. So too was rum.

Almost as soon as they arrived in Georgia, the settlers complained. The colonists demanded slaves, pointing out to the trustees that unless the new planters possessed an unfree labor force,

they could not compete economically with their South Carolina neighbors. The settlers also wanted a voice in local government. In 1738, 121 people living in Savannah petitioned for fundamental reforms in the colony's constitution. Oglethorpe responded angrily, "The idle ones are indeed for Negroes. If the petition is countenanced, the province is ruined." The settlers did not give up. In 1741 they again petitioned Oglethorpe, this time addressing him as "our Perpetual Dictator."

While the colonists grumbled about various restrictions, Oglethorpe tried and failed to capture the Spanish fortress at Saint Augustine (1740). This personal disappointment coupled with the growing popular unrest destroyed his interest in Georgia. The trustees were forced to compromise their principles. In 1738 they eliminated all restrictions on the amount of land a man could own; they allowed women to inherit land. In 1750 they permitted the settlers to import slaves. Soon Georgians could drink rum. In 1751 the trustees returned Georgia to the king, undoubtedly relieved to be free of what had become a hard-drinking, slave-owning plantation society much like that in South Carolina. The king

Indian chiefs visiting the trustees of Georgia in London, 1734. When settlements expanded, relationships between whites and Indians deteriorated. The settlers soon became restive under the rule of the trustees.

authorized an assembly in 1751, but even with these social and political changes, Georgia attracted very few new settlers.

King George's War and Its Aftermath

In 1743 the Americans were dragged once again into the imperial conflict. During King George's War (1743–1748), known in Europe as the War of Austrian Succession, the colonists scored a magnificent victory over the French. Louisbourg, a gigantic fortress on Cape Breton Island, the easternmost promontory of Canada, guarded the approaches to the Gulf of Saint Lawrence and Quebec. It was described as the "Gibralter of the New World." An army of New England troops under the command of William Pepperrell captured Louisbourg in June 1745, a feat that demonstrated that the British colonists were able to fight and to mount effective joint operations. The Americans, however, were in for a shock. When the war ended with the signing of the Treaty of Aix-la-Chapelle in 1748, the British government handed Louisbourg back to the French in exchange for

concessions elsewhere. New Englanders saw this as a slight, an insult they did not soon forget.

By the conclusion of King George's War, the goals of the conflict had clearly changed. Americans no longer aimed simply at protecting their territory from attack. They now wanted to gain complete control over the West, a region obviously rich in economic opportunity. Trade with the Indians was quite lucrative. There was also land. Speculators looked at maps of the Ohio Valley, and where others saw only empty space, they saw potential fortunes. Long before the French and Indians had been driven out of this territory, rival land companies were lobbying the English Crown for title to vast western tracts. In Virginia, the Ohio Company (1747) recruited wealthy Chesapeake planters in an effort to gain 200,000 acres on the Ohio River. Another speculative enterprise based in Virginia, the Loyal Land Company, acquired rights to 800,000 acres of western land in 1748.

The French were not prepared to surrender an inch. But as they recognized, time was running against them. Not only were the English colonies growing more populous, they also possessed a seemingly inexhaustible supply of manufactured

■ *The faded battle flag carried by the New Englanders who captured Louisbourg in 1745.*

goods to trade with the Indians. The French decided in the early 1750s, therefore, to seize the Ohio Valley before the Virginians could do so. They established forts throughout the region, the most formidable being Fort Duquesne, located at the strategic fork in the Ohio River near the modern city of Pittsburgh.

Although France and England had not officially declared war, British officials advised the governor of Virginia to "repell force by force." The Virginians, of course, needed no encouragement. They were eager to make good their claim to the Ohio Valley, and in 1754 several militia companies under the command of a promising young officer, George Washington, constructed Fort Necessity not far from Fort Duquesne. The plan failed. French and Indian troops overran the badly exposed outpost (July 3, 1754). Among other things, this humiliating setback revealed that a single colony could not defeat the French.

Albany Congress and Braddock's Defeat

Benjamin Franklin, for one, understood the need for intercolonial cooperation. When British officials invited representatives from the northern colonies to Albany (June 1754) to discuss rela-

tions with the Iroquois, Franklin used the occasion to present a bold blueprint for colonial union. His so-called Albany Plan envisioned the formation of a Grand Council, made up of elected delegates from the various colonies, to oversee matters of common defense, western expansion, and Indian affairs. A President General appointed by the king would preside. Franklin's most daring suggestion involved taxation. He insisted that the council be authorized to collect taxes to cover military expenditures.

First reaction to the Albany Plan was enthusiastic. To take effect, however, it required the support of the separate colonial assemblies as well as Parliament. It received neither. The assemblies were jealous of their fiscal authority, and the English thought the scheme undermined the Crown's power of American affairs. As Franklin noted wistfully in his *Autobiography*, "Its fate was singular: the assemblies did not adopt it, as they all thought there was too much *prerogative* in it, and in England it was judg'd to have too much of the *democratic*."

In 1755 the Ohio Valley again became the scene of fierce fighting. Even though there was still no formal declaration of war, the British resolved to destroy Fort Duquesne, and to that end, they dispatched units of the regular army to America. In command was Major General Edward Braddock, who inspired neither fear nor respect. One colonist described Braddock as ". . . very indolent, Slave to his passions, women & wine, as great an Epicure as could be in his eating, tho a brave man."

■ *The first political cartoon to appear in an American newspaper. By Benjamin Franklin (1754).*

On July 9 Braddock led a joint force of twenty-five hundred British redcoats and colonists into one of the worst defeats in British military history. The French and Indians opened fire as Braddock's army was wading over the Monongahela River, about eight miles from Fort Duquesne. Along a narrow road already congested with heavy wagons and confused men, Braddock ordered a counterattack, described by one of his officers as "without any form or order but that of a parcell of school boys coming out of s[c]hool." Nearly 70 percent of Braddock's troops were either killed or wounded in western Pennsylvania. The general himself died in battle. The French, who suffered only light casualties, remained in firm control of the Ohio Valley. The entire affair profoundly angered Washington, who fumed, "We have been most scandalously beaten by a trifling body of men."

French and Indian War

Britain's imperial war effort had hit bottom. No one in England or America seemed to possess the leadership necessary to drive the French from the Mississippi Valley. The cabinet of George II (1727–1760) lacked the will to organize and finance a sustained military campaign in the New World, and colonial assemblies balked every time the mother country asked them to raise men and money. On May 18, 1756, the British finally declared war on the French, a conflict called the French and Indian War in America and the Seven Years' War in Europe. Yet despite Britain's apparent determination to fight, confusion and mismanagement still reigned on the American battlefront.

Had it not been for William Pitt, the most powerful minister in George's cabinet, the military stalemate might have continued. This arrogant Englishman believed he was the only person capable of saving the British empire, an opinion he publicly expressed. When he became effective head of the Ministry in December 1756, Pitt had an opportunity to prove his mettle.

In the past, great battles on the European continent had worked mainly to France's advantage. Pitt saw no point in continuing to concentrate upon Europe and in 1757 he advanced a bold, new imperial policy, one based on mercantilist as-

<table>
<tr><td colspan="2">Chronology</td></tr>
<tr><td>1689</td><td>William and Mary accede to the English throne</td></tr>
<tr><td>1702</td><td>Anne becomes queen of England</td></tr>
<tr><td>1706</td><td>Birth of Benjamin Franklin</td></tr>
<tr><td>1714</td><td>George I of Hanover becomes monarch of Great Britain</td></tr>
<tr><td>1727</td><td>George II accedes to the British throne</td></tr>
<tr><td>1732</td><td>Colony of Georgia is established
Birth of George Washington</td></tr>
<tr><td>1734–1736</td><td>First expression of the Great Awakening at Northampton, Massachusetts</td></tr>
<tr><td>1740</td><td>George Whitefield electrifies his listeners at Boston</td></tr>
<tr><td>1745</td><td>Colonial troops capture Louisbourg</td></tr>
<tr><td>1754</td><td>Albany Congress meets</td></tr>
<tr><td>1755</td><td>Braddock is defeated by the French and Indians in western Pennsylvania</td></tr>
<tr><td>1756</td><td>French and Indian War (Seven Years' War) is formally declared</td></tr>
<tr><td>1759</td><td>British are victorious at Quebec. Wolfe and Montcalm are killed in battle</td></tr>
<tr><td>1760</td><td>George III becomes king of Great Britain</td></tr>
<tr><td>1763</td><td>Peace of Paris ending French and Indian War is signed</td></tr>
</table>

sumptions. In Pitt's judgment, the critical confrontation would take place in North America, where Britain and France were struggling to control colonial markets and raw materials. Indeed, according to Pitt, America was "where England and Europe are to be fought for." He was determined, therefore, to expel the French from the continent, however great the cost.

To effect this ambitious scheme, Pitt took personal command of the army and navy. He mapped strategy. He even promoted young promising officers over the heads of their superiors. He also recognized that the success of the war effort could not depend upon the generosity of the colonial assemblies. Great Britain would have to foot most of the bill. Pitt's military expenditures, of course, created an enormous national debt that would soon haunt both Britain and its colonies, but at the time, no one foresaw the fiscal consequences of victory in America.

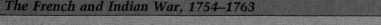

Major battle sites. The conflict ended with Great Britain driving the French from mainland North America.

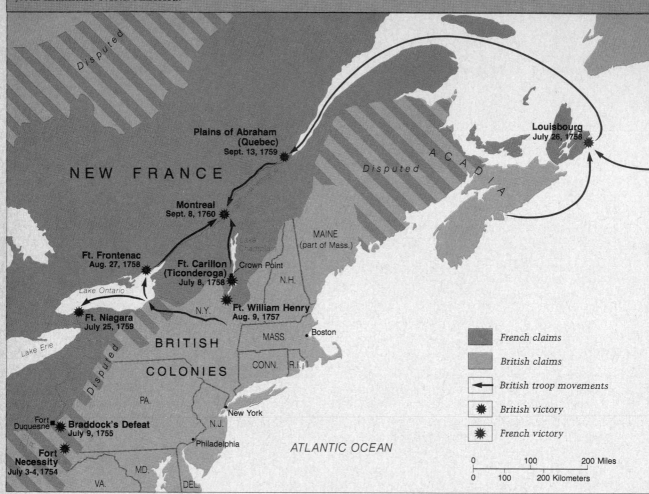

To direct the grand campaign, Pitt selected two relatively obscure colonels, Jeffrey Amherst and James Wolfe. It was a masterful choice, one that a less self-confident man than Pitt would never have dared to make. Both officers were young, talented, and ambitious, and on July 26, 1758, forces under their direction captured Louisbourg, the same fortress that the colonists had taken a decade earlier!

This victory cut the Canadians' main supply line with France. The small population of New France could no longer meet the military demands placed on it. Poor harvests in 1756 and 1757 added to the growing problems. As the situation became increasingly desperate, the French forts of the Ohio Valley and the Great Lakes began to fall. Duquesne was simply abandoned late in 1758 as French and Indian troops under the brilliant Marquis de Montcalm retreated toward Quebec and Montreal. During the summer of 1759 the French surrendered key forts at Ticonderoga, Crown Point, and Niagara.

The climax to a century of war came dramatically in September 1759. Wolfe, now a major general, assaulted Quebec with nine thousand men. But it was not simply force of arms that brought victory. Wolfe proceeded as if he were preparing to attack the city directly, but under cover of darkness, his troops scaled a cliff to dominate a less well defended position. At dawn

■ *The British stormed Quebec in 1759 and defeated the French decisively on the Plains of Abraham overlooking the city.*

on September 13, 1759, they took the French from the rear by surprise. The decisive action occurred on the Plains of Abraham, a bluff high above the Saint Lawrence River. Both Wolfe and Montcalm were mortally wounded. When an aide informed Wolfe that the French had been routed, he sighed, "Now, God be praised, I will die in peace." On September 8, 1760, Amherst accepted the final surrender of the French army at Montreal.

The Peace of Paris signed on February 10, 1763, almost fulfilled Pitt's grandiose dreams. Great Britain took possession of an empire that stretched around the globe. Only Guadeloupe and Martinique, the Caribbean sugar islands, were given back to the French. After a century-long struggle, the French had been driven from the mainland of North America. Even Louisiana passed out of France's control into Spanish hands. The treaty gave Britain title to Canada, Florida, and all the land east of the Mississippi River. Moreover, with the stroke of a diplomat's pen, eighty thousand French-speaking Canadians, most of them Catholic, became the subjects of George III. The colonists were overjoyed. It was a time of good feelings and national pride. Together, the English and the Americans had thwarted the "Gallic peril." Samuel Davies, a Presbyterian who had brought the Great Awakening to Virginia, announced confidently that the long-awaited

victory would inaugurate "*a new heaven and a new earth.*"

The Seven Years' War made a deep impression upon American society. Even though Franklin's Albany Plan had failed, the military struggle had forced the colonists to cooperate on an unprecedented scale. It also drew them into closer contact with the mother country. They became aware of being part of a great empire, but in the very process of waging war, they acquired a more intimate sense of an America that lay beyond the plantation and the village. Conflict had carried men across colonial boundaries, exposing them to a vast territory full of opportunities for a booming population. Moreover, the war trained a corps of American officers, people like George Washington, who learned from firsthand experience that the British were not invincible.

Forging an Identity

In 1754 a young American found himself in Great Britain on the eve of a parliamentary election. The prospect excited John Dickinson, for as he explained in letters to his father, he would have the opportunity to hear "some of the greatest men in England, perhaps in the world." But the

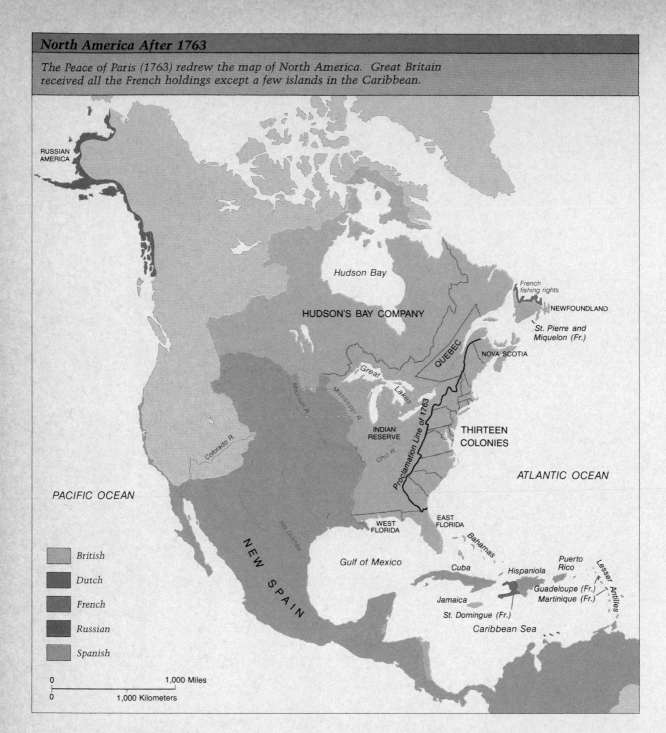

The Peace of Paris (1763) redrew the map of North America. Great Britain received all the French holdings except a few islands in the Caribbean.

RUSSIAN
AMERICA

Hudson Bay

HUDSON'S BAY COMPANY

French
fishing rights

NEWFOUNDLAND

St. Pierre and
Miquelon (Fr.)

QUEBEC

NOVA SCOTIA

Great

Lakes

Mississippi R.

Missouri R.

INDIAN
RESERVE

Ohio R.

Proclamation Line of 1763

THIRTEEN
COLONIES

ATLANTIC OCEAN

Colorado R.

PACIFIC OCEAN

Rio Grande

WEST
FLORIDA

EAST
FLORIDA

NEW SPAIN

Bahamas

Gulf of Mexico

Cuba

Hispaniola

Puerto
Rico

Lesser Antilles

Jamaica

Guadeloupe (Fr.)
Martinique (Fr.)

St. Domingue (Fr.)

Caribbean Sea

British

Dutch

French

Russian

Spanish

0   1,000 Miles
0   1,000 Kilometers

corruption that this provincial visitor witnessed quickly destroyed whatever illusions he may have possessed about the superiority of the British political system. Candidates openly bribed electors; drunkards were encouraged to vote.

The experience deeply shocked Dickinson, a man who was by temperament no prude. "It is grown a vice here to be virtuous," he reported to his father. "People are grown too polite to have an old-fashioned religion, and are too weak to find out a new, from whence follows the most unbounded licentiousness and utter disregard of virtue, which is the unfailing cause of the destruction of all empires."

More than a decade later, Dickinson penned one of the most influential pamphlets of the American Revolution, *Letters from a Farmer in Pennsylvania*. How much his earlier experiences in the mother country shaped his political views is impossible to judge. It was clear, however, that Dickinson had made a choice. He was proud to be an American.

Dickinson's intellectual odyssey was not unusual. After 1760, other provincials, persons who had been attracted to Great Britain by the chance to advance their careers, denounced the luxury and corruption that seemed to have swept the mother country. Perhaps they resented being treated as cultural inferiors; perhaps they reflected the spirit of the Great Awakening. Whatever their personal motives, many colonial leaders had become convinced that Britain's rulers threatened what one Marylander called "the reign of American freedom."

Recommended Reading

The most comprehensive examination of Anglo-American relations in the late colonial period is Lawrence H. Gipson, *British Empire Before the American Revolution*, 8 vols. (1936–1949). A much shorter, but well-written introduction to the topics discussed in this chapter is Richard Hofstadter, *America at 1750: A Social Portrait* (1971). James A. Henretta, *Evolution of American Society, 1700–1815* (1973), devotes more attention to economic change, but he also provides provocative sections on culture and religion. For the wars of empire, see Howard H. Peckham, *The Colonial Wars, 1689–1762* (1964), an entertaining and well-organized book. The state of eighteenth-century religion, not just evangelical religion, is examined in Sydney E. Ahlstrom's encyclopedic *Religious History of the American People* (1972). A useful discussion of the revivals can be found in Edwin S. Gaustad, *Great Awakening in New England* (1957). Anyone curious about intellectual history should read Henry F. May, *The Enlightenment in America* (1976). And finally, the most imaginative analysis of eighteenth-century colonial politics is Bernard Bailyn, *The Origins of American Politics* (1968).

Additional Bibliography

The growth of the American population in this period is traced in Robert V. Wells, *The Population of the British Colonies in America Before 1776* (1975) and James G. Leyburn, *The Scotch-Irish: A Social History* (1962). See also Carl Bridenbaugh, *Myths and Realities, Societies in the Colonial South* (1952); James T. Lemon, *The Best Poor Man's Country* (1972); Gary B. Nash, *The Urban Crucible* (1979); and Carl Bridenbaugh, *Cities in the Wilderness* (1938). The economic development of colonial America and England is discussed in Jacob M. Price, *Capital and Credit in British Overseas Trade* (1980); Gary M. Walton and James F. Shepherd, *The Economic Rise of Early America* (1979); Edwin J. Perkins, *The Economy of Colonial America* (1980); and E. J. Hobsbawm, *Industry and Empire* (1968). For the story of the line of forts, see Michael D. Coe, "The Line of Forts: Archeology of Mid-Eighteenth Century on the Massachusetts Frontier," in Peter Benes, ed., *New England Historical Archeology* (1977).

The most entertaining account of the imperial wars is Francis Parkman's nineteenth-century work, *France and England in North America*. More recent studies include Douglas E. Leach, *Arms for Empire: A Military History of the British Colonies in North America, 1607–1763* (1973) and Verner W. Crane, *The Southern Frontier, 1670–1732* (1929). On the founding of Georgia, Kenneth Coleman, *Colonial Georgia: A History* (1976) and Harold E. Davis, *The Fledgling Province: Social and Cultural Life in Colonial Georgia, 1733–1776* (1976).

Verner W. Crane, *Benjamin Franklin and a Rising People* (1952) is a good biography, but there is really no adequate substitute for Franklin himself. Several excellent editions of his *Autobiography* are available. The American Enlightenment is explored in Carl Bridenbaugh, "Philosophy Put to Use: Voluntary Associations for Propagating the Enlightenment in Philadelphia, 1727 to 1776," *Pennsylvania Magazine of History and Biography* 101 (1977): 70–88. See also Richard L. Bushman, "American High Style and Vernacular Cultures Before the Revolution," in Jack Greene and Jack Pole, eds., *Colonial Anglo-America, 1607–1763* (1983).

On the Great Awakening, see George Whitefield's *Journals* (1969) as well as *The Great Awakening* (1967), edited by Alan Heimert and Perry Miller; and Jon Butler, "Enthusiasm Described and Decried: The Great Awakening as Interpretive Fiction," *Journal of American History* 69 (1982): 305–25.

Eighteenth-century English politics is the subject of J. H. Plumb, *Sir Robert Walpole*, 2 vols. (1956–1960); Isaac Kramnick, *Bolingbroke and His Circle: The Politics of Nostalgia in the Age of Walpole* (1968); W. A. Speck, *Stability and Strife; England, 1714–1760* (1977); Leonard W. Labaree, *Royal Government in America* (1930); Robert E. Brown, *Middle-Class Democracy and the Revolution in Massachusetts, 1691–1780* (1955); and Chilton Williamson, *American Suffrage: From Property to Democracy, 1760–1860* (1960). See also J. R. Pole, *Political Representation* (1966). The politics of specific colonies and governors are examined in Jack P. Greene, *The Quest for Power* (1963); Patricia Bonomi, *A Factious People: Politics and Society in Colonial New York* (1977); William Pencak, *War, Politics and Revolution in Provincial Massachusetts* (1981); A. Roger Ekirch, *"Poor Carolina," Politics and Society in Colonial North Carolina, 1729–1776* (1981); and John A. Schutz, *William Shirley* (1961).

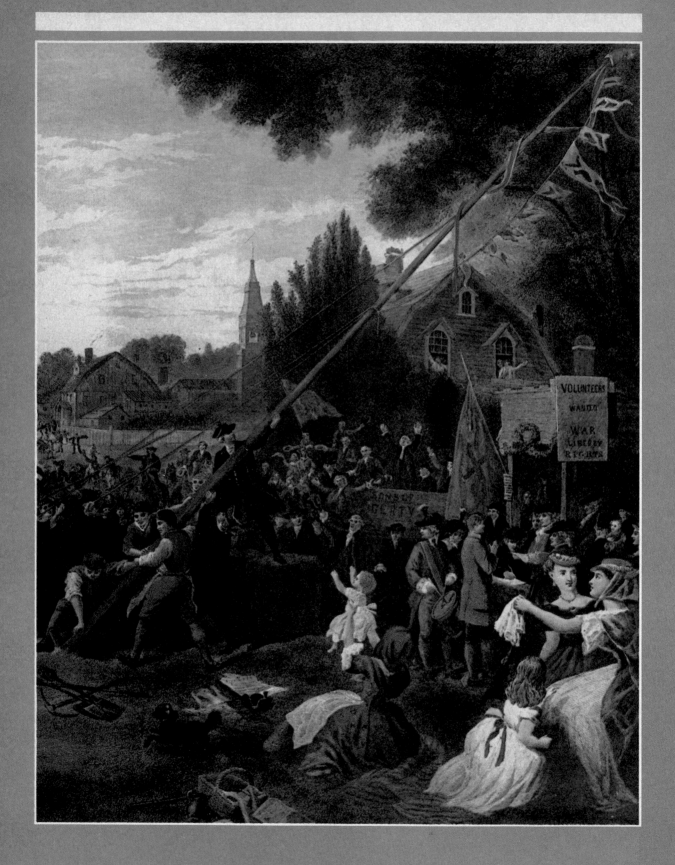

chapter 5

THE AMERICAN REVOLUTION: FROM PROTEST TO INDEPENDENCE, 1763–1783

During the revolutionary war, a captured British officer spent some time at the plantation of Colonel Thomas Mann Randolph, a leader of Virginia's gentry. The Englishman described the arrival of three farmers who were members of the local militia. He characterized the militiamen as "peasants," for without asking their host's permission, the Americans drew chairs up to the fire, pulled off their muddy boots, and began spitting. The British officer was appalled; after the farmers departed, he observed that they had not shown Randolph proper deference. The colonel responded that such behavior had come to be expected, for "the spirit of independency" had been transformed into "equality." Indeed, every American who "bore arms" during the Revolution considered himself as good as his neighbors. "No doubt," Randolph remarked to the officer, "each of these men conceives himself, in every respect, my equal."

This chance encounter illuminates the character of the American Revolution. The initial stimulus for rebellion came from the gentry, from the rich and wellborn, who resented Parliament's efforts to curtail their rights within the British empire. They voiced their unhappiness in published statements and in speeches before elected assemblies. Passionate rhetoric made them uneasy. But as these influential planters, wealthy merchants, and prominent clergymen discovered, the revolutionary movement generated a momentum that they could not control. As relations with the mother country deteriorated, the traditional leaders of colonial society were forced to invite the common folk to join the protest—as rioters, as petitioners, and finally, as soldiers. Newspapers, sermons, and pamphlets helped transform what had begun as a squabble among the gentry into a mass movement, and as Randolph learned, once the common people had become involved in shaping the nation's destiny, they could never again be excluded.

The incident at Randolph's plantation reveals a second, often overlooked, aspect of the American Revolution. It involved a massive military commitment. If common American soldiers had not been willing to stand up to seasoned British troops, to face the terror of the bayonet charge, independence would have remained a dream of intellectuals. Proportionate to the population, a greater percentage of Americans died in military service during the Revolution than in any war in American history, with the exception of the Civil War. The concept of liberty so magnificently expressed in revolutionary pamphlets was not, therefore, simply an abstraction, an exclusive concern of political theorists like Thomas Jefferson and John Adams. It also motivated the common folk—mud-covered Virginia militiamen, for example—to take up weapons and risk death in their quest for independence. Those who survived the ordeal were never quite the same, for the very experience of fighting, of assuming responsibility in battle, and perhaps even of taking the lives of British officers gave dramatic new meaning to social equality.

Imperial Crisis

No one consciously set out in 1763 to achieve independence. What Americans came to regard as "common sense" in 1776, they would have seen as madness or treason a decade earlier. The bonds of loyalty that had cemented the British empire dissolved slowly. It is only with the benefit of hindsight that the confrontations of this period seem to have led inexorably to the Revolution. The men and women who lived through these difficult years, however, did not know what the future would bring. At several points British rulers and American colonists could have compromised. They could have attempted in some way to ease growing tensions. Their failure to do so was the result of thousands of separate decisions, errors, and misunderstandings. The Revolution was, in fact, a complex series of events, full of unexpected turns, extraordinary creativity, and great personal sacrifice.

Failure of Imagination

Ultimate responsibility for preserving the empire fell to George III. When he became king of England in 1760, he was a young man, only twenty-two years of age. In public, contemporaries praised the new monarch. In private, however, they expressed grave reservations. The youth had led a sheltered, loveless life; his father, an irresponsible playboy, died in 1751. Young George had not received a good education, and even though he demonstrated considerable mechanical ability, his grandfather, George II, thought his grandson dull-witted, an opinion widely shared. As one might expect, George grew up hating not only his grandfather, but almost everyone associated with the reign of George II.

To hide his intellectual inadequacies, the new king adopted a pedantic habit of correcting people for small faults, a characteristic made all the more annoying by his obvious inability to grasp the larger implications of government policy. Unfortunately, the king could not be ignored, and during a difficult period that demanded imagination, generosity, and wisdom, George muddled along as best he could.

The new monarch was determined to play an aggressive role in government. This decision caused considerable dismay among England's political leaders. For decades a powerful, though loosely associated, group of men who called themselves "Whigs" had set policy and controlled patronage. George II accepted this situation, and so long as the Whigs in Parliament did not meddle with his beloved army, the king let them rule the nation.

In one stroke, George III destroyed this cozy relationship. He selected as his chief minister the Earl of Bute, a Scot whose only qualification for office appeared to be his friendship with the young king and the young king's mother. The Whigs who dominated Parliament were outraged. Bute had no ties with the members of the House of Commons; he owed them no favors. It seemed to the Whigs that with the appointment of Bute George was trying to turn back the clock, to reestablish a personal Stuart monarchy free from traditional constitutional restraints. The Whigs blamed Bute for every wrong, real or imagined. George did not, in fact, harbor such arbitrary

■ *Despite his insecurity over an inadequate education, George III was determined to take an active role in reigning over Parliament and the colonies.*

ambitions, but his actions threw customary political practices into doubt.

By 1763 Bute had despaired of public life. His departure, however, neither restored the Whigs to preeminence nor dampened the king's enthusiasm for domestic politics. Everyone agreed that George had the right to select whomever he desired for cabinet posts, but until 1770 no one seemed able to please the monarch. Ministers came and went, often for no other reason than George's personal distaste. Because of this chronic instability, subministers, minor bureaucrats who directed routine colonial affairs, did not know what was expected of them. In the absence of long-range policy, some ministers made narrowly based decisions; others did nothing. Most devoted their energies to finding a political patron capable of satisfying the fickle king. Talent played little part in the scramble for office, and incompetent hacks were advanced as frequently as were men of vision.

The king does not bear the sole blame for England's loss of empire in America. The members of Parliament, the men who actually drafted the statutes that drove a wedge between the colonists and the mother country, failed to respond creatively to the challenge of events. With rare exception, they clung doggedly to the principle of parliamentary sovereignty, and when Americans questioned whether that legislative body in London should govern colonial affairs, parliamentary spokesmen provided no constructive basis for compromise. The establishment of a separate American commonwealth bound to Britain only by commerce and common allegiance to the monarch received no support in the House of Commons. As Thomas Hutchinson, royal governor of Massachusetts, explained, there was no middle ground "between the supreme authority of Parliament and the total independence of the colonies: it is impossible there should be two independent legislatures in one and the same state."

Parliament's attitude was in part a product of ignorance. Few men active in English government had visited America. For those who attempted to follow colonial affairs, accurate information proved extremely difficult to obtain. Packet boats carrying passengers and mail sailed regularly between London and the various colonial ports, but the voyage across the Atlantic required at least four weeks. One could not expect to receive an answer from America to a specific question in less than three months. And of course, all correspondence was laboriously copied in longhand by overworked clerks serving in understaffed offices. As a result of the lag in communication between England and America, rumors sometimes passed for true accounts, and misunderstanding influenced the formulation of colonial policy.

American Perspective on Imperial Politics

At the conclusion of the French and Indian War, it seemed inconceivable that the colonists would challenge the supremacy of Parliament. But the crisis in imperial relations that soon developed forced the Americans first to define and then to defend principles that were rooted deeply in the colonial political culture.

For more than a century, the colonists' ideas about their role within the British empire had remained a vague, untested bundle of assumptions about personal liberties, property rights, and representative institutions. By 1763, however, certain fundamental American beliefs had become clear. From Massachusetts to Georgia, colonists affirmed the importance of representative government. They also accepted the authority of local assemblies to tax their constituents. To declare that the House of Commons in London enjoyed the same right made no sense to them. Parliament was too distant; its members could not possibly comprehend American interests.

The colonists also rejected the distinction that English officials sometimes made between "internal" and "external" taxes, in other words, between taxes imposed directly upon a person's estate and taxes upon trade. Merchants could obviously pass "external" taxes on to consumers. As the New York Assembly explained in a petition to Parliament, "all Impositions, whether they be internal Taxes, or Duties paid, for what we consume, equally diminish the Estates upon which we are charged." In America, a tax was a tax by whatever name. Admittedly, Parliament might regulate trade for the good of the empire, but it could not collect revenue on this side of the Atlantic. While Americans generally admired the British constitution, few colonists ever seriously advocated sending their own representatives to the House of Commons. Such persons, the colonists assumed, would quickly lose touch with the voters who had selected them.

Political thought in the colonies contained a strong moral component, one that British rulers and American Loyalists (people who sided with the king during the Revolution) never fully understood. The origins of this highly religious perspective on civil government are difficult to locate with precision. Certainly, the Great Awakening raised men's and women's consciousness of an obligation to conduct themselves according to Scripture in public as well as in private affairs. At the same time, many Americans who were not swept up by the evangelical fervor adopted the "Commonwealthman" tradition, a body of political assumptions generally identified with two eighteenth-century English publicists, John Trenchard and Thomas Gordon (see chapter 4). Whatever the intellectual sources may have been, colonists viewed *power* as extremely dangerous, a force that would surely destroy liberty unless it was countered by *virtue*. According to Samuel Adams, Boston's radical leader, the American goal was the creation of a "Christian Sparta," an ideal commonwealth in which vigilant citizens would constantly guard against the spread of corruption, degeneracy, and luxury. Persons who shared this moral outlook regarded bad policy not only as the result of human error but as evidence of sin or corruption.

Insistence upon public virtue—sacrifice of self-interest to the public good—became the dominant theme of revolutionary political writing. American pamphleteers seldom took a dispassionate, legalistic approach to their analysis of power and liberty. More commonly, they exposed plots hatched by corrupt courtiers, such as the Earl of Bute. None of them—nor their readers—had any doubt that Americans were more virtuous than were the people of England.

During the 1760s, however, popular writers were not certain how long the colonists could hold out against arbitrary taxation, standing ar-

■ *Firebrand Samuel Adams, seen here in a portrait by Copley, was a fervent revolutionary whose oratory galvanized Boston street crowds.*

mies, Anglican bishops—in other words, against a host of external threats designed to crush American liberty. In 1774, for example, the people of Farmington, Connecticut, declared that "the present ministry, being instigated by the devil and led by their wicked and corrupt hearts, have a design to take away our liberties and properties, and to enslave us forever." Indeed, these Connecticut farmers described Britain's leaders as "pimps and parasites." This highly emotional, conspiratorial rhetoric sometimes shocks modern readers who assume that America's revolutionary leaders were products of the Enlightenment, persons who relied solely upon reason to solve social and political problems. Whatever the origins of their ideas may have been, the colonial pamphleteers successfully roused common men and women to resist Britain with force of arms.

Colonial newspapers spread these ideas through a large, dispersed population. A majority of adult white males—especially in the northern colonies—were literate, and it is not surprising that the number of journals published in this country increased dramatically during the revolutionary period. For the first time in American history, persons living in various parts of the continent could closely follow events that occurred in distant American cities. Because of the availability of newspapers, the details of Bostonians' confrontations with British authorities were known throughout the colonies, and these shared political experiences drew Americans more closely together, making it possible—in the words of John Adams—for "Thirteen clocks . . . to strike together—a perfection of mechanism which no artist had ever before effected."

Eroding the Bonds of Empire: Challenge and Resistance

Following the Seven Years' War, more than seven thousand British troops, members of the regular army, remained in North America. Their alleged purpose was to protect Indians from predatory frontiersmen and to preserve order in the newly conquered territories of Florida and Quebec. But no one person in the British government actually

Legislation	Date	Provisions	Colonial Reaction
Sugar Act	April 5, 1764	Increased duties on sugar; reduced duty on molasses; expanded jurisdiction of vice-admiralty courts	Several assemblies protest taxation for revenue
Stamp Act	March 22, 1765; repealed March 18, 1766	Printed documents (deeds, newspapers, marriage licenses, etc.) issued only on special stamped paper purchased from stamp collectors	Riots in cities; collectors forced to resign; Stamp Act Congress (October 1765)
Quartering Act	May 1765	Colonists must supply British troops with housing and other items (candles, salt, rum, etc.)	Protest in assemblies; New York Assembly punished for failure to comply (1767)
Declaratory Act	March 18, 1766	Parliament declares its sovereignty over the colonies "in all cases whatsoever"	Ignored in celebration over repeal of the Stamp Act
Townshend Revenue Acts	June 26, 29, July 2, 1767; all repealed except duty on tea, March 1770	Duties on glass, lead, paper, paints, tea; customs collections tightened in America	Nonimportation of British goods; assemblies protest; newspapers attack British policy
Tea Act	May 10, 1773	Parliament gives East India Company right to sell tea directly to Americans; some duties on tea reduced	Protests against favoritism shown to monopolistic company; tea destroyed in Boston (December 16, 1773)
Coercive Acts (Intolerable Acts)	March–June 1774	Closed port of Boston; restructured Massachusetts government; restricted town meetings; troops quartered in Boston; British officials accused of crimes sent to England or Canada for trial	Boycott of British goods; First Continental Congress convenes (September 1774)
Prohibitory Act	December 22, 1775	Declares British intention to coerce Americans into submission; embargo on American goods; American ships seized	Drives Continental Congress closer to decision for independence

made the decision to keep an army in the colonies. This unexpected circumstance occurred because various officials in London assumed that someone else had issued the order and thus, what was in fact a nondecision, a result of bureaucratic confusion and inertia, provided the initial catalyst for Anglo-American hostility.

The war had saddled Britain with a national debt so huge that over one half of the annual budget went to interest payments. A peacetime army, so far from the mother country, fueled the budgetary crisis; it cost a great deal of money to maintain scattered, often inaccessible, military posts on the American frontier. The growing financial burden weighed heavily on restive English taxpayers and sent government leaders scurrying in search of new sources of revenue.

For their part, colonists doubted the value of this very expensive army. First, Britain did not leave enough troops in America to maintain peace effectively. The weakness of the army was dramatically demonstrated in the spring of 1763. An Ottawa chief named Pontiac sparked a general uprising among the western Indian tribes that had been allied with the French during the war and who hated all British people, even those sent to protect them from land-grabbing colonists. Pontiac attacked Detroit, while other Indians harassed the Pennsylvania and Virginia frontier. At the end of the year, after his followers began deserting, Pontiac sued for peace. During this brief outbreak, the British army proved unable to defend exposed colonial settlements, and several thousand Americans lost their lives.

Second, the colonists fully intended to settle the fertile region west of the Appalachian Mountains. After the British government issued the Proclamation of 1763, which prohibited governors from granting land beyond the headwaters of rivers flowing into the Atlantic, disappointed Americans viewed the army as an obstruction to legitimate economic development, a domestic police force that cost too much money.

The task of reducing England's debt fell to George Grenville, the rigid, somewhat unimaginative chancellor of the exchequer who replaced Bute in 1763 as the king's first minister. After carefully reviewing the state of Britain's finances, Grenville concluded that the colonists would have to contribute to the maintenance of the army. The first bill he steered through Parliament was the Revenue Act of 1764, known as the Sugar Act.

This legislation represented a major break with the Navigation Acts that had governed the flow of colonial commerce for almost a century (see chapter 3). Those acts had forced Americans to trade with the mother country; their primary purpose was not to raise money. The Sugar Act—and the acts that soon followed—redefined the relationship between America and Great Britain. The colonies were now expected to generate revenues. The preamble of the Sugar Act proclaimed explicitly: "It is just and necessary that a revenue be raised . . . in America for defraying the expenses of defending, protecting, and securing the same." The act also created a great deal of new paperwork. To discourage smuggling, bribery, and other illegalities, Parliament reduced the duty on molasses (set originally by the Molasses Act of 1733) from six to three pence per gallon. At so low a rate, Grenville reasoned, colonial merchants would have little incentive to corrupt customs collectors or to give navy patrol boats the slip. Just in case the Americans tried to circumvent the law, Grenville added tough new enforcement procedures. The new act expanded the jurisdiction of vice-admiralty courts over commerce and gave customs officers broader powers in searching for contraband.

American reaction, though muted, came swiftly. According to the members of the Rhode Island Assembly, the Sugar Act taxed the colonists in a manner "inconsistent with their rights and privileges as British subjects." James Otis, a fiery orator from Massachusetts, exclaimed that the legislation deprived Americans of "the rights of assessing their own taxes." The protest involved no violence, but to Grenville and persons of his temperament, even petitions smacked of ingratitude. After all, they reasoned, had not the mother country saved the Americans from the French? But Grenville and his colleagues—and many modern historians—viewed the problem from a narrow perspective. They overlooked the importance of colonial staples such as rice and tobacco in promoting the prosperity of the mother country. Moreover, American markets helped sustain British industry (see chapter 4). The empire had run well enough before the Seven Years' War, and the colonists saw no justification for Grenville's aggressive new policy now that the military emergency had passed.

The Stamp Act Precipitates a Political Crisis

Even before the Sugar Act had gone into effect, Grenville put the final touches on a second revenue measure, the Stamp Act. He had little fear of parliamentary opposition. The majority of the House of Commons assumed that Parliament possessed the right to tax the colonists, and so when the chancellor of the exchequer announced a plan to squeeze £60,000 annually out of the Americans, the members responded with enthusiasm. The Stamp Act was scheduled to go into effect on November 1, 1765, and in anticipation of brisk sales, Grenville appointed stamp distributors for every colony.

During the debate in Parliament, several members warned that the act would raise a storm of protest in the colonies. Colonel Isaac Barré, a veteran of the Seven Years' War, reminded his colleagues that the Americans were "sons of liberty" and would not surrender their rights without a fight. But Barré's appeal fell upon deaf ears. Britain's rulers were so sure of themselves, so self-righteous, that they cut off any possibility of constructive debate with persons of contrary opinion.

■ *The Stamp Act required the purchase of special seals to validate legal documents (left). Colonists' protests were expressed in many interesting ways (right).*

Word of the Stamp Act reached America in May, and it was soon clear that Barré had gauged the colonists' response correctly. The most dramatic incident occurred in Virginia's House of Burgesses. Patrick Henry, young and eloquent, whom contemporaries compared in fervor to evangelical preachers, introduced five resolutions protesting the Stamp Act on the floor of the assembly. He timed his move carefully. It was late in the session; many of the more conservative burgesses had already departed for their plantations. Even then, Henry's resolves declaring that Virginians had the right to tax themselves as they alone saw fit passed by narrow margins. A fifth resolution, stricken almost immediately from the legislative records, announced that any attempt to collect stamp revenues in America was "illegal, unconstitutional, and unjust, and has a manifest tendency to destroy British as well as American liberty." Henry was carried away by the force of his own rhetoric. He reminded his fellow Virginians that Caesar had had his Brutus, Charles I his Cromwell, and he hoped that "some good American would stand up for his country . . ." An astonished speaker of the house cut Henry off in midsentence, accusing him of treason.

The Virginia Resolves might have remained a local matter had it not been for the colonial press. Newspapers throughout America printed Henry's resolutions, but perhaps because editors did not really know what had happened in Williamsburg, they reported that all five resolutions had received the burgesses' full support. Several journals even carried two resolves that Henry had not dared to introduce. The result of this misunderstanding, of course, was that the Virginians appeared to have taken an extremely radical position on the issue of the supremacy of Parliament, one that other Americans now trumpeted before their own assemblies. No wonder that Francis Bernard, royal governor of Massachusetts, called the Virginia resolves an "alarm bell."

Not to be outdone by Virginia, Massachusetts called a general meeting to protest Grenville's policy. Nine colonies sent representatives to the Stamp Act Congress that convened in New York City in October 1765. It was the first intercolonial gathering held since the abortive Albany Congress of 1754; if nothing else, the new congress provided leaders from different regions with an opportunity to discuss common problems. The delegates drafted petitions to the king and Parliament which restated the colonists' belief "that no taxes should be imposed on them, but with their own consent, given personally, or by their representatives." The tone of the meeting was restrained, even conciliatory. The congress studiously avoided any mention of independence or disloyalty to the Crown.

Resistance to the Stamp Act soon spread from the assemblies to the streets. Anonymous artisans and seamen, angered by Parliament's apparent insensitivity and fearful that the statute would increase unemployment and poverty, organized mass protests in the major colonial ports. In Boston, the "Sons of Liberty" burned in effigy the local stamp distributor, Andrew Oliver, and when that action failed to bring about his resignation, they tore down one of his office buildings. Even after he resigned, the mob nearly demolished the elegant home of Oliver's close associate, Lieutenant Governor Thomas Hutchinson. The violence frightened colonial leaders, yet evidence suggests that they encouraged the lower classes to intimidate royal officials. Popular participation in these protests was an exciting experience for people who had traditionally deferred to their social betters. After 1765, it was impossible for either royal governors or patriot leaders to take the common folk for granted.

By November 1, 1765, stamp distributors in almost every American port had publicly resigned, and without distributors, the hated revenue stamps could not be sold. With one exception, daily life in the colonies was undisturbed. The courts soon reopened; most newspapers were published. However the Sons of Liberty persuaded—some said coerced—colonial merchants to boycott British goods until Parliament repealed the Stamp Act. The merchants showed little enthusiasm for such tactics, but talk of tar and feathers stimulated cooperation.

In July 1765 Grenville fell from power, not because the king thought his policies inept, but rather because George did not like the man. His replacement as first lord of the treasury, Lord Rockingham, was young, inexperienced, and terrified of public speaking, a serious handicap to launching a brilliant parliamentary career. The Rockinghamites—as his followers were called—envisioned a prosperous empire founded upon an expanding commerce and local government under the gentle guidance of Parliament. In this unified structure, it seemed improbable that Parliament would ever be obliged to exercise control in a manner likely to offend the Americans. Rockingham wanted to repeal the Stamp Act, but because of the shakiness of his own political coalition, he could not announce such a decision until it enjoyed broad national support. He, therefore, urged merchants and manufacturers throughout England to petition Parliament for repeal of the act, claiming that the American boycott would soon drive them into bankruptcy.

Grenville, now simply a member of Parliament, would tolerate no retreat on the issue of supremacy. He urged his colleagues in the House of Commons to be tough, to condemn "the outrageous tumults and insurrections which have been excited and carried on in North America." But William Pitt, the architect of victory in the Seven Years' War and a hero throughout America, eloquently defended the colonists' position, and after the Rockingham ministry gathered additional support from prominent figures such as Benjamin Franklin, it felt strong enough to recommend repeal. On February 22, 1766, the House of Commons voted 275–167 to rescind the Stamp Act.

Lest its retreat on the Stamp Act be interpreted as weakness, the House of Commons passed the Declaratory Act (March 1766), a shrill defence of parliamentary supremacy over the Americans "in all cases whatsoever." The colonists' insistence upon no taxation without representation failed to impress British rulers. England's merchants, supposedly America's allies, claimed sole responsibility for the Stamp Act repeal. The colonists had only complicated the task, the merchants lectured, and if the Americans knew what was good for them, they would keep quiet. To George Mason, a leading political figure in Virginia, such advice sounded patronizing. The British merchants seemed to be saying, "We have with infinite difficulty and fatigue got you excused this one time; pray be a good boy for the future, do what your papa and mama bid you, and hasten to return them your most grateful acknowledgements for condescending to let you keep what is your own." To this, Mason snapped "ridiculous!"

The Stamp Act crisis also eroded the colonists' respect for imperial officeholders in America.

Suddenly, these men—royal governors, customs collectors, military personnel—appeared alien, as if their interests were not those of the people over whom they exercised authority. One person who had been forced to resign the post of stamp distributor for South Carolina noted several years later that "The Stamp Act had introduc'd so much Party Rage, Faction, and Debate that the ancient Harmony, Generosity, and Urbanity for which these People were celebrated is destroyed, and at an End." Similar reports came from other colonies, and it is testimony to the Americans' lingering loyalty to the British Crown and constitution that rebellion did not occur in 1765.

Townshend's Boast: Tea and Sovereignty

Rockingham's ministry soon gave way to a government headed once again by William Pitt, who was now the Earl of Chatham. The aging Pitt suffered horribly from gout, and during his long absences from London, Charles Townshend, his chancellor of the exchequer, made important policy decisions. Townshend was an impetuous man whose mouth often outran his mind. During a parliamentary debate in January 1767, he surprised everyone by blithely announcing that he knew a way to obtain revenue from the Americans. The members of the House of Commons were so pleased with the news that they promptly voted to lower English land taxes, an action that threatened fiscal chaos.

A budgetary crisis forced Townshend to make good on his extraordinary boast. His plan turned out to be a grab bag of duties on American imports of paper, glass, paint, and tea which collectively were known as the Townshend Revenue Acts (May 1767). The chancellor recognized that without tough instruments of enforcement, his duties would not generate the promised revenue. Therefore, he created an American Board of Customs Commissioners, a body based in Boston and supported by reorganized vice-admiralty courts located in Boston, Philadelphia, and Charleston. And for good measure, Townshend induced Parliament to order the governor of New York to veto all bills passed by that colony's assembly until it supplied resident British troops

in accordance with the Quartering Act (May 1765) that required the colonies to house and supply the army. The Americans regarded this as more taxation without representation, and in New York at least, they refused to pay.

Americans were no more willing to pay Townshend's duties than they had been to buy Grenville's stamps. No congress was called; none was necessary. Recent events had taught the colonists how to coordinate protest and they moved to resist the unconstitutional revenue acts. In major ports, the Sons of Liberty organized boycotts of British goods. Imported finery came to symbolize England's political corruption. Americans prided themselves on wearing homespun clothes, a badge of simplicity and virtue. Women were enthusiastic supporters of the boycott. They worked hard to produce more homespun and refrained from patronizing uncooperative Loyalist merchants.

On February 11, 1768, the Massachusetts House of Representatives drafted a circular letter which it then sent to other colonial assemblies. The letter requested suggestions on how best to thwart the Townshend Acts; not surprisingly, legislators in other parts of America, busy with local matters, simply ignored this general appeal. But not Lord Hillsborough, England's secretary for American affairs. This rather mild action struck him as gross treason, and he ordered the Massachusetts representatives to rescind their "seditious paper." After considering Hillsborough's demand, the legislators voted ninety-two to seventeen to defy him.

Suddenly, the circular letter became a *cause célèbre*. The royal governor of Massachusetts hastily dissolved the House of Representatives. That decision compelled the other colonies to demonstrate their support for Massachusetts. Assembly after assembly now felt obligated to take up the circular letter, an action Hillsborough had specifically forbidden. Assemblies in other colonies were dissolved, creating a much broader crisis of representative government. Throughout America, the number 92 immediately became a symbol of patriotism. In fact, Parliament's challenge had brought about the very results it most wanted to avoid: a foundation for intercolonial communication and a strengthening of conviction among the colonists of the righteousness of their position.

AGRARIAN WORK IN EARLY AMERICA

"A lazy man's crop," said a Swedish visitor in the 1740s about American corn. This reaction to cultivation of maize is understandable—an acre of good soil often yielded fifty bushels of the crop while marginal land could produce as much as twenty-five bushels. All farmers planted some corn, and for most of the colonial period it was a staple of the American diet. Farmers of the seventeenth and eighteenth centuries, however, cannot be characterized as lazy. Farming demanded energy, skill, enterprise, and self-reliance for few tasks were so difficult and time-consuming as plowing, harrowing, and cultivating the soil.

The sweat and toil of agrarian work was a crucial part of the lives of most colonial Americans and shaped their society. Until recently, historians gave little attention to work in the colonial period, al-

though they have long assumed the importance of labor in industrial America. Yet farm labor played as powerful a role in shaping early America as factory work was to do later. Indeed, what the settlers grew and where they grew it determined their pattern of existence. Crops were the arbiter of time for the colonial farmer, providing the farm family with both seasonal and daily schedules. Historian James Henretta has noted that most babies in farm families were born in the harvest season, following the cycle of the agricultural year.

By 1757, the settlement of Bethlehem, Pennsylvania, founded by the Moravian sect, was already thriving and self-sufficient. It was organized as an agrarian community, incorporating a bakery, tailor shop, shoemaker, blacksmith, saw and grist mills, carpentry shop, spinning and weaving mills, and even a brewery.

The Van Bergen homestead, a seemingly successful farm in the Hudson River valley of New York, includes four black slaves and two white servants, with two Indians apparently passing by.

The demands of agricultural work influenced social relations and cultural values as well. The predominance of mixed grain farming in the northern and middle colonies, tobacco in the Chesapeake region, and rice in South Carolina shaped societies in each region that were uniquely suited to their product. In New England, for example, a short growing season and labor scarcity fostered cooperation among farmers. Joshua Hempstead of Stonington, Connecticut, recorded in 1715 that he was "all day with all ye boys & benja[min] Fox & Peter Latimer breaking up and planting at Jo Lesters." With a borrowed plow and eight oxen these men plowed one and a half acres in two days.

*C*ooperation of this sort was commonplace throughout New England. In fact, a 1646 Massachusetts Bay law required neighbors to assist one another at times of harvest because "hay, corn, flax and hemp comes usually so near together that much loss can hardly be avoided." Though centered on hard work, these communal gatherings often developed into corn-husking contests, log-rolling bees, and other events that formed the heart of rural social life.

In this corn-husking scene of the early 1800s, a young boy holds up an ear of red corn, which, according to New England tradition, entitles him to kiss the nearest girl.

*T*obacco helped shape a vastly different culture in the Chesapeake colonies. Work in any year's crop extended from before seedtime to beyond seedtime of the next year with no long intervals. Whereas in the northern and middle colonies, slack time between harvest and planting enabled many farmers to take up other pursuits, such as lumbering, which fostered the development of a diversified economy, tobacco farmers had few such opportunities. Moreover, tobacco required such detailed attention that a single laborer could not tend more than three or four acres. As a result, the Chesapeake region quickly developed a staple one-crop economy. A traveler commented in 1698 that "[tobacco] swallows up all other things." Even itinerant skilled laborers were paid with "straggling parcels of Tobacco."

*R*ice cultivation in South Carolina required similar levels of activity. Once the rice plants had sprouted, labor centered on a continual process of flooding, draining, and weeding the fields. Work involved brawn and endurance rather than skill. Indeed, throughout the colonial period it was generally believed that whites could not survive the conditions of labor required by rice. Digging irrigation ditches in a hot, swampy environment seemed better suited to blacks. The rice fields were, in fact, deadly for both blacks and whites. Mortality rates were exceedingly high.

The uninterrupted series of tasks and the large fields involved in tobacco and rice cultivation were more conducive to plantation organization than to the small family farms found in the north. Unlike grain farms, plantations developed into almost self-sufficient communities. Slaves not only produced rice and tobacco but grew foodstuffs, raised livestock, and served as craftsmen as well. William Boyd II of Virginia boasted that planters "live in a kind of Independence of Every one but Providence."

Hampton, shown here in 1799, was typical of the elaborate plantation houses of Tidewater Virginia and Maryland. The smaller buildings housed the kitchen, servants' quarters, and vegetable cellars.

*H*istorians are just beginning to investigate the complex web of relationships that existed between agrarian work culture, group behavior, politics, and religion. By learning more about how farmers approached their work, an understanding of seventeenth- and eighteenth-century American culture will be greatly enhanced.

Rice Hope was a plantation in an area particularly suited to growing rice, on the Cooper River in South Carolina's low country. A system of tidal cultivation banked the silt in the riverbeds by building ditches and dikes and using floodgates. The system required hundreds of slaves to work on the banks, do the planting and successive hoeing, and then harvest and husk the crop. One successful Carolina planter owned 47,532 acres and 490 slaves; by 1790, 1300 families in the rural Charleston area owned 43,000 slaves.

In the backcountry, life was very different from life on the eastern seaboard. Isolated from other homesteads, the farm family had to be self-sufficient. They felled the trees to build their cabin and farmed a plot of land amid the tree stumps.

The Boston Massacre
Heightens Tensions

In October 1768 British rulers made another mistake, one that raised tensions almost to the pitch they had reached during the Stamp Act riots. The issue was the army. In part to save money and in part to intimidate colonial troublemakers, the ministry transferred four thousand regular troops from Nova Scotia and Ireland to Boston. Most of the army had already been withdrawn from the frontier to the seacoast to save revenue, thereby raising more acutely than ever the issue of why troops were in America at all. The armed strangers camped on Boston Commons, and when citizens passed the site, redcoats shouted obscenities. Sometimes in accordance with martial law, an errant soldier was whipped within an inch of his life, a bloody sight that sickened Boston civilians. To make relations worse, redcoats—men who were ill-treated and underpaid—competed in their spare time for jobs with local dockworkers and artisans. Work was already in short supply, and the streets crackled with tension.

When colonists questioned why the army had been sent to a peaceful city, pamphleteers responded that it was there to further a conspiracy originally conceived by Bute to oppress Americans, to take away their liberties, to collect illegal revenues. Grenville, Hillsborough, Townshend; they were all, supposedly, part of the plot. Such rhetoric sounds excessive, but to Americans who had absorbed the political theories of the Commonwealthmen, a pattern of tyranny seemed obvious.

Colonists had no difficulty interpreting the violence that erupted in Boston on March 5, 1770. In the gathering dusk of that afternoon, young boys and street toughs bombarded a small isolated patrol outside the offices of the hated customs commissioners in King Street with rocks and snowballs. The details of this incident are obscure, but it appears that as the mob grew and became more threatening, the soldiers panicked. In the confusion, the troops fired, leaving five Americans dead.

Pamphleteers promptly labeled the incident a "massacre." The victims were seen as martyrs and were memorialized in extravagant terms. In

■ *Outrage over the Boston Massacre was fanned by the propaganda of this etching by Paul Revere, which showed British redcoats firing on well-dressed men and women.*

one eulogy, Joseph Warren addressed the dead men's widows and children, dramatically recreating the gruesome scene in King Street. "Behold thy murdered husband gasping on the ground," Warren cried, " . . . take heed, ye orphan babes, lest, whilst your streaming eyes are fixed upon the ghastly corpse, your feet slide on the stones bespattered with your father's brains." Apparently to propagandists like Warren, it mattered little that the five civilians had been bachelors! Paul Revere's engraving of the massacre, appropriately splattered with blood, became an instant best seller. Confronted with such intense reaction and with the possibility of massive armed resistance, Crown officials wisely moved the army to an island in Boston harbor.

At this critical moment, the king's new first minister restored a measure of tranquillity. Lord North, congenial, well-meaning, but not very talented, became chancellor of the exchequer following Townshend's death in 1767. North became the first minister in 1770, and for the next twelve years—indeed, throughout most of the American crisis—he managed to retain his office. His secret formula seems to have been an ability to get along with George III and to build an effective majority in Parliament.

One of North's first recommendations to Parliament was the repeal of the Townshend duties. Not only had these ill-conceived duties unnecessarily angered the colonists, they also hurt English manufacturers, a cardinal sin in the mercantilist system. By taxing British exports such as glass and paint, Parliament had only encouraged the Americans to develop their own industries; thus without much prodding, the House of Commons dropped all the Townshend duties—with the notable exception of tea. The tax on tea was retained not for revenue purposes, North insisted, but as a reminder that England's rulers still subscribed to the principles of the Declaratory Act. They would not compromise the supremacy of Parliament. In mid-1770, however, the matter of tea seemed trivial to most Americans. They had drawn back from the precipice, a little frightened by the events of the past two years, and desperately hoped to head off future confrontation.

An Interlude of Order, 1770–1773

For a brief moment, American colonists and British officials put aside their recent animosities. Colonial merchants returned to familiar patterns of trade, pleased no doubt to end the local boycotts that had depressed the American economy. British goods flooded into colonial ports; the level of American indebtedness soared to new highs. In this period of apparent reconciliation, the people of Massachusetts—even of Boston—decided that they could accept their new royal governor, Thomas Hutchinson. After all, he was an American.

But appearances were deceiving. The bonds of imperial loyalty remained fragile, and even as Lord North attempted to win the colonists' trust, Crown officials in America created new strains. Customs Commissioners whom Townshend had appointed to collect his duties remained in the colonies long after his Revenue Acts had been repealed. If they had been honest, unobtrusive

administrators, perhaps no one would have taken notice of their behavior. But the Customs Commissioners regularly abused their powers of search and seizure and in the process lined their own pockets. In Massachusetts, Rhode Island, and South Carolina—to cite the most notorious cases—these officials drove local citizens to distraction by enforcing the Navigation Acts with such rigor that a skiff could not cross Narragansett Bay with a load of firewood without first obtaining a sheaf of legal documents. One slip, no matter how minor, could bring confiscation of ship and cargo.

The commissioners were not only corrupt, they were also foolish. If they had restricted their extortion to the common folk, they might have avoided becoming a major American grievance. But they could not control their greed. Some customs officers harassed the wealthiest, most powerful men around, men like John Hancock of Boston and Henry Laurens of Charleston. The commissioners' actions drove members of the colonial ruling class into opposition to the king's government. When in the summer of 1772 a group of disguised Rhode Islanders burnt a customs vessel, the *Gaspee*, Americans cheered. A special royal commission sent to arrest the culprits discovered that not a single Rhode Islander had the slightest idea how the ship could have come to such an unhappy end.

Samuel Adams (1722–1803) refused to accept the notion that the repeal of the Townshend duties had secured American liberty. During the early 1770s, while colonial leaders turned to other matters, Adams kept the cause alive with a drumfire of publicity. He reminded the people of Boston that the tax on tea remained in force. He organized public anniversaries commemorating the repeal of the Stamp Act and the Boston Massacre. Adams was a genuine revolutionary, an ideologue filled with a burning sense of indignation at the real and alleged wrongs suffered by his countrymen. To his contemporaries, this man resembled a figure out of New England's Puritan past. He seemed obsessed with the preservation of public virtue, as if he really believed that traditional values could protect Americans from British oppression. With each new attempt by Parliament to assert its supremacy over the colonists, more and more Bostonians listened to what Adams had to say. He observed ominously that

The American Revolution: From Protest to Independence

the British intended to use the tea revenue to pay judicial salaries, thus freeing the judges from dependence upon the assembly. When in November 1772 Adams suggested the formation of a committee of correspondence to communicate grievances to villagers throughout Massachusetts, he received broad support. Americans living in other colonies soon copied his idea. It was a brilliant stroke. Adams developed a structure of political cooperation completely independent of royal government.

The Boston Tea Party Provokes Punishment

In May 1773 Parliament resumed its old tricks. It passed the Tea Act, a strange piece of legislation that one might think the colonists would have welcomed. The statute was not intended as a revenue measure. Rather, Parliament wanted to save the floundering East India Company, a trading house burdened with eighteen million pounds of unsold tea. The House of Commons reasoned that if this tea were shipped directly to America by the company's own agents, eliminating the colonial middlemen, Americans could buy their tea at bargain rates, and the company would survive. But Parliament's logic was flawed. First, since the Townshend duties remained in effect, this new act seemed like a devious way to win popular support for Parliament's right to tax the colonists without representation. Second, the act threatened to undercut tea smugglers and powerful groups in Boston. Considering the American reaction, the British government might have been well advised to find another way to rescue the ailing company. In Philadelphia, and then at New York City, colonists turned back the tea ships before they could unload.

But in Boston the issue was not so easily resolved. Governor Hutchinson, a strong-willed man, would not permit the vessels to return to England. Local patriots would not let them unload. And so, crammed with the East India Company's tea, the ships sat in Boston Harbor waiting for the colonists to make up their minds. On the night of December 16, 1773, they did so in dramatic style. A group of men in Indian dress boarded the ships and pitched 340 chests of tea worth £10,000 over the side. Whether Samuel

Adams organized the famed "Tea Party" is not known. No doubt, he and his allies were not taken by surprise. Even at the time, John Adams, Samuel's distant cousin, sensed the event would have far-reaching significance. "This Destruction of the Tea," he scribbled in his diary, "is so bold, so daring, so firm, intrepid, and inflexible, and it must have so important consequences, and so lasting, that I can't but consider it as an epocha in history."

When news of the Tea Party reached London in January 1774, the North ministry was stunned. The people of Boston had treated parliamentary supremacy with utter contempt, and British rulers saw no humor whatsoever in the destruction of private property by subjects of the Crown dressed in costume. To quell such rebelliousness, Parliament passed a series of laws called the Coercive Acts. (In America they were referred to as the Intolerable Acts.) This legislation (1) closed

■ *The colonists' destruction of private property at the Boston Tea Party attracted foreign attention, as shown by this engraving from a German almanac.*

the port of Boston until the city fully compensated the East India Company for the lost tea, (2) restructured the Massachusetts government by transforming the upper house from an elective to an appointed body restricting the number of legal town meetings to one a year, (3) allowed the royal governor to transfer British officials arrested for offenses committed in the line of duty to England where there was little likelihood they would be convicted, and (4) authorized the army to quarter troops wherever they were needed, even if this required the compulsory requisition of uninhabited private buildings. George III enthusiastically supported this tough policy; he appointed General Thomas Gage to serve as the colony's new royal governor. Gage apparently won the king's favor by announcing that in America "Nothing can be done but by forcible means."

This sweeping denial of constitutional liberties confirmed the colonists' worst fears. To men like Samuel Adams, it seemed as if Britain really intended to enslave the American people. Colonial moderates found their position shaken by the vindictiveness of the Coercive Acts. Edmund Burke, one of America's last friends in Parliament, noted sadly on the floor of Commons, "this is the day, then, that you wish to go to war with all America, in order to conciliate that country to this . . ."

In the midst of this constitutional crisis, Parliament announced plans to establish a new civil government for the Canadian province of Quebec (Quebec Act, June 22, 1774). This territory had been ruled by military authority following the Seven Years' War. The Quebec Act not only failed to create an elective assembly—an institution the Americans regarded as essential for the protection of liberty—but also awarded French Roman Catholics a large voice in local political affairs. Moreover, since Quebec extended all the way to the Ohio River and west to the Mississippi, Americans concluded that Parliament wanted to deny the settlers and traders in this fast developing region their constitutional rights, a threat that affected all colonists, not just those of Massachusetts Bay.

If in 1774 the House of Commons thought it could isolate Boston from the rest of America, it was in for a rude surprise. Colonists living in other parts of the continent recognized immediately that the principles at stake in Boston affect-

ed all Americans. As one Virginian explained, ". . . there were no Heats and Troubles in Virginia till the Blockade of Boston." Few persons advocated independence, but they could not remain passive while Boston was destroyed. They sent food and money and, during the fall of 1774, reflected more deeply than ever on what it meant to be a colonist in the British empire.

The sticking point remained—as it had been in 1765—the sovereignty of Parliament. No one in the mother country could think of a way around this constitutional impasse. In 1773 Benjamin Franklin had offered a suggestion. "The Parliament," he observed, "has no right to make any law whatever, binding on the colonies . . . the king, and not the king, lords, and commons collectively, is their sovereign." But so long as it still seemed possible to coerce the Americans into obedience, to punish these errant children, Britain's rulers had little incentive to accept such a humiliating compromise.

Decision for Independence

Samuel Adams had prepared Americans for this moment. During the summer of 1774, committees of correspondence analyzed the perilous situation in which the colonists found themselves. Something, of course, had to be done. But what? Would the southern colonies support resistance in New England? Would Pennsylvanians stand up to Parliament? Not surprisingly, the committees endorsed a call for a continental congress, a gathering of fifty-five elected delegates from twelve colonies (Georgia sent none but agreed to support the action taken). This momentous gathering convened in Philadelphia on September 5. It included some of America's most articulate, respected leaders; among the group were John and Samuel Adams, Patrick Henry, Richard Henry Lee, Christopher Gadsden, and George Washington.

But the delegates were strangers to one another. They knew little about the customs and values, the geography and economy of Britain's other provinces. As John Adams explained on September 18, "It has taken Us much Time to get acquainted with the Tempers, Views, Characters, and Designs of Persons and to let them into the

Circumstances of our Province." During the early sessions of the Congress, the delegates eyed each other closely, trying to gain a sense of the strength and integrity of the men with whom they might commit treason.

Differences of opinion soon surfaced. Delegates from the Middle Colonies—Joseph Galloway of Pennsylvania, for example—wanted to proceed with caution, but before they knew what had happened, Samuel Adams maneuvered these moderates into a position far more radical than they found comfortable. Boston's master politician engineered congressional commendation of the Suffolk Resolves, a bold statement drawn up in Suffolk County, Massachusetts, that encouraged Americans to resist the Coercive Acts forcibly.

After this decision, the tone of the meeting was established. Moderate spokesmen introduced conciliatory measures, which received polite discussion but failed to win a majority vote. Just before returning to their homes, the delegates created the "Association," an intercolonial agreement to halt all commerce with the mother country until Parliament repealed the Intolerable Acts. They also agreed to meet in the coming year. George III sneered at these activities. "I am not sorry," he confided, "that the line of conduct seems now chalked out . . . the New England Governments are in a state of Rebellion, blows must decide whether they are to be subject to this country or independent."

Shots Heard Around the World

The king was correct. Before Congress reconvened, "blows" fell at Lexington and Concord, two small farm villages in eastern Massachusetts. One the evening of April 18, 1775, General Gage dispatched troops from Boston to seize rebel supplies. Paul Revere, a renowned silversmith and active patriot, warned the colonists that the redcoats were coming. The militia of Lexington, a collection of ill-trained farmers, boys as well as old men, decided to stand on the village green on the following morning, April 19, as the British soldiers passed on the road to Concord. No one planned to fight, but in a moment of confusion someone (probably a colonist) fired; the redcoats discharged a volley, and eight Americans lay dead.

Word of the incident spread rapidly, and by the time the British force reached its destination, the countryside swarmed with "minutemen," special companies of Massachusetts militia prepared to

■ *This 1775 engraving by Amos Doolittle, who was on the scene, shows the attack on the British regulars as they marched from Concord back to Boston. The minutemen fired from cover. It is not certain who fired the first shot at Lexington.*

respond instantly to military emergencies. The redcoats found nothing of significance in Concord; the long march back to Boston turned into a rout. Lord Percy, a British officer who brought up reinforcements, remarked more in surprise than bitterness, "whoever looks upon them [the American solders] as an irregular mob, will find himself much mistaken." On June 17 colonial militiamen again held their own against seasoned troops at the battle of Bunker Hill (actually Breed's Hill). The British finally took the hill, but after this costly "victory" in which he lost 10 percent of his troops, Gage complained that the Americans had displayed "a conduct and spirit against us, they never showed against the French."

The Second Continental Congress Directs the War Effort

Members of the Second Continental Congress gathered in Philadelphia in May 1775. They faced an awesome responsibility. British government in the mainland colonies had almost ceased to function, and with Americans fighting redcoats, the country desperately needed strong central leadership. Slowly, often reluctantly, Congress took control of the war. The delegates formed a Continental army and appointed George Washington its commander, in part because he seemed to have greater military experience than anyone else available and in part because he looked like he should be commander in chief. The delegates were also eager to select someone who did not come from Massachusetts, a colony that seemed already to possess too much power in national councils. The members of Congress purchased military supplies and, to pay for them, issued paper money. But while they were assuming the powers of a sovereign government, the congressmen refused to declare independence. They debated and fretted, listened to the appeals of moderates who played upon the colonists' remaining loyalty to Britain, and then did nothing.

Indecision drove men like John Adams nearly mad. In one tirade against his timid colleagues, he exclaimed that they possessed "the vanity of the ape, the tameness of the ox, or the stupid servility of the ass." Haste, however, would have been a terrible mistake. While Adams and Richard Henry Lee of Virginia were willing to sever ties

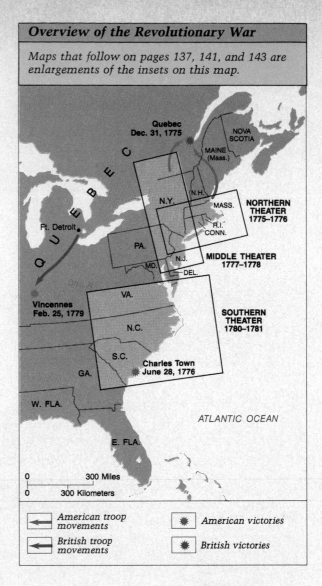

Overview of the Revolutionary War

Maps that follow on pages 137, 141, and 143 are enlargements of the insets on this map.

Quebec
Dec. 31, 1775

NOVA SCOTIA

MAINE (Mass.)

QUEBEC

N.Y.   N.H.
            MASS.

Ft. Detroit

R.I.
CONN.

NORTHERN THEATER 1775–1776

PA.
            N.J.
MD.   DEL.

MIDDLE THEATER 1777–1778

Vincennes
Feb. 25, 1779

VA.

SOUTHERN THEATER 1780–1781

N.C.

S.C.

GA.   Charles Town
            June 28, 1776

W. FLA.

ATLANTIC OCEAN

E. FLA.

0   300 Miles
0   300 Kilometers

American troop movements

British troop movements

American victories

British victories

with the mother country, many Americans were not convinced that such a step was either desirable or necessary. If Congress had moved too quickly, it might have become vulnerable to charges of extremism, in which case the rebellion would have seemed more like an overthrow by a faction or clique than an expression of popular will.

The British government appeared intent upon transforming colonial moderates into angry rebels. In December 1775 Parliament passed the Prohibitory Act, declaring war on American commerce. Until the colonists begged for pardon, they could not trade with the rest of the world. The British navy blockaded their ports and seized

American ships on the high seas. Lord North also hired German mercenaries (the Russians drove too hard a bargain) to put down the rebellion. And in America, royal governors like Lord Dunmore further undermined the possibility of reconciliation by urging Virginia's slaves to take up arms against their masters. Few did so, but the effort to stir up black rebellion infuriated the Virginia gentry.

Thomas Paine (1737–1809) pushed the colonists even closer to independence. Nothing in this man's background suggested that he would write the most important pamphlet in American history. In England, Paine had tried and failed in a number of jobs, and exactly why he elected to move to America in 1774 is not clear. While still in England, Paine had the good fortune to meet Benjamin Franklin, who presented him with letters of introduction to the leading patriots of Pennsylvania. At the urging of his new American friends, Paine produced *Common Sense*, an essay that became an instant best-seller. In only three months it sold over 120,000 copies. Paine confirmed in forceful prose what the colonists had been thinking but had been unable to state in coherent form. "My motive and object in all my political works," he declared, " . . . have been to rescue man from tyranny and false systems of government, and enable him to be free."

Common Sense systematically stripped kingship of historical and theological justification. For centuries, the English had maintained the fiction that the monarch could do no wrong. When the government oppressed the people, the royal counselors received the blame. The Crown was above suspicion. To this, Paine cried nonsense. Monarchs ruled by force. Goerge III was simply a "royal brute," who by his arbitrary behavior had surrendered his claim to the colonists' obedience. The pamphlet also attacked the whole idea of a mixed and balanced constitution. Indeed, *Common Sense* was a powerful democratic manifesto.

Paine's greatest contribution to the revolutionary cause was persuading common folk to sever their ties with Great Britain. It was not reasonable, he argued, to regard England as the mother country. "Europe, and not England," he explained, "is the parent country of America. This new world hath been the asylum for the persecuted lovers of civil and religious liberty from *every part* of Europe." No doubt that message made a

■ *The message of Thomas Paine's pamphlet,* Common Sense *(title page shown), was easy to follow. His stark phrases calling for "The Free and Independent States of America" reverberated in people's hearts and minds.*

deep impression on Pennsylvania's German population. The time had come for the colonists to form an independent republic. "We have it in our power," Paine wrote in one of his most moving statements, "to begin the world over again . . . the birthday of a new world is at hand."

On July 2, 1776, after a long and tedious debate, Congress finally voted for independence. The motion passed; twelve states for, none against. Thomas Jefferson, a young Virginia lawyer and planter who enjoyed a reputation as a graceful writer, drafted a formal declaration which was accepted with only minor alterations two days later. Much of the Declaration of Independence consisted of a list of specific grievances against George III and his government. Like the skilled lawyer he was, Jefferson presented the evidence for independence. But the document did not become famous for those passages. Long after the establishment of the new Republic, the declaration challenged Americans to make good on the principle that "all men are created equal." John Adams nicely expressed the patriots' fervor when he wrote on July 3: "Yesterday the greatest question was decided, which ever was debated in America, and a greater perhaps, never was or will be decided among men."

The committee appointed by Congress to draft a declaration of independence included (left to right) John Adams, Roger Sherman, Robert Livingston, Thomas Jefferson, and Benjamin Franklin. In this painting, they are shown submitting Jefferson's draft to the Speaker.

War for Independence

Only fools and visionaries were optimistic about America's prospects of winning independence in 1776. The Americans had taken on a formidable military power. The population of the mother country was perhaps four times that of its former colonies. England also possessed a strong industrial base, a well-trained regular army supplemented by thousands of hired German troops (Hessians), and a navy that dominated the world's oceans. Many British officers had battlefield experience. They already knew what the Americans would slowly learn, that waging war requires great discipline, money, and sacrifice.

The British government entered the conflict fully confident that it could beat the Americans. In 1776, Lord North and his colleagues regarded the war as a police action. They anticipated that a mere show of armed force would intimidate the upstart colonists. As soon as the rebels in Boston had been humbled, the British argued, people living in other colonies would desert the cause for independence. General Gage, for example, told the king that the colonists "will be Lions, whilst we are Lambs, . . . if we take a resolute part they will undoubtedly prove very weak." Since this advice confirmed George's views, he called Gage "an honest determined man."

As later events demonstrated, of course, Britain had become involved in an impossible military situation, in some ways analogous to that in which the United States found itself recently in Vietnam. Three separate elements neutralized advantages held by the larger power over its adversary. First, the British had to transport men and supplies across the Atlantic, a logistic challenge of unprecedented complexity. Unreliable lines of communication broke down under the strain of war.

Second, America was too vast to be conquered by conventional military methods. Redcoats might gain control over the major port cities, but as long as the Continental army remained intact, the rebellion continued. As Washington explained, " . . . the possession of our Towns, while we have an Army in the field, will avail them little . . . It is our Arms, not defenceless Towns, they have to subdue." Even if England had recruited enough soldiers to occupy the entire country, it would still have lost the war. As one Loyalist instructed the king, "if all America becomes a garrison, she is not worth your attention." Britain could only win by crushing the American will to resist.

And third, British strategists never appreciated the depth of the Americans' commitment to a political ideology. In the wars of eighteenth-century Europe such beliefs had seldom mattered. Troops served because they were paid or because the military was a vocation, but most certainly not because they hoped to advance a set of constitutional principles. Americans were different. They fought for liberty. As one French officer reported from the United States, "It is incredible that soldiers composed of men of every age, even of children of fifteen, of whites and blacks, almost naked, unpaid, and rather poorly fed, can march so well and withstand fire so steadfastly."

During the earliest months of rebellion, American soldiers—especially those of New England—suffered no lack of confidence. Indeed, they interpreted their courageous stands at Concord and Bunker Hill as evidence that brave, yeomen farmers could lick British regulars on any battlefield. George Washington spent the first years of the war disabusing the colonists of this foolishness, for as he had learned during the French and Indian War, military success depended upon endless drill, careful planning, and tough discipline—

qualities that did not characterize the minutemen.

Washington insisted upon organizing a regular, well-trained field army. Some advisers urged the commander in chief to wage a guerrilla war, one in which small partisan bands would sap Britain's will to rule Americans. But Washington rejected that course. He recognized that the Continental army served not only as a fighting force but also as a symbol of the republican cause. Its very existence would sustain American hopes, and so long as the army survived, American agents could plausibly solicit foreign aid. This thinking shaped Washington's wartime strategy; he studiously avoided "general actions" in which the Continental army might be destroyed. Critics complained about Washington's caution, but as they soon discovered, he understood better than they what independence required.

If the commander in chief was correct about the army, however, he failed to comprehend the importance of the militia. These scattered, al-

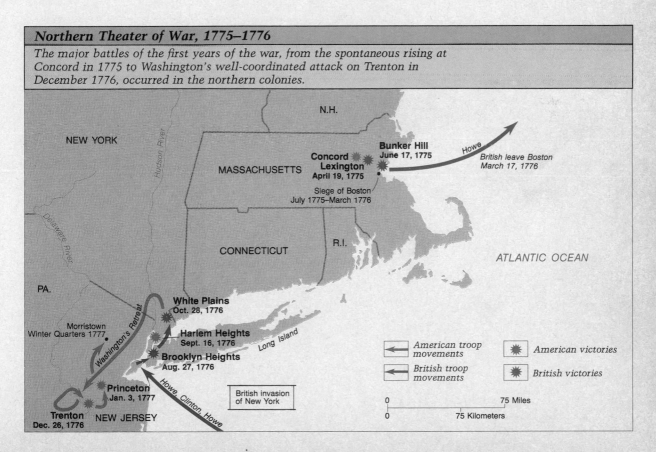

Northern Theater of War, 1775–1776

The major battles of the first years of the war, from the spontaneous rising at Concord in 1775 to Washington's well-coordinated attack on Trenton in December 1776, occurred in the northern colonies.

■ *This portrait of General George Washington, a miniature by Charles Willson Peale, was painted during the winter of 1777–1778. After more than two trying years as commander in chief, Washington's appearance had become careworn.*

After the embarrassing defeats in Massachusetts, the king appointed General Sir William Howe to replace the ill-fated Gage. British rulers now understood that a simple police action would not be sufficient to crush the American rebellion. Parliament authorized sending over fifty thousand troops to the mainland colonies, and after evacuating Boston—an untenable strategic position—the British forces stormed ashore at Staten Island in New York harbor on July 3, 1776. From this more central location, Howe believed he could cut the New Englanders off from the rest of America. He enjoyed the powerful support of the British navy under the command of his brother, Admiral Lord Richard Howe.

When Washington learned that the British were digging in at New York, he transferred many of his inexperienced soldiers to Long Island where they suffered a major defeat (August 26, 1776). In a series of disastrous engagements for the Americans, Howe drove the Continental army across the Hudson River into New Jersey. Because of his failure to take full advantage of the situation, however, General Howe lost what seemed in retrospect an excellent opportunity to annihilate Washington's entire army. Nevertheless, the Americans were on the run, and in the fall of 1776, contemporaries predicted that the rebels would soon capitulate.

"Times that Try Men's Souls"

Swift victories in New York and New Jersey persuaded General Howe that few Americans enthusiastically supported independence. He issued a general pardon, therefore, to anyone who would swear allegiance to George III. The results were encouraging. Over three thousand men and women who lived in areas occupied by the British army took the oath. This group included one signer of the Declaration of Independence. Howe perceived that a lasting peace in America would require his troops to treat "our enemies as if they might one day become our friends." A member of Lord North's cabinet grumbled that this was "a sentimental manner of making war," a short-

most amateur, military units seldom altered the outcome of battle, but they did maintain control over large areas of the country not directly affected by the British army. Throughout the war, they compelled men and women who would rather have remained neutral to support actively the American effort. In 1777, for example, the militia of Farmington, Connecticut, visited a group of suspected Tories, as Loyalists were called, and after "educating" these people in the fundamentals of republican ideology, a militia spokesman announced, "They were indeed grossly ignorant of the true grounds of the present war with Great Britain . . . [but] They appeared to be penitent of their former conduct, [and] professed themselves convinced . . . that there was no such thing as remaining neuters." Without local political coercion, Washington's task would have been considerably more difficult.

In this painting of the battle of Princeton, George Washington (left, on horseback) directs American cannon fire with his sword. Shouting "It's a fine fox chase, my boys!" he led the rout of the British rear guard.

sighted view considering England's experience in attempting to pacify the Irish. The pardon plan eventually failed not because Howe lacked toughness but because his soldiers and officers regarded loyal Americans as inferior provincials, an attitude that did little to promote good relations. In any case, as soon as the redcoats left a pardoned region, the rebel militia retaliated against those who had deserted the patriot cause.

In December 1776, Washington's bedraggled army retreated across the Delaware River into Pennsylvania. American prospects appeared bleaker than at any other time during the war. The Continental army lacked basic supplies, and many men who had signed up for short-term enlistments prepared to go home. "These are the times that try men's souls," Paine wrote in a pamphlet entitled *American Crisis*. "The summer soldier and the sunshine patriot will, in this crisis, shrink from the service of their country, but he that stands it *now* deserves . . . love and thanks . . ." Before winter, Washington determined to attempt one last desperate stroke.

Howe played into Washington's hands. The British forces were dispersed in small garrisons across the state of New Jersey, and while the Americans could not possibly have defeated the combined British army, they did possess the capacity—with luck—to capture an exposed post. On the night of December 25, Continental soldiers slipped over the ice-filled Delaware River and at Trenton took nine hundred sleeping Hessian mercenaries by complete surprise.

Cheered by success, Washington returned a second time to Trenton, but on this occasion the Continental army was not so fortunate. A large British force under Lord Cornwallis trapped the Americans. Instead of standing and fighting— really an impossible challenge—Washington secretly, by night, marched his little army around Cornwallis' left flank. On January 3, 1777, the Americans surprised a British garrison at Princeton. Washington then went into winter quarters. The British, fearful of losing any more outposts, consolidated their troops, thus leaving much of the state in the hands of the patriot militia.

Victory in a Year of Defeat

In 1777 England's chief military strategist, Lord George Germain, still perceived the war in conventional European terms. A large field army would somehow maneuver Washington's Continental troops into a decisive battle in which the British would enjoy a clear advantage. Complete victory over the Americans certainly seemed within England's grasp. Unfortunately for the men who advocated this plan, the Continental forces proved extremely elusive, and while one British army vainly tried to corner Washington in Pennsylvania, another was forced to surrender in the forests of upstate New York.

In the summer of 1777 General John Burgoyne, a dashing though overbearing officer, descended from Canada with a force of over seven thousand troops. They intended to clear the Hudson Valley of rebel resistance, join Howe's army which was to come up to Albany, and thereby cut New England off from the other states. Burgoyne fought in a grand style. Accompanied by a German band, thirty carts filled with the general's liquor and belongings, and two thousand dependents and camp followers, the British set out to thrash the Americans. The campaign was a disaster. Military units, mostly from New England, cut the enemy force apart in the deep woods north of Albany. At the battle of Bennington (August 16), the New Hampshire militia under Brigadier General John Stark overwhelmed a thousand German mercenaries. After this setback, Burgoyne's forces struggled forward, desperately hoping that Howe would rush to their rescue, but when it became clear that their situation at Saratoga was hopeless, the haughty Burgoyne was forced to surrender fifty-eight hundred men to the American General Horatio Gates (October 17).

Soon after Burgoyne left Canada, General Howe quite unexpectedly decided to move his main army from New York City to Philadelphia. Exactly what he hoped to achieve was not clear, even to Britain's rulers, and of course, when Burgoyne called for assistance, Howe was sitting in the new nation's capital still trying to devise a way to destroy the Continental army. Howe's campaign began in late July. The British forces sailed to the head of the Chesapeake Bay and then marched north to Philadelphia. Washington's troops obstructed the enemy's progress, first at Brandywine Creek (September 11) and then at Paoli (September 20), but the outnumbered Americans could not stop the British from entering Philadelphia.

Anxious lest these defeats discourage Congress and the American people, Washington attempted one last battle before the onset of winter. In a curious engagement at Germantown (October 4), the Americans launched a major counterattack on a fog-covered battlefield, but just at the moment when success seemed assured, the Americans broke off the fight. "When every thing gave the most flattering hopes of victory," Washington complained, "the troops began suddenly to retreat." Bad luck, confusion, and incompetence contributed to the failure. A discouraged Continental army dug in at Valley Forge, twenty miles outside of Philadelphia, where camp diseases took twenty-five hundred American lives. In their misery, few American soldiers realized that their situation was not nearly as desperate as it had been in 1776.

The French Alliance

Even before the Americans declared their independence, agents of the government of Louis XVI began to explore ways to aid the colonists, not so much because the French monarchy favored the republican cause, but because it hoped to embarrass the English. The French deeply resented the defeat they had sustained during the Seven Years' War. During the early months of the Revolution, the French covertly sent tons of essential military supplies to the Americans. The negotiations for these arms involved secret agents and fictitious trading companies, the type of clandestine operation more typical of modern times than of the eighteenth century. But when American representatives, Benjamin Franklin for one, pleaded for official recognition of American independence or for outright military alliance, the French advised patience. The international stakes were too great for the king openly to back a cause that had little chance of success.

The American victory at Saratoga convinced the French that the rebels had formidable forces and were serious in their resolve. Indeed, Lord North drew the same conclusion. When news of

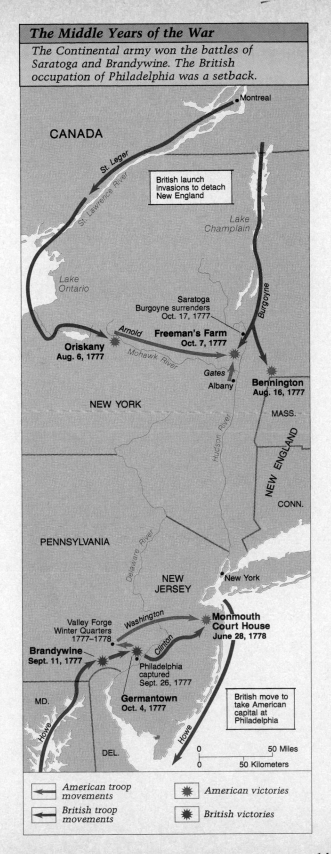

The Middle Years of the War

The Continental army won the battles of Saratoga and Brandywine. The British occupation of Philadelphia was a setback.

Montreal

CANADA

St. Leger

St. Lawrence River

British launch invasions to detach New England

Lake Champlain

Lake Ontario

Saratoga
Burgoyne surrenders
Oct. 17, 1777

Arnold

Freeman's Farm
Oct. 7, 1777

Oriskany
Aug. 6, 1777

Mohawk River

Burgoyne

Gates

Albany

Bennington
Aug. 16, 1777

NEW YORK

MASS.

Hudson River

NEW ENGLAND

CONN.

PENNSYLVANIA

Delaware River

NEW JERSEY

New York

Valley Forge
Winter Quarters
1777–1778

Washington

Monmouth
Court House
June 28, 1778

Clinton

Brandywine
Sept. 11, 1777

Philadelphia
captured
Sept. 26, 1777

Germantown
Oct. 4, 1777

MD.

Howe

British move to take American capital at Philadelphia

DEL.

Howe

| | 0 | 50 Miles |
| 0 | 50 Kilometers |

→ American troop movements

→ British troop movements

✴ American victories

✴ British victories

Saratoga reached London, North muttered, "this damned war." In private conversation he expressed doubts about England's ability to win the contest, knowing that the French would soon enter the contest.

In April 1778 North tried to avert a greatly expanded war by sending a peace commission to America. He instructed this group, headed by the Earl of Carlisle, to bargain with the Continental Congress "as if it were a legal body." If the colonists would agree to drop their demand for independence, they could turn the imperial calendar back to 1763. Parliament belatedly conceded the right of Americans to tax themselves, even to elect their own governors. It also promised to remove all British troops in times of peace. The proposal might have gained substantial support back in 1776. The war, however, had hardened American resolve; the Congress refused to deal with Carlisle.

In Paris, Franklin performed brilliantly. In meetings with French officials, he hinted that the Americans might accept a British peace initiative. If the French wanted the war to continue, if they really wanted to embarrass their old rival, then they had to do what the English refused, formally recognize the independence of the United States.

The stratagem paid off handsomely. On February 6, 1778, the French presented American representatives with two separate treaties. The first, called the Treaty of Amity and Commerce, established commercial relations between France and the United States. It tacitly accepted the existence of a new, independent republic. The Treaty of Alliance was even more generous, considering America's obvious military and economic weaknesses. In the event that France and England went to war (they did so on June 14 as everyone expected), the French agreed to reject "either Truce or Peace with Great Britain . . . until the independence of the United States shall have been formally or tacitly assured by the Treaty or Treaties that shall terminate the War." Even more amazing, France surrendered its claim to all territories formerly owned by Great Britain east of the Mississippi River. The Americans pledged that they would not sign a separate peace with Britain without first informing their new ally. And in return, France made no claim to Canada, asking only for the right to take possession of certain

Franklin's wit and charm made him a pet to the ladies of the French court of Versailles. Here he receives a crown of laurel from an admirer. King Louis XVI and Queen Marie Antionette are seated at right.

British islands in the Caribbean. Never had Franklin worked his magic to greater effect.

French intervention instantly transformed British military strategy. What had been a colonial rebellion suddenly became a world conflict, a continuation of the great wars for empire of the late seventeenth century (see chapter 4). Scarce military resources, especially newer fighting ships, had to be diverted from the American theater to guard the English Channel. In fact, there was talk in London of a possible French invasion. While the threat of such an assault was not very great until 1779, the French navy posed a serious challenge to the overextended British fleet. By concentrating their warships in a specific area, the French could hold off or even defeat British squadrons, an advantage that would figure significantly in the American victory at Yorktown.

The Final Campaign

British General Henry Clinton replaced Howe, who resigned after the battle of Saratoga. Clinton was a strangely complex individual. As a subordi-

nate officer, he had impressed his superiors as imaginative but easily provoked to anger. When he took command of the British army, his resolute self-confidence suddenly dissolved. Perhaps he feared failure? Whatever the explanation for his vacillation, Clinton's record in America was little better than Howe's or Gage's.

Military strategists calculated that Britain's last chance of winning the war lay in the southern colonies, a region largely untouched in the early years of fighting. Intelligence reports reaching London indicated that Georgia and South Carolina contained a sizable body of Loyalists, men who would take up arms for the Crown if only they received support and encouragement from the regular army. The southern strategy devised by Germain and Clinton in 1779 turned the war into a bitter guerrilla conflict, and during the last months of battle, British officers worried that their search for an easy victory had inadvertently opened a Pandora's box of uncontrollable partisan furies.

The southern campaign opened in the spring of 1780. Savannah had already fallen, and Clinton reckoned that if the British could take Charleston, they would be able to control the entire

Major battles from the fall of Savannah to the final victory at Yorktown.

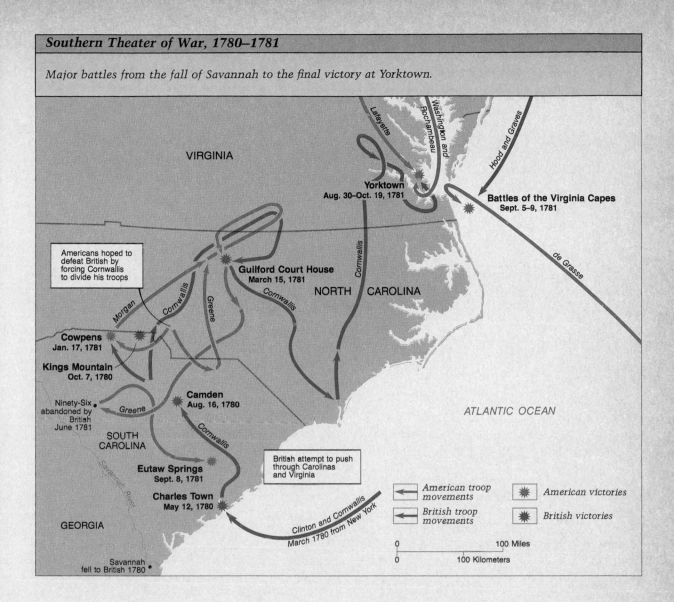

VIRGINIA

Lafayette

Washington and Rochambeau

Hood and Graves

Yorktown
Aug. 30–Oct. 19, 1781

Battles of the Virginia Capes
Sept. 5–9, 1781

de Grasse

Americans hoped to defeat British by forcing Cornwallis to divide his troops

Cornwallis

Guilford Court House
March 15, 1781

NORTH CAROLINA

Cornwallis

Morgan

Cornwallis

Greene

Cowpens
Jan. 17, 1781

Kings Mountain
Oct. 7, 1780

Ninety-Six abandoned by British June 1781

Greene

Camden
Aug. 16, 1780

ATLANTIC OCEAN

SOUTH CAROLINA

Cornwallis

Eutaw Springs
Sept. 8, 1781

British attempt to push through Carolinas and Virginia

Charles Town
May 12, 1780

Savannah River

GEORGIA

Clinton and Cornwallis
March 1780 from New York

Savannah fell to British 1780

American troop movements

British troop movements

American victories

British victories

0   100 Miles
0   100 Kilometers

South. A large fleet carrying nearly eight thousand redcoats reached South Carolina in February. Complacent Americans had allowed the city's fortifications to decay, and in a desperate, last-minute effort to preserve Charleston, General Benjamin Lincoln's forces dug trenches and reinforced walls, but to no avail. Clinton and his second in command, General Cornwallis, gradually encircled the city, and on May 12, Lincoln surrendered an American army of almost six thousand men.

The defeat took Congress by surprise, and with-out making proper preparations, it dispatched a second army to South Carolina under Horatio Gates, the hero of Saratoga. He too failed. At Camden, Cornwallis outmaneuvered the raw American recruits, capturing or killing 750 during the course of battle (August 16). Poor Gates galloped from the scene and did not stop until he reached Hillsboro, North Carolina, two hundred miles away.

Even at this early stage of the southern campaign, the dangers of partisan warfare had become evident. Tory raiders showed little interest in

Popular Culture and Revolutionary Ferment

No one knows exactly why men and women rebel against governments. Economic deprivation and political frustration contribute to unrest, but the spark that ignites popular passions, that causes common people to risk their lives in battle, often arises from a society's most basic traditions and beliefs.

The American Revolution illustrates this complex process of revolt. The educated elite in the colonies may have found their inspiration in reading classical history or political pamphlets, but the common people, those who protested British taxation in the streets, seem to have gained resolution from a deep Protestant tradition, a set of religious values recently reinforced during the Great Awakening (see chapter 4). For ordinary men and women, the American Revolution may have seemed a kind of morality play, a drama that transformed complicated issues of representation and sovereignty into a stark conflict between American good and British evil.

Even before colonial protests against British taxation led to bloodshed, religious passions helped draw thousands of people into the streets of Boston on Pope's Day, a traditional anti-Catholic holiday celebrated on November 5. (In England,

the holiday was known as Guy Fawkes Day and commemorated exposure of the Gunpowder Plot of 1605, a conspiracy organized by English Catholics to blow up Parliament which was thwarted at the last minute.) For the holiday, Bostonians arranged elaborate processions, complete with effigies of the pope and the devil, which they burned at the climax of the festivities. Sometimes the annual celebration turned ugly, as rival gangs from the north and south ends of the city tried to disrupt each other's parade. During the French and Indian War, the crowds grew increasingly unruly, as the pageantry triggered an outpouring of emotions that sprang from the New Englanders' fervent commitment to the Reformation and their desire to rid Canada of Catholic domination.

The Pope's Day celebrations provided a model for demonstrations against the Stamp Act. The first public protest against the British law in Boston, on August 14, 1765, began with a rally under a large elm, the original colonial "Liberty Tree." Hanging from its branches were effigies of Andrew Oliver, Boston's first stamp collector, and the devil, whose pitchfork menaced Oliver. A Label attached to the effigy of Oliver read:

Fair Freedom's glorious cause I've meanly quitted
For the sake of self;
But ah! the Devil had me outwitted,
And instead of stamping others, I've hang'd myself

As night fell, a diverse crowd of gentlemen, workers, and even a few women carried the effigies through the streets of Boston. After destroying a building owned by Oliver, they marched to Fort Hill where "they made a burnt offering of the effigies for these sins of the people which had caused such heavy judgments as the Stamp Act, etc. to be laid upon them." This symbolic protest ended with a sort of conversion; in much the same way that anxious sinners renounced evil at evangelical meetings, Oliver announced publicly that he would resign as stamp collector.

The devil was a familiar feature in American political cartoons. In one famous illustration, published in 1774, the devil held a list of crimes committed by Governor Thomas Hutchinson of Massachusetts, as the viper of death prepared to punish the royal official for his sins. This gruesome imagery revealed that patriots thought of Hutchinson not only as a political opponent but also as a moral traitor. No one who saw these macabre figures could fail to appreciate the accompanying warning: "Let the destroyers of mankind behold and tremble!"

A similar message was at the heart of the patriot practice of tarring and feathering. Crowds in Boston usually reserved this humiliating punishment for informers who reported violations to the hated customs officers. The victim became the main actor in a public morality play, in which he was wheeled in a cart before jeering crowds and forced to repent. This spectacle recalled a verse often repeated on Pope's Day:

See the informer how he stands
If anyone now takes his part
An enemy to all the Land
He'll go to Hell without a cart.

Patriots regarded military traitors as the worst of sinners. When General Benedict Arnold, who had been a hero during the early stages of the war, went over to the British in 1780, Americans accused him of selling out to the devil. A huge parade held in Philadelphia included a two-faced Arnold riding in front of Satan. The devil held a bag of gold—presumably the source of Arnold's fall—and a pitchfork which he used to prod the traitor along the path to Hell.

Revolutionary leaders also tapped long-standing Puritan hostility to the theater. Puritans and other strict Protestants indicted the theater for encouraging idleness, hypocrisy, deceit, and even effeminacy, since men usually played women's roles. But their greatest objection was that the stage appealed to those emotions and lusts that God-fearing men and women tried to restrain through knowledge of Scripture. Theaters, they believed, were nothing less than enemies of the church. "Those therefore who serve the Devill in Playes and Play-houses; its impossible for them to serve the Lord in prayers and Churches," asserted one Puritan thinker.

Patriot leaders also considered the stage a rival for popular loyalties. In 1766 the Sons of Liberty in New York City demolished a theater. And in 1774 the First Continental Congress resolved to "discountenance and discourage every species of extravagance and dissipation, especially . . . shews, plays and other expensive diversions and entertainments." Such proclamations helped to channel Protestant moral fervor into a commitment to the patriot cause.

During the war itself—when soldiers were actually fighting and dying—religion helped sustain patriotism. In 1775, for example, a company of Massachusetts soldiers on their way to Quebec, camped briefly at Newburyport, where George Whitefield had been buried. Before the troops resumed their long march to Canada, some of them opened the minister's tomb and cut off small pieces of Whitefield's collar and wristband, an act that seems ghoulish only to those who do not fully comprehend the importance of religion in the lives of the common soldiers.

Religious symbol and ritual thus galvanized common men and women by expressing the issues that divided the colonies from England in moral terms. The Great Awakening had prepared the colonists to view the contest in terms of American virtue and English vice, of God and the devil. By appealing to the strong Protestant tradition in the colonies, patriots mobilized the American people for revolution.

serving as regular soldiers in Cornwallis' army. They preferred night riding, indiscriminate plundering or murdering of neighbors against whom they harbored ancient grudges. The British had unleashed a horde of banditti across South Carolina. Men who genuinely supported independence or who had merely fallen victim to the Loyalist guerrillas bided their time. They retreated westward waiting for their enemies to make a mistake. Their chance came on October 7 at King's Mountain, North Carolina. The backwoodsmen decimated a force of British regulars and Tory raiders who had strayed too far from base. This was the most vicious fighting of the Revolution. One witness reported that when a British officer tried to surrender, he was summarily shot down by at last seven American soldiers.

Cornwallis, badly confused and poorly supplied, proceeded to squander his strength chasing American forces across the Carolinas. Whatever military strategy had compelled him to leave Charleston had long since been abandoned, and in early 1781, Cornwallis informed Clinton that "Events alone can decide the future Steps." Events, however, did not run in the British favor. Congress sent General Nathanael Greene to the South with a new army. This young Rhode Islander was the most capable general on Washington's staff. Greene joined Daniel Morgan, leader of the famed Virginia Riflemen, and in a series of tactically brilliant engagements, they sapped the strength of Cornwallis' army, first at Cowpens, South Carolina (January 17, 1781), and later at Guilford Courthouse, North Carolina (March 15). Clinton fumed in New York City. In his estimation, the inept Cornwallis had left "two valuable colonies behind him to be overrun and conquered by the very army which he boasts to have completely routed but a week or two before."

Cornwallis pushed north into Virginia, planning apparently to establish a base of operations on the coast. He selected Yorktown, a sleepy tobacco market town located on a peninsula bounded by the York and James rivers. Washington watched these maneuvers closely. The canny Virginia planter knew this territory intimately, and he sensed that Cornwallis had made a serious blunder. When Washington learned that the French fleet could gain temporary dominance in the Chesapeake Bay, he rushed south from New Jersey. With him marched thousands of well-trained French troops under Marquis de Lafayette and Comte de Rochambeau. All the pieces fell into place. The French admiral, Comte de Grasse, cut Cornwallis off from the sea, while Washington and his lieutenants encircled the British on land. On October 19, 1781, Cornwallis surrendered his entire army of six thousand men. When Lord North heard of the defeat at Yorktown, he moaned, "Oh God! It is all over." The British still controlled New York City and Charleston, but except for a few skirmishes, the fighting ended. The task of securing the independence of the United States was now in the hands of the diplomats.

The Losers: The American Loyalists

The war lasted longer than anyone had predicted in 1776. While the nation won its independence, many Americans paid a terrible price. Indeed, a large number of men and women decided that however much they had loved colonial society, they could not accept the new government.

No one knows for certain how many Americans supported the Crown during the Revolution. Some Loyalists undoubtedly kept silent and avoided making a public commitment that might have led to banishment or loss of property. But for many persons, neutrality proved impossible. Over one hundred thousand men and women permanently left America. While a number of these exiles had served as British officeholders—men like Thomas Hutchinson, for example—in the main, they came from all ranks and sections of society and included farmers, merchants, and tradesmen. These people subscribed to certain political principles as strongly as did their adversaries. A sizable refugee community settled in London. Many of these exiles, usually persons who had held positions of power in the empire, begged for pensions from the king. Other, more humble individuals drawn from every state of the Union relocated in Canada or the West Indies.

The Loyalists were caught in a difficult squeeze. The British never quite trusted them. After all, they were Americans. During the early stages of the war, Loyalists organized militia companies and hoped to pacify large areas of the

■ *The fate of the Tories was an unhappy one. The patriots meted out harsh and summary punishments to those who did not flee to England or Canada.*

England, and its body in America, and its neck ought to be stretched."

Long after the victorious Americans turned their attentions to the business of building a new republic, Loyalists remembered a receding colonial past, a comfortable, ordered world that had been lost forever at Yorktown. Many lonely individuals wanted desperately to return. Perhaps the most poignant testimony came from a young mother living in exile in Nova Scotia. "I climbed to the top of Chipman's Hill and watched the sails disappear in the distance," she recounted, "and such a feeling of loneliness came over me that though I had not shed a tear through all the war I sat down on the damp moss with my baby on my lap and cried bitterly."

Winning the Peace

Congress appointed a splendid delegation to negotiate a peace treaty: Benjamin Franklin, John Adams, and John Jay. According to their official instructions, they were to insist only upon the recognition of the independence of the United States. On other issues, Congress ordered its delegates to defer to the counsel of the French government.

But the political environment in Paris was much different than the diplomats had been led to expect. The French had formed a military alliance with Spain, and French officials announced that they could not consider the details of an American settlement until after the Spanish had recaptured Gibraltar from the British. The prospects for a Spanish victory were not good, and in any case, it was well known that Spain coveted the lands lying between the Appalachian Mountains and the Mississippi River. Indeed, there were even rumors afloat in Paris that the great European powers might intrigue to deny the United States its independence.

While the three American delegates publicly paid their respects to French officials, they secretly entered into negotiations with an English agent. These actions, of course, violated their instructions. The French were not fooled. Their spies kept them informed of what occurred at these meetings, and while they could have protested the American breach of faith, they did not do so.

countryside with the support of the regular army. The British generals were unreliable partners, however, for no sooner had they called upon loyal Americans to come forward than the redcoats marched away, leaving the Tories exposed to rebel retaliation. And in England, the exiles found themselves treated as second-class citizens. While many of them received monetary compensation for their sacrifice, they were never regarded as the equals of native-born English citizens. Not surprisingly, the Loyalist community in London was gradually transformed into a bitter collection of men and women who felt unwelcome on both sides of the Atlantic.

Americans who actively supported independence saw these people as traitors who deserved their fate of constant, often violent, harassment. In many states—but especially in New York—revolutionary governments confiscated Loyalist property. Other friends of the king received beatings, or as the rebels called them, "grand Toory [sic] rides." A few were even executed. According to one patriot, "A Tory is a thing whose head is in

Chronology

1763	Peace of Paris ends the Seven Years' War
1764	Parliament passes Sugar Act to collect American revenue
1765	Stamp Act receives support of House of Commons (March) Stamp Act Congress meets in New York City (October)
1766	Stamp Act repealed the same day that Declaratory Act becomes law (March 18)
1767	Townshend Revenue Acts stir American anger (June-July)
1768	Massachusetts assembly refuses to rescind circular letter (February)
1770	Parliament repeals all Townshend duties except one on tea (March) British troops "massacre" Boston civilians (March)
1772	Samuel Adams forms committee of correspondence
1773	Lord North's government passes Tea Act (May) Bostonians hold Tea Party (December)
1774	Parliament punishes Boston with Coercive Acts (March-June) First Continental Congress convenes (September)
1775	Patriots take stand at Lexington and Concord (April) Second Continental Congress gathers (May) Americans hold their own at Bunker Hill (June)
1776	Congress votes for independence; Declaration of Independence is signed British defeat Washington at Long Island (August) Americans score victory at Trenton (December)
1777	General Burgoyne surrenders at Saratoga (October)
1778	French treaties recognize independence of the United States (February)
1780	British take Charleston (May)
1781	Washington forces Cornwallis to surrender at Yorktown (October)
1783	Peace treaty signed (September) British evacuate New York City (November)

The peacemakers drove a remarkable bargain, a much better one than Congress could have expected. The preliminary agreement signed on September 3, 1783, not only guaranteed the independence of the United States, it also transferred all the territory east of the Mississippi River, except Florida which remained under Spanish sovereignty, to the new Republic. The treaty established generous boundaries on the north and south and gave the Americans important fishing rights in the North Atlantic. In exchange, Congress promised to help British merchants collect debts contracted before the Revolution and compensate Loyalists whose lands had been confiscated by the various state governments. Even though the Americans negotiated separately with the British, they did not sign a separate peace. The preliminary treaty did not become effective until France reached its own agreement with Great Britain. Thus did the Americans honor the French alliance. It is difficult to imagine how Franklin, Adams, and Jay could have negotiated a more favorable conclusion to the war. In the fall of 1783, the last redcoats sailed from New York City, ending 176 years of colonial rule.

Republican Challenge

The American people had waged war against the most powerful nation in Europe and emerged victorious. The treaty marked the conclusion of a colonial rebellion, but it remained for the men and women who had resisted taxation without representation to work out the full implications of republicanism. What would be the shape of the new government? What powers would be delegated to the people, the states, the federal authorities? How far would the wealthy, well-born leaders of the rebellion be willing to extend political, social, and economic rights? No wonder that Dr. Benjamin Rush explained: "There is nothing more common than to confound the terms of American Revolution with those of the late American war. The American war is over, but this is far from being the case with the American Revolution. On the contrary, nothing but the first act of the great drama is closed."

The American Revolution: From Protest to Independence

Recommended Reading

The revolutionary era is one of the most heavily analyzed periods of American history. No sooner had the fighting stopped than the participants began to interpret the meaning of the Revolution, and the torrent of books and articles continues unabated. Two of the more readable syntheses of this vast literature are Merrill Jensen, *The Founding of a Nation: A History of the American Revolution, 1763–1789* (1968) and Robert Middlekauff, *The Glorious Cause: The American Revolution 1763–1789* (1982). Middlekauff provides an especially good account of the military side of the Revolution. Edmund S. Morgan, *The Birth of the Republic 1763–1789* (1956) is a short but provocative examination of the revolutionary era. Morgan argues that during this period Americans took ideas seriously, that they fought for abstract principles as well as economic issues. The best introduction to military history remains Howard H. Peckham, *The War for Independence: A Military History* (1958). There are several fine document collections available; a good one is Jack P. Greene, ed., *Colonies to Nation, 1763–1789: A Documentary History of the American Revolution* (1967).

Additional Bibliography

The literature dealing with British politics on the eve of the American Revolution is particulary rich. One important study is John Brooke, *King George III* (1974). For information on the development of political associations, see John Brewer, *Party Ideology and Popular Politics at the Accession of George III* (1976); Bernard Donoughue, *British Politics and the American Revolution: The Path to War, 1773–1775* (1964); and L. B. Namier, *The Structure of Politics at the Accession of George III* (1929).

The American interpretation of changing British politics is imaginatively discussed in Bernard Bailyn, *The Ideological Origins of the American Revolution* (1967). Also valuable are H. Trevor Colbourn, *The Lamp of Experience: Whig History and the Intellectual Origins of the American Revolution* (1965) and Pauline Maier, *From Resistance to Revolution: Colonial Radicals and the Development of American Opposition to Britain, 1765–1776* (1972).

The most perceptive work on the events leading to the Revolution is Edmund S. and Helen M. Morgan, *The Stamp Act Crisis* (1953), a book that provides an excellent account of American society in 1765. Other studies of these difficult years are John Shy, *Toward Lexington* (1965); David Ammerman, *In The Common Cause: American Response to the Coercive Acts of 1774* (1974); Benjamin W. Labaree, *The Boston Tea Party* (1964); Oliver M. Dickerson, *The Navigation Acts and the American Revolution* (1951); and Richard D. Brown, *Revolutionary Politics in Massachusetts: The Boston Committee of Correspondence and the Towns, 1772–1774* (1970). Robert A. Gross, *The Minutemen and their World* (1976) is a fine study of Concord. Edward Countryman explores the complex events in New York in *A People in Revolution: The American Revolution and Political Society in New York, 1760–1790* (1982). For information on Thomas Paine see Eric Foner, *Tom Paine and Revolutionary America* (1976). Two excellent essay collections on the coming of revolution are Alfred F. Young, ed., *The American Revolution: Explorations in American Radicalism* (1976) and Stephen G. Kurtz and James H. Hutson, eds., *Essays on the American Revolution* (1973). An imaginative study of the changing ways in which Anglo-Americans viewed the structure of society during this period is Jay Fliegelman, *Prodigals and Pilgrims: The American Revolution Against Patriarchical Authority, 1750–1800* (1982).

The most detailed study of the war is Don Higginbotham, *The War of American Independence* (1971), but see also Christopher Ward, *The War of the Revolution* (1952). The British side of the story is well told in Piers Mackesy, *The War for America, 1775–1783* (1964). For an innovative interpretation of the militia see John Shy, *A People Numerous and Armed* (1976). There are biographical studies of almost all the generals, but a good starting place is George A. Billias, ed., *George Washington's Generals* (1964). Another helpful book is Ira D. Gruber, *The Howe Brothers and the American Revolution* (1972). The Americans' changing attitudes toward the Continental army are traced in Charles Royster, *A Revolutionary People at War* (1979). Also see Benjamin Quarles, *The Negro in the American Revolution* (1961) and Mary Beth Norton, *Liberty's Daughters: The Revolutionary Experience of American Women, 1750–1800* (1980).

The Loyalists are examined in Wallace Brown, *The King's Friends: The Composition and Motives of the American Loyalist Claimants* (1965) and William H. Nelson, *The American Tory* (1961). A sensitive biography of one reflective Loyalist is Bernard Bailyn, *The Ordeal of Thomas Hutchinson* (1974). Richard B. Morris, *The Peacemakers: The Great Powers and American Independence* (1965) provides a comprehensive study of the peace negotiations. Samuel Flagg Bemis, *The Diplomacy of the American Revolution* (1935) remains a useful examination.

A bizarre controversy shattered the harmony of Boston in 1785. The dispute broke out soon after a group of young adults, sons and daughters of the city's wealthiest families, announced the formation of a tea assembly or "Sans Souci Club." The members of this select group gathered once a week for the pleasure of good conversation, a game of cards, some dancing, and perhaps a glass of Madeira wine.

These meetings outraged other Bostonians, many of them old patriots. Samuel Adams, who dreamed of creating a "Christian Sparta," a virtuous society committed to republican purity, sounded the alarm. "Say, my country," he thundered, "why do you suffer all the intemperances of Great Britain to be fostered in our bosom, in all their vile luxuriance?" The club's very existence threatened the *"republican principles"* for which Americans had so recently fought a revolution.

To the superficial observer the assembly's activities may have appeared innocent, but vigilant republicans—Americans who not only rejected monarchy but also held the people themselves responsible for preserving liberty—explained that these "foolish gratifications" would erode public morality, substituting "luxury, prodigality, and profligacy" for "prudence, virtue, and economy." When the young people defended the propriety of their behavior, their opponents responded darkly, "Rome, Athens, and all ye cities of renown, whence came your fall?"

However ridiculous it may now appear, this local tempest reflected deep tensions within postrevolutionary American society. Victory over the British forced people to translate abstract notions about republicanism—in other words, about popular constitutional government—into daily practice. The effort proved considerably more difficult than anyone had predicted in 1776. As students of classical history understood, republican government required public virtue, a commitment to self-sacrifice.

Yet during the 1780s, citizens of the new nation seemed caught up in a wild, destructive scramble for material wealth. Revolutionary leaders had boldly declared that all men were created equal,

and yet black Americans languished in bondage. The patriots had condemned colonialism, and yet some Americans thought that people who settled west of the Appalachian Mountains should remain dependent upon the original thirteen states. Indeed, when the dispute over the "Sans Souci Club" occurred, it was not even clear whether the Americans would establish a strong central government or divide themselves into smaller, autonomous republics.

These challenges generated an outpouring of political genius. At other times in American history, persons of extraordinary talent have been drawn to theology, commerce, or science, but during the 1780s, the country's intellectual leaders—Thomas Jefferson, James Madison, Alexander Hamilton, and John Adams among others—focused their creative energies on the problem of how a free people ought to govern themselves.

The Limits of Revolutionary Change

Revolution changed American society, often in ways that no one had planned. This phenomenon is not surprising. The great revolutions of modern times produced radical transformations in French, Russian, and Chinese society. By comparison, the immediate results of the American Revolution appear much tamer, less wrenching. Nevertheless, national independence compelled people to reevaluate social relations that they had taken for granted during the colonial period. However faltering their first steps, they raised fundamental questions about the meaning of equality in American society that still have not been answered to everyone's satisfaction.

Social and Political Reform

Following the war, Americans aggressively ferreted out and, with republican fervor, denounced any traces of aristocratic pretense. As colonists, they had long resented the claims that certain Englishmen made to special privilege simply because of noble birth. When revolutionary officers formed the Society of the Cincinnati in 1783 (see pp. 172–73), their action provoked a howl of protest. A society based on artificial status was contrary to republican principles. Men dropped honorific titles such as "esquire." Lawyers of republican persuasion chided judges who wore great flowing wigs to court.

The appearance of equality was as important as its actual achievement. In fact, the distribution of wealth in postwar America was more uneven than it had been in the mid-eighteenth century. The sudden accumulation of large fortunes by new families made other Americans particularly sensitive to aristocratic display, for it seemed intolerable that a revolution waged against a monarchy should produce a class of persons legally, or even visibly, distinguished from their fellow citizens.

In an effort to root out the notion of a privileged class, states abolished laws of primogeniture and entail. In colonial times these laws allowed a landholder either to pass his entire estate to his eldest son or to declare that his property could never be divided, sold, or given away. Jefferson claimed that the repeal of these practices would eradicate "antient [sic] and future aristocracy; a foundation [has been] laid for a government truly republican." Jefferson exaggerated the social impact of this reform. In neither Virginia nor North Carolina did the abolition of primogeniture greatly affect local custom. The great tobacco planters had seldom encumbered their estates with entail, and they generally provided all their children— daughters as well as sons—with land. Nonetheless, republican legislators wanted to cleanse traces of the former feudal order from the statute books.

Republican ferment also encouraged many states to lower property requirements for voting. After the revolutionary experience, such a step seemed logical. As one group of farmers declared, no man can be "free & independent" unless he possesses "a voice . . . in the choice of the most important Officers in the Legislature." Pennsylvania and Georgia allowed all taxpayers to participate in elections. Other states were less democratic, but with the exception of Massachusetts, they reduced property qualifications. These re-

■ *The aristocratic finery adorning the women in this portrait by James Peale (c. 1793) offended many fervent republicans, who decried "luxury" in dress.*

forms, however, did not significantly expand the American electorate. Long before the Revolution, an overwhelming percentage of free males had owned enough land to vote. In any case, during the 1780s republican lawmakers were not prepared to experiment with universal manhood suffrage, for as John Adams observed, if the states pushed these reforms too far, "New claims will arise: women will demand a vote . . . and every man who has not a farthing, will demand an equal vote with any other."

The most important changes in voting patterns were the result of western migration. As Americans moved to the frontier, they received full political representation in their state legislatures, and because new districts tended to be poorer than established coastal settlements, their inhabitants selected representatives who seemed less cultured, less well trained than those sent by eastern voters. Moreover, western delegates resented traveling so far to attend legislative meetings, and they lobbied successfully to transfer state capitals to more convenient locations. During this period, Georgia moved the seat of its government from Savannah to Augusta, South Carolina from Charleston to Columbia, North Carolina from New Bern to Raleigh, Virginia from Williamsburg to Richmond, New York from New York City to Albany, and New Hampshire from Portsmouth to Concord.

After independence, Americans also reexamined the relation between church and state. Republican spokesmen like Thomas Jefferson insisted that rulers had no right to interfere with the free expression of an individual's religious beliefs. As governor of Virginia, he strenuously advocated the disestablishment of the Anglican church, an institution that had received tax monies and other benefits during the colonial period. Jefferson and his allies regarded such special privilege not only as a denial of religious freedom—after all, rival denominations did not receive tax money—but also as a vestige of aristocratic society.

When in 1786 Virginia struck down the last ties between church and state, Madison announced that the legislature "extinguished forever the ambitious hope of making laws for the human minds." Other southern states disestablished the Anglican church, but in Massachusetts and Connecticut, Congregational churches continued to enjoy special legal status. Moreover, while Americans championed toleration, they seldom favored irreligion or secularism, philosophies that radically challenged Christian values.

Slavery in the New Republic

Revolutionary fervor even forced Americans to confront the most appalling contradiction to the republican principles—slavery. Abolitionist sentiment ran high during the 1780s, especially among the Quakers of the middle states. They were supported by other persons who formed antislavery societies. By the 1790s groups dedicated to ending slavery in this country had been established in all the states from Massachusetts to Virginia. They included such prominent figures as Alexander Hamilton, John Jay, and Benjamin Franklin. Their activities made a profound impact upon many Americans who had never thought seriously about the institution of slavery. James Madison, a Virginia planter as well as a politician, explained that he was persuaded to free his slave Billey because he could not deny a black man "that liberty for which we have paid the price of so much blood, and have proclaimed so often to be the right . . . of every human being."

In several states north of Virginia the attack on slavery took a number of different forms. The Vermont constitution of 1777 specifically prohibited slavery. In 1780 the Pennsylvania legislature abolished the practice. While other state legislatures did not directly address the problem, the results were similar. A court in Massachusetts ruled slavery unconstitutional and thereby freed "a Grate [sic] number of Blacks . . . who . . . are held in a state of slavery within the bowels of a

Slave auctions (such as this one from Lewis Miller's sketchbook of a slightly later time) were an abomination to many Americans and an embarrassment to many more.

free and christian Country." By the decade after 1800 slavery was well on the road to extinction in the northern states.

Even in the South, where blacks made up a large percentage of the population, slavery embarrassed thoughtful republicans. Like Madison, some planters simply freed their slaves, and by 1790 the number of free blacks living in Virginia had increased sharply. Richard Randolph, for example, stated in his will that he freed his slaves "over whom my ancestors have usurped and exercised the most lawless and monstrous tyranny." Other whites whose economic well-being was dependent upon slave labor rejected such reasoning, but in the era of republican experimentation, no southern leader defended slavery as a positive social good, an argument planters throughout the South preached with great vehemence in the nineteenth century.

Despite these promising beginnings, however, the southern states did not abolish slavery. The economic incentives to maintain a servile labor force, especially after the invention of the cotton gin in 1793 and the opening up of the Alabama and Mississippi frontier, overwhelmed the abolitionist impulse. An opportunity to translate the rhetoric of the American Revolution into social practice had been lost, at least temporarily. Jefferson reported sadly in 1805, "I have long since given up the expectation of any early provision for the extinction of slavery among us." Unlike some contemporary Virginians, the man who wrote the Declaration of Independence could not bring himself to free his own slaves.

Rising Expectations of Women

The currents of republicanism also raised the expectations of American women. Abigail Adams, one of the generation's most articulate women, instructed her husband, John, as he set off for the opening of the Continental Congress: "I desire you would Remember the Ladies, and be more generous and favourable to them than your ancestors. Do not put such unlimited power into the hands of the Husbands." Men like John were not much more receptive to such pleas than their forefathers had been.

During this period women began to petition for divorce on new grounds. One case is particularly

■ *Abigail Adams, wife of patriot John Adams, was a spirited woman whose plea to limit the power of husbands gained little sympathetic attention.*

instructive concerning changing attitudes toward women and the family. In 1784 John Backus, an obscure Massachusetts silversmith, was hauled before a local court and asked why he beat his wife. He responded that "it was Partly owing to his Education for his father treated his mother in the same manner." The difference was that Backus' wife refused to tolerate such abuse, and she sued successfully for divorce. According to Nancy Cott, a historian who has closely studied divorce patterns in late eighteenth-century Massachusetts, "women were able to obtain divorce with freedom to remarry and after 1773 did so on approximately the same terms as men."

The war itself presented some women with fresh opportunities to employ their talents. In 1780 Esther DeBerdt Reed founded a large, volunteer woman's organization in Philadelphia—the first of its kind in the United States—that raised over $300,000 for Washington's army. Other women ran family farms and businesses while their husbands fought the British. And in 1790 the New Jersey legislature explicitly allowed women who owned property to vote.

Despite these scattered gains, republican society still defined women's roles exclusively in terms of mother, wife, and homemaker. Other pursuits seemed unnatural, even threatening, and it is perhaps not surprising, therefore, that in 1807 the New Jersey lawmakers repealed female suffrage in the interests of "the safety, quiet, and good order and dignity of the state."

Taking Stock of Revolutionary Reform

The Revolution did not bring about a massive restructuring of American society, at least not in the short term. Nevertheless, republican spokesmen like Samuel Adams and Thomas Jefferson raised issues of immense significance for the later history of the United States. They insisted that equality, however narrowly defined, was an essential element of republican government, and even though they failed to abolish slavery or institute universal manhood suffrage, they vigorously articulated a set of assumptions about people's rights and liberties that challenged future generations of Americans to make good on the promise of the Revolution.

And if the Revolution seems less radical than those of other nations, particularly that of France, it may be because eighteenth-century Americans had fewer entrenched barriers to overcome in the first place. Despite their sensitivity to aristocratic privilege, the colonists did not overthrow a powerful ruling class. Indeed, the Revolution confirmed many rights that colonial Americans had long enjoyed—broad suffrage, religious toleration, and freedom of movement. During the 1780s they aggressively took advantage of new economic opportunities, and perhaps the most pointed evidence of social change in this period was the complaint of one wealthy Bostonian who remarked in 1779 that "Fellows who would have cleaned my shoes five years ago, have amassed fortunes, and are riding chariots."

Experimenting with Self-Government

In May 1776 the Second Continental Congress urged the states to adopt constitutions. The old colonial charters filled with references to king and Parliament were clearly no longer adequate, and within a few years, most states had taken action. Rhode Island and Connecticut already enjoyed republican government by virtue of their unique seventeenth-century charters that allowed the voters to select both governors and legislators. Eleven other states plus Vermont created new political structures, and their deliberations reveal how Americans living in different regions and reacting to different social pressures defined fundamental republican principles.

Several constitutions were frankly experimental, and some states later rewrote documents that had been drafted in the first flush of independence. But if these early constitutions were provisional, they nevertheless provided the framers of the federal Constitution of 1787 with invaluable insights into the strengths and weaknesses of government based on the will of the people.

Blueprints for State Government

Despite disagreements over details, Americans who wrote the various state constitutions shared certain political assumptions. First, they insisted upon preparing *written* documents. For many of them, of course, this seemed a natural step. As colonists, they had lived under royal charters, documents that described the workings of local government in detail. The Massachusetts Bay Charter of 1629, for example (see chapter 2), guaranteed that the Puritans would enjoy the rights of Englishmen even after they had moved to the New World. And in New England, Congregationalists drew up church covenants stating in clear, contractual language the rights and responsibilities of the entire congregation.

However logical the decision to produce written documents may have seemed to the Americans, it represented a major break with English practice. Political philosophers in the mother country had long boasted of Britain's unwritten constitution, a collection of judicial reports and parliamentary statutes. But this highly vaunted system had not protected the colonists from oppression; hence, after declaring independence, Americans demanded that their state constitutions explicitly define the rights of the people as well as the powers of their rulers.

After 1776, public officials' assurances of good faith were no longer regarded as sufficient safeguards to liberty. In fact, one particularly vocal group who espoused republican principles, the so-called Berkshire Constitutionalists of western Massachusetts, informed state authorities that the Revolution had returned them to "a state of Nature," and they refused to obey state laws until the people of Massachusetts formally agreed to "a fundamental Constitution as the Basis and ground work of Legislation."

Guaranteeing Natural Rights in the States

The authors of the state constitutions believed that men and women possessed certain natural rights over which government exercised no control whatsoever. So that future rulers—potential tyrants—would know the exact limits of their authority, these fundamental rights were carefully spelled out. Indeed, the people of Massachusetts rejected the proposed state constitution of 1778 largely because it lacked a full statement of their basic rights. They demanded a guarantee of "rights of conscience, and . . . security of persons and property, which every member in the State hath a right to expect from the supreme power."

Eight state constitutions contained specific Declarations of Rights. The length and character of these lists varied, but in general, they affirmed three fundamental freedoms: religion, speech, and press. They protected citizens from unlawful searches and seizures; they upheld trial by jury. George Mason, a shrewd political thinker who had written important revolutionary pamphlets, penned the most influential Declaration of Rights. It was appended to the Virginia Constitution of 1776, and Mason's words were incorporated not only into other state constitutions but also into the famed Bill of Rights of the federal Constitution.

In almost every state, delegates to constitutional conventions drastically reduced the power of the governor. The constitutions of Pennsylvania and Georgia abolished the governor's office. In four other states terms like president were substituted for governor. Even when those who designed the new state governments provided for a governor, they severely circumscribed his authority. He was allowed to make almost no political appointments, and while the state legislators closely monitored his activities, he possessed no veto over their decisions (Massachusetts being the lone exception). Most early constitutions lodged nearly all effective power in the legislature. In fact, the writers of the state constitutions were so fearful of the concentration of power in the hands of one person that they failed to realize that governors—like the representatives—were servants of a free people.

The legislature dominated early state government. The constitutions of Pennsylvania and Georgia provided for an unicameral or one-house system, and since any taxpayer could cast a ballot in these states, their legislatures became the nation's most democratic. Other states authorized the creation of two houses, but even as they did so, some of the more radical republicans wondered why Americans needed a senate or upper house. What concerns, they asked, did that body represent that could not be more fully and directly voiced in the lower house? After all, America had just freed itself of an aristocracy. The two-house form survived the Revolution largely because it was familiar and because some persons had already begun to suspect that certain checks upon the popular will, however arbitrary they might appear, were necessary to preserve minority rights.

Defining the Will of the People

Massachusetts did not adopt a constitution until 1780, several years after the other states had done so. The experience of the people of Massachusetts is particularly significant because in their efforts to establish a workable system of republican government, they hit upon a remarkable political innovation. After the rejection of two constitutions drafted by the state legislature, the responsibility fell to a specially elected convention of delegates whose sole purpose was the "formation of a new Constitution."

John Adams served as the chief architect of the governmental framework of Massachusetts. It included a house and senate, a popularly elected governor who—unlike the chief executives of the other states—possessed a veto over legislative bills, and property qualifications for officeholders as well as voters. The most striking aspect of the 1780 constitution, however, was its opening sentence: "We . . . the people of Massachusetts . . . agree upon, ordain, and establish." This powerful vocabulary would be echoed in the federal Constitution. The Massachusetts experiment reminded Americans that ordinary officeholders could not be trusted to define fundamental rights. That important task required a convention of delegates who could legitimately claim to speak for the people.

In 1780 no one knew whether the state experiments would succeed. There was no question that a different type of person had begun to appear in public office. When one Virginian surveyed the newly elected House of Burgesses in 1776, he discovered that it was "composed of men not quite so well dressed, nor so politely educated, nor so highly born as some Assemblies I have formerly seen." This particular Virginian approved of such change, for he believed that "the People's men," however plain they might appear, possessed honesty and sincerity. They were, in fact, representative republicans.

Other Americans were less optimistic about the nation's immediate prospects. The health of a small republic depended entirely upon the virtue of its people. If they or their elected officials succumbed to material temptation, if they failed to comprehend the moral dimensions of political power, then the state constitutions were no more than worthless pieces of paper. The risk of excess was great. In 1778 a group of New Englanders, fearful that unbridled freedom would create political anarchy, observed, "The idea of liberty has been held up in so dazzling colours that some of us may not be willing to submit to that subordination necessary in the freest states."

Creating a New National Government

When the Second Continental Congress convened in 1775, the delegates found themselves waging war in the name of a country that did not yet exist. As the military crisis deepened, Congress gradually—often reluctantly—assumed greater authority over national affairs, but everyone agreed that such narrowly conceived measures were a poor substitute for a legally constituted government. The separate states could not possibly deal with the range of issues that now confronted the American people. Indeed, if independence meant anything in a world of sovereign nations, it implied the creation of a central authority capable of conducting war, borrowing money, regulating trade, and negotiating treaties.

Unenthusiastic Reception for the Articles of Confederation

The first attempt to produce a framework for national government failed miserably. Congress appointed a committee headed by John Dickinson, a lawyer who had written an important revolutionary pamphlet entitled *Letters from a Farmer in Pennsylvania*. Dickinson envisioned the creation of a strong central government, and the report his committee presented on July 12, 1776, shocked delegates who assumed that the constitution would authorize a loose confederation of states. Dickinson's plan placed the western territories, land claimed by the separate states, under congressional control. In addition, Dickinson's committee called for equal state representation in Congress.

Since some states such as Virginia and Massachusetts were more populous than others, the plan fueled tensions between large and small states. Also unsettling was Dickinson's recommendation that taxes be paid to Congress on the basis of a state's total population, black as well as white, a formula that angered Southerners who did not think that slaves should be counted. Indeed, even before the British evacuated Boston, Dickinson's committee raised many hard political issues that would divide Americans for several decades.

Not surprisingly, the draft that Congress finally approved in November 1777 bore little resemblance to Dickinson's original plan. The Articles of Confederation jealously guarded the sovereignty of the states. The delegates who drafted this framework shared a general republican conviction that power—especially power so far removed from the people—was inherently dangerous and that the only way to preserve liberty was to place

■ *John Dickinson, a London-trained lawyer, conceived a bold plan for a strong central government.*

as many constraints as possible upon federal authority.

They succeeded marvelously; Congress created a government that many people regarded as powerless. The Articles provided for a single legislative body, consisting of representatives selected annually by the state legislatures. Each state possessed a single vote in Congress. It could send as many as seven delegates, as few as two, but if they divided evenly on a certain issue, the state lost its vote. There was no independent executive, and of course, no veto over legislative decisions. The Articles also denied Congress the power of taxation, a serious oversight in time of war. The national government could obtain funds only by asking the states for contributions, called requisitions, but if a state failed to cooperate— and many did—Congress limped along without financial support. Amendments to this constitution required unanimous assent by all thirteen states. The authors of the new system apparently expected a powerless national government to handle foreign relations, military matters, Indian affairs, and interstate disputes. They most emphatically did not award Congress ownership of the lands west of the Appalachian Mountains.

The new constitution sent to the states for ratification was greeted with a mixture of apathy and hostility. Most Americans were far more interested in local affairs than in the actions of Congress. When a British army marched through a state, creating a need for immediate military aid, people spoke positively about central government, but as soon as the threat had passed, they sang a different tune. During this period, even the slightest encroachment upon state sovereignty rankled the extreme republicans.

Who Owns the West?

The major bone of contention, however, was the disposition of the vast, unsurveyed territory west of the Appalachians that everyone hoped the British would soon surrender. Some states, such as Virginia and Georgia, claimed land all the way from the Atlantic Ocean to the elusive "South Sea" by virtue of royal charters. State legislators —their appetites whetted by aggressive land speculators—anticipated generating large revenues through land sales. Connecticut, New York, Pennsylvania, and North Carolina also announced intentions to seize blocks of western land.

Other states were not blessed with vague or ambiguous royal charters. The boundaries of Maryland, Delaware, and New Jersey had been established many years earlier, and it seemed as if people living in these states would be permanently cut off from the anticipated bounty. In protest, these "landless" states stubbornly refused to ratify the Articles of Confederation. Marylanders were particularly vociferous. All the states had made sacrifices for the common good during the Revolution, they complained, and it appeared only fair that all states should profit from the fruits of victory, in this case, from the sale of western lands. Maryland's spokesmen feared that if Congress did not void Virginia's excessive claims to all of the Northwest Territory (the land west of Pennsylvania and north of the Ohio River) as well as a large area south of the Ohio, beyond the Cumberland Gap, known as Kentucky, then Marylanders would desert their home state in

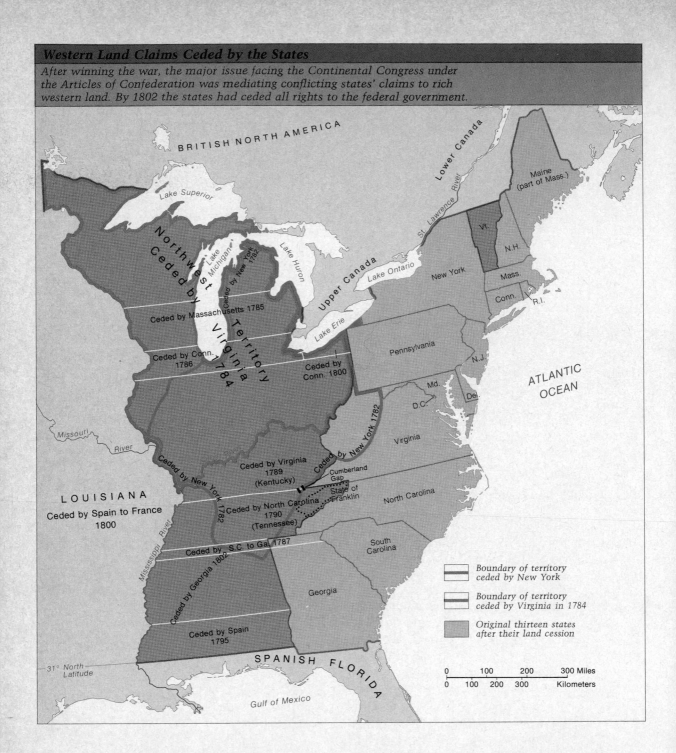

Western Land Claims Ceded by the States

After winning the war, the major issue facing the Continental Congress under the Articles of Confederation was mediating conflicting states' claims to rich western land. By 1802 the states had ceded all rights to the federal government.

BRITISH NORTH AMERICA

Lake Superior

Northwest Territory Ceded by Virginia 1784

Ceded by New York 1782

Ceded by Massachusetts 1785

Ceded by Conn. 1786

Ceded by Conn. 1800

Lake Michigan

Lake Huron

Lake Ontario

Lake Erie

Upper Canada

Lower Canada

St. Lawrence River

Maine (part of Mass.)

Vt.

N.H.

New York

Mass.

Conn.

R.I.

Pennsylvania

N.J.

Md.

Del.

D.C.

ATLANTIC OCEAN

Missouri River

LOUISIANA
Ceded by Spain to France 1800

Ceded by New York 1782

Ceded by Virginia 1789 (Kentucky)

Ceded by New York 1782

Cumberland Gap

State of Franklin

Virginia

North Carolina

Ceded by North Carolina 1790 (Tennessee)

Mississippi River

Ceded by S.C. to Ga. 1787

Ceded by Georgia 1802

South Carolina

Georgia

Ceded by Spain 1795

31° North Latitude

SPANISH FLORIDA

Gulf of Mexico

Boundary of territory ceded by New York

Boundary of territory ceded by Virginia in 1784

Original thirteen states after their land cession

0   100   200   300 Miles
0 100 200 300 Kilometers

search of cheap Virginia farms, leaving Maryland an underpopulated wasteland.

Virginians scoffed at these pleas for equity. They knew that behind the Marylanders' statements of high purpose lay the greed of speculators. Private land companies had sprung up before the Revolution and purchased large tracts from the Indians in areas claimed by Virginia. Their agents petitioned Parliament to legitimate these questionable transactions. That effort failed. After the Declaration of Independence, however, the companies shifted the focus of their lobbying to Congress, particularly to the representatives of landless states like Maryland. By liberally distributing shares of stock, officials of the Indiana, Illinois, and Wabash companies gained powerful supporters such as Benjamin Franklin, Robert Morris, and Thomas Johnson, governor of Maryland. These activities had little effect upon the leaders of Virginia; they remained firm. Why, they asked, should Virginia surrender its historic claims to western lands to enrich a handful of selfish speculators? Delaware and New Jersey modified their demands and joined the Confederation, but Maryland held out for five years.

The states resolved this bitter controversy in 1781 as much by accident as by design. Virginia agreed to cede its holdings north of the Ohio River to the Confederation on condition that Congress nullify the land companies' earlier purchases from the Indians. A practical consideration softened Virginia's resolve. Republicans such as Jefferson worried about expanding their state beyond the mountains; with poor transportation links, it seemed impossible to govern such a large territory effectively from Richmond. The western settlers might even come to regard Virginia as a colonial power insensitive to their needs. Marylanders who dreamed of making fortunes on the land market grumbled, but when a British army appeared on their border, they prudently accepted the Articles (March 1, 1781). Congress required another three years to work out the details of the Virginia cession. Other landed states followed Virginia's example. These transfers established an important principle, for after 1781 there was no question that the West belonged not to the states but to the United States. In this matter at least, the national government now exercised full sovereignty.

No one greeted ratification of the Articles with jubilation. Americans were still fully occupied with winning independence. In 1781 the new government began setting up a bureaucracy. It created the Departments of War, Foreign Affairs, and Finance. By far the most influential figure in the Confederation government was Robert Morris (1734–1806), a freewheeling Philadelphia merchant who was appointed the first superintendent of finance. His decisions provoked controversy. Contemporaries who feared the development of a strong national government identified Morris with efforts to undermine the authority of the

■ *Those who opposed the policies of Robert Morris called him the most dangerous man in America.*

states, to seize the power of taxation, and at least one congressional critic labeled him a "pecuniary dictator."

The Confederation's Major Achievement

Whatever the weaknesses of Congress may have been, it scored one impressive triumph. Congressional action brought order to western settlement, especially in the Northwest Territory, and incorporated frontier Americans into an expanding federal system. In 1781 the prospects for success did not seem promising. For years, colonial authorities had ignored people who migrated far inland, sending neither money nor soldiers to protect them from Indian attack. Tensions between the seaboard colonies and the frontier regions had sometimes flared into violence. In 1763 a group of Scotch-Irish frontiersmen calling themselves the "Paxton Boys" protested Pennsylvania's inadequate defenses by killing several innocent Indians and marching on the colonial capital. Similar disorders occurred in South Carolina in 1767, in North Carolina in 1769, and in Vermont in 1777. With thousands of men and women, most of them squatters, pouring across the Appalachian Mountains, Congress had to act quickly to avoid the past errors of royal and colonial authorities.

The initial attempt to deal with this explosive problem came in 1784. Jefferson, then serving as a member of Congress, drafted an ordinance that became the basis for later, more enduring legislation. Jefferson recommended carving ten new states out of the western lands located north of the Ohio River and recently ceded to the United States by Virginia. He specified that each new state establish a republican form of government. When the population of a territory equaled that of the smallest state already in the Confederation, the region could apply for full statehood. In the meantime, free adult males could participate in local government, a democratic guarantee that frightened several of Jefferson's more conservative colleagues.

■ *The Land Ordinance of 1785 established procedures for dividing the western territory into townships, such as the one in Ohio shown on this survey map.*

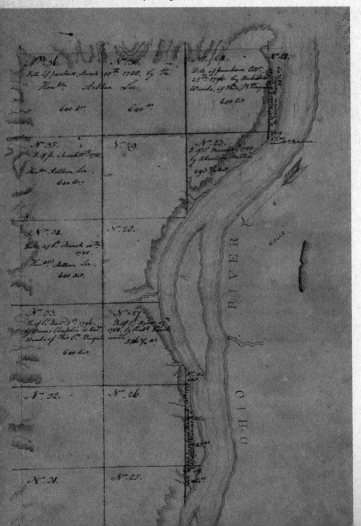

The impoverished Congress was eager to sell off the western territory as quickly as possible. After all, the frontier represented a source of income that did not depend upon the unreliable generosity of the states. A second ordinance, passed in 1785 and called the Land Ordinance, established an orderly process for laying out new townships and marketing public lands.

The 1785 scheme possessed geometric elegance. Surveyors marked off townships, each running directly from east to west. These units, 6 miles square, were subdivided into 36 separate sections of 640 acres (1 square mile) each. This grid pattern survived long after the Confederation had passed into history. The government planned to auction off its holdings at prices of not less than a dollar an acre. Congress set the minimum purchase at 640 acres, and paper money was not accepted in payment. Section sixteen was set aside for the support of public education; the federal government reserved four other sections for its own use.

Public response disappointed Congress. Surveying the lands took far longer than anticipated, and few persons possessed enough hard currency to make even the minimum purchase. Finally, a solution to the problem came from Manasseh Cutler, a New England minister turned land speculator and congressional lobbyist, and his associates, who included several former officers of the Continental army.

Cutler and his companions, representing the Ohio and Scioto companies, offered to purchase more than six million unsurveyed acres of land located in present-day southeastern Ohio by persuading Congress to accept at full face value government loan certificates that had been issued to soldiers during the Revolution. On the open market, the Ohio company could pick up these certificates for as little as 10 percent of their face value; thus, the company stood to make a fortune. Like so many other get-rich-quick schemes, however, this one failed to produce the anticipated millions.

Congress also had reservations about frontier democracy. In the 1780s the West seemed to be filling up with people who by eastern standards were uncultured. Timothy Pickering, a New Englander, declared that "the emigrants to the frontier lands are the least worthy subjects in the United States. They are little less savage than the

Grid Pattern of a Township
36 sections of 640 acres (1 square mile each)

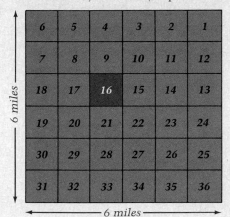

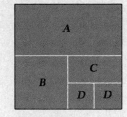

A   Half-section   320 acres
B   Quarter-section   160 acres
C   Half-quarter section   80 acres
D   Quarter-quarter sections   40 acres

Income of one section reserved for the support of public education

Indians; and when possessed of the most fertile spots, for want of industry, live miserably." The charge was as old as the frontier itself. Indeed, seventeenth-century Englishmen had said the same things of the earliest Virginians. The lawless image stuck, however, and even a sober observer like Washington insisted that the West crawled with "banditti." The Ordinance of 1784 placed the government of the territories in the hands of people about whom congressmen and speculators had second thoughts.

These various currents shaped the Ordinance of 1787, one of the final acts passed under the Confederation. This bill, also called the Northwest Ordinance, provided a new structure for government of the Northwest Territory. The plan authorized the creation of between three and five territories, each to be ruled by a governor, a secretary, and three judges appointed by Congress. When the population reached five thousand, voters who owned property could elect an assembly, but its decisions were subject to the governor's absolute veto. Once sixty thousand persons resided in a territory, they could write a constitution and petition for full statehood. While these procedures represented a retreat from Jefferson's original proposal, the Ordinance of 1787 contained several significant features. A bill

of rights guaranteed the settlers the right to trial by jury, freedom of religion, and due process of law. In addition, this act outlawed slavery, a prohibition that freed the future states of Ohio, Indiana, Illinois, Michigan, and Wisconsin from the curse of human bondage.

By contrast, settlement south of the Ohio River seemed chaotic. Long before the end of the war, thousands of Americans streamed through the Cumberland Gap into a part of Virginia known as Kentucky. The most famous of these settlers was Daniel Boone. In 1775 the population of Kentucky was approximately one hundred; by 1784 it had jumped to thirty thousand. Speculators purchased large tracts from the Indians, planning to resell this acreage to settlers at handsome profits. In 1776 one land company asked Congress to reorganize its holdings into a new state called Transylvania. While nothing came of this self-serving request, another, even more aggressive, group of speculators in 1784 carved the state of Franklin out of a section of present-day Tennessee then claimed by North Carolina. Rival speculators prevented formal recognition of Franklin's government. By 1790 the entire region south of the Ohio River had been transformed into a crazy quilt of claims and counterclaims that generated lawsuits for many years to come.

The widespread land speculation in the territory south of the Ohio River did not go unnoticed by European political cartoonists of the day. The French caption explains that "Citizen Mignard signs today for some English companions who are selling imaginary lands in the United States. The better to ensnare dupes, they draw geological maps, converting rocky deserts into fertile plains, show roads cutting through impassable cliffs, and offer shares in lands which do not belong to them."

Weaknesses of the Confederation

Throughout the country, men and women became increasingly critical of the Articles of Confederation. Complaints varied from region to region, from person to person, but most disappointment reflected economic frustration. Americans assumed that peace would restore prosperity. But recovery following the Revolution was slow. Families that had postponed purchases of imported goods—either because of British blockade or personal hardship—now rushed to buy European finery. Even before England signed a treaty, its merchants flooded American ports with consumer items and offered easy credit.

Weak Congress Blamed for Economic Problems

The sudden renewal of trade with Great Britain on such a large scale undermined the stability of the American economy. Specie flowed back across the Atlantic, leaving the United States desperately short of hard currency, and when British merchants called in their debts, thriftless American buyers often fell into bankruptcy. "The disagreeable state of our commerce," observed James Wilson, an advocate of strong national government, has been the result "of extravagant and injudicious importation . . . we seemed to have forgot that to pay was as necessary in trade as to purchase." To blame the Confederation alone for the economic depression would be unfair. Nevertheless, during the 1780s many people agreed that a stronger government could somehow have softened the blow. In their rush to acquire imported luxuries, Americans seemed to have deserted republican principles, and a weak Congress was helpless to restore national virtue.

Critics pointed to the government's inability to regulate trade. Whenever a congressman suggested restricting British access to American markets, southern representatives who feared any controls on the export of tobacco, rice, and cotton bellowed in protest. They anticipated that navigation acts written by the Confederation would put planters under the yoke of northern shipping interests.

The country's chronic fiscal instability increased public anxiety. During the war, Congress printed over $200 million in paper currency, but because of an extraordinarily high rate of inflation, the rate of exchange for Continental bills soon declined to a fraction of their face value. In 1781 Congress turned to the states for help. They were asked to retire the worthless money. Instead, several states not only recirculated the continental bills, they also issued worthless currency of their own.

A heavy burden of state and national debt compounded the general sense of economic crisis. Revolutionary soldiers had yet to be paid. Citizens who had loaned money and goods to the government clamored for reimbursement. Foreign creditors demanded interest on funds advanced during the Revolution. These pressures grew, but Congress was unable to respond. The Articles specifically prohibited it from taxing the American people. It required little imagination to see that the Confederation would soon default on its legal obligations unless something was done quickly.

In response, an aggressive group of men announced that they knew how to save the Confederation. The "nationalists"—persons like Alexander Hamilton, James Madison, and Robert Morris—called for major constitutional reforms, the chief of which was an amendment allowing Congress to collect a 5 percent tax on imported goods. Revenues generated by the proposed Impost of 1781 would be used by the Confederation to reduce the national debt. On this point they were adamant. The nationalists recognized that whoever paid the public debt would gain the public trust. If the states assumed that responsibility, then the country could easily fragment into separate republics. "A national debt," Hamilton explained in 1781, "if it is not excessive, will be to us a national blessing. It will be a powerful cement of our union." Twelve states accepted the Impost, but Rhode Island resolutely refused to cooperate. One negative vote and the taxing plan was dead.

The nationalists sparked fierce opposition. Many Americans were apprehensive of their plans, especially those of Robert Morris. His wheelings and dealings as superintendent of finance appeared to threaten the moral fiber of the young Republic. Richard Henry Lee and Samuel Adams, men of impeccable patriotic credentials, decried Morris' efforts to create a national bank. Such an institution would bring forth a flock of

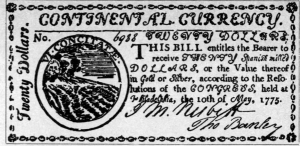

■ *"Not worth a Continental" became a common oath when inflation eroded the value of the Continental currency. Currency issued by the states was equally valueless.*

social parasites, the kind of persons that Americans associated with corrupt monarchical government. One person declared that if an impost ever passed, Morris "will have all [the money] in his Pocket."

The nationalists regarded their opponents as economically naive. A country with the potential of the United States required a complex, centralized fixcal system. But for all their pretensions to realism, the nationalists of the early 1780s were politically inept. They underestimated the depth of republican fears, and in their rush to strengthen the Articles, they overplayed their hand.

A group of extreme nationalists even appealed to the army for support. To this day, no one knows the full story of the Newburgh Conspiracy of 1783. Officers of the Continental army stationed at Newburgh, New York, worried that Congress would disband them without funding their pensions and began to lobby intensively for relief. In March, they scheduled general meetings to protest the weakness and duplicity of Congress. The officers' initial efforts were harmless enough, but frustrated nationalists such as Morris and Hamilton decided that if the army exerted sufficient pressure on the government, perhaps even threatened a military takeover, then stubborn Americans might be compelled to amend the Articles.

The conspirators failed to take George Washington's integrity into account. No matter how much he wanted a strong central government, he would not tolerate insubordination by the military. In a surprise visit, Washington confronted the officers directly at Newburgh. He intended to read a prepared statement. Fumbling with his glasses before his men, he commented, "Gentlemen, you must pardon me. I have grown gray in your service and now find myself growing blind." The unexpected vulnerability of this great soldier reduced the troops to tears, and in an instant, the rebellion was broken. Washington deserves credit for preserving civilian rule in this country. "The idea of a redress by force," he told Hamilton, "is too chimerical to have a place in the imagination of any serious mind in the Army . . . The Army is a dangerous instrument to play with."

In April 1783 Congress proposed a second impost, but it too failed to win unanimous ratification. Even a personal appeal by Washington could not save the amendment. As one opponent explained, if "permanent Funds are given to Congress, the aristocratic Influence, which predominates in more than a major part of the United States, will fully establish an arbitrary Government." With this defeat, nationalists gave up on the Confederation. Morris retired from government, and Madison returned to Virginia utterly depressed by what he had witnessed.

Difficulties in Confederation Diplomacy

In foreign affairs, Congress endured further embarrassment. It could not even enforce the provisions of its own peace treaty. American negotiators had promised Great Britain that its citizens could collect debts contracted before the Revolution. The states, however, dragged their heels, and several even passed laws obstructing the settlement of legitimate prewar claims. Congress was powerless to force compliance. The British responded to this apparent provocation by refusing to evacuate troops from posts located in the Northwest Territory. A strong national government would have driven the redcoats out, but without adequate funds, the weak Congress could not provide soldiers for such a mission.

Congress' postrevolutionary dealings with Spain were equally humiliating. That nation refused to accept the southern boundary of the United States established by the Treaty of Paris. Spain claimed sovereignty over much of the land located between Georgia and the Mississippi River, and its agents schemed with Indian tribes in this region to resist American expansion. On July 21, 1784, Spain fueled the controversy by closing the lower Mississippi River to citizens of the United States.

This unexpected decision devastated western farmers. Free use of the Mississippi was essential to the economic development of the entire Ohio Valley. Because of the prohibitively high cost of transporting freight for long distances over land, western settlers—and southern planters eyeing future opportunities in this area—demanded a secure water link with the world's markets. Their spokesmen in Congress denounced anyone who claimed that navigation of the Mississippi was a negotiable issue.

In 1785 a Spanish official, Don Diego de Gardoqui, opened talks with John Jay, a New Yorker appointed by Congress to obtain rights to navigation of the Mississippi. Jay soon discovered that Gardoqui would not compromise. After making little progress, Jay seized the initiative. If Gardoqui would allow American merchants to trade directly with Spain, thus opening up an important new market to ships from New England and the middle states, then the United States might forgo navigation of the Mississippi for twenty-five years. When southern delegates heard of Jay's concessions, they were outraged. It appeared to them as if representatives of northern commerce were ready to abandon the southern frontier. Angry congressmen accused New Englanders of attempting to divide the United States into separate confederations, for as one Virginian exclaimed, the proposed Spanish treaty "would weaken if not destroy the union by disaffecting the Southern States . . . to obtain a trivial commercial advantage." Congress wisely terminated the negotiations with Spain.

By the mid-1780s, Congress had squandered whatever respect it may once have enjoyed. It met irregularly. Some states did not even bother to send delegates and pressing issues often had to be postponed for lack of a quorum. The nation even lacked a permanent capital, and Congress drifted from Philadelphia to Princeton, to Annapolis to New York City, prompting one humorist to suggest that the government purchase an air balloon. This newly invented device, he explained, would allow the members of Congress to "float along from one end of the continent to the other" and "suddenly pop down into any of the states they please."

Restructuring the Republic

Thoughtful Americans, especially those who had provided leadership during the Revolution, agreed that something had to be done. By 1785 the country seemed to have lost direction. The buoyant optimism that sustained revolutionary patriots had dissolved into pessimism and doubt. In 1786 Washington bitterly observed: "What astonishing changes a few years are capable of producing. Have we fought for this? Was it with these expectations that we launched into a sea of trouble, and have bravely struggled through the most threatening dangers?"

Diagnosing the Nation's Ills

The country's problems could be traced in part to the republicans' own ideology. During the 1770s, they insisted that the greatest threat to the American people was concentration of power in the hands of unscrupulous rulers. With this principle in mind, they transformed state governors into mere figureheads and emasculated the Confederation in the name of popular liberties.

Yet despite these precautions, the United States was in trouble. The people—from whom so much civic virtue had been expected—failed to fulfill the hopes of the early advocates of republicanism. The states had been plagued not by executive tyranny but by an excess of democracy, by a failure of the majority to preserve the legitimate rights of the minority, by an unrestrained individualism that led to anarchy rather than good order.

Confronted with economic chaos, many states blithely churned out worthless currency, while others passed laws impeding the collection of debt. In Rhode Island the situation became absurd. State legislators made it illegal for merchants to reject Rhode Island money even though everyone knew it had no value. No wonder Governor William Livingston of New Jersey declared in 1787, "We do not exhibit the virtue that is necessary to support a republican government."

As Americans tried to interpret these experiences within a republican framework, they were checked by the most widely accepted political wisdom of the age. Baron de Montesquieu (1689–1755), a French political philospher of immense international reputation, declared flatly that a republican government could not flourish in a large territory. The reasons were clear. If the people lost direct control over their representatives, they would fall prey to tyrants. Large distances allowed rulers to hide their corruption; physical separation presented aristocrats with opportunities to seize power.

In the United States, most learned men treated Montesquieu's theories as self-evident truths. His writings seemed to demonstrate the importance of preserving the sovereignty of the states, for however much these small republics abused the rights of property and ignored minority interests, it was plainly unscientific to maintain that a republic consisting of thirteen states, several million people, and thousands of acres of territory could long survive.

James Madison rejected Montesquieu's argument, and in so doing, helped Americans to think of republican government in exciting new ways. This soft-spoken, rather unprepossessing Virginian was the most brilliant American political thinker of his generation. One French official described Madison as "a man one must study a long time in order to make a fair appraisal." Those who listened carefully to what Madison had to say, however, soon recognized his genius for translating theory into practice.

Madison delved into the writings of a group of Scottish philosophers, the most prominent being David Hume (1711–1776), and from their works he concluded that Americans need not fear a greatly expanded republic. Madison perceived that "the inconveniences of popular States contrary to prevailing Theory, are in proportion not to the extent, but to the narrowness of their limits." Indeed, it was in small states like Rhode Island that legislative majorities tyrannized the propertied minority. In a large republic, these injustices could be avoided. With so many people scattered over a huge area, no one faction would be able to form an effective majority. In a large territory, Madison explained, "the Society becomes broken into a greater variety of interests, of pursuits, of passions, which check each other, whilst those who may feel a common sentiment have less opportunity of communication and contact."

Madison did not, however, advocate a modern "interest-group" model of political behavior. The contending parties were incapable of working for the common good. They were too mired in their own local, selfish concerns. Rather, Madison thought that competing factions would neutralize each other, leaving the business of governing the republic to the ablest, most virtuous persons that the nation could produce. In other words, Madison's federal system was not a small state writ large; it was something entirely different, a government based on the will of the people and yet detached from their narrowly based demands. This thinking formed the foundation of Madison's most famous political essay, *The Federalist* No. 10.

■ *Among the framers of the Constitution, James Madison, not yet forty, was the most effective advocate of a strong central government.*

Movement Toward Constitutional Reform

A concerted movement to overhaul the Articles of Confederation began in the mid-1780s. The Massachusetts legislature asked Congress to call a convention for the purpose of revising the entire constitution. Nothing came of the suggestion until 1786 when Madison and his friends persuaded the Virginia assembly to recommend a convention to explore the creation of a unified system of "commercial regulations." Congress supported the idea. In September delegates from five states arrived in Annapolis, Maryland, to discuss issues that extended far beyond commerce. The small turnout was disappointing, but the occasion provided strong nationalists with an opportunity to hatch an even bolder plan. The Annapolis delegates advised Congress to hold a second meeting in Philadelphia "to take into consideration the situation of the United States, to devise such further provisions as shall appear to them necessary to render the constitution of the Federal Government adequate to the exigencies of the Union." Whether staunch states' rights advocates in Congress knew what was afoot is not clear. In any case, Congress authorized a grand convention to gather in May 1787.

Events played into Madison's hands. Soon after the Annapolis meeting, an uprising known as Shays' Rebellion, involving several thousand impoverished farmers, shattered the peace of western Massachusetts. No matter how hard these men worked the soil, they always found themselves in debt to eastern creditors. They complained of high taxes, of high interest rates, and most of all, of a state government insensitive to their problems. In 1786 Daniel Shays, a veteran of the battle of Bunker Hill, and his armed neighbors closed a county courthouse where creditors were suing to foreclose farm mortgages. At one point, the rural insurgents marched to Springfield, site of a federal arsenal, and Congress dispatched an army of thirteen hundred soldiers to put down Shays' Rebellion. Long before the United States troops arrived, however, state militiamen had restored order in the region.

Nationalists throughout the United States overreacted to news of Shays' Rebellion. From their perspective, the incident symbolized the breakdown of law and order that they had long

■ *The farmers' uprising led by Daniel Shays was easily put down, but it frightened the citizenry and strengthened the demand for a strong new government.*

the nature of government. They were practical people, lawyers, merchants, and planters, many of whom had fought in the Revolution and served in the Congress of the Confederation. The majority were in their thirties or forties. The gathering included George Washington, James Madison, George Mason, Robert Morris, James Wilson, John Dickinson, Benjamin Franklin, and Alexander Hamilton, just to name some of the more prominent participants. Absent were John Adams and Jefferson, who were conducting diplomacy in Europe; Patrick Henry stayed home in Virginia because he "smelled a rat."

As soon as the convention opened on May 25, the delegates made several procedural decisions of the utmost importance. First, they ruled that their discussions would be kept absolutely secret. There were no official journals, no newspaper accounts. This determination allowed delegates to speak their minds freely, without fear of criticism from people who had not actually witnessed the debates. Even in private correspondence, Madison did not tell his close friend Jefferson what was happening in Philadelphia. The delegates also decided to vote by state, but to avoid the kinds of problems that had plagued the Confederation, they ruled that key proposals needed the support of only a majority instead of the nine states required under the Articles.

predicted. "Great commotions are prevailing in Massachusetts," Madison wrote. "An appeal to the sword is exceedingly dreaded." The time had come for sensible people to speak up for a strong national government. The unrest in Massachusetts persuaded persons who might otherwise have ignored the Philadelphia meeting to participate in drafting a new constitution.

Constitutional Convention Convenes at Philadelphia

In the spring of 1787 fifty-five men representing twelve states traveled to Philadelphia. Rhode Island refused to take part in the proceedings, a decision that Madison attributed to its "wickedness and folly." Thomas Jefferson described the convention as an "assembly of demi-Gods," but this flattering depiction is misleading. However much modern Americans revere the Constitution, they should remember that the individuals who wrote it did not possess divine insight into

Plans for a Government Framework

Madison understood that whoever sets the agenda, controls the meeting. Even before all the delegates had arrived, he drew up a framework for a new federal system known as the "Virginia Plan." Madison wisely persuaded Edmund Randolph, Virginia's popular governor, to present this scheme to the convention on May 29. Randolph claimed that the Virginia Plan merely revised sections of the Articles, but everyone, including Madison, knew better. "My ideas," he observed, "strike . . . deeply at the old Confederation." He advocated a strong central government, one that possessed "a negative in all cases whatsoever on the local Legislatures."

The Virginia Plan envisioned a national legislature consisting of two houses, one elected directly by the people, the other chosen by the first

■ *Paintings like this, in which Washington appears enthroned in a radiant aura, contributed to the mythic reputations of the men who framed the Constitution at the 1787 Convention in Independence Hall, Philadelphia.*

house from nominations made by the state assemblies. Representation in both houses was proportional to the state's population. The Virginia Plan provided for an executive elected by Congress. To the surprise of the states' rights supporters, the entire package carried easily, and the convention found itself discussing the details of "a *national* Government . . . consisting of a *supreme* Legislature, Executive, and Judiciary."

The Virginia Plan had been pushed through the convention so fast that opponents hardly had an opportunity to present their objections. On June 15 they spoke up. William Paterson, a New Jersey lawyer, advanced the so-called New Jersey Plan, a scheme that preserved the fundamental spirit of the Articles of Confederation. Paterson's proposal retained the unicameral legislature in which each state possessed one vote, and at the same time, gave Congress extensive new powers to tax and regulate trade. Paterson argued that these revisions, while more modest that Madison's plan, would have greater appeal for the American people. "I believe," he said, "that a little practical virtue is to be preferred to the finest theoretical principles, which cannot be carried into effect."

The delegates listened politely and then soundly rejected the New Jersey Plan on June 19. Indeed, only New Jersey, New York, and Delaware voted in favor of Paterson's scheme.

Rejection of this framework did not resolve the most controversial issue before the convention. Paterson and others feared that under the Virginia Plan, small states would lose their separate identities. These delegates maintained that unless each state possessed an equal vote in Congress, the small states would find themselves at the mercy of their larger neighbors.

This argument outraged the delegates who favored a strong federal government. It awarded too much power to the states. "For whom [are we] forming a Government?" Wilson cried. "Is it for men, or for the imaginary beings called States?" It seemed absurd to claim that Rhode Island with only 68,000 people should have the same voice in Congress as Virginia's 747,000 inhabitants. "The States," Madison lectured, "never possessed the essential rights of sovereignty . . . The State of Maryland voted by counties—did this make the counties sovereign?" This analysis, however logical it may have been, failed to sway any votes.

170

The Republican Experiment

Compromise Saves the Convention

The mood of the convention was tense. Hard work and frustration, coupled with Philadelphia's sweltering summer heat, frayed nerves, and some members predicted that this meeting would accomplish nothing of significance. But despite the growing pessimism, the gathering did not break up. The delegates desperately wanted to produce a constitution, and they refused to give up until they had explored every avenue of reconciliation. Perhaps cooler heads agreed with Washington: "To please all is impossible, and to attempt it would be vain. The only way, therefore, is . . . to form such a government as will bear the scrutinizing eye of criticism, and trust it to the good sense and patriotism of the people."

Mediation clearly offered the only way to overcome what Roger Sherman, a Connecticut delegate, called "a full stop." On July 2 a "grand committee" of one person from each state was elected by the convention to resolve persistent differences between the large and small states. Franklin, at eighty-one the oldest delegate, served as chairman. The two fiercest supporters of proportional representation, Madison and Wilson, were left off the "grand committee," a sure sign that the small states would salvage something from compromise.

The committee recommended that the states be equally represented in the upper house of Congress, while representation was to be proportionate in the lower house. Only the lower house could initiate money bills. Franklin's committee also decided that one member of the lower house should be selected for every forty thousand inhabitants of a state, and for this purpose, a slave was to be counted as three fifths of a freeman. As with most compromise solutions, this one fully satisfied no one. It did, however, overcome a major impasse, and after the small states gained an assured voice in the upper house, later named the Senate, they cooperated in efforts to create a strong central government.

On July 26, the convention formed a Committee of Detail, a group that prepared a rough draft of the Constitution. After it completed its work—writing a document that preserved the fundamental points of the Virginia Plan—the delegates debated each article. The task required the better part of a month.

During these sessions, the members of the convention concluded that the president, as they now called the executive, should be selected by an electoral college, a body of prominent men in each state chosen by local voters. The number of "electoral" votes held by each state equaled its number of representatives and senators. This awkward device guaranteed that the president would not be indebted to Congress for his office. Whoever received the second largest number of votes in the electoral college automatically became vice-president. In the event that no person received a majority of the votes, the election would be decided by the lower house—the House of Representatives—with each state casting a single vote.

Delegates also armed the chief executive with a veto power over legislation as well as the right to nominate judges. Both privileges, of course, would have been unthinkable a decade earlier, but the state experiments revealed the importance of having an independent executive to maintain a balanced system of republican government. The Philadelphia convention telescoped into four months the process of constitutional education that had taken over four years to learn at the state level. It began with a nearly omnipotent parliament (the Virginia Plan) and ended with the separation of powers (as in the Massachusetts constitution of 1780). If nothing else, the constitutional convention demonstrated that when so many able people from different states are brought together, they actually learn something.

Hints of Future Controversy

During the final days of August, two new issues suddenly disrupted the convention. One was a harbinger of the great sectional crisis of the nineteenth century. Many northern representatives detested the slave trade and wanted to end it immediately. "It seemed now to be pretty well understood," Madison jotted in his private notes, "that the real difference of interest lay, not between the large and small but between the N. and Southn. States. The institution of slavery and its consequences formed a line of discrimination."

Republican Nightmare

One of the more alarming threats to American liberties arose during the 1780s from an unlikely source, an organization of revolutionary officers headed by George Washington. This Society of the Cincinnati, its members insisted, was nothing more than a fraternal organization. Frightened citizens, however, protested that the society endangered republican principles that the Continental army had defended on the battlefield.

Fraternity and benevolence, not subversion, inspired the founding of the Society of the Cincinnati in 1783. Organized by Washington's trusted lieutenant, Henry Knox, the society extended membership to all former officers who had served for three years or who were fighting at the close of the revolutionary war. It aimed at perpetuating wartime ties among the officer corps and helping those veterans who suffered misfortune. That spirit of camaraderie is manifest in *Washington's Farewell to His Officers*, painting on facing page. The organization took its name from the ancient Roman warrior Cincinnatus, who defended his country and then exchanged his sword for a plow.

Yet, despite Washington's presence, many Americans considered the society an affront to egalitarian principles. Membership passed to the oldest male heir of each officer, a practice that smacked of European aristocracy. One critic asserted that the establishment of the society was "as rapid a Stride towards an hereditary Military Nobility as was ever made in so short a Time." Another outraged citizen warned, "It is in reality and will turn out to be an *hereditary peerage*." The society, it seemed to these impassioned observers, was nothing less than a royalist plot.

Even more alarming was the society's potential political power. Members might not fade back into society as had Cincinnatus but would become a sort of reserve force, which, when mobilized, could crush a rebellion or topple the government. Some critics even maintained that the society's charitable fund could be used to finance nefarious political schemes. To many anxious republicans, the Society of the Cincinnati already resembled far too closely the military organizations of Europe. Benjamin Franklin, for example, charged that the members had "been too much struck with the Ribbands and Crosses they have seen . . . hanging to the buttonholes of Foreign Officers."

The outcry against the society reached fever pitch by 1784. A committee of the Massachusetts legislature concluded that the society was "dangerous to the peace, liberty and safety of the United States in General, and this Commonwealth in particular." Throughout New England, many people feared that the organization was in league with foreign powers.

This controversy especially disturbed Washington. Eager to calm the furor, Washington asked the advice of Thomas Jefferson, who was representing Virginia in Congress. Jefferson reported that opposition to the organization was almost unanimous in Congress, and even though there was no cause for alarm while Washington was president-general, "his successor . . . may adopt a more mistaken road to glory." Washington, however, rejected Jefferson's plea for dissolution of the society. Believing in the fraternal and benevolent purposes that inspired the Cincinnati, Washington determined instead to reform the organization.

At the society's general convention in Philadelphia in 1784, Washington introduced a series of sweeping proposals. He appealed to the delegates to strike from their charter "every word, sentence, and clause which has a political tendency." Furthermore, he urged an end to hereditary membership and a ban on contributions from foreign sources. The convention, however, balked at Washington's recommendations, and even the general's arm-twisting failed to sway many members. Not until Washington threatened to resign as president-general did the convention approve almost all his reforms, provided the state societies concurred.

Despite scattered efforts to turn the society into a political pressure group, the dire predictions of the critics were never fulfilled. The meetings of the organization became primarily social affairs and remain so to this day.

Although short-lived, this controversy illustrated the strength of revolutionary ferment after independence. Republicanism promised nothing less than a new social order, one free of artificial or hereditary distinctions. This ideology, however, was as fragile as it was revolutionary. Those who studied the history of Greece and Rome knew that subversion had destroyed those ancient republics. Threats to republican principles could arise from innocuous or improbable sources—tea societies or veterans' organizations. The price of liberty, republicans maintained, was constant vigilance.

The delegates reached an uneasy compromise. Southerners feared that the new Congress would pass commercial regulations adversely affecting the planters. They demanded, therefore, that no trade laws be passed without a two-thirds majority of the legislature. They agreed to back down on this point, however, in exchange for guarantees that the legislature would not interfere with the slave trade until 1808 (see chapter 8). It was a bitter pill for Northerners to swallow, but they conceded that establishing a strong national government was of greater immediate importance than ending the slave trade. "Great as the evil is," Madison confessed, "a dismemberment of the union would be worse."

The second issue was the absence in the Constitution of a bill of rights. Such declarations had been included in most state constitutions, and Virginians like George Mason insisted that the states and their citizens needed explicit protection from possible excesses by the federal government. While many delegates sympathized with Mason's appeal, they noted that the hour was late and in any case, that the proposed constitution provided sufficient security for individual rights. During the hard battles over ratification, the delegates to the convention may have regretted passing over the issue so lightly.

The delegates adopted an ingenious procedure for ratification. Instead of submitting the Constitution to the various state legislatures, all of which had a vested interest in maintaining the status quo and most of which had two houses either of which could block approval, they called for the election of thirteen state conventions especially chosen to review the new federal government. The delegates may have picked this idea up from the Massachusetts experiment of 1780. Moreover, the Constitution would take effect after the assent of only nine states. There was no danger, therefore, that the proposed system would fail simply because a single state like Rhode Island withheld approval.

The convention asked Gouverneur Morris, a delegate from Pennsylvania noted for his urbanity, to make final stylistic changes in the wording of the Constitution. When Morris examined the working draft, he discovered that it spoke of the collection of states forming a new government. This wording presented problems. Ratification required only nine states. No one knew whether all the states would accept the Constitution, and if not, which nine would. A strong possibility existed that several New England states would reject the document. Morris' brilliant phrase, "We, the People of the United States," eliminated this difficulty. The new nation was a republic of the people, not of the states.

On September 17, thirty-nine men signed the Constitution. A few members of the convention like Mason could not support the document. Others had already gone home. For over three months, Madison had served as the convention's driving intellectual force. He now generously summarized the experience: "there never was an assembly of men, charged with a great and arduous trust, who were more pure in their motives, or more exclusively or anxiously devoted to the object committed to them."

Battle for Ratification

Supporters of the Constitution recognized that ratification would not be easy. After all, the convention had been authorized only to revise the Articles, but instead, it produced a radical new plan that fundamentally altered relations between the states and the central government. The delegates dutifully dispatched copies of the Constitution to the Congress of Confederation, then meeting in New York City, and that powerless body referred the document to the separate states without any specific recommendation. The fight for ratification had begun.

Federalists and Anti-Federalists

Proponents of the Constitution enjoyed great advantages over the unorganized opposition. In the contest for ratification, however, they took no chances. Their most astute move was the adoption of the label *Federalist*. This term cleverly suggested that they stood for a confederation of states rather than for the creation of a supreme national authority. Critics of the Constitution, who tended to be somewhat poorer, less urban, and less well-educated than their opponents, cried foul, but there was little they could do. They were stuck with the name *Anti-Federalist*, an awkward term that made their cause seem far more obstructionist than it actually was.

The Federalists recruited the most prominent public figures of the day. In every state convention, speakers favoring the Constitution were more polished, better educated, more fully prepared than were their opponents. In New York the campaign to win ratification sparked publication of *The Federalist*, a remarkable series of essays written by Madison, Hamilton, and Jay during the fall and winter of 1787 and 1788. The nation's newspapers threw themselves overwhelmingly behind the new government. In fact, few journals even bothered to carry Anti-Federalist writings. In some states, the Federalists adopted tactics of questionable propriety in order to gain ratification. In Pennsylvania, for example, they achieved a legal quorum for a crucial vote by dragging several opposition delegates off the streets. In New York, Hamilton intimidated upstate Anti-Federalists with threats that New York City would secede from the state unless it ratified the Constitution.

With so many factors working against them, the Anti-Federalists still came amazingly close to victory. Indeed, the Constitution **was ratified** in New York by a vote of 30 to 27, in Massachusetts by 187 to 168, and in Virginia by 89 to 79. According to historian Herbert J. Storing, scholars have generally dismissed the Anti-Federalists "as narrow-minded local politicians, unwilling to face the utter inadequacy of the Articles of Confederation or incapable of seeing beyond the boundaries of their own states or localities." But considering the close votes in some large states, it would appear that the men who resisted ratification were not so far removed from the political mainstream as has sometimes been suggested.

The Anti-Federalists spoke the language of the Commonwealthmen (see chapter 4). Like the extreme republicans who wrote the first state constitutions, the Anti-Federalists were deeply suspicious of political power. During the debates over ratification, they warned that public officials, however selected, would be constantly scheming to expand their authority.

The preservation of liberty required constant vigilance. It seemed obvious that the larger the republic, the greater the opportunity for political corruption. Local voters could not possibly know what their representatives in a distant capital were doing. The government outlined in the Constitution invited precisely the kinds of problems that Montesquieu had described in his famous essay. "In so extensive a republic," one Anti-Federalist declared, "the great officers of government would soon become above the control of the people, and abuse their power."

Anti-Federalists possessed a narrow view of representation. They argued that elected officials should reflect the character of their constituents as closely as possible. In a typical Anti-Federalist statement, Mason explained that republican representatives "ought to mix with the people, think as they think, feel as they feel,—ought to be perfectly amendable to them, and thoroughly acquainted with their interest and condition." It seemed unlikely that in large congressional districts, the people would be able to preserve such close ties with their representatives. According to the Anti-Federalists, the Constitution favored persons wealthy enough to have forged a reputation that extended beyond a single community. Samuel Chase told the members of the Maryland ratifying convention that under the new system "the distance between the people and their representatives will be so great that there is no probability of a farmer or planter being chosen . . . only the *gentry*, the *rich* and the well born will be elected."

Federalist speakers mocked their opponents' limited perspective. The Constitution deserved general support precisely because it insured that future Americans would be represented by "natural aristocrats," individuals possessing greater insights, skills, and training than did the average citizen. These talented leaders, Federalists insisted, could discern the interests of the entire population. They were not tied to the selfish needs of local communities. "The little demagogue of a petty parish or county will find his importance annihilated [under the Constitution] and his intrigues useless," predicted Charles Cotesworth Pinckney, a South Carolina Federalist.

The Anti-Federalist Legacy

The first ten amendments to the Constitution are the major legacy of the Anti-Federalist argument. The absence of a bill of rights troubled many people. In almost every state convention, opponents of the Constitution pointed to the need for greater protection of individual liberties, rights that people presumably possessed naturally. "It is necessary," wrote one Anti-Federalist, "that the sober and industrious part of the community should be defended from the rapacity and violence of the vicious and idle. A bill of rights, therefore, ought to set forth the purposes for which the compact is made, and serves to secure the minority against the usurpation and tyranny of the majority." The list of fundamental rights varied from state to state, but most Anti-Federalists demanded specific guarantees for jury trial and freedom of religion. They wanted prohibitions against cruel and unusual punishments. There was also considerable, though not universal, support for freedom of speech and freedom of the press.

Many Federalists found this a telling complaint. After all, they had attacked the Confederation for its inability to secure minority rights. While ratification was still in doubt, however, the Federalists resisted changes in the Constitution for fear that opponents of a strong central government would undo the work of the Philadelphia convention. Madison and others pledged to present a bill of rights to Congress as soon as the Constitution was ratified.

The Constitution drew support from many different types of people. In fact, historians have been unable to discover sharp correlations be-

Ratification of the Constitution

State	Date	Vote For	Vote Against
Delaware	December 8, 1787	30	0
Pennsylvania	December 12, 1787	46	23
New Jersey	December 18, 1787	38	0
Georgia	January 2, 1788	26	0
Connecticut	January 9, 1788	128	40
Massachusetts	February 16, 1788	187	168
Maryland	April 26, 1788	63	11
South Carolina	May 23, 1788	149	73
New Hampshire	June 21, 1788	57	47
Virginia	June 25, 1788	89	79
New York	July 26, 1788	30	27
North Carolina	November 21, 1789	194	77
Rhode Island	May 29, 1790	34	32

tween wealth and occupation on the one hand and attitudes toward the proposed system of government on the other. In general, Federalists lived in more commercialized areas than did their opponents. In the cities, artisans as well as merchants called for ratification, while those farmers who were only marginally involved in commercial agriculture frequently voted Anti-Federalist.

Despite passionate pleas from Patrick Henry and other Anti-Federalists, most state conventions quickly adopted the Constitution. Delaware

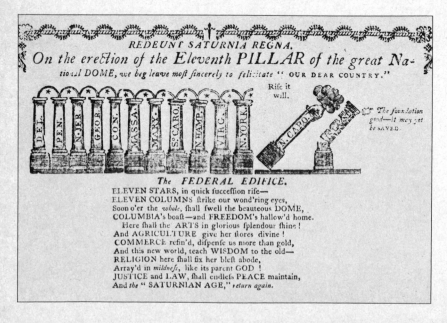

According to this 1788 cartoon, once the powerful states of Virginia and New York ratified the Constitution, the nation would enter a "golden age", without the support of dilatory North Carolina and Rhode Island.

acted first (December 7, 1787), and a number of other states soon followed. Within eight months of the Philadelphia meeting, eight of the nine states required to launch the government had ratified the document. The contests in New York, Virginia, and New Hampshire (June 1788) were close, but they too joined the union, leaving only North Carolina and Rhode Island outside the United States. Eventually (November 21, 1789, and May 29, 1790), even these states ratified the Constitution. While the state conventions generated angry rhetoric, Americans soon closed ranks behind the new government. An Anti-Federalist who represented one small Massachusetts village explained that "he had opposed the adoption of this Constitution; but that he had been overruled . . . by a majority of wise and understanding men [and that now] he should endeavor to sow the seeds of union and peace among the people he represented."

Adding a Bill of Rights

During the ratification debates, several states suggested amendments to the Constitution. Madison and others regarded these proposals with little enthusiasm. In *The Federalist* No. 84, Hamilton bluntly reminded the American people that "the constitution is itself . . . a BILL OF RIGHTS." But after the adoption of the Constitution had been assured, Madison moderated his stand. If nothing else, passage of a bill of rights would appease able men like Mason and Edmund Randolph, who might otherwise remain alienated from the new federal system. "We have in this way something to gain," Madison observed, "and if we proceed with caution, nothing to lose."

The crucial consideration was caution. A number of people throughout the nation advocated calling a second constitutional convention, one that would take Anti-Federalist criticism into account. Madison wanted to avoid such a meeting, and he feared that some members of the first Congress might use the bill of rights as an excuse to revise the entire Constitution or to promote a second convention.

Madison carefully reviewed the state recommendations as well as the various declarations of rights that had appeared in the early state constitutions, and on June 8, 1789, he placed before the

Chronology

1776	Second Continental Congress authorizes colonies to create republican governments (May)
	Eight states draft new constitutions; two others already enjoy republican government by virtue of former colonial charters
1777	Congress accepts Articles of Confederation after long debate (November)
1780	Massachusetts finally ratifies state constitution
1781	States ratify Articles of Confederation following settlement of Virginia's western land claims
	British army surrenders at Yorktown (October)
1782	States fail to ratify proposed Impost tax
1783	Newburgh Conspiracy thwarted (March)
	Society of the Cincinnati raises a storm of criticism
	Treaty of peace signed with Great Britain (September)
1785	Land Ordinance for Northwest Territory passed by Congress
1786	Jay-Gardoqui negotiations over Mississippi navigation anger southern states
	Annapolis Convention suggests second meeting to revise the Articles of Confederation (September)
	Shays' Rebellion frightens American leaders
1787	Constitutional Convention convenes in Philadelphia (May)
	Northwest Ordinance passed by Congress; restructures territorial government
1787–1788	The federal Constitution is ratified by all states except North Carolina and Rhode Island
1791	Bill of Rights (first ten amendments of the Constitution) ratified by states

House of Representatives a set of amendments designed to protect individual rights from government interference. Madison told the members of Congress that the greatest dangers to popular liberties came from "the majority [operating] against the minority." A committee compressed and revised his original ideas into twelve amendments, ten of which were ratified and became known collectively as the Bill of Rights. For many

■ *In this chamber of Federal Hall in New York City, the first capital of the United States, the Bill of Rights was presented to Congress in 1789. Within two years, these ten amendments were ratified by three fourths of the states.*

modern Americans these amendments are the most important section of the Constitution. Madison had hoped that additions would be inserted into the text of the Constitution at the appropriate places, not tacked onto the end, but he was overruled.

The Bill of Rights protected the freedoms of assembly, speech, religion, and the press; guaranteed speedy trial by an impartial jury; preserved the people's right to bear arms; and prohibited unreasonable searches. Other amendments dealt with legal procedure. Some opponents of the Constitution urged Congress to provide greater safeguards for states' rights, but Madison had no intention of backing away from a strong central government. Only the Tenth Amendment addressed the states' relation to the federal system. This crucial article, designed to calm Anti-Federalist fears, specified that those "powers not delegated to the United States by the Constitution, nor prohibited by it to the States, are reserved to the States respectively, or to the people."

On September 25, 1789, the Bill of Rights passed both houses of Congress, and by December 15, 1791, these amendments had been ratified by three fourths of the states. Madison was justly proud of his achievement. He had effectively secured individual rights without undermining the Constitution. When he asked his friend Jefferson for his opinion of the Bill of Rights, Jefferson responded with typical republican candor: "I like [it] . . . as far as it goes; but I should have been for going further."

A New Beginning

By 1789 one phase of American political experimentation had come to an end. During these exciting years, the people gradually, often haltingly, learned that in a republican society they themselves were sovereign. They could no longer blame the failure of government on inept monarchs or greedy aristocrats. They bore a great responsibility. Americans had demanded a government of the people only to discover during the 1780s that in some situations the people cannot be trusted with power, that majorities can tyrannize minorities, that the best of governments can abuse individual rights. They had the good sense, therefore, to establish a marvelous system of checks and balances that protected the people from themselves.

The country's prospects seemed bright. Franklin captured the national temper during the final moments of the constitutional convention. As the delegates came forward to sign the document, he observed that there was a sun carved on the back of George Washington's chair. "I have," the aged philosopher noted, " . . . often in the course of the session . . . looked at [the sun] behind the President without being able to tell whether it was rising or setting: but now at length I have the happiness to know that it is a rising and not a setting sun."

Recommended Reading

The best general accounts of this period have been written by Merrill Jensen and Jackson Turner Main. See especially Jensen's *Articles of Confederation*, rev. ed. (1959) and *The New Nation, A History of the United States During the Confederation, 1781–1789* (1950) as well as Main's *The Sovereign States, 1775–1783* (1973) and *The Anti-Federalists, Critics of the Constitution, 1781–1788* (1961). Gordon S. Wood provides a penetrating analysis in *The Creation of the American Republic, 1776–1787* (1969). The failure of Congress during the 1780s is the subject of Jack N. Rakove's monograph, *The Beginnings of National Politics: An Interpretive History of the Continental Congress* (1979).

Additional Bibliography

The social effects of the Revolution are covered in J. Franklin Jameson, *The American Revolution Considered as a Social Movement* (1926). Additional insights are presented in Edmund S. Morgan, "The American Revolution Considered as an Intellectual Movement," in Morton White and Arthur M. Schlesinger, Jr., eds., *Paths of American Thought* (1963) and in Robert E. Shalhope, "Toward a Republican Synthesis: The Emergence of an Understanding of Republicanism in American Historiography," *William and Mary Quarterly*, 3d ser. 29 (1975): 49–80 and "Republicanism and Early American Historiography," *ibid.* 39 (1982): 334–57.

The changing basis of political participation is discussed in Chilton Williamson, *American Suffrage from Property to Democracy, 1760–1860* (1960) and J. R. Pole, *Political Representation in England and the Origins of the American Republic* (1966). On black Americans, see Winthrop Jordan, *White Over Black: American Attitudes toward the Negro, 1550–1812* (1968); Benjamin Quarles, *The Negro in the American Revolution* (1961); Arthur Zilversmit, *The First Emancipation* (1961); and William W. Freehling, "The Founding Fathers and Slavery," *American Historical Review* 77 (1972): 81–93. On women, see Linda K. Kerber, *Women of the Republic: Intellect and Ideology in Revolutionary America* (1980); Mary Beth Norton, *Liberty's Daughters: The Revolutionary Experience of American Women, 1750–1800* (1980); and Nancy F. Cott, "Divorce and the Changing Status of Women in Eighteenth-Century Massachusetts," *William and Mary Quarterly*, 3rd ser. 33 (1976): 586–614.

The early state constitutions are discussed in Gordon Wood, *Creation of the American Republic* (1972) and Willi Paul Adams, *The First American Constitutions: Republican Ideology and the Making of the State Constitutions* (1980). On the individual states, see Edward Countryman, *A People in Revolution: The American Revolution and Political Society in New York, 1760–1790* (1981); Richard P. McCormick, *Experiment in Independence: New Jersey in the Critical Period, 1781–1789* (1950); Robert J. Taylor, *Western Massachusetts in the Revolution* (1954); and Oscar Handlin and Mary Handlin, *Commonwealth: A Study of the Role of Government in the American Economy: Massachusetts, 1774–1861*, rev. ed. (1969).

The Newburgh Conspiracy is covered in Richard H. Kohn, *Eagle and Sword: The Federalists and the Creation of the Military Establishment in America, 1783–1802* (1975). On the financial problems that beset the Confederation, see E. J. Ferguson, *The Power of the Purse: A History of American Public Finance 1776–1790* (1961) and Clarence L. Ver Steeg, *Robert Morris* (1954). The day-to-day workings of Congress are examined in H. J. Henderson, *Party Politics in the Continental Congress* (1974). A good survey of western settlement is Thomas D. Clark, *Frontier America: The Story of the Western Movement* (1959). Several good books on diplomacy are Frederick Marks, *Independence on Trial: Foreign Affairs and the Making of the Constitution* (1973); Charles R. Ritcheson, *Aftermath of Revolution: British Policy Toward the United States, 1783–1795* (1969); and Arthur P. Whitaker, *The Spanish-American Frontier* (1927).

The best source on the Constitution is Max Farrand, ed., *Records of the Federal Convention of 1787*, 4 vols. (1911–1937). Charles A. Beard's *Economic Interpretation of the Constitution of the United States* (1913) caused a generation of historians to examine the financial accounts of convention delegates, but as Forrest McDonald demonstrates in *We The People* (1958), Beard's thesis simply does not hold water. The intellectual background of the Founders is examined in Garry Wills, *Explaining America: The Federalist* (1981). To understand Madison's thinking about a large republic, see the essays in Douglass Adair, *Fame and the Founding Fathers*, edited by Trevor Colbourn (1974) and Irving Brant, *The Fourth President, A Life of James Madison* (1970).

On the debates over ratification, see Jonathan Elliot, ed., *The Debates in the Several State Conventions on the Adoption of the Federal Constitution*, 5 vols, (1876); Herbert J. Storing, ed., *The Complete Anti-Federalist*, 7 vols. (1981); John P. Kaminski and Gaspare J. Saladino, eds., *The Documentary History of the Ratification of the Constitution* (1982); and, of course, *The Federalist*, edited by J. E. Cooke (1961). The Anti-Federalist mind is reconstructed in Cecelia M. Kenyon, "Men of Little Faith: The Anti-Federalists on the Nature of Representative Government," *William and Mary Quarterly*, 3d ser. 12 (1955): 3–43.

chapter 7

REPUBLICAN GOVERNMENT ON TRIAL, 1788–1800

While presiding over the first meeting of the United States Senate in 1789, Vice-President John Adams called the senators' attention to a pressing procedural question. How would they address George Washington, the newly-elected president? Adams insisted that Washington deserved an impressive title, a designation lending dignity and weight to his office. The vice-president warned the senators that if they called Washington simply "President of the United States," the "common people of foreign countries [as well as] the sailors and soldiers [would] despise him to all eternity." Adams recommended "His Highness, the President of the United States, and Protector of their Liberties," but some senators favored "His Elective Majesty" or "His Excellency."

Adams' initiative caught many persons, including Washington, completely by surprise. They regarded the entire debate as ridiculous. James Madison, a member of the House of Representatives, announced that pretentious European titles were ill-suited to the "genius of the people" and "the nature of our Government." Thomas Jefferson, who was then residing in Paris, could not comprehend what motivated the Vice-President, and in private correspondence, he repeated Benjamin Franklin's judgment that Adams "means well for his Country, is always an honest Man, often a wise one, but sometimes, and in some things, absolutely out of his senses." When the senators learned that their efforts embarrassed Washington, they dropped the topic. The leader of the new Republic would be called President of the United States. One wag, however, dubbed the portly Adams, "His Rotundity."

The comic-opera quality of this debate should not obscure the participants' seriousness. During the 1790s, decisions about the use of power, about actual government policies and positions, had the potential to set a lasting precedent and thus to reinforce or imperil the Revolution itself. American leaders who only a few months earlier had worked together for ratification of the Constitution suddenly found themselves at odds over how best to put widely shared republican principles into practice. Public figures increasingly gravitated to Alexander Hamilton or Thomas Jefferson, the two most powerful personalities of the decade, and before Washington retired from the presidency, these loose political affiliations had hardened into open party identification, either Federalist or Republican, a development that no one in 1787 had anticipated or desired.

The process was painful. Political competition generated angry, even violent confrontation. Contemporaries associated parties with faction, with conspiratorial efforts to undermine public virtue. The United States had not yet developed the concept of loyal political opposition. In the 1790s, therefore, sensible and honorable people sometimes mistook simple disagreement over policy for treason. Since Federalists and Republicans both claimed to speak for the common good, for a revolutionary heritage, people assumed that one group or the other had to be lying. Suspicion, verging on paranoia, permeated political discussion; before the end of this difficult decade, party spokesmen advocated blatantly partisan actions that could have involved the United States in international war, shattered the Union, and destroyed constitutional liberties. Few times in this country's history has politics—the use of power by officials of the central government—so fully occupied the attention of the American people.

The Young Republic Is Launched

In 1788 George Washington enjoyed great popularity throughout the nation. The people remembered him as the selfless leader of the Continental army, and even before the states had ratified the Constitution, everyone assumed that he would be chosen president of the United States. He received the unanimous support of the electoral college, an achievement that no subsequent president has duplicated. Adams, a quick-tempered New Englander who championed national independence in 1776, was selected vice-president. As Washington left his beloved Virginia plantation,

Mount Vernon, for New York City, he recognized that the people—now so vocal in their support—could be fickle. "I fear," he explained with mature insight, "if the issue of public measures should not correspond with their sanguine expectations, they will turn the extravagant . . . praise . . . into equally extravagant . . . censures."

Washington bore great responsibility. The political stability of the young Republic depended in large measure on how he handled himself in office. In the eyes of his compatriots, he had been transformed into a living symbol of the new government, and during his presidency (1789–1797), he carried himself with studied dignity and reserve—never ostentatious, the embodiment of classical republican values. Contemporaries sensed that although Washington put himself forward for elective office, he somehow stood above the hurly-burly of routine politics. A French diplomat who witnessed Washington's first inauguration in New York City reported in awe: "He has the soul, look and figure of a hero united in him." But the adulation of Washington—however well meant—seriously affected the conduct of public affairs, for criticism of his administration was regarded as an attack on the President and by extension, on the Republic itself. During the early years of Washington's presidency, therefore, American public opinion discouraged partisan politics.

Washington created a strong, independent presidency. While he discussed pressing issues with the members of his cabinet—indeed, solicited their opinions—he left no doubt that he alone made policy. Moreover, the first President resisted congressional efforts to restrict executive authority, especially in foreign affairs.

The first Congress quickly established executive departments. Some congressmen wanted to prohibit presidents from dismissing cabinet-level appointees without Senate approval, but James Madison—still a voice for a strong, independent executive—led a successful fight against this restriction upon presidential authority. Madison recognized that the chief executive could not function unless he had personal confidence in the people with whom he worked. In 1789 Congress created the Departments of War, State, and the Treasury, and as secretaries, Washington nominated Henry Knox, Thomas Jefferson, and Alexander Hamilton respectively. Edmund Randolph

The figurative first meeting of Washington's cabinet, shown here in an engraving from a painting by Alonzo Chappell, took place at Washington's Mount Vernon home.

served as part-time attorney general, a position that ranked slightly lower in prestige than the head of a department. Since the secretary of the treasury oversaw the collection of customs and other future federal taxes, he could anticipate having several thousand jobs to dispense, an obvious source of political patronage.

To modern Americans accustomed to a large federal bureaucracy, the size of Washington's government seems amazingly small. When Jefferson arrived in New York to take over the State Department, for example, he found two chief clerks, two assistants, and a part-time translator. With this tiny staff, he not only maintained contacts with the representatives of foreign governments, collected information about world affairs, and communicated with United States officials living overseas but also organized the entire federal census! Jefferson immediately recognized that his new job would allow him little leisure for personal interests. The situation in other departments was similar. Overworked clerks scribbled madly just to keep up with the press of correspondence. John Adams, reviewing a bundle of letters and memos, grumbled "often the handwriting is almost illegible." Considering these working conditions, it is not surprising that the President had difficulty persuading able people to accept positions in the new government. It is even more astonishing that Hamilton and Jefferson were able to accomplish as much as they did with so little assistance.

Congress also provided for a federal court system. The Judiciary Act of 1789, the work primarily of Connecticut Congressman Oliver Ellsworth, created a Supreme Court staffed by a chief justice and five associate justices. In addition, the statute set up thirteen district courts authorized to review the decisions of the state courts. John Jay, a leading figure in New York politics, agreed to serve as chief justice, but since federal judges in the 1790s were expected to travel hundreds of miles over terrible roads to attend sessions of the inferior courts, few persons of outstanding talent and training joined Jay on the federal bench. One who did, Judge James Iredell, complained that service on the Supreme Court had transformed him into a "travelling postboy."

Remembering the financial insecurity of the old Confederation government, the newly elected congressmen passed the tariff of 1789, a tax of approximately 5 percent on imports. Even before it went into effect, however, the act sparked controversy. Southern planters, who relied heavily upon European imports, claimed the tariff discriminated against their interests in favor of those of northern merchants. The new levy generated considerable revenue for the young Republic, but responsibility for shaping the economy of the new nation fell mainly to Alexander Hamilton, the first secretary of the treasury.

Opposing Views on the Destiny of America

Washington's first cabinet included two extraordinary personalities, Alexander Hamilton and Thomas Jefferson. Both had served the country with distinction during the Revolution, were rec-ognized by contemporaries as men of special genius as well as high ambition, and brought to public office a powerful vision of how the American people could achieve greatness. The story of their opposing views during the decade of the 1790s provides insight into the birth and development of political parties. It also reveals how a common political ideology, republicanism, could be interpreted in such vastly different ways that decisions about government policy turned former friends into bitter adversaries. Indeed, the falling out of Hamilton and Jefferson reflected deep, potentially explosive, political divisions within American society.

Hamilton was a brilliant, dynamic young lawyer who had distinguished himself as Washington's aide-de-camp during the Revolution. Born in the West Indies, the child of an adulterous relationship, Hamilton employed charm, courage, and intellect to fulfill his inexhaustible ambition. He strove not for wealth but for reputation. Men and women who fell under his spell found him almost irresistible, but to enemies, Hamilton appeared a dark, calculating, even evil, genius. He advocated a strong central government and refused to be bound by the strict wording of the Constitution, a document Hamilton once called "a shilly shally thing." While he had fought for American independence, he admired British culture and during the 1790s, he advocated closer commercial and diplomatic ties with the former mother country with whom "we have a similarity of tastes, language, and general manners."

Jefferson possessed a profoundly different temperament. This tall Virginian was more reflective and shone less brightly in society than did Hamilton. Contemporaries sometimes interpreted his retiring manner as lack of ambition. They misread Jefferson. He thirsted not for power or wealth but for an opportunity to advance the democratic principles that he had stated so eloquently in the Declaration of Independence. When Jefferson became secretary of state in January 1790, he had just returned from Paris where he witnessed the first, exhilarating moments of the French Revolution. These earthshaking events, he believed, marked the beginning of a worldwide republican assault on absolute monarchy and aristocratic privilege. His European experiences biased Jeffer-

During the first years of Washington's administration, neither Hamilton (left) nor Jefferson recognized the full extent of their differences. But as events forced the federal government to make decisions on economic and foreign affairs, the two secretaries increasingly came into open conflict.

son in favor of France over Great Britain when the two nations clashed.

The contrast between these two powerful figures during the early years of Washington's administration should not be exaggerated. They shared many fundamental beliefs. Indeed, both Hamilton and Jefferson insisted that they were working for the creation of a strong, prosperous republic. Hamilton was publicly accused of being a secret monarchist, but he never repudiated the ideals of the American Revolution. Rather than seeing them as spokesmen for competing ideologies, one should view Hamilton and Jefferson as different kinds of republicans who during the 1790s attempted as best they could to cope with unprecedented political challenges.

However much these two men had in common, serious differences emerged. Washington's secretaries disagreed on precisely how the United States should fulfill its destiny. As head of the Treasury department, Hamilton urged his fellow citizens to think in terms of bold commercial development, of farms and factories embedded within a complex financial network that would reduce the nation's reliance upon foreign trade. Because Great Britain had already established an elaborate system of banking and credit, the secretary looked to that country for economic models that might be reproduced on this side of the Atlantic.

Hamilton also voiced concerns about the role of the people in shaping public policy. His view of human nature caused him to fear total democracy. He assumed that in a republican society, the gravest threat to political stability was anarchy rather than monarchy. "The truth," he claimed, "unquestionably is, that the only path to a subversion of the republican system of the Country is, by flattering the prejudices of the people, and exciting their jealousies and apprehensions, to throw affairs into confusion and bring on civil commotion." The best hope for the survival of the Republic, Hamilton believed, lay with the country's monied classes. If the wealthiest people could be persuaded that their economic self-interest could be advanced—or at least made less insecure—by the central government, then they would work to strengthen it, and by so doing, bring a greater measure of prosperity to the common people. From Hamilton's perspective, there was no conflict between private greed and public good; one was the source of the other.

On almost every detail, Jefferson challenged Hamilton's analysis. The secretary of state assumed that the strength of the American economy lay not in its industrial potential, but in its agricultural productivity. The "immensity of land" represented the country's major economic resource. Contrary to the claims of some critics. Jefferson did not advocate agrarian self-sufficiency or look back nostalgically to a golden age dominated by simple yeomen. He recognized the necessity of change, and while he thought that persons who worked the soil were more responsible citizens than were those who labored in factories for wages, he encouraged the nation's farmers to participate in an expanding international market. Americans could exchange raw materials "for finer manufactures than they are able to execute themselves."

Unlike Hamilton, Jefferson expressed faith in the ability of the American people to shape policy. Throughout this troubled decade, even when the very survival of constitutional government seemed in doubt, Jefferson maintained a boundless optimism in the judgment of the common folk. He instinctively trusted the people, feared that uncontrolled government power might destroy their liberties, and insisted that public officials follow the letter of the constitution, a frame of government he described as "the wisest ever presented to men." The greatest threat to the young Republic, he argued, came from the corrupt activities of pseudo-aristocrats, persons who placed the protection of "property" and "civil order" above the preservation of "liberty." To tie the nation's future to the selfish interests of a privileged class—bankers, manufacturers, speculators—seemed cynical as well as dangerous. He despised speculators who encouraged "the rage of getting rich in a day," since such "gaming" activities inevitably promoted the kinds of public vice that threatened republican government. To mortgage the future of the common people by creating a large national debt struck Jefferson as particularly insane.

Hamilton's Grand Design

The unsettled state of the nation's finances presented the new government with a staggering challenge. In August 1789 the House of Representatives announced that "adequate provision for the support of public credit [is] a matter of high importance to the national honor and prosperity." However pressing the problem appeared, no one was prepared to advance a solution, and the House asked the secretary of the treasury to make suggestions.

Congress may have received more than it bargained for. Hamilton threw himself into the task. He read deeply in abstruse economic literature. He even developed a questionnaire designed to find out how the United States economy really worked and sent it to scores of commercial and political leaders throughout the country. But when Hamilton's reports were complete, they bore the unmistakable stamp of his own creative genius. The secretary synthesized a vast amount of information into an economic blueprint so complex, so innovative that even his allies were slightly baffled. Theodore Sedgwick, a congressman who supported Hamilton's program, explained weakly that the Secretary's ideas were "difficult to understand . . . while we are in our infancy in the knowledge of Finance." Certainly, Washington never fully grasped the subtleties of Hamilton's plan.

The secretary presented his *Report on Public Credit* to Congress on January 14, 1790. His research revealed that the nation's outstanding debt stood at approximately $54 million. This sum represented various obligations that the United States government had incurred during the revolutionary war. In addition to foreign loans, the figure included loan certificates that the government had issued to its own citizens and soldiers. But that was not all. The states still owed creditors approximately $25 million. During the 1780s, Americans desperate for cash had been forced to sell government certificates to speculators at greatly discounted prices, and it was estimated that approximately $40 million of the nation's debt was owed to twenty thousand people, only 20 percent of whom were the orginal creditors.

Funding and Assumption

Hamilton's *Report on the Public Credit* contained two major recommendations covering the areas of funding and assumption. First, under his plan the United States promised to fund its foreign and domestic obligations at full face value. Current holders of loan certificates, whoever they were and no matter how they obtained them, could exchange the old certificates for new government bonds bearing a moderate rate of interest. Second, the secretary urged the federal government to assume responsibility for paying the remaining state debts.

Hamilton reasoned that his credit system would accomplish several desirable goals. It would significantly reduce the power of the individual states in shaping national economic policy, something Hamilton regarded as essential in maintaining a strong federal government. Moreover, the creation of a fully funded national debt signaled to investors throughout the world that the United States was now solvent, that its bonds represented a good risk. Hamilton argued that investment capital, which might otherwise flow to Europe, would remain in this country, providing a source of money for commercial and industrial investment. In short, Hamilton invited the country's wealthiest citizens to invest in the future of the United States. Critics claimed that the only people who stood to profit from the scheme were Hamilton's friends—some of whom sat in Congress and who had purchased great numbers of public securities at very low prices.

To Hamilton's great surprise, Madison—his friend and collaborator in writing *The Federalist* —attacked the funding scheme in the House of Representatives. The Virginia congressman agreed that the United States should honor its debts. He worried, however, about the citizens and soldiers who, because of personal financial hardship, had been compelled to sell their certificates at prices far below face value. Why should wealthy speculators now profit from their hardship? If the government treated the current holders of certificates less generously, Madison declared, then there might be sufficient funds to provide equitable treatment for the distressed patriots. Whatever the moral justification for

Madison's plan may have been, it proved unworkable. Far too many records had been lost since the Revolution for the Treasury Department to be able to identify all the original holders. In February 1790 Congress soundly defeated Madison's proposal.

Assumption unleashed even greater criticism. Some states had already paid their revolutionary debts, and Hamilton's program seemed designed to reward certain states—Massachusetts and South Carolina, for example—simply because they had failed to put their finances in order. In addition, the secretary's opponents in Congress became suspicious that assumption was merely a ploy to increase the power and wealth of Hamilton's immediate friends. "The Secretary's people scarce disguise their design," observed William Maclay, a crusty Scotch-Irish senator from Pennsylvania, "which is to create a mass of debts which will justify them in seizing all the sources of government."

No doubt, Maclay and others expressed genuine fears. It is also true that some congressmen who fought assumption were looking after their own investments. As speculators in state-owned lands, they stood to lose a great deal of money if the federal government assumed responsibility for the outstanding state debts. These congressmen bought up depreciated state securities, exchanged them at face value for state-owned lands, and pocketed the difference. Hamilton's plan threatened to destroy these lucrative transactions by cutting off the supply of cut-rate state securities. On April 12 a rebellious House led by Madison defeated assumption.

The victory was short-lived. Hamilton and congressional supporters resorted to legislative horse-trading to revive his foundering program. In exchange for locating the new federal capital on the Potomac River, a move that would stimulate the depressed economy of northern Virginia, several key congressmen who shared Madison's political philosophy changed their votes on assumption. Hamilton may also have offered to give the state of Virginia more federal money that it actually deserved. Whatever the details of these negotiations may have been, in August Washington signed assumption and funding into law. The first element of Hamilton's design was now securely in place.

Republican Capital
Rises from a Swamp

The location chosen for America's permanent capital better suited hunters and farmers than statesmen. As late as 1800, a congressman on his way from the Capitol to the executive mansion might have shot a pheasant, hooked a perch, or killed a black snake. Pennsylvania Avenue cut through a swampy wilderness that nourished snipes and partridges. Fish teemed in the Tiber River south of the unpaved avenue, and bullfrogs filled the woods with their croaking. "So very thinly is the city peopled, and so little is it frequented," wrote one surprised visitor, "that quails and other birds are constantly shot within a hundred yards of the Capitol, and even during the sitting of the houses of Congress." Less than a century later, another visitor marveled that this area had become a "vast labyrinth of streets, drives, and parks ornamented with fountains, [and] statues . . ." This transformation from swamp to splendid city began in 1790 when Congress asked President George Washington to select a site for a new national capital.

In 1790 the members of Congress agreed to meet in Philadelphia for ten years and then move to a permanent location on the Potomac River.

With his choice limited to a 150-mile strip along the Potomac, President Washington chose a site east of the river between Alexandria, Virginia, and Georgetown, Maryland. Local tobacco planters who were experiencing a prolonged depression were pleased to cede their lands to the United States government. Maryland and Virginia surrendered their claims to the land and thereby set the national government outside established state boundaries. The removal of the central government to its own federal district reflected the spirit of the new Constitution. State legislatures had elected delegates to the Congress of the Confederation, but now citizens voted directly for the members of the House of Representatives. States no longer controlled the central government. Believing that this autonomous national government deserved a grand capital, the President began to plan the federal city in 1791.

To design a capital worthy of America's bold republican experiment, President Washington commissioned Pierre Charles L'Enfant. Architect, engineer, and artist, L'Enfant pursued his charge with such single-minded determination that city commissioners and local landowners found him a difficult colleague. Suspicious of land speculators, the Frenchman refused to show his city plan to potential land buyers until an engraved copy made the design available to all citizens. And when an important local landowner built a house that conflicted with L'Enfant's master plan (an engraved version of the plan is shown on p. 188), the angry designer ordered the house destroyed. While such incidents eventually forced Washington to dismiss L'Enfant, the President pushed ahead with the plan.

The capital reflected the nation's republican ideology. Having served in America's revolutionary war, L'Enfant relished the opportunity to translate the United States Constitution into a city plan. Since the Constitution established a government with three branches, L'Enfant designed a city with three focal points. A house for Congress supplied the first focus and sat on a small hill, emphasizing the legislature's superiority over the other branches. Buildings for the executive and judiciary formed the other foci. Wide avenues radiated to the city limits from both the congressional and the executive sites to facilitate communication between voters and their representatives. In contrast, no avenue served the Court. This isolation was meant to protect the judiciary's disinterested judgment from political pressures.

But the ambitious French planner also envisioned the capital as a commercial center and an inspiration to republican virtue. Diagonal avenues extended like rays from the city's important buildings and districts, intersecting the staid gridiron pattern of streets. Parks and a mall broke the monotony of buildings; statues, fountains, and a national church sought to inspire republican heroism. L'Enfant situated the major commercial district southeast of the Capital at Navy Yard, and he suggested that a canal move goods through the city. Though the nation could scarcely afford to implement L'Enfant's extravagant dream in 1792, his design guided later generations and remains the recognizable basis of twentieth-century Washington.

Just as L'Enfant planned a city to glorify republican government, so architects designed buildings to dignify the Republic. Patriotic designers deemed classical architecture the only style worthy of the American achievement. Designs for public buildings inevitably recommended columns, porticoes, and pediments that reminded viewers of the nation's ties to the great republics of antiquity. Indeed, the insistence on classical architecture demonstrated the conviction that destiny would lift the United States to greatness equal to that of ancient Greece and Rome.

This boxlike north wing of the Capitol was the only portion of the building completed by November 1800.

By 1800 the city of Washington had attracted only 3200 people. The city had been selling lots for nine years. At the first public auction of Washington lands, only 35 of 10,000 lots sold. Subsequent public auctions produced even fewer cash sales. Because the city commissioners needed land sales to finance improvements in the capital, the failure to dispose of land at public auction convinced them to sell to speculators. But even the speculators fell into debt, leaving the city with few houses, fewer streets, and no glory.

By fits and starts Washington eventually grew into L'Enfant's dazzling republican capital. For much of the nineteenth century, cattle roamed the mall. During the War of 1812 British marines burnt much of the city to the ground; other national crises, such as the Civil War, slowed development. Not until the end of the nineteenth century did the District of Columbia reflect the grandeur that L'Enfant and others had envisioned —a unique monument to both city planning and republican government.

The Controversial Bank of the United States

The persistent Hamilton submitted his second report to Congress in January 1791. He proposed that the United States government charter a national bank, much like the Bank of England. This privately owned institution would be funded in part by the federal government. Indeed, since the bank would own millions of dollars of new United States bonds, its financial stability was tied directly to the strength of the federal government and, of course, to the success of the Hamiltonian program. The secretary of the treasury argued that a growing financial community required a central bank to facilitate increasingly complex commercial transactions. The institution not only would serve as the main depository of the United States government but also would issue currency acceptable in payment of federal taxes. Because of that guarantee, the money would maintain its value while in circulation.

Madison and others in Congress immediately raised a howl of protest. While they were not oblivious to the many important services that a national bank might provide for a growing country, they suspected that banks—especially those

■ *The National Bank of the United States, an important part of Hamilton's economic plan for a strong central government, opened in Philadelphia in 1791.*

modeled on British institutions—might "perpetuate a larged monied interest" in this country. And what about the Constitution? That document said nothing specifically about chartering financial corporations, and they warned that if Hamilton and his supporters were allowed to stretch fundamental law on this occasion, they could not be held back in the future. Popular liberties would be at the mercy of whoever happened to be in office. "To take a single step," Jefferson warned, "beyond the boundaries thus specifically drawn around the powers of Congress is to take possession of a boundless field of power, no longer susceptible to definition." On this issue Hamilton stubbornly refused to compromise, announcing angrily, "This is the first symptom of a spirit which must either by killed or will kill the constitution of the United States."

This intense controversy involving his closest advisers worried the President. Even though the bank bill passed Congress (February 8), Washington seriously considered vetoing the legislation on constitutional grounds. Before doing so, however, he requested written opinions from the members of his cabinet. Jefferson's rambling, wholly predictable attack on the bank was not one of his more persuasive performances. By contrast, in only a few days, Hamilton prepared a masterful essay entitled "Defense of the Constitutionality of the Bank." He assured the President that Article I, Section 8 of the Constitution— "The Congress shall have Power . . . To make all Laws which shall be necessary and proper for carrying into Execution the foregoing Powers"— justified issuing charters to national banks. The "foregoing Powers" upon which Hamilton placed so much weight were taxation, regulation of commerce, and making war. He boldly articulated a doctrine of *implied powers*, an interpretation of the constitution that neither Madison nor Jefferson had anticipated. Hamilton's so-called loose construction carried the day, and on February 25, 1791, Washington signed the bank act into law.

Hamilton triumphed in Congress, but the general public looked upon his actions with growing fear and hostility. Many persons associated huge national debts and privileged banks with the decay of public virtue. Men of Jefferson's temperament believed that Great Britain—a country that Hamilton held in high regard—had compromised the purity of its ancient constitution by allowing speculators to worm their way into positions of political power.

Hamilton seemed intent on reproducing this corrupt system in the United States. When news of his proposal to fund the national debt at full face value leaked out, urban speculators rushed to rural areas where they purchased loan certificates from unsuspecting citizens at bargain prices. An anonymous New Yorker who signed a newspaper article "A Dutchess County Farmer" claimed that the certificates had been taken up by "brokers, speculators, Jews, members of Congress and foreigners." To backcountry farmers, making money without actually engaging in physical labor appeared immoral, unrepublican, and certainly, un-American. When the greed of a former Treasury Department official led to several serious bankruptcies in 1792, people began to listen more closely to what Madison, Jefferson, and their associates were saying about growing corruption in high places.

Setback for Hamilton

In his third major report, *Report on Manufactures*, submitted to Congress in December 1791, Hamilton revealed the final details of his grand design for the economic future of the United States. This lengthy document suggested ways by which the federal government might stimulate manufacturing. If the country wanted to free itself from dependence upon European imports, Hamilton observed, then it had to develop its own industry, textile mills for example. Without direct government intervention, however, the process would take decades. Americans would continue to invest in agriculture. But, according to the secretary of the treasury, protective tariffs and special industrial bounties would greatly accelerate the growth of a balanced economy, and with proper planning, the United States would soon hold its own with England and France.

In Congress the battle lines were clearly drawn. Hamilton's opponents—not yet a disciplined party but a loose coalition of men who shared Madison's and Jefferson's misgivings about the secretary's program—ignored his economic arguments. Instead, they engaged him on moral and political grounds. Madison railed against the dangers of "consolidation", a process that threatened to concentrate all power in the federal government, leaving the states defenseless. Under the Confederation, of course, Madison had stood with the nationalists against the advocates of extreme states' rights (see chapter 6). His disagreements with Hamilton over economic policy, coupled with the necessity of pleasing the voters of his Virginia congressional district every two years, transformed Madison into a spokesman for the states.

Jefferson attacked the *Report on Manufactures* from a different angle. He assumed—largely because he had been horrified by Europe's urban poverty—that cities bred vice. The government, Jefferson argued, should do nothing to promote their development. He believed that Hamilton's proposal guaranteed that American workers would leave the countryside and crowd into urban centers. "I think our government will remain virtuous for many centuries," Jefferson explained, "as long as they [the people] are chiefly agricultural . . . When they get piled upon one another in large cities, as in Europe, they will become corrupt as in Europe." And southern congressmen saw tariffs and bounties as vehicles for enriching Hamilton's northern friends at the planters' expense. The recommendations in the *Report on Manufactures* were soundly defeated in the House of Representatives.

Washington detested political squabbling. The President, of course, could see that the members of his cabinet disagreed on many issues, but in 1792 he still believed that Hamilton and Jefferson —and the people who looked to them for advice— could be reconciled. In August, he begged them personally to rise above the "internal dissensions [which are] . . . harrowing and tearing at our vitals." The appeal came too late. Hamilton's reports eroded the good will of 1788, and by the conclusion of Washington's first term, neither secretary trusted the other's judgment. Their sparring had produced congressional factions but as yet no real political parties with permanent organization which engaged in campaigning. As yet, Hamilton and Jefferson only dimly appreciated the force of public opinion in shaping federal policy.

Foreign Affairs: A Catalyst to the Birth of Political Parties

During Washington's second term (1793–1797), war in Europe dramatically thrust foreign affairs into the forefront of American life. The impact of this development upon the conduct of domestic politics was devastating. Officials who had formerly disagreed on economic policy now identified their interests with either Britain or France, the world's most powerful nations. Differences of political opinion, however trivial, were suddenly cited as evidence that one group or the other had entered into treasonous correspondence with external enemies eager to compromise the independence and prosperity of the United States. As Jefferson observed in the troubled summer of 1793, European conflict "kindled and brought forward the two parties with an ardour which our own interests merely, could never excite."

Formal political organizations—the Federalists and Republicans—were born in this poisonous atmosphere. The clash between these groups developed over how best to preserve the new Republic. The Republicans advocated states' rights, strict interpretation of the Constitution, friendship with France, and vigilance against "the avaricious, monopolizing Spirit of Commerce and Commercial Men." The Federalists urged a strong national government, central economic planning, closer ties with Great Britain, and maintenance of public order, even if that meant calling out federal troops.

Threats to United States Neutrality

Great Britain treated the United States with arrogance. The colonists had defeated the redcoats on land, but on the high seas, the Americans were no match for the British navy, the strongest in the world. Indeed, the young Republic could not even compel its old adversary to comply with the Treaty of 1783, in which the British had agreed to vacate military posts in the Northwest Territory. In 1794 approximately a thousand British soldiers still occupied American land, an obstruction that

Governor George Clinton of New York claimed had excluded United States citizens "from a very valuable trade to which their situation would naturally have invited them." Moreover, even though 75 percent of American imports came from Great Britain, that country refused to grant the United States full commercial reciprocity. Among other provocations, it barred American shipping from the lucrative West Indian trade.

France presented a very different challenge. In May 1789 Louis XVI, desperate for revenue, authorized a meeting of a representative assembly known as the Estates General, and by so doing, the king unleashed explosive revolutionary forces that toppled the monarchy and cost him his life (January 1793). The men who seized power—and they came and went rapidly—were militant republicans, ideologues eager to liberate all Europe from feudal institutions. In the early years of the Revolution, France drew upon the American experience, and Thomas Paine and the Marquis de Lafayette enjoyed great popularity. But the French found that they could not stop the Revolution. Constitutional reform turned into bloody purges, and one radical group, the Jacobins, guillotined thousands of people—many wrongfully—who were suspected of monarchist sympathies during the so-called Reign of Terror (October 1793–July 1794). These events left Americans confused. While those who shared Jefferson's views cheered the spread of republicanism, those who sided with Hamilton condemned French expansionism and political violence.

In the face of growing international tension, neutrality seemed the most prudent course for the United States. But that policy was easier for a weak country to proclaim than to defend. In February 1793 France declared war on Great Britain—what the leaders of revolutionary France called the "war of all peoples against all kings"— and these powerful European rivals immediately challenged the official American position on shipping: "free ships make free goods," meaning that belligerents should not interfere with the shipping of neutral carriers. To make matters worse, no one was certain whether the Franco-American Treaties of 1778 (see chapter 5) legally bound the United States to support its old ally against Great Britain.

Both Hamilton and Jefferson wanted to avoid war. The secretary of state believed that nations

■ *The execution of Louis XVI by French revolutionaries served to deepen the growing political division in America. Republicans, although they deplored the excesses of the Reign of Terror, continued to support the French people. Federalists feared that the violence and lawlessness would spread to the United States.*

desiring American goods should be forced to honor American neutrality. In other words, if Britain treated the United States as a colonial possession, if the Royal Navy stopped American ships on the high seas and forced seamen to serve the king—in other words, if it impressed American sailors—then the United States should award France special commercial advantages. Hamilton thought Jefferson's scheme insane. He pointed out that Britain possessed the largest navy in the world and was not likely to be coerced by American threats. The United States, he counseled, should appease the former mother country even if that meant swallowing national pride.

A newly appointed French minister to the United States, Edmond Genêt, precipitated the first major diplomatic crisis. This unstable young man arrived in Charleston, South Carolina, in April 1793. He found considerable popular enthusiasm for the French Revolution and, buoyed by this reception, he authorized privately owned, American vessels to seize British ships in the name of France. Such actions clearly violated United States neutrality and invited British retaliation. When government officials warned Genêt to desist, he threatened to take his appeal directly to the American people. They presumably loved France more than the Washington administration did.

This confrontation particularly embarrassed Jefferson, the most outspoken pro-French member of the cabinet. He described Genêt as "hot headed, all imagination, no judgment, passionate, disrespectful and even indecent towards the President." Washington did not wait to discover if the treaties of 1778 were still in force. Before he had formally received the impudent French minister, the President issued a Proclamation of Neutrality (April 22). Ironically, when Genêt learned that the Jacobins intended to cut off his head, he requested asylum and spent the remainder of his life in New York.

Jay's Treaty Divides the Nation

Great Britain failed to take advantage of Genêt's insolence. Instead, it pushed the United States to the brink of war. British forts in the Northwest Territory remained a constant source of tension. In June 1793 a new element was added. The

London government closed French ports to neutral shipping, and in November, its navy captured several hundred American vessels trading in the French West Indies. The British had not even bothered to give the United States advance warning of a change in policy. Outraged members of Congress, especially those who identified with Jefferson and Madison, demanded retaliation, an embargo, a stoppage of debt payment, even war.

Before this rhetoric produced violence, Washington made one final effort to preserve peace. In May 1794 he sent Chief Justice John Jay to London to negotiate a formidable list of grievances. Jay's major objectives were removal of the British forts, payment for ships taken in the West Indies, improved commercial relations, and acceptance of the American definition of neutral rights.

Jefferson's supporters—by now openly called the "Republican interest"—anticipated a treaty favorable to the United States. After all, they explained, the war with France had not gone well for Great Britain, and the British people were surely desperate for American foodstuffs. Even before Jay departed, however, his mission stood little chance of success. Hamilton had already secretly informed British officials that the United States would compromise on most issues.

Not surprisingly, when Jay reached London, he encountered polite but firm resistance. The chief justice did persuade the British to abandon their frontier posts and to allow small American ships to trade in the British West Indies, but they rejected out of hand the United States position on neutral rights. The Royal Navy would continue to search American vessels on the high seas for contraband and to impress sailors suspected of being British citizens. Moreover, there would be no compensation for the ships seized in 1793 until the Americans paid British merchants for debts contracted before the Revolution. And to the particular annoyance of Southerners, not a word was said about the slaves that the British army had carried off at the conclusion of the war. While Jay salvaged the peace, he appeared to have betrayed the national interest.

News of Jay's Treaty—perhaps more correctly called Hamilton's Treaty—produced an angry outcry in the nation's capital. Even Washington was apprehensive. He submitted the document to the Senate without recommending ratification, a sign that the President was not entirely happy with the results of Jay's mission. After an extremely bitter debate, the upper house, controlled by Federalists, accepted a revised version of the treaty (June 1795). The vote was 20 to 10, a bare two-thirds majority.

The details of the Jay agreement soon leaked to the press. Throughout the country, people who had generally been apathetic about national politics were swept up in a wave of protest. Urban mobs condemned Jay's alleged sellout; rural settlers burned him in effigy. Jay jokingly told friends that he could find his way across the country simply by following the light of these fires. Southerners announced they would not pay prerevolutionary debts to British merchants. The

■ *John Jay was burned in effigy by angry mobs, who viewed the terms of his agreement with Great Britain as a betrayal of American interests.*

Virginia legislature proposed a Constitutional amendment reducing the Senate's role in the treaty-making process. As Fisher Ames, a Federalist congressman, noted darkly, "These little whirlwinds of dry leaves and dirt portend a hurricane."

His prediction proved accurate. The storm broke in the House of Representatives. Republican congressmen thought they could stop Jay's Treaty by withholding funds for its implementation. As part of their plan, they demanded that Washington show the House state papers relating to Jay's mission. Washington refused to comply. He angrily lectured the representatives, telling them that "The nature of foreign negotiations requires caution; and their success must often depend on secrecy."

The President still had a trump card to play. He raised the possibility that the House was really contemplating his impeachment. Such an action was, of course, unthinkable. Even criticizing Washington in public was politically dangerous, and as soon as he redefined the issue before Congress, petitions supporting the President flooded into the nation's capital. The Maryland legislature, for example, declared its "unabated reliance on the integrity, judgment, and patriotism of the President of the United States," a statement that clearly called into question the patriotism of certain Republican congressmen. The Federalists won a stunning tactical victory over the opposition. Had a less popular man than Washington occupied the presidency, however, they would not have fared so well. The division between the two parties was beyond repair. The Republicans labeled the Federalist "the British party"; the Federalists believed that the Republicans were in league with the French.

By the time that Jay's Treaty became law (June 14, 1795), the two giants of Washington's first cabinet had retired. Late in 1793 Jefferson returned to his Virginia plantation, Monticello, where despite his separation from day-to-day political affairs, he remained the chief spokesman for the Republican party. His rival, Hamilton, left the Treasury in January 1795 to practice law in New York City. He maintained close ties with important Federalist officials, and even more than Jefferson, Hamilton concerned himself with the details of party organization.

Diplomacy in the West

Before Great Britain finally withdrew its troops from the western forts, its military officers encouraged local tribes—the Shawnee, Chippewa, and Miami—to attack settlers and traders from the United States. The Indians won several impressive victories over federal troops in the area that would become western Ohio and Indiana. In 1790 General Josiah Harmar led his soldiers into an ambush. The following year, an army under General Arthur St. Clair suffered more than nine hundred casualties near the Wabash River. But

British Military Posts

White settlement in the Northwest Territory during Washington's administration precipitated several major battles with the Indians.

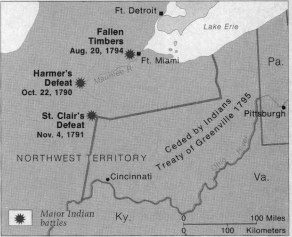

the Indians were actually more vulnerable than they realized, for when confronted with a major United States army under the command of General Anthony Wayne, they received no support from their former British allies. At the battle of Fallen Timbers (August 20, 1794), Wayne's forces crushed Indian resistance in the Northwest Territory, and the tribes were compelled to sign the Treaty of Greenville, formally ceding to the United States government the land that became Ohio. In 1796 the last British soldiers departed for Canada.

Shrewd negotiations mixed with pure luck helped secure the nation's southwestern frontier. Fo complex reasons having to do with the state of European diplomacy, Spanish officials in 1795 encouraged the United States representative in Madrid to discuss the navigation of the Mississippi River. Before this initiative, the Spanish government not only had closed the river to American commerce but also had incited the Indians of

the region to harass United States settlers (see chapter 6). Relations between the two countries would probably have deteriorated further had the United States not signed Jay's Treaty. The Spanish assumed—quite erroneously—that Great Britain and the United States had formed an alliance to strip Spain of its North American possessions.

To avoid this imagined disaster, officials in Madrid offered the American envoy, Thomas Pinckney, extraordinary concessions: the opening of the Mississippi, the right to deposit goods in New Orleans without paying duties, a secure southern boundary on the thrity-first parallel (a line roughly parallel to the Northern boundary of Florida and running west to the Mississippi), and a promise to stay out of Indian affairs. An amazed Pinckney signed the Treaty of San Lorenzo (also called Pinckney's Treaty) on October 27, 1795, and in March the Senate ratified the document without a single dissenting vote. Pinckney, who came from a prominent South Carolina family, instantly became the hero of the Federalist party.

Popular Political Culture

More than any other event during Washington's administration, ratification of Jay's Treaty generated intense political strife. Even as members of Congress voted as Republicans or Federalists, they condemned the rising partisan spirit as a grave threat to the stability of the United States. Popular writers equated "party" with "faction," and faction with conspiracy to overthrow legitimate authority. Party conflict also suggested that Americans had lost the sense of common purpose that had united them during the Revolution. Contemporaries did not appreciate the beneficial role that parties could play by presenting alternative solutions to foreign and domestic problems. Organized opposition smacked of disloyalty and therefore had to be eliminated by any means—fair or foul. These intellectual currents coupled with the obvious existence of two parties created an atmosphere that bred suspicion. In the name of national unity, Federalists as well as Republicans advocated the destruction of political adversaries.

GEORGE WASHINGTON
PRESIDENT.
1792.

■ *This engraved medallion is typical of the commemorative medals the United States presented to the chiefs of the Indian tribes with whom it signed treaties.*

The Partisan Role of Newspapers and Political Clubs

More than any other single element, newspapers transformed the political culture of the United States. Americans were voracious readers. In 1789 a foreign visitor observed, "The common people [here] are on a footing, in point of literature, with the middle ranks of Europe. They all read and write, and understand arithmetic;—almost every little town now furnishes a circulating library."

A rapidly expanding number of newspapers appealed to this large, literate audience. John Fenno established the *Gazette of the United States* (1789), a journal that supported Hamilton's political philosophy. The Republicans responded in October 1790 with Philip Freneau's influential *National Gazette*. While the format of these publications was similar to that of the colonial papers, their tone was quite different. These fiercely partisan journals presented rumor and opinion as fact. Public officials were regularly dragged through the rhetorical mud. Jefferson, for example, was accused of cowardice; Hamilton vilified as an adulterer. As party competition became more bitter, editors showed less restraint. One Republican paper even suggested that George Washington had been a British agent during the Revolution. No wonder Fisher Ames announced in 1801, "The newspapers are an overmatch for any government."

Even poets and essayists were caught up in the political fray. The better writers—and this was not a period of outstanding artistic achievement in the United States—often produced party propaganda. However much Freneau aspired to fame as a poet, he is remembered today chiefly as a champion of the Republican cause. Noah Webster, who later published *An American Dictionary of the English Language* (1828), spent the 1790s editing a strident Federalist journal, *American Minerva*, in New York City. And Joel Barlow, a Connecticut poet of modest talent, celebrated the French Revolution in verse, thus clearly identifying himself with the party of Jefferson. American writers sometimes complained that the culture of the young Republic was too materialistic, too unappreciative of the subtler forms of art then popular in Europe. But it was clear that poets who ignored patriotism and politics simply did not sell well in the United States.

This decade also witnessed the birth of political clubs. These "Democratic" or "Republican" associations, as they were called, first appeared in 1793 and were modeled on the political debating societies that sprang up in France during the early years of the French Revolution. Perhaps because of the French connection, Federalists assumed that the American clubs represented the interests of the Republican party. Their purpose was clearly political indoctrination. The Philadelphia Society announced that it would "cultivate a just knowledge of rational liberty." A "Democratic" club in New York City asked each member to declare himself a "firm and steadfast friend of the EQUAL RIGHTS OF MAN."

By 1794 at least twenty-four clubs were holding regular meetings. How many Americans actually attended their debates is not known, but regardless of the number, the clubs obviously complemented the newspapers in providing the common people with highly partisan political information.

Whiskey Rebellion Linked to Republican Incendiaries

In 1794 the Federalists accused the political clubs of triggering real violence. The farmers of western Pennsylvania regularly distilled their grain into whiskey, a hard liquor highly prized by the Scotch-Irish settlers. Not only did these people enjoy strong drink, they also claimed that barrels of liquor were easier to transport to distant markets than were sacks of wheat. In any case, they hated paying the federal excise tax on distilled whiskey that Congress had imposed in 1791.

A minor tax revolt occurred in the Pittsburgh region in 1794, and local farmers threatened a federal excise collector with bodily harm. In response to this local incident, President Washington raised thirteen thousand troops. Hamilton, who thirsted for military fame, volunteered to lead the soldiers into battle, but after marching around the Pennsylvania countryside for several weeks, the army could find only twenty troublemakers. Of these, two were convicted of high crimes against the United States government, one reportedly a "simpleton" and the other insane.

■ *Tarring and feathering federal officials was one way in which western Pennsylvanians protested the tax on whiskey in 1794. Washington's call for troops to put down the insurrection drew more volunteers than he had been able to raise during most of the American Revolution.*

Washington eventually pardoned both rebels, and peace returned to the frontier.

In the national political forum, however, the Whiskey Rebellion had just begun. Spokesmen for both parties offered sinister explanations for this seemingly innocuous affair. Washington blamed the "Republican" clubs for promoting civil unrest. He apparently believed that the opposition party had dispatched French agents to western Pennsylvania to undermine the authority of the federal government. In November 1794 Washington informed Congress that these "self-created societies"—in other words, the Republican political clubs—had inspired "a spirit inimical to all order." Indeed, the Whiskey Rebellion had been "fomented by combinations of men who . . . have disseminated, from an ignorance or perversion of facts, suspicions, jealousies, and accusations of the whole Government."

The President's interpretation of this rural tax revolt was no less charitable than the conspiratorial explanation offered by the Republicans. Jefferson labeled the entire episode a Hamiltonian device to create an army for the purpose of intimidating Republicans. How else could one explain the administration's gross overreaction to a few disgruntled farmers? "An insurrection was announced and proclaimed and armed against," Jefferson noted, "but could never be found." The response of both parties reveals a pervasive fear of some secret, evil design to destroy the Republic. The clubs and newspapers—as yet unfamiliar tools for mobilizing public opinion—fanned these anxieties, convincing many government officials that the First Amendment should not be interpreted as protecting political dissent.

In September 1796 Washington published his famed "Farewell Address," formally declaring his intention to retire from the presidency. In the address, which was printed in newspapers throughout the country, Washington warned against all political faction. Written in large part by Hamilton, who drew upon a draft prepared several years earlier by Madison, the address served narrowly partisan ends. The product of growing political strife, it sought to advance the Federalist cause in the forthcoming election. By waiting until September to announce his retirement, Washington denied the Republicans valuable time to organize an effective campaign. There was an element of irony in this initiative. Washington had always maintained that he stood above party. While he may have done so in the early years of his presidency, events such as the signing of Jay's Treaty and the suppression of the Whiskey Rebellion transformed him in the eyes of many Americans into a spokesman solely for Hamilton's Federalist party.

Washington also spoke to foreign policy matters in the address. He counseled that the United States avoid making any permanent alliances with distant nations that had no real interest in promoting American security. This statement guided foreign relations for many years and became the credo of later American isolationists, who argued that the United States should steer clear of foreign entanglements.

Federalists in Power

The election of 1796 took place in an atmosphere of mutual distrust. Jefferson, soon to be the vice-president, informed a friend that "an Anglican and aristocratic party has sprung up, whose avowed object is to draw over us the substance, as they have already done the forms, of British government." On their part, the Federalists were convinced that their Republican opponents wanted to hand the government over to French radicals. By modern standards, the structures of both political parties were still primitive. Leaders of national stature such as Madison and Hamilton wrote letters encouraging local gentlemen around the country to support a certain candidate, but no one attempted to canvass the voters in advance of the election.

During the campaign the Federalists sowed the seeds of their eventual destruction. Party stalwarts agreed that John Adams should run against the Republican candidate, Thomas Jefferson. Hamilton, however, could not leave well enough alone. From his law office in New York City, he schemed to deprive Adams of the presidency. His motives are obscure. He apparently feared that an independent-minded Adams would be difficult to manipulate. He was correct.

Hamilton exploited an awkward feature of the electoral college. In accordance with the Constitution, each elector cast two ballots, and the person who gained the most votes became president. The runner-up, regardless of party affiliation, served as vice-president. Ordinarily the Fed-

The Election of 1796		
Candidate	Party	Electoral Vote
J. Adams	Federalist	71
Jefferson	Republican	68
Pinckney	Federalist	59

eralist electors would have cast one vote for Adams and one for Thomas Pinckney, the hero of the negotiations with Spain and the party's choice for vice-president. Everyone hoped, of course, that there would be no tie. Hamilton secretly urged southern Federalists to support only Pinckney if that meant throwing away an elector's second vote. If everything had gone according to plan, Pinckney would have received more votes than Adams. The strategy backfired when New Englanders loyal to Adams heard of Hamilton's maneuvering. They dropped Pinckney, and when the votes were counted, Adams had 71, Jefferson 68, and Pinckney 59. Hamilton's treachery not only angered the new President but also heightened tensions within the Federalist party.

Adams assumed the presidency under intolerable conditions. He found himself saddled with the members of Washington's old cabinet, a group of second-raters who regularly consulted with Hamilton behind Adams' back. The two most offensive were Timothy Pickering, secretary of state, and James McHenry, secretary of war. But to have dismissed them summarily would have called Washington's judgment into question, and Adams was not publicly prepared to take that risk.

Adams also had to work with a Republican vice-president. Adams hoped that he and Jefferson could cooperate as they had done during the Revolution—they had served together on the committee that prepared the Declaration of Independence—but partisan pressures soon overwhelmed the President's good intentions. Jefferson recorded their final attempt at reconciliation. Strolling home one night after dinner, Jefferson and Adams reached a place "where our road separated, his being down Market Street, mine along Fifth, and we took leave; and he [Adams] never after that . . . consulted me as to any measure of the government."

The XYZ Affair and Domestic Politics

Foreign affairs immediately occupied Adams' full attention. The French government regarded Jay's Treaty as an affront. By allowing Great Britain to define the conditions for neutrality, the United States had in effect sided with that nation against the interests of France.

Relations between the two countries steadily deteriorated. The French dismissed Charles Cotesworth Pinckney, the United States representative in Paris. Pierre Adet, the French minister in Philadelphia, openly tried to influence the 1796 election in favor of the Republicans. His stupid meddling not only embarrassed Jefferson, it also offended the American people. The situation then took a violent turn. In 1797 French privateers began seizing Americn ships; within a year, they captured more than three hundred vessels. During this period, neither country both-

ered to declare war, and for that reason the hostilities came to be known as the Quasi-War.

Hamilton and his friends welcomed a popular outpouring of anti-French sentiment. The "High Federalists"—as Hamilton's wing of the party was called—counseled the President to prepare for all-out war, hoping that war would purge the United States of French influence. Adams was not persuaded to escalate the conflict. He dispatched a special commission in a final attempt to remove the sources of antagonism. This famous negotiating team consisted of Charles Pinckney, John Marshall, and Elbridge Gerry. They were instructed to obtain compensation for the ships seized by French privateers as well as release from the treaties of 1778. Federalists still worried that this old agreement might oblige the United States to defend French colonies in the Caribbean against British attack, something they were extremely reluctant to do. In exchange, the commission offered France the same commercial privileges granted to Great Britain in Jay's Treaty.

■ *This cartoon captures the anti-French sentiment many Americans felt after President Adams disclosed the papers of the XYZ affair. America—depicted as a young maiden—is being plundered by five Frenchmen, who represent the five Directors of the French government.*

While the diplomats negotiated for peace, Adams talked of strengthening American defenses, rhetoric that pleased the militant members of his own party.

The commission was shocked by the outrageous treatment it received in France. Instead of dealing directly with Talleyrand, the minister of foreign relations, they met with obscure intermediaries who demanded a huge bribe. The commission reported that Talleyrand would not open negotiations unless he was given $250,000. In addition, the French government expected a "loan" of millions of dollars. The Americans refused to play this insulting game. Pinckney angrily sputtered, "No, no, not a sixpence," and with Marshall he returned to the United States. When they arrived home, Marshall offered his much-quoted toast: "Millions for defense, but not one cent for tribute."

Diplomatic humiliation set off a domestic political explosion. When Adams presented the commission's official correspondence before Congress—the names of Talleyrand's lackeys were labeled X, Y, and Z—the Federalists burst out with a war cry. At last, they would be able to even old scores with the Republicans. In April 1798, a Federalist newspaper in New York City announced ominously that any American who refused to censure France " . . . must have a soul black enough to be *fit* for *treasons, strategems,* and *spoils*." Rumors of conspiracy spread throughout the country. Personal friendships between Republicans and Federalists were shattered. Jefferson described the tense political atmosphere in a letter to an old colleague: "You and I have formerly seen warm debates and high political passions. But gentlemen of different politics would then speak to each other, and separate the business of the Senate from that of society. It is not so now. Men who have been intimate all their lives, cross the streets to avoid meeting, and turn their heads another way, lest they should be obliged to touch their hats."

Crushing Political Dissent

In the spring of 1798 High Federalists assumed that it was just a matter of time until Adams asked Congress for a formal declaration of war. In the meantime, they pushed for a general rearma-

■ *The thirty-six-gun frigate* Philadelphia, *shown here under construction in a Philadelphia shipyard in 1799, was later captured by Barbary pirates (see p. 215).*

(see p. 215)

ment, new fighting ships, additional harbor fortifications, and most important, a greatly expanded United States Army. About the need for land forces, Adams remained understandably skeptical. He saw no likelihood of French invasion.

The President missed the political point. The army the Federalists wanted was intended not to thwart French aggression but to stifle internal opposition. Indeed, militant Federalists used the XYZ affair as the occasion to institute what Jefferson termed the "reign of witches." The threat to the Republicans was not simply a figment of the vice-president's overwrought imagination. When Theodore Sedgwick, now a Federalist senator from Massachusetts, first learned of the commission's failure, he observed in words that capture the High Federalists' vindictiveness, "It will afford a glorious opportunity to destroy faction. Improve it."

During the summer of 1798 a provisional army gradually came into existence. George Washington agreed to lead the troops, but he would do so only on condition that Adams appoint Hamilton as second-in-command. This demand placed the President in a terrible dilemma. Several revolutionary veterans—Henry Knox, for example—

outranked Hamilton. Moreover, the former secretary of the treasury had consistently undermined Adams' authority, and to give Hamilton a position of real power in the government seemed awkward at best. When Washington insisted, however, Adams was forced to support Hamilton.

The chief of the High Federalists threw himself into the task of recruiting and supplying the troops. No detail escaped his attention. He and Secretary of War McHenry made certain that in this political army only loyal Federalists received commissions. They even denied Adams' son-in-law a post. The entire enterprise took on an air of unreality. Hamilton longed for military glory, and he may have contemplated attacking Spain's Latin American colonies. His driving obsession, however, was the restoration of political order. No doubt, he agreed with a Federalist senator from Connecticut who predicted that the Republicans "never will yield till violence is introduced; we must have a partial civil war . . . and the bayonet must convince some, who are beyond the reach of other arguments."

Hamilton should not have treated Adams with such open contempt. After all, the Massachusetts statesman was still the President, and without presidential cooperation, Hamilton could not fulfill his grand military ambitions. Whenever pressing questions concerning the army arose, Adams was nowhere to be found. He let commissions lie on his desk unsigned; he took overlong vacations to New England. He made it quite clear that his first love was the navy. In May 1798, the President persuaded Congress to establish the Navy Department. For this new cabinet position, he selected Benjamin Stoddert, a person who did not take orders from Hamilton. Moreover, Adams further infuriated the High Federalists by refusing to ask Congress for a formal declaration of war. When they pressed him, Adams threatened to resign, making Jefferson president. As the weeks passed, the American people increasingly looked upon the idle army as an expensive extravagance.

Silencing Political Opposition: The Alien and Sedition Acts

The Federalists did not rely solely upon the army to crush political dissent. During the summer of 1798, the party's majority in Congress passed a group of bills known collectively as the Alien and Sedition Acts. This legislation authorized the use of federal courts and the powers of the presidency to silence the Republicans. The acts were born of fear and vindictiveness, and in their efforts to punish the followers of Jefferson, the Federalists created the nation's first major crisis over civil liberties.

Congress drew up three separate Alien Acts. The first, the Alien Enemies Law, vested the President with extraordinary wartime powers. On his own authority he could detain or deport foreigners who behaved in a manner he thought suspicious. Since Adams refused to ask for a declaration of war, this legislation never went into effect. A second act, the Alien Law, empowered the President to expel any foreigner from the United States simply by executive decree. Congress limited the act to two years, and while Adams did not attempt to enforce it, the mere threat of arrest caused some Frenchmen to flee the country. The third act, the Naturalization Law, was the most flagrantly political of the group. The act established a fourteen-year probationary period before foreigners could apply for full United States citizenship. Federalists recognized that recent immigrants, especially the Irish, tended to vote Republican. The Naturalization Law, therefore, was designed to keep "hordes of wild Irishmen" away from the polls for as long as possible.

The Sedition Law struck at the heart of free political exchange. It defined criticism of the United States government as criminal libel; citizens found guilty by a jury were subject to fines and imprisonment. Congress entrusted enforcement of the act to the federal courts. Republicans were justly worried that the Sedition Law undermined rights guaranteed by the First Amendment. When they protested, however, the High Federalists dismissed their complaints. The Constitution, they declared, did not condone "the most groundless and malignant lies, striking at the safety and existence of the nation." They were determined to shut down the opposition press and were willing to give the government what seemed almost dictatorial powers to achieve that end. The Jeffersonians also expressed concern over the federal judiciary's expanded role in punishing sedition. They believed that such matters were best left to state officials.

Americans living in widely scattered regions of the country soon witnessed political repression firsthand. District courts staffed by Federalist appointees indicted seventeen people for criticizing the government. Several cases were absurd. In Newark, New Jersey, for example, a drunkard staggered out of a tavern to watch a sixteen-gun salute fired in honor of President Adams. When the man expressed the hope that a cannonball might lodge in Adam's ample posterior, he was arrested. No wonder that a New York City journal declared, "joking may be very dangerous even to a free country."

The most celebrated trial occurred in Vermont. A Republican congressman, Matthew Lyon, who was running for reelection, publicly accused the Adams' administration of mishandling the Quasi-War. This was not the first time that this Irish immigrant had angered the Federalists. On the floor of the House of Representatives, Lyon once spit in the eye of a Federalist congressman from Connecticut. Lyon was immediately labeled the "Spitting Lyon," and one Bostonian declared, "I feel grieved that the saliva of an Irishman should be felt upon the face of an American & he, a New Englandman." A Federalist court was pleased to have the opportunity to convict him of libel. But Lyon enjoyed the last laugh. While he served his term in jail, his constituents reelected him to Congress.

As this and other cases demonstrated, the federal courts had become political tools. While the fumbling efforts at enforcement of the Sedition Law did not silence opposition—indeed, they sparked even greater criticism and created martyrs—the actions of the administration persuaded Republicans that the survival of free government was at stake. Time was running out. "There is no event," Jefferson warned, " . . . however atrocious, which may not be expected."

The Republicans Appeal to the States

By the fall of 1798 Jefferson and Madison were convinced that the Federalists envisioned the creation of a police state. According to Madison, the Sedition Law "ought to produce universal alarm." It threatened the free communication of ideas which he "deemed the only effectual guardian of every other right." Some extreme Republicans such as John Taylor of Virginia recommended secession from the Union; others advocated armed resistance. But Jefferson wisely counseled against such extreme strategies. "This is not the kind of opposition the American people will permit," he reminded his desperate supporters. The last best hope for American freedom lay in the state legislatures.

■ In the early years of the Republic, political dissent sometimes escalated to physical violence. This fistfight on the floor of Congress took place on February 15, 1798. The combatants are Republican Matthew Lyon and Federalist Roger Griswold.

As the crisis deepened, Jefferson and Madison drafted separate protests known as the Virginia and Kentucky Resolutions. Both statements vigorously defended the right of individual state assemblies to interpret the constitutionality of federal law. Jefferson wrote the Kentucky Resolutions in November 1798, and in an outburst of partisan anger, he flirted with a doctrine as dangerous to the survival of the United States as anything advanced by Hamilton and his High Federalist friends.

In the Kentucky Resolutions, Jefferson described the federal union as a compact. The states transferred certain explicit powers to the national government, but in his opinion, they retained full authority over all matters not specifically mentioned in the Constitution. Jefferson rejected Hamilton's broad interpretation of the "general welfare" clause. "Every state," Jefferson argued, "has a natural right in cases not within the compact . . . to *nullify* of their own authority all assumptions of power within their limits." Carried to an extreme, this logic could have led to the breakup of the federal government, and in 1798 Kentucky legislators were not prepared to take such a radical stance. While they diluted Jefferson's prose, they fully accepted his belief that the Alien and Sedition Acts were unconstitutional and ought to be repealed.

When Madison drafted the Virginia Resolutions in December, he took a stand more temperate than Jefferson's. While Madison urged the states to defend the rights of the American people, he resisted the notion that a single state legislature could or should have the authority to overthrow federal law.

The Virginia and Kentucky Resolutions must be viewed in proper historical context. They were not intended as statements of abstract principles and most certainly not as a justification for southern secession. They were pure political party propaganda. Jefferson and Madison dramatically reminded American voters during a period of severe domestic tension that the Republicans offered a clear alternative to Federalist rule. No other state legislatures passed the Resolutions, and even in Virginia where the Republicans enjoyed broad support, several important figures such as John Marshall and George Washington censured the states' rights argument.

■ *John Adams, in the pearl gray suit and sword he wore for his 1797 inauguration. The portrait is by English artist William Winstanley, 1798. Party difficulties plagued Adams throughout his presidency.*

Adams' Finest Hour

In February 1799 President Adams belatedly declared his independence from the Hamiltonian wing of the Federalist party. Throughout the confrontation with France, Adams had shown little enthusiasm for war. Following the XYZ debacle, he began to receive informal reports that Talleyrand had changed his tune. The French foreign minister told Elbridge Gerry and other Americans that the bribery episode had been an unfortunate misunderstanding and that if the United States sent new representatives, he was prepared to negotiate in good faith. The High Federalists ridiculed this report. But Adams, still brooding over Hamilton's appointment to the army, decided to throw his own waning prestige behind peace. In February he suddenly asked the Senate to confirm William Vans Murray as United States representative to France.

The move caught the High Federalists totally by surprise. They sputtered with outrage. "It is solely the President's act," Pickering cried, "and we were all thunderstruck when we heard of it." Adams was just warming to the task. In May he fired Pickering and McHenry, an action he should have taken months earlier. With peace in the offing, American taxpayers complained more and more about the cost of maintaining an unnecessary army. The President was only too happy to dismantle Hamilton's dream.

When the new negotiators—Oliver Ellsworth and William Davie joined Murray—finally arrived in France in November, 1799, they discovered that yet another group had come to power. This government, headed by Napoleon Bonaparte, cooperated in drawing up an agreement known as the Convention of Mortefontaine. The French refused to compensate the Americans for vessels taken during the Quasi-War, but they did declare the treaties of 1778 null and void. Moreover, the convention removed annoying French restrictions on United States commerce. Not only had Adams avoided war, he had also created an atmosphere of mutual trust that paved the way for the purchase of the Louisiana Territory. The President declared with considerable justification that the second French mission was "the most disinterested, the most determined and the most successful [act] of my whole life." It also cost him reelection.

The Peaceful Revolution: The Election of 1800

On the eve of the election of 1800, the Federalists were fatally divided. Adams enjoyed wide popularity among the Federalist rank and file, especially in New England, but articulate party spokesmen like Hamilton vowed to punish the President for his betrayal of their militant policies. Hamilton even composed a scathing pamphlet entitled *Letter Concerning the Public Con-*

	Chronology
1787	Constitution of the United States signed (September)
1789	George Washington inaugurated (April) Louis XVI of France calls meeting of the Estates General (May)
1790	Congress approves Hamilton's plan for funding and assumption (July)
1791	Bank of the United States is chartered (February) Hamilton's *Report on Manufactures* rejected by Congress (December)
1793	France's revolutionary government announces a "war of all people against all kings" (February) Genêt affair strains relations with France (April) Washington issues Proclamation of Neutrality (April) Spread of "Democratic" clubs alarms Federalists Jefferson resigns as secretary of state (December)
1794	Whiskey Rebellion put down by United States Army (July–November) General Anthony Wayne defeats Indians at Battle of Fallen Timbers (August)
1795	Hamilton resigns as secretary of the treasury (January) Jay's Treaty divides the nation (June) Pinckney's Treaty with Spain is a welcome surprise (October)
1796	Washington publishes "Farewell Address" (September) John Adams elected president (December)
1797	XYZ Affair poisons United States relations with France (October)
1798–1800	Quasi-War with France
1798	Congress passes the Alien and Sedition Acts (June and July) Provisional army is formed Virginia and Kentucky Resolutions protest the Alien and Sedition Acts (November and December)
1799	George Washington dies (December)
1800	Convention of Mortefontaine is signed with France, ending Quasi-War (September)
1801	House of Representatives elects Thomas Jefferson president (February)

duct and Character of John Adams, an essay that questioned Adams' ability to hold high office.

Once again the former secretary of the treasury attempted to rig the voting in the electoral college so that the party's vice-presidential candidate, Charles Cotesworth Pinckney, would receive more ballots than did Adams. As in 1796, the conspiracy backfired. The Republicans gained 73 votes, while the Federalists trailed with 65.

But to everyone's surprise, the election was not resolved in the electoral college. When the ballots were counted, Jefferson and his running mate, Aaron Burr, had tied. This accident—a Republican elector should have thrown away his second vote—sent the selection of the next president to the House of Representatives, a body still controlled by members of the Federalist party.

As the House began its work on February 27, 1801, excitement ran high. Each state delegation cast a single vote, with nine votes needed to be elected. On the first ballot Jefferson received the support of eight states, Burr six, and two states divided evenly. People predicted a quick victory for Jefferson, but after dozens of ballots, the House had still not selected a president. "The scene was now ludicrous," observed one witness. "Many had sent home for night-caps and pillows, and wrapped in shawls and great-coats, lay about the floor of the committee-rooms, or sat sleeping in their seats." The drama dragged on for days. To add to the confusion, Burr unaccountably refused to withdraw. Contemporaries thought his ambition had overcome his good sense.

The logjam finally broke when leading Federalists decided that Jefferson, whatever his faults, would make a more responsible president than would the shifty Burr. Even Hamilton labeled Burr "the most dangerous man of the community." On the thirty-sixth ballot, Representative James A. Bayard of Delaware announced that he no longer supported Burr. This decision, coupled with Burr's inaction, gave Jefferson the presidency, ten states to four.

THE PROVIDENTIAL DETECTION

■ *In the election of 1800, both Republicans and Federalists distributed broadsides, like the one shown here, to urge voters to support their party's candidates.*

The Twelfth Amendment, ratified in 1804, saved the American people from repeating this potentially dangerous turn of events. Henceforth, the electoral college cast separate ballots for president and vice-president.

During the final days of his presidency, Adams appointed as many Federalists as possible to the federal bench. Jefferson protested the hasty manner in which these "midnight judges" were selected. One of them, John Marshall, became chief justice of the United States, a post he held with distinction for thirty-four years. But behind the last-minute flurry of activity lay bitterness and disappointment. Adams never forgave Hamilton. "No party," the Federalist President wrote, "that ever existed knew itself so little or so vainly overrated its own influence and popularity as

The Election of 1800		
Candidate	Party	Electoral Vote
Jefferson	Republican	73
J. Adams	Federalist	65

ours. None ever understood so ill the causes of its own power, or so wantonly destroyed them." On the morning of Jefferson's inauguration, Adams slipped away from the capital—now located in Washington—unnoticed and unappreciated.

In the address that Adams missed, Jefferson attempted to quiet partisan fears. "We are all republicans; we are all federalists," the new President declared. By this statement he did not mean to suggest that party differences were no longer important. Jefferson reminded his audience that whatever the politicians might say, the people shared a deep commitment to a federal Union based upon republican ideals set forth during the American Revolution. Indeed, the President interpreted the election of 1800 as a revolutionary episode, a fulfillment of the principles of 1776.

Recent battles, of course, colored Jefferson's judgment. The contests of the 1790s had been hard fought; the outcome often in doubt. Jefferson looked back at this period as a confrontation between the "advocates of republican and those of kingly government," and he believed that only the vigilance of his own party had saved the country from Federalist "liberticide."

From a broader historical perspective, however, the election of 1800 seems noteworthy for what did not occur. There were no riots in the streets, no attempted coup by military officers, no secession from the Union, nothing except the peaceful transfer of government from the leaders of one party to those of the opposition. That in itself was a remarkable achievement.

Recommended Reading

John C. Miller, *The Federalist Era 1789–1801* (1960), provides the best political survey of this exciting period. Forrest McDonald has reinterpreted the politics of the 1790s in *The Presidency of George Washington* (1974) and *Alexander Hamilton* (1979). See also Merrill D. Peterson, *Thomas Jefferson and the New Nation: A Biography* (1970). Drew McCoy, *The Elusive Republic: Political Economy in Jeffersonian America* (1980), provides important insights into the issues that divided Hamilton and Jefferson. Richard Hofstadter avoided taking sides in *The Idea of a Party System: The Rise of Legitimate Opposition in the United States, 1780–1840* (1969). A solid account of Adams' presidency is Stephan G. Kurtz, *The Presidency of John Adams: The Collapse of Federalism 1795–1800* (1957).

Additional Bibliography

Some of the best biographies of Hamilton and Jefferson include Dumas Malone, *Jefferson and the Rights of Man* (1951) and *Jefferson and the Ordeal of Liberty* (1962); Gerald Stourzh, *Alexander Hamilton and the Idea of Republican Government* (1970); Broadus Mitchell, *Alexander Hamilton: A Concise Biography* (1976); and Jacob Ernest Cooke, *Alexander Hamilton* (1982). For the politics of this decade, see the papers of George Washington, John Adams, Thomas Jefferson, Alexander Hamilton, John Jay, and James Madison.

Political ideologies of this period are discussed in Lance Banning, *The Jeffersonian Persuasion: Evolution of Party Ideology* (1978); Richard Buel, Jr., *Securing the Revolution: Ideology in American Politics, 1789–1815* (1972); and Joyce Appleby, "Commercial Farming and the 'Agrarian Myth' in the Early Republic," *Journal of American History* 68 (1982): 833–49.

The problems associated with the developing political parties are examined in Joseph Charles, *The Origins of the American Party System* (1956); William N. Chambers, *Political Parties in a New Nation: The American Experience, 1776–1809* (1963); and Noble E. Cunningham, Jr., *The Jeffersonian Republicans: The Formation of Party Organization, 1789–1801* (1957). Two studies merit special attention: Alfred F. Young, *The Democratic Republicans of New York: The Origins 1763–1797* (1967) and Norman Risjord, *Chesapeake Politics, 1781–1800* (1978). Leland D. Baldwin provides a fully detailed account in *Whiskey Rebels: The Story of a Frontier Uprising* (1939). Also helpful is John R. Howe, Jr., "Republican Thought and the Political Violence of the 1790s," *American Quarterly* 19 (1967): 147–65. See also Joseph J. Ellis, *After the Revolution: Profiles of Early American Culture* (1979) and Emory Elliott, *Revolutionary Writers: Literature and Authority in the New Republic 1725–1810* (1982).

The most detailed treatments of the major negotiations and treaty fights are Samuel F. Bemis, *Jay's Treaty: A Study in Commerce and Diplomacy* (1923) and *Pinckney's Treaty: A Study of America's Advantage from Europe's Distress* (1926). More recent studies include Alexander De Conde, *Entangling Alliance: Politics and Diplomacy Under George Washington* (1958) and *The Quasi-War: Politics and Diplomacy of the Undeclared War with France 1797–1801* (1966); Gerald A. Combs, *The Jay Treaty: Political Battleground of the Founding Fathers* (1970); Albert H. Bowman, *The Struggle for Neutrality: Franco-American Diplomacy during the Federalist Era* (1974); and William Stinchcombe, *The XYZ Affair* (1980).

President Adams' estrangement from the Hamiltonians is examined in Manning J. Dauer, *The Adams Federalists* (1953). The new government's attempt to restrict civil rights is covered in James Morton Smith, *Freedom's Fetters: The Alien and Sedition Laws and American Civil Liberties* (1956). Richard H. Kohn, *Eagle and Sword: The Federalists and the Creation of the Military Establishment in America 1783–1803* (1975), describes the plans to form a Federalist army.

chapter 8

REPUBLICAN
ASCENDANCY

British visitors often disliked Jeffersonian society. Wherever they traveled in the young Republic, they met ill-mannered people inspired with a ruling passion for liberty and equality. Charles William Janson, an Englishman who lived in the United States for thirteen years, recounted an exchange he found particularly unsettling that had occurred at the home of an American acquaintance. "On knocking at the door," he reported, "it was opened by a servant maid, whom I had never before seen." The woman's behavior astonished Janson. "The following is the dialogue, word for word, which took place on this occasion:—'Is your master at home?'—'I have no master.'—Don't you live here?'—'I *stay* here.'—'And who are you then?'—'Why, I am Mr. _____'s *help*. I'd have you know, *man*, that I am no *sarvant* [sic]; none but *negers* [sic] are *sarvants.*'"

Standing on his friend's doorstep, Janson encountered the authentic voice of Jeffersonian republicanism—self-confident, assertive, blatantly racist, and having no intention of being relegated to low social status. The maid believed that she was her employer's equal, perhaps not in wealth but surely in character. She may have even dreamed of someday owning a house staffed with *"help."* American society fostered such ambition. In the early nineteenth century, thousands of settlers poured across the Appalachian Mountains or moved to cities in search of opportunity. Thomas Jefferson and individuals who ran for public office under the banner of the Republican party spoke for these people.

The limits of the Jeffersonian vision were obvious even to contemporaries. The people who spoke most nobly about equality often owned slaves. Blacks, who represented one fifth of the population of the United States, were totally excluded from the new opportunities opening up in the cities and the West. Indeed, the maid in the incident described above insisted—with no apparent sense of inconsistency—that her position was superior to that of blacks, who were brought to lifelong servitude involuntarily. It is not surprising that leaders of the Federalist party accused the Republicans, especially those who lived in the South, of hypocrisy, and in 1804 one Massachusetts Federalist sarcastically defined Jeffersonian democracy as "an Indian word, signifying '*a great tobacco planter, who had herds of black slaves.*'" The race issue simply would not go away. Beneath the political maneuvering over the acquistion of the Louisiana Territory and the War of 1812 lay fundamental disagreement about the spread of slavery to the western territories.

In other areas the Jeffersonians did not fulfill even their own high expectations. As members of an opposition party during the presidency of John Adams, they insisted upon a strict interpretation of the Constitution, upon peaceful foreign relations, and upon a reduction of the role of the federal government in the lives of the average citizens. But following the election of 1800, Jefferson and his supporters discovered that unanticipated pressures, foreign and domestic, forced them to moderate these goals. Before he retired from public office, Jefferson interpreted the Constitution in a way that permitted the government to purchase the Louisiana Territory when the opportunity arose; he regulated the national economy with a rigor that would have made Alexander Hamilton blush, and he led the country to the brink of war. Some Americans praised the President's pragmatism; others felt betrayed. For a man who had played a leading role in the revolt against George III, it must have been shocking in 1807 to find himself labeled a "despot" in a popular New England newspaper. "Give ear no longer to the siren voice of democracy and Jeffersonian liberty," the editor shrieked. "It is a cursed delusion, adopted by traitors, and recommended by sycophants."

Burgeoning Population and Economy

During the early decades of the nineteenth century, the population of the United States experienced substantial growth. The 1810 census counted 7,240,000 Americans, a jump of almost 2 million in just ten years. Of this total, approximately 20 percent were blacks, the majority of whom lived in the South. The large population increase in the nation was the result primarily of natural reproduction, since during Jefferson's presidency few immigrants moved to the New World. The largest single group in this society was children, boys and girls who were born after Washington's administration and who came of age at a time when the nation's boundaries were rapidly expanding.

Even as Americans defended the rights of individual states, they were forming strong regional identifications. In commerce and politics they perceived themselves as representatives of distinct subcultures—Southerners, New Englanders, or Westerners. No doubt, the broadening geographic horizons reflected improved transportation links that enabled people to travel more easily within the various sections. But the growing regional mentality was also the product of defensiveness. While local writers celebrated New England's cultural distinctiveness, for example, they were clearly uneasy about the region's rejection of the democratic values that were sweeping the rest of the nation. Moreover,

during this period people living south of the Potomac River began describing themselves as Southerners, not as citizens of the Chesapeake or the Carolinas as they had done in colonial times.

This shifting focus of attention resulted not only from an awareness of shared economic interests but also from a sensitivity to outside attacks upon slavery. Several times during the first fifteen years of the nineteenth century, conspirators actually advocated secession, and while these harebrained schemes failed, they revealed the powerful sectional loyalties that undermined national unity.

Peopling the West

The most striking changes occurred in the West. Before the end of the American Revolution, only Indian traders and a few hardy settlers had ventured across the Appalachians. After 1790, however, a flood of people rushed west to stake out farms on the rich soil. Many settlers followed the so-called northern route across Pennsylvania or New York into the old Northwest Territory. Pittsburgh and Cincinnati, both strategically lo-

■ First settled in 1788, by 1800 Cincinnati—a busy trading center on the Ohio River—included a post office, a Presbyterian church, and the Green Tree Hotel.

CINCINNATI-1800.

cated on the Ohio River, became important commercial ports. In 1803 Ohio joined the Union, and territorial governments were formed in Indiana (1800), Louisiana (1805), Michigan (1805), Illinois (1809), and Missouri (1812). Southerners poured into the new states of Kentucky (1792) and Tennessee (1796). Wherever they located, Westerners depended upon water transportation. Because of the extraordinarily high cost of hauling goods over land, riverboats represented the only economical means of carrying agricultural products to distant markets. The Mississippi River was the crucial commercial link for the entire region, and Westerners did not feel secure so long as New Orleans remained under Spanish control.

Families who moved west attempted to transplant familiar Eastern customs to the frontier. In some areas such as the Western Reserve, a narrow strip of land along Lake Erie in northern Ohio, the influence of New England remained strong. In general, however, a creative mixing of peoples of different backgrounds in a strange environment generated distinctive folkways. Westerners developed their own heroes like Mike Fink, the legendary keelboatman of the Mississippi River; Daniel Boone, the famed trapper and Indian fighter; and the eye-gouging "alligatormen" of Kentucky and Tennessee. Americans who crossed the mountains were ambitious and self-confident, excited by the challenge of almost unlimited geographic mobility. A French traveler observed in 1802 that in the entire region he visited there were no farms "where one cannot with confidence ask the owner from whence he had emigrated, or, according to the light manners of the Americans, 'What part of the world do you come from?'" These rootless people, he explained "incline perpetually toward the most distant fringes of American settlement."

Only one obstacle barred the way. At the beginning of the nineteenth century a substantial number of Native Americans still lived in the region. Indeed, they insisted that the land belonged to them. The tragedy was that the Indians, many of them dependent upon trade with the white people and ravaged by disease and alcohol, lacked unity. Small groups allegedly representing the interests of an entire tribe sold off huge pieces of land, often for whiskey and trinkets.

These fraudulent transactions disgusted the

■ *The Prophet provided spiritual leadership for the union of Indian tribes he and his brother Tecumseh organized to resist white encroachment upon Indian lands.*

brilliant Shawnee leaders, Tecumseh, and his brother, Tenskwatawa (known as the Prophet). These men desperately attempted to revitalize tribal cultures, and against overwhelming odds, they briefly persuaded Native Americans living in the Indiana Territory to avoid contact with whites, to resist alcohol, and most important, to hold on to their land. Frontiersmen saw Tecumseh as a threat to progress, and during the War of 1812, they shattered the Indians' dream of cultural renaissance. The populous Creek nation located in the modern states of Alabama and Mississippi also resisted the settlers' advance, but its warriors were crushed by Andrew Jackson's Tennessee militia at the battle of Horseshoe Bend (March 1814).

Well-meaning Jeffersonians did not intend to destroy the Indians. The President talked of creating a vast reservation beyond the Mississippi River, just as the British had talked before the Revolution of a sanctuary beyond the Appalachian Mountains. He sent federal agents to "civilize" the Indians, to transform them into yeoman farmers. But even the most enlightened thinkers of the day did not believe that the Indians possessed a culture worth preserving.

Commercial Capitalism

Before 1820 the prosperity of the United States depended primarily upon its agriculture and trade. Jeffersonian America was by no stretch of the imagination an industrial economy. The overwhelming majority of the population—84 percent in 1810—was directly involved in agriculture. Southerners concentrated upon staple crops, tobacco, rice, and cotton, which they sold on the European market. In the North people generally produced livestock and cereal crops. Regardless of location, however, the nation's farmers followed a back-breaking work routine that did not differ substantially from that of their parents and grandparents. Except for the cotton gin, important chemical and mechanical inventions did not appear in the fields for another generation. Probably the major innovation of this period was the agricultural fair, an idea first advanced in 1809 by a Massachusetts farmer, Elkanah Watson. In hopes of improving animal breeding, he offered prizes for the best livestock in the county. The experiment was a great success, for as Watson reported, "Many farmers, and even women, were excited by curiosity to attend this first novel, and humble exhibition."

The merchant marine represented an equally important element in America's preindustrial economy. At the turn of the century, ships flying the Stars and Stripes transported a large share of the world's trade. Merchants in Boston, New York, and Philadelphia received handsome profits from this commerce. Their ships provided essential links between European countries and their Caribbean colonies. France, for example, relied heavily upon American vessels for its sugar. These lucrative transactions, coupled with the export of domestic staples, especially cotton, generated great fortunes. Between 1793 and 1807, the year that Jefferson imposed the embargo, American commerce enjoyed a more than 500 percent increase in the value of exports and in net earnings. Unfortunately, the boom did not last. The success of the "carrying trade" depended in large measure upon friendly relations between the United States and the major European powers. When England and France began seizing American ships—as they both did after 1805—national prosperity suffered.

The cities of Jeffersonian America functioned chiefly as depots for international trade. Only about 7 percent of the nation's population lived in urban centers, and most of these people owed

■ *George Crowinshield, Sr., commissioned artist George Ropes to paint this scene of Crowninshield's Wharf in Salem harbor. The warehouses on the wharf are filled with treasures from the Indies—silks from China, and gold and ivory from the Guinea Coast.*

To the Shores of Tripoli

Long before Korea and Vietnam, the United States dealt with undeclared war in faraway places. During the early years of Jefferson's first administration, efforts to protect American commerce brought the United States into such a war with the potentates of four Muslim states of North Africa, known as the Barbary States. This unusual conflict represented the earliest example of an American effort to "destablize" a foreign government. It also featured heroics by the fledgling U.S. Marine Corps. At the time of professed neutrality, this distant war with alien people demonstrated how extensively the United States had been drawn into interests overseas.

Problems with the Barbary States began soon after the American Revolution. Pirates from Morocco, Algiers, Tripoli, and Tunis had long preyed on European shipping, and American vessels became easy targets once they lost the protection of the British navy. Neither side in this strange conflict knew much about the other. In one letter the dey of Algiers referred to "the President and ruler of the American people living on the island called America, belonging to the islands of the ocean." Most Americans could not have even located the Barbary States on a map.

Diplomatic efforts to guarantee that American ships would not be molested in Mediterranean waters produced only temporary settlements.

The Barbary potentates' extravagant price for peace rose to a level of tribute that the United States found intolerable. During the 1790s the American government sent more than $100,000 to "protect" merchant ships from seizure. But as soon as the payments stopped, the pirates captured vessels flying the Stars and Stripes and demanded huge ransoms for American sailors who languished in prison. One outraged poet exclaimed:

Great God! The rovers who infest the waves
Have seiz'd our ships, and made our freemen
slaves.

Frustrated American leaders concluded that force might accomplish what talk and money could not. After impassioned debate in the mid-1790s, Congress approved the construction of frigates for use against Algiers. In 1801, President Thomas Jefferson ordered a naval task force to the Mediterranean, and in February 1802—after the bashaw of Tripoli had declared war against the United States—Congress authorized the navy to take offensive action, in effect, to wage war. No longer would the United States pay tribute to the Barbary States, except as one commander promised, "through the mouth of a cannon."

Talking tough was considerably easier than

waging war so far from home. The American task force mounted an ineffective blockade of the Barbary coast, winning only a few scattered victories. An aggressive new American commander, Commodore Edward Preble, forced Morocco to quit the war, but the United States suffered a major setback when Tripoli captured the frigate *Philadephia*, anchored it in the harbor, and imprisoned its crew. Only a daring naval raid on the harbor of Tripoli, in which a small expedition led by Stephen Decatur successfully boarded and burned the vessel, prevented the pirates from turning the warship to use against its former owners. Freeing the crew cost Jefferson's government another $60,000!

With the President's approval, American representatives in North Africa now hatched a bizarre scheme of intrigue to end the war. Their goals were to overthrow the bashaw of Tripoli and replace him with a ruler friendly to the United States. In Egypt, the American diplomat William Eaton made an agreement with the bashaw's exiled rival and organized a force of American marines and Arab mercenaries to install this claimant on the throne. After a five hundred-mile trek on camels through the Libyan desert, the expedition captured the Tripolitan city of Derna. But this legendary expedition "to the shores of Tripoli"—hence the words of the Marine hymn—ended in fiasco. Without consulting Eaton, another American negotiator made peace with the bashaw.

However confusing the end of the war, Ameri-cans exulted in the exploits of their maritime heroes. Victories over the Barbary States—no matter how transitory—brought an outpouring of patriotic rhetoric and a new sense of national self-confidence. With more than a hint of smugness and cultural arrogance, Americans congratulated themselves on succeeding where Europe had failed. "It must be mortifying to some of the neighboring European powers," wrote one diplomat of the American triumph, "to see that the Barbary states have been taught their first lessons of humiliation from the Western World."

The war and eventual victory over the Barbary States also confirmed the principles that guided American foreign policy. Freedom of the seas and unrestricted commerce were most important. Not only did unhindered trade bring prosperity to American farmers and merchants, but according to republican ideology, it also encouraged the spread of liberty and human progress. If commerce were freed, Jefferson explained, "the greatest mass possible would then be produced of those things which contribute to human life and human happiness; the numbers of mankind would be increased, and their condition bettered."

Until the end of the nineteenth century, the navy acted primarily as a police force, as it had during the Barbary wars, to protect American trade with Europe, Asia, Africa, and Latin America. Americans did not turn inward after independence, rather they looked outward to a world transformed by commerce and republicanism.

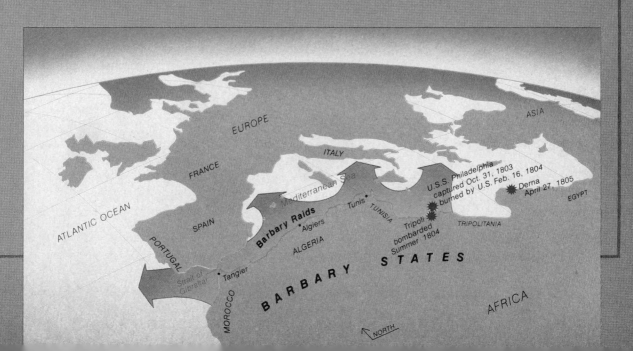

their livelihoods either directly or indirectly to the "carrying trade." Artisans maintained the fleet; skilled workers produced new ships; laborers loaded cargoes. And as some merchant families became wealthy, they demanded luxury items such as fine furniture. This specialized market drew a small, but highly visible, group of master craftsmen, and their extraordinarily beautiful and intricate pieces—New England clocks, for example—were perhaps the highest artistic achievement of the period.

Despite these accomplishments, American cities exercised only a marginal influence upon the nation's vast hinterland. Because of the high cost of land transportation, urban merchants seldom purchased goods for export—flour and meat, for example—from a distance of more than 150 miles. The separation between rural and urban Americans was far more pronounced during Jefferson's presidency than it was after the development of canals and railroads a few decades later.

The booming carrying trade may actually have retarded the industrialization of the United States. The lure of large profits drew investment capital—a scarce resource in a developing society —into commerce. By contrast, manufacturing seemed too risky. One contemporary complained, "The brilliant prospects held out by commerce, caused our citizens to neglect the mechanical and manufacturing branches of industry."

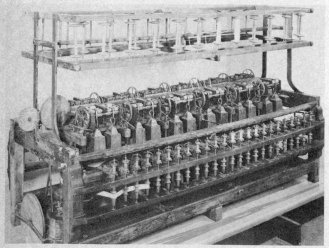

■ *Because drawing plans of the Arkwright spinning frame was a criminal offense in England, Samuel Slater memorized the design before he came to America in 1789.*

He may have exaggerated slightly to make his point. Samuel Slater, an English-born designer of textile machinery, did establish several cotton spinning mills in New England, but before the 1820s these plants employed only a small number of workers. In fact, during this period far more cloth was produced in individual households than in factories. Another farsighted inventor, Robert Fulton, sailed the first American steamship up the Hudson River in 1807. In time, this marvelous innovation opened new markets for domestic manufacturers, especially in the West. At the conclusion of the War of 1812, however, few people anticipated how greatly steam power would eventually transform the character of the American economy.

Republicans in Power

The District of Columbia seemed an appropriate capital for a Republican president. At the time of Jefferson's first inauguration, Washington was still an isolated rural village, a far cry from the cosmopolitan centers of Philadelphia and New York. Jefferson fit comfortably into Washington society. He despised formal ceremony and sometimes shocked foreign dignitaries by meeting them in his slippers or a threadbare jacket. He spent as much time as his official duties allowed in reading and reflection. Isaac, one of Jefferson's slaves, recounted, "Old master had abundance of books: sometimes would have twenty of 'em down on the floor at once; read fust one then tother."

The President was a poor public speaker. He wisely refused to deliver annual addresses before Congress. In personal coversation, however, Jefferson exuded considerable charm. His dinner parties were major social events, and in this forum, the President regaled politicians with his knowledge of literature, philosophy, and science. According to Margaret Bayard Smith, the wife of a congressman, the President "has more ease than grace—all the winning softness of politeness, without the artificial polish of courts."

Notwithstanding his commitment to the life of the mind, Jefferson was a politician to the core. He ran for presidency in order to achieve specific goals: the reduction of the size and cost of federal government, the repeal of obnoxious Federalist legislation such as the Alien Acts, and the maintenance of international peace. To accomplish his program, Jefferson realized that he required the full cooperation of congressional Republicans, some of whom were fiercely independent men. Over such figures Jefferson exercised political mastery. He established close ties with the leaders of both Houses of Congress, and while he seldom announced his plans in public, he made certain that his legislative lieutenants knew exactly what he desired. Contemporaries who described Jefferson as a weak president—and some Federalists did just that—did not read the scores of memoranda he sent to political friends or witness the informal meetings he held at the executive mansion with important Republicans. In two terms as president, Jefferson never had to veto a single act of Congress.

Jefferson carefully selected the members of his cabinet. During Washington's administration, he had witnessed—even provoked—severe infighting; as president, he nominated only those who enthusiastically supported his programs. James Madison, the leading figure at the Constitutional Convention, became secretary of state. For the Treasury, Jefferson chose Albert Gallatin, a Swiss-born financier who understood the complexities of the federal budget. Henry Dearborn, secretary of war, and Levi Lincoln, attorney general, were less impressive individuals, but they both came from Massachusetts, a Federalist stronghold in which Jefferson hoped to win Republican support. Robert Smith agreed to serve as secretary of the navy. "If I had the universe to choose from," the President announced, "I could not change one of my associates to my better satisfaction."

Jeffersonian Reforms

A top priority of the new government was cutting the national debt. Throughout American history, presidents have advocated such reductions, but in the twentieth century, few have achieved them. Jefferson succeeded. He and Gallatin regarded a large federal deficit as dangerous to the health of republican institutions. In fact, both men associated debt with Alexander Hamilton's Federalist financial programs (see chapter 7), measures they considered harmful to republicanism. Jefferson

claimed that legislators elected by the current generation did not have the right to mortgage the future of unborn Americans.

Jefferson also wanted to diminish the activities of the federal government. He urged Congress to repeal all direct taxes, including the hated Whiskey Tax that had sparked an insurrection in 1794. Secretary Gallatin linked federal income to the carrying trade. He calculated that the entire cost of national government could be borne by customs receipts. As long as commerce flourished, revenues provided sufficient sums. When international war closed foreign markets, however, the flow of funds dried up.

To help pay the debt inherited from the Adams administration, Jefferson ordered substantial cuts in the national budget. The President closed several American embassies in Europe. He also slashed military spending. In his first term Jefferson reduced the size of the United States Army by 50 percent. This decision left only three thousand soldiers to guard the entire frontier. In addition, he retired a majority of the navy's warships. When New Englanders claimed that these cuts left the country defenseless, Jefferson countered with a disarming argument. As ships of the United States Navy sailed the world's oceans, he claimed, they were liable to provoke hostilities, perhaps even war; hence by reducing the size of the fleet, he promoted peace.

More than budgetary considerations prompted Jefferson's military reductions. He was deeply suspicious of standing armies. In the event of foreign attack, he reasoned, the militia would rise in defense of the Republic. No doubt, his experiences during the Revolution influenced his thinking on military affairs, for in 1776 an aroused populace had taken up arms against the British. To ensure that the citizen soldiers would receive professional leadership in battle, Jefferson created the Army Corps of Engineers and the military academy at West Point in 1802.

Political patronage greatly annoyed the new President. Loyal Republicans throughout the United States had worked hard for Jefferson's victory, and as soon as he took office, they stormed the executive mansion seeking federal employment. While the President controlled several hundred jobs, he refused to dismiss all the Federalists. To be sure, he acted quickly to remove the so-called midnight appointees, highly partisan selections that Adams had made after learning of Jefferson's election. But to transform federal hiring into an undisciplined spoils system, especially at the highest levels of the federal bureaucracy, seemed to Jefferson to be shortsighted. Moderate Federalists might be converted to the Republican party, and in any case, there was a good chance that they possessed the expertise needed to run the government. At the end of his first term, one half of the people holding office were appointees of Washington and Adams.

Jefferson's political moderation helped hasten the demise of the Federalist party. This loose organization had nearly destroyed itself during the election of 1800 (see chapter 7), and following Adams' defeat, prominent Federalist spokesmen such as Fisher Ames and John Jay withdrew from national affairs. They refused to adopt the popular forms of campaigning that the Republicans had developed so successfully during the late 1790s. The mere prospect of flattering the common people was odious enough to drive some Federalists into political retirement.

Many of them also sensed that national expansion worked against their interests. The creation of new states and congressional reapportionment inevitably seemed to increase the number of Republican representatives in Washington. By 1805 the Federalists retained only a few seats in New England and Delaware. "The power of the [Jefferson] Administration," confessed John Quincy Adams in 1802, "rests upon the support of a much stronger majority of the people throughout the Union than the former administrations ever possessed since the first establishment of the Constitution."

After 1804 a group of younger Federalists belatedly attempted to pump life into the dying party. They experimented with popular election techniques. In some states they tightened party organization, held nominating conventions, and campaigned energetically for office. These were essential reforms, for as one Federalist explained, the party would surely die if its leaders did no more than write "private letters to each other." But with the exception of a brief Federalist revival in the Northeast between 1807 and 1814, the results of these activities were disappointing. Even the younger Federalists felt it was demeaning to appeal for votes. The diehards like Timothy Pickering promoted wild secessionist schemes in New England, while the most promising moderates—John Quincy Adams and William Plumer, for example—joined the Republicans.

Louisiana Purchase

When Jefferson first took office, he was confident that Louisiana as well as Florida would eventually become part of the United States. After all, Spain owned the territory, and Jefferson assumed that he could persuade the rulers of that notoriously weak nation to sell their colonies. If that peaceful strategy failed, the President was prepared to threaten forceable occupation.

In May 1801, however, prospects for the easy or inevitable acquisition of Louisiana suddenly darkened. Jefferson learned that Spain had secretly transferred title to the entire region to France, its powerful northern neighbor. To make matters worse, the French leader Napoleon seemed intent upon reestablishing an empire in North America. Even as Jefferson sought additional information concerning the details of the transfer, Napoleon was dispatching a large army to put down a rebellion in France's sugar-rich Caribbean colony, Santo Domingo. From that island stronghold in the West Indies, French troops could seize New Orleans and close the Mississippi River to American trade.

A sense of crisis enveloped Washington. Some congressmen urged Jefferson to prepare for war against France. Tensions increased when the Spanish officials who still governed New Orleans announced the closing of that port to American commerce (October 1802). Jefferson and his advisers assumed that the Spanish had acted upon orders from France, but despite this serious provocation, the President preferred negotiations to war. In January 1803 he asked James Monroe, a loyal Republican from Virginia, to join the American Minister, Robert Livingston, in Paris. The President instructed the two men to explore the possibility of purchasing the city of New Orleans. Lest they underestimate the importance of their diplomatic mission, Jefferson reminded them, "There is on the globe one single spot, the possessor of which is our natural and habitual enemy. It is New Orleans." If Livingston and Monroe failed, Jefferson realized that he would be forced to turn to Great Britain for military assistance. Depen-

■ *By 1803, when this view was painted, New Orleans was already a thriving port and an important outlet for products from the growing frontier. President Jefferson recognized the strategic location of the city and determined to buy it from France.*

dence upon that country seemed repellent, but he recognized that as soon as French troops moved into Louisiana, "we must marry ourselves to the British fleet and nation."

By the time Monroe joined Livingston in France, Napoleon had lost interest in establishing an American empire. The army he sent to Santo Domingo defeated the rebels but succumbed to tropical diseases. By the end of 1802 over thirty thousand veteran troops had died. In a fit of disgust, Napoleon announced, "Damn sugar, damn coffee, damn colonies . . . I renounce Louisiana." The diplomats from the United States knew nothing of these developments. They were taken by complete surprise, therefore, when they learned that Talleyrand, the French minister for foreign relations, had offered to sell the entire Louisiana Territory in April 1803. For only $15 million the Americans doubled the size of the United States. In fact, Livingston and Monroe were not certain how much land they had actually purchased. When they asked Talleyrand whether the deal included Florida, he responded ambiguously, "You have made a noble bargain for yourselves, and I suppose you will make the most of it." Even at that moment, Livingston realized that the transaction would alter the course of

American history. "From this day," he wrote, "the United States take their place among the powers of first rank."

In the midst of the Louisiana controversy, Jefferson dispatched a secret message to Congress requesting $2500 for the exploration of the Far West (January 1803). How closely this decision was connected to the Paris negotiations is not clear. Whatever the case may have been, the President asked his talented private secretary, Meriwether Lewis, to discover whether the Missouri River "may offer the most direct & practicable water communication across this continent for the purposes of commerce." The President also regarded the expedition as a wonderful opportunity to collect precise data about flora and fauna. He personally instructed Lewis in the latest techniques of scientific observation. While preparing for this great adventure, Lewis' second-in-command, William Clark, assumed such a prominent role that the effort became known as the Lewis and Clark Expedition. The exploring party set out from St. Louis in May 1804, and after barely surviving crossing the snow-covered Rocky Mountains, with their food supply running dangerously low Americans reached the Pacific Ocean in November 1805. The group re-

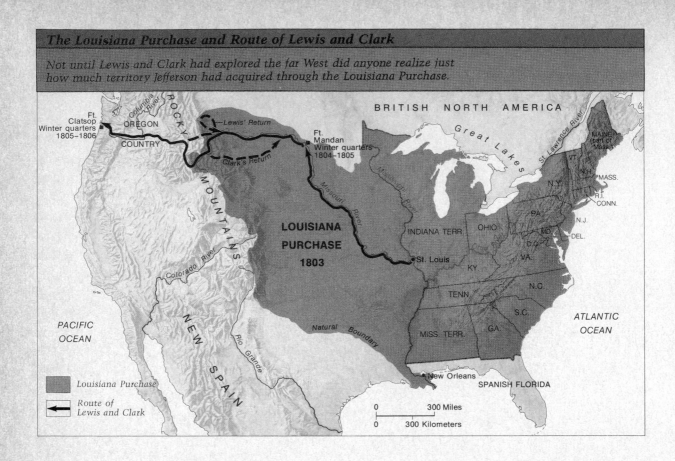

The Louisiana Purchase and Route of Lewis and Clark

Not until Lewis and Clark had explored the far West did anyone realize just how much territory Jefferson had acquired through the Louisiana Purchase.

turned safely the following September. The results of this expedition not only fulfilled Jefferson's scientific expectations, but also reaffirmed his faith in the future economic prosperity of the United States.

The American people responded enthusiastically to news of the Louisiana purchase. The only criticism came from a few disgruntled Federalists in New England who thought that the United States was already too large. Jefferson, of course, was immensely relieved. The nation had avoided war with France. Nevertheless, he worried that the treaty might be unconstitutional. The President pointed out that the Constitution did not specifically authorize the acquisition of vast new territories and the incorporation of thousands of foreign citizens. To escape this apparent legal dilemma, Jefferson proposed an amendment to the Constitution. Few persons, even his closest advisers, shared the President's scruples. Events in France soon forced Jefferson to adopt a more pragmatic course. When he heard that Napoleon had become impatient for his money, Jefferson

rushed the treaty to a Senate eager to ratify the agreement and nothing more was said about amending the Constitution.

Jefferson's fears about the incorporation of this new territory were not unwarranted. The area that eventually became the state of Louisiana (1812) contained many people of French and Spanish background who possessed no familiarity with representative institutions. Their laws had been autocratic; their local government corrupt. To allow such persons to elect a representative assembly struck the President as dangerous. He did not even know whether the population of Louisiana would remain loyal to the United States. Jefferson, therefore, recommended to Congress a transitional government consisting entirely of appointed officials. In March 1804 the Louisiana Government Bill narrowly passed the House of Representatives. Members of the President's own party attacked the plan. After all, it imposed taxes on the citizens of Louisiana without their consent. According to one outspoken Tennessee congressman, the bill "establishes a

The drawing above is from the 1812 edition of Patrick Gass' Journal, one of the first authentic accounts of Lewis and Clark's Expedition. To the left is the elk-skin bound diary that Clark used to take field notes. Samples of Clark's drawings include a diagram showing how the Chinook Indians flattened their infants' heads by binding them between two boards; a salmon trout; and a map of the area near the Great Falls of Columbia.

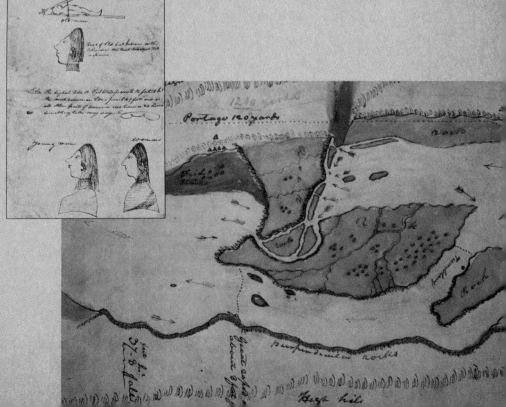

The Election of 1804		
Candidate	Party	Electoral Vote
Jefferson	Republican	162
Pinckney	Federalist	14

complete despotism." Most troubling perhaps was the fact that the legislation ran counter to Jefferson's well-known republican principles.

Nonetheless, Jefferson concluded his first term on a wave of popularity. He had maintained the peace, reduced taxes, and expanded the boundaries of the United States. Not surprisingly, he overwhelmed his Federalist opponent in the presidential election of 1804. In the electoral college Jefferson received 162 votes to Charles Cotesworth Pinckney's 14. Republicans controlled Congress. John Randolph, the most articulate member of the House of Representatives, exclaimed, "Never was there an administration more brilliant than that of Mr. Jefferson up to this period. We were indeed in 'the full tide of successful experiment!'"

Sources of Political Dissension

At the moment of Jefferson's greatest electoral victory, a perceptive person might have seen signs of serious division within the Republican party and within the country. The President's heavy-handed attempts to reform the federal courts stirred deep animosities. Republicans had begun sniping at other Republicans, and one leading member of the party, Aaron Burr, became involved in a bizarre plot to separate the West from the rest of the nation. Congressional debates over the future of the slave trade revealed the existence of powerful sectional loyalties and profound disagreement on the issue.

Attack on the Judges

Jefferson's controversy with the federal bench commenced the moment he first became president. The Federalists, realizing that they would soon lose control over the executive branch, passed the Judiciary Act of 1801. This bill created

several circuit courts and sixteen new judgeships. Through his "midnight" appointments, Adams quickly filled these positions with stalwarts of the Federalist party. Such blatantly partisan behavior angered Jefferson. In the courts, he explained, the Federalists hoped to preserve their political influence, and "from that battery all the works of Republicanism are to be beaten down and erased." Even more infuriating was Adams' appointment of John Marshall as the new chief justice. This shrewd, largely self-educated Virginian of Federalist background, whose training in the laws consisted of a series of lectures he attended at William and Mary College in 1780, was clearly a man who could hold his own against the new President.

In January 1802 Jefferson's congressional allies called for repeal of the Judiciary Act. In public debate they studiously avoided the obvious political issue. They argued that the new circuit courts should be closed not only because they were staffed by Federalists but also because they were needlessly expensive. The judges did not hear enough cases to warrant continuance. The Federalists mounted an able defense. The Constitution, they observed, provided for the removal of federal judges only when they were found guilty of high crimes and misdemeanors. By repealing the Judiciary Act, the legislative branch would in effect be dismissing judges without a trial, a clear violation of their constitutional rights. This argument made little impression upon the Republican party. In March Congress voted overwhelmingly for repeal.

While Congress debated the Judiciary Act, another battle suddenly erupted. One of Adams' "midnight" appointees, William Marbury, complained that the new administration would not give him his commission for the office of justice of the peace for the District of Columbia. He sought redress before the Supreme Court, demanding that the federal justices compel James Madison, the secretary of state, to deliver the necessary papers. When they learned that Marshall had agreed to hear this case, the Republicans were furious. Apparently the chief justice wanted to provoke a confrontation with the executive branch.

Marshall was too clever to jeopardize the independence of the Supreme Court over this relatively minor issue. In his celebrated *Marbury* v.

Madison decision (February 1803), Marshall berated the secretary of state for withholding Marbury's commission. Nevertheless, he concluded that the Supreme Court did not possess jurisdiction over such matters. Poor Marbury was out of luck. The Republicans proclaimed victory. In fact, they were so pleased with the outcome that they failed to examine the logic of Marshall's decision. He had ruled that part of the earlier act of Congress, the one on which Marbury based his appeal, was unconstitutional. This was the first time that the Supreme Court asserted its right to judge the constitutionality of congressional acts, and while contemporaries did not fully appreciate the significance of Marshall's doctrine, *Marbury* v. *Madison* later served as an important precedent for judicial review of federal statutes.

Neither Marbury's defeat nor repeal of the Judiciary Act placated extreme Republicans. They insisted that federal judges should be made more responsive to the will of the people. One solution, short of electing federal judges, was impeachment. This clumsy device provided the legislature with a way of removing particularly obnoxious individuals. Early in 1803, John Pickering, an incompetent judge from New Hampshire, presented the Republicans with a curious test case. This Federalist appointee suffered from alcoholism as well as insanity. While his outrageous behavior on the bench embarrassed everyone, Pickering had not committed any high crimes against the United States government. Ignoring such legal niceties, Jefferson's congressional allies pushed for impeachment. Although the Senate convicted Pickering (March 1804), many senators refused to compromise the letter of the Constitution and were conspicuously absent on the day of the final vote.

Jefferson was apparently so eager to purge the courts of Federalists that he failed to heed these warnings. By the spring of 1803 he had set his sights on a target far more important than John Pickering. In a Baltimore newspaper, the President stumbled upon the transcript of a speech allegedly delivered before a federal grand jury. The words seemed almost treasonous. The person responsible was Samuel Chase, a justice of the Supreme Court, who had frequently attacked Republican policies. Jefferson leapt at the chance to remove Chase from office. Indeed, the moment he learned of Chase's actions, the President wrote

to a leading Republican congressman, asking, "Ought the seditious and offical attack on the principles of our Contitution . . . go unpunished?" The congressman took the hint. In a matter of weeks, the Republican-controlled House of Representatives indicted Chase.

Even at this early stage of the impeachment, some members of Congress expressed uneasiness. The charges drawn up against the judge were purely political. There was no doubt that the judge's speech had been indiscreet. He had told the Baltimore jurors that "our late reformers"—in other words, the Republicans—threatened "peace and order, freedom and property." But while Chase lacked good judgment, his attack on the Jefferson administration hardly seemed criminal. Nathaniel Macon, a powerful Republican con-

■ *Presiding officer Aaron Burr ordered extra seating installed in the Senate chamber to accommodate the spectators who attended Justice Chase's impeachment trial.*

REPORT

OF THE

T R I A L

OF THE

HON. SAMUEL CHASE,

ONE OF THE ASSOCIATE JUSTICES

OF THE

SUPREME COURT OF THE UNITED STATES,

BEFORE THE

HIGH COURT OF IMPEACHMENT,

COMPOSED OF THE

Senate of the United States,

FOR CHARGES EXHIBITED AGAINST HIM BY THE

HOUSE OF REPRESENTATIVES,

In the name of themselves, and of all the People of the United States,

FOR

HIGH CRIMES & MISDEMEANORS,

SUPPOSED TO HAVE BEEN BY HIM COMMITTED;

WITH THE NECESSARY

DOCUMENTS AND OFFICIAL PAPERS,

From his Impeachment to final Acquital.

TAKEN IN SHORT HAND,

BY CHARLES EVANS,

AND THE ARGUMENTS OF COUNSEL REVISED BY THEM

FROM HIS MANUSCRIPT.

BALTIMORE:

PRINTED FOR SAMUEL BUTLER AND GEORGE KEATINGE.

1805.

gressman from North Carolina, wondered aloud, "Is error of opinion to be dreaded where enquiry is free?" This was the sort of question that Jefferson himself had asked the Federalists following passage of the Alien and Sedition Acts, but in 1804 Macon went unanswered. It was clear that if the Senate convicted Chase, every member of the Supreme Court, including Marshall, might also be dismissed.

Chase's trial before the United States Senate was one of the most dramatic events in American legal history. Aaron Burr, the vice-president, organized the proceedings, and for reasons known only to himself, Burr redecorated the Senate chamber so that it looked more like the British House of Lords than the meeting place of a republican legislature. In this luxurious setting, Chase and his lawyers conducted a masterful defense. By contrast, John Randolph, the congressman who served as chief prosecutor, behaved in an erratic manner, betraying repeatedly his ignorance of relevant points of law. While most Republican senators personally disliked the arrogant Chase, they refused to expand the constitutional definition of impeachable offenses to suit Randolph's argument, and on March 1, 1805, the Senate acquitted the justice of all charges. The experience apparently convinced Chase of the need for greater moderation. After returning to the federal bench, he refrained from attacking Republican policies. His Jeffersonian opponents also learned something important. American politicians do not like tampering with the Constitution in order to get rid of specific judges, even an imprudent one like Chase.

Critics and Conspirators

The collapse of the Federalists on the national level encouraged dissension within the Republican party. Extremists in Congress insisted upon monopolizing the President's ear, and when he listened to political moderates, they rebelled. The members of the most vociferous faction called themselves "the *good old* republicans"; the newspapers labeled them the "Tertium Quids," literally translated a "third something." During Jefferson's second term, the Quids argued that the President's policies, foreign and domestic, sacrificed virtue for pragmatism. Their chief spokes-

men were two members from Virginia, John Randolph and John Taylor of Caroline (the name of his plantation), both of whom were convinced that Jefferson had betrayed the republican purity of the Founding Fathers. They both despised commercial capitalism. Taylor urged Americans to return to a simple agrarian way of life. Randolph's attacks were particularly shrill. He saved his sharpest barbs for Gallatin and Madison, Republican moderates who failed to appreciate the congressman's self-righteous posturing.

The Yazoo controversy raised the Quids from political obscurity. Randolph and his friends transformed the issue into a moral crusade, and contemporaries reported that at the height of the dispute, Randolph could destroy a rival merely by labeling him a "Yazoo" man. This complex legal battle began in 1795 when a throroughly corrupt Georgia assembly sold 35 million acres of western land, known as the Yazoo claims, to private companies at bargain prices. It soon became apparent that every member of the legislature had been bribed, and in 1796 state lawmakers rescinded the entire agreement. Unfortunately, some land had already changed hands. When Jefferson became president a specially appointed federal commission attempted to settle the mess. It recommended that Congress set aside 5 million acres for buyers who had unwittingly purchased land from the discredited companies.

Randolph immediately cried foul. Such a compromise, however well-meaning, condoned fraud. Republican virtue hung in the balance. For months the Quids harangued Congress about the Yazoo business, but in the end their impassioned oratory accomplished nothing. The Marshall Supreme Court upheld the rights of the original purchasers in *Fletcher* v. *Peck* (1810). The justices unanimously declared that legislative fraud did not impair private contracts and that the Georgia assembly of 1796 did not have authority to take away lands already sold to innocent buyers. This important case upheld the Supreme Court's authority to rule on the constitutionality of state laws.

Vice-President Aaron Burr created far more serious difficulties for the President. The two men had never been close. Burr's strange behavior during the election of 1800 (see chapter 7) raised suspicions that he had conspired to deprive Jefferson of the presidency. Whatever the truth may

■ *Frustrated in his attempt to win national political power, Aaron Burr initiated a series of maneuverings that led eventually to his downfall.*

have been, the vice-president entered the new administration under a cloud. He played only a marginal role in shaping policy, a situation extremely frustrating for a person as ambitious as Burr.

In the spring of 1804 Burr decided to run for the governorship of New York. Although he was a Republican, he entered into political negotiations with High Federalists who were plotting the secession of New England and New York from the Union. In a particularly scurrilous contest—and New York politics were always abusive— Alexander Hamilton described Burr as " . . . a dangerous man . . . who ought not to be trusted with the reins of government" and urged Federalists in the state to vote for another candidate.

Whether Hamilton's appeals influenced the voters is not clear. Burr, however, blamed Hamilton for his subsequent defeat and challenged his tormentor to a duel. Even though Hamilton condemned this form of violence—his own son had recently been killed in a duel—he accepted Burr's "invitation." On July 11, 1804, at Weehawken, New Jersey, the vice-president shot and killed the former secretary of the treasury. Both New York and New Jersey indicted Burr for murder. If he returned to either state, he would immediately be arrested. His political career lay in shambles.

In his final weeks as vice-president, Burr hatched a scheme so audacious that the people with whom he dealt could not decide whether he was a genius or a madman. Burr covered his tracks well. No two contacts ever heard the same story. On a trip down the Ohio River in April 1805 after his term as vice-president was over, he hinted broadly that he was planning a filibustering operation against a Spanish colony, perhaps Mexico. Burr also suggested that he envisioned separating the western states and territories from the Union. The region certainly seemed ripe for secession. The citizens of New Orleans acted as if they wanted no part of the United States. Wherever Burr traveled, he recruited adventurers; he mingled with the leading politicians of Kentucky, Ohio, and Tennessee. James Wilkinson, commander of the United States Army in the Mississippi Valley, accepted an important role in this vaguely defined conspiracy. The general was a thoroughly corrupt opportunist. Randolph described him as "the only man that I ever saw who was from bark to the very core a villain."

In the late summer of 1806 Burr put his ill-defined plan into action. A small group of volunteers constructed riverboats on a small island in the Ohio River owned by Harman Blennerhassett, an Irish immigrant who found Burr's charm irresistible. By the time this armed band set out to join Wilkinson's forces, however, the general had experienced a change of heart. He frantically dispatched letters to Jefferson denouncing Burr. Wilkinson's betrayal destroyed any chance of success, and conspirators throughout the West rushed pell-mell to save their own skins. Facing certain defeat, Burr tried to escape to Spanish Florida. It was already too late. Federal authorities arrested Burr in February 1807 and took him to Richmond to stand trial for treason. The prospect of humiliating his old rival was hardly displeasing to the President. Even before a jury had been called, Jefferson announced publicly that Burr's guilt "is placed beyond all question."

Jefferson spoke prematurely. John Adams wisely observed, if Burr's "guilt is as clear as the Noon day Sun, the first Magistrate ought not to have pronounced it so before a Jury had tryed him."

The trial judge was John Marshall, a strong Federalist not likely to do the Republican administration any favors. During the entire proceedings, Marshall insisted upon a narrow constitutional definition of treason. He refused to hear testimony regarding Burr's supposed intentions. "Troops must be embodied," Marshall thundered, "men must be actually assembled." He demanded two witnesses to each overt act of treason.

Burr, of course, had been too clever to leave this sort of evidence. While Jefferson complained bitterly about the miscarriage of justice, the jurors declared on September 1, 1807, that the defendant was "not proved guilty by any evidence submitted to us." The public was outraged, and Burr prudently went into exile in Europe. The President threatened to introduce an amendment to the Constitution calling for the election of federal judges. Nothing came of his proposal. And Marshall, who behaved in an undeniably partisan manner, inadvertently helped protect the civil rights of all Americans. If the chief justice had allowed circumstantial evidence into the Richmond courtroom, if he had listened to rumor and hearsay, he would have made it much easier for later presidents to use trumped-up conspiracy charges to silence legitimate political opposition.

Trying to End the Slave Trade

Slavery sparked angry debate at the Constitutional Convention of 1787. If delegates from the northern states had refused to compromise on this issue, Southerners would not have supported the new government. The slave states demanded a great deal in return for cooperation. According to an agreement that determined the size of a state's congressional delegation, a slave counted as three-fifths of a free white male (see chapter 6). This political formula meant that while blacks did not vote, they helped increase the number of southern representatives. The South in turn gave up very little, agreeing only that after 1808 Congress *might consider* banning the importation of slaves into the United States. Slaves even influenced the outcome of national elections. Had the three-fifths rule not been in effect in 1800, for example, Adams would surely have had the votes to defeat Jefferson in the electoral college.

In an annual message sent to Congress in December 1806, Jefferson urged the representatives to prepare legislation outlawing the slave trade. During the early months of 1807, congressmen debated various ways of ending this embarrassing commerce. It was clear that the issue cut across party lines. Northern representatives generally favored a strong bill; some even wanted to make smuggling slaves into the country a capital offense. But there was a serious problem. The northern congressmen could not figure out what to do with black people captured by the customs agents who would enforce the legislation. To sell these Africans would involve the federal government in slavery, something which many Northerners found morally repugnant. Nor was there much sympathy for freeing them. Ignorant of the English language and lacking personal possessions, it seemed unlikely that these blacks could long survive free in the American South.

Southern congressmen responded with threats and ridicule. They explained to their northern colleagues that no one in the South regarded slavery as evil. It appeared naive, therefore, to expect local planters to enforce a ban on the slave trade or to inform federal agents when they spotted a smuggler. The notion that these culprits deserved capital punishment seemed viciously inappropriate. At one point in the debate, Peter Early, a congressman from Georgia, announced that the South wanted "no civil wars, no rebellions, no insurrections, no resistance to the authority of government." All he demanded, in fact, was to let the states regulate slavery. To this, a Republican congressman from western Pennsylvania retorted that Americans who hated slavery would not be "terrified by the threat of civil war."

The bill that Jefferson finally signed in March 1807 probably pleased no one. The law prohibited the importation of slaves into the United States after the new year. Whenever customs officials captured a smuggler, the slaves were turned over to state authorities and disposed of according to local custom. Southerners did not cooperate, and for many years African slaves continued to pour into southern ports. Ironically, even more blacks would have been imported had Great Britain not outlawed the slave trade in 1807. Ships of the Royal Navy seized American smugglers off the coast of Africa, and when anyone complained, the British explained that they were merely enforcing the laws of the United States.

Failure of Foreign Policy

During Jefferson's second term (1805–1809), the United States found itself in the midst of a world at war. A brief peace in Europe ended abruptly in 1803, and the two military giants of the age, France and Great Britain, fought for supremacy on land and sea. This was a kind of total war unknown in the eighteenth century. Napoleon's armies carried the ideology of the French Revolution across the continent. The emperor—as Napoleon Bonaparte called himself after December 1804—transformed conquered nations into French satellites. Only Britain offered effective resistance. On October 21, 1805, Admiral Horatio Nelson destroyed the main French fleet at the battle of Trafalgar, demonstrating decisively the absolute supremacy of the Royal Navy. But only a few weeks later (December 2, 1805), Napoleon crushed British forces at the battle of Austerlitz and confirmed his clear superiority on land.

During the early stages of the war, the United States profited from European adversity. As "neutral carriers," American ships transported goods to any port in the world where they could find a buyer, and American merchants grew wealthy serving Britain and France. Since the Royal Navy did not allow direct trade between France and its colonies, American captains conducted "broken voyages." Vessels sailing out of French ports in the Caribbean would put in briefly in the United States, pay nominal customs, and then leave for France. For several years, the British did little to halt this obvious subterfuge.

Napoleon's successes on the battlefield, however, quickly strained Britain's economic resources. In July 1805 a British admiralty court announced in the *Essex* decision that henceforth "broken voyages" were illegal. The Royal Navy began seizing American ships in record number. Moreover, as the war continued, the British stepped up the impressment of sailors on ships flying the United States flag. Estimates of the number of men impressed ranged as high as nine thousand.

Beginning in 1806, the British government issued a series of trade regulations known as "Orders in Council." These proclamations forbade neutral commerce with the Continent and threatened any ship that violated these orders with seizure. The declarations created what were in

■ *American sailors faced the danger of impressment—being removed from American merchant ships and forced into labor on British war vessels.*

effect "paper blockades," for even the powerful British navy could not monitor the activities of every Continental port.

Napoleon responded to Britain's commercial regulations with his own "paper blockade," called the Continental System. In the Berlin Decree of November 1806 and the Milan Decree of December 1807, he announced the closing of all Continental ports to British trade. Since French armies occupied most of the territory between Spain and Germany, the decrees obviously cut the British out of a large market. The French emperor also declared that neutral vessels carrying British goods were liable to seizure. For the Americans there was no escape. They were caught between two conflicting systems. The British ordered American ships to stop off on the way to the Continent; Napoleon was determined to seize any vessel that obeyed the British.

This unhappy turn of international events baffled Jefferson. He had assumed that civilized countries would respect neutral rights; justice obliged them to do so. Appeals to reason, however, made little impression upon states at war. "As for France and England," the President growled, " . . . the one is a den of robbers, the other of pirates." In a desperate attempt to avoid hostilities for which the United States was ill-prepared, Jefferson ordered James Monroe and William Pinckney to negotiate a commercial treaty with Great Britain. The document they signed on December 31, 1806, said nothing about the obnoxious practice of impressment, and an angry President refused to submit the treaty to the Senate for ratification.

The United States soon suffered an even greater humiliation. A ship of the Royal Navy, the *Leopard*, sailing off the coast of Virginia, commanded an American warship to submit to a search for deserters (June 21, 1807). When the captain of the *Chesapeake* refused to cooperate, the *Leopard* opened fire, killing three men and wounding eighteen. The attack clearly violated the sovereignty of the United States. Official protests received only a perfunctory apology from the British government, and the American people demanded revenge.

Despite the pressure of public opinion, however, Jefferson played for time. He recognized that the United States was unprepared for war against a powerful nation like Great Britain. The President worried that an expensive conflict with Great Britain would quickly undo the fiscal reforms of his first term. As Gallatin explained, in the event of war the United States "will be poorer, both as a nation and as a government, our debt and taxes will increase, and our progress in every respect be interrupted."

Embargo Divides the Nation

Jefferson found what he regarded as a satisfactory way to deal with European predators with a policy he called "peaceable coercion." If Britain and France refused to respect the rights of neutral carriers, then the United States would keep its ships at home. Not only would this action protect them from seizure, it would also deprive the European powers of much needed American goods, especially food. The President predicted that a total embargo of American commerce would soon force Britain and France to negotiate with the United States in good faith. "Our commerce is so valuable to them," he declared, "that

■ *Many people opposed the embargo. This cartoonist, for example, saw it as a policy that allowed both England and France to take advantage of the United States.*

they will be glad to purchase it when the only price we ask is to do us justice." Congress passed the Embargo Act on December 22, 1807.

"Peaceable coercion" turned into a Jeffersonian nightmare. The President apparently believed that the American people would enthusiastically support the embargo. That was a naive assumption. Compliance required a series of enforcement acts that over fourteen months became increasingly harsh.

By the middle of 1808, Jefferson and Gallatin were involved in the regulation of the smallest details of American economic life. Indeed, in the words of one of Jefferson's biographers, Merrill D. Peterson, the President assumed the role of "commissar of the nation's economy." The federal government supervised the coastal trade, lest a ship sailing between two states slip away to Europe or the West Indies. Overland trade with Canada was proscribed. When violations still occurred, Congress gave customs collectors the right to seize a vessel merely on suspicion of wrongdoing. A final desperate act, passed in January 1809, prohibited the loading of any United States vessel, regardless of size, without authorization from a customs officer who was supported by the army, navy, and local militia. Jefferson's eagerness to pursue a reasonable foreign policy blinded him to the fact that he and a Republican Congress would have had to establish a police state to make it work.

Northerners hated the embargo. Persons living near Lake Champlain in upper New York State simply ignored the regulations, and they roughed up collectors who interfered with the Canadian trade. The administration was determined to stop the smugglers. Jefferson urged the governor of New York to call out the militia. "I think it so important," the President explained in August 1808, "... to crush these audacious proceedings, and to make the offenders feel the consequences of individuals daring to oppose a law by force, that no effort should be spared to compass the object." In a decision that George III might have applauded, Jefferson dispatched federal troops—led by the conspiratorial General Wilkinson—to overawe the citizens of New York.

New Englanders regarded the embargo as lunacy. Merchants of the region were willing to take their chances on the high seas, but for reasons that few people understood, the President insisted that it was better to preserve ships from possible seizure than to make profits. Sailors and artisans were thrown out of work. The popular press maintained a constant howl of protest. One writer observed that embargo in reverse spelled "O grab me!" A poem published in July 1808 captured the growing frustration:

> Our ships, all in motion,
> Once whitened the ocean,
>   They sail'd and returned with a cargo;
> Now doom'd to decay
> They have fallen a prey
>   To Jefferson, worms, and Embargo.

Not surprisingly, the Federalist party experienced a brief revival in New England, and a few extremists suggested the possibility of state assemblies nullifying federal law.

By 1809 the bankruptcy of Jefferson's foreign policy was obvious. The embargo never seriously damaged the British economy. In fact, British merchants rushed to take over the lucrative markets that the Americans had been forced to abandon. Napoleon liked the embargo, since it seemed to harm Great Britain more than it did France. Faced with growing popular opposition, the Republicans in Congress panicked. One newly elected representative declared that "peaceful coercion" was a "miserable and mischievous failure" and joined his colleagues in repealing the embargo a few days before James Madison's inauguration. Relations between the United States and the great European powers were much worse in 1809 than they had been in 1805. During his second term, the pressures of office weighed heavily upon Jefferson, and after so many years of public service, he welcomed retirement to Monticello.

Fumbling Toward War

As president, James Madison suffered from several personal and political handicaps. Although his intellectual abilities were great, he lacked the qualities necessary for effective leadership. In public gatherings, he impressed people as being "exceedingly modest," and one foreign visitor claimed that the new President " . . . always seems to grant that the one with whom he talks is his superior in mind and training." Critics argued that Madison's humility revealed a weak, vacillating character.

During the election of 1808, Randolph and the Quids tried unsuccessfully to persuade James Monroe to challenge Madison's candidacy. Jefferson favored his old friend Madison. In the end, a caucus of Republican congressmen gave the official nod to Madison, the first time in American history that such a congressional group controlled a presidential nomination. While the former secretary of state defeated his Federalist rival, Charles Cotesworth Pinckney, in the electoral college by the margin of 122 to 47, the Federalists made impressive gains in the House of Representatives. Madison compounded his difficulties by appointing cabinet members who actively opposed his policies.

The Election of 1808		
Candidate	Party	Electoral Vote
Madison	Republican	122
Pinckney	Federalist	47

■ *Dolley Madison, a charming and vivacious woman, hosted popular informal entertainments at the White House and set the standard for future First Ladies.*

The new President confronted the same foreign policy problems that had occupied his predecessor. Neither Britain nor France showed the slightest interest in respecting American neutral rights. Threats against either nation rang hollow so long as the United States failed to develop its military strength. Out of weakness, therefore, Madison was compelled to put the Non-Intercourse Act into effect. Congress passed this clumsy piece of legislation at the same time that it repealed the Embargo (March 1, 1809). The new bill authorized the resumption of trade between the United States and all nations of the world *except* Britain and France. Either of these countries could restore full commercial relations simply by promising to observe the rights of neutral carriers.

The British immediately took advantage of this offer. Their minister to the United States, David M. Erskine, informed Madison that the British government had modified its position on a number of sensitive commercial issues. The President was so encouraged by these talks that he publicly announced that trade with Great Britain could resume on June 10, 1809. Unfortunately, Erskine had not conferred with his superiors on the details of these negotiations. George Canning, the

foreign secretary, rejected the agreement out of hand, and while an embarrassed Madison fumed in Washington, the Royal Navy seized the American ships that had already put to sea.

Canning's apparent betrayal led the artless Madison straight into a French trap. In May 1810 Congress passed Macon's Bill Number Two, an act sponsored by Nathanial Macon of North Carolina. In a complete reversal of strategy, this poorly drafted legislation reestablished trade with *both* England and France. It also contained a curious carrot-and-stick provision. As soon as either of these European states repealed restrictions upon neutral shipping, the United States goverment promised to halt all commerce with the other.

Napoleon spotted a rare opportunity. He informed the United States minister in Paris that France would no longer enforce the hated Berlin and Milan Decrees. Again, Madison acted impulsively. Without waiting for further information from Paris, he announced that unless Britain repealed the Orders in Council by November, the United States would cut off commercial relations. Only later did the President learn that Napoleon had no intention of living up to his side of the bargain; his agents continued to seize American ships. Madison, who had been humiliated by the Erskine experience, decided to ignore the French provocations, to pretend that the Emperor was behaving in an honest manner. The British could not explain why the United States tolerated such obvious deception. No one in London suspected that the President really had no options left.

Events unrelated to international commerce fueled anti-British sentiment in the newly settled parts of the United States. Westerners believed— incorrectly as it turned out—that British agents operating out of Canada had persuaded Tecumseh's warriors to resist the spread of American settlement. According to the rumors that ran through the region, the British dreamed of monopolizing the fur trade. In any case, General William Henry Harrison, governor of the Indiana Territory, marched an army to the edge of a large Shawnee Village at the mouth of Tippecanoe Creek near the banks of the Wabash River. On the morning of November 7, 1811, the American troops routed the Indians at the battle of Tippecanoe. Harrison immediately became a national hero, and several decades later the American people rewarded "Tippecanoe" by electing him president. This incident forced Tecumseh to seek British military assistance, something he probably would not have done had Harrison left him alone.

In 1811 the anti-British mood of Congress intensified. A group of militant representatives, some of them elected to Congress for the first time in the election of 1810, announced that they would no longer tolerate national humiliation. They called for action, for resistance to Great Britain, for any course that promised to achieve respect for the United States and security for its republican institutions. These aggressive nationalists, many of them elected in the South and West, have sometimes been labeled the "War Hawks." The group included Henry Clay, an earthy Kentucky congressman who served as Speaker of the House, and John C. Calhoun, a brilliant South Carolinian. These fiery orators spoke of honor and pride, as if foreign relations were a sort of duel between gentlemen. While the War Hawks were Republicans, they repudiated Jefferson's policy of peaceful coercion.

Madison surrendered to the "War Hawks." On June 1, 1812, he sent Congress a declaration of war against Great Britain. The timing of his action was peculiar. Over the preceding months, tensions between the two nations had relaxed. No new attacks had occurred. Indeed, at the very moment that Madison called for war, the British government was suspending the Orders in Council, a conciliatory gesture that certainly would have preserved the peace. Because of the slowness of transatlantic communication, however, the President did not learn of this decision until Americans had already taken up arms.

Even contemporaries expressed confusion about the causes of the War of 1812. Madison's formal message to Congress listed Great Britain's violation of maritime rights, impressment of American seamen, and provocation of Indians. No doubt, the President was sincere, but since western and southern congressmen had no direct interest in neutral rights, one suspects that the War Hawks had other goals in mind. Some probably hoped to conquer Canada. For others the whole affair may have truly been a matter of national pride. Andrew Jackson wrote, *"For what are we going to fight? . . . we are going to fight for the reestablishment of our national character, misunderstood and vilified at home and abroad."*

■ *While Tecumseh was away, Shawnee tribesmen attacked the U.S. troops led by General William Henry Harrison. Although his troops lost more men than did the Indians, Harrison claimed the victory.*

The Election of 1812

Candidate	Party	Electoral Vote
Madison	Republican	128
Clinton	Republican* (antiwar faction)	89

*Clinton was nominated by a convention of antiwar Republicans and endorsed by the Federalists.

New Englanders in whose commercial interests the war would supposedly be waged ridiculed such chauvinism. The vote in Congress was close, 79 to 49 in the House, 19 to 13 in the Senate. With this doubtful mandate, the country marched to war against the most powerful maritime nation in Europe. Division over the war question was reflected in the election of 1812. A faction of antiwar Republicans nominated De Witt Clinton of New York, who was endorsed by the Federalists. Nevertheless Madison, the Republican candidate, won reelection, gaining 128 electoral votes to Clinton's 89.

The Strange War of 1812

Optimism ran high. The War Hawks apparently believed that even though the United States possessed only a small army and navy, it could easily sweep the British out of Canada. Such predictions flew in the face of political and military realities. Not only did the Republicans fail to appreciate how unprepared the country was for war, they also refused to mobilize needed resources. The House rejected proposals for direct taxes and authorized naval appropriations only with the greatest reluctance. Indeed, even as they planned for battle, the Republicans were haunted by the consequences of their political and economic convictions. They did not seem to understand that a weak, highly decentralized government— the one that Jeffersonians championed—was incapable of waging an expensive war against the world's greatest sea power.

New Englanders refused to cooperate with the war effort. In July 1812, one clergyman in Massachusetts urged the people of the region to "proclaim an honourable neutrality." Many persons did just that. New Englanders carried on a lucrative, though illegal, commerce with the enemy.

When the United States Treasury appealed for loans to finance the war, wealthy northern merchants failed to respond. The British government apparently believed that the New England states might negotiate a separate peace, and during the first year of war, the Royal Navy did not bother to blockade the major northern ports.

American military operations focused initially upon the western forts. The results were discouraging. On August 16, 1812, Major General William Hull surrendered an entire army to a smaller British force at Detroit. Michilimackinac was lost. Poorly coordinated marches against the enemy at Niagara and Montreal achieved nothing. These experiences demonstrated that the militia, no matter how enthusiastic, was no match for well-trained European veterans. On the sea, the United States did much better. In August, Captain Isaac Hull's *Constitution* defeated the H.M.S. *Guerriere* in a fierce battle, and American privateers destroyed or captured a number of British merchantmen. These successes were somewhat deceptive, however. So long as Napoleon threatened the Continent, Great Britain could spare few warships for service in America. As soon as peace returned to Europe in the spring of 1814, Britain redeployed its fleet and easily blockaded the tiny United States Navy.

The campaigns of 1813 revealed that conquering Canada would be more difficult than the War Hawks ever imagined. Both sides in this war recognized that whoever controlled the Great Lakes controlled the West. On Lake Erie the Americans won the race for naval superiority. On September 10, 1813, Oliver Hazard Perry destroyed a British fleet at Put-in-Bay, and in a much quoted letter written immediately after the battle, Perry exclaimed, "We have met the enemy; and they are ours." On October 5, General Harrison overran an army of British troops and Indian warriors at the battle of Thames River. During this engagement Tecumseh was killed. On the other fronts, however, the war went badly for the Americans. General Wilkinson suffered an embarrasing defeat near Montreal (battle of Chrysler's Farm, November 11), and the British navy held its own on Lake Ontario.

In 1814 the British took the offensive. Following their victory over Napoleon, British strategists planned to increase pressure on three separate American fronts: the Canadian frontier,

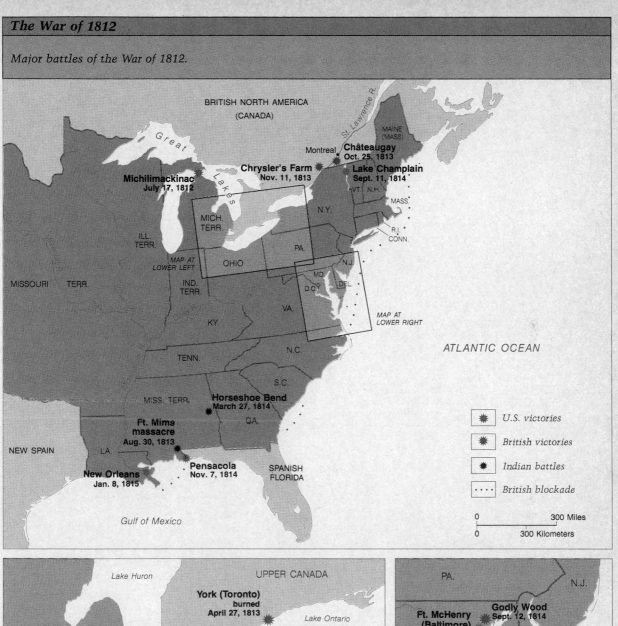

The War of 1812

Major battles of the War of 1812.

BRITISH NORTH AMERICA
(CANADA)

St. Lawrence R.

MAINE
('MASS)

Great Lakes

Montreal

Châteaugay
Oct. 25, 1813

Chrysler's Farm
Nov. 11, 1813

Lake Champlain
Sept. 11, 1814

Michilimackinac
July 17, 1812

VT. N.H.

N.Y.

MASS.

MICH.
TERR.

ILL.
TERR.

PA.

R.I.
CONN.

*MAP AT
LOWER LEFT*

OHIO

N.J.

MD.

D.C.

DEL.

MISSOURI   TERR.

IND.
TERR.

VA.

*MAP AT
LOWER RIGHT*

KY.

ATLANTIC OCEAN

TENN.

N.C.

S.C.

Horseshoe Bend
March 27, 1814

MISS. TERR.

GA.

**Ft. Mims
massacre**
Aug. 30, 1813

NEW SPAIN

LA.

Pensacola
Nov. 7, 1814

SPANISH
FLORIDA

New Orleans
Jan. 8, 1815

✸	*U.S. victories*
✸	*British victories*
✸	*Indian battles*
....	*British blockade*

Gulf of Mexico

0 ———— 300 Miles
0 ———— 300 Kilometers

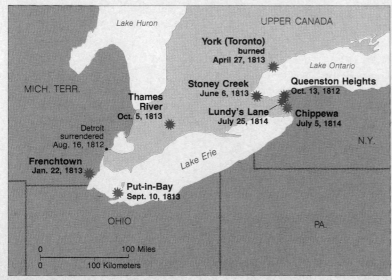

Lake Huron

UPPER CANADA

York (Toronto)
burned
April 27, 1813

Lake Ontario

MICH. TERR.

Stoney Creek
June 6, 1813

Queenston Heights
Oct. 13, 1812

**Thames
River**
Oct. 5, 1813

Lundy's Lane
July 25, 1814

Chippewa
July 5, 1814

Detroit
surrendered
Aug. 16, 1812

N.Y.

Frenchtown
Jan. 22, 1813

Lake Erie

Put-in-Bay
Sept. 10, 1813

OHIO

PA.

0 ———— 100 Miles
0 ———— 100 Kilometers

PA.

N.J.

Godly Wood
Sept. 12, 1814

**Ft. McHenry
(Baltimore)**
Sept. 13–14, 1814

Bladensburg
Aug. 24, 1814

Washington, D.C.
burned Aug. 24, 1814

DEL.

MD.

Chesapeake Bay

VA.

ATLANTIC
OCEAN

Craney I.
June 20, 1813

Same scale as
map at left

■ *Although the* Constitution's *defeat of the H.M.S.* Guerriere *was not a great strategic victory, it did provide the Americans with a much needed boost in morale.*

Chesapeake coastal settlements, and New Orleans. Sir George Prevost, commander of the British forces in Canada, marched his army south into upper New York State, the route taken by General John Burgoyne during the American Revolution. Prevost was even less successful than Burgoyne had been. A hastily assembled American fleet led by Captain Thomas Macdonough turned back a British flotilla off Plattsburg on Lake Champlain (September 11, 1814). When Prevost learned of this setback, he retreated quickly into Canada. Although the Americans did not realize the full significance of this battle, the triumph accelerated peace negotiations, for after news of Plattsburg reached London, the British government concluded that major land operations along the Canadian border were futile.

Throughout the year, British warships harassed the Chesapeake coast. To their surprise, the British found the region almost totally undefended, and on August 24, 1814, in retaliation for the Americans' destruction of the capital of Upper Canada (York, Ontario), a small force of British marines burned the nation's capital, a victory more symbolic than strategic. Encouraged by their easy success and contemptuous of America's ragtag soldiers, the British launched a full-scale attack on Baltimore (September 14). To everyone's surprise, the fort guarding the harbor held out against a heavy naval bombardment, and the British gave up the operation. The survival of Fort McHenry inspired Francis Scott Key to write "The Star-Spangled Banner."

The battle of New Orleans should never have occurred. The British landed a large assault force under General Edward Pakenham at precisely the same time that diplomats in Europe were preparing the final drafts of a peace treaty. The combatants, of course, knew nothing of these distant developments. An unusual army of Tennessee riflemen, city residents, and French pirates blocked the British route to New Orleans. On January 8, 1815, Pakenham foolishly ordered a frontal attack against General Andrew Jackson's well-defended positions, and in a matter of hours, the entire British force had been destroyed. The Americans suffered only light casualties. The victory not only transformed Jackson into a national folk hero, it also provided the people of the United States with a much needed source of pride. Even in military terms, the battle was significant, for if the British had managed to occupy New Orleans, they would have been difficult to dislodge regardless of the specific provisions of the peace treaty.

Hartford Convention: The Demise of the Federalists

In the fall of 1814, a group of leading New England politicians, most of them moderate Federalists, gathered in Hartford to discuss relations between the people of their region and the federal government. The delegates were angry and hurt by the Madison administration's seeming insensitivity to the economic interests of the New England states. The embargo had soured New Englanders on Republican foreign policy, but the events of the War of 1812 added insult to injury. When British troops occupied the coastal villages of Maine, then part of Massachusetts, the President did nothing to drive out the enemy. Of course, the self-righteous complaints of convention organizers overlooked New England's tepid support for the war effort.

The men who met at Hartford on December 15 did not advocate secession from the Union. Although people living in other sections of the

■ *This scene of the battle of New Orleans, painted from sketches drawn during the engagement, shows the Americans standing their ground against the British frontal assault. The Americans suffered only light casualties in the battle, but more than two thousand British soldiers were killed or wounded.*

country cried treason, the convention delegates only recommended changes in the Constitution. They drafted a number of amendments that reflected the New Englanders' growing frustration. One proposal suggested that congressional representation should be calculated on the basis of the number of white males living in a state. New England congressmen were tired of the three-fifths rule that gave southern slaveholders a disproportionally large voice in the House. The convention also wanted to limit each president to a single term in office, a reform that New Englanders hoped might end Virginia's monopoly of the executive mansion. And finally, the delegates insisted that a two-thirds majority was necessary before Congress could declare war, pass commercial regulations, or admit new states to the Union. The moderate Federalists of New England were confident that these constitutional changes would protect their region from the tyranny of southern Republicans.

The convention dispatched its resolutions to Washington, but soon after an official delegation reached the federal capital, the situation became extremely awkward. Everyone was celebrating the victory of New Orleans and the announcement of peace. Republican leaders in Congress accused the hapless New Englanders of disloyal-

ty, and people throughout the country were persuaded that a group of wild secessionists had attempted to destroy the Union. The Hartford Convention accelerated the final demise of the Federalist party.

Treaty of Ghent Ends the War

The czar of Russia originally offered to mediate the Anglo-American conflict. His fumbling efforts only wasted time, and it was not until August 8, 1814, that serious talks began in the Belgian city of Ghent. The United States sent a distinguished negotiating team: John Quincy Adams, Albert Gallatin, Henry Clay, James A. Bayard, and Jonathan Russell. The members of the British delegation were both more arrogant and more obscure. During the early weeks of discussions, they made impossible demands. They insisted upon territorial concessions from the United States, the right to navigate the Mississippi River, and the creation of a large Indian buffer state in the Northwest Territory. The Americans listened to this presentation, more or less politely, and then rejected the entire package. In turn, they lectured their British counterparts about maritime rights and impressment.

Chronology

1800 Thomas Jefferson elected president

1801 Adams makes "midnight" appointments of federal judges

1802 Judiciary Act is repealed (March)

1803 Chief Justice John Marshall rules on *Marbury* v. *Madison* (February); sets precedent for judicial review
Louisiana Purchase concluded with France (May)

1803–1806 Lewis and Clark explore the Northwest

1804 Aaron Burr kills Alexander Hamilton in a duel (July)
Jefferson elected to second term

1805 Justice Samuel Chase acquitted by Senate (March)

1807 American warship *Chesapeake* fired upon by British *Leopard* (June)
Burr is tried for conspiracy (August–September)
Embargo Act passed (December)

1808 Slave trade is ended (January)
Madison elected president

1809 Embargo is repealed; Non-Intercourse Act passed (March)

1810 Macon's Bill Number Two reestablishes trade with Britain and France (May)

1811 Harrison defeats Indians at Tippecanoe (November)

1812 Declaration of war against Great Britain (June)
Madison elected to second term, defeating De Witt Clinton of New York

1813 Perry destroys British fleet at battle of Put-in-Bay (September)
Harrison wins again at battle of Thames River (October)

1814 Jackson crushes Creek Indians at Horseshoe Bend (March)
British marines burn Washington, D.C. (August)
Americans turn back British at Plattsburg (September)
Hartford Convention meets to recommend constitutional changes (December)
Treaty of Ghent ends War of 1812 (December)

1815 Jackson routs British at battle of New Orleans (January)

Fatigue finally broke the diplomatic deadlock. The British government realized that no amount of military force could significantly alter the outcome of hostilities in the United States. When one important minister asked the Duke of Wellington, the hero of the Napoleonic Wars, for his assessment of British prospects following the battle of Plattsburg, the general replied, "I do not know where you could carry on . . . an operation which would be so injurious to the Americans as to force them to sue for peace."

Weary negotiators signed the Treaty of Ghent on Christmas Eve 1814. The document dealt with virtually none of the topics contained in Madison's original war message. Neither side surrendered territory; Great Britain refused even to discuss the topic of impressment. In fact, after more than two years of hostilities, the adversaries merely agreed to end the fighting, postponing the vexing issues of neutral rights until a later date. The Senate apparently concluded that stalemate was preferable to continued conflict and ratified the treaty 35 to 0.

Most Americans—except perhaps the diehard Federalists of New England—thought the War of 1812 an important success. Even though the country's military accomplishments had been unimpressive, the people of the United States had been swept up in a contagion of nationalism. The Hartford debacle served to discredit secessionist fantasies for several decades. Americans had waged a "second war of independence" and in the process transformed the Union into a symbol of national destiny. "The war," reflected Gallatin, "has renewed and reinstated the national feelings and character which the Revolution had given, and which were daily lessened . . . They are more Americans; they feel and act more as a nation; and I hope that the permanency of the Union is thereby better secured."

Jeffersonian Legacy

A remarkable coincidence occurred on July 4, 1826, the fiftieth anniversary of the Declaration of Independence. On that day, Thomas Jefferson died at Monticello. His last words were "Is it the Fourth?" On the same day several hundred miles to the north, John Adams also passed his last day on earth. His mind was on his old friend and sometimes adversary, and during his final moments, Adams found comfort in the assurance that "Thomas Jefferson still survives."

Adams was correct. The political battles that occupied both men during their presidencies had already passed into history and were largely forgotten by a nation eager to exploit its abundant natural resources. But the spirit of the Declaration of Independence survived, and despite his obvious shortcomings as a man and politician, Jefferson's vision of a society in which "all men are created equal" challenged later Americans to make good on the promise of 1776.

Recommended Reading

The best-written and in many ways the fullest account of the first two decades of the nineteenth century remains Henry Adams' classic *History of the United States During the Administrations of Jefferson and Madison*, 9 vols. (1889–1891). A fine abridged edition has been prepared by Ernest Samuels (1967). A good general account of the period is Marshall Smelser, *The Democratic Republic, 1801–1815* (1968). Anyone interested in the problems that Jefferson faced as president should read Merrill D. Peterson, *Thomas Jefferson and the New Nation: A Biography* (1970) and Forrest McDonald, *The Presidency of Thomas Jefferson* (1976). George Dangerfield provides a quite readable narrative of the major events of the War of 1812 in *The Era of Good Feelings* (1952).

Additional Bibliography

The economic developments of this period are the subject of several interesting studies. The most provocative is Thomas C. Cochran, *Frontiers of Change: Early Industrialization of America* (1981). Also see Stuart Bruchey, *The Roots of American Economic Growth, 1607–1861* (1965); Douglass C. North, *The Economic Growth of the United States 1790–1860* (1961); James A. Henretta, *The Evolution of American Society, 1700–1815: An Interdisciplinary Analysis* (1973); and David Montgomery, "The Working Classes of the Pre-Industrial American City, 1780–1830," *Labor History* 9 (1968): 3–22. Charles W. Janson's account of American society along with other valuable contemporary documents can be found in Gordon S. Wood, ed., *The Rising Glory of America 1760–1820* (1971). A good introduction to history of the western settlements is Reginald Horsman, *The Frontier in the Formative Years, 1783–1815* (1970). Richard Lyle Power analyzes the culture of this expanding region in *Planting Corn Belt Culture, The Impress of the Upland Southerners and Yankee in the Old Northwest* (1953). Rising sectionalism is the focus of Thomas P. Abernethy, *The South in the New Nation 1789–1819* (1961). Bernard W. Sheehan explores the government's inability to deal constructively with the Indians in *Seeds of Extinction: Jeffersonian Philanthropy and the American Indian* (1973).

The challenges confronting Jefferson as president are discussed in Dumas Malone, *Jefferson and His Time*, vols. 4 and 5 (1970, 1974). Several works focus more narrowly upon political problems: Noble E. Cunningham, Jr., *The Process of Government Under Jefferson* (1978); James Sterling Young, *The Washington Community, 1800–1828* (1966); Robert M. Johnstone, Jr., *Jefferson and the Presidency: Leadership in the Young Republic* (1978); and Carl E. Prince, "The Passing of the Aristocracy: Jefferson's Removal of the Federalists, 1801–1805," *Journal of American History* 57 (1970): 563–75. See also Richard. E. Ellis' masterful *The Jeffersonian Crisis: Courts and Politics in the Young Republic* (1971). A good introduction to the political philosophy of the Jeffersonians is Daniel Boorstin, *The Lost World of Thomas Jefferson* (1948).

The Louisiana Purchase is the subject of Alexander DeConde, *The Affair of Louisiana* (1976). On the Lewis and Clark Expedition see David Freeman Hawke, *Those Tremendous Mountains: The Story of the Lewis and Clark Expedition* (1980) and John Logal Allen, *Passage Through the Garden: Lewis and Clark and the Image of the American Northwest* (1975).

Two Republicans who gave Jefferson so much trouble are discussed in Robert E. Shalhope, *John Taylor of Caroline: Pastoral Republican* (1980) and Robert Dawidoff, *The Education of John Randolph* (1979). See also Noble E. Cunningham, Jr., "Who Were the Quids?," *Mississippi Valley Historical Review* 50 (1963): 252–63. The Burr conspiracy is discussed in Thomas P. Abernathy, *The Burr Conspiracy* (1954); but see also Milton Lomask's biography *Aaron Burr*, vols. 1 and 2 (1979, 1982). The most thoughtful exploration of the relation of slavery to politics is Donald L. Robinson, *Slavery in the Structure of American Politics 1765–1820* (1971).

The country's foreign policy problems are treated in Bradford Perkins, *Prologue to War, England and the United States, 1805–1812* (1961); Louis M. Sears, *Jefferson and the Embargo* (1927); and Buron Spivak, *Jefferson's English Crisis: Commerce, Embargo, and the Republican Revolution* (1979).

For the details of this period see Irving Brant, *James Madison*, vols. 4–6 (1953–1961) as well as Ralph Ketcham, *James Madison: A Biography* (1971). There are several good accounts of the War of 1812: Roger H. Brown, *The Republic in Peril: 1812* (1964); Harry L. Coles, *The War of 1812* (1965); Reginal Horsman, *The Causes of the War of 1812* (1962); and J. A. C. Stagg, "James Madison and the 'Malcontents': The Political Origins of the War of 1812," *William and Mary Quarterly* 33 (1976): 556–85.

The problems facing the Federalist party are the subject of Samuel Eliot Morison, *Harrison Gray Otis, 1765–1848: The Urbane Federalist* (1962); David Hackett Fischer, *The Revolution of American Conservatism* (1965); Linda K. Kerber, *Federalists in Dissent: Imagery and Ideology in Jeffersonian America* (1970); and James M. Banner, Jr., *To The Hartford Convention* (1970).

chapter 9

A
NATION
EMERGES

When the Marquis de Lafayette revisited the United States in 1824, he marveled at how the country had changed in the more than forty years since he had served with George Washington. During his grand tour of thirteen months, the great French hero of the American Revolution traveled to all parts of the country. He was greeted by adoring crowds in places that had been unsettled or beyond the nation's borders four decades earlier. Besides covering the eastern seaboard, Lafayette went west to New Orleans, then up the Mississippi and the Ohio by steamboat. He thus sampled a new mode of transportation that was helping to bring the far-flung outposts and settlements of a much enlarged nation into regular contact with each other. Such travel was still hazardous. LaFayette had to be rescued from a sinking steamboat on the Ohio before he could complete his journey to Cincinnati, hub city of the newly settled trans-Appalachian West.

Everywhere Lafayette was greeted with patriotic oratory celebrating the liberty, prosperity, and progress of the new nation. Speaking before a joint session of both houses of Congress, the old hero responded in kind, telling his hosts exactly what they wanted to hear. He hailed "the immense improvements" and "admirable communications" that he had witnessed and declared himself deeply moved by "all the grandeur and prosperity of these happy United States, which, at the same time they nobly seem the complete assertion of American independence, reflect on every part of the world the light of a far superior political civilization."

There were good reasons why Americans made LaFayette's return visit the occasion for patriotic celebration and reaffirmation. Since the War of 1812, the nation had been free from serious foreign threats to its independence and way of life. It was growing rapidly in population, size, and wealth. Its republican form of government, which many had considered a risky experiment at the time of its origin, was apparently working well. James Monroe, the current president, had proclaimed in his first inaugural address that "the

United States have flourished beyond example. Their citizens individually have been happy and the nation prosperous." Expansion "to the Great Lakes and beyond the sources of the great rivers which communicate through our whole interior," meant that "no country was ever happier with respect to its domain." As for the government itself, it was so near to perfection that "in respect to it we have no essential improvement to make."

Beneath the optimism and self-confidence, however, there were undercurrents of doubt and anxiety about the future. The visit of the aged Lafayette signified the passing of the Founding Fathers into the mists of memory. Less than a year after his departure, Jefferson and Adams, the last of the great Founders, would die within hours of each other on the fiftieth anniversary of the Declaration of Independence. Could their example of republican virtue and self-sacrifice be maintained in an increasingly prosperous and materialistic society? Many in fact believed public virtue had declined since the heroic age of the Revolution. And what about the place of slavery in a "perfect" democratic republic? Lafayette himself noted with disappointment that the United States had not yet extended freedom and equality to the black slaves of the southern states.

But the peace following the War of 1812 did open the way for a great surge of nation-building. Nationalism was more than pious rhetoric during an era when firm foundations were being laid for economic growth. As soon as new lands were acquired or opened up for settlement, hordes of pioneers rushed in. Improvements in transportation soon gave many of them access to distant markets, and advances in the processing of raw materials led to the first stirrings of industrialization. Political leadership provided little active direction for this process of growth and expansion, but an active judiciary took up part of the slack in a series of decisions that served to promote economic development and assert the priority of national over state and local interests. To guarantee the peace and security essential for internal progress, statesmen proclaimed a foreign policy designed to insulate America from external involvements. A new nation of great potential wealth and power was emerging.

Expansion and Migration

The peace concluded with Great Britain in 1815 allowed the American people to shift their attention from Europe and the Atlantic to the vast lands of North America that lay before them. Although the British had withdrawn from the region north of the Ohio, they continued to lay claim to the Pacific Northwest. Spain still possessed Florida and much of the present-day American West. Between the Appalachians and the Mississippi settlement had already begun in earnest, especially in the new states of Ohio, Kentucky, and Tennessee. In the lower Mississippi Valley, the former French colony of Louisiana had been admitted as a state in 1812, and a thriving settlement existed around Natchez in the Mississippi Territory. Elsewhere, however, the trans-Appalachian West was only sparsely settled by whites, and much good land remained in Indian hands. Diplomacy, military action (or at least the threat of it), and the westward movement of vast numbers of settlers were all needed before the continent would yield up its wealth.

Extending the Boundaries

The first goal of postwar expansionists was to obtain Florida from Spain. In the eyes of the Spanish, their possession extended along the Gulf Coast to the Mississippi, but in 1812 the United States had annexed the area between the Mississippi and the Perdido rivers in what became Alabama. The remainder, known as East Florida, became a prime object of territorial ambition for President James Monroe and his energetic secretary of state, John Quincy Adams. Adams had a grand design for continental expansion that required nullifying or reducing Spanish claims west of the Mississippi as well as east of it; he eagerly awaited an opportunity to apply pressure for that purpose.

General Andrew Jackson provided such an op-

portunity. In 1816 United States troops first crossed into East Florida in pursuit of hostile Seminole Indians and the fugitive slaves that they were harboring. This raid touched off a wider conflict, and after taking command in late 1817, Jackson went beyond his official orders and occupied East Florida in April and May of 1818. In addition, he court-martialed and executed two British subjects whom he accused of being enemy agents. These aggressive acts were condemned by all the members of Monroe's cabinet except Adams and by a report of the House of Representatives. But no disciplinary action was taken, mainly because public opinion rallied behind the hero of New Orleans.

In November 1818, Secretary Adams informed the Spanish government that the United States had acted in self-defense and that further conflict would be avoided only if East Florida was ceded to the United States. The Madrid government, weakened by Latin American revolutions and the resulting disintegration of its empire, was in no position to resist American bullying. As part of the Adams-Onís Treaty, signed on February 22, 1819, Spain relinquished Florida to the United States. In return the United States assumed $5 million of the claims of American citizens against Spain.

A strong believer that the United States had a continental destiny, Adams also used the confrontation over Florida to divest the Spanish of their claim to the Pacific coast north of California, thus opening a path for future American expansion to the Pacific. Taking advantage of Spain's desire to keep its title to Texas—which the United States had previously claimed as part of the Louisiana purchase—Adams induced the Spanish minister Luis de Onís to agree to a dividing line between American and Spanish territory that ran north of Texas but extended all the way to the Pacific. Great Britain and Russia still had competing claims to the Pacific Northwest, but the United States was now poised to acquire some frontage on a second ocean. These understandings were included in the Adams-Onís Treaty, which also became known as the Transcontinental Treaty. As Adams described this achievement in his diary, "The acknowledgement of a definite line of boundary to the South Sea [Pacific] forms a great epoch in our history."

Historian Henry Adams described the North American continent as "an uncovered ore bed." Much had to be done, however, before its riches could be mined.

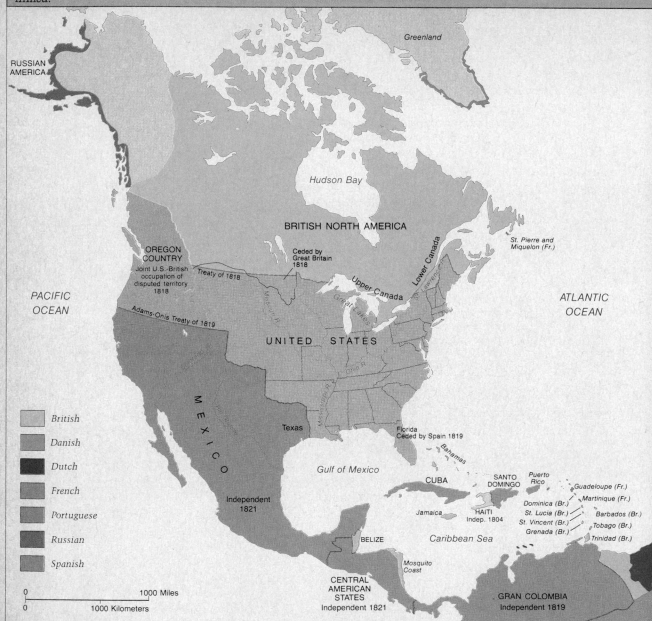

Interest in exploitation of the Far West continued to grow during the second and third decades of the nineteenth century. In 1811 a New York merchant, John Jacob Astor, founded the fur trading post of Astoria at the mouth of the Columbia River in the Oregon country. Astor's American Fur Company later sold its interests to a British firm, but in the 1820s and '30s fur traders operating out of St. Louis worked their way up the Missouri to the northern Rockies and beyond. First they limited themselves to trading for furs with the Indians, but the Rocky Mountain Fur

Company, founded in 1822, relied on white trappers or "mountain men" who went after game on their own and sold the furs to agents of the company at an annual "rendezvous."

These colorful characters, who included such legendary figures as Jedediah Smith, Jim Bridger, Kit Carson, and Jim Beckwourth (one of the many Afro-Americans who contributed to the opening of the West), accomplished prodigious feats of survival under harsh natural conditions. They explored many parts of the Rockies and the Great Basin for the first time. They often married Indian women and assimilated much of the culture and technology of the Native Americans. Although they actually depleted the animal resources on which the Indians depended, these mountain men projected an image of being part of their environment rather than destroyers of it. To later generations they typified a romantic ideal of lonely self-reliance in harmony with unspoiled nature.

The reports of military expeditions provided better information about the Far West than the tales of the mountain men, most of whom were illiterate. The most notable of the postwar expeditions was mounted by Major Stephen S. Long in 1819–1820. Long mapped some of the rivers of the Great Plains and discovered the peak in the Rockies that bears his name. He also endorsed the misleading view that the plains beyond the Missouri was a "great American desert" unfit for cultivation or settlement. For the time being, the Far West remained beyond American dreams of agrarian expansion and economic development. The real focus of attention between 1815 and the 1840s was the nearer West, the rich agricultural lands between the Appalachians and the Mississippi that were being opened up for settlement.

■ *Mountain men like Jim Beckwourth (right) and Indians met at rendezvous to trade their furs to company agents in exchange for food, ammunition, and other goods. Feasting, drinking, gambling, and sharing exploits were also part of the annual event. The moccasins (far right), trimmed with trade beads and worn by both Indians and trappers, show how trade influenced both cultures.*

Complete occupation and exploitation of the trans-Appalachian interior required displacing the many Indian communities still inhabiting that region in 1815. In the Ohio Valley and the Northwest Territory, military defeat had already made Native Americans only a minor obstacle to the ambitions of white settlers and land speculators. When the British withdrew from the Old Northwest in 1815, they left their former Indian allies virtually defenseless before the tide of whites who rushed into the region. Consigned by treaty to reservations outside the main lines of white advance, most of the tribes were eventually forced west of the Mississippi. The last stand of the woodland Indians of the Midwest occurred in 1831–1832, when a faction of the confederated Sac and Fox Indians under Chief Black Hawk attempted to reoccupy lands east of the Mississippi previously ceded by another tribal faction. Federal troops and Illinois state militia pursued Black Hawk's band and drove it back to the river where it was almost exterminated while attempting to cross to the western bank.

Uprooting the once populous Indian communities of the Old Northwest was part of a national program for removing Indians of the eastern part of the country to an area beyond the Mississippi. Whites of the time viewed Indian society and culture as radically inferior to their own and doomed by the march of "progress." Furthermore, the fact that Indians held land communally and not in private parcels was regarded as an insuperable obstacle to economic development. As originally conceived by Thomas Jefferson, removal would have allowed those Indians who became "civilized" to remain behind on individually owned farms and qualify for American citizenship. This policy would reduce Indian holdings without appearing to violate American standards of justice. But during the Monroe era it became clear that white settlers wanted nothing less than the removal of all Indians, "civilized" or not. The issue was particularly pressing in the South. Greed combined with racism as land-grabbing state governments pressed for the total extinction of Indian land titles within their borders.

In the South, as in the Old Northwest, a series of treaties negotiated between 1815 and 1830 reduced tribal holdings and provided for the eventual removal of most Indians to the trans-Mississippi West. But some southern tribes held on tenaciously to their homelands. The so-called five civilized tribes—the Cherokees, Creeks, Seminoles, Choctaws, and Chickasaws—had become settled agriculturalists. It was no easy task to induce the "civilized tribes" to give up the substantial and relatively prosperous enclaves in Georgia, Florida, Alabama, and Mississippi still held in the 1820s and '30s. But the pressure continued to mount. The federal government used a combination of deception, bribery, and threats to induce land cessions. When federal action did not yield results fast enough to suit southern whites who coveted Indian land for

Representatives of eight Indian tribes met with government agents at Prairie du Chien, Wisconsin, in 1825 to define the boundaries of their respective land claims. The United States claimed the right to make "an amicable and final adjustment" of the claims. Within twenty-five years most of the tribes present at Prairie du Chien had ceded their land to the government.

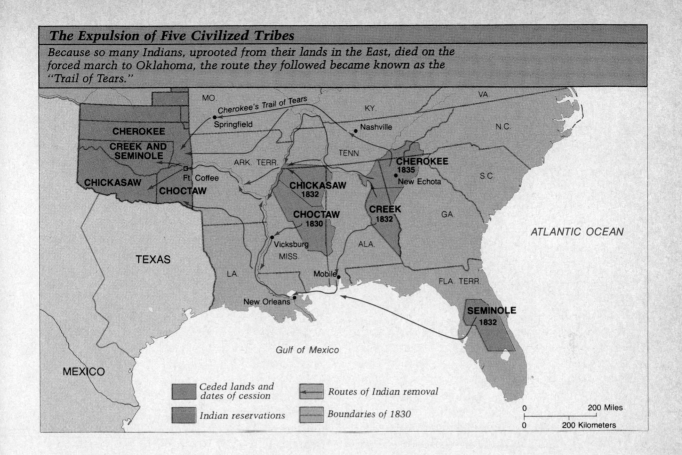

The Expulsion of Five Civilized Tribes

Because so many Indians, uprooted from their lands in the East, died on the forced march to Oklahoma, the route they followed became known as the "Trail of Tears."

mining, speculation, and cotton production, state governments began to act on their own proclaiming state jurisdiction over lands still allotted by federal treaty to Indians within the state's borders. The stage was thus set for the forced removal of the five civilized tribes to Oklahoma during the administration of Andrew Jackson. (See chapter 10 for a more complete discussion.)

While Indians were being hustled or driven beyond the Mississippi, settlers poured across the Appalachians and filled the agricultural heartland of the United States. This movement was the most dramatic and significant phase of the great westward expansion of population and settlement that began in the early colonial period and lasted until the 1880s. In 1810 only about one seventh of the American population lived beyond the Appalachians; by 1840 more than a third did. During that period Illinois grew from a territory with 12,282 inhabitants to a state with 476,183; Mississippi's population of about 40,000 increased tenfold; and Michigan grew from a remote frontier area with less than 5000 people into

a settled region with more than 200,000. Eight new western states were added to the Union during this period. Because of the government's removal policies, few of the settlers actually had to fight Indians. But they did have to obtain possession of land and derive a livelihood from it. For many, this was no easy task.

Much of the vast acreage opened up by the westward movement passed through the hands of land speculators before it reached those of the farmers and planters. Government lands in the western territories were first surveyed and then sold at auction. After a financial panic in 1819 brought ruin to many who had purchased tracts on credit, the minimum price was lowered from $2.00 to $1.25 an acre, but full payment was required in cash. Since few settlers could afford the necessary outlays, wealthy speculators continued to acquire most of the good land. In the prosperous period following the War of 1812, and again during the boom of the early- to mid-1830s, speculation in public lands proceeded at a massive and feverish rate.

Eventually most of the land did find its way into the hands of actual cultivators. In some areas squatters arrived before the official survey and formed claims associations which policed land auctions to prevent "outsiders" from bidding up the price and buying their farms out from under them. Squatters also agitated for formal "preemption" rights from the government. Between 1799 and 1830 Congress passed a number of special acts which granted squatters in specific areas the right to buy the land that they had already improved at the minimum price. In 1841 the right to farm on public lands with the assurance of a *future* preemption right was formally acknowledged by Congress.

Settlers who arrived after speculators had secured title had to deal with land barons. Fortunately for the settlers, most speculators operated on credit and were forced to obtain a quick return on their investment. They did this by selling land at a profit to settlers who had some capital, renting out farms until the tenants had earned enough to buy them, or loaning money to squatters until they were in a position to pay for the land in installments. As a result, the family farm or owner-operated plantation became the characteristic unit of western agriculture.

Since the pioneer family was likely to be saddled with debt of one kind or another, it was usually forced from the beginning to do more than simply raise enough food to subsist. Farmers also had to produce something for market. Not surprisingly, most of the earliest settlement was along rivers which provided a natural means of transportation for flatboats loaded with corn, wheat, cotton, or cured meat. From more remote areas, farmers drove livestock over primitive trails and roads to eastern markets. One way to turn bulky grain, especially corn, into a more easily transportable commodity was to distill it into whiskey. To meet the needs of farmers local marketing centers quickly sprung up, usually at river junctions. Some of these grew into small cities virtually overnight. In the Midwest, the rapid rise of towns and cities serving surrounding farming areas greatly accelerated regional development.

Not all frontier people had the chance, or even the desire, to become market farmers dependent on town-based merchants. In the backcountry of the South and the southernmost parts of the Midwest, many came to prefer the independence of a basically subsistence form of agriculture and resisted the spread of money and commerce. Their relative isolation allowed them to live free of market relationships for an extended period.

The People and Culture of the Frontier

Most of the hundreds of thousands of settlers who populated the West were farmers from the seaboard states. They migrated for all sorts of reasons, but prominent among them were overpopulation, rising land prices, and declining fertility of the soil in the older regions. Few sought to escape or repudiate the "civilized" and settled way of life that they had known in the East. Most of them moved in family units and tried to recreate their former way of life as soon as possible. Women were often reluctant to migrate in the first place, and when they arrived in new areas, they strove valiantly to recapture the comfort and stability that they had left behind.

New Englanders moving to western New York or northern Ohio, Indiana, and Illinois brought with them their churches, schools, notions of community uplift, and Puritan ideals of hard work and self-denial. The Southerners who emigrated from Virginia and the Carolinas to Kentucky, Tennessee, and the Southwest retained their devotion to family honor, personal independence, and ideas of white supremacy. So did their cousins who settled in the lower part of the Old Northwest.

In general, the pioneers sought out the kind of terrain and soil with which they were already familiar. People from the eastern uplands favored the hill country of the West. Piedmont and tidewater farmers or planters usually made for the lower and flatter areas. The fertile prairies of the Midwest were avoided by early settlers, who preferred river bottoms or wooded sections because they were more like "home" and could be farmed by tried-and-true methods. Rather than being the bold and deliberate innovators of myth, the typical agricultural pioneers were deeply averse to changing their traditional habits.

Yet some adjustments were necessary simply to survive under frontier conditions. Initially, at least, a high degree of self-sufficiency was required on isolated homesteads. Men cut down trees, built cabins, broke the soil, and put in crops; besides cooking, keeping house, and caring for children, women made clothes, manufactured soap and other household necessities, churned butter, preserved food for the winter, and worked in the fields at busy times. Crops had to be planted, harvested, and readied for home consumption with simple tools brought in wagons from the East—often no more than an axe, a spade, and a spinning wheel.

But this picture of frontier self-reliance is not the whole story. Most settlers in fact found it

On the frontier, women were responsible for preparing all the food, even sometimes for slaughtering the animals (top). Quilting bees (bottom) offered men and women a rare opportunity to socialize.

extremely difficult to accomplish all these tasks using only family labor. A more common practice was the sharing of work by a number of pioneer families. Except in parts of the Southwest, where frontier planters had taken slaves with them, the normal way to get heavy labor done in the newly settled regions was through mutual aid. Assembling the neighbors to raise a house, burn the woods, roll logs, harvest wheat, husk corn, pull flax, or make quilts helped turn collective work into a festive social occasion. Passing the jug was a normal feature of these "bees," and an uproarious good time was often the result of the various contests or competitions that speeded the work along. These communal events represented a creative response to the shortage of labor and at the same time provided a source for communal solidarity. They probably tell us more about the "spirit of the frontier" than the conventional image of the pioneer as a lonely individualist.

While some settlers remained in one place and "grew up with the country," many others moved on after a relatively short time. The wandering of young Abraham Lincoln's family from Kentucky to Indiana and finally to Illinois between 1816 and 1830 was fairly typical. The physical mobility characteristic of nineteenth-century Americans in general was particularly pronounced in frontier regions. Improved land could be sold at a profit and the proceeds used to buy new acreage beyond the horizon where the soil was reportedly richer. The temptations of small-scale land speculation and the lure of new land further west induced a large proportion of new settlers to pull up stakes and move on after only a few years. Hence few early nineteenth-century American farmers developed the kind of attachment to the land that often characterized rural populations in other parts of the world.

Transportation and the Market Economy

It took more than spread of settlement to bring prosperity to new areas and ensure that they would identify with older regions or with the country as a whole. Along the eastern seaboard land transportation was so primitive that in 1813 it took seventy-five days for one wagon of goods drawn by four horses to make a trip of about a thousand miles from Worcester, Massachusetts, to Charleston, South Carolina. But coastal shipping eased the problem to some extent in the East and stimulated the growth of port cities. Traveling west over the mountains meant months on the trail.

After the War of 1812 political leaders realized that national security, economic progress, and political unity were all more or less dependent on binding the nation together through a greatly improved transportation network. Accordingly, President Madison called for a federally supported program of "internal improvements" in 1815. Recommending such a program in Congress, Congressman John C. Calhoun described it as a great nationalizing enterprise: "Let us, then, bind the nation together with a perfect system of roads and canals. Let us conquer space." In the ensuing decades, Calhoun's vision of a transportation revolution was realized to a considerable extent, although the direct role of the federal government proved to be less important than anticipated.

A Revolution in Transportation: Roads and Steamboats

Americans who wished to get from place to place rapidly and cheaply needed, as a bare minimum, new and improved roads. The first great federal transportation project was the building between 1811 and 1818 of the National Road between Cumberland, Maryland, on the Potomac, and Wheeling, Virginia, on the Ohio. This impressive toll road had a crushed stone surface and immense stone bridges. It was subsequently extended and reached Vandalia, Illinois, in 1838. Another thoroughfare to the west completed during this period was the Lancaster Turnpike connecting Philadelphia and Pittsburgh. Other major cities were also linked by "turnpikes"—privately owned toll roads chartered by the states. By about 1825, southern New England, upstate New York, much of Pennsylvania, and northern New Jersey were crisscrossed by thousands of miles of turnpikes.

By themselves, however, the toll roads failed to meet the demand for low-cost transportation over long distances. For the most part, travelers benefited more than did transporters of bulky freight. The latter usually found that total expenses—toll plus the cost and maintenance of heavy wagons and great teams of horses—were too high to guarantee a satisfactory profit from haulage. Hence traffic was less than anticipated, and the tolls collected were insufficient to provide an adequate return to investors. On the whole, therefore, the turnpikes were a losing proposition and did little to "conquer space" in the sense of linking up the settled seaboard areas with the new West.

The National Road itself had severe limitations. Although it was able to carry a substantial east-west traffic of settler parties and wagonloads of manufactured goods, as well as a reverse flow of livestock being driven to market, it could not offer the low freight costs required for the long-distance hauling of wheat, flour, and the other

On their way west to the Alleghenies, a party of settlers lead their Conestoga wagons, loaded with freight, past the Fairview Inn on the National Road near Baltimore. Heading east is a herd of cattle being driven to market.

bulky agricultural products of the Ohio valley. For these commodities, water transportation of some sort was clearly required.

The fact that the United States had a great natural transportation system in its river network was one of the most significant reasons for the country's rapid economic development. The Ohio-Mississippi system in particular provided ready access to the rich agricultural areas of the interior and a natural outlet for their products. By 1815, large numbers of flatboats loaded with wheat, flour, and salt pork were making the two thousand-mile trip from Pittsburgh to New Orleans. On the lower Mississippi and its main tributaries cotton could be loaded from plantation or town wharfs onto river craft or small seagoing vessels and carried to the same destination. Even after the coming of the steamboat, flatboats continued to carry a major share of the downriver trade.

But the flatboat trade was necessarily a one-way traffic. A farmer from Ohio or Illinois, or someone hired to do the job, could float down to New Orleans easily enough but there was generally no way to get back except by walking overland through rough country. Keelboats and barges could fight their way upriver but the journey was so difficult and time-consuming that few attempted it. Until the problem of upriver navigation was solved, the Ohio-Mississippi could not carry the manufactured goods that farmers desired in exchange for their crops.

Fortunately, a solution was readily at hand—the use of steam power for river transportation. Late in the eighteenth century a number of American inventors had experimented with mounting steam engines on river boats. John Fitch even exhibited an early model to delegates at the Constitutional Convention. But making a commercially successful craft required further refinement. In 1807 inventor Robert Fulton, backed by Robert R. Livingston—a New Yorker of great wealth and political prominence—demonstrated the full potential of the steamboat by successfully propelling the *Clermont* 150 miles up the Hudson River. The first steamboat launched in the West was the *New Orleans*, which made the long trip from Pittsburgh to New Orleans in 1811–1812. Besides becoming a principal means of passenger travel on the inland waterways of the East, the river steamboat revolutionized the commerce of the West. In 1815 the *Enterprise* made the first return trip from New Orleans to Pittsburgh. Within five years, 69 steamboats with a total tonnage of 13,890 were plying western waters.

Steam transport was a great boon for farmers and merchants. It reduced costs, increased the speed of moving goods and people, and allowed a two-way commerce on the Mississippi and Ohio. Eastern manufacturers and merchants now had a

■ *Although some called his Clermont (above) "Fulton's Folly," Robert Fulton immediately turned a profit from his fleet of steamboats, which reduced the cost and increased the speed of river transport.*

■ *Man-made canals temporarily filled the gap in a developing transportation system of rivers and roads. This scene of the junction of the Erie and Northern canals (c. 1835) shows mules walking alongside the canal towing the boats and barges. The locks are seen in the background.*

better way to reach the interior markets than the old method of hauling everything over the Appalachians by road.

The steamboat quickly captured the American imagination. The great paddle wheelers became luxurious floating hotels, the natural habitats of gamblers and confidence men. For the pleasure of passengers and onlookers, steamboats sometimes raced against each other, and their more skillful pilots became folk heroes. But the boats also had a lamentable safety record, frequently running aground, colliding, or blowing up. The most publicized disasters of antebellum America were a series of spectacular boiler explosions that claimed the lives of hundreds of passengers. As a result of such accidents, the federal government began in 1838 to regulate steamboats and monitor their construction and operation. This legislation stands as the only instance in the pre-Civil War period of direct federal regulation of domestic transportation.

The Canal Boom

A transportation system based solely on rivers and roads had one enormous gap—it did not provide an economical way to ship western farm produce directly east to the growing urban market of the seaboard states. The solution offered by the politicians and merchants of the Middle Atlantic and midwestern states was to build a system of canals which linked seaboard cities directly to the Great Lakes, the Ohio, and ultimately the Mississippi.

The best natural location for a canal between a river flowing into the Atlantic and one of the Great Lakes was between Albany and Buffalo, a relatively flat stretch of 364 miles. The potential value of such a project had long been recognized, but when it was actually approved by the New York legislature in 1817 it was justly hailed as an enterprise of breathtaking boldness. At that time, no more than about 100 miles of canal existed in the entire United States, and the longest single canal extended only 26 miles. Credit for the project belongs mainly to New York's vigorous and farsighted governor, De Witt Clinton. He persuaded the New York state legislature to underwrite the project by issuing bonds, and construction began in 1818. In less than two years, 75 miles were already finished, and the first tolls were being collected. In 1825 the entire canal was opened with great public acclaim and celebration.

At 364 miles long, 40 feet wide, 4 feet deep, and containing 84 locks, the Erie Canal was the most spectacular engineering achievement of the young Republic. Furthermore, it was a great economic success. It reduced the cost of moving goods from Buffalo to Albany to one twelfth the previous rate. It not only lowered the cost of western products in the East but caused an even sharper decline in the price of goods imported from the East by Westerners. It also helped to make New York City the unchallenged commercial capital of the nation.

The great success of the Erie Canal inspired other states to extend public credit for canal building. Between 1826 and 1834, Pennsylvania constructed an even longer and more elaborate canal, covering the 395 miles from Philadelphia to Pittsburgh and requiring twice as many locks as its New York competitor. But the Pennsylvania Main Line Canal did not do as well as the Erie, partly because of the bottleneck that developed at the crest of the Alleghenies where canal boats had to be hauled over a high ridge on an inclined-plane railroad. Ohio also embarked on an ambitious program of canal construction, completing

an artificial waterway from the Ohio River to Cleveland on Lake Erie in 1833. Shorter canals were built in many other states connecting navigable rivers with sea or lake ports. The last of these was the Illinois and Michigan Canal, completed in 1848. It linked Chicago and the Great Lakes with the Illinois River and the Mississippi.

The canal boom ended when it became apparent in the 1830s and '40s that most of these waterways were unprofitable. State credit had been overextended, and the panic and depression of the late '30s and early '40s forced retrenchment. Moreover, by this time railroads were beginning to compete successfully for the same traffic, and a new phase in the transportation revolution was beginning.

Transportation and Trade

Rivers, roads, and canals carried both goods and people over the east-west and north-south routes of trade and transportation.

Images of the West in American Culture

"American democracy was born of no theorist's dream; it was not carried in the *Susan Constant* to Virginia, or in the *Mayflower* to Plymouth. It came stark and strong and full of life out of the American forest, and it gained new strength each time it touched a new frontier." So wrote historian Frederick Jackson Turner in 1914. Turner's "frontier thesis"—his view that American character and institutions resulted from the pioneer experience—was the most influential interpretation of American history ever offered. Today most historians find other themes of American development of equal or even greater importance. But Turner's vision of the West as the cradle of democracy, individualism, and other distinctive and valuable American characteristics was the climax of a major trend in cultural history. From the eighteenth century to the twentieth, Americans concerned with the nation's character and destiny looked to the virgin land of the West for insight and inspiration.

Two main ideas, first expressed in the colonial period, influenced thinking about the West throughout the nineteenth century. One was that the center of world civilization was ever moving toward the setting sun: "Westward the course of empire takes its way." This meant that the United States would eventually eclipse Europe in power and cultural achievement and that a westward movement of Americans was the extension of civilization along its preordained path. From the time that Jefferson sent Lewis and Clark to explore the Pacific Northwest in 1803 until California was acquired in 1848, expansionists advocated movement to the Pacific in order to open a "passage to India" and complete the march of civilization around the globe.

The second idea was that each frontier that opened up would repeat the social evolution of the entire human race. In its simplest form, this theory held that humankind had developed through a series of stages from "savagery"—when subsistence was derived from hunting and fishing—to "barbarism"—which saw the first introduction of agriculture and a settled way of life—and finally to "civilization," which is based on a complex urban and industrial economy. On each successive frontier, as Jefferson predicted and Turner later observed, a way of life based on hunting and trapping was followed by subsistence farming and ultimately by the rise of towns, commerce, and manufacturing. The development of frontiers exemplified the belief in gradual and predictable progress that was so central to nineteenth-century American hopes and expectations.

The American Indian, according to this vision, represented the "savage" or primitive stage of human development. A traveler, viewing Indian life in 1831, concluded that "the aborigines . . . resemble the people of the earliest ages of the world." Whites in effect offered Native Americans the choice of becoming "civilized" or getting out of the path of progress. But many doubted that Indians were capable of civilization and callously predicted that the passing of the "savage stage" on the frontier would also mean the total extinction of the original inhabitants.

The image of the West as the great arena for the advance of civilization did not, however, reveal the full range and depth of attitudes toward the frontier. The prevailing models for civilized life were the advanced societies of western Europe, and American nationalism seemed to require that something new and distinctive arise from developments on this side of the Atlantic. Frederick Jackson Turner's notion that democracy was born in the wilderness was rooted in the long-standing efforts of American writers and thinkers to find virtue and strength in the frontier experience itself.

James Fenimore Cooper was the first major American writer to use frontier settings and characters. Beginning in 1823, he wrote a series of novels featuring the character of Natty Bumppo or "Leatherstocking"—a figure who became the prototype for the Western hero of popular fiction. Leatherstocking is a hunter and scout who prefers the freedom of living in the forest to the constraints of a settled, domesticated existence. In the *Pioneers*, the first novel in the series, he responds to the criticism that his way of life cuts him off from "the influences of more sacred things": "I have lived in the woods for forty long years and have five years at a time without seeing the light of a clearing . . . and I should like to know where you'll find a man . . . who can get an easier living, . . . and as for honesty, or doing what's right between man and man, I'll not turn

my back to the longest winded deacon." Through Leatherstocking Cooper was expressing a main theme of American romanticism—the claim that a solitary experience of untamed nature inspired a higher kind of wisdom than life among families, schools, and churches.

Henry David Thoreau made the same point in *Walden* (1854) when he described the West as "another name for the wild" and affirmed that "in Wildness is the preservation of the World. . . . From the forest and wilderness come tonics and barks which brace mankind." But the attitude of romantic writers toward the unspoiled West was not really as favorable as these quotations suggest. Cooper implied that Natty Bumppo was a rare phenomenon; most of Cooper's other frontier characters were rude and immoral.

In fact, the literary image of the virtuous frontiersman did not really mean that educated Easterners idolized western pioneers. The image was a projection of their fantasies and not a serious proposal for dismantling modern society in favor of a simpler, more primitive way of life. Furthermore, the typical pioneer was not a solitary hunter; he was a struggling farmer with a hardworking wife, both of whom valued society and order. When finally discovered by a new school of realistic novelists in the late nineteenth century, the western farmer was portrayed as the hapless victim of harsh economic conditions.

Hence the idea that frontier conditions brought out what was good and strong in the American character never really took deep root in our culture. Even the popular "Wild West" fiction that first emerged in the dime novels of the 1860s and '70s portrayed a violent way of life that was fun to read about but that few people would actually want to experience. The image of the frontier was escapism for Easterners and something to conquer as quickly as possible for most actual settlers in the West. It was only after "the West was won" and the frontier closed that true glorification could occur. Perhaps the experience of settling new lands did make Americans more enterprising and self-reliant, as Frederick Jackson Turner claimed. But for most nineteenth-century Americans, the frontier was a place of hardship and deprivation that had to be endured in order to make way for something better.

But canals should not be written off as economic failures that contributed little to the improvement of transportation. Some of them continued to be important arteries up to the time of the Civil War and well beyond. Furthermore, the "failure" of many of the canals was due solely to their inability to yield an adequate return on the money invested in them. This problem of financing tells us little or nothing about their public usefulness. Concerning one failing canal, a contemporary argued that it "has been more useful to the public, than to the owners." Had the canals been thought of as providing a service rather than yielding a profit—in the manner, for example, of modern interstate highways—they might have maintained a high reputation for serving the economic interests of the nation. As it was, they contributed enormously to creating vital economic ties between the agricultural West and the industrializing Northeast.

Emergence of a Market Economy

The desire to reduce the costs and increase the speed of shipping heavy freight over great distances laid the groundwork for a new economic system. Canals made it less expensive and more profitable for Western farmers to ship their wheat and flour to New York and Philadelphia and also gave manufacturers in the East ready access to an interior market. Steamboats reduced shipping costs on the Ohio and Mississippi, and put farmers in the enviable position of receiving more for their crops and paying less for the goods they needed to import. Hence improved transport led to an increase in farm income and provided a stimulus for commercial agriculture.

At the beginning of the nineteenth century, the typical farming household consumed most of what it produced and sold only a small surplus in nearby markets. Most manufactured articles were produced at home. Easier and cheaper access to distant markets caused a decisive change in this pattern. Between 1800 and 1840, agricultural output increased at an annual rate of approximately 3 percent a year, and a rapidly growing portion of this production consisted of commodities grown for sale rather than consumed at home. This rise in productivity was partly due to technological advances. Iron or steel plows proved better than

wooden ones, the grain cradle displaced the scythe for harvesting, and better varieties or strains of crops, grasses, and livestock were introduced. But the availability of good land and the revolution in marketing were the most important spurs to profitable commercial farming. Good land made for high yields, at least for a time; and when the soil was worn out by excessive planting, a farmer could simply migrate to more fertile lands farther west. The existence or extension of transportation facilities made distant markets available and plugged farmers into a commercial network that provided credit and relieved them of the need to do their own selling.

This emerging exchange network encouraged a movement away from diversified farming and toward regional concentration on staple crops. Wheat was the main cash crop of the North, and the center of its cultivation moved westward as soil depletion, pests, and plant diseases lowered yields in older regions. In 1815 the heart of the wheat belt was New York and Pennsylvania. By 1839, Ohio was the leading producer and Indiana

Agriculture in the Late 1830s

Good land, technological improvements, and a new marketing system contributed to increasing agricultural productivity during the first half of the nineteenth century.

Predominantly cropland

Forest with scattered cropland and pasture

Sparsely populated or nonproductive land

Cotton Kingdom

and Illinois were beginning to come into their own. On the rocky hillsides of New England, sheep raising was displacing the mixed farming of an earlier era. But the prime example of successful staple production in this era was the rise of the cotton kingdom in the South.

A number of factors made the South the world's greatest producer of cotton. First was the great demand generated by the rise of textile manufacturing in England and, to a lesser extent, in New England. Second was the effect of the cotton gin on processing. Invented by Eli Whitney in 1793, this simple device cut the labor costs involved in cleaning short-staple cotton, thus making it an easily marketable commodity.

A third reason for the rise of cotton was the availability of good land in the Southwest. As yields fell in the original areas of cultivation—mainly South Carolina and Georgia—the opening of the rich and fertile plantation areas or "black belts" of Alabama, Mississippi, and Louisiana shifted the Cotton Kingdom westward and resulted in a vast increase in total production. In 1816 New Orleans, the great marketing center for Western crops, received 37,000 bales; by 1830 428,000 arrived; and in 1840, the number had reached 923,000. Between 1817 and 1840, the amount of cotton produced in the South tripled from 461,000 bales to 1,350,000.

A fourth factor—the existence of slavery, which provided a flexible system of forced labor—permitted operations on a scale impossible for the family labor system of the agricultural North. Finally, the cotton economy benefited from the South's splendid natural transportation system—its great network of navigable rivers extending deep into the interior from the cotton ports of Charleston, Savannah, Mobile, and, of course, New Orleans. The South had less need than other agricultural regions for artificial "internal improvements" such as canals and good roads. Planters could simply establish themselves on or near a river and ship their crops to market via natural waterways.

Commerce and Banking

As regions specialized in the growing of commercial crops, a new system of marketing emerged. During an early or pioneer stage in many areas,

farmers did their marketing personally, even when it required long journeys overland or by flatboat. With the growth of country towns, local merchants took over the crop near the source, bartering clothing and other manufactured goods for produce. These intermediaries shipped the farmers' crops to larger local markets like Pittsburgh, Cincinnati, and St. Louis. From there the commodities could be sent on to Philadelphia, New York, or New Orleans. Cotton growers in the South were more likely to deal directly with factors or agents in the port cities from which their crop was exported. But even in the South commission merchants in such inland towns as Macon, Atlanta, Montgomery, Shreveport, and Nashville became increasingly important as intermediaries.

The extension of credit was a crucial element in the whole system. Farmers borrowed from local merchants, who received an advance of their own when they consigned the crop to a commission house or factor. The commission agents relied on credit from merchants or manufacturers at the ultimate destination, which might be Liverpool or New York City. The intermediaries all charged fees and interest but the net cost to the farmers was less than when they had handled their own marketing. The need for credit encouraged the growth of money and banking.

Before the revolutions in transportation and marketing, small-scale local economies could survive to a considerable extent on barter. Farmers could give grain to their blacksmiths who could in turn exchange the grain for iron from a local forge. But long-distance transactions involving credit and deferred payment required money and lots of it. Under the Constitution the United States government is the only agency authorized to issue money. But in the early to mid-nineteenth century the government printed no paper money and produced gold and silver coins in such small quantities that it utterly failed to meet the expanding economy's need for a circulating currency.

Private or state banking institutions filled the void by issuing bank notes, promises to redeem their paper in *specie*—gold or silver—on the bearer's demand. After Congress failed to recharter the Bank of the United States in 1811, state-chartered banks took up the slack. But many of them lacked adequate reserves and were forced to suspend specie payments during the War of 1812. The demand for money and credit during the immediate postwar boom led to a vast increase in the number of state banks—from 88 to 208 within two years. The resulting flood of state bank notes caused this form of currency to depreciate well below its face value and threatened a runaway inflation. In an effort to stabilize the currency, Congress established a second Bank of the United States in 1816. Besides serving as a repository of federal funds, the Bank was authorized to issue notes, which the government would accept in payment of taxes or for the purchase of public lands. It was also expected to serve as a check on the state banks by forcing them to resume specie payments.

Whenever the national bank tried to enforce tight money policies by requiring that banks have adequate specie reserves to back their notes, state banks in the South and West—where national bank notes were in short supply and the demand for credit was heavy—resisted vigorously. The result was a running battle in which state and private banks responded to local pressures by printing bank notes in excessive quantities only to confront efforts by the national bank to call them to account. The state banks were not as irresponsible or as out of tune with the real economic needs of their regions as they are often pictured as being. Their notes may have circulated at less than face value, but they nevertheless met a genuine need for currency and credit.

Early Industrialism

The growth of a market economy also created new opportunities for industrialists. In 1815 most manufacturing in the United States was carried on in households, in the workshops of skilled artisans, or in small mills, which used waterpower to turn wheat into flour or timber into boards. The factory form of production, in which supervised workers tended or operated machines under one roof, was rare. It was found mainly in southern New England where a number of small spinning mills, relying heavily on the labor of women and children, accomplished one step in the manufacture of cotton textiles. But most spinning of thread, as well as the weaving, cutting, sewing of cloth, was still done by women working at home.

As late as 1820, about two thirds of the clothing worn by Americans was made entirely in households by female family members—wives and daughters. But a growing proportion was produced for market, rather than direct home consumption. Under the "putting-out system" of manufacturing, merchant capitalists provided raw material to people in their own homes, picked up the finished or semifinished products, paid the workers, and took charge of distribution. Besides textiles, items such as shoes and hats were made under the putting-out system. Home manufacturing of this type was centered in the Northeast and often involved farm families making profitable use of their slack seasons. It did not usually present a direct challenge to the economic preeminence of agriculture or seriously disrupt a rural pattern of life.

The making of articles that required greater skill—such as high quality shoes and boots, carriages or wagons, mill wheels, and barrels or kegs—was mostly carried on by artisans working in small shops in towns. But in the decades after 1815, the merchants who purchased from these workers gained greater control over production. Shops expanded in size, masters tended to become entrepreneurs rather than working artisans, and journeymen often became wage earners rather than aspiring masters. At the same time, the growing market for low-priced goods led to a stress on speed, quantity, and standardization in the methods of production. Even where no substantial mechanization was involved, shops dealing in handmade goods for a local clientele tended to become small factories turning out mass-produced items for a wider public.

A fully developed factory system emerged first in textile manufacturing. The establishment of the first cotton mills utilizing the power loom as well as spinning machinery—thus making it possible to turn fiber into cloth in a single factory—resulted from the efforts of a trio of Boston merchants, Francis Cabot Lowell, Nathan Appleton, and Patrick Tracy Jackson. On a visit to England in 1810 and '11, Lowell succeeded in memorizing the closely guarded industrial secret of how a power loom was constructed. Returning to Boston, he joined with Appleton and Jackson to acquire a water site at Waltham and obtain a corporate charter for textile manufacturing on a new and expanded scale.

Under the name of the Boston Manufacturing Company, the associates began their Waltham operation in 1813. Its phenomenal success led to the erection of a larger and even more profitable mill at Lowell in 1822 and another at Chicopee in 1823. Lowell became the great showplace for early American industrialization. Its large and seemingly contented work force of unmarried young women residing in supervised dormitories, its unprecedented scale of operation, its successful mechanization of almost every stage of the production process—all captured the American middle-class imagination in the 1820s and '30s. Other mills using similar methods sprang up throughout New England, and the region became the first important manufacturing area in the United States.

The shift in textile manufacture from domestic to factory production was primarily a shift in the locus of female economic activity. As the New England textile industry grew, the putting-out system rapidly declined. Between 1824 and 1832, household production of textiles dropped from 50 to 90 percent in most parts of New England. The shift to factory production changed the course of capitalistic activity in the region. Before the 1820s, New England merchants concentrated mainly on international trade, and it was in the mercantile houses of Boston that the great profits were being made. A major source of capital was the lucrative China trade carried on by fast, well-built New England vessels. When the success of Waltham and Lowell became clear, many merchants shifted their capital away from oceanic trade and into manufacturing. This change had important political consequences, as leading politicians like Daniel Webster no longer advocated a low tariff that favored exporters over importers. They now became leading proponents of a high duty rate designed to protect manufacturers from foreign competition.

The development of other "infant industries" of the postwar period was less dramatic and would not come to fruition until the 1840s and '50s. Technology to improve the rolling and refining of iron was imported from England; it gradually encouraged the growth of a domestic iron industry centered in Pennsylvania. The use of interchangeable parts in the manufacture of small arms, pioneered by Eli Whitney and Simeon North, not only helped to modernize the weapons

New England became a center for textile manufacturing during the Industrial Revolution. This machinery was used for spinning and winding cotton yarn on bobbins.

industry but also contributed more generally to the growth of new forms of mass production.

Although most manufacturing was centered in the Northeast, the West also experienced a modest industrial progress. Increasing rapidly in number and size were facilities for processing farm products, such as grist mills, slaughterhouses, and tanneries. Distilleries in Kentucky and Ohio began during the 1820s to produce vast quantities of corn whiskey for a seemingly insatiable public.

One should not assume, however, that America had already experienced an industrial revolution by 1840. In that year, 63.4 percent of the nation's labor force was still employed in agriculture. Only 8.8 percent were directly involved in factory production. This represented a major shift since 1810 when the figures were 83.7 and 3.2 percent. But the numbers would have to change a good deal more before it could be said that industrialization had really arrived. The revolution that did occur during these years was essentially one of distribution rather than production. The growth of a market economy of national scope—still based mainly on agriculture but involving a rapid flow of capital, commodities, and services from region to region—was the major economic development of this period. And it was one that had vast repercussions for all aspects of American life.

Technological Development, 1750–1860
(Dates refer to patent or first successful use)

Year	Inventor	Contribution	Importance/Description
1787	John Fitch	Steamboat	First successful American steamboat
1793	Eli Whitney	Cotton gin	Simplified process of separating fiber from seeds; helped make cotton a profitable staple of southern agriculture
1798	Eli Whitney	Jig for guiding tools	Facilitated manufacture of interchangeable parts
1802	Oliver Evans	Steam engine	First American steam engine; led to manufacture of high-pressure engines used throughout eastern United States
1813	Richard B. Chenaworth	Cast-iron plow	First iron plow to be made in three separate pieces, thus making possible replacement of parts
1830	Peter Cooper	Railroad locomotive	First steam locomotive built in America
1831	Cyrus McCormick	Reaper	Mechanized harvesting; early model could cut six acres of grain a day
1836	Samuel Colt	Revolver	First successful repeating pistol
1837	John Deere	Steel plow	Steel surface kept soil from sticking; farming thus made easier on rich prairies of Midwest
1839	Charles Goodyear	Vulcanization of rubber	Made rubber much more useful by preventing it from sticking and melting in hot weather
1842	Crawford W. Long	First administered ether in surgery	Reduced pain and risk of shock during operations
1844	Samuel F. B. Morse	Telegraph	Made long-distance communication almost instantaneous
1846	Elias Howe	Sewing machine	First practical machine for automatic sewing
1846	Norbert Rillieux	Vacuum evaporator	Improved method of removing water from sugar cane; revolutionized sugar industry and was later applied to many other products
1847	Richard M. Hoe	Rotary printing press	Printed an entire sheet in one motion, vastly speeded up printing process
1851	William Kelly	"Air-boiling process"	Improved method of converting iron into steel (usually known as Bessemer process because English inventor had more advantageous patent and financial arrangements)
1853	Elisha G. Otis	Passenger elevator	Improved movement in buildings; when later electrified, stimulated development of skyscrapers
1859	Edwin L. Drake	First American oil well	Initiated oil industry in the United States
1859	George M. Pullman	Pullman car	First sleeping-car suitable for long-distance travel

Source: From *Freedom and Crisis: An American History, Third Edition,* by Allen Weinstein and Frank Otto Gotell. Copyright © 1974, 1978, 1981 by Random House, Inc. Reprinted by permission of the publisher.

The Politics of Nation-Building After the War of 1812

Geographic expansion, economic growth, and the changes in American life that accompanied them were bound in the long run to generate political controversy. Farmers, merchants, manufacturers, and laborers were affected by the changes in different ways. So were Northerners, Southerners, and Westerners. Federal and state policies meant to encourage or control growth and expansion did not benefit all these groups or sections equally, and unavoidable conflicts of interest and ideology occurred. But the temporary lack of a party system meant that politicians did not have to band together and offer the voters a choice of programs and ideologies. A myth of national harmony prevailed, culminating in the "Era of Good Feeling" during James Monroe's two terms as president.

Behind this facade, individuals and groups fought for advantage, as always, but without the public accountability and need for broad popular approval that a party system would have required. As a result, popular interest in national politics fell to a low ebb.

The absence of party discipline and programs did not completely immobilize the federal government. Congress did manage to legislate on some matters of national concern. Although the President had little control over Congressional action, he could still take important initiatives in foreign policy. The third branch of government—the Supreme Court—was in a position to make far-reaching decisions affecting the relationship between the federal government and the states. The common theme of the public policies that emerged between the War of 1812 and the Age of Jackson was an awakening nationalism—a sense of American pride and purpose that reflected the physical expansionism and material progress of the period.

The Republicans in Power

By the end of the War of 1812, the Federalist party was no longer a significant force in national politics. The party of Jefferson, now known simply as the Republicans, was so completely domi-

nant that it no longer had to distinguish itself from its opponents. Retreating from their original philosophy of states' rights and limited government, party leaders now openly embraced some of the programs of their former Federalist rivals—policies that seemed dictated by postwar conditions. In December 1815, President Madison proposed to Congress that it consider such measures as the reestablishment of a national bank, a protective tariff for industry, and a program of federally financed internal improvements to bind "more closely together the various parts of our extended confederacy." Thus did Jefferson's successor endorse a program enunciated by Alexander Hamilton.

In Congress, Henry Clay of Kentucky took the lead in advocating that the government take action to promote economic development. The keystone of what Clay called the "American system" was a high protective tariff to stimulate industrial growth and provide a "home market" for the farmers of the West, making the nation economically self-sufficient and free from a dangerous dependence on Europe.

In 1816 Congress took the first step toward establishing a neo-Federalist "American System." It enacted a tariff raising import duties an average of 20 percent. This legislation was deemed necessary because a flood of British manufactured goods was beginning to threaten the infant industries that had sprung up during the period when imports had been shut off by the embargo and the war. The tariff had substantial support in all parts of the country. It was supported by a large majority of congressmen from New England and the Middle Atlantic states, and by a respectable minority of the southern delegation. In 1816 manufacturing was not so much a powerful interest as a patriotic concern. Many Americans believed that the preservation of political independence and victory in future wars required industrial independence for the nation. Furthermore, important sectors of the agricultural economy also felt the need of protection—especially the hemp growers of Kentucky, the sugar planters of Louisiana, and the wool producers of New England.

Later the same year, Congress voted to establish the second Bank of the United States. The new national bank had a twenty-year charter, an authorized capital of $35 million, and the right to establish branches throughout the country as needed. Organized much like the first bank, it was a mixed public-private institution, with the federal government owning one fifth of the stock and appointing five of its twenty-five directors. The Bank served the government by providing a depository for its funds, an outlet for marketing its securities, and a source of redeemable bank notes that could be used for the payment of taxes or the purchase of public lands. The bank bill was opposed by state banking interests and strict constructionists, but the majority of Congress found it a necessary and proper means for promoting financial stability and meeting the constitutional responsibility of the federal government to raise money from taxation and loans.

Legislation dealing with internal improvements made less headway in Congress, because it aroused stronger constitutional objections and invited disagreements among sectional groups over who would benefit from specific projects. Except for the National Road, the federal government undertook no major transportation projects during the Madison and Monroe administrations. Both presidents believed, as did Jefferson before them, that internal improvements were desirable but that a constitutional amendment was required before federal monies could legally be used for the building of roads and canals within individual states. In 1817, just before leaving office, Madison vetoed a bill that would have distributed $1,500,000 among the states for local transportation projects.

The following year, there was a lengthy debate in the House of Representatives on the question of whether Congress had the authority to make appropriations for internal improvements. Although a preliminary vote approved the principle, further discussion led to its rejection. In 1822 Monroe vetoed legislation for the repair and administration of the National Road, arguing that even this modest activity was beyond the constitutional powers of Congress. Consequently, public aid for the building of roads and canals continued to come almost exclusively from state and local governments.

Monroe as President

As had Jefferson before him, President Madison chose his own successor in 1816. James Monroe thus became the third successive Virginian to occupy the White House for a full two terms. Monroe was well qualified in terms of experience, having been an officer in the Revolution, governor of Virginia, a special emissary to France, and secretary of state. He was a stolid and unimaginative man, lacking the intellectual depth and agility of his predecessors, but he was reliable, dignified, and high-principled. He projected an image of a disinterested statesman in the tradition of the Founders. (He even dressed in the outmoded fashions of the revolutionary era.) Nominated, as was the custom of the time, by a caucus of Republicans in the House of Representatives, he faced only nominal Federalist opposition in the general election.

The Election of 1816

Candidate	Party	Electoral Vote
Monroe	Republican	183
King	Federalist	34

The Election of 1820

Candidate	Party	Electoral Vote
Monroe	Republican	231
J. Q. Adams		1

The keynote of Monroe's presidency was national harmony, which meant that he went out of his way to avoid controversy. His first inaugural expressed the complacency and optimism of the time, and he followed it up with a goodwill tour of the country, the first made by a president since Washington. A local newspaper was so impressed with Monroe's warm reception in Federalist Boston that it announced that party strife was a thing of the past and that an "era of good feelings" had begun.

A principal aim of Monroe's administrations was to see that these good feelings persisted. He hoped to accommodate or conciliate all the sectional or economic interests of the country and devote his main attention to the task of asserting American power and influence on the world stage. His choice of a cabinet was well calculated to serve these purposes. His secretary of state, John Quincy Adams, was not only a diplomat of great experience and skill but also a New

■ *President James Monroe presided over the "era of good feelings," but serious economic and political difficulties beset the country during his term of office.*

Englander. If recent precedent was to be followed, he would succeed Monroe as president. This expectation served to blunt New England's dissatisfaction with the continuation of the "Virginia dynasty." As secretary of war, Monroe chose John C. Calhoun, a leading Southerner who was also at this time a fervent nationalist. To accommodate the old-line states' rights wing of the party, he appointed William C. Crawford of Georgia—Monroe's opponent in the nominating caucus of 1816—as secretary of the treasury.

The first challenge to Monroe's hopes for domestic peace and prosperity was the panic of 1819, which brought an abrupt end to the postwar boom. After a period of rampant inflation, easy credit, and massive land speculation, the Bank of the United States pricked the bubble by calling in loans and demanding the immediate redemption in specie of the state bank notes in its possession. This retrenchment brought a drastic downturn in the economy, as prices fell sharply, businesses failed, and land bought on credit was foreclosed upon.

In 1821 Congress responded weakly to the resulting depression by passing a relief act that eased the terms for paying debts owed on public land. But Monroe himself had no program to relieve the economic crisis because he did not feel called upon to exert this kind of leadership. The one-party system then prevailing left the Presi-

dent without the ability to work through an organized majority party in Congress; one-party rule had in fact degenerated into a chaotic "no-party" system. Monroe was thus able to remain above the battle and persuade the American public that he was in no way responsible for the state of the economy nor was he in a position to do anything about it. Unlike a modern president, Monroe could retain his full popularity during hard times—the depression was in full swing at the time of his nearly unanimous reelection.

Monroe prized national harmony even more than economic prosperity. But during his first administration a bitter controversy developed between the North and the South over the admission of Missouri to the Union. Once again Monroe remained above the battle and suffered little damage to his own prestige. It was left entirely to the legislative branch of the government to deal with the nation's most serious domestic political crisis between the War of 1812 and the late 1840s.

The Missouri Compromise

In 1817, the Missouri territorial assembly applied for statehood. Since there were two to three thousand slaves already in the territory and the petition made no provision for their emancipation or for curbing further introduction of slaves, it was clear that Missouri would enter the Union as a slave state unless Congress took special action. Missouri was slated to be the first state, other than Louisiana, to be carved out of the Louisiana Purchase, and resolution of the status of slavery there would have implications for the rest of the trans-Mississippi West.

When the question came before Congress in early 1819, submerged sectional fears and anxieties came bubbling to the surface. Many Northerners were resentful of southern control of the presidency and of the fact that the three-fifths clause of the Constitution by which every five slaves were counted as three persons in figuring the state's population, gave the South's free population added weight in the House of Representatives and the electoral college. The South, on the other hand, feared for the future of what they regarded as a necessary balance of power between the sections. Up until 1819 a strict equality had been maintained by alternately admitting slave and free states; in that year there were eleven of each. But northern population was growing more rapidly than southern, and the North had built up a decisive majority in the House of Representatives. Hence the South saw its equal vote in the Senate as essential for preservation of the balance.

In February 1819, Congressman James Tallmadge of New York introduced an amendment to the statehood bill banning further introduction of slaves into Missouri and providing for the gradual emancipation of those already there. After a heated debate, the House approved the Tallmadge amendment by a narrow margin. The Senate, however, voted it down. The issue remained unresolved until a new Congress convened in December 1819. In the great debate that ensued in the Senate, the Federalist leader Rufus King of New York argued that Congress was within its rights to require prohibition of slavery before Missouri could become a state. Southern senators protested that denying Missouri's freedom in this matter was an attack on the principle of equality among the states and that the Tallmadge amendment was a northern power play intended to upset the balance of power.

A separate statehood petition from the people of Maine, who were seeking to be separated from Massachusetts, suggested a way out of the impasse. In February 1820, the Senate voted to couple the admission of Missouri as a slave state with the admission of Maine as a free state. A further amendment was also passed prohibiting slavery in the rest of the Louisiana Purchase north of the southern border of Missouri, or above the latitude of 36°30′. The Senate's compromise then went to the House where it was initially rejected. But through the adroit maneuvering of Henry Clay—who broke the proposal into three separate bills—it eventually won House approval. The measure authorizing Missouri to frame a constitution and apply for admission as a slave state passed by a razor-thin margin of 90 to 87.

A major sectional crisis had been resolved. But

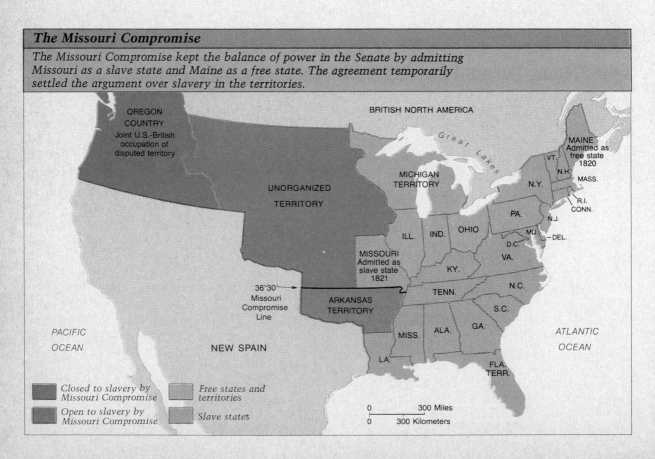

The Missouri Compromise

The Missouri Compromise kept the balance of power in the Senate by admitting Missouri as a slave state and Maine as a free state. The agreement temporarily settled the argument over slavery in the territories.

OREGON COUNTRY
Joint U.S.-British occupation of disputed territory

BRITISH NORTH AMERICA

Great Lakes

MAINE Admitted as free state 1820

UNORGANIZED TERRITORY

MICHIGAN TERRITORY

VT.
N.H.
MASS.
N.Y.
R.I.
CONN.
PA.
N.J.
ILL. IND. OHIO
MD.
DEL.
D.C.
VA.
MISSOURI Admitted as slave state 1821
KY.
36°30′ Missouri Compromise Line
ARKANSAS TERRITORY
TENN.
N.C.
S.C.
GA.
MISS. ALA.
LA.
FLA. TERR.

PACIFIC OCEAN

NEW SPAIN

ATLANTIC OCEAN

Closed to slavery by Missouri Compromise
Open to slavery by Missouri Compromise
Free states and territories
Slave states

0   300 Miles
0   300 Kilometers

the Missouri affair had ominous overtones for the future of North-South relations. Thomas Jefferson described the controversy as "a fire bell in the night," threatening the peace of the Union. In 1821, he wrote prophetically of future dangers: "All, I fear, do not see the speck on our horizon which is to burst on us as a tornado, sooner or later. The line of division lately marked out between the different portions of our confederacy is such as will never, I fear, to be obliterated." The congressional furor had shown that when the issue of slavery or its extension came directly before the people's representatives, regional loyalties took precedence over party or other considerations. An emotional rhetoric of morality and fundamental rights issued from both sides, and votes followed sectional lines much more closely than on any other issue. If the United States were to acquire any new territories in which the status of slavery had to be determined by Congress, renewed sectional strife would be inevitable.

Postwar Nationalism and the Supreme Court

While the Monroe administration was proclaiming national harmony and congressional leaders were struggling to reconcile sectional differences, the third branch of government—the Supreme Court—was making a more substantial and enduring contribution to the growth of nationalism and a strong federal government. Much of this achievement was due to the firm leadership and fine legal mind of the chief justice of the United States, John Marshall.

A Virginian, a Federalist, and the devoted disciple and biographer of George Washington, Marshall served as chief justice from 1801 to 1835, and during that entire period he dominated the Court as no other chief justice has ever done. Discouraging dissent and seeking to hammer out a single opinion on almost every case that came before the Court, he played a role that has been compared to that of a symphony conductor who is also composer of the music and principal soloist.

As the author of most of the major opinions issued by the Supreme Court during its formative period, Marshall gave shape to the Constitution and clarified the crucial role of the Court in the American system of government. He placed the protection of individual liberty, especially the right to acquire property, above the attainment of political, social, or economic equality. Ultimately he was a nationalist, believing that the strength, security, and happiness of the American people depended mainly on economic growth and the creation of new wealth. As he saw it, the Constitution existed to provide the political ground rules for a society of industrious and productive individuals who could enrich themselves while adding to the strength of the nation as a whole.

The role of the Supreme Court, in Marshall's view, was to interpret and enforce these ground rules, especially against the efforts of state legislatures to interfere with the constitutionally protected rights of individuals or combinations of individuals to acquire property through productive activity. To limit state action, he cited the contract clause of the Constitution which prohibited a state from passing a law "impairing the obligation of contracts." As the legal watchdog of an enterprising, capitalistic society, the Court could also approve a liberal grant of power for the federal government so that the latter could fulfill its constitutional responsibility to promote the general welfare by encouraging economic development and national prosperity.

In a series of major decisions between 1819 and 1824, the Marshall Court enhanced the power of the judicial branch and used the contract clause of the Constitution to limit the power of state legislatures. It also strengthened the federal government by sanctioning a broad or loose construction of its constitutional powers and by clearly affirming its supremacy over the states.

In *Dartmouth College v. Woodward* (1819) the Court was asked to rule on whether the legislature of New Hampshire had the right to convert Dartmouth from a private college into a state university. Daniel Webster, arguing for the college and against the state, contended that Dartmouth's original charter of 1769 was a valid and irrevocable contract. The Court accepted his argument. Speaking for all the justices, Marshall made the far-reaching determination that any charter granted by a state to a private corporation was fully protected by the contract clause.

In practical terms, the Court's ruling in the Dartmouth case meant that the kind of business

As chief justice, John Marshall affirmed the Supreme Court's authority to interpret the Constitution and to nullify state laws in conflict with it.

enterprises then being incorporated by state governments—such as turnpike or canal companies and textile manufacturing firms—could hold on indefinitely to any privileges or favors that had been granted in their original charters. The decision therefore increased the power and independence of business corporations by weakening the ability of the states to regulate them or withdraw their privileges. This ruling helped foster the growth of the modern corporation as a profit-making enterprise with only limited public responsibilities.

About a month after the Dartmouth ruling, in March 1819, the Marshall Court handed down its most important decision. The case of *McCulloch* v. *Maryland* arose because the state of Maryland had levied a tax on the Baltimore branch of the Bank of the United States. The unanimous opinion of the Court, delivered by Marshall, was that the Maryland tax was unconstitutional. The two main issues were whether Congress had the right to establish a national bank and whether a state had the power to tax or regulate an agency or institution created by Congress.

In response to the first question, Marshall set forth his doctrine of "implied powers." Conceding that no specific authorization to charter a bank could be found in the Constitution, the chief justice argued that such a right could be deduced from more general powers and from an understanding of the "great objects" for which the federal government had been founded. Marshall thus struck a blow for "loose construction" of the Constitution and a broad grant of power to the federal government to encourage economic growth and stability.

In answer to the second question—the right of a state to tax or regulate a federal agency—Marshall held that the Bank was indeed such an agency and that the power to tax it involved the power to destroy it. In an important assertion of the supremacy of the national government, Marshall argued that the American people "did not design to make their government dependent on the states." This opinion ran counter to the view of many Americans, particularly in the South, that the Constitution did not in fact take away sovereignty from the states. This debate over federal-state relations was not finally resolved until the northern victory in the Civil War decisively affirmed the dominance of federal authority. But Marshall's decision gave great new weight to a nationalist constitutional philosophy.

The case of *Gibbons* v. *Ogden* in 1824 led to a decision that bolstered the power of Congress to regulate interstate commerce. A steamboat monopoly granted by the state of New York was challenged by a competing ferry service operating between New York and New Jersey. The Court declared the New York grant unconstitutional because it amounted to state interference with Congress' exclusive right to regulate interstate commerce. Until this time, it had not been clearly established that "commerce" included navigation, and the Court's ruling went a long way toward freeing private interests engaged in furthering the transportation revolution from state interference.

This case clearly showed the dual effect of Marshall's decision-making. It broadened the power of the federal government at the expense of the states while at the same time encouraging the growth of a national market economy. The actions of the Supreme Court provide the clearest and most consistent example of the main nationalistic trends of the postwar period—the acknowledgment of the federal government's major role in promoting the growth of a powerful and prosperous America and the rise of a nationwide capitalist economy.

Nationalism in Foreign Policy: The Monroe Doctrine

The new spirit of nationalism was also reflected in foreign affairs. The main diplomatic challenge facing Monroe after his reelection in 1820 was how to respond to the successful revolt of most of Spain's Latin American colonies after the Napoleonic wars. In Congress Henry Clay was calling for immediate recognition of the new republics. In doing so he expressed the belief of many Americans that their neighbors to the south were simply following the example of the United States in its own struggle for independence.

Before 1822, the administration stuck to a policy of neutrality. Monroe and Secretary of State Adams feared that recognizing the revolutionary governments would antagonize Spain and impede negotiations to acquire Florida. But pressure for recognition grew in Congress; in 1821 the House of Representatives, responding to Clay's impassioned oratory, passed a resolution of sympathy for the Latin American revolutionaries and made it clear to the President that he would have the support of Congress if and when he decided to accord recognition. After the Florida treaty had been formally ratified in 1821, Monroe agreed to recognition and the establishment of diplomatic ties with the Latin American republics. Mexico and Colombia were recognized in 1822, Chile and Argentina in 1823, Brazil (which had separated from Portugal) and the Federation of Central American States in 1824, and Peru in 1826.

Recognizing the republics put the United States on a possible collision course with the major European powers. Austria, Russia, and Prussia were committed to rolling back the tides of liberalism, self-government, and national self-determination that had arisen during the French Revolution and its Napoleonic aftermath. After Napoleon's first defeat in 1814, the monarchs of Europe had joined in an alliance to protect "legitimate" authoritarian governments from democratic challenges. Originally Great Britain was a member of this concert of nations but withdrew when it found its own interests conflicted with those of the other members. In 1822 the remaining alliance members, joined now by the restored French monarchy, met in Verona to deal with the deteriorating Spanish situation. Although the re-

actionary "Grand Alliance" did not undertake direct intervention in Latin America, it did give France the green light to invade Spain and restore a Bourbon regime that might be disposed to reconquer the empire. Both Great Britain and the United States were alarmed by this prospect.

Particularly troubling to American policymakers was the role of Tsar Alexander I of Russia in these maneuverings. Not only was the tsar an outspoken and active opponent of Latin American independence, but he was attempting to extend Russian claims on the Pacific coast of North America south to the fifty-first parallel—into the Oregon country that the United States wanted for itself. The fear that Russia would become a major influence in the Western Hemisphere weighed heavily on the mind of Secretary of State Adams as he formulated foreign policy during Monroe's second term.

The threat from the Grand Alliance pointed to a need for American cooperation with Great Britain, which had its own reasons for wanting to prevent a restoration of Spanish or French power in the New World. Independent nations offered better and more open markets for British manu-

Chronology

1813	Boston Manufacturing Company founds cotton mill at Waltham, Massachusetts
1815	War of 1812 ends
1816	James Monroe elected president
1818	Andrew Jackson invades Florida
1819	Supreme Court hands down far-reaching decision in Dartmouth College case and in *McCulloch* v. *Maryland* Adams-Onís treaty cedes Spanish territory to the United States Financial panic is followed by a depression lasting until 1823
1820	Missouri Compromise resolves nation's first sectional crisis Monroe reelected president unanimously
1823	Monroe Doctrine proclaimed
1824	LaFayette revisits the United States Supreme Court decides *Gibbons* v. *Ogden*
1825	Erie Canal completed; Canal Era begins

factured goods than the colonies of other nations, and the spokesmen for a burgeoning industrial capitalism anticipated a profitable economic dominance over Latin America. In early 1823 the British foreign secretary, George Canning, tried to exact from the French a pledge that they would make no attempt to acquire territories in Spanish America. When that venture failed, he sought to involve the United States in a joint policy to prevent the Grand Alliance from intervening in Latin America.

In August 1823 Canning broached the possibility of joint Anglo-American action against the designs of the Alliance to Richard Rush, U.S. minister to Great Britain, and Rush referred the suggestion to the president. Monroe welcomed the British initiative because he believed that the United States should play an active role in transatlantic affairs by playing off one European power against another. His inclination to go along with Canning was strengthened by the advice of former presidents Jefferson and Madison, both of whom favored open cooperation with the British.

When Monroe presented the question to his cabinet, however, he encountered the opposition of Secretary of State Adams, who favored a different approach. Adams distrusted the British and differed from the president in his general view of proper relations between the United States and Europe. Adams believed that the national interest would best be served by avoiding all entanglements in European politics while at the same time discouraging European intervention in the Americas. Hence he opposed support for the Greek revolutionaries who were in revolt against Turkish domination, but regarded Latin American independence as essential for the safety and security of the United States.

Political ambition also predisposed Adams against joint action with Great Britain; he hoped to be the next president and did not wish to give his rivals the chance to label him as pro-British. He therefore advocated unilateral action by the United States rather than some kind of joint declaration with the British. As he told the cabinet in November, "It would be more candid, as well as more dignified, to avow our principles explicitly to Russia and France, than to come in as a cock-boat of the British man-of-war."

In the end, Adams managed to swing Monroe and the cabinet around to his viewpoint. In his

John Quincy Adams, secretary of state under James Monroe, advocated a policy of national self-interest and freedom from entanglement in European affairs.

annual message to Congress on December 2, 1823, Monroe included a far-reaching statement on foreign policy that was actually written mainly by Adams. What came to be known as the Monroe Doctrine solemnly declared that the United States opposed any further colonization in the Americas or any effort by European nations to extend their political systems outside of their own hemisphere. In return, the United States pledged not to involve itself in the internal affairs of Europe or to take part in European wars. The statement envisioned a North and South America composed entirely of independent republics—among which the United States would be preeminent.

Although the Monroe Doctrine made little impression on the great powers of Europe at the time it was proclaimed, it signified the rise of a new sense of independence and self-confidence in American attitudes toward the Old World. The United States would now go its own way free of involvement in European conflicts and would energetically protect its own sphere from European interference. The Doctrine also reflected the inward-looking nationalism that had arisen after the War of 1812. The refusal of Congress to recognize Greek independence revealed the extent to which America had detached itself from active involvement in a worldwide struggle against tyranny. America came close to denying a part of its revolutionary heritage in favor of a more conventional patriotism and sense of national interest.

The Monroe Doctrine was the capstone of an era that celebrated American strength, prosperity, and independence. Self-satisfaction, geographic expansion, and solid economic achievement were the keynotes of the age. The wider world was receding from view, but as Americans shifted their attention to internal matters the spirit of harmony and consensus that President Monroe had tried to call forth could not sustain itself. A more competitive climate was emerging, as revealed by the fact that several candidates actively sought the presidency in 1824. By that time the era of consensus nationalism, one-party dominance, and political "good feelings" was about to give way to partisan politics and bitter conflict. To a considerable extent these controversies involved the fruits of "progress"—the question of who would reap the benefits—or pay the price—of a growing economy and a changing society.

Recommended Reading

The standard surveys of the period between the War of 1812 and the Age of Jackson are two works by George Dangerfield: *The Era of Good Feelings* (1952) and *Awakening of American Nationalism, 1815–1828* (1965). A lively narrative of westward expansion is Dale Van Every, *The Final Challenge: The American Frontier, 1804–1845* (1964); but Malcolm J. Rohrbough, *The Trans-Appalachian Frontier* (1978), is more comprehensive and authoritative. Outstanding studies of economic transformation and the rise of a market economy are George R. Taylor, *The Transportation Revolution, 1815–1860* (1951); Paul W. Gates, *The Farmer's Age: Agriculture, 1815–1860* (1960); Stuart Bruchey, *Growth of the Modern American Economy* (1975); and Douglas C. North, *The Economic Growth of the United States, 1790–1860* (1961). An incisive study of the Marshall Court's decisions is Robert K. Faulkner, *The Jurisprudence of John Marshall* (1968). Samuel F. Bemis, *John Quincy Adams and the Foundations of American Policy* (1949), provides the classic account of the statesmanship that led to the Monroe Doctrine. But see also Ernest May, *The Making of the Monroe Doctrine* (1976), for a persuasive new interpretation of how the doctrine originated.

Additional Bibliography

Good accounts of LaFayette's visit and what Americans made of it can be found in Fred Somkin, *Unquiet Eagle: Memory and Desire in the Idea of American Freedom, 1815–1860* (1967) and Anne C. Loveland, *Emblem of Liberty: The Image of Lafayette in the American Mind* (1971). For general accounts of the westward movement, see Frederick Jackson Turner, *The Frontier in American History* (1920) and Ray A. Billington, *Westward Expansion* (1974). On the removal of Native Americans, see Grant Foreman, *Indian Removal*, rev. ed. (1953); A. H. DeRosier, *The Removal of the Choctau Indians* (1970); Francis P. Prucha, *American Indian Policy in the Formative Years* (1962); and Dale Van Every, *Disinherited: The Lost Birthright of the American Indian* (1966). Life on the frontier is covered in Frank Owsley, *Plain Folk of the Old South* (1948); Allen G. Bogue, *From Prairie to Corn Belt* (1963); Richard L. Power, *Planting Corn Belt Culture* (1953); and R.C. Buley, *The Old Northwest: Pioneer Period*, 2 vols. (1950). On exploration and fur-trading in the West, see William H. Goetzmann, *Exploration and Empire* (1966) and David J. Wishart, *The Fur Trade of the American West, 1817–1840* (1979).

Major works on the development of internal waterways are Carter Goodrich, *Government Promotion of American Canals and Railroads* (1960); Harry N. Schieber, *Ohio Canal Era* (1969); Ronald E. Shaw, *Erie Water West* (1966); Erik E. Haites et al., *Western River Transportation* (1975); and Louis C. Hunter, *Steamboats on Western Rivers* (1949). On agricultural development, see Percy W. Bidwell and John I. Falconer, *History of Agriculture in the Northern United States* (1925) and Lewis C. Gary, *History of Agriculture in the Southern United States to 1860*, 2 vols. (1933). The early growth of manufacturing is treated in Caroline F. Ware, *The Early New England Cotton Manufacture*, 2 vols. (1926); Arthur H. Cole, *The American Wool Manufacture*, 2 vols. (1926); Peter Tenin, *Iron and Steel in Nineteenth Century America* (1964); H. J. Habakkuk, *American and British Technology in the Nineteenth Century* (1962); and David J. Jeremy, *Transatlantic Industrial Revolution* (1981).

The politics of postwar nationalism are examined in Shaw Livermore, Jr., *The Twilight of Federalism* (1962); Harry Ammon, *James Monroe* (1971); James S. Young, *The Washington Community, 1800–1828* (1966); and Clement Eaton, *Henry Clay and the Art of American Politics* (1957). The Marshall Court is covered in Leonard Baker, *John Marshall* (1974); Albert J. Beveridge, *John Marshall*, 4 vols. (1916–1919); R. Kent Newmyer, *The Supreme Court under Madison and Taney* (1968); and Morton J. Horwitz, *The Transformation of American Law, 1780–1860* (1977).

On diplomacy and the Monroe Doctrine, see Philip C. Brooks, *Diplomacy and the Borderlands* (1939); Walter LaFeber, ed., *John Quincy Adams and American Continental Empire* (1965); and Dexter Perkins, *The Monroe Doctrine, 1823–1826* (1927) and *Hands off: A History of the Monroe Doctrine* (1941).

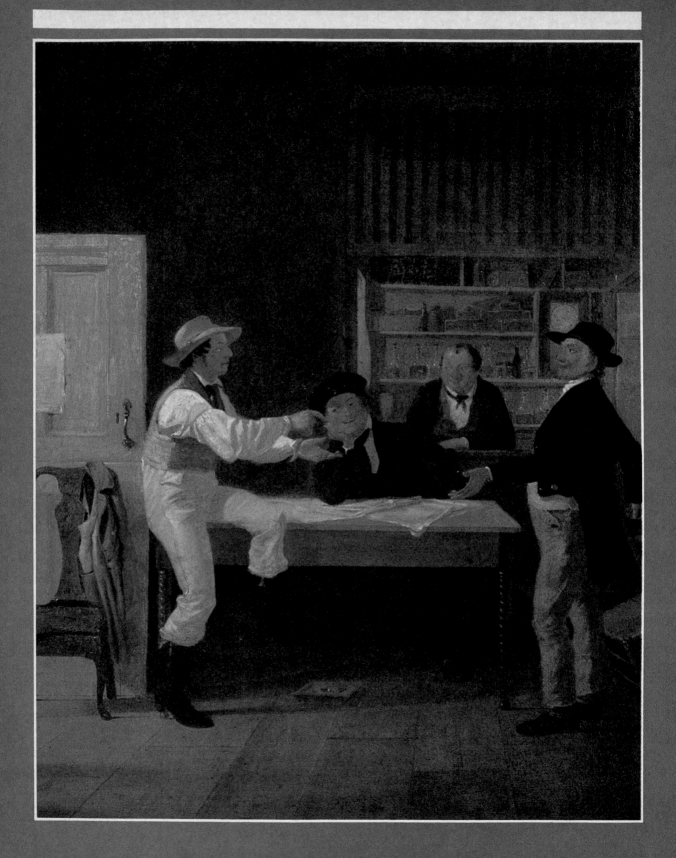

chapter 10

THE
TRIUMPH
OF DEMOCRACY

So many Americans were moving about in the 1820s and '30s that new ways had to be devised to meet their needs. To service the rising tide of travelers, transients, and new arrivals, businessmen erected large hotels in the center of major cities. There they provided lodging, food, and drink on an unprecedented scale. These establishments were as different from the inns of the eighteenth century as the steamboat was from the flatboat. A prototype of the new hotel was the Boston Exchange Hotel with its 8 stories and 300 rooms. Opened in 1809, the Exchange burned down nine years later; and the depression that followed the financial panic of 1819 put a damper on hotel building. After the return of prosperity in 1825, the "first-class hotel" soon became a prominent feature of the American scene. The splendor and comforts of the Baltimore City Hotel, Gadsby's National Hotel in Washington, and the Tremont House of Boston—all of which opened in the late 1820s—dazzled travelers and local residents alike. By the 1830s, imposing hotels were springing up in commercial centers all over the country.

According to the historian Doris Elizabeth King, "the new hotels were so obviously 'public' and 'democratic' in their character that foreigners were often to describe them as a true reflection of American society." These hotels were indeed indicative of the democratic tendencies of the age. Their very existence showed that people were on the move geographically and socially. Among their patrons were traveling salesmen, ambitious young men seeking to establish themselves in a new city, and restless pursuers of "the main chance" not yet ready to put down roots.

Hotel managers shocked European visitors by failing to enforce traditional social distinctions among their clientele. Under the "American plan," guests were required to pay for their meals, and this meant eating at a common "table d'hôte" with anyone who happened to be there, including servants traveling with their employers. Ability to pay was the only requirement for admission (unless one happened to be an unescorted female or be dark-skinned), and every patron, regardless of social background and occupation, enjoyed the kind of personal service previously available only to a privileged class. Because a large proportion of the population stayed in hotels at one time or another, foreigners inferred that there was widespread prosperity and a much

■ *The democratic mingling of social classes was especially apparent in the dining rooms of major hotels that sprang up during the early nineteenth century. Under the "American plan," guests paid for each meal and chose their food from hearty menus like the "Ladies' ordinary menu from the City Hotel in Washington, D.C., in 1848 (right). Of course, dining at long tables with strangers of uncertain breeding and table manners did have its hazards, as illustrated by the contemporary cartoon, "Pass the mustard."*

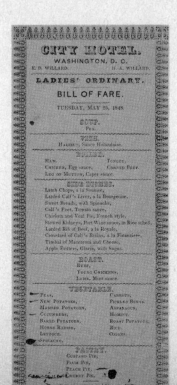

greater "equality of condition" than existed in Europe.

But the hotel culture also revealed some of the limitations of the new era of democratic ideals and aspirations. Blacks and women were excluded or discriminated against, just as they were denied the suffrage at a time when it was being extended to all white males. The genuinely poor —of whom there were more than met the eye of most European visitors—simply could not afford to patronize the hotels and were consigned to squalid rooming houses. If the social equality *within* the hotel reflected a decline in traditional rigid class lines, the broad gulf between potential patrons and those who could not pay the rates signaled the growth of inequality based squarely on wealth rather than inherited status.

The hotel life also reflected the emergence of democratic politics. Professional politicians of a new breed, pursuing the votes of a mass electorate, spent much of their time in hotels as they traveled about. Those elected to Congress or a state legislature often stayed in hotels during the session. The political deals and bargains required for effective party organization or legislative success were sometimes concluded in the private dining rooms of these establishments.

When Andrew Jackson arrived in Washington to prepare for his administration in 1829, he took residence at the new National Hotel. After a horde of well-wishers had made a shambles of the White House during his inaugural reception, Jackson retreated to the National for peace and quiet. The hotel was more than a public and "democratic" gathering place; it was also a haven where the rising men of politics and business could find rest and privacy. In its lobbies, salons, and private rooms the spirit of an age was expressing itself.

■ *A painting of Andrew Jackson in the heroic style by Thomas Sully. The painting shows the President as the common people saw him.*

Democracy in Theory and Practice

Historians have often viewed Andrew Jackson's coming to power—his election in 1828 and the boisterous "people's" inauguration that followed —as the critical moment when a democratic spirit took possession of American culture and public life. But the democratic movement was too broad and deep to be reflected adequately in the rise of a single leader, however influential. Before turning directly to Jackson's role—and to the national political arena where he played it—we need to understand the wider ferment and changing climate of opinion that turned America in a more democratic direction and made Jackson's rise possible.

During the 1820s and '30s the term *democracy* first became generally acceptable as a way of describing how American institutions were supposed to work. Most of the Founders had viewed democracy as a dangerous tendency that needed to be held in check within a well-balanced republic. Too much direct popular influence over government and society allegedly led to instability and even anarchy since the general public was more liable than a cultivated elite to be ruled by passion or corrupted by unscrupulous leaders. For champions of popular government in the Jacksonian period, however, the people were truly sovereign and could do no wrong. "The voice of the people is the voice of God" was their clearest expression of this principle. Conservatives were less certain of the wisdom of the common folk. But even they were coming to recognize that public opinion had to be won over before major policy decisions could be made.

Besides evoking a heightened sense of "popular sovereignty," the democratic impulse stimulated a process of social leveling—an equalization of status for all citizens. Earlier Americans had usually assumed that the rich and wellborn should be treated with special respect and recognized as natural leaders of the community and guardians of its culture and values. By the 1830s the disappearance of inherited social ranks and clearly defined aristocracies or privileged groups struck European visitors like Alexis de Tocqueville as the most radical feature of democracy in America. Historians have described this development as a decline of the spirit of deference.

The decline of deference meant that "self-made men" of lowly origins could now rise more readily to positions of power and influence and that exclusiveness and aristocratic pretensions were likely to provoke popular hostility or scorn. But economic equality, in the sense of an equitable sharing of wealth, was not part of the agenda of mainstream Jacksonianism. This was, after all, a competitive capitalistic society. The watchword was equality of opportunity not equality of rewards. Life was a race, and so long as everyone appeared to have an equal start, there could be no complaint if some were winners and some were losers.

The Democratic Ferment

The supremacy of democracy was most obvious in the new politics of universal manhood suffrage and mass political parties. By the 1820s, most states had removed the last remaining barriers to participation by all white males. In frontier states it proved impractical to base the vote on property because of uncertainty over land titles; in the older states of the East reformers worked successfully to end the suffrage restrictions on all or most of the white men previously excluded. This change was not as radical or controversial as it would be later in nineteenth-century Europe; ownership of land was so common in the United

■ *Democratic fervor inspired creative measures to keep the candidates' names before the voters. This life-sized cast-iron bullfrog is from Jackson's campaign.*

States that a general suffrage did not mean that men without property became a voting majority.

Accompanying this broadening of the electorate was a rise in the proportion of public officials who were elected rather than appointed. More and more judges, as well as legislative and executive officeholders, were chosen by the people. A new style of politicking developed. Politicians had to get out and campaign, demonstrating in their speeches on the stump that they could mirror the fears and concerns of the voters. Electoral politics began to assume a more festive and dramatic quality.

Skillful and farsighted politicians—like Martin Van Buren in New York—began in the 1820s to build stable statewide political organizations out of what had been loosely organized factions of the Republican party. Before the rise of effective national parties, politicians created true party organizations on the state level by dispensing government jobs to their friends and supporters, and by attacking their rivals as enemies of popular aspirations. Van Buren in particular knew exactly what he was doing. Earlier politicians had regarded parties as a threat to republican virtue and had embraced them only as a temporary expedient, but Van Buren regarded a permanent two-party system as an essential to democratic government. In his opinion, regular parties were an effective check on the temptation to abuse power, a tendency deeply planted in the human heart. The major breakthrough in American political thought during the 1820s and '30s was the idea of a "loyal opposition," ready to capitalize politically on the mistakes or excesses of the "ins," without denying their right to act in the same way when the "ins" became the "outs."

Changes in the method of nominating and electing a president fostered the growth of a two-party system on the national level. By 1828 presidential electors were chosen by popular vote rather than by state legislature in all but two of the twenty-four states. The new need to mobilize grass-roots voters behind particular candidates required some form of national organization. Coalitions of state parties which could agree on a single standard-bearer gradually evolved into the great national parties of the Jacksonian era—the Democrats and the Whigs. When national nominating conventions made their appearance in 1831, the choice of candidates became a matter for representative party assemblies rather than congressional caucuses or ad hoc political alliances.

New political institutions and practices encouraged a great upsurge of popular interest and participation. In the presidential election of 1824, the proportion of adult males voting was less than 27 percent. In 1828, it rose sharply to 55 percent, held at about the same level for the elections of 1832 and '36, and then shot up to 78 percent in 1840—the first election in which two fully organized national parties each nominated a single candidate and campaigned for their choices in every state in the Union.

Economic questions dominated the political controversies of the 1820s and '30s. The panic of 1819 and the subsequent depression heightened popular interest in government economic policy, first on the state and then on the national level. No one really knew how to solve the problems of a market economy that went through cycles of boom and bust, but many people thought they had the answer. Some, especially small farmers, favored a return to a simpler and more "honest" economy without banks, paper money, and the easy credit that encouraged speculation. Others, particularly emerging enterpreneurs, saw salvation in government aid and protection for venture capital. Business owners appealed to state governments for charters that granted special privileges

to banks, transportation enterprises, and manufacturing corporations. Politicians attempted to respond to these conflicting views about the best way to restore and maintain prosperity. Out of the economic distress of the early 1820s came a rapid growth of state-level political activity and organization that foreshadowed the rise of national parties organized around economic programs.

The party disputes that arose over corporations, tariffs, banks, and internal improvements involved more than the direct economic concerns of particular interest groups. The republican ideology of the revolutionary period survived in the form of widespread fears of conspiracy against American liberty and equality. Whenever any group appeared to be exerting decisive influence over public policy, people who did not identify with that group's aspirations were quick to charge them with corruption and impending tyranny.

The notion that the American experiment was a fragile one, constantly threatened by power-hungry conspirators, eventually took two principal forms. For Jacksonians, it was "the money power" that endangered the survival of republicanism; for their opponents it was men like Jackson himself—alleged "rabble-rousers" who gulled the electorate into ratifying high-handed and tyrannical actions contrary to the true interests of the nation.

An object of increasing concern for both sides was the role of the federal government. Should it take positive steps to foster economic growth, as the National Republicans and later the Whigs contended, or should it simply attempt to destroy what Jacksonians decried as "special privilege" or "corporate monopoly"? Almost everyone favored equality of opportunity, but there was serious disagreement over whether this goal could best be achieved by active governmental support of commerce and industry or by divorcing the government from the economy in the name of laissez-faire and free competition.

For one group of dissenters, democracy took on a more radical meaning. Workingmen's parties and trade unions emerged in eastern cities during the late '20s and early '30s, and their leaders condemned the growing gap between the rich and the poor resulting from early industrialization and the growth of a market economy. They argued that an expansion of low-paying wage labor

Even workers with little education could grasp the meaning of this Workingmen's Party cartoon, in which a millionaire conspires with the devil to buy an election, while the honest workingman attempts to follow the banner of Liberty by casting his ballot.

was putting working people under the dominance of their employers to such an extent that the American tradition of "equal rights" was in grave danger. Society, in their view, was divided between "producers"—laborers, artisans, farmers, and small business owners who ran their own enterprises—and nonproducing "parasites"— bankers, speculators, and merchant capitalists. Their aim was to give the producers greater control over the fruits of their labor.

These radicals called for a number of reforms to achieve their goal of equal rights. Thomas Skidmore, a founder of the New York Workingman's Party, advocated the abolition of inheritance and a redistribution of land. Champions of the rights of labor also demanded greatly extended and improved systems of public education. But educational reform, however radical or extensive, could only provide equal opportunities to future generations. To relieve the plight of adult workers at a time when their economic and social status was deteriorating, labor reformers and trade unionists experimented with cooperative production and called for a ten-hour workday, abolition of imprisonment for debt, and a currency system based exclusively on hard money so that workers could no longer be paid in depreciated bank notes.

Northern abolitionists and early proponents of women's rights made another kind of effort to extend the meaning and scope of democracy. Radical abolitionists sought an immediate end to southern slavery and supported extension of the franchise and other civil rights for the free blacks of the North. A women's rights movement also developed, partially out of the involvement of women in the abolitionist crusade of the 1830s and the enlarged conception of equal rights that this experience had fostered. But Jacksonian America was too permeated with racism and male chauvinism to give much heed to claims that the equal rights prescribed by the Declaration of Independence should be extended to blacks and women. In many ways, the civil and political situation of both groups deteriorated during an era when white males were claiming their full democratic birthright. (See chapter 11 for a more detailed discussion of these movements.)

Democracy and Society

Although some inequalities persisted or even grew during the age of democracy, they did so in the face of a growing belief that equality was the governing principle of American society. What this meant in practice was that no one could expect special privileges because of family connections. The plain folk, who in an earlier period would have known their place and deferred to their betters, were now likely to greet claims for special treatment with indifference or scorn. The popular hero was "the self-made man" who had climbed the ladder of success through his own efforts without forgetting his origin. European nobles who traveled in America were constantly affronted by democratic attitudes and manners. One was rudely rebuffed when he tried to hire an entire stagecoach for himself and his valet. On other occasions these blue-blooded tourists were forced to eat at the same table as teamsters and stagecoach drivers or share rooms in country inns with rough characters of all kinds. Another irritation was the absence of special first-class accommodations on steamboats and railroads.

Except for southern slaveholders, wealthy Americans could not depend on a distinctive social class for domestic service. Instead of keeping "servants," they hired "help"—household workers who refused to wear livery, agreed to work for only short periods of time, and sometimes insisted on eating at the same table as their employers. As noted in the maid's comments quoted in chapter 8, no true American was willing to be considered as a member of a servant class, and those who engaged in domestic work regarded it as a temporary stopgap. Except as a euphemistic substitute for the word *slave*, the term *servant* virtually disappeared from the American vocabulary.

Another sign of equality was the decline of distinctive modes of dress for upper and lower classes. The elaborate periwigs and knee breeches worn by eighteenth-century gentlemen gave way to short hair and pantaloons, a style that was adopted by men of all social classes. Fashionable dress among women also ceased to be a sure index of gentility; serving girls on their day off wore the same kind of finery as the wives and daughters of the wealthy. Those with a good eye for detail might detect subtle differences in taste or in the quality of materials, but the casual observer or crowds in a large city could easily conclude that all Americans belonged to a single social class.

But of course Americans were not all of one social class. In fact, inequality based on control of productive resources was increasing during the Jacksonian period. A growing percentage of the population, especially in urban areas, possessed no real estate and little other property. The rise of industrialization was creating a permanent class of low-paid wage earners. In rural areas there was a significant division between successful commercial farmers and those who subsisted on marginal land, to say nothing of the enormous inequality of status between southern planters and their black slaves. But most foreign observers overlooked the widening gap between the propertied middle class and the laboring population; their attention was riveted on the fact that all white males were equal before the law and at the polls, a situation that was genuinely radical by European standards.

Furthermore, traditional forms of privilege and elitism were indeed under strong attack, as evidenced by changes in the organization and status of the learned professions. Under Jacksonian pressure, state legislatures abolished the licensing requirements for physicians previously adminis-

The distinction between social classes was further blurred by a change in fashion, as shown by this New York company's advertisement for fall and winter fashions for 1837 and 1838.

Philadelphia's Working People in the Age of Jackson

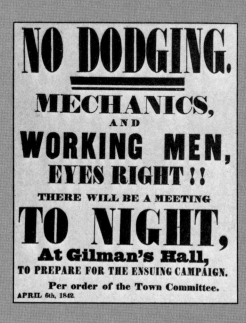

NO DODGING.

MECHANICS, AND WORKING MEN, EYES RIGHT!! THERE WILL BE A MEETING TO NIGHT, At Gilman's Hall, TO PREPARE FOR THE ENSUING CAMPAIGN. Per order of the Town Committee. APRIL 6th, 1842.

Between 1800 and 1850, Philadelphia grew rapidly and changed enormously. From a seaport and commercial center with 81,000 residents it developed into an industrial metropolis with a population of 408,000. The new factories were located mainly on the outskirts of the city, and most were small in comparison to New England's great textile mills. Furthermore, the great majority of the working-class men and women, even at the end of the period, were not actually employed within the factories. They were paid to operate hand looms in their own cottages, worked as artisans in relatively small shops, cut and sewed cloth and leather in garrets and sweatshops, or did the unskilled lifting and hauling necessary in every bustling city.

Before the beginnings of massive immigration in the 1840s, most of Philadelphia's working people were native-born Americans. Some were born in the city but more had recently migrated from the countryside. (More rural Americans moved to the city in pre–Civil War America than went west in search of better farmland.) Less than 10 percent of the workers of the 1820s and '30s were European immigrants. But the fact that they came from more or less similar backgrounds did not mean that working people had a uniform culture and outlook on life.

In his research on working-class men, historian Bruce Laurie has identified three distinct cultural styles among them. Some were evangelical Christians, strongly affected by a recent series of revivals. Their religious orientation encouraged regular and sustained work, abstention from alcohol, and hopes for upward mobility through individual effort. Another group he calls the "traditionalists." They had attitudes characteristic of workers from preindustrial times. They worked only when necessary and at their own pace. It was important, they insisted, to allow ample time for such communal recreations as drinking, gaming, and brawling. A tailor, found conspicuously lounging in public on a working day, summed up this ethic to a shocked Presbyterian minister. Asked if he and a companion were unemployed, the tailor replied: "Not at all. We are only enjoying the *Tailor's Vacation*. Pressure is well enough, as I can testify when the last dollar is about to be pressed out of me, but *Vacation* is capital. It tickles one's fancy with the notion of choice. 'Nothing on compulsion' is my motto."

A third group of working people rejected both evangelical religion and the devil-may-care attitude of the traditionalists. These were the working-class radicals. Self-made intellectuals devoted to serious reading and discussion, they carried on the tradition of free thought in religion and politics associated with Thomas Paine and other radicals of the revolutionary period. They valued discipline and efficiency in the work place —most of them were skilled artisans and proud of their handiwork; but they objected vigorously to the loss of personal independence that the new industrialism was bringing in its wake. From their ranks came most of the leaders of the militant labor movement that arose in Philadelphia during the Jacksonian period.

A spokesman for the radical position was William Heighton, an English immigrant. In 1827 and '28, he spoke out in favor of labor's right to all the wealth it produced. In strong language, he denounced an economic system that allowed the mere "accumulators" of wealth—merchants, bankers, landlords, and professionals—to get progressively richer, while the "producers" of it— artisans, laborers, and farmers—lived in deepening poverty. He was right to complain; modern studies show that the most affluent 10 percent of Philadelphia's population was greatly increasing its share of the community's total wealth during this period.

Ideas similar to Heighton's helped make Philadelphia a center for political and trade union activity among the working class beginning in the late 1820s. Philadelphia radicals founded and dominated the first genuine labor movement in American history—the Mechanics' Union of Trade Associations, founded in 1827 as a federation of societies previously formed by craftsmen in particular trades. But this organization included only skilled artisans and was therefore in no position to speak for the working class as a whole. The same activists also organized the Workingmen's Party to compete in local elections, but their effort to translate labor militancy into effective political action failed dismally at the polls.

In 1834 Philadelphia's labor militants met to establish a new organization that would include more workers and avoid the treacherous shoals of electoral politics. The General Trades' Union of the City and County of Philadelphia soon grew into the most successful local labor federation of the time, incorporating fifty craft associations with a total of ten thousand members.

In 1835 the General Trades' Union took a leading role in America's first general strike. The walkout began spontaneously when coal heavers on the Schuylkill River docks suddenly deserted their jobs to protest long hours. Shoemakers, carpenters, and members of most other trades soon joined them in the streets. Eventually about twenty thousand workers—skilled and unskilled alike—were on strike. They demanded a ten-hour workday for all industrial employees and higher wages for those who took work into their homes. The strike was spectacularly successful; except in the textile mills where workers accepted management's offer of an eleven-hour day, a norm of ten hours on the job was accepted everywhere. Membership in the General Trades' Union soared during and after the strike, and it appeared that a vigorous and effective labor movement had been born in Philadelphia.

But the panic of 1837 and the deep depression that followed caused mass unemployment and crippled efforts to organize working men. Times were so hard in Philadelphia that a third to a fourth of the working population left the city hoping to find employment elsewhere. The General Trades' Union simply collapsed under the weight of joblessness and despair. But this first major effort to unionize American workers and exert mass pressure for better working conditions left an enduring legacy of ideas and experience for future champions of labor.

tered by local medical societies. As a result, practitioners of unorthodox modes of healing were permitted to compete freely with established medical doctors. One popular therapy was Thomsonianism, a form of treatment based entirely on the use of common herbs and roots. The Thomsonians identified themselves openly with Jacksonian Democracy, attacked the "monopolistic" tendencies of the medical profession, and argued that their own form of medicine would make every man his own physician. The democratic tide also struck the legal profession. Local bar associations continued to set the qualifications for practicing attorneys, but in many places they lowered standards and admitted persons with little or no formal training and only the most rudimentary knowledge of the law.

For the clergy, "popular sovereignty" meant that they were increasingly under the thumb of the laity. The growing dependence of ministers on the support and approval of their congregations forced them to develop a more popular and emotional style of preaching. Ministers had ceased to command respect merely because of their office. To succeed in their calling they had to please the public, in much the same way that a politician had to satisfy the electorate.

Members of the old upper class who could not adapt to the new politics and democratic rhetoric often found themselves stripped of the offices they had once held almost as a matter of right. Denied direct political power, they sought to exert influence through their control of philanthropic and charitable activities. But even here they were seriously challenged by national reform movements and philanthropic organizations that employed professional traveling agents and experimented with new forms of mass appeal. "Gentlemen of property and standing" joined the northern mobs who attacked abolitionists in the 1830s partly because the antislavery movement bypassed the local notables who had previously held a monopoly on the sanctioning and promoting of worthy causes.

Democratic Culture

The democratic spirit also found expression in the rise of new forms of literature and art directed at a mass audience. The intentions of individual artists and writers varied considerably. Some sought success by pandering to popular taste in defiance of traditional standards of high culture. Others tried to capture the spirit of the age by portraying the everyday life of ordinary Americans rather than the traditional subjects of "aristocratic" art. A notable few hoped to use literature and art as a way of improving popular taste and instilling deeper moral and spiritual values. But all of them were aware that their audience was the broad citizenry of a democratic nation rather than a refined elite.

A mass market for popular literature was made possible by a rise in literacy and a revolution in the technology of printing. An increase in potential readers and a decrease in publishing costs led to a flood of lurid and sentimental novels, some of which became the first American best-sellers. By the 1840s and '50s writers like George Lippard, Mrs. Southworth, and Augusta Jane Evans had perfected the formulas that led to surefire commercial success. Gothic horror and the perils of virtuous heroines threatened by dastardly villains were among the ingredients that readers came to expect from popular fiction. Many of the new sentimental novels were written by and for women. Some women implicitly protested against their situation by portraying men in general as tyrannical, unreliable, or vicious and the women they abandoned or failed to support as resourceful individualists capable of making their own way in a man's world. But the standard happy endings sustained the convention that a woman's place was in the home; for a virtuous and protective man always turned up and saved the heroine from independence.

In the theater, melodrama became the dominant genre. Despite religious objections, theatergoing was a popular recreation in the cities during the Jacksonian era. The standard fare involved the inevitable trio of beleaguered heroine, mustachioed villain, and a hero who asserted himself in the nick of time. Patriotic comedies extolling the common sense of the rustic Yankee who foiled the foppish European aristocrat were also popular and served to arouse the democratic sympathies of the audience. Men and women of all classes went to the theater, and those in the cheap seats often behaved raucously and even violently when they did not like what they saw. Unpopular actors or plays could even provoke serious riots. In an

1849 incident in New York, 134 people were killed in disorders stemming from hostility toward an English actor who was the rival of Edwin Forrest, the most popular American thespian of the time.

The spirit of "popular sovereignty" expressed itself less dramatically in the visual arts, but its influence was nonetheless felt. Beginning in the 1830s there was a vogue of democratic genre painting that featured scenes from everyday life, usually with a comic twist. (See the photo essay on democratic genre art following page 288.)

Architecture and sculpture reflected the democratic spirit in a different way; they were viewed as civic art forms meant to glorify the achievements of the Republic. In the 1820s and '30s, the Greek style with its columned façades not only predominated in the architecture of public buildings but was also favored for banks, hotels, and private dwellings. Besides symbolizing an identification of the United States with the democracy of ancient Greece, it was a way of achieving monumental impressiveness at a fairly low cost. Even in newly settled frontier communities, it was relatively easy and inexpensive to put up a functional square building and then add a classical façade. Not everyone could live in structures that looked like Greek temples, but almost everyone could admire them from the outside or conduct business within their walls.

Sculpture was intended strictly for public admiration or inspiration, and its principal subjects were the heroes of the Republic. The sculptors who accepted public commissions had to make sure that their work met the expectations of politicians and taxpayers, who favored stately, idealized images. Horatio Greenough, the greatest of sculptor of the pre–Civil War era, got into trouble when he unveiled a seated George Washington, dressed in classical grab and nude from the waist up. Much more acceptable was the equestrian figure of Andrew Jackson executed for the federal government by Clark Mills and unveiled in 1853. What most impressed the public was that Mills had succeeded in balancing the horse on two legs.

Serious exponents of a higher culture and a more refined sensibility sought to reach the new public in the hope of enlightening or uplifting it. The "Brahmin poets" of New England—Henry Wadsworth Longfellow, James Russell Lowell,

■ *A performance of the farce* Monsieur Tonson *at the Park Theater, New York, 1822. Both men and women attended the theater, but only men were seated on the main floor.*

and Oliver Wendell Holmes—offered lofty sentiments and moral messages to a receptive middle class; Ralph Waldo Emerson carried his philosophy of spiritual self-reliance to lyceums and lecture halls across the country, and great novelists like Nathaniel Hawthorne and Herman Melville experimented with the popular romantic genres. But Hawthorne and Melville failed to gain a large readership. The ironic and pessimistic view of life that pervaded their work clashed with the optimism of the age.

The great landscape painters of the period—Thomas Cole, Asher Durand, and Frederic Edwin Church—believed that their representations of untamed nature would elevate popular taste and convey moral truths. The ideal of art for art's sake was utterly alien to the instructional spirit of mid-nineteenth-century American culture. The responsibility of the artist in a democratic society, it was generally assumed, was to contribute to the general welfare by encouraging virtue and

■ *Asher Durand's paintings, such as* In the Catskills *(above), helped establish an image of a young and optimistic republic, as noble as its wilderness.*

proper sentiments. Only Edgar Allen Poe seemed to fit the European image of romantic genius rebelling against middle-class pieties. But in his own way, Poe exploited the popular fascination with death in his verse and used the conventions of Gothic horror in his tales. The most original of the antebellum poets, Walt Whitman, sought to be a direct mouthpiece for the rising democratic spirit, but his abandonment of traditional verse forms and his freedom in dealing with the sexual side of human nature left him isolated and unappreciated during his most creative years.

Jackson and the Politics of Democracy

The public figure who came to symbolize the triumph of democracy was Andrew Jackson, who came out a loser in the presidential election of 1824. His victory four years later, his actions as President, and the great political party that formed around him refashioned national politics in a more democratic mold. It may be an exaggeration to call the whole period from the 1820s to the '40s "the age of Jackson," but Old Hickory occupied the center of the public stage during much of that turbulent and eventful era.

The Election of 1824 and J. Q. Adams' Administration

The election of 1824 was one of the most complicated and controversial in American history. As Monroe's second term ended, the ruling Republican party was in disarray and could not agree on who should succeed to the presidency. The party's congressional causus chose William Crawford Georgia, an old-line Jeffersonian. But a majority of congressmen showed their disapproval of this outmoded method of nominating candidates by refusing to attend the caucus. Monroe himself favored John Quincy Adams of Massachusetts. This gave the New England statesman an important boost but did not discourage others from entering the contest. Supporters of Henry Clay and John C. Calhoun mounted campaigns for their favorites, and a group of local leaders in his home state of Tennessee tossed Jackson's hat into the ring.

Initially Jackson was not given much of a chance. Unlike the other aspirants he had not played a conspicuous role in national politics; his sole claim to fame was as a military hero, and not even his original supporters believed that this would be sufficient to catapult him into the White House. But after testing the waters, Calhoun withdrew and chose instead to run for vice-president. Then Crawford suffered a debilitating stroke that weakened his chances. With one Southerner out of the race and another disabled, Jackson began to pick up support in the slaveholding states. He also found favor among those in the North and West who were disenchanted with the economic nationalism of Clay and Adams. At this time Jackson did not openly oppose Clay's "American system"—indeed he appeared to give it a qualified endorsement—but

The Election of 1824			
Candidate	Party	Popular Vote	Electoral Vote*
J. Q. Adams	No party	113,122	84
Jackson	designations	151,271	99
Clay		47,531	37
Crawford		40,856	41

No candidate received a majority of the electoral votes. Adams was elected by the House of Representatives.

he was not strongly identified with it in the public mind.

In the election Jackson won a plurality of the electoral votes. But since he lacked the necessary majority, the contest was thrown into the House of Representatives where the legislators were to choose from among the three top candidates. Here Adams emerged victorious over Jackson and Crawford. Clay, who had just missed making the final three, provided the winning margin by persuading his supporters to vote for Adams. When Adams proceeded to appoint Clay as his secretary of state, the Jacksonians charged that a "corrupt bargain" had deprived their favorite of the presidency. Although there was no evidence that Clay had bartered votes for the promise of a high office that often led to the White House, the corrupt-bargain charge was widely believed. As a result, Adams assumed office under a cloud of suspicion.

Although he was a man of integrity and vision, Adams was an inept politician. The political winds were blowing against nationalistic programs, partly because the country was just recovering from a depression that many thought had been caused or worsened by federal banking and tariff policies. Adams refused to bow to public opinion and called instead for an expansion of governmental activity. Advocates of states' rights and a strict construction of the Constitution were aghast, and the opposition that developed in Congress turned the administration's domestic program into a pipe dream.

The new Congress that was elected in 1826 was clearly under the control of men hostile to the administration and favorable to the presidential aspirations of Andrew Jackson. The main business before Congress was the tariff issue. Pressure for greater protection came not only from manu-

facturers but also from many farmers, especially wool and hemp growers. The cotton-growing South—the only section where tariffs of all kinds were unpopular—was already safely in the general's camp. As for Jackson himself, he had never categorically opposed protective tariffs so long as they were "judicious."

As it turned out, however, the resulting tariff law was anything but judicious. The operating principle in the congressional give-and-take was something for everybody. Those favoring protection for farmers agreed to protection for manufacturers and vice versa. The substantial, across-the-board increase in duties that resulted angered southern free traders and became known as the "tariff of abominations." But historians long erred in explaining the 1828 tariff as a complex Jacksonian plot that backfired; it was in fact an early example of how special interest groups can achieve their goals in democratic politics through the process of legislative bargaining known as logrolling.

■ *Popular belief that John Quincy Adams had bought the support of Henry Clay cast doubt on Adams' integrity. This enamel miniature of Clay was worn as a pin.*

Jackson Comes to Power

The campaign of 1828 actually began early in the Adams administration. Rallying around the charge of a corrupt bargain between Adams and Clay, Jackson's supporters began to organize on the state and local level with an eye to reversing the outcome of the 1824 election. By late 1827 a Jackson committee was functioning in virtually every county and important town or city in the nation. Influential state or regional leaders who had supported other candidates in 1824 now rallied behind the Tennessean to create a formidable coalition.

The most significant of these were Vice-President Calhoun, who now spoke for the militant states' rights sentiment of the South; Senator Martin Van Buren, who dominated New York politics through the political machine known as the Albany Regency; and two Kentucky editors, Francis P. Blair and Amos Kendall, who worked to mobilize opposition to Henry Clay and his "American system" in the West. As they prepared themselves for the canvass of 1828, these leaders and their many local followers laid the foundations for the first modern American political party—the Democrats. The fact that the Democratic party was founded to promote the cause of a particular presidential candidate revealed a central characteristic of the emerging two-party system. From this time on, according to historian Richard P. McCormick, national parties existed primarily "to engage in a contest for the presidency." Without this great prize, there would have been little incentive to create national organizations out of the parties and factions developing in the several states.

The election of 1828 saw the birth of a new era of mass democracy. The mighty effort on behalf of Jackson featured the widespread use of such electioneering techniques as huge public rallies, torchlight parades, and lavish barbecues or picnics paid for by the candidate's supporters. Personalities and mudslinging dominated the campaign. The Democratic party press and a legion of pamphleteers bombarded the public with praise of Old Hickory and vicious personal attacks on Adams. The supporters of Adams responded in kind; they even sunk to the level of accusing Jackson's wife Rachel of bigamy and adultery because she had unwittingly married Jackson before being officially divorced from her first husband. The Democrats then came up with the utterly false charge that Adams' wife was born out of wedlock!

What gave Jacksonians the edge was their success in portraying their candidate as an authentic man of the people, despite his substantial fortune in land and slaves. His backwoods upbringing, his record as a popular military hero and Indian fighter, and even his lack of education were touted as evidence that he was a true representative of the common people, especially the plain folk of the South and the West. In the words of one of his supporters, Jackson had "a judgment unclouded by the visionary speculations of the academician." Adams, according to Democratic propagandists, was the exact opposite—an over-educated aristocrat, more at home in the salon and the study than among plain people. As on some other occasions in American history, anti-intellectualism was a potent force. It was nature's nobleman against the aloof New England Brahmin, and Adams never really had a chance.

The result had the appearance of a landslide for Old Hickory. Jackson won 642,553 popular votes and 178 electoral votes to 500,897 popular votes and 83 electoral votes for Adams. Clearly Jackson's organization had been more effective and his popular appeal substantially greater. But the

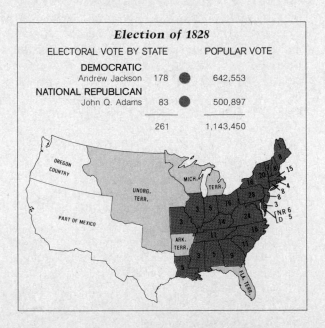

Election of 1828

verdict of the people was not as decisive as these figures might suggest. Although Jackson had piled up massive majorities in some of the slave states, the voters elsewhere divided fairly evenly. Furthermore, it was not clear what kind of a mandate he had won. Most of the politicians in his camp favored states' rights and limited government as against the nationalism of Adams and Clay, but the general himself had never taken a clear public stand on such issues as banks, tariffs, and internal improvements. His victory was more a triumph of image and personality than the popular endorsement of a particular set of programs.

Jackson turned out to be one of the most forceful and domineering of American presidents. His most striking character traits were an indomitable will, an intolerance of opposition, and a prickly pride that would not permit him to forgive or forget an insult or supposed act of betrayal. It is sometimes hard to determine whether his political actions were motivated by principle or personal spite. His troubled childhood and difficult early life—his father died before he was born and his mother when he was fourteen—clearly affected his personality. As a young man on his own in a frontier environment, he had learned to fight his own battles. Somewhat violent in temper and action, he fought a number of duels and served in wars against the British, the Spanish, and the Indians with a zeal that his critics found excessive. His experiences had made him tough and resourceful but had also deprived him of the flexibility normally associated with successful politicians. Yet he generally got what he wanted. He may have been prone to neurotic obsession, but if so there was method in his madness.

Jackson's presidency commenced with his open endorsement of rotation of officeholders or what his critics called "the spoils system." Although he did not actually depart radically from his predecessors in the degree to which he removed federal officeholders and replaced them with his supporters, he was the first president to defend this practice as a legitimate application of democratic doctrine. He proclaimed in his first annual message that "the duties of all public officers are . . . so plain and simple that men of intelligence may readily qualify themselves for their performance" and that "no man has any more intrinsic claim to office than another."

Jackson's resigning cabinet members were, according to this cartoon, rats deserting a crumbling house.

Jackson also established a new kind of relationship with his cabinet. Under previous administrations, cabinet officers had frequently acted on their own responsibility, making major policy decisions and advising Congress on legislation without presidential direction. Normally they had served for the full term of the president who selected them. Key questions affecting the government as a whole had often been decided by a majority vote of the cabinet. All that changed with the inauguration of Jackson. Old Hickory regarded himself as "the direct representative of the people" and his cabinet as an interchangeable set of administrators whose sole function was to carry out the will of the chief executive. He used his cabinet members more for consultation than for policymaking, and he diluted their influence even further by relying heavily on the advice of an unofficial and confidential set of advisors known as the Kitchen Cabinet.

Midway in his first administration Jackson completely reorganized his cabinet, replacing almost all of his original appointees. The apparent cause of this upheaval was the Peggy Eaton affair. Peggy O'Neale Eaton was the daughter of a Washington tavern owner who married Secretary of War John Eaton in 1829. Because of gossip about her moral character, the wives of other cabinet members refused to receive her socially. Jackson became her fervent champion, partly because he found the charges against her reminiscent of the slanders against his late wife Rachel. When he raised the issue of Mrs. Eaton's social status at a cabinet meeting, only Secretary of State Van Buren, a widower, supported his stand. This seemingly trivial incident led to the resignation of all but one of the cabinet members, and the President was able to begin again with a fresh slate. Although Van Buren resigned with the rest, his loyalty was rewarded by his appointment as minister to England and strong prospects of future favor.

■ *Sequoyah's invention of the Cherokee alphabet enabled thousands of Cherokees to read and write primers and newspapers published in their own language.*

Indian Removal

The first major policy question facing the Jackson administration concerned the fate of Native Americans. Jackson had long favored removing eastern Indians to lands beyond the Mississippi. In his military service on the southern frontier, he had been directly involved in coercing or persuading tribal groups to emigrate. Jackson's support of removal was no different from the policy of previous administrations. The only real issue was how rapidly and thoroughly the process should be carried out and by what means. At the time of Jackson's election, the states of Georgia, Alabama, and Mississippi, distressed by the federal government's failure to eliminate the substantial Indian enclaves remaining within their boundaries, were clamoring for quick action. President Adams had recently quarreled with the state of Georgia over the terms of removal treaties involving the Creek Indians.

The greatest obstacle to voluntary relocation, however, was the Cherokee nation which held land in Georgia, Alabama, North Carolina, and Tennessee. The Cherokees not only refused to move but had instituted a republican form of government for themselves, achieved literacy in their own language, and made considerable progress toward adopting a settled agrarian way of life similar to that of southern whites. The professed aim of the government's Indian policy was the "civilization" of the Indians, and the official reason given for removal was that this aim could not be accomplished in areas surrounded by white settlements and subject to demoralizing frontier influences. But missionaries and northeastern philanthropists argued that the Cherokees were a major exception to the rule and should be allowed to remain where they were.

The southern states disagreed. Immediately after Jackson's election, Georgia extended its state laws over the Cherokees. Before he was inaugurated, Alabama and Mississippi took similar action by asserting state authority over the tribes in their own states. This legislation defied provisions of the Constitution giving the federal government exclusive jurisdiction over Indian affairs and also violated specific treaties. As anticipated, Jackson quickly gave his endorsement to the state actions. His own attitude toward Indians was that they were children when they did the white man's bidding and savage beasts when they resisted. He was also keenly aware of his political debt to the land-hungry states of the South.

Consequently, in his December 1829 message to Congress he advocated a new and more coercive removal policy. He denied Cherokee autonomy, asserted the primacy of states' rights over Indian rights, and called for the speedy and thorough removal of all eastern Indians to designated areas beyond the Mississippi.

Early in 1830 the President's congressional supporters introduced a bill to implement this policy. The ensuing debate was vigorous and heated. Opponents took up the cause of the Cherokees in particular and charged that the President had defied the Constitution by removing federal protection from the southeastern tribes. But Jackson and his supporters were determined to ride roughshod over humanitarian or constitutional objections to Indian dispossession. With strong support from the South and the western border states, the removal bill passed the Senate by a vote of 28 to 19 and the House by the narrow margin of 102 to 97.

Jackson then moved quickly to conclude the necessary treaties, using the threat of unilateral state action to bludgeon the tribes into submission. In 1832 he condoned Georgia's defiance of a Supreme Court decision (*Worcester* v. *Georgia*) that denied the right of a state to extend its jurisdiction over tribal lands. By 1833 all the southeastern tribes except the Cherokees had agreed to evacuate their ancestral homes. In 1838 a stubbornly resisting majority faction of the Cherokees were rounded up by federal troops and forcibly marched to Oklahoma. This trek— known as the "Trail of Tears"—was made under such harsh conditions that almost a quarter of the marchers died on the way. A ruthless land grab, the Cherokee removal exposed the prejudiced and greedy side of Jacksonian democracy.

The Nullification Crisis

During the 1820s Southerners became increasingly fearful of federal encroachment on the rights of the states. Behind this concern, in South Carolina at least, was a strengthened commitment to the preservation of slavery and a resulting anxiety about possible uses of federal power to strike at the "peculiar institution." Hoping to keep the explosive slavery issue out of the political limelight, South Carolinians seized on another genuine grievance—the protective tariff—as the issue on which to take their stand in favor of a state veto power over federal actions that they viewed as contrary to their interests. As a staple-producing and exporting region, the South had

Cherokee Indians, carrying their few possessions, are prodded along by U.S. soldiers on the "Trail of Tears." Several thousand Indians died on the ruthless forced march from their homelands in the East to the newly established Indian Territory in Oklahoma.

sound economic reasons for favoring free trade. Tariffs increased the prices that southern agriculturalists paid for manufactured goods and threatened to undermine their foreign markets by inciting counterprotection.

Vice-President John C. Calhoun emerged as the leader of the states' rights insurgency in South Carolina, abandoning his earlier support of nationalism and the "American system." After the passage of the "tariff of abominations" in 1828, the state legislature declared the new duties unconstitutional and endorsed a lengthy disquisition—written anonymously by Calhoun—that affirmed the right of an individual state to nullify federal law. Calhoun supported Jackson in 1828 and expected to serve amicably as his vice-president because he did not expect Jackson to desert his native region on questions involving the tariff and states' rights. He also entertained hopes of succeeding Jackson as president. Early in his administration, Jackson appeared well attuned to the southern slave-holding position on state versus federal authority. Besides acquiescing in Georgia's de facto nullification of federal treaties upholding Indian tribal rights, he vetoed a major internal improvements bill in 1830, invoking a strict construction of the Constitution to deny federal funds for the building of the Maysville Road in Kentucky.

In the meantime, however, a bitter personal feud developed between Jackson and Calhoun. The vice-president and his wife were viewed by Jackson as prime movers in the ostracism of Peggy Eaton. Furthermore, evidence came to light that Calhoun, as secretary of state in Monroe's cabinet in 1818, had favored punishing Jackson for his incursion into Florida. As Calhoun lost favor with Jackson, it became clear that Van Buren rather than the vice-president would be Jackson's designated successor. The personal breach between Jackson and Calhoun colored and intensified their confrontation over nullification and the tariff.

But there were also differences of principle. Although generally a defender of states' rights and strict construction of the Constitution, Jackson opposed the theory of nullification as a threat to the survival of the Union. In his view, federal power should be held in check, but this did not mean that the states were truly sovereign. His nationalism was that of a military man who had fought for the United States against foreign enemies and was not about to permit the nation's disintegration at the hands of domestic dissidents. The differences between Jackson and Calhoun came into the open at the Jefferson Day Dinner in 1830, when Jackson offered the toast "Our Union: It must be preserved"; to which Calhoun responded: "The Union next to Liberty most dear. May we always remember that it can only be preserved by distributing equally the benefits and the burdens of the Union."

In 1830 and '31 the movement against the tariff gained strength in South Carolina. Calhoun openly took the lead, elaborating further on his view that states had the right to set aside federal laws.

Vice-President John C. Calhoun (right) emerged as a champion of states' rights during the nullification crisis, when cartoons showed the emaciated South burdened by tariffs while the North grew fat at southern expense.

In 1832 Congress passed a new tariff that lowered the rates slightly but retained the principle of protection. Supporters of nullification argued that the new law simply demonstrated that no genuine relief could be expected from Washington. They then succeeded in persuading the South Carolina state legislature to call a special convention. When the convention met in November 1832, the members voted overwhelmingly to nullify the tariffs of 1828 and '32 and to forbid the collection of customs duties within the state.

Jackson reacted with characteristic decisiveness. He alerted the secretary of war to prepare for possible military action, issued a proclamation denouncing nullification as a treasonous attack on the Union, and asked Congress to vote him the authority to use the army to enforce the tariff. At the same time, he sought to pacify the nullifiers somewhat by recommending a lower tariff. Congress responded by enacting the Force Bill—which gave the President the military powers he sought—and the compromise tariff of 1833. The latter was primarily the work of Jackson's political enemy Henry Clay, but the President signed it anyway. Faced with Jackson's clear intention to use force if necessary and somewhat appeased by the prospect of a lower tariff, South Carolina suspended the nullification ordinance in late January 1833 and formally rescinded it in March, after the new tariff had been enacted. To demonstrate that they had not conceded their constitutional position, the convention delegates concluded their deliberations by nullifying the Force Bill.

The nullification crisis revealed that Southerners would not tolerate any federal action that seemed contrary to their interests or raised doubts about the institution of slavery. The nullifiers' principle of state sovereignty implied the right of secession as well as the right to declare laws of Congress null and void. As subsequent events would clearly show, a fear of northern meddling with slavery was the main spur to the growth of a militant states' rights philosophy in the South. Outside of South Carolina, such anxieties were still relatively weak at the time of the nullification crisis. Jackson was himself a Southerner and a slaveholder, a man who detested abolitionists and everything they stood for. In many ways, he was a proslavery president; later he would use his executive power to stop anti-slavery literature from being carried by the U.S. mails.

But some far-sighted southern loyalists were alarmed by the Unionist doctrines Jackson propounded in his proclamation against nullification. More strongly than any previous president, he had asserted that the federal government was supreme over the states and that the Union was indivisible. What was more, he had justified the use of force against states that denied federal authority.

The Bank War and the Second Party System

Jackson's most important and controversial use of executive power was his successful attack on the Bank of the United States. "The Bank War" revealed some of the deepest concerns of Jackson and his supporters and expressed their concept of democracy in a dramatic way. It also aroused intense opposition to the President and his policies, an opposition that crystallized in a new national party—the Whigs. The destruction of the Bank and the economic disruption that followed brought to the forefront the issue of the government's relationship to the nation's financial system. Differences on this question helped to sustain the new two-party system and provided the stuff of political controversy during the administration of Jackson's handpicked successor—Martin Van Buren.

Mr. Biddle's Bank

The Bank of the United States had long been embroiled in public controversy. Its role in precipitating the panic of 1819 by suddenly calling in its loans had led many, especially in the South and the West, to blame the Bank for the subsequent depression. But after Nicholas Biddle took over the Bank's presidency in 1823, it regained public confidence. Biddle was an able manager who probably understood the mysteries of banking and currency better than any other American of his generation. A Philadelphia gentleman of broad culture, extensive education, and some political experience, his major faults were his arrogance and his vanity. He was inclined to rely too much on his own judgment and refused to admit his mistakes until it was too late to correct them. But his record prior to the confrontation with Jackson was a good one. In 1825 and again in 1828, he acted decisively to curb an overextension of credit by state banks and helped avert a recurrence of the boom-and-bust cycle.

The actual performance of the Bank was not the only source of criticism. Old-line Jeffersonians had always opposed it on principle, both because they viewed its establishment as unconstitutional and because it placed too much power in the hands of a small, privileged group. The Bank was a chartered monopoly, an essentially private corporation that performed public services in return for exclusive economic rights. "In 1828," according to historian Robert Remini, "the Bank was a financial colossus, entrenched in the nation's economy, possessing the means of draining specie from state banks at will and regulating the currency according to its own estimate of the nation's needs."

Because of the Bank's great influence, it was easy to blame it for anything that went wrong with the economy. In an era of rising democracy, the most obvious and telling objection to the Bank was simply that it possessed great power and privilege without being under popular control.

The Bank Veto and the Election of 1832

Jackson came into office with strong reservations about banking and paper money in general—the result in part of his own brushes with bankruptcy after accepting promissory notes or depreciated currency. He also harbored suspicions that branches of the Bank of the United States had illicitly used their influence on behalf of his opponent in the presidential election. In his annual messages in 1829 and 1830, Jackson called on Congress to begin discussing "possible modification of a system which cannot continue to exist in its present form without . . . perpetual apprehensions and discontent on the part of the States and the People."

Biddle began to worry about the fate of the Bank's charter when it came up for renewal in 1836. At the same time, Jackson was listening to the advice of some members of his Kitchen Cabinet, especially Amos Kendall and Francis P. Blair, who thought that an attack on the Bank would provide a good party issue for the election of 1832. Biddle then made a fateful blunder. Panicked by the presidential messages and the anti-Bank oratory of congressional Jacksonians like Senator Thomas Hart Benton of Missouri, he determined to seek recharter by Congress in 1832, four years ahead of schedule. Senator Henry Clay, leader of the antiadministration forces on Capitol Hill, encouraged this move because he was convinced that Jackson had chosen the unpopular side of the issue and would be embarrassed or even discredited by a congressional endorsement of the Bank.

The bill to recharter, which was introduced in the House and Senate in early 1832, aroused Jackson and unified his administration and party against renewal. The bill found many supporters in Congress, however, as a number of legislators had received loans from the Bank. Furthermore, the economy seemed to be prospering under the Bank's guidance. As a result, the bill to recharter passed Congress with ease.

The next move was Jackson's, and he made the most of the opportunity. He vetoed the bill and defended his action with ringing statements of principle. After repeating his opinion that the Bank was unconstitutional, notwithstanding the Supreme Court's ruling on the issue, he went on to argue that it violated the fundamental rights of the people in a democratic society: "In the full enjoyment of the gifts of Heaven and the fruits of superior industry, economy, and virtue, every man is equally entitled to protection by law; but when the laws undertake to add to those natural and just advantages artificial distinctions, to grant . . . exclusive privileges, the humble members of society—the farmer, mechanics, and laborers—who have neither the time nor the means of securing like favors to themselves, have a right to complain of the injustice of their government." Government, he added, should "confine itself to equal protection. . . . In the act before me there seems to be a wide and unnecessary departure from these just principles."

Jackson thus called on the common people to join him in fighting the "monster" corporation. His veto message was the first ever delivered by a president that went beyond strictly constitution-

George Caleb Bingham, *The Verdict of the People*. After 1855.

DEMOCRATIC GENRE ART: EVERYDAY LIFE IN JACKSONIAN AMERICA

The spirit of "popular sovereignty" expressed itself in the visual arts, as well as in literature. Beginning in the 1830s a vogue of democratic genre painting began, featuring scenes from everyday life, usually with a comic twist. The first notable practitioner of this style was William S. Mount, who specialized in lively rural scenes. His aesthetic credo was simple: "Paint pictures that will take with the public—never paint for the few but the many." Yet Mount was an accomplished artist who left paintings of enduring value. It was his country folk dancing, gambling, playing music, or horse-trading that appealed strongly to contemporaries, but art historians have found much to praise in his ability to use architecture, particularly that of the common barn, to achieve striking compositional effects.

William Sidney Mount, *Rustic Dance After a Sleigh Ride*. 1830.

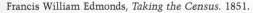

Mount's great successor was George Caleb Bingham of Missouri, who graphically portrayed riverboatmen, politicians, and domestic scenes. His colorful paintings of election settings, such as *The Verdict of the People* (see the preceding page), are perhaps the best artistic representations of Jacksonian politics in action. (What many historians have overlooked, however, is that Bingham was a conservative Whig bent on satirizing the excesses of democratic politics.)

Other painters glorify democracy through their portrayals of common people in everyday activities. Francis Edmonds frequently portrayed rustic domestic scenes that extolled the simple life. *Taking the Census* also has the humorous touch so often seen in genre painting. The duck hunters—and the dog—in William T. Ranney's *Duck Hunters on the Hoboken Marshes* catch the keen anticipation and the spirit of the sport in their avid, even

Francis William Edmonds, *Taking the Census*. 1851.

Tompkins Harrison Matteson, *Sugaring Off*. 1845.

Richard Caton Woodville, *The Card Players*. 1846.

exaggerated, concentration. Sporting subjects were extremely popular and were widely distributed as lithographs.

An interesting juxtaposition of city and country types is depicted in Tompkins Harrison Matteson's *Sugaring Off*. Well-dressed city sophisticates are introduced to a rustic event—collecting the sap of maple trees and boiling it down to syrup and then sugar. The elegant city folk stand in marked contrast to an unpretentious country fellow.

Great attention to detail was characteristic of the anecdotal scenes favored by genre artists. In *The Card Players* by Richard Caton Woodville, the scene is carefully set. Trunk, food basket, hanging timetables, liquid refreshment, and washbasin with towel—all signify travelers at a way station. Players, standing observer, and a non-participant with an understandably pensive expression are skillfully arranged for high dramatic quality.

William Tylee Ranney, *Duck Hunters on the Hoboken Marshes*. 1849.

Albertus D. O. Browere, *Mrs. McCormick's General Store*. 1844.   Lilly Martin Spencer, *Kiss Me and You'll Kiss the 'Lasses*. 1856.

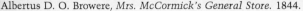

Quaintness and sentimentality were stock-in-trade for a number of democratic genre painters. Albertus Browere strove for a comic effect in *Mrs. McCormick's General Store*. The infuriated proprietress stands up gamely to the shoplifting juvenile rowdies, but the rendering is inoffensive, without any menacing undertones. Lilly Martin Spencer's *Kiss Me and You Kiss the 'Lasses* portrays a coquettish, but somewhat less saccharine, subject than the demure young women doing "woman's work" depicted in many genre paintings. Spencer was one of very few recognized female painters of the age.

A true vulgarization of democratic genre art came with the flood of cheap engravings in the 1850s. The firm of Currier and Ives, formed in 1857, hired a legion of artists to turn out blatantly sentimental scenes of rural and domestic life and the workingman, grotesque caricatures of black people, and lurid depictions of public disasters, as in *The Life of a Fireman*. Currier and Ives produced almost 70,000 prints in the seventy years they were in business.

The Life of a Fireman, a Currier and Ives lithograph.

al arguments to deal directly with social and economic issues. Congressional attempts to override the veto failed, and Jackson resolved to take the entire issue to the people in the upcoming presidential election, which he viewed as a referendum to decide whether he or the Bank would prevail.

The 1832 election, the first in which candidates were chosen by national nominating conventions, pitted Jackson against Henry Clay, standard-bearer of the National Republicans. Although the Democrats did not adopt a formal platform, the party stood firmly behind Jackson in his opposition to rechartering the Bank. Clay and the National Republicans attempted to marshal the pro-Bank sentiment that was strong in many parts of the country. But Jackson won a great personal triumph, garnering 219 electoral votes to 49 for Clay. His share of the popular vote was not quite as high as it was in 1828, but it was substantial enough to be interpreted as a mandate for continuing the war against the Bank.

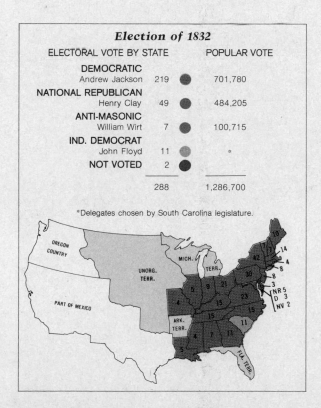

Election of 1832

ELECTORAL VOTE BY STATE		POPULAR VOTE
DEMOCRATIC		
Andrew Jackson	219	701,780
NATIONAL REPUBLICAN		
Henry Clay	49	484,205
ANTI-MASONIC		
William Wirt	7	100,715
IND. DEMOCRAT		
John Floyd	11	*
NOT VOTED	2	
	288	1,286,700

*Delegates chosen by South Carolina legislature.

Killing the Bank

Not content with preventing the Bank from getting a new charter, the victorious Jackson now resolved to attack it directly by removing federal deposits from Biddle's vaults. Jackson told Van Buren, "The bank . . . is trying to kill me, but I will kill it." The Bank had indeed used all the political influence it could muster in an attempt to prevent Jackson's reelection. But this was clearly an act of self-defense. Old Hickory regarded Biddle's actions as a personal attack, part of a devious plot to destroy the President's reputation and deny him the popular approval that he deserved. Although he presided over the first modern American political party, Jackson did not really share Van Buren's belief in the legitimacy of a competitive party system. His opponents were not merely wrong, they were evil and deserved to be destroyed. Furthermore, the election results convinced him that he was the people's chosen instrument in the struggle against corruption and privilege, the only man who could save the pure republicanism of Jefferson and the Founding Fathers from the "monster bank."

In order to remove the deposits from the Bank, Jackson had to overcome strong resistance in his own cabinet. When one secretary of the treasury refused to support the policy, he was shifted to another cabinet post. When a second balked at carrying out removal, he was replaced by Roger B. Taney, a Jackson loyalist and dedicated opponent of the Bank. Beginning in late September 1833, Taney ceased depositing government money in the Bank of the United States and began to withdraw the funds already there. Although Jackson had earlier suggested that the government keep its money in some kind of public bank, he had never worked out the details and made a specific proposal to Congress. The problem of how to dispose of the funds was therefore resolved by an ill-advised decision to place them in selected state banks. By the end of 1833, twenty-three state banks had been chosen as depositories. Opponents charged that the banks had been chosen for political rather than fiscal reasons and dubbed them Jackson's "pet banks."

The Bank counterattacked by calling in outstanding loans and instituting a policy of credit contraction that helped bring on an economic recession. Biddle hoped to win support for rechar-

■ *Aided by Van Buren (center) and Major Downing (right), a stock character, Jackson wields his veto rod against the monster bank, whose heads represent the directors of the state branches. Biddle is wearing the top hat.*

who originally defended Jackson's veto now became disenchanted with the President because they thought he had gone too far in asserting the powers of his office.

The Emergence of the Whigs

The coalition that passed the censure resolution in the Senate provided the nucleus for a new national party—the Whigs. The leadership of the new party and a majority of its support came from National Republicans associated with Clay and ex–New England Federalists led by Senator Daniel Webster of Massachusetts. But the Whigs picked up critical support from southern proponents of states' rights who had been upset by the political nationalism of Jackson's stand on nullification and now saw an unconstitutional abuse of power in his withdrawal of federal deposits from the Bank of the United States. Even Calhoun and his nullifiers moved temporarily into the Whig camp. This initial rallying cry for this diverse anti-Jackson coalition was "executive usurpation." The Whig label was chosen because of its associations with both English and American revolutionary opposition to royal power and prerogatives. In their propaganda, the Whigs portrayed the tyrannical designs of "King Andrew" and his court.

The Whigs also gradually absorbed the Anti-Masonic party, a surprisingly strong political movement that had arisen in the northeastern states in the late 1820s and early '30s. Capitalizing on the hysteria aroused by the 1826 disappearance and apparent murder of a New Yorker who had threatened to reveal the secrets of the Masonic order, the Anti-Masons exploited traditional American fears of secret societies and conspiracies. They also appealed successfully to the moral concerns of the northern middle class under the sway of an emerging evangelical Protestantism. (For more on the evangelical movement, see the next chapter.) Anti-Masons detested Jacksonianism mainly because it stood for a toleration of diverse life-styles. Democrats did not think government should be concerned because people drank, gambled, or found better things to do than going to church on Sundays. Their opponents from the Anti-Masonic tradition believed that government should restrict such "sinful" behav-

ter by demonstrating that weakening the Bank's position would be disastrous for the economy. But all he showed, at least to the President's supporters, was that they had been right all along about the Bank's excessive power. With some justice, they accused Biddle of deliberately and unnecessarily causing economic distress out of personal resentment and a desire to maintain his unchecked powers and privileges. The Bank never did regain its charter.

Even more serious than the conflict over the Bank was the strong opposition to Jackson's fiscal policies that developed in Congress. Henry Clay and his supporters contended that the President had violated the Bank's charter and exceeded his constitutional authority when he removed the deposits. They eventually persuaded the Senate to approve a motion of censure. Jacksonians in the House were able to block such action, but the President was further humiliated when the Senate refused to confirm Taney as secretary of the treasury. Not all of this criticism and obstructionism can be attributed to sour grapes on the part of pro-Bank politicians. Some congressmen

ior. This desire for moral and religious uniformity contributed an important cultural dimension to northern Whiggery.

As the election of 1836 approached, the government's fiscal policies also provoked a localized rebellion among the urban, working-class elements of the Democratic coalition. In New York City, a dissident faction broke with the regular Democratic organization mainly over issues involving banking and currency. These radicals—called "Loco-Focos" after the matches they used for illumination when their opponents turned off the gaslights at a party meeting—favored a strict hard-money policy and condemned Jackson's transfer of federal deposits to the state banks as inflationary. Because they wanted working people to be paid in specie rather than inflated bank notes, the Loco-Focos went beyond opposition to the Bank of the United States and attacked state banks as well. Seeing no basis for cooperation with the Whigs, they established the independent Equal Rights Party and nominated a separate state ticket for 1836.

Jackson himself had hard-money sentiments and probably regarded the "pet bank" solution as a temporary expedient. Somewhat reluctantly, he surrendered to congressional pressure in early 1836 and signed legislation allocating surplus federal revenues to the deposit banks, increasing their numbers, and weakening federal controls over them. The result was a runaway inflation. State banks in the South and West responded to demands from land-speculating interests by issuing a new flood of paper money. Reacting somewhat belatedly to the speculative mania he had helped to create, Jackson pricked the bubble on July 11, 1836. He issued his "specie circular," requiring that after August 15 only gold and silver would be accepted in payment for public lands. This action served to curb inflation and land speculation but did so in such a sudden and drastic way that it helped precipitate the financial panic of 1837.

The Rise and Fall of Van Buren

As his successor, Jackson chose Martin Van Buren, who had served him loyally as vice-president during his second term and was probably the greatest master of practical politics in the

■ *An adroit politician and a loyal vice-president to Jackson, Martin Van Buren was Jackson's choice and the Democratic party's nominee for president in 1836.*

Democratic party. The Democratic National Convention of 1835 unanimously confirmed Jackson's choice. In accepting the nomination, Van Buren promised to "tread generally in the footsteps of General Jackson."

The newly created Whig party, reflecting the diversity of its constituency, was unable to decide on a single standard-bearer and chose instead to run three regional candidates—Daniel Webster in the East, William Henry Harrison of Ohio (also the Anti-Masonic nominee) in the Old Northwest, and Hugh Lawson White of Tennessee (a former Jackson supporter) in the South. The Whigs hoped to deprive Van Buren of enough electoral votes to throw the election into the House of Representatives where one of the Whigs might stand a chance.

This stratagem proved unsuccessful. Van Buren carried fifteen of the twenty-six states and won a clear majority in the electoral college. But the election foreshadowed future trouble for the Democrats, particularly in the South. There the Whigs ran virtually even, erasing the enormous majorities that Jackson had run up in 1828 and 1832. The emergence of a two-party system in the previously solid South resulted from two factors —opposition to some of Jackson's policies and the image of Van Buren as an unreliable Yankee politician.

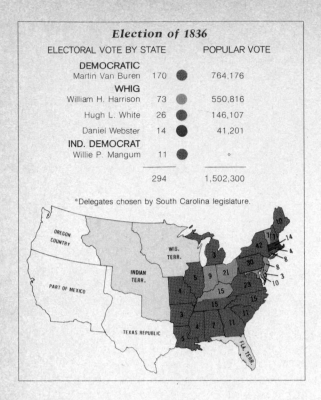

The main business of Van Buren's administration was to straighten out the financial disorder resulting from the destruction of the Bank of the United States and the issuing of Jackson's specie circular. As he took office Van Buren was immediately faced with a catastrophic depression. The price of cotton fell by almost 50 percent, banks all over the nation suspended specie payments, many businesses went bankrupt, and unemployed persons demonstrated in several cities. The sale of public lands fell off so drastically that the federal surplus, earmarked in 1836 for distribution to the states, now became a deficit.

Economic historians have concluded that the panic of 1837 was not exclusively, or even primarily, the result of government policies. It was in fact international in scope and reflected some complex changes in the world economy that were beyond the control of American policymakers. But the Whigs were quick to blame the state of the economy on Jacksonian finance, and the administration had to make a politically effective response. Since Van Buren and his party were committed to a policy of laissez-faire on the federal level, there was little or nothing they could do to relieve economic distress through subsidies or relief measures. If anything, Van Buren was a more dedicated proponent of limited government and strict constructionism than Jackson had been. But he could at least try to salvage the federal funds deposited in shaky state banks and devise a new system of public finance that would not contribute to future panics by fueling speculation and credit expansion.

Van Buren's solution was to establish a public depository for government funds with no connections whatsoever to commercial banking. His proposal for an "independent subtreasury" aroused intense opposition from the congressional Whigs, who strongly favored the reestablishment of a national bank as the only way to restore economic stability. Whig resistance stalled the subtreasury bill for three years; it was not until 1840 that it was enacted into law. In the meantime the economy had temporarily revived in 1838 only to sink again into a deeper depression the following year.

Van Buren's chances for reelection in 1840 were undoubtedly hurt by the state of the economy. But the principal reason for his defeat was that he lacked the charisma of a Jackson and was thus unable to overcome the extremely effective campaign mounted by the Whigs. In 1836 the Whigs had been disorganized and had not fully mastered the new democratic politics. But in 1840, they settled on a single nominee and outdid the Democrats in grass-roots organization and popular electioneering. The Whigs passed over the true leader of their party, Henry Clay, because he was identified with too many controversial positions. Instead they found their own Jackson in William Henry Harrison, a military hero of advanced age, who was associated in the public mind with the battle of Tippecanoe and the winning of the West.

Harrison's views on public issues were little known, and the Whigs ran him without a platform to avoid distracting the electorate from his personal qualities. They pretended that Harrison had been born in a log cabin—actually it was a pillared mansion—and that he preferred hard cider to more effete beverages. To balance the ticket and increase its appeal in the South they chose John Tyler of Virginia, a converted states' rights Democrat, to be Harrison's running mate.

■ *A charismatic leader, a folksy man of the people—that was the image conveyed by the campaign banners the Whig party created for the 1840 campaign of William Henry Harrison, the hero of Tippecanoe.*

Using the slogan, "Tippecanoe and Tyler, Too," the Whigs pulled out all stops in their bid for the White House. Rallies and parades were organized in every locality, complete with posters, placards, campaign hats and emblems, special songs, and even movable log cabins filled with coonskin caps and barrels of cider for the faithful. Imitating the Jacksonian propaganda against Adams in 1828, they portrayed Van Buren as a luxury-loving aristocrat and compared him with their own homespun candidate. The Democrats countered by using many of the same methods, but they simply could not project an image of Van Buren that rivaled Harrison's grass-roots appeal. There was an enormous turnout on election day—78 percent of those eligible to vote. When it was over, Harrison had parlayed a narrow edge in the popular vote into a landslide in the electoral college. He carried 19 of the 26 states and won 234 electoral votes to 60 for Van Buren. The Whigs also won control of both houses of Congress.

Heyday of the Second Party System

America's "second party system" came of age in the election of 1840. Unlike the earlier competition between Federalists and Jeffersonian Repub-

licans, the rivalry of Democrats and Whigs made the two-party pattern a permanent feature of electoral politics in the United States. During the 1840s, the two national parties competed on fairly equal terms for the support of the electorate. Allegiance to one party or the other became an important source of personal identity for many Americans and increased their interest and participation in politics.

In addition to drama and entertainment, the parties offered the voters a real choice of programs and ideologies. Whigs stood for a "positive liberal state"—which meant that government had the right and duty to subsidize or protect enterprises that could contribute to general prosperity and economic growth. Democrats normally advocated a "negative liberal state." According to them, government should keep its hands off the economy; only by doing nothing could it avoid favoring special interests and interfering with free competition. They charged that granting subsidies or special charters to any group would create pockets of privilege or monopoly and put ordinary citizens under the thumb of the rich and powerful.

Conflict over economic issues helped determine each party's base of support. In the Whig

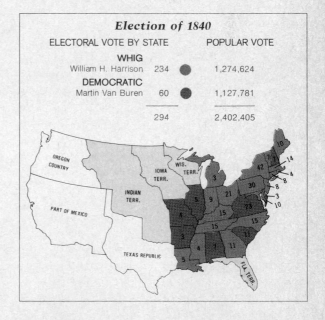

Election of 1840

ELECTORAL VOTE BY STATE		POPULAR VOTE
WHIG		
William H. Harrison	234	1,274,624
DEMOCRATIC		
Martin Van Buren	60	1,127,781
	294	2,402,405

Chronology

1824	House of Representatives elects John Quincy Adams president
1828	Congress passes "tariff of abominations" Jackson elected president over J. Q. Adams
1830	Jackson vetoes the Maysville Road bill Congress passes Indian Removal Act
1831	Jackson reorganizes his cabinet First national nominating conventions meet
1832	Jackson vetoes the bill rechartering the Bank of the United States Jackson reelected, defeating Henry Clay (National Republican candidate)
1832–1833	Crisis erupts over South Carolina's attempt to nullify the tariff of 1832
1833	Jackson removes federal deposits from the Bank of the United States
1834	Whig party comes into existence
1836	Jackson issues "specie circular" Martin Van Buren elected president
1837	Financial panic occurs, followed by depression lasting until 1843
1840	Congress passes the Independent Subtreasury Bill Harrison (Whig) defeats Van Buren (Democrat) for the presidency

camp were most industrialists and merchants, plus a large proportion of those farmers and planters who had adapted successfully to a market economy. Democrats appealed mainly to smaller farmers, workers, declining gentry, and emerging entrepreneurs who were excluded from the established commercial groups that stood to benefit most from Whig programs. To some extent, this division pitted richer and more privileged Americans against those who were poorer and less economically or socially secure. But it did not follow class lines in any simple or direct way. Many business owners were Democrats, and large numbers of wage earners voted Whig. Merchants engaged in the import trade had no use for Whiggish high tariffs, while workers in industries clamoring for protection often concluded that their jobs depended on such duties.

Economic interest was not the only factor behind the choice of parties. Life-styles and ethnic or religious identities strongly affected party loyalties during this period. In the northern states, one way to tell the typical Whig from the typical Democrat was to see what each did on Sunday. A person who went to one of the evangelical Protestant churches was very likely to be a Whig. Or the other hand, the person who attended a ritualized service—Catholic, Lutheran or Episcopalian—or did not go to church at all was most probably a Democrat.

The Democrats were the favored party of immigrants, Catholics, freethinkers, backwoods farmers, and those of all classes who enjoyed traditional amusements condemned by the new breed of moral reformers. One thing that all these groups had in common was a desire to be left alone, free of restrictions on their freedom to think and behave as they liked. The Whigs enjoyed particularly strong support among Protestants of old stock living in smaller cities, towns, and prosperous rural areas devoted to market farming. In general the Whigs welcomed a market economy but wished to restrain the individualism and disorder it created by enforcing cultural and moral values derived from the Puritan tradition. Most of those who sought to be "their brothers' keepers" were Whigs. Some of the roots of party allegiance can be found in local divisions over such matters as temperance, keeping the Sabbath, and reading the Bible in public schools.

Nevertheless, party conflict in Congress continued to center on national economic policy. Whigs stood firm for a loose construction of the Constitution and positive federal guidance and support for business and economic development. The Democrats persisted in their defense of strict construction, states' rights, and laissez-faire. Debates over tariffs, banking, and internal improvements remained vital and vigorous during the 1840s.

True believers in both parties saw a deep ideological or moral meaning in the clash over economic issues. Whigs and Democrats had conflicting views of the good society, and their policy positions reflected these differences. The Democrats were the party of individualism and personal liberty. They perceived the American people as a collection of self-sufficient atoms. The role of government was to remove obstacles to individual rights, which could mean the right to rise economically, the right to drink hard liquor, or the right to be unorthodox in religion. The Whigs, on the other hand, were the party of community. They believed that the propertied, the well-educated, and the pious were responsible for guiding the masses toward the common good. For many of them the common good required moral and humanitarian reform as well as controlled economic growth.

Each, in a sense, reflected one side of a broader democratic impulse. The Jacksonian legacy was a stress on individual freedom and ethnic or cultural tolerance (except for blacks). The Whigs, despite their elitist tendencies, perceived that in a republic strong government could serve the general interest and further a spirit of national unity. Later generations of progressive Americans would seek to create a balance between freedom and community, liberty and order. In doing so, they would necessarily draw on both of the political cultures of the second party system.

Recommended Reading

Arthur M. Schlesinger, Jr., *The Age of Jackson* (1945), sees Jacksonian Democracy as a progressive protest against big business and stresses the participation of urban workers. Marvin Meyers, *The Jacksonian Persuasion: Politics and Belief* (1960), argues that Jacksonians appealed to nostalgia for an older America—"an idealized ancestral way" which they believed was threatened by commercialization. Lee Benson, *The Concept of Jacksonian Democracy: New York as a Test Case* (1964), finds an ethnocultural basis for democratic allegiance. A sharply critical view of Jacksonian leadership—one which stresses opportunism, greed, and demagoguery—can be found in Edward Pessen, *Jacksonian America: Society, Personality, and Politics*, rev.ed. (1979). This work also offers a comprehensive survey of the social, economic, and political developments of the period.

The classic study of the new party system is Richard P. McCormick, *The Second Party System: Party Formation in the Jacksonian Era* (1966). On what the anti-Jacksonians stood for, see especially Daniel Walker Howe, *The Political Culture of the American Whigs* (1979). James C. Curtis, *Andrew Jackson and the Search for Vindication* (1976), provides a good introduction to Jackson's career and personality. On Jackson's popular image, see John William Ward, *Andrew Jackson: Symbol for an Age* (1955). The culture of the period is well surveyed in Russel B. Nye, *Society and Culture in America, 1830–1860* (1960). Alexis de Tocqueville, *Democracy in America*, 2 vols. (1945), is a foreign visitor's analysis of American life in the 1830s.

Additional Bibliography

On the hotel as a symbolic institution, see Doris Elizabeth King, "The First Class Hotel and the Age of the Common Man," *Journal of Southern History* 23 (1957); 173–88. On the new politics, see Chilton Williamson, *American Suffrage from Property to Democracy* (1960) and Richard Hofstadter, *The Idea of a Party System* (1970). On radical, working-class movements, see Walter Hugins, *Jacksonian Democracy and the Working Class: A Study of the New York Workingmen's Movement* (1960); Edward Pessen, *Most Uncommon Jacksonians: The Radical Leaders of the Early Labor Movement* (1967); and Bruce Laurie, *Working People of Philadelphia, 1800–1850* (1980). Social manifestations of the democratic character are covered in Joseph F. Kett, *The Formation of the American Medical Profession* (1968); Daniel H. Calhoun, *Professional Lives in America: Structure and Aspiration, 1750–1850* (1965); and Donald M. Scott, *From Office to Profession: The New England Ministry, 1750–1850* (1978). On democratic culture, see E. Douglas Branch, *The Sentimental Years, 1836–1860* (1934); Oliver W. Larkin, *Art and Life in America* (1960); Neil Harris, *The Artist in American Society: The Formative Years, 1790–1860* (1966); and Henry Nash Smith, *Democracy and the Novel: Popular Resistance to Classic American Writers* (1978).

The emergence of Andrew Jackson and the Democratic party is described in Samuel F. Bemis, *John Quincy Adams and the Union* (1956) and in Robert V. Remini, *Martin Van Buren and the Making of the Democratic Party* (1959), *The Election of Andrew Jackson* (1964), and *Andrew Jackson* (1966). Jackson's presidency is examined in Richard B. Latner, *The Presidency of Andrew Jackson: White House Politics, 1829–1837* (1979). On Jackson's Indian policy, see Bernard W. Sheehan, *The Seeds of Extinction: Jeffersonian Philanthropy and the American Indian* (1973); Michael Paul Rogin, *Fathers and Children: Andrew Jackson and the Subjugation of the American Indian* (1975); and Ronald N. Satz, *American Indian Policy in the Jacksonian Era* (1975). On nullification, see William W. Freehling, *Prelude to Civil War: The Nullification Controversy in South Carolina, 1816–1836* (1966).

The Bank War is discussed in Bray Hammond, *Banks and Politics in America from the Revolution to the Civil War* (1957); Thomas P. Govan, *Nicholas Biddle* (1959); Robert V. Remini, *Andrew Jackson and the Bank War* (1967); and John M. Paul, *The Politics of Jacksonian Finance* (1972). On Van Buren, see James C. Curtis, *The Fox at Bay: Martin Van Buren and the Presidency* (1970).

For more on the rise of the Whigs, see Clement Eaton, *Henry Clay and the Art of American Politics* (1957) and Richard N. Current, *Daniel Webster and the Rise of National Conservatism* (1955). The growth of a two-party system in the South is described in William J. Cooper, Jr., *The South and the Politics of Slavery* (1978). The politics of the 1840s is surveyed in William R. Brock, *Parties and Political Conscience, 1840–1850* (1979).

chapter 11

THE
PURSUIT
OF PERFECTION

In the winter of 1830–1831 a wave of religious revivals swept the northern states. The most dramatic and successful took place in Rochester, New York. Large audiences, composed mostly of respectable and prosperous citizens, heard evangelist Charles G. Finney preach that every man or woman had the power to choose Christ and a godly life. For six months Finney held prayer meetings almost daily, putting intense pressure on those who had not experienced salvation. Hundreds came forth to declare their faith, and church membership doubled during his stay. The newly awakened Christians of Rochester were urged to convert relatives, neighbors, and employees. If enough people enlisted in the evangelical crusade, Finney proclaimed, the millennium would be achieved within months.

Finney's call for religious and moral renewal fell on fertile ground in Rochester. This bustling boom town on the Erie Canal was suffering from severe growing pains and tensions arising from rapid economic development. Leading families were divided into quarreling factions, and workingmen were breaking free from the control that their employers had previously exerted over their daily lives. Most of the early converts were from the middle class. Businessmen who had been heavy drinkers and irregular churchgoers now abstained from alcohol and went to church at least twice a week. They also pressured the employees in their workshops, mills, and stores to do likewise. More rigorous standards of proper behavior and religious conformity unified Rochester's elite and increased its ability to control the rest of the community. As in other cities swept by the revival, evangelical Protestantism provided the middle class with a stronger sense of identity and purpose.

But the war on sin was not limited to such safe ground. Among those converted in Rochester and elsewhere were some who could not rest easy until the nation as a whole conformed to the pure Christianity of the Sermon on the Mount. Finney expressed such a hope himself, but he concentrated on the religious conversion and moral uplift of the individual, trusting that the purification of

American society and politics would automatically follow. Other religious and moral reformers were inspired to crusade against those social and political institutions that failed to measure up to the standards of Christian perfection. They proceeded to attack such collective "sins" as the liquor traffic, war, slavery, and even government. Religiously inspired reformism cut two ways. On the one hand, it brought a measure of order and cultural unity to previously divided and troubled communities like Rochester. But it also inspired a variety of more radical movements or experiments that threatened to undermine established institutions and principles. One of these —abolitionism—would trigger political upheaval and help to bring on the Civil War.

According to some historians, the evangelical revival and the reform movements it inspired reflected the same spirit as the new democratic politics. In a sense this is true: politicians and evangelists both sought popular favor and assumed that individuals were free agents capable of self-direction and self-improvement. But they made different kinds of demands on ordinary people. Jacksonians idealized common folk pretty much as they found them and saw no danger to the community if individuals pursued their worldly interests. Evangelical reformers, on the other hand, believed that the common people needed to be redeemed and uplifted—committed to a higher goal than self-interest. They did not trust a democracy of unbelievers and sinners. The Republic would be safe, they insisted, only if a right-minded minority preached, taught, and agitated until the mass of ordinary citizens was reborn into a higher life.

The Rise of Evangelicalism

American Protestantism was in a state of constant ferment during the early nineteenth century. The separation of church and state, a process that began during the Revolution, was now complete. Government sponsorship and funding had ended for the established churches of the colonial era, such as the Congregationalists of New England and the Episcopalians of the South. Dissenting groups, like the Baptists and Methodists, welcomed full religious freedom because it offered a better chance to win new converts. But all pious Protestants were concerned about the spread of "infidelity"—their word for secular-humanistic beliefs. The Founders had set a troubling example by their casual or even unfriendly attitude toward religious orthodoxy. Secular ideas drawn from the Enlightenment (see chapter 4) had achieved wide acceptance as a basis for the establishment of a democratic republic, and opposition to mixing religion with public life remained strong during the age of Jackson.

Revivalism provided the best way to extend religious values and build up church membership. The Great Awakening of the mid-eighteenth century had shown the wonders that evangelists could accomplish, and the new revivalists repeated this success by greatly increasing the proportion of the population that belonged to Protestant churches. They also capitalized on the growing willingness of Americans to form effective voluntary organizations. Spiritual renewals were often followed by mobilization of the faithful into associations to spread the gospel and reform American morals.

Lithographs like this graphic portrayal of good and evil reminded people of the evangelists' message—that wicked ways led to everlasting punishment.

The Second Great Awakening: The Frontier Phase

The Second Great Awakening began in earnest on the southern frontier around the turn of the century. In 1801 a crowd estimated at nearly fifty thousand gathered at Cane Ridge, Kentucky. According to a contemporary observer:

> The noise was like the roar of Niagara. The vast sea of human beings seemed to be agitated as if by a storm. I counted seven ministers all preaching at once. . . . Some of the people were singing, others praying, some crying for mercy . . . while others were shouting most vociferously. . . . At one time I saw at least five hundred swept down in a moment, as if a battery of a thousand guns had been opened upon them, and then followed immediately shrieks and shouts that rent the heavens.

Highly emotional camp meetings, organized usually by Methodists or Baptists, soon became a regular feature of religious life in the South and the lower Midwest (see the photo on p. 296). On the frontier the camp meeting met social as well as religious needs. In the sparsely settled southern backcountry it was difficult to sustain local churches with regular ministers. The Methodists solved part of the problem by sending out circuit riders, and the Baptists licensed uneducated farmers to preach to their neighbors. But for many people the only way to get baptized, married, or have a communal religious experience was to attend a camp meeting.

Rowdies and scoffers also attended. Mostly they drank whiskey, caroused, and fornicated on the fringes of the small city of tents and wagons. But sometimes they were "struck down" by a mighty blast from one of the pulpits. Evangelists loved to tell stories of such conversions or near-conversions. According to Methodist preacher Peter Cartwright, one scoffer was seized by the "jerks"—a set of involuntary bodily movements often observed at camp meetings. Normally such an exercise would lead to conversion, but this particular sinner had such a hard heart that he

The Rise of Evangelicalism

refused to surrender to God. The result was that he kept on "jerking" until his neck was broken.

Camp meetings obviously provided an emotional outlet for rural people whose everyday lives were often lonely and tedious. But they could also promote a sense of community and social discipline. Conversion at a camp meeting could be a rite of passage, signifying that a young man or woman had outgrown wild or antisocial behavior and was now ready to become a respectable member of the community. But for the most part frontier revivalism remained highly individualistic. It strengthened personal piety and morality but did not stimulate organized benevolence or social reform.

The Second Great Awakening in the North

Reformist tendencies were more evident in the distinctive kind of revivalism that originated in New England and western New York. The northern evangelists were mostly Congregationalists and Presbyterians, strongly influenced by the traditions of New England Puritanism. Their greatest successes were not in rural or frontier areas but in small- to medium-sized towns and cities. Their revivals could be stirring affairs but were less extravagantly emotional than the camp meetings of the frontier South. The northern brand of evangelism resulted in the formation of societies devoted to the redemption of the human race in general and American society in particular.

The reform movement began in New England as an effort to defend Calvinism against the liberal views of religion fostered by the Enlightenment. The Reverend Timothy Dwight, who became president of Yale College in 1795, was alarmed by the younger generation's growing acceptance of the belief that the Deity was the benevolent master architect of a rational universe rather than an all-powerful, mysterious God. During the late eighteenth century, some Congregationalist clergy began to exalt human reason above religious faith, thus turning their backs on the traditional Calvinist sense of sin and depravity. When their rationalism reached the point of denying the doctrine of the Trinity, they proclaimed themselves to be "Unitarians."

To Dwight's horror, the Unitarians captured some of the more fashionable and sophisticated New England congregations and even won control of the Harvard Divinity School. He fought back by preaching to Yale undergraduates that they were "dead in sin" and succeeded in provoking a series of campus revivals. But the harshness and pessimism of orthodox Calvinist doctrine, with its stress on original sin and predestination, had limited appeal in a Republic committed to human freedom and progress.

Dwight himself made some concessions to the spirit of the age by agreeing that human beings had a limited control over their spiritual destinies. But a younger generation of Congregational ministers reshaped New England Puritanism to increase its appeal to people who shared the prevailing optimism about human capabilities.

The main theologian of early nineteenth-century neo-Calvinism was Nathaniel Taylor, a disciple of Dwight, who also held forth at Yale. Taylor softened the doctrine of predestination almost out of existence by contending that every individual was a "free agent" who had the ability to overcome a natural inclination to sin. His reconciliation of original sin with "free agency" enabled neo-Calvinist evangelists to resist Unitarianism and to compete successfully with the revival denominations—such as the Methodists and the "free will" branch of the Baptists—who also believed that sinners had the ability to choose salvation.

The first great practitioner of the new evangelical Calvinism was Lyman Beecher, another of Dwight's pupils. In the period just before and after the War of 1812, Beecher helped to promote a series of revivals in the Congregational churches of New England. Using his own homespun version of Taylor's doctrine of free agency, Beecher induced thousands—in his home church in Litchfield, Connecticut, and in other churches that offered him their pulpits—to acknowledge their sinfulness and surrender to God. One of his cohorts, Asahel Nettleton, became Congregationalism's first itinerant evangelist.

During the late 1820s Beecher was forced to confront the new and more radical form of revivalism being practiced in western New York by Charles G. Finney. Upstate New York was a seedbed for religious enthusiasms of various kinds. A majority of its population were trans-

The Beecher family contributed four influential members to the reform movement. Lyman Beecher (seated center) was a successful preacher and a master strategist in the organized campaign against sin and infidelity. His eldest daughter, Catharine (on his left) was a leader in the movement supporting higher education for women. Another daughter, Harriet (seated far left) wrote the abolitionist novel Uncle Tom's Cabin. Lyman's son, Henry Ward Beecher (standing far right) was an ardent antislavery advocate and later became one of the most celebrated preachers of the post-Civil War era.

planted New Englanders who had left behind their close-knit village communities and ancestral churches but not their Puritan consciences. Troubled by rapid economic changes and the social dislocations that went with them, they were ripe for the assurances of a new faith and a sense of moral direction.

Although he worked within the Congregational and Presbyterian churches (which were then cooperating under a plan of union established in 1804), Finney departed radically from traditional Calvinist doctrines. In his hands, the doctrine of free agency became unqualified freewill. One of his sermons was entitled "Sinners Bound To Change Their Own Hearts." Basically, Finney was indifferent to theological issues. His appeal was strictly to emotion or to "the heart" rather than to doctrine or reason. He simply wanted his converts to feel the power of Christ and become new men and women. He eventually adopted the extreme view that it was possible for redeemed Christians to be totally free of sin—to be perfect as their Father in Heaven is perfect.

Beginning in 1823, Finney conducted a series of highly successful revivals in the towns and cities of western New York, culminating in the aforementioned triumph in Rochester in 1830–1831.

Even more controversial than his freewheeling approach to theology were the means he used to win converts. Finney sought instantaneous conversions through a variety of new methods. These included protracted meetings lasting all night or for several days in a row, the placing of an "anxious bench" in front of the congregation where those in the process of repentance could receive special attention, and encouraging women to pray publicly for the souls of their male relatives.

The results could be dramatic. Sometimes listeners fell to the floor in fits of excitement. "If I had had a sword in my hand," Finney recalled, "I could not have cut them off as fast as they fell." Although he appealed to emotion, Finney had a practical, almost manipulative, attitude toward the conversion process: It "is not a miracle or dependent on a miracle in any sense. . . . It is purely a philosophical result of the right use of constituted means."

Beecher and the eastern evangelicals were disturbed by Finney's new methods and by the hysteria that they produced. They were also upset because he violated long-standing Christian tradition by allowing women to pray aloud in church. An evangelical summit meeting between Beecher and Finney, held at New Lebanon, New York, in 1827, failed to reach agreement on this and other issues. Beecher even threatened to stand on the state line if Finney attempted to bring his crusade into Connecticut. But it soon became clear that Finney was not merely stirring people to temporary peaks of excitement; he was also leaving strong and active churches behind him, and eastern opposition gradually weakened. Finney eventually founded a tabernacle in New York City that became a rallying point for evangelical efforts to reach the urban masses.

From Revivalism to Reform

The northern wing of the Second Great Awakening inspired a great movement for social reform. Converts were organized into voluntary associations that sought to stamp out sin and social evil and win the world for Christ. It was an activist and outgoing Christianity that was being advanced, rather than one that called for withdrawal from a sinful world. Most of the converts of northern revivalism were middle-class citizens already active in the lives of their communities. They were seeking to adjust to the bustling world of the market revolution in ways that would not violate their traditional moral and social values. Given the generally optimistic and forward-looking attitudes of such Americans, it is understandable that a wave of conversions would lead to hopes for the salvation of the nation and the world.

In New England, Beecher and his evangelical associates were behind the establishment of a great network of missionary and benevolent societies. In 1810 Presbyterians and Congregationalists founded a Board of Commissioners for Foreign Missions and soon dispatched two missionaries to India. In 1816 the Reverend Samuel John Mills took the leading role in organizing the American Bible Society. By 1821, the society had distributed 140,000 Bibles, mostly in parts of the West where there was a scarcity of churches and clergymen.

Another major effort went into the publication and distribution of religious tracts, mainly by the American Tract Society, founded in 1825. Groups beyond the reach of regular churches were the target of special societies, such as missions to seamen, Indians, and the urban poor. In 1816–1817 middle-class women in New York, Philadelphia, Charleston, and Boston formed societies to spread the gospel in lower-class wards—where, as one of their missionaries put it, there was "a great mass of people beyond the restraints of religion."

Evangelicals founded moral reform societies as well as missions. Some of these aimed at curbing irreligious activity on the Sabbath; others sought to stamp out dueling, gambling, and prostitution. In New York in 1831, a zealous young clergyman published a sensational report claiming that there were ten thousand prostitutes in the city laying their snares for innocent young men. As a result of this exposé, an asylum was established for the redemption of "abandoned women." When middle-class women became involved in this crusade, attention was shifted to the men who patronized the prostitutes, and it was proposed that teams of observers record and publish the names of those seen entering brothels. But this plan was abandoned because it offended those who thought that the cause of virtue would be better served by suppressing public discussion and investigation of sexual vices.

Beecher was especially influential in the temperance crusade, the most successful of the reform movements; his published sermons against drink were the most important and widely distributed of the early tracts calling for total abstinence from "demon rum." The temperance movement was directed at a real social evil, more serious in many ways than the drug problem of today. Since the Revolution, whiskey had become the most popular American beverage. Made from corn by individual farmers or, by the 1820s, in commercial distilleries, it was cheaper than milk or beer and safer than water (which was often contaminated). In some parts of the country rum and brandy were also popular. Hard liquor was frequently consumed with food as a table beverage, even at breakfast, and children sometimes imbibed along with adults. Per capita annual consumption of distilled beverages in the 1820s was almost triple what it is today, and alcoholism had reached epidemic proportions.

The temperance reformers viewed indulgence in alcohol as a threat to public morality. Drunkenness was seen as a loss of self-control and moral responsibility that spawned crime, vice, and disorder. Above all, it threatened the family. The

■ *Temperance propaganda, like this broadside, warned that "demon rum"*
would lead the drinker down the direct path to poverty and wretchedness
and would bring about the ruin of his entire family.

main target of temperance propaganda was the husband and father who abused, neglected, or abandoned his wife and children because he was a slave to the bottle. The drinking habits of the poor or laboring classes also aroused great concern. Particularly in urban areas, the "respectable" and propertied elements lived in fear that lower-class mobs, crazed with drink, would attack private property and destroy the social order.

Many of the evangelical reformers regarded intemperance as the greatest single obstacle to the achievement of a republic of God-fearing, self-disciplined citizens. In 1826 a group of clergymen previously active in mission work organized the American Temperance Society to coordinate and extend the work already begun by local churches and moral reform societies. The original aim was to encourage abstinence from "ardent spirits" or hard liquor; there was no agreement on the evils of beer and wine. The society sent out lecturers, issued a flood of literature, and sponsored essay contests. Its agents organized revival meetings and called on those in attendance to sign a pledge promising abstinence from spirits.

The campaign was enormously effective. By 1834 there were five thousand local branches with more than a million members. Although it may be doubted whether large numbers of confirmed drunkards were actually cured, the movement did succeed in altering the drinking habits of middle-class Americans by making temperance a mark of respectability. Per capita consumption of hard liquor declined more than 50 percent during the 1830s.

Cooperating missionary and reform societies—collectively known as "the benevolent empire"—were a major force in American culture by the early 1830s. Efforts to modify American attitudes and institutions seemed to be bearing fruit. A new ethic of self-control and self-discipline was being instilled in the middle class that equipped individuals to confront a new world of economic growth and social mobility without losing their cultural and moral bearings.

But some evangelicals felt frustrated because they failed to exert direct political influence, especially over the federal government. In 1828–1829, the General Union for Promoting the Observance of the Christian Sabbath mounted a campaign to ban the transporting of U.S. mail on Sunday. Jacksonians in Congress sharply rejected the proposal and warned against clerical meddling in politics. This unsuccessful crusade was based on a misunderstanding of why churches and church-sponsored organizations were thriving. The success of the evangelical movement was due to voluntarism and the freedom to exert a purely moral or spiritual influence.

By the 1830s the French traveler Alexis de Tocqueville could marvel at the power of Christian faith and morality in a land without an established church. "Religion in America," he wrote, "takes no direct part in the government of society, but it must be regarded as the first of their political institutions; for if it does not impart a taste for freedom, it facilitates the use of it." It seemed that voluntaristic religion produced moral and law-abiding citizens without the need for governmental coercion. In 1829 an evangelical journal made the same point: " ' What has religion to do with the State?' you ask. In the form of ecclesiastical alliances nothing; but in its operation as a controlling, purifying power in the consciences of the people, we answer it has everything to do, it is the last hope of republics. . . ."

Domesticity and Changes in the American Family

The evangelical culture of the 1820s and '30s influenced the family as an institution and inspired new conceptions of its role in American society. For many parents, child-rearing was viewed as essential preparation for the self-disciplined Christian life, and they performed their nurturing duties with greater seriousness and self-consciousness. Women—who were regarded as particularly susceptible to religious and moral influences—assumed a greater importance within the domestic circle. Home and family were glorified to such an extent that people could lose sight of the fact that a market society was weakening traditional kinship ties and setting many people adrift in an impersonal world of economic relationships.

Marriage and Sex Roles

The American family underwent major changes in the decades between the revolution and the mid-nineteenth century. One was the triumph of marriage for love. Parents now exercised even less control over their children's selection of mates than they had in the colonial period. The desire to protect family property and maintain social status remained strong, but mutual affection was now considered absolutely essential to a proper union. Beginning in the late eighteenth century, romantic novels popularized the idea that marriage should be based exclusively on the promptings of the heart. Careful studies of mar-

riage patterns show that it was becoming easier for sons to marry while their fathers were still alive and for younger daughters to wed before their oldest sisters—trends that reflected a weakening of the traditional parental role.

It seems likely, too, that relations between husbands and wives were becoming more affectionate. In the main, eighteenth-century correspondence between spouses had been formal and distant in tone. The husband often assumed a patriarchal role, even using such salutations as "my dear child" and rarely confessing that he missed his wife or craved her company. One patronizing husband, for example, urged his wife to read more, warning her that "my good opinion depends on the *amiable accomplishments* of your *mind.*" Letters from women to their husbands were highly deferential and did not usually give advice or express disapproval.

By the early nineteenth century first names, pet names, and terms of endearment like "honey" or "darling" were increasingly used by both sexes, and absent husbands frequently confessed that they felt lost without their mates. In their replies, wives assumed a more egalitarian tone and offered counsel on a wide range of subjects. One wrote to a husband who had admitted to flirting with pretty women that she was more than "a little jealous." She asked him angrily how he would feel if she made a similar confession— "would it be more immoral in me than in you?"

At its best, marriage had become more a matter of companionship and less an exertion of male dominance. But the change should not be exaggerated or romanticized. In law, and in cases of conflict between spouses, the husband remained the unchallenged head of the household. True independence or equality for women was impossible at a time when men held exclusive legal authority over a couple's property and children. Divorce was difficult for everyone, but the double standard made it easier for husbands than wives to dissolve a marriage on grounds of adultery.

Such power as women exerted within the home came from their ability to affect the decisions of men who had learned to respect their moral qualities and good sense. The evangelical movement encouraged this quiet expression of feminine influence. The revivals not only gave women a role in converting men but made a

According to the Cult of True Womanhood, the proper sphere for woman was her home—the place where she could instill goodness in her family as she practiced the cardinal virtues of piety, purity, submissiveness, and domesticity.

feminized Christ the main object of worship. A nurturing, loving, merciful saviour, mediating between a stern father and his erring children, provided the model for woman's new role as spiritual head of the home.

Historians have described the new conception of woman's role as the "Cult of True Womanhood" or the "ideology of domesticity." Woman's place was in the home and on a pedestal. The ideal wife and mother was "an angel in the house," a model of piety and virtue who exerted a wholesome moral and religious influence over members of the coarser sex. A masculine view of the true woman was well expressed in a poem published in 1846:

I would have her as pure as the snow on the mount—
*   As true as the smile that to infamy's given—*
As pure as the wave of the crystalline fount,
*   Yet as warm in the heart as the sunlight of heaven.*

The sociological reality behind the Cult of True Womanhood was an increasing division between the working lives of men and women. In the eighteenth century and earlier most economic activity had been centered in the home and nearby, and husbands and wives often worked together in a common enterprise. By the early to mid-nineteenth century this way of life was limited mainly to rural areas. In towns and cities, the rise of factories and countinghouses severed the home from the workplace. Men went forth every morning to their places of labor, leaving their wives at home to tend the house and the children. Married women were therefore increasingly deprived of a productive economic role. The cult of domesticity made a virtue of the fact that men were solely responsible for running the affairs of the world and building up the economy.

A new conception of sex roles justified and glorified this pattern. The "doctrine of two spheres"—as set forth in novels, advice literature, and the new ladies' magazines—sentimentalized the woman who kept a spotless house, nurtured her children, and offered her husband a refuge from the heartless world of commerce and industry. From a modern point of view, it is easy to condemn the cult of domesticity as a rationalization for male dominance—and to a considerable extent it obviously was. But most women of the early to mid-nineteenth century probably did not feel oppressed or degraded by the new arrangement. The earlier pattern of cooperation had not implied sexual equality—normally men had been very much in charge of farms or home industries and had often treated their wives more like servants than partners. The new norm of confinement to the home did not necessarily imply that women were inferior. By the standards of evangelical culture, women in the domestic sphere could be viewed as superior to men since women were in a good position to cultivate the "feminine" virtues of love and self-sacrifice and thus act as official guardians of religious and moral values.

The domestic ideology had real meaning only for relatively affluent women. Working-class wives were not usually employed outside the home during this period, but they labored long and hard within the household. Besides cleaning, cooking, and taking care of large numbers of children, they often took in washing or piece work to supplement a meager family income. Their endless domestic drudgery made a sham of the notion that women had the time and energy for the "higher things of life."

For middle-class women whose husbands earned a good income, however, freedom from industrial or farm labor offered tangible benefits. They now had the leisure to read extensively in the new literature directed primarily at housewives and to cultivate deep and lasting friendships with other women. The result was a distinctively feminine subculture emphasizing "sisterhood" or "sorority." This growing sense of solidarity with other women and of the importance of sexual identity could transcend the private home and even the barriers of social class. Beginning in the 1820s urban women of the middle and upper classes organized societies for the relief and rehabilitation of poor or "fallen women." The aim of these organizations was not economic and political equality with men but the elevation of all females to true womanhood.

For some women, the domestic ideal even sanctioned ladylike efforts to extend their sphere until it conquered the masculine world outside the home. This domestic feminism was reflected in women's involvement in crusades to stamp out such masculine sins as intemperance, gambling, and sexual vice. It was also the motivating force behind Catharine Beecher's campaign to make schoolteaching a women's occupation. A prolific and influential writer on the theory and practice of domesticity, this unmarried daughter of Lyman Beecher saw the role of the spinster-teacher as equivalent to that of mother. By instilling in young males the virtues that only women could teach, the schoolmarm could help redeem America from corruption and materialism.

But Beecher and other domestic feminists knew that the main responsibility for remaking the world in the image of the home fell on those married women who understood what they could accomplish simply by being wives and mothers. Reforming husbands was difficult: they were away so much of the time and tended to be preoccupied with business. But this very fact gave women primary responsibility for the rearing of children—an activity to which nineteenth-century Americans attached almost cosmic significance. Since women were considered particularly well qualified to transmit piety and morality to future citizens of the Republic, the cult of domesticity exalted motherhood and encouraged a new concern with childhood as the time of life when "character" was formed.

The Discovery of Childhood

The nineteenth century has been called "the century of the child." More than before, childhood was seen as a distinct stage of life requiring the special and sustained attention of adults. The family now became "child-centered," which meant that the care, nurture, and rearing of children was viewed as the family's main function. In earlier times, adults treated children in a more casual way, often sending them away from home for education or apprenticeship at a very early age. Among the well-to-do, children spent more time with servants or tutors than with their parents.

By the early decades of the nineteenth century, however, children were staying at home longer and receiving much more attention from parents, especially mothers. "Increasingly," according to historian Carl Degler, "children were viewed as individuals, as persons in their own right. The new attitude is reflected, for example, in the decline of the practice of naming children after their parents." Almost completely abandoned was the colonial custom—nearly inconceivable today—of naming a living child after a sibling who had died in infancy. Each child was now looked upon as a unique and irreplaceable individual.

New customs and fashions heralded the "discovery" of childhood. Books aimed specifically at juveniles began to roll off the presses. Parents became more self-conscious about their responsibilities and sought help from a new literature providing expert advice on child-rearing. One early nineteenth-century mother wrote that "There is scarcely any subject concerning which I feel more anxiety than the proper education of my children. It is a difficult and delicate subject, the more I feel how much is to be learnt by myself."

The new concern for children resulted in more intimate relations between parents and children. The ideal family described in the advice manuals and sentimental literature was bound together by affection rather than authority. Firm discipline remained at the core of "family government," but there was a change in the preferred method of enforcing good behavior. Corporal punishment declined, partially displaced by shaming or withholding of affection. Disobedient middle-class children were now more likely to be confined to their rooms to reflect on their sins than to receive a good thrashing. Discipline could no longer be justified as the constant application of physical force over naturally wayward beings. In an age of moral perfectionism, its role was to induce repentance and change basic attitudes. The intended result was often described as "self-government"; and to achieve it parents used guilt, rather than fear, as their main source of leverage. A mother's sorrow or a father's stern and prolonged silence were deemed more effective in forming character than blows or angry words.

Child-centered families also meant smaller families. If nineteenth-century families had remained as large as those of earlier times, it would have been impossible to lavish so much care and attention on individual offspring. For reasons that are still not completely understood, the average number of children born to each woman during her fertile years dropped from 7.04 in 1800 to 5.42 in 1850. As a result, average family size declined about 25 percent, beginning a long-range trend lasting to the present day.

The practice of various forms of birth control undoubtedly contributed to this demographic revolution. Ancestors of the modern condom and diaphragm were openly advertised and sold during the pre–Civil War period, but it was likely that most couples controlled family size by practicing the withdrawal method or limiting the frequency of intercourse. Abortion was also surprisingly common and was on the rise. One historian has estimated that by 1850 there was one abortion for every five or six live births.

Parents seemed to understand that having fewer children meant that they could provide their offspring with a better start in life. Such attitudes were appropriate to a society that was beginning to shift from agriculture to commerce and industry. For rural households short of labor, large families were an economic asset. For urban couples who hoped to send their children into a competitive world that demanded special talents and training, they were a distinct liability.

Institutional Reform

The family could not carry the whole burden of socializing and reforming individuals. Children needed schooling as well as parental nurture, and many lacked the advantage of a real home environment. Some adults, too, seemed to require special kinds of attention and treatment. Seeking to extend the advantages of "family government" beyond the domestic circle, reformers worked to establish or improve public institutions that were designed to shape individual character and instill a capacity for self-discipline.

The Extension of Education

The period from 1820 to 1850 saw an enormous expansion of free public schools. The new resolve to put more children in school for longer periods reflected many of the same values that exalted the child-centered family. Up to a certain age children could be effectively nurtured and educated at home. But after that they needed formal training at a character-molding institution that would prepare them to make a living and bear the burdens of republican citizenship. Purely intellectual training at school was regarded as less important than moral indoctrination.

The Shakers

One of the communitarian religious movements that sprang up in the pre-Civil War period had a special fascination for outsiders. The Shakers—officially known as the Millennial Church or the United Society of Believers—welcomed curious travelers to their settlements, and many of the visitors reported in great detail on the unusual way of life that they observed there.

The Shakers were descended from a small English sect of the same name that appeared in the early to mid-eighteenth century. The English Shakers were radical millennialists, which meant that they expected Christ's Second Coming to occur momentarily. They got their name from the fact that they expressed their religious fervor through vigorous bodily movements, which eventually took the form of a ritualized dance. Most of the Shakers were from the working class, and one of their converts was a woman named Ann Lee, who joined the sect in 1758.

After she had been jailed several times for preaching strange and unorthodox doctrines in public places, Lee emigrated to America in 1774. Mother Ann, as she was known to her followers, came to believe that she was the one sent by God to save the world. It would not be farfetched to call her the great feminist of Christian millennialism. She preached that God was both masculine and feminine and that Christ had incarnated only the masculine side. It was her vocation to bring on the millennium by embodying the feminine attributes of the Almighty. Hence the American Shakers worshiped Ann Lee and expressed belief in a new theology based squarely on the principle of sexual equality.

Mother Ann died in 1784, but not before she had made enough American converts to establish a permanent sect. Taking advantage of all the land available in America, the Shakers drew apart from the rest of society and established communities where they could practice their own version of Christian perfectionism free of harassment. The mother colony was at Mount Lebanon, New York, but other Shaker communities were established in the New England states before 1800 and in Ohio and Kentucky thereafter. By the 1830s, twenty settlements in seven states had a combined membership of approximately six thousand.

In the Shaker communities all property was owned in common and political authority was vested in a self-perpetuating group of ministers. Hence the Shakers practiced a form of "theocratic communism." Reflecting their belief in sexual equality, they required that the ministry of each community be composed of a equal number of elders and elderesses. What most attracted the interest of outsiders, however, was the fact that Shakers banned sexual intercourse and marriage, requiring strict celibacy of all members. To enforce this rule they segregated men and women in most social and economic activities. This novel arrangement resulted from a belief that the end of the world was at hand; thus there was no need to reproduce the human race, and those anticipating salvation should begin to live in the pure spiritual state that would arrive with the millennium. The rule of chastity obviously limited the growth of the Shaker communities, but a willingness to adopt orphans and to accept converts allowed some of them to survive well into the twentieth century.

Visitors to the Shaker settlements were, for the most part, impressed with the order, decorum, cleanliness, and quiet prosperity that prevailed. But beginning in 1837 religious services in the communities suddenly became wildly ecstatic. Relatively formalized dancing was replaced by spontaneous and violent "shaking and turning exercizes." Shakers had always believed in spiritualism, or direct communication with departed

souls, but now there was an epidemic of spiritual possession. In almost every service, members fell into trances, conveyed messages from the spirit world, and spoke in what were thought to be foreign tongues. Some observers concluded that the Shakers had literally gone mad, and for a time the ministers thought it advisable to close their services to the public.

It was a time when religious revivalism had recently swept the country as a whole, and the Shakers were simply having their own outburst of enthusiasm, showing perhaps that they were not completely cut off from the outside world. Since Shakers were already intensely religious, their

revivals were even more violent and frantic than those taking place elsewhere. Modern psychologists might attribute this frenzy to sexual frustration, but such an interpretation would not explain why the Shaker ecstatic revival ended about 1845. After that time, the calm and sober spirit of earlier years again prevailed.

The Shakers, despite their isolation and singularity, made some important contributions to American culture. They valued simplicity in all things, and this ideal became a basis for creative achievement. The virtue of simplicity was expressed in the words of the hauntingly beautiful Shaker hymn (which later became the theme for Aaron Copland's twentieth-century symphonic work *Appalachian Spring*), "'Tis a gift to be simple." Their aesthetic ideal of simplicity inspired Shaker artisans to design buildings and furnishings that were purely functional and without ornamentation. In the eyes of modern art critics and historians, Shaker handiwork achieved an elegance and purity of form that ranks it among the most beautiful ever produced in America. The Tree of Life emblem (opposite page) is from a Shaker spirit drawing that was received as a vision by Sister Hannah Cohoon and recorded in 1854.

Besides being an extension of the family, the school could also serve as a substitute for it. Educational reformers were alarmed at the masses of poor and immigrant children who allegedly lacked a proper home environment. It was up to the schools to make up for this disadvantage. Otherwise, the Republic would be in danger from masses of people "incapable of self-government."

Before the 1820s, schooling in the United States was a haphazard affair. The wealthy sent their children to private schools, and some of the poor sent their children to charity or "pauper" schools that were usually financed in part by state or local governments. Public education was most highly developed in New England states, where towns were required by law to support elementary schools. It was weakest in the South where almost all education was private. Between the 1820s and the 1850s, the movement for publicly supported common schools made great headway in the North and had limited success in parts of the South. In theory, the common school was an egalitarian institution providing a free basic education for children of all social backgrounds.

The agitation for expanded public education began in the 1820s and early '30s as a central demand of the workingmen's movements in eastern cities. These hard-pressed artisans and craftsmen viewed free schools open to all as a way of countering the growing gap between rich and poor. Initially, strong opposition came from more affluent taxpayers who did not see why they should pay for the education of other people's children. But middle-class reformers soon seized the initiative, shaped educational reform to their own end of social discipline, and provided the momentum needed for legislative success.

The most influential spokesman for the common school movement was Horace Mann of Massachusetts. As a lawyer and member of the state legislature, Mann worked tirelessly for the establishment of a state board of education and adequate tax support for local schools. In 1837 he persuaded the state legislature to enact his proposals, and he subsequently resigned his seat to become the first secretary of the new board, an office he held with great distinction until 1848. His philosophy of education was based on the premise that children were clay in the hands of teachers and school officials and could be molded

to a state of perfection. Like the advocates of child-rearing through moral influence rather than physical force, he discouraged corporal punishment except as a last resort. His position on this issue led to a bitter controversy with Boston schoolmasters who retained a Calvinist sense of original sin and favored a freer use of the rod.

Against those who argued that school taxes violated the rights of property, Mann contended that private property was actually held in trust for the good of the community. "The property of this commonwealth," he wrote in his annual report of 1846, "is pledged for the education of all its youth up to such a point as will save them from poverty and vice, and prepare them for the adequate performance of their social and civil duties." Mann's conception of public education as a means of social discipline converted the middle and upper classes to the cause. By teaching middle-class morality and respect for order, the schools could turn potential rowdies and revolutionaries into law-abiding citizens. They could also encourage social mobility by opening doors for lower-class children who were determined to do better than their parents.

In practice, the new or improved public schools often alienated working-class pupils and their families rather than reforming them. The compulsory attendance laws that were passed in Massachusetts and other states deprived poor families of needed wage earners without guaranteeing new occupational opportunities for those with an elementary education. As the laboring class became increasingly immigrant and Catholic in the 1840s and '50s, dissatisfaction arose over the evangelical Protestant tone of "moral instruction" in the schools. Quite consciously, Mann and his disciples were trying to impose a uniform culture on people who valued differing traditions.

In addition to the "three Rs" of reading, writing, and arithmetic, the essence of what was being taught in the public schools of the mid-nineteenth century was the "Protestant ethic"—industry, punctuality, sobriety, and frugality. These were the virtues stressed in the famous McGuffey readers, which first appeared in 1836. Millions of children learned to read by digesting McGuffey's parables about the terrible fate of those who gave in to sloth, drunkenness, or wastefulness. Such moral indoctrination helped produce generations of Americans with personalities

■ *The lessons and examples in* McGuffey's
Readers *upheld the basic virtues of thrift,
honesty, and charity, and taught that evil deeds
never went unpunished.*

and beliefs adapted to the needs of an industrializing society—people who could be depended upon
to adjust to the precise and regular routines of the
factory or the office. But as an education for
"self-government"—in the sense of learning to
think for oneself—it left much to be desired.

Fortunately, however, education was not limited to the schools nor devoted solely to children.
Every city and almost every town or village had a
lyceum, debating society, or mechanic's institute
where adults of all social classes could broaden
their intellectual horizons. The lyceums featured
discourses on such subjects as "self-reliance" or
"the conduct of life" by creative thinkers such as
Ralph Waldo Emerson, explanations and demonstrations of the latest scientific discoveries, and
debates among members on controversial issues.

Young Abraham Lincoln, who had received less
than two years of formal schooling as a child in
backwoods Indiana, sharpened his intellect in the
early 1830s as a member of the New Salem
(Illinois) debating society. In 1838, after moving
to Springfield, he set forth his political principles
when he spoke at the local lyceum on "The
Perpetuation of Our Political Institutions." Unlike the public schools, the lyceums and debating
societies fostered independent thought and the
spread of new ideas.

Discovering the Asylum

Some segments of the population were obviously
beyond the reach of family government and character training provided in homes and schools. In
the 1820s and '30s, reformers became acutely
aware of the danger to society posed by an apparently increasing number of criminals, lunatics,
and paupers. Their answer was to establish special institutions to house those deemed incapable
of self-discipline. Their goals were humanitarian;
they believed that reform and rehabilitation were
possible if the right kind of controlled environment could be created.

In earlier times, the existence of paupers, law-
breakers and insane persons had been taken for
granted. Their presence was viewed as the consequence of divine judgment or original sin. For the
most part these people were dealt with in ways
that did not isolate them from local communities. The insane were allowed to wander about if
harmless, confined at home if they were dangerous; the poor were supported by private charity or
the dole provided by towns or counties; convicted
criminals were whipped, held for limited periods
in local jails, or—in the case of very serious
offenses—executed.

By the early nineteenth century these traditional methods had come to seem both inadequate and unenlightened. Dealing with deviants
in a neighborly way broke down as economic
development and organization disrupted community life. At the same time, reformers were concluding that all defects of mind and character
were correctable—that the insane could be cured,
criminals reformed, and paupers taught to pull
themselves out of destitution. The result was
what historian David Rothman termed "the dis-

covery of the asylum"—the invention and establishment of special institutions for the confinement and reformation of deviants.

The 1820s and '30s saw the emergence of state-supported prisons, insane asylums, and poorhouses. New York and Pennsylvania led the way in prison reform. Institutions at Philadelphia and Auburn, New York, attracted international attention as model penitentiaries, mainly because of their experiments in isolating inmates from one another. Solitary confinement was viewed as a humanitarian and therapeutic policy because it gave inmates a chance to reflect on their sins free from the corrupting influence of other convicts. In theory, prisons and asylums substituted for the family. The custodians were intended to act as parents by providing moral advice and training.

In practice, these institutions were far different from the affectionate families idealized by the cult of domesticity. Most of them accommodated only a single sex or maintained a strict segregation of male and female inmates. Their most prominent feature was the imposition of a rigid daily routine. The early superintendents and wardens believed that the enforcement of an inflexible and demanding set of rules and procedures would encourage self-discipline. The French observers, Alexis de Tocqueville and Gustave de Beaumont summed up these practical expectations after a tour of American prisons in 1831 and '32: "The habits or order to which the prisoner is subjected for several years . . . the obedience of every moment to inflexible rules, the regularity of a uniform life . . . are calculated to produce a deep impression upon his mind. Perhaps, leaving the prison he is not an honest man, but he has contracted honest habits. . . ."

In retrospect, it is clear that the prisons, asylums, and poorhouses did not achieve the aims of their founders. Public support was inadequate to meet the needs of a growing inmate population; the result was overcrowding and the use of brutality to keep order. For the most part, prisons failed to reform hardened criminals, and the primitive psychotherapy known as "moral treatment" failed to cure most asylum patients. The poorhouses rapidly degenerated into sinkholes of despair. A combination of naive theories and poor performance doomed these institutions to a custodial rather than a reformatory role.

But conditions would have been even worse had it not been for the efforts of one individual—Dorothea Dix. Between 1838 and the Civil War this remarkable woman devoted her considerable energies and skills to publicizing the inhumane treatment prevailing in prisons, almshouses, and insane asylums and lobbying for corrective action. As a direct result of her activities fifteen states opened new hospitals for the insane and others improved their supervision of penitentiaries, asylums, and poorhouses. Dix ranks as one of the most practical and effective of all the reformers of the pre–Civil War era.

In this woodcut, prisoners—in hand-on-shoulder lockstep—march into the dining room at Sing Sing Prison in New York. Rigid discipline and extensive rules restricting the inmates' movements, speech, and actions were thought to be important elements in reforming criminals. In most prisons, a strict silence was enforced at all times to allow the prisoners to reflect on the error of their ways.

■ *The crowded conditions in asylums like Blackwell's Island in New York stirred the sympathies of Dorothea Dix, one of the most effective reformers of this period.*

Reform Turns Radical

During the 1830s, internal dissension split the great reform movement spawned by the Second Great Awakening. Efforts to promote evangelical piety, improve personal and public morality, and shape character through familial or institutional discipline continued and even flourished. But bolder spirits went beyond such goals and set their sights on the total liberation and perfection of the individual. Especially in New England and the upper North, a new breed of reformers, prophets, and utopians attacked established institutions and rejected all compromise with what they viewed as a corrupt society.

Divisions in the Benevolent Empire

Early nineteenth-century reformers were, for the most part, committed to gradually changing existing attitudes and practices in ways that would not invite conflict or disrupt the fabric of society. But by the mid-1830s a new mood of impatience and perfectionism surfaced within the benevolent societies. In 1836, for example, the Temperance Society split over two issues—whether the absti-

nence pledge should be extended to include beer and wine and whether pressure should be applied to producers and sellers of alcoholic beverages as well as to consumers. Radicals insisted on a total commitment to "cold water" and were prepared to clash head-on with an important economic interest. Moderates held back from such goals and tactics because they wished to avoid hostility from prominent citizens who drank wine or had money invested in the liquor business.

A similar rift occurred in the American Peace Society, an antiwar organization founded in 1828 by clergymen seeking to promote Christian concern for world peace. Most of the founders admitted the propriety of "defensive wars" and were shocked when some members of the society began to denounce all use of force as a violation of the Sermon on the Mount. The dissidents, who called themselves "nonresistants," withdrew from the organization in 1838. Led by Henry C. Wright, they formed the New England Non-Resistant Society to promote an absolute pacifism, which denied the right of self-defense to nations or individuals and repudiated all forms of governmental coercion.

The new perfectionism realized its most dramatic and important success within the antislavery movement. Before the 1830s most people who expressed religious and moral concern over slavery were affiliated with the American Colonization Society, a benevolent organization founded in 1817. Most colonizationists admitted that slavery was an evil, but they also viewed it as a deeply rooted social and economic institution that could only be eliminated very gradually and with the cooperation of slaveholders. Reflecting the power of racial prejudice, they proposed to transport freed blacks to Africa as a way of relieving southern fears that a race war would erupt if slaves were simply released from bondage and allowed to remain in America. In 1821 the society established the colony of Liberia in West Africa, and during the next decade a few thousand American blacks were settled there.

Colonization proved to be grossly inadequate as a step toward the elimination of slavery. Many of the blacks taken to Africa were already free, and those liberated by masters influenced by the movement represented only a tiny percentage of the natural increase of the southern slave population. Northern blacks denounced this enterprise

In the inaugural issue of his antislavery weekly, The Liberator, *William Lloyd Garrison (left) announced that he was launching a militant battle against the evil and sin of slavery. The stirring words that appeared in that first issue are repeated on the Liberator Banner (above).*

because it denied the prospect of racial equality in America. Black opposition to colonizationism helped persuade William Lloyd Garrison and other white abolitionists to repudiate the Colonization Society and support immediate emancipation without emigration.

Garrison launched a new and more radical antislavery movement in 1831 when he began to publish a journal called the *Liberator* in Boston. Most of the small number of early subscribers to Garrison's *Liberator* were free blacks, and radical abolitionists depended heavily on black support from then on. Black orators, especially escaped slaves like Frederick Douglass, were featured at antislavery meetings, and some Afro-Americans became officers of antislavery societies.

Garrison denounced colonization as a slaveholder's plot to remove troublesome free blacks and an ignoble surrender to un-Christian prejudices. His rhetoric was as severe as his proposals were radical. As he wrote in the first issue of the *Liberator*, "I will be as harsh as truth and as uncompromising as justice. . . . I am in earnest—I will not equivocate—I will not excuse—I will not retreat a single inch—AND I WILL BE HEARD."

Heard he was. In 1833 Garrison and other abolitionists founded the American Anti-Slavery Society. "We shall send forth agents to lift up the voice of remonstrance, of warning, of entreaty, and of rebuke," its Declaration of Sentiments proclaimed. The colonization movement was placed on the defensive, and during the 1830s many of its most active northern supporters became abolitionists.

Black leaders in the abolitionist movement included Frederick Douglass (left) and William Whipper (right). Douglass, who escaped from slavery in 1838, became one of the most effective voices in the crusade against slavery. In 1837, twelve years before Thoreau's essay "Civil Disobedience," Whipper published an article in The Colored Times *entitled "An Address on Non-Resistance to Offensive Aggression." Whipper was also one of the founders of the American Moral Reform Society, a black abolitionist organization.*

The Abolitionist Enterprise

The abolitionist movement, like the temperance crusade, was a direct outgrowth of the Second Great Awakening. Many leading abolitionists had undergone conversion experiences in the 1820s and were already committed to a life of Christian activism before they dedicated themselves to freeing the slaves. Several were ministers or divinity students seeking a mission in life that would fulfill their spiritual and professional ambitions.

The career of Theodore Dwight Weld exemplified the connection between revivalism and abolitionism. Weld came from a long line of New England ministers. After dropping out of divinity school because of a combination of physical and spiritual ailments, he migrated to western New York. There he fell under the influence of Charles G. Finney and, after a long struggle, underwent a conversion experience in 1826. He then became an itinerant lecturer for various reform causes. By the early 1830s, his attention was focused on the moral issues raised by the institution of slavery. After a brief flirtation with the colonization movement, Weld was converted to abolitionism in 1832. A critical factor in his decision was the recognition that colonizationists did not really accept blacks as equals or "brothers-in-Christ." In 1834 he instigated what amounted to a series of abolitionist revivals at Lane Theological Seminary in Cincinnati. When the trustees of the seminary attempted to suppress further discussion of the case for immediate emancipation, Weld led a mass walkout of most of the students. "The Lane rebels" subsequently founded Oberlin College as a center for abolitionist activity.

In 1835 and '36 Weld toured Ohio and western New York preaching abolitionism. He also supervised and trained other agents and orators as part of a campaign to convert the entire region to the cause of immediate emancipation. The tried and true methods of the revival—fervent preaching, protracted meetings, and the call for individuals to come forth and announce their redemption—were put at the service of the antislavery movement. Weld and his associates often had to face angry mobs, but they left behind them tens of thousands of new abolitionists and hundreds of local antislavery societies. As a result of their efforts, northern Ohio and western New York became hotbeds of abolitionist sentiment.

In general, antislavery orators and organizers enjoyed their greatest successes in the small- to medium-sized towns of the upper North. The typical convert came from an upwardly mobile family engaged in small business, the skilled trades, or market farming. In larger towns and cities, or when they ventured close to the Mason-Dixon line, abolitionists encountered fierce and effective opposition. In 1835 Garrison was mobbed in the streets of Boston and almost lynched. Weld himself suffered a disillusioning setback in 1836 when riots forced him to cancel his appearances in Troy, New York. In New York City, the Tappan brothers—Lewis and Arthur—were frequent objects of threats and violence. These two successful merchants were key figures in the movement because they used their substantial wealth to finance antislavery activities. In 1835–1836 they supported a massive effort to print antislavery pamphlets and distribute them through the U.S. mails. But they made relatively few converts in their own city; most New Yorkers regarded them as dangerous radicals.

Abolitionists who thought of taking their message to the fringes of the South had reason to pause, given the fate of the antislavery editor Elijah Lovejoy. In 1837 while attempting to defend himself and his printing press from a mob in Alton, Illinois, just across the Mississippi River from slaveholding Missouri, Lovejoy was shot and killed.

Racism was a major cause of antiabolitionist violence in the North. Rumors that abolitionists advocated or practiced interracial marriage could easily incite an urban crowd. If it could not find white abolitionists, the mob was likely to turn on local blacks. Working-class whites tended to fear that economic and social competition with blacks would increase if abolitionists succeeded in freeing the slaves and making them citizens. But a striking feature of many of the mobs was that they were dominated by "gentlemen of property and standing." Solid citizens resorted to violence, it would appear, because abolitionism threatened their conservative notions of social order and hierarchy.

By the end of the 1830s, the abolitionist movement was under great stress. Besides the burden of external repression, there was dissension with-

in the movement. Becoming an abolitionist required an exacting conscience and an unwillingness to compromise on matters of principle. These character traits also made it difficult for abolitionists to work together and maintain a united front against their opponents. Relations between black and white abolitionists were, for the most part, tense and uneasy. Blacks protested that they did not have a fair share of leadership positions or influence over policy. Not even abolitionists were entirely free of the prejudices rife in the larger white society, and blacks resented the paternalism and condescension that often resulted.

During the late 1830s, Garrison, the most visible spokesman for the cause, began to adopt positions that other abolitionists found extreme and divisive. He embraced the nonresistant or "no-government" philosophy of Henry C. Wright and urged abolitionists to abstain from voting or otherwise participating in a corrupt political system. He also attacked the clergy and the churches for refusing to take a strong antislavery stand and encouraged his followers to "come out" of the established denominations rather than continuing to work within them.

These positions alienated those members of the Anti-Slavery Society who continued to hope that organized religion and the existing political system could be influenced or even taken over by abolitionists. But it was Garrison's stand on women's rights that led to an open break at the national convention of 1840. Following their leader's principle that women should be equal partners in the crusade, a Garrison-led majority elected a female abolitionist to the executive committee of the Anti-Slavery Society. A minority, led by Lewis Tappan, then withdrew to form a competing organization—the American and Foreign Anti-Slavery Society.

The new organization never amounted to much, but the schism did weaken Garrison's influence within the movement. When he later repudiated the United States Constitution as a proslavery document and called for northern secession from the Union, few antislavery people in the mid-Atlantic or midwestern states went along. Outside of New England, most abolitionists worked *within* the churches and avoided controversial side issues like women's rights and nonresistant pacifism. Some antislavery advocates chose the path of political action. The Liberty party, organized in 1840, was their first attempt to enter the electoral arena under their own banner; it signaled a new effort to turn antislavery sentiment into political power.

Historians have debated the question of whether the abolitionist movement of the 1830s and early '40s was a success or failure. It obviously failed to convert a majority of Americans to its position that slavery was a sinful institution that should be abolished immediately. Since that position implied that blacks should be granted equality as American citizens, it ran up against the powerful conviction of white supremacy prevailing in all parts of the country. In the South, abolitionism caused a strong counterreaction and helped inspire a more militant and uncompromising defense of slavery. The belief that peaceful agitation, or what abolitionists called "moral suasion," would convert slaveholders and their northern sympathizers to abolition was obviously unrealistic.

But in another sense the crusade was successful. It brought the slavery issue to the forefront of public consciousness and convinced a substantial and growing segment of the northern population that the South's peculiar institution was morally wrong and a potential danger to the American way of life. The politicians who later mobilized the North against the expansion of slavery into the territories drew strength from the reservoir of antislavery attitudes and sentiment created by the abolitionists.

From Abolitionism to Women's Rights

Abolitionism also served as a catalyst for the women's rights movement. From the beginning women were active participants in the abolitionist crusade. Between 1835 and 1838, the American Anti-Slavery Society bombarded Congress with petitions, mostly calling for abolition of slavery in the District of Columbia. Over half of the thousands of antislavery petitions sent to Washington had women's signatures on them.

Some antislavery women went further and defied conventional ideas of their proper sphere by becoming public speakers and demanding an equal role in the leadership of antislavery socie-

ties. The most famous of these were the Grimké sisters, Sarah and Angelina, who attracted enormous attention because they were the rebellious daughters of a South Carolina slaveholder. When some male abolitionists objected to their speaking in public, Garrison came to their defense and helped forge a link between black and female struggles for equality.

The battle to participate equally in the antislavery crusade made a number of female abolitionists acutely aware of male dominance and oppression. For them, the same principles that justified the liberation of the slaves also applied to the emancipation of women from all restrictions on their rights as citizens. In 1840 Garrison's American followers withdrew from the first World's Anti-Slavery Convention in London because the sponsors refused to seat the female members of their delegation. Among the women thus excluded were Lucretia Mott and Elizabeth Cady Stanton.

Elizabeth Cady Stanton, a leader of the woman's rights movement, reared seven children. In addition to her pioneering work for woman's rights and especially for woman suffrage, she also lectured frequently on family life and child care.

Wounded by male reluctance to extend the cause of emancipation to include women, Stanton and Mott organized a new and independent movement for women's rights. The high point of their campaign was the famous convention at Seneca Falls, New York, in 1848. The "Declaration of Sentiments" issued by this first national gathering of feminists charged that "The history of mankind is a history of repeated injuries and usurpations on the part of man toward woman, having in direct object the establishment of an absolute tyranny over her." It went on to demand that all women be given the right to vote and that married women be freed from unjust laws giving husbands control of their property, persons, and children. Rejecting the cult of domesticity with its doctrine of separate spheres, these women and their male supporters launched the modern movement for sexual equality.

Radical Ideas and Experiments

Hopes for individual or social perfection were not limited to reformers inspired by evangelicalism. Between the 1820s and '50s, a great variety of schemes for human redemption came from those who had rejected orthodox Protestantism. Some were secular humanists carrying on the free-thinking tradition of the Enlightenment, but most were seeking new paths to spiritual or religious fulfillment. These philosophical and religious radicals attacked established institutions, prescribed new modes of living, and founded utopian communities to put their ideas into practice.

A radical movement of foreign origin that gained a toehold in Jacksonian American was utopian socialism. In 1825–1826, the British manufacturer and reformer Robert Owen visited the United States and founded a community based on common and equal ownership of property at New Harmony, Indiana. About the same time, Owen's associate Frances Wright gathered a group of slaves at Nashoba, Tennessee, and set them to work earning their freedom in an atmosphere of "rational cooperation." The rapid demise of both of these model communities suggested that utopian socialism did not easily take root in American soil.

But the impulse survived. In the 1840s, a number of Americans, including the prominent editor Horace Greeley, became interested in the ideas of the French utopian theorist Charles Fourier. Fourier called for cooperative communities in which everyone did a fair share of the work and tasks were allotted to make use of the natural abilities and instincts of the members. Between forty and fifty Fourieristic "phalanxes" were subsequently established in the mid-Atlantic and midwestern states. These communities were not purely socialistic; in fact they were organized as joint stock companies. But they did give the members

■ *The utopian community Bishop Hill was founded in Illinois by Eric Janson, who left the orthodoxy of the Swedish Lutheran Church for a return to a simpler form of Christianity. This painting by Olaf Krans, a member of the community, shows men and women working together to harvest wheat.*

an opportunity to live and work in a communal atmosphere. Like the Owenite communities, they were short-lived, surviving for an average of only two years. The common complaint of the founders was that Americans were too individualistic to cooperate in the ways that Fourier's theories required.

The most successful and long-lived of the pre–Civil War utopias was established in 1848 at Oneida, New York, and was inspired by an unorthodox brand of Christian perfectionism. Its founder, John Humphrey Noyes, believed that the Second Coming of Christ had already occurred; hence human beings were totally free from sin and were no longer obliged to follow the moral rules that their previously fallen state had required. At Oneida, traditional marriage was outlawed and a form of "free love" was put into practice. But life at Oneida bore no resemblance to a perpetual orgy. The choosing or changing of sexual partners was closely regulated by an elaborate set of rules. Birth control was practiced, and a couple could have children only if they seemed likely to produce healthy and intelligent offspring. Systematic calculation was also applied to the economic life of the community, and the result was sustained prosperity. As a business enterprise, Oneida functioned very much like an efficient modern corporation.

Brook Farm, near Roxbury, Massachusetts, is the best remembered of the utopian experiments because of its close connection with the literary and philosophical movement known as transcendentalism. Most transcendentalists were Unitarians or ex-Unitarians who were dissatisfied with the sober rationalism of their denomination and sought a more intense kind of spiritual experience. Unable to embrace evangelical Christianity because of intellectual resistance to its doctrines, they sought inspiration from a philosophical and literary idealism of German origin. Their prophet was Ralph Waldo Emerson, a brilliant essayist and lecturer who preached that each individual could commune directly with a benign spiritual force that animated nature and the universe—he called it the "oversoul." In the vicinity of Emerson's home in Concord, Massachusetts, a group of like-minded seekers for truth and spiritual fulfillment gathered during the 1830s and '40s.

There was something self-contradictory about the notion of a transcendentalist community.

Chronology	
1801	Massive revival held at Cane Ridge, Kentucky
1826	American Temperance Society organized
1830–1831	Charles G. Finney evangelizes Rochester, New York
1831	William Lloyd Garrison publishes first issue of the *Liberator*
1833	Abolitionists found American Anti-Slavery Society
1836	American Temperance Society splits into factions
1836–1837	Theodore Weld advocates abolition in Ohio and upstate New York
1837	Massachusetts establishes a state board of education Abolitionist editor Elijah Lovejoy killed by a proslavery mob
1840	American Anti-Slavery Society splits over women's rights and other issues
1841	Transcendentalists organize a model community at Brook Farm
1848	Feminists gather at Seneca Falls, New York, and found the women's rights movement
1854	Henry David Thoreau's *Walden* published

Emerson himself was a radical individualist committed to "self-culture" and "the sufficiency of the private man." He carefully avoided all involvement in organized movements or associations because they limited the freedom of the individual to develop inner resources and find a personal path to spiritual illumination. But the group at Brook Farm, led by the Reverend George Ripley, went ahead anyway and attempted to set up a community that would provide an ideal environment for self-fulfillment.

Between 1841 and 1845, they worked the land in common, conducted an excellent school on the principle that spontaneity rather than discipline was the key to education, and allowed ample time for conversation, meditation, communion with nature, and artistic activity of all kinds. Visitors and guest lecturers included such luminaries as Emerson; Margaret Fuller, the brilliant feminist writer; and Theodore Parker, the Unitarian theologian and radical reformer. The great fiction writer Nathaniel Hawthorne was in residence for a time and later provided a gently satirical portrait of the experiment in his novel *The Blithedale Romance.* In 1845 Brook Farm was reconstituted as a Fourieristic phalanx, but some of the original spirit persisted until its dissolution in 1849.

Another experiment in transcendental living adhered more closely to the individualistic spirit of the movement. Between 1845 and 1847, Henry David Thoreau, a young disciple of Emerson, lived by himself in the woods along the shore of Walden Pond and carefully recorded his thoughts and impressions. In a sense, he pushed the ideal of "self-culture" to its logical outcome—a utopia of one. The result was *Walden* (published in 1854), one of the greatest achievements in American literature.

■ *Thoreau (left) explained that he went to live in solitude in the woods because he wished to "front only the essential facts of life." The sketch below appeared on the title page of the first edition of* Walden, *the remarkable record of his experiment in living.*

Fads and Fashions

Not only venturesome intellectuals experimented with new beliefs and life-styles. Between the 1830s and '50s, a number of fads, fashions, and medical cure-alls appeared on the scene, indicating that a large segment of the middle class was obsessed with the pursuit of personal health, happiness, and moral perfection. Dietary reformers like Sylvester Graham convinced many people to give up meat, coffee, tea, and pastries in favor of fruit, vegetables, and whole wheat bread. Some women, especially feminists, began to wear loose-fitting pantalettes or "bloomers," popularized by Amelia Bloomer. These clothes were more convenient and less restricting than the elaborate structure of corsets, petticoats, and hooped skirts currently in fashion. A concern with understanding and improving personal character and abilities was reflected in the craze for phrenology—a popular pseudoscience that involved studying the shape of the skull to determine natural aptitudes and inclinations.

In an age of perfectionism, even the dead could be enlisted on the side of universal reform. In the 1850s spiritualists like Andrew Jackson Davis and the Fox sisters—Margaret, Leah, and Catharine—convinced an extraordinary number of people that it was possible to make direct contact with the departed, who were viewed as having "passed on" to a purer state of being and a higher wisdom. Seances were held in parlors all over the nation, and large crowds turned out for demonstrations of "spirit-rapping" and other psychic manifestations. Spiritualist beliefs were a logical outgrowth (some might say to the point of absurdity) of the perfectionist dream pursued so ardently by antebellum Americans.

Pre-Civil War reform was both a criticism of American reality and a celebration of America's promise. It condemned the materialism, self-seeking, and opportunistic politics of the age. It sought, perhaps unrealistically, to purify society and politics by appealing directly to the spiritual or rational capabilities of individuals. It was long on inspirational rhetoric but somewhat short on practical programs. But it did show that pursuit of the ideal was deeply rooted in American culture.

Recommended Reading

Alice Felt Tyler, *Freedom's Ferment: Phases of American Social History from the Colonial Period to the Outbreak of the Civil War* (1944), gives a lively overview of the varieties of pre–Civil War reform activity. Ronald G. Walters, *American Reformers, 1815–1860* (1978), provides a modern interpretation of these movements. A particularly useful selection of articles and essays is David Brion Davis, ed., *Ante-Bellum Reform* (1967). The best general work on the revivalism of the Second Great Awakening is William G. McLoughlin, *Modern Revivalism* (1959). Paul E. Johnson, *A Shopkeeper's Millennium: Society and Revivals in Rochester, New York, 1815–1837* (1978), incisively describes the impact of the revival on a single community. A good introduction to the changing roles of women and the family in nineteenth-century America is Carl N. Degler, *At Odds: Women and the Family in America From the Revolution to the Present* (1980). David J. Rothman, *The Discovery of the Asylum: Social Order and Disorder in the New Republic* (1971), provides a penetrating analysis of the movement for institutional reform. For an up-to-date survey of abolitionism, see James Brewer Stewart, *Holy Warriors: The Abolitionists and American Slavery* (1976).

Additional Bibliography

The various dimensions of evangelical religion are covered in William G. McLoughlin, *Revivals, Awakenings, and Reform: An Essay on Religion and Social Change in America, 1607–1977* (1978); John B. Boles, *The Great Revival* (1972); Donald G. Mathews, *Religion in the Old South* (1977); Charles A. Johnson, *The Frontier Camp Meeting* (1955); Whitney R. Cross, *The Burned-Over District* (1950); Perry Miller, *The Life of the Mind in America from the Revolution to the Civil War* (1965); and Charles C. Cole, *The Social Ideas of the Northern Evangelists* (1954). The connection between revivalism and organized benevolence is treated in Clifford Griffen, *Their Brothers' Keepers: Moral Stewardship in the United States, 1800–1865* (1960); Charles I. Foster, *An Errand of Mercy: The Evangelical United Front* (1960); John R. Bodo, *The Protestant Clergy and Public Issues, 1812–1848* (1954); and Timothy I. Smith, *Revivalism and Social Reform in Mid-Nineteenth-Century America* (1957). On the temperance movement, see John A. Krout, *The Origins of Prohibition* (1925); Joseph R. Gusfield, *Symbolic Crusade: Status, Politics, and the American Temperance Movement* (1963); W. J. Rorabaugh, *The Alcoholic Republic: An American Tradition* (1979); and Ian R. Tyrrell, *Sobering Up: From Temperance to Prohibition in Antebellum America, 1800–1860* (1979).

The cult of domesticity is the subject of Barbara Welter, "The Cult of True Womanhood," *American Quarterly* 18 (1966): 217–40; Nancy F. Cott, *The Bonds of Womanhood: "Woman's Sphere" in New England 1780–1835* (1977); and Kathryn Kish Sklar, *Catharine Beecher: A Study in American Domesticity* (1973).

Bernard Wishy, *The Child and the Republic: The Dawn of Modern American Child Nurture* (1968), treats childhood and child-rearing. Light is shed on the limitation of family size in James Reed, *From Private Vice to Public Virtue: The Birth Control Movement and American Society since 1830* (1978) and James C. Mohr, *Abortion in America: The Origins and Evolution of National Policy, 1800–1900* (1978). On educational reform, see Lawrence Cremin, *American Education: The National Experience, 1783–1876* (1980); Rush Welter, *Popular Education and Democratic Thought* (1962); and Michael B. Katz, *The Irony of Early School Reform: Educational Innovation in Mid-Nineteenth-Century Massachusetts* (1968). The emergence of modern prisons is described in Blake McKelvy, *American Prisons* (1936) and W. David Lewis, *From Newgate to Dannemora: The Rise of the Penitentiary in New York* (1965). On the rise of asylums, see Gerald N. Grob, *Mental Institutions in America: Social Policy to 1875* (1973).

There is a vast literature on the abolitionist movement. Among the most significant works are Gilbert H. Barnes, *The Antislavery Impulse* (1934); Louis Filler, *The Crusade Against Slavery, 1830–1860* (1960); John L. Thomas, *The Liberator: William Lloyd Garrison* (1963); Martin Duberman, ed., *The Antislavery Vanguard: New Essays on the Abolitionists* (1965); Aileen S. Kraditor, *Means and Ends in American Abolitionism: Garrison and His Critics on Strategy and Tactics* (1967); Bertram Wyatt-Brown, *Lewis Tappan and the Evangelical War Against Slavery* (1969); Lewis Perry, *Radical Abolitionism: Anarchy and the Government of God in Antislavery Thought* (1973); Ronald G. Walters, *The Antislavery Appeal: American Abolitionists after 1830* (1976); Robert H. Abzug, *Passionate Liberator: Theodore Dwight Weld and the Dilemma of Reform* (1980); and Lawrence J. Friedman, *Gregarious Saints: Self and Community in American Abolitionism* (1982), Leonard L. Richards, "Gentlemen of Property and Standing": Anti-Abolition Mobs in Jacksonian America (1970), interprets violence against the abolitionists. On the connection between abolition and women's rights, see Gerda Lerner, *The Grimké Sisters from South Carolina: Rebels Against Slavery* (1967) and Blanche Glassman Hersh, *The Slavery of Sex: Feminist Abolitionists in America* (1978).

The utopian impulse is the subject of Arthur Bestor, *Backwoods Utopias* (1950); Mark Holloway, *Heavens on Earth* (1951); and Michael Fellman, *The Unbounded Frame: Freedom and Community in Nineteenth-Century Utopianism* (1973). The best approach to Brook Farm and the transcendentalists is by way of two excellent collections of original sources: Henry W. Sams, ed., *Autobiography of Brook Farm* (1958) and Perry Miller, ed., *The American Transcendentalists* (1956). See also Anne C. Rose, *Transcendentalism as a Social Movement, 1830–1850* (1981). On spiritualism, see R. Laurence Moore, *In Search of White Crows: Spiritualism, Parapsychology, and American Culture* (1977).

chapter 12

MASTERS
AND SLAVES

On August 22, 1831, the worst nightmare of southern slaveholders became reality. A group of slaves in Southampton County, Virginia, rose in open and bloody rebellion. Their leader was Nat Turner, a preacher and prophet who believed that God had given him a sign that the time was ripe to strike for freedom; a vision of black and white angels wrestling in the sky had convinced him that divine wrath was about to be visited upon the white oppressor.

Beginning with a few followers and rallying others as he went along, Turner led his band from plantation to plantation and oversaw the killing of nearly sixty whites. But the rebellion was short-lived; after only forty-eight hours, white forces dispersed the rampaging slaves. The rebels were then rounded up and executed, along with dozens of other slaves who were vaguely suspected of complicity. Nat Turner was the last to be captured, and he went to the gallows unrepentant, convinced that he had acted in accordance with God's will.

After the initial panic and rumors of a wider insurrection had passed, white Southerners went about the grim business of making sure that such an incident would never happen again. Their anxiety and determination were strengthened by the fact that 1831 also saw the emergence of a more militant northern abolitionism. Nat Turner and William Lloyd Garrison were viewed as two prongs of a revolutionary attack on the southern way of life. Although no evidence came to light that Turner was directly influenced by abolitionist propaganda, many whites believed that he must have been or that future rebels might be. Consequently, they launched a massive campaign to quarantine the slaves from possible exposure to antislavery ideas and attitudes.

A series of new laws severely restricted the rights of slaves to move about, assemble without white supervision, or learn to read and write. The wave of repression did not stop at the color line; laws and the threat of mob action prevented white dissenters from publicly criticizing or even questioning the institution of slavery. The South rapidly became a closed society with a closed mind. Loyalty to the region was firmly identified with defense of its peculiar institution, and proslavery agitators sought to create a mood of crisis and danger requiring absolute unity and single-mindedness among the white population. This embattled attitude lay behind the growth of a more militant sectionalism and inspired threats to secede from the Union if security for slaveholding seemed to require it.

The campaign for repression apparently achieved its original aim. Between 1831 and the Civil War there were no further uprisings resulting in the mass killing of whites. This fact has led some historians to conclude that Afro-American slaves were brainwashed into a state of docility. But resistance to slavery simply took other and less dangerous forms than open revolt. The brute force employed in response to the Turner rebellion and the elaborate precautions taken against its recurrence provided slaves with a more realistic sense of the odds against direct confrontation with white power. As a result they sought or perfected other methods of asserting their humanity and maintaining their self-esteem. This heroic effort to endure slavery without surrendering to it gave rise to an Afro-American culture of lasting value.

Slavery and the Southern Economy

Slavery would not have lasted as long as it did—and Southerners would not have reacted so strongly to real or imagined threats to its survival—if an influential class of whites had not had a vital and growing economic interest in this form of human exploitation. Since the early colonial period, forced labor had been essential to the South's plantation economy. In the period between the 1790s and the Civil War, plantation agriculture expanded enormously and so did dependence on slave labor; for unfree blacks were the only workers readily available to landowners who sought to profit from expanding market opportunities by raising staple crops on a large scale.

By the time of the Civil War 90 percent of the South's four million slaves worked on plantations and farms. In the seven cotton-producing states of the lower South (see the map in chapter 9, p. 254) slaves constituted close to half the total population and were responsible for producing 90 percent of the cotton and almost all of the rice and sugar. In the upper South whites outnumbered slaves by more than three to one and were less dependent on their labor. To understand southern thought and behavior it is necessary to bear in mind these major differences between the cotton kingdom with its entrenched one-crop plantation system and the upper South, which was actually moving away from this pattern during the pre–Civil War period.

Economic Adjustment in the Upper South

Tobacco, the original plantation crop of the colonial period, continued to be the principal slave-cultivated commodity of the upper tier of southern states during the pre–Civil War era. But markets were often depressed, and profitable tobacco cultivation was hard to sustain for very long in one place because it rapidly depleted the soil. As a result, there were continual shifts in the areas of greatest production and much experimentation with new crops and methods of farming in the older regions. This process began immediately after the Revolution when soil exhaustion and declining prices induced the planters of tidewater Virginia and Maryland to shift from tobacco to wheat. Further west, in the upland areas known as the Piedmont, tobacco continued to be the money crop for a longer period because of the availability of rich soils.

After a brief boom following the War of 1812, prices again collapsed and many upland planters shifted to wheat, only to find that their new crop was soon ravaged by plant pests and diseases. Some reverted to tobacco—in the words of historian Avery Craven, "the old hopeless shifting from one crop to another began again." Despite the problems associated with tobacco, the crop moved westward; by 1860 more was grown in the new western states than in the older eastern ones, and Kentucky had emerged as a major producer.

During the lengthy depression of the tobacco market that lasted from the 1820s to the 1850s, agricultural experimentation was widespread in Virginia and Maryland. Increased use of fertilizer, systematic rotation of tobacco with other crops, and the growth of diversified farming based on a mix of wheat, corn, and livestock contributed to a gradual revival of agricultural prosperity. Such changes increased the need for capital but reduced the demand for labor. Improvements were financed in part by selling surplus slaves in regions of the lower South where staple crop production was more profitable. The interstate slave trade, which sent hundreds of thousands of slaves in a southwesterly direction between 1815 and 1860, was thus a godsend to the slaveowners of

These slaves were walking from Virginia to a new home in Tennessee when they were observed by the artist, Lewis Miller. Farmers in the upper South—the soil-exhausted regions of Virginia, for example—sometimes sold their excess slaves to finance ventures into diversified farming.

Arise! Arise! and weep no more dry up your tears, we Shall part no more. Come rose we go to Tennessee. that happy Shore. to old virginia never — never — return.

the upper South and a key to their survival and returning prosperity.

Some economic historians have concluded that the most important crop produced in the tobacco kingdom was not the "stinking weed" but human beings cultivated for the auction block. Respectable planters tended to sell slaves reluctantly, usually only when debts or the need to make changes seemed to require it. But the economic effect was clear: the natural increase of their slaves beyond what the planters needed for their operations provided them with a crucial source of capital in a period of transition and innovation.

Nevertheless, the fact that slave labor was declining in importance in the upper South meant that the peculiar institution had a weaker hold on public loyalty there than in the cotton states. Diversification of agriculture was accompanied by a more rapid rate of urban and industrial development than was occurring elsewhere in the South. As a result, Virginians, Marylanders, and Kentuckians were seriously divided on whether their ultimate future lay with the Deep South's plantation economy or with the industrializing, free labor system that was flourishing just north of their borders.

The Rise of the Cotton Kingdom

The warmer climate and good soils of the lower tier of southern states made it possible to raise crops more naturally suited than tobacco or cereals to the plantation form of agriculture and the heavy use of slave labor. Since the colonial period, rice and a special variety of fine cotton (known as "long staple") had been grown profitably on vast estates along the coast of South Carolina and Georgia. In lower Louisiana, between New Orleans and Baton Rouge, sugar was the cash crop. As in the West Indies, sugar production required a large investment and a great deal of back-breaking labor: or, in other words, large, well-financed plantations and small armies of slave laborers. But cultivation of rice, long-staple cotton, and sugar was limited by natural conditions to peripheral, semitropical areas. It was the rise of "short-staple" cotton as the South's major crop that strengthened the hold of slavery and the plantation on the southern economy.

Short-staple cotton differed from the long-staple variety in two important ways: its bolls contained seeds that were much more difficult to extract by hand, and it could be grown almost anywhere south of Virginia and Kentucky—the main requirement was a guarantee of two hundred frost-free days. Before 1793, the seed extraction problem had prevented short-staple cotton from becoming a major market crop. But the invention of the cotton gin resolved that difficulty, and the subsequent westward movement opened vast areas for its cultivation. Unlike rice and sugar, cotton could be grown on small farms as well as on plantations. But large planters enjoyed certain advantages that made them the main producers. Only relatively large operators could afford their own gins or possessed the capital to acquire the fertile bottomlands that brought the highest yields. They also had lower transportation costs because they were able to monopolize the land along the rivers and streams that were the South's natural arteries of transportation.

Cotton was well suited to a plantation form of production. The required tasks were relatively simple and could be performed by supervised gangs of unfree workers. Furthermore, there was enough work to be done in all seasons to keep the force occupied throughout the year. Unlike cereals, which have only to be planted, allowed to grow, and then harvested rapidly, cotton requires constant weeding or "chopping" while growing and can be picked over an extended period. The relative absence of seasonal variations in work needs made the use of slave laborers highly practical.

The first major cotton-producing regions were inland areas of Georgia and South Carolina that were already thinly settled at the time the cotton gin was introduced. The center of production shifted rapidly westward during the nineteenth century. By the 1830s, Alabama and Mississippi had surpassed Georgia and South Carolina. By the 1850s, Arkansas, northwest Louisiana, and east Texas were the most prosperous and rapidly growing plantation regions. The rise in total production that accompanied this geographical expansion was phenomenal. Between 1792 and 1817, the South's output of cotton rose from about 13,000 bales to 461,000; by 1840 it was 1,350,000; nine years later it had risen to 2,850,000; and in 1860 production peaked at the

■ *Field slaves answered the call to labor at dawn and ended their workday only when there was too little daylight left to continue. Daily tasks were assigned by a slave driver, whose duty it was to see that the work was done. On large plantations slave labor was also used to run the cotton gin, which combed out the embedded seeds, and to row the keelboats, which carried the master's cotton to market.*

colossal figure of 4,800,000 bales. Most of this cotton went to supply the booming textile industry of Great Britain. Lesser proportions went to the manufacturers of continental Europe and the northeastern United States.

"Cotton is king!" proclaimed a southern orator in the 1850s, and he was right. By that time, three quarters of the world's supply of cotton came from the American South, and this single commodity accounted for over half of the total dollar value of American exports. Cotton growing and the network of commercial and industrial enterprises that marketed and processed this crop constituted the most important economic interest in the United States on the eve of the Civil War. Since slavery and cotton seemed inextricably linked, it appeared self-evident to many Southerners that their peculiar institution was the keystone of national wealth and economic progress.

Despite its overall success, however, the rise of the cotton kingdom did not bring a uniform or steady prosperity to the lower South. Many planters worked the land until it was exhausted and then took their slaves westward to richer soils, leaving depressed and ravaged areas in their wake.

Planters were also beset and sometimes ruined by fluctuations in markets and prices. Boom periods or flush times were followed by falling prices and a wave of bankruptcies. The great periods of expansion and bonanza profits were 1815–1819, 1832–1837, and 1849–1860. The first two booms were deflated by a fall in cotton prices resulting from overproduction. During the eleven years of rising output and high prices preceding the Civil War the planters gradually forgot their earlier troubles and began to imagine that they were immune to future economic disasters.

Despite the insecurities associated with cotton production, most of the time this crop represented the best chance for profitable investment that existed in the Old South. Prudent planters who had not borrowed too heavily during flush times could survive periods of depression by cutting costs and making their plantations self-sufficient. Instead of buying food and clothing for their slaves, as they normally did when cotton prices were high, they could shift acreage away from cotton and plant subsistence crops. For those with worn-out land, two options existed: they could sell their land and move west or they could

sell their slaves to raise capital for fertilization, crop rotation, and other improvements that could help them survive where they were. Hence planters had little incentive to seek alternatives to slavery, the plantation, and dependence on a single cash crop. From a purely economic point of view they had every reason to rally to the defense of slavery.

Slavery and Industrialization

As the sectional quarrel with the North intensified, Southerners became increasingly alarmed by their region's lack of economic self-sufficiency. Dependence on the North for capital, marketing facilities, and manufactured goods was seen as evidence of a dangerous subservience to "external" economic interests. Southern nationalists like J. D. B. DeBow, editor of the influential *DeBow's Review*, called during the 1850s for the South to develop its own industries, commerce, and shipping. As a fervent defender of slavery, DeBow did not believe that such diversification would require a massive shift to free wage labor. He saw no reason why slaves could not be used as the main work force in an industrial revolution. But his call for a diversified economy went unanswered. Men with capital were doing too well in plantation agriculture to risk their money in other ventures.

It is difficult to determine whether it was some inherent characteristic of slavery as a labor system or simply the strong market demand for cotton and the South's capacity to meet it that kept most slaves working on plantations and farms. A minority—about 5 percent during the 1850s—were, in fact, successfully employed in industrial tasks. Besides providing most of the labor for mining, lumbering, and constructing roads, canals, and railroads, slaves also worked in cotton mills and tobacco factories.

In the 1840s and '50s, a debate raged among white capitalists over whether the South should industrialize, using free whites or enslaved blacks. William Gregg of South Carolina, the foremost promoter of cotton mills in the Old South, defended a white labor policy, arguing that factory work would provide new economic opportunities for a degraded class of poor whites. But other advocates of industrialization feared that the growth of a free working class would lead to social conflict among whites and preferred using slaves for all supervised manual labor. In practice, some factories employed slaves, others white workers, and a few even experimented with integrated work forces. As nearly as can be determined, mills that hired or purchased slave labor were just as profitable and efficient as those paying wages to whites.

It is clear, however, that the union of slavery and cotton that was central to the South's prosperity impeded industrialization and left the region dependent on a one-crop agriculture and on the North for capital and marketing. Slaves were the only available workers who could be employed on plantations; rural whites refused to work for low wages when they had the alternative of subsistence farming on marginal lands in the southern backcountry. Industry, on the other hand, was concentrated in towns and cities where white labor was more readily available. When agriculture was booming—as it was during the 1850s—urban and industrial slaves tended to be displaced by whites and shifted to farming. So long as plantations yielded substantial profits, there could be no major movement of slaves from agriculture to industry. If anything, the trend was in the opposite direction.

The "Profitability" Issue

Some Southerners were obviously making money, and a great deal of it, using slave labor to raise cotton. The great mansions of the Alabama "black belt" and the lower Mississippi could not have been built if their owners had not been successful. But did slavery yield a good return for the great majority of slaveholders who were not large planters? Did it provide the basis for general prosperity and a relatively high standard of living for the southern population in general, or at least for the two thirds of it who were white and free? These questions have been hotly debated by economic historians. Some knowledge of the main arguments regarding its "profitability" is helpful to an understanding of the South's attachment to slavery.

For many years historians believed that slave-based agriculture was, on the average, not very lucrative. Planters' account books seemed to show at best a modest return on investment. In the 1850s, the price of slaves rose at a faster rate than the price of cotton, allegedly squeezing many operators. Some historians even concluded that slavery was a dying institution by the time of the Civil War. Profitability, they argued, depended on access to new and fertile land suitable for plantation agriculture, and virtually all such land within the limits of the United States had already been taken up by 1860. Hence slavery had reached its natural limits of expansion and was on the verge of becoming so unprofitable that it would fall of its own weight in the near future.

A more recent interpretation, based on modern economic theory, holds that slavery was in fact still an economically sound institution in 1860 and showed no signs of imminent decline. A reexamination of planters' records using modern accounting methods shows that during the 1850s planters could normally expect an annual return of 8 to 10 percent on capital invested. This yield was roughly equivalent to the best that could then be obtained from the most lucrative sectors of northern industry and commerce.

Furthermore, it is no longer clear that plantation agriculture had reached its natural limits of expansion by 1860. Production in Texas had not yet peaked, and construction of railroads and levees was opening up new areas for cotton growing elsewhere in the South. With the advantage of hindsight, economic historians have pointed out that improvements in transportation and flood control would enable the post–Civil War South to double its cotton acreage. Those who now argue that slavery was profitable and had an expansive future have made a strong and convincing case.

But the larger question remains: what sort of economic development did a slave plantation system foster? The system may have made slaveholders wealthy, but did the benefits trickle down to the rest of the population—to the majority of whites who owned no slaves and to the slaves themselves? Did it promote efficiency and progressive change? Economists Robert Fogel and Stanley Engerman have argued that slave plantation agriculture was much more efficient than northern family farming. They came to this conclusion using a measure of productivity involving a ratio of "input"—capital, labor, and land—to "output"—the dollar value of the crop when sold. Critics have pointed out that the higher efficiency rate for plantation agriculture may be due entirely to market conditions, or, in other words, to the fact that cotton was in greater demand than such northern commodities as wheat and livestock. Hence, Fogel and Engerman's calculations do not prove their assertion that the plantation was an internally efficient enterprise with good managers and industrious, well-motivated workers.

Other evidence suggests that small slaveholders and nonslaveholders shared only to a very limited extent in the bonanza profits of the cotton economy. Because of various insecurities—lack of credit, high transportation costs, and a greater vulnerability to market fluctuations—

they had to devote a larger share of their acreage to subsistence crops, especially corn and hogs, than did the planters. They were thus able to survive, but their standard of living was lower than that of most northern farmers. Slaves benefited from planter profits to the extent that they were better fed, housed, and clothed than they would have been had their owners been less prosperous. But to suggest that they were better-off than northern wage laborers is proslavery propaganda rather than documented fact.

The South's economic development was skewed in favor of a single route to wealth, open only to the minority possessing both a white skin

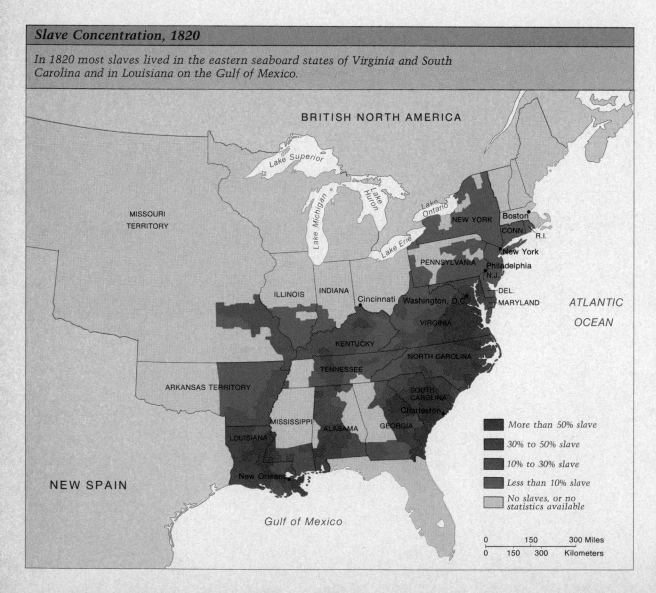

Slave Concentration, 1820

In 1820 most slaves lived in the eastern seaboard states of Virginia and South Carolina and in Louisiana on the Gulf of Mexico.

Legend:
- More than 50% slave
- 30% to 50% slave
- 10% to 30% slave
- Less than 10% slave
- No slaves, or no statistics available

and access to capital. The concentration of capital and business energies on cotton production foreclosed the kind of diversified industrial and commercial growth that would have provided wider opportunities. Thus, in comparison to the industrializing North, the South was an underdeveloped region in which neither slaves nor lower-class whites had much incentive to work hard. A lack of public education for whites and the denial of even minimal literacy to slaves represented a critical failure to develop human resources. Good ground exists for concluding that the South's economy was condemned to backwardness so long as it was based on slavery.

The Slaveholding Society

If the precise effect of slavery on the South's economic life remains debatable, there is less room for disagreement concerning its impact on social arrangements and attitudes. More than any other factor, the ownership of slaves determined gradations of social prestige and influence among whites. The large planters were the dominant class, and nonslaveholders were of lower social rank. But the fact that all whites were free and that most blacks were slaves created a sharp cleavage between the races that could create the

Slave Concentration, 1860

By 1860 slavery had extended throughout the southern states, with the greatest concentrations of slaves in the states of the Deep South. There were also sizable slave populations in the new states of Missouri, Arkansas, Texas, and Florida.

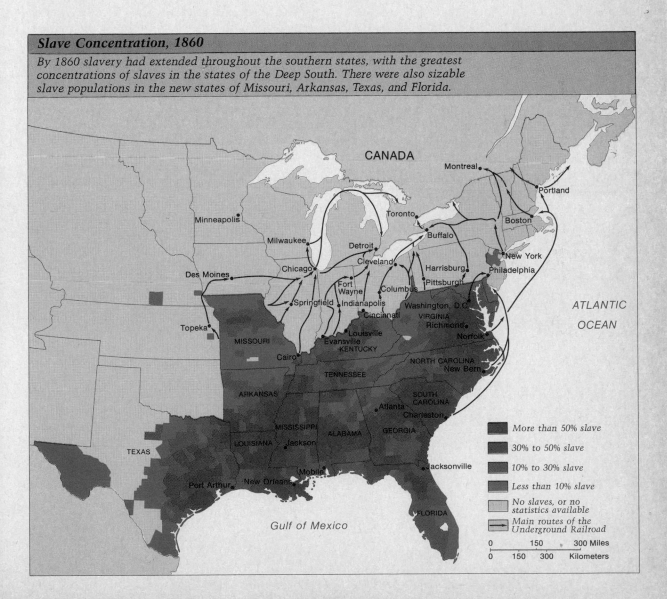

More than 50% slave
30% to 50% slave
10% to 30% slave
Less than 10% slave
No slaves, or no statistics available
Main routes of the Underground Railroad

0   150   300 Miles
0   150   300   Kilometers

impression (some would say the illusion) of a basic equality within "the master race." In the language of sociologists, inequality in the Old South was determined in two ways: by "class"—differences in status resulting from unequal access to wealth and productive resources—and by "caste"—the inherited advantages or disadvantages associated with racial ancestry. An awareness of both systems of social ranking is necessary for an understanding of southern society.

The Planters' World

Those who know the Old South only from modern novels, films, and television programs are likely to envision a land filled with majestic plantations. Pillared mansions behind oak-lined carriageways are portrayed as scenes of aristocratic splendor, where courtly gentlemen and elegant ladies, attended by hordes of uniformed black servants, lived in refined luxury. It is easy to conclude from such images that the typical white Southerner was an aristocrat who belonged to a family that owned large numbers of slaves.

The great houses existed—many of them can still be seen in places like the low country of South Carolina and the lower Mississippi Valley—and some wealthy slaveholders did maintain as aristocratic a life-style as was ever seen in the United States. But census returns indicate that this was the world of only a small percentage of slaveowners and a minuscule portion of the total white population.

In 1850 only 30 percent of all white Southerners belonged to families owning slaves; by 1860 the proportion had shrunk to 25 percent. Even in the cotton belt of the Deep South, slaveholders were a minority of whites on the eve of the Civil War—about 40 percent. Planters, defined by the census takers as agriculturalists owning twenty or more slaves, were the minority of a minority. In 1860 planters and their families constituted about 12 percent of all slaveholders and less than 4 percent of the total white population of the South. But even the master of twenty to fifty slaves could rarely live up to the popular image of aristocratic grandeur. To build a great house and entertain lavishly, a planter had to own at least fifty slaves and preferably many more. In 1860

■ Portraits such as these, of two wealthy South Carolina families, helped perpetuate the myth that all southern whites were rich planters who owned many slaves. In fact, only a small number of Southerners belonged to the planter class.

these substantial planters comprised less than 3 percent of all slaveholders and less than 1 percent of all whites.

Although few in numbers, the great planters had a weighty influence on southern life. They set the tone and values for much of the rest of society, especially for the smaller slaveowners who sought to imitate the planters' style of living to the extent that resources allowed. Although many of them were too busy tending to their plantations to become openly involved in politics, they held more than their share of high offices and often exerted a decisive influence on public policy. Within those regions of the South where plantation agriculture predominated, they were a ruling class in every sense of the term.

Contrary to legend, most of the great planters of the pre–Civil War period were self-made rather than descendants of the old colonial gentry. For example, one Irish immigrant started out with a log cabin and a few acres in upland South Carolina around 1800. Gradually acquiring more land, he planted cotton at a time when the boom was just beginning. Eventually he bought slaves and tore down the log cabin to put up a frame house. Within five years, he was able to build a "big house" with columns, set up his own cotton gin, buy a carriage, and become a local magistrate. At the time of his death in 1854, he had served in the state legislature and had built up an estate of 2000 acres, 114 slaves, and 4 cotton gins. Despite his humble origins, the local newspapers referred to him as "a gentleman of the old school."

As the cotton kingdom spread westward from South Carolina and Georgia to Alabama, Mississippi, and Louisiana, the men who became the wealthiest planters were even less likely to have genteel backgrounds. A large proportion of them began as hard-driving businessmen who built up capital from commerce, land speculation, banking, and even slave-trading. They then used their profits to buy plantations. The highly competitive, boom-or-bust economy of the Southwest put a greater premium on sharp dealing and business skills than on genealogy. Stephen Duncan, probably the most prosperous cotton planter in the South during the 1850s (he owned 8 plantations and 1018 slaves), had invested the profits from his banking operations. Among the largest sugar planters of southern Louisiana at this time were Maunsel White and John Burnside, immigrants who had prospered as New Orleans merchants, and Isaac Franklin, former king of the slave traders.

To be successful, a planter had to be a shrewd businessman who kept a careful eye on the market, the prices of slaves and land, and the extent of his indebtedness. Reliable "factors"—the agents who marketed the crop and provided advances against future sales—could assist him in making decisions, but a planter who failed to spend a good deal of time with his account books could end up in serious trouble. Managing the slaves and plantation production was also difficult and time-consuming, even when overseers were available to supervise day-to-day activities. Hence few planters could be the men of leisure featured in the popular image of the Old South.

Some of the richest and most secure did aspire to live in the manner of a traditional landed aristocracy. A few were so successful that they were accepted as equals by visiting English nobility. "Big houses," elegant carriages, fancy-dress balls, and excessive numbers of house servants all reflected aristocratic aspirations. The romantic cult of chivalry, described in the popular novels of

■ *The planter's need to keep track of all expenses was evident on ration day, when field slaves received their weekly food allotment, usually corn meal and three to four pounds of meat, frequently bacon.*

Dueling in the Old South

In the midst of the nullification controversy of 1832, a South Carolina newspaper editor employed sarcasm in condemning a rival editor's attitude in the campaign against the protective tariff (see chapter 10). The result of the exchange was a meeting on "the field of honor"—in this case an island in the river dividing South Carolina from Georgia. In the ensuing duel, the editor who favored restraint shot and killed the supporter of nullification. Such deadly combat between men of differing political views was a common occurrence in the Old South. The victor in this duel, Benjamin F. Perry, later noted in his autobiography that the affair had forced his political opponents to treat him with respect and courtesy: "When a man knows that he is to be held accountable for his want of courtesy, he is not so apt to indulge in abuse. In this way dueling produces a greater courtesy in society & a higher refinement."

Perry's comments give us a clue to the persistence of dueling in the Old South after it had died out elsewhere in the United States. Violence in word and deed was a strong tendency in southern culture. Owning slaves who could be whipped at

will could make men arrogant and quick-tempered. Each planter—the unchallenged lord of his own domain—had to watch himself in dealing with his peers. Any hint of the high-handed manner used with slaves could be taken as a grave insult and lead to violence, although southern customs of hospitality and extreme courtesy helped check the propensity toward anger and violence that lurked beneath the surface of social intercourse.

Dueling, strange as it may seem, can also be viewed as a form of restraint, a way of checking more spontaneous and disruptive acts of violence. Instead of leaping immediately into a fight with whatever weapons were at hand, southern gentlemen who had insulted each other submitted to an elaborate procedure that might end in bloodshed, but often did not. Friends of each party would first attempt to reconcile the quarrel. If they failed, the duel took place; but there was still a good chance that it would be bloodless. As in the famous duel of 1845 between Congressmen Thomas Clingman of North Carolina and William Yancey of Alabama, the participants might decide that honor had been satisfied after both men had fired and missed. Most duels seem to have ended this way or with one participant taking a nonlethal wound. But where the antagonism was very deep and intense, the duelists would fire away until one was killed. Andrew Jackson once fought a duel with a man he utterly despised who was known to be a better marksman. Jackson allowed his rival to fire first and was severely wounded. But he stood his ground, carefully took aim, and coolly dispatched his opponent.

Dueling also functioned as a means of affirming southern ideas of social status and hierarchy. Only gentlemen—or those who aspired to be gentlemen—fought duels. Lower-class whites had their own sense of honor, but they satisfied it in cruder and more direct ways. They fought spontaneously, slashing at each other with bowie knives or wrestling with no holds barred. It was the mark of the gentleman to forgo such rough methods of asserting personal or family honor by submitting to the *code duello*. Consequently, men of dubious background who aspired to "aristocratic" status were likely to welcome being challenged to a formal duel. Robert Bailey, an illiterate Virginia cockfighter, was delighted when a fellow militia officer called him to account. He viewed the resulting "affair of honor" as a sign that he had won acceptance as a member of the gentry.

Not all influential Southerners approved of dueling. In fact the official attitude was one of condemnation. Every southern state prohibited the practice, and most Christian demoninations considered it sinful. But neither laws nor preaching could stamp out dueling in the Old South. Duelists who broke the law were usually acquitted by juries of their peers. As in so many aspects of southern life, there was a substantial gap between law and custom, between official ethical standards and the values that actually governed conduct. Public opinion virtually required a gentleman to violate the law and defy the churches if he received a challenge (unless, of course, he was known to be a fervent Christian. Pious Christian planters were rarely challenged to duels; and when they were, no one thought worse of them if they refused to participate for reasons of conscience.)

This dueling scene in New Orleans was witnessed by the artist on a visit to that city in 1866.

A Mississippi politician who fought several duels without loss of power and influence summed up the prevailing attitude: "I am no advocate of dueling, and shall always from principle avoid such a thing . . . but when a man is placed in a situation where if he does not fight, life will be rendered valueless to him, both in his own eyes and those of the community," then he has no choice but to fight. Dueling might be wrong in the abstract, but it was nonetheless necessary. It could not be avoided because it reflected the deepest values of a society that placed manhood and "honor" above the middle-class standards of civilized behavior that held sway in the northern states.

It was no accident that some of the "fire-eating" secessionists of the 1840s and '50s—men like William L. Yancey of Alabama and Louis T. Wigfall of Texas—were frequently involved in duels. They projected into sectional politics the same prickly sense of honor that led them to counter personal insults with challenges to combat. For them the quarrel between North and South was very much an "affair of honor," and they were ready to pursue it to the point of shedding blood.

Sir Walter Scott, was in vogue in some circles and even led to the nonviolent reenactment of medieval tournaments. Dueling, despite some efforts to repress it, remained the standard way to settle "affairs of honor" among gentlemen (see the special feature in this chapter, pp. 334–35). Another sign of gentility was the tendency of planters' sons to avoid "trade" as a primary or secondary career in favor of law or the military. Planters' daughters were trained from girlhood to play the piano, speak French, dress in the latest fashions, and sparkle in the drawing room or on the dance floor. The aristocratic style originated among the older gentry of the seaboard slave states, but by the 1840s and '50s it had spread southwest as a second generation of wealthy planters began to displace the rough-hewn pioneers of the cotton kingdom.

Planters and Slaves

No assessment of the planters' outlook or "world view" can be made without considering their relations with their slaves. Planters, by the census definition, owned more than half of all the slaves in the South and set the standards for treatment and management of them. Most of the planters, it is clear from their private letters and journals, as well as from proslavery propaganda, liked to think of themselves as kindly and paternalistic. Often they referred to their slaves as if they were members of an extended patriarchal family—a favorite phrase was "our people." Blacks in general were described as a race of perpetual children requiring constant care and supervision by superior whites. Paternalistic rhetoric increased greatly after abolitionists began to charge that most slaveholders were sadistic monsters. To some extent, the response was part of a defensive effort to redeem the South's reputation and self-respect.

There was, nevertheless, an element of truth in the planters' claim that their slaves were relatively well treated. Recent comparative studies have suggested that North American slaves of the pre–Civil War period enjoyed a higher standard of living that those in other New World slave societies such as Brazil and the West Indian sugar islands. Food, clothing, and shelter were normally sufficient to sustain life and labor at above a bare

subsistence level; family life was encouraged and to some extent flourished; and average life expectancy, birth rate, and natural growth in population were only slightly below the average for southern whites. The rapid increase of the slave population in the Old South stands in sharp contrast to the usual failure of slave populations to reproduce themselves.

But relatively good physical conditions for slaves do not demonstrate that planters put ethical considerations ahead of self-interest. The ban on the transatlantic slave trade in 1808 was effective enough to make the domestic reproduction of the slave force an economic necessity if the system were to be perpetuated. Rising slave prices thereafter inhibited extreme physical abuse and deprivation. Slaves were valuable property and the main tools of production for a booming economy, and it was in the interest of masters to see that their property remained in good enough condition to work hard and bear large numbers of children. Furthermore, a good return on their investment enabled southern planters to divert a significant portion of their profits to slave maintenance—a luxury not available to masters in less prosperous plantation economies.

The testimony of slaves themselves and of some independent white observers suggests that masters of large plantations generally did not have close and intimate relationships with the mass of field slaves. The kind of affection and concern associated with a father figure appears to have been limited mainly to relationships with a few favored house servants or other elite slaves, such as drivers and highly skilled craftsmen. The field hands on large estates dealt mostly with overseers who were hired or fired on their ability to meet production quotas.

When they were being most realistic, planters conceded that the ultimate basis of their authority was force and intimidation, rather than the natural obedience due to a loving parent. Scattered among their statements are admissions that they must rely on the "principle of fear," "more and more on the power of fear," or—most graphically—that it was necessary "to make them stand in fear." Devices for inspiring fear including whipping—a common practice on most plantations—and the threat of sale away from family and friends. Planters' manuals and instructions to overseers reveal that certain and

■ *This photograph of a slave with the instruments of torture used to punish slaves was widely distributed to raise money "for the benefit of colored people . . . ."*

holders were not as sadistic and brutish as Simon Legree. But—and this was her real point—there was something terribly wrong with an institution that made a Simon Legree possible.

The World of the Common Whites

As we have seen, 88 percent of all slaveholders in 1860 owned fewer than twenty slaves and thus were not planters in the usual sense of the term. Of these, the great majority had fewer than ten. Some of the small slaveholders were urban merchants or professional men who needed slaves only for domestic service, but more typical were farmers who used one or two slave families to ease the burden of their own labor. Relatively little is known about life on these small slaveholding farms; unlike the planters, the owners left few records behind. But we do know that life was relatively spartan. Masters lived in log cabins or small frame cottages and slaves in lofts or sheds that were not usually up to plantation housing standards.

For better or worse, relations between owners and their slaves were more intimate than on larger estates. Unlike planters, these farmers often worked in the fields alongside their slaves and sometimes ate at the same table or slept under the same roof. But such closeness did not necessarily result in better treatment. Slave testimony reveals that both the best and the worst of slavery could be found on these farms, depending on the character and disposition of the master. Given a choice, most slaves preferred to live on plantations because they offered the sociability, culture, and kinship of the quarters, as well as better prospects for adquate food, clothing, and shelter. Marginal slaveholders often sank into poverty and were forced either to sell their slaves or give them short rations.

Just below the small slaveholders on the social scale was a substantial class of yeoman farmers who owned land that they worked themselves. Contrary to another myth about the Old South, most of these people did not fit the image of the degraded, shiftless "poor white." Such poor whites did exist, mainly as squatters on stretches of barren or sandy soil that no one else wanted. But they were a minority of the nonslaveholding rural population. The majority were proud, self-

swift punishment for any infraction of the rules or even for a surly attitude was the preferred method for maintaining order and productivity.

Despite economic considerations, some masters inevitably yielded to the temptations of power or to their bad tempers and tortured or killed their slaves. Others raped slave women or forced them into sexual relationships. Slaves had little legal protection against such abuse because slave testimony was not accepted in court. Abolitionists were correct in condemning slavery on principle because it gave one human being nearly absolute power over another. Human nature being what it is, such a situation was bound to result in atrocities. Even Harriet Beecher Stowe acknowledged in *Uncle Tom's Cabin*, her celebrated antislavery novel of 1852, that most slave-

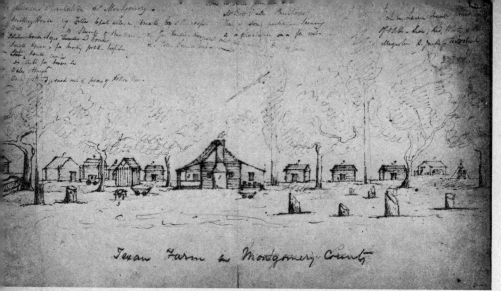

This drawing of a backwoods farm in Texas around 1850 illustrates the typical living accommodations of the small slaveholding farmer. The master lived in the log house in the center, while his slaves occupied the smaller cabins. Other buildings included a smokehouse, a corncrib, and a honey stand. This farmer must have been at least moderately prosperous because he owned his own cotton gin and press.

reliant farmers whose way of life did not differ markedly from that of family farmers in the Midwest during the early stages of settlement. If they were disadvantaged in comparison with farmers elsewhere in the United States, it was because the lack of economic development and urban growth perpetuated frontier conditions and denied them the opportunity to produce a substantial surplus for market.

The yeomen were mostly concentrated in the backcountry where slaves and plantations were rarely seen. In every southern state, there were hilly sections unsuitable for plantation agriculture. The foothills or interior valleys of the Appalachians and the Ozarks offered reasonably good soils for mixed farming, and long stretches of "piney barrens" along the Gulf Coast were suitable for raising livestock. In such regions slaveless farmers concentrated, giving rise to the "white counties" that complicated southern politics. A somewhat distinct group were the genuine mountaineers, who lived too high up to succeed at farming and relied heavily on hunting, lumbering, and distilling whiskey.

The lack of transportation facilities, more than some failure of energy or character, limited the prosperity of the yeomen. A large part of their effort was devoted to growing subsistence crops, mainly corn. They raised a small percentage of the South's cotton and tobacco, but production was severely limited by the difficulty of marketing. Their main source of cash was livestock, especially hogs. Hogs could walk to market over long distances, and massive droves from the back-country to urban markets were commonplace. But southern livestock, which was generally allowed to forage in the woods rather than being fattened on grain, was of poor quality and did not bring high prices or big profits to raisers.

Although they did not benefit directly from the peculiar institution, most yeomen and other non-slaveholders tolerated slavery and were fiercely opposed to abolitionism in any form. A few antislavery Southerners, most notably Hinton R. Helper of North Carolina, tried to convince the yeomen that they were victimized by planter dominance and should work for its overthrow. These dissenters presented a plausible set of arguments, emphasizing that slavery and the plantation system created a privileged class and severely limited the economic opportunities of the nonslaveholding white majority.

Most yeomen were staunch Jacksonians who resented aristocratic pretensions and feared concentrations of power and wealth in the hands of the few. When asked about the gentry, they commonly voiced their disdain of "cotton snobs" and rich planters generally. In state and local politics, they sometimes expressed these feelings by voting against planter interests on issues involving representation, banking, and internal improvements. Why, then, did they fail to respond to antislavery appeals that called on them to strike at the real source of planter power and privilege?

One reason was that some nonslaveholders hoped to get ahead in the world, and in the South this meant acquiring slaves of their own. Just enough of the more prosperous yeomen broke into the slaveholding classes to make this dream seem believable. Planters, anxious to ensure the loyalty of nonslaveholders, strenuously encouraged the notion that every white man was a potential master.

But the main reason why most nonslaveholders went along with the proslavery leadership was their intense fear and dislike of blacks. Although they had no natural love of planters and slavery, they believed—or could be induced to believe—that abolition would lead to disaster. In part their anxieties were economic; freed slaves would compete with them for land or jobs. But their racism went deeper than this. "Now suppose they was free," a nonslaveholder told a northern traveler, "you see they'd think themselves just as good as we ... just suppose you had a family of children, how would like to hev a niggar feeling just as good as a white man? how'd you like to hev a niggar steppin' up to your darter?" Emancipation was unthinkable because it would remove the pride and status that automatically went along with a white skin in this acutely race-conscious society. Slavery, despite its drawbacks, served to keep blacks "in their place" and to make all whites however poor or underprivileged they might be, feel that they were superior to somebody.

A Closed Mind and a Closed Society

Despite the tacit assent of most nonslaveholders, the dominant class never lost its fear that lower-class whites would turn against slavery. They felt threatened from two sides: from the slave quarters where a new Nat Turner might be gathering his forces, and from the backcountry where yeomen and poor whites might heed the call of abolitionists and rise up against planter domination. Beginning in the 1830s, the ruling element tightened the screws of slavery and used their control of government and communications to create a mood of impending catastrophe designed to ensure that all southern whites were of a single mind on the slavery issue.

Before the 1830s, open discussion of the rights or wrongs of slavery had been possible in many parts of the South. Apologists commonly described the institution as "a necessary evil." In the upper South, as late as the 1820s, there had been significant support for the American Colonization Society with its program of gradual, voluntary emancipation accompanied by deportation of the freedmen. In 1831 and '32—in the wake of the Nat Turner uprising—the Virginia state legislature debated a gradual emancipation plan. Major support for ensuring white safety by getting rid of both slavery and blacks came from representatives of the yeoman farmers living west of the Blue Ridge Mountains. But the defeat of the proposal effectively ended the discussion. The argument that slavery was "a positive good"—rather than an evil slated for gradual elimination —won the day.

The "positive good" defense of slavery was an answer to the abolitionist charge that the institution was inherently sinful. The message was carried in a host of books, pamphlets, and newspaper editorials published between the 1830s and the Civil War. Who, historians have asked, was it meant to persuade? Partly, the argument was aimed at the North, as a way of bolstering the strong current of antiabolitionist sentiment. But Southerners themselves were a prime target; the message was clearly calculated to resolve the kind of doubts and misgivings that had been freely expressed before the 1830s. Much of it may have been over the heads of nonslaveholders, many of whom were semiliterate, but some of the arguments, in popularized form, were used to arouse racial anxieties that tended to neutralize antislavery sentiment among the lower classes.

The proslavery argument was based on three main propositions. The first and foremost was that enslavement was the natural and proper status for people of African descent. Blacks, it was alleged, were innately inferior to whites and suited only for slavery. Biased scientific and historical evidence was presented to support this claim. Secondly, slavery was held to be sanctioned by the Bible and Christianity—a position made necessary by the abolitionist appeal to Christian ethics. Ancient Hebrew slavery was held up as a divinely sanctioned model, and Saint Paul was quoted endlessly on the duty of servants to obey their masters. Southern churchmen took the lead in reconciling slavery with religion and also made renewed efforts to convert the slaves as a way of showing that enslavement could be a means for spreading the gospel.

■ *This proslavery cartoon of 1841 contends that the black slave in America had a better life than did the working-class white in England. Supposedly, the grateful slaves were clothed, fed, and cared for in their old age by kindly and sympathetic masters, while starving English workers were mercilessly exploited by factory owners.*

Finally, efforts were made to show that slavery was consistent with the humanitarian spirit of the nineteenth century. The premise that blacks were naturally dependent led to the notion that they needed some kind of "family government" or special regime equivalent to the asylums that existed for the small numbers of whites who were also incapable of caring for themselves. The plantation allegedly provided such an environment, as benevolent masters guided and ruled this race of perpetual children.

By the 1850s, the proslavery argument had gone beyond mere apology for the South and its peculiar institution and featured an ingenious attack on the free labor system of the North. According to the Virginian George Fitzhugh, the master-slave relationship was *more* humane than the one prevailing between employers and wage laborers in the North. Slaves had security against unemployment and a guarantee of care in old age,

while free workers might face destitution and even starvation at any time. Worker insecurity in free societies led inevitably to strikes, bitter class conflicts, and the rise of socialism; slave societies, on the other hand, could more effectively protect property rights and maintain other traditional values because its laboring class was both better treated, and at the same time, more firmly controlled.

In addition to arguing against the abolitionists, proslavery Southerners attempted to seal off their region from antislavery ideas and influences. Whites who were bold enough to criticize slavery publicly were mobbed or persecuted. One of the last and bravest of the southern abolitionists, Cassius M. Clay of Kentucky, armed himself with a brace of pistols when he gave speeches until the threat of mob violence finally forced him across the Ohio. In 1856 a University of North Carolina professor was fired because he admitted that he would vote for the moderately antislavery Republican Party if he had a chance. Clergymen who questioned the morality of slavery were driven from their pulpits, and northern travelers suspected of being abolitionist agents were tarred and feathered. When abolitionists tried to send their literature through the mails during the 1830s, it was seized in southern post offices and publicly burned.

Such flagrant denials of free speech and civil liberties were inspired by fears that nonslaveholding whites and slaves would get the wrong ideas. Hinton R. Helper's book, *The Impending Crisis of the South*, an 1857 appeal to nonslaveholders to resist the planter regime, was suppressed with particular vigor; those found with copies were beaten up or even lynched. But the deepest fear was that slaves would hear the abolitionist talk or read antislavery literature and be inspired to rebel. Such anxieties rose to panic pitch after the Nat Turner rebellion. Consequently, new laws were passed making it a crime to teach slaves to read and write. Other repressive legislation aimed at slaves banned meetings unless a white man was present, severely restricted the activities of black preachers, and suppressed independent black churches. Free blacks, who were thought to be possible instigators of slave revolt, were denied basic civil liberties and were the object of growing surveillance and harassment.

All these efforts at thought control and internal security did not allay the fears of abolitionist subversion, lower-class white dissent, and, above all, slave revolt. The persistent barrage of proslavery propaganda and the course of national events in the 1850s created a mood of panic and desperation. By this time an increasing number of Southerners had become convinced that safety from abolitionism and its associated terrors required a formal withdrawal from the Union—secession.

The Black Experience Under Slavery

Most blacks, if not most whites, experienced slavery on plantations; the majority of slaves lived on units owned by planters who had twenty or more slaves. The masters of these agrarian communities sought to ensure their personal

■ *This woman is believed to be the granddaughter of Marie Therese, a freed slave who married Thomas Metoyer, a Frenchman, and built Melrose Plantation in Louisiana. By 1847 the plantation had passed to white ownership.*

safety and the profitability of their enterprises by using all the means—physical and psychological—at their command to make slaves docile and obedient. By word and deed, they tried to convince the slaves that whites were superior and had a right to rule over blacks. Masters also drew constant attention to their awesome power and ability to deal harshly with rebels and malcontents. As increasing numbers of slaves were converted to Christianity and attended white-supervised services, they were forced to hear, over and over again, that God had commanded slaves to obey their masters.

It is a great tribute to the resourcefulness and spirit of Afro-Americans that most of them resisted these pressures and managed to retain an inner sense of their own worth and dignity. When conditions were right, they openly asserted their desire for freedom and equality and showed their disdain for white claims that slavery was "a positive good." But the struggle for freedom involved more than the confrontation of master and slave; free blacks, in both the North and the South, did what they could to speed the day when all Afro-Americans would be free.

How Slaves Resisted

Open rebellion, the bearing of arms against the oppressors by organized groups of slaves, was the most dramatic and clear-cut form of slave resistance. In the period between 1800 and 1831, a number of slaves participated in revolts that showed their willingness to risk their lives in a desperate bid for liberation. In 1800 a Virginia slave named Gabriel Prosser mobilized a large band of his fellows to march on Richmond. But a violent storm dispersed "Gabriel's army" and enabled whites to suppress the uprising without any loss of white life.

In 1811 several hundred Louisiana slaves marched on New Orleans brandishing guns, waving flags, and beating drums. It took three hundred soldiers of the U.S. Army, aided by armed planters and militiamen, to stop the advance and to end the rebellion. In 1822 whites in Charleston, South Carolina, uncovered an extensive and well-planned conspiracy, organized by a free black man named Denmark Vesey, to seize local armories, arm the slave population, and take possession of the city. Although the Vesey conspiracy was nipped in the bud, it convinced South Carolinians that blacks were "the Jacobins [a reference to the terrorists of the French Revolution] of the country against whom we should always be on guard."

Only a year after the Vesey affair, whites in Norfolk County, Virginia, complained of the activities of a marauding band of runaway slaves that had killed several whites. The militia was sent out and captured the alleged leader—a fugitive of several years standing named Bob Ferebee. Groups of runaways, who hid for years in places like the Great Dismal Swamp of Virginia, continued to raid plantations throughout the antebellum period and were inclined to fight to death rather than be recaptured.

As we have already seen, the most bloody and terrifying of all slave revolts was the Nat Turner insurrection of 1831. Although it was the last slave rebellion of this kind during the pre–Civil War period, armed resistance had not ended. Indeed, the most sustained and successful effort of slaves to win their freedom by force of arms took place in Florida between 1835 and 1842 when hundreds of black fugitives fought in the Second Seminole War alongside the Indians who had given them a haven. The Seminoles were resisting removal to Oklahoma, but for the blacks who took part, the war was a struggle for their own freedom, and the treaty that ended it allowed most of them to accompany their Indian allies to the trans-Mississippi West.

Only a tiny fraction of all slaves ever took part in organized acts of violent resistance against white power. Most realized that the odds against a successful revolt were very high, and bitter experience had shown them that the usual outcome was death to the rebels. As a consequence, therefore, they characteristically devised safer or more ingenious ways to resist white dominance.

One way of protesting against slavery was to run away, and thousands of slaves showed their discontent and desire for freedom in this fashion. Most fugitives never got beyond the neighborhood of the plantation; after "lying out" for a time, they would return, often after negotiating immunity from punishment. But many escapees remained free for years by hiding in swamps or other remote areas, and a fraction made it to freedom in the North or Mexico. Some fugitives stowed away aboard ships heading to northern ports; others traveled overland for hundreds of miles, avoiding patrols and inquisitive whites by staying off the roads and moving only at night. Light-skinned blacks sometimes made it to freedom by passing for whites, and one resourceful slave even had himself packed in a box and shipped to the North.

For the majority of slaves, however, flight was not a real option. Either they lived too deep in the South to have any chance of reaching free soil, or they were reluctant to leave family and friends behind. The typical fugitive was a young, unmarried male from the upper South. Slaves who did not or could not leave the plantation had to register their opposition to the masters' regime while remaining under the yoke of bondage.

The normal way of expressing discontent was engaging in a kind of indirect or passive resistance. Many slaves worked slowly and inefficiently, not because they were naturally lazy (as whites supposed), but as a gesture of protest or alienation. In the words of a popular slave song, "You may think I'm working/But I ain't." Others withheld labor by feigning illness or injury. Stealing provisions—a very common activity on most plantations—was another way to show contempt

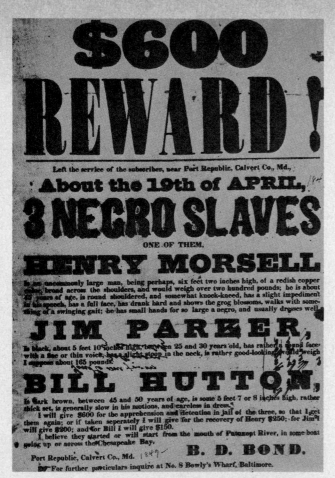

$600 REWARD !

Left the service of the subscriber, near Port Republic, Calvert Co., Md.,

About the 19th of APRIL,

3 NEGRO SLAVES

ONE OF THEM,

HENRY MORSELL

Is an uncommonly large man, being perhaps, six feet two inches high, of a redish copper color, broad across the shoulders, and would weigh over two hundred pounds; he is about 40 years of age, is round shouldered, and somewhat knock-kneed, has a slight impediment in his speech, has a full face, has drank hard and shows the grog blossoms, walks with something of a swinging gait; he has small hands for so large a negro, and usually dresses well.

JIM PARKER,

Is black, about 5 feet 10 inches high, between 25 and 30 years old, has rather a round face, with a fine or thin voice, has a slight stoop in the neck, is rather good-looking, would weigh I suppose about 165 pounds.

BILL HUTTON,

Is dark brown, between 45 and 50 years of age, is some 5 feet 7 or 8 inches high, rather thick set, is generally slow in his motions, and careless in dress.

I will give $600 for the apprehension and detention in jail of the three, so that I get them again; or if taken seperately I will give for the recovery of Henry $250; for Jim I will give $200; and for Bill I will give $150.

I believe they started or will start from the mouth of Patuxent River, in some boat going up or across the Chesapeake Bay.

B. D. BOND.

Port Republic, Calvert Co., Md. 1849

For further particulars inquire at No. 8 Bowly's Wharf, Baltimore.

Running away was one way to escape slavery, but for most slaves flight was impossible. They sought instead other means by which they could improve their condition as slaves.

for authority. According to the code of ethics prevailing in the slave quarters, theft from the master was no sin; it was simply a way for slaves to get a larger share of the fruits of their own labors.

Substantial numbers of slaves committed acts of sabotage. Tools and agricultural implements were deliberately broken, animals were willfully neglected or mistreated, and barns or other out-buildings were set afire. Often masters could not identify the culprits because slaves did not readily inform on one another. The ultimate act of clandestine resistance was poisoning the master's food. Some slaves, especially the "conjure men" who practiced a combination of folk medicine and witchcraft, knew how to mix rare, virtually untraceable poisons; and a suspiciously large number of plantation whites became suddenly

and mysteriously ill. Sometimes whole families died from obscure "diseases" that did not infect the slave quarters.

The basic attitude behind such actions was revealed in the folk tales that slaves passed down from generation to generation. The famous Bruh Rabbit stories showed how a small, apparently defenseless animal could overcome a bigger and stronger one through cunning and deceit. Although these tales often had an African origin, they also served as an allegory for the black view of the master-slave relationship. Other stories—which were not told in front of whites—openly portrayed the slave as a clever trickster outwitting the master. In once such tale a slave reports to his master that seven hogs have died of "malitis." Thinking that this is a dread disease, the master agrees to let the slaves have all the meat. What really happened, however, was that "One of the strongest Negroes got up early in the morning" and "skitted to the hog pen with a heavy mallet in his hand. When he tapped Mister Hog 'tween the eyes with that mallet, 'malitis' set in mighty quick."

The Struggles of Free Blacks

In addition to the four million blacks in bondage, there were approximately five hundred thousand free Afro-Americans in 1860, about half of them living in slave states. Whether they were in the North or in the South, "free Negroes" were treated as social outcasts and denied legal and political equality with whites. Public facilities were strictly segregated, and after the 1830s blacks in the United States could vote only in four New England states. Nowhere but in Massachusetts could they testify in court cases involving whites.

Free blacks had difficulty finding decent jobs; most employers preferred immigrants or other whites over blacks, and the latter were usually relegated to menial and poorly paid occupations: casual day labor or domestic service. Many states excluded blacks entirely from public schools, and the federal government barred them from the militia, the postal service, and full access to public lands. Free blacks were even denied U.S. passports; in effect they were stateless persons even before the 1857 Supreme Court ruling that no Negro could claim American citizenship.

In the South, free blacks were subject to a set of direct controls that tended to make them semi-slaves. They were often forced to register or have white guardians who were responsible for their behavior. Invariably they were required to carry papers proving their free status, and in some states they had to obtain official permission to move from one county to another. Licensing laws were invoked to exclude blacks from several occupations, and attempts by blacks to hold meetings or form organizations were frequently restricted or denied by the authorities. Sometimes vagrancy and apprenticeship laws were used to force free blacks into a state of economic dependency barely distinguishable from outright slavery. Just before the outbreak of the Civil War, a campaign developed in some southern states to carry this pattern of repression and discrimination to its logical conclusion. Several state legislatures proposed laws giving free Negroes the choice of emigrating from the state or being enslaved.

Although beset by special problems of their own, most free blacks identified with the suffering of the slaves; when circumstances allowed, they protested against the peculiar institution and worked for its abolition. Many of them had once been slaves themselves or were the children of slaves; often they had close relatives who were still in bondage. Furthermore, they knew that the discrimination from which they suffered was rooted in slavery and the racial attitudes that accompanied it. So long as slavery existed, their own rights were likely to be denied and even their freedom was at risk; former slaves who could not prove they had been legally freed were subject to reenslavement. This threat existed even in the North; under federal fugitive slave laws, escaped slaves could be returned to bondage. Even blacks who were born free were not perfectly safe. Kidnaping or fraudulent seizure by slave-catchers was always a possibility.

Because of the elaborate system of control and surveillance, free blacks in the South were in a relatively weak position to work against slavery. The case of Denmark Vesey showed that a prosperous and well-situated free black might give his life in the struggle for freedom, but it also revealed the dangers of revolutionary activity and the odds against success. The wave of repression against the free black population that followed the Vesey conspiracy heightened the dangers and increased the odds. Consequently, most free blacks found that survival depended on creating the impression of loyalty to the planter regime. In some parts of the lower South, groups of relatively privileged free Negroes, mostly of racially mixed origin, were sometimes persuaded that it was to their advantage to preserve the status quo. As skilled craftsmen and small businessmen dependent on white favors and patronage, they had little incentive to risk everything by taking the side of the slaves. In southern Louisiana, there was even a small group of mulatto planters who lived in luxury, supported by the labor of other Afro-Americans.

Free blacks in the North were in a better position to join the struggle for freedom. Despite all the prejudice and discrimination that they faced, they still enjoyed some basic civil liberties denied to southern blacks. They could protest publicly against slavery or white supremacy and could form associations for the advancement and liberation of Afro-Americans. The Negro convention movement, which sponsored national meetings of black leaders beginning in 1830, provided an important forum for independent black expression. Their most eloquent statement came in 1854, when black leaders met in Cleveland to declare their faith in a separate racial identity, proclaiming, "We pledge our integrity to use all honorable means, to unite us, as one people, on this continent."

Black newspapers, such as *Freedom's Journal*, first published in 1827, and *The North Star*, founded by Frederick Douglass in 1847, gave black writers a chance to preach their gospel of liberation to black readers. Afro-American authors also produced a stream of books and pamphlets attacking slavery, refuting racism, and advocating various forms of resistance. One of the most influential publications was David Walker's *Appeal . . . to the Colored Citizens of the World*, which appeared in 1829. Walker denounced slavery in the most vigorous language possible and called for a black revolt against white tyranny.

Free blacks in the North did more than make verbal protests against racial injustice. They were also the main conductors on the fabled "underground railroad" that opened a path for fugitives from slavery. It used to be supposed that benevolent whites were primarily responsible for organ-

Harriet Tubman, on the extreme left, is shown here with some of the slaves she helped escape on the underground railroad. Born a slave in Maryland, she escaped to Philadelphia in 1849. She is said to have helped as many as three hundred blacks flee slavery. Many of them she led all the way to Canada, where they would be beyond the reach of the Fugitive Slave Law.

ized efforts to guide and assist fugitive slaves, but modern research has shown that the underground railroad was largely a black-operated enterprise. Courageous ex-slaves like Harriet Tubman and Josiah Henson made regular forays into the slave states to lead other blacks to freedom, and many of the "stations" along the way were manned by free Negroes. In northern towns and cities, free blacks organized "vigilance committees" to protect fugitives and thwart the slave catchers. Groups of blacks even used force to rescue recaptured fugitives from the authorities. In Boston in 1851 one such group seized a slave named Shadrack from a U.S. marshal who was in the process of returning him to bondage. In deeds as well as words, free blacks showed their unyielding hostility to slavery and racism.

Afro-American Religion

Afro-Americans could not have resisted or even endured slavery if they had been utterly demoralized by its oppressiveness. What made the struggle for freedom possible were inner resources and patterns of thought that gave dignity to their lives and hopes for a brighter future. From the realm of culture and fundamental beliefs blacks drew the strength to hold their heads high and look beyond their immediate condition.

Religion was the cornerstone of this emerging Afro-American culture, especially among the slaves. Black Christianity may have owed its original existence to the efforts of white missionaries, but it was far from being a mere imitation of white religious forms and beliefs. It was rather a distinctive variant of evangelical Protestantism that incorporated elements of African religion and stressed those portions of the Bible that spoke to the aspirations of an enslaved people thirsting for freedom.

Free blacks formed the first independent black churches by seceding from white congregations that discriminated against them in seating and church governance. Out of these secessions came a variety of autonomous Baptist groups and the highly successful African Methodist Episcopal (A. M. E.) Church, organized as a national denomination under the leadership of Reverend Richard Allen of Philadelphia in 1816. But the mass of blacks did not have access to these independent churches. Mostly they served only free blacks and urban slaves with indulgent masters. In the deep South, whites regarded A.M.E. churches with suspicion and sometimes suppressed them; a thriving congregation in Charleston was forced to close its doors in 1822 after some of its members had been implicated in the Vesey conspiracy.

Plantation slaves who were exposed to Christianity either attended neighboring white churches

Plantation Burial *depicts slaves gathering in a forest to bury a fellow slave. Many spirituals sung by the slaves pictured death as a welcome release from bondage and created an image of an afterlife where the trials and cares of this life were unknown. "I Know Moonrise," a well-known funeral song, expressed the slaves' longing for peace and deliverance: "I'll lie in my grave and stretch out my arms/I'll go to judgment in the evening of the day/And my soul and thy soul shall meet that day/When I lay this body down."*

or worshiped at home. On large estates masters or white missionaries often conducted regular Sunday services. But the narratives and recollections of exslaves reveal that white-sanctioned religious activity was only a superficial part of the slaves' spiritual life. The true slave religion was practiced at night, often secretly, and was led by black preachers. Historian Albert J. Raboteau has described this underground black Christianity as "the invisible institution."

This covert slave religion was a highly emotional affair that featured singing, shouting, and dancing. In some ways the atmosphere resembled a backwoods revival meeting. But much of what went on was actually an adaptation of African religious beliefs and customs. The chanting mode of preaching—with the congregation responding at regular intervals—and the expression of religious feelings through rhythmical movements, really a form of dance, were clearly African in origin. The black conversion experience was normally a state of ecstasy more akin to possession by spirits—a major form of African religious expression—than to the agony of those "struck down" at white revivals. The emphasis on sinfulness and fear of damnation that were core themes of white evangelicalism played a lesser role among blacks. For them, religion was more an

affirmation of the joy of life than a rejection of worldly pleasures and temptations.

Slave sermons and religious songs spoke directly to the plight of a people in bondage and implicitly asserted their right to be free. The most popular of all biblical subjects was the deliverance of the children of Israel from slavery in Egypt. The book of Exodus provided more than its share of texts for sermons and images for songs. In one moving spiritual, God commands Moses to "tell Old Pharaoh" to "let my people Go." In another, Mary is told that she can stop weeping and begin to rejoice because "Pharaoh's army got drownded" trying to cross the Red Sea. Many sermons and songs referred to the crossing of Jordan and the arrival in the Promised Land. "Oh Canaan, sweet Canaan, I am bound for the land of Canaan" and "Oh brothers, don't get weary . . . We'll land on Canaan's shore" are typical of lines from spirituals known to have been sung by slaves. Other songs invoked the liberation theme in different ways. One recalled that Jesus had "set poor sinners free," and another prophesied that "We'll soon be free, when the Lord will call us home."

Most of the songs of freedom and deliverance can be interpreted as referring exclusively to religious salvation and the afterlife—and this was undoubtedly how slaves hoped their masters would understand them. But the slaves did not forget that God had once freed a people from slavery in this life and punished their masters. The Bible thus gave Afro-Americans the hope that they, as a people, would repeat the experience of the Israelites and be delivered from bondage. During the Civil War, observers noted that freed slaves seemed to regard their emancipation as something that had been preordained and were inclined to view Lincoln as the reincarnation of Moses.

Besides being the basis for a deep-rooted hope for eventual freedom, religion helped the slaves endure bondage without losing their sense of inner worth. Unless their masters were unusually pious, religious slaves could regard themselves as superior to their owners. Some slaves even believed that all whites were damned because of their unjust treatment of blacks, while all slaves would be saved because any sins they committed were the involuntary result of their condition.

More importantly, "the invisible institution" gave blacks a chance to create and control a world of their own. Preachers, elders, and other leaders of unofficial slave congregations could acquire a sense of status within their own community that had not been conferred by whites. The singers who improvised the spirituals found an outlet for independent artistic expression. Although religion did not inspire slaves to open rebellion (except in the case of Nat Turner), it must be regarded as a prime source of resistance to the dehumanizing effects of enslavement. It helped create a sense of community, solidarity, and self-esteem among slaves by giving them something of their own that they found infinitely precious.

Chronology

1793	Eli Whitney invents the cotton gin
1800	Gabriel Prosser leads abortive slave rebellion in Virginia
1811	Slaves revolt in Point Coupeé section of Louisiana
1822	Denmark Vesey conspiracy uncovered in Charleston, South Carolina
1829	David Walker publishes *Appeal* calling for slave insurrection
1830	First National Negro Convention meets
1831	Slaves under Nat Turner rebel in Virginia, killing almost sixty whites
1832	Virginia legislature votes against gradual emancipation
1835–1842	Blacks fight alongside Indians in the Second Seminole War
1837	Panic of 1837 is followed by major depression of the cotton market
1847	Frederick Douglass publishes *The North Star*, a black antislavery newspaper
1849	Cotton prices rise, and a sustained boom commences.
1851	Group of free blacks rescues escaped slave Shadrack from federal authorities in Boston
1852	Harriet Beecher Stowe's antislavery novel *Uncle Tom's Cabin* is published and becomes a best-seller
1857	Hinton R. Helper attacks slavery on economic grounds in *The Impending Crisis of the South*; the book is suppressed in the southern states
1860	Cotton prices and production reach all-time peak

The Slave Family

The black family was the other institution that prevented slavery from becoming unendurable and utterly demoralizing. Contrary to what historians and sociologists used to believe, the majority of slaves lived in two-parent households. Although slave marriages were not legally binding, many masters encouraged stable unions, and the slaves themselves apparently preferred monogamy to more casual or promiscuous relationships. Plantation registers reveal that many slave marriages lasted for as long as twenty or thirty years and were more often broken by death or sale than by dissolution of the union. The black sexual ethic valued marital fidelity, an attitude strongly influenced by Christian teachings. But slaves did not attach the same importance as whites to chastity among unmarried females. Premarital sex was tolerated, and it was common for a slave woman to bear one child out of wedlock before settling into a permanent union.

An invoice of ten negroes sent this day to John B Williamson by Geo Kremer named & cost as follows

To wit. Betsey Kackley	$410.00
Nancy Aulick	515.00
Harry & Helen Miller . . .	1200.00
Mary Kootz	600.00
Betsey Ott	566.00
Isaac & Fanny Brent . .	992.00
Lucinda Luckett	467.50
George Smith	510.00
Amount of my traveling expences & boarding	5254.50
of lot No 9 not included in the other bill .	39.50
Kremers expences transporting lot No 9 to Richd	51.00
Carryall hire . .	6.00
	$5351.00

I have this day delivered the above named negroes costing including my expences and other expences five thousand three hundred & fifty dollars this May 26th 1835—

John W. Pittman

I did intend to leave Nancy child but she made such a damned fuss I had to let her take it I could of got fifty Dollars for so you must add forty Dollars to the above

■ *Some slave families managed to stay together, as shown by the footnote to this 1835 bill of sale: "I did intend to leave Nancy child but she made such a damned fuss I had to let her take it . . ."*

Relations between spouses and between parents and children were normally close and affectionate. Slave husbands and fathers did not, of course, have the same power and authority as free heads of families; they could not play the role of breadwinner or even protect their wives and children from harsh punishment or sexual abuse by masters or overseers. But they did what they could, and this included supplementing the family diet by hunting, fishing, or pilfering plantation stores. Husbands and wives usually interacted on a basis of rough equality and did everything possible to relieve each other's burdens; together they taught their children how to survive slavery and plantation life.

The terrible anguish that usually accompanied the breakup of families through sale showed the depth of kinship feelings. Masters knew that the first place to look for a fugitive was in the neighborhood of a family member who had been sold away. After emancipation, thousands of freed slaves wandered about looking for spouses, children, or parents from whom they had been forcibly separated years before. The famous spiritual, "Sometime I feel like a motherless child," was far more than an expression of religious need; it also reflected the family anxieties and personal tragedies of many slaves.

Feelings of kinship and mutual obligation extended beyond the nuclear family. Grandparents, uncles, aunts, and even cousins were known to slaves through direct contact or family lore. A sense of family continuity over three or more generations was revealed in the names that slaves gave to their children or took for themselves. Infants were frequently named after grandparents, and those slaves who assumed surnames often chose that of an ancestor's owner rather than the family name of a current master. The historian Herbert G. Gutman has found further evidence of extended family ties in an apparent taboo against the marriages of first cousins. Since unions between close cousins were common among planter families, such a ban could not have been an imitation of white practice: it was either an independent invention of slave culture of an adaptation of African kinship systems.

Kinship ties were not limited to blood relations. When families were broken up by sale, individual members who found themselves on plantations far from home were likely to be "adopted" into new kinship networks. Orphans or children without responsible parents were quickly absorbed without prejudice into new families.

What becomes apparent from studies of the slave family is that kinship provided a model for personal relationships and the basis for a sense of community. For some purposes, all the slaves on a plantation were in reality members of a single extended family, as their forms of address clearly reveal. Edlerly slaves were addressed by everyone else as "uncle" and "aunty," and younger unrelated slaves commonly called each other "brother" or "sister." Slave culture was a family culture, and this was one of its greatest sources of strength and cohesion. Strong kinship ties, whether real or fictive, meant that slaves could depend on one another in times of trouble. The kinship network also provided a vehicle for the transmission of Afro-American folk traditions from one generation to the next. Together with slave religion, kinship gave Afro-Americans a feeling that they were members of a community, not just a collection of individuals victimized by oppression.

The sense of being part of a community was the key to black survival under slavery. Although slave culture did not normally sanction violent resistance to the slaveholder's regime, the inner world that slaves made for themselves gave them the spiritual strength to thwart the masters' efforts to dominate their hearts and minds. After emancipation, this rich and resilient cultural heritage would continue to give meaning to the lives of Afro-Americans. When combined with the tradition of open protest created by rebellious slaves and free black abolitionists, it would inspire and sustain new struggles for equality.

Recommended Reading

Major works that take a broad view of slavery are Kenneth M. Stampp, *The Peculiar Institution: Slavery in the Ante-Bellum South* (1956), which stresses its coercive features; John W. Blassingame, *The Slave Community: Plantation Life in the Ante-Bellum South* (1972), which focuses on slave culture and psychology; and Eugene D. Genovese, *Roll, Jordan, Roll: The World the Slaves Made* (1974), which probes the paternalistic character of the institution and the way in which slaves made a world for themselves within its bounds.

On the economics of slavery, see Gavin Wright, *The Political Economy of the Cotton South: Households, Markets, and Wealth in the Nineteenth Century* (1978). Clement Eaton, *The Growth of Southern Civilization, 1790–1860* (1961), provides a good introduction to life in the Old South.

Black resistance to slavery is described in Vincent Harding, *There is a River: The Black Struggle for Freedom in America* (1981). Slave culture and community are examined in Albert J. Raboteau, *Slave Religion* (1978); Herbert G. Gutman, *The Black Family in Slavery and Freedom, 1750–1925* (1976); and Lawrence W. Levine, *Black Culture and Consciousness: Afro-American Folk Thought from Slavery to Freedom* (1977).

Additional Bibliography

General works on slavery and the Old South include Ulrich B. Phillips, *American Negro Slavery* (1918) and *Life and Labor in the Old South* (1929); Eugene D. Genovese, *The Political Economy of Slavery: Studies in the Economy and Society of the Slave South* (1965);

and Leslie Howard Owens, *This Species of Property: Slave Life and Culture in the Old South* (1976). The classic account of southern agriculture is Lewis C. Gray, *History of Agriculture in the Southern United States to 1860*, 2 vols. (1941). On the economics of slavery, see Robert William Fogel and Stanley L. Engerman, *Time on the Cross: The Economics of American Negro Slavery*, 2 vols. (1974); Paul A. David et al., *Reckoning with Slavery: A Critical Study of the Quantitative History of American Negro Slavery* (1976); and Herbert G. Gutman, *Slavery and the Numbers Game: A Critique of Time on the Cross* (1975).

Nonagricultural slavery is examined in Robert S. Starobin, *Industrial Slavery in the Old South* (1970); Richard C. Wade, *Slavery in the Cities* (1964); and Claudia Dale Goldin, *Urban Slavery in the American South, 1820–1860: A Quantitative History* (1976). See also Frank Tannenbaum, *Slave and Citizen: The Negro in the Americas* (1946) and Carl N. Degler, *Neither Black Nor White: Slavery and Race Relations in Brazil and the United States* (1971).

On the society and culture of the southern white population, see W. J. Cash, *The Mind of the South* (1941); Frank L. Owsley, *Plain Folk of the Old South* (1949); Dickson D. Bruce, Jr., *Violence and Culture in the Antebellum South* (1979); Clement Eaton, *The Mind of the Old South* (1964); Drew Gilpin Faust, *A Sacred Circle: The Dilemma of the Intellectual in the Old South, 1840–1860* (1977); Bertram Wyatt-Brown, *Southern Honor: Ethics and Behavior in the Old South* (1982); and John McCardell, *The Idea of a Southern Nation: Southern Nationalists and Southern Nationalism, 1830–1860* (1979).

Proslavery consciousness is treated in William Sumner Jenkins, *Pro-Slavery Thought in the Old South* (1935); George M. Fredrickson, *The Black Image in the White Mind: The Debate on Afro-American Character and Destiny, 1817–1914* (1971); Eugene D. Genovese, *The World the Slaveholders Made: Two Essays in Interpretation* (1969); and H. Shelton Smith, *In His Image, But . . . : Racism in Southern Religion, 1780–1910* (1972). Southern dissent and efforts to repress it are well covered in Carl N. Degler, *The Other South: Southern Dissenters in the Nineteenth Century* (1974).

On slave revolts, see Herbert Aptheker, *American Negro Slave Revolts* (1943) and Eugene D. Genovese, *From Rebellion to Revolution: Afro-American Slave Revolts in the Making of the Modern World* (1979). The plight of Southern free blacks is covered in Ira Berlin, *Slaves Without Masters: The Free Negro in the Antebellum South* (1974), and racial discrimination in the North is described in Leon Litwack, *North of Slavery: The Free Negro in the Free States, 1790–1860* (1961). Benjamin Quarles, *Black Abolitionists* (1969), and Jane H. Pease and William H. Pease, *They Who Would Be Free* (1974), treat the involvement of northern blacks in the antislavery movement. On life in the slave quarters, see George P. Rawick, *From Sundown to Sunup: The Making of the Black Community* (1972) and Thomas L. Webber, *Deep Like Rivers: Education in the Slave Quarters, 1831–1865* (1978).

chapter 13

AN AGE
OF EXPANSIONISM

Orators and writers, responding to the surging nationalism of the 1840s, hailed the emergence of a mood or movement known as "Young America." The rhetoric of the Young Americans was as extravagant as their ambitions. "The spirit of Young America," noted a Boston newspaper in 1844, "will not be satisfied with what has been attained but plumes its young wings for a higher and more glorious flight. The hopes of America, the hopes of Humanity must rest on this spirit. . . . The steam is up, the young overpowering spirit of the country will press onward." Nothing, the newspaper continued, could "stop the advancement of this truly democratic and omnipotent spirit of the age." This identification of Young America with the extension of democracy reveals its roots in the Jacksonianism of the previous decade; the major voices for the expansionist spirit were young Democrats seeking a new way to recapture the political magic of Old Hickory. Their current hero was a "Young Hickory," who also came out of Tennessee to become a strong president—James K. Polk.

Those who identified with this image of an adolescent nation awakening to maturity favored an aggressive foreign policy, territorial acquisitions, and rapid economic growth. They called in turn for annexation of Texas, assertion of an American claim to all of Oregon, and the appropriation of vast new territories from Mexico. They also celebrated the technological advances that would knit this new empire together, especially the telegraph and the railroad. Telegraphs, according to one writer, would "flash sensation and volition backward and to and from towns and provinces as if they were organs and limbs of a single organism"; while railroads provided "a vast system of iron muscles which, as it were, move the limbs of the mighty organism."

Young America was an intellectual as well as a political movement. In 1845, a Washington journal hailed the election of Polk as a sign that youth will "dare to take antiquity by the beard, and tear the cloak from hoary-headed hypocrisy. Too young to be corrupt . . . it is Young America, awakened to a sense of her own intellectual greatness by her soaring spirit. It stands in strength, the voice of the majority." During the Polk administration, "Young American" writers and critics—mostly based in New York—called for a new and distinctive national literature, free of subservience to European themes or models and expressive of the democratic spirit. Their organ was the *Literary World*, founded in 1847, and its ideals influenced two of the greatest writers the nation has ever produced—Walt Whitman and Herman Melville.

Whitman captured much of the exuberance and expansionism of Young America in his "Song of the Open Road":

From this hour I ordain myself loos'd of limits and imaginary lines,
Going where I list, my own master total and absolute,
. . . .
I inhale great draughts of space,
The east and the west are mine, and the north and the south are mine.

I am larger, better than I thought.

In *Moby Dick*, Herman Melville produced a novel sufficiently original in form and conception to more than fulfill the demand of Young Ameri-

■ *A native of New York, Herman Melville shaped knowledge gained as a merchant sailor into* Moby Dick, *a cautionary saga about the dark side of human ambition.*

cans for "a New Literature to fit the New Man in the New Age." But Melville was too deep a thinker not to see the perils that underlay the soaring ambition and aggressiveness of the new age. In the character of Ahab, the whaling captain who brings destruction on himself and his ship by his relentless pursuit of the white whale, he symbolized—among other things—the dangers facing a nation that was overreaching itself by indulging its pride and exalted sense of destiny with too little concern for the moral and practical consequences.

Movement to the Far West

In the 1830s and '40s the westward movement of population left the valley of the Mississippi behind and penetrated the Far West all the way to the Pacific. Pioneers pursued fertile land and economic opportunity beyond the existing boundaries of the United States and thus helped set the stage for the annexations and international crises of the 1840s. Some went for material gain, others for adventure, and a significant minority sought freedom from religious persecution. But whatever their reasons for migrating, they brought American attitudes and loyalties into regions that were already occupied or at least claimed by Mexico or Great Britain. Whether they realized it or not, these pioneers were the vanguard of American expansionism.

Borderlands of the 1830s

Territorial ambition lured Americans northward as well as westward, and for a time it seemed that Canada might be a new frontier for expansionism. Conflicts over the border between America and British North America led periodically to calls for diplomatic or military action to wrest the northern half of the continent from the English.

Since the birth of the Republic there had been a major dispute over the boundary between Maine and the Canadian province of New Brunswick. The United States and Great Britain submitted their claims to the king of the Netherlands for arbitration, but the Senate rejected his compromise proposal in 1832. In 1839 fighting broke out between Canadian lumberjacks and the Maine

militia. This long-festering border controversy poisoned Anglo-American relations until 1842, when Secretary of State Daniel Webster concluded an agreement with the British government, represented by Lord Ashburton. The Webster-Ashburton Treaty gave over half of the disputed territory to the United States and established a definite northeastern boundary with Canada. (See the map of America in the mid-nineteenth century in the front pages of the book for the territorial expansion discussed in this chapter.)

On the other side of the continent, the United States and Britain both laid claim to Oregon, a vast unsettled area that lay between the Rockies and the Pacific from the forty-second parallel (the northern boundary of California) to the latitude of 54°40' (the southern boundary of Alaska). In 1818 the two nations agreed to joint occupation for ten years, an agreement that was renewed indefinitely in 1827. Meanwhile, the Americans had strengthened their claim by acquiring Spain's rights to the Pacific Northwest in the Adams-Onís Treaty (see chapter 9), and the British had gained effective control of the northern portion of the Oregon country through the activities of the Hudson's Bay Company, a well-financed fur-trading concern. Blocking an equitable division was the reluctance on both sides to surrender access to the Columbia River basin and the adjacent territory extending north to the forty-ninth parallel (which later became the northern border of the state of Washington).

The Oregon country was virtually unpopulated before 1840, but the same could not be said of the Mexican borderlands that lay directly west of Jacksonian America. Spanish settlements in present-day New Mexico dated from the end of the sixteenth century. By 1827 this province had about forty-four thousand people, engaged mainly in sheep-raising and mining. Mexican peasant villages and Indian pueblos coexisted in relative harmony, but most of the wealth was siphoned off by a small class of large landowners who also dominated the provincial government. To save the province from economic stagnation, the Mexican authorities decided in 1822 to encourage trade between Santa Fe, the capital of New Mexico, and the United States. They succeeded in stimulating commercial prosperity, but they also whetted expansionist appetites on the Anglo side of the border.

California in the 1820s and '30s was a more colorful, turbulent, and fragile northward extension of Mexican civilization. It was little more than a half-century since Spanish missionaries and soldiers had taken control of the region. Much less populous than New Mexico—there were only about four thousand Hispanic inhabitants in 1827—California was a land of huge estates and enormous herds of cattle. At the beginning of the 1830s most of the land and the wealth of the province was controlled by the chain of twenty-one mission stations that stretched from San Diego to San Francisco. Thirty thousand converted Indians herded cattle and raised wheat on the vast mission holdings. Great as these numbers may seem, they represented only a small fraction of the original indigenous population; there had been a dramatic and catastrophic decline in Indian population during the previous sixty years of Spanish rule. Exposure to European diseases and the stresses and strains of forced labor on the missions had taken an enormous toll among the Native Americans.

In 1833 the Mexican government confiscated the Church's lands and released the Indians from semislavery, but this in fact made their plight even worse. Rather than giving the land to Indian peasants, the government awarded immense tracts to Mexican citizens, and a new class of large landowners or *rancheros* replaced the *padres* as the rulers of Old California. Seven hundred grantees took possession of *ranchos* ranging up to nearly fifty thousand acres in size and proceeded to subject the Indians to a new and harsher form of servitude. During the fifteen years that they held sway, the rancheros created an American legend through their lavish hospitality, extravagant dress, superb horsemanship, and taste for violent and dangerous sports. Their flamboyant life-style and devotion to the pursuit of pleasure captured the fancy and aroused the secret envy of many American visitors and traders.

The Americans who saw California in the 1830s (and conveyed to the rest of the nation a romatic image of this sun-baked land of beautiful scenery and senoritas) were mostly merchants and sailors involved in the oceanic trade between Boston and California ports. New England clipper ships sailed around Cape Horn at the southern tip of South America to barter manufactured goods for cowhides. One Boston firm came away with

■ *Elegant Don José Sepulveda was typical of the Mexican rancheros who took over the California cattle industry and ruled Old California after 1833.*

over five hundred thousand hides in a twenty-year period. By the mid-1830s, several Yankee merchants had taken up permanent residence in towns like Monterey and San Diego in order to conduct the California end of the business. The reports that they sent back about the Golden West sparked great interest in eastern business circles.

The Texas Revolution

At the same time that some Americans were trading with California, others were taking possession of Texas. After Mexico became independent in 1821, it inherited Spain's claim to Texas, which the United States had conceded in the Adams-Onís Treaty of 1819 (see chapter 9). Both Adams and Jackson tried to buy Texas from Mexico, but their offers were firmly rebuffed. Beginning in the early 1820s, however, American settlers began to move into Texas at the invitation of the Mexican government.

In 1823 Mexican officials agreed to the proposal of two Americans—Moses Austin and his son Stephen F. Austin—to populate Texas by granting huge tracts of land to a few individuals who would then act as colonizing agents. The younger Austin received the earliest and largest of these grants for himself. In 1823, 300 American families were settled on the Austin grant, and within a year the colony's population had swelled to 2021. American immigrants were drawn by the offer of fertile and inexpensive land, and those from the southwestern states often brought slaves with them in the hope of extending the cotton kingdom.

Friction soon developed between the Mexican government and the American colonists over such issues as the status of slavery and the Catholic Church. In 1829 Mexico formally freed all slaves under its jurisdiction, but the Texans simply ignored the decree. Mexican law also required that immigrants accept the Catholic faith, but this regulation also became a dead letter. A Mexican government commission reported in 1829 that Americans were the great majority of the Texas population and were flagrantly violating Mexican law—refusing to emancipate their slaves, evading import duties on goods from the United States, and failing to convert to Catholicism. The following year the Mexican Congress prohibited further American immigration and importation of slaves to Texas.

But enforcement of the new law was feeble, and the flow of settlers, slaves, and smuggled goods continued virtually unabated. A long-standing complaint of the Texans was the failure of the Mexican constitution to grant them local self-government. Under the Mexican federal system, Texas was joined to the state of Coahuila, and Texan representatives were outnumbered three to one in the state legislature. In 1832 Texans showed their displeasure with Mexican rule by rioting in protest against the arrest of several Americans by the commander of the Galveston garrison.

Stephen F. Austin went to Mexico City in 1833 to present the Texans' grievances and seek concessions from the central government. He succeeded in having the ban against American immigration lifted, but got only vague promises about tariff relief, and failed to win agreement to the separation of Texas from Coahuila. As he was about to return to Texas, Austin was arrested and imprisoned for writing a letter recommending that Texans set up a state government without Mexico City's consent.

The spark that ignited a full-scale revolt in 1835 was a comic-opera incident involving the collection of Mexican export duties in the port of Galveston. An American prankster marked a box of sawdust for export, and the angry customs official who inspected it sought to arrest the perpetrator of the joke. When his efforts were resisted by a mob of Texans, he summoned troops, and the settlers rose in rebellion. This uprising received the blessings of Stephen F. Austin, who had just returned from his imprisonment in Mexico.

■
After his father's death, Stephen F. Austin carried out his father's dream of populating Texas with American families, beginning in 1823. By 1835, his inability to win concessions from the Mexican government forced Austin to support rebellion.

During the revolution that followed the Texans claimed that they were fighting for freedom against a long experience of oppression. Actually, Mexican rule had not been harsh; the worst that can be said was that it was inefficient, inconsistent, and sometimes corrupt. Furthermore, the Texans' devotion to "liberty" did not prevent them from defending slavery against Mexico's attempt to abolish it. Texans had done pretty much what they pleased, despite laws to the contrary and angry rumblings from south of the Rio Grande.

A more plausible justification for revolution was the Texans' fear of what might happen in the future under the latest regime to be established in

355

Mexico City. In 1834 General Antonio López de Santa Anna made himself dictator of Mexico and abolished the federal system of government. When news of these developments reached Texas late in the year, they were accompanied by rumors of the impending disfranchisement and even expulsion of American immigrants. The rebels, already aroused by the sawdust incident, were influenced by these rumors and put a very sinister construction on Santa Anna's new policy of enforcing tariff regulations by military force.

When he learned that the Texans were resisting customs collections, Santa Anna sent reinforcements. On June 30, 1835, before any additional troops could arrive, a band of settlers led by W. B. Travis captured the Mexican garrison at Anahuac without firing a shot. The settlers first engaged Mexican troops at Gonzales in October and forced the retreat of a cavalry detachment. Shortly thereafter, Stephen F. Austin laid siege to San Antonio with a force of five hundred men and after six weeks forced its surrender, thereby capturing most of the Mexican troops then in Texas.

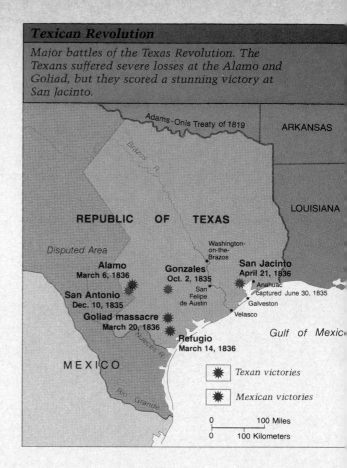

Texican Revolution

Major battles of the Texas Revolution. The Texans suffered severe losses at the Alamo and Goliad, but they scored a stunning victory at San Jacinto.

The Republic of Texas

While this early fighting was going on, delegates from the American communities met in convention and after some hesitation voted overwhelmingly to declare their independence on March 1, 1836. A constitution, based closely on that of the United States, was adopted for the new Republic of Texas, and a temporary government was installed to carry on the military struggle.

Within days after Texas declared itself a republic, 4000 Mexican soldiers were in San Antonio assaulting the Alamo, an abandoned mission where 187 Texas defenders had taken refuge. The Texans literally fought to the last man, exacting a heavy price from the enemy. Their martyrdom gave the Texas revolution new inspiration and the rallying cry, "Remember the Alamo." A few days later another Texas detachment was surrounded and captured in an open plain near the San Antonio River and was marched to the town of Goliad where all 350 of its members were summarily executed. The "Goliad massacre" provoked the Texas rebels to even more desperate resistance.

The main Texas army, under General Sam Houston, moved quickly to avenge these early defeats. On April 20, 1836, Houston led his force of 700 men in a daring assault on Santa Anna's encampment near the San Jacinto River. Within fifteen minutes the battle was over; 630 Mexicans were killed and 730 were captured—including Santa Anna himself. The Texans lost only a handful of men. Santa Anna was marched to Velasco, the meeting place of the Texas government, where he was forced to sign treaties recognizing the independence of Texas and its claim to territory all the way to the Rio Grande. The Mexican government declared these agreements null and void and attempted to send forth a new army of conquest. But by this time the Texas army had grown to such a size that Mexican commanders prudently avoided a direct engagement, and Mexico City conceded the autonomy of the Texas republic while continuing to protest its illegality.

Sam Houston, the hero of San Jacinto, became the first president of the Texas republic. His platform sought annexation to the United States, and one of his first acts in office was to send an emissary to Washington to test the waters. Houston's agent found much sympathy for Texas independence but little appetite for immediate annexation. He was told by Andrew Jackson and others that domestic politics and fear of a war with Mexico made such action impossible. The most that he could win from Congress and the Jackson administration was formal recognition of Texas sovereignty.

In its short career as the "Lone Star Republic," Texas drew settlers from the United States at an accelerating rate. The panic of 1837 impelled many debt-ridden and land-hungry farmers to take advantage of the free grants of 1280 acres that Texas offered to immigrating heads of families. In the decade after independence, the population of Texas soared, from 30,000 to 142,000. Most of the newcomers assumed, as did the old settlers, that they would soon be annexed and restored to American citizenship.

Trails of Trade and Settlement

After New Mexico opened its trade to American merchants, a thriving commerce developed along the trail that ran from Independence, Missouri, to Santa Fe. The first of these merchants to reach the New Mexican capital was William Becknell, who arrived with his train of goods in January 1822. Others followed rapidly. To protect themselves from the hostile Indians whose territory they had to cross, the traders traveled in large caravans, one or two of which would arrive in Santa Fe every summer. The federal government assisted them by providing troops when necessary and by appropriating money to purchase rights of passage from various tribes. Even so, the trip across the Cimarron desert and the southern Rockies was often difficult and hazardous. But profits from the exchange of textiles and other manufactured goods for furs, mules, and precious metals were substantial enough to make the risk worth taking.

■ *After the battle of San Jacinto, its hero Sam Houston, lying wounded under a tree, accepts the surrender of Santa Anna, at left in white breeches. The man cupping his ear at right is Erastus "Deaf" Smith, a famous scout and important man in Houston's army.*

Indians and Whites on the Overland Trail

It is a familiar scenario. The covered wagons are drawn into a tight circle and the pioneers are just ready to settle down for the night. A lonely sentinel or two patrols the area, warily watching for a surprise Indian attack. Suddenly, hundreds of Indians on horseback appear, yelling out blood-curdling war whoops as they charge forward. Arrows, some of them flaming, fly over and into the wagons. Hastily, the heroic pioneers grab their rifles, and from behind their defenses, they fire on the Indians. Occasionally, an Indian brave or his horse falls. This image of violence on the overland trail may make for exciting cinema, but it conveys a false impression of the relations between whites and Indians during the great westward trek that brought a quarter of a million settlers to Oregon and California during the 1840s and '50s.

For one thing, it leaves out the kind of interaction that a Jesuit missionary observed in 1846 and described as "mutual aid." Indians assisted the emigrants in a variety of ways. Sometimes they gave directions or recommended the best routes to overlanders who were lost or uncertain about the best trail to follow. Often they helped wagon trains ford wide and dangerous rivers, acting as swimming stock-herders or as boatmen to convey goods and people to the opposite bank.

Trade was by far the most significant form of "mutual aid"; it provided the overlanders with items essential to their survival. To replace horses that died or were stolen, the overlanders bartered blankets and clothing for Indian ponies. When immigrants were running short of food, they were often able to get fresh vegetables, fish, and meat from Indians. Whites also obtained and used such products of Indian handicraft as moccasins and buffalo robes. Almost all trade took the form of bartering goods because Indians had little use for money. Sometimes they demanded whiskey, but most overlanders were reluctant to provide it, and "firewater" never became a major trade item on the trails.

Although peaceful exchange was the dominant form of relations between Indians and whites on the overland trail, tension was inevitable in certain situations. The Plains Indians in particular often demanded tribute from the whites who were passing through their lands. As the flow of wagon trains increased during the 1840s, grass was overgrazed, game was killed or frightened away, and such scarce resources as timber and water were depleted. Indians therefore thought that they had a perfect right to impose a kind of tax on the overlanders. The emigrants, however, often refused to recognize such rights, and if they paid tribute at all, they did so only under duress. Overlanders were also annoyed because Indians frequently took possession of bridges built by earlier emigrant parties and charged tolls for their use. Confrontations over tributes and tolls became more tense as time went on but did not usually result in violent clashes. In most cases the physically weaker side had the common sense to back down.

Although the incidence of violence along the trail has been much exaggerated in popular accounts, it did occur. Indians occasionally attacked wagon trains, mostly during the 1850s. Rarely, however, did they mass in large numbers to assault a group of wagons drawn up in a circle. Usually they attacked relatively small parties of emigrants while their Conestoga wagons were stretched out along the trail. The most dangerous situation for the overlanders occurred when small groups of them left their encampments and wandered into the surrounding countryside. If such scouting parties encountered unfriendly Indians, they might be robbed of everything and sent back to camp stark naked. If they resisted, some or all of them might be killed.

Recent historical investigation has shown that whites often provoked such incidents by their own casual violence against Indians. Statistics on the killings that occurred on the trail reveal that Indians were more often the victims than the perpetrators of violence. According to the calculations of historian John D. Unruh, Jr., Indians killed 362 emigrants between the years of 1840 and 1860. During the same period 426 Native Americans died at the hands of whites. Unruh also cites several instances when overlanders

murdered Indians without provocation. One emigrant, for example, shot an Indian whose only offense had been to frighten the white man's horse. In 1847 an entire party reacted in a genocidal way to the theft of some of its livestock. "After that," its leader recalled, "we shot at every Indian we saw—this soon cleared the way." It is not surprising that such behavior could provoke Indians to retaliate. Unruh concludes that violence was made worse by "the callous attitude of cultural and racial superiority so many overlanders exemplified . . . ."

Some of the worst atrocities attributed to Indians may actually have been committed by white bandits disguised as red men. In 1859 a group of emigrants from Iowa was attacked by men dressed as Indians who had painted their skins but could not conceal their light brown hair and perfect command of the English language. These desperadoes scalped and killed eight members of the party after torturing and mutilating some of them. In another incident, a pioneer woman who was raped and then shot by five "Indians" lived long enough to reveal that "they were all white men. They had not taken the precaution to paint the whole body."

Despite the occasional violence, most whites received more help than hostility from Indians and never had to defend themselves against attack. The Native Americans, unfortunately, derived little or no long-range benefit from permitting whites to cut a highway to the Pacific through their lands. Their economy and way of life were disrupted, and they would find it increasingly difficult to defend their independence against white encroachment and domination.

Relations between the United States and Mexico soured following the Texas revolution, and this had a devastating effect on the Santa Fe trade. Much of the ill feeling was caused by the Texans' blundering efforts to get a piece of the Santa Fe action. A Texas expedition of 1841 appeared more military than commercial to the rulers of Santa Fe, and they arrested all its members. In retaliation, a volunteer force of Texas avengers expressed their wrath by attacking and killing Mexican troops along the Sante Fe Trail. The Mexican government then moved to curtail the Santa Fe trade. In April 1842 it passed a new tariff banning the importation of many of the goods sold by American merchants and prohibiting the export of gold and silver. Further restrictions in 1843 denied most American traders access to the Santa Fe market.

The famous Oregon Trail was the great overland route that brought the wagon trains of American migrants to the West Coast during the 1840s. Extending for two thousand miles across the northern Great Plains and the mountains beyond,

it crossed the Rockies at the South Pass and then forked; the main northern route led to the Willamette Valley of Oregon, but various alternative trails were opened during the decade for overlanders heading for California. The journey took about six months; most parties departed in May, hoping to arrive in November before the great snows hit the last mountain barriers.

After small groups had made their way to both Oregon and California in 1841 and '42, a mass migration—mostly to Oregon—began in 1843. Within two years, five thousand Americans, living in the Willamette Valley south of the Columbia River, were demanding the extension of full American sovereignty over the Oregon country.

The Mormon Trek

An important and distinctive group of pioneers followed the Oregon Trail as far as the South Pass and then veered southwestward to establish a thriving colony in the region of the Great Salt

Western Trails

Hollywood to the contrary, Indians were not much of a danger on the western trails. Most wagon trains completed the journey westward without experiencing an Indian attack.

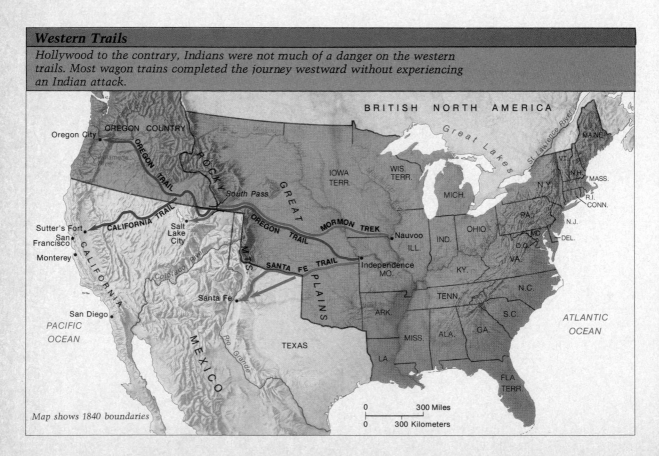

Map shows 1840 boundaries

In July 1847, the vanguard of Mormon pioneers (143 men, 3 women, and 2 children) built an irrigation dam that would turn the desert of Great Salt Lake into farmland. Within a few years, Great Salt Lake had a population of 8000.

Lake. These were Mormons, members of the most successful religious denomination founded exclusively on American soil—the Church of Jesus Christ of Latter Day Saints.

The background of the Mormon trek was a history of persecution in the eastern states. Joseph Smith, founder of Mormonism, encountered strong opposition from the time he announced a new divine revelation in Palmyra, New York, in 1830. According to this new revelation, the lost tribes of Israel had come to the new world in ancient times. One group had founded a Christian civilization, only to be exterminated by the heathen tribes which survived as the American Indians. Smith and those he converted to his new faith were committed to restoring the pure religion that had once thrived on American soil by founding a western Zion where they could practice their faith unmolested and carry out their special mission to convert the Native Americans.

In the 1830s the Mormons established communities in Ohio and Missouri, but the former went bankrupt in the panic of 1837 and the latter was the target of angry mobs and vigilante violence. After the Mormons lost the "war" they fought against the Missourians in 1839, Smith led his followers back across the Mississippi to Illinois, where he received a liberal charter from the state legislature to found a town at Nauvoo. Here the Mormons had a temporary measure of security and self-government, but Smith soon reported new revelations which engendered dissension among his followers and hostility from neighboring "gentiles." Most controversial was his authorization of polygamy, or plural marriage. In 1844 Smith was killed by a mob while being held in jail in Carthage, Illinois, on a charge stemming from his high-handed treatment of some dissident Mormons who objected to his new policies.

The death of Smith confirmed the growing conviction of the Mormon leadership that they needed to move further west to establish their Zion in the wilderness. In late 1845, Smith's successor, Brigham Young, decided to send a party of fifteen hundred men to assess the chances of a colony in the vicinity of the Great Salt Lake. Nauvoo was quickly depopulated as twelve thousand Mormons took to the trail in 1846. The following year Young himself arrived in Utah and sent back word to the thousands encamped along the trail that he had found the promised land.

The Mormon community that Young established in Utah is one of the great success stories of western settlement. In contrast to the extreme individualism and disorder that characterized the mining camps and other new communities, "the state of Deseret" (as Utah was originally called) was a model of discipline and cooperation. Because of its communitarian form of social organization, its centralized government, and the religious dedication of its inhabitants, this frontier society was able to expand settlement in a planned and efficient way and develop a system of irrigation that "made the desert bloom."

Utah's main problem was the determination of its political status. When the Mormons first arrived, they were encroaching illegally into Mexican territory. After Utah came under American sovereignty in 1848, the state of Deseret fought to maintain its autonomy and its custom of polygamy against the efforts of the federal government to extend American law and set up the usual type of territorial administration. In 1857 President Buchanan sent a military force to bring Utah to heel, and the Mormons prepared to repel this "invasion." But after a heavy snow prevented the army from crossing the Rockies, Buchanan offered an olive branch in the form of a general "pardon" for Mormons who had violated federal law but would agree to cooperate with U.S. authorities in the future. In return, Brigham Young called off his plan to resist the army by force and accepted the nominal authority of an appointed territorial governor.

Manifest Destiny and the Mexican War

The rush of settlers beyond the nation's borders in the 1830s and '40s inspired politicians and propagandists to call for annexation of those areas which the migrants were occupying. Some went further and proclaimed that it was the "manifest destiny" of the United States to expand until it had absorbed all of North America, including Canada and Mexico. Such ambitions—and the policies they inspired—led to a major diplomatic confrontation with Great Britain and a war with Mexico.

Tyler and Texas

President John Tyler initiated the politics of Manifest Destiny. He was vice-president when William Henry Harrison died in office in 1841 after serving scarcely a month. The first of our "accidental presidents," Tyler was a states' rights, proslavery Virginian who had been picked as Harrison's running mate to broaden the appeal of the Whig ticket. Profoundly out of sympathy with the mainstream of his own party, he soon broke with the Whigs in Congress, who had united behind Henry Clay's nationalistic economic program. Despite the fact that he lacked a base in either of the major parties, Tyler hoped to be elected president in his own right in 1844. To accomplish this difficult feat, he needed a new issue around which he could build a following that would cut across established party lines.

In 1843 Tyler decided to put the full weight of his administration behind the annexation of Texas. He anticipated that incorporation of the Lone Star Republic would be a popular move, especially in the South where it would feed the appetite for additional slave states. With the South solidly behind him, Tyler expected to have a good chance in the election of 1844.

To achieve his objective, Tyler enlisted the support of John C. Calhoun, the leading political defender of slavery and southern rights. Calhoun saw the annexation issue as a way of uniting the South and taking the offensive against the abolitionists. Success or failure in this effort would constitute a decisive test of whether the North was willing to give the southern states a fair share of national power and adequate assurances for the future of their way of life. If antislavery sentiment succeeded in blocking the acquisition of Texas, the Southerners would at least know where they stood and could begin to "calculate the value of the union."

To prepare the public mind for annexation, the Tyler administration launched a propaganda campaign in the summer of 1843 based on reports of British designs on Texas. According to information supplied by Duff Green, an unofficial American agent in England, the British were preparing to guarantee Texas independence and make a loan to the financially troubled republic in return for the abolition of slavery. In fact, the British had no such intentions, but the stories were believed and used to give urgency to the annexation cause.

Secretary of State Abel Upshur, a protégé of Calhoun, began negotiating an annexation treaty. When Upshur was killed in an accident, Calhoun replaced him and carried the negotiations to a successful conclusion. When the treaty was brought before the Senate in 1844, Calhoun denounced the British for attempting to subvert the South's essential system of labor and racial control by using Texas as a base of abolitionist operations. According to the supporters of Tyler and Calhoun, the South's security and well-being —and by extension that of the nation—required the immediate incorporation of Texas into the Union.

The strategy of linking annexation explicitly to the interests of the South and slavery backfired politically. Northern antislavery Whigs charged that the whole scheme was a proslavery plot meant to advance the interest of one section of the nation against the other—an allegation that has more substance than most historians have been willing to acknowledge. Consequently, the Senate rejected the treaty by a decisive vote of 35 to 16 in June 1844. Tyler then attempted to bring Texas into the Union through an alternative means—a joint resolution of both houses of Congress admitting it as a state. But Congress adjourned before the issue came to a vote, and the whole question hung fire in anticipation of the election of 1844.

The Triumph of Polk and Annexation

Tyler's initiative made the future of Texas the central issue in the 1844 campaign. But party lines held firm, and the President himself was unable to capitalize on it. Tyler tried to run as an independent, but his failure to gain significant support eventually forced him to step aside.

If the Democratic party convention had been held in 1843—as originally scheduled—ex-President Martin Van Buren would have won the

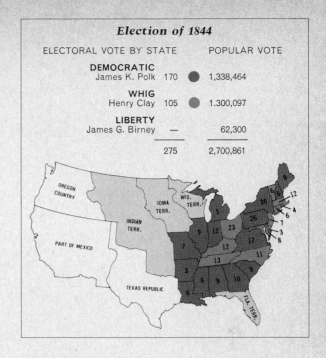

Election of 1844

ELECTORAL VOTE BY STATE			POPULAR VOTE
DEMOCRATIC James K. Polk	170		1,338,464
WHIG Henry Clay	105		1.300,097
LIBERTY James G. Birney	—		62,300
	275		2,700,861

nomination easily. But postponement of the Democratic conclave until May 1844 weakened his chances. In the meantime the annexation question came to the fore, and Van Buren was forced to take a stand on it. He persisted in the view he had held as president—that incorporation of Texas would arouse sectional strife and destroy the unity of the Democratic party, an opinion that seemed confirmed in 1844 when the dominant party faction in Van Buren's home state of New York came out against Tyler's Texas policy. In an effort to keep the issue out of the campaign, Van Buren struck a gentleman's agreement with Henry Clay, the overwhelming favorite for the Whig nomination, that both of them would publicly oppose immediate annexation.

Van Buren's letter opposing annexation appeared shortly before the Democratic convention

The Liberty Party Swings an Election

Candidate	Party	Actual Vote in New York	National Electoral Vote	If Liberty Voters Had Voted Whig	Projected Electoral Vote
Clay	Whig	232,482	105	**248,294**	**141**
Birney	Liberty	15,812	0		
Polk	Democrat	237,588	170	237,588	134

and it cost him the nomination. Angry southern delegates used the rule requiring approval by a two-thirds vote to block Van Buren's nomination. After several ballots a dark horse candidate—James K. Polk of Tennessee—emerged triumphant. Polk, a protégé of Andrew Jackson, had been Speaker of the House of Representatives and governor of Tennessee. A shrewd if somewhat devious politician, he had persuaded other presidential aspirants to stand aside by promising that he would serve only one term if elected.

Polk was an avowed expansionist, and he ran on a platform calling for the simultaneous annexation of Texas and assertion of American claims to all of Oregon. He identified himself and his party with the popular cause of turning the United States into a continental nation, an aspiration that attracted support in the North as well as in the South. His was a much more astute political strategy than the overtly prosouthern expansionism advocated by Tyler and Calhoun. The Whig nominee, Henry Clay, was basically antiexpansionist, but his sense of the growing popularity of Texas annexation among southern Whigs caused him to waffle on the issue during the campaign. This in turn cost Clay the support of a small but crucial group of northern antislavery Whigs, who defected to the abolitionist Liberty Party.

Polk won the fall election by a relatively narrow popular margin. His triumph in the electoral college—170 votes to 105—was secured by victories in New York and Michigan, where the Liberty party candidate, James G. Birney, had taken away enough votes from Clay to affect the outcome. (See the map and the chart of the election of 1844 on p. 363.) The closeness of the election meant that the Democrats had something less than a clear mandate to implement their expansionist policies, but this did not prevent them from claiming that the people had backed an aggressive campaign to extend the borders of the United States.

After the election, Congress reconvened to consider the annexation of Texas. The mood had changed as a result of Polk's victory, and some leading Democratic senators who had initially opposed Tyler's scheme for annexation by joint resolution of Congress now modified their position. As a result, annexation was approved a few days before Polk took office.

The Doctrine of Manifest Destiny

The expansionist mood that accompanied Polk's election and the annexation of Texas was given a name and a rationale in the summer of 1845. John L. O'Sullivan, a proponent of the "Young America" movement and editor of the influential *United States Magazine and Democratic Review*, charged that foreign governments were conspiring to block the annexation of Texas in an effort to thwart "the fulfillment of our manifest destiny to overspread the continent alloted by providence for the free development of our yearly multiplying millions."

Besides coining the phrase *Manifest Destiny*, O'Sullivan pointed to the three main ideas that lay behind it. One was that God was on the side of American expansionism. This notion came naturally out of the long tradition of identifying the growth of America with the divinely ordained success of a chosen people. A second idea, implied in the phrase *free development*, was that the spread of American rule meant what other propagandists for expansion described as "extending the area of freedom." Democratic institutions and local self-government would follow the flag if areas claimed by autocratic foreign governments were annexed to the United States. O'Sullivan's third premise was that population growth required the outlet that territorial acquisitions would provide. Behind this notion lurked a fear that growing numbers would lead to diminished opportunity and European-type socioeconomic class divisions if the restless and the ambitious were not given new lands to settle and exploit.

In its most extreme form, Manifest Destiny meant that the United States would someday occupy the entire North American continent, that nothing less would appease its land-hungry population. "Make way, I say, for the young American Buffalo," bellowed a Democratic orator in 1844, "—he has not yet got land enough . . . I tell you we will give him Oregon for his summer shade, and the region of Texas as his winter pasture. (Applause) Like all of his race, he wants salt, too. Well, he shall have the use of two oceans—the mighty Pacific and the turbulent Atlantic . . . He shall not stop his career until he slakes his thirst in the frozen ocean. (Cheers)"

The only question in the minds of fervent expansionists and "Young Americans" was whether the United States would acquire its vast new domain through a gradual, peaceful process of settler infiltration or through active diplomacy backed by force and the threat of war. The decision was up to President Polk.

Polk and the Oregon Question

In 1845 and '46 the United States came closer to armed conflict with Great Britain than at any time since the War of 1812. The willingness of some Americans to go to war over Oregon was expressed in the rallying cry "fifty-four forty or fight." This slogan was actually coined by Whigs seeking to ridicule Democratic expansionists, but Democrats later took it over as a vivid expression of their demand for what is now British Columbia. Polk fed this expansionist fever by laying claim in his inaugural address to all of the Oregon country. Privately, however, he was willing to accept the forty-ninth parallel. What made the situation so tense was that Polk was dedicated to an aggressive diplomacy of bluff and bluster. As historian David M. Pletcher has put it, Polk "set forth on a foreign policy of strong stands, overstated arguments, and menacing public announcements, not because he wanted war but because he felt that this was the only policy which his foreign adversaries would understand."

In July 1845 Polk authorized Secretary of State James Buchanan to reply to the latest British request for terms by offering a boundary along the forty-ninth parallel. Because this did not meet the British demand for all of Vancouver Island and free navigation of the Columbia River, the British ambassador rejected the proposal out-of-hand. This rebuff infuriated Polk; in his view the offer was a generous and conciliatory retreat from his public position. He subsequently withdrew it and refused a British request of December 1845 that he renew the offer and submit the dispute to international arbitration. Instead he called on Congress to terminate the agreement providing for joint occupation of the Pacific Northwest. Congress complied in April 1846, and Polk submitted the required year's notice to the British on May 21.

Since abrogation of the joint agreement implied that the United States would attempt to extend its jurisdiction north to 54°40', the British government decided to take the diplomatic initiative in an effort to avert war, while at the same time dispatching warships to the Western Hemisphere in case conciliation failed. Their new proposal accepted the forty-ninth parallel as the border to a point where the boundary would veer south so that Britain could retain Vancouver Island. It also provided for British navigation rights on the Columbia River. When the draft treaty was received in June, Polk refused either to endorse or reject it and took the unusual step of submitting it directly to the Senate for advice. The Senate recommended that the treaty be accepted with the single change that British rights to navigate the Columbia be made temporary. It was ratified in that form on June 15.

Polk was prompted to settle the Oregon question because he now had a war with Mexico on his hands. His reckless diplomacy had brought

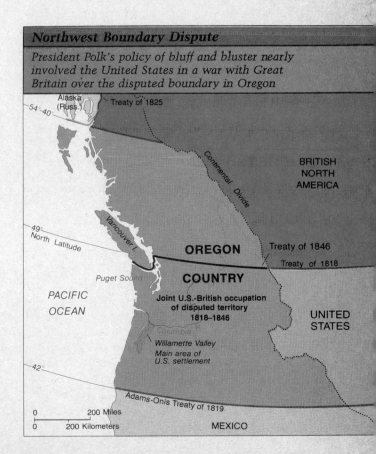

Northwest Boundary Dispute

President Polk's policy of bluff and bluster nearly involved the United States in a war with Great Britain over the disputed boundary in Oregon

Alaska (Russ.)

Treaty of 1825

54°-40'

BRITISH NORTH AMERICA

Continental Divide

49° North Latitude

Vancouver I.

OREGON

Treaty of 1846

Treaty of 1818

Puget Sound

COUNTRY

PACIFIC OCEAN

Joint U.S.-British occupation of disputed territory 1818–1846

UNITED STATES

Columbia

Willamette Valley
Main area of
U.S. settlement

42°

Adams-Onís Treaty of 1819

0   200 Miles
0   200 Kilometers

MEXICO

■ *This 1846 cartoon entitled "This Is the House That Polk Built" shows President Polk sitting forlornly in a house of cards, which represent the delicately balanced issues facing him.*

War with Mexico

While the United States was avoiding a war with Great Britain, it was getting into one with Mexico. Although they had recognized Texas independence in 1845, the Mexicans rejected the Lone Star Republic's unjustified claim to the unsettled territory between the Nueces River and the Rio Grande. When the United States annexed Texas and assumed its claim to the disputed area, Mexico broke off diplomatic relations and prepared for armed conflict.

Polk responded by placing troops in Louisiana on the alert and by dispatching John Slidell as an emissary to Mexico City in the hope that he could resolve the boundary dispute and also persuade the Mexicans to sell New Mexico and California to the United States. The Mexican government refused to receive Slidell because the nature of his appointment ignored the fact that regular diplomatic relations were suspended. While Slidell was waiting in Mexico City in January 1846, Polk ordered General Zachary Taylor, commander of American forces in the Southwest, to advance well beyond the Nueces and proceed toward the Rio Grande, thus invading Mexican territory.

By April, Taylor had taken up a position near Matamoros on the Rio Grande. On the opposite bank of the river, Mexican forces had assembled and erected a fort. On April 24, sixteen hundred Mexican troops crossed the river and the following day met and attacked a small American detachment, killing eleven and capturing the rest. After learning of the incident, Taylor sent word to the President: "Hostilities," he reported, "may now be considered as commenced."

This news was neither unexpected nor unwelcome. Polk in fact was already preparing his war message to Congress when he learned of the fighting on the Rio Grande. A short and decisive war, he had concluded, would force the cession of California and New Mexico to the United States. When Congress declared war on May 13, American agents and an "exploring expedition" under John C. Fremont were already in California stirring up dissension against Mexican rule, and ships of the U.S. Navy lay waiting expectantly off the shore. Two days later, Polk ordered a force under Colonel Stephen Kearny to march to Santa Fe and take possession of New Mexico.

the nation within an eyelash of being involved in two wars at the same time. American policymakers got what they wanted from the Oregon treaty, which was Puget Sound and the strait south of Vancouver Island that led into it. Acquisition of this splendid natural harbor gave the United States its first deep-water port on the Pacific. Polk's initial demand for all of Oregon was made partly for domestic political consumption and partly to bluff the British into making more concessions. It was a dangerous game on both fronts. When Polk finally agreed to the solution, he alienated expansionist advocates in the Old Northwest who had supported his call for all of Oregon.

For many Northerners, the promise of new acquisitions in the Pacific Northwest was the only thing that made annexation of Texas palatable. They hoped that new free states could be created to counterbalance the admission of slaveholding Texas to the Union. As this prospect receded, the charge of antislavery defenders that Texas annexation was a southern plot drew more support; to Northerners Polk began to look more and more like a president concerned mainly with furthering the interests of his native region.

The war lasted much longer than expected because the Mexicans refused to make peace despite a succession of military defeats. In the first major campaign of the conflict, Taylor followed up his victory in two battles fought north of the Rio Grande by crossing the river, taking Matamoros and marching on Monterrey. In September, his forces assaulted and captured this major city of northern Mexico after overcoming fierce resistance.

But Taylor's controversial decision to allow the Mexican garrison to go free and his unwillingness or inability to advance further into Mexico angered Polk and led him to adopt a new strategy for winning the war and a new commander to implement it. General Winfield Scott was ordered to prepare an amphibious attack on Vera Cruz with the aim of placing an American army within striking distance of Mexico City itself. With half his forces detached for the new invasion, Taylor was left to hold his position in northern Mexico. But this did not deprive him of a final moment of glory. At Buena Vista, in February 1847, he defeated a sizable Mexican army sent northward to dislodge him. Despite his unpopularity with the administration, Taylor was hailed as a national hero and a possible candidate for president.

Meanwhile, the Kearney expedition captured

The Mexican War

The Mexican War added half a million square miles of territory to the United States, but the cost was high: $100 million and thirteen thousand lives.

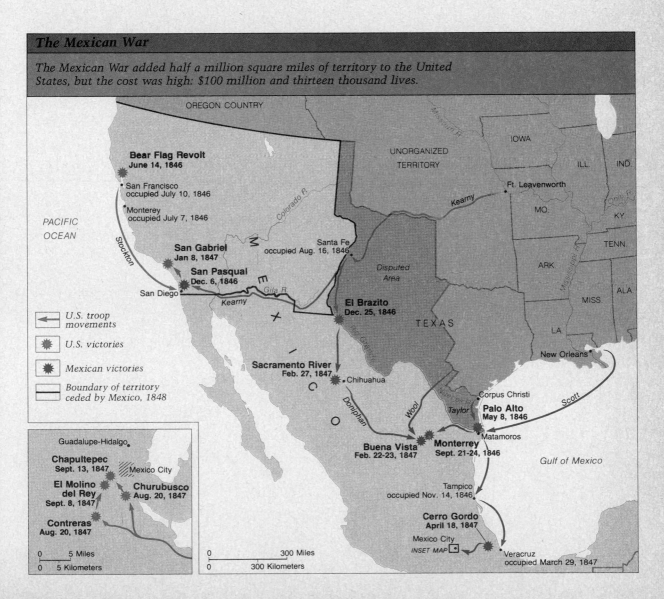

Although General Zachary Taylor (below) was popularly perceived as a national hero, his inability to win a quick victory over the Mexicans angered Polk.

After a decisive victory at Vera Cruz, General Winfield Scott led the troops at the fierce battle of Cerro Gordo (above). More than 1000 Mexican soldiers were killed and over 3000 were captured. The United States forces lost 417 soldiers but gained the road to Mexico City. Within a few months, Scott's forces were massed outside the Mexican capital. On September 14 the city fell, and a triumphant Scott rode into the center of Mexico City (below).

Santa Fe, proclaimed the annexation of New Mexico by the United States, and set off for California. There they found that American settlers, in cooperation with John C. Fremont's exploring expedition, had revolted against Mexican authorities and declared their independence as the "Bear Flag Republic." The navy had also captured the port of Monterey. With the addition of Kearney's troops, a relatively small number of Americans were able to take possession of California against scattered and disorganized Mexican opposition, a process that was completed by the beginning of 1847.

The decisive Vera Cruz campaign was slow to develop because of the massive and careful preparations required. But in March 1847 the main American army under General Scott finally landed near that crucial port city and laid siege to it. Vera Cruz fell after eighteen days, and then Scott began his advance on Mexico City. In the most important single battle of the war, Scott met forces under General Santa Anna at Cerro Gordo on April 17 and 18. The Mexicans occupied an apparently impregnable position on high ground blocking the way to Mexico City. A daring flanking maneuver that required soldiers to scramble up the mountainsides enabled Scott to win the decisive victory that opened the road to the Mexican capital. By August American troops were drawn up in front of Mexico City. After a temporary armistice, a brief respite that was actually used by the Mexicans to regroup and improve their defenses, Scott ordered the massive assault that captured the city on September 14.

Settlement of the Mexican War

Accompanying Scott's army was a diplomat, Nicholas P. Trist, who was authorized to negotiate a peace treaty whenever the Mexicans decided they had had enough. Despite a sequence of American victories and the imminent fall of Mexico City, Trist made little progress. No Mexican leader was willing to invite the wrath of an intensely proud and nationalistic citizenry by agreeing to the kind of terms that Polk wanted to impose. Even after the United States had achieved a total military victory, Trist found it difficult to exact an acceptable treaty from the Mexican government. By November, Polk was so irked by the delay that he ordered Trist to return to Washington. Radical adherents of Manifest Destiny were now clamoring for the annexation of all Mexico, and Polk himself may have been momentarily tempted by the chance to move from military occupation to outright annexation.

Trist, to his credit, ignored Polk's instructions and continued to negotiate. On February 2, 1848, he signed a treaty that gained all the concessions he had been commissioned to obtain. The Treaty of Guadalupe Hidalgo ceded New Mexico and California to the United States for $15 million, established the Rio Grande as the border between Texas and Mexico, and promised that the United States government would assume the substantial claims of American citizens against Mexico. When the agreement reached Washington, Polk censured Trist for disobeying orders but approved of his treaty, which he sent to the Senate for ratification. Senate approval by a vote of 38 to 14 came on March 10.

As a result of the Mexican War the United States gained half a million square miles of territory. The treaty of 1848 enlarged the size of the nation by about 20 percent, adding to its domain the present states of California, Utah, and New Mexico, most of Arizona, and parts of Colorado and Wyoming. But one intriguing question remains. Why, given the expansionist spirit of the age, did the campaign to acquire all of Mexico fail?

According to the historian Frederick Merk, a major factor was the peculiar combination of racism and anticolonialism that dominated American opinion. It was one thing to acquire thinly populated areas that could be settled by "Anglo-Saxon" pioneers. It was something else again to incorporate a large population that was mainly of mixed Spanish and Indian origin. These "half-breeds," charged racist opponents of the "All Mexico" movement, could never be fit citizens of a self-governing republic. They would have to be ruled in the way that the British governed India, and the possession of colonial dependencies was contrary to American ideals and traditions.

Merk's thesis sheds light on why the general public had little appetite for swallowing all of Mexico, but those actually making policy had more mundane and practical reasons for being satisfied with what was obtained at Guadalupe

Hidalgo. What they had really wanted all along, historian Norman Graebner contends, were the great California harbors of San Francisco and San Diego. From these ports Americans could trade directly with the Orient and dominate the commerce of the Pacific. Once acquisition of California had been assured, policymakers had little incentive to press for more Mexican territory.

The war with Mexico divided the American public and provoked political dissension. A majority of the Whig party opposed the war in principle, arguing (correctly) that the United States had no valid claims to the area south of the Nueces. Whig congressmen voted for military appropriations while the conflict was going on, but they constantly criticized the President for starting it. More ominous was the charge of antislavery Northerners from both parties that the real purpose of the war was to spread the institution of slavery and increase the political power of the southern states. While battles were being fought in Mexico, Congress was debating a proposal to prohibit slavery in any territories that might be acquired from Mexico. A bitter sectional quarrel over the status of slavery in new areas was a major legacy of the Mexican War.

The domestic controversies aroused by the war and the propaganda of Manifest Destiny revealed the limits of mid-nineteenth-century American expansionism and put a damper on additional efforts to extend the nation's boundaries. Concerns about slavery and race impeded acquisition of new territory in Latin America and the Caribbean (see chapter 14). Resolution of the Oregon dispute clearly indicated that the United States was not willing to go to war with a powerful adversary to obtain large chunks of British North America, and the old ambition of incorporating Canada rapidly faded. After 1848, American growth usually took the form of populating and developing the vast territory already acquired.

Internal Expansionism

The expansionists of the 1840s saw a clear link between acquisition of new territory and other forms of material growth and development. In 1844 Samuel F. B. Morse perfected and demonstrated his electric telegraph, a device that would make it possible to communicate rapidly over the expanse of a continental nation. Simultaneously, the railroad was becoming increasingly important as a means of moving people and goods over the same great distances. Improvements in manufacturing and agricultural methods led to an upsurge in the volume and range of internal trade, and the beginnings of mass immigration were providing human resources for the exploitation of new areas and economic opportunities.

After gold was discovered in newly acquired California in 1848, a flood of emigrants from the East and several foreign nations arrived by ship or wagon train, their appetites whetted by the thought of striking it rich. The gold they unearthed spurred the national economy, and the rapid growth of population centers on the Pacific Coast inspired projects for transcontinental telegraph lines and railroad tracks.

When the spirit of Manifest Destiny and the thirst for acquiring new territory waned after the Mexican War, the expansionist impulse turned inward. The technological advances and population increase of the 1840s continued during the '50s. The result was an acceleration of economic growth, a substantial increase in industrialization, and the emergence of a new American working class.

The Triumph of the Railroad

More than anything else, it was the rise of the railroad that transformed the American economy during the 1840s and '50s. The technology came from England, where steam locomotives were first used to haul cars along tracks at the beginning of the century. In 1830 and '31 two American railroads began commercial operation—the Charleston and Hamburg in South Carolina and the Baltimore and Ohio in Maryland. After these pioneer lines had shown that steam locomotion was practical and profitable, several other railroads were built and began to carry passengers and freight during the 1830s.

But canals proved to be strong competitors, especially for the freight business. By 1840 railroads had 2818 miles of track—a figure almost equal to the combined length of all canals—but the latter still carried a much larger volume of goods. Passengers might prefer the speed of trains, which reached astonishing velocities of twenty to thirty miles an hour, but the lower unit cost of freight on the canal boats prevented most shippers from changing their habits. Furthermore, states like New York and Pennsylvania that had invested heavily in canals resisted chartering a competitive form of transportation. Most of the early railroads reached out from port cities, like Boston and Baltimore, that did not have good canal routes to the interior. For them, steam locomotion provided a chance to cut into the enormous commerce that flowed along the Erie Canal and gave New York an advantage in the scramble for western trade.

During the 1840s rails extended beyond the northeastern and Middle Atlantic states, and mileage increased more than threefold, reaching a total of more than nine thousand miles by 1850. Expansion was even greater in the following decade when about twenty thousand miles of additional track were laid. By 1860 all the states east of the Mississippi had rail service, and a traveler could go by train from New York to Chicago and return by way of Memphis. Throughout the 1840s and '50s, railroads cut deeply into the freight business of the canals and succeeded in driving many of them out of business. The cost of hauling goods by rail decreased dramatically because of improved track construction and the introduction of powerful locomotives that could haul more cars. New York and Pennsylvania were slow to encourage rail transportation because of their early commitment to canals, but by the 1850s both states had accepted the inevitable and were promoting massive railroad building.

The development of railroads had an enormous effect on the economy as a whole. Although the burgeoning demand for iron rails was initially met mainly by importation from England, it eventually spurred development of the domestic iron industry. Since railroads required an enormous outlay of capital, their promoters pioneered new methods for financing business enterprise. At a time when most manufacturing and mercantile concerns were still owned by families or partnerships, the railroad companies sold stock to the general public and helped to set the pattern for the separation of ownership and control that characterizes the modern corporation. They also developed new types of securities, such as "preferred stock" with no voting rights but the assurance of a fixed rate of return and long-term bonds at a set rate of interest.

But the gathering and control of private capital did not fully meet the needs of the early railroad barons. State and local governments, convinced that railroads were the key to their future prosperity, loaned the railroads money, bought their stock, and guaranteed their bonds. Despite the dominant policy of laissez-faire, the federal government became involved by surveying the routes of projected lines and providing land

Railroad Mileage, ca. 1860

Area	Miles
New England	3,660
Middle Atlantic	6,353
Old Northwest	9,592
Southeast	5,463
Southwest	4,072
Far West	1,495
Total	30,636

Source: Adapted from George R. Taylor and Irene D. Neu, The American Railroad Network, 1861 to 1890 (1956; reprint ed., Salem, N.H.: Arno, 1981).

Railroads, 1850 and 1860

During the 1840s and '50s railroad lines moved rapidly westward. By 1860 more than thirty thousand miles of track had been laid.

grants. In 1850, for example, several million acres of public land were granted to the Illinois Central. In all, forty companies received such aid before 1860, and a precedent was set for the massive land grants of the post–Civil War era.

The Industrial Revolution Takes Off

While railroads were initiating a revolution in transportation, American industry was entering a new phase of rapid and sustained growth. The factory mode of production, which had originated before 1840 in the cotton mills of New England, was extended to a variety of other products. Woolen manufacturing was concentrated in single production units beginning in the 1830s, and by 1860 the largest textile mills in the country were producing wool cloth. In the coal and iron regions of eastern Pennsylvania, iron was being forged and rolled in factories by 1850. Among the other industries that adopted the factory system during this period were those producing shoes, firearms, clocks, and sewing machines.

The essential features of this mode of production were the gathering of a supervised work force in a single place, the payment of cash wages to workers, the use of interchangeable parts, and manufacture by "continuous process." Within a factory setting, standardized parts, manufactured separately and in bulk, could be efficiently and rapidly assembled into a final product by an ordered sequence of continuously repeated operations. Mass production, which involved the division of labor into a series of relatively simple and repetitive tasks, contrasted sharply with the traditional craft mode of production, in which a single worker produced the entire product out of raw materials. The transformation of a craft into a modern industry is well illustrated by the evolution of shoemaking. The independent cobbler producing shoes for order was first challenged by a putting-out system involving the assignment of various tasks to physically separated workers—and then virtually displaced by the great shoe factories that by the 1850s were operating in cities like Lynn, Massachusetts.

New technology played an important role in the transition to mass production. Just as power looms and spinning machinery had made textile mills possible, the development of new and more reliable machines or industrial techniques revolutionized other industries. Elias Howe's invention of the sewing machine in 1846 laid the basis for the ready-to-wear clothing industry and also contributed to the mechanization of shoemaking. During the 1840s, iron manufacturers adopted the British practice of using coal rather than charcoal for smelting and thus produced a metal better suited to industrial needs. Charles Goodyear's discovery of the process for the vulcanization of rubber in 1839 made a new range of manufactured items available to the American consumer, most notably the overshoe.

Perhaps the greatest triumph of American technology during the mid-nineteenth century was the development of the world's most sophisticated and reliable machine tools. Such advances as the invention of the extraordinarily accurate measuring device known as the *vernier caliper* in 1851 and the first production of turret lathes in 1854 were signs of a special American aptitude for the kind of precision toolmaking that was essential to efficient industrialization.

Progress in industrial technology and organization did not mean that the United States had become an industrial society by 1860. Agriculture retained first place both as a source of livelihood for individuals and as a contributor to the gross national product. Nearly 60 percent of the gainfully employed still worked on the land. But farming itself, at least in the North, was undergoing a technological revolution of its own. John Deere's steel plow, invented in 1837 and mass produced by the 1850s, enabled midwestern farmers to cultivate the tough prairie soils that had resisted cast iron implements. The mechanical reaper, patented by Cyrus McCormick in 1834, offered an enormous saving in the labor required for harvesting grain; by 1851 McCormick was producing more than a thousand reapers a year in his Chicago plant. Other new farm implements that came into widespread use before 1860 included seed drills, cultivators, and threshing machines.

A dynamic interaction between advances in transportation, industry, and agriculture gave great strength and resiliency to the economy of the northern states during the 1850s. Railroads

Young women who worked in factories like Thomson's Skirt Manufactory (left) used 100,000 feet of whalebone and 150,000 yards of muslin to produce 90,000 hoopskirts each month.

A technological revolution in farming followed the introduction of new farm implements like Cyrus McCormick's reaper (below). The reaper could cut six times as much grain per day as could a man using a scythe.

Using coal to fire the furnaces produced a more malleable, less brittle type of iron that could be used for a wide variety of industrial applications. A coal delivery at the Kensington Iron Works and Rolling Mills in Philadelphia in about 1845 (left) shows a water wheel in the center of the building being used to generate power for rolling the molten iron.

offered western farmers better access to eastern markets. After Chicago and New York were linked by rail in 1853, the flow of most midwestern farm commodities shifted from the North-South direction based on river-borne traffic that had still predominated in the 1830s and '40s, to an East-West pattern.

The mechanization of agriculture did more than lead to more efficient and profitable commercial farming; it also provided an additional impetus to industrialization, and its labor-saving features released manpower for other economic activities. The growth of industry and the modernization of agriculture can thus be seen as mutually reinforcing aspects of a single process of economic growth.

Mass Immigration Begins

The original incentive to mechanize northern industry and agriculture came in part from a shortage of cheap labor. Compared with the industrializing nations of Europe, the United States of the early nineteenth century was a labor-scarce economy. Since it was difficult to attract able-bodied men to work for low wages in factories or on farms, women and children were used extensively in the early textile mills, and commercial farmers had to rely heavily on the labor of their family members. In the face of such limited and uncertain labor supplies, producers were greatly tempted to experiment with labor-saving machinery. By the 1840s and '50s, however, industrialization had reached a point where it could readily absorb a new influx of unskilled workers. Factories required increasing numbers of unskilled operatives, and railroad builders needed construction gangs. The growth of industrial work opportunities helped attract a multitude of European immigrants during the two decades before the Civil War.

Between 1820 and 1840, an estimated 700,000 immigrants arrived in the United States, mainly from the British Isles and German-speaking areas of continental Europe. During the 1840s this substantial flow suddenly became a flood. No less than 4,200,000 crossed the Atlantic between 1840

Composition of Immigration, 1840–1860

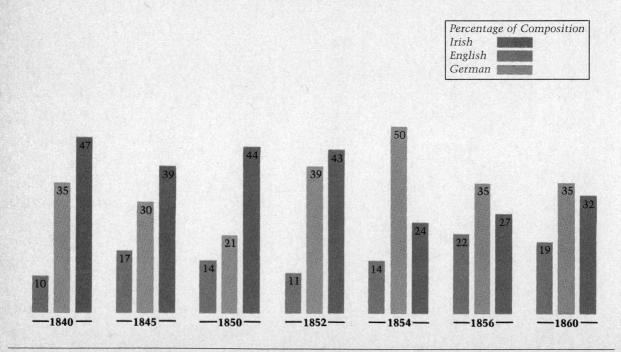

Percentage of Composition
Irish
English
German

Source: U.S. Bureau of the Census, Historical Statistics of the United States, Colonial Times to 1970, Bicentennial Edition, Washington, D.C., 1975.

and 1860, and about 3 million of these arrived in the single decade between 1845 and 1855. This was the greatest influx in proportion to total population—then about 20 million—that the nation has ever experienced. The largest single source of the new mass immigration was Ireland, but Germany was not far behind. Smaller contingents came from Switzerland, Norway, Sweden, and the Netherlands.

This massive transatlantic movement had many causes; some people were "pushed" out of their homes, while others were "pulled" toward America. The great "push" factor that caused a million and a half Irish to forsake the Emerald Isle between 1845 and 1854 was the great potato famine. When a series of blights hit the potato crop—the principal source of subsistence for Irish peasants—the choice for many was emigration or starvation. Escape to America was made possible by the low fares then prevailing on sailing ships bound from England to North America. Ships involved in the timber trade carried their bulky cargoes from Boston or Halifax to Liverpool; as an alternative to returning to America partly in ballast, they packed Irish immigrants into their holds. The squalor and misery in these "steerage" accommodations were almost beyond belief.

Because of the ports involved in the lumber trade—Boston, Halifax, Saint John's, and Saint Andrews—the Irish usually arrived in Canada or the northeastern states. Immobilized by poverty and a lack of the skills required for pioneering in the West, most of them remained in the northeast. By the 1850s, they constituted a substantial portion of the total population of Boston, New York, Philadelphia, and many smaller cities of the New England and Middle Atlantic states. Forced to subsist on low-paid menial labor and crowded into festering urban slums, they were looked down upon by most native-born Americans. Their devotion to Catholicism aroused Protestant resentment and mob violence, and employers sometimes showed their anti-Irish sentiment by advertising jobs for which "No Irish Need Apply." (See chapter 14 for a discussion of the growth of nativism and anti-Catholicism.)

The million or so Germans who also came in the late 1840s and early '50s were somewhat

Immigration to the United States, 1820–1860

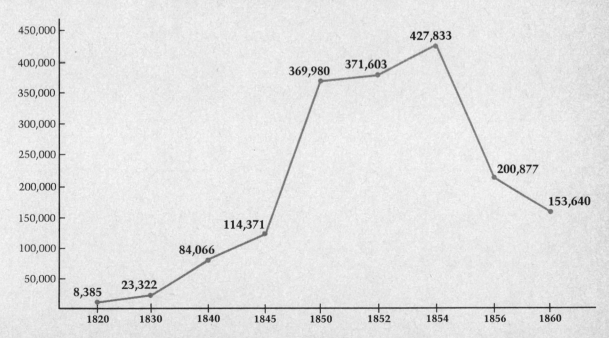

Source: U.S. Bureau of the Census, Historical Statistics of the United States, Colonial Times to 1970, Bicentennial Edition, Washington, D.C., 1975.

(a) Baron Biesele, upon his arrival in America (in German): "Hey, fellow countryman, where can we find a German tavern?"
Countryman (in German): "Damme. Do you think I'm a no-good like you? I am an American."

(b) Baron Biesele, first week after arrival (in German to another recently arrived German): "Well, Marianel, how do you like it in America?"
Marianel (in German): "Oh, Baron, the language, the language. I'll never learn it in all my life."

(c) Baron Biesele, two weeks after arrival (in German): "Can you tell us—Hey, beautiful Marianel, isn't that you?"
Marianel (in English): "You are mistaken. I don't talk Dutch."

■ *These lithographs from the* Fliegende Blatter *(Cincinnati, 1847) feature the antics of Baron Biesele, a popular cartoon character in the German prototype of this short-lived Cincinnati periodical of the same name.*

more fortunate. Most of them were also peasants, but they fled hard times rather than outright catastrophe. Changes in German landholding patterns and the rise of a fluctuating market economy put pressure on small operators. Those whose mortgages were foreclosed—or who could no longer make the regular payments to landlords that were the price of emancipation from feudal obligations—frequently opted for immigration to America. Unlike the Irish, they often escaped with a small amount of capital with which to make a fresh start in the New World.

Many German immigrants were artisans and sought to ply their trades in cities like New York, St. Louis, Cincinnati and Milwaukee—all of which became centers of German-American population. But a large portion of those with peasant backgrounds went back to the land. The possession of diversified agricultural skills and small amounts of capital enabled many Germans to become successful midwestern farmers. In general, they encountered less prejudice and discrimination than the Irish. For those who were Protes-

tant, religious affinity with their American neighbors made for relative tolerance. But even Germans who were Catholic normally escaped the virulent scorn heaped upon the Irish, perhaps because they did not carry the added burden of being members of an ethnic group Americans had learned to despise from their English ancestors and cousins.

What attracted or "pulled" most of the Irish, German, and other European immigrants to America was the promise of economic opportunity. A minority, like some of the German revolutionaries of 1848, chose the United States because they admired its democratic political system. But most immigrants were more interested in the chance to make a decent living than in voting or running for office. The force of the economic motive can be seen in the fact that peak periods of immigration—1845 to 1855 is a prime example—coincided very closely with times of domestic prosperity and high demand for labor. During depression periods, such as 1839 to 1842 and 1857 to 1859, immigration dropped off significantly.

The New Working Class

A majority of the immigrants ended up as wage workers in factories, mines, and construction camps, or as casual day laborers doing the many unskilled tasks required by urban and commercial growth. By providing a vast pool of cheap labor, they fueled and accelerated the Industrial Revolution. During the 1850s factory production in Boston and other port cities previously devoted to commerce grew—mainly because thousands of recent Irish immigrants were willing to work for the kind of low wages that almost guaranteed large profits for entrepreneurs.

In the established industries and older mill towns of the Northeast, immigrants gradually displaced the native-born workers who had predominated in the 1830s and '40s. The changing work force of the textile mills in Lowell, Massachusetts, provided a striking example of this process. In 1836 only 3.7 percent of the workers in one Lowell mill were foreign-born; most members of the labor force at that time were young, unmarried women from New England farms. By 1860 immigrants constituted 61.7 percent of the work force. A related development was a great increase in the number of men who tended machines in textile and other factories. Irish males, employers found, were willing to perform tasks that native-born men had generally regarded as women's work.

This trend reveals much about the changing character of the American working class. In the 1830s most male workers were artisans, while unskilled factory work was still largely the province of women and children. Both groups were predominantly of American stock. In the 1840s the proportion of men engaged in factory work increased, although the work force in the textile industry remained predominantly female. During that decade work conditions in many mills deteriorated. Workdays of twelve to fourteen hours were not new, but the paternalism that had earlier evoked a spirit of cooperation from workers was replaced by a more impersonal and cost-conscious form of management. During the depression that followed the panic of 1837, the bosses attempted to reduce expenses and increase productivity by cutting wages, increasing the speed of machinery, and "stretching out"—giving each worker more machinery to operate.

■ A strictly regimented work week of eleven-hour days, six days a week, left the women workers at the Lowell textile mills little free time of their own.

The result was a new upsurge of labor militancy involving female as well as male factory workers. Mill girls in Lowell, for example, formed a union of their own—the Female Labor Reform Association—and engaged in an unsuccessful strike action. On a broader front, workers' organizations petitioned state legislatures to pass laws limiting the workday to ten hours. Some such laws were actually passed, but they turned out to be ineffective because employers could still require a prospective worker to sign a special contract agreeing to longer hours.

The employment of immigrants in increasing numbers between the mid-1840s and the late '50s made it more difficult to organize industrial workers. Impoverished fugitives from the Irish potato famine tended to have lower economic expectations and more conservative social attitudes than native-born workers. Consequently the Irish immigrants were willing to work for less and were not so prone to protest bad working conditions. Most industrial laborers remained unorganized and resisted appeals for solidarity along class lines.

But the new working class of former rural folk did not make the transition to industrial wage labor easily or without protesting in subtle and indirect ways. Tardiness, absenteeism, drunkenness, loafing on the job, and other forms of resistance to factory discipline reflected deep hostility to the unaccustomed and seemingly unnatural routines of "continuous-process" production. The adjustment to new styles and rhythms of work was painful and took time. Historians are only now beginning to examine the inner world of the early generations of industrial workers, and they are finding evidence of discontent rather than docility, cultural resistance rather than easy adaptation.

By 1860 industrial expansion and immigration had created a working class of men and women who seemed destined for a life of low-paid wage labor. This reality stood in contrast to America's self-image as a land of opportunity and upward mobility. Wage labor was popularly viewed as a temporary condition from which workers were supposed to extricate themselves by hard work and frugality. According to Abraham Lincoln, speaking in 1850 of the North's "free labor" society, "there is no such thing as a freeman being fatally fixed for life, in the condition of a hired laborer." This ideal still had some validity in rapidly developing regions of the western states, but it was mostly myth when applied to the increasingly foreign-born industrial workers of the Northeast.

Both internal and external expansion had come at a heavy cost. Tensions associated with class and ethnic rivalries were only one part of the price of rapid economic development. The acquisition of new territories would soon lead to a catastrophic sectional controversy. From the late 1840s to the Civil War, the United States was a divided society in more sense than one, and the need to control or resolve these conflicts presented politicians and statesmen with a monumental challenge.

Recommended Reading

The best overview of expansion to the Pacific is Ray A. Billington, *The Far Western Frontier, 1830–1860* (1956). The impulse behind Manifest Destiny has been variously interpreted. Albert K. Weinberg's classic *Manifest Destiny: A Study of National Expansionism in American History* (1935) describes and stresses the ideological rationale. Frederick Merk, *Manifest Destiny and Mission in American History* (1963), analyzes public opinion and shows how divided it was on the question of territorial acquisitions. Norman A. Graebner, *Empire on the Pacific: A Study in American Continental Expansionism* (1956), highlights the desire for Pacific harbors as a motive for adding new territory. The most complete and authoritative account of the diplomatic side of expansionism in this period is David M. Pletcher, *The Diplomacy of Annexation: Texas, Oregon, and the Mexican War* (1973). Charles G. Sellers, *James K. Polk: Continentalist, 1843–1846* (1966) is the definitive work on Polk's election and the expansionist policies of his administration. For a lively narrative of Manifest Destiny at its climax, see Bernard De Voto, *The Year of Decision, 1846* (1943). A good brief account of the main events of the Mexican War is Otis A. Singletary, *The Mexican War* (1960).

Economic developments of the 1840s and '50s are well covered in George R. Taylor, *The Transportation Revolution, 1815–1960* (1952) and Albert Fishlow, *American Railroads and the Transformation of the Ante-Bellum Economy* (1965). A good short introduction to immigration is Maldwyn Allen Jones, *American Immigration* (1960). Oscar Handlin, *Boston Immigrants: A Study in Acculturation*, rev. ed. (1959) is a classic study of immigration to one city. Still a standard work on the antebellum working class is Norman J. Ware, *The Industrial Worker, 1840–1860* (1924); for the new approach to labor history that emphasizes working-class culture, see Herbert G. Gutman, *Work, Culture, and Society in Industrializing America* (1976). A pathbreaking and insightful study of workers in the textile industry is Thomas Dublin, *Women at Work: The Transformation of Work and Community in Lowell, Massachusetts, 1826–1860* (1979).

Additional Bibliography

Other important works on American penetration and settlement of the Far West include William H. Goetzmann, *Exploration and Empire: The Explorer and the Scientist in the Winning of the American West* (1966); W. C. Binkley, *The Texas Revolution* (1952); John D. Unruh, Jr., *The Plains Across: The Overland Immigrants and the Trans-Mississippi West, 1840–1860* (1979); Thomas O'Dea, *The Mormons* (1957); Wallace Stegner, *The Gathering of Zion: The Story of the Mormon Trail* (1964); and R. W. Paul, *California Gold* (1947). The politics and diplomacy of expansionism are treated in two books by Frederick Merk: *Slavery and the Annexation of Texas* (1972) and *The Monroe Doctrine and American Expansion, 1843–1849* (1966). For further insight into the expansionist motives of the Tyler administration, see William J. Cooper, *The South and the Politics of Slavery, 1828–1856* (1978). On military aspects of the Mexican War, see K. Jack Bauer, *The Mexican War, 1846–1848* (1974). John H. Schroeder, *Mr. Polk's War: American Opposition and Dissent* (1973), treats the domestic controversy aroused by the conflict. The Mexican side of the struggle for the Southwest is well presented in David J. Weber, *The Mexican Frontier, 1821–1846: The American Southwest Under Mexico* (1982). The ideas associated with Manifest Destiny and "Young America" are further explored in Reginald Horsman, *Race and Manifest Destiny* (1981) and Perry Miller, *The Raven and the Whale* (1956).

Economic growth and technological development in the late antebellum period are covered in Douglass C. North, *The Economic Growth of the United States, 1790–1860* (1961); Thomas C. Cochran and William Miller, *The Age of Enterprise: A Social History of Industrial America* (1942); Robert W. Fogel, *Railroads and American Economic Growth* (1964); Stuart Bruchey, *The Roots of American Economic Growth, 1607–1861* (1965); Albert D. Chandler, Jr., *The Visible Hand: Managerial Revolution in American Business* (1977); Peter Temin, *Iron and Steel in Nineteenth Century America* (1964); and Merritt Roe Smith, *Harpers Ferry Armory and the New Technology* (1977). For further insight into immigration, see Marcus L. Hansen, *The Atlantic Migration, 1607–1860* (1940); Carl Wittke, *The Irish in America* (1956); Katherine Neils Conzen, *Immigrant Milwaukee, 1836–1860* (1976); Robert Ernst, *Immigrant Life in New York City, 1825–1863* (1949); and Philip Taylor, *The Distant Magnet: European Immigration to the United States of America* (1971). Important recent works that deal with the working-class experience include Alan Dawley, *Class and Community: The Industrial Revolution in Lynn* (1976) and Bruce Laurie, *Working People of Philadelphia, 1800–1850* (1980).

chapter 14

THE
SECTIONAL
CRISIS

On May 22, 1856, Representative Preston Brooks of South Carolina suddenly appeared on the floor of the Senate. With fire in his eyes and a cane in his hand he approached Charles Sumner, the antislavery senator from Massachusetts. Brooks was enraged because Sumner had recently given a fiery oration condemning the South for plotting to extend slavery to the Kansas Territory. What was worse, the speech had included insulting references to Senator Andrew Butler of South Carolina, a kinsman of Brooks. When he found Sumner seated at his desk, Brooks proceeded to batter him over the head. Amazed and stunned, Sumner made a desperate effort to rise and ripped his bolted desk from the floor. He then collapsed under a continued torrent of blows.

Sumner was so badly injured by the assault that he did not return to the Senate for three years. But his home state reelected him in 1857 and kept his seat vacant as testimony against southern brutality and "barbarism." In parts of the North that were up in arms against the expansion of slavery, Sumner was hailed as a martyr to the cause of "free soil." Brooks, denounced in the North as a bully, was lionized by his fellow Southerners. When he resigned from the House after a vote of

■ *After his constituents learned of Preston Brooks' caning of Senator Sumner, they sent Brooks a gold-handled cowhide whip to use on other antislavery advocates.*

censure had narrowly failed because of solid southern opposition, his constituents reelected him unanimously.

These contrasting reactions show how bitter sectional antagonism had become by 1856. Sumner spoke for the radical wing of the new Republican party, which was making a bid for national power by mobilizing the North against the alleged aggressions of "the slave power." Southerners viewed the very existence of this party as an insult to their section of the country and a threat to its vital interests. Sumner came closer to being an abolitionist than any other member of Congress, and nothing created greater fear and anxiety among Southerners than their belief that antislavery forces were plotting against their way of life. To many Northerners, "bully Brooks" stood for all the arrogant and violent slaveholders who were allegedly conspiring to extend their barbaric labor system. By 1856, therefore, the sectional cleavage that would lead to the Civil War was already corroding the foundations of national unity.

The crisis of the mid-1850s came only a few years after the elaborate compromise of 1850 had seemingly resolved the dispute over the future of slavery in the territories acquired as a result of the Mexican War. The renewed agitation over the extension of slavery that led to Brooks' attack on Sumner was set in motion by the Kansas-Nebraska Act of 1854. This legislation revived the sectional conflict and led to the emergence of the Republican party. From that point on, a dramatic series of events heightened the mood of sectional confrontation and destroyed the prospects for a new compromise. The caning of Charles Sumner was one of these events, and violence on the Senate floor foreshadowed violence on the battlefield.

The Compromise of 1850

Conflict over slavery in the territories first arose in the late 1840s. The positions taken on this issue between 1846 and 1850 established the range of options that would reemerge after 1854. But during this earlier phase of the sectional controversy, the leaders of two strong national parties, each with substantial followings in both the North and the South, had a vested interest in resolving the crisis. Efforts to create uncompromising sectional parties failed to disrupt what historians call the second party system—the vigorous competition between Whigs and Democrats that had characterized elections since the 1830s. Furthermore, the less tangible features of sectionalism—emotion and ideology—were not as divisive as they would later become. Hence a fragile compromise was achieved through a kind of give-and-take that would not be possible in the changed environment of the mid-1850s.

The Problem of Slavery in the Mexican Cession

As the price of union between states committed to slavery and those in the process of abolishing it, the Founders had attempted to exclude the slavery issue from national politics. The Constitution gave the federal government no definite authority to regulate or destroy the institution where it existed under state law. Although many of the Founders hoped for the eventual demise of slavery, they provided no means to achieve this end except voluntary state action. These ground rules limited the effect of northern attacks on the South's peculiar institution. It was easy to condemn slavery in principle but very difficult to develop a practical program to eliminate it without defying the Constitution.

Radical abolitionists saw this problem clearly and resolved it by rejecting the law of the land in favor of a "higher law" prohibiting human bondage. In 1844 William Lloyd Garrison publicly burned the Constitution, condemning it as "A COVENANT WITH DEATH, AN AGREEMENT WITH HELL." But Garrison spoke for a small minority dedicated to freeing the North, at whatever cost, from the sin of condoning slavery.

During the 1840s the majority of Northerners showed that while they disliked slavery, they also detested abolitionism. They were inclined to view slavery as a backward and unwholesome institution, much inferior to their own free labor system, and could be persuaded that slaveholders were power-hungry aristocrats seeking more than their share of national political influence. But they regarded the Constitution as a binding contract between slave and free states and were likely to be prejudiced against blacks and reluctant to accept large numbers of them as free citizens. Consequently, they saw no legal or desirable way to bring about emancipation within the southern states.

But the Constitution had not predetermined the status of slavery in *future* states. Since Congress had the power to admit new states to the Union under any conditions it wished to impose, a majority could require the abolition of slavery as the price of admission. An effort to use this power had led to the Missouri crisis of 1819–1820 (see chapter 9). The resulting compromise was designed to decide future cases and maintain a rough parity between slave and free states by drawing a line between them and extending it westward through the unsettled portions of what was then American soil. When specific territories were settled, organized, and prepared for statehood, slavery would be permitted south of the line and prohibited north of it. This policy followed the earlier precedent of the Northwest Ordinance of 1787, which had banned slavery in territories north of the Ohio river, thus allowing it to expand into the regions that became the cotton kingdom of the nineteenth century.

This tradition of providing both the free North and the slave South with opportunities for expansion and the creation of new states broke down when new territories were wrested from Mexico in the 1840s. When Texas was admitted as a slave state, northern expansionists could still look forward to the admission of Oregon as a counterbalancing free state. But the Mexican War raised the prospect that California and New Mexico would also be acquired. Since it was generally assumed in the North that Congress had the power to prohibit slavery in new territories, a movement developed in Congress to do just that.

The Wilmot Proviso Launches the Free-Soil Movement

The "free-soil" crusade began in August 1846, only three months after the start of the Mexican War, when Congressman David Wilmot, a Pennsylvania Democrat, proposed an amendment to the military appropriations bill that would ban slavery in any territory that might be acquired from Mexico.

Wilmot spoke for the large number of northern Democrats who felt neglected and betrayed by the policies of the Polk administration. Pennsylvanians like Wilmot were upset because the tariff of 1846 reduced duties to a level unacceptable to the manufacturing interests of their state. Others, especially midwesterners, were annoyed that Polk had vetoed a bill to provide federal funds for the improvement of rivers and harbors. Democratic expansionists also felt betrayed because Polk had gone back on his pledge to obtain "all of Oregon" up to 54°40' and then had proceeded to wage war to win all of Texas. This twist in the course of Manifest Destiny convinced them that the South and its interests were dominating the party and the administration. David Wilmot expressed these feelings when he wrote that "I am jealous of the power of the South."

Nevertheless, these pioneer free-soilers had a genuine interest in the issue actually at hand—the question of who would control and settle the new territories. Combining an appeal to racial prejudice with opposition to slavery as an institution, Wilmot defined his cause as involving the "rights of white freemen" to go to areas where they could live "without the disgrace which association with negro slavery brings on white labor." In other words, give the common folk of the North a fair chance by excluding unfair competition with slavery and blacks from territory obtained in the Mexican cession. By linking racism with resistance to the spread of slavery, Wilmot appealed to a broad spectrum of northern opinion.

Northern Whigs backed Wilmot's Proviso because they shared his concern about the outcome of an unregulated competition between slave and free labor in the territories. Furthermore, voting for the measure provided a good outlet for their frustration at being unable to halt the annexation of Texas and the Mexican War. The preferred position of some Whig leaders was no expansion at all, but when expansion seemed inevitable the northern wing of the party endorsed the view that acquisition of Mexican territory should not be used to increase the power of the slave states.

In the first House vote on the Wilmot Proviso, party lines crumbled and were replaced by a sharp sectional cleavage. Every northern congressman with the exception of two Democrats voted for it, and every Southerner except two Whigs went on record against it. After passing the House, the Proviso was blocked in the Senate by a combination of southern influence and Democratic loyalty to the administration. When the appropriation bill went back to the House without the Proviso, the adminstration's arm-twisting succeeded in changing enough northern Democratic votes to send the Proviso down to defeat.

Reactions to the Proviso on the state and local level provided further evidence of the polarizing effect of the territorial issue. Northern state legislatures, with one exception, endorsed the Proviso, while southern orators proclaimed that its passage would insult their section and violate the principle of equality among the states by denying slaveholding citizens access to federal territories.

The end of the Mexican War, the formal acquisition of New Mexico and California, and the approaching election of 1848 gave new urgency to a search for politically feasible solutions to the crisis. The extreme alternatives—the Proviso policy of "free soil" and the radical southern response that slavery could be extended to any territory—threatened to destroy the national parties because there was no bisectional support for either of them.

Popular Sovereignty and the Election of 1848

After a futile attempt was made to extend the Missouri Compromise line to the Pacific—a proposal that was unacceptable to Northerners because most of the Mexican cession lay south of the line—a new approach was devised that appealed especially to Democrats. Its main proponent was Senator Lewis Cass of Michigan, an aspirant for the party's presidential nomination. Cass, who described his formula as "squatter sovereignty," would leave the determination of the status of slavery in a territory to the actual settlers. From the beginning this proposal contained an ambiguity that allowed it to be interpreted differently in the North and the South. For northern Democrats squatter sovereignty—or "popular sovereignty" as it was later called—meant that the settlers could vote slavery up or

■ *In this cartoon, Democrats Lewis Cass and John C. Calhoun and abolitionist Whigs Horace Greeley, William Lloyd Garrison, and Abby Folsom look on as Martin Van Buren, the Free-Soil party candidate in the election of 1848, attempts to bridge the chasm between the Democratic platform and that of the antislavery Whigs. The Free-Soil influence was decisive in the election; it split the Democratic vote, thus allowing Whig candidate Zachary Taylor to win the presidency.*

down at the first meeting of a territorial legislature. For the southern wing of the party, it meant that a decision would only be made at the time a convention drew up a constitution and applied for statehood. It was in the interest of national Democratic leaders to leave this ambiguity unresolved for as long as possible.

Congress failed to resolve the future of slavery in the Mexican cession in time for the election of 1848, and the issue entered the arena of presidential politics. The Democrats nominated Cass on a platform of squatter sovereignty. The Whigs evaded the question by running General Zachary Taylor—the hero of the battle of Buena Vista—without a platform. Taylor refused to commit himself on the status of slavery in the territories, but northern Whigs favoring restriction took heart from the general's promise not to veto any territorial legislation passed by Congress. Southern Whigs went along with Taylor mainly because he was a Southerner who owned slaves and would presumably defend the interests of his native region.

Northerners who strongly supported the Wilmot Proviso—and felt betrayed that neither the Whigs nor the Democrats were supporting it—were attracted by a third party movement. In August a tumultuous convention in Buffalo nominated former President Van Buren to carry the banner of the Free-Soil party. Support for the Free-Soilers came from antislavery Whigs dis-

mayed by their party's nomination of a slaveholder and its evasiveness on the territorial issue, disgruntled Democrats who had backed the Proviso and resented southern influence in their party, and some of the former adherents of the abolitionist Liberty party. Van Buren himself was motivated less by antislavery zeal than by bitterness at being denied the Democratic nomination in 1844 because of southern obstructionism. The

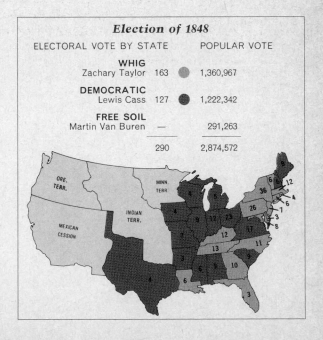

Election of 1848		
ELECTORAL VOTE BY STATE		POPULAR VOTE
WHIG Zachary Taylor	163	1,360,967
DEMOCRATIC Lewis Cass	127	1,222,342
FREE SOIL Martin Van Buren	—	291,263
	290	2,874,572

founding of the Free-Soil party was the first significant effort to create a broadly based sectional party addressing itself to voters' concerns about the extension of slavery.

After a noisy and confusing campaign, Taylor came out on top, winning a majority of the electoral votes in both the North and the South and a total of 1,361,000 popular votes to 1,222,000 for Cass and 291,000 for Van Buren. The Free-Soilers failed to carry a single state but were strong enough to run second behind Taylor in New York, Massachusetts, and Vermont.

Taylor Takes Charge

Once in office, Taylor devised a bold plan to decide the fate of slavery in the Mexican cession. A brusque military man who disdained political give-and-take, he tried to engineer the immediate admission of California and New Mexico to the Union as states, thus bypassing the territorial stage entirely and eliminating the whole question of the status of slavery in the federal domain. This proposal made practical sense in regard to California which was filling up rapidly with settlers drawn there by the lust for gold. Under the administration's urging, Californians convened a constitutional convention and applied for admission to the Union as a free state. In New Mexico, where American settlers were few and vastly outnumbered by conquered Mexicans, it proved impossible to get a statehood movement off the ground.

Instead of resolving the crisis, President Taylor's initiative only worsened it. Once it was clear that California was going to be a free state, the administration's plan aroused intense opposition in the South. Fearing that New Mexico would also be free because Mexican law had prohibited slavery there, Southerners of both parties accused the President of trying to impose the Wilmot Proviso in a new form. The prospect that only free states would emerge from the entire Mexican cession inspired serious talk of secession.

In Congress, Senator John C. Calhoun of South Carolina saw a chance to achieve his long-standing goal of creating a southern voting bloc that would cut across regular party lines. State legislatures and conventions throughtout the South denounced "northern aggression" against the rights of the slave states. As signs of southern fury increased, Calhoun rejoiced that the South had never been so "united . . . bold, and decided." In the fall and winter of 1849–1850 several southern states agreed to participate in a convention, to be held in Nashville in June, where grievances could be aired and demands made. For an increasing number of southern political leaders the survival of the Union would depend on the North's response to the demands of the southern rights movement.

Forging a Compromise

When it became clear that the President would not abandon or modify his plan in order to appease the South, independent efforts began in Congress to arrange a compromise. Hoping that he could again play the role of "great pacificator" as he had in the Missouri Compromise of 1820, Senator Henry Clay of Kentucky offered a series of resolutions meant to restore sectional harmony. He hoped to reduce tension by providing mutual concessions on a range of divisive issues. On the critical territorial question, his solution was to admit California as a free state and organize the rest of the Mexican cession with no explicit prohibition of slavery—in other words, without the Wilmot Proviso. Pointing to the arid climate of the New Mexico region, which made it unsuitable for cotton culture and slavery, Clay told Northerners, "You have got nature itself on your side." He also sought to resolve a major boundary dispute between New Mexico and Texas by granting the disputed region to New Mexico while compensating Texas through federal assumption of its state debt. As a concession to the North on another issue—the existence of slavery in the District of Columbia—he recommended prohibiting the buying and selling of slaves in the nation's capital. He called for more vigorous enforcement of the fugitive slave law.

The compromise plan, which was proposed in February 1850, took several months to get through Congress. One obstacle was President Taylor's firm resistance to the proposal; another was the difficulty of getting congressmen to vote for it in the form of a single package or "omnibus bill." Few politicians were willing to go on record as supporting the key concessions to the *other*

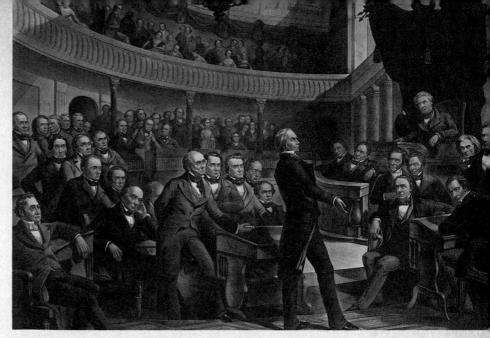

■ *In the Senate chamber, its balconies overflowing with spectators, Henry Clay pleads for passage of the Compromise of 1850. John C. Calhoun (standing third from right) was by this time mortally ill; his speech denouncing the compromise was read by Senator James Mason of Virginia. Daniel Webster (seated at left with his head resting on his hand), himself ailing, argued in favor of the compromise plan.*

section. The logjam was broken in July. President Taylor died and was succeeded by Millard Fillmore, who favored the compromise. Also, a decision was made to abandon the omnibus strategy in favor of a series of measures that could be voted on separately. After the breakup of the omnibus bill, Democrats replaced the original Whig sponsors as leaders of the compromise movement. Senator Stephen A. Douglas, a Democrat from Illinois, was particularly influential in maneuvering the separate provisions of the plan through Congress.

As finally approved, the Compromise of 1850 differed somewhat from Clay's original proposals. As the price of Democratic support, the popular sovereignty principle was included in the bills organizing New Mexico and Utah. Territorial legislatures in the Mexican cession were explicitly granted power over "all rightful subjects of legislation," which were presumed to include slavery. Half of the compensation to Texas for giving up its claims to New Mexico was paid directly to holders of Texas bonds, a decision that reflected intense lobbying by interested parties.

Abolition of the slave trade in the District of Columbia and a new fugitive slave law were also enacted. The latter was a particularly outrageous piece of legislation. As the result of southern pressures and amendments, suspected fugitives were now denied a jury trial, the right to testify in their own behalf, and other minimal constitutional rights. As a result, there were no effective safeguards against false identification and the kidnaping of blacks who were legally free.

The compromise passed because its key measures were supported by both northern Democrats and southern Whigs. No single bill was backed by a majority of the congressmen from both sections, and few senators or representatives actually voted for the entire package. Many northern Whigs and southern Democrats thought the end result conceded too much to the other section. Doubts therefore persisted over the value or workability of a "compromise" that was really more like an armistice or a cease-fire.

Yet the Compromise of 1850 did serve for a time as a basis for sectional peace. In southern state elections in 1850–1851 moderate coalitions won out over the radicals who viewed the compromise as a sellout to the North. But this emerging "unionism" was conditional. Southerners demanded strict northern adherence to the compromise, especially to the Fugitive Slave Law, as the price for keeping threats of secession suppressed. In the North, the compromise was backed by virtually the entire Democratic party and by one faction of the Whigs. Despite the unpopularity of the Fugitive Slave Law in some areas, it was generally well enforced during the early 1850s. By 1852, when the Democrats endorsed the compromise in their platform and the Whigs acceded to it in theirs, it appeared that sharp differences on the slavery issue had once again been banished from national politics.

Resistance to the Fugitive Slave Law

The Fugitive Slave Law of 1850 required that the full authority of the federal government be placed at the service of slaveowners seeking the return of any of their slaves who had escaped. Presidents Fillmore, Pierce, and Buchanan took this responsibility seriously as did the federal courts charged with enforcing the law. (The men with rifles shown above are federal marshals.) Of the 191 escaped slaves claimed by their masters during the 1850s, more than 80 percent were actually returned.

But these figures are deceptive. The sometimes violent resistance that developed in parts of the North made enforcement of the law difficult and expensive. In a minority of the cases, white and black abolitionists attempted forcible rescues of slaves in custody. In a few spectacular instances they succeeded. But even when they failed, they caused the slave catchers enough trouble and expense to discourage further efforts to extradite fugitives in areas where antislavery sentiment was strong. In all of New England only four claims were made for the return of fugitives during the 1850s, and none after 1854—when one case brought Boston to the verge of a popular insurrection against federal authority.

In 1854 northern state legislatures began to pass "personal liberty laws" barring the use of state law enforcement officers and facilities for the apprehension and return of fugitives. This legislation added to the difficulty of applying the law. Southerners grew increasingly angry at the combination of violent resistance and legal obstruction that seemed to be nullifying a part of the Compromise of 1850 to which they attached particular importance. The claim that the South's constitutional right to have its fugitives returned was being grossly violated was one of the main grievances that fed the secession movement.

Actual rescues of captured fugitives, although few in number, provided dramatic evidence that at least some Northerners were ready to risk life and limb in the cause of black freedom. In 1851 the first such rescue occurred when a group of free blacks broke into a Boston courtroom and spirited away a fugitive named Shadrack. Eight men were indicted for helping in the escape—four blacks and four white abolitionists. None were convicted. Later the same year, a slaveholder from Maryland tried with the help of federal marshals to recapture a fugitive living in Christiana, Pennsylvania. A group of blacks fought back, assisted by a number of local white Quakers. In the ensuing riot the slaveholder was shot and killed. Once again, efforts to prosecute the resisters under federal law failed to win a single conviction.

A third famous rescue in 1851 occurred in Syracuse, New York. Abolitionists were gathering for a Liberty party convention when word was received that an accused runaway known as Jerry was being held in a local jail. A crown of free blacks and white abolitionists assembled outside the police station to demand Jerry's release. As the mob was dispersing, a group of the protesters, acting on a plan conceived earlier in the day, succeeded in entering the police station, releasing Jerry, and whisking him to a waiting carriage. Only one of the several perpetrators brought to trial was actually convicted.

Similar actions succeeded in restoring fugitives to liberty in Racine, Wisconsin (1854), Mechanicsburg, Ohio (1857), and Wellington, Ohio (1858). Attempts to prosecute one of the leaders in the Racine rescue led to a serious confrontation between state courts arguing that the Fugitive State Act was unconstitutional and federal courts upholding the law. In the Mechanicsburg incident, state and federal authorities again clashed. Local officials arrested and indicted United States marshals trying to enforce the Fugitive Slave Law and in turn were arrested and charged by federal authorities.

Successful rescues probably did less to stiffen northern opposition to the Fugitive Slave Law than attempts that failed. Two unsuccessful ventures occurred in Boston, the hub of abolitionism,

and they aroused intense anger and frustration among the increasing number of Northerners who saw the forcible return of fugitives as a sign that the "slave power" was threatening northern liberties.

In 1851 a black named Thomas Sims was brought before a United States commissioner on the charge that he had escaped from slavery in Georgia. Abolitionists held public rallies in his defense, packed the courtroom and the square outside, and planned to rescue him—by force if necessary. But after the commissioner decided against Sims' claim to freedom, three hundred armed men marched him to a waiting ship before the abolitionists could devise a plan of action. (The broadside displayed after that incident is shown below.)

In 1854 the victim was Anthony Burns, claimed by a Virginia slaveholder. This time the abolitionists were ready; they used a huge public meeting in order to launch a rescue attempt before Burns' hearing could take place. The plan was to announce at the meeting that a mob of blacks was attacking the courthouse. It was expected that the entire audience would then rush to the courthouse and gain Burns' release through sheer force of numbers. The result was a scene that recalled Boston on the eve of the American Revolution. A huge mob stormed the locked courthouse, breaking windows and battering doors. Eventually one door gave way, and several armed abolitionists rushed in. In the fighting that followed, one of the men guarding Burns was killed but the fugitive himself could not be reached. The mayor then called out a company of artillery to protect the courthouse. Faced with cannons, the mob dispersed.

During Burns' actual hearing, thousands gathered in Court Square but were intimidated by the troops massed in front of the courthouse. When Burns was finally declared a fugitive and taken from the courthouse, United States artillery and infantry units cleared Court Square, then lined the streets leading to the wharf. A mob estimated at twenty thousand gathered to hiss and groan. Burns was returned to bondage, but at a heavy price to defenders of slavery. Abolitionism became even more popular in Boston, and no further attempts were made to enforce the Fugitive Slave Law in New England.

CAUTION!!
COLORED PEOPLE
OF BOSTON, ONE & ALL,
You are hereby respectfully CAUTIONED and advised, to avoid conversing with the
Watchmen and Police Officers of Boston,
For since the recent ORDER OF THE MAYOR & ALDERMEN, they are empowered to act as
KIDNAPPERS
AND
Slave Catchers,
And they have already been actually employed in KIDNAPPING, CATCHING, AND KEEPING SLAVES. Therefore, if you value your LIBERTY, and the *Welfare of the Fugitives* among you, *Shun* them in every possible manner, as so many *HOUNDS* on the track of the most unfortunate of your race.

Keep a Sharp Look Out for KIDNAPPERS, and have TOP EYE open.
APRIL 24, 1851.

THEODORE PARKER'S PLACARD

Placard written by Theodore Parker and printed and posted by the Vigilance Committee of Boston after the rendition of Thomas Sims to slavery in April, 1851.

Political Upheaval, 1852–1856

The second party system—Democrats versus Whigs—survived the crisis over slavery in the Mexican cession, but in the long run the Compromise of 1850 may have weakened it. Although both national parties had been careful during the 1840s not to take stands on the slavery issue that would alienate their supporters in either section of the country, they had in fact offered voters alternative ways of dealing with the question. Democrats had endorsed headlong territorial expansion with the promise of a fair division of the spoils between slave and free states. Whigs had generally opposed annexations or acquisitions that were likely to bring the slavery question to the fore and threaten sectional harmony. With some shifts of emphasis and interpretation, each strategy could be presented to southern voters as a good way to protect slavery and to Northerners as a good way to contain it.

The consensus of 1852 meant that the parties had to find other issues on which to base their distinctive appeals. Their failure to do so encouraged voter apathy and a disenchantment with the major parties. When the Democrats sought to revive the Manifest Destiny issue in 1854, they inadvertently reopened the explosive issue of slavery in the territories. By this time, the Whigs were too weak and divided to respond with a policy of their own, and a purely sectional free-soil party—the Republicans—gained prominence. The collapse of the second party system released sectional agitation from the earlier constraints imposed by the competition of strong national parties.

The Party System in Crisis

The presidential campaign of 1852 was singularly devoid of major issues. With the slavery question ignored, some Whigs tried to revive interest in the nationalistic economic policies that were the traditional hallmarks of their party. But convincing arguments in favor of a protective tariff, a national bank, and internal improvements were hard to make in a period of sustained prosperity. Business was thriving under the Democratic program of laissez-faire.

Another tempting issue was immigration. Many Whigs were upset by the massive influx from Europe, partly because most of the new

■ *Davenport, Iowa, was a thriving center of trade in 1856, enjoying a busy riverboat and rail traffic. Logs shipped down the Mississippi were sawn into lumber in the city's sawmills, then the lumber was shipped by rail to the frontier. Grain, hogs, and cattle were also shipped out of Davenport.*

arrivals were Catholics, and the Whig following was largely evangelical Protestant. For office-seeking Whig politicians a more urgent problem was the fact that immigrants voted overwhelmingly for their Democratic opponents. The Whig leadership was divided on whether to compete with the Democrats for the immigrant vote or respond to the prejudices of the party rank and file by calling for restrictions on immigrant voting rights.

The Whigs nominated General Winfield Scott of Mexican War fame who supported the faction that resisted nativism and sought to broaden the appeal of the party. The fact that Scott's daughters were being raised as Catholics was publicized to demonstrate his good intentions toward immigrant communities. This strategy backfired and contributed to disaster at the polls. For the most part, Catholic immigrants retained their Democratic allegiance, and some nativist Whigs apparently sat out the election to protest their party's disregard of their cultural prejudice.

But the main cause for Scott's crushing defeat was the support he lost in the South when he allied himself with the northern antislavery wing of the party, led by Senator William Seward of New York. The Democratic candidate, Franklin Pierce of New Hampshire, was a colorless nonentity compared to his rival, but he swept the Deep South by enormous majorities and edged out Scott in most of the free states. In the most one-sided election since 1820, Pierce received 254 electoral votes from 27 states while Scott carried only 4 states with 42 electoral votes. The outcome revealed that the Whig party was in deep trouble because it lacked a program that would distinguish it from the Democrats and would appeal to voters in both sections of the country.

Despite their overwhelming victory in 1852, the Democrats also had reasons for anxiety about the loyalty of their supporters. Because the major parties had ceased to offer clear-cut alternatives to the electorate, voter apathy or alienation was a growing trend in the early '50s. The Democrats won majorities in both North and South in 1852 primarily because the public viewed them as the most reliable supporters of the Compromise of 1850. Most of the northern Democrats who had bolted to the Free-Soil party in 1848 returned to the fold, but any future tilt toward the South would inevitably result in new desertions.

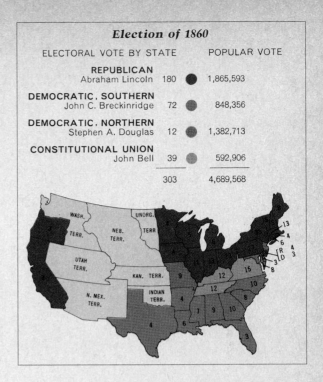

Election of 1860

ELECTORAL VOTE BY STATE		POPULAR VOTE
REPUBLICAN Abraham Lincoln	180	1,865,593
DEMOCRATIC, SOUTHERN John C. Breckinridge	72	848,356
DEMOCRATIC, NORTHERN Stephen A. Douglas	12	1,382,713
CONSTITUTIONAL UNION John Bell	39	592,906
	303	4,689,568

The Kansas-Nebraska Act Raises a Storm

In January 1854, Senator Stephen A. Douglas proposed a bill to organize the territory west of Missouri and Iowa. Since this region fell within the area where slavery had been banned by the Missouri Compromise, Douglas anticipated objections from Southerners concerned about the creation of more free states. To head off this opposition and keep the Democratic party united, Douglas disregarded the compromise line and sought to set up territorial government in Kansas and Nebraska on the basis of popular sovereignty, relying on the precedent set in the Compromise of 1850.

Douglas wanted to organize the Kansas-Nebraska area quickly because he was a strong supporter of the expansion of settlement and commerce. Along with other midwestern promoters of the economic development of the frontier, he hoped that a railroad would soon be built to the Pacific with Chicago (or another midwestern city) as its eastern terminus. Since the railroad would have to pass through the territory in question, a long controversy over the status of slavery there would slow down the process of organization and settlement. As a leader of the Democratic party, Douglas also hoped that his Kansas-Nebraska bill would revive the spirit of Manifest Destiny which had given the party cohesion and electoral success in the mid-1840s (see chapter 13). As the main spokesman for a new expansionism, he expected to win the Democratic nomination and the presidency.

The price of southern support, Douglas soon discovered, was the addition of an amendment explicitly repealing the Missouri Compromise. Although he realized that this would "raise a hell of a storm," he reluctantly agreed. In this more provocative form, the bill made its way through Congress, passing the Senate by a large margin and the House by a narrow one. The vote in the House showed that Douglas had split his party rather than uniting it; exactly half of the northern Democrats voted against the legislation.

The Democrats who broke ranks were responding to the storm Douglas had predicted but underestimated. A manifesto of "independent Democrats" denounced the bill as "a gross violation of a sacred pledge." A memorial from three thousand New England ministers described it as a craven and sinful surrender to the slave power. For many Northerners, probably a majority, the Kansas-Nebraska Act was an abomination because it appeared to permit slavery in an area where it had previously been prohibited. Southerners had not proposed the act or even shown much interest in it; now they felt obligated to support it. They gave deadly ammunition to those who were seeking to convince the northern public that there was a conspiracy to extend slavery.

Douglas' bill had a catastrophic effect on the prospects for sectional harmony. It repudiated a compromise that many in the North regarded as a binding sectional compact, almost as sacred and necessary to the survival of the Union as the Constitution itself. In defiance of the whole compromise tradition, it made a concession to the South on the issue of slavery extension without providing an equivalent concession to the North. It also shattered the fragile sectional accommodation of 1850 and made future compromises less

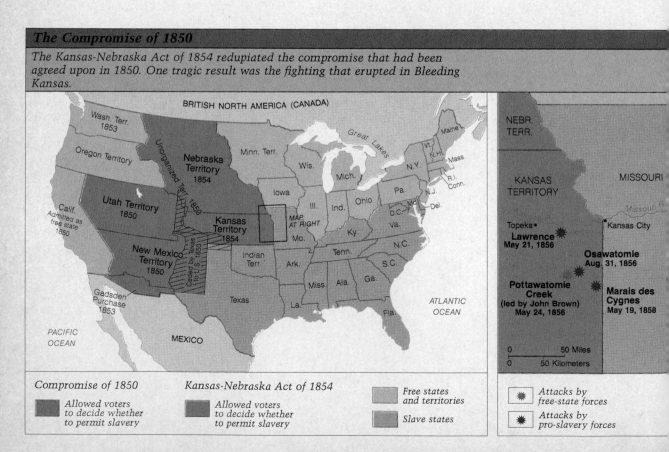

The Compromise of 1850

The Kansas-Nebraska Act of 1854 redupiated the compromise that had been agreed upon in 1850. One tragic result was the fighting that erupted in Bleeding Kansas.

likely. From now on, northern sectionalists would be fighting to regain what they had lost, while Southerners would battle to maintain rights already conceded.

The act also destroyed what was left of the second party system. The already weakened and tottering Whig party totally disintegrated when its congressional representation split cleanly along sectional lines on the Kansas-Nebraska issue. The Democratic party survived, but its ability to act as a unifying national force was seriously impaired. Northern desertions and southern gains (resulting from the recruitment of proslavery Whigs) combined to destroy the sectional balance within the party and place it under firm southern control.

The congressional elections of 1854 revealed the political chaos Douglas had created. In the North, "anti-Nebraska" coalitions of Whigs, dissident Democrats, and Free-Soilers swept regular Democrats out of office. Most congressmen who had voted for the act were decisively defeated, and sixty-six of the ninety-one House seats held by northern Democrats were lost to opponents running under various labels. In some states, these anti-Democratic coalitions would evolve directly into a new and stronger free-soil party— the Republicans. In the Deep South, however, the Democrats routed the remaining Whigs and came close to ending two-party competition on the state level.

The furor over Kansas-Nebraska also doomed the efforts of the Pierce administration to revive an expansionist foreign policy. Pierce and Secretary of State William Marcy were committed to acquiring Cuba from Spain. In October 1854, the American ministers to England, France, and Spain met in Ostend, Belgium, and drew up a memorandum for the administration urging acquisition of Cuba by any means necessary —including force, if Spain refused to sell the island. The "Ostend Manifesto" became public in the midst of the controversy resulting from the Kansas-Nebraska Act, and those Northerners who were convinced that the administration was trying to extend slavery to the Great Plains were enraged to discover that it was also scheming to fulfill the southern expansionist dream of a "Caribbean slave empire." The resulting storm of protest forced Pierce and his cohorts to abandon their scheme.

An Appeal to Nativism: The Know-Nothing Episode

The collapse of the Whigs created the opening for a new political party. The anti-Nebraska coalitions of 1854 suggested that such a party might be organized on the basis of northern opposition to the extension of slavery to the territories. Before such a prospect could be realized, however, an alternative emerged in the form of a major political movement based on hostility to immigrants. For a time, it appeared that the Whigs would be replaced by a nativist party rather than an antislavery one.

Massive immigration of Irish and Germans (see chapter 13), most of whom were Catholic, led to increasing tension between ethnic groups during the 1840s and early '50s. The fact that most of these new arrivals clustered in their own separate communities or neighborhoods helped arouse the suspicion and distrust of older-stock Americans. Native-born and even immigrant Protestants viewed the newcomers as bearers of an alien culture. Their fears were demonstrated in bloody anti-Catholic riots, church and convent burnings, and in a barrage of propaganda and lurid literature trumpeting the menace of "popery" to the American way of life. Nativist agitators charged that immigrants were agents of a foreign despotism, based in Rome, that was bent on overthrowing the American Republic.

Political nativism first emerged during the 1840s in the form of local "American" parties protesting immigrant influence in cities like New York and Philadelphia. In 1849 a secret fraternal organization, the Order of the Star-Spangled Banner, was founded in New York as a vehicle for anti-immigrant attitudes. When members were asked about the organization, they were instructed to reply, "I know nothing." The order grew rapidly in size, and in 1854 it had a membership of somewhere between 800,000 and 1,500,000. The political objective of the Know-Nothings was to extend the period of naturalization in order to undercut immigrant voting strength and to keep aliens in their place.

In 1854–1855 the movement surfaced as a major political force, calling itself the American party. Most of its backing came from Whigs looking for a new home, but it also attracted some ex-Democrats. Know-Nothingism also appealed to native-born workers fearful of competition from low-paid immigrants. But many people supported the American party simply because it was against the Democrats and was an available alternative.

The success of the new party was so dramatic that it was compared to a hurricane. In 1854 it won complete control in Massachusetts, capturing the governorship, most of the seats in the legislature, and the entire congressional delegation. In 1855 the Know-Nothings took power in three more New England states, swept Maryland, Kentucky, and Texas, and emerged as the principal opposition to the Democrats everywhere else, except in the Midwest. By late 1855 the Know-Nothings showed every sign of displacing the Whigs as the nation's second party.

Yet, almost as rapidly as it had arisen, the Know-Nothing movement collapsed. Its demise in 1856 is one of the great mysteries of American political history. As an intersectional party, its failure is understandable enough. When the Know-Nothings attempted to hold a national convention in 1856, northern and southern delegates split on the question of slavery in the territories, showing that former Whigs were still at odds over the same issue that had destroyed their old party.

Less clear is why the Know-Nothings failed to become the major opposition party to the Democrats in the North. One possible reason was that their free-soil Republican rivals, who were seeking to build a party committed to the containment of slavery, had an issue with wider appeal. But political nativism probably contained the seeds of its own extinction. Know-Nothingism was in part a grass-roots protest against the professional politicians who had led the Whig and Democratic parties. Concern about the effects of immigration on American culture and society would not have generated a mass political movement had it not been coupled with a belief that political bosses were "voting" immigrants for their own corrupt purposes. Most Know-Nothing spokesmen and elected officials were neither professional politicians nor established community leaders—their very inexperience was a major source of their original attraction to voters.

Furthermore, the Know-Nothings were never a real party; their distrust of conventional politics made it hard for them to develop organizational discipline. With inexperienced leaders and a lack of cohesion, the Know-Nothings were unable to make use of power once they had it. Their common cause—restriction of immigrant voting rights—did not provide answers to most of the problems facing the country. Once voters discovered that the Know-Nothings also *did* nothing, or at least failed to do anything that a more conventional party could not do better, they recovered from their antipolitical binge and looked for more competent leadership.

■ *Know-Nothings often charged that immigrant voters were stealing American elections. In the cartoon at left, German and Irish immigrants, represented by German beer and Irish whiskey, are stealing the ballot box. An anti–Know-Nothing cartoon (right) portrays the Know-Nothings as gun-wielding ruffians.*

Kansas and the Rise of the Republicans

The new Republican party was an outgrowth of the anti-Nebraska coalition of 1854. The Republican name was first used in midwestern states like Wisconsin and Michigan where Know-Nothingism failed to win a mass following. A new political label was required, because free-soil Democrats—who were an especially important element in the midwestern coalitons—refused to march under the Whig banner or even support any candidate for high office who called himself a Whig.

When the Know-Nothing party split over the Kansas-Nebraska issue in 1856, most of the northern nativists went over to the Republicans. The Republican argument that "the slave power conspiracy" was a greater threat to American liberty and equality than an alleged "Popish plot" proved to be persuasive. But nativists did not have to abandon their ethnic and religious prejudices to become Republicans. Although Republican leaders generally avoided taking anti-immigrant positions—some out of strong principle and others with an eye to the votes of the foreign-born—the party had a distinct flavor of evangelical Protestantism. On the local level Republicans sometimes supported causes that reflected an anti-immigrant or anti-Catholic bias —such as prohibition of the sale of alcoholic beverages, observance of the Sabbath, defense of Protestant Bible-reading in schools, and opposition to state aid for parochial education.

Unlike the Know-Nothings, the Republican party was led by seasoned professional politicians, men who had earlier been prominent Whigs or Democrats. Adept at organizing the grass roots, building durable coalitions, and employing all the techniques of popular campaigning, they built up an effective party apparatus in an amazingly short time. By late 1855, the party had won the adherence of two thirds of the anti-Nebraska congressmen elected in 1854. One of these, Nathaniel Banks of Massachusetts, was elected Speaker of the House after a lengthy struggle. By early 1856 the new party was well established throughout the North and was preparing to make a serious bid for the presidency.

Underlying the rapid growth of the Republican party was the strong and growing appeal of its position on slavery in the territories. Republicans viewed the unsettled West as a land of opportunities, a place to which the ambitious and hard-working could migrate in the hope of improving their social and economic position. Free soil would serve as a guarantee of free competition or "the right to rise." But if slavery was permitted to expand, the rights of "free labor" would be denied. Slaveholders would monopolize the best land, use their slaves to compete unfairly with free white workers, and block efforts at commercial and industrial development. Some Republicans also pandered to race prejudice: they presented their policy as a way to keep blacks out of the territories, thus preserving the new lands for exclusive white occupancy.

Although passage of the Kansas-Nebraska Act raised the territorial issue and gave birth to the Republican party, it was the turmoil associated with attempts to implement popular sovereignty in Kansas that kept the issue alive and enabled the Republicans to increase their following throughout the North. When Kansas was organized in the fall of 1854, a bitter contest began for control of the territorial government. New Englanders founded an Immigrant Aid Society to encourage antislavery settlement in Kansas, but the earliest arrivals came from slaveholding Missouri. In the first territorial elections proslavery settlers were joined at the polls by thousands of Missouri residents who crossed the border to vote illegally. The result was a decisive victory for the slave-state forces. The legislature then proceeded to pass laws that not only legalized slavery but made it a crime to speak or act against it.

Settlers favoring free soil, most of whom came from the Midwest, were already a majority of the actual residents of the territory when the fraudulently elected legislature stripped them of their civil liberties. To defend themselves and their convictions, they took up arms and established a rival territorial government under a constitution that outlawed slavery. The Pierce administration and its appointed local agents refused to recognize this "free-state" initiative, but Republicans in Congress defended it.

A small-scale civil war then broke out between the rival regimes, culminating in May 1856 when proslavery adherents raided the free-state capital at Lawrence. Portrayed in Republican propaganda as "the sack of Lawrence," this incursion resulted

■ *Free-soil settlers in Kansas, outraged by the manner in which the proslavery forces had seized control of the territorial legislature, called for a new state convention to draw up a constitution outlawing slavery.*

■ *Violence swept Bleeding Kansas in the mid-1850s. In the Marais des Cygnes massacre (below), five free-soilers were killed by proslavery forces seeking revenge for the murders committed by fanatic abolitionist John Brown and his followers at Pottawatomie Creek.*

in substantial property damage but no loss of life. More bloody was the reprisal carried out by the antislavery zealot John Brown. Upon hearing of the attack on Lawrence, Brown and a few followers murdered five proslavery settlers in cold blood. During the next few months—until a truce was arranged by an effective territorial governor in the fall of 1856—a hit-and-run guerrilla war raged between free-state and slave-state factions. (See the map of Bleeding Kansas on p. 392.)

The national Republican press had a field day with the events in Kansas, exaggerating the ex-tent of the violence but correctly pointing out that the federal government was favoring rule by a proslavery minority over a free-soil majority. Since the "sack of Lawrence" occurred at about the same time that Charles Sumner was assaulted on the Senate floor, the Republicans launched their 1856 campaign under the twin slogans, "Bleeding Kansas and Bleeding Sumner." The image of an evil and aggressive "slave power," using violence to deny constitutional rights to its opponents, was a potent device for arousing northern sympathies and winning votes.

Sectional Division in the Election of 1856

The Republican nominating convention revealed the strictly sectional nature of the new party. Only a handful of the delegates attended from the slave states, and all of these were from the upper South. The platform called for liberation of Kansas from the slave power and congressional prohibition of slavery in all territories. The nominee was John C. Frémont, explorer of the West and participant in the conquest of California during the Mexican War.

The Democratic convention dumped the ineffectual Pierce, passed over Stephen A. Douglas, and nominated James Buchanan of Pennsylvania who had a long career in public service. The Democrats' platform endorsed popular sovereignty in the territories. The American party, a Know-Nothing remnant that survived mainly as the rallying point for anti-Democratic conservatives in the border states and parts of the South, chose ex-President Millard Fillmore as its standard-bearer and received the backing of those northern Whigs who resisted the Republicans and hoped to revive the tradition of sectional compromise.

The election was really two separate races—one in the North, where the main contest was between Frémont and Buchanan, and the other in the South, which pitted Fillmore against Buchanan. The Pennsylvania Democrat emerged victorious because he outpolled Fillmore in all but one of the slave states (Maryland) and edged out Frémont in four crucial northern states—Pennsylvania, New Jersey, Indiana, and Illinois. But the Republicans did remarkably well for a party that was scarcely more than a year old. Frémont won eleven of the sixteen free states, sweeping the upper North with substantial majorities and winning a larger proportion of the northern popular vote than either of his opponents. Since the free states had a substantial majority in the electoral college, a future Republican candidate could win the presidency simply by overcoming a slim Democratic edge in the lower North.

In the South, where the possibility of a Frémont victory had revived talk of secession, the results of the election brought a momentary sense of relief tinged with deep anxiety about the future. For Southerners, the very existence of a sectional party committed to restricting the expansion of slavery constituted an insult to their way of life.

■ *This 1856 campaign poster credits Republican candidate John C. Frémont with securing the admission of California as a free state and derides his Democratic opponent, James Buchanan, for endorsing the Ostend Manifesto, which urged U.S. seizure of Cuba.*

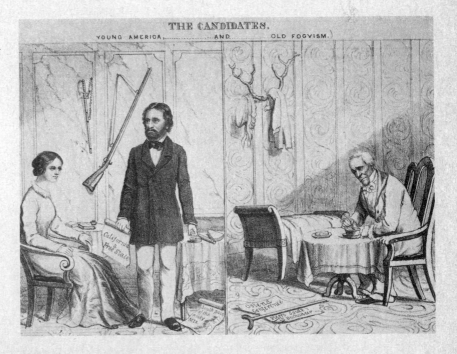

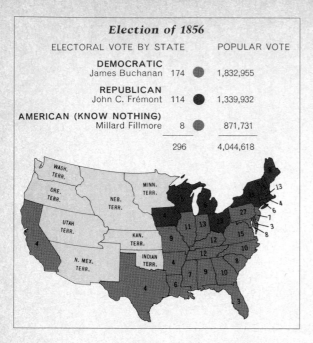

Cultural Sectionalism

Signs of cultural and intellectual cleavage had appeared well before the triumph of sectional politics. In the mid-1840s, the Methodist and Baptist churches split into northern and southern denominations because of differing attitudes toward slaveholding. Presbyterians remained formally united, but northern and southern factions went their separate ways on the slavery issue. Instead of unifying Americans around a common Protestant faith, the churches became nurseries of sectional discord. Increasingly, northern preachers and congregations denounced slaveholding as a sin, while most southern church leaders rallied to a biblical defense of the peculiar institution and became influential apologists for the southern way of life. Prominent religious leaders—such as Henry Ward Beecher, George B. Cheever, and Theodore Parker in the North; and James H. Thornwell, Leonidas Polk, and Bishop Stephen Elliott in the South—were in the forefront of sectional mobilization. As men of God, they helped to turn political questions into moral issues and reduced the prospects for a compromise.

American literature also became sectionalized during the 1840s and '50s. Southern men of letters, including such notable figures as William Gilmore Simms and Edgar Allen Poe, wrote proslavery polemics. Simms and many lesser novelists produced a flood of "plantation romances" glorifying southern civilization and sneering at that of the North. The notion that planter "cavaliers" were superior to money-grubbing Yankees was the message that most Southerners derived from the homegrown literature that they read. In the North, prominent men of letters—Emerson, Thoreau, James Russell Lowell and others—expressed strong antislavery sentiments in prose and poetry, particularly after the outbreak of the Mexican War.

Literary abolitionism reached a climax in 1852 when Harriet Beecher Stowe published *Uncle Tom's Cabin*, an enormously successful novel (it sold more than three hundred thousand copies in a single year) that fixed in the northern mind the image of the slaveholder as a brutal Simon Legree. Much of its emotional impact came from the book's portrayal of slavery as a threat to the

That such a party was genuinely popular in the North was profoundly alarming and raised grave doubts about the security of slavery within the Union. The continued success of a unified Democratic party under southern influence or control was widely viewed as the last hope for the maintenance of sectional balance and "southern rights."

The House Divided, 1857–1860

The sectional quarrel deepened and became virtually "irreconcilable" in the years between the election of Buchanan in 1856 and Lincoln's victory in 1860. A series of incidents provoked one side or the other, heightened the tension, and ultimately brought the crisis to a head. Behind the panicky reaction to public events lay a growing sense that the North and South were so different in culture and so opposed in basic interests that they could no longer coexist in the same nation.

■ *The propaganda effect of* Uncle Tom's Cabin *was tremendous. The story was retold on the stage, in the schoolroom, and in the lecture hall. This illustration is from a London edition, published November 1, 1852.*

family and the cult of domesticity. When the saintly Uncle Tom was sold away from his adoring wife and children, Northerners shuddered with horror and some Southerners felt a painful twinge of conscience.

Southern defensiveness gradually hardened into cultural and economic nationalism. Northern textbooks were banished from the schools in favor of those with a prosouthern slant, young men of the planter class were induced to stay in the South for higher education rather than going North (as had been the custom), and a movement developed to encourage southern industry and commerce as a way of reducing dependence on the North. A major vehicle for encouraging nationalistic sentiments, defending slavery, and promoting self-sufficiency was *De Bow's Review*, an influential journal published in New Orleans. Almost without exception, prominent southern educators and intellectuals of the late 1850s rallied behind the idea of a southern nation.

The Dred Scott Case

When James Buchanan was inaugurated on March 4, 1857, the dispute over the legal status of slavery in the territories was an open door through which sectional fears and hatreds could enter the political arena. Buchanan hoped to close that door by encouraging the Supreme Court to resolve the constitutional issue once and for all.

The Court was then about the render its decision in the case of *Dred Scott* v. *Sanford*. The plaintiff in this case was a Missouri slave whose owner had taken him to the Wisconsin Territory during the 1830s. Several years later they returned to Missouri. After his master's death, Dred Scott sued for his freedom on the grounds that he had lived for many years in an area where slavery had been outlawed by the Missouri Compromise. The case got into the federal courts because Scott's subsequent owner had moved to New York, leaving his slave in Missouri. The Supreme Court could have decided the issue on the narrow ground that a slave was not a citizen and therefore had no right to sue in federal courts. Indeed, it did make that determination, and a majority of the justices were at one point inclined to stop there. But President-elect Buchanan, in the days just before the inauguration, encouraged the Court to reconsider the case and render a broader decision that would settle the slavery issue.

On March 6, Chief Justice Roger B. Taney announced that the majority had ruled against Scott, basing their decision on several arguments. One was that Scott could not sue because he was not a citizen. Taney, in fact, argued further that no Afro-American—slave or free—could be a citizen of the United States. But the real bombshell in the decision was the ruling that Dred Scott would not have won his case even if he had been a legal plaintiff. His residence in the Wisconsin Territory established no right to freedom because Congress had no power to prohibit slavery there. The Missouri Compromise was thus declared unconstitutional and so, implicitly, was the main plank in the Republican platform.

If Buchanan expected the decision to reduce sectional tension, he was quickly proved wrong. In the North, and especially among Republicans, the Court's verdict was viewed as the latest diabolical act of the "slave power conspiracy."

■ A newspaper account of the Supreme Court's decision on the Dred Scott case (left). Scott's wife and two daughters are also pictured.

■ Chief Justice Roger B. Taney (above) handed down the Dred Scott decision. Northerners decried Taney's ruling that Negroes "had no rights which the white man is bound to respect."

The charge that the decision was a political maneuver rather than a disinterested interpretation of the Constitution was supported by strong circumstantial evidence. Five of the six judges who voted in the majority were proslavery Southerners, and their "resolution" of the territorial issue was close to the extreme southern rights position long advocated by John C. Calhoun. Furthermore, the fact that Buchanan had played a role in the decision was widely known, and it was suspected that he had conspired with the justices in response to pressure from the prosouthern wing of the Democratic party.

Republicans denounced the decision as "a wicked and false judgment" and as "the greatest crime in the annals of the republic"; but they managed to avoid open defiance of the Supreme Court's authority by denying that the justices had formally decided the territorial question. According to their interpretation of what the Court had

done, the overthrow of the Missouri Compromise was *obiter dicta*, a judicial opinion that was not binding because it had not been necessary to decide the case at hand. Their legal reasoning has been judged faulty by constitutional scholars, but it served to reassure the moderates in the party they were not going against the law of the land by continuing to demand a congressional ban on slavery in the territories. The decision actually helped the Republicans build support since it lent credence to their claim that an aggressive slave power was dominating all branches of the federal government and attempting to use the Constitution to achieve its own ends.

The Lecompton Controversy

While the Dred Scott case was being decided, leaders of the proslavery faction in Kansas concluded that the time was ripe to draft a constitution and seek admission to the Union as a slave state. Since settlers with free-state views were now an overwhelming majority in the territory, the success of the plan required a rigged, gerrymandered election for convention delegates. When it became clear that the election was fixed, the free-staters boycotted it, and the proslavery forces won complete control. The resulting constitution, drawn up at Lecompton, was certain to be voted down if submitted to the voters in a fair election, and sure to be rejected by Congress if no referendum of any kind was held.

To resolve this dilemma, supporters of the constitution decided to permit a vote on the slavery provision alone, giving the electorate the narrow choice of allowing or forbidding the future importation of slaves. Since there was no way to vote for total abolition, the free-state majority again resorted to a boycott, thus allowing ratification of a constitution that protected existing slave property and placed no restriction on importations. Meanwhile, however, the free-staters had finally gained control of the territorial legislature, and they authorized a second referendum on the constitution as a whole. This time, the proslavery party boycotted the election, and the Lecompton constitution was overwhelmingly rejected.

The Lecompton constitution was such an obvious perversion of popular sovereignty that Stephen A. Douglas spoke out against it. But the Buchanan administration, bowing to southern pressure, tried to push it through Congress in early 1858, despite overwhelming evidence that the people of Kansas did not wish to enter the Union as a slave state. The resulting debate in Congress became so bitter and impassioned that it provoked fist fights between northern and southern members. Buchanan, using all the political muscle he could command, scored a victory in the Senate, which voted to admit Kansas under the Lecompton constitution on March 23. But the administration was stymied in the House, where the bill went down to defeat on April 1. A face-saving compromise was then devised that allowed resubmission of the constitution to the Kansas voters on the pretext that a change in the provisions for a federal land grant was required. Finally, in August 1858, the people of Kansas killed the Lecompton constitution when they voted it down by a margin of six to one.

The Lecompton controversy seriously aggravated the sectional quarrel. For Republicans, the administration's frantic efforts to admit Kansas as a slave state exposed southern dominance of the Democratic party and the lengths to which proslavery conspirators would go to achieve their ends. Among Democrats, the affair opened a deep rift between the followers of Douglas and the backers of the Buchanan administration. Because of his anti-Lecompton stand, Douglas gained popularity in the North, and some Republicans even flirted with the idea of joining forces with him against the "doughfaces"—prosouthern Democrats—who stood with Buchanan.

For Douglas himself, however, the affair was a disaster; it destroyed his hopes of uniting the Democratic party and defusing the slavery issue through the application of popular sovereignty. What had happened in Kansas suggested that popular sovereignty in practice was no less than an invitation to civil war. Furthermore, the Dred Scott decision implied that the voters of a territory could not legally decide the fate of slavery at any time before the constitution-making stage. Hence, the interpretation of popular sovereignty favored in the North was undermined, and Southerners could insist on full protection of their right to own human property in all federal territories. For his stand against Lecompton, Douglas was denounced as a traitor in the South, and his hopes of being elected president were seriously diminished.

Debating the Morality of Slavery

Douglas' more immediate problem was to win reelection to the Senate from Illinois in 1858. Here he faced surprisingly tough opposition from a Republican candidate who, in defiance of precedent, was nominated by a party convention. (At this time senators were elected by state legislatures.) Douglas' rival, former Whig Congressman Abraham Lincoln, set out to convince the voters that Douglas could not be relied upon to oppose the extension of slavery, even though he had opposed the admission of Kansas under a proslavery constitution.

In the famous speech that opened his campaign, Lincoln tried to distance himself from his

■ *Stephen A. Douglas, the "Little Giant" from Illinois, won election to Congress when he was just thirty years old. Four years later he was elected to the Senate.*

opponent by taking a more radical position. He argued that the nation had reached the crisis point in the struggle between slavery and freedom: "'A house divided against itself cannot stand.' I believe this government cannot endure, permanently half *slave* and half *free*." He then described the chain of events between the Kansas-Nebraska Act and the Dred Scott decision as evidence of a plot to extend and nationalize slavery and called for defensive actions to stop the spread of slavery and place it "where the

public mind shall rest in the belief that it is in the course of ultimate extinction." He tried to link Douglas to this proslavery conspiracy by pointing to his rival's unwillingness to take a stand on the morality of slavery, to his professed indifference whether slavery was voted up or down in the territories. For Lincoln, the only security against the triumph of slavery and the slave power was moral opposition to human bondage. Neutrality on the moral issue would lull the public into accepting the expansion of slavery until it was legal everywhere.

In the subsequent series of debates that focused national attention on the Illinois senatorial contest, Lincoln hammered away at the theme that Douglas was a covert defender of slavery because he was not a principled opponent of it. Douglas responded by accusing Lincoln of endangering the Union by his talk of putting slavery on the path to extinction. Denying that he was an abolitionist, Lincoln made a distinction between tolerating slavery in the South, where it was protected by the Constitution, and allowing it to expand to places where it could legally be prohibited. Restriction of slavery, he argued, had been the policy of the Founders, and it was Douglas and the Democrats who had departed from the great tradition of containing an evil that could not be immediately eliminated.

In the debate at Freeport, Illinois, Lincoln questioned Douglas on how he could reconcile popular sovereignty with the Dred Scott decision. The Little Giant, as Douglas was called by his admirers, responded that slavery could not exist without supportive legislation to sustain it and that territorial legislatures could simply refrain from passing a slave code if they wanted to keep it out. Douglas' "Freeport doctrine" did not suddenly alienate his southern supporters, as historians used to believe, because his anti-Lecompton stand had already undermined his popularity in the slave states. But it undoubtedly hardened southern opposition to his presidential ambitions.

Douglas' most effective debating point was to charge that Lincoln's moral opposition to slavery implied a belief in racial equality. Lincoln, facing an intensely racist electorate, vigorously denied this charge and affirmed his commitment to white supremacy. He would grant blacks the right to the fruits of their own labor while deny-

■ *Abraham Lincoln, shown here in his first full-length portrait. Although Lincoln lost the contest for the Senate seat in 1858, the Lincoln-Douglas debates established his reputation as a rising star of the Republican party.*

■ *Lincoln and Douglas would meet as rivals again, in the contest for the presidency in 1860. In that fight, the prize would be the White House.*

ing them the "privileges" of citizenship. This was an inherently contradictory position, and Douglas made the most of it.

Although Republican candidates for the state legislature won a majority of the popular votes, the Democrats carried more counties and thus were able to send Douglas back to the Senate. Lincoln lost an office, but he won respect in Republican circles throughout the country. By stressing the moral dimension of the slavery question and undercutting any possibility of fusion between Republicans and Douglas Democrats, he had sharpened his party's ideological focus and had stiffened its backbone against any temptation to compromise its free-soil position.

The South's Crisis of Fear

After Kansas became a free territory instead of a slave state in August 1858, slavery in the territories became a symbolic issue rather than a practical and substantive one. The remaining unorganized areas, which were in the Rockies and northern Great Plains, were unlikely to attract slaveholding settlers. Southern expansionists still dreamed of annexations in the Caribbean and Central America but had little hope of winning congressional approval. Nevertheless, Southerners continued to demand the "right" to take their slaves into the territories, and Republicans persisted in denying it to them. Although the Republicans repeatedly promised that they would not interfere with slavery where it already existed, Southerners refused to believe them and interpreted their unyielding stand against the extension of slavery as a threat to southern rights and security.

A chain of events in late 1859 and early 1860 turned southern anxiety about northern attitudes and policies into a "crisis of fear." These events alarmed slaveholders because they appeared to threaten their safety and dominance in a new and direct way.

The first of these incidents was John Brown's raid on Harpers Ferry, Virginia, in October 1859. Brown was a fervent abolitionist who had shown in Kansas that he was prepared to use violence and terrorism against the enemies of black freedom. He had the appearance and manner of an Old Testament prophet (see the photo on p. 380) and thought of himself as God's chosen instrument "to purge this land with blood" and eradicate the sin of slaveholding. On October 16, he led eighteen men from his band of twenty-two (which included five free blacks) across the Potomac River from his base in Maryland and seized the federal arsenal and armory in Harpers Ferry.

Brown's aim was to arm the local slave population to commence a guerrilla war from havens in the Appalachians that would eventually extend to the plantation regions of the lower South. But the neighboring slaves did not rise up to join him, and Brown's raiders were driven out of the armory and arsenal by the local militia and forced to take refuge in a fire-engine house. There they held out until their bastion was stormed by a force of United States Marines commanded by Colonel Robert E. Lee. In the course of the fighting, ten of Brown's men were killed or mortally wounded, along with seven of the townspeople and soldiers who opposed them.

The wounded Brown and his remaining followers were put on trial for treason against the state of Virginia. The subsequent investigation produced evidence that several prominent northern abolitionists had approved of Brown's plan—to the extent that they understood it—and had raised money for his preparations. This revelation seemed to confirm southern fears that abolitionists were actively engaged in fomenting slave insurrection.

After Brown was sentenced to be hanged, Southerners were further stunned by the outpouring of sympathy and admiration that his impending fate aroused in the North. As Ralph Waldo Emerson expressed it, Brown "would make the gallows as glorious as the cross." His actual execution on December 2 completed Brown's elevation to the status of a martyred saint of the antislavery cause. The day of his death was marked in parts of the North by the tolling of bells, the firing of cannons, and the holding of memorial services.

Although Republican politicians were quick to denounce John Brown for his violent methods, Southerners interpreted the wave of northern sympathy as an expression of the majority opinion and the Republicans' "real" attitude. According to historian James McPherson, "They identified Brown with the abolitionists, the abolitionists with Republicans, and Republicans with the whole North." Within the South, the raid and its aftermath touched off a frenzy of fear, repression, and mobilization. Witch-hunts searched for the agents of a vast, imagined conspiracy to stir up slave rebellion; vigilance committees were organized in many localities to resist subversion and insure control of slaves, and orators pointed increasingly to secession as the only way to protect southern safety.

Brown was scarcely in his grave when another set of events put southern nerves on edge once more. Next to abolitionist-abetted rebellions, the slaveholding South's greatest fear was that the nonslaveholding majority would turn against the master class and that the solidarity of southern whites behind the peculiar institution would crumble. When Congress met to elect a Speaker of the House on December 5, the Republican candidate—John Sherman of Ohio—was bitterly denounced by Southerners because he had endorsed as a campaign document Hinton Rowan Helper's *Impending Crisis of the South*. Helper's book, which called upon lower-class whites to resist planter dominance and abolish slavery in their own interest, was regarded by slaveholders as even more seditious than *Uncle Tom's Cabin*, and they feared the spread of "Helperism" among poor whites almost as much as the effect of "John Brownism" on the slaves.

The ensuing contest over the Speaker's office lasted almost two months. As the balloting went on, southern congressmen threatened secession if Sherman was elected, and feelings became so heated that some representatives began to carry weapons on the floor of the House. Since the Republicans did not have an absolute majority and needed the votes of a few members of the American party, it eventually became clear that Sherman could not be elected, and his name was withdrawn in favor of a moderate Republican who had refrained from endorsing Helper's book. The impasse over the speakership was thus resolved, but the contest helped persuade Southerners that the Republicans were committed to stirring up class conflict among southern whites.

The identification of Republicans with Helper's ideas may have been decisive in convincing many conservative planters that a Republican victory in the presidential election of 1860 would be intolerable. Anxiety about the future allegiance of nonslaveholding whites had been growing during the 1850s because of changes in the pattern of slave ownership. A dramatic rise in the price of slaves was undermining the ambition of slaveless farmers to join the slaveholding ranks. During the decade the proportion of white heads of families owning slaves had shrunk from 30 to 25 percent in all the slave states and from 50 to 40 percent in the cotton belt of the lower South. Perceiving in this trend the seeds of class conflict, proslavery extremists had called for the reopening of the Atlantic slave trade as a way to reduce the price of slaves and make them more widely available. Although the interest of large owners in preserving the appreciated value of their human property had helped prevent this "proslavery crusade" from gaining broad support, many slaveholders were concerned about the social and political consequences of their status as a shrinking minority. Even those most strongly committed to the Union were terrified by the prospect that a Republican party in control of the federal government would use its power to foster "Helperism" among the South's non-slaveholding majority.

The Election of 1860

The Republicans, sniffing victory and generally unaware of the depth of southern feeling against them, met in Chicago on May 16 to nominate a presidential candidate. The initial front-runner, Senator William H. Seward of New York, had two strikes against him: he had a reputation for radicalism and a long record of strong opposition to the nativist movement. What a majority of the delegates wanted was a less controversial nominee who could win two or three of the northern states that had been in the Democratic column in 1856. Abraham Lincoln met their specifications: he was from Illinois, a state that the Republicans needed to win, he had a more moderate image than Seward, and he had kept his personal distaste for Know-Nothingism to himself. In addition, he was a self-made man, whose rise from frontier poverty to legal and political prominence embodied the Republican ideal of equal opportunity for all. After trailing Seward by a large margin on the first ballot, Lincoln picked up enough strength on the second to pull virtually even and was nominated on the third.

The platform, like the nominee, was meant to broaden the party's appeal in the North. Although a commitment to halt the expansion of slavery remained, economic matters received more attention than they had in 1856. With an eye on Pennsylvania, the delegates called for a high protective tariff; other planks included endorsement of free homesteads, which was popular in the Midwest, and federal aid for internal improvements, especially a transcontinental railroad. The platform was cleverly designed to bring most ex-Whigs into the Republican camp while also accommodating enough renegade Democrats to give the party a solid majority in the northern states.

The Democrats failed to present a united front against this formidable challenge. When the party first met in the sweltering heat of Charleston in late April, Douglas commanded a majority of the delegates but was unable to win the two-thirds required for nomination because of unyielding southern opposition. He did succeed in getting the convention to endorse popular sovereignty as its slavery platform, but the price was a walkout by southern delegates who favored a federal slave code for the territories.

■ In this cartoon from the 1860 election, candidates Lincoln and Douglas struggle for control of the Western section of the country, while Breckenridge tears away the South. John Bell of the constitutional Union party futilely attempts to repair the damage to the torn nation.

Unable to agree on a nominee, the convention adjourned to reconvene in Baltimore in June. The next time around, a fight developed over whether to seat newly selected pro-Douglas delegations from some southern states in place of the bolters from the first convention. When the Douglas forces won most of the contested seats, another and more massive southern walkout took place. The result was a fracture of the Democratic party. The delegates who remained nominated Douglas and reaffirmed the party's commitment to popular sovereignty, while the bolters convened elsewhere to nominate John Breckenridge of Kentucky on a platform of federal protection for slavery in the territories.

By the time the campaign got underway, four parties were running presidential candidates. In addition to the Republicans, the Douglas Democrats, and the "Southern Rights" Democrats, a remnant of conservative Whigs and Know-Nothings nominated John Bell of Tennessee under the banner of the Constitutional Union party. Taking no explicit stand on the issue of slavery in the territories, the Constitutional Unionists tried to represent the spirit of sectional accommodation that had led to compromise in 1820 and 1850. In effect, the race became a separate two-party contest in each section: in the North the real choice was between Lincoln and Douglas, and in the South the only candidates with a fighting chance were Breckenridge and Bell. Douglas alone tried to carry on a national campaign, visiting all parts of the country and gaining some support in every state. But only in Missouri did he actually win.

When the results came in, the Republicans had achieved a stunning victory. By gaining the electoral votes of all the free states except a fraction of New Jersey's, Lincoln won a decisive majority —180 to 123 for his combined opponents. In the North, his 54 percent of the popular vote annihilated Douglas. In the South, where Lincoln was not even on the ballot, Breckenridge triumphed everywhere except in Virginia, Kentucky, and Tennessee, which went for Bell and the Constitutional Unionists. The Republican strategy of seeking power by trying to win decisively in the majority section was brilliantly successful. Although less than 40 percent of those who went to the polls throughout the nation actually voted for Lincoln, his support in the North was so solid that he would have won in the electoral college

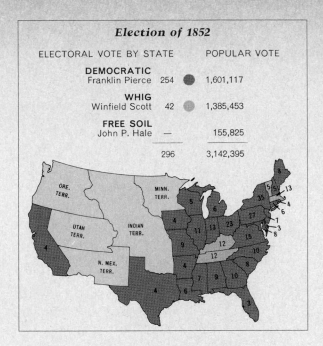

even if his opponents had been unified behind a single candidate.

Most Southerners saw the result of the election as a catastrophe. A candidate and a party with no support in their own section had won the Presidency on a platform viewed as insulting to southern honor and hostile to vital southern interests. Since the birth of the Republic, Southerners had either sat in the White House or exerted considerable influence over those who did. Those days might now be gone forever. Rather than accepting permanent minority status in American politics and face the resulting dangers to black slavery and white "liberty," the political leaders of the lower South launched a movement for immediate secession from the Union.

Explaining the Crisis

Generations of historians have searched for the underlying causes of the crisis leading to disruption of the Union but have failed to agree on exactly what they were. Some have stressed the clash of economic interests between agrarian and industrializing regions. But this interpretation does not reflect the way people at the time expressed their concerns. The main issues in the sectional debates of the 1850s were whether slavery was right or wrong and whether it should be extended or contained. Disagreements over protective tariffs and other economic measures allegedly benefiting one section or the other were clearly secondary. Furthermore, it has never been clear why the interests of northern industry and those of the South's commercial agriculture were irreconcilable. From a purely economic point of view, there was no necessity for producers of raw materials to go to war with those who marketed or processed them.

Another group of historians have blamed the crisis on "irresponsible" politicians and agitators on both sides of the Mason-Dixon line. Public opinion, they argue, was whipped into a frenzy over issues that competent statesmen could have resolved. But this viewpoint has been sharply criticized for failing to acknowledge the depths of feeling that could be aroused by the slavery question and for underestimating the obstacles to a peaceful solution.

The dominant modern view is that the crisis was rooted in profound ideological differences over the morality and utility of slavery as an institution. Most interpreters are now agreed that the roots of the conflict lay in the fact that the South was a slave society and determined to stay that way, while the North was equally committed to a free labor system. In the words of historian David Potter, "slavery really had a polarizing effect, for the North had no slaveholders—at least not of resident slaves—and the South had virtually no abolitionists." No other differences divided the regions in this decisive way, and it is hard to imagine that secessionism would have developed if the South had followed the North's example and abolished slavery in the postrevolutionary period.

Nevertheless, the existence or nonexistence of slavery will not explain why the crisis came when it did and in the way that it did. Why did the conflict become "irreconcilable" in the 1850s and not earlier or later? Why did it take the form of a political struggle over the future of slavery in the territories? Adequate answers to both questions require an understanding of political developments that were not directly caused by tensions over slavery.

By the 1850s, the established Whig and Democratic parties were in trouble because they no longer offered the voters clear-cut alternatives on the economic issues that had been the bread and butter of politics during the heyday of the second party system. This situation created an opening for new parties and issues. After the Know-Nothings failed to make attitudes toward immigrants the basis for a political realignment, the Republicans used the issue of slavery in the territories to build the first successful sectional party in American history. They called for "free soil" rather than freedom for blacks because abolitionism conflicted with the northern majority's commitment to white supremacy and its respect for the original constitutional compromise that established a hands-off policy toward slavery in the southern states. For Southerners, the Republican party now became the main issue, and they fought against it from within the Democratic party until it ceased to function as a national organization in 1860.

If politicians seeking new ways to mobilize an apathetic electorate are seen as the main instigators of sectional crisis, the reasons why certain appeals were more effective than others must still be explained. Why did the slavery extension issue arouse such strong feelings in the two sections during the 1850s? The same issue had arisen earlier and had proved adjustable, even in 1820 when the second party system—with its vested interest in compromise—had not yet emerged. If the expansion of slavery had been as vital and emotional a question in 1820 as it was in the 1850s, the declining Federalist party would presumably have revived in the form of a northern sectional party adamantly opposed to the admission of slave states to the Union.

Ultimately, therefore, the crisis of the 1850s must be understood as having a deep social and cultural dimension as well as a purely political one. The North and South had diverged significantly in basic beliefs and values between the 1820s and the 1850s. In the free states, the rise of reform-minded evangelicalism had given a new sense of moral direction and purpose to a rising middle class adapting to the new market economy (see chapter 11). Such evangelical virtues as self-help, thriftiness, sobriety, and diligence were well suited to the growth of a dynamic capitalis-

MISTRESS COLUMBIA, WHO HAS BEEN TAKING A NAP, SUDDENLY WAKES UP AND CALLS HER NOISY SCHOLARS TO ORDER.

■ As the decade of the 1850s ended, the future of the Union appeared uncertain. In this cartoon, published in January 1860, Mistress Columbia attempts to call her unruly scholars to order, but legislators on both sides of the Mason-Dixon line continue to fight as they study the Constitution, looking for justification for their conflicting claims.

■ A "Wide-Awakes" torchlight parade in New York City, 1860. In the
presidential campaign of 1860, the Republicans organized their supporters
into "Wide-Awake Clubs," whose uniformed members marched in small
towns and large cities to drum up support for Lincoln and a Republican
victory.

tic economy still based primarily on small producers. In much of the South, the slave plantation
system prospered, and the notion that white
liberty and equality depended on having enslaved
blacks to do menial labor became more deeply
entrenched.

When politicians appealed to sectionalism during the 1850s, therefore, they could evoke conflicting views of what constituted the good society. The South—with its allegedly idle masters,
degraded unfree workers, and shiftless poor
whites—seemed to a majority of Northerners to
be in flagrant violation of the Protestant work
ethic and the ideal of open competition in "the
race of life." From the dominant southern point
of view, the North was a land of hypocritical
money-grubbers who denied the obvious fact that
dependent laboring classes—especially racially
inferior ones—had to be kept under the kind of
rigid control that only slavery could provide.
According to the ideology of northern Republicans, the freedom of the individual depended on
equality of opportunity for everyone; in the
minds of Southern sectionalists, it required that
part of the population be enslaved. Once these
contrary views of the world had become the main
themes of political discourse, sectional compromise was no longer possible.

Recommended Reading

The best general account of the politics of the sectional
crisis is David M. Potter, *The Impending Crisis, 1848–
1861* (1976). This well-written and authoritative work
combines a vivid and detailed narrative of events with a
shrewd and detailed interpretation of them. A provocative new analysis of the party system in crisis is
Michael F. Holt, *The Political Crisis of the 1850s*
(1978). Holt incorporates the social-scientific approaches and methods of the "new political history." The
most important studies of northern political sectionalism are Eric Foner, *Free Soil, Free Labor, Free Men: The
Ideology of the Republican Party before the Civil War*
(1970) on the Republican party generally, and Don E.

Chronology

1846 David Wilmot introduces proviso banning slavery in the Mexican cession

1848 Free-Soil party is founded
Zachary Taylor (Whig) elected president, defeating Lewis Cass (Democrat) and Martin Van Buren (Free-Soil)

1849 California seeks admission to the Union as a free state

1850 Congress debates sectional issues and enacts Compromise of 1850

1852 Harriet Beecher Stowe publishes *Uncle Tom's Cabin*
Franklin Pierce (Democrat) elected president by a large majority over Winfield Scott (Whig)

1854 Congress passes Kansas-Nebraska Act, repealing Missouri Compromise
Republican party founded in several northern states.
Anti-Nebraska coalitions score victories in congressional elections in the North

1854–1855 Know-Nothing party achieves stunning successes in state politics

1854–1856 Free-state and slave-state forces struggle for control of Kansas Territory

1856 Preston Brooks assaults Charles Sumner on Senate floor
James Buchanan wins presidency despite strong challenge in the North from John C. Frémont

1857 Supreme Court decides Dred Scott case and legalizes slavery in all territories

1858 Congress refuses to admit Kansas to Union under the proslavery Lecompton constitution.
Lincoln and Douglas debate slavery issue in Illinois

1859 John Brown raids Harpers Ferry, is captured and executed

1859–1860 Fierce struggle takes place over election of a Republican as Speaker of the House (December–February)

1860 Republicans nominate Abraham Lincoln for presidency (May)
Democratic party splits into northern and southern factions with separate candidates and platforms (June)
Lincoln wins the presidency over Douglas (northern Democrat), Breckenridge (southern Democrat), and Bell (Constitutional Unionist)

Fehrenbacher, *Prelude to Greatness: Lincoln in the 1850's* (1962) on Lincoln's rise to prominence. Both works take ideas and ideologies seriously. There are no general works of comparable quality on the background of southern separatism, but William L. Barney, *The Road to Secession: A New Perspective on the Old South* (1972) is a good introduction to the subject.

Additional Bibliography

The most detailed and thorough discussion of the events leading up to the Civil War is Allan Nevins, *The Ordeal of the Union*, vols. 1–4 (1947–1950). A more concise effort to cover the same ground is Avery Craven, *The Coming of the Civil War*, 2d ed. (1957). Craven has also produced the most extensive study of southern responses to the events of the crisis period in *The Growth of Southern Nationalism, 1848–1861* (1953). Conflicting explanations of what caused the breakup of the Union can be found in Kenneth M. Stampp, ed., *The Causes of the Civil War*, rev. ed. (1974).

There are good books on most of the specific political events and personalities of the period. On developments between 1846 and 1850, see Chaplain W. Morrison, *Democratic Politics and Sectionalism: The Wilmot Proviso Controversy* (1967) and Holman Hamilton, *Prologue to Conflict: The Crisis and Compromise of 1850* (1964). Enforcement of the Fugitive Slave Law is the subject of Stanley W. Campbell, *The Slave Catchers* (1970). The rise of antislavery politics in the 1840s and '50s is well described in Richard H. Sewell, *Ballots for Freedom: Antislavery Politics in the United States, 1837–1860* (1976). Eugene H. Berwanger, *The Frontier Against Slavery: Western Anti-Negro Prejudice in the Slavery Extension Controversy* (1967), stresses the role of racial attitudes in the free-soil movement. Insights into the origin and nature of the Republican party—and specifically its relation to nativism—can be derived from Ronald P. Formisano, *The Birth of Mass Political Parties: Michigan, 1827–1861* (1971) and Michael F. Holt, *Forging a New Majority: The Formation of the Republican Party in Pittsburgh, 1848–1860* (1969). On nativism generally, see Ray Allen Billington, *The Protestant Crusade, 1800–1860* (1938) and Carleton Beales, *Brass Knuckles Crusade: The Great Know-Nothing Conspiracy* (1960). James A. Rawley, *Race and Politics: "Bleeding Kansas" and the Coming of the Civil War* (1969), deals with the struggle over slavery in the Kansas Territory. Stephen A. Douglas, a key participant in the crisis of the 1850s, is the subject of a major biography by Robert W. Johannsen: *Stephen A. Douglas* (1973). David Donald, *Charles Sumner and the Coming of the Civil War* (1960), puts another important political figure into context. Don E. Fehrenbacher, *The Dred Scott Case: Its Significance in American Law and Politics* (1978) is the definitive work on the subject, but see also Vincent C. Hopkins, *Dred Scott's Case* (1951). An incisive analysis of the "great debates" is Harry V. Jaffa, *Crisis of the House Divided: An Interpretation of* the *Lincoln-Douglas Debates* (1959). A stimulating psychoanalytic interpretation of the Lincoln-Douglas rivalry is George B. Forgie, *Patricide in the House Divided: A Psychological Interpretation of Lincoln and His Age* (1979). Roy Franklin Nichols, *The Disruption of American Democracy* (1948), treats the breakdown of the Democratic party between 1856 and 1860. On John Brown and his raid, see Stephen B. Oates, *To Purge This Land with Blood: A Biography of John Brown* (1970). Stephen A. Channing, *Crisis of Fear: Secession in South Carolina*, details the hysteria that seized one southern state after Brown's raid. On the controversy over Helper's inflammatory book, see the introduction to Hinton R. Helper, *The Impending Crisis of the South: How to Meet It*, edited by George M. Fredrickson (1968).

Perspectives on the intellectual and cultural aspects of the sectional conflict can be derived from William R. Taylor, *Cavalier and Yankee: The Old South and American National Character* (1961); John McCardell, *The Idea of a Southern Nation: Southern Nationalists and Southern Nationalism, 1830–1860* (1979); Major L. Wilson, *Space and Freedom: The Quest for Nationality and the Irrepressible Conflict* (1974); Paul C. Nagel, *One Nation Indivisible: The Union in American Thought* (1964); Perry Miller, *The Life of the Mind in America: From the Revolution to the Civil War* (1965); Donald G. Mathews, *Slavery and Methodism: A Chapter in American Morality, 1780–1845* (1965); and Ronald T. Takaki, *A Pro-Slavery Crusade: The Agitation to Reopen the African Slave Trade* (1971). See also works cited in the bibliographies of earlier chapters dealing with evangelicalism, abolitionism, and the pro-slavery argument.

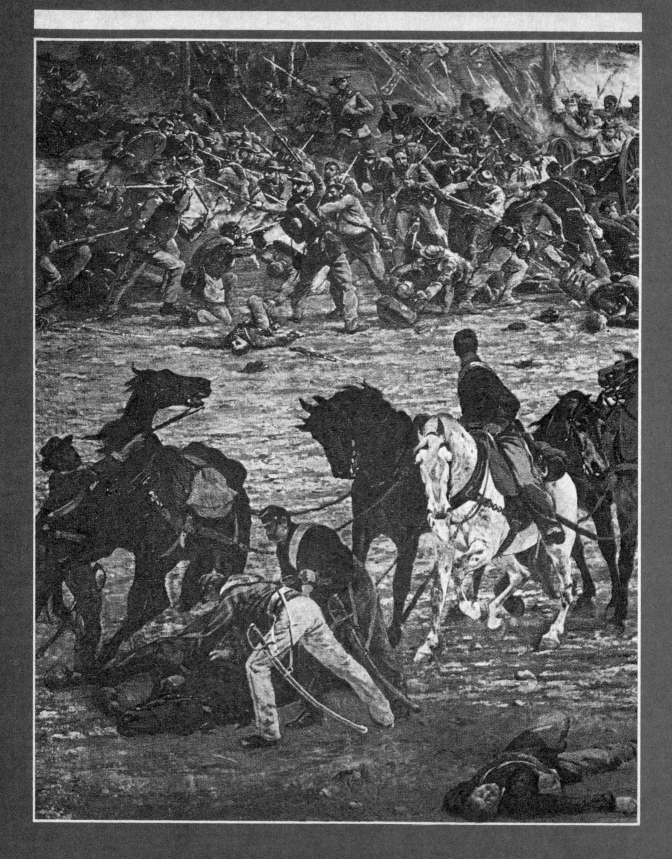

chapter 15

SECESSION
AND THE
CIVIL WAR

The man elected to the White House in 1860 was striking in appearance—he was six feet four inches in height and seemed even taller because of his disproportionately long legs and his habit of wearing a high silk "stovepipe" hat. But Abraham Lincoln's previous career provided no guarantee that he would tower over most of our other presidents in more than physical height. When Lincoln sketched the main events of his life for a campaign biographer in June 1860, he was modest almost to the point of self-depreciation. Especially regretting his "want of education," he assured the biographer that "he does what he can to supply the want."

Born to poor and illiterate parents on the Kentucky frontier in 1809, Lincoln received a few months of formal schooling in Indiana after the family moved there in 1816. But mostly he educated himself, reading and rereading a few treasured books by firelight. In 1831, when the family migrated to Illinois, he left home to make a living for himself in the struggling settlement of New Salem, where he worked as a surveyor, shopkeeper, and local postmaster. His brief career as a merchant was disastrous: he went bankrupt and was saddled with debt for years to come. But he eventually found a path to success in law and politics. While studying law on his own in New Salem, he managed to get elected to the state legislature. In 1837, he moved to Springfield, a growing town that offered bright prospects for a young lawyer-politician. Lincoln combined exceptional political and legal skills with a down-to-earth, humorous way of addressing jurors and voters. Consequently, he became a leader of the Whig party in Illinois and one of the most sought-after of the lawyers who rode the central Illinois judicial circuit.

The high point of his political career as a Whig was one term in Congress (1847–1849). Lincoln did not seek reelection, but he would have faced certain defeat had he done so. His strong stand against the Mexican War alienated much of his constituency, and the voters expressed their disaffection in 1848 by electing a Democrat over the Whig who tried to succeed him. An even greater disappointment followed in 1849 when President Zachary Taylor, for whom Lincoln had campaigned vigorously and effectively, failed to appoint him to a patronage job he coveted. Having been repudiated by the electorate and ignored by the national leadership of a party he had served loyally and well, Lincoln retired from active politics and concentrated on building his law practice.

The Kansas-Nebraska Act of 1854, with its advocacy of popular sovereignty, provided Lincoln with a heaven-sent opportunity to return to politics with a stronger base of support. For the first time, his driving ambition for political success and his personal convictions about what was best for the country were easy to reconcile. Lincoln had long believed that slavery was an unjust institution that should be tolerated only to the extent that the Constitution and the tradition of sectional compromise required. He attacked Douglas' plan of popular sovereignty because it broke with precedents for federal containment or control of the growth of slavery. After trying in vain to rally free-soilers around the Whig standard, Lincoln threw in his lot with the Republicans, assumed leadership of the new party in Illinois, attracted national attention in his bid for Douglas' Senate seat in 1858, and turned out to have the right qualifications when the Republicans chose a presidential nominee in 1860.

After Lincoln's election provoked southern secession and plunged the nation into the greatest crisis in its history, there was understandable skepticism about him in many quarters: was the former rail-splitter from Illinois up to the responsibilities he faced? Lincoln had less experience that would be relevant to a wartime presidency than any previous chief executive—never having been a governor, senator, cabinet officer, vice-president, or high-ranking military officer. But some of his training as a prairie politician would prove extremely useful in the years ahead.

Lincoln had shown himself adept at the art of party leadership, which meant being able to accommodate various factions and define party issues and principles in a way that would encourage unity and dedication to the cause. Since the Republican party would serve during the war as the main vehicle for mobilizing and maintaining devotion to the Union effort, these political skills assumed crucial importance. Holding the party together by persuasion and patronage was essential to unifying the nation by force, and Lincoln succeeded in doing both.

Another reason for Lincoln's effectiveness as a war leader was that he identified wholeheartedly with the northern cause and could inspire others to make sacrifices for it. In his view, the issue in the conflict was nothing less than the survival of the kind of political system that gave men like himself a chance for high office. In addressing a special session of Congress in 1861, Lincoln provided a powerful statement of what the war was all about.

And this issue embraces more than the fate of these United States. It presents to the whole family of man, the question of whether a constitutional republic, or a democracy—a government of the people by the same people— can or cannot, maintain its territorial integrity against its own domestic foes. . . . It forces us to ask: . . . "Must a government, of necessity be too strong for the liberties of its own people, or too weak to maintain its own existence?"

The Civil War not only tested the ability of American democracy to function in an orderly and constitutional manner, it also put on trial the very principle of democracy at a time when most European nations had rejected political liberalism and accepted the conservative view that popular government would inevitably collapse into anarchy. As Lincoln put it in the Gettysburg Address, the only cause great enough to justify the enormous sacrifice of life on the battlefields was the struggle to preserve the democratic ideal, or to ensure that "government of the people, by the people, for the people, shall not perish from the earth."

The Storm Gathers

Lincoln's election provoked the secession of seven states of the Deep South but did not lead immediately to armed conflict. Before the sectional quarrel turned from a cold war into a hot

■ This Matthew Brady photograph of Abraham Lincoln was taken when Lincoln arrived in Washington for his inauguration. In his inaugural address, Lincoln appealed for preservation of the Union.

one, two things had to happen: a final effort to defuse the conflict by compromise and conciliation had to fail, and the North needed to develop a firm resolve to maintain the Union by military action. Both of these developments may seem inevitable to us, but for most of those living at the time it was not clear until the guns blazed at Fort Sumter that the sectional crisis would have to be resolved on the battlefield.

The Deep South Secedes

South Carolina, which had long been in the forefront of southern rights and proslavery agitation, was the first state to secede. On December 20, 1860, a convention meeting in Charleston declared unanimously that "the union now subsisting between South Carolina and other states, under the name of the 'United States of America,' is hereby dissolved." The constitutional theory behind secession was that the Union was a "compact" among sovereign states, each of

CHARLESTON

MERCURY

EXTRA:

Passed unanimously at 1.15 o'clock, P. M. December 20th, 1860.

AN ORDINANCE

To dissolve the Union between the State of South Carolina and other States united with her under the compact entitled "The Constitution of the United States of America."

We, the People of the State of South Carolina, in Convention assembled, do declare and ordain, and it is hereby declared and ordained,

That the Ordinance adopted by us in Convention, on the twenty-third day of May, in the year of our Lord one thousand seven hundred and eighty-eight, whereby the Constitution of the United States of America was ratified, and also, all Acts and parts of Acts of the General Assembly of this State, ratifying amendments of the said Constitution, are hereby repealed; and that the union now subsisting between South Carolina and other States, under the name of "The United States of America," is hereby dissolved.

THE

UNION

IS

DISSOLVED!

■ *A South Carolina newspaper announces the dissolution of the Union. South Carolina's secession was celebrated in the South with bonfires, parades, and fireworks.*

which could withdraw from the Union by the vote of a convention similar to the one that had ratified the Constitution in the first place. The South Carolinians justified seceding at this time by charging that "a sectional party" had elected a president "whose opinions and purposes are hostile to slavery."

In other states of the cotton kingdom there was similar outrage at Lincoln's election but less certainty about how to respond to it. Those who advocated immediate secession by each state were opposed by the "cooperationists," who believed that the slave states should act as a unit rather than individually. If the cooperationists had triumphed, secession would have been delayed until a southern convention had agreed upon it. Some of these moderates hoped that a delay would provide time to extort major concessions from the North and thus remove the need for dissolving the Union. But South Carolina's unilateral action set a precedent that weakened their cause.

When conventions in six other states of the Deep South met during January 1861, delegates favoring immediate secession were everywhere in the majority; only in Alabama and Georgia did the cooperationists even come close to stemming the tide. By February 1, seven states had removed themselves from the Union—South Carolina, Alabama, Mississippi, Florida, Georgia, Louisiana, and Texas. In the upper South, however, calls for immediate secession were unsuccessful; majority opinion in Virginia, North Carolina, Tennessee, and Arkansas did not subscribe to the view that Lincoln's election was a sufficient reason for breaking up the Union.

Without waiting for their sister slave states to the north, delegates from the Deep South met in Montgomery, Alabama, on February 4 to establish the Confederate States of America. The convention acted as a provisional government while at the same time drafting a permanent constitution. Relatively moderate leaders, most of whom had not supported secession until *after* Lincoln's election, dominated the proceedings and defeated or modified some of the pet schemes of a radical faction composed of extreme southern nationalists. Voted down were proposals to reopen the Atlantic slave trade, to abolish the three-fifths clause (in favor of counting all slaves in determining congressional representation), and to prohibit the admission of free states to the new Confederacy.

The resulting constitution was surprisingly similar to that of the United States. Most of the differences merely spelled out traditional southern interpretations of the federal charter: the central government was denied the authority to impose protective tariffs, subsidize internal improvements, or interfere with slavery in the states, and was required to pass laws protecting slavery in the territories. As provisional president and vice-president, the convention chose Jefferson Davis of Mississippi and Alexander Stephens of Georgia, men who had previously resisted secessionist agitation. Stephens, in fact, had led the cooperationist forces in his home state. Radical "fire eaters" like William Yancey of Alabama and Robert Barnwell Rhett of South Carolina were denied positions of authority in the new government.

The moderation shown in Montgomery resulted in part from a desire to win support for the cause of secessionism in the reluctant states of the upper South, where such radical measures as

IMAGES OF SLAVERY

*H*istorians understand the past mainly through written documents. But much can also be learned by looking at visual materials—drawings, etchings, paintings, and photographs. A particularly rich pictorial record has survived illustrating the slave experience in the Old South.

There is no better way to appreciate the physical environment of slavery than to look at representations of the plantation. We quickly discover that some plantations were large, carefully laid-out estates, with "great houses" that are among the most impressive examples of American domestic architecture. Others, however, were essentially backwoods farms, with modest log structures arranged in a haphazard fashion. Slave quarters, too, were variable in form and construction. But it is significant that virtually all American slaves lived in individual family cabins, rather than in barracks or dormitories as in many other slave societies. This arrangement

provided a physical basis for the strong and affectionate families that most slaves struggled to establish and maintain.

But slave families could never be sure that they would not be torn apart. To enforce discipline or to pay their debts, masters frequently sold one spouse without the other or children without their parents. The cruelty and callousness inherent in slavery is well conveyed in the many contemporary depictions of the slave auction. Here we can get a sense of what it meant to treat men and women like articles of trade, denying their humanity and family feelings.

The main house, or plantation, was surrounded by the kitchen, smokehouse, well, gardens, and, sometimes, the domestic slaves' quarters. Further out, but still within the vicinity of the main house were the field slaves' quarters.

After the Sale: Slaves Going South from Richmond. *Slaves are being loaded into carts. An infant is being handed to a woman who may be the baby's mother; or, perhaps the child has been taken from the woman who holds a blanket hanging from the boxcar window.*

An Austrian artist traveling the South in the 1850s and '60s sketched the following scenes: A service in a Catholic church at which "the singing was astonishingly fine"; slaves' cabins, each occupied by only one family; wild-rice plantations along the Arkansas River; and a Louisiana sugar plantation, where the hundreds of slaves wore striped clothes for high visibility.

From other drawings and paintings we can derive some sense of the day-to-day conditions on the plantation. The kind of work that slaves did—chopping cotton, cutting sugar cane, caring for the master's house and children, performing a range of odd jobs and menial tasks—can be seen in revealing detail. We notice that slaves were sometimes supervised by black drivers rather than white overseers.

Slave work was not all drudgery; some of it even permitted the expression of strong creative impulses. Slave craftsmen produced articles of great beauty, sometimes to serve their masters and sometimes to please themselves. Art historians have found strong African influences in some of the fine pottery, wood carving, metalwork, and leatherwork that slaves produced.

Another aspect of slavery can be understood from pictures showing how slaves were dressed. Field slaves wore simple garments made of coarse cloth while house servants were often dressed quite fashionably. Differences in apparel reflected differences in status; for whites sought to "divide and conquer" by setting off the more privileged slaves from those consigned mainly to field work.

Slaves did much of the craftwork as well as the field work. Shown here are a brass servant's bell made in Natchez, Mississippi, in 1815, and a Louisiana clock dated 1833.

In Godey's Lady's Book *of 1858 slave lady's maids wore clothes that reflected the status of their fashionable mistresses.*

This black slave driver on a plantation in South Carolina was described by the artist as "a man of information, and really very well bred—though he could neither read nor write. I did not suppose it possible that a negro in the situation of a slave-driver, could be so much like a gentleman—but so it was."

Life under slavery was not all work, and some artists have left behind vivid and sometimes sympathetic illustrations of how slaves used their precious leisure time. Their images of slaves relaxing and playing music give some hint of the rich folk culture and the capacity for making the best of a bad situation that helped blacks endure servitude.

"Preparation for the enjoyment of a fine Sunday" is the notation made by Latrobe on this watercolor of the early 1800s. He carefully observed and sketched the homemade musical instruments of the slaves (below). One, a guitarlike example, had a carved figure at the end of the fingerboard. Latrobe mistakenly thought it was imported from Africa.

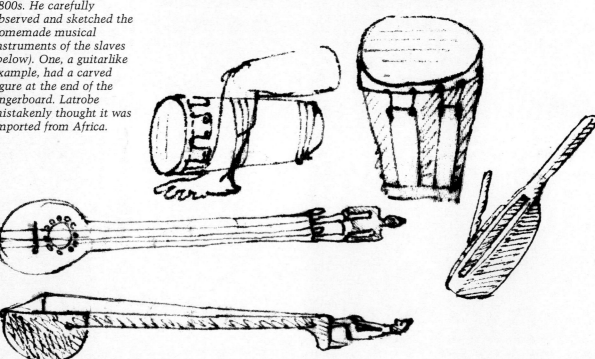

reopening the slave trade were unpopular. But it also revealed something important about the nature of the separatist impulse even in the lower South. Extremists, who were totally lacking in reverence for the Union and wished to create a new order that would carry the proslavery argument to its logical extreme of southern nationalism, had never succeeded in getting a majority behind them. Most Southerners were staunchly proslavery but had been opposed to dissolving the Union and repudiating their traditional patriotic loyalties so long as there had been good reasons to believe that slavery was safe from northern interference.

The panic following Lincoln's election destroyed that sense of security; but it was clear from the actions of the Montgomery convention that the goal of the new converts to secessionism was not to establish a slaveholders' reactionary utopia. What they really wanted was to recreate the Union as it had been before the rise of the new Republican party, and they opted for secession only when it seemed clear that separation was the only way to achieve their aim. The decision to allow free states to join the Confederacy reflected a hope that much of the old Union could be reconstituted under southern direction. Some optimists even predicted that all of the North except New England would eventually transfer their loyalty to the new government.

Secession and the formation of the Confederacy thus amounted to a very conservative and defensive kind of "revolution." The only justification for southern independence upon which a majority could agree was the need for greater security for the "peculiar institution." Vice-President Stephens spoke for all the founders of the Confederacy when he described the "cornerstone" of the new government as "the great truth that the negro is not equal to the white man—that slavery —subordination to the superior race—is his natural condition."

The Failure of Compromise

While the Deep South was opting for independence, moderates in the North and the border slave states were trying to devise a compromise that would stem the secessionist tide before it could engulf the entire South. When the lame-duck Congress reconvened in December 1860, strong sentiment existed, even among some Republicans, to seek an adjustment of sectional differences. Senator John Crittenden of Kentucky presented a plan that served as the focus for discussion. Crittenden's proposal, which resembled Henry Clay's earlier compromises, advocated extending the Missouri Compromise line to the Pacific to guarantee the protection of slavery in the southwestern territories. It also recommended federal compensation to the owners of escaped slaves and a constitutional amendment that would forever prohibit the federal government from abolishing or regulating slavery in the states. But this action was not really a concession to the South, because Republicans had always acknowledged that the federal government had no constitutional authority to meddle with slavery in the states.

Initially, congressional Republicans showed some willingness to give ground and take these proposals seriously. At one point William Seward of New York, the leading Republican in the Senate, seemed on the verge of supporting the Crittenden plan. Somewhat confused about how firmly they should support the party position that slavery must be banned in all territories, Republicans in Congress turned for guidance to the President-elect, who had remained in Springfield and was refusing to make public statements on the secession crisis. An emissary brought back word that Lincoln was adamantly opposed to the extension of the compromise line. In the words of one of his fellow Republicans, he stood "firm as an oak."

This resounding no to the central provision of the Crittenden plan stiffened the backbone of the congressional Republicans, and they voted against the compromise in committee. Also voting against it, and thereby ensuring its defeat, were the remaining senators and congressmen of the seceding states, who had vowed in advance to support no compromise unless the majority of Republicans also endorsed it. Their purpose in taking this stand was to obtain guarantees that the northern sectional party would end their attacks on "southern rights." The Republicans did in the end agree to support Crittenden's "unamendable" amendment.

Some historians have blamed Lincoln and the Republicans for causing an unnecessary war by rejecting a compromise that would have appeased southern pride without, on the face of it, providing any practical opportunities for the expansion of slavery. But it is questionable whether approval of the compromise would have halted secession of the Deep South. If we take the secessionists at their word, they would have been satisfied with nothing less than federal protection of slavery in *all* territories and the active suppression of antislavery agitation in the North.

Furthermore, Lincoln and those who took his advice had what they considered to be very good reasons for not making territorial concessions. One of these derived from the mistaken notion that the secession movement was a conspiracy that reflected the will of only a minority of Southerners. Concessions would allegedly demoralize southern Unionists and moderates by showing that the "rule-or-ruin" attitude of the radical sectionalists paid dividends. But it is doubtful that Lincoln and the dedicated freesoilers for whom he spoke would have given ground even if they had realized that the secession movement was now genuinely popular in the Deep South. In their view, extending the Missouri Compromise line of 36° 30′ to the Pacific would not halt agitation for extending slavery to new areas. South of the line were Cuba and Central America, long the target of southern expansionists who dreamed of a "Caribbean slave empire." The only way to resolve the crisis over the future of slavery and reunite "the house divided" was to remove any chance that slaveholders could enlarge their domain.

And the War Came

By the time of Lincoln's inauguration, seven states had seceded, formed an independent confederacy, and seized most federal forts and other installations in the Deep South without firing a shot. Lincoln's predecessor, James Buchanan, had denied the right of secession but had also refused to use "coercion" to maintain federal authority. His doubts whether a Union held together by force was worth keeping were for a time widely shared in the North. Besides the business community, fearful of breaking commercial links with the cotton-producing South, some antislavery Republicans and abolitionists opposed coercive action because they thought that the nation might be better off if "the erring sisters" of the Deep South were allowed "to go in peace."

The collapse of compromise efforts narrowed the choice to peaceful separation or war between the sections. By early March, the tide of public opinion was beginning to shift in favor of strong action to preserve the Union. Once the business community realized that conciliation would not keep the cotton states in the Union, it put most of its weight behind coercive measures, reasoning that a temporary disruption of commerce was better than the permanent loss of the South as a market and source of raw materials.

In his inaugural address, Lincoln called for a cautious and limited use of force. He would defend federal forts and installations not yet in Confederate hands but would not attempt to recapture the ones already taken. He thus tried to shift the burden for beginning hostilities to the Confederacy, which would have to attack before it would be attacked.

As Lincoln spoke, only four military installations within the seceded states were still held by United States forces. Two of these were in the remote Florida Keys and thus attracted little attention. The others were Fort Pickens in northern Florida, which was safely located on an island outside of the port of Pensacola, and Fort Sumter inside Charleston harbor. Attention focused on the South Carolina installation because the Confederacy was demanding the surrender of a garrison that was within easy reach of shore batteries and running low on supplies. Shortly after taking office, Lincoln was informed that Sumter could not hold out much longer and that he would have to decide whether to reinforce it or let it fall.

Initially, the majority of Lincoln's cabinet opposed efforts to reinforce or provision Sumter on the grounds that it was indefensible anyway. Secretary of State Seward was so certain that this would be the ultimate decision that he so advised representatives of the Confederacy. Lincoln kept his options open in regard to Sumter. On April 4, he ordered that an expedition be prepared to bring food and other provisions to the beleaguered troops in Charleston harbor. Two days later, he discovered that his orders to reinforce Fort Pickens had not been carried out. Later that same day, he sent word to the governor of South Carolina that the relief expedition was being sent.

At 4:30 in the morning of April 12, 1861, a Confederate battery at Fort Johnson opened fire on the Union forces at Fort Sumter in Charleston harbor. Residents of Charleston watched from their rooftops as the bombardment continued.

It sailed on April 8 and 9, but before it ever arrived, Confederate authorities decided that the sending of provisions was a hostile act and proceeded to attack the fort. Early on the morning of April 12, shore batteries opened fire; the bombardment continued for forty hours without loss of life but with heavy damage to the walls of the fort. Finally, on April 13, the Union forces under Major Robert Anderson surrendered, and the Confederate flag was raised over Fort Sumter. The South had won a victory but had also assumed responsibility for firing the first shot. Lincoln had taken pains to ensure that if the South was really determined to fight for its independence, it would have to begin by taking an aggressive action.

On April 15, Lincoln proclaimed that an insurrection existed in the Deep South and called upon the militia of the loyal states to provide seventy-five thousand troops for short-term service to put it down. Two days later, a sitting Virginia convention, which had earlier rejected secession, reversed itself and voted to join the Confederacy. Within the next five weeks, Arkansas, Tennessee, and North Carolina followed suit. These slave states of the upper South had been unwilling to secede just because Lincoln was elected, but

when he called upon them to provide troops to "coerce" other southern states, they had to choose sides. Believing that secession was a constitutional right, they were quick to cut their ties with a government that opted for the use of force to maintain the Union and called on them to join in the effort.

In the North, the firing on Sumter evoked strong feelings of patriotism and dedication to the union. "It seems as if we were never alive till now; never had a country till now," wrote a New Yorker; and a Bostonian noted that "I never before knew what a popular excitement can be." Stephen A. Douglas, Lincoln's former political rival, pledged his full support for the crusade against secession and literally worked himself to death rallying midwestern Democrats behind the government. By firing on the flag, the Confederacy united the North. Everyone assumed that the war would be short and not very bloody; it remained to be seen whether Unionist fervor could be sustained through a long and costly struggle.

The entire Confederacy, which now moved its capital from Montgomery to Richmond, Virginia, contained only eleven of the fifteen states in which slavery was lawful. In the border slave states of Maryland, Delaware, Kentucky, and Missouri, secession was thwarted by a combination of local Unionism and federal intervention. Kentucky, the most crucial of these states, greeted the outbreak of war by proclaiming its neutrality. It ended up on the Union side mainly because Lincoln was carefully to respect this tenuous neutrality and provoked the South into being the first to violate it by sending regular troops into the state. Maryland, which surrounded the nation's capital and provided it with access to the free states, was kept in the Union by more ruthless methods, which included the use of martial law to suppress Confederate sympathizers. In Missouri, the presence of regular troops, aided significantly by a staunchly pro-Union German immigrant population, stymied the secession movement.

Hence the Civil War was not, strictly speaking, a struggle between slave and free states. Nor did it simply pit states that could not tolerate Lincoln's election against those that could. More than anything else, conflicting views on the right of secession determined the ultimate division of states and the choices of individuals in areas where sentiment was divided. General Robert E. Lee, for example, was neither a defender of slavery nor a southern nationalist. But he followed Virginia out of the Union because he was the loyal son of a "sovereign state." General George Thomas, another Virginian, chose the Union because he believed that it was indissoluble. Although concern about the future of slavery had driven the Deep South to secede in the first place, the actual lineup of states and supporters meant that the two sides would define the war less as a struggle over slavery than as a contest to determine whether the Union was indivisible. (See the map of secession in the front pages of the book.)

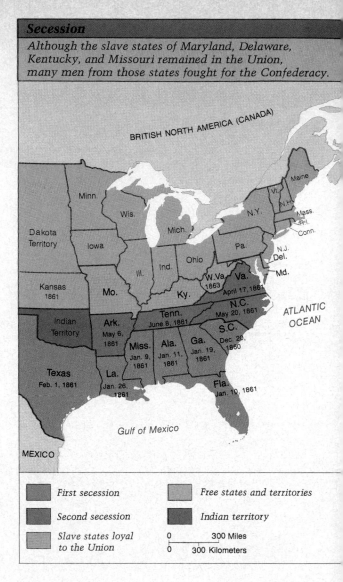

Secession

Although the slave states of Maryland, Delaware, Kentucky, and Missouri remained in the Union, many men from those states fought for the Confederacy.

Legend:
- First secession
- Second secession
- Slave states loyal to the Union
- Free states and territories
- Indian territory

0 — 300 Miles
0 — 300 Kilometers

societies, economies, and political systems, as well as a battle of wits between generals and military strategists—and the Civil War was no exception.

Adjusting to Total War

The Civil War was a "total war" because the North could achieve its aim of restoring the Union only if the South was so thoroughly defeated that its separatist government was overthrown. It was a long war because the Confederacy put up "a hell of a fight" before it would agree to be put to death. A total war is a test of

Prospects, Plans, and Expectations

If the war was to be decided by sheer physical strength, then the North had an enormous edge in population, industrial capacity, and railroad mileage (see the chart on p. 421). Nevertheless, the South had some advantages that went a long way toward counterbalancing the North's demograph-

Resources of the Union and the Confederacy, 1861

	Union	Confederacy
Population	23,000,000	8,700,000*
Real and personal property	$11,000,000,000	$5,370,000,000
Banking capital	$330,000,000	$27,000,000
Capital investment	$850,000,000	$95,000,000
Manufacturing establishments	110,000	18,000
Value of production (annual)	$1,500,000,000	$155,000,000
Industrial workers	1,300,000	110,000
Railroad mileage	22,000	9,000

*40 percent were slaves (3,500,000)

Source: From *Freedom and Crisis: An American History*, Third Edition, by Allen Weinstein and Frank Otto Gatell. Copyright © 1974, 1978, 1981 by Random House, Inc. Reprinted by permission of the publisher.

ic and industrial superiority. It could do more with less, because its armies faced an easier task. To achieve its aim of independence, the Confederacy needed only to defend its own territory successfully. The North, on the other hand, had to invade and conquer the South. Consequently, the Confederacy faced a less serious supply problem, had a greater capacity to choose the time and place of combat, and could take advantage of familiar terrain and a friendly civilian population.

The nature of the war meant that southern leaders could define their cause as defense of their homeland against an alien invader and thus appeal to the fervid patriotism of a white population that viewed Yankee domination as a form of slavery. It seemed doubtful in 1861 that Northerners would be willing to make an equal sacrifice for the relatively abstract principle that the Union was sacred and perpetual.

Confederate optimism on the eve of the war was also fed by other—and more dubious—calculations. It was widely assumed that Southerners would make better fighting men than Yankees. Farm boys used to riding and shooting could allegedly whip several times their number among the clerks and factory workers (many of them immigrants) who would make up a large part of the Union army. When most of the large proportion of high-ranking officers in the U. S. Army who were of southern origin resigned to accept Confederate commands, Southerners confidently anticipated that their armies would be better led. If external help was needed, such major foreign powers as England and France might come to the aid of the Confederacy because industrial

economies of those European nations depended on southern cotton.

As they thought about strategy in the weeks and months after Fort Sumter, the leaders of both sides tried to find the best way to capitalize on their advantages and compensate for their limitations. The choice before President Davis, who assumed personal direction of the Confederate military effort, was whether to stay on the defensive or seek a sudden and dramatic victory by invading the North. He chose to wage an essentially defensive war in the hope that he could make the Union pay so dearly for its incursions into the South that the northern populace would soon tire of the effort.

Northern military planners had greater difficulty in working out a basic strategy, and it took a good deal of trial and error (mostly error) before there was a clear sense of what had to be done. Some optimists believed that the war could be won quickly and easily by sending an army to capture the Confederate capital of Richmond, scarcely a hundred miles from Washington. The "On to Richmond" solution died on the battlefields of Virginia when it soon became clear that difficult terrain and an ably led, hard-fighting Confederate army blocked the way. Aware of the costs of invading the South at points where its forces were concentrated, the aged General Winfield Scott—who commanded the Union army during the early months of the war—recommended an "anaconda policy." Like a great boa constrictor, the North would squeeze the South into submission by blockading the southern coasts, seizing control of the Mississippi, and

left the Confederacy. His basic plan of applying pressure and probing for weaknesses at several points simultaneously was a good one because it took maximum advantage of the North's superiority in manpower and matériel. But it required better military leadership than the North possessed at the beginning of the war and took a painfully long time to put into effect.

Mobilizing the Home Fronts

The North and South faced very similar problems in trying to create the vast support systems needed by armies in the field. At the beginning of the conflict, both sides had more volunteers than could be armed and outfitted. The South was forced to reject about two hundred thousand men in the first year of the war, and the North could commit only a fraction of its forces to battle. Further confusion resulted from the fact that recruiting was done primarily by the states, which were reluctant to surrender control of the forces they had raised. Both Lincoln and Davis had to deal with governors who resisted centralized direction of the military effort.

As it became clear that hopes for a short and easy war were false, the pool of volunteers began to dry up. Many of the early recruits, who had been enrolled for short terms, showed a reluctance to reenlist. To resolve this problem, the Confederacy passed a conscription law in April 1862, and the Union edged toward a draft in July when Congress gave Lincoln the power to assign manpower quotas to each state and resort to conscription if they were not met. (See the special feature in this chapter, pp. 424–25.)

To produce the materials of war, both governments relied mainly on private industry. In the North, especially, the system of contracting with private firms and individuals to supply the army resulted in much corruption and inefficiency. The government at times bought "shoddy" uniforms that disintegrated in a heavy rain, defective rifles, and broken-down horses unfit for service. But the North's economy was strong at the core, and by 1863 its factories and farms were producing more than enough to provision the troops without significantly lowering the living standards of the civilian population.

The southern economy was much less adapta-

■ *Industrial superiority was one of the North's advantages. This gun factory at West Point, New York, supplied some three thousand cannons for Union armies.*

cutting off supplies of food and other essential commodities. This plan pointed to the West as the main locus of military operations.

Eventually Lincoln decided on a two-front war. He would keep the pressure on Virginia in the hope that a breakthrough would occur there, while at the same time he would authorize an advance down the Mississippi Valley with the aim of isolating Texas, Arkansas, and Louisiana. Lincoln also attached great importance to the coastal blockade and expected naval operations to seize the ports through which goods entered and

ble to the needs of a total war. Because of the weakness of its industrial base, the South of 1861 depended on the outside world for most of its manufactured goods. As the Union blockade became more effective, the Confederacy had to rely increasingly on a government-sponsored crash program to produce the war materials. In addition to encouraging and promoting private initiative, the government built its own munitions plants, including a gigantic powder factory at Augusta, Georgia. Astonishingly, the Confederate Ordinance Bureau, under the able direction of General Josiah Gorgas, succeeded in producing or procuring sufficient armaments to keep southern armies well supplied throughout the conflict.

Southern agriculture, however, failed to meet the challenge. Part of the problem resulted from reluctance of planters to shift from staples that could not longer be exported to foodstuffs that were urgently needed. But more significant was the inadequacy of the South's internal transportation system. Its limited rail network was designed to link plantation regions to port cities rather than connect food-producing areas with centers of population, as was the pattern in the North. New railroad construction during the war did not resolve the problem; most of it aimed to facilitate the movement of troops rather than the distribution of food.

When northern forces penetrated parts of the South, they created new gaps in the system. As a result, much of the corn or livestock that was raised could not reach the people who needed it. Although well armed, Confederate soldiers were increasingly undernourished, and by 1863 civilians in urban areas were rioting to protest shortages of food. To supply the troops, the Confederate commissary resorted to the impressment of available agricultural produce at below the market price, a policy that was resisted so vigorously by farmers and local politicians that it eventually had to be abandoned.

Another challenge faced by both sides was how to finance an enormously costly struggle. Although special war taxes were imposed, neither side was willing to resort to the heavy taxation that was needed to maintain fiscal integrity. Americans, it seems, were more willing to die for their government than to pay for it. Besides floating loans and selling bonds, both treasuries

■ *Confederate volunteers (left) at the start of the war and a young Union soldier (above). The soldiers' misconceptions of one another vanished when they met on the battlefield.*

Soldiering Through the Civil War

It took massive volunteering to make the Civil War the bloodiest in American history. Some young men joined the fight out of pure patriotism; others to prove their manhood to family, friends, or sweethearts. A rush to enlist began immediately after the attack on Fort Sumter had infected both sections with war fever. Ministers and churches gave their blessings to the righteous outrage sweeping the common folk of both sections. Stump speeches and newspaper editorials conveying the same message reached an even greater number of listeners and readers. Wherever people met in public, young men heard the call to come to the defense of the Union or the Confederacy.

Initially, the creation and supply of Union and Confederate army units was in the hands of local communities. A politician—or some other leading citizen—would search for men to fill a company or regiment. Once a unit was assembled, it elected its own officers and chose a commander—usually the man who had led the recruiting drive. The entire procedure, with its solicitation of votes and promises of patronage, was much like a peacetime local election.

But officer-politicians rarely knew the first thing about training and equipping troops, even less about commanding them in battle. Shortages of clothing and other essentials created problems that could not be solved by local initiative. Simply moving soldiers from one place to another proved a major undertaking, as calls for more than half a million troops on each side swamped the railroads and put an impossible burden on the tiny corps of professional officers who tried to coordinate the movement of men and supplies.

Early Union defeats and a strategic stalemate not only dashed the hopes on both sides for a "short engagement filled with glory" but also dampened volunteer enthusiasm. Inactivity, poor living conditions, and letters from home pleading for help with the harvest led to disillusionment.

On both sides enlistment and re-enlistment bounties were quickly instituted to maintain the ranks of the original volunteers. Terms of service were lengthened, in most cases to three years.

Even after the introduction of conscription laws in 1862–1863, volunteers vastly outnumbered draftees. Most, however, were not eager recruits. They preferred to join local units rather than be drafted and risk fighting alongside total strangers. Although the South passed the first conscription law, it maintained its army largely by inducing veterans to reenlist. By 1865, the Union had two million men under arms; the Confederacy, five hundred thousand.

Despite high rates of desertion, the armies did not disappear under the strain of war—but neither did the problems of maintaining and handling them. Discipline was a pressing concern on both sides. The early battles were contests between armed mobs that might break and run with little provocation.

The solution hit upon by both sides, but used most effectively by the Union, was the army training camp. With its "50,000 pup tents and wigwams," the camp was the volunteer's way station between home and battlefield. Many recruits spent their entire terms of service shuttling between these tent cities, forming a huge reserve upon which field commanders could call to replace casualties. Fewer men died of wounds than of dysentery, typhoid fever, and other waterborne diseases contracted in the camps, which were often located on swampy land without adequate fresh water. Food became steadily more plentiful in the Union camps. But men in the field were condemned to a steady diet of "hardtack and half-cooked beans," which produced its own set of diseases, particularly scurvy.

Despite the cost in human life, the camps were essential to the final Union victory. Professional noncommissioned officers from the peacetime army were used to turn men into soldiers who could fire a rifle and understand simple commands. Bored soldiers starved for reading material formed a ready audience for camp newspapers, which harped on the theme of obedience and the need to trust regular Army officers. The liberal use of the court-martial and the board of review enabled the professional soldiers to rid the army of its most incompetent officer-politicians and instill discipline in the ranks. Camp newspapers reported these proceedings, which ran into the hundreds each month, and spread the word that disobedience and disloyalty would not be tolerated. Discipline also benefited the common soldier's health, as doctors, officers, and agents of the United States Sanitary Commission teamed up to improve camp cleanliness and reduce disease.

Soldiers in camp and in the field retained a keen interest in politics. In the North, soldier support was crucial for Lincoln. Although voting was often difficult, military men who had the chance consistently gave overwhelming majorities to the Republican party. (The sketch on p. 424 shows soldiers voting in the 1864 election near the Petersburg lines.)

While the Union soldier's experience moved toward a higher standard of living and acceptable discipline, "Johnny Reb" had to survive under steadily worsening conditions. The Confederate supply system did not improve significantly during the course of the war and grew worse wherever the North invaded or blockaded. Friction resulting from class differences between gentlemen planters and yeoman farmers placed an additional burden on command and morale.

Although the training and supply of northern troops became increasingly superior to what Southerners could expect, the battlefield performance of fighting men on the two sides remained roughly on a par throughout the war. Camp lessons were often forgotten in the heat of battle, particularly by green troops who "saw the elephant" (went into battle for the first time) and ran from it. The Union's ability to call more new men into service may have guaranteed ultimate victory, but it meant that battle-hardened Confederate veterans faced large numbers of raw northern recruits in every major battle. Since experience often counted for more than basic training and equipment, southern troops could expect to engage the enemy on fairly equal terms. Furthermore, lapses of discipline on either side did not always produce negative results. At the battle of Chattanooga (1863), Union troops ordered to make a cautious advance instead stormed a strategic ridge under murderous fire and routed the entrenched enemy. When General Grant demanded to know by whose order this was done, a subordinate replied, "Their own, I fancy."

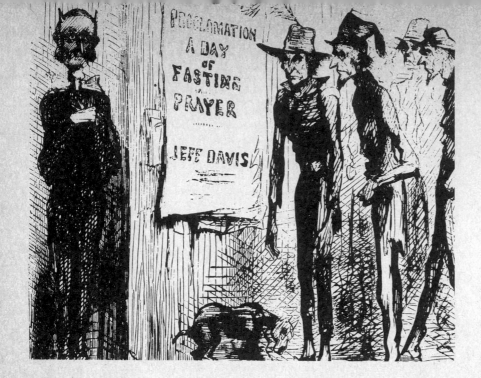

Gaunt southern citizens stare unbelievingly at a poster announcing a day of fasting proclaimed by a horned Jefferson Davis. Davis' insistent demands for supplies for his army aroused the hard-pressed Southerners' anger.

deliberately inflated the currency by printing large quantities of paper money that could not be redeemed in gold and silver. In August 1861 the Confederacy issued $100 million of such currency, and the Union followed suit by printing $150 million in early 1862. The presses rolled throughout the war, and runaway inflation was the inevitable result. But the problem was much less severe in the North, because of the overall strength of its economy. War taxes on income were more readily collectable than in the South, and bond issues were more successful.

The Confederacy was hampered from the outset by a severe shortage of readily disposable wealth that could be tapped for public purposes. Land and cotton could not easily be turned into rifles and cannons, and the southern treasury had to accept payments "in kind." As a result, Confederate "assets" eventually consisted mainly of bales of cotton that were unexportable because of the blockade. As the Confederate government fell deeper and deeper into debt and printed more and more paper money, its rate of inflation soared out of sight. By August 1863 a Confederate dollar was worth only eight cents in gold. Late in the war, it could be said with little exaggeration that it took a wheelbarrow full of money to buy a purse full of goods.

Political Leadership: Northern Success and Southern Failure

Total war also forced political adjustments, and both the Union and the Confederacy had to face the question of how much democracy and individual freedom could be permitted when military success required an unprecedented exercise of governmental authority. Since both constitutions made the president commander in chief of the army and navy, Lincoln and Davis took actions that would have been regarded as arbitrary or even tyrannical in peacetime. But "politics as usual"—in the form of free elections, public political controversy, and the maneuverings of parties, factions, and interest groups—persisted to a surprising degree.

Lincoln was especially bold in assuming new executive powers. After the fighting started at Fort Sumter, he expanded the regular army and advanced public money to private individuals without authorization by Congress. On April 27, 1861, he declared martial law, which enabled the military to arrest civilians suspected of aiding the enemy, and suspended the writ of habeas corpus in the area between Philadelphia and Washington, an action deemed necessary because of mob attacks on Union troops passing through Baltimore.

Suspension of the writ enabled the government to arrest Confederate sympathizers and hold them without trial, and in September 1862 Lincoln extended this authority to all parts of the United States where "disloyal" elements were active. Such executive interference with civil liberties was unprecedented and possibly unconstitutional, but Lincoln argued that "necessity" justified a flexible interpretation of his war powers. For critics of suspension he had a question: "are all the laws, *but one*, to go unexecuted, and the government itself to go to pieces, lest that one be violated?" During the war approximately ten thousand suspected subversives were detained by northern military authorities, despite a storm of protest from Democrats and civil libertarians.

For the most part, however, the Lincoln administration showed restraint and tolerated a broad spectrum of political dissent. Although the government closed down a few newspapers for brief periods, antiadministration journals were allowed to criticize the President and his party almost at will. "Peace Democrats"—who called for restoration of the Union by negotiation rather than force—ran for office, sat in Congress and in state legislatures, and thus had ample opportunity to present their views to the public. Lincoln's hand was in fact strengthened by the persistence of vigorous two-party competition in the North during the Civil War. Since his war policies were also the platform of his party, he could usually rely on unified partisan backing for his most controversial decisions.

Jefferson Davis, most historians agree, was a less effective war leader than Lincoln. He defined his powers as commander in chief narrowly and literally, which meant that he assumed personal direction of the armed forces but left policymaking for the mobilization and control of the civilian population primarily to the Confederate Congress. Unfortunately, he overestimated his capacities as a strategist and lacked the tact to handle field commanders who were as proud and testy as he was. Two of the South's best generals —Joseph E. Johnston and P. G. T. Beauregard— were denied the commands that they deserved because they could not get along with Davis. One of the worst—Braxton E. Bragg—happened to be a personal favorite of the President and was allowed to keep a major command even after he had clearly demonstrated his incompetence.

■ *Jefferson Davis, inaugurated as president of the Confederacy on February 18, 1861, was a West Point graduate and had served as secretary of war under President Franklin Pierce.*

Davis' greatest failing, however, was his lack of initiative and leadership in dealing with the problems of the home front. He devoted little attention to a deteriorating economic situation that caused great hardship and sapped Confederate morale. Although the South had a much more serious problem of internal division and disloyalty than the North, he refrained from declaring martial law on his own authority. The Confederate Congress grudgingly voted him such power when he asked for it but allowed it to be applied only in limited areas and for short periods.

As the war dragged on, Davis' political and popular support eroded. He was opposed and obstructed by state governors—such as Joseph E. Brown of Georgia and Zebulon Vance of North Carolina—who resisted conscription and other Confederate policies that violated the tradition of states' rights. The Confederate Congress served as a forum for bitter attacks on the administration's conduct of the war, and by 1863 a majority of southern newspapers were taking an anti-Davis line. Even if he had been a more able and inspiring leader, Davis would have had difficulty maintaining his authority and credibility. Unlike Lincoln, he did not have an organized party behind him, for the Confederacy never developed a two-party system. As a result, it was difficult to mobilize the support required for hard decisions and controversial policies.

Early Campaigns and Battles

The first campaign of the war was a minor triumph for the Union, as forces under General George McClellan succeeded in driving Confederate troops out of the Kanawha Valley of western Virginia during May and June 1861. McClellan's victory ensured that this region of predominantly Unionist sentiment remained under northern control; out of it came the new "loyal" state of West Virginia, organized and admitted to the Union in 1863.

But the war's first major battle was a disaster for northern arms. Against his better judgment, General Winfield Scott responded to the "On to Richmond" clamor and ordered poorly trained Union troops under General Irvin McDowell to advance against the Confederate forces gathered at Manassas Junction, Virginia. They attacked the enemy position near Bull Run Creek on July 21 and seemed on their way to victory until Confederate reinforcements arrived from the Shenandoah Valley. After General Thomas J. Jackson had earned the nickname "Stonewall" for holding the line against the northern assault, the augmented southern army counterattacked and routed the invading force. As they retreated toward Washington, the raw Union troops gave way to panic and broke ranks in their stampede to safety.

The humiliating defeat at Bull Run led to a shake-up of the northern high command. The man of the hour was George McClellan, who first replaced McDowell as commander of troops in the Washington area and then became general in chief when Scott was eased into retirement. A cautious disciplinarian, McClellan spent the fall and winter drilling his troops and whipping them into shape. President Lincoln, who could not understand why McClellan was taking so long to

go into the field, became increasingly impatient and finally tried to order the army into action.

Before McClellan could make his move, Union forces in the West won some important victories. In February 1862, a joint military-naval operation, commanded by General Ulysses S. Grant, captured Fort Henry on the Tennessee River and Fort Donelson on the Cumberland. Fourteen thousand prisoners were taken at Donelson, and the Confederate army was forced to withdraw from Kentucky and middle Tennessee. Southern forces in the West then massed at Corinth, Mississippi, just across the border from Tennessee. When a slow-moving Union army arrived just north of the Mississippi state line, the South launched a surprise attack on April 6. In the battle of Shiloh, one of the bloodiest of the war, only the timely arrival of reinforcements prevented the annihilation of Union troops backed up against the Tennessee River. After a second day of fierce fighting, the Confederates retreated to Corinth, leaving the enemy forces battered and exhausted.

Although the military effort to seize control of the Mississippi Valley was temporarily halted at Shiloh, the Union navy soon contributed dramatically to the pursuit of that objective. On April 26 a fleet under Flag Officer David Farragut, coming up from the Gulf, captured the port of New Orleans after boldly running past the forts below the city. The occupation of New Orleans, besides securing the mouth of the Mississippi, climaxed of a series of naval and amphibious operations around the edges of the Confederacy that had already succeeded in capturing South Carolina's Sea Islands and North Carolina's Roanoke Island. Strategically located bases were thus provided to enforce a blockade of the southern coast. The last serious challenge to the North's naval supremacy ended on March 9, 1862, when the Confederate ironclad vessel *Virginia* (originally the U.S.S. *Merrimack*)—which had demolished wooden-hulled northern ships in the vicinity of Hampton Roads, Virginia—was driven back by the *Monitor*, an armored and turreted Union gunship.

Successes around the edges of the Confederacy did not relieve northern frustration at the inactivity or failure of Union forces on the eastern front. Only after Lincoln had relieved him of supreme command and ordered him to take the offensive at the head of the Army of the Potomac did

■ *The battle of the ironclads between the huge* Merrimack *and the smaller* Monitor *ended in a draw. Both ships were later lost; the* Merrimack *was blown up in Norfolk harbor in May 1862 and the* Monitor *went down in a gale in December.*

McClellan start campaigning. Spurning the treacherous overland route to Richmond, he moved his forces by water to the peninsula southeast of the Confederate capital. After landing at Fortress Monroe, which had remained in Union hands, McClellan began moving up the peninsula in early April 1862. For a month he was bogged down before Yorktown, which he chose to besiege rather than assault directly. After Yorktown fell on May 4, he pushed ahead to a point twenty miles from Richmond, where he awaited the additional troops that he expected Lincoln to send.

These reinforcements were not forthcoming because the President concluded that they were needed to defend Washington. While McClellan was inching his way up the peninsula, a relatively small southern force under Stonewall Jackson was on the rampage in the Shenandoah Valley, where it succeeded in pinning down a much larger Union army and defeating its detached parts in a series of lightning moves. When it appeared by late May that Jackson might be poised to march east and attack the Union capital, Lincoln decided to withhold troops from McClellan.

If McClellan had moved more boldly and decisively, he probably could have captured Richmond with the forces he had. But a combination of faulty intelligence reports and his own natural caution led him to falter in the face of what he wrongly believed to be superior numbers. At the end of May, the Confederates under Joseph E. Johnston took the offensive when they discovered that McClellan's army was divided on either side of the Chickahominy River. In the battle of Seven Pines, McClellan was barely able to hold his ground on the side of the river under attack until a corps from the other side crossed over just in time to save the day. During the battle, General Johnston was severely wounded; succeeding him in command of the Confederate Army of Northern Virginia was native Virginian and West Point graduate Robert E. Lee.

Toward the end of June, Lee began an all-out effort to expel McClellan from the outskirts of Richmond. In a series of battles that lasted for seven days, the two armies clawed at each other indecisively. Although McClellan repulsed Lee's final assaults at Malvern Hill, the Union general decided to retreat down the peninsula to a more secure base. This backward step convinced Lincoln that the peninsula campaign was an exercise in futility.

On July 11 Lincoln appointed General Henry W. Halleck, who had been in overall command in the western theater, to be the new general in chief and through him ordered McClellan to withdraw his army from the peninsula to join a force under General John Pope that was preparing to move on Richmond by the overland route. As usual, McClellan was slow in responding, and the Confederates got to Pope before he did. At the end of August, in the second battle fought near Bull Run, Lee established his reputation for brilliant generalship; he sent Stonewall Jackson to Pope's rear, provoked the rash Union general to attack Jackson with full force, and then threw the main Confederate army against the Union's flank. Badly beaten, Pope retreated to the defenses of Washington where he was stripped of command. Out of sheer desperation, Lincoln reappointed McClellan to head the Army of the Potomac.

Lee proceeded to lead his exuberant troops on an invasion of Maryland, in the hope of isolating Washington from the rest of the North. McClellan caught up with him near Sharpsburg, and the bloodiest one-day battle of the war ensued. When the smoke cleared at Antietam on September 17, almost five thousand men had been killed on the two sides and more than eighteen thousand wounded. The result was a draw, but Lee was forced to fall back south of the Potomac to protect his dangerously extended supply lines. McClellan was slow in pursuit, and Lincoln blamed him for letting the enemy escape.

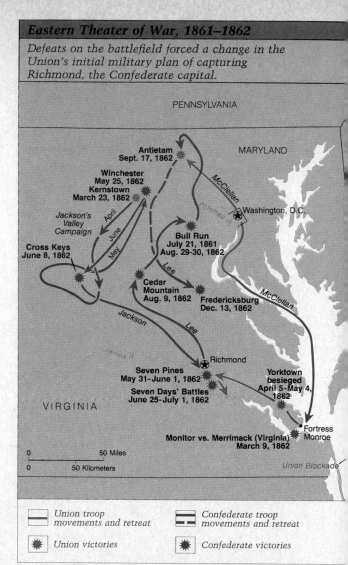

Eastern Theater of War, 1861–1862

Defeats on the battlefield forced a change in the Union's initial military plan of capturing Richmond, the Confederate capital.

PENNSYLVANIA

MARYLAND

Antietam
Sept. 17, 1862

Winchester
May 25, 1862

Kernstown
March 23, 1862

Jackson's Valley Campaign

Washington, D.C.

Bull Run
July 21, 1861
Aug. 29-30, 1862

Cross Keys
June 8, 1862

Cedar Mountain
Aug. 9, 1862

Fredericksburg
Dec. 13, 1862

James R.

Richmond

Yorktown besieged
April 5-May 4, 1862

Seven Pines
May 31-June 1, 1862

Seven Days' Battles
June 25-July 1, 1862

VIRGINIA

Monitor vs. Merrimack (Virginia)
March 9, 1862

Fortress Monroe

Union Blockade

0 ___ 50 Miles
0 ___ 50 Kilometers

	Union troop movements and retreat		Confederate troop movements and retreat
	Union victories		Confederate victories

In this Matthew Brady photograph (right), taken after the furious and brutal fighting at Antietam, the unburied body of a young rebel soldier lies next to the fresh grave of a fallen Union opponent.

After Antietam, Lincoln visited McClellan's field headquarters (far right) to urge the general to take action. McClellan is on the left facing the President.

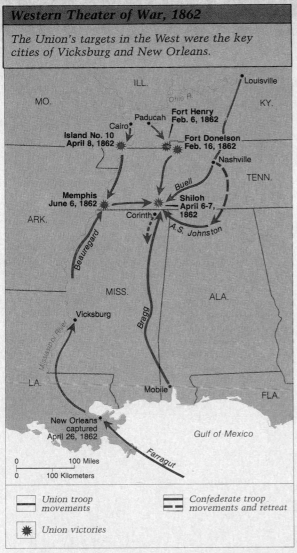

Convinced that McClellan was fatally infected with "the slows," Lincoln once again sought a more aggressive general and put Ambrose E. Burnside in command of the Army of the Potomac. Burnside was aggressive enough, but he was also rather dense. His limitations were disastrously revealed at the battle of Fredericksburg, Virginia, on December 13, 1862, when he launched a direct assault to try to capture an entrenched and elevated position. Throughout the Civil War such uphill charges almost invariably failed because of the range and deadly accuracy of small arms fire when concentrated on exposed troops. The debacle at Fredericksburg, where Union forces suffered more than twice as many casualties as their opponents, ended a year of bitter failure for the North on the eastern front.

The Diplomatic Struggle

The critical period of Civil War diplomacy was 1861–1862, when the South was making every effort to induce major foreign powers to recognize its independence and break the Union blockade. The hope that England and France could be persuaded to involve themselves in the war on the Confederate side stemmed from the fact that these nations depended on the South for three quarters of their cotton supply. In the case of Britain, the uninterrupted production of cotton textiles appeared essential to economic prosperity; an estimated 20 to 25 percent of its entire

population was supported directly or indirectly by this single industry.

The Confederate commissioners sent to England and France in May 1861 succeeded in gaining recognition of southern "belligerency," which meant that the new government could claim some of the international rights of a nation at war. The North protested vigorously, but by declaring a blockade of southern ports, it had undermined its official position that the rebellion was merely a domestic insurrection. The main advantage of belligerent status was that it permitted the South to purchase and outfit privateers in neutral ports. As a result, Confederate raiders, built and armed in British shipyards, like the *Alabama*—which single-handedly sunk sixty-two vessels—devastated northern shipping to such an extent that insurance costs eventually forced most of the American merchant marine off the high seas for the duration of the war.

In the fall of 1861 the Confederate government dispatched James M. Mason and John Slidell to be its permanent envoys to England and France respectively and instructed them to push for full recognition of the Confederacy. They took passage on the British steamer *Trent*, which was stopped and boarded in international waters by a United States warship. Mason and Slidell were taken into custody by the Union captain, causing a diplomatic crisis that nearly led to war between England and the United States. Refusing to tolerate this flagrant violation of its maritime rights, Britain threatened war if the Confederate emissaries were not released. After a few weeks of ferocious posturing by both sides, Lincoln and Secretary of State Seward made the prudent decision to allow Mason and Slidell to proceed to their destinations.

These envoys may as well have stayed at home; they failed in their mission to obtain full recognition of the Confederacy from either England or France. The anticipated cotton shortage was slow to develop, for the bumper crop of 1860 had created a large surplus in British and French warehouses. Recognition did seem likely for a brief period in the fall of 1862. Napoleon III, the emperor of France, personally favored the southern cause, mainly because he was trying to set up a puppet government in Mexico and saw the chance to trade French support of the Confederacy for an acceptance of his regime south of the

Lord Punch: "That was Jeff Davis . . . Don't you recognize him?" Lord Pam (Palmerston): "Not exactly—may have to do so some of these days." In fact, Britain never recognized the Confederacy.

border. But he was unwilling to risk war with the United States unless the British would cosponsor his plan to offer European mediation of the American conflict and then recognize the Confederacy if—as expected—the North refused to go along.

British opinion, both official and public, was seriously divided on how to respond to the American conflict. In 1861 and '62 Lord Palmerston, the prime minister, and Lord Russell, the foreign secretary, played a cautious waiting game. Their government was sympathetic to the South but wary of the danger of war with the North if they acted on their preferences. Northern diplomats knew how to play on these fears: Secretary of State Seward and Charles Francis Adams, the American minister to Great Britain, could be relied upon to threaten war at any hint of British recognition or support of the Confederacy.

In September 1862 the British cabinet debated mediation and recognition as serious possibilities. Lord Russell pressed for a pro-Confederate policy because he was convinced that the South was now strong enough to secure its independence. But when word arrived that Lee had failed to win a clear victory at Antietam and was retreating, Lord Palmerston overruled the foreign secretary and decided to maintain a hands-off policy. The British would intervene, his decision suggested, only if the South won decisively on the battlefield.

The cotton famine finally hit in late 1862, causing massive unemployment in the British textile industry. But, contrary to southern hopes, public opinion did not force the government to abandon its neutrality and use force to break the Union blockade. Historians used to believe that unselfish pro-Union sympathy among the suffering mill workers was a main cause of restraint, but this theory ignored the fact that the British working class still lacked the right to vote and thus had little influence over policy.

Influential interest groups, which actually benefited from the famine, provided the crucial support for continuing a policy of nonintervention. Among these groups were owners of large cotton mills who had made bonanza profits on their existing stocks and were happy to see weaker competitors go under while they awaited new sources of supply. By early 1863 cotton from Egypt and India put the industry back on the track toward full production. Other obvious beneficiaries of nonintervention were manufacturers of wool and linen textiles, munition-makers who supplied both sides, and shipping interests who profited from the decline of American competition on the world's sea lanes. Since the British economy as a whole gained more than it lost from neutrality, it is not surprising that there was little effective pressure for a change in policy.

By early 1863, when it was clear that "King Cotton Diplomacy" had failed, the Confederacy broke off formal relations with Great Britain. Its hopes for foreign intervention came to nothing because the European powers acted out of self-interest and calculated that the advantages of getting involved were not worth the risk of a war with the United States. Only a decisive military victory would have gained recognition for southern independence, and if the Confederacy had actually won such a victory, it would not have needed foreign backing.

Fight to the Finish

The last two and a half years of the struggle saw the implementation of more radical war measures. The most dramatic and important of these was the North's effort to follow through on Lincoln's decision to free the slaves and bring the black population into the war on the Union side. The tide of battle turned in the summer of 1863, but the South continued to resist valiantly for two more years, until finally overcome by the sheer weight of the North's advantages in manpower and resources.

The Coming of Emancipation

At the beginning of the war, when the North still hoped for a quick and easy victory, only dedicated abolitionists favored turning the struggle for the Union into a crusade against slavery. In the summer of 1861 Congress voted almost unanimously for a resolution affirming that the war was being fought only to preserve the Union and not to change the domestic institutions of any state. But as it became clear how hard it was going to be to subdue the "rebels," sentiment developed for striking a blow at the South's economic and social system by freeing its slaves. In a tentative move toward emancipation, Congress in July 1862 authorized the government to confiscate the slaves of masters who supported the Confederacy.

Although Lincoln favored freedom for blacks as an ultimate goal, he was reluctant to commit his administration to a policy of immediate emancipation. In the fall of 1861 and again in the spring of 1862, he disallowed the orders of field commanders who sought to free slaves in areas occupied by their forces, thus angering abolitionists and the strongly antislavery Republicans known as "Radicals." Lincoln's caution stemmed from a fear of alienating Unionist elements in the border slave states and from his own preference for a gradual, compensated form of emancipation. He hoped that such a plan could be put into effect in loyal slaveholding areas and then extended to the rebellious states as the basis for a voluntary restoration of the Union.

Lincoln was also aware that one of the main obstacles to any program leading to emancipation was the strong racial prejudices of most whites in both the North and the South. Although personally more tolerant than many, Lincoln was pessimistic about the prospects of equality for blacks in the United States. He therefore coupled his moderate proposals with a plea for government subsidies to support the voluntary "colonization" of freed blacks outside of the United States, and he actively sought places that would accept them.

But the slaveholding states that remained loyal to the Union refused to endorse Lincoln's gradual plan, and the failure of Union arms in the spring and summer of 1862 increased the public clamor for striking directly at the South's peculiar institution. In July Lincoln drafted an emancipation proclamation and read it to his cabinet but was persuaded by Secretary of State Seward not to issue it until the North had won a victory and could not be accused of acting out of sheer desperation. Later in the summer Lincoln responded publicly to critics of his cautious policy, indicating that he would take any action in regard to slavery that would further the Union cause.

Finally, on September 22, 1862, Lincoln issued his preliminary Emancipation Proclamation. Mc-

Clellan's success in stopping Lee at Antietam provided the occasion, but the President was also responding to growing political pressures. Most Republican politicians were now firmly committed to an emancipation policy, and many were on the verge of repudiating the administration for its inaction. Had Lincoln failed to act, his party would have been badly split, and he would have been in the minority faction. The proclamation gave the Confederate states one hundred days to give up the struggle without losing their slaves. There was little chance that they would do so, but Lincoln was still leaving the door open for a more conservative and peaceful way of ending slavery than sudden emancipation at the point of a gun. In December Lincoln proposed to Congress that it approve a series of constitutional amendments providing for gradual, compensated emancipation and subsidized colonization.

Since there was no response from the South and little enthusiasm in Congress for Lincoln's gradual plan, the President went ahead on January 1, 1863, declaring that all slaves in those areas under Confederate control "shall be . . . thenceforward, and forever free." He justified the final proclamation as an act of "military necessity" sanctioned by the war powers of the president and authorized the enlistment of freed slaves in the Union army. The language and tone of the

EMANCIPATION

A romanticized engraving (left) celebrating the Emancipation Proclamation for breaking the chains of slavery.

The 54th Massachusetts Colored Regiment charging Fort Wagner, South Carolina, July 1863. The 54th was the first black unit recruited during the war. Charles and Lewis Douglass, sons of Frederick Douglass, served with this regiment.

document—one historian has described it as having "all the moral grandeur of a bill of lading"—made it clear that blacks were being freed for reasons of state and not out of humanitarian conviction.

Despite its uninspiring origin and limited application—it did not extend to loyal slave states or to occupied areas—the proclamation did commit the Union to the abolition of slavery as a war aim. It also accelerated the breakdown of slavery as a labor system, a process that was already well under way by early 1863. The blacks who had remained in captured areas or deserted their masters to cross Union lines before 1863 had been kept in a kind of way station between slavery and freedom, in accordance with the theory that they were "contraband of war." As word spread among the slaves that emancipation was now official policy, larger numbers of them were inspired to run off and seek the protection of approaching northern armies. One slave who crossed the Union lines summed up their motives: "I wants to be free. I came in from the plantation and don't want to go back; . . . I don't want to be a slave again." Approximately one quarter of the slave population gained freedom during the war under the terms of the Emancipation Proclamation and thus deprived the South of an important part of its agricultural work force.

The Black Role in the War

Amost two hundred thousand Afro-Americans, most of them newly freed slaves, eventually served in the Union armed forces and made a vital contribution to the North's victory. Although they were enrolled in segregated units under white officers, initially paid less than their white counterparts, and used disproportionately for garrison duty or heavy labor behind the lines, "blacks in blue" fought heroically in several major battles during the last two years of the war. The assistant secretary of war observed them in action at Millikin's Bend on the Mississippi in June 1863 and reported that "the bravery of blacks in the battle . . . completely revolutionized the sentiment of the army with regard to the employment of Negro troops."

Wartime freedmen who avoided military service were often conscripted to serve as contract wage laborers on cotton plantations owned or leased by "loyal" white planters within the occupied areas of the Deep South. Abolitionists protested that the coercion used by military authorities to get blacks back into the cotton fields amounted to slavery in a new form, but those in power argued that the necessities of war and the northern economy required such "temporary" arrangements. To some extent, regimentation of

E.W. McINTOSH Co. E. 141
Being Exchanged at Vicks
mach for from 1865
Andersonville Prison

■ *The prison camps of the North (like Point
Lookout, Maryland, above) and the South (like
Andersonville, Georgia, right) were equally
deadly. Nearly fifty thousand prisoners died in
the camps during the war.*

the freedmen within the South was a way of
assuring racially prejudiced Northerners, especially in the Midwest, that emancipation would
not result in a massive migration of black refugees to their region of the country.

The heroic performance of Afro-American
troops and the easing of northern fears of being
swamped by black migrants led to a deepening
commitment to emancipation as a permanent
and comprehensive policy. Realizing that his
proclamation had a shaky constitutional foundation and might apply only to slaves actually freed
while the war was going on, Lincoln sought to
organize and recognize loyal state governments
in southern areas under Union control on condition that they abolish slavery in their constitutions. He also encouraged local campaigns to
emancipate the slaves in the border states and
saw them triumph in Maryland and Missouri in
1864.

Finally, Lincoln pressed for an amendment to
the federal constitution outlawing involuntary
servitude. After supporting its inclusion as a
central plank in the Republican platform of 1864,
Lincoln used all his influence to win congressional approval for the new Thirteenth Amendment.
On January 31, 1865, the House approved the

amendment by a narrow margin. There was an
explosion of joy on the floor and in the galleries,
and then the House voted to adjourn for the rest
of the day "in honor of this immortal and sublime
event." The cause of freedom for blacks and the
cause of the Union had at last become one and the
same. Lincoln, despite his earlier hesitations and
misgivings, had earned the right to go down in
history as "the great emancipator."

The Tide Turns

By early 1863 the Confederate economy was in
shambles and its diplomacy had collapsed. The
social order of the South was also showing signs
of severe strain. Masters were losing control of
their slaves, and nonslaveholding whites were
becoming disillusioned with the hardships of a
war that some of them described as a "rich man's
war and a poor man's fight." As slaves fled from
the plantations, increasing numbers of lower-
class whites deserted the army or refused to be
drafted in the first place. Whole counties in the
southern backcountry became "deserter havens,"
which Confederate officials could enter only at
the risk of their lives. Appalachian mountaineers,

who had remained loyal to the Union, resisted the Confederacy more directly by mounting a small-scale guerrilla war behind southern lines.

Yet the North was slow to capitalize on the South's internal weaknesses; it had its own serious morale problems. The long series of defeats on the eastern front had engendered war weariness, and the new policies that "military necessity" forced the government to adopt encountered fierce opposition.

Although popular with Republicans, emancipation was viewed by most Democrats as a betrayal of northern war aims. Racism was a main ingredient in their opposition to freeing blacks. According to one Democratic senator, "We mean that the United States . . . shall be the white man's home . . . and the nigger shall never be his equal." Riding a backlash against the preliminary proclamation, Democrats made significant gains in the congressional elections of 1862, especially in the Midwest where they also captured several state legislatures.

The Enrollment Act of March 1863, which provided for outright conscription, provoked a violent response from those unwilling to "fight for the niggers." A series of antidraft riots broke out, culminating in the bloodiest domestic disorder in American history—the New York riot of July 1863. The New York mob, composed mainly of Irish-American laborers, burned the draft office, the homes of leading Republicans, and an orphanage for black children. They also lynched more than a dozen defenseless blacks who fell into their hands. At least 120 people died before federal troops restored order.

To fight dissension and "disloyalty," the government used its martial law authority to arrest the alleged ringleaders, including one prominent Democratic congressman. Patriotic private organizations also issued a barrage of propaganda aimed at what they believed was a vast secret conspiracy to undermine the northern war effort. Historians disagree about the real extent of covert and illegal antiwar activity, but militant advocates of "peace at any price"—popularly known as Copperheads —were certainly active in some areas, especially among the immigrant working classes of large cities and in southern Ohio, Indiana, and Illinois.

The only effective way to overcome the disillusionment that fed the peace movement was to start winning battles and thus convince the

An 1863 draft call in New York provoked a riot when the draftees learned that rich men had been able to buy exemptions from the draft.

northern public that victory was assured. But before this could happen the North suffered one more humiliating defeat on the eastern front. In early May 1863, Union forces under General Joseph Hooker were routed at Chancellorsville, Virginia, by a Confederate army less than half its size. Once again, Robert E. Lee demonstrated his superior generalship, this time by dividing his forces and sending Stonewall Jackson to make a devastating surprise attack on the Union right. But the Confederacy did suffer one major loss: Jackson himself died as a result of wounds he received in the battle.

In the West, however, a major Union triumph was taking shape. For over a year, General Ulysses S. Grant had been trying to put his forces in position to capture Vicksburg, Mississippi, the almost inaccessible Confederate bastion that stood between the North and control of the Mississippi River. Finally, in late March 1863, he crossed the river north of the city and moved his forces to a point south of it, where he joined up

■ *Bold and decisive, Confederate General Robert E. Lee (above) often combated an enemy army that greatly outnumbered his own troops. Union General Ulysses S. Grant (right) demonstrated a remarkable capacity to capitalize on his opponents' mistakes.*

with naval forces that had run the Confederate batteries mounted on Vicksburg's high bluffs. In one of the boldest campaigns of the war, Grant crossed the river, deliberately cutting himself off from his sources of supply, and marched into the interior of Mississippi. Living off the land and out of communication with an anxious and perplexed Lincoln, his troops won a series of victories over two separate Confederate armies and advanced on Vicksburg from the east. After unsuccessfully assaulting the city's defenses, Grant settled down for a siege on May 22.

The Confederate government considered and rejected proposals to mount a major offensive into Tennessee and Kentucky in the hope of drawing Grant away from Vicksburg. Instead, President Davis approved Robert E. Lee's plan for an all-out invasion of the Northeast. Although this option provided no hope for relieving Vicksburg, it might lead to a dramatic victory that would more than

compensate for loss of the Mississippi stronghold. Lee's army crossed the Potomac in June and kept going until it reached Gettysburg, Pennsylvania. There Lee confronted a Union army that had taken up strong defensive positions on Cemetery Ridge and Culp's Hill. This was one of the few occasions in the war when the North could capitalize on the tactical advantage of choosing its ground and then defending it against an enemy whose supply lines were extended.

On July 2 a series of Confederate attacks failed to dislodge General George Meade's troops from the high ground they occupied. The following day Lee faced the choice of retreating to protect his lines of communcation or launching a final, desperate assault. With more boldness than wisdom, he chose to make a direct attack on the strongest part of the Union line. The resulting charge on Cemetery Ridge was disastrous; advancing Confederate soldiers dropped like flies under the

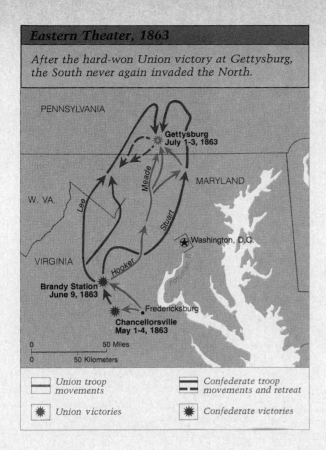

Eastern Theater, 1863

After the hard-won Union victory at Gettysburg, the South never again invaded the North.

PENNSYLVANIA

Gettysburg
July 1–3, 1863

Meade

MARYLAND

W. VA.

Lee

Stuart

Washington, D.C.

VIRGINIA

Hooker

Brandy Station
June 9, 1863

Fredericksburg

Chancellorsville
May 1–4, 1863

| 0 | 50 Miles |
| 0 | 50 Kilometers |

□ Union troop movements
□ Union victories
■ Confederate troop movements and retreat
✸ Confederate victories

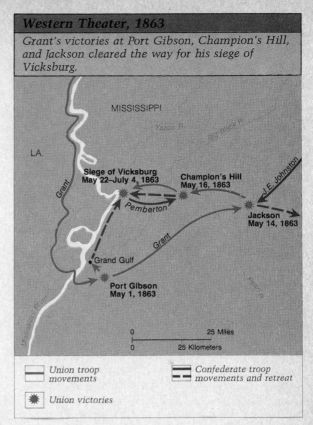

Western Theater, 1863

Grant's victories at Port Gibson, Champion's Hill, and Jackson cleared the way for his siege of Vicksburg.

MISSISSIPPI

Yazoo R.

Big Black R.

LA.

Siege of Vicksburg
May 22–July 4, 1863

Champion's Hill
May 16, 1863

J. E. Johnston

Grant

Pemberton

Jackson
May 14, 1863

Grand Gulf

Grant

Port Gibson
May 1, 1863

Pearl R.

Mississippi River

| 0 | 25 Miles |
| 0 | 25 Kilometers |

□ Union troop movements
□ Union victories
■ Confederate troop movements and retreat

barrage of Union artillery and rifle fire. Only a few made it to the top of the ridge, and they were killed or captured.

Retreat was now inevitable, and Lee withdrew his battered troops to the Potomac, only to find that the river was at flood stage and could not be crossed for several days. But Meade failed to follow up his victory with a vigorous pursuit, and Lee was allowed to escape a trap that could have resulted in his annihilation. Vicksburg fell to Grant on July 4, the same day that Lee began his withdrawal, and Northerners rejoiced at the twin Independence Day victories that turned the tide of the war. The Union had secured control of the Mississippi and had at last won a major battle in the East. But Lincoln's joy turned to frustration when he learned that his generals had missed the chance to capture Lee's army and bring a quick end to the war.

Last Stages of the Conflict

Later in 1863 the North finally gained control of the middle South, an area where indecisive fighting had been going on since the beginning of the conflict. The main Union target was Chattanooga, "the gateway to the Southeast." In September, troops under General William Rosecrans managed to maneuver the Confederates out of the city only to be outfought and driven back at Chickamauga. The Union army then retreated into Chattanooga where it was surrounded and besieged by southern forces. After Grant arrived from Vicksburg to take command, the encirclement was broken by daring assaults upon the Confederate positions on Lookout Mountain and Missionary Ridge. As a result of its success in the battle of Chattanooga, the North was poised for an invasion of Georgia.

Grant's victories in the West earned him promotion to general in chief of all the Union armies. After assuming that position in March 1864, he ordered a multipronged offensive to finish off the Confederacy. The main movements were a march on Richmond under his personal command and a thrust by the western armies, now led by General William T. Sherman, in the direction of Atlanta and the heart of Georgia.

In May and early June, Grant and Lee fought a series of bloody battles in northern Virginia that tended to follow a set pattern. Lee would take up an entrenched position in the path of the invading force, and Grant would attack it, sustaining heavy losses but also inflicting casualties that the shrinking Confederate army could ill afford. When his direct assault had failed, Grant would move to his left, hoping in vain to maneuver Lee into a less defensible position. In the battles of the Wilderness, Spotsylvania, and Cold Harbor the Union lost about sixty thousand men—more than twice the number of Confederate casualties —without defeating Lee or opening the road to Richmond. After losing twelve thousand men in a single day at Cold Harbor, Grant decided to change his tactics and moved his army to the south of Richmond. There he drew up before Petersburg, a rail center that linked Richmond to the rest of the Confederacy; after failing to take it by assault, he settled down for a siege.

The siege of Petersburg was a long-drawn-out affair, and the resulting stalemate in the East caused northern morale to plummet during the summer of 1864. Lincoln was facing reelection, and his failure to end the war dimmed his prospects. Although nominated with ease in June —with Andrew Johnson, a proadministration Democrat from Tennessee, as his running mate— Lincoln confronted growing opposition within his own party, especially from Radicals who disagreed with his apparently lenient approach to the future restoration of seceded states to the Union. After Lincoln vetoed a congressional reconstruction plan in July, some Radicals began to call for a new convention to nominate another candidate.

The Democrats seemed in a good position to capitalize on Republican divisions and made a strong bid for the White House. Their platform appealed to war weariness by calling for a ceasefire followed by negotiations to reestablish the Union. The party's nominee, General George

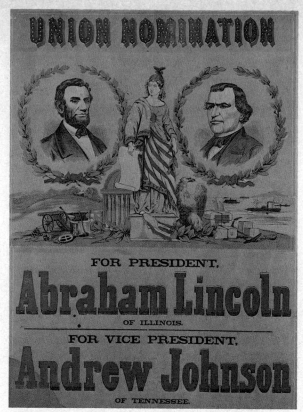

A campaign poster for the 1864 election. The Republican platform promised a quick end to the fighting.

McClellan, announced that he would not be bound by the peace plank and would pursue the war. But he promised to end the conflict sooner than Lincoln could because he would not insist on emancipation as a condition for reconstruction. By late summer Lincoln confessed privately that he would probably be defeated.

Northern military successes changed the political outlook. Sherman's invasion of Georgia went well; between May and September he employed a series of skillful flanking movements to force the Confederates to retreat to the outskirts of Atlanta. On September 2, the city fell, and northern forces occupied the hub of the Deep South. The news unified the Republican party behind Lincoln and improved his chances for defeating McClellan in November. The election itself was almost an anticlimax: Lincoln won 212 of a possible 233 electoral votes and 55 percent of the popular vote. The Republican cause of "liberty and Union" was secure.

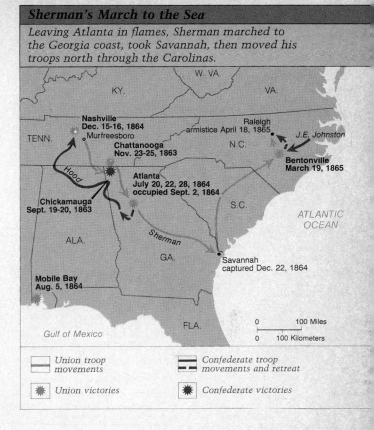

Sherman's March to the Sea

Leaving Atlanta in flames, Sherman marched to the Georgia coast, took Savannah, then moved his troops north through the Carolinas.

The concluding military operations revealed the futility of further southern resistance. Cutting himself off from his supply lines and living off the land, Sherman marched almost unopposed through Georgia to the sea, destroying almost everything of possible military or economic value in a corridor three hundred miles long and sixty miles wide. The Confederate army that had opposed him at Atlanta moved northward into Tennessee, where it was defeated and almost destroyed by Union forces under General George Thomas at Nashville in mid-December. Sherman captured Savannah on December 22 and presented the city to Lincoln as a Christmas present.

■ An Atlanta mansion destroyed by Sherman's troops. After Atlanta fell, Sherman and his sixty thousand troops marched unopposed to the sea, leaving in their wake a trail of burned homes and barns, demolished bridges and railroads.

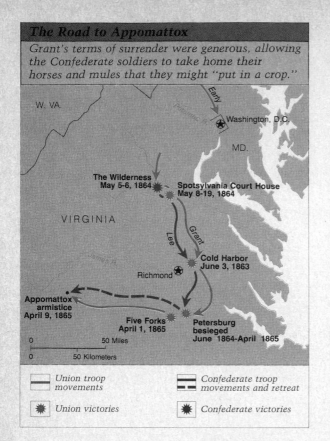

The Road to Appomattox

Grant's terms of surrender were generous, allowing the Confederate soldiers to take home their horses and mules that they might "put in a crop."

W. VA.

Washington, D.C.

MD.

The Wilderness
May 5-6, 1864

Spotsylvania Court House
May 8-19, 1864

VIRGINIA

Lee

Grant

Cold Harbor
June 3, 1863

Richmond

Appomattox
armistice
April 9, 1865

Five Forks
April 1, 1865

Petersburg
besieged
June 1864-April 1865

0   50 Miles

0   50 Kilometers

Union troop movements

Confederate troop movements and retreat

Union victories

Confederate victories

He then turned north and marched through the Carolinas with the aim of joining up with Grant at Petersburg.

While Sherman was tearing up the Carolinas, Grant finally ended the stalemate at Petersburg. When Lee's starving and exhausted army tried to break through the Union lines, Grant renewed his attack and forced the Confederates to abandon Petersburg and Richmond on April 2, 1865. He then pursued them westward for a hundred miles, placing his forces in position to cut off their line of retreat to the south. Recognizing the hopelessness of further resistance, Lee surrendered his army at Appomattox Courthouse on April 9.

But the joy of the victorious North turned to sorrow and anger when John Wilkes Booth assassinated Abraham Lincoln at Ford's Theater in Washington on April 14. Booth, a pro-Confederate actor, shot Lincoln in the head while the President was taking in a light comedy. Although Booth had a few accomplices—one of whom attempted to murder Secretary of State Seward—popular theories that the assassination was the result of a vast conspiracy involving Confederate leaders or (according to another version) Radical Republicans have never been substantiated and are extremely implausible.

With the surrenders of Lee at Appomattox and Johnston in North Carolina, the Civil War ended. The Confederate flag— the Stars and Bars—was furled and the guns were laid down. The work of reconstructing the Union, however, still lay ahead.

Large rewards were offered for the capture of Lincoln's assassin, John Wilkes Booth, and his accomplices (above). On April 26, Booth was trapped in a burning barn in Virginia and shot.

During the war many women replaced skilled male workers in the manufacturing labor force. These women (right) are filling cartridges in the United States Arsenal at Watertown, New York.

The man who had spoken of the need to sacrifice for the Union cause at Gettysburg had himself given "the last full measure of devotion" to the cause of "government of the people, by the people, for the people." Four days after Lincoln's death the only remaining Confederate force of any significance, the troops under Joseph E. Johnston who had been opposing Sherman in North Carolina, laid down their arms. The Union was saved.

Effects of the War

The nation that emerged from four years of total war was not the same America that had split apart in 1861. Nearly 640,000 young men who would otherwise have married, raised families, and contributed their talents to building up the country were in their graves, the victims of enemy fire or the diseases that spread rapidly in military encampments in this era before the rise of modern medicine and sanitation. The widows and sweethearts they left behind temporarily increased the proportion of unmarried women in the population, and some members of this generation of involuntary "spinsters" sought new opportunities for making a living or serving the community that went beyond the purely domestic roles previously prescribed for women. The large number who had served as nurses or volunteer workers during the war were especially responsive to calls for broadening "the woman's sphere."

At enormous human and economic cost, the nation had emancipated four million Afro-

Americans from slavery, but it had not yet resolved that they would be equal citizens. At the time of Lincoln's assassination, most northern states still denied blacks equality under the law and the right to vote. Whether the North would extend more rights to southern freedmen than it had granted to its own "free Negroes" was an open question.

The impact of the war on white working people was also unclear. Those in the industrializing parts of the North had suffered and lost ground economically because prices had risen much faster than wages during the conflict. But Republican rhetoric stressing "equal opportunity" and the "dignity of labor" raised hopes that the crusade against slavery could be broadened into a movement to improve the lot of working people in general. Foreign-born workers had additional reason to be optimistic; the fact that so many immigrants had fought and died for the Union cause had—for the moment—weakened nativist sentiment and encouraged ethnic tolerance.

What the war definitely decided was that the federal government was supreme over the states and had a broad grant of constitutional authority to act on matters affecting "the general welfare." The southern principle of state sovereignty and strict construction died at Appomattox, and the United States was on its way to becoming a true nation-state with an effective central government. But it retained a federal structure; although states could no longer claim the right to secede or nullify federal law, they still had primary responsibility for most functions of government. Everyone agreed that the Constitution placed limits on what the national government could do, and questions would continue to arise about where federal authority ended and states' rights began.

A broadened definition of federal powers had its greatest impact in the realm of economic policy. During the war, Republican-dominated Congresses passed a rash of legislation designed to give encouragement and direction to the nation's economic development. Taking advantage of the absence of southern opposition, Republicans rejected the pre–Civil War tradition of laissez-faire and enacted a Whiggish program of active support for business and agriculture. In 1862 Congress passed a high protective tariff, approved a home-

■ *Members of the U.S. Sanitary Commission at Fredericksburg, Virginia, in 1864. The Sanitary Commission distributed food, clothing, and medicine to the army and sent inspectors to field camps to instruct the soldiers in matters of sanitation, water supplies, and cooking.*

stead act intended to encourage settlement of the West by providing free land to settlers, granted huge tracts of public land to railroad companies to support the building of a transcontinental railroad, and gave the states land for the establishment of agricultural colleges. The following year, Congress set up a national banking system that required member banks to keep adequate reserves and invest a third of their capital in government securities. The notes that the national banks issued became the country's first standardized and reliable circulating currency.

These wartime achievements added up to a decisive and permanent shift in the relationship between the federal government and private enterprise. The Republicans took a limited government that did little more than seek to protect the marketplace from the threat of monopoly and changed it into an activist state that promoted and subsidized the efforts of the economically industrious and ambitious.

The most pervasive effect of the war on northern society was to encourage an "organizational revolution." Aided by government policies, venturesome businessmen took advantage of the new national market created by military procurement to build larger firms that could operate across state lines; some of the huge corporate enterprises of the postwar era began to take shape. Philanthropists also developed more effective national associations; the most notable of these were the Sanitary and Christian Commissions that ministered to the physical and spiritual needs of the troops. Both the men who served in the army and those men and women who supported them on the home front became accustomed to working in large, bureaucratic organizations of a kind that had scarcely existed before the war. The result was that an individualistic society of small producers began to be transformed into the more highly organized and "incorporated" America that would emerge during the Gilded Age.

Recommended Reading

Two general surveys of the Civil War era stand out from among the vast number that have been published: J. G. Randall and David Donald, *The Civil War and Reconstruction*, 2d ed. (1969), and James M. McPherson, *Ordeal by Fire: The Civil War and Reconstruction* (1981). An excellent shorter account is David Herbert Donald, *Liberty and Union* (1978). The Confederate experience is well covered in Clement Eaton, *A History of the Southern Confederacy* (1954), and Emory M. Thomas, *The Confederate Nation: 1861–1865* (1979). Eaton stresses internal problems and weaknesses, while Thomas highlights achievements under adversity. The best one-volume introduction to the military side of the conflict is Bruce Catton, *This Hallowed Ground* (1956).

Lincoln's career and wartime leadership are treated in two excellent biographies: Benjamin P. Thomas, *Abraham Lincoln* (1954), and Stephen B. Oates, *With Malice toward None: The Life of Abraham Lincoln* (1977). A penetrating analysis of events immediately preceding the fighting is Kenneth M. Stampp, *And the War Came: The North and the Sectional Crisis* (1950). John Hope Franklin, *The Emancipation Proclamation* (1963) is a good short account of the North's decision to free the slaves. Five leading historians offer conflicting interpretations in their attempts to explain the south's defeat in *Why the North Won the Civil War*, edited by David Donald (1960). A brilliant study of the writings of those who experienced the war is Edmund Wilson, *Patriotic Gore: Studies in the Literature of the American Civil War* (1962).

Additional Bibliography

The most thorough modern history of the Civil War is Allan Nevins, *The War for the Union*, 4 vols. (1959–1971). Bruce Catton, *Centennial History of the Civil War*, 3 vols, (1961–1965) is the most detailed account of the military aspects of the conflict. The day-to-day drama of the war is well conveyed in Shelby Foote, *The Civil War: A Narrative*, 3 vols, (1958–1974). One-volume studies that provide useful general perspectives on the conflict include Robert H. Jones, *Disrupted Decades: The Civil War and Reconstruction Years* (1973); Emory M. Thomas, *The American War and Peace, 1860–1877* (1973); David Lindsey, *Americans in Conflict: The Civil War and Reconstruction* (1974); William L. Barney, *Flawed Victory: A New Perspective on the Civil War* (1975); Robert Cruden, *The War That Never Ended: The American Civil War* (1973); and Thomas H. O'Connor, *The Disunited States: The Era of the Civil War and Reconstruction*, 2d ed. (1978). Among the many collections of essays that deal with general issues of the period are George M. Fredrickson, ed., *A Nation Divided: Problems and Issues of the Civil War and Reconstruction* (1975); Allan Nevins, *The Statesmanship of the Civil War* (1962); David Donald, *Lincoln Reconsidered: Essays on the Civil War Era* (1956); Eric Foner, *Politics and Ideology in the Age of the Civil War* (1980); and David M. Potter, *The South and the Sectional Conflict* (1968).

Further insight into the Confederate side of the struggle can be derived from E. Merton Coulter, *The Confederate States of America* (1950); Charles P. Roland, *The Confederacy* (1960); Frank E. Vandiver, *Their Tattered Flags: The Epic of the Confederacy* (1970); Emory M. Thomas, *The Confederacy as a Revolutionary Experience* (1971); and Bell I. Wiley, *The Road to Appomattox* (1956). Jefferson Davis' leadership is assessed in Paul D. Escott, *After Secession: Jefferson Davis and the Failure of Confederate Nationalism* (1978); Hudson Strode, *Jefferson Davis*, 3 vols. (1955–1964); Clement Eaton, *Jefferson Davis* (1977); and Frank E. Vandiver, *Jefferson Davis and the Confederate States* (1964). The most detailed works on Lincoln's stewardship of the Union cause are James G. Randall, *Lincoln the President*, 4 vols. (1945–1955, vol. 4 completed by Richard N. Current) and Carl Sandburg's less reliable *Abraham Lincoln: The War Years*, 4 vols. (1939).

Events leading up to the outbreak of hostilities are covered in Dwight L. Dumond, *The Secession Movement* (1931); Ralph Wooster, *The Secession Conventions of the South* (1962); Charles R. Lee, *The Confederate Constitutions* (1963); David M. Potter, *Lincoln and His Party in the Secession Crisis*, 2d ed. (1962); and Richard N. Current, *Lincoln and the First Shot* (1963).

The literature on military commanders, campaigns, and battles is enormous, but mention must be made of Douglas Southall Freeman's outstanding works on southern generalship: *R. E. Lee: A Biography*, 4 vols. (1934–1935) and *Lee Lieutenants*, 3 vols. (1942–1944). Also of exceptional merit is Bruce Catton's trilogy on the Army of the Potomac: *Mr. Lincoln's Army* (1951), *Glory Road* (1952), and *A Stillness at Appomattox* (1953). On the common soldier's experience of the war, see two books by Bell I. Wiley: *The Life of Johnny Reb* (1943) and *The Life of Billy Yank* (1952).

Major works on northern politics during the war are William B. Hesseltine, *Lincoln and the War Governors* (1948); T. Harry Williams, *Lincoln and the Radicals* (1941); Hans Trefousse, *The Radical Republicans: Lincoln's Vanguard for Racial Justice* (1969); David Donald, *Charles Sumner and the Rights of Man* (1970); Joel Silbey, *A Respectable Minority: The Democratic Party in the Civil War Era* (1977); Wood Gray, *The Hidden Civil War: The Story of the Copperheads* (1942); Frank L. Klement, *Copperheads in the Middle West* (1960); and Leonard P. Curry, *Blueprint for Modern America: Non-Military Legislation of the First Civil War Congress* (1968). On legal and constitutional issues, see James G. Randall, *Constitutional Problems under Lincoln*, rev. ed. (1961); Harold M. Hyman, *A More Perfect Union: The Impact of the Civil War and Reconstruction on the Constitution* (1973); and Philip S. Paludan, *A Covenant with Death: The Constitution, the Law, and Equality in the Civil War Era* (1975).

Other aspects of northern life during the war are treated in Emerson D. Fite, *Social and Economic Conditions in the North during the Civil War* (1910); Paul

Secession and the Civil War

W. Gates, *Agriculture and the Civil War* (1965); George M. Fredrickson, *The Inner Civil War: Northern Intellectuals and the Crisis of the Union* (1965); Daniel Aaron, *The Unwritten War: American Writers and the Civil War* (1973); and James H. Morehead, *American Apocalypse: Yankee Protestants and the Civil War* (1978).

For an understanding of the South's internal problems, see Frank Owsley, *States Rights in the Confederacy* (1925); Curtis A. Amlund, *Federalism in the Southern Confederacy* (1966); Wilfred B. Yearns, *The Confederate Congress* (1960); Richard C. Todd, *Confederate Finance* (1954); and Bell I. Wiley, *The Plain People of the Confederacy* (1943).

Emancipation and the role of blacks in the war are the subject of a number of excellent studies, including Benjamin Quarles, *The Negro in the Civil War* (1953) and *Lincoln and the Negro* (1962); Bell I. Wiley, *Southern Negroes, 1861–1865* (1938); James M. McPherson, *The Struggle for Equality: Abolitionists and the Negro in the Civil War and Reconstruction* (1964); LaWanda Cox, *Lincoln and Black Freedom* (1981); V. Jacque Voegeli, *Free but not Equal: The Midwest and the Negro during the Civil War*; Forrest G. Wood, *Black Scare: The Racist Response to the Civil War and Reconstruction* (1968); Louis Gerteis, *From Contraband to Freedman: Federal Policy toward Southern Blacks 1861–1865* (1973); Willie Lee Rose, *Rehearsal for Reconstruction: The Port Royal Experiment* (1964); Herman Belz, *A New Birth of Freedom: The Republican Party and Freedmen's Rights, 1861–1866* (1976); and Robert F. Durden, *The Gray and the Black: The Confederate Debate on Emancipation* (1972).

On wartime diplomacy, see David P. Crook, *The North, the South and the Powers, 1861–1865* (1974); Frank Owsley, *King Cotton Diplomacy*, rev. ed (1959); Donaldson Jordan and Edwin J. Pratt, *Europe and the American Civil War* (1931); Brian Jenkins, *Britain and the War for the Union* (1974); and Mary Ellison, *Support for Secession: Lancashire and the American Civil War* (1972).

HARPER'S WEEKLY.

A JOURNAL OF CIVILIZATION.

Vol. XI.—No. 568.]   NEW YORK, SATURDAY, NOVEMBER 16, 1867.   [SINGLE COPIES TEN CENTS.
[$4.00 PER YEAR IN ADVANCE.

Entered according to Act of Congress, in the Year 1867, by Harper & Brothers, in the Clerk's Office of the District Court for the Southern District of New York.

chapter 16

THE AGONY OF RECONSTRUCTION

D. W. Griffith's *Birth of a Nation* (1915) was the most ambitious film yet made by the fledgling American film industry. An epic of the Civil War and Reconstruction produced a half-century after the events it portrays, the movie remains a technical masterpiece, combining impressive, realistic battle scenes with a heavy dose of political and racial propaganda. The villains are vindictive northern politicians, corrupt carpetbaggers, and ignorant ex-slaves lusting for power over their former masters. To make the message clear, words are flashed on the screen describing Reconstruction as a callous attempt to *"put the white South under the heel of the black South."* Later in the film leering blacks carry signs reading "Equality/Equal Rights/Equal Politics/Equal Marriage."

Lincoln is depicted as a wise statesman who would have spared the South the horrors of black rule, but his assassination gives power to a vengeful Republican congressman, meant to represent Thaddeus Stevens. Under the urging of his mulatto mistress, the congressman hatches a devilish plot to oppress and humiliate the white South. The fruits of this scheming are revealed in a scene portraying the South Carolina state legislature as a mob of grinning, barefooted blacks, carousing at the taxpayers' expense.

The melodramatic plot features two climactic episodes. In the first a southern maiden throws herself from a cliff to escape the embraces of a "renegade Negro," and in the second the Ku Klux Klan rescues the daughter of a northern Republican from a forced marriage with a mulatto politician. Even the father, a professed champion of black equality, rejoices in this triumph of racial purity. The message is unmistakable—the Klan saved the South and white civilization from a fate worse than death.

At a special White House screening, then President Woodrow Wilson, who was of southern birth and a professional historian as well as a politician, found the film impressive and rooted in fact. "It is like writing history with lightning," he announced. "And my only regret is that it is all so terribly true." The movie, undoubtedly helped by the presidential blurb, was a spectacular popular success. Black protests, organized by the recently founded National Association for the Advancement of Colored People (NAACP), forced censors in some northern cities to delete some of the more blatantly racist scenes, but millions of Americans saw and applauded the uncut version.

The picture of Reconstruction presented in *Birth of a Nation* developed from the image projected by the southern leaders who had overthrown Radical rule in the 1870s and then proceeded to put blacks "in their place" by stripping them of rights supposedly guaranteed by the Fourteenth and Fifteenth Amendments. Over the next forty years many Northerners became persuaded that their forebears made a terrible mistake in trying to enforce equal rights for blacks after the Civil War.

During the period between the 1890s and the 1940s, most professional historians agreed; they concluded that Reconstruction was one of the most disgraceful episodes in American history—a "tragic era" when misguided or opportunistic northern politicians had enfranchised a black population obviously unfit for citizenship, thereby condemning the long-suffering South to an orgy of misrule and corruption. Some black scholars of the 1920s and '30s disagreed vehemently with this view, notably W. E. B. Du Bois in his massive work *Black Reconstruction in America*, but not until the 1950s and '60s did a majority of Reconstruction historians reject the exaggerations, distortions, and racist assumptions of this image. Because they dissented vigorously from the old orthodoxy, these historians became known as "revisionists." Even today, however, some of the myths reflected in *Birth of a Nation* have a strong hold on the popular historical imagination.

Retelling the story of Reconstruction from a modern revisionist perspective does not require setting up a new myth of saintly Radical Republicans, model black officeholders, and totally vicious southern whites to replace the stereotypes in *Birth of a Nation*. Mixed motives, hypocrisy, blunders, and corruption were important aspects of the complex drama that unfolded between the end of the Civil War and the final collapse of Reconstruction in 1877. But there was another side, involving the heroic struggle of blacks and their white allies to achieve racial justice and equality against overwhelming odds. If Reconstruction was "tragic," it was not because what was attempted was wrong; it was rather because those who tried to form a more egalitarian society in the South lacked the sustained support and unfaltering will to achieve their aims.

The President Versus Congress

The problem of how to reconstruct the Union in the wake of the South's military defeat was one of the most difficult and perplexing challenges ever faced by American policymakers. The Constitution provided no firm guidelines, for the framers had not anticipated a division of the country into warring sections. Once emancipation became a northern war aim, the problem was compounded by a new issue: how far should the federal government go to secure freedom and civil rights for four million former slaves?

The debate that evolved led to a major political crisis. Advocates of a minimal Reconstruction policy favored quick restoration of the Union with no protection for the freed slaves beyond the prohibition of slavery. Proponents of a more radical policy wanted readmission of the southern states to be dependent on guarantees that "loyal" men would displace the Confederate elite and that blacks would acquire some of the basic rights of American citizenship. The White House favored the minimal approach, while Congress came to endorse the more radical and thoroughgoing form of Reconstruction. The resulting struggle between Congress and the chief executive was the most serious clash between two branches of government in the nation's history.

Wartime Reconstruction

Tension between the President and Congress over how to reconstruct the Union began during the war. Occupied mainly with achieving victory,

■ *"The Union Christmas Dinner" appeared in Harper's Weekly in 1864. The cartoon illustrates the spirit of forgiveness and reconciliation that marked Lincoln's policy toward the South.*

Lincoln never set forth a final and comprehensive plan for bringing the rebellious states back into the fold. But he did take some initiatives that indicated he favored a lenient and conciliatory policy toward Southerners who would give up the struggle and repudiate slavery. In December 1863 he issued a Proclamation of Amnesty and Reconstruction; it offered a full pardon to all Southerners (with the exception of certain classes of Confederate leaders) who would take an oath of allegiance to the Union and acknowledge the legality of emancipation. Once 10 percent or more of the voting population of any occupied state had taken the oath, they were authorized to set up a loyal government. Efforts to establish such regimes were quickly undertaken in states that were wholly or partially occupied by Union troops; by 1864 Louisiana and Arkansas had fully functioning Unionist governments.

Lincoln's policy was meant to shorten the war. The President hoped that granting pardon and political recognition to oath-taking minorities would weaken the southern cause by making it easy for disillusioned or lukewarm Confederates to switch sides. He also hoped to further his emancipation policy by insisting that the new governments abolish slavery, an action that might prove crucial if—as seemed possible before Lincoln's reelection in 1864 and Congress' subsequent passage of the Thirteenth Amendment—the courts or a future Democratic administration were to disallow or revoke the Emancipation Proclamation. When constitutional conventions operating under the 10 percent plan in Louisiana and Arkansas dutifully abolished slavery in 1864, emancipation came closer to being irreversible.

But Congress was unhappy with the President's reconstruction experiments and in 1864 refused to seat the Unionists elected to the House and Senate from Louisiana and Arkansas. A minority of congressional Republicans—the strongly anti-slavery Radicals—favored strong protection for black rights as a precondition for the readmission of southern states. These Republican militants were upset because Lincoln had not insisted that the constitution-makers provide for black suffrage. But a larger group in Congress was not yet prepared to implement civil and political equality for blacks. Most of these moderates also opposed Lincoln's plan, but they did so primarily because they did not trust the repentant Confederates who would play a major role in the new governments. No matter what their position on black rights, most congressional Republicans feared that hypocritical oath-taking would allow the old ruling class to return to power and cheat the North of the full fruits of its impending victory.

Also disturbing Congress was a sense that the President was exceeding his authority by using executive powers to restore the Union. Lincoln operated on the theory that secession, being illegal, did not place the Confederate states outside the Union in a constitutional sense. Since individuals and not states had defied federal authority, the President could use his pardoning power to certify a loyal electorate, which could then function as the legitimate state government.

The dominant view in Congress, on the other hand, was that the southern states had definitely withdrawn from the Union and that it was up to Congress to decide when and how they would be readmitted. The most popular justification for congressional responsibility was based on the clause of the Constitution providing that "the United States shall guarantee to every State in this Union a Republican Form of Government." By seceding, it was argued, the Confederate states had ceased to be republican, and it was now Congress' job to set the conditions to be met before they could be readmitted.

After refusing to recognize Lincoln's 10 percent governments, Congress passed a Reconstruction bill of its own in July 1864. Known as the Wade-Davis bill, this legislation required that 50 percent of the voters must take an oath of future loyalty before the restoration process could begin. Once this had occurred, those who could swear that they had never willingly supported the Confederacy could vote in an election for delegates to a constitutional convention. The bill in its final form did not require black suffrage, but it did give federal courts the power to enforce emancipation. Faced with this attempt to nullify his own program, Lincoln exercized a pocket veto by refusing to sign the bill before Congress adjourned. He justified his action by announcing that he did not wish to be committed to any single reconstruction plan. The sponsors of the bill responded with an angry manifesto, and Lincoln's relations with Congress reached their lowest ebb.

Congress and the President remained stalemated on the Reconstruction issue for the rest of the war. During his last months in office, however, Lincoln showed some willingness to compromise. He persisted in his efforts to obtain full recognition for the governments he had nurtured in Louisiana and Arkansas but seemed receptive to the setting of other conditions—perhaps including black suffrage—for readmission of those states where wartime conditions had prevented execution of his plan. However, he died without clarifying his intentions, leaving historians to speculate on whether his quarrel with Congress would have worsened or been resolved. Given Lincoln's past record of political flexibility, the best bet is that he would have come to terms with the majority of his party.

Andrew Johnson at the Helm

Andrew Johnson, the man suddenly made president by an assassin's bullet, attempted to put the Union back together on his own authority in 1865. But his policies eventually put him at odds with Congress and the Republican party and provoked the most serious internal crisis in the history of the federal government.

Johnson's approach to Reconstruction was shaped by his background. Born in dire poverty in North Carolina, he migrated as a young man to

■ *Nearly insurmountable problems with a Congress determined to enact its own Reconstruction policy plagued Andrew Johnson through his presidency. Impeached in 1868, he escaped conviction by a single vote.*

the privilege of a wealthy minority. He revealed his basic attitude when he expressed the extraordinary wish that "every head of family in the United States had one slave to take the drudgery and menial service off his family."

During the war, while acting as military governor of Tennessee, Johnson endorsed Lincoln's emancipation policy and carried it into effect. But he viewed it primarily as a means of destroying the power of the hated planter class rather than as a recognition of black humanity. He was chosen as Lincoln's running mate in 1864 because putting a proadministration Democrat, who was a southern Unionist in the bargain, on the ticket would broaden its appeal. No one expected Johnson to succeed to the presidency; it is one of the strange accidents of American history that a southern Democrat, a fervent white supremacist, came to preside over a Republican administration immediately after the Civil War.

What may seem even stranger is the fact that some Radical Republicans initially welcomed Johnson's ascent to the nation's highest office. But their hopes make sense in the light of Johnson's record of fierce loyalty to the Union and his apparent agreement with the Radicals that ex-Confederates should be severely treated. More than Lincoln, who had spoken of "malice toward none and charity for all," Johnson seemed likely to punish southern "traitors" and prevent them from regaining political influence. Only gradually did the deep disagreement between the President and the Republican majority in Congress become evident.

The Reconstruction policy that Johnson initiated on May 29, 1865, created some uneasiness among the Radicals, but most other Republicans, moderate and conservative, were willing to give it a chance. Johnson placed North Carolina and eventually other states under appointed provisional governors chosen from among prominent southern politicians who had opposed the secession movement and had rendered no conspicuous service to the Confederacy. The governors were responsible for calling constitutional conventions and ensuring that only "loyal" whites were permitted to vote for delegates. Participation required taking the oath of allegiance that Lincoln had prescribed earlier. Once again Confederate leaders and former officeholders who had participated in the rebellion were excluded. To regain

eastern Tennessee where he made his living as a tailor. Lacking formal schooling, he was barely able to read until adult life and subsequently entered politics as a Jacksonian Democrat. His effectiveness as a stump speaker railing against the planter aristocracy made him the spokesman for Tennessee's nonslaveholding whites and the most successful politician in the state. He advanced from state legislator to congressman to governor and in 1857 was elected to the United States Senate.

When Tennessee seceded in 1861, Johnson was the only senator from a Confederate state who remained loyal to the Union and continued to serve in Washington. But his Unionism and defense of the common people did not include antislavery sentiments. Nor was he friendly to blacks. While campaigning in Tennessee, he had objected only to the fact that slaveholding was

their political and property rights, those in the exempted categories had to apply for individual presidential pardons. Johnson made one significant addition to the list of the excluded: all those possessing taxable property exceeding $20,000 in value. In this fashion, he sought to prevent his longtime adversaries—the planter class—from participating in the reconstruction of southern state governments.

Once the conventions met, Johnson urged them to do three things: declare the ordinances of secession illegal, repudiate the Confederate debt, and ratify the Thirteenth Amendment abolishing slavery. After governments had been reestablished under constitutions meeting these conditions, the President assumed that the process of Reconstuction would be complete and that the ex-Confederate states could regain their full rights under the Constitution.

The conventions, dominated by prewar Unionists and representatives of backcountry yeoman farmers, did their work in a way satisfactory to the President but troubling to many congressional Republicans. Rather than quickly accepting Johnson's recommendations, the delegates in several states approved them begrudgingly or with qualifications. Furthermore, all the resulting constitutions limited the suffrage to whites, disappointing the large number of Northerners who hoped, as Lincoln had, that at least some blacks—perhaps those who were educated or had served in the Union army—would be given the vote. Johnson on the whole seemed eager to give southern white majorities a free hand in determining the civil and political status of the freed slaves.

Republican uneasiness turned to disillusionment and anger when the state legislatures elected under the new constitutions proceeded to pass "Black Codes" subjecting the former slaves to a variety of special regulations and restrictions on their freedom. Especially troubling were vagrancy and apprenticeship laws that forced blacks to work and denied them a free choice of employers. Blacks in some states were also prevented from testifying in court against whites and were subject to a separate penal code. To Radicals, the Black Codes looked suspiciously like slavery under a new guise. More upsetting to northern public opinion in general was the fact that a number of prominent ex-Confederate leaders were elected to Congress in the fall of 1865.

Johnson himself was partly responsible for this turn of events. Despite his lifelong feud with the planter class, he was generous in granting pardons to members of the old elite who came to him, hat in hand, and asked for them. When former Confederate Vice-President Alexander Stephens and other proscribed ex-rebels were elected to Congress although they had not been pardoned, Johnson granted them special amnesty so that they could serve.

The growing rift between the President and Congress came into the open in December when the House and Senate refused to seat the recently elected southern delegation. Instead of endorsing Johnson's work and recognizing the state governments he had called into being, Congress established a joint committee, chaired by Senator William Pitt Fessenden of Maine, to review Reconstruction policy and set further conditions for readmission of the seceded states.

Congress Takes the Initiative

The struggle over how to reconstruct the Union ended with Congress doing the job all over again. The clash between Johnson and Congress was a matter of principle and could not be reconciled. Johnson's personality—his prickly pride, sharp tongue, intolerance of opposition, and stubborn refusal to give an inch—did not help his political cause. But the root of the problem was that he disagreed with the majority of Congress on what Reconstruction was supposed to accomplish. An heir of the Democratic states' rights tradition, he wanted to restore the prewar federal system as quickly as possible, with the single change that states would no longer have the right to legalize slavery.

Most Republicans, on the other hand, believed that the sectional conflict would not be resolved until there were firm guarantees that the old southern ruling class would not regain regional power and national influence by devising new ways to subjugate blacks. Since emancipation had nullified the three-fifths clause of the Constitution by which slaves had been counted as three fifths of a person, all blacks were now to be counted in determining representation. Consequently, unlike Johnson, the Republicans worried about increased southern strength in Congress

■ *According to this cartoon, Congress' plan of Reconstruction was a bitter dose for the South, and the President, "Naughty Andy," urged Southerners not to accept the plan. Mrs. Columbia insisted, however, that Dr. Congress knew what was best.*

and the electoral college. Congress favored a reconstruction policy that would give the federal government authority to limit the political role of ex-Confederates and provide some protection for black citizenship.

Republican leaders—with the exception of a few extreme Radicals like Charles Sumner—lacked any firm conviction that blacks were inherently equal to whites. They *did* believe, however, that a modern democratic state should provide the same basic rights and opportunities for all citizens, regardless of their natural abilities. Principle coincided easily with political expediency; southern blacks, whatever their alleged shortcomings, were likely to be loyal to the Republican party that had emancipated them. They could be used, if necessary, to counteract the influence of resurgent ex-Confederates, thus preventing the Democrats from returning to national dominance through control of the South.

The disagreement between the President and Congress became irreconcilable in early 1866 when Johnson vetoed two bills that had passed with overwhelming Republican support. The first

extended the life of the Freedmen's Bureau—a temporary agency set up to aid the former slaves by providing relief, education, legal help, and assistance in obtaining land or employment. The second was a civil rights bill meant to nullify the black codes and guarantee to the freedmen "full and equal benefit of all laws and proceedings for the security of person and property as is enjoyed by white citizens."

The vetoes shocked moderate Republicans who had expected Johnson to accept these relatively modest measures as a way of heading off more radical proposals, such as black suffrage and a prolonged denial of political rights to ex-Confederates. Presidential opposition to policies that represented the bare minimum of Republican demands on the South alienated the moderates in the party and ensured a wide opposition to Johnson's plan of Reconstruction. Johnson succeeded in blocking the Freedmen's Bureau bill, although a modified version later passed. But the Civil Rights Act won the two-thirds majority necessary to override his veto, signifying that the President was now hopelessly at odds with most of the congressmen from what was supposed to be his own party.

Johnson soon revealed that he intended to abandon the Republicans and place himself at the head of a new conservative party uniting the small minority of Republicans who supported him with a reviving Democratic party that was rallying behind his Reconstruction policy. In preparation for the elections of 1866, Johnson helped found the National Union movement to promote his plan to readmit the southern states to the Union without further qualifications. A National Union convention meeting in Philadelphia in August 1866 called for the election to Congress of men who endorsed the presidential plan for Reconstruction.

Meanwhile, the Republican majority on Capitol Hill, fearing that Johnson would not enforce civil rights legislation or that the courts would declare such federal laws unconstitutional, passed the Fourteenth Amendment. This, the most important of all our constitutional amendments, gave the federal government responsibility for guaranteeing equal rights under the law to all Americans. The first section defined national citizenship for the first time as extending to "all persons born or naturalized in the United States."

The states were prohibited from abridging the rights of American citizens and could not "deprive any person of life, liberty, or property, without due process of law; nor deny to any person . . . equal protection of the laws."

The other sections of the amendment were important in the context of the time but had fewer long-term implications. Section two sought to encourage extension of voting rights to blacks by reducing the congressional representation of any state that formally deprived a portion of its male citizens of the right to vote. The third section denied federal office to those who had taken an oath of office to support the United States Constitution and then had supported the Confederacy, and the fourth repudiated the Confederate debt. The amendment was sent to the states with an implied understanding that Southerners would be readmitted to Congress only if their states ratified it.

The congressional elections of 1866 served as a referendum on the Fourteenth Amendment. Johnson opposed it on the grounds that it created a "centralized" government and denied the states the right to manage their own affairs; he also counselled southern state legislatures to reject it, and all except Tennessee followed his advice. The President's case for state autonomy was weakened by the publicity resulting from bloody race riots in New Orleans and Memphis. These and other reported atrocities against the former slaves made it clear that the existing southern state governments were failing abysmally to protect the "life, liberty, or property" of the ex-slaves.

Johnson further weakened his cause by taking the stump on behalf of candidates who supported his policies. In his notorious "swing around the circle," he toured the nation, slandering his opponents in crude language and engaging in undignified exchanges with hecklers. Enraged by southern inflexibility and the antics of a president who acted as if he were still campaigning in the backwoods of Tennessee, northern voters repudiated the administration. The Republican majority in Congress increased to a solid two thirds in both houses, and the radical wing of the party gained strength at the expense of moderates and conservatives.

Congressional Reconstruction Plan Enacted

Congress was now in a position to implement its own plan of Reconstruction. In 1867 it passed a series of acts that nullified the President's initiatives and reorganized the South on a new basis. Generally referred to as "Radical Reconstruc-

Reconstruction Amendments, 1865–1870

Amendment	Main Provisions	Congressional Passage (⅔ majority in each house required)	Ratification Process (¾ of all states including ex-Confederate states required)
13	Slavery prohibited in United States	January 1865	December 1865 (twenty-seven states, including eight southern states)
14	1. National citizenship 2. State representation in Congress reduced proportionally to number of voters disfranchised 3. Former Confederates denied right to hold office	June 1866	Rejected by twelve southern and border states, February 1867 Radicals make readmission of southern states hinge on ratification Ratified July 1868
15	Explicit prohibition of denial of franchise because of race, color, or past servitude	February 1869	Ratification required for readmission of Virginia, Texas, Mississippi, Georgia Ratified March 1870

The Agony of Reconstruction

tion," these measures actually represented a compromise between genuine Radicals and the more moderate elements within the party.

Consistent Radicals like Senator Charles Sumner of Massachusetts and Congressmen Thaddeus Stevens of Pennsylvania and George Julian of Indiana wanted to shape southern society before readmitting ex-Confederates to the Union. Their program of "regeneration before reconstruction" required an extended period of military rule, confiscation and redistribution of large landholdings among the freedmen, and federal aid for schools that would educate blacks for citizenship. But the majority of Republican congressmen found such a program unacceptable because it broke with American traditions of federalism and regard for property rights.

The First Reconstruction Act, passed over Johnson's veto on March 2, 1867, did place the South under military rule—but only for a short period. The act opened the way for the readmission of any state that framed and ratified a new constitution providing for black suffrage. Ex-Confederates disqualified from holding federal office under the Fourteenth Amendment were prohibited from voting for delegates to the constitutional conventions or in the elections to ratify the conventions' work. Since blacks were allowed to participate in this process, Republicans thought they had found a way to ensure that

"loyal" men would dominate the new governments. Speed was essential because some Republican leaders anticipated that they would need votes from the reconstructed South in order to retain control of Congress and the White House in 1868.

"Radical Reconstruction" was based on the false assumption that once blacks had the vote, they would have the power to protect themselves against the efforts of white supremacists to deny them their rights. The Reconstruction Acts thus signaled a retreat from the true Radical position that a sustained use of federal authority was needed to complete the transition from slavery to freedom and prevent the resurgence of the South's old ruling class. The majority of Republicans were unwilling to embrace centralized government and an extended period of military rule over civilians. Such drastic steps went beyond the popular northern consensus on necessary and proper Reconstruction measures. Thus, despite strong reservations, Radicals like Thaddeus Stevens supported the plan of readmitting the southern states on the basis of black suffrage when they realized that this was as far as the party and the northern public were willing to go.

Even so, congressional Reconstruction did have a radical aspect. Although the program won Republican support partly because it promised practical political advantages, a genuine spirit of dem-

■ *Among the most influential of the Radicals was Congressman Thaddeus Stevens of Pennsylvania. He advocated seizing a portion of the property of southern whites and distributing it among the freed blacks.*

ocratic idealism gave legitimacy and fervor to the cause of black suffrage. The principle that even the poorest and most underprivileged should have access to the ballot box was a noble and enlightened one. The problem was how to enforce it under conditions then existing in the postwar South.

The Impeachment Crisis

The first obstacle to enforcement of congressional Reconstruction was resistance from the White House. Johnson thoroughly disapproved of the new policy and sought to thwart the will of Congress by administering the plan in his own obstructive fashion. He immediately began to dismiss officeholders who sympathized with Radical Reconstruction, and he countermanded the orders of generals in charge of southern military districts who were zealous in their enforcement of the new legislation. Some Radical generals were transferred and replaced by conservative Democrats. Congress responded by passing laws designed to limit presidential authority over Reconstruction matters. One of these measures was the Tenure of Office Act, requiring Senate approv-

al for the firing of cabinet officers and other officials whose appointment had needed the consent of the Senate. Another measure—a rider to an army appropriations bill—sought to limit Johnson's authority to issue orders to military commanders.

Johnson objected vigorously to these restrictions on the ground that they violated the constitutional doctrine of the separation of powers. When it became clear that the President was resolute in fighting for his powers and using them to resist the establishment of Radical regimes in the southern states, some congressmen began to call for his impeachment. A preliminary effort foundered in 1867, but when Johnson tried to discharge Secretary of War Edwin Stanton—the only Radical in the cabinet—and persisted in his efforts despite the disapproval of the Senate, the proimpeachment forces gained in strength.

In January 1868 Johnson ordered General Grant, who already commanded the army, to replace Stanton as head of the War Department. But Grant had his eye on the Republican presidential nomination and refused to defy Congress. Johnson subsequently appointed General Lorenzo Thomas, who agreed to serve. Faced with this apparent violation of the Tenure of Office Act, the House voted overwhelmingly to impeach the President on February 24, and he was placed on trial before the Senate.

Johnson narrowly avoided conviction and removal from office. Seven Republican senators broke with the party leadership and voted for acquittal. Thus, the impeachment effort fell one vote short of the necessary two thirds. This outcome resulted in part from a skillful defense. Attorneys for the President argued for a narrow interpretation of the constitutional provision that a president can be impeached only for a "high crime and misdemeanor," asserting that this referred only to an indictable crime. Responding to the charge that Johnson had deliberately violated the Tenure of Office Act, the defense contended that the law did not apply to the removal of Stanton because he had been appointed by Lincoln, not Johnson.

The prosecution countered with a different interpretation of the Tenure of Office Act, but the core of their case was that Johnson had abused the powers of his office in an effort to sabotage the congressional Reconstruction policy. Obstructing the will of the legislative branch, they claimed, was sufficient grounds for conviction even if no crime had been committed. The Republicans who broke ranks to vote for acquittal could not endorse such a broad view of the impeachment power. They feared that removal of a president for essentially political reasons would threaten the constitutional balance of powers and open the way to legislative supremacy over the executive.

Although Johnson's acquittal by the narrowest of margins protected the American presidency from congressional domination, the impeachment episode helped create an impression in the public mind that the Radicals were ready to turn the Constitution to their own use to gain their objectives. Conservatives were again alarmed when Congress took action in 1868 to deny the Supreme Court's appellate jurisdiction in cases involving the military arrest and imprisonment of anti-Reconstruction activists in the South. But the evidence of congressional ruthlessness and illegality is not as strong as most historians used to think. Modern legal scholars have found merit in the Radicals' claim that their actions did not violate the Constitution.

The failed impeachment effort was an embarrassment to congressional Republicans, but the episode did ensure that Reconstruction in the South would proceed as the majority in Congress intended. During the trial Johnson helped influence the verdict by pledging to enforce the Reconstruction Acts, and he held to this promise during his remaining months in office. Unable to depose the President, the Radicals had at least succeeded in neutralizing his opposition to their program.

Reconstruction in the South

The Civil War left the South devastated, demoralized, and destitute. Slavery was dead, but what this meant for future relationships between whites and blacks was still in doubt. The overwhelming majority of southern whites wanted to keep blacks adrift between slavery and freedom—without rights, in a status resembling that of the "free Negroes" of the Old South. Blacks sought to be independent of their former masters and viewed the acquisition of land, education, and the vote as the best means of achieving this goal. The

Political cartoonist Thomas Nast entitled this cartoon on Johnson's impeachment "The Political Death of the Bogus Caesar." Johnson was not convicted, but neither did his party nominate him for the presidency in 1868. It was not the end of his political career, however; he was elected to the Senate from Tennessee in 1874.

thousands of Northerners who went south after the war for economic or humanitarian reasons hoped to extend Yankee "civilization" to what they viewed as an unenlightened and barbarous region. For most of them this reformation required the aid of the freedmen; not enough southern whites were willing to accept the new order and embrace northern middle-class values.

The struggle of these groups to achieve their conflicting goals bred chaos, violence, and instability. Unsettled conditions meant that there were many opportunities for corruption, crime, and terrorism. This was scarcely an ideal setting for an experiment in interracial democracy, but one was attempted nonetheless. Its success depended on massive and sustained support from the federal government. To the extent that this was forthcoming, progressive reform could be achieved. When it faltered, the forces of reaction and white supremacy were unleashed.

Social and Economic Adjustments

The Civil War scarred the southern landscape and wrecked its economy. Central South Carolina looked to one 1865 observer "like a broad black streak of ruin and desolation"; the Tennessee Valley, according to another, "consists for the most part of plantations in a state of semi-ruin and plantations of which the ruin is for the present complete and total." Several major cities —including Atlanta, Columbia, and Richmond— were gutted by fire. Most factories were dismantled or destroyed, and long stretches of railroad were torn up.

Physical ruin would not have been so disastrous if investment capital had been available for rebuilding. But the substantial wealth represented by Confederate currency and bonds had melted away, and emancipation of the slaves had divested the propertied classes of their most valuable and productive assets. According to some estimates, the South's per capita wealth in 1865 was only about half what it had been in 1860.

Recovery could not even begin until a new labor system replaced slavery. It was widely assumed in both the North and the South that southern prosperity would continue to depend on cotton and that the plantation was the most efficient unit for producing the crop. But rebuild-

ing the plantation economy was hindered by lack of capital to pay wages, the deep-rooted belief of southern whites that blacks would work only under compulsion, and the freedmen's resistance to labor conditions that recalled slavery.

Blacks strongly preferred to be small independent farmers rather than plantation laborers, and for a time they had reason to hope that the federal government would support their ambitions. General Sherman, hampered by the huge numbers of black fugitives that followed his army on its famous march, issued an order in January 1865 that set aside the islands and coastal areas of Georgia and South Carolina for exclusive black occupancy on forty-acre plots. Furthermore, the Freedmen's Bureau, as one of its many responsibilities, was given control of hundreds of thousands of acres of abandoned or confiscated land and authorized to make forty-acre grants to black settlers for three-year periods, after which they would have the option to buy at low prices. By June 1865, forty thousand black farmers were at work on three hundred thousand acres of what they thought would be their own land.

But the dream of "forty acres and a mule" was not to be realized. President Johnson pardoned the owners of most of the land consigned to the ex-slaves by Sherman and the Freedmen's Bureau, and proposals for an effective program of land confiscation and redistribution failed to get through Congress. Consequently, most blacks in physical possession of small farms failed to acquire title, and the mass of freedmen were left with little or no prospect of becoming landowners. Recalling the plight of southern blacks in 1865, an ex-slave later wrote that "they were set free without a dollar, without a foot of land, and without the wherewithal to get the next meal even."

For most ex-slaves no alternative remained except to return to the white-owned cotton fields. By mid to late 1865 the majority of freedmen had accepted this fate. The most common form of agricultural employment in 1865 and '66 was a contract labor system. Under this system workers committed themselves for a year in return for fixed wages, a substantial portion of which were withheld until after the harvest. Since many planters were inclined to drive hard bargains, abuse their workers, or cheat them at the end of the year, the Freedmen's Bureau assumed the role

For many former slaves, conditions were little changed after the Civil War. Lacking their own property, many blacks—like the cotton pickers above—were forced to work the lands of their former owners.

■ *Below, a William Aiken Walker painting of a sharecropper's cabin. Too often freed blacks discovered that sharecropping led to a new form of economic servitude.*

of reviewing the contracts and enforcing them. But bureau officials had differing notions of what it meant to protect blacks from exploitation. Some stood up strongly for the rights of the freedmen; others served as allies of the planters, rounding up available workers, coercing them to sign contracts for low wages, and then helping keep them in line.

After 1867, when the bureau's influence was waning (it was phased out completely by 1869), a new arrangement evolved out of direct negotiations between planters and freedmen. Unhappy with gang labor and constant white supervision, blacks demanded sharecropper status—in other words, the right to work a small piece of land independently in return for a fixed share of the crop produced on it, usually one half. Many landowners accepted this arrangement because it did not require much capital and forced the tenant to share the risks of crop failure or a fall in cotton prices. These considerations loomed larger after disastrous harvests in 1866 and '67.

Blacks initially viewed sharecropping as a step up from wage labor in the direction of landownership. But during the 1870s this form of tenancy evolved into a new kind of servitude. Croppers had to live on credit until their cotton was sold, and planters or merchants seized the chance to "provision" them at high prices and exorbitant rates of interest. Creditors were entitled to deduct what was owed to them out of the tenant's share of the crop and this left most sharecroppers with no net profit at the end of the year—more often than not with a debt that had to be worked off in subsequent years. Various methods, legal and extralegal, were eventually devised to bind indebted tenants to a single landlord for extended periods, and a system of virtual peonage resulted.

While landless blacks in the countryside were being reduced to economic dependence, those in towns and cities found themselves living in an increasingly segregated society. The Black Codes of 1865 attempted to require separation of the races in public places and facilities; when most of the codes were set aside by federal authorities as violations of the Civil Rights Act of 1866, the

Education was one route through which the former slaves believed they could escape the harsh economic and social conditions of the Reconstruction South. The earliest schools for the freedmen, like this primary school at Vicksburg, Mississippi, were usually staffed by white women from one of the northern abolitionist or missionary societies.

same end was often achieved through private initiative and community pressure. In some cities blacks successfully resisted being consigned to separate streetcars by appealing to the military during the brief period when it exercised authority or by organizing boycotts. But they found it almost impossible to gain admittance to most hotels, restaurants, and other privately owned establishments catering to whites. On railroads, separate black, or "Jim Crow," cars were not yet the rule, but Afro-Americans were normally denied first-class accommodations. When black-supported Republican governments came to power in 1868, some of them passed civil rights acts requiring equal access to public facilities, but little effort was made to enforce the legislation.

Some forms of racial separation were not openly discriminatory, and blacks accepted or even endorsed them. Freedmen who had belonged to white churches as slaves welcomed the chance to join all-black denominations like the African Methodist Episcopal Chuch, which provided freedom from white dominance and a more congenial style of worship. The first schools for ex-slaves were all-black institutions established by the Freedmen's Bureau and various northern missionary societies. Having been denied any education at all during the antebellum period, most blacks viewed separate schooling as an opportunity rather than as a form of discrimination. When the Radical governments set up public school systems, they condoned de facto educational segregation. Only in the city schools of New Orleans

and at the University of South Carolina were there serious attempts during Reconstruction to bring white and black students together in the same classrooms.

The upshot of all forms of racial separatism—whether produced by white prejudice or black accommodation—was to create a divided society, one in which blacks and whites lived much of the time in separate worlds. But there were two exceptions to this pattern: one was at work, where blacks necessarily dealt with white employers; the other was in the political sphere, where blacks sought to exercise their rights as citizens of a democracy.

Political Reconstruction in the South

The state governments that emerged in 1865 had little or no regard for the rights of the freed slaves. Some of their codes even made black unemployment a crime, which meant that blacks had to make long-term contracts with white employers or face judicial punishment. Others limited the rights of blacks to own property or engage in occupations other than those of servant or laborer. The codes were set aside by the actions of Congress, the military, and the Freedmen's Bureau, but private violence and discrimination against blacks continued on a massive scale unchecked by state authorities. Hundreds, perhaps thousands, of blacks were murdered by whites in

1865–1866, and few of the perpetrators were brought to justice.

The imposition of military rule in 1867 was designed in part to protect former slaves from violence and intimidation, but the task was beyond the capacity of the few thousand troops stationed in the South. When new constitutions were approved and states readmitted to the Union under the congressional plan in 1868, the problem became more severe. White opponents of Radical Reconstruction adopted systematic terrorism as a means of keeping blacks away from the polls. Yet the military presence was progressively reduced, leaving the new Republican regimes to fight a losing battle against armed white supremacists. In the words of historian William Gillette, "there was simply no federal force large enough to give heart to black Republicans or to bridle southern white violence."

Hastily organized in 1867, the southern Republican party dominated the constitution making of 1868 and the regimes that came out of it. The party was an attempted coalition of three social groups (which of course varied in their relative strength from state to state). One was the same class that was becoming the backbone of the Republican party in the North—businessmen with an interest in enlisting government on the side of private enterprise. Many Republicans of this stripe were recent arrivals from the North—so-called carpetbaggers—but some were former Whig planters or merchants who were born in the South or had immigrated to the region before the war and now saw a chance to realize their dreams for commercial and industrial development.

Poor white farmers, especially those from upland areas where Unionist sentiment had been strong during the Civil War, were a second element in the original coalition. These owners of small farms expected the party to favor their interests at the expense of the wealthy landowners and to come to their aid with special legislation when—as was often the case in this period of economic upheaval—they faced the loss of their homesteads to creditors. Newly enfranchised blacks were the third group to which the Republicans appealed. Blacks formed the vast majority of the Republican rank and file in most states and were concerned mainly with education, civil rights, and landownership.

Under the best of conditions, these coalitions

Race riots erupted in several southern cities as white Southerners turned to violence to keep black voters from exercising their right of suffrage. The scene above is from the Memphis riots of 1868.

would have been difficult to maintain. Each group had its own distinct goals and did not fully support the aims of the other segments. White yeomen, for example, had a bred-in-the-bone resistance to black equality. And for how long could one expect essentially conservative businessmen to support costly measures for the elevation or relief of the lower classes of either race? In some states, astute Democratic politicians exploited these divisions by appealing to disaffected white Republicans. As a result, Republican coalitions split, opening the way for the overthrow of Radical rule.

But during the relatively brief period when they were in power in the South—it varied from one to nine years depending on the state—the Republicans chalked up some notable achievements. They established (on paper at least) the South's first adequate systems of public education, democratized state and local government, and appropriated funds for an enormous expansion of public services and welfare responsibilities. They also sought to foster economic development by subsidizing the construction of railroads and other internal improvements.

These activities—particularly the grants to railroads—were often accompanied by inefficiency, waste, and corruption. Although the Radical regimes brought needed reforms to the South, it can scarcely be claimed that they were model governments. Embezzlement of public funds and bribery of state lawmakers or officials were common occurrences. State debts and tax burdens rose enormously, mainly because governments had undertaken heavy new responsibilities, but partly as a result of waste and graft. But the situation varied from state to state; ruling cliques in Louisiana and South Carolina were guilty of much wrongdoing, yet Mississippi had a relatively honest and frugal regime.

Furthermore, southern corruption was not exceptional, nor was it a special result of the extension of suffrage to uneducated blacks, as critics of Radical Reconstruction have claimed. It was part of a national pattern during an era when private interests considered buying government favors a part of the cost of doing business, and many politicians expected to profit by obliging them. The Louisiana governor who pocketed $100,000 in a single year on an $8000 salary was a small-time operator compared to Boss Tweed of New York City, whose notorious "Ring" probably stole more than was embezzled in all the southern states combined. If railroad magnate Jay Gould could bribe the majority of the New York state legislature to gain concessions for the Erie Railroad, it should come as no surprise that "Honest John" Patterson, representing the Blue Ridge Railroad, could do the same in South Carolina.

Blacks bore only a limited responsibility for the dishonesty of the Radical governments. Although sixteen blacks served in Congress—two in the Senate—between 1869 and 1880, only in South Carolina did blacks constitute a majority of even one house of the state legislature. Furthermore, no black governors were elected during Reconstruction (although P. B. S. Pinchback served for a time as acting governor of Louisiana). The biggest grafters were opportunistic whites—some of the most notorious were carpetbaggers but others were native Southerners. Businessmen offering bribes included members of the prewar gentry who were staunch opponents of Radical programs. Some black legislators went with the tide and accepted "loans" from those railroad lobbyists who would pay most for their votes, but the same men could usually be depended upon to vote the will of their constituents on civil rights or educational issues.

It was unfortunate, however, that blacks first entered American politics at a time when public ethics were at a low point. They served or supported corrupt and wasteful regimes because they had no alternative. Although the Democrats, or "Conservatives" as they called themselves in some states, made sporadic efforts to attract black voters, it was clear that if they won control, they would attempt to strip blacks of their civil and political rights. But opponents of Radical Reconstruction were able to capitalize on racial prejudice and persuade many Americans that "good government" was synonymous with white supremacy.

Contrary to myth, the small number of blacks elected to state or national office during Reconstruction demonstrated on the average more integrity and competence than their white counterparts. Most were fairly well educated, having been free Negroes or unusually privileged slaves before the war. Among the most capable were Senator Blanche K. Bruce of Mississippi—elected to the Senate in 1874 after rising to deserved prominence in the Republican party of his home state; Congressman Robert Brown Elliott of South Carolina—an adroit politician who was also a consistent champion of civil rights; and Congressman James T. Rapier of Alabama, who stirred Congress and the nation in 1873 with his eloquent appeals for federal aid to southern education and new laws to enforce equal rights for Afro-Americans.

The Age of Grant

Ulysses S. Grant was the only president between Jackson and Wilson to serve two full and consecutive terms. But unlike other chief executives so favored by fortune and the electorate, Grant is commonly regarded as a failure. Historians used to blame him mainly for the corruption that surfaced in his administration. More recently he has been condemned for the inconsistency and ultimate failure of his southern policy. The charges are valid, and no one is likely to make the case that he was a great statesman. Faced with the demands of the presidency, Grant found that he had no strong principles to guide him except

■ *In the Senate, Blanche K. Bruce (left) championed the causes of citizenship for the American Indians and improvement of the Mississippi River. Electioneering in the South, a sketch by W. L. Sheppard, depicts a black politician campaigning for votes among newly enfranchised freedmen.*

loyalty to old friends and to politicians who supported him. But the problems he faced were difficult, if not insoluble. A president with a clearer sense of duty and purpose might have done little better.

Rise of the Money Question

The impeachment crisis of 1868 represented the high point of popular interest in Reconstruction issues. Already competing for public attention was the question of how to manage the nation's currency, and more specifically, what to do about the greenbacks—paper money issued during the war. Hugh McCulloch, secretary of the Treasury under Johnson, favored a return to "sound" money and in 1866, he had initiated a policy of withdrawing greenbacks from circulation until they were on a par with gold, thus allowing a return to payments in silver or gold. Opposition to this hard-money policy and the resulting deflation came from a number of groups; it split both the major parties. In general, the "greenbackers"

were strongest in the credit-hungry West and among expansionist-minded manufacturers. Defenders of hard money were mostly the commercial and financial interests in the East; they received crucial support from intellectuals who regarded government-sponsored inflation as immoral or contrary to the natural laws of classical economics.

In 1868 the money question surged briefly to the forefront of national politics. Faced with a business recession blamed on McCulloch's policy of contracting the currency, Congress voted to stop the retirement of greenbacks. The Democratic party, responding to midwestern pressure, included in its platform a plan calling for the redemption of much of the Civil War debt in greenbacks rather than gold, despite the fact that bondholders had been assured of specie payment. But divisions within the parties prevented the money question from becoming a central issue in the presidential campaign. The Democrats nominated Governor Horatio Seymour of New York, a sound-money supporter, thus nullifying their progreenback platform. Republicans based their

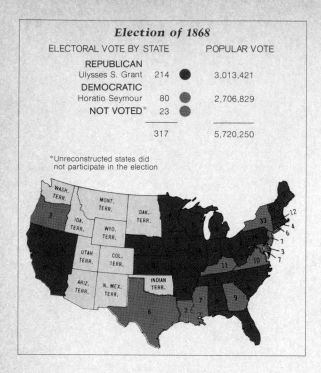

campaign mainly on a defense of their reconstruction policy and a celebration of their popular candidate. With the help of votes from the Republican-dominated southern states, Grant won a decisive victory.

In 1869 and '70 a Republican-controlled Congress passed laws that assured payment in gold to most bondholders but eased the burden of the huge Civil War debt by refunding it, which meant that bonds soon coming due were exchanged for those that would not be payable for ten, fifteen, or thirty years. In this way the public credit was protected, but at the same time those who had purchased bonds during the war with depreciated paper currency were assured of great profits.

Still unresolved was the problem of what to do about the $356 million in greenbacks that remained in circulation. Hard-money proponents wanted to retire them quickly, while inflationists thought more should be issued to stimulate the economy. Both opinions were held by leading Republicans. The Grant administration followed the middle course of allowing the greenbacks to float until economic expansion would bring them to a par with gold, thus permitting a painless return to specie payments. But the panic of 1873, which brought much of the economy to its knees, led to a revival of agitation to inflate the curren-

cy. Debt-ridden farmers, who would be the backbone of the greenback movement for years to come, now joined the easy-money clamor for the first time.

Responding to the money and credit crunch, Congress moved in 1874 to authorize a modest issue of new greenbacks. But Grant, influenced by the opinions of hard-money financiers, vetoed the bill. In 1875, Congress, led by Senator John Sherman of Ohio, enacted the Specie Resumption Act which provided for a limited reduction of greenbacks leading to full resumption of specie payments by January 1, 1879. Although Congress softened the blow by permitting an expanded issue of national bank notes, its action was widely interpreted as deflation in the midst of depression. Farmers and workers, who were already suffering acutely from deflation, reacted with dismay and anger.

The Democratic party could not capitalize adequately on these sentiments because of the influence of its own hard-money faction, and in 1876 an independent Greenback party entered the national political arena. The party's nominee for president, Peter Cooper, received an insignificant number of votes, but in 1878 the Greenback Labor party polled more than a million votes and elected fourteen congressmen. Greenbackers kept the money issue alive through the next decade.

Retreat from Reconstruction

The Republican effort to make equal rights for blacks the law of the land culminated in the Fifteenth Amendment. Passed by Congress in 1869 and ratified by the states in 1870, the amendment prohibited any state from denying a citizen the right to vote because of race, color, or previous condition of servitude. A more radical version, requiring universal manhood suffrage, was rejected because it departed too sharply from traditional views of federal-state relations. States therefore could still limit the suffrage by imposing literacy tests, property qualifications, or poll taxes allegedly applying to all racial groups; such devices would eventually be used to strip southern blacks of the right to vote. But the makers of the amendment did not foresee this result. They believed that their action would prevent future Congresses or southern constitutional conven-

An engraving celebrating the
passage of the Fifteenth
Amendment, which provided
for universal male suffrage.
Passage of the amendment
was troubling to many
feminists since women were
still denied the right to vote
(see pp. 470–471).

THE RESULT OF THE FIFTEENTH AMENDMENT,
And the Rise and Progress of the African Race in America and its final Accomplishment, and Celebration on May 19ᵗʰ A.D. 1870.

tions from repealing or nullifying the provisions for black suffrage included in the Reconstruction Acts. A secondary aim was to enfranchise blacks in those northern states that still denied them the vote.

The Grant administration was charged with enforcing the amendment and protecting black voting rights in the reconstructed states. Since survival of the Republican regimes depended on black support, political partisanship dictated federal action, even though the North's emotional and ideological commitment to black citizenship was waning.

Between 1868 and 1872, the main threat to southern Republican regimes came from the Ku Klux Klan and other secret societies bent on restoring white supremacy by intimidating blacks who sought to exercise their political rights. First organized in Tennessee in 1866, the Klan spread rapidly to other states, adopting increasingly lawless and brutal tactics. A grassroots vigilance movement and not a centralized conspiracy, the Klan thrived on local initiative and gained support from whites of all social classes. Its secrecy, decentralization, popular support, and utter ruthlessness made it very difficult to suppress. As soon as blacks had been granted the right to vote, hooded night riders began to visit the cabins of those who were known to be active Republicans; some victims were only threatened, but others were whipped or even murdered. A typical incident was related by a black Georgian: "They broke my door open, took me out of bed, took me to the woods and whipped me three hours or more and left me for dead. They said to me, 'Do you think you will vote for another damned radical ticket?'"

These methods were first used effectively in the presidential election of 1868. Grant lost Louisiana and Georgia mainly because the Klan—or the Knights of the White Camelia as the Louisiana variant was called—launched a reign of terror to prevent prospective black voters from exercising their right. In Louisiana political violence claimed more than a thousand lives, and in Arkansas, which Grant managed to carry, more than two hundred Republicans, including a congressman, were assassinated.

Thereafter, Klan terrorism was directed mainly at Republican state governments. Virtual insurrections broke out in Arkansas, Tennessee, North Carolina, and parts of South Carolina. Republican governors called out the state militia to fight the Klan, but only the Arkansas militia succeeded in bringing it to heel. In Tennessee, North Carolina, and Georgia Klan activities helped undermine

Above, a member of the Ku Klux Klan, a secret white supremacist organization, in typical regalia. Before any election, hooded Klansmen terrorized blacks to discourage them from voting.

The White League was another organization formed to deny blacks their rights. Above, armed White Leaguers guard a ballot box to prevent black voters from depositing their ballots.

Republican control, thus allowing the Democrats to come to power in all of these states by 1870.

Faced with the violent overthrow of the southern Republican party, Congress and the Grant administration were forced to act. A series of laws passed in 1870–1871 sought to enforce the Fifteenth Amendment by providing federal protection for black suffrage and authorizing use of the army against the Klan. These "Ku Klux Klan" or "Force" Acts made interference with voting rights a federal crime and established provisions for government supervision of elections. In addition, the legislation empowered the president to call out troops and suspend the writ of habeas corpus to quell insurrection. In 1871–1872, thousands of suspected Klansmen were arrested by the military or U.S. marshals, and the writ was suspended in nine counties of South Carolina which had been virtually taken over by the secret order. Although most of the accused Klansmen either were never brought to trial, were acquitted, or received suspended sentences, the enforcement effort was vigorous enough to put a damper on hooded terrorism and ensure relatively fair and peaceful elections in 1872.

Radical Reconstruction in the South was obviously tottering by 1872, and further outbreaks of violence helped bring its total collapse. The surviving Republican governments were riddled by factionalism and tainted by charges of corruption, and the northern public became increasingly disenchanted with federal intervention on behalf of these regimes, even when their opponents were resorting to riot and murder.

Grant did intervene militarily in Louisiana in 1874 when an overt paramilitary organization known as the White League staged an armed insurrection against a Republican government accused of stealing an election. But when another unofficial militia—the White Line of Mississippi—instigated a series of bloody race riots prior to the state elections of 1875, Grant refused the governor's request for federal troops. As a result, black voters were successfully intimidated—one county registered only seven Republican votes where there had been a black majority of two thousand, and Mississippi fell to the Conservatives. According to one account, Grant decided to withhold troops because he had been warned that intervention might cost the Republicans the crucial state of Ohio in the same off-year elections.

By 1876 Republicans held on to only three southern states—South Carolina, Louisiana, and Florida. Partly because of Grant's hesitant and inconsistent use of presidential power but mainly because the northern electorate would no longer tolerate military action to sustain Republican governments and black voting rights, Radical Reconstruction was falling into total eclipse.

Spoilsmen Versus Reformers

One reason Grant found it increasingly difficult to take strong action to protect southern Republicans was the bad odor surrounding his stewardship of the federal government and the Republican party. Reformers charged that a corrupt national administration was propping up bad governments in the South for personal and partisan advantage. An apparent case in point was Grant's intervention in Louisiana in 1872 on behalf of an ill-reputed Republican faction headed by his wife's brother-in-law, who controlled federal patronage as collector of customs in New Orleans.

The Republican party in the Grant era was rapidly losing the idealism and high purpose associated with the crusade against slavery. By the beginning of the 1870s, the men who had been the conscience of the party—old-line radicals like Thaddeus Stevens, Charles Sumner, and Benjamin Wade—were either dead, out of politics, or at odds with the administration. New leaders of a different stamp, whom historians have dubbed "spoilsmen" or "politicos" were taking their place. When he made common cause with hard-boiled manipulators like Senators Roscoe Conkling of New York and James G. Blaine of Maine, Grant lost credibility with reform-minded Republicans.

During Grant's first administration, an aura of scandal surrounded the White House but did not directly implicate the President. In 1869 the financial buccaneer Jay Gould enlisted the aid of a brother-in-law of Grant to further his incredible scheme to corner the gold market. Gould failed in the attempt, but he did manage to save himself and come away with a huge profit.

Grant's first-term vice-president, Schuyler Colfax of Indiana, was directly involved in the notorious Crédit Mobilier scandal. Crédit Mobilier was a construction company that actually served as a fraudulent device for siphoning off profits that should have gone to the stockholders of the Union Pacific Railroad, which was the beneficiary of massive federal land grants. In order to forestall government inquiry into this arrangement, Crédit Mobilier stock was distributed to influential congressmen, including Colfax (who was Speaker of the House before he was elected vice-president). The whole business came to light just before the campaign of 1872.

Republicans who could not tolerate such corruption or had other grievances against the administration broke with Grant in 1872 and formed a third party committed to "honest government" and "reconciliation" between the North and the South. Led initially by high-minded reformers like Senator Carl Schurz of Missouri, the "Liberal Republicans" endorsed reform of the civil service to curb the corruption-breeding patronage system and advocated strict laissez-faire economic policies—which meant low tariffs, an end to government subsidies for railroads, and hard money. Despite their rhetoric of idealism and reform, the Liberal Republicans were extremely conservative in their notions of what government should do to assure justice for blacks and other underprivileged Americans.

The Liberal Republicans' national convention nominated Horace Greeley, editor of the respected *New York Tribune*. This was a curious and divisive choice since Greeley was at odds with the founders of the movement on the tariff question and indifferent to civil service reform. The Democrats also endorsed Greeley, mainly because he promised to end Radical Reconstruction by restoring "self-government" to the South.

But the journalist turned out to be a poor campaigner who failed to inspire enthusiasm from lifelong supporters of either party. Most

The Election of 1872

Candidate	Party	Popular Vote	Electoral Vote*
Grant	Republican	3,598,235	286
Greeley	Democrat and Liberal Republican	2,834,761	Greeley died before the electoral college voted.

Out of a total of 366 electoral votes. Greeley's votes were divided among the four minor candidates.

Woman's Rights and the Fifteenth Amendment

Extending citizenship and the right to vote to the newly freed slaves marked a milestone in their passage from slavery to freedom. The Fourteenth Amendment, adopted in 1868, defined citizenship and forbade the states from abridging the rights of citizens or denying them "equal protection of the laws." The amendment, in effect, extended to blacks the rights, privileges, and immunities of citizenship. The Fifteenth Amendment, proposed by Congress in 1869 and ratified by the states within a year, prohibited federal and state governments from denying the vote to anyone "on account of race, color, or previous condition of servitude." Of course, states could still restrict the right to vote, by property and literacy requirements, for example; hence the amendment prohibited one type of disfranchisement rather than requiring universal manhood suffrage.

Nonetheless, the amendment seemed to offer something to everyone with a stake in the Union's victory. For the abolitionists and other reformers, it meant the triumph of principles of human rights and the admission of blacks into political equality with whites. For Republican party leaders, it created a bloc of black voters in the South likely to be grateful to its northern liberators—and to demonstrate its gratitude at

the polls. And to the slaves themselves, it gave some protection from their former masters, a chance to defend themselves against southern political action aimed at returning them to a form of slavery. But to the many women who had worked for emancipation, the amendment offered little. Congress had neglected their demands for woman suffrage while enfranchising the male members of a group that remained at the bottom of society in status and wealth.

Feminists and abolitionists had a long history of intermittent periods of cooperation and conflict. Women were active in the abolition movement from the first, forming female auxiliaries to the antislavery societies, collecting signatures on antislavery petitions, and raising money for the cause. As long as the women were willing to work behind the scenes, abolitionist leaders welcomed their support. But in the late 1830s, inspired by concern for the slaves and belief in their own abilities, women began to lecture against slavery in public, to take part in abolitionist debates, and to serve on abolitionist committees. Abolitionists then began to argue among themselves over the proper role of women in their organizations.

The women's issue divided abolitionists into

three main camps. William Lloyd Garrison and his radical followers saw abolitionism as part of a larger crusade for human rights and welcomed women's participation in the movement. They did not actively work for woman suffrage or make it a part of their program, but they insisted that anyone who wished might speak out on behalf of the slave. More conservative abolitionists like Lewis Tappan saw emancipation as removing the main blemish from a generally healthy society and feared the disruption of too much change. Both custom and divine law told them that women belonged at home in the family, under the protection of a husband or father. These conservatives believed that womankind neither needed nor deserved a public voice and thus had no place in official abolitionist activity. A third, smaller group of men, like Theodore Weld, endorsed feminism but urged caution and prudence on the radicals. The northern public, they reasoned, would not support emancipation if it were linked to other reforms. Women should keep silent until the slaves were freed, and then they could work for their own liberation.

The women who had started the controversy were drawn into a stronger commitment to their own rights. "What *then* can *woman* do for the slave," asked Angelina Grimké, "when she herself is under the feet of man and shamed into silence?" Continuing to work in the cause of the slave, these women developed a separate feminist movement as well, demanding—among other things—the vote.

These divisions reemerged in the late 1860s when Congress debated the future of the freedmen. Male antislavery advocates at last had a chance to influence national policy, and their doubts about how far reform should be carried took on a new importance. A few men supported the most radical position, that the demands of blacks and women were inseparable and must be met together. The more conservative abolitionists, who had never supported woman's rights, continued to work only for black men's suffrage. They found powerful allies among the many Republicans in Congress who saw no political advantage in giving the vote to women. But even former radicals now heeded the counsel of expediency, concluding that women must wait to act until black freedom had been secured. It was "the Negro's hour," and the first priority of Reconstruction government must be to guarantee the black man's status as an American citizen. Blacks, as part of an enlarged and liberal voting public, would later aid the passage of woman suffrage.

Women were not so sure. Upset by language in the Fourteenth Amendment limiting its protections to "male citizens," they campaigned hard for a suffrage amendment that would include women as well as blacks. Their defeat caused a new division within their own ranks. Differences over the Fifteenth Amendment split feminists into two factions, each with its own organization. One, represented by Lucy Stone (p. 470 right), Julia Ward Howe, and the American Woman Suffrage Association, sided with the advocates of expediency and supported the Fifteenth Amendment. Though the amendment had been a disappointment, "I will be thankful in my soul if *any* body can get out of this terrible pit," proclaimed Lucy Stone. Susan B. Anthony (p. 470 left) disagreed, threatening to "cut off this right arm of mine before I will ever work for or demand the ballot for the Negro and not the woman." Anthony and Elizabeth Cady Stanton broke their ties with the abolitionists and Radical Republicans, who they felt had betrayed them. Speaking out vehemently against the amendment, they organized a movement led by women that concentrated on women's goals. In 1869 they formed the National Woman Suffrage Association, committed to passing a sixteenth amendment that would enfranchise women.

Leaders of both factions—Stanton and Anthony as well as Stone and Howe—had worked to bring about emancipation; Stanton and Anthony had even led a petition drive for the Thirteenth Amendment freeing the slaves. But their success as abolitionists convinced them of their abilities as women, and to see the black man given rights denied themselves seemed a brutal slap in the face. Women of education and status could not vote; freed*men* could. Feminists were faced with a painful choice between full loyalty to their own cause and full support for the rights of blacks. The decisions they made divided the women suffrage movement for a generation to come.

Belknap was impeached by the House after an investigation revealed that he had taken bribes for the sale of Indian trading posts. He avoided conviction in the Senate only by resigning from office before his trial. Grant fought hard to protect Belknap, to the point of participating in what a later generation might call a "cover-up."

There is no evidence that Grant profited personally from any of the misdeeds of his subordinates. Yet he is not entirely without blame for the corruption in his administration. He failed to take action against the malefactors, and even after their guilt had been clearly established, he tried to shield them from justice.

Reunion and the New South

Congressional Reconstruction prolonged the sense of sectional division and conflict for a dozen years after the guns had fallen silent. Its final liquidation in 1877 opened the way to a reconciliation of North and South that some historians have celebrated as a culminating achievement of American nationalism. But the costs of reunion were high for less privileged groups in the South. The civil and political rights of blacks, left unprotected, were progressively and relentlessly stripped away by white supremacist regimes. Lower-class whites saw their interests sacrificed to those of capitalists and landlords. Despite the rhetoric hailing a prosperous "New South," the region remained poor and open to exploitation by northern business interests.

The Compromise of 1877

The election of 1876 pitted Rutherford B. Hayes of Ohio, a Republican governor untainted by the scandals of the Grant era, against Governor Samuel J. Tilden of New York, a Democratic reformer who had battled against Tammany Hall and the Tweed Ring. (For more on the Tweed Ring, see chapter 19.) Honest government was apparently the electorate's highest priority. When the returns came in, Tilden had clearly won the popular vote and seemed likely to win a narrow victory in the electoral college. But the result was placed in

"In for It," a rare anti-Grant cartoon by Thomas Nast, shows the President falling headlong into the barrel of scandals that tainted his administration.

Republicans stuck with Grant, despite the corruption issue, because they still could not stomach the idea of ex-rebels returning to power in the South. Many Democrats, recalling Greeley's previous record as a staunch Republican, simply stayed away from the polls. The result was a decisive victory for Grant, whose 56 percent of the popular vote was the highest percentage won by any candidate between Andrew Jackson and Theodore Roosevelt.

Grant's second administration bore out the reformers' worst suspicions about corruption in high places. In 1875 the public learned that federal revenue officials had conspired with distillers to defraud the government of millions of dollars in liquor taxes. Grant's private secretary, Orville E. Babcock, was indicted as a member of the "Whiskey Ring" and was saved from conviction only by the President's personal intercession. The next year, Grant's Secretary of War William E.

be ratified by both houses of Congress. The Republican-dominated Senate readily approved it, but Democrats in the House planned a filibuster to delay the final counting of the electoral votes until after inauguration day. If the filibuster succeeded, neither candidate would have a majority and, as provided in the Constitution, the election would be decided by the House, where the Democrats controlled enough states to elect Tilden.

To ensure Hayes' election, Republican leaders negotiated secretly with conservative southern Democrats, some of whom seemed willing to abandon the filibuster if the last troops were withdrawn and "home rule" was restored to the South. Eventually an informal bargain was struck, which historians have dubbed "the Compromise of 1877." In a sense, Hayes did not really concede anything, because he had already decided to end federal support for the crumbling Radical regimes. But southern negotiators were heartened by firm assurances that this would indeed be the policy. Some were also influenced by vaguer promises involving federal support for southern railroads and internal improvements.

Rutherford B. Hayes (above) was awarded the presidency in the disputed election of 1876 even though he won fewer popular votes than his opponent, Democrat Samuel Tilden.

doubt when the returns from the three southern states still controlled by the Republicans—South Carolina, Florida, and Louisiana—were contested. If Hayes were to be awarded these three states, plus one contested electoral vote in Oregon, Republican strategists realized, he would triumph in the electoral college by a single vote.

The outcome of the election remained undecided for months, plunging the nation into a major political crisis. To resolve the impasse, Congress appointed a special electoral commission of fifteen members to determine who would receive the votes of the disputed states. Originally composed of seven Democrats, seven Republicans, and an independent, it fell under Republican control when the independent member resigned to run for the Senate, and a Republican was appointed to take his place. The commission split along party lines and voted 8 to 7 to award Hayes the disputed states. But this decision still had to

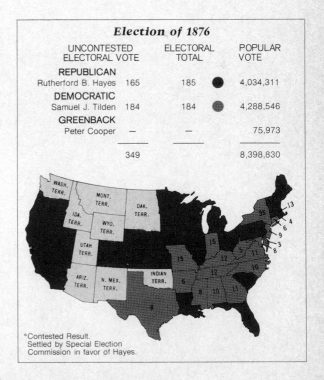

Election of 1876

	UNCONTESTED ELECTORAL VOTE	ELECTORAL TOTAL		POPULAR VOTE
REPUBLICAN				
Rutherford B. Hayes	165	185	●	4,034,311
DEMOCRATIC				
Samuel J. Tilden	184	184	●	4,288,546
GREENBACK				
Peter Cooper	—	—		75,973
		349		8,398,830

*Contested Result.
Settled by Special Election
Commission in favor of Hayes.

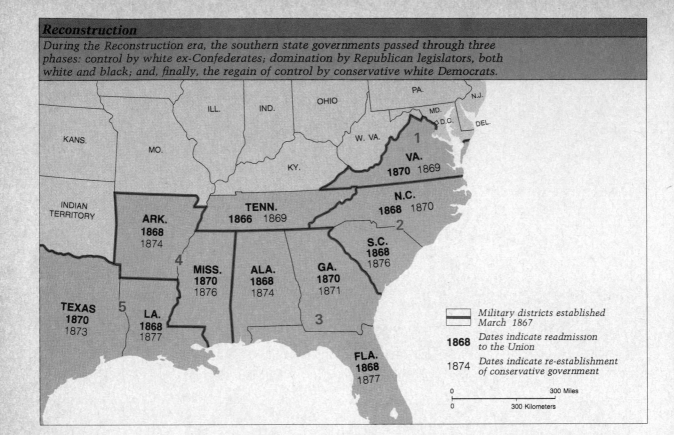

Reconstruction

During the Reconstruction era, the southern state governments passed through three phases: control by white ex-Confederates; domination by Republican legislators, both white and black; and, finally, the regain of control by conservative white Democrats.

Map labels:

KANS. · ILL. · IND. · OHIO · PA. · N.J. · MD. · D.C. · DEL. · MO. · KY. · W. VA.

1 — VA. **1870** 1869

INDIAN TERRITORY · ARK. **1868** 1874 · TENN. **1866** 1869 · N.C. **1868** 1870

2 — S.C. **1868** 1876

4 · MISS. **1870** 1876 · ALA. **1868** 1874 · GA. **1870** 1871

TEXAS **1870** 1873 · 5 · LA. **1868** 1877 · 3

FLA. **1868** 1877

Legend:

Military districts established March 1867

1868 Dates indicate readmission to the Union

1874 Dates indicate re-establishment of conservative government

0 ———— 300 Miles

0 ———— 300 Kilometers

With southern Democratic acquiescence, the filibuster was broken and Hayes took the oath of office. He immediately ordered the army not to resist a Democratic takeover in South Carolina and Louisiana. Thus fell the last of the Radical governments, and the entire South was firmly under the control of white Democrats. The trauma of the war and Reconstruction had destroyed the chances for a renewal of two-party competition among white Southerners.

Northern Republicans soon reverted to denouncing the South for its crimes against black suffrage. But this "waving of the bloody shirt" soon degenerated into an empty campaign ritual aimed at northern voters who could still be moved by sectional antagonism.

The New South

The men who led the crusade against Radical Reconstruction in the South and came to power after it fell in one state after another are usually referred to as the "Redeemers." They were predominantly upper class in origins and loyalties, but the elite that they represented was not identical to the ruling group of the Old South. Although planters who had been large slaveholders were conspicuous in their ranks, most Redeemers favored commercial and industrial interests over those that were strictly agrarian. Some were sharp-witted men who had seized the political and economic opportunities created by disordered conditions in the postwar South. Others were prewar aristocrats who had made the adjustment to a new age by adopting the values and practices of tough-minded businessmen.

The ideology of the Redeemers rested on two bases—white supremacy and industrial progress. The first was the principal rallying cry that brought them to power in the first place. Once the Redeemers were in office they found that they could stay there by charging that opponents of ruling Democratic cliques were trying to divide "the white man's party" and open the way to a

■ *The first industries of the New South were usually processing plants for the agricultural products of the region. Above, blacks working on a sugar plantation in Louisiana are cutting sugar cane to be processed in the plantation's refinery.*

return of "black domination." The gospel of industrial progress—the image of a "New South" where factories and railroads would bring prosperity to all—served to mask policies that favored employers over workers, landlords over tenants, and creditors over debtors. It also opened the doors to northern capital and encouraged absentee ownership of important segments of the southern economy.

The new governments were more economical than those of Reconstruction, mainly because they cut back drastically on appropriations for schools and other needed public services. But they were scarcely more honest—embezzlement of funds and bribery of officials continued to occur to an alarming extent. Louisiana, for example, suffered for decades from the flagrant corruption associated with a state-chartered lottery.

The Redeemer regimes of the late 1870s and '80s badly neglected the interests of small white farmers. Whites, as well as blacks, were suffering from the notorious "crop lien" system, which gave local merchants who advanced credit at high

rates of interest during the growing season the right to take possession of the harvested crop on terms that buried farmers deeper and deeper in debt. As a result, increasing numbers of whites lost title to their homesteads and were reduced to tenancy. When a depression of world cotton prices added to the burden of a ruinous credit system, agrarian protesters began to challenge the ruling elite, first through the Southern Farmers' Alliance of the late 1880s and then by supporting its political descendant—the Populist party of the 1890s.

But the greatest hardships imposed by the new order were reserved for blacks. The Redeemers promised, as part of the understanding that led to the end of federal intervention in 1877, that they would respect the rights of blacks as set forth in the Fourteenth and Fifteenth amendments. Governor Wade Hampton of South Carolina was especially vocal in pledging that Afro-Americans would not be reduced to second-class citizenship by the new regimes. But when blacks tried to vote Republican in the "redeemed" states, they encountered renewed violence and intimidation. "Bulldozing" Afro-American voters remained common practice in state elections during the late 1870s and early '80s; those blacks who withstood the threat of losing their jobs or being evicted from tenant farms if they voted for the party of Lincoln were visited at night and literally whipped into line. The message was clear—vote Democratic or vote not at all.

Furthermore, white Democrats now controlled the electoral machinery and were able to manipulate the black vote by stuffing ballot boxes, discarding unwanted votes, or reporting fraudulent totals. Some states also imposed complicated new voting requirements to discourage black participation. Full-scale disfranchisement did not occur until literacy tests and other legalized obstacles to voting were imposed in the period from 1890 to 1910, but by that time less formal and comprehensive methods had already made a mockery of the Fifteenth Amendment.

Nevertheless, blacks continued to vote freely in some localities until the 1890s; a few districts even elected black Republicans to Congress during the immediate post-Reconstruction period.

The last of these, Representative George H. White of North Carolina, served until 1901. His farewell address eloquently conveyed the agony of southern blacks in the era of Jim Crow (strict segregation).

These parting words are in behalf of an outraged, heart-broken, bruised, and bleeding but God-fearing people, faithful, industrious, loyal people—rising people, full of potential force . . . The only apology that I have to make for the earnestness with which I have spoken is that I am pleading for the life, the liberty, the future happiness, and manhood suffrage of one-eighth of the entire population of the United States.

The dark night of racism that fell on the South after Reconstruction seemed to unleash all the baser impulses of human nature. Between 1889 and 1899 an average of 187 blacks were lynched every year for alleged offenses against white supremacy. Those convicted of petty crimes against property were often little better off; many were condemned to be leased out to private contractors

■ *Lynching was responsible for more than three thousand deaths between 1889 and 1918. Nor were lynchings confined to the South. During that thirty-year-period, only seven states reported no lynchings.*

Supreme Court Decisions Affecting Black Civil Rights, 1875–1900

Hall v. *DeCuir* (1878)	Struck down Louisiana law prohibiting racial discrimination by "common carriers" (railroads, steamboats, buses). Court declares the law a "burden" on interstate commerce, over which states had no authority.
United States v. *Harris* (1882)	Federal laws to punish crimes such as murder and assault declared unconstitutional. Such crimes declared to be the sole concern of local government. Court ignores the frequent racial motivation behind such crimes in the South.
Civil Rights Cases (1883)	Struck down Civil Rights Act of 1875. Congress may not legislate on civil rights unless a *state* passes a discriminatory law. Court declares the Fourteenth Amendment silent on racial discrimination by private citizens.
Plessy v. *Ferguson* (1896)	Louisiana statute requiring "separate but equal" accommodations on railroads upheld. Court declares that segregation is *not* necessarily discrimination.
Williams v. *Mississippi* (1898)	State law requiring a literacy test to qualify for voting upheld. Court refuses to find any implication of racial discrimination in the law. Using such laws, southern states rapidly disenfranchise blacks.

whose brutality rivaled that of the most sadistic slaveholders. (Annual death rates in the convict camps ranged as high as 25 percent.) Finally, the dignity of blacks was cruelly affronted by the wave of segregation laws passed in the 1890s, which served to remind them constantly that they were deemed unfit to associate with whites on any basis that implied equality.

The North and the federal government did little or nothing to stem the tide of racial oppression in the South. A series of Supreme Court decisions between 1875 and 1896 gutted the Reconstruction amendments and the legislation passed to enforce them, leaving blacks virtually defenseless against political and social discrimination.

At the same time, the wounds of the Civil War were healing, and white Americans were seized by the spirit of sectional reconciliation. By the late 1880s, Union and Confederate veterans were tenting together and celebrating their common Americanism. "Reunion" was becoming a cultural as well as political reality. But whites could come back together only because Northerners had tacitly agreed to give Southerners a free hand in their efforts to reduce blacks to a new form of servitude. It was the "outraged, heart-broken, bruised, and bleeding" Afro-Americans of the South who paid the heaviest price for sectional reunion.

Recommended Reading

Two excellent short accounts of what happened during Reconstruction are Kenneth Stampp, *The Era of Reconstruction, 1865–1877* (1965), and John Hope Franklin, *Reconstruction: After the Civil War* (1961). Both incorporate modern "revisionist" interpretations. W. E. B. DuBois, *Black Reconstruction in America, 1860–1880* (1935) is not altogether reliable but remains brilliant and provocative. The section on Reconstruction in J. G. Randall and David Donald, *The Civil War and Reconstruction*, 2d ed. (1969) is valuable because it seeks a middle ground between traditional views of Reconstruction and revisionist interpretations. The latest reconsiderations of Reconstruction issues can be found in J. Morgan Kousser and James M. McPherson, eds. *Region, Race, and Reconstruction: Essays in Honor of C. Vann Woodward* (1982). Morton Keller, *Affairs of State: Public Life in Late Nineteenth Century America* (1977), provides a brilliant analysis of American government and politics during Reconstruction and afterward.

Chronology

1863 Lincoln sets forth 10 percent Reconstruction plan

1864 Wade-Davis Bill passes Congress, is pocket-vetoed by Lincoln

1865 Johnson moves to reconstruct the South on his own initiative
Congress refuses to seat representatives and senators elected from states reestablished under presidential plan (December)

1866 Johnson vetoes Freedmen's Bureau Bill (February)
Johnson vetoes Civil Rights Act; it passes over his veto (April)
Congress passes Fourteenth Amendment (June)
Republicans increase their congressional majority in the fall elections

1867 First Reconstruction Act is passed over Johnson's veto (March)

1868 Johnson is impeached; he avoids conviction by one vote (February-May)
Southern blacks vote and serve in constitutional conventions
Grant wins presidential election, defeating Horatio Seymour

1869 Congress passes Fifteenth Amendment, granting blacks the right to vote

1870–1871 Congress passes Ku Klux Klan Acts to protect black voting rights in the South

1872 Grant relected president, defeating Horace Greeley, candidate of Liberal Republicans and Democrats

1873 Financial panic plunges nation into depression

1875 Congress passes Specie Resumption Act "Whiskey Ring" scandal exposed

1876–1877 Disputed presidential election resolved in favor of Republican Hayes over Democrat Tilden

1877 "Compromise of 1877" results in end to military intervention in the South and fall of the last Radical governments

Particular phases of Reconstruction are covered in Eric L. McKitrick, *Andrew Johnson and Reconstruction, 1865–1867* (1960); W. R. Brock, *An American Crisis: Congress and Reconstruction, 1865–1867* (1963); and William Gillette, *Retreat from Reconstruction, 1869–1879* (1979). Leon F. Litwack, *Been in the Storm So Long: The Aftermath of Slavery* (1979), provides a moving portrayal of the black experience of emancipation. The best introduction to the Grant era is William S. McFeeley, *Grant: A Biography* (1981). On the end of Reconstruction and the character of the post-Reconstruction South, see two classic works by C. Vann Woodward: *Reunion and Reaction*, rev. ed. (1956) and *Origins of the New South, 1877–1913* (1951).

Additional Bibliography

The Reconstruction era is surveyed in Rembert W. Patrick, *The Reconstruction of the Nation* (1967); Avery O. Craven, *Reconstruction: The Ending of the Civil War* (1969); and Harold M. Hyman, ed., *New Frontiers of the American Reconstruction* (1966).

The conflict between the President and Congress is examined in David Donald, *The Politics of Reconstruction, 1863–1867* (1965); Michael Les Benedict, *A Compromise of Principle: Congressional Republicans and Reconstruction* (1974) and *The Impeachment and Trial of Andrew Johnson* (1973); and Hans L. Trefousse, *Impeachment of a President* (1975). On constitutional issues, Stanley I. Kutler, *Judicial Power and Reconstruction Politics* (1968), and Harold M. Hyman, *A More Perfect Union: The Impact of the Civil War and Reconstruction on the Constitution* (1973), are useful.

Reconstruction in the South is surveyed in E. Merton Coulter, *The South During Reconstruction* (1947). Michael Perman, *Reunion Without Compromise: The South and Reconstruction, 1865–1868* (1973), deals effectively with southern politics in the immediate postwar years. On the Freedmen's Bureau, see George R. Bentley, *A History of the Freedmen's Bureau* (1965); William McFeeley, *Yankee Godfather: General O. O. Howard and the Freedmen* (1968); and Donald G. Nieman, *To Set the Law in Motion: The Freedmen's Bureau and Legal Rights for Blacks, 1865–1868* (1979).

Harold O. Rabinowitz, *Race Relations in the Urban South, 1865–1890* (1977); Roger A. Fischer, *The Segregation Struggle in Louisiana, 1862–1877* (1974); and C. Vann Woodward, *The Strange Career of Jim Crow*, 3d rev. ed. (1974) cover race relations in the postwar South. Economic adjustments are analyzed in Lawrence N. Powell, *New Masters: Northern Planters During the Civil War and Reconstruction* (1980); Roger L. Ransom and Richard Sutch, *One Kind of Freedom: The Economic Consequences of Emancipation* (1977); Stephen J. DeCanio, *Agriculture in the Postbellum South* (1974); and Daniel A. Novak, *The Wheel of Servitude: Black Forced Labor After Emancipation* (1978).

American labor during Reconstruction is the subject

of David Montgomery, *Beyond Equality: Labor and the Radical Republicans, 1861–1872* (1967). Liberal republicanism is examined in Ari A. Hoogenboom, *Outlawing the Spoils: A History of Civil Service Reform* (1961), and John G. Sproat, *"The Best Men": Liberal Reformers in the Gilded Age* (1968).

Keith I. Polakoff, *The Politics of Inertia* (1977), challenges C. Vann Woodward's interpretation of the Compromise of 1877. Woodward's conclusions on the Redeemer period have been confirmed or disputed in Paul M. Gaston, *The New South Creed* (1970); William Cooper, *The Conservative Regime: South Carolina,* *1877–1890* (1968); Jonathan M. Weiner, *Social Origins of the New South: Alabama, 1860–1885* (1978); and J. Morgan Kousser, *The Shaping of Southern Politics: Suffrage Restriction and the Establishment of the One-Party South* (1974). Post-Reconstruction northern attitudes toward the South and blacks are treated in Vincent de Santis, *Republicans Face the Southern Question* (1959); Stanley P. Hirshson, *Farewell to the Bloody Shirt: Northern Republicans and the Southern Negro, 1877–1893* (1962); and Rayford W. Logan, *The Betrayal of the Negro: From Rutherford B. Hayes to Woodrow Wilson,* rev. ed. (1965).

THE WEST: EXPLOITING AN EMPIRE

chapter 17

In the last three decades of the nineteenth century a flood of settlers ventured into America's newest and last West. James H. Kyner, a railroad contractor in Oregon, saw in the 1880s "an almost unbroken stream of emigrants from horizon to horizon. . . . Teams and covered wagons, horsemen, little bunches of cows, more wagons, some drawn by cows, men walking, women and children riding—an endless stream of hardy, optimistic folk, going west to seek their fortunes and to settle an empire."

Prospectors poured into unsettled areas in search of "paydirt," railroads crisscrossed the continent, eastern and foreign capitalists invested in cattle and land bonanzas, and farmers took up the promise of free western lands. In 1867 Horace Greeley, editor of the New York *Tribune*, told New York City's unemployed: "If you strike off into the broad, free West, and make yourself a farm from Uncle Sam's generous domain, you will crowd nobody, starve nobody, and neither you nor your children need evermore beg for something to do."

With the end of the Civil War, white Americans again claimed a special destiny to expand across the continent. In the process they crushed the culture of the American Indians and ignored the special contributions of those of other nationalities, such as the Chinese miners and laborers and the Mexican herdsmen. As millions moved west, the states of Colorado, Washington, Montana, the Dakotas, Idaho, Wyoming, and Utah were carved out of the vast lands across the Mississippi. At the turn of the century only Arizona, New Mexico, and Oklahoma remained as territories.

The West became a great colonial empire, harnessed to eastern capital and tied increasingly to national and international markets. Western economies depended to an unusual degree on the federal government, which subsidized their railroads, distributed their land, and spent millions of dollars for the upkeep of soldiers and Indians. Regional variations persisted; and Westerners remained proud of their hardy, individualistic traditions. Yet they imitated the East's social, cultural, and political patterns.

By the 1890s the West of the buffalo and Indian was gone, and instead there were cities and towns, health resorts, Paris fashions, and the latest magazines. As Francis Parkman, a New Englander who had made the dangerous crossing to Oregon in 1846, reflected sadly in 1892: "The Wild West is tamed, and its savage charms have withered."

Beyond the Frontier

The frontier line had reached the edge of the timber country of Missouri by 1840. Beyond lay an enormous land of rolling prairies, parched deserts, and rugged, majestic mountains. Emerging from the timber country, travelers first encountered the Great Plains—treeless, nearly flat, an endless "sea of grassy hillocks." The Prairie Plains, the eastern part of the region, enjoyed rich soil and good rainfall; it included parts of present-day Wisconsin, Minnesota, the Dakotas, Nebraska, Kansas, Oklahoma, and Texas. To the west—covering Montana, Wyoming, Colorado, New Mexico, and Arizona—were the High Plains, rough, semiarid, rising gently to the foothills of the Rocky Mountains.

Running from Alaska to central New Mexico, the Rockies presented a formidable barrier. There were valuable beaver in the streams and gold near Pike's Peak. But most travelers hurried through the northern passes, emerging in the desolate basin of present-day southern Idaho and Utah. Indians lived there—the Utes, Paiutes, Bannocks, and Shoshoni—scrabbling out a bare subsistence by digging for roots, seeds, and berries. Scornful whites called them "Digger Indians," a stern judgment on people trying their best to survive. On the west the lofty Coast ranges, the Cascades and Sierra Nevada, held back rainfall; beyond were the temperate lands of the Pacific Coast.

Early explorers like Zebulon Pike thought the country beyond the Mississippi was uninhabitable, fit only, Pike said, for "wandering and uncivilized aborigines." Mapmakers agreed; between 1825 and 1860 American maps showed this land as "The Great American Desert." Settlement paused on the edge of the Plains, and most settlers headed directly for California and Oregon.

The Plains daunted even those hurrying across them. "You look on, on, on, out into space, out almost beyond time itself," John Noble, a painter reared in Kansas, remarked.

You see nothing but the rise and swell of land and grass, and then more grass—the monotonous, endless prairie! A stranger traveling on the prairie would get his hopes up, expecting to see something different on making the next rise. To him the disappointment and monotony were terrible. "He's got loneliness," we would say of such a man.

Few rivers cut through the Plains; those that did raged in the winter and trickled in the summer. Rainfall usually did not reach fifteen inches a year, not enough to support extensive agriculture. There was little lumber for homes and fences, and the tools of eastern settlement—the cast-iron plow, the boat, and the ax—were virtually useless on the tough and treeless Plains soil. "East of the Mississippi," historian Walter Prescott Webb noted, "civilization stood on three legs—land, water, and timber; west of the Mississippi not one but two of these legs were withdrawn,—water and timber,—and civilization was left on one leg—land."

Hot winds seared the Plains in summer, and northers, blizzards, and hailstorms froze them in

Physiographic Map of the United States

In the Great Plains and Rocky Mountains, the topography, climate, altitudes, crops, and, especially, the drought led to changes in a mode of settlement that had been essentially uniform from the Atlantic Coast through Kentucky and Ohio and on to Missouri. The rectangular land surveys and the quarter-section lots that were traditional in woods and prairie could not accommodate Great Plains conditions.

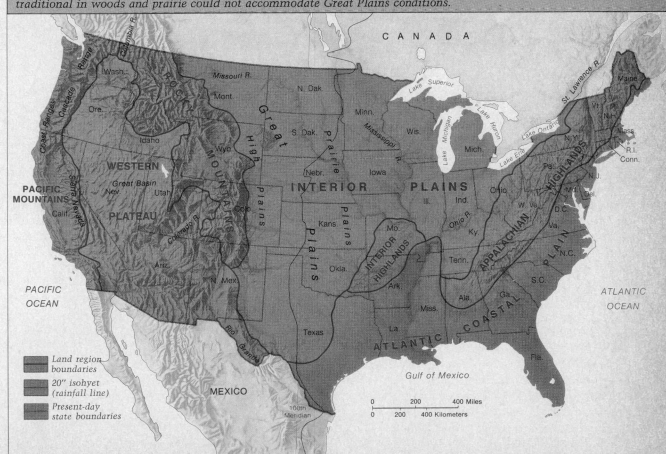

Land region boundaries
20" isohyet (rainfall line)
Present-day state boundaries

winter. Wildlife roamed in profusion. Antelope shared the open prairies with wolves, coyote, and millions of jack rabbits and prairie dogs. The American bison, better known as the buffalo, grazed in enormous herds from Mexico to Canada. In 1865 perhaps fifteen million buffalo lived on the Plains, so many they seemed like "leaves in a forest" to an early observer. A single herd sighted in 1871 had four million head.

Crushing the Indians

When Greeley urged New Yorkers to move West and "crowd nobody," he—like almost all his white countrymen—ignored the fact that large numbers of people already lived there. At the close of the Civil War Indians inhabited nearly half the United States. By 1880 they had been driven onto smaller and smaller reservations and were no longer an independent people. A decade later even their culture had crumbled under the impact of white domination.

In 1865 nearly a quarter of a million Indians lived in the western half of the country. Tribes like the Winnebago, Menominee, Cherokee, and Chippewa were resettled there, forced out of their eastern lands by advancing white settlement. Other tribes were native to the region. In the Southwest there were the Pueblo groups, including the Hopi, Zuni, and Rio Grande Pueblos. Peaceful farmers and herders, they had built up complex traditions around a settled way of life.

The Pueblo groups were cultivators of corn. They lived on the subdesert plateau of present-day western New Mexico and eastern Arizona. Harassed by powerful neighboring tribes, they built communal houses of adobe brick on high mesas or in cracks in the cliffs. More nomadic were the Camp Dwellers, the Navajo and Jicarilla Apache who roamed eastern New Mexico and western Texas. Blending elements of the Plains and Plateau environments, they lived in teepees or mud huts, grew some crops to supplement their hunting, and moved readily from place to place. The Navajo herded sheep and produced beautiful ornamental silver, baskets, and blankets. Fierce fighters, Apache horsemen were feared by whites and fellow Indians across the southwestern Plains.

Farther west were the short, stout, dark-skinned natives of present-day California. Divided into many small bands, they eked out a difficult existence living on roots, grubs, berries, and small game. In the Pacific Northwest, where fish and forest animals made life easier, the Klamath, Chinook, Yurok, and Shasta tribes developed a rich civilization. They built plank houses and canoes, worked extensively in wood, and evolved a complex social and political organization. Settled and determined, they resisted the invasion of the whites.

By the 1870s most of these tribes had been destroyed or beaten into submission. The powerful Ute, crushed in 1855, ceded most of their Utah lands to the United States and settled on a small reservation near Great Salt Lake. The Navajo and Apache fought back desperately, but between 1865 and 1873 they too were confined to reservations. The California Indians succumbed to the contagious diseases carried by whites during the Gold Rush of 1849. Miners burned their villages and by 1880 there were less than twenty thousand Indians in California.

Life of the Plains Indians

Nearly two thirds of the Indians lived on the Great Plains. The Plains tribes included the Sioux of present-day Minnesota and the Dakotas, the Blackfoot of Idaho and Montana, the Cheyenne, Crow, and Arapaho of the central Plains, the Pawnee of western Nebraska, and the Kiowa, Apache, and Comanche of present-day Texas and New Mexico.

Nomadic and warlike, the Plains Indians depended on the buffalo and horse. The modern horse, first brought by Spanish explorers in the 1500s, spread north from Mexico onto the Plains, and by the 1700s had changed the Plains Indians' way of life. They gave up farming almost entirely to hunt the buffalo, ranging widely over the rolling plains. They also became superb warriors and horsemen, among the best light cavalry in the world.

Equipped with stout wood bows, three feet or less in length, Plains tribes made fierce warriors. Hiding their bodies behind their racing ponies, they drove deadly arrows clear through a buffalo. Against white troops or settlers, the skillful Co-

(Below) The Buffalo Hunt *by Charles M. Russell. At first the Plains Indians hunted the buffalo on foot; then, with the arrival of the horse, on horseback. After the buffalo was killed, women skinned the hide, cut up the meat, and then cured the hide as shown in the painting (right) by George Catlin. Women also decorated the teepees and preserved the meat by drying it on racks in the sun.*

manche rode three hundred yards and shot twenty arrows in the time it took a soldier to load his firearm once. The introduction of the new Colt six-shooters during the 1850s gave white troops a rapid-fire weapon but did not entirely offset the Indians' advantage.

Migratory in culture, the Plains Indians formed tribes of several thousand people but lived in smaller "bands" of three to five hundred. The Comanche, who numbered perhaps seven thousand, had thirteen bands with such names as Burnt Meat, Making Bags While Moving, and Those Who Move Often. Each band was governed by a chief and a council of elder men, and Indians of the same tribe transferred freely from band to band. Bands acted independently, making it difficult for the United States government to deal with the fragmented tribes.

The bands followed and lived off the buffalo. Buffalo provided food, clothing, and shelter; and the Indians, unlike later white hunters, used every part of the animal. The meat was dried or "jerked" in the hot Plains air. The skins made teepees, blankets, and robes. Buffalo bones became knives; tendons were made into bow strings; horns and hooves were boiled into glue. Buffalo "chips"—dried manure—were burned as fuel.

Warfare between tribes usually took the form of brief raids and skirmishes. Plains Indians fought few prolonged wars and rarely coveted territory. Most conflicts involved only a few warriors intent on stealing horses or "counting coups"—touching an enemy's body with the hand or a special stick. Tribes developed a fierce and trained warrior class, recognized for achievements in battle. Speaking different languages, Indians of various tribes were nevertheless able to communicate with one another through a highly developed sign language.

The Plains tribes divided labor tasks according to sex. Men hunted, traded, supervised ceremonial activities, and cleared ground for planting. Women were responsible for child-rearing and artistic activity. They also performed the camp work, grew vegetables, prepared buffalo meat and hides, and gathered berries and roots. Among tribes like the Sioux, there was little difference in status. Men were respected for hunting and war, women for their artistic skills with quill and paint.

Before the Civil War Americans used the land west of the Mississippi as "one big reservation." The government named the area "Indian Country," moved eastern tribes there with firm treaty guarantees, and in 1834 passed the Indian Intercourse Act which prohibited any white person from entering Indian country without a license.

The situation changed in the 1850s. Wagon trains wound their way to California and Oregon, miners pushed into western gold fields, and there was talk of a transcontinental railroad. To clear the way for settlement, the federal government in 1851 abandoned "One Big Reservation" in favor of a new policy of "concentration." For the first time it assigned definite boundaries to each tribe. The Sioux, for example, were given the Dakota country north of the Platte River, the Crows a large area near the Powder River, and the Cheyenne and Arapaho the Colorado foothills between the North Platte and Arkansas rivers for "as long as waters run and the grass shall grow."

The "concentration" policy lasted only a few years. Accustomed to hunt widely for buffalo, many Indians refused to stay within their assigned areas. White settlers poured into Indian lands, then called on the government to protect them. Indians were pushed out of Kansas and Nebraska in the 1850s, even as white reformers fought to hold those territories open for free blacks. In 1859 gold miners moved into the Pike's Peak country, touching off warfare with the Cheyenne and Arapaho.

In 1864, tired of the fighting, the two tribes asked for peace. Certain that the war was over, Chief Black Kettle led his seven hundred followers to camp on Sand Creek in southeastern Colorado. Early on the morning of November 29, 1864, a group of Colorado militia led by Colonel John M. Chivington attacked the sleeping Indians. "Kill and scalp all, big and little," Chivington told his men. "Nits make lice." Black Kettle tried to stop the ambush, raising first an American flag and then a white flag. Neither worked. Indian men, women, and children were clubbed, stabbed, and scalped.

The Chivington massacre set off angry protests in Colorado and the East. Congress appointed an investigating committee, and the government concluded a treaty with the Cheyenne and Arapaho condemning "the gross and wanton outrages." Still, the two tribes were forced to surrender their Sand Creek reservation in exchange for lands elsewhere. The Kiowa and Comanche were also ousted from areas they had been granted "forever" only a few years before. As the Sioux chief Spotted Tail said: "Why does not the Great Father put his red children on wheels so that he can move them as he will?"

Before long the powerful Sioux were on the warpath in the great Sioux War of 1865–1867. Once again an invasion of gold miners touched off the war, which flared even more intensely when the federal government announced plans to connect the various mining towns by building the Bozeman Trail through the heart of the Sioux hunting grounds in Montana. Red Cloud, the Sioux chief, determined to stop the trail. In December 1866, pursued by an army column under Captain William J. Fetterman, he lured the incautious Fetterman deep into the wilderness, ambushed him, and wiped out all eighty-two soldiers in his command.

The Fetterman massacre, coming so soon after the Chivington massacre, sparked a public debate over the nation's Indian policy. Like the policy itself, the debate reflected differing white views of the Indians. In the East some reform, humanitarian, and church groups wanted a humane peace policy, directed toward educating and "civilizing" the tribes. Many people, East and West, questioned this approach, convinced that Indians were savages unfit for civilization. Westerners in general favored firm control over the Indians, including swift punishment of any who rebelled.

In 1867 the peace advocates won the debate. Halting construction on the Bozeman Trail, Congress created a Peace Commission of four civilians and three generals to end the Sioux War and eliminate permanently the causes of Indian wars. Setting out for the West, the Peace Commissioners agreed that only one policy offered a permanent solution: a policy of "small reservations" to isolate the Indians on distant lands, teach them to farm, and gradually "civilize" them.

The commissioners chose two areas to hold all the Plains Indians. The fifty-four thousand Indi-

Indians in the West: Major Battles and Reservations

"They made us many promises, more than I remember, but they never kept but one; they promised to take our land, and they took it." So said Red Cloud of the Ogala Sioux, summarizing Indian-white relations in the 1870s.

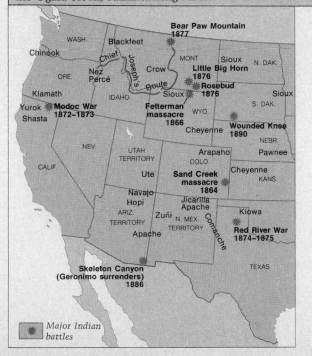

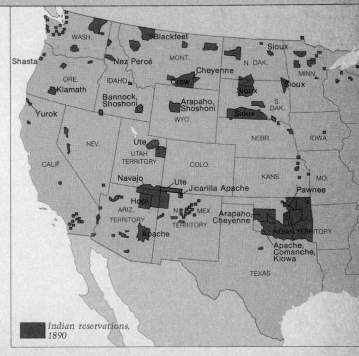

Crushing the Indians

ans on the northern Plains would be moved north of the Black Hills in Dakota Territory, far from prospective white settlement. On the southern Plains the eighty-six thousand Indians would be moved into present-day Oklahoma, a region also considered unattractive to whites. In both areas tribes would be assigned specific reservations where government agents could supervise them.

The Kiowa, Comanche, Cheyenne, and Arapaho agreed to the plan in 1867, the Sioux in 1868. Extending the policy beyond the Plains, the Ute, Shoshoni, Bannock, Navajo, and Apache also accepted small reservations. "We have now selected and provided reservations for all, off the great road," an army commander wrote. "All who cling to their old hunting-grounds are hostile and will remain so till killed off."

Final Battles on the Plains

Few Indians settled peacefully into life on the new reservations. Young warriors and minor chiefs denounced the treaties and drifted back to the open countryside. In late 1868 warfare broke out again, and it took over a decade of violence to beat the Indians into submission. The Kiowa and Comanche rampaged through the Texas Panhandle, looting and killing, until the army crushed them in the Red River War of 1874–1875 and ended warfare in the Southwest.

On the northern Plains fighting resulted from the Black Hills Gold Rush of 1875. As prospectors tramped across Indian hunting grounds, the Sioux gathered to stop them. They were led by Rain-in-the-Face, the great war chief Crazy Horse, and the famous medicine man Sitting Bull. The army sent several columns of troops after the Indians, but one, under flamboyant Lieutenant Colonel George A. Custer, pushed recklessly ahead, eager to claim the victory. On the morning of June 25, 1876, thinking he had a small band of Indians surrounded on the banks of the Little Bighorn River in Montana, Custer divided his column and took 265 men toward the Indian village. Instead of finding a small band, he discovered that he had stumbled on the main Sioux camp with 2500 warriors.

By mid-afternoon it was over; Custer and his men were dead. Custer was largely responsible for the loss, but "Custer's Last Stand," set in blazing

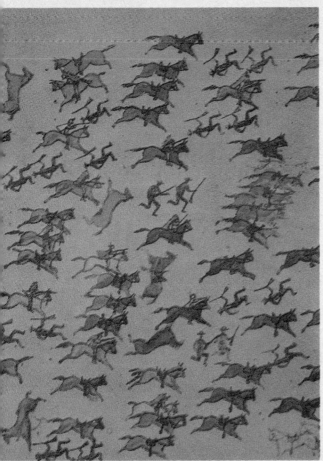

Sitting Bull (far left) led the Sioux against the U.S. cavalry at the Little Bighorn. The pictograph (below left), by Ogala Sioux Amos Bad Heart Bull, is an Indian version of that battle. Left, a photograph of Crow Indians taken prisoner after an unsuccessful uprising in Montana in 1877. Below is the mass grave of the two hundred Indian men, women, and children massacred at Wounded Knee. Twenty-nine soldiers also died in the battle. There was another victim at Wounded Knee. Black Elk, an Ogala Sioux, later recalled, "A people's dream died there."

headlines across the country, signaled a nation-wide demand for revenge. Within a few months the Sioux were surrounded and beaten, 3000 of them surrendering in October 1876. Sitting Bull and a few followers who had fled to Canada gave up in 1881.

The Sioux War ended the major Indian warfare in the West, but occasional outbreaks occurred for several years thereafter. In 1877 the Nez Percé tribe of Oregon, a people who had warmly welcomed Lewis and Clark in 1805, rebelled against government policy. Hoping to reach Canada, Chief Joseph led the tribe on a courageous flight covering 75 days and 1321 miles. They defeated the pursuing army at every turn but then ran out of food, horses, and ammunition. Surrendering, they were sent to barren lands in the Indian Country of Oklahoma, and there, most of them died from disease.

In 1890 the Teton Sioux of South Dakota, bitter and starving, became restless. Many of them turned to the "Ghost Dances," a set of dances and rites that grew from a vision of a Paiute messiah named Wovoka. Performance of the dances, Wovoka said, would bring back Indian lands and cause the whites to disappear. All Indians would reunite, the earth would be covered with dust, and a new earth would come upon the old. The vanished buffalo would return in great herds.

The army intervened to stop the dancing, touching off violence that killed Sitting Bull and a number of other warriors. Frightened Indians fled southwest to join other Ghost Dancers under the aging chief Big Foot. Moving quickly, troops of the Seventh Cavalry, Custer's old regiment, caught up with Big Foot's band who agreed to come to the army camp on Wounded Knee Creek in South Dakota. An Indian, it is thought, fired the first shot, returned by the army's new machine guns. Firing a shell a second, they shredded tepees and people. About two hundred men, women, and children were massacred in the snow.

The End of Tribal Life

The final step in Indian policy came in the 1870s and '80s. Some reformers had long argued against segregating the Indians on reservations, urging instead that the nation assimilate them individu-

Tom Torlino, a Navajo Indian photographed before and after his "assimilation." Torlino attended the Carlisle Indian School in Pennsylvania.

ally into white culture. These "assimilationists" wanted to use education, land policy, and federal law to eradicate tribal society.

Congress began to adopt the policy in 1871 when it ended the practice of treaty-making with Indian tribes. Since tribes were no longer separate nations, they lost many of their political and judicial functions, and the power of the chiefs was weakened. In 1882 Congress created a Court of Indian Offenses to try Indians who broke government rules, and soon thereafter it made Indians answerable in regular courts for certain crimes.

While Congress worked to break down the tribes, educators trained young Indians to adjust to white culture. In 1879 fifty Pawnee, Kiowa, and Cheyenne youths were brought east to the new Carlisle Indian School in Carlisle, Pennsylvania. Other Indian schools soon opened, including the Haskell Institute in Kansas and numerous day schools on the western reservations. The schools taught students to fix machines and farm; they forced them to trim their long hair, made them speak English, banned the wearing of tribal paint or clothes, and forbade tribal ceremonies and dances. "Kill the Indian and save the man," said Richard H. Pratt, the army officer who founded the Carlisle School.

Land ownership was the final and most important link in the new policy. Indians who owned land, it was thought, would become responsible, self-reliant citizens. Deciding to give each Indian a farm, Congress in 1887 passed the Dawes Severalty Act, the most important legal development in Indian-white relations in over three centuries.

Aiming to end tribal life, the Dawes Act divided tribal lands into small plots for distribution among members of the tribe. Each family head received 160 acres, single adults 80 acres, and children 40 acres. Once the land was distributed, any surplus was sold to white settlers, with the profits going to Indian schools. To keep the Indians' land from falling into the hands of speculators, the federal government held it in trust for twenty-five years. Finally, American citizenship was granted to Indians who accepted their land, lived apart from the tribe, and "adopted the habits of civilized life."

Through the Dawes Act, 47 million acres of land were distributed to Indians and their families. There were another 90 million acres in the reservations, and these lands, often the most fertile, were sold to white settlers. Speculators evaded the twenty-five-year rule, leasing rather than purchasing the land from the Indians. Many

Indians knew little about farming. Their tools were rudimentary, and in the culture of the Plains Indians, farming was women's work. In 1934 the government returned to the idea of tribal land ownership, but by then 138 million acres of Indian land had shrunk to 48 million acres, half of which was barren.

The final blow to tribal life came not in the Dawes Act but in the virtual extermination of the buffalo, the Plains Indians' chief resource and the basis for their unique way of life. The killing began in the 1860s as the transcontinental railroads pushed west, but in 1871 a Pennsylvania tannery discovered that buffalo hides made valuable leather. Professional hunters like William F. "Buffalo Bill" Cody swarmed across the Plains, killing millions of the helpless beasts.

Buffalo hunting became a favorite pastime. Churches and schools raised money by sponsoring hunts, such as the one, three hundred strong, that left Lawrence, Kansas, in October 1868. Chartering a train, the group took along the Lawrence Cornet Band for entertainment. For two days they saw no buffalo until suddenly the horizon filled with them. As the train chugged along, a hundred rifles fired and fired again; finally a buffalo fell. The train stopped, and the

A pile of forty thousand buffalo hides, Dodge City, Kansas, 1874. Before the arrival of white settlers, immense herds of millions of buffalo roamed the western Plains. By 1883 only a few thousand of the animals were left. When the buffalo disappeared, the way of life of the Plains Indians also came to an end.

Blacks in Blue:
The Buffalo Soldiers in the West

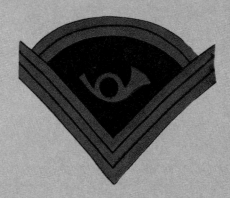

On Saturday afternoons youngsters used to sit in darkened movie theaters and cheer the victories of the United States cavalry over the Indians. Typically, the Indians were about to capture a wagon train, when army bugles suddenly sounded. Then the blue-coated cavalry charged over the hill. Few in the theaters cheered for the Indians; fewer still noticed the absence of black faces among the on-charging cavalry. But in fact, more than 2000 black cavalrymen served on the western frontier between 1867 and 1890. Known as the "buffalo soldiers," they made up a fifth of the U.S. cavalry.

Black troops were first used on a large scale during the Civil War (see chapter 15). Organized in segregated units, with white officers, they fought with distinction. Nearly 180,000 blacks served in the Union army; 34,000 of them died. When the war ended in 1865, Congress for the first time authorized black troops to serve in the regular peacetime army. In addition to infantry, it created two cavalry regiments—the Ninth and Tenth, which became known as the famous buffalo soldiers.

Like other black regiments, the Ninth and Tenth Cavalry had white officers who took special examinations before they could serve. The chaplains were assigned not only to preach but to teach reading, writing, and arithmetic. The food was poor; racism was widespread. The army stocked the first black units with worn-out horses, a serious matter to men whose lives depended on the speed and stamina of their mounts. "Since our first mount in 1867 this regiment has received nothing but broken down horses and repaired equipment," an officer said in 1870.

Many white officers refused to serve with black troops. George A. Custer, the handsome "boy general," turned down a position in the Ninth and joined the new Seventh Cavalry, headed for disaster at Little Bighorn. The *Army and Navy Journal* carried ads that told a similar story:

**A FIRST LIEUTENANT
OF INFANTRY**
(white)
stationed at a
very desirable post
in the Department of the South
desires a transfer with
an officer of the same grade
on equal terms
if in a white regiment
but if in a colored regiment
a reasonable bonus
would be expected.

There was no shortage of black troops for the officers to lead. Blacks enlisted because the army offered some advancement in a closed society. It also paid $13 a month, plus room and board.

In 1867 the Ninth and Tenth Cavalry were posted to the West, where they remained for two decades. Under Colonel Benjamin H. Grierson, a Civil War hero, the Tenth went to Fort Riley, Kansas; the regiment arrived in the midst of a great Indian war. Kiowas, Comanches, Cheyennes, Arapahoes, and Sioux were on the warpath. Troopers of the Tenth defended farms, stages, trains, and work crews building railroad tracks to the west. Cornered by a band of Cheyennes, they beat back the attack and won a new name. Earlier known as the "brunettes" or "Africans," the Cheyenne now called them the buffalo soldiers, a name that soon applied to all black soldiers in the West (some of the "buffalo soldiers" of the Tenth Cavalry are shown in the photo right).

From 1868 to 1874 the Tenth served on the Kansas frontier. The dull winter days were filled with drills and scouting parties outside the post. In spring and summer the good weather brought forth new forays. Indian bands raided farms and ranches and stampeded cattle herds on the way north from Texas. They struck and then melted back into the reservations.

The Ninth Cavalry also had a difficult job. Commanded by Colonel Edward Hatch, who had served with Grierson in the Civil War, it was stationed in West Texas and along the Rio Grande. The summers were so hot that men collapsed with sunstroke, the winters so cold that water froze in the canteens. Indians from outside the area frequently raided it. From the north Kiowa and Comanche warriors rode down the Great Comanche War Trail; Kickapoos crossed the Rio Grande from Mexico. Gangs of Mexican bandits and restless Civil War veterans roamed and plundered at will.

In 1874–1875 the Ninth fought in the great Red River War, in which the Kiowas and Comanches, fed up with conditions on the reservations, revolted against Grant's peace policy. Marching, fighting, then marching again, the soldiers harried and wore out the Indians, who finally surrendered in the spring of 1875. Herded into a new

and desolate reservation, the Mescalero Apaches of New Mexico took to the warpath in 1877 and again in 1879. Each time it took a year of grueling warfare to effect their surrender. In 1886 black cavalrymen surrounded and captured the famous Apache chief Geronimo. In that and other campaigns, several buffalo soldiers won the Congressional Medal of Honor.

Black troops hunted Big Foot and his band before the slaughter at Wounded Knee in 1890 (see p. 490), and they served in many of the West's most famous Indian battles. While a third of all army recruits deserted between 1865 and 1890, the Ninth and Tenth Cavalry had few desertions. In 1880 the Tenth had the fewest desertions of any regiment in the country.

It was ironic that in the West black men fought red men to benefit white men. Once the Indian wars ended, the buffalo soldiers worked to keep illegal settlers out of Indian or government land; much of this land was later opened to settlement. Both regiments saw action in the Spanish-American War, the Ninth at San Juan Hill, the Tenth in the fighting around Santiago. The old buffalo soldiers were forgotten in retirement, although some of them had the satisfaction of settling on the western lands they had done so much to pacify.

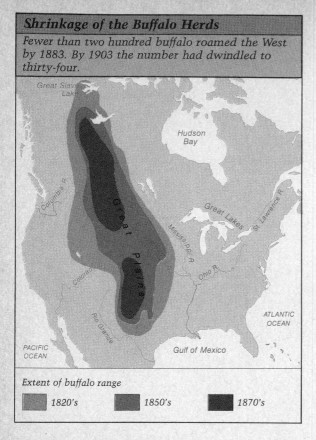

Shrinkage of the Buffalo Herds

Fewer than two hundred buffalo roamed the West by 1883. By 1903 the number had dwindled to thirty-four.

Extent of buffalo range

1820's   1850's   1870's

guests swarmed off. A hunter stood atop the kill. An observer described the scene: "Then came the ladies; a ring was formed; the cornet band gathered around, and, as if to tantalize the spirits of all departed buffalo, as well as Indians, played Yankee Doodle."

Between 1872 and 1874 professional hunters slaughtered three million buffalo a year. In a frontier form of a factory system, riflemen, skinners, and transport wagons pushed through the vast herds, which shrank steadily behind them. A good hunter killed a hundred buffalo a day; skinners took off the hides, removed the tongue, hump, and tallow, and left the rest. "I have seen their bodies so thick after being skinned," a hunter said, "that they would look like logs where a hurricane had passed through a forest."

By 1883 the buffalo were almost gone. When the government set out to produce the famous "buffalo nickel," the designer had to go to the Bronx Zoo in New York City to find a buffalo.

By 1900 there were only two hundred thousand Indians in the country, most of them on reservations. Many lived in poverty. Alcoholism and unemployment were growing problems, and Indians, no longer able to live off the buffalo, became wards of the state. They lost their special distinctiveness as a culture. Once possessors of the entire continent, they had been crowded into smaller and smaller areas, overwhelmed by the demand to become settled, literate, and English-speaking. "Except for the internment of the West Coast Japanese during World War II," said historian Roger L. Nichols, "Indian removal is the only example of large-scale government-enforced migration in American history. For the Japanese, the move was temporary; for the Indians it was not."

Even as the Indians lost their identity, they entered the romantic folklore of the West. Dime novels, snapped up by readers young and old, told tales of Indian fighting on the Plains. Buffalo Bill Cody turned it all into a profitable business. Beginning in 1883, his Wild West Show ran for over three decades, playing to millions of viewers in the United States, Canada, and Europe. It featured Plains Indians chasing buffalo, performing a war dance, and attacking a settler's cabin. In 1885 Sitting Bull himself, victor over Custer at the battle of Little Big Horn, performed in the show.

Settlement of the West

Between 1870 and 1900 white—and some black—Americans settled the enormous total of 430 million acres west of the Mississippi; they occupied more land than in all the years before 1870.

People moved West for many reasons. Some sought adventure; others wanted to escape the drab routine of factory or city life. Many moved to California for their health. The Mormons settled Utah to escape religious persecution. Others followed the mining camps, the advancing railroads, and the farming and cattle frontier. "Most of the time we were solitary adventurers in a great land as fresh and new as a spring morning, and we were free and full of the zest of darers," said Charles Goodnight, a Texas cattleman and founder of the famous Goodnight Trail.

Whatever the specific reason, most people moved West to better their lot. On the whole, their timing was good, for as a nation's population grew, so did demand for the livestock and the agricultural, mineral, and lumber products of the expanding West. Contrary to older historical views, the West did not act as a major "safety valve," an outlet for social and economic tensions. The poor and unemployed did not have the means to move there and establish farms. "Moreover," as Douglass C. North, an economic historian, said, "most people moved West in good times . . . in periods of rising prices, of expanding demand, when the prospects for making money from this new land looked brightest; and this aspect characterized the whole pattern of settlement."

Men and Women on the Overland Trail

The first movement west aimed not for the nearby Plains but for California and Oregon on the continent's far shore. It started in the 1849 Gold Rush to California, and in the next three decades perhaps as many as half a million individuals made the long journey. Some walked; others rode horses alone or in small groups. About half joined great caravans, numbering 150 wagons or more, that inched across the 2000 miles between the Missouri River and the Pacific Coast.

More often than not, men made the decision to make the crossing. Wives either went with their husbands or faced being left behind. Four out of five men on the overland trail had picked up stakes and moved before, some of them several times. Most had little cash, but they needed only strong legs, a few staples, and a willingness to tighten the belt when game was scarce. The majority of people traveled in family groups, including in-laws, grandchildren, aunts, and uncles. As one historian said: "The quest for something new would take place in the context of the very familiar."

Individuals and wagon trains set out from various points along the Missouri River. Leaving in the spring and traveling through the summer, they hoped to reach their destination before the first snowfall. During April, travelers gradually assembled in spring camp just across the Missouri River, waiting for the new grass to ripen into forage. They packed and repacked the wagons and elected the train's leaders, who would set the line of march, look for water and campsites, and impose discipline. Some trains adopted detailed rules, fearing a lapse into savagery in the wild lands across the Missouri. "Every man to carry with him a Bible and other religious books, as we hope not to degenerate into a state of barbarism," one agreement said.

Setting out in early May, travelers divided the enormous route into manageable portions. The first leg of the journey followed the Platte River west to Fort Kearney in central Nebraska Territory, a distance of about three hundred miles. The land was even, with good supplies of wood, grass, and water. From a distance the white-topped wagons seemed driven by a common force, but in fact, internal discipline broke down almost immediately. Arguments erupted over the pace of the march, the choice of campsites, the number of guards to post, whether to rest or push on. Elected leaders quit; new ones were chosen. Every train was filled with individualists, and as the son of one train captain said, "if you think it's any snap to run a wagon train of 66 wagons with every man in the train having a different idea of what is the best thing to do, all I can say is that some day you ought to try it."

Men, women, and children had different tasks on the trail. Men concerned themselves almost entirely with hunting, guard duty, and transportation. They rose at four A.M. to hitch the wagons, and after breakfast began the day's march. At noon they stopped and set the teams to graze, while the women prepared the midday meal. The march continued until sunset. Then, while the men relaxed, the women fixed dinner and the next day's lunch, and the children kindled the fire, brought water to camp, and searched for wood or other fuel. Walking fifteen miles a day, in searing heat and mountain cold, travelers were exhausted by late afternoon. "We can all, as soon as we stop, lie down on the grass or anywhere and be asleep in less than no time almost," Rebecca Ketcham, an Oregon-bound emigrant, reported.

For women the trail was lonely, and they worked to exhaustion. Before long they adjusted their clothing to the harsh conditions, adopting the new bloomer pants, shortening their skirts, or wearing regular "wash dresses"—so called because they had shorter hemlines that did not drag on the wet ground on washday. Men hunted buffalo and antelope for fresh meat. Both men and women carried firearms in case of Indian attacks, but most emigrants saw few Indians en route.

Not every one was a crack shot. "The young men of our party . . . went out this morning for the purpose of hunting buffalo," Harriet Ward noted sardonically in her diary. "They soon discovered a herd of a hundred and fifty, rushed into their midst, fired their guns without effect and finally succeeded in capturing a cow."

The first stage of the journey was deceptively easy, and travelers usually reached Fort Kearney by late May. The second leg led another 300 miles up the Platte River to Fort Laramie on the eastern edge of Wyoming Territory. The heat of June had burned the grass, and there was no wood. Anxious to beat the early snowfalls, travelers rested a day or two at the fort, then hurried on to South Pass, 280 miles to the west, the best route through the forbidding Rockies. The land was barren. It was now mid-July, but the mountain nights were so cold that ice formed on top of the water buckets.

Beyond South Pass, some emigrants turned south to the Mormon settlements on Great Salt Lake, but most headed 340 miles north to Fort Hall on the Snake River in Idaho. It took another three months to cover the remaining 800 miles. California-bound travelers followed the Humboldt River through the summer heat of Nevada. Well into September they began the final arduous push: first, a 55-mile stretch of desert; then 70 difficult miles up the eastern slopes of the Sierra Nevada, hoisting wagons laboriously over massive outcrops of rock; and finally the last 100 miles down the western slopes to the welcome October greenness of the Sacramento Valley.

Under the best of conditions the trip took six months, sixteen hours a day, dawn to dusk, of hard, grueling labor. Walking halfway across the continent was no easy task, and it provided a never-to-be-forgotten experience for those who did it. The wagon trains, carrying the dreams of thousands of individuals, reproduced society in small focus: individualistic, hopeful, mobile, divided by age and sex roles, apprehensive, yet willing to strike out for the distant and new.

Land for the Taking

As railroads pushed west in the 1870s and '80s, locomotive trains replaced wagon trains, but the shift was gradual, and until the end of the century emigrants often combined both modes of travel. Into the 1890s travelers could be seen making their way across the West by any available means. Early railroad transportation was expensive, and the average farm family could not afford to buy tickets and ship supplies. Many Europeans traveled by rail to designated outfitting places, and then proceeded West with wagons and oxen. Traffic flowed in all directions. Eager settlers heading West passed defeated ones returning East.

Why did they come? "The motive that induced us to part with the pleasant associations and the dear friends of our childhood days," explained Phoebe Judson, an early emigrant, "was to obtain from the government of the United States a grant of land that 'Uncle Sam' had promised to give to the head of each family who settled in this new country." A popular camp song reflected the same motive:

Come along, come along—don't be alarmed,
Uncle Sam is rich enough to give us all a farm.

Uncle Sam owned about 1 billion acres of land in the 1860s, much of it mountain and desert land unsuited for agriculture. By 1900 the various land laws had distributed half of it. Between 1862 and 1890 the government gave away 48 million acres under the Homestead Act of 1862, sold about 100 million acres to private citizens and corporations, granted 128 million acres to railroad companies to tempt them to build across the unsettled West, and sold huge tracts to the states.

The Homestead Act of 1862, a law of great significance, gave 160 acres of land to anyone who would pay a $10 registration and pledge to live on it and cultivate it for five years. The offer set off a mass migration of land-hungry Europeans, dazzled by a country that gave its land away. Americans also seized on the act's provisions, and between 1862 and 1900 nearly 400,000 families claimed free homesteads under it.

Yet the Homestead Act did not work as Congress had hoped. Few farmers and laborers had the cash to move to the frontier, buy farm equipment, and wait out the year or two before the farm became self-supporting. Tailored to the timber and water conditions of the East, the act did not work as well in the semiarid West. In the fertile valleys of the Mississippi, 160 acres provided a generous farm. A farmer on the Great Plains needed either a larger farm for dry farming or a smaller one for irrigation.

The Timber Culture Act of 1873 attempted to adjust the Homestead Act to western conditions. It allowed homesteaders to claim an additional 160 acres if they planted trees on a quarter of it within four years. A successful act, it distributed 10 million acres of land, encouraged needed forestation, and enabled homesteaders to expand their farms to a workable size. Cattle ranchers lobbied for another law, the Desert Land Act of 1877, which allowed individuals to obtain 640 acres in the arid states for $1.25 an acre, provided they irrigated part of it within three years. This act invited fraud. Irrigation sometimes meant a bucket of water dumped on the ground, and ranchers used their hired hands to claim large tracts. More than 2.6 million acres was distributed, much of it fraudulently.

The Timber and Stone Act of 1878, applied only to lands "unfit for cultivation" and valuable chiefly for timber or stone. It permitted anyone in California, Nevada, Oregon, and Washington to buy up to 160 acres of forestland for $2.50 an acre. Like ranchers, lumber companies used employees to file false claims. Company agents rounded up seamen on the waterfront, marched them to the land office to file their claims, took them to a notary public to sign over the claims to the company, and then marched them back to the waterfront for payment in beer or cash. By 1900, 3.6 million acres of rich forest land had been claimed under the measure.

Speculators made ingenious use of the land laws. Sending agents in advance of settlement, they moved along choice river bottoms or irrigable areas, accumulating large holdings to be held for high prices. In the arid West, where control of water meant control of the surrounding land, shrewd ranchers plotted their holdings accordingly. In Colorado one cattleman, John F. Iliff, owned only 105 small parcels of land, but by placing them around the few waterholes, he effectively dominated an empire stretching over 6000 square miles.

As beneficiaries of the government's policy of land grants for railway construction, the railroad companies were the West's largest landowners. Eager to have immigrants settle on the land they owned near the railroad right-of-way, and eager to boost their freight and passenger business, the companies sent agents to the East and Europe. Attractive brochures touted life in the West. The Union Pacific called the rocky Platte Valley in Nebraska "a flowery meadow of great fertility, clothed in nutritious grasses." The Burlington Railroad reminded women of the West's many unmarried men: "when a daughter of the East is once beyond the Missouri she rarely recrosses it except on a bridal tour."

Railroad lines set up Land Departments and Bureaus of Immigration. The Land Department priced the land, arranged credit terms, and even gave free farming courses to immigrants. The

■ *Railroad companies distributed elaborately illustrated brochures and broadsides to lure people to the West, where they would settle on land owned by the railroad.*

Bureau of Immigration employed agents in Europe, met immigrants at eastern seaports, and ran special cars for land-seekers heading West. In 1874 the Santa Fe Railroad convinced 1900 Russian Mennonites to bring $2 million in gold drafts and settle on the fertile plains of Kansas.

Half a billion acres of western land were given or sold to speculators and corporations. At the same time only 600,000 homestead patents were issued, covering 80 million acres. Thus, only one acre in every nine initially went to individual pioneers, the intended beneficiaries of the nation's largesse.

Territorial Government

As new areas of the West opened, they were organized as territories under the control of Congress and the president. The territorial system started with the famous Northwest Ordinance of 1787 (see chapter 6), which established the rules by which territories became states. Washington ran the territories like "a passive group of colonial mandates." The president appointed the governor and judges in each territory; Congress detailed their duties, set their budgets, and oversaw their activities. Territorial officials had almost absolute power over the territories.

Until statehood, then, the territories depended on the federal government for their existence. They became an important part of the patronage system, a place to give jobs to deserving politicians. Lew Wallace of Indiana, a Civil War hero, was named governor of New Mexico Territory in the 1870s. Unable to sleep in the stuffy governor's residence, Wallace wrote the bestselling novel *Ben Hur.*

The national political parties, especially the Republicans, funneled government funds into the territorial economies, and in areas like Wyoming and the Dakotas, where resources were scarce, economic growth depended on them. Many early settlers held patronage jobs or hoped for them, traded with government-supported Indians, sold supplies to army troops, and speculated in government lands.

As his advertisement suggested, E. P. Caldwell, a small-town attorney in Huron, Dakota Territory, made a living the way many Westerners did, by serving Washington and the East:

MONEY LOANED
for Eastern Capitalists
Taxes Paid for Nonresidents

INVESTMENTS
CAREFULLY MADE
for Eastern Capitalists

GENERAL LAW,
Land and Collection Business
Transacted

Buy and Sell Real Estate
U.S. Land Business
Promptly Attended to

In a large portion of the trans-Mississippi West, a generation grew up under territorial rule. Inevitably, they developed distinct ideas about politics, government, and the economy.

The Spanish-Speaking Southwest

In the nineteenth century almost all Spanish-speaking people in the United States lived in California, Arizona, New Mexico, Texas, and Colorado. Their numbers were small—California had only 8086 Mexican residents in 1900—but the influence of their culture and institutions was large. In some respects the Southwestern frontier was more Spanish-American than Anglo-American.

Pushing northward from Mexico, the Spanish brought to the Southwest irrigation, stock raising, weaving, and the rule of law. After winning independence in the 1820s, the Mexicans brought additional laws, ranching methods, chaps, and the burro. Both Spanish and Mexicans created the legal framework for distributing land and water, a precious resource in the Southwest. They gave large grants of land to communities for grazing, to individuals as rewards for service, and to the various Indian pueblos.

In Southern California the Californios, descendants of the original colonizers, began after the 1860s to lose their once vast landholdings to drought and mortgages. Some turned to crime and became feared bandidos; others, like José María Amador, lived in poverty and remembered better days:

> When I was but a little boy I drained the chocolate pot,
> But now I am a poor man and am condemned to slop.

In 1875 Romualdo Pacheco, an aristocratic native son, served as governor of California and then went on to Congress. But as the Californios died out, Mexican-Americans continued the Spanish-Mexican influence. In 1880 one quarter of the residents of Los Angeles County were Spanish speaking.

In New Mexico Spanish-speaking citizens remained the majority ethnic group until 1928, and the Spanish-Mexican culture dominated the territory. Contests over land grants became New Mexico's largest industry; lawyers who dealt in them amassed huge holdings. After 1888 *Las Gorras Blancas*, The White Caps, a secret organization of Spanish-Americans, attacked the movement of Anglo ranchers into the Las Vegas community land grant. Armed and hooded like a Ku Klux Klan, they rode at night—but to defend civil rights instead of stifle them.

Throughout the Southwest the Spanish-Mexican heritage gave a distinctive shape to society. It fostered a modified economic caste system, a strong Roman Catholic influence, and the primary use of the Spanish language. Spanish names and customs spread, even among Anglos. David Starr Jordan, arriving from Indiana to become the first president of Stanford University in California, bestowed Spanish names on streets, houses, and a Stanford dormitory. Spanish was the region's first or second language. Confronted by Sheriff Pat Garrett in a darkened room, New Mexico's famous outlaw, Billy the Kid, died saying *"Quien es? Quien es?"* ("Who is it? Who is it?")

The Bonanza West

Between 1850 and 1900 wave after wave of newcomers swept over the trans-Mississippi West. There were riches for the taking, hidden in gold-washed streams, spread lushly over grass-covered prairies, or available in the gullible minds of greedy newcomers. The nineteenth-century West took shape in the search for mining, cattle, and land bonanzas that drew eager settlers from the East and around the world.

As with all bonanzas, the consequences in the West were uneven growth, boom-and-bust economic cycles, and wasted resources. As a society it seemed constantly in the making. People moved here and there, following river bottoms, gold strikes, railroad tracks, and other opportunities. "Instant cities" arose. San Francisco, Salt Lake City, and Denver were the most spectacular examples, but every cow town and mining camp witnessed a similar phenomenon. San Francisco needed a little more than two decades to attract a third of a million people; Boston needed more than two centuries to do the same.

Most Westerners came to get rich quickly, and they adopted institutions that reflected that goal. As a contemporary poem said:

> Love to see the stir an' bustle
> In the busy town,
> Everybody on the hustle

*Saltin' profits down.
Everybody got a wad a'
Ready cash laid by;
Ain't no flies on Colorado—
Not a cussed fly.*

In their lives the West was an idea as well as a region, and the idea molded them as much as they molded it.

The Mining Bonanza

Mining was the first important magnet to attract people to the West. Many came to "strike it rich" in gold and silver, but at least half the newcomers had no intention of working in the mines. Instead, they provided food, clothing, and services to the thousands of miners. Leland Stanford and Collis P. Huntington, who later built the Central Pacific Railroad, set up a general store in Sacramento where they sold shovels and supplies. Stephen J. Field, later a prominent justice of the United States Supreme Court, followed the Gold Rush to California to practice law.

The California Gold Rush of 1849 began the mining boom and set the pattern for subsequent experience. Individual prospectors made the first strikes, discovering pockets of gold along streams flowing westward from the Sierra Nevada. To get the gold, they used a simple process called placer mining, which required little skill, technology, or capital. A placer miner needed only a shovel, washing pan, and a good claim. As the placers gave out, a great deal of gold remained, but it was locked in quartz or buried deep in the earth. Mining became an expensive business, far beyond the reach of the average miner.

Large corporations moved in to dig the deep shafts and finance costly equipment. Quartz mining required heavy rock crushers, mercury vats to dissolve the gold, and large retorts to recapture it. Eastern and European financiers assumed control, labor became unionized, and mining towns took on some of the characteristics of the industrial city. Individual prospectors meanwhile dashed on to the next find. Unlike other frontiers, the mining frontier moved from west to east, as the original California miners—the "yonder-siders," they were called—hurried eastward in search of the big strike.

In 1859 fresh strikes were made near Pike's Peak in Colorado and in the Carson River Valley of Nevada. News of both discoveries set off wild migrations—100,000 miners were in Pike's Peak country by June 1859. The gold there quickly played out, but the Nevada find uncovered a

With the "long tom," miners washed placer gold from pay dirt. These prospectors, photographed in 1852, are working at a stream bed near Auburn, California.

thick, bluish black ore that was almost pure silver and gold. A quick-witted drifter named Henry T. P. Comstock talked his way into partnership in the claim, and word of the Comstock Lode—with ore worth $3876 a ton—flashed over the mountains.

Thousands of miners climbed the Sierra Nevada that summer. On the rough slopes of Davidson Mountain they created Virginia City, the prototype of the tumultuous western mining town. Mark Twain was there and described the scene in *Roughing It* (1872): "The sidewalks swarmed with people. . . . Joy sat on every countenance, and there was a glad, almost fierce, intensity in every eye, that told of the money-getting schemes that were seething in every brain and the high hope that held sway in every heart."

The biggest strike was yet to come. In 1873 John W. Mackay and three partners formed a company to dig deep into the mountain, and at 1167 feet they hit the Big Bonanza, a seam of gold and silver more than 54 feet wide. It was the richest discovery in the history of mining. Between 1859 and 1879 the Comstock Lode produced gold and silver worth $306 million. Most of it went to financiers and corporations. Mackay himself became the richest person in the world, earning (according to a European newspaper) $25

a minute, $5 a minute more than Czar Alexander II of Russia.

In the 1860s and '70s important strikes were made in Washington, Idaho, Nevada, Colorado, Montana, Arizona, and Dakota. Extremely mobile, miners flocked from strike to strike, and new camps and mining towns sprang up overnight. "The miners of Idaho were like quicksilver," said Hubert Howe Bancroft, an early historian. "A mass of them dropped in any locality, broke up into individual globules, and ran off after any atom of gold in their vicinity. They stayed nowhere longer than the gold attracted them."

The final fling came in the Black Hills rush of 1874–1876. The army had tried to keep miners out of the area, the heart of the Sioux hunting grounds, and even sent a scientific party under Colonel George A. Custer to disprove the rumors of gold. Instead, Custer found gold all over the hills, and the rush was on. Miners, gamblers, desperadoes, and prostitutes flocked to Deadwood, the most lawless of all the mining camps. There, Martha Jane Canary—a crack shot who, as Calamity Jane, won fame as a scout and teamster —fell in love with Wild Bill Hickok; and Hickok himself—a western legend who had tamed Kansas cow towns, killed an unknown number of men, and toured in Buffalo Bill's Wild West Show

■ *Martha Jane Canary—Calamity Jane—in the uniform of a U.S. Army scout. She boasted of her marksmanship and her exploits as a pony express rider and a scout.*

—died, shot in the back of the head. Hickok was thirty-nine.

Towns such as Deadwood, in the Dakota Territory; Virginia City, Nevada; Leadville, Colorado; and Tombstone, Arizona, began a new process in the frontier experience. The farming frontier naturally took place in a rural setting. On the mining frontier, the camp—the germ of a city—appeared almost simultaneously with the first "strike." Periodicals, the latest fashions, theaters, schools, literary clubs, and lending libraries came quickly to the camps, providing civilized refinements not available on other frontiers. But urbanization also created the need for municipal government, sanitation, and law enforcement.

Mining camps were governed by a simple democracy. Soon after a strike, the miners in the area met to organize a mining "district" and adopted rules governing behavior in it. Rules regulated the size and boundaries of claims, established procedures for settling disputes, and set penalties for crimes. Petty criminals were banished from the district; serious offenders were hanged. In the case of a major dispute, the whole camp gathered, chose legal counsel for both sides, and heard the evidence. If all else failed, miners formed secret vigilance committees to hang a few offenders as a lesson to the rest. Early visitors to the mining country were struck by the way miners, solitary and competitive, joined together, founded a camp, and created a society.

The camps were mostly male, made up of "men who can rough it" and a few ladies of "spirit and energy." In 1870 men outnumbered women in the mining districts by more than two to one; there were few children. Prostitutes followed the camps around the West, and "respectable" women were an object of curiosity. Four arrived in Nevada City in 1853, and as one observed: "The men stand and gaze at us with mouth and eyes wide open, every time we go out." Some women worked claims, but more often they took jobs as cooks, housekeepers, and seamstresses—for wages considerably higher than in the East. There were advantages in scarcity. "I lead a life of great variety—full of agreeable, and stirring incidents," one woman said. "I think that I should find any other country very dull after this."

In most camps between one quarter and one half of the population was foreign-born. The lure of gold drew large numbers of Chinese, Chileans, Peruvians, Mexicans, French, Germans, and English. Experienced miners, the Latin Americans brought valuable mining techniques. At least six thousand Mexicans joined the California rush of 1849, and by 1852 there were twenty-five thousand Chinese in California. Painstaking, the Chinese profitably worked claims others had abandoned. In the 1860s almost one third of the miners in the West were Chinese.

Hostility often surfaced against foreign miners, particularly the French, Latin Americans, and Chinese. In 1850 California passed a Foreign Miners' Tax that charged foreign miners a $20 monthly licensing fee. As intended, it drove out Mexican and other miners. Riots against Chinese laborers occurred in the 1870s and '80s in Los Angeles, San Francisco, Seattle, Reno, and Denver. Responding to pressure, Congress passed the Chinese Exclusion Act of 1882, which suspended immigration of Chinese laborers for ten years. The number of Chinese in the United States fell drastically.

By the 1890s the early mining bonanza was over. All told, the western mines contributed billions of dollars to the economy. They helped finance the Civil War and provided needed capital for industrialization. The vast boost in silver production from the Comstock Lode changed the relative value of gold and silver, the base of American currency. Bitter disputes over the currency affected politics and led to the famous "battle of the standards," the presidential election of 1896 (see chapter 20).

The mining frontier populated portions of the West and sped its political organization. Nevada, Idaho, and Montana were granted early statehood because of mining. Merchants, editors, lawyers, and ministers accompanied the frontier and established permanent settlements. But the industry also left behind painful scars in the form of invaded Indian reservations, pitted hills, and lonely ghost towns.

Gold from the Roots Up

"There's gold from the grass roots down," said California Joe, a guide in the gold districts of Dakota in the 1870s, "but there's more gold from the grass roots up." Ranchers began to recognize the potential of the vast grasslands of the West. The Plains were covered with buffalo or grama grass, a wiry variety with short, hard stems. Cattle thrived on it.

For twenty years after 1865, cattle ranching dominated the "open range," a vast, fenceless

Mining Camps and Cattle Trails

Opportunistic, materialistic, and exploitative Westerners were always ready to seize the main chance. Lucky miners extracted gold from beneath the ground and cattle ranchers made fortunes from the grasslands above the ground.

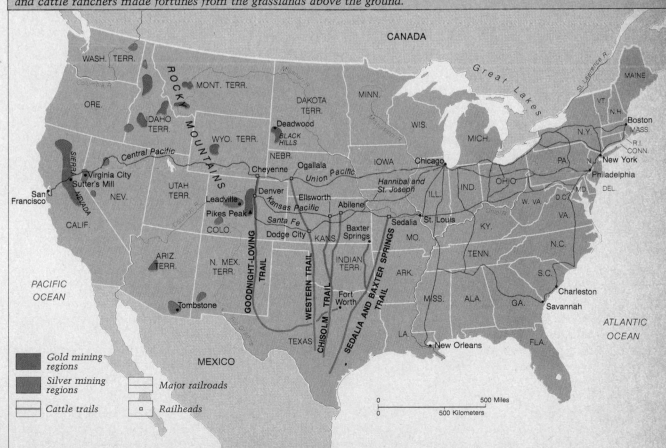

Cowboys roping longhorns, a painting by James Walker. Roping was often the most difficult part of a cowboy's job. It required expert horsemanship, a good sense of timing, and great skill with the rope or lariat.

area extending from the Texas Panhandle north into Canada. The techniques of the business came from Mexico, where long before American cowboys moved herds north, their Mexican counterparts, the *vaqueros*, developed the essential techniques of branding, roundups, and roping. The cattle themselves, the famous Texas longhorns, also came from Mexico. Spreading over the grasslands of southern Texas, the longhorns multiplied rapidly. Although their meat was coarse and stringy, they fed a nation hungry for beef at the end of the Civil War.

The problem was to get the beef to eastern markets, and Joseph G. McCoy, a livestock shipper from Illinois, solved it. Looking for a way to market Texas beef, McCoy conceived the idea of taking the cattle to railheads in Kansas. He talked first with the president of the Missouri Pacific, who ordered him out of his office, and then with the head of the Kansas Pacific, who laughed at the idea. The persistent McCoy finally signed a contract in 1867 with the Hannibal and St. Joseph Railroad. Searching for an appropriate rail junction, he settled on the sleepy Kansas town of Abilene, "a very small, dead place," he remembered, with about a dozen log huts and one near-bankrupt saloon.

In September 1867, McCoy shipped the first train of twenty cars of longhorn cattle. By the end of the year a thousand carloads had followed, all headed for Chicago markets. In 1870 three hundred thousand head of Texas cattle reached Abilene, and the following year—the peak year—seven hundred thousand head. The Alamo Saloon, crowded with tired cowboys at the end of the drive, now employed seventy-five bartenders, working three eight-hour shifts.

The profits were enormous. Drivers bought cheap Texas steers for $7 a head and sold them for $60 or $70 a head at the northern railhead. The most famous trail was the Chisholm, running from southern Texas through Oklahoma Territory to Ellsworth and Abilene, Kansas, on the Kansas Pacific Railroad. Dodge City, Kansas, became the prime shipping center between 1875 and 1879.

Cowboys pushed steers northward in herds of two to three thousand. Novels and films have portrayed them as white, but at least a quarter were black and possibly another quarter were Mexicans. A typical crew on the trail north might have eight men, half of them black or Mexican. Most of the trail bosses were white; they earned about $125 a month. As James "Jim" Perry, a renowned black cowboy who worked for more than twenty years as a rider, roper, and cook for the XIT ranch, said: "If it weren't for my damned old black face, I'd have been a boss long ago."

Like miners, cattlemen lived beyond the formal reach of the law and so established their own. Before each drive Charles Goodnight drew up rules governing behavior on the trail. A cowboy who shot another was hanged on the spot. Ranchers adopted rules for cattle ownership, branding, roundups, and drives; and they formed associations to enforce them. The Wyoming Stock Growers' Association, the largest and most formidable, had four hundred members owning two million cattle; its reach extended well beyond Wyoming into Colorado, Nebraska, Montana, and the Dakotas. Throughout this vast territory the "laws" of the association were often the law of the land.

Hollywood to the contrary, there was little violence in the booming cow towns. The number of homicides in a year never topped five in any town, and in many years no one was killed. Doc Holliday and William B. (Bat) Masterson never killed anyone. John Wesley Hardin, a legendary teen-aged gunman, shot only one man, firing blindly through a hotel room wall to stop him from snoring. Famous western sheriffs had everyday duties. Wild Bill Hickok served as Abilene's street commissioner, and the Wichita city council made its lawmen, including Wyatt Earp, repair streets and sidewalks before each cattle season.

By 1880 more than six million cattle had been driven to northern markets. But the era of the great cattle drive was ending. Farmers were planting wheat on the old buffalo ranges; barbed wire, a recent invention, cut across the trails and divided up the big ranches. Mechanical improvements in slaughtering, refrigerated transportation, and cold storage modernized the industry. Ranchers bred the Texas longhorns with heavier Hereford and Angus bulls, and as the new breeds proved profitable, more and more ranches opened on the northern ranges.

By the mid-1880s some 4.5 million cattle grazed the High Plains, reminding people of the once great herds of buffalo. Stories of vast profits circulated, attracting outside capital. Large investments transformed ranching into big business, often controlled by absentee owners and subject to new problems.

By 1885 experienced cattlemen were growing alarmed. A presidential order that year forced stockmen out of the Indian Territory in Oklahoma, adding 200,000 cattle to the overcrowded northern ranges. The winter of 1885–1886 was cold, and the following summer was one of the hottest on record. Waterholes dried up; the grass turned brown. Beef prices fell. The *Rocky Mountain Husbandman* urged ranchers to sell: "Beef is low, very low, and prices are tending downward. . . . But for all that, it would be better to sell at a low figure, than to endanger the whole herd by having the range overstocked."

The winter of 1886–1887 was one of the worst in western history. Temperatures dropped to 45 degrees below zero, and cattle that once would have saved themselves by drifting ahead of the storms, came up against the new barbed wire fences. Herds jammed together, pawing the frozen ground or stripping bark from trees in search of food. Cattle died by the tens of thousands. In

■ *Nat Love, born a slave in Tennessee in 1854, claimed to be the original "Deadwood Dick," having won the title—he said—in a cowboy contest in Deadwood, South Dakota, in 1876.*

■ *Cowboys' lives were brutal with long hours, dangerous conditions, and low pay. They earned between $25 and $40 a month and managed herds worth fortunes.*

the spring of 1887, when the snows thawed, ranchers found stacks of carcasses piled up against the fences.

The melting snows did produce a lush crop of grass for the survivors. The cattle business recovered, but it took different directions. Outside capital, so plentiful in the boom years, dried up. Ranchers began fencing their lands, reducing the size of their herds, and growing hay for winter food. To the dismay of cowboys, mowing machines and hay rakes became as important as chuck wagons and branding irons. "I tell you times have changed,"one cowboy said sadly.

The last roundup on the northern ranges took place in 1905. Ranches grew smaller, and some ranchers, mainly in the scrub country of the Southwest, switched to raising sheep. In Wyoming the number of cattle shrank from nine million in 1886 to three million in 1895, the same number as when the boom began. Homesteaders, armed with barbed wire and new strains of wheat, pushed onto the Plains, and the day of the open range was over.

Farming on the Frontier

Like miners and cattlemen, millions of farmers moved West in the decades after 1870 to seek crop bonanzas and new ways of life. Some realized their dreams; many fought just to survive.

Said a folk song from Greer County, Oklahoma:

Hurrah for Greer County! The land of the free,
The land of the bedbug, grasshopper, and flea;
I'll sing of its praises, I'll tell of its fame,
While starving to death on my government claim.

Between 1870 and 1900 farmers cultivated more land than ever before in American history. They peopled the Plains from Dakota to Texas, pushed the Indians out of their last sanctuary in Oklahoma, and poured into the basins and foothills of the Rockies. By 1900 the western half of the nation contained almost 30 percent of the population, compared to less than 1 percent just a half-century earlier.

Sodbusters on the Plains

Unlike mining, farm settlement often followed predictable patterns, taking population from states east of the frontier line and moving gradually westward. Crossing the Mississippi, farmers settled first in South Dakota, Minnesota, western Iowa, Nebraska, Kansas, and Texas. The movement slumped during the depression of the 1870s, but then a new wave of optimism carried thousands more west. Several years of above-average rainfall convinced farmers that the Dakotas, western Nebraska and Kansas, and eastern Colorado were the "rain belt of the Plains." Between 1870 and 1900 the population on the Plains tripled.

Farming there presented new problems. There was little surface water, and wells ranged between fifty and five hundred feet deep. Well drillers charged up to $2 a foot. Taking advantage of the steady Plains winds, windmills brought the water to the surface, but they too were expensive, and until 1900 many farmers could not afford them. Lumber for homes and fences was also scarce. Some settlers imported it from distant Wisconsin, but a single homestead of 160 acres cost $1000 to fence, an amount few could pay.

Unable to afford wood, farmers often started out in dreary sod houses. Cut into three-foot sections, the thick prairie sod was laid like brick, with space left for two windows and a door. Since glass was scarce, cloth hung over the windows; a blanket was hung from the ceiling to make two rooms. Sod houses were small, provided little light and air, and were impossible to keep clean. When it rained, water seeped through the roof. Yet a sod house cost only $2.78 to build.

Outside, the Plains environment sorely tested the men and women who moved there. Neighbors were distant; the land stretched on as far as the eye could see. Always the wind blew. "As long as I live I'll never see such a lonely country," a woman said of the Texas Plains; a Nebraska woman said: "These unbounded prairies have such an air of desolation—and the stillness is very oppressive."

In the winters savage storms swept the open grasslands. Ice caked on the cattle until their heads were too heavy to hold up. Summertime temperatures stayed near 110 degrees for weeks at a time. Fearsome rainstorms, building in the summer's heat, beat down the young corn and wheat. The summers also brought grasshoppers,

■ *A Nebraska farm couple plowing the corn in the dooryard of their sod house in 1888. Corn, which could fight its way through tough prairie grass, was often the prairie farmer's first crop.*

arriving without warning, flying in clouds so huge they shut out the sun. The grasshoppers ate everything in sight: crops, clothing, mosquito netting, tree bark, even plow handles. In the summer of 1874 they devastated the whole Plains from Texas to the Dakotas, eating everything "but the mortgage," as one farmer said.

New Farming Methods

Farmers adopted new techniques to meet these conditions. For one thing, they needed cheap and effective fencing material, and in 1874 Joseph F. Glidden, a farmer from De Kalb, Illinois, provided it with the invention of barbed wire. By 1883 his factory was turning out 600 miles of barbed wire every day, and farmers were buying it faster than it could be produced.

Dry farming, a new technique, helped compensate for the lack of rainfall. By plowing furrows twelve to fourteen inches deep, and creating a dust mulch to fill the furrow, farmers loosened the soil and slowed evaporation. Wheat farmers imported European varieties that could withstand the harsh Plains winters. Hard-kerneled varieties like "Turkey Red" wheat from Russia required new milling methods, developed during the 1870s. By 1881 Minneapolis, St. Louis, and Kansas City had become milling centers for the rich "New Process" flour.

Farm technology changed long before the Civil War, but later developments improved it. In 1877 James Oliver of Indiana patented a chilled-iron plow with a smooth-surface mold board that did not clog in the thick prairie soils. The spring-tooth harrow (1869) sped soil preparation; the grain drill (1874) opened furrows and scientifically fed seed into the ground. The lister (1880) dug a deep furrow, planted corn at the bottom, and covered the seed—all in one operation.

The first baling press was built in 1866, and the hay loader was patented in 1876. The first successful harvester, the cord binder (1878), cut and tied bundles of grain, enabling two men and a team of horses to harvest twenty acres of wheat a day. Invented earlier, threshers grew larger; employing as many as nine men and ten horses, they threshed three hundred bushels of grain a day.

In 1890 over 900 corporations manufactured farm machinery. Scientific agriculture flourished under new discoveries linking soil minerals and plant growth. Samuel Johnson of Yale University wrote books on *How Crops Grow* (1868) and *How Crops Feed* (1870), and one of his students pioneered work on nitrogen, the base of many modern fertilizers. The Hatch Act, passed in 1887, supported agricultural experiment stations that spread the discoveries among farmers. Four years later, these stations employed over 450 persons and distributed more than 300 published reports annually to some 350,000 readers.

In the late 1870s huge bonanza farms rose, run by the new machinery and financed with outside capital. Oliver Dalrymple, the most famous of the bonanza farmers, headed an experiment in North Dakota's Red River Valley in 1875, then moved on to manage the Grandin Bonanza of 61,000 acres, five times the size of Manhattan Island. Dalrymple hired armies of workers, bought machinery by the carload, and planted on a scale that dazzled the West. "You are in a sea of wheat," said one visitor to the Grandin Bonanza. "The railroad train rolls through an ocean of grain. . . . We encounter a squadron of war chariots . . . doing the work of human hands."

The bonanza farms—thanks to their size and machinery—captured the country's imagination. Using 200 pairs of harrows, 155 binders, and 16 threshers, Dalrymple produced 600,000 bushels of wheat in 1881. He and other bonanza managers profited from the economies of scale, buying materials at wholesale prices and receiving rebates from the railroads. Then a period of drought began. Rainfall dropped between 1885 and 1890, and the large-scale growers found it hard to compete with smaller farmers who diversified their crops and cultivated more intensively. Many of the large bonanzas slowly disintegrated, and Dalrymple himself went bankrupt in 1896.

Discontent on the Farm

Like the cattle boom, the farming boom ended sharply after 1887. A severe drought that year cut harvests, and other droughts followed in 1889 and 1894. Thousands of new farmers were wiped out on the western Plains. Between 1888 and 1892 more than half the population of western Kansas left. In the 1890s Nebraska lost fifteen thousand people and six thousand farms.

■ *Thirty-two horses pull a harvester-thresher combine through a wheat field in Oregon. The huge machines combined the work of binding and threshing into one operation. Soon the animals were replaced by steam power.*

Farmers grew angry and restless. They complained about declining crop prices, rising railroad rates, and heavy mortgages. In the wheat-growing Plains the economic problems were persistent. Returning home to Iowa in 1889, the author Hamlin Garland found his farming friends caught up "in a sullen rebellion against the government and against God."

Every house I visited had its individual message of sordid struggle and half-hidden despair. . . . All the gilding of farm life melted away. The hard and bitter realities came back upon me in a flood. Nature was as bountiful as ever . . . but no splendor of cloud, no grace of sunset, could conceal the poverty of these people.

Touring the South in the 1860s, Oliver H. Kelley, a clerk in the Department of Agriculture, was struck by the drabness of rural life. In 1867 he founded the National Grange of the Patrons of Husbandry, known simply as the Grange. The Grange provided social, cultural, and educational activities for its members. Its constitution

banned involvement in politics, but Grangers often ignored it and supported railroad regulation and other measures.

The Grange grew rapidly during the depression of the 1870s, and by 1875 it had over 800,000 members in 20,000 local Granges. Most were in the Midwest and South. The Granges set up cooperative stores, grain elevators, warehouses, insurance companies, and farm machinery factories. Many failed, but in the meantime the organization made its mark. Farm-oriented groups like the Farmers' Alliance, with branches in both South and West, began to attract followers. Discontent grew, spilling over into the turbulent Populist movement of the 1890s. (See chapter 20 for a more detailed discussion.)

The peopling of the West transformed American agriculture. The states beyond the Mississippi became the garden land of the nation. California sent fruit, wine, and wheat to eastern markets. Under the Mormons, Utah flourished with irrigation. Texas beef stocked the country's tables, and vast wheat fields, stretching to the horizon, covered Minnesota, the Dakotas, Mon-

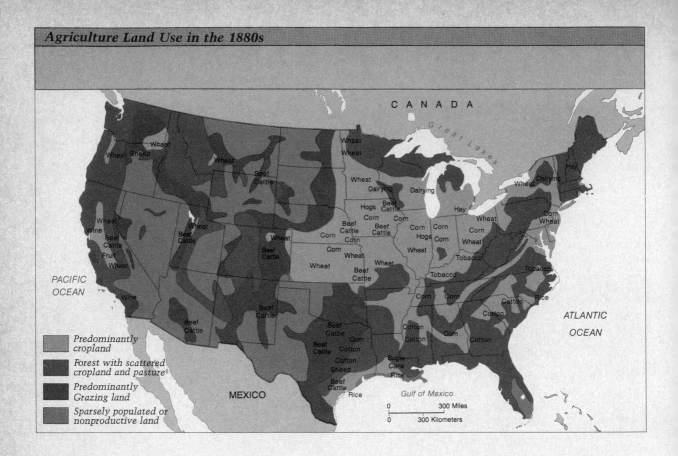

CANADA

Great Lakes

PACIFIC
OCEAN

ATLANTIC
OCEAN

MEXICO

Gulf of Mexico

- Predominantly cropland
- Forest with scattered cropland and pasture
- Predominantly Grazing land
- Sparsely populated or nonproductive land

0   300 Miles

0   300 Kilometers

tana, and eastern Colorado. All produced more than Americans could consume. By 1890 American farmers were exporting large amounts of wheat and other crops.

Farmers became more commercial and scientific. They needed to know more and work harder. Mail-order houses and rural free delivery diminished their isolation and tied them ever closer to the national future. "This is a new age to the farmer," said a statistician in the Department of Agriculture in 1889. "He is now, more than ever before, a citizen of the world."

The Final Fling

As the West filled in with people, pressure mounted on the president and Congress to open the last Indian territory, Oklahoma, to settlers. In March 1889 Congress acted and forced the Creeks and Seminoles, two tribes who had been moved into Oklahoma in the 1820s, to surrender their rights. The arrangements complete, President Benjamin Harrison announced the opening of the Oklahoma District as of noon, April 22, 1889.

Preparations were feverish all along the frontier. "From all the West," historian Ray Allen Billington noted, "the homeless, the speculators, the adventurers, flocked to the still forbidden land." On the morning of April 22, nearly 100,000 people lined the Oklahoma borders; "for miles on end horsemen, wagons, hacks, carriages, bicycles, and a host of vehicles beggaring description stood wheel to wheel awaiting the signal." Fifteen Santa Fe trains were jammed with people from platform to roof.

At noon the starting flag dropped. Bugles and cannon signaled the opening of the "last" territory. Horsemen lunged forward, overloaded wagons collided and overturned. The trains steamed slowly forward, forced to keep a pace that would not give their passengers an undue advantage.

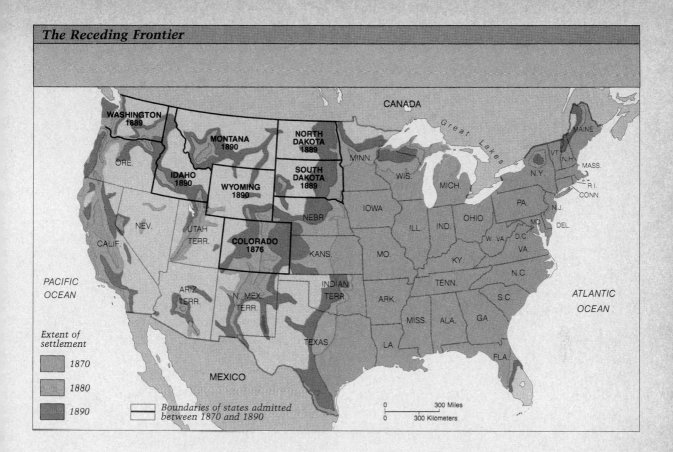

By sunset that day settlers claimed 12,000 homesteads, and the 1,920,000 acres of the Oklahoma District were officially settled. Homesteaders threw up shelters for the night. By evening, Oklahoma City, that morning merely a spot on the prairie with cottonwoods and grass, had 10,000 people; Guthrie to the north had 15,000. Speculators swiftly erected pay toilets, and drinking water cost as much as a beer.

The "Boomers" and "Sooners"—those who had jumped the gun—reflected the speed of western settlement. "Creation!" a character in Edna Ferber's novel *Cimarron* declared. "Hell! That took six days. This was done in one. It was History made in an hour—and I helped make it."

Between the Civil War and 1900 the West witnessed one of the greatest migrations in history. With the Indians driven into smaller and smaller areas, farms, ranches, mines, and cities took over the vast lands from the Mississippi to

the Pacific. The 1890 census noted that for the first time in the country's history, "there can hardly be said to be a frontier line." Picking up the theme, Frederick Jackson Turner, a young history instructor at the University of Wisconsin, examined its importance in an influential 1893 paper, "The Significance of the Frontier in American History."

"The existence of an area of free land," Turner wrote, "its continuous recession, and the advance of American settlement westward, explain American development." It shaped customs and character; gave rise to independence, self-confidence, and individualism; and fostered invention and adaptation. Historians have substantially modified Turner's thesis by pointing to frontier conservatism and imitativeness, the influence of varying racial groups, and the persistence of European ideas and institutions. Yet there can be no doubt that the frontier and the West influenced American development.

Western lands attracted European, Latin American, and Asian immigrants, adding to the society's talent and diversity. The mines, forests, and farms of the West fueled the economy, sent raw materials to eastern factories, and fed the growing cities. Though defeated in warfare, Indian and Spanish influence persisted in art, architecture, law, and western folklore. The West was the first American empire, and it had a profound impact on the American mind and imagination.

Recommended Reading

The best general account of the movement West is Ray Allen Billington, *Westward Expansion* (1967), which also has a first-rate bibliography. See also Frederick Merk, *History of the Westward Movement* (1978). Frederick Jackson Turner's influential interpretation of frontier development, "The Significance of the Frontier in American History," is in his *Frontier in American History* (1920). Walter Prescott Webb, *The Great Plains* (1931), offers a fascinating analysis of development on the Plains.

Rodman W. Paul gives a thorough survey of the mining bonanza in *Mining Frontiers of the Far West* (1963), while Fred A. Shannon provides similar coverage for agriculture in *The Farmer's Last Frontier* (1945). Lewis Atherton, *The Cattle Kings* (1961), and E. S. Osgood, *The Day of the Cattleman* (1929), cover the cattle industry. Louis B. Wright, *Culture on the Moving Frontier* (1955), argues that settlers did not give up books and other cultural assets as they moved West; Henry Nash Smith, *Virgin Land: The American West as Symbol and Myth* (1950) is superb on the literary images of the West in the nineteenth century.

Recent authors have taken fresh and stimulating looks at older or ignored questions. Robert R. Dykstra, *The Cattle Towns* (1968), examines five Kansas cattle towns, with interesting results. Gunther Barth traces the rapid rise of San Francisco and Denver in *Instant Cities* (1975), and Earl Pomeroy, *The Pacific Slope* (1965), looks at urban and other developments in the Far West. Julie Roy Jeffrey, *Frontier Women: The Trans-Mississippi West* (1979), and Joanna L. Stratton, *Pioneer Women: Voices from the Kansas Frontier* (1981), are perceptive works on a neglected topic, and John Mack Faragher, *Women and Men on the Overland Trail* (1979), examines social and other relationships on the trails west.

Additional Bibliography

On the Indians, there are a number of valuable works, including William T. Hagan, *American Indians* (1961); Wilcomb E. Washburn, *The Indian in America* (1975); Robert M. Utley, *The Last Days of the Sioux Nation* (1963) and *Frontier Regulars: The United States Army* and the Indian (1973); and R. K. Andrist, *The Long Death: The Last Days of the Plains Indians* (1964). Helen Hunt Jackson, *A Century of Dishonor* (1881) is a stinging contemporary account.

Dwight W. Hoover, *The Red and the Black* (1976), and Leonard Dinnerstein, Roger L. Nichols, and David M. Reimers, *Natives and Strangers* (1979), contrast Indian policy with the treatment of other minorities. Leonard Pitt looks at *The Decline of the Californios: A Social History of the Spanish-Speaking Californians* (1966); Mario T. Garcia at the Mexican immigrants to El Paso in *Desert Immigrants* (1981); and Gunther Barth at the treatment of the Chinese in *Bitter Strength* (1964).

George R. Stewart, *The California Trail* (1962) and John D. Unruh, Jr., *The Plains Across: The Overland Emigrants and the Trans-Mississippi West, 1840–1860* (1979) are good, but read some of the extraordinary diaries, including David M. Potter, ed., *The Trail to California* (1962) and Dale Morgan, ed., *Overland in 1846* (1963). A. B. Guthrie, Jr., *The Way West* (1949) is an excellent fictional account based on considerable research.

Books on the mining bonanza include Rodman W. Paul, *California Gold* (1948); Charles H. Shinn, *Mining Camps* (1885); William T. Jackson, *Treasure Hill: Portrait of a Silver Mining Camp* (1963); Odie B. Faulk, *Tombstone: Myth and Reality* (1972); D. A. Smith, *Rocky Mountain Mining Camps: The Urban Frontier* (1967); Dan DeQuille, *History of the Big Bonanza* (1876); Eliot Lord, *Comstock Mining and Miners* (1883); and Mark Twain, *Roughing It* (1872).

The best works on the cowboy are E. E. Dale, *Cow Country* (1942); Andy Adams, *The Log of a Cowboy* (1902); and J. B. Franz and J. E. Choate, *The American Cowboy: The Myth and Reality* (1955). Ralph P. Bieber's edited version of Joseph G. McCoy, *Historic Sketches of the Cattle Trade of the West and Southwest* (1940) is indispensable on the man who claimed to start the great herds north. Gene M. Gressley, *Bankers and Cattlemen* (1966), details outside investment in cattle.

Federal land policy is surveyed in Roy M. Robbins, *Our Landed Heritage* (1942), and Paul Wallace Gates, *Fifty Million Acres* (1954). Valuable studies of farming include Gilbert C. Fite, *The Farmer's Frontier* (1966); Allan G. Bogue, *From Prairie to Corn Belt* (1963); Everett Dick, *The Sod-House Frontier* (1937); and H. M. Drache, *The Day of the Bonanza* (1964). Solon J. Buck, *The Granger Movement* (1913), studies early farm discontent and the Grange.

chapter 18

THE
INDUSTRIAL
SOCIETY

In 1876 Americans celebrated their first century of independence. Survivors of a recent civil war, they observed the centenary proudly and rather self-consciously, in song and speech, and above all in a grand Centennial Exposition held in Philadelphia, Pennsylvania.

Spread over thirteen acres of land, the exposition focused more on the present than the past. Fairgoers strolled through exhibits of life in colonial times, then hurried off to see the main attractions: machines, inventions, and new products. They saw linoleum, a new, easy-to-clean floor covering. For the first time they tasted root beer, supplied by a young druggist named Charles Hires, and the rare banana, wrapped in foil and selling for a dime. They saw their first bicycle, an awkward high-wheeled contraption with solid tires.

A Japanese Pavilion generated widespread interest in the culture of Japan. There was also a Women's Building, the first ever in a major exposition. Inside were displayed paintings and sculpture by women artists, along with rows of textile machinery staffed by female operators.

In the entire exposition, machinery was the focus and Machinery Hall the most popular building. Here were the products of an ever improving civilization. Long lines of the curious waited to see the telephone, Alexander Graham Bell's new device. ("My God, it talks!" the emperor of Brazil exclaimed.) Thomas A. Edison displayed several recent inventions, while nearby, whirring machines turned out bricks, chewing tobacco, and other products. Fairgoers saw the first public display of the typewriter, Elisha Otis' new elevator, and the Westinghouse railroad air brake.

But above all, they crowded around the mighty Corliss engine, the focal point of the exposition. A giant steam engine, it dwarfed everything in Machinery Hall, its twin vertical cylinders towering almost four stories in the air. Alone it supplied power for the eight thousand other machines, large and small, on the exposition grounds. Poorly designed, the Corliss was soon obsolete, but for the moment it captured the nation's imagination. It symbolized swift movement toward an industrial and urban society. John Greenleaf Whittier, the aging rural poet, likened it to the snake in the Garden of Eden and refused to see it.

As Whittier feared, the United States was fast becoming an industrial society. Developments earlier in the century laid the basis, but the most spectacular advances in industrialization came during the three decades after the Civil War. At the start of the war the country lagged well behind industrializing nations such as Great Britain, France, and Germany. By 1900 it had vaulted far into the lead, with a manufacturing output that exceeded the *combined* output of its three European rivals. Over the same years cities grew, technology advanced, and farm production rose. Developments in manufacturing, mining, agriculture, transportation, and communication changed society.

Many Americans eagerly sought the change. William Dean Howells, a leading novelist, visited

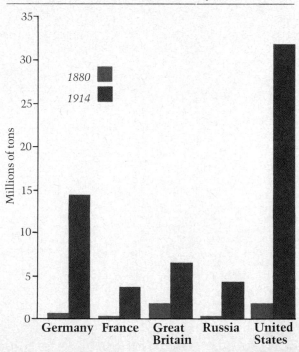

International Steel Production, 1880–1914

the Centennial Exposition and stood in awe before the Corliss. Comparing it to the paintings and sculpture on display, Howells preferred the machine: "It is in these things of iron and steel," he said, "that the national genius most freely speaks."

Industrial Development

American industry owed its remarkable growth to several considerations. It fed on an abundance of natural resources: coal, iron, timber, petroleum, waterpower. An iron manufacturer likened the nation to "a gigantic bowl filled with treasure." Labor was also abundant, drawn from American farm families and the hosts of European immigrants who flocked to American mines, cities, and factories. Nearly eight million immigrants arrived in the 1870s and 1880s; another fifteen million came between 1890 and 1914.

The burgeoning population led to expanded markets, which new devices like the telegraph and telephone helped to exploit. The swiftly growing urban populations devoured goods, and the railroads, spreading pell-mell across the land, linked the cities together and opened a national market. Within its boundaries the United States had the largest free-trade market in the world, while tariff barriers partially protected its producers from outside competition.

Expansive market and labor conditions buoyed the confidence of investors, European and American, who provided large amounts of capital. Technological progress, so remarkable in these years, doomed some older industries (tallow, for example) but increased productivity in others, such as the kerosene industry, and created entirely new industries as well. Through inventions like the harvester and the combine, it also helped foster a firm agricultural base, on which industrialization depends.

Eager to promote economic growth, government at all levels—federal, state, and local—gave manufacturers money, land, and other resources. Other benefits, too, flowed from the American system of government: stability, commitment to the concept of private property, and initially at least, a reluctance to regulate industrial activity. Unlike their European counterparts, American manufacturers faced few legal or social barriers, and their main domestic rivals, the southern planters, had lost political power in the Civil War.

In this atmosphere entrepreneurs flourished. Taking steps crucial for industrialization, they organized, managed, and assumed the financial risks of the new enterprises. Admirers called them "captains of industry"; foes labeled them "robber barons." To some degree they were both —creative *and* acquisitive. If sometimes they seemed larger than life, they dealt in concepts, distances, and quantities often unknown to earlier generations.

Industrial growth, it must be remembered, was neither a simple nor steady nor inevitable process. It involved human decisions and brought with it large social benefits and costs. Growth varied from industry to industry and from year to year. It was concentrated in the North and East, from where in 1890 more than 85 percent of America's manufactured goods originated. The more sparsely settled West provided raw materi-

■ *A sectional view of the "beehive" headquarters of Montgomery Ward & Co., one of the emerging retail and mail-order giants of the '90s (see p. 530).*

als, while the South, although making major gains in iron, textiles, and tobacco, had to rebuild after wartime devastation. In 1890 the industrial production of the entire South amounted in value to about half that of the state of New York.

Still, industrial development proceeded at an extraordinary pace. Between 1865 and 1914 the real Gross National Product (GNP)—the total monetary value of all goods and services produced in a year, with prices held stable—grew at a rate of more than 4 percent a year, increasing about eightfold overall. As Robert Higgs, an economic historian, noted: "Never before had such rapid growth continued for so long."

An Empire on Rails

Genuine revolutions happen rarely, but a major one occurred in the nineteenth century: a revolution in transportation and communications. When the century began, people traveled and communicated much as they had for centuries; when it ended, the railroad, the telegraph, the telephone, and the ocean-going steamship had wrought enormous changes.

The steamship sliced in half the time of the Atlantic crossing and, not dependent on wind and tide, introduced new regularity in the movement of goods and passengers. The telegraph, flashing messages almost instantaneously along miles of wire (four hundred thousand miles of it in the early 1880s), transformed communications, as did the telephone a little later. But the railroad worked the largest changes of all. Along with Bessemer steel, it was the most significant technical innovation of the century.

"Emblem of Motion and Power"

More than most such innovations, the railroad dramatically affected economic and social life. Economic growth would have occurred without it, of course; canals, inland steamboats, and the country's superb system of interior waterways already provided the outlines of an effective transportation network. But the railroad added significantly to the network and contributed advantages all its own.

Those advantages included more direct routes, greater speed, greater safety and comfort than other modes of land travel, more dependable schedules, a larger volume of traffic, and year-round service. A day's land travel on stagecoach or horseback might cover fifty miles. The railroad covered fifty miles in about an hour, seven hundred miles in a day. It went where canals and rivers did not go—directly to the loading platforms of great factories or across the arid West. As construction crews pushed tracks onward, vast areas of the continent opened for settlement.

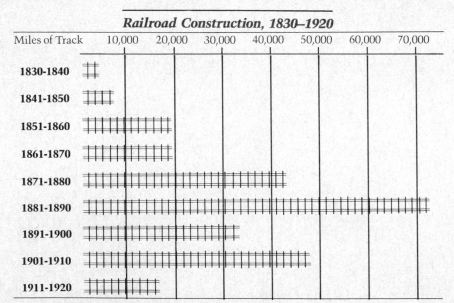

Railroad Construction, 1830–1920

Source: U.S. Bureau of the Census, Historical Statistics of the United States, Colonial Times to 1970, Bicentennial Edition, Washington, D.C., 1975.

Linking widely separated cities and villages, the railroad ended the relative isolation and self-sufficiency of the country's "island communities." It tied people together, brought in outside products, fostered greater interdependence, and encouraged economic specialization. Under its stimulus, Chicago supplied meat to the nation; Minneapolis, grain; and Saint Louis, beer. For these and other communities the railroad made possible a national market and in so doing pointed the way toward mass production and mass consumption, two of the hallmarks of twentieth-century society.

It also pointed the way toward later business development. The railroad, as Alfred D. Chandler, the historian of business, has written, was "the nation's first big business"; it worked out "the modern ways of finance, management, labor relations, competition, and government regulation."

A railroad corporation, far-flung and complex, was a new kind of business. It stretched over thousands of miles, employed thousands of people, dealt with countless customers, and required a scale of organization and decision making unknown in earlier business. Railroad managers never met most customers or even many employees; thus arose new problems in marketing and labor relations. Year by year railroad companies consumed large quantities of iron, steel, coal, lumber, and glass; purchases stimulated growth and employment in numerous industries.

No wonder, then, that the railroad captured so completely the country's imagination. Walt Whitman, the poet who celebrated American achievement, chanted the locomotive's praises:

Thy black cylindric body, golden brass and silvery steel . . .
Thy great protruding head-light fix'd in front,
Thy long, pale, floating vapor-pennants, tinged with delicate purple . . .
Thy knitted frame, thy springs and valves, the tremulous twinkle of thy wheels,
Thy train of cars behind, obedient, merrily following . . .
Type of the modern—emblem of motion and power—pulse of the continent . . .
Fierce-throated beauty!

For nearly a hundred years—the railroad era lasted through the 1940s—children gathered as de-

pots, paused in the fields to wave as the fast express flashed by, listened at night to far-off whistles, and wondered what lay down the tracks. They lived in a world grown smaller.

Building the Empire

When Lee surrendered at Appomattox in 1865, the country already had 35,000 miles of track, and much of the railroad system east of the Mississippi River was in place (see chapter 13). Farther west, the rail network stood poised on the edge of settlement. Although southern railroads were in shambles from the war, the United States had nearly as much railroad track as the rest of the world.

After the Civil War, rail construction increased by leaps and bounds. From 35,000 miles in 1865, the network expanded to 93,000 miles in 1880; 166,000 in 1890; and 193,000 in 1900—more than in all Europe including Russia. Mileage peaked at 254,037 miles in 1916, just before the industry began its long decline into the mid-twentieth century.

To build such an empire took vast amounts of capital—over $4.5 billion by 1880, before even half of it was complete. American and European investors provided some of the money; government supplied the rest. In all, local governments gave railroad companies about $300 million, and

■ *The* Fast Mail, *with its hook out to seize the mail pouch, its brave engineer, its gleaming brass and belching smoke, fascinated Americans.*

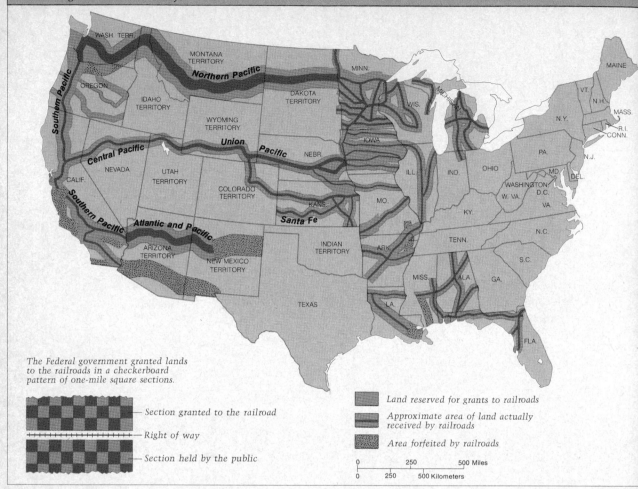

The Federal government granted lands to the railroads in a checkerboard pattern of one-mile square sections.

Section granted to the railroad

Right of way

Section held by the public

Land reserved for grants to railroads

Approximate area of land actually received by railroads

Area forfeited by railroads

state governments added $228 million more. The federal government loaned nearly $65 million to a half dozen western railroads and donated millions of acres of the public domain. Between 1850 and 1871, some eighty railroads received more than 170 million acres of land.

Almost 90 percent of the federal land grants lay in twenty states west of the Mississippi River. Federal land grants helped build 18,738 miles of track, less than 8 percent of the system. The land was frequently distant and difficult to market. Railroad companies sometimes sold it to raise cash but more often used it as security for bonds or loans.

Beyond doubt, the grants of cash and land promoted waste and corruption. The companies built fast and wastefully, eager to collect the subsidies that went with each mile of track. Wanting quick profits, some owners formed separate construction companies to which they awarded lavish contracts. In this way the notorious Crédit Mobilier, a constuction company controlled by an inner ring on the Union Pacific, enriched its owners in the 1860s, while the Contract and Finance Company did the same on the Central Pacific. The Crédit Mobilier bribed congressmen and state legislators in order to avoid congressional investigation of its activities (see chapter 16).

Yet, on balance, the grants probably worked

more benefits than evils. As Congress had hoped, the grants were the lure for railroad building across the rugged, unsettled West, where it would be years before revenues would repay construction. Farmers, ranchers, and merchants poured into the newly opened areas, settling the country and boosting the value of government and private land nearby. The grants seemed necessary in a nation which, unlike Europe, expected private enterprise to build the railroads. In return for aid, Congress required the railroads to carry government freight, troops, and mail at substantially reduced rates—resulting in savings to the government of almost $1 billion between 1850 and 1945. In no other cases of federal subsidies to carriers—canals, highways, and airlines—did Congress exact specific benefits in return.

Linking the Nation via Trunk Lines

The early railroads may seem to have linked different regions, but in fact they did not. Built with little regard for through traffic, they were designed more to protect local interests than to tap outside markets. Many extended fewer than fifty miles. To avoid cooperating with other lines, they adopted conflicting schedules, built separate depots, and above all, used different gauges. Gauges, the distance between the rails, ranged from 4 feet 8½ inches, which became the standard gauge, to 6 feet. Without special equipment, trains of one gauge could not run on tracks of another.

The Civil War showed the value of fast, long-distance transportation, and after 1865 railroad managers worked to provide it. In a burst of consolidation the large swallowed the small; integrated rail networks became a reality. Railroads also adopted standard schedules, signals, equipment, and finally in 1886, the standard gauge. In 1866, in a dramatic innovation to speed traffic, railroad companies introduced fast freight lines which pooled cars for service between cities.

In the Northeast four great trunk lines took shape, all intended to link eastern seaports with the rich traffic of the Great Lakes and western rivers. Like a massive river system, trunk lines drew traffic from dozens of tributaries (feeder lines) and carried it to major markets. The Baltimore and Ohio (B & O), which reached Chicago in 1874, was one; the Erie Railroad was another. Running from New York City to Chicago, the

This poster advertised the Erie Railroad as a great trunk line, renowned for its "double-tracked steel rails, scenic route, and well-appointed passenger cars, equipped with the celebrated Pullman hotel, drawing room and sleeping coaches."

An Empire on Rails

Erie paralleled the route of Cornelius Vanderbilt —the "Commodore"—a crusty old multimillionaire from the shipping business who put together a third trunk line of his own.

Nearly seventy years old when he first entered railroading, Vanderbilt wasted no time. In 1867 he took over the New York Central Railroad and merged it with other lines to provide a track from New York City to Buffalo. When he died in 1877, his Central operated over forty-five hundred miles of track.

J. Edgar Thomson and Thomas A. Scott built the fourth trunk line, the Pennsylvania Railroad, which initially ran from Philadelphia to Pittsburgh. Restless and energetic, they dreamed of a rail empire stretching through the South and West. A brilliant business leader, Scott expanded the Pennsylvania system to Cincinnati, Indianapolis, Saint Louis, and Chicago in 1869, New York City in 1871, and Baltimore and Washington soon thereafter.

In the war-damaged South, consolidation took longer. As Reconstruction waned, northern and European capital rebuilt and integrated the southern lines, especially during the 1880s when rail construction in the South led the nation. By 1900 the South had five large systems: the Illinois Central, linking Chicago, New Orleans, and Savannah, Georgia; the Atlantic Coast Line and the Seaboard Air Line, both running from Virginia to Florida; the Louisville & Nashville, tapping the iron and coal regions of the middle South; and the Southern Railway, which ran from Washington, D.C., to New Orleans. Just four decades after the secession crisis, these systems tied the South into a national transportation network.

Over that rail system, passengers and freight moved in relative speed, comfort, and safety. Automatic couplers (1868), air brakes (1869), refrigerator cars (1867), dining cars, heated cars, electric switches, and stronger locomotives transformed railroad service. George Pullman's lavish sleeping cars became popular. Handsome depots, like New York's Grand Central and Washington's Union Station, were erected at major terminals. Passenger miles per year increased from five billion in 1870 to sixteen billion in 1900.

In November 1883, the railroads even changed time. Ending the crazy quilt jumble of local times that caused scheduling difficulties, the American Railway Association divided the country into four time zones and adopted the modern system of standard time. Congress took thirty-five years longer; it adopted standard time in 1918 in the midst of World War I.

Rails Across the Continent

The dream of a transcontinental railroad, linking the Atlantic and Pacific oceans, stretched back many years but had always succumbed to sectional quarrels over the route. In 1862 and 1864, with the South out of the picture, Congress passed legislation to build the first transcontinental. The act incorporated the Union Pacific Railroad Company to build westward from Nebraska to meet the Central Pacific Railroad Company, building eastward from the Pacific Coast. For each mile built, the two companies received from Congress twenty square miles of land in alternate sections along the track. For each mile they also received a thirty-year loan of $16,000, $32,000, or $48,000, depending on the difficulty of the terrain over which they built.

Construction began simultaneously at Omaha and Sacramento in 1863, lagged during the war, and moved vigorously ahead after 1865. It became a race, each company vying for land, loans, and potential markets. General Grenville M. Dodge, a tough Union army veteran, served as construction chief for the Union Pacific, while Charles Crocker, a former Sacramento dry-goods merchant, led the Central Pacific crews. Dodge organized an army of ten thousand workers, many of them ex-soldiers and Irish immigrants. Pushing rapidly westward, he encountered frequent Indian attacks but had the advantage of building over flat prairie.

Crocker faced more trying conditions in the high Sierra Nevada along California's eastern border. After several experiments he decided that Chinese laborers worked best, and he hired six thousand of them, most brought directly from China. "I built the Central Pacific," Crocker enjoyed boasting, but the Chinese crews did the awesome work. Under the most difficult conditions they dug, blasted, and pushed their way slowly east.

On May 10, 1869, the two lines met at Promontory Point, Utah, near the northern tip of the Great Salt Lake. Dodge's crews had built 1086

■ *After the last spike was hammered in at Promontory Point, the pilots of the two locomotives touched and exchanged champagne toasts. The chief engineers of the two lines are seen shaking hands.*

miles of track, Crocker's 689. The Union Pacific and Central Pacific presidents hammered in a golden spike (both missed it on the first try), and the dreamed-of connection was made. The telegraph flashed the news east and west, setting off wild celebrations.

The transcontinental railroad symbolized American unity and progress. Along with the Suez Canal, completed the same year, it helped knit the world together. Bret Harte, the exuberant poet of the West, wrote of Promontory Point:

What was it the Engines said,
Pilots touching,—head to head
Facing on the single track,
Half a world behind each back?

In the next twenty-five years four more railroads reached the coast: the Northern Pacific (completed in 1883), running from Minnesota to Oregon; the Atchison, Topeka and Santa Fe (1883), connecting Kansas City and Los Angeles; the powerful Southern Pacific (1883), running from San Francisco and Los Angeles to New Orleans; and James J. Hill's superbly built Great Northern Railway (1893), running from Minneapolis-Saint Paul to Seattle, Washington.

By the 1890s business leaders talked comfortably of railroad systems stretching deep into South America and across the Bering Strait to Asia, Europe, and Africa. In an age of progress, anything seemed possible. "The American," said the Chicago *Tribune,* "intelligent and self-reliant, has banished forever the impossible from his philosophy."

Problems of Growth

Overbuilding during the 1870s and '80s caused serious problems for the railroads. Lines paralleled each other, and where they did not, speculators like Jay Gould often laid one down to force a rival line to buy it at inflated prices. While many managers worked to improve service, Gould and others bought and sold railroads like toys, watered their stock, and milked their assets. By

1885, almost one third of railroad stock represented "water," that is, stock distributed in excess of the real value of the assets.

Competition was severe, and managers fought desperately for traffic. They offered special rates and favors: free passes for large shippers; low rates on bulk freight, carload lots, and long hauls; and above all, rebates—secret, privately negotiated reductions below published rates. Fierce rate wars broke out frequently, convincing managers that ruthless competition helped no one. Rebates made more enemies than friends.

Managers like Albert Fink, the brilliant vice-president of the Louisville & Nashville, tried first to control competition by sharing traffic. Fink directed the Eastern Trunk Line Association (1877), which divided westbound traffic among the four trunk lines. Similar associations pooled traffic in the South and West, but none survived the intense pressures of competition. Customers grew adept at bargaining for rebates and other privileges, and railroads rarely felt able to refuse them. In the first six months of 1880 the New York Central alone granted six thousand special rates.

Failing to cooperate, railroad owners next tried to consolidate. Through purchase, lease, and merger, they gobbled up competitors and built "self-sustaining systems" that dominated entire regions. But many of these systems, expensive and unwieldy, collapsed in the panic of 1893. By mid-1894 a quarter of the railroads were bankrupt. The victims of the panic included such legendary names as the Erie, B & O, Santa Fe, Northern Pacific, and Union Pacific.

Needing money, railroads turned naturally to bankers, who finally imposed order on the industry. J. Pierpont Morgan, head of the New York investment house of J. P. Morgan and Company, took the lead. Massively built, with eyes so piercing they seemed like the headlights of an onrushing train, Morgan was the most powerful figure in American finance. He liked efficiency, combination, and order. He disliked "wasteful" competition. In 1885, during a bruising rate war between the New York Central and the Pennsylvania, Morgan invited the combatants to a conference aboard his palatial steam yacht, *Corsair*. Cruising on Long Island Sound, he arranged a traffic-sharing agreement and collected a million-dollar fee. Bringing peace to an industry could be profit-

A 1903 photograph of J. P. Morgan by Edward Steichen. The photographer captured Morgan's awesome presence, the embodiment of power.

able. It also satisfied Morgan's passion for stability.

After 1893 Morgan and a few other bankers refinanced ailing railroads, and in the process they took control of the industry. Their methods were direct: fixed costs and debt were ruthlessly cut; new stock was issued to provide capital; rates were stabilized; rebates and competition were eliminated; and control was vested in a "voting trust" of hand-picked trustees. Between 1894 and 1898 Morgan reorganized—critics said "Morganized"—the Southern Railway, the Erie, the Northern Pacific, and the B & O. In addition, he took over a half dozen other important railroads. By 1900 he dominated American railroading.

As the new century began, the railroads had pioneered the patterns followed by most other industries. Seven giant systems controlled nearly two thirds of the mileage, and they in turn answered to a few investment banking firms like the house of Morgan. For good and ill, a national transportation network, centralized and relatively efficient, was now in place.

An Industrial Empire

Along with railroads, the new industrial empire was based on steel. Harder and more durable than other kinds of iron, steel wrought changes in manufacturing, agriculture, transportation, and architecture. It permitted longer bridges, taller buildings, stronger railroad track, newer weapons, better plows, heavier machinery, and faster ships. Made in great furnaces by strong men, it symbolized the tough, often brutal nature of industrial society. From the 1870s onward, steel output became the worldwide accepted measure of industrial progress, and nations around the globe vied for leadership.

The Bessemer process, developed in the late 1850s by Henry Bessemer in England and independently by William Kelly in the United States, made it possible. Both Bessemer and Kelly discovered that a blast of air through molten iron burned off carbon and other impurities, resulting in steel of a more uniform and durable quality. The discovery transformed the industry. While earlier methods produced amounts a person could lift, a Bessemer converter dealt with five tons of molten metal at a time. The mass production of steel was now possible.

Carnegie and Steel

Bessemer plants demanded extensive capital investment, abundant raw materials, and sophisticated production techniques. Using chemical and other processes, they required research departments, which became critical components of later American industries. Costly to build, they limited entry into the industry to the handful who could afford them.

Great steel districts arose in Pennsylvania, Ohio, and Alabama—especially near Pittsburgh, which became the center of the industry. Output shot up. In 1874 the United States produced less than half the pig iron produced in Great Britain. By 1890 it took the lead, and in 1900 it produced four times as much as Britain.

Iron ore abounded in the fabulous deposits near Lake Superior, the greatest deposits in the world. In the mines of the Mesabi Range in Minnesota, giant steam shovels loaded ore on railroad cars for

The Jones & Laughlin Steel Mills in Pittsburgh, around 1905. The haze of factory smoke darkens the sky and the horizon.

transport to ships on the Great Lakes. Powered lifts, self-loading devices, and other innovations sped the process. "By the turn of the century," historian Peter Temin noted, "the transport of Lake ores had become an intricate ballet of large and complex machines."

Like the railroads, steel companies grew larger and larger. In 1880 only nine companies could produce more than 100,000 tons a year. By the early 1890s several companies exceeded 250,000 tons, and two—including the great Carnegie Steel Company—produced over a million tons a year. As operations expanded, managers needed greater skills. Product development, marketing, and consumer preferences became important. Competition was fierce, and steel companies, like the railroads, tried secret agreements, pools, and consolidation. During the 1880s and '90s they moved toward vertical integration, a type of organization in which a single company owns and controls the entire process from the unearthing of the raw materials to the manufacture and sale of the finished product. Such companies combined coal and iron mines, transportation companies, blast furnaces, and rolling mills into integrated networks.

525

An Industrial Empire

■ *Of all the great industrial tycoons, Carnegie best combined intelligence, luck, and personal charm.*

Andrew Carnegie emerged as the undisputed master of the industry. Born in Scotland, he came to the United States in 1848 at the age of twelve. Settling near Pittsburgh, he went to work as a bobbin boy in a cotton mill, earning $1.20 a week. He soon took a job in a telegraph office, where in 1852 his hard work and skill caught the eye of Thomas A. Scott of the Pennsylvania Railroad. Starting as Scott's personal telegrapher, Carnegie spent a total of twelve years on the Pennsylvania, a training ground for company managers. By 1859 he had become a divisional superintendent. He was twenty-four.

Soon rich from shrewd investments, Carnegie plunged into the steel industry in 1872. On the Monongahela River south of Pittsburgh he built the giant J. Edgar Thomson Steel Works, named after the president of the Pennsylvania Railroad, his biggest customer. With his warmth and salesmanship, he attracted able subordinates such as Henry Clay Frick and Charles M. Schwab, whom he drove hard and paid well. Although he had written magazine articles defending the rights of workers, Carnegie kept the wages of the laborers in his mills low, disliked unions, and crushed a violent strike at his Homestead works in 1892 (see p. 539).

In 1878 he won the steel contract for the Brooklyn Bridge. During the next decade, as city building boomed, he converted the huge Homestead works near Pittsburgh to the manufacture of structural beams and angles, which went into the New York City elevated railway, the first skyscrapers, and the Washington Monument. Carnegie profits mounted: from $2 million in 1888 to $40 million in 1900. That year Carnegie Steel alone produced more steel than Great Britain. Employing twenty thousand people, it was the largest industrial company in the world.

In 1901 Carnegie sold it. Believing that wealth brought social obligations, he wanted to devote his full time to philanthropy. He found a buyer in J. Pierpont Morgan, who in the late 1890s had put together several steel companies, including Federal Steel, Carnegie's chief rival. Carnegie Steel had blocked Morgan's well-known desire for control, and in mid-1900, when a war loomed between the two interests, Morgan decided to buy Carnegie out. In early January 1901 Morgan told Charles M. Schwab: "Go and find his price." Schwab cornered Carnegie on the golf course, Carnegie listened, and the next day handed Schwab a note, scribbled in blunt pencil, asking almost a half billion dollars. Morgan glanced at it and said: "I accept this price."

Drawing other companies into the combination, Morgan on March 3, 1901, announced the creation of the United States Steel Corporation. The new firm was capitalized at $1.4 billion, the first billion-dollar company. It absorbed over 200 other companies, employed 168,000 people, and produced 9 million tons of iron and steel a year. It controlled three fifths of the country's steel business. Soon there were other giants, including Bethlehem Steel, Republic Steel, and National Steel. As the nineteenth century ended, steel products—rare just thirty years before—had altered the landscape. Huge firms, investment bankers, and professional managers dominated the industry.

Rockefeller and Oil

Petroleum worked comparable changes in the economic and social landscape, although mostly after 1900. Distilled into oil, it lubricated the machinery of the industrial age. There seemed

■ *This 1902 cartoon, hostile toward Morgan's control of railroads, steel, and shipping, labels him "Alexander the Great" looking for more worlds to conquer.*

refineries cost little, competition flourished. Output fluctuated dramatically; prices rose and fell with devastating effect. Refineries—usually a collection of wooden shacks and tanks—were centered in Cleveland and Pittsburgh, near the original oil-producing regions.

A young merchant from Cleveland named John D. Rockefeller imposed order on the industry. "I had an ambition to build," he later recalled, and beginning in 1863, at the age of twenty-four, he built the Standard Oil Company, soon to become one of the titans of corporate business. Like Morgan, Rockefeller considered competition wasteful, small-scale enterprise inefficient, and consolidation the path of the future. Consolidation "revolutionized the way of doing business all over the world," he said. "The time was ripe for it. It had to come, though all we saw at the moment was the need to save ourselves from wasteful conditions."

Methodically, Rockefeller absorbed or destroyed competitors in Cleveland and elsewhere. As ruthless in his methods as Carnegie, he lacked the steel master's spontaneous charm. He was distant and taciturn, a man of deep religious beliefs who taught Bible classes at Cleveland's Erie Street Baptist Church. Like Carnegie, he demanded efficiency, relentless cost-cutting, and the latest technology. He attracted exceptional lieutenants—although, as one said, he could see further ahead than any of them, "and then see around the corner."

"Nothing in haste, nothing ill-done," Rockefeller often said to himself. "Your future hangs on every day that passes." Paying careful attention to detail, he counted the stoppers in barrels, shortened barrel hoops to save metal, and in one famous incident, reduced the number of drops of solder on kerosene cans from forty to thirty-nine. In large-scale production, Rockefeller realized, even small reductions meant huge savings. Research uncovered other ways of lowering costs and improving products, and Herman Frasch, a brilliant Standard chemist, solved problem after problem in the refining of oil.

In the end, Rockefeller triumphed over his competitors by marketing products of high quality at the lowest unit cost. But he employed other, less savory methods as well. He threatened rivals and bribed politicians. He exploited railroad rebates, extorted other privileges, and employed

little use for gasoline (the internal combustion engine had only just been developed), but kerosene, another major distillate, brought inexpensive illumination into almost every home. Whale oil, cottonseed oil, and even tallow candles were expensive to burn; consequently, many people went to bed at nightfall. Kerosene lamps opened the evenings to activity, which altered the patterns of life.

Like other changes in these years, the oil boom happened with surprising speed. In the mid-1850s petroleum was a bothersome, smelly fluid that occasionally rose to the surface of springs and streams. Clever entrepreneurs bottled it in patent medicines; a few scooped up enough to burn. Other entrepreneurs soon found that drilling reached pockets of oil beneath the earth. In 1859 Edwin L. Drake drilled the first oil well near Titusville in northwest Pennsylvania, and the "black gold" fever struck. Chemists soon discovered ways to make lubricating oil, grease, paint, wax, varnish, naphtha, and paraffin. Within a few years there was a world market in oil.

At first, growth of the oil industry was chaotic. Early drillers and refiners produced for local markets, and since drilling wells and even erecting

■ *John D. Rockefeller, satirized in a 1901* Punch *cartoon, is enthroned on oil, the base of his empire; his crown is girdled by other holdings.*

which dividends were paid. On January 2, 1882, the first of the modern trusts was born. As Dodd intended, it immediately centralized control of Standard's far-flung empire.

Competition almost disappeared; profits soared. A trust movement swept the country, as industries with similar problems—whiskey, lead, and sugar, among others—followed Standard's example. The word *trust* became synonymous with monopoly, amid vehement protests from the public. Antitrust became a watchword for a generation of reformers from the 1880s through the era of Woodrow Wilson. But Rockefeller's purpose had been *management* of a monopoly, not monopoly itself, which he had already achieved.

In 1897 Rockefeller retired with a fortune of nearly $900 million, but for Standard Oil and petroleum in general, the most expansive period was yet to come. The great oil pools of Texas and Oklahoma had not yet been discovered. Plastics and other oil-based synthetics were several decades in the future. There were only four usable automobiles in the country, and the day of the gasoline engine, automobile, and airplane lay just ahead.

The Business of Invention

"America has become known the world around as the home of invention," boasted the Commissioner of Patents in 1892. It had not always been so; until the last third of the nineteenth century, the country imported most of its technology. Then an extraordinary group of inventors and tinkerers—"specialists in invention," Thomas A. Edison called them—began to study the world around them. Some of their inventions gave rise to new industries; a few actually changed the quality of life.

The number of patents issued to inventors reflected the trend. During the 1850s fewer than 2000 patents were issued each year. By the 1880s and '90s, the figure reached more than 20,000 a year. Between 1790 and 1860 the Patent Office issued just 36,000 patents; in the decade of the 1890s alone, it issued more than 200,000.

Some of the inventions transformed communications. In 1866 Cyrus W. Field improved the transatlantic cable linking the telegraph net-

spies to harass the customers of competing refiners. By 1879 he controlled 90 percent of the country's oil-refining capacity.

Vertically integrated, Standard Oil owned wells, timberlands, barrel and chemical plants, refineries, warehouses, pipelines, and fleets of tankers and oil cars. Its marketing organization served as the model for the industry. Standard exported oil to Asia, Africa, and South America; and its five-gallon kerosene tin, like Coca-Cola during a later era, was a familiar sight in the most distant parts of the world.

To manage it all, the company developed a new plan of business organization, the trust, which had profound significance for American business. In 1881 Samuel T. C. Dodd, Standard's attorney, set up the Standard Oil Trust, with a board of nine trustees empowered "to hold, control, and manage" all Standard's properties. Stockholders exchanged their stock for trust certificates, on

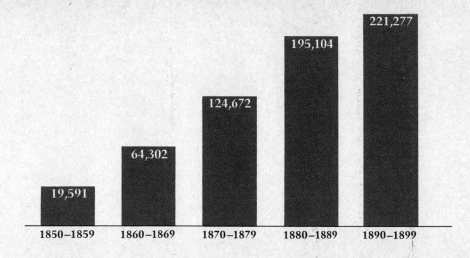

Patents Issued, by Decade, 1850–1899 (in thousands)

1850–1859	1860–1869	1870–1879	1880–1889	1890–1899
19,591	64,302	124,672	195,104	221,277

Source: U.S. Bureau of the Census, Historical Statistics of the United States, Colonial Times to 1970, Bicentennial Edition, Washington, D.C. 1975.

works of Europe and the United States. By the early 1870s land and submarine cables ran to Brazil, Japan, and the China coast; in the next two decades they reached Africa and spread across South America. Diplomats and business leaders could now "talk" to their counterparts in Johannesburg or Saigon. Even before the telephone, the cables quickened the pace of foreign affairs, revolutionized journalism, and allowed businesses to expand and centralize.

The typewriter (1867), stock ticker (1867), cash register (1879), calculating machine (1887), and adding machine (1888) helped business transactions. High-speed spindles, automatic looms, and electric sewing machines transformed the clothing industry, which for the first time in history turned out ready-made clothes for the masses. In 1890 the Census Bureau first used machines to sort and tabulate data on punched cards, a portent of a new era of information storage and treatment.

In 1879 George Eastman patented a process for coating gelatine on photographic dry plates, which led to celluloid film and the motion pictures. By 1888 he was marketing the Kodak, which weighed 35 ounces, took 100 exposures, and cost only $25. Even though early Kodaks had to be returned to the factory, camera and all, for film developing, they revolutionized photogra-

phy. Now almost anyone could snap a picture. In the mid-1890s Eastman Kodak was an $8 million company which had changed the leisure habits of millions of Americans.

Other innovations improved the diet. There were new processes for flour, canned meat, vegetables, condensed milk, and even beer—an offshoot of Louis Pasteur's discoveries about bacteria. Packaged cereals appeared on breakfast tables. Refrigerated railroad cars, ice-cooled, brought fresh fruit from Florida and California to all parts of the country. In the 1870s Gustavus F. Swift, a Chicago meatpacker, hit on the idea of using the cars to distribute meat nationwide. Setting up "dissembly" factories to butcher meat (Henry Ford later copied them for his famous "assembly" lines), he started an "era of cheap beef," as a newspaper said.

No innovation, however, rivaled in importance the telephone and the use of electricity for light and power. The telephone was the work of Alexander Graham Bell, a shrewd and genial Scotsman who settled in Boston in 1871. Interested in the problems of the deaf, Bell experimented with ways to transmit speech electrically, and after several years developed electrified metal disks that, much like the human ear, converted sound waves to electrical impulses and back again. On March 10, 1876, he transmitted the first sentence

over a telephone: "Mr. Watson, come here; I want you." Later that year he exhibited the new device to excited crowds at the Centennial Exposition in Philadelphia.

In 1878—the year a telephone was installed in the White House—the first telephone exchange opened in New Haven, Connecticut. Fighting off competitors who challenged the patent, the young Bell Telephone Company dominated the growing industry. By 1895 there were about 310,000 phones; a decade later, there were 10 million—one for almost every ten people. In 1915 Bell himself opened the first transcontinental telephone line from New York to San Francisco. By then American Telephone and Telegraph Company, formed by the Bell interests in 1885, had become a vast holding company, consolidating over a hundred local systems.

If the telephone dissolved communications barriers as old as the human race, Thomas Alva Edison, the "Wizard of Menlo Park," invented processes and products of comparable significance. Born in 1847, Edison had little formal education, although he was an avid reader. Like Carnegie, he went into the new field of telegraphy. Tinkering in his spare time, he made several important improvements, including a telegraph capable of sending four messages over a single wire. Gathering teams of specialists to work on specific problems, Edison built at Menlo Park, New Jersey, the first modern research laboratory. It may have been his most important invention.

The laboratory, Edison promised, would turn out "a minor invention every ten days and a big thing every six months or so." In 1877 it turned out a big thing. Worried about a telephone's high cost, Edison set out to invent a "telephone repeater," which became the phonograph. Those unable to afford a phone, he thought, could record their voices for replay from a central telephone station. Using tin foil wrapped around a grooved, rotating cylinder, he shouted the verses of "Mary had a little lamb" and then listened in awe as the machine played them back. "I was never so taken aback in all my life," he later said. "Everybody was astonished. I was always afraid of things that worked the first time."

In 1896 records made of hard rubber and shellac appeared on the market; the following year a phonograph sold for $20. In 1904 someone had the idea of recording on both sides of the record,

■ *Alexander Graham Bell (top) is seen making the first telephone call between New York City and Chicago in 1892. Thomas A. Edison (bottom) with his incandescent lamps. His discovery of the "Edison effect" revealed the basic principle on which modern electronics rests.*

and the phonograph record in its modern form was born. For the first time in history, people could listen again and again to a favorite symphony or piano solo. The phonograph made human experience repeatable in a way never before possible.

In 1879 came an even larger triumph, the incandescent lamp. Sir Joseph William Swan, an English inventor, had already experimented with the carbon filament, but Edison's task involved more than finding a durable filament. He set out to do nothing less than change light. A trial-and-error inventor, Edison tested sixteen hundred materials before producing, late in 1879, the carbon filament he wanted. Then he had to devise a complex system of conductors, meters, and generators, by which electricity could be divided and distributed to homes and businesses.

With the financial backing of J. Pierpont Morgan, he organized the Edison Illuminating Company and built the Pearl Street power station in New York City, the testing ground of the new apparatus. On September 4, 1882, as Morgan and others watched, Edison threw a switch and lit the house of Morgan, the stock exchange, the *New York Times*, and a number of other buildings. Power stations soon opened in Boston, Philadelphia, and Chicago. By 1900 there were 2774 stations, lighting some 2 million electric lights around the country. In a nation alive with light, the habits of centuries changed. A flick of the switch lit homes and factories at any hour of the day or night.

In a rare blunder, Edison based his system on low-voltage direct current, which could be transmitted only about two miles. George Westinghouse, the inventor of the railroad air brake, demonstrated the advantages of high-voltage alternating current, transmitted over great distances. In 1886 he formed the Westinghouse Electric Company and with the inventor Nikola Tesla, a Hungarian immigrant, developed an alternating-current motor that could convert electricity into mechanical power. Electricity could light a lamp or illuminate a skyscraper; pull a streetcar or drive an entire railroad; run a sewing machine or power a mammoth assembly line. Transmitted easily over long distances, it freed factories and cities from location near water or coal. Electricity, in short, brought a revolution.

Taking advantage of the new devices, Frank J. Sprague, a young engineer, electrified the Richmond, Virginia, streetcar system in 1887. Other cities quickly followed. Electric-powered subway systems opened in Boston in 1897 and New York City in 1904. Overhead wires and third-rails made urban transportation quieter, faster, and cleaner. Buried under pavement or strung from pole to pole, wires of every description—trolley, telephone, and power—marked the birth of the modern city.

The Sellers

The increased output of the industrial age was one thing, but the products still had to be sold, and that gave rise to a new "science" of marketing. Some business leaders—like Swift in meatpacking, James B. Duke in tobacco, and Rockefeller in oil—built extensive marketing organizations of their own. Others relied on retailers, merchandising techniques, and advertising, developing a host of methods to convince consumers to buy.

In 1867 businesses spent about $50 million on advertising; in 1900 they spent over $500 million, and the figure was increasing rapidly. The first advertising agency, N. W. Ayer and Son, of Philadelphia, began to service businesses in the mid-1870s, and it was followed by numerous imitators. The rotary press (1875) churned out newspapers and introduced a new era in newspaper advertising. Woodcuts, halftones, and photoengraving added illustrations to catch the consumer's eye. Brand names became popular, and already Kellogg was promising cornflake eaters "Genuine Joy, Genuine Appetite, Genuine Health and therefore Genuine Complexion."

Bringing producer and consumer together, nationwide advertising was the final link in the national market. Humorist Finley Peter Dunne's Irish characters poked fun at the ads for breakfast cereals:

Guff . . . ye've seen th' advertisement: "Out iv th' house wint Lucky Joe; Guff was th' stuff that made him go." Mother prefers Almostfood, a scientific preparation iv burlap. I used to take Sawd Ust . . . later I had a peeryod iv Hungareen, a chimically pure diet, made iv th' exterryor iv bath towels. We all have our little tastes an' enthusyasms in th' matter iv break-fast foods, dependin' on what pa-a-pers we read an' what billboords we've seen iv late.

R. H. Macy in New York, John Wanamaker in Philadelphia, and Marshall Field in Chicago turned the department store into a national institution. There people could browse (a relatively new concept) and buy. Innovations in pricing, display, and advertising helped customers develop wants they did not know they had. In 1870 Wanamaker took out the first full-page newspaper ad, and Macy, an aggressive advertiser, touted "goods suitable for the millionaire at prices in reach of the millions."

The "chain store"—an American term—spread across the country. The A & P grocery stores, begun in 1859, numbered sixty-seven by 1876, all marked by the familiar red-and-gold facade. By 1915 there were a thousand of them. In 1880 F. W. Woolworth, bored with the family farm, opened the first "Five and Ten Cent Store" in Utica, New York. He had fifty-nine stores in 1900, the year he adopted the bright red storefront and heaping counters to lure customers in and persuade them to buy.

In similar fashion, Sears, Roebuck and Montgomery Ward sold to rural customers through mail-order catalogs—a means of selling that depended on effective transportation and a high level of customer literacy. As a traveler for a dry-goods firm, Aaron Montgomery Ward had seen an unfulfilled need of people in the rural West. He started the mail-order trend in 1872, with a one-sheet price list offered from a Chicago loft. By 1884 he offered almost 10,000 items in a catalog of 240 pages.

Richard W. Sears also saw the possibilities in the mail-order business. Starting with watches and jewelry, he gradually expanded his list. In the early 1880s he moved to Chicago, and with Alvah C. Roebuck, founded Sears, Roebuck and Company. Sears sold anything and everything, prospering in a business that relied on mutual faith between unseen customers and distant distributors. Sears catalogs, soon over 500 pages long, exploited four-color illustrations and other new techniques. By the early 1900s, Sears distributed 6 million catalogs annually.

Advertising, brand names, chain stores, and mail-order houses brought Americans of all varieties into a national market. Even as the country grew, a certain homogeneity of goods bound it together, touching cities and farms, East and West, rich and poor. There was a common language of consumption. The market, some con-

■ *An early store of the Great Atlantic & Pacific Tea Company chain, 1898. Displayed on the counters and shelves are lamps and fans to be given to customers as premiums. Note the sandwichboard man—a walking advertisement.*

temporaries thought, also bridged ethnic and other differences. Alfred Marshall, a prominent English economist, wrote in 1919: "Widely as the Scandinavians are separated from the Italians, and the native Americans from the Poles, in sentiment, in modes of living, and even in occupations, they are yet purchasers of nearly the same goods. . . . [T]hey buy similar clothes, furniture, and implements."

The theory had limits, as Marshall himself knew; ethnic and racial differences remained deep in the society. But Americans *had* become a community of consumers, surrounded by goods unavailable just a few decades before, and able to purchase them. They had learned to make, want, and buy. "Because you see the main thing today is—shopping," Arthur Miller, a twentieth-century playwright, said in *The Price*.

Years ago a person, he was unhappy, didn't know what to do with himself—he'd go to church, start a revolution—something. Today you're unhappy? Can't figure it out? What is the salvation? Go shopping.

The Wage Earner

While entrepreneurs were important, it was the labor of millions of men and women that built the new industrial society. In their individual stories, nearly all unrecorded, lay much of the achievement, drama, and pain of these years.

In a number of respects, their lot improved during the last quarter of the nineteenth century. Real wages rose, working conditions got better, and the workers' influence in national affairs increased. Between 1880 and 1914, wages of the average worker rose about $7 a year, measured in constant dollars. Like others, workers also benefited from expanding health and educational services.

But life was not easy. Before 1900 most wage earners worked ten hours a day, six days a week. If skilled, they earned about 20¢ an hour; if unskilled, just half that. On average they earned between $400 and $500 a year. It took about $600 to live decently. Construction workers, machinists, government employees, printers, clerical workers, and western miners made more than the average. Eastern coal miners, agricultural work-

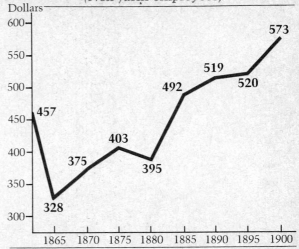

Average Annual Earnings, 1865–1900
(Non-farm employees)

Dollars

600 —
550 —   573
500 —   519
450 —   457   492   520
400 —   403
350 —   375   395
300 —   328

1865 1870 1875 1880 1885 1890 1895 1900

Source: U.S. Bureau of the Census, Historical Statistics of the United States, Colonial Times to 1970, *Bicentennial Edition, Washington, D.C., 1975.*

ers, garment workers, and unskilled factory hands made considerably less.

There were few holidays or vacations and little respite from the grueling routine. Skilled workers could turn the system to their own ends—New York City cigarmakers, for example, paid someone to read to them while they worked—but the unskilled seldom had such luxury. They were too easily replaced. "A bit of advice to you," said a guidebook for immigrant Jews in the 1890s: "do not take a moment's rest. Run, do, work, and keep your own good in mind."

Work was not only grueling; it was highly dangerous. Safety standards were low, and accidents were common. On the railroads, 1 in every 26 workers was injured, 1 in every 399 killed per year. Thousands suffered from chronic illness, unknowing victims of dust, chemicals, and other pollutants. In the early 1900s Dr. Alice Hamilton established a link between jobs and disease, but meanwhile, illness weakened or struck down many a breadwinner.

The breadwinner might be a woman or child; both worked in increasing numbers. In 1870 about 15 percent of women over the age of sixteen were employed for wages; in 1900 20 percent (5.3 million women) were. Of 303 occupations listed in the 1900 census, women were represented in 296. Between 1870 and 1900 the number of working children rose nearly 130 percent to 1.8 mil-

In the early 1900s, photographer Lewis Hine documented many poignant scenes of child labor. These mill boys (left) had to climb up the machine frames to reach their work. A business office in 1907 (below). The female stenographer earned about $6 a week.

lion. In Paterson, New Jersey, an important industrial city, about half of all boys and girls aged eleven to fourteen had jobs.

Most working women were young and single. Many began work at sixteen or seventeen, worked a half-dozen years or so, married, and quit. In 1900 only 5 percent of all married women were employed outside the home, although black women were an important exception. Among them, 25 percent of married women worked in 1900, usually on southern farms or as low-paid laundresses and domestic servants. As clerical work expanded, women learned new skills like typing and stenography. Moving into formerly male occupations, they became secretaries, bookkeepers, typists, telephone operators, and clerks in the new department stores.

A few women—very few—became ministers, lawyers, and doctors. Arabella Mansfield, admitted to the Iowa bar in 1869, was the first woman lawyer in the country. But change was slow, and in the 1880s some law schools were still refusing to admit women because they "had not the mentality to study law." Among women entering the professions, the overwhelming majority became nurses, schoolteachers, and librarians. In such professions a process of *feminization* occurred, in which women became a majority of the workers, a small number of men took the management roles, and most men left for other jobs, lowering the profession's status.

In most jobs, status and pay were divided unequally between men and women. Many of both sexes thought a woman's place was in the home, "queen of a little house—no matter how humble —where there are children rolling on the floor." When employed in factories, women tended to occupy jobs that were viewed as natural extensions of household activity. They made clothes and textiles, processed food, and made cigars, tobacco, and shoes. In the ladies' garment industry, which employed large numbers of women, they were the sewers and finishers, jobs that paid less; men were the higher-paid cutters and pressers.

In *The Long Day: The Story of a New York Working Girl as Told by Herself* (1906), the girl, a young schoolteacher, earned $2.50 a week, paid $1.00 for her room, and had $1.50 for food, clothes, carfare, and any social life. For breakfast she had bread, butter, and coffee; for lunch bread and butter; for dinner potato soup, bread, and butter. In Pittsburgh a worker in a pickle factory said of her day: "I have stood ten hours; I have fitted 1,300 corks; I have hauled and loaded 4,000 jars of pickles. My pay is seventy cents." Exhausted, such workers fell into bed at night and crawled out again at dawn to begin another "long day."

In general, adults earned more than children, the skilled more than the unskilled, native-born more than foreign-born, Protestants more than Catholics or Jews, and whites more than blacks and Asians. On average, women made a little more than half as much as men, according to contemporary estimates. In some cases, employers defended the differences—the foreign-born, for example, might not speak English—but most simply reflected bias against race, creed, or sex. In the industrial society white, native-born Protestants—the bulk of the population—reaped the greatest rewards.

Blacks labored on the fringes, usually in menial occupations. The last hired and first fired, they earned less than other workers at almost every level of skill. On the Pacific Coast, the Chinese—and later the Japanese—lived in enclaves and

This anti-Chinese cartoon in a weekly newspaper in San Francisco in 1877 shows the depth of workingmen's prejudice against Asians.

suffered periodic attacks of discrimination. In 1879 the Workingmen's party of California got a provision in the state constitution forbidding corporations to employ Chinese, and in 1882 Congress prohibited the immigration of Chinese workers for ten years.

Culture of Work

Among almost all groups, industrialization shattered age-old patterns, including work habits and the culture of work, as Herbert G. Gutman, a social historian, has noted. It made people adapt "older work routines to new necessities and strained those wedded to premodern patterns of labor." Adaptation was difficult and often demeaning. Virtually everyone went through it, and newcomers repeated the experiences of those who came before.

Men and women fresh from farms were not accustomed to the factory's disciplines. Now they worked indoors rather than out, paced themselves to the clock rather than the movements of the sun, and followed the needs of the market rather than the natural rhythms of the seasons. They had foremen and hierarchies and strict rules. Piece work determined wages, and always —as Morris Rosenfeld, a clothing presser, wrote— there was the relentless clock:

The Clock in the workshop,—it rests not a moment;
It points on, and ticks on: eternity-time;
Once someone told me the clock had a meaning,—
In pointing and ticking had reason and rhyme. . . .
At times, when I listen, I hear the clock plainly;—
The reason of old—the old meaning—is gone!
The maddening pendulum urges me forward
To labor and still labor on.
The tick of the clock is the boss in his anger.
The face of the clock has the eyes of the foe.
The clock—I shudder—Dost hear how it draws me?
It calls me "Machine" and it cries [to] me "Sew"!

As industries grew larger, work became more impersonal. Machines displaced skilled artisans, and the unskilled tended them for employers they never saw. Workers picked up and left their jobs with startling frequency, and factories drew on a churning, highly mobile labor supply. Historian Stephan Thernstrom, who has carefully studied the census records, found that only about half the people recorded in any census still lived in the same community ten years later. "The country had an enormous reservoir of restless and foot-loose men, who could be lured to new destinations when opportunity beckoned."

Thernstrom and others have also found substantial economic and social mobility. The Horatio Alger stories, of course, had always said so, and careers like Andrew Carnegie's—the impoverished immigrant boy who made good— seemed to confirm it. The actual record was considerably more limited. Most business leaders in the period came from well-to-do or middle-class families of old American stock. Of 360 iron and steel barons in Pittsburgh, Carnegie's own city, only 5 fit the Carnegie characteristics, and one of those was Carnegie himself. Still, if few workers became steel magnates, many workers made major progress during their lifetimes. In Thernstrom's study, he discovered that a quarter of the manual laborers rose to middle-class posi-

tions, and working-class children were even more likely to move up the ladder. In Boston about half the Jewish immigrants rose from manual to middle-class jobs, and English, Irish, and Italian immigrants were not far behind.

The chance for advancement played a vital role in American industrial development. It gave workers hope, wedded them to the system, and tempered their response to the appeal of labor unions and working-class agitation. Very few workers rose from rags to riches, but a great many rose to better jobs and higher status.

Labor Unions

Weak throughout the nineteenth century, labor unions never included more than 2 percent of the total labor force nor more than 10 percent of industrial workers. To many workers, unions seemed "foreign," radical, and out of step with the American tradition of individual advancement. Craft, ethnic, and other differences fragmented the labor force, and its extraordinary mobility made organization difficult. Employers opposed unions. "I have always had one rule," said an executive of U.S. Steel. "If a worker sticks up his head, hit it."

As the national economy emerged, however, national labor unions gradually took shape. The early unions often represented skilled workers in local areas, but in 1866 William H. Sylvis, a Pennsylvania iron-molder, united several unions into a single national organization, the National Labor Union. Like many of the era's labor leaders, Sylvis sought long-range humanitarian reforms, such as the establishment of workers' cooperatives, rather than specific, bread-and-butter goals. A talented propagandist, he attracted many members—some 640,000 by 1868—but he died in 1869, and the organization did not long survive him.

The year Sylvis died, Uriah S. Stephens and a group of Philadelphia garment workers founded a far more successful organization, the Noble and Holy Order of the Knights of Labor. A secret fraternal order, it grew slowly through the 1870s, until Terence V. Powderly, the new Grand Master Workman elected in 1879, ended the secrecy and embarked on an aggressive program. Wanting to unite all labor, the Knights welcomed everyone who "toiled," regardless of skill, creed, sex, or color. Unlike most unions they organized female workers, and at their peak they had 60,000 black members.

Harking back to the Jacksonians, the Knights set the "producers" against monopoly and special privilege. As members they excluded only "nonproducers"—bankers, lawyers, liquor dealers, and gamblers. Since employers were "producers," they could join; and since workers and employers had common interests, workers should not strike. The order's platform included the eight-hour day and the abolition of child and prisoner labor, but more often it focused on uplifting, utopian reform. Powderly, the eloquent and idealistic leader, spun dreams of a new era of harmony and cooperation. He wanted to sweep away trusts and end drunkenness. Workers should pool their resources, establish worker-run factories, railroads, and mines, and escape from the wage system. "The aim of the Knights of Labor— properly understood—is to make each man his own employer," Powderly said.

Membership grew steadily—from 42,000 in 1882 to 110,000 in 1885. In March 1885, ignoring Powderly's dislike of strikes, local Knights in Saint Louis, Kansas City, and other cities won a victory against Jay Gould's Missouri Pacific Railroad, and membership soared. It soon reached almost 730,000 but neither Powderly nor the union's loose structure could handle the growth. In 1886 the wily Gould struck back, crushing the

■ *Women delegates at a national meeting of the Knights of Labor in 1886. Women belonged to separate associations affiliated with local all-male unions.*

Knights on the Texas and Pacific Railroad, and the boom was over. By 1890 the order had shrunk to 100,000 members, and a few years later it was virtually defunct.

Even as the Knights waxed and waned, another organization emerged that was to endure. Founded in 1881, the American Federation of Labor (AFL) was a loose alliance of national craft unions. Unlike the Knights, the AFL rejected industrial unionism. It organized only skilled workers along craft lines, avoided politics, and worked for specific practical objectives. "I have my own philosophy and my own dreams," Samuel Gompers, the founder and longtime president, said, "but first and foremost I want to increase the workingman's welfare year by year."

Born in a London tenement in 1850, Gompers was a child of the union movement. Settling in New York, he worked as a cigarmaker, took an active hand in union activities, and flirted for a time with socialism and working-class politics. As leader of the AFL, he adopted a pragmatic approach to labor's needs. Gompers accepted capitalism and did not argue for fundamental chang-

Rise and Decline of the Knights of Labor

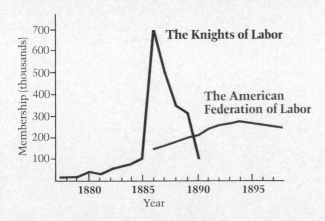

Source: From Leo Wolman, The Growth of American Trade Unions, *1924.*

es in it. For labor he wanted simply a recognized place within the system and a greater share of the rewards.

Unlike Powderly, Gompers and the AFL assumed that most workers would remain workers throughout their lives. The task, then, lay in improving lives in "practical" ways: higher wages, shorter hours, and better working conditions. They offered some attractive assurances to employers. As trade unionists, they would use the strike and boycott, but only to achieve limited gains, and if treated fairly, they would provide a stable labor force. They would not oppose monopolies and trusts, as Gompers said, "so long as we obtain fair wages."

By the 1890s the AFL was the most important labor group in the country, and Gompers, the guiding spirit, stayed its president, except for one year, until his death in 1924. Membership expanded from 140,000 in 1886, past 250,000 in 1892, to over a million by 1901. The AFL then included almost a third of the country's skilled workers. By 1914 it had over 2 million members. The great majority of workers—skilled and unskilled—remained unorganized, but Gompers and the AFL had become a significant force in national life.

Few unions allowed women to join. The Knights of Labor had a Department of Woman's Work headed by Leonora M. Barry, a shrewd, enthusiastic organizer who established a dozen women's locals and investigated the condition of women's labor. The AFL either ignored or opposed women workers. Only two of its national affiliates—the Cigar Makers' Union and the Typographical Union—accepted women as members; others prohibited them outright, and Gompers himself often complained that women workers undercut the pay scales for men. Conditions improved after 1900, but even then unions were largely a man's world. The AFL did not expressly forbid black workers from joining, but member unions used high initiation fees, technical examinations, and other means to discourage black membership.

Labor Unrest

Workers used various means to adjust to the factory age. To the dismay of managers and "effi-ciency" experts, they often dictated the pace and quality of their work, and they set the tone of the workplace. Newly arrived immigrants got jobs for friends and relatives, taught them how to deal with factory conditions, and humanized the workplace.

Many employers believed in an "iron law of wages" in which supply and demand, not the welfare of their workers, dictated wages. "If I wanted boiler iron," a steelmaker said, "I would go out on the market and buy where I could get it the cheapest, and if I wanted to employ men I would do the same thing." Wanting a docile labor force, employers fired workers who joined unions, hired scabs to replace strikers, and used a powerful new weapon, the court injunction, to quell strikes. The injunction, which forbade workers to interfere with their employers' business, was used to break the great Pullman strike of 1894 (see chapter 20), and the Supreme Court upheld use of the injunction in *In re Debs* (1895). Court decisions also affected the legal protection offered to workers. In *Holden* v. *Hardy* (1896), the Court upheld a law limiting working hours for miners, but in *Lochner* v. *New York* (1905) it struck down a law limiting bakery workers to a sixty-hour week and ten-hour day.

As employers' attitudes hardened, strikes and violence broke out. Between 1880 and 1900 there were more than 23,000 strikes involving 6.6 million workers. The railroad strike of 1877 (see the special feature in this chapter) paralyzed railroads from West Virginia to California, resulted in the deaths of over 100 workers, and required federal troops to suppress it. Another outburst of labor unrest occurred during the mid-1880s; in 1886, the peak year, 610,000 workers were off the job because of strikes and lockouts.

The worst incident took place at Haymarket Square in Chicago. In early May 1886 police, intervening in a strike at the McCormick Harvester works, shot and killed two workers. The next evening, May 4, labor leaders called a protest meeting at Haymarket Square near downtown Chicago. The meeting was peaceful, even a bit dull; about three thousand people were there. Police ordered them to disperse; someone threw a dynamite bomb which instantly killed one policeman and fatally wounded six others. Police fired into the crowd and killed four people.

No one ever discovered who threw the bomb,

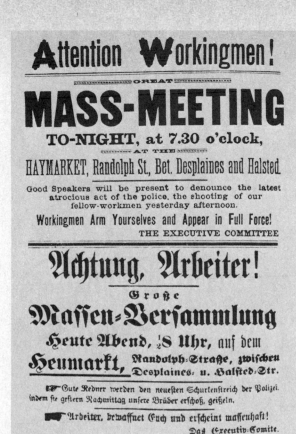

■ *Anarchists called for a protest meeting and distributed these bilingual handbills on the day of the Haymarket Square bombing in 1886.*

Steel Workers, an AFL affiliate, struck, and Frick responded by locking the workers out of the plant. The workers surrounded it, and Frick, furious, hired a small private army of Pinkerton detectives to drive them off. But alert workers spotted the approaching detectives, pinned them down with gunfire, and forced them to surrender. Three detectives and ten workers died in the battle.

A few days later the Pennsylvania governor ordered the state militia to impose peace at Homestead. On July 23 an anarchist named Alexander Berkman, who was not one of the strikers, walked into Frick's office and shot him. He fired twice, then stabbed him several times. Incredibly, Frick survived, watched the police take Berkman away, called in a doctor to bandage his wounds, and stayed in the office until closing time. "I do not think I shall die," he told reporters. "But if I

but many Americans—not just business leaders—demanded action against labor "radicalism." Cities strengthened their police forces and armories. In Chicago donors helped to establish nearby Fort Sheridan and the Great Lakes Naval Training Station to curb social turmoil. Uncertain who threw the bomb, Chicago police rounded up eight anarchists who were found guilty of murder. Four were hanged, one committed suicide, and three remained in jail until pardoned by the governor in 1893. Linking labor and anarchism in the public mind, the Haymarket Riot weakened the national labor movement.

Violence again broke out in the unsettled conditions of the 1890s. In 1892 federal troops crushed a strike of silver miners in the Coeur d'Alene district of Idaho. That same year Carnegie and Henry Clay Frick, his partner and manager, lowered wages nearly 20 percent at the Homestead steel plant. The Amalgamated Iron and

■ *This engraving in* Harper's Weekly, *July 16, 1892, depicts the surrender of Pinkerton detectives after a bloody battle with Homestead strikers. Thirteen men lay dead; ten strikers and three detectives. The strikers' victory was only temporary.*

The Great Railroad Strike of 1877

On May 24, 1877, in the midst of a nationwide depression, the Pennsylvania Railroad announced a 10 percent cut in pay. At the time engineers made about $3.25 a day for a twelve-hour day, conductors $2.75, firemen $1.90, and brakemen $1.75. Other railroads also cut pay; the Baltimore & Ohio announced cuts totaling 20 percent. For firemen and brakemen on the B & O, that meant a wage of $.90 a day.

Those wages hurt. As a worker on the B & O said: "We eat our hard bread and tainted meat two days on the sooty cars up the road, and when we come home, find our children gnawing bones and our wives complaining that they cannot even buy hominy and molasses for food."

When pay cuts on the B & O took effect on July 16, anger erupted. In Martinsburg, West Virginia, after one train crew walked off the job leaving their cattle train standing on the tracks, the stoppage spread to other crews. Trains backed up for two miles east and west of town, and at the request of B & O officials, the governor of West Virginia called out the state militia.

The next day, the militia stood guard as another crew took over the cattle train. Strikers boarded the train, and one of them fired a pistol. His fire was returned, and he fell, mortally wounded. The militiamen, many of them sympathetic to the strike, turned and left the yards. Alarmed,

West Virginia's governor called for federal troops to protect railroad property. President Rutherford B. Hayes hesitated, but on July 18 he issued the orders. For the first time since the 1830s the army was ordered out in peacetime to quell a strike.

As the strike spread along the B & O, jeering crowds threw stones at passing freights. At Cumberland, Maryland, west of Martinsburg, only one freight in sixteen got through. On July 20 the governor of Maryland, too, ordered out the state militia. As one regiment emerged from the Garden Street Armory in Baltimore, the city's factories let out for the day. Homeward-bound workers pelted the bewildered soldiers with stones. Blocks away, several thousand people penned up another regiment. Shooting started, and when it ended, eleven civilians were dead and forty were wounded. At the request of Maryland's governor, President Hayes that night sent army units to Baltimore. Portions of two states were now under federal protection.

The strike spread westward through New York, Pennsylvania, and Ohio. In each one of those states the militia was called out. Workers on the giant Pennsylvania system stayed on the job until Robert Pitcairn, the aggressive superintendent of the Pittsburgh division, ordered double-headers—trains with two locomotives—on all eastbound freights. Double-headers pulled more freight and required fewer crewmen, but they were difficult to handle.

The morning the order took effect, Augustus Harris, a veteran flagman, refused to take out the 8:40 double-header. Workers and sympathizers blocked the 9:40 trains; incoming crews joined the shutdown. At noon men from the steel mills mingled in the crowd.

During the night Pennsylvania state officials ordered in two trainloads of militia from Philadelphia to clear the key Twenty-eighth Street railroad crossing. Several thousand people massed at the crossing and on the hillsides above. There were revolver shots, and the militia opened fire. Within minutes, twenty people lay dead, including a woman and three small children. Fifteen soldiers were hurt.

The strike spread. On Monday, July 23, the New York Central, a vital link between New York City and Chicago, shut down. Cleveland, Buffalo, and other cities were cut off from fuel and supplies. The next day, a general strike paralyzed Saint Louis, and strikes hit major railroads to the West. That night, all freight traffic in and out of Chicago, a vital railroad hub, came to a halt.

Chicago factories closed; angry crowds paraded through the streets. Bankers and lawyers armed themselves with Springfield rifles from nearby government arsenals. On Wednesday evening, July 25, violence broke out when excited policemen fired into a crowd. Citizens' militias and working people battled across the city. Shooting continued through the next day; eighteen people died.

Determined to stop the violence, President Hayes sent six companies of soldiers to Chicago and ordered the army to open the Pennsylvania line between Philadelphia and Pittsburgh. On Saturday, July 28, the break came. Nine days after the original order, the first double-header left Pittsburgh with thirty-four cars of cattle and two cars of troops.

Within a matter of days the anger was spent and the Great Strike was over. It lasted about two weeks, touched eleven states, and affected two thirds of the country's railroad track. According to one estimate, it involved over 80,000 railroad workers and 500,000 workers in other occupations. More than a hundred people died.

Some employers responded to the strike by tightening hiring procedures, cracking down on labor unions, and stengthening police forces. Others, eager to avert another conflict, took measures to alleviate grievances. By 1880 most of the railroads had raised pay scales to earlier levels.

Many people here and abroad studied the significance of the strike. Did it mean, as some suggested, that war between capital and labor had begun? Did industrialization inevitably involve class dislocation, class tensions, and violence? Were federal troops required to maintain peace in the new industrial society?

Railroad strike violence: (above) devastation in Pittsburgh's railroad yards after a night of bloodshed; (opposite) Cincinnati's Union Station on fire.

Answers differed. One response was heightened demands for government intervention to regulate railroads and thereby lessen the hardships brought on by rapid industrial growth.

But like most events, the strike had the greatest impact on ordinary individuals whose opinions went unrecorded. In moments of individual decision, they stranded trains in Martinsburg, closed factories in Chicago, and shut down entire railroad networks.

Chronology

1859 First oil well drilled near Titusville, Pennsylvania

1866 William Sylvis establishes National Labor Union

1869 Transcontinental railroad completed at Promontory Point, Utah
Knights of Labor organize

1876 Alexander Graham Bell invents the telephone
Centennial Exposition held in Philadelphia

1877 Railroads cut workers' wages, leading to bloody and violent strike

1879 Thomas A. Edison invents the incandescent lamp

1881 Samuel Gompers founds American Federation of Labor (AFL)

1882 Rockefeller's Standard Oil Company becomes nation's first trust
Edison opens first electric generating station in New York

1883 Railroads introduce standard time zones

1886 Labor protest erupts in violence in Haymarket Riot in Chicago
Railroads adopt standard gauge

1892 Workers strike at Homestead steel plant in Pennsylvania

1901 J. P. Morgan announces formation of U.S. Steel Corporation, nation's first billion-dollar company

the American promise of abundance. National wealth grew from $16 billion in 1860 to $88 billion in 1900; wealth per capita more than doubled. For the bulk of the population, the standard of living—a particularly American concept—rose.

But industrialization also meant rapid change, social instability, exploitation of labor, and growing disparity in income between rich and poor. Industry flourished, but control rested in fewer and fewer hands. Maturing quickly, the young system became a new corporate capitalism: giant businesses, interlocking in ownership, managed by a new professional class, and selling an expanding variety of goods in an increasingly controlled market. As goods spread through the society, so did a sharpened, aggressive materialism. Workers felt the strains of the shift to a new social order. Now, in the last three decades of the century, Americans had to learn how to adjust to life in the industrial society.

Recommended Reading

Samuel P. Hays, *The Response to Industrialism: 1885–1914* (1957) is an influential interpretation of the period. A detailed survey is Edward C. Kirkland, *Industry Comes of Age: Business, Labor, and Public Policy, 1860–1897* (1967). Douglass C. North, *Growth and Welfare in the American Past: A New Economic History* (1966) is stimulating. Other valuable overviews include Stuart Bruchey's brief *Growth of the Modern Economy* (1975), W. Elliot Brownlee's more detailed *Dynamics of Ascent: A History of the American Economy* (1974), and Robert Higgs, *The Transformation of the American Economy, 1865–1914* (1971).

For stimulating interpretations of the period, see Robert H. Wiebe, *The Search for Order, 1877–1920* (1968) and John A. Garraty, *The New Commonwealth, 1877–1890* (1968). Thomas C. Cochran and William Miller, *The Age of Enterprise* (1942) and Alfred D. Chandler, *The Visible Hand: The Managerial Revolution in American Business* (1978) are perceptive. The railroad empire is treated in G. R. Taylor and I. D. Neu, *The American Railroad Network, 1861–1890* (1956) and John F. Stover, *American Railroads* (1961). On the steel industry, see Peter Temin, *Iron and Steel in Nineteenth-Century America* (1964) and Joseph F. Wall, *Andrew Carnegie* (1970).

For the techniques of selling, see Daniel J. Boorstin, *The Americans: The Democratic Experience* (1973). Two superb books by Sam B. Warner, Jr., *Streetcar Suburbs: The Process of Growth in Boston, 1870–1900* (1962) and *The Urban Wilderness: A History of the American City* (1973), examine technology and city

do or not, the company will pursue the same policy and it will win." In late July the Homestead works reopened under military guard, and in November the strikers gave up.

Events like those at Homestead troubled many Americans who wondered whether industrialization, for all its benefits, might carry a heavy price in social upheaval, class tensions, and even outright warfare. Most workers did not share in the immense profits of the industrial age, and as the nineteenth century came to a close, there were some who rebelled against the inequity.

In the half-century after the Civil War, the United States became an industrial nation—the leading one, in fact, in the world. On one hand, industrialization meant "progress," growth, world power, and in some sense, fulfillment of

development. The wage earner is examined in Herbert G. Gutman, *Work, Culture, and Society in Industrializing America* (1976) and in two books by Stephan Thernstrom: *Poverty and Progress: Social Mobility in the Nineteenth-Century City* (1964) and *The Other Bostonians: Poverty and Progress in the American Metropolis, 1880–1970* (1973). Philip S. Foner, *Women and the American Labor Movement*, 2 vols. (1979); Lois W. Banner, *Women in Modern America: A Brief History* (1974); and Milton Cantor and Bruce Laurie, eds., *Class, Sex, and the Woman Worker* (1977) are excellent.

Additional Bibliography

Alfred D. Chandler, *The Railroads: The Nation's First Big Business* (1965), stresses the railroads' importance; Robert Fogel, *Railroads in American Economic Growth* (1964), questions it. Julius Grodinsky, *Jay Gould* (1957) and Albro Martin, *James J. Hill and the Opening of the Northwest* (1976) are superb.

For steel, see Carnegie's *Autobiography of Andrew Carnegie* (1920); Harold C. Livesay, *Andrew Carnegie and the Rise of Big Business* (1975); and John Ingham, *The Iron Barons: A Social Analysis of an American Urban Elite, 1874–1965* (1978). For the oil industry, see Carl Solberg, *Oil Power* (1976); H. F. Williamson and A. R. Daum, *The American Petroleum Industry: Age of Illumination* (1959); and Allan Nevins, *Study in Power: John D. Rockefeller*, 2 vols. (1953). For Morgan, see Lewis Corey, *The House of Morgan* (1930) and Frederick Lewis Allen, *The Great Pierpont Morgan* (1949).

On technological developments, Lewis Mumford, *Technics and Civilization* (1934); Charles Singer et al., eds., *History of Technology*, vol. 5, *The Late Nineteenth Century, c. 1850 to c. 1900* (1958); and W. P. Strassmann, *Risk and Technological Innovation: American Manufacturing Methods During the Nineteenth Century* (1959) are the places to begin. Useful studies include Matthew Josephson, *Edison* (1959); H. G. Prout, *A Life of George Westinghouse* (1921); John Brooks, *Telephone: The First Hundred Years* (1976); and Robert V. Bruce, *Alexander Graham Bell and the Conquest of Solitude* (1973).

Frank Presbrey, *The History and Development of Advertising* (1929) is the best general account; others include J. P. Wood, *The Story of Advertising* (1958); Ralph M. Hower, *History of Macy's of New York, 1858–1919* (1943); John K. Winkler, *Five and Ten: The Fabulous Life of F. W. Woolworth* (1940); and Boris Emmet and John E. Jeuck, *Catalogues and Counters: A History of Sears, Roebuck and Company* (1950). Also, David M. Potter, *People of Plenty: Economic Abundance and the American Character* (1954).

On labor, see David Brody, *Steelworkers in America: The Nonunion Era* (1960); Gerald N. Grob, *Workers and Utopia: A Study of Ideological Conflict in the American Labor Movement, 1865–1900* (1961); N. J. Ware, *The Labor Movement in the United States, 1860–1893* (1929); and S. B. Kaufman, *Samuel Gompers and the Origins of the American Federation of Labor* (1973). John Laslett, *Labor and the Left: A Study of Socialist and Radical Influences in the American Labor Movement, 1881–1924* (1970) is illuminating. Terence V. Powderly, *Thirty Years of Labor* (1889) and Samuel Gompers, *Seventy Years of Life and Labor*, 2 vols. (1925), give the flavor of their thought.

chapter 19

TOWARD AN URBAN SOCIETY:
1877–1890

Life in the United States, said the perceptive English statesman and historian James Bryce in the 1880s, "is in most ways pleasanter, easier, simpler than in Europe; it floats in a sense of happiness like that of a radiant summer morning."

Between 1877 and 1890 factories poured out consumer goods, and the newly invented cash registers rang up sale after sale. Electric lights and telephones enhanced social life. People eager for amusement discovered baseball, bicycling, and the great traveling circus. Public and private educational systems burgeoned; illiteracy declined. Life expectancy increased. "The old nations of the earth creep on at a snail's pace," wrote Andrew Carnegie in *Triumphant Democracy* (1886), "the Republic thunders past with the rush of an express."

Other voices raised somber warnings. "The time was," said Congressman John Reagan of Texas in 1877, "when none were poor and none rich. . . . Then the few became fabulously rich, the many wretchedly poor . . . and the poorer we are the poorer they would make us." In the 1870s and '80s social critics and reformers like Henry George, Edward Bellamy, Jacob Riis, and others poked among the dark corners of American life and questioned what they saw.

Opportunity was not open to all; wealth was an elusive goal. Corruption strained the political system, hard-pressed to respond to the extraordinary pace of change. Crime and violence were everywhere on the rise—among urban street gangs, Western bandits and vigilantes, and Southern night riders. Cities virtually exploded in population, and immigrants crowded by the millions into slums. Men, women, and children worked in factories from dawn to dusk; work-related accidents took an appalling toll of lives and limbs.

"Amid the greatest accumulations of wealth," wrote Henry George in *Progress and Poverty* (1879), one of the era's most influential books, "men die of starvation, and puny infants suckle dry breasts. . . . The promised land flies before us like a mirage." George described America as "the House of Have and the House of Want," almost in paraphrase of Lincoln's earlier metaphor of the "house divided." Could this house, unlike that one, stand?

Life in America, 1877

From 1877 to the 1890s the nation underwent sweeping changes that affected economic, political, and social life. Technology changed mores; bright lights and new careers drew young men and women to the cities; family ties loosened. Cities, suburbs, and factories took new forms. While many people worked harder and harder, others had increased leisure time. The roles of women and children changed in a number of ways, and immigrants molded the society and in turn were molded by it.

"We are in a period," President Rutherford B. Hayes said in 1878, "when old questions are settled, and the new ones are not yet brought forward." Old questions—questions of racial, social and economic justice, and of federal-state relations—were not settled, but people wanted new directions. Political issues lost the sharp focus of the Civil War and Reconstruction. For men and women of middle age in 1877, the issues of the Union and slavery had been the overriding public concerns throughout their adult lives. Now, with the end of Reconstruction, it seemed time for new concerns.

Change and movement were everywhere, in cities and factories, on farms that sprinkled the Western prairies, and along railroad tracks pushing into unsettled domain. Thanks to advancing technology, news flashed quickly across the oceans, and for the first time in history people shook open their evening newspapers to read of that day's events in distant lands.

In 1877 the country had 47 million people. A little more than a decade later there were nearly 63 million. Nine tenths of the population was white; just under one tenth was black. There were 66,000 Indians, 108,000 Chinese, and 148 Japanese. The bulk of the white population, most of whom were Protestant, came from the so-called Anglo-Saxon countries of northern Europe. WASPs—White Anglo-Saxon Protestants—dominated American society.

Most people still lived on farms or in small towns. Their lives revolved around the farm, the church, and the general store. In 1880 nearly 75 percent of the population lived in communities of fewer than twenty-five hundred people. In 1900, in the midst of city growth, 60 percent still did. The average family in 1880 had three children, and life expectancy was about forty-three years. By 1900 it had risen to forty-seven years, the result of improved health care. For blacks and other minorities, often living in unsanitary rural areas, life expectancy was substantially lower: thirty-three years in 1900.

Houses were usually made of wooden shingles or clapboard, set back from unpaved streets, whose dusty surfaces muffled the sounds of passing horses. Life was quiet. Many homes had a front porch for summertime sitting. In the backyard there were numerous outbuildings, including one—at the end of a well-worn path—with a

■ *State Street, Jacksonville, 1889. The quiet, tree-lined street reflects the unhurried pace of life in small-town America in the late nineteenth century.*

distinctive half-moon carved in the door. There was a vegetable garden and often a chicken coop or cowshed; families—even in the cities—needed backyard produce to supplement their diet. Inside the house, life centered in the kitchen with its enormous wood or coal stove.

Meals tended to be heavy and so did people. Even breakfast had several courses and could include steak, eggs, fish, potatoes, toast, and coffee. Food prices were low. Families ate fresh homegrown produce in the summer, and "put up" fruits and vegetables for the long winters. Toward the end of the century eating habits changed. New packaged breakfast cereals became popular; fresh fruit and vegetables came in on fast trains from Florida and California, and commercially canned food processing became safer and cheaper. The newfangled icebox, cooled by blocks of ice, kept food fresher and added new treats like ice cream.

Medical science was in the midst of a major revolution. Louis Pasteur's recent discovery that germs cause infection and disease created the new science of microbiology and led the way to the development of vaccines and other preventive measures. But tuberculosis, typhoid, diphtheria, and pneumonia—all are now curable—were still the leading causes of death. Many families knew the wrenching pain of a child's death. Infant mortality declined between 1877 and 1900, but the decline was gradual; the great drop did not come until after 1920.

1890 Retail Prices: Food

BACON	1 lb.	**15.5¢**
BUTTER	1 lb.	**25.5¢**
EGGS	1 dozen	**20.8¢**
FLOUR	5 lbs.	**14.5¢**
MILK	½ gal. delivered	**13.6¢**
PORK CHOPS	1 lb.	**10.7¢**
POTATOES	10 lbs.	**16¢**
ROUND STEAK	1 lb.	**12.3¢**
SUGAR	5 lbs.	**34.5¢**

Source: U.S. Bureau of the Census, Historical Statistics of the United States, Colonial Times to 1970, *Bicentennial Edition, Washington, D.C., 1975.*

There were few hospitals and no hospital insurance. Most patients stayed at home, although medical practice, especially surgery, expanded rapidly. Once brutal and dangerous, surgery in these years became relatively safe and painless. Anesthetics—ether and chloroform—eliminated pain, and antiseptic practices helped prevent postoperative infections. Antiseptic practices at childbirth also cut down on puerperal fever, an infection that for centuries had killed many women and newborn infants. An earlier discovery—nitrous oxide, called laughing gas—eased the discomfort of dentistry. The new science of psychology began to explore the mind, hitherto uncharted (see the special feature on pp. 564–65). William James, a leading American psychologist and philosopher, laid the foundations of modern behaviorist psychology, which stressed the importance of the environment on human development.

Manners and Mores

The code of Victorian morality, its name derived from the British queen who reigned throughout the period, set the tone for the era. The code prescribed stern standards of dress, manners, and sexual behavior. It was both obeyed and disobeyed, and it reflected the tensions of a generation that was undergoing a change in moral standards.

In 1877 children were to be seen and not heard. They spoke when spoken to, listened rather than chattered—or at least that was the rule. Older boys and girls were often chaperoned, although they could always find moments alone. They played post office and spin the bottle; they puffed cigarettes behind the barn. William Allen White, later a famous journalist, recalled the high jinks of his boyhood. He and his friends smeared their naked bodies with mud and leaped out in full view of passengers on passing trains. Counterbalancing such youthful exuberance was strong pride in virtue and self-control. "Thank heaven I am absolutely pure," Theodore Roosevelt, the future president, wrote in 1880 after proposing to Alice Lee. "I can tell Alice everything I have ever done."

Gentlemen of the middle class dressed in heavy black suits, derby hats, and white shirts with

■ *The slightest exertion on the part of women who wore the fashionable, tightly laced, steel-and-whalebone corset was likely to bring on a fainting spell.*

paper collars. Women wore tight corsets, long, dark dresses, and black shoes reaching well above the ankles. As with so many things, styles changed dramatically toward the end of the century, spurred in part by new sporting fads such as golf, tennis, and bicycling, which required looser clothing. By the 1890s a middle-class woman wore a tailored suit or a dark skirt and a blouse, called a "shirtwaist," modeled after men's shirts. Her skirts still draped about the ankles, but more and more she removed or loosened the corset, the dread device that squeezed skin and internal organs into fashionable eighteen-inch waistlines.

Religious and patriotic values were strong. One of the centers of community life, the church often set the tenor for family and social relationships. On Sundays the family dressed in Sunday-best and attended a long morning service, followed by Sunday dinner, naps, reading, and another church service in the evening. In the 1880s eight out of ten church members were Protestants; most of the rest were Roman Catholics. Evangelists like Dwight L. Moody, a former Chicago shoe salesman, and Ira B. Sankey, an organist and singer, conducted mass revival meetings across the country. Enormously successful, Moody preached to millions and sparked a spiritual awakening on American college campuses.

With slavery abolished, reformers turned their attention to new moral and political issues. One group, known as the Mugwumps, worked to end corruption in politics. Drawn mostly from the educated and upper class, they included individuals like Thomas Nast, the famous political cartoonist, George William Curtis, editor of *Harper's Weekly*, and E. L. Godkin, editor of the influential *Nation*. Other zealous reformers campaigned for prohibition of the sale of intoxicating liquors, hoping to end the social evils that stemmed from drunkenness. In 1874, women who advocated total abstinence from alcoholic beverages formed the Women's Christian Temperance Union. Their leader, Frances E. Willard, served as president of the group from 1879 until her death in 1898. By then the WCTU had 10,000 branches and 500,000 members.

In New York City, Anthony Comstock formed the Society for the Suppression of Vice, which supervised public morality. At his request Congress passed the Comstock Law (1873) prohibiting the mailing or transporting of "obscene, lewd or lascivious" articles. The law was not successful; within a few years Comstock reported finding 64,094 "articles for immoral use," 700 pounds of "lead moulds for making obscene matter," 202,679 obscene photographs, and 26 "obscene pictures, framed on walls of saloons."

Leisure and Entertainment

In the 1870s people tended to rise early. On getting up, they washed from the pitcher and bowl in the bedroom, first breaking the layer of ice if it was winter. In winter, they often left their clothes in the kitchen near the warmth of the stove. After dressing and eating, they went off to work and school; without large refrigerators, housewives marketed almost daily. In the evenings, families gathered in the "second parlor" or living room, where the children did their lessons, played games, sang around the piano, and listened to that day's verse from the Bible.

Popular games included cards, dominoes, backgammon, chess, and checkers. Many homes had a packet of "author cards" that required knowledge of books, authors, and noted quotations. The latest fad was the stereopticon or "magic lantern," which brought three-dimensional life to art, history, and nature. Like "author cards" and other games, it was instructional as well as entertaining.

The newest outdoor game was croquet, so popular that candles were mounted on the wickets to allow play at night. Croquet was the first outdoor game designed for play by both sexes, and it frequently served as a setting for courtship. Early manuals advised girls how to assume attractive poses while hitting the ball. A popular song of the period told of a pair seated side by side as the

mallets and balls unheeded lay . . .
and I thought to myself, is that Croquet?

American taste in the theater ran to intrigue, swordplay, melodrama, and grandiloquent language. New York's Broadway—known as the Great White Way because of the sparkling new gaslights—had seventeen theaters in the early 1870s. Road shows took popular plays to many cities and towns; in 1887 Edwin Booth, the period's most acclaimed actor (and the brother of Lincoln's assassin), played to packed houses all across the Midwest. Most plays were imported from Europe; the United States had few serious playwrights.

Sentimental ballads such as "Silver Threads Among the Gold" (1873) remained the most popular musical form, but the insistent syncopated rhythms of ragtime were being heard. By the time the strains of Scott Joplin's "Maple Leaf Rag" (1899) popularized ragtime, critics complained that "a wave of vulgar, filthy and suggestive music has inundated the land." Classical music flourished. The New England Conservatory (1867), the Cincinnati College of Music (1878), and the Metropolitan Opera (1883) were new sources of civic pride; New York, Boston, and Chicago launched first-rate symphony orchestras between 1878 and 1891.

In the hamlets and small towns of America traveling circuses were enormously popular. Hamlin Garland, an author who grew up in small Iowa villages, recalled how the circus came "trailing clouds of glorified dust and filling our minds with the color of romance. . . . It brought to our ears the latest band pieces and taught us the

■ *Below, the third baseman makes a bare-handed catch as the runner slides safely into base. Right, the high-wheeled bicycles the men are riding were called "ordinaries."*

popular songs. It furnished us with jokes. It relieved our dullness. It gave us something to talk about." Larger circuses, run by entrepreneurs like P. T. Barnum and James A. Bailey, played the cities, but every town attracted its own smaller version. When the circus was not in town, Buffalo Bill's Wild West Show was, reenacting Indian battles and displaying frontier marksmanship.

Fairs, horse races, balloon ascensions, bicycle tournaments, and football and baseball contests attracted avid fans. The years between 1870 and 1900 saw the rise of organized spectator sports, a trend reflecting the new uses of leisure. Baseball's first professional team, the Cincinnati Red Stockings, appeared in 1869, and baseball soon became the preeminent national sport. Fans sang songs about it ("Take Me Out to the Ballgame"), wrote poems about it ("Casey at the Bat"), and made up riddles about it ("What has eighteen feet and catches flies?"). Modern rules were adopted. Umpires were designated to call balls and strikes; catchers wore masks and chest protectors and moved closer to the plate instead of staying back to catch the ball on the bounce. Fielders had to catch the ball on the fly rather than on one

bounce in their caps. By 1890 professional baseball teams were drawing crowds of sixty thousand daily.

In 1869 Princeton and Rutgers played the first intercollegiate football game. Soon other schools picked up the sport, and by the early 1890s crowds of fifty thousand or more attended the most popular contests. Basketball, invented in 1891, gained a large following. Boxing, a popular topic of conversation in saloons and schoolyards, was outlawed in most states. For a time championship prizefights were held in secret, with news of the result spread rapidly by word-of-mouth. Matches were long and bloody, fought with bare knuckles until the invention in the 1880s of the five-ounce boxing glove. John L. Sullivan, the Boston Strong Boy and the era's most popular champion, won the heavyweight title in 1882 in a brutal seventy-five-round victory over the stubborn Jake Kilrain.

As gas and electric lights brightened the night, and streetcars crisscrossed city streets, leisure habits changed. Delighted with the new technology, people took advantage of an increasing variety of things to do. They stayed home less often.

Steam, steel, and electricity transformed cities. In this W. Louis Sonntag, Jr., watercolor of New York City's Bowery in 1895, electric streetcars travel up and down the street while the elevated railroad rumbles overhead. Bright incandescent lamps light up the night.

New York City's first electric sign—"Manhattan Beach Swept by Ocean Breezes"—appeared in 1881, and people filled the streets on their way to the theater, vaudeville shows, dance halls, or just out for an evening stroll.

Family Life

In 1873 a writer said: "Whatever tends to deteriorate the marriage relation and consequently the home, tends to deteriorate the whole machinery of life, whether social or political." Nonetheless, under the impact of industrialization and urbanization, family relationships were changing. On the farm parents and children worked more or less together, and the family was a producing unit. In factories, family members rarely worked together. In working-class families, mothers, fathers, and children separated at dawn and returned, ready for sleep, at dark. Morris Rosenfeld, a clothing presser, lamented in "My Boy":

I have a little boy at home,
A pretty little son;

I think sometimes the world is mine
In him, my only one. . . .

'Ere dawn my labor drives me forth;
Tis night when I am free;
A stranger am I to my child;
And stranger my child to me.

Middle-class fathers began to move their families out of the city to the suburbs, while they commuted to work on the new streetcars, leaving wives and children at home and school.

As the middle-class family's economic function declined, it took on increased emotional significance. "In the old days," said a woman in 1907, "a married woman was supposed to be a frump and a bore and a physical wreck. Now you are supposed to keep up intellectually, to look young and well and be fresh and bright and entertaining." Magazines like the *Ladies' Home Journal*, which started in 1889, glorified motherhood and the home, but its articles and ads featured women as homebound, child-oriented consumers. While society's leaders spoke fondly of the value of homemaking, the status of housewives declined under the factory system, which emphasized money rewards and devalued household labor.

In and out of the family, there was growing recognition of the self-sufficient working woman, employed in factory, telephone exchange, and business office, who was entering the work force in increasing numbers. In 1880 there were 2.6 million women gainfully employed; in 1890, 4 million. In 1882 the Census Bureau took the first census of working women; most were single and worked out of necessity rather than choice.

This "New Woman" was seen by many as a corruption of the ideal vision of the American woman, in which man worshipped "a diviner self than his own," innocent, helpless, and good. Women were to be better than the world around them. They were brought up, said Ida Tarbell, a leading political reformer who went through it herself, "as if wrongdoing were impossible to them."

■ *Women operators, called "Hello Girls," were hired to work telephone switchboards after it was discovered that male operators tended to argue too much with the subscribers.*

Views changed, albeit slowly. One important change occurred in the legal codes pertaining to women, particularly in the common law doctrine of *femme couverte*. Under that doctrine, wives were chattel of their husbands; they could not legally control their own earnings, property, or children unless they had drawn up a specific contract before marriage. By 1890 many states had substantially revised the doctrine to allow wives control of their earnings and inherited property. In cases of divorce, the new laws also recognized women's rights to custody or joint custody of their children. Although divorce was still far from being socially acceptable, divorce rates more than doubled during the last third of the century. By 1905 one in twelve marriages was ending in divorce.

In the 1870s and '80s a growing number of women were asserting their own humanness. They fought for the vote, lobbied for equal pay, and sought self-fulfillment. The new interest in psychology and medicine strengthened their cause. Charlotte Perkins Gilman, author of *Women and Economics* (1898), joined other women in questioning the ideal of womanly "innocence," which, she argued, actually meant ignorance. In medical and popular literature, menstruation, sexual intercourse, and childbirth were becoming viewed as natural functions instead of taboo topics.

Edward Bliss Foote's *Plain Home Talk of Love, Marriage, and Parentage*, a best-seller that went through many editions between the 1880s and 1900s, challenged Victorian notions that sexual intercourse was unhealthy and intended solely to produce children. In *Plain Facts for Old and Young* (1881), Dr. John H. Kellogg urged parents to recognize the early awakening of sexual feelings in their children. Still, such matters were avoided in many American homes. Rheta Childe Dorr, a journalist, remembered that when a girl reached the age of fourteen, new rules were introduced, "and when you asked for an explanation you met only embarrassed silence."

Women espoused causes with new fervor. Susan B. Anthony, a veteran of many reform campaigns, tried to vote in the 1872 presidential election and was fined $100, which she refused to pay. In 1890 she helped form the National American Woman Suffrage Association to work for the enfranchisement of women (see chapter 22). On

New York's Lower East Side, the Ladies Anti-Beef Trust Association, formed to protest increases in the price of meat, established a boycott of butcher shops. When their demands were ignored, the women invaded the shops, poured kerosene on the meat, and set fire to it. "We don't riot," Rebecca Ablowitz told the judge. "But if all we did was to weep at home, nobody would notice it; so we have to do something to help ourselves."

Educating the Masses

Continuing a trend that stretched back a hundred years, childhood was becoming a distinct time of life. There was still only a vague concept of adolescence—the special nature of the teen-age years—but the role of children was changing. Less and less were children perceived as "little adults," valued for the additional financial gain they might bring into the family. Now children were to grow and learn and be nurtured rather than rushed into adulthood.

As a result, schooling became more important and American educators came closer than ever before to universal education. By 1900, thirty-one states and territories (out of fifty-one) had enacted laws making school attendance compulsory. In 1870 there were only 160 public high schools; in 1900 there were 6000. In the same years, public school budgets rose from $63 million to $253 million; illiteracy declined from 20 percent to just over 10 percent of the population. Still, even as late as 1900, the average adult had only five years of schooling.

Most schools stressed a highly structured curriculum, focused on discipline and routine. In 1892 Joseph Rice, a pediatrician, toured twelve hundred classrooms in thirty-six cities. In a typical classroom, he reported, the atmosphere was "damp and chilly," the teacher strict. "The unkindly spirit of the teacher is strikingly apparent; the pupils being completely subjugated to her will, are silent and motionless." One teacher asked her pupils, "How can you learn anything with your knees and toes out of order?"

School began early; boys attended all day, but girls often stayed home after lunch, since it was thought they needed less in the way of learning. On the teacher's command, students stood and recited from *Webster's Spellers* and *McGuffey's*

■ *Although education was growing in importance, in most schools the emphasis continued to be on conformity and deportment with the teacher acting as drillmaster and disciplinarian.*

Readers, the period's most popular textbooks. The work of William Holmes McGuffey, a professor of languages at Miami University in Ohio, *McGuffey's Readers* had been in use since 1836 (see chapter 11); 100 million copies were sold in the last half of the nineteenth century. Nearly every child read them; they taught not only reading but also ethics, values, and religion. In the *Readers* boys grew up to be heroes, girls to be mothers, and hard work always meant success:

Shall birds, and bees, and ants, be wise,
* While I my moments waste?*
O let me with the morning rise,
* And to my duty haste.*

The South lagged far behind in education. Family size was about twice as large as in the North, and a greater proportion of the population lived in isolated rural areas. State and local authorities mandated fewer weeks in the average school year, and many southern states refused to adopt compulsory education laws. Most important, Southerners insisted on maintaining separate school systems to segregate the races. Supported by the

United States Supreme Court decision in *Plessy v. Ferguson* (1896), segregated schooling added a devastating financial burden to education in the South.

North Carolina and Alabama mandated segregated schools in 1876, South Carolina and Louisiana in 1877, Mississippi in 1878, and Virginia in 1882. The laws often implied that the schools would be "separate but equal," but they rarely were. Black schools were usually dilapidated, the teachers in them paid considerably less than white teachers. In 1890 only 35 percent of black children attended school in the South; 55 percent of white children did. That year nearly two thirds of the country's black population was illiterate.

Educational techniques changed after the 1870s. Educators paid more attention to early elementary education, a trend that placed young children in school and helped the growing number of mothers who worked outside the home. The kindergarten movement, started in Saint Louis in 1873, spread across the country. In kindergartens, four- to six-year olds learned by playing, not by keeping their knees and toes in order. For older children, Jane Addams and other reformers advocated "practical" courses in manual training and homemaking. "We are impatient with the schools which lay all stress on reading and writing," Addams said, for "they fail to give the child any clew to the life about him."

For the first time education became a field of university study. European theorists like Johann Friedrich Herbart, a German educator, argued that learning occurred best in an atmosphere of freedom and confidence between teachers and pupils. Teacher training became increasingly professional. Only 10 normal schools, or teacher-training institutions, existed in the United States before the Civil War. By 1900 there were 345, and one in every five elementary teachers had graduated from a professional school.

Higher Education

Nearly 150 new colleges and universities opened in the twenty years between 1880 and 1900. The Morrill Land Grant Act of 1862 gave large grants of land to the states for the establishment of colleges to teach "agriculture and the mechanic arts." The act fostered 69 "land-grant" institutions, including the great state universities of Wisconsin, California, Minnesota, and Illinois.

Private philanthropy, born of the large fortunes of the industrial age, also spurred growth in higher education. Leland Stanford gave $24 million to endow Stanford University on his California ranch, and John D. Rockefeller, founder of the Standard Oil Company, gave $34 million to found the University of Chicago. Other industrialists established Cornell (1865), Vanderbilt (1873), and Tulane (1884).

As colleges expanded, their function changed, and their curriculum broadened. No longer did they exist primarily to train young men for the ministry. They moved away from the classical curriculum of rhetoric, mathematics, Latin, and Greek toward "reality and practicality," as President David Starr Jordan of Stanford University said. The Massachusetts Institute of Technology (M.I.T.), founded in 1861, focused on science and engineering.

Influenced by the new German universities, which emphasized specialized research, Johns Hopkins University in Baltimore opened the nation's first separate graduate school in 1876. Under President Daniel Coit Gilman, Johns Hopkins stressed the seminar and laboratory as teaching tools, bringing together student and teacher in close association. By 1900 more than nine thousand Americans had studied in Germany, and some of them returned home to become presidents of institutions such as Harvard, Yale, Columbia, the University of Chicago, and Johns Hopkins.

One of them, Charles W. Eliot, who became president of Harvard in 1869 at the age of thirty-five, moved to end, as an admirer said, the "old fogyism" that marked the institution. Revising the curriculum, Eliot set up the elective system in which students chose their own courses rather than following a rigidly prescribed curriculum. Lectures and discussions replaced rote recitation, and courses in the natural and social sciences, fine arts, and modern languages multiplied. In the 1890s Eliot's Harvard moved to the forefront of educational innovation.

Before the Civil War, only three private colleges admitted women to study with men. After the war educational opportunities increased for women. A number of women's colleges opened, including Vassar (1865), Wellesley (1875), Smith

Unlike these Smith College chemistry students, most women who attended college in the 1870s and '80s were urged to take home economics rather than science courses.

W. E. B. Du Bois (top) argued against the accommodationist approach of Booker T. Washington and the emphasis on vocational training at Washington's Tuskegee Institute. Students in the wheelwright shop at Tuskegee are shown in the photo at bottom.

(1875), Bryn Mawr (1885), Barnard (1889), and Radcliffe (1893). The land-grant colleges of the Midwest, open to women from the outset, spurred a nationwide trend toward coeducation, although some physicians, like Harvard Medical School's Dr. Edward H. Clarke in his popular *Sex in Education* (1873), continued to argue that the strain of learning made women sterile. By 1900 women made up about 40 percent of college students, and four out of five colleges admitted them.

Fewer opportunities existed for blacks and other minorities. Mrs. Jane Stanford encouraged the Chinese who had worked on her husband's Central Pacific Railroad to apply to Stanford University, but her policy was unusual. Most colleges did not accept minorities, and few applied. W. E. B. Du Bois, the brilliant black sociologist and civil rights leader, attended Harvard in the late 1880s but found the society of Harvard Yard closed against him. Disdained and disdainful, he "asked no fellowship of my fellow students." Chosen as one of the commencement speakers, Du Bois picked as his topic, "Jefferson Davis," treating it, said an onlooker, with "an almost contemptuous fairness."

Black students turned to black colleges such as the Hampton Normal and Industrial Institute in Virginia and the Tuskegee Institute in Alabama. Booker T. Washington, an ex-slave, put into practice his educational ideas at Tuskegee, which opened in 1881. Washington began Tuskegee with limited funds, four run-down buildings, and only thirty students; by 1900 it was a model industrial and agricultural school. Spread over forty-six buildings, it offered instruction in thirty trades to fourteen hundred students.

Washington stressed patience, manual training, and hard work. "No race," he said in 1895, "can prosper till it learns that there is as much dignity in tilling a field as in writing a poem. It is at the bottom of life we must begin, and not at the top." Rather than fighting for equal rights, blacks should acquire property, improve themselves through self-help, and show they were worthy of their rights. Many whites and blacks welcomed this philosophy; Du Bois, on the other hand, charged that Washington would simply create a black working class to till the farms and tend the machines of white society. But Washington did believe in black equality, and he bespoke a racial pride that contributed to the rise of black nationalism in the twentieth century.

Throughout higher education there was increased emphasis on professional training, particularly in medicine, dentistry, and law. Enrollments swelled, even as standards of admission tightened. The number of medical schools in the country rose from 75 in 1870 to 160 in 1900, and the number of medical students—including more and more women—almost tripled. Schools of nursing grew from only 15 in 1880 to 432 in 1900. Doctors, lawyers, and others became part of a growing middle class that shaped the concerns of the Progressive era (see chapter 22).

Although fewer than 5 percent of the college-age population attended college during the 1877–1890 period, the new trends had great impact. A generation of men and women encountered new ideas that changed their views of themselves and society. Courses never before offered, like Philosophy II at Harvard, "The Ethics of Social Reform," which students called "drainage, drunkenness, and divorce," heightened interest in social problems and the need for reform. Some graduating students burned with a desire to cure society's ills. "My life began . . . at Johns Hopkins University," Frederic C. Howe, an influential reformer, recalled. "I came alive, I felt a sense of responsibility to the world, I wanted to change things."

The Lure of the City

William Allen White left the small Kansas town of his boyhood in 1891 to go to the "gilded metropolis" of Kansas City. White was twenty-three years old, and the experience affected him for the rest of his life. He rode the cable cars and used the newfangled telephone—"always with the consciousness that I was tampering with a miracle," he said of the phone. He purchased a second-hand dress suit, listened to the music of a sixty-piece orchestra, attended plays, and heard James Whitcomb Riley recite poetry. "Life was certainly one round of joy in Kansas City," White said.

Between 1870 and 1900 the city—like the factory—became a symbol of a new America. Drawn from farms, small towns and foreign lands, newcomers swelled the population of older cities and created new ones almost overnight. At the beginning of the Civil War only one sixth of the American people lived in cities of 8,000 people or more. By 1900, one third did; by 1910, one half. "We live in the age of great cities," wrote the Reverend Samuel Lane Loomis in 1887. "Each successive year finds a stronger and more irresistible current sweeping in towards the centers of life."

The current brought growth of an explosive sort. Thousands of years of history had produced only a handful of cities with more than a half-million in population. In 1900 the United States

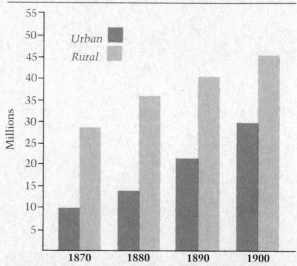

Urban and Rural Population, 1870–1900 (in millions)

Urban
Rural

Source: U.S. Bureau of the Census, Historical Statistics of the United States, Colonial Times to 1970, *Bicentennial Edition*, Washington, D.C., 1975.

had six such cities, including three—New York, Chicago, and Philadelphia—with a population over a million.

Strangers in a New Land

While some of the new city dwellers came from farms and small towns, many of them came from abroad. Most came from Europe, where unemployment, food shortages, and increasing threats of war sent millions fleeing across the Atlantic to make a fresh start in the United States. Italians first came in large numbers to escape an 1887 cholera epidemic in southern Italy; tens of thousands of Jews sought refuge from the anti-Semitic pogroms that swept Russia and Poland after 1880.

All told, the immigration figures were staggering. Between 1877 and 1890 more than 6.3 million people entered the United States. In one year alone, 1882, almost 789,000 people came. By 1890 about 15 percent of the population, 9 million people, were foreign-born.

Most newcomers were job seekers. Nearly two thirds were males, and the majority were between the ages of fifteen and forty. Most were unskilled laborers. Most settled on the eastern seaboard. In 1901 the Industrial Relocation Office was established to relieve overcrowding in the eastern cities; opening Galveston, Texas as a port of entry, it attracted many Russian Jews to Texas and the Southwest. But most immigrants preferred the shorter, more familiar journey to New York, and they tended to crowd into northern and eastern cities, settling in areas where others of their nationality or religion had settled.

They were often dazzled by what they saw. They stared at electric lights, indoor plumbing, soda fountains, streetcars, plush train seats for all classes, ice cream, lemons, and bananas. Relatives whisked them off to buy new "American" clothes and showed them the teeming markets, department stores, and Woolworth's new five and dime stores. "It seemed quite advanced compared with our home in Khelm," said a young Polish girl. "There was a sense of safety and hope that we had never felt in Poland."

Cities had increasingly large foreign-born populations. In 1900 three fourths of Chicago's population was foreign-born or of foreign-born parentage, two thirds of Boston's, and one half of Philadelphia's. New York City, where most immigrants arrived and many stayed, had more Italians than lived in Naples, more Germans than

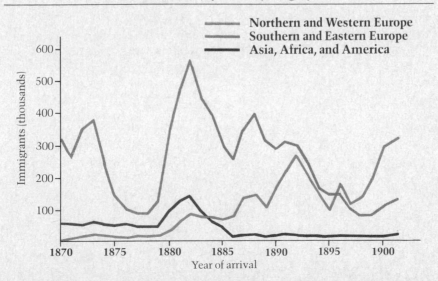

Immigration to the United States, 1870–1900 (by area of origin)

Northern and Western Europe
Southern and Eastern Europe
Asia, Africa, and America

Immigrants (thousands)

Year of arrival

Source: U.S. Bureau of the Census, Historical Statistics of the United States, Colonial Times to 1970, Bicentennial Edition, Washington, D.C., 1975.

In a Puck cartoon entitled "Looking Backward," the shadows of their immigrant origins loom over the rich and powerful who wanted to deny the "new" immigrants from central and southern Europe admission to America. The caption on the cartoon reads, "They would close to the newcomer the bridge that carried them and their fathers over."

lived in Hamburg, and twice as many Irish as lived in Dublin. Four out of five New York City residents in 1890 were of foreign birth or foreign parentage.

Beginning in the 1880s, the sources of immigration shifted dramatically away from northern and western Europe, the chief source of immigration for over two centuries. More and more immigrants came from southern and eastern Europe: Italy, Greece, Austro-Hungary, Poland, and Russia. Between 1880 and 1910 approximately 8.4 million people came from these lands. The "new" immigrants tended to be Catholics or Jews rather than Protestants, unskilled rather than skilled, and they often spoke "strange" languages. Most were poor and uneducated; sticking together in closeknit communities, they clung to their native customs, languages, and religions.

More than any previous group, the so-called new immigrants troubled the mainstream society. Could they be assimilated? Did they share "American" values? Such questions preoccupied groups like the American Protective Association, which arose in the 1890s and worked to limit or end immigration. Sneering epithets became part of the national vocabulary: "wop" and "dago" for Italians, "bohunk" for Bohemians, Hungarians, and other Slavs, "grease-ball" for Greeks, and "kike" for Jews. "You don't call . . . an Italian a white man?" a congressman asked a railroad construction boss in 1890. "No, Sir," the boss replied. "An Italian is a Dago."

Anti-Catholicism and anti-Semitism flared up again, as they had in the 1850s (recall chapter 14).

Edward A. Ross, a prominent sociologist, publicly decried "the lower class of Jews of Eastern Europe [who] reach here [as] moral cripples, their souls warped and dwarfed." In 1889 the head of the Fresh Air Fund, a program that sent New York City children on vacations to the suburbs, noted that "no one asked for Italian children." The Immigration Restriction League, founded in 1894, demanded a literacy test for immigrants from southern and eastern Europe. Congress passed such a law in 1896, but President Cleveland vetoed it.

Immigrants and the City

Industrial capitalism—the world of factories and foremen and grimy machines—tested the immigrants and placed an enormous strain upon their families. Many immigrants came from peasant societies where life proceeded according to outdoor routine and age-old tradition. In their new city homes, they found both new freedoms and new confinements, a different language, and a novel set of customs and expectations. Historians have only recently begun to discover the remarkable ways in which they learned to adjust.

Like native-born families, most immigrant families were nuclear in structure—they consisted of two parents and their children. Though variations occurred from group to group, men and women occupied roles similar to those in native families; men were wage earners, women housekeepers and mothers. Margaret Boyington, who studied steelworkers' homes in Homestead in the early 1900s, learned that the father played relatively little role in child-rearing or managing the family's finances. "His part of the problem is to earn and hers to spend." In Chicago Jane Addams discovered that immigrant women made it "a standard of domestic virtue that a man must not touch his pay envelope, but bring it home unopened to his wife."

Although patterns varied between ethnic groups, and between economic classes within ethnic groups, immigrants tended to marry within the group more than did the native-born. In one New York community, only 2 percent of French Canadian and 7 percent of Irish working men married outside their ethnic group in 1880, compared to almost 40 percent of native-born working men. Immigrants also tended to marry at a later age than natives, and they tended to have more children, a fact that worried nativists opposed to immigration.

Immigrants shaped the city as much as it shaped them. Most of them tried to retain their traditional culture for themselves and their children while at the same time adapting to life in their new country. To do this, they spoke their native language, practiced their religious faith, read their own newspapers, and established special parochial or other schools. They observed traditional holidays and formed a myriad of social organizations to maintain ties between members of the group.

Immigrant associations—there were many of them in every city—offered fellowship in a strange land. They helped newcomers find jobs and homes; they provided important services such as unemployment and health insurance. In a Massachusetts textile town, the Irish Benevolent Society said: "We visit our sick, and bury our dead." Some groups were no larger than a neighborhood; others spread nationwide. In 1914 the Deutsch-Amerikanischer Nationalbund, the largest of them, had more than two million members in dozens of cities and towns. Many women belonged to and participated in the work of the immigrant associations; in addition, there were groups exclusively for women such as the Polish Women's Alliance, the Jednota Ceskyck Dam (Society of Czech Women), and the National Council of Jewish Women.

The Polish National Alliance (PNA), a typical

Ethnic Neighborhoods in Chicago, 1870

Immigrants coming to a big city settled in neighborhoods where people were familiar with the customs and traditions of their native land.

Blacks
Czech/Slovak
German
Irish
Italian
Polish
Scandinavian

immigrant association, was founded in 1880. Like other organizations, it helped new immigrants on their arrival, offered insurance plans, established libraries and museums, sponsored youth programs, fielded baseball teams, and organized trips back to Poland. Each year the PNA published a sought-after calendar filled with Polish holidays, information, and proverbs. Extolling Poles' contributions to their new country, it erected monuments to distinguished Americans of Polish descent.

Every major city had dozens of foreign-language newspapers, with circulations large and small. The first newspaper published in the Lithuanian language appeared in the United States, not in Lithuania. Eagerly read, the papers carried news of events in the homeland, but they also reported on local ethnic leaders, told readers how to vote and become citizens, and gave practical tips on adjusting to life in the United States. In similar fashion, the Swedes, Poles, Czechs, and Germans established ethnic theaters that performed national plays and music. The Yiddish

(Jewish) Theater, the most famous, started in the 1880s in New York City and lasted for over fifty years.

The church and the school were the most important institutions in every immigrant community. East European Jews established synagogues and religious schools wherever they settled; they taught the Hebrew language and raised their children in a heritage they did not want to leave behind. Among groups like the Irish and the Poles, the Roman Catholic Church provided spiritual and educational guidance. In the parish schools, Polish priests and nuns taught Polish-American children about Polish as well as American culture in the Polish language.

Church, school, and fraternal societies shaped the way in which immigrants adjusted to life in America. By preserving language, religion, and heritage, they also shaped the country itself.

■ The ten-story Home Insurance Building, designed by William LeBaron Jenney, showed that with elevators and a steel frame buildings could soar to almost any height.

Skyscrapers and Suburbs

Beginning in the 1880s a revolution in technology transformed American cities. The age of steel and glass produced the skyscraper; the streetcar produced the suburbs and new residential patterns.

On the eve of the change, American cities were a crowded jumble of small buildings. Church steeples stood out on the skyline, clearly visible above the roofs of factories and office buildings. Buildings were usually made of masonry, and since the massive walls had to support their own weight, they could be no taller than a dozen or so stories. Steel frames and girders ended that limitation and allowed buildings to soar higher and higher. "Curtain walls," which concealed the steel framework, were no longer load-bearing; they were pierced by many windows that let in fresh air and light. Completed in 1885, the Home Insurance Building in Chicago was the country's first metal-frame structure.

To a group of talented Chicago architects the new trends served as a springboard for innovative forms. The leader of the movement was Louis H. Sullivan, who had studied at M.I.T. and in Paris before settling in Chicago, attracted by the chance to rebuild the city after the great fire of 1871. In 1886, at the age of thirty, he began work on the Chicago Auditorium, one of the last great masonry buildings. "Then came the flash of imagination which saw the single thing," he later said. "The trick was turned; and there swiftly came into being something new under the sun." Sullivan's skyscrapers, the "flash of imagination," changed the urban skyline.

In the Wainwright Building in Saint Louis (1890), the Schiller Building (1892) and the Carson, Pirie, and Scott department store (1899) in Chicago, and the Prudential Building in Buffalo (1895), Sullivan developed the new forms. Architects must discard "books, rules, precedents," he announced; responding to the new, they should design for a building's function. "Form follows function," Sullivan believed, and he passed the idea on to a talented disciple, Frank Lloyd Wright. The modern city should stretch to the sky. A skyscraper "must be every inch a proud and soaring thing, rising in sheer exaltation . . . from bottom to top . . . a unit without a single dissenting line."

Electric elevators carried passengers upward in the new skyscrapers. During the same years streetcars carried them outward to expanded boundaries that transformed urban life.

Cities were no longer largely "walking cities," confined to a radius of two or three miles, the distance an individual might walk. Streetcar systems extended the radius and changed the urban map. Cable lines, electric surface lines, and elevated rapid transit brought shoppers and workers into central business districts and sped them home again. Offering the cheap five-cent fare with a free transfer, these mass transit systems fostered commuting; widely separated business and residential districts sprang up. The middle class moved farther and farther out to the leafy greenness of the suburbs.

As the middle class moved out of the cities, the immigrants and working class poured in. They took over the older brownstones, row houses, and workers' cottages, turning them under the sheer weight of numbers into the slums of the central city. In the cities of the past classes and occupations had been thrown together; without streetcars and subways there was no other choice. The streetcar city, sprawling and specialized, became a more fragmented and stratified society with middle-class residential rings surrounding a business and working-class core.

Tenements and Privies

In the shadow of the skyscrapers grimy rows of tenements filled the central city. Exploring them in words and photographs, Jacob Riis described them in *How the Other Half Lives* (1890).

Be a little careful, please! The hall is dark and you might stumble. . . . Here where the hall turns and dives into utter darkness is . . . a flight of stairs. You can feel your way, if you cannot see it. Close? Yes! What would you have? All the fresh air that enters these stairs comes from the hall-door that is forever slamming. . . . Here is a door. Listen! That short, hacking cough, that tiny, helpless wail — what do they mean? . . . The child is dying of measles. With half a chance it might have lived; but it had none. That dark bedroom killed it.

Tenement houses on small city lots crowded people into cramped apartments. In the late 1870s architect James E. Ware won a competition for tenement design with the "dumbbell tenement." Rising seven or eight stories in height, the dumb-bell tenement packed about thirty four-room apartments on a lot only 25 by 100 feet. Between four and sixteen families lived on a floor; two toilets in the hall of each floor served their needs. Narrowed at the middle, the tenement resembled a giant dumbbell in shape. The indented middle created an air shaft between adjoining buildings that provided a little light and ventilation. It also carried flames from one story to the next, making these buildings notorious firetraps. In 1890 nearly half the dwellings in New York City were tenements.

That year more than 1.4 million people lived on Manhattan Island, one of whose wards had a population density of 334,000 people per square mile. Many people lived in alleys and basements so dark they could not be photographed until flashlight photography was invented in 1887. Exploring the city, William Dean Howells, the prominent author, inhaled "the stenches of the neglected street . . . [and] the yet fouler and dreadfuller poverty smell which breathes from the open doorways."

Howells smelled more than poverty. In the 1870s and '80s cities stank. One problem was horse manure, hundreds of tons of it a day in every city. Another was the privy, "a single one of which," said a leading authority on public health, "may render life in a whole neighborhood almost unendurable in the summer."

Baltimore smelled "like a billion polecats," recalled H. L. Mencken, who grew up there. Said one New York City resident: "The stench is something terrible." Another wrote that "the stink is enough to knock you down." In 1880 the Chicago *Times* said that a "solid stink" pervaded the city. "No other word expresses it so well as stink. A stench means something finite. Stink reaches the infinite and becomes sublime in the magnitude of odiousness." In 1892 one neighborhood of Chicago, covering a third of a square mile, had only three bathtubs.

Cities dumped their wastes into the nearest body of water, then drew drinking water from the same site. Many built modern, purified waterworks but could not keep pace with spiraling growth. In 1900 fewer than one in ten city dwellers drank filtered water. Factories, the pride of the era, polluted the urban air. At night Pittsburgh looked and sounded like "Hell with the lid off," according to contemporary observers. Smoke

A WARNING TO LANDLORDS.

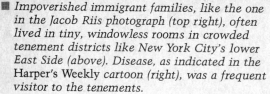

■ *Impoverished immigrant families, like the one in the Jacob Riis photograph (top right), often lived in tiny, windowless rooms in crowded tenement districts like New York City's lower East Side (above). Disease, as indicated in the Harper's Weekly cartoon (right), was a frequent visitor to the tenements.*

poured from seventy-three glass factories, forty-one iron and steel mills, and twenty-nine oil refineries. The choking air helped prevent lung diseases and malaria—or so the city's advertising claimed.

Crime was another growing problem. The nation's homicide rate nearly tripled in the 1880s, much of the increase coming in the cities. Slum youths formed street gangs with names like the Hayes Valley gang in San Francisco or the Baxter Street Dudes, the Daybreak Boys, and the Alley Gang in New York. The Daybreak Boys, all under

twelve years of age, rose up early to rob ships in the harbor. In San Francisco the gangs gave rise to the new word "hoodlums," described by a disgusted English traveler as "young embryo criminals" who robbed and murdered at night.

After remaining constant for many decades, the suicide rate rose steadily between 1870 and 1900, according to a recent study of Philadelphia. Alcoholism also rose, especially among men. A 1905 survey of Chicago counted as many saloons as grocery stores, meat markets, and dry goods stores combined.

The House That Tweed Built

Closely connected with explosive urban growth was the emergence of the powerful city political machine. As cities grew, lines of responsibility in city governments became hopelessly confused, increasing the opportunity for corruption and greed. Burgeoning populations required streets, buildings, and public services; immigrants needed even more services. In this situation party machines played an important role.

The machines traded services for votes. Loosely knit, they were headed by a strong, influential leader—the "boss"—who tied together a network of ward and precinct captains, each of whom looked after his local constituents. In New York "Honest" John Kelley, Richard Croker, and Charles F. Murphy led Tammany Hall, the famous Democratic party organization that dominated city politics from the 1850s to the 1930s. Other bosses included "Hinky Dink" Kenna and "Bathhouse John" Coughlin in Chicago, James McManes in Philadelphia, and Christopher A. Buckley—the notorious "Blind Boss," who used an exceptional memory for voices to make up for failing eyesight—in San Francisco.

William M. Tweed, head of the famed Tweed Ring in New York, provided the model for them all. Nearly six feet tall, weighing almost three hundred pounds, Tweed rose through the ranks of Tammany Hall. He served in turn as city alderman, member of Congress, and New York State assemblyman. A man of culture and warmth, he moved easily between the rough back alleys of New York and the parlors and clubs of the city's elite. Behind the scenes he headed a ring that plundered New York for tens of millions of dollars.

The New York County Courthouse—"The House that Tweed Built"—was his masterpiece. Nestled in City Hall Park in downtown Manhattan, the three-story structure was designed to cost $250,000, but the bills ran a bit higher. Furniture, carpets, and window shades alone came to more than $5.5 million. Three tables and forty chairs cost the city $180,000. Tweed's own quarry supplied the marble; the plumber got almost $1.5 million for fixtures. Andrew Garvey, the "Prince of Plasterers," charged $500,000 for plaster work, and then $1 million to repair the

same work. His total bill came to $2,870,464.06. (The *New York Times* suggested that the six cents be donated to charity.) In the end the building cost over $13 million—and in 1872, when Tweed fell, it was still not finished.

Some bosses were plainly corrupt; others believed in "honest graft," a term Tammany's George Washington Plunkitt coined to describe "legitimate" profits made from advance knowledge of city projects. Why did voters keep them in power? The answers are complex, involving skillful political organization and the type of constituency. Most immigrants had little experience with democratic government and proved easy prey for well-oiled machines. For the most part, however, the bosses stayed in power because they paid attention to the needs of the least privileged city voters. They offered valued services in an era when neither government nor business lent a hand.

If an immigrant, tired and bewildered after the long crossing, came looking for a job, bosses like Tweed, Plunkitt, or Buckley found him one in city offices or local businesses. If a family's breadwinner died or was injured, the bosses donated food and clothing and saw to it that the family made it through the crisis. If the winter was particularly cold, they provided free coal to heat tenement apartments. They ran picnics for slum children on hot summer days and contributed to hospitals, orphanages, and dozens of worthy neighborhood causes.

Most bosses became wealthy; they were not Robin Hoods who took from the rich to give to the poor. They took for themselves as well. Reformers occasionally ousted them. Tweed fell from power in 1872, "Blind Boss" Buckley in 1891, Croker in 1894. But reformers rarely stayed in power long. Drawn mainly from the middle and upper classes, they had little understanding of the needs of the poor. Before long they returned to private concerns, and the bosses, who had known it would happen all along, cheerily took power again.

"What tells in holdin' your grip on your district," the engaging Plunkitt once said, "is to go right down among the poor families and help them in the different ways they need help. . . . It's philanthropy, but it's politics, too—mighty good politics. . . . The poor are the most grateful people in the world."

Charles J. Guiteau and the Controversial Insanity Defense

Charles J. Guiteau was thirty-nine years old in 1881. Short and slightly built, he sported a mustache and a trim, dark beard. He did not smoke or drink, and he took particular pride in his neat appearance. In 1879 he had published a religious volume bearing the modest title, *The Truth, A Companion to the Bible*. "I had ideas but no reputation," he later said. A desire for political recognition and a hope of lasting fame were among his ideas. Although without political influence of any kind, he supported James A. Garfield in the presidential election of 1880, then persuaded himself that he deserved a handsome reward. He wrote Garfield to say that he would be happy to accept an ambassadorship in Europe.

Soon after taking office, Garfield became entangled in a fight with Senator Roscoe Conkling of New York and the Conkling wing of the Republican party (see chapter 20). The intraparty struggle disturbed Guiteau. "Like a flash" the idea came to him (he testified at his trial) that all would be well if only Garfield were "removed." On June 6, Guiteau purchased for $10 a British Bull Dog revolver and a box of cartridges. He chose a bone-handled revolver, thinking it would look

nice in the museum case it was destined to occupy.

For three weeks in June, Guiteau stalked Garfield through the streets of Washington. Finally, on July 2, Guiteau could wait no longer. Garfield was scheduled to leave that day for Williams College, his alma mater, to deliver a commencement address. With his revolver in his pocket, Guiteau set out for the Baltimore and Potomac Railroad depot. As Garfield walked toward the train, Guiteau ran up behind him and fired two shots, hitting the President in the arm and lower back. "My God! What is that?" cried Garfield as he fell, partly conscious, to the depot floor.

An alert policeman arrested Guiteau immediately. In his pocket was the gun, and in the railway station, where he had left them for later discovery, were a copy of his book, *The Truth*, a biographical sketch for the convenience of the newspapers, and a letter addressed "To the White House," dated July 2. "The President's death," the letter stated, "was a sad necessity, but it will unite the Republican party and save the Republic. Life is a fleeting dream, and it matters little when one goes. A human life is of small value."

Taken to the White House, Garfield lay gravely ill throughout the summer as doctors probed unsuccessfully to find the bullet that had entered his back. Day by day this once powerful man wasted away, ravaged by internal infection. On September 19, 1881, eighty days after the shooting, he died.

Americans were horrified by the assassination. Many people assumed it was the work of a madman. Garfield himself thought Guiteau must be crazy. There was no other explanation.

Madman. Crazy. These were deceptively simple words in the 1880s when little was known about the mind and mental illness. In the weeks following the shooting, professionals in the developing field of psychology took a deep interest in Guiteau and his impending trial. Guiteau was likely, it seemed, to plead not guilty by reason of insanity. But much of the public viewed such a plea as the "insanity dodge," and American psychiatry itself was sharply divided over the proper definition of insanity and criminal responsibility.

In 1881 most psychologists agreed that mental illness was a physical disease, but one that could be caused by emotional pressures. They differed, however, over the interpretation of the *symptoms* of mental illness. So-called conservative psychologists like John P. Gray, the influential editor of the *American Journal of Insanity*, played down the emotional and behaviorial symptoms. Liberal psychologists, like Edward C. Spitzka, trained in Germany, stressed their importance.

The insanity defense often hinged on a defendant's previous record. If the record showed criminal activity, then it was believed that the crime at issue in the trial resulted most likely from evil impulses, not mental illness. If it showed, however, a blameless life (Guiteau, for example, boasted that he neither smoked nor drank), then the crime was thought to result from a disease that led to mental illness. Trials involving an insanity defense often became lengthy sessions in "competitive biography," as opposing psychiatrists recited the telling factors in the defendant's life and family background.

Guiteau's trial (the sketch opposite shows the defendant entertaining the jury with a comic story) became a test of the era's conflicting theories of mental illness. From the outset, government attorneys stressed the M'Naghten Rule, a legal rule that held a defendant responsible if he understood the nature of his act and knew it to be against the law. The prosecutors claimed that Guiteau's self-seeking motives and methodical planning could not be the products of a fevered, disordered mind.

The defense called eight psychiatrists, Spitzka among them, to the stand. Seven had little effect on the jury, but Spitzka was different. After examining Guiteau, he concluded that the defendant was, beyond all doubt, insane. "I concluded that I had an insane man to deal with on sight, before I asked him any questions. He has got the insane manner as well marked as I have ever seen it in an asylum." Guiteau's illness was hereditary, Spitzka testified, and very likely his brain from birth had unequal sides.

Taken aback by Spitzka's testimony, the prosecution called a flood of rebuttal witnesses to attest to Guiteau's sanity. Gray himself took the stand in the trial's final days and reported on a two-day interview with Guiteau from which he determined that Guiteau was obviously sane. Insanity was not hereditary. It was a physical disease whose symptoms reflected the disease itself, and in Guiteau there was no evidence of brain disease or anything except a sinful, dissolute life.

On January 5, 1882, the trial ended. The jury retired at 4:35 P.M., and at 5:40 it returned with a verdict of guilty. After the legal appeals were exhausted, Guiteau was hanged on June 30, 1882.

Guiteau's death allowed a closer look at the controversy. In apparent verification of Spitzka's theory, the autopsy showed that the left hemisphere of Guiteau's brain was larger than the right. Twentieth-century psychiatrists who have studied the case tend to agree that Guiteau was mentally ill, but by then insanity had become a common legal defense. "There is no such thing as a science of insanity, any more than a science of health," *The Nation*, an influential journal, reported in 1882.

As the years passed, heredity and emotional symptoms became more important in the diagnosis of mental illness. In 1981—one hundred years after Garfield and Guiteau—at the trial of John Hinckley, who shot and wounded President Ronald Reagan, Hinckley was found not guilty by reason of insanity.

When Henry George asked a friend what could be done about the problem of political corruption in American cities, his friend replied: "Nothing! You and I can do nothing at all. . . . We can only wait for evolution. Perhaps in four or five thousand years evolution may have carried men beyond this state of things."

This stress on the slow pace of change reflected the doctrine of Social Darwinism, based on the evolutionary theories of Charles Darwin and the writings of English social philosopher Herbert Spencer. In several influential books Spencer applied Darwinian principles of natural selection to society, combining biology and sociology in a theory of "social selection" that explained human progress. Like animals, society evolved, slowly, by adapting to the environment. The "survival of the fittest"—a term Spencer, not Darwin, invented—preserved the strong and weeded out the weak. "If they are sufficiently complete to live, they *do* live, and it is well they should live. If they are not sufficiently complete to live, they die, and it is best they should die."

Social Darwinism had a number of influential followers in the United States, including William Graham Sumner, a professor of political and social science at Yale University. One of the country's best-known academic figures, Sumner was forceful and eloquent. In writings such as *What Social Classes Owe to Each Other* (1883) and "The Absurd Effort to Make the World Over" (1894), he argued that government action on behalf of the poor or weak interfered in evolution and sapped the species. Reform tampered with the laws of nature. "It is the greatest folly of which a man can be capable to sit down with a slate and pencil to plan out a new social world," Sumner said.

The influence of Social Darwinism on American thinking has been exaggerated, but in the powerful hands of Sumner and others it did influence some journalists, ministers, and policymakers. Between 1877 and the 1890s, however, it came under increasing attack. In fields like religion, economics, politics, literature, and law, thoughtful people raised questions about established conditions and suggested the need for reform.

Read and reread, passed from hand to hand, Henry George's nationwide best-seller, *Progress and Poverty* (1879), led the way to a more critical appraisal of American society in the 1880s and beyond. The book jolted traditional thought. "It was responsible," one historian has said, "for starting along new lines of thinking an amazing number of the men and women" who became leaders of reform.

Born in 1839, the child of a poor Philadelphia family, George had little formal schooling. As a boy he went to sea, then worked as a prospector, printer, and journalist. Self-educated as an economist, he moved to San Francisco in the late 1850s and began to study "the fierce struggle of our civilized life." Disturbed by the depression of the 1870s and labor upheavals like the great railroad strikes of 1877, George saw modern society—rich, complex, with material goods hitherto unknown—as sadly flawed.

"The present century," he wrote "has been marked by a prodigious increase in wealth-producing power. . . . It was natural to expect, and it was expected, that . . . real poverty [would become] a thing of the past." Instead, he argued

it becomes no easier for the masses of our people to make a living. On the contrary, it is becoming harder. The wealthy class is becoming more wealthy; but the poorer class is becoming more dependent. The gulf between the employed and the employer is growing wider; social contrasts are becoming sharper; as liveried carriages appear, so do barefooted children.

George proposed a simple solution. Land formed the basis of wealth; a "single tax" on it, replacing all other taxes, would equalize wealth and raise revenue to help the poor. "Single-tax" clubs sprang up around the country, but George's solution, simplistic and unappealing, had much less impact than his analysis of the problem itself. He raised questions a generation of readers set out to answer.

New Currents in Social Thought

George's emphasis on deprivation in the environment excited a young country lawyer in Ashtabu-

■ *The rich and poor of Victorian America: Mrs. Cornelia Ward Hall and her children (above) and a tenement mother and her children trying to eke out a living by making paper roses (right).*

la, Ohio, Clarence Darrow. Unlike the Social Darwinists, Darrow was sure that criminals were made and not born. They grew out of "the unjust condition of human life." In the mid-1880s he left for Chicago and a forty-year career working to convince people that poverty lay at the root of crime. "There is no such thing as crime as the word is generally understood . . . ," he told a group of startled prisoners in the Cook County jail. "If every man, woman and child in the world had a chance to make a decent, fair, honest living there would be no jails and no lawyers and no courts."

As Darrow rejected the implications of Social Darwinism, in similar fashion did Richard T. Ely and a group of young economists poke holes in traditional economic thought. Fresh from graduate study in Germany, Ely in 1884 attacked classical economics for its dogmatism, simple faith in laissez-faire, and reliance on self-interest as a guide for human conduct. The "younger" economics, he said, must no longer be "a tool in the hands of the greedy and the avaricious for keeping down and oppressing the laboring classes. It does not acknowledge laissez-faire as an excuse for doing nothing while people starve."

Accepting a post at Johns Hopkins University, Ely assigned graduate students to study labor conditions in Baltimore and other cities; one of them, John R. Commons, went on to publish a massive four-volume study, *History of Labour in the United States*. In 1885 Ely led a small band of rebels in founding the American Economic Association, which linked economics to social problems and urged government intervention in economic affairs. Social critic Thorstein Veblen saw economic laws as a mask for human greed. In *The Theory of the Leisure Class* (1899), Veblen analyzed the "predatory wealth" and "conspicuous consumption" of the business class.

Edward Bellamy dreamed of a cooperative society where poverty, greed, and crime no longer existed. A lawyer from western Massachusetts, Bellamy published *Looking Backward, 2000–1887*, in 1887 and became a national reform figure virtually overnight. The novel's protagonist, Julian West, falls asleep in 1887 and awakes in the year 2000. Wide-eyed, he finds himself in a socialist utopia; the government owns the means of production, and citizens share the material rewards. Cooperation, rather than competition, is the watchword.

The world of *Looking Backward* had limits; it was regimented, paternalistic, and filled with the gadgets and material concerns of Bellamy's own day. But it had a dramatic effect on many readers. The book sold at the rate of ten thousand copies a week, and its followers formed Nationalist Clubs to work for its objectives. By 1890 there were such clubs in twenty-seven states, all calling for the nationalization of public utilities and a wider distribution of wealth.

Walter Rauschenbusch, a young Baptist minister, read widely from the writings of Bellamy and George, along with the works of other social reformers. When he took his first church post in Hell's Kitchen, a blighted area of New York City, he soon discovered the weight of the slum environment. "One could hear," he said, "human virtue cracking and crushing all around." In the 1890s Rauschenbusch became a professor at the Rochester Theological Seminary, and he began to expound on the responsibility of organized religion to advance social justice.

Traditional doctrines of Protestantism stressed individual salvation and a better life in the next world, not in this one. Poverty was evidence of sinfulness; the poor had only themselves to blame. "God has intended the great to be great and the little to be little," said Henry Ward Beecher, the country's best-known pastor. Wealth and destitution, suburbs and slums — all formed part of God's plan.

Challenging those traditional doctrines, a number of churches in the 1880s began establishing missions in the city slums. William Dwight Porter Bliss, an Episcopal clergyman, founded the Church of the Carpenter in a working-class district of Boston. Lewis M. Pease worked in the grim Five Points area of New York; Alexander Irvine, a Jewish missionary, lived in a flophouse in the Bowery. Irvine walked his skid row neighborhood every afternoon to lend a hand to those in need. Living among the poor and homeless, the urban missionaries grew impatient with religious doctrines that endorsed the status quo.

Many of the new trends were reflected in an emerging religious philosophy known as the "Social Gospel." As the name suggests, the Social Gospel focused on society as well as individuals, on improving living conditions as well as saving souls. Sermons in Social Gospel churches called upon church members to fulfill their social obligations, and adults met before and after the regular service to discuss social and economic problems. Children were excused from sermons, organized into age groups, and encouraged to make the church a center for social as well as religious activity. Soon, churches included dining halls, gymnasiums, and even theaters.

The most active Social Gospel leader was Washington Gladden, a Congregational minister and prolific writer. Linking Christianity to the social and economic environment, Gladden spent a lifetime working for "social salvation." He saw Christianity as a fellowship of love and the church as a social agency. In *Applied Christianity* (1886) and other writings, he denounced competition, urged an "industrial partnership" between employers and employees, and called for efforts to help the poor.

The Settlement Houses

A growing number of social workers, living in the urban slums, shared Gladden's concern. Like Tweed and Plunkitt, they appreciated the dependency of the poor; unlike them, they wanted to eradicate the conditions that underlay it.

Youthful, idealistic, and mostly middle-class, these social workers took as their model Toynbee Hall, founded in 1884 in the slums of East London. Stanton Coit, a moody and poetic graduate of Amherst College, was the first American to borrow the settlement-house idea; in 1886 he opened the Neighborhood Guild on the Lower East Side of New York. The idea spread swiftly. By 1900 there were over a hundred settlements in the country; five years later there were over two hundred, and by 1910 more than four hundred.

The settlements included Jane Addams' famous Hull House in Chicago (1889); Robert A. Woods' South End House in Boston (1892); and Lillian Wald's Henry Street Settlement in New York (1893). These reformers wanted to bridge the socioeconomic gap between rich and poor and to bring education, culture, and hope to the slums. They sought to create in the heart of the city the values and sense of community of small-town America. Of settlement workers, Wald said in *The House on Henry Street* (1915): "We were to live in a neighborhood . . . identify ourselves with it socially, and, in brief, contribute to it our citizenship."

Many of the settlement workers were women, some of them college graduates who found that society had little use for their talents and energy. Jane Addams, a graduate of Rockford College in Illinois, opened Hull House on South Halsted Street in the heart of the Chicago slums. Twenty-nine years old, endowed with a forceful and winning personality, she intended "to share the lives of the poor" and humanize the industrial city. "American ideals," she said, "crumbled under the overpowering poverty of the over-crowded city."

Occupying an old rundown mansion, Hull House had a "plainness that just escaped barrenness and just touched the artistic." Its staff stressed education, offering classes in elementary English and Shakespeare, lectures on ethics and the history of art, and courses in cooking, sewing, and manual skills. Hull House had university extension classes for college credit; John Dewey and Frank Lloyd Wright lectured there. Gradually it expanded to occupy a dozen buildings sprawling over more than a city block.

Like settlement workers in other cities, Addams and her colleagues studied the immigrants in nearby tenements. Laboriously they identified the background of every family in a one-third square mile area around Hull House. Finding people of eighteen different nationalities, they taught them American history and the English language, yet also encouraged them—through folk festivals and art—to preserve their heritage.

In Boston, Robert Woods of South End House focused on the problem of school dropouts. He offered manual training, formed clubs to get young people off the streets, and established a cheap restaurant where the hungry could eat. Lillian Wald, the daughter of a wealthy family and herself a graduate nurse, concentrated on providing health care for the poor. In 1898 the first Catholic-run settlement house opened in New York, and in 1900 Bronson House opened in Los Angeles to work in the Mexican-American community.

Florence Kelley, a spirited young graduate of Cornell, taught night school one winter in Chicago. Watching children break under the burden of poverty, she devoted her life to the problem of child labor. Convinced of the need for political activism, she worked with Addams and others to push through the Illinois Factory Act of 1893, which prohibited the employment of children under the age of fourteen for longer than eight hours a day.

A Crisis in Social Welfare

When the depression of 1893 struck (see chapter 20), it jarred the young settlement workers, many

The first public playground in Chicago was started by Hull House in 1893. Medical care and day care nurseries were among the services offered at Hull House.

of whom had just begun their work. Addams and the Hull House workers helped form the Chicago Bureau of Charities to coordinate emergency relief. Kelley, recently appointed the chief factory inspector of Illinois, worked even harder to end child labor, and in 1899 she moved to New York City to head the National Consumers League, which marshaled the buying power of women to encourage employers to provide better working conditions.

In cities and towns across the country traditional methods of helping the needy foundered in the crisis. Churches, Charity Organization Societies, and Community Chests did what they could, but their resources were limited, and they functioned on traditional lines. Many of them still tried to reform rather than aid individual families, and people were often reluctant to call on them for help.

Gradually, a new class of professional social workers arose to fill the need. Unlike the church and charity volunteers, these social workers wanted not only to feed the poor but to study their condition and alleviate it. Revealingly they called themselves "case workers" and daily collected data on the income, housing, jobs, health, and habits of the poor. Prowling tenement districts, they gathered information about the number of rooms, number of occupants, ventilation, and sanitation, putting together a fund of useful data.

Studies of the poor popped up everywhere. Walter Wyckoff, a graduate of Princeton University, embarked in 1891 on what he called "an experiment in reality." For eighteen months he worked as an unskilled laborer in jobs from Connecticut to California. "I am vastly ignorant of the labor problems and am trying to learn by experience," he said as he set out. After working as a ditch digger, farmhand, and logger, Wyckoff summarized his findings in *The Workers* (1897), a book immediately hailed as a major contribution to sociology.

To investigate living issues, Wyckoff felt, one must investigate life, and so many others followed his example that sometimes it seemed the observers outnumbered those being observed. Lillian Pettengill took a job as a domestic servant to see "the ups and downs of this particular dog-life from the dog's end of the chain." Others became street beggars, miners, lumberjacks, and factory laborers. Bessie and Marie Van Vorst's *The Woman Who Toils: Being the Experiences of Two Gentlewomen as Factory Girls* (1903) studied female workers, as did Helen Campbell's *Women Wage-Earners: Their Past, Their Present and Their Future* (1893), which suggested that the conditions of factory employment prepared women mainly "for the hospital, the workhouse, and the prison."

William T. Stead, a prominent British editor, visited the Chicago World's Fair in 1893 and stayed to examine the city. He roamed the flophouses and tenements and dropped in at Hull House to drink hot chocolate and talk over conditions with Jane Addams. Later he wrote an influential book *If Christ Came to Chicago* (1894), and in a series of mass meetings during 1893, he called for a civic revival. In response, Chicagoans formed the Civic Federation, a group of forty leaders who aimed to make Chicago "the best governed, the healthiest city in this country." Setting up task forces for philanthropy, moral improvement, and legislation, the new group helped spawn the National Civic Federation (1900), a nationwide organization devoted to reform of urban life.

"The United States was born in the country and moved to the city," historian Richard Hofstadter said. Much of that movement occurred during the nineteenth century when the United

States was the most rapidly urbanizing nation in the western world. American cities bustled with energy; they absorbed millions of migrants from Europe and other parts of the world. That migration, and the urban growth that accompanied it, reshaped American politics and culture.

By 1920 the census showed that, for the first time, most Americans lived in cities. By then, too, almost half the population was descended from people who arrived after the American Revolution. As European, African, and Asian cultures met in the American city, a culturally pluralistic society emerged. Dozens of nationalities produced a hyphenated culture whose members considered themselves Polish-Americans, Afro-Americans, and Irish-Americans. The melting pot sometimes melted, but it only partially blended.

"Ah, Vera," said a character in Israel Zangwill's popular play, *The Melting Pot* (1908), "what is the glory of Rome and Jerusalem where all nations and races come to worship and look back, compared with the glory of America, where all races and nations come to labour and look forward!" Critics scorned the play as "romantic claptrap," and indeed it was. But the metaphor of the melting pot clearly depicted a new national image. In the decades after the 1870s a jumble of ethnic and racial groups responded to the challenges of industrialization and urbanization.

Recommended Reading

On urban America, see Sam Bass Warner, Jr.: *Streetcar Suburbs* (1962) and *The Urban Wilderness* (1972). Arthur M. Schlesinger, *The Rise of the City, 1878–1898* (1933) is a pioneering study; Blake McKelvey, *The Urbanization of America, 1860–1915* (1963); Constance M. Green, *The Rise of Urban America* (1965); and Howard P. Chudacoff, *The Evolution of American Urban Society*, rev. ed. (1981) are also valuable.

Russel B. Nye, *The Unembarrassed Muse: The Popular Arts in America* (1970), covers popular culture; Neil Harris, *Humbug: The Art of P. T. Barnum* (1973), is superb on both Barnum and the era. For family life, see Carl N. Degler, *At Odds: Women and the Family in America from the Revolution to the Present* (1980); Joseph Kett, *Rites of Passage: Adolescence in America* (1977); and Tamara K. Hareven and Maris Vinovskis, eds., *Family and Population in Nineteenth Century America* (1978). For education, see L. A. Cremin, *The Transformation of the School: Progressivism in American Education, 1876–1956* (1961); Lawrence Veysey, *The Emergence of the American University* (1965); and

David B. Tyack, *The One Best System: A History of American Urban Education* (1974).

Oscar Handlin, *The Uprooted*, 2d ed. (1973) and John Higham, *Strangers in the Land: Patterns of American Nativism* (1955) are classic studies. Robert H. Bremner, *From the Depths: The Discovery of Poverty in the United States* (1956); Allen F. Davis, *Spearheads for Reform: The Social Settlements and the Progressive Movement, 1890–1914* (1967); and *American Heroine: The Life and Legend of Jane Addams* (1973), also by Allen F. Davis, examine urban reform.

Treatments of intellectual currents include Richard Hofstadter, *Social Darwinism in American Thought*, rev. ed. (1955); Sidney Fine, *Laissez Faire and the General Welfare State* (1956); and Eric F. Goldman, *Rendezvous with Destiny* (1952).

Additional Bibliography

Robert H. Walker, *Life in the Age of Enterprise, 1865–1900* (1967), examines everyday life. On leisure and entertainment, see Gunther Barth, *City People* (1980); Harold Seymour, *Baseball*, 2 vols. (1960–1971); Foster R. Dulles, *America Learns to Play* (1966); and Ronald L. Davis, *A History of Music in American Life*, vol. 2: *The Gilded Years, 1865–1920* (1980). David J. Pivar, *Purity Crusade: Sexual Morality and Social Control, 1868–1900* (1973); Susan Estabrook Kennedy, *If All We Did Was To Weep At Home: A History of White Working Class Women in America* (1979); Barbara Mayer Wertheimer, *We Were There: The Story of Working Women in America* (1977); and Lois W. Banner, *Women in Modern America: A Brief History* (1974), are helpful.

On education, see Sidney Hook, *John Dewey* (1939); Frederick Rudolph, *The American College and University* (1962); C. W. Dabney, *Universal Education in the South* (1936); Donald Spivey, *Schooling for the New Slavery: Black Industrial Education, 1868–1915* (1978); and Louis R. Harlan, *Booker T. Washington: The Making of a Black Leader, 1865–1901* (1972).

For immigration and urban growth, consult Barbara Solomon, *Ancestors and Immigrants* (1956); Josef J. Barton, *Peasants and Strangers: Italians, Rumanians, and Slovaks in an American City* (1975); Leonard Dinnerstein, Roger L. Nichols, and David M. Reimers, *Natives and Strangers* (1979); Moses Rischin, *The Promised City: New York's Jews* (1962); David Ward, *Cities and Immigrants* (1971); Thomas L. Philpott, *The Slum and the Ghetto* (1978); William A. Bullough, *The Blind Boss and His City* (1979); and Leo Hershkowitz, *Tweed's New York: Another Look* (1977).

See also Dorothy Rose Blumberg, *Florence Kelley: The Making of a Social Pioneer* (1971); Roy M. Lubove, *The Progressives and the Slums: Tenement House Reform in New York City* (1962); Martin J. Schiesl, *The Politics of Efficiency: Municipal Administration and Reform in America* (1977); Henry F. May, *Protestant Churches and Industrial America* (1949); and R. C. White, Jr., and C. H. Hopkins, *The Social Gospel: Religion and Reform in Changing America* (1976).

chapter 20

POLITICAL REALIGNMENTS AND THE DECADE OF DECISION: THE 1890s

In mid-February 1893, panic suddenly hit the New York stock market. In one day investors dumped a million shares of a leading company, the Philadelphia and Reading Railroad, and it went bankrupt. Business investment dropped sharply in the railroad and construction industries, touching off the worst economic downturn to that point in the country's history.

Frightened, people hurriedly sold stocks and other assets to buy gold. The overwhelming demand depleted the gold reserve of the United States Treasury. Eroding almost daily in March 1893, the Treasury's reserve slumped toward the $100 million mark, an amount that stood for the government's commitment to maintain the gold standard. On April 22, for the first time since the 1870s, it fell below $100 million.

The news shattered business confidence—the stock market broke. On Wednesday, May 3, railroad and industrial stocks plummeted, and the next day several major firms went bankrupt.

When the market opened on Friday, crowds filled the galleries, anticipating a panic. Within minutes, leading stocks plunged to record lows, and there was pandemonium on the floor and in the streets outside. May 5, 1893, Wall Street's worst day until the Great Crash of 1929, became "Industrial Black Friday," "a day of terrible strain long remembered on the market."

Afterward, banks cut back on loans. Unable to get capital, businesses failed at an average rate of two dozen a day during the month of May. "The papers are full of failures—banks are breaking all over the country, and there is a tremendous contraction of credits and hoarding of money going on everywhere," an observer noted. On July 26 the Erie Railroad, one of the leading names in railroading history, failed.

August 1893 was the worst month. Across the country factories and mines shut down. In Orange, New Jersey, Thomas A. Edison, the symbol of the country's ingenuity, laid off 240 employees

■ *A run on a New York City bank during the Panic of 1895 (left). In Chicago the economic downturn and the Pullman strike forced many of the poor to live in hastily thrown-together shantytowns (right).*

at the Edison Phonograph Works. On August 15 the Northern Pacific Railroad went bankrupt; the Union Pacific and the Santa Fe soon followed. Some economists estimated unemployment at 2 million people or nearly 15 percent of the labor force.

"There are thousands of homeless and starving men in the streets," reported a young journalist in Chicago. "I have seen more misery in this last week than I ever saw in my life before." Charity societies and churches tried to help, but they could not handle the huge numbers of needy in the cities, and they did not even reach the farms. Susan Orcutt, a farm woman from Kansas, wrote in June 1894: "I take my pen in hand to let you know we are starving. . . . My husband went away to find work and came home last night and told me that he would have to starve. He has been in 10 counties and did not get no work. . . . I haven't had nothing to eat today and it is 3 o'clock."

Continuing through 1897, the depression was the decisive event of the decade. At its height, three million people were unemployed. The human costs were enormous, even among the well-to-do. "They were for me years of simple Hell," shattering "my whole scheme of life," said Charles Francis Adams, the descendant of two American presidents. "I was sixty-three years old and a tired man when at last the effects of the 1893 convulsion wore themselves out."

Thanks to city lights and new entertainment, the decade became known as the Gay Nineties, but it was hardly that. When it was over, prosperity had returned, and the United States had crushed Spain in a brief and popular war (see chapter 21). Yet the depression had profound and lasting effects. Attitudes changed and ideas were reshaped in many fields, above all in politics. A realignment of the American political system, which had been developing since the end of Reconstruction, finally reached its fruition in the 1890s, establishing new patterns that lasted well into the twentieth century.

Politics of Stalemate

Electoral politics was a major fascination of the Gilded Age, its mass entertainment and favorite sport. There were few other distractions, and politics was the arena for action and reform. Millions of Americans read party newspapers, listened to three-hour speeches by party leaders, and in elections turned out in enormous numbers to vote. In the six presidential elections from 1876 to 1896, an average of almost 79 percent of the electorate voted, a higher percentage than voted before or after.

White males made up the bulk of the electorate; until after the turn of the century women could vote in national elections only in Wyoming, Utah, Idaho, and Colorado. The National Woman Suffrage Association early sued for the vote, but in 1875 the Supreme Court (*Minor* v. *Happersett*) upheld the power of the states to deny this right to women. On several occasions Congress refused to pass a constitutional amendment for woman's suffrage, and between 1870 and 1910 nearly a dozen states defeated referenda to grant women the vote.

Black men were increasingly kept from the polls. In 1877 Georgia adopted the poll tax to make voters pay an annual tax for the right to vote. The technique, aimed at impoverished blacks, was quickly copied across the South. In 1882 South Carolina adopted the "eight box" law, also copied elsewhere, that required ballots for separate offices to be placed in separate boxes, a difficult task for illiterate voters.

In 1890 Mississippi required voters to be able to read and interpret the federal Constitution to the satisfaction of registration officials, all of them white. Eight years later Louisiana adopted the famous "grandfather clause," demanding a literacy test for all voters except the sons and grandsons of those who had voted in the state before 1867—a time, of course, when no blacks could vote. The number of black voters decreased dramatically. In 1896 there were 130,334 registered black voters in Louisiana; in 1904 there were 1342.

The Party Deadlock

The 1870s and '80s were still dominated by the Civil War generation, the unusual group of people who rose to power in the turbulent 1850s. In both the North and South they had ruled longer than most generations, with a consciousness that the war experience had set them apart. Five of the six presidents elected between 1865 and 1900 had served in the war, as had many civic, business, and religious leaders. In 1890 there were well over a million veterans of the Union army still alive, and Confederate veterans numbered in the hundreds of thousands.

Party loyalties—rooted in Civil War traditions, ethnic and religious differences, and perhaps class distinctions—were remarkably strong. Voters clung to their old parties, shifts were infrequent, and there were relatively few "independent" voters. Although linked to the defeated Confederacy, the Democrats revived quickly after the war. In 1874 they gained control of the House of Representatives, which they maintained for all but four of the succeeding twenty years. The Democrats rested on a less sectional base than did the Republicans. While identification with civil rights and military rule cut Republican strength in the South, the Democratic party's principles of states' rights, decentralization, and limited government won supporters everywhere.

If Democrats offered "the master-wisdom of governing little," the Republicans pursued policies in which local interests merged into nationwide patterns, and government became an instrument to promote moral and material wealth. The Republicans passed the Homestead Act (1862), granted subsidies to the transcontinental railroads, and pushed other measures to encourage economic growth. They enacted legislation and constitutional amendments to protect civil rights. They advocated a high protective tariff as a tool of economic policy, to keep out foreign products while "infant industries" grew.

In national elections, sixteen states, mostly in New England and the North, consistently voted Republican; fourteen states, mostly in the South, consistently voted Democratic. Elections, therefore, depended on a handful of "doubtful" states, which could swing elections either way. These states—New York, New Jersey, Connecticut, Ohio, Indiana, and Illinois—received special attention at election time. Politicians lavished money and time on them; presidential candidates usually came from them. From 1868 to 1912 eight of the nine Republican presidential candidates and six of the seven Democratic candidates came from the "doubtful" states, especially New York and Ohio.

The two parties were evenly matched, and elections were closely fought. In three of the five presidential elections from 1876 to 1892, the victor won by less than 1 percent of the vote; in 1876 and 1888 the losing candidates actually had more popular votes than the winners but lost in the electoral college. Knowing that small mistakes could lose elections, politicians became extremely cautious; it was difficult to govern. Only twice during these years did one party control both the presidency and the two houses of Congress—the Republicans in 1888 and the Democrats in 1892.

Historians once believed that politicians accomplished little between 1877 and 1900, but they were looking in the wrong location. With the impeachment of Andrew Johnson, the authority of the presidency dwindled in relation to congressional strength. For the first time in many years attention shifted away from Washington itself. North and South, people who were weary of the centralization brought on by war and Reconstruction looked first to state and local governments to deal with issues.

Experiments in the States

Across the country, state bureaus and commissions were established to regulate the new industrial society. Commodities shippers, especially farmers and merchants, in protest against the railroads' policies of rate discrimination and other corrupt practices—bribes and free passes given to public officials in exchange for favors—turned to the states for government action. In 1869 Massachusetts established the first commission to oversee the railroads; by 1900 twenty-eight states had taken such action. Most of the early commissions were advisory in nature; they collected statistics and published reports on rates and practices—serving, one commissioner said, "as a sort of lens" to focus public attention. Impatient with the results, legislatures in the Midwest and on the Pacific Coast established commissions with greater powers to fix rates, outlaw rebates, and investigate rate discrimination. These commissions, experimental in nature, served as models for later policy at the federal level.

Illinois had one of the most thoroughgoing provisions. Responding to local merchants who

"WHITE CITY" THE COLUMBIAN EXPOSITION OF 1893

On May 1, 1893, the World's Columbian Exposition opened in Chicago. A focal event of the decade, the Exposition commemorated the four-hundredth anniversary of Columbus' voyage to the New World. It also celebrated modern industrial progress and featured the latest mechanical inventions in acres of white plaster buildings modeled on Greek and Roman patterns. Called the White City, the Exposition cost $31 million and attracted twenty-seven million visitors.

Artists, architects, and engineers flocked to Chicago to participate in its creation. In contrast to the normal jumble of urban growth, the Exposition offered one of the first examples of a planned city. Ten leading architects set out to design it. Frederic Law Olmstead, the designer of New York's famed Central Park, produced his last major public landscape for it, a large lagoon and park along Lake Michigan. It touched off city-planning and "city-beautiful" movements that affected cities as far apart as Washington, Manila, and San Francisco. Chicago transformed itself under the farsighted Chicago Plan (1907–1909) of Daniel H. Burnham, one of the Exposition's chief architects. "City-beautiful" designers integrated transportation, sanitation, and urban architecture in a more "human" city; parks, playgrounds, and tree-lined boulevards proliferated.

The Grand Court at Night. *The Administration Building looms above the gondolas and illuminated fountains that shimmer in the lagoon at the main entrance to the Fair.*

Visitors stroll amid parkways, islands, commemorative columns, and shining white palaces mirrored in wide lagoons.

Louis Sullivan's Transportation Building. *Unique in its deviation from the Fair's classic style of porticoes and pillars.*

The Palace of Electricity. *Many fairgoers saw their first electric lamp here—a great pillar of light studded with colored globes that flashed kaleidoscopic patterns.*

Machinery Hall. *Bethlehem Iron Works' full-sized model of a 125-ton steam hammer, the largest in the world.*

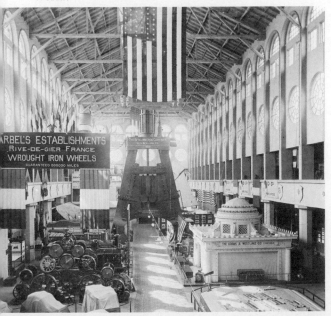

Opening day attracted a crowd of two hundred thousand strong, eager to see the marvels. Jane Addams' purse was snatched; the crowd on the Midway saw the first Ferris wheel, commissioned as a feat of American engineering to rival the recently erected Eiffel Tower in Paris; visitors tasted the first grapefruit brought in on refrigerated railroad cars from Florida and California; American Bell Telephone, a fast-growing young company, offered the first long-distance calls to New York and Boston; Edison showed his latest phonographs and, more fascinating, his new Kinetoscope, a peep-show device that ran short motion pictures on the just-invented celluloid film. (The first Kinetoscope parlor opened the next month on Broadway in New York.)

Machinery at the Exposition went far beyond the famous Corliss steam engine that had impressed the world at the Philadelphia Exposition only seventeen years earlier. A much more "up-to-date" wonder—the new magic of electricity—generated the power for the marvels of machinery exhibited in Chicago. For the first time, visitors saw the electric dynamo and George Westinghouse's alternating-current generator. The Westinghouse Company tucked Edison's incandescent light bulbs in every nook and cranny. Opening the Exposition, President Grover Cleveland touched an ivory telegraph key and the electric current unfurled flags, lit ten thousand electric lights, and started engines throughout the grounds of the fair. In Machinery Hall, the thirty-seven steam engines started at once, producing, in a reporter's words, "a sound that will thrill every observer."

The Exposition represented "the transformation of power into beauty," one onlooker said. Elaborate in its symbolism, the White City celebrated social harmony, the union of architects, engineers, inventors, businessmen, and laborers to create the industrial society. It fused timeless classical forms with the turbulent progress of the new civilization.

For a dazzling moment in Chicago an era paid homage to its accomplishments. A moment was all it had. Three days after the opening ceremonies, the stock market broke, rallied, then broke again. The American economy, so lovingly celebrated by the White City in Chicago, was about to collapse into the worst depression in the history of the nation.

Midway Plaisance. *A favorite with visitors, the entertainment area of the Fair featured foreign villages where a babel of tongues could be heard. When feet gave out, wheeled chairs and "pushers" were available to drive people around.*

Ferris Wheel. *A 264-foot high wheel. Each glass car held sixty passengers. Several couples tried unsuccessfully to get married on the top car!*

Little Egypt. *She scored a triumph on the Midway despite debate about "whether the customs of Cairo would undermine the morals of the public."*

Phoenix House. *This exquisite small Japanese structure, erected by workmen sent by the emperor of Japan, influenced young American architects, notably Frank Lloyd Wright, whose "prairie style" incorporated features of Japanese architecture.*

This cartoon, entitled "The Scourge of the West" (1885) satirizes railroad monopolists. The robber baron astride his iron horse brandishes his weapons—land grants and federal funds—and shoots down workers and farmers.

were upset with existing railroad rate policies, the Illinois state constitution of 1870 declared railroads to be public highways and authorized the legislature to pass laws establishing maximum rates and preventing rate discrimination. In the important case of *Munn* v. *Illinois* (1877), the Supreme Court upheld the Illinois legislation, declaring that private property "affected with the public interest . . . must submit to being controlled by the public for the common good."

But the Court soon weakened that judgment. In the *Wabash* case of 1886 (*Wabash, St. Louis, & Pacific Railway Co.* v. *Illinois*), it narrowed the *Munn* rule and held that states could not regulate commerce extending beyond their borders. Only Congress could. The *Wabash* decision spurred Congress to pass the Interstate Commerce Act (1887), which created the Interstate Commerce Commission to investigate and oversee railroad activities. The act outlawed rebates and pooling agreements, and the ICC became the prototype of the federal commissions that today regulate many parts of the economy.

Reestablishing Presidential Power

Johnson's impeachment, the scandals of the Grant administrations, and the controversy surrounding the 1876 election (see chapter 16) weakened the presidency. During the last two decades of the nineteenth century presidents fought to reassert their authority, and by 1900, under William McKinley, they had succeeded to a remarkable degree. The late 1890s, in fact, marked the birth of the modern powerful presidency.

Rutherford B. Hayes entered the White House with his title clouded by the disputed election of 1876 (see chapter 16). Opponents called him "His Fraudulency" and "Rutherfraud B. Hayes," but soon he began to reassert the authority of the presidency. Hayes worked for reform in the civil service, placed well-known reformers in high offices, and ordering the last troops out of South Carolina and Louisiana, ended military Reconstruction. He hoped to revive the Republican party in the South by persuading business-oriented ex-Whigs to join a national party that would support their economic interests more effectively than the Democrats did. In this attempt, however, he failed. Committed to the gold standard—the only basis, Hayes thought, of a sound currency—in 1878 he vetoed the Bland–Allison Silver Purchase bill, which called for the partial coinage of silver, but Congress passed it over his veto.

James A. Garfield, a Union army hero and long-time member of Congress, succeeded Hayes. Winning by a handful of votes in 1880, he took office energetically, determined to unite the Republican party (which had been split by personality differences and disagreement over policy to-

The Election of 1880		Popular Vote	Electoral Vote
Candidate	Party		
Garfield	Republican	4,446,158	214
Hancock	Democrat	4,444,260	155
Weaver	Greenback	305,997	0

ward the tariff and the South) lower the tariff to reduce surplus revenues, and assert American economic and strategic interests in Latin America. Ambitious and eloquent, Garfield had looked forward to the presidency, yet within a few weeks he said to friends: "My God! What is there in this place that a man should ever want to get into it?"

Office seekers, hordes of them, evoked Garfield's anguish. Each one wanted a government job, and each one thought nothing of cornering the President on every occasion. The problem of government jobs also provoked a bitter fight with the powerful senator from New York, Roscoe Conkling, who resented some of Garfield's choices. On the verge of victory over Conkling, Garfield planned to leave Washington on July 2, 1881, for a vacation in New England. Walking toward his train, he was shot in the back by Charles J. Guiteau, a deranged lawyer and disappointed office seeker (see the special feature in chapter 19). Suffering through the summer, Garfield succumbed on September 19, 1881, and Vice-President Chester A. Arthur—an ally of Senator Conkling—became president.

Arthur was a better president than many had expected. Deftly he established his independence of Conkling. Conservative in outlook, he reversed Garfield's foreign policy initiatives in Latin America, but he approved the construction of the modern American navy. Arthur worked to lower the tariff, and in 1883, with his backing, Congress passed the Pendleton Act to reform the civil service. In part a reaction against Garfield's assassination, the act created a bipartisan Civil Service Commission to administer competitive examinations and appoint officeholders on the basis of merit.

In the election of 1884 Grover Cleveland, the Democratic governor of New York, narrowly defeated Republican nominee James G. Blaine, largely because of the continuing divisions in the Republican party. The first Democratic president

since 1861, Cleveland was slow and ponderous, known for his honesty, stubbornness, and hard work. His term in the White House from 1885 to 1889 reflected the Democratic party's desire to curtail federal activities. Cleveland vetoed over two thirds of the bills presented to him, more than all his predecessors combined.

The Election of 1884		Popular Vote	Electoral Vote
Candidate	Party		
Cleveland	Democrat	4,874,621	219
Blaine	Republican	4,848,936	182
Butler	Greenback	175,096	0
St. John	Prohibition	147,482	0

Forthright and sincere, he brought a new respectability to a Democratic party still tainted by its link with secession. Working long into the night, he reviewed veterans' pensions and civil service appointments. He continued Arthur's naval construction program and forced railroad, lumber, and cattle companies to surrender millions of acres of fraudulently occupied public domain. Late in 1887 he devoted his annual message to an attack on the tariff, "the vicious, inequitable, and illogical source of unnecessary taxation," and committed himself and the Democratic party to lower the tariff.

Election of 1888

ELECTORAL VOTE BY STATE   POPULAR VOTE

REPUBLICAN
Benjamin Harrison   233   ●   5,447,129

DEMOCRATIC
Grover Cleveland   168   ●   5,537,857

MINOR PARTIES   —   396,441

401   11,381,427

The Republicans accused him of undermining American industries, and in 1888 they nominated for the presidency Benjamin Harrison, a defender of the tariff. Cleveland garnered 90,000 more popular votes than Harrison but won the electoral votes of only two northern states and the South. Harrison won the rest of the North, most of the "doubtful" states, and the election.

Republicans in Power: The Billion-Dollar Congress

Despite Harrison's narrow margin, the election of 1888 was the most sweeping victory for either party in almost twenty years; it gave the Republicans the presidency and both houses of Congress. Eager to block Republican-sponsored laws, the Democrats in Congress used minority tactics, especially the "disappearing quorum" rule, which let members of the House of Representatives join in debate but then refuse to answer the roll call to determine if a quorum was present.

For two months the Democrats used the rule to bring Congress to a halt. The Republicans grew angry and impatient. On January 29, 1890, they fell two votes short of a quorum, and Speaker of the House Thomas B. Reed, a crusty veteran of Maine politics, made congressional history. "The Chair," he said, "directs the Clerk to record the following names of members present and refusing to vote." Democrats shouted "Czar! Czar!" a title that stuck to Reed for the rest of his life. Tumult continued for days, but in mid-February 1890 the Republicans adopted the Reed rules and proceeded to enact the party's program.

Tariffs, Trusts, and Silver

As if a dam had burst, law after law poured out of the Republican Congress during 1890. The Republicans passed the McKinley Tariff Act, which raised tariff duties about 4 percent, higher than ever before; it also included a novel reciprocity provision that allowed the president to lower duties if other countries did the same. In addition, the act used duties to promote new industries, like tinplate for packaging the new "canned" foods appearing on grocery-store shelves. A De-

pendent Pensions Act granted pensions to Civil War veterans, their widows, and children. The pensions were modest—$6 to $12 a month—but the number of pensioners doubled by 1893, when nearly one million individuals received about $160 million in pensions.

The Republicans also passed the Sherman Antitrust Act, the first federal attempt to regulate big business. As the initial attempt to deal with the problem of trusts and industrial growth, the act shaped all later antitrust policy. It declared illegal "every contract, combination in the form of trust or otherwise, or conspiracy, in restraint of trade or commerce." Penalties for violation were stiff, including fines and imprisonment and the dissolution of guilty trusts. Experimental in nature, the act's terms were often vague and left precise interpretation to later experience and the courts.

One of the most important laws Congress has passed, the Sherman Antitrust Act made the United States virtually the only industrial nation to regulate business combinations. It tried to harness big business without harming it. The Supreme Court crippled the act in *U.S.* v. *E. C. Knight Co.* (1895), ruling that it applied only to commerce and not to manufacturing. But after the turn of the century it gained fresh power.

Another measure, the Sherman Silver Purchase Act, tried to end the troublesome problem of silver. As one of the two precious metals, silver had once played a large role in currencies around the world, but by the mid-1800s, it had slipped into disuse. With the discovery of the great bonanza mines in Nevada (see chapter 17), American silver production quadrupled between 1870 and 1890, glutting the world market and persuading many European nations to demonetize silver in favor of the scarcer metal, gold. The United States kept a limited form of silver coinage with congressional passage of the Bland-Allison Act in 1878.

Support for silver coinage was especially strong in the South and West, where people thought it might inflate the currency, raise wages and crop prices, and challenge the hated power of the gold-oriented Northeast. Eager to avert the free coinage of silver, which would require the coinage of all silver presented at the United States mints, President Harrison and other Republican leaders pressed for a compromise that took shape in the Sherman Silver Purchase Act of 1890.

The act directed the Treasury to purchase 4.5 million ounces of silver a month and to issue legal tender in the form of Treasury notes in payment for it. The act was a compromise; it satisfied both sides. Opponents of silver were pleased that it did not include free coinage. Silverites, on the other hand, were delighted that the monthly purchases would buy up most of the country's silver production. The Treasury notes, moreover, could be cashed for either gold or silver at the bank, a gesture toward a true bimetallic system based on silver and gold.

As a final measure, Republicans in the House passed a federal elections bill to protect the voting rights of blacks in the South. Although restrained in language and intent, it set off a storm of denunciation among the Democrats, who called it a "force bill" that would station army troops in the South. Because of the outcry, the bill failed in the Senate; it was the last major effort until the 1950s to enforce the Fifteenth Amendment to the Constitution.

The 1890 Elections

The Republican Congress of 1890 was one of the most important Congresses in American history, both because of the number of laws it passed and because many of the laws were so influential in shaping later policy. This Congress also asserted federal authority to a degree the country would not then accept. It passed a record number of significant laws, but the Democrats labeled it the "Billion-Dollar Congress" for spending that much in appropriations and grants.

"This is a billion-dollar country," Speaker Reed replied, but the voters disagreed. The 1890 elections crushed the Republicans, who lost seventy-eight seats in the House, an extraordinary loss. The elections also crushed Republicans in the Midwest where, again enlarging government authority, they had passed state laws prohibiting the sale of alcoholic beverages, requiring the closing of businesses on Sunday, and mandating the use of English in the public schools. Roman Catholics, German Lutherans, and other groups resented such laws, and they angrily deserted the Republicans.

Political veterans went down to defeat, and new leaders vaulted into sudden prominence.

Nebraska elected a Democratic governor for the first time in its history. The state of Iowa, once so staunchly Republican that a local leader had predicted that "Iowa will go Democratic when Hell goes Methodist," went Democratic in 1890.

The Rise of the Populist Movement

The elections of 1890 drew attention to a fast-growing movement among farmers that soon came to be known far and wide as Populism. The movement had begun rather quietly, in places distant from normal centers of attention, and for a time it went almost unnoticed in the press. But during the summer of 1890 wagonloads of farm families in the South and West converged on campgrounds and picnic areas to socialize and discuss common problems. They came by the thousands, weary of drought, mortgages, and low crop prices. At the campgrounds they picnicked, talked, and listened to recruiters from an organization called the National Farmers' Alliance and Industrial Union, which promised unified action to solve agricultural problems.

Farmers were joining the Alliance at the rate of a thousand a week; the Kansas Alliance alone claimed 130,000 members in 1890. The summer of 1890 became "that wonderful picnicking, speech-making Alliance summer," a time of fellowship and spirit long remembered by farmers.

The Farm Problem

Farm discontent was a worldwide phenomenon between 1870 and 1900. With the new means of transportation and communication, farmers everywhere were caught up in a complex international market they neither controlled nor entirely understood.

American farmers complained bitterly about declining prices for their products, rising railroad rates for shipping them, and burdensome mortgages. Some of the grievances were valid. Farm profits were certainly low; agriculture in general tends to produce low profits because of the ease of entry into the industry. The prices of farm commodities fell between 1865 and 1890—corn sold

Selected Commodity Prices

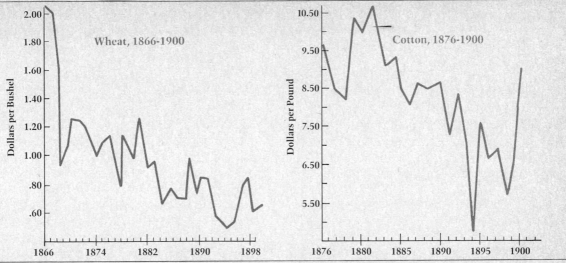

Source: U.S. Bureau of the Census, Historical Statistics of the United States, Colonial Times to 1970, Bicentennial Edition, Washington, D.C., 1975.

at sixty-three cents a bushel in 1881 and twenty-eight cents in 1890—but they did not fall as low as did other commodity prices. Farmers received less for their crops, yet their purchasing power increased.

Neither was the farmers' second grievance—rising railroad rates—entirely justified. Railroad rates actually fell during these years, benefiting shippers of all products. Farm mortgages, while certainly burdensome, were common since many farmers mortgaged their property to expand their holdings or buy new farm machinery. Most mortgages were short, with a term of four years or less, after which farmers could renegotiate at new rates, and the new machinery enabled farmers to triple their output and increase their income.

The actual situation varied from area to area and year to year. New England farmers suffered from overworked land; many southern farmers were trapped in the lien system that kept them always in debt. A study of farms in the Midwest between 1860 and 1900 suggests that farm income rose substantially in the 1860s, fell during the devastating depression of the '70s, rose in the '80s, and remained roughly constant in the '90s. There were also large variations in farm profits from county to county, again indicating the absence of clear nationwide patterns. Farmers who had good land close to railroad transportation did well; others did not.

Still, many farmers were sure their condition had declined, and this perception sparked a growing anger. Everyone in the 1870s and '80s seemed excited about factories, not farms. Farmers were now "hayseeds," a word that first appeared in 1889, and they watched their offspring leave for city lights and new careers. Books like *The Spider and the Fly: or, Tricks, Traps, and Pitfalls of City Life by One Who Knows* (1873) warned against such a move, but still the children went. A literature of disillusionment emerged, most notably Hamlin Garland's *Son of the Middle Border* (1890) and *Main-Travelled Roads* (1891) which described the ugliness of farm life.

The Fast-Growing Farmers' Alliance

Originally a social organization for farmers, the Grange lost many of its members as it turned more and more toward politics in the late 1870s. In its place, a multitude of farm societies sprang into existence. By the end of the 1880s they had formed into two major organizations: the National Farmers' Alliance, located on the Plains west of the Mississippi and known as the Northwestern Alliance; and the Farmers' Alliance and Industrial Union, based in the South and known as the Southern Alliance.

■ *The Grange, personified as a farmer, rouses the sleeping citizenry to the dangers of the trusts in this 1880 engraving.*

The Southern Alliance began in Texas in 1875 but did not assume major proportions until Dr. Charles W. Macune, an energetic and farsighted leader, took over the leadership in 1886. Rapidly expanding, the Alliance absorbed other agricultural societies. Its agents spread across the South where farmers were fed up with crop liens, depleted lands, and sharecropping. They "seem like unto ripe fruit," an Alliance organizer said, "you can garner them by a gentle shake of the bush." In 1890 the Southern Alliance claimed more than a million members.

An effective organization, it published a newspaper, distributed Alliance material to hundreds of local newspapers, and in five years sent lecturers to forty-three states and territories where they spoke to two million farm families. It was "the most massive organizing drive by any citizen institution of nineteenth-century America." Like the Grange, the Alliance also established cooperative grain elevators, marketing associations, and retail stores—all designed to bring farmers to-

gether to make greater profits. Most of the projects were short-lived, but for a time between 1886 and 1892 cooperative enterprises blossomed in the South.

Loosely affiliated with the Southern Alliance, a separate Colored Farmers' National Alliance and Cooperative Union enlisted black farmers in the South. Claiming over a million members, it probably had closer to 250,000, but even that figure was sizable in an era when "uppity" blacks faced not merely defeat, but death. In 1891 black cotton pickers struck for higher wages near Memphis, Tennessee. Led by Ben Patterson, a thirty-year-old picker, they walked off several plantations, but a posse hunted them down and, following violence on both sides, lynched fifteen strikers, including Patterson. The abortive strike ended the Colored Farmers' Alliance.

On the Plains, the Northwestern Alliance, a smaller organization, was formed in 1880 by Milton George of Chicago. Its objectives were similar to those of the Southern Alliance, but it disagreed with the Southerners' emphasis on secrecy, centralized control, and separate organizations for blacks. In 1889 the Southern Alliance changed its name to the National Farmers' Alliance and Industrial Union and persuaded the three strongest state alliances on the plains— those in North Dakota, South Dakota, and Kansas —to join. Thereafter, the new organization dominated the Alliance movement.

The Alliance mainly sponsored social and economic programs, but it turned early to politics. In the West its leaders rejected both the Republicans and Democrats and organized their own party. In June 1890, Kansas organizers formed the first major People's party. The Southern Alliance resisted the idea of a new party for fear it might divide the white vote, thus undercutting white supremacy. The Southerners instead followed leaders such as Benjamin F. Tillman of South Carolina who wanted to capture control of the dominant Democratic party.

Thomas E. Watson and Leonidas L. Polk, two politically minded Southerners, reflected the high quality of Alliance leadership. Georgia-born, Watson was a talented orator and organizer; he urged Georgia farmers, black and white, to unite against their oppressors. The president of the National Farmers' Alliance, Polk believed in scientific farming and cooperative action. Jeremiah Simpson of Kansas, probably the most able of the western leaders, was reflective and well-read. A follower of reformer Henry George, he pushed for major social and economic change. Mary E. Lease—Mary Ellen to her friends, "Mary Yellin'" to her opponents—helped head a movement remarkably open to female leadership. A captivating speaker, she made 160 speeches during the summer of 1890, calling on farmers to rise against Wall Street and the industrial East.

Populist Mary E. Lease advised farmers to "raise less corn and more hell." She also said ". . . if one man has not enough to eat three times a day and another man has $25 million, that last man has something that belongs to the first."

Meeting in Ocala, Florida, in 1890, the Alliance adopted the Ocala Demands, the platform it pushed for as long as it existed. First and foremost, the demands called for the creation of a "sub-treasury system," which would allow farmers to store their crops in government warehouses. In return, they could claim Treasury notes for up to 80 percent of the local market value of the crop, a loan to be repaid when the crops were sold. Farmers could thus hold their crops for the best price. The Ocala Demands also urged the free coinage of silver, an end to protective tariffs and national banks, a federal income tax, the direct election of senators, and tighter regulation of railroad companies.

The Alliance strategy worked well in the elections of 1890. In Kansas the Alliance-related People's party, organized just a few months before, elected four congressmen and a United States senator. Across the South the Alliance won victories based on "the Alliance Yardstick," a demand that Democratic party candidates pledge support for Alliance measures. Alliance leaders claimed thirty-eight Alliance supporters elected to Congress, with at least a dozen more pledged to Alliance principles.

The People's Party

After the 1890 elections, Northern Alliance leaders urged the formation of a national third party to promote reform, although the Southerners remained reluctant, still hopeful of capturing control of the Democratic party. Plans for a new party were discussed at Alliance conventions in 1891 and the following year. In July 1892, a convention in Omaha, Nebraska, formed the new People's party. Southern Alliance leaders joined in, convinced now that there was no reason to cooperate with the Democrats who exploited Alliance popularity but failed to adopt its reforms.

In the South the Populists had worked to unite black and white farmers. "They are in the ditch just like we are," a white Texas Populist said. Blacks and whites served on Populist election committees; they spoke from the same platforms, and they ran on the same tickets. Populist sheriffs called blacks for jury duty, an unheard-of practice in the close-of-the-century South. In 1892 a black Populist was threatened with lynching; he took refuge with Tom Watson, and two thousand white farmers, some of whom rode all night to get there, guarded Watson's house until the threat passed.

Many of the delegates at the Omaha convention had planned to nominate Leonidas L. Polk for president, but he died suddenly in June, and the convention turned instead to James B. Weaver of Iowa, a former congressman, Union army general, and third-party candidate for president in 1880 (on the Greenback-Labor party ticket). As its platform, the People's party adopted many of the Ocala Demands.

Weaver waged an active campaign but with mixed results. He won 1,039,000 votes, the first third-party presidential candidate ever to attract more than a million votes. He carried Kansas, Idaho, Nevada, and Colorado, along with portions of North Dakota and Oregon, for a total of twenty-two electoral votes. The Populists elected

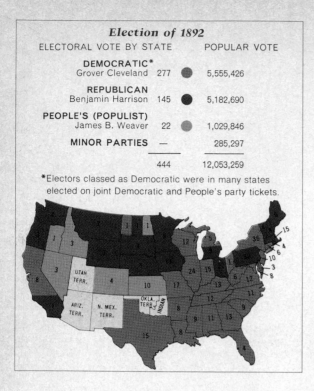

Election of 1892

ELECTORAL VOTE BY STATE		POPULAR VOTE
DEMOCRATIC*		
Grover Cleveland	277	5,555,426
REPUBLICAN		
Benjamin Harrison	145	5,182,690
PEOPLE'S (POPULIST)		
James B. Weaver	22	1,029,846
MINOR PARTIES	—	285,297
	444	12,053,259

*Electors classed as Democratic were in many states elected on joint Democratic and People's party tickets.

The Crisis of the Depression

Building on the Democratic party's sweeping triumph in the midterm elections of 1890, Grover Cleveland decisively defeated incumbent President Benjamin Harrison in 1892. He won by nearly 400,000 votes, a large margin by the standards of the era, and the Democrats increased their strength in the cities and among working-class voters. For the first time since the 1850s, they controlled the White House and both branches of Congress.

Unfortunately for Cleveland, the panic of 1893 struck almost as he took office. The economy had expanded too rapidly in the 1870s and '80s. Railroads had overbuilt, gambling on future growth. Companies had grown beyond their markets; farms and businesses had borrowed heavily for expansion. The mood changed early in 1893. Business confidence sagged, and investors became timid and uneasy. Panic hit the stock market. During 1893 fifteen thousand business firms and more than six hundred banks closed.

The year 1894 was even worse. The gross national product dropped again, and by mid-year the number of unemployed stood at three million. One out of every five workers was unemployed. Unprecedented numbers of needy people taxed the ability of churches and charities to help. "Famine is in our midst," said the head of one city's relief committee. In the summer a heat wave and drought struck the farm belt west of the Mississippi River, creating conditions unmatched until the devastating Dust Bowl of the 1930s. Corn withered in the fields. In the South the price of cotton fell below five cents a pound, far under the break-even point.

People became restless and angry. As one newspaper said in 1896: "On every corner stands a man whose fortune in these dull times has made him an ugly critic of everything and everybody." There was even talk of revolution and bloodshed. "Everyone scolds," Henry Adams, the historian, wrote a British friend. "Everyone also knows what ought to be done. Everyone reviles everyone who does not agree with him, and everyone differs, or agrees only in contempt for everyone else. As far as I can see, everyone is right."

governors in Kansas and North Dakota, ten congressmen, five senators, and about fifteen hundred members of state legislatures.

Despite the Populists' victories, the election brought disappointment. Using fraud and manipulation, Southern Democrats deflected the Populists' efforts and simply wrote them off. Weaver was held to less than a quarter of the vote in every southern state except Alabama. In most of the country he lost heavily in urban areas with the exception of some mining towns in the Far West. He also failed to win over farmers in the settled Midwest. In no midwestern state did he win as much as 5 percent of the vote.

In the election of 1892 many voters switched parties, but they tended to switch to the Democrats rather than the Populists, whose platform on silver and other issues had no appeal among city dwellers or factory workers. Although the Populists did run candidates in the next three presidential elections, their heyday was over. In 1892 Farmers' Alliance membership dropped for the second year in a row, and the organization, once the breeding ground of the People's party, was broken.

Coxey's Army and the Pullman Strike

Some of the unemployed wandered across the country—singly, in small groups, and in small armies. In February 1894, police ejected six hundred unemployed men who stormed the State House in Boston demanding relief. During 1894 there were some fourteen hundred strikes involving more than a half million workers.

On Easter Sunday, 1894, an unusual "army" of perhaps three hundred people left Massillon, Ohio. At its head rode "General" Jacob S. Coxey, a mild-looking, middle-aged businessman who wanted to put the nation's jobless to work building roads. Coxey wanted Congress to pass the Coxey Good Roads bill, which would authorize the printing of $500 million in paper money to finance road construction. His march to Washington—"a petition in boots," he called it— drew nationwide attention. Forty-three newspaper correspondents accompanied him, reporting every detail of the march.

Other armies sprang up around the country, and all headed for Washington to persuade the government to provide jobs on irrigation, road construction, or other projects. In the West they commandeered freight trains and headed east. Coxey himself reached Washington on May 1, 1894, after a difficult, tiring march. Police were everywhere, lining the streets and blocking the approaches to the Capitol. Coxey made it to the foot of the Capitol steps, but before he could do anything, the police were on him. He and a companion were clubbed, then arrested for trespassing. A week later Coxey was sentenced to twenty days in jail.

The armies melted away, but discontent did not. The great Pullman strike—one of the largest strikes in the country's history—began just a few days after Coxey's arrest when the employees of the Pullman Palace Car Company, living in a company town (a town in which everything was owned and everything was provided by the company) struck to protest wage cuts, continuing high rents, and layoffs. On June 26, 1894, the American Railway Union (ARU) under Eugene V. Debs joined the strike by refusing to handle trains that carried Pullman sleeping cars.

Within hours the strike paralyzed the western

■ The march on Washington by Coxey's "army" of unemployed men was an indication of the strength of Populist sentiment and the widespread unrest of the decade.

half of the nation. Grain and livestock could not reach markets. Factories shut down for lack of coal. The strike extended into twenty-seven states and territories, tying up the economy and renewing talk of class warfare. In Washington, President Cleveland decided to break it because it obstructed delivery of the mail.

On July 2 he secured a court injunction against the ARU, and he ordered troops to Chicago. When they arrived on the morning of Independence Day, the city was peaceful. Before long, however, violence broke out, and mobs composed mostly of nonstrikers overturned freight cars, looted, and burned. Restoring order, the army occupied railroad yards in Illinois, California, and other points. By late July the strike was over; Debs was jailed for violating the injunction. Many people applauded Cleveland's action, "nominally for the expedition of the mails," a newspaper said, but "really for the preservation of society."

The Pullman strike had far-reaching consequences for the development of the labor move-

Above, army cavalry troopers clear the way for a train to pass through the strikers' lines during the 1894 Pullman strike in Chicago. Eugene V. Debs (left), leader of the American Railway Union. When troops were ordered to Chicago, Debs' hopes for a nonviolent strike were dashed.

ment. Upholding Debs' sentence in *In re Debs* (1895), the Supreme Court endorsed the use of the injunction in labor disputes, thus giving business and government an effective antilabor weapon that hindered union growth in the 1890s. The strike's failure catapulted Debs into prominence. Working people resented Cleveland's actions in the strike, particularly as it became apparent that he sided with the railroads.

The Miners of the Midwest

The plight of coal miners in the Midwest illustrated the personal and social impact of the depression. Even in the best of times, mining was a dirty and dangerous business. One miner in twelve died underground; one in three suffered injury. Mines routinely closed for as long as six months a year, and wages fell with the depression. An Illinois miner earned $.97 per ton in 1889 and only $.80 in 1896. A bituminous coal miner made $282 a year.

Midwestern mining was often a family occupation, passed down from father to son. It demanded delicate judgments about when to blast, where to follow a seam, and how to avoid rockfalls. Until 1890 English and Irish immigrants dominated the business. They migrated from mine to mine, but nearly always lived in flimsy shacks owned by the company. Time and again the miners struck for higher wages—between 1887 and 1894 there were 116 major coal strikes in Illinois, 111 in Ohio.

After 1890 immigration from southern and eastern Europe, hitherto a trickle, became a flood. Italians, Lithuanians, Poles, Slovaks, Magyars, Russians, Bohemians, and Croatians came to the mines to find work. In three years nearly a thousand Italians settled in Coal City, Illinois; they comprised more than a third of the population. In other mining towns, Italian and Polish miners soon comprised almost half the population.

As the depression deepened, tensions grew between miners and their employers and between "old" miners and the "new." Many "new" miners spoke no English, and often they were "birds of passage," transients who had come to the United States to make money to take back home. Lacking the skills handed down by the "old" miners, they were often blamed for accidents, and they worked longer hours for less pay. At many a tavern after work, "old" miners grumbled about the different-looking newcomers and considered ways to get rid of them.

In April 1894 a wave of wage reductions sparked an explosion of labor unrest in the mines. The United Mine Workers, a struggling union formed just four years earlier, called for a strike of bituminous coal miners, and on April 21 virtually all Midwestern and Pennsylvania miners—some 170,000 in all—quit working. The flow of crucial coal slackened; cities faced blackouts; factories closed.

The violence that soon broke out followed a significant pattern. Over the years the English and Irish miners had built up a set of unspoken understandings with their employers. The "new" miners had not, and they were more prone to violent action to win a strike. The depression hit them especially hard, frustrating their plans to earn money and return home. In many areas, anger and frustration turned the 1894 strikes into outright war.

For nearly two weeks in June 1894 fighting rocked the Illinois, Ohio, and Indiana coalfields. Mobs ignited mine shafts, dynamited coal trains, and defied the state militias. While miners of all backgrounds participated in the violence, it often divided "old" miners and "new." In Spring Valley, Illinois, exiled Italian anarchists took over the strike leadership and incited rioting despite the opposition of the "old" miners. Elsewhere, a mine fired by arsonists burned because the "new" miners prevented the "old" ones from extinguishing the blaze.

Shocked by the violence, public opinion shifted against the strikers. The strike ended in a matter of weeks, but its effects lingered. English and Irish miners moved out into other jobs or up into supervisory positions. Jokes and songs poked cruel fun at the "new" immigrants, and the Pennsylvania and Illinois legislatures adopted laws to keep them out of the mines. Thousands of "old" miners voted Populist in 1894—the Populist platform called for restrictions on immigration—in one of the Populists' few successes that year. The United Mine Workers, dominated by the older miners, began in 1896 to urge Congress to stop the "demoralizing effects" of immigration.

Occurring at the same time, the Pullman strike pulled attention away from the crisis in the coalfields, yet the miners' strike involved three times as many workers and provided a revealing glimpse of the tensions within American society. The miners of the Midwest were the first large group of skilled workers seriously affected by the flood of immigrants from southern and eastern Europe. Buffeted by depression, they reflected the social and economic discord that permeated every industry.

A Beleaguered President

President Cleveland was sure that he knew the cause of the depression. The Sherman Silver Purchase Act of 1890, he believed, had damaged business confidence, drained the Treasury's gold reserve, and caused the panic. The solution to the depression was equally simple: repeal the act.

In June 1893, Cleveland summoned Congress into special session. India had just closed its mints to silver, and Mexico was now the only country in the world with free silver coinage. The silverites were on the defensive, although they pleaded for a compromise. Rejecting the pleas, Cleveland pushed the repeal bill through Congress, and on November 1, 1893, he signed it into law. Always sure of himself, he had staked everything on a single measure—a winning strategy if he succeeded, a devastating one if he did not.

Repeal of the Sherman Silver Purchase Act was probably a necessary action. It responded to the realities of international finance, reduced the flight of gold out of the country, and over the long run boosted business confidence. Unfortunately, it contracted the currency at a time when inflation might have helped. It also did not bring economic revival. The stock market remained listless, businesses continued to close, unemployment spread, and farm prices dropped. "We are hourly expecting the arrival of the benevolent man who is to pay ten cents a pound for cotton," a Virginia newspaper said.

The repeal battle of 1893, discrediting the conservative Cleveland Democrats who had dominated the party since the 1860s, reshaped the politics of the country. It confined the Democratic party largely to the South, helped the Republicans become the majority party in 1894, and strengthened the position of the silver Democrats in their bid for the presidency in 1896. It also focused national attention on the silver issue and thus intensified the silver sentiment Cleveland intended to dampen. In the end, repeal did not even solve the Treasury's gold problem. By January 1894, the reserve had fallen to $65 million. A year later it fell to $44.5 million.

In January 1894 Cleveland desperately resorted to a sale of $50 million in gold bonds to replenish the gold reserve; the following November he again sold bonds; and in February 1895, arousing outrage among many, he agreed to a third bond sale that allowed financier J. Pierpont Morgan and other bankers to reap large profits. A fourth bond sale in January 1896 also failed to stop the drain on the reserve, although it further sharpened the silverites' hatred of President Cleveland.

Depression Politics

In 1894 Cleveland and the Democrats tried to fulfill their long-standing promise to reduce the tariff. The Wilson-Gorman Tariff Act, passed by Congress in August 1894, contained only modest reductions in duties. It reduced the tariff on coal, iron ore, wool, and sugar, ended the McKinley Tariff Act's popular reciprocity agreements with other countries, and moved some duties higher than before. It also imposed a small income tax, a provision the Supreme Court overturned in 1895. Discouraged, Cleveland let the bill become law without his signature.

The Democrats were buried in the elections of 1894. Suffering the greatest defeat in congressional history, they lost 113 House seats, while the Republicans gained 117. In twenty-four states not a single Democrat was elected to Congress. Only one Democrat (Boston's John F. Fitzgerald, the grandfather of President John F. Kennedy) came from all of New England. The Democrats even lost some of the "Solid South," and in the Midwest, a crucial battleground of the 1890s, the party was virtually destroyed.

Wooing labor and the unemployed, the Populists made striking inroads in parts of the South and West, yet it was far from enough. In a year in which thousands of voters switched parties, the People's party elected only four senators or congressmen. Southern Democrats again used fraud and violence to keep the Populists' totals down. In the Midwest the Populists won double the number of votes they had received in 1894, yet still attracted less than 7 percent of the vote. Across the country the discontented tended to vote for the Republicans, not the Populists, a discouraging sign for the Populist party.

For millions of people, Grover Cleveland became a scapegoat for the country's economic ills. Fearing attack, he placed new police barracks on the White House grounds. The Democratic party split, and southern and western Democrats deserted him in droves. At Democratic conventions Cleveland's name evoked jeers. "He is an old bag of beef," Democratic Congressman "Pitchfork" Ben Tillman told a South Carolina audience, "and I am going to go to Washington with a pitchfork and prod him in his old fat ribs."

The elections of 1894 marked the end of the party deadlock that had existed since the 1870s. The Democrats lost, the Populists gained somewhat, and the Republicans became the majority party in the country. The Republican doctrines of activism and national authority, repudiated in the elections of 1890, became more attractive in the midst of depression.

Changing Attitudes

Across the country people were rethinking older ideas about government, the economy, and society. The depression, brutal and far-reaching, undermined traditional views. As men and women concluded that established ideas had failed to deal with the depression, they looked for new ones. There was, the president of the University of Wisconsin said, "a general, all-pervasive, restless discontent with the results of current political and economic thought."

In prosperous times Americans had thought of unemployment as the result of personal failure, affecting primarily the lazy and immoral. Now, in the midst of depression, everyone knew people who were both worthy *and* unemployed. Next door a respected neighbor might be laid off, down the block an entire factory shut down. People debated issues they had long taken for granted. New and reinvigorated local institutions—discussion clubs, women's clubs, reform societies, university extension centers, church groups, farmer's societies—gave people a place to discuss alternatives to the existing order. Pressures for reform increased, and demand grew for government intervention to help the poor and unemployed.

Everybody Works but Father

As husbands and fathers lost their jobs, more and more women and children went to work. Even as late as 1901, well after the depression had ended, a study of working-class families showed that more than half the principal breadwinners were out of work. So many women and children worked that in 1905 there was a popular song, "Everybody Works but Father."

During the 1890s the number of working women rose from 4 million to 5.3 million. Trying to make ends meet, they took in boarders and found jobs as laundresses, cleaners, or domestics. Where possible they worked in offices and factories. Far more black urban women than white worked to supplement their husbands' meager earnings. In New York City in 1900, nearly 60 percent of black women worked compared to 27 percent of the foreign-born and 24 percent of native-born white women. Men still dominated business offices, but during the 1890s more and more employers noted the relative cheapness of female labor. Women telegraph and telephone operators nearly tripled in number during the decade. Women worked as clerks in the new five-and-tens and department stores and as nurses; in 1900 half a million were teachers. They increasingly entered office work as stenographers and typists, occupations in which they earned between $6.00 and $15.00 a week, compared to factory wages of $1.50 to $8.00 a week.

The depression also caused an increasing number of children to work. During the 1890s the number of children employed in southern textile mills jumped more than 160 percent, and boys and girls under sixteen years of age made up nearly a third of the labor force of the mills. Youngsters of eight and nine years worked twelve hours a day for pitiful wages. In most cases children worked not in factories but in farming and city street trades like peddling and shoe-shining. In 1900 the South had more than half the child laborers in the nation.

■ *Tiny barefoot children peddling newspapers and female domestics serving the rich—their meager earnings were desperately needed.*

Concerned about child labor, middle-class women in 1896 formed the League for the Protection of the Family, which called for compulsory education to get children out of factories and into classrooms. The Mothers Congress of 1896 gave rise to the National Congress of Parents and Teachers, the spawning-ground of thousands of local PTAs. The National Council of Women and the General Federation of Women's Clubs took up similar issues. By the end of the 1890s the Federation had 150,000 members who worked for various civic reforms in the fields of child welfare, education, and sanitation.

Changing Themes in Literature

The depression also gave point to a growing movement in literature toward realism and naturalism. In the years after the Civil War, literature often reflected the mood of romanticism—sentimental and unrealistic. Walt Whitman called it "ornamental confectionary" and "copious dribble," but it remained popular through the end of the century.

After the 1870s a number of talented authors rejected romanticism and turned instead to realism. Determined to portray life as it was, they studied local dialects, wrote regional stories, and emphasized the "true" relationships between people. In doing so, they reflected broader trends in the society, such as industrialism, evolutionary theory which emphasized the effect of the environment on humans, and the new philosophy of pragmatism which stressed the relativity of values. (See chapter 22 for a more detailed discussion of pragmatism.)

Regionalist authors like Joel Chandler Harris and George Washington Cable depicted life in the South; Hamlin Garland described the grimness of life on the Great Plains; and Sarah Orne Jewett wrote about everyday life in rural New England. Another regionalist, Bret Harte, achieved fame with stories that portrayed the local color of the California mining camps, particularly in his popular tale, "The Outcasts of Poker Flat."

Harte was joined by a more talented writer, Mark Twain, who became the country's most outstanding realist author. Growing up along the Mississippi River in Hannibal County, Missouri, the young Samuel Langhorne Clemens observed life around him with a humorous and skeptical eye. Adopting a pen name from the river term "mark twain" (two fathoms), he wrote a number of important works that drew on his own experiences. *Life on the Mississippi* (1883) described his career as a steamboat pilot. *The Adventures of Tom Sawyer* (1876) and *The Adventures of Huckleberry Finn* (1884) gained international prominence. In these books, Twain used dialect and common speech instead of literary language, touching off a major change in American prose style.

William Dean Howells—after Twain, the country's most famous author—came more slowly to the realist approach. At first he wrote about the happier sides of life, but he grew worried about the impact of industrialization. *A Traveler from Altruria* (1894), a utopian novel, described an industrial society that consumed lives. The poem, "Society" (1895), written in the midst of the depression, compared society to a splendid ball in which men and women danced on flowers covering the bodies of the poor:

> *And now and then from out the dreadful floor*
> *An arm or brow was lifted from the rest,*
> *As if to strike in madness, or implore*
> *For mercy; and anon some suffering breast*
> *Heaved from the mass and sank; and as before*
> *The revellers above them thronged and prest.*

Other writers became impatient even with realism. Pushing Darwinian theory to its limits, they wrote of a world in which a cruel and merciless environment determined human fate. Often focusing on economic hardship, naturalist writers studied the poor, the lower classes, and the criminal mind; they brought to their writing the social workers' passion for direct and honest experience.

Stephen Crane spent a night in a seven-cent lodging house on the Bowery and in "An Experiment in Misery" captured the smells and sounds of the poor. Crane depicted the carnage of war in *The Red Badge of Courage* (1895) and the impact of poverty in *Maggie: A Girl of the Streets* (1893). His poetry suggested the unimportance of the individual in an uncaring world:

> *A man said to the universe*
> *"Sir, I exist!"*
> *"However," replied the universe,*
> *"The fact has not created in me*
> *A sense of obligation."*

Frank Norris assailed the power of big business in two dramatic novels, *The Octopus* (1901) and *The Pit* (1903), both the story of individual futility in the face of the heartless corporations. Norris' *McTeague* (1899) studied the disintegration of character under economic pressure. Jack London, another naturalist author, traced the power of nature over civilized society in novels like *The*

■ *Illustrations from popular literary works of the time: Mark Twain (top left) created an idyllic setting for the adventures of the irrepressible Tom Sawyer, shown here convincing a gullible friend of the joys of whitewashing a fence (bottom left). A powerful drawing entitled "From the Depths" (above) illustrated J. Ames Mitchell's* The Silent Way *(1906), which dealt with the class struggle. The tenement house alley gang (below) illustrated Stephen Crane's* Maggie.

Sea Wolf (1904) and *The Call of the Wild* (1903), his classic tale of a sled dog that preferred the difficult life of the wilderness to the world of human beings.

Theodore Dreiser, the foremost naturalist writer, grimly portrayed a dark world in which human beings were tossed about by forces beyond their understanding or control. "My own ambition," Dreiser said, "is to represent my world, to conform to the large, truthful lines of life." In his great novel, *Sister Carrie* (1901), he followed a young farm girl who took a job in a Chicago shoe factory. He described the exhausting nature of factory work: "Her hands began to ache at the wrists and then in the fingers, and towards the last she seemed one mass of dull, complaining muscle, fixed in an eternal position, and performing a single mechanical movement."

Like other naturalists, Dreiser focused on environment and character. He thought writers should tell the truth about human affairs, not fabricate romance, and *Sister Carrie*, he said, was "not intended as a piece of literary craftsmanship, but was a picture of conditions."

The Presidential Election of 1896

The election of 1896 was known as " the battle of the standards" because it involved the gold and silver standards of value in the monetary system of the nation. New voting patterns replaced the old, a new majority party confirmed its control of the country, and national policy shifted to suit the new realities.

The Mystique of Silver

Sentiment for free silver coinage grew swiftly after 1894, dominating the South and West, appearing even in the farming regions of New York and New England. Prosilver literature flooded the country (see the special feature in this chapter on pp. 594–95). Pamphlets issued by the millions argued silver's virtues.

People wanted quick solutions to the economic crisis. During 1896 unemployment shot up; farm income and prices fell to the lowest point in the

decade. "I can remember back as far as 1858," an Iowa hardware dealer said in February 1896, "and I have never seen such hard times as these are." The silverites offered a solution, simple but compelling: the free and independent coinage of silver at the ratio of sixteen to one. Free coinage meant that the United States mints would coin all the silver offered to them. Independent coinage meant that the country would coin silver regardless of the policies of other nations, nearly all of which were on the gold standard.

Above all, the silverites believed in a quantity theory of money: the amount of money in circulation determined the level of activity in the economy. A shortage of money meant declining activity and depression. Silver meant more money and thus prosperity. Added to the currency, it would increase the money supply and stir new economic activity. Farm prices would rise. "It means the reopening of closed factories, the relighting of fires in darkened furnaces; it means hope instead of despair; comfort in place of suffering; life instead of death."

By 1896 silver was a symbol. It had moral and patriotic dimensions and stood for a wide range of popular grievances. For many, it reflected rural values rather than urban ones, suggested a shift of power away from the Northeast, and spoke for the downtrodden instead of the well–to–do. Silver represented the common people, as the vast literature of the movement showed.

William H. Harvey's *Coin's Financial School* (1894), the most popular of all silver pamphlets, had the eloquent Coin, a wise but unknown youth, tutoring famous people on the currency. Bankers, lawyers, and scholars came to argue for gold, but left shaken, leaning toward silver. *Coin's Financial School* sold five thousand copies a day at its peak in 1895, with tens of thousands of copies distributed free by silver organizations. It "is being sold on every railroad train by the newsboys and at every cigar store . . . ," a Mississippi congressman said. "It is being read by almost everybody."

Silver was a social movement, one of the largest in American history, but its life span turned out to be brief. As a mass phenomenon, it flourished between 1894 and 1896, then succumbed to electoral defeat, the return of prosperity, and the onset of fresh concerns. But in its time it bespoke a national mood and won millions of followers.

The Republicans and Gold

Scenting victory over the discredited Democrats, numerous Republicans fought for the party's presidential nomination, including "Czar" Thomas B. Reed of the Billion-Dollar Congress. Reed picked up early support but suffered from his reputation for biting wit. William McKinley of Ohio, his chief rival, soon passed him in the race for the nomination.

Able, calm, and affable, McKinley had served in the Union army during the Civil War. In 1876 he won a seat in Congress where he became the chief sponsor of the tariff act named for him. In the months before the 1896 national convention, Marcus A. Hanna, his campaign manager and trusted friend, built a powerful national organization that featured McKinley as "the Advance Agent of Prosperity." When the convention met in June, McKinley had the nomination in hand, and he backed a platform that favored the gold standard against the free coinage of silver.

Republicans favoring silver proposed a pro-silver platform, but the convention overwhelmingly defeated it. Twenty-three silverite Republicans, far fewer than prosilver forces had hoped, marched out of the convention hall. The remaining delegates waved handkerchiefs and flags and shouted "Good-bye" and "Put them out." Hanna stood on a chair screaming "Go! Go! Go!" William Jennings Bryan, who was there as a special correspondent for a Nebraska newspaper climbed on a desk to get a better view.

■ *Supporters of William McKinley's gold-standard platform in 1896 sported handsome goldbug pins like the one shown here.*

The Democrats and Silver

Despite President Cleveland's opposition, more than twenty Democratic state platforms came out for free silver in 1894. Power in the party shifted to the South, where it remained for decades. The party's base narrowed; its outlook increasingly reflected southern views on silver, race, and other issues. In effect, the Democrats became a sectional—no longer a national—party.

The anti-Cleveland Democrats had their issue, but they lacked a leader. Out in Nebraska, Bryan saw the opportunity. He was barely thirty-six years old and had relatively little political experience. But he had spent months wooing support, and he was a captivating public speaker—tall, slender, and handsome, with a resounding voice that in an era without microphones projected easily into every corner of an auditorium. Practicing at home before a mirror, he rehearsed his speeches again and again, as his wife, Mary, a bright, sharp, and politically astute woman, listened for errors.

From the outset of the 1896 Democratic convention, the silver Democrats were in charge, and they put together a platform that stunned the Cleveland wing of the party. It demanded the free coinage of silver, attacked Cleveland's actions in the Pullman strike, and censured his gold bond sales. On July 9, as delegates debated the platform, Bryan's moment came. Striding to the stage, he stood for an instant, a hand raised for silence, waiting for the applause to die down. He would not contend with the previous speakers, he began, for "this is not a contest between persons. The humblest citizen in all the land, when clad in the armor of a righteous cause, is stronger than all the hosts of error. I come to speak to you in defense of a cause as holy as the cause of liberty—the cause of humanity."

The delegates were captivated. Like a trained choir, they rose, cheered each point, and sat back to listen for more. They were there, Bryan said, "to enter up the judgment already rendered by the plain people of this country." The country praised businessmen but forgot that laborers, miners, and farmers were businessmen, too. Shouts rang through the hall and delegates pounded on chairs. Savoring each cheer, Bryan defended silver. Then came the famous closing: "Having behind us the producing masses of this

The Wonderful Wizard of Oz

A restless dreamer, Frank Baum tried his hand at several careers before he gained fame and fortune as a writer of children's literature. From 1888 to 1891 he ran a store and newspaper in South Dakota, where he experienced the desolation and grayness that accompanied agrarian discontent. An avid supporter of William Jennings Bryan in the "battle of the standards," Baum wrote an enduring allegory of the silver movement, *The Wonderful Wizard of Oz.* Published in April 1900, it was an immediate success.

The book opens with a grim description of Kansas:

When Dorothy stood in the doorway and looked around, she could see nothing but the great gray prairie on every side. Not a tree nor a house broke the broad sweep of flat country that reached the edge of the sky in all directions. The sun had baked the plowed land into a gray mass, with little cracks running through it. Even the grass was not green, for the sun had burned the tops of the long blades until they were the same gray color to be seen everywhere. Once the house had been painted, but the sun blistered the paint and the rains washed it away, and now the house was as dull and gray as everything else.

Kansas had not always seemed that way. After 1854, when the Kansas-Nebraska Act opened to settlement its fifty million acres of rich grassland, people poured into the state to stake their claims. Many came from the hilly, timbered country to the east, and breaking onto the prairie, they saw "a new world, reaching to the far horizon without break of trees or chimney stack; just sky and grass and grass and sky . . . . The hush was so loud . . . . The heavens seemed nearer than ever before and awe and beauty and majesty over all."

In later years railroads crisscrossed the state, and advertisements touted the fertile soil. Land was plentiful, rainfall somehow seemed to increase each year, crop prices held at levels high enough to pay, new farming implements yielded larger crops, and property values increased.

Yet life on the prairie was never an easy matter. Flat, lonely, and windswept, the land affected people in ways that were hard to describe to the folks back East. When Aunt Em, Dorothy's aunt, came to Kansas to live, she was young and pretty, but the sun and wind soon changed her. "They had taken the sparkle from her eyes and left them a sober gray; they had taken the red from her cheeks and lips, and they were gray also." Like Aunt Em, Uncle Henry never laughed. "He worked hard from morning till night and did not know what joy was."

After 1887 a series of droughts struck Kansas, and as many as three out of four farms were mortgaged in some Kansas counties. Thousands of settlers like Aunt Em and Uncle Henry gave up and retraced their steps East; others trusted in the Farmers' Alliance and pinned their hopes on the free coinage of silver. While gold as a standard of currency symbolized the idle rich of the industrial Northeast, silver stood for the common folk. Added to the currency in the form of silver dollars, it meant more money, higher crop prices, and a return of prosperity.

Or so the supporters of silver coinage believed. In *The Wonderful Wizard of Oz*, Dorothy (every person) is carried by a cyclone (a victory of the silver forces at the polls) from drought-stricken Kansas to a marvelous land of riches and witches. Unlike dry, gray Kansas, Oz is beautiful, with rippling brooks, stately trees, colorful flowers, and bright-feathered birds. On arrival, Dorothy disposes of one witch, the Wicked Witch of the East (the Eastern money power and those favoring gold), and frees the Munchkins (the common people) from servitude. To return to Kansas, she must first go to the Emerald City (the national capital, greenback-colored).

Dorothy wears magical silver slippers and follows the yellow brick road, thus achieving a proper relationship between the precious metals, silver and gold. Like many of her countrymen, she does not at first recognize the power of the silver slippers, but a kiss from the Good Witch of the North (Northern voters) protects her on the road. Dorothy meets the Scarecrow (the farmer) who has been told he has no brain but actually possesses great common sense (no "hick" or "hayseed," he); the Tin Woodman (the industrial worker) who fears he has become heartless but discovers the spirit of love and cooperation; and the Cowardly Lion (reformers, particularly Wil-

liam Jennings Bryan) who turns out not to be very cowardly at all.

When the four companions reach the Emerald City, they meet the "Great and Terrible" Wizard who tells them that, to gain his help, they must destroy the Wicked Witch of the West (mortgage companies, heartless nature, and other things opposing progress there). Courageously, they set forth. Dorothy dissolves the witch with a bucket of water (what else for drought-ridden farmers?), but when they return to the Emerald City, they find that the Wizard (the money power) is only a charlatan, a manipulator, whose power rests on myth and illusion. "I thought Oz was a great Head," said Dorothy . . . "And I thought Oz was a terrible Beast," said the Tin Woodman. "And I thought Oz was a Ball of Fire," exclaimed the Lion. "No; you are all wrong," said the little man meekly. "I have been making believe."

Dorothy unmasks the wizard, and with the help of Glinda, the Good Witch of the South (support for silver was strong in the South), uses the silver slippers to return home to Kansas. Sadly, the shoes are lost in flight. Back in Oz, the Scarecrow rules the Emerald City (the triumph of the farmers), and the Tin Woodman reigns in the West (industrialism moves West). "Oz" was a familiar abbreviation to those involved in the 16 (ounces) to 1 fight over the ratio of silver to gold.

Baum wanted to write American fairy tales to "bear the stamp of our times and depict the progressive fairies of today." The land of Oz reflected his belief in the American values of freedom and independence, love of family, self-reliance, individualism, and sympathy for the underdog. *Oz*, he said in the original introduction, "aspires to being a modernized fairy tale, in which the wonderment and joy are retained and the heartaches and nightmares are left out."

The *Oz* stories have remained popular, and they still rest on many children's bookshelves. A 1939 film starring Judy Garland as Dorothy, with Ray Bolger as the Scarecrow, Jack Haley as the Tin Woodman, Bert Lahr as the Cowardly Lion, and Frank Morgan as the Wizard was spectacularly successful. Released in the midst of another depression, the film included songs designed, as Dorothy once had, to escape hardship "Somewhere Over the Rainbow."

nation and the world . . . we will answer their demand for a gold standard by saying to them: 'You shall not press down upon the brow of labor this crown of thorns, you shall not crucify mankind upon a cross of gold.'"

Bryan moved his fingers down his temples, suggesting blood trickling from his wounds. He ended with his arms outstretched as on a cross. Letting the silence hang, he dropped his arms, stepped back, then started to his seat. Suddenly, there was pandemonium. Delegates shouted and cheered. When the tumult subsided, they adopted the anti-Cleveland platform, and the next day, Bryan won the presidential nomination.

Campaign and Election

The Democratic convention presented the Populists with a dilemma. The People's party had staked everything on the assumption that neither major party would endorse silver. Now it faced a painful choice: nominate an independent ticket and risk splitting the silverite forces or nominate Bryan and give up its separate identity as a party.

The choice was unpleasant, and it shattered the People's party. Meeting late in July, the party's national convention nominated Bryan, but rather

■ *Although William Jennings Bryan was acclaimed enthusiastically as he campaigned throughout the nation, he failed to win the election.*

than accept the Democratic candidate for vice-president, it named Tom Watson instead. The Populists' endorsement probably hurt Bryan as much as it helped. It won him relatively few votes, since many Populists would have voted for him anyway. It identified him as a Populist, which he was not, and allowed the Republicans to accuse him of heading a ragtag army of malcontents. The squabble over Watson seemed to prove that the Democratic-Populist alliance could never stay together long enough to govern.

In August 1896, Bryan set off on a campaign that became an American legend. Much of the conservative eastern press had deserted him, and he took his campaign directly to the voters, the first presidential candidate in history to do so in a systematic way. By his own count, Bryan traveled 18,009 miles, visited 27 states, and spoke 600 times to a total of some 3 million people. He built skillfully on a new "merchandising" style of campaign in which he worked to educate and persuade voters.

Bryan summoned voters to an older America: a land where farms were as important as factories, where the virtues of rural and religious life outweighed the doubtful lure of the city, where common people still ruled, and opportunity existed for all. He drew on the Jeffersonian tradition of rural virtue, distrust of central authority, and abiding faith in the powers of human reason.

Urged to take the stump against Bryan, McKinley replied: "I might just as well put up a trapeze on my front lawn and compete with some professional athlete as go out speaking against Bryan." The Republican candidate let voters come to him. Railroads brought them by the thousands into McKinley's hometown of Canton, Ohio, and he spoke to them from his front porch. Through use of the press, he reached fully as many people as Bryan's more strenuous effort. Appealing to labor, immigrants, wealthy farmers, businessmen, and the middle class, McKinley defended economic nationalism and the advancing urban-industrial society.

On election day, voter turnout was extraordinarily high, a measure of the intense interest. By nightfall the outcome was clear: McKinley won 50 percent of the vote to Bryan's 46 percent. He won the Northeast and Midwest and carried four border states. In the cities McKinley crushed Bryan.

The election struck down the Populists, whose

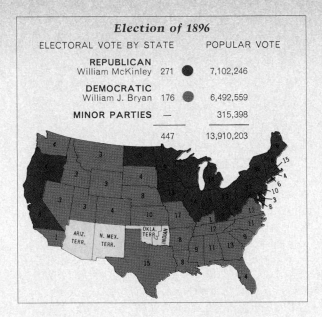

Election of 1896

ELECTORAL VOTE BY STATE		POPULAR VOTE
REPUBLICAN William McKinley	271	7,102,246
DEMOCRATIC William J. Bryan	176	6,492,559
MINOR PARTIES	—	315,398
	447	13,910,203

totals sagged nearly everywhere. Many Populist proposals were later adopted under different leadership. The graduated income tax, crop loans to farmers, the secret ballot, and direct election of United States senators all were early Populist ideas. But the People's party never could win over a majority of the voters, and failing that, it vanished after 1896.

The McKinley Administration

The election of 1896 cemented the voter realignment of 1894 and initiated a generation of Republican rule. For more than three decades after 1896, with only a brief Democratic resurgence under Woodrow Wilson, the Republicans remained the country's majority party.

McKinley took office in 1897 under favorable circumstances. To everyone's relief, the economy had begun to revive. The stock market rose, factories once again churned out goods, and farmers prospered. Farm prices climbed sharply during 1897 on bumper crops of wheat, cotton, and corn. Discoveries of gold in Australia and Alaska—together with the development of a new cyanide process for extracting gold from ore—enlarged the world's gold supply, decreased its price, and inflated the currency as the silverites had hoped.

For the first time since 1890, the 1897 Treasury statements showed a comfortable gold reserve.

McKinley and the Republicans basked in the glow. They became the party of progress and prosperity, an image that helped them win victories until another depression hit in the 1930s. McKinley's popularity soared. Open and accessible in contrast to Cleveland's isolation, he rode the Washington streetcars, walked the streets, and enjoyed looking in department store windows. Cleveland's special police barracks vanished from the White House lawn. McKinley became the first president to ride in an automobile, reaching the speed of eighteen miles an hour.

An activist president, he set the policies of the administration. Conscious of the limits of power, he maintained close ties with Congress and worked hard to educate the public on national choices and priorities. McKinley struck new relations with the press and traveled far more than previous presidents. In some ways he began the modern presidency.

Shortly after taking office, he summoned Congress into special session to revise the tariff. In July 1897 the Dingley Tariff passed the House and Senate. It raised average tariff duties to a record level, and as the final burst of nineteenth-century protectionism, it caused trouble for the Republican party. By the end of the 1890s consumers, critics, and the Republicans themselves were wondering if the tariff had outlived its usefulness in the maturing American economy.

From the 1860s to the '90s the Republicans had built their party on a pledge to *promote* economic growth through the use of state and national power. By 1900, with the industrial system firmly in place, the focus had shifted. The need to *regulate*, to control the effects of industrialism, became a central public concern of the new century. McKinley prodded the Republicans to meet that shift, but he died before his plans matured.

McKinley toyed with the idea of lowering the tariff, but one obstacle always stood in the way: the government needed revenue, and tariff duties were one of the few taxes the public would support. The Spanish-American War of 1898 (see chapter 21) persuaded people to accept greater federal power and, with it, new forms of taxation. In 1899 McKinley spoke of lowering tariff barriers in a world that technology had made smaller.

Chronology

1876 Mark Twain publishes *The Adventures of Tom Sawyer*; sets off major change in American literary style

1877 Disputed election of 1876 results in awarding of presidency to Republican Rutherford B. Hayes

1880 Republican James A. Garfield elected president

1881 Garfield assassinated; Vice-President Chester A. Arthur becomes president

1884 Democrat Grover Cleveland elected president, defeating Republican James G. Blaine

1887 Cleveland calls for lowering of tariff duties

1888 Republican Benjamin Harrison wins presidential election

1889 National Farmers' Alliance and Industrial Union formed to address problems of farmers

1890 Republican-dominated "Billion-Dollar" Congress enacts McKinley Tariff Act, Sherman Antitrust Act, and Sherman Silver Purchase Act
Farmers' Alliance adopts the Ocala Demands

1892 Democrat Cleveland defeats Republican Harrison for presidency
People's Party formed

1893 Financial panic touches off depression lasting until 1897
Sherman Silver Purchase Act repealed
World Columbian Exposition opens in Chicago

1894 Coxey's army marches on Washington
Employees of Pullman Palace Car Company strike

1896 Republican McKinley defeats William Jennings Bryan, Democratic and Populist candidate, in "Battle of the Standards"

1897 Gold discovered in Alaska
Dingley Tariff Act raises tariff duties

1900 McKinley reelected, again defeating Bryan
Gold Standard Act establishes gold as standard of currency

1901 McKinley assassinated; Vice-President Theodore Roosevelt assumes presidency
Naturalist writer Theodore Dreiser publishes *Sister Carrie*

"God and man have linked the nations together . . . ," he said in his last speech at Buffalo, New York, in 1901. "Isolation is no longer possible or desirable."

In 1898 and '99, the McKinley administration focused on the war with Spain, the peace treaty that followed, and the dawning realization that the war had thrust the United States into a position of world power (see chapter 21). In March 1900, Congress passed the Gold Standard Act, which declared gold the standard of currency and ended the silver controversy that had dominated the 1890s.

The presidential campaign of 1900 was a replay of the McKinley-Bryan fight of 1896. Bryan stressed the issues of imperialism and the trusts; McKinley stressed his record at home and abroad. The result in 1900 was a landslide.

The Election of 1900

Candidate	Party	Popular Vote	Electoral Vote
McKinley	Republican	7,218,039	292
Bryan	Democrat	6,358,345	155
Woolley	Prohibition	209,004	0
Debs	Socialist	86,935	0

On September 6, 1901, a few months after his second inauguration, McKinley stood in a receiving line at the Pan-American Exposition in Buffalo. Leon Czolgosz, a twenty-eight-year-old unemployed laborer and anarchist, moved through the line and, reaching the President, shot him. Surgeons probed the wound but could find nothing. A recent discovery called the X-ray was on display at the exposition, but it was not used. On September 14, McKinley died, and Vice-President Theodore Roosevelt became president. A new century had begun.

Reform movements begun in the 1890s flowered in the Progressive period after 1900. Political patterns shifted, the presidency acquired fresh power, and massive unrest prompted social change. The war with Spain brought worldwide responsibilities.

Technology continued to alter the way Americans lived. In 1896 Henry Ford produced a two-cylinder, four-horsepower car, the first of the

■ *Gold triumphs over silver in this* Puck *cartoon referring to the Gold Standard Act of 1900.*

famous line that bore his name. In 1899 the first automobile salesroom opened in New York, and some innovative thinkers were already imagining a network of service stations to keep the new cars running. At Kitty Hawk, North Carolina, Wilbur and Orville Wright, two bicycle manufacturers, neared the birth of powered flight.

The realignments that reached their peak in the 1890s seem distant, yet they are not. Important decisions in those years shaped nearly everything that came after them. In character and influence, the 1890s are as much a part of the twentieth century as of the nineteenth.

Recommended Reading

The most thorough account of the 1890s is in Harold U. Faulkner, *Politics, Reform and Expansion, 1890–1900* (1959), but see also Robert H. Wiebe, *The Search for Order, 1877–1920* (1967) and Samuel P. Hays, *The Response to Industrialism 1855–1914* (1957). David P. Thelen, *The New Citizenship: Origins of Progressivism in Wisconsin, 1885–1900* (1972), stresses the impact of the depression on ideas and attitudes.

The best study of the 1890s depression is Charles Hoffman, *The Depression of the Nineties: An Economic*

History (1970). On politics, see H. Wayne Morgan, *From Hayes to McKinley: National Party Politics, 1877-1896* (1969), and Richard J. Jensen, *The Winning of the Midwest: Social and Political Conflict, 1888-1896* (1971). C. Vann Woodward examines the South in *Origins of the New South, 1887–1913* (1951).

Larzer Ziff, *The American 1890s: Life and Times of a Lost Generation* (1966); Henry Steele Commager, *The American Mind* (1950); and Justin Kaplan, *Mr. Clemens and Mark Twain: A Biography* (1966), examine literary currents. On Populism, see John D. Hicks, *The Populist Revolt: A History of the Farmers' Alliance and the People's Party* (1931) and Lawrence Goodwyn, *Democratic Promise: The Populist Moment in America* (1976). C. Vann Woodward, *Tom Watson: Agrarian Rebel* (1938), is a superb biography.

Additional Bibliography

On politics, see Morton Keller, *Affairs of State: Public Life in Late Nineteenth Century America* (1977); Paul John Kleppner, *The Cross of Culture: A Social Analysis of Midwestern Politics, 1850–1900* (1970); Robert D. Marcus, *Grand Old Party: Political Structure in the Gilded Age, 1880–1896* (1971); and R. Hal Williams, *Years of Decision: American Politics in the 1890s* (1978).

Biographies of the era's personalities include Allan Nevins, *Grover Cleveland: A Study in Courage* (1932); Paola E. Coletta, *William Jennings Bryan*, 3 vols. (1964–1969); Lewis L. Gould, *The Presidency of William McKinley* (1981); Stuart Noblin, *Leonidas Lafayette Polk* (1949); Peter H. Argersinger, *Populism and Politics: William Alfred Peffer and the People's Party* (1974); and Martin Ridge, *Ignatius Donnelly: The Portrait of a Politician* (1962).

On Populism, see Robert C. McMath, Jr., *Populist Vanguard: A History of the Southern Farmers' Alliance* (1975); James E. Wright, *The Politics of Populism: Dissent in Colorado* (1974); O. Gene Clanton, *Kansas Populism: Ideas and Men* (1969); Robert W. Larson, *New Mexico Populism* (1974); and Stanley B. Parsons, *The Populist Context: Rural Versus Urban Power on a Great Plains Frontier* (1973).

Social and labor unrest is covered in Almont Lindsey, *The Pullman Strike: The Story of a Unique Experiment and of a Great Labor Upheaval* (1942); Stanley Buder, *Pullman: An Experiment in Industrial Order and Community Planning, 1880–1930* (1967); Ray Ginger, *The Bending Cross: A Biography of Eugene Victor Debs* (1969); and Donald L. McMurry, *Coxey's Army: A Study of the Industrial Army Movement of 1894* (1929). Walter T. K. Nugent, *Money and American Society* (1968) and Allen Weinstein, *Prelude to Populism: Origins of the Silver Issue, 1867–1878* (1970), explain the silver-gold controversy.

Stanley L. Jones, *The Presidential Election of 1896* (1964); Paul W. Glad, *McKinley, Bryan, and the People* (1964); and Robert F. Durden, *The Climax of Populism: The Election of 1896* (1965) examine that election.

chapter 21

TOWARD EMPIRE

When war with Spain began in April 1898, many Americans regretted it, but many others welcomed it. War was different then, shorter and more personal than the all-encompassing, lengthy, and mechanistic wars of the twentieth century. There were many people—highly respected people—who thought that nations must fight every now and then to prove their power and test the national spirit.

Theodore Roosevelt, thirty-nine years old in 1898, was one of them. Nations needed to fight in order to survive, he thought. For months Roosevelt argued strenuously for war with Spain, first on grounds of freeing Cuba and expelling Spain from the hemisphere; second, because of "the benefit done to our people by giving them something to think of which isn't material gain"; and third, because the army and navy needed the practice.

In April 1898 Roosevelt was serving in the important post of assistant secretary of the navy. When war broke out he quickly resigned to join the army, rejecting the advice of the secretary of the navy who warned he would only "ride a horse and brush mosquitoes from his neck in the Florida sands." The secretary was wrong—dead wrong—and later had the grace to admit it. "Roosevelt was right," he said. "His going into the Army led straight to the Presidency."

In 1898 officers supplied their own uniforms, and Roosevelt, the son of well-to-do parents, wanted his to be stylish. He wired Brooks Brothers, the expensive New York clothier, for a "regular Lieutenant-Colonel's uniform without yellow on the collar and with leggings," to be ready in a week. Joining a friend, he chose to enlist his own regiment, and after a few telephone calls to friends and telegrams to the governors of Arizona, New Mexico, and Oklahoma asking for "good shots and good riders," he had more than enough men. The First United States Volunteer Cavalry, an intriguing mixture of Ivy League athletes and western frontiersmen, was born.

Known as the Rough Riders, it included men from the Harvard, Yale, and Princeton clubs of New York City, the Somerset Club of Boston, and New York's exclusive Knickerbocker Club. Former college athletes—football players, tennis players, and track stars—enlisted. Woodbury Kane, a wealthy yachtsman, signed up and promptly volunteered for kitchen duty.

Other volunteers came from the West—natural soldiers, Roosevelt called them, "tall and sinewy, with resolute, weather-beaten faces, and eyes that looked a man straight in the face without flinching." Among the cowboys, hunters, and prospectors, there was Bucky O'Neill, a legendary Arizona sheriff and Indian fighter, a half-dozen other sheriffs and Texas Rangers, a large number of Indians, a famous broncobuster, and an ex-marshal of Dodge City, Kansas.

Eager for war, the men trained hard, played harder, and rarely passed up a chance for an intellectual discussion—if Roosevelt's memoir of the war is to be believed. Once, he overheard Bucky O'Neill and a Princeton graduate "discussing Aryan word-roots together, and then sliding off into a review of the novels of Balzac, and a discussion as to how far Balzac could be said to be the founder of the modern realistic school of fiction." Roosevelt himself spent his spare time reading *Superiorité des Anglo-Saxons*, a French work that strove to prove the superiority of English-speaking peoples. In such a camp discipline was lax, and enlisted men got on easily with the officers.

The troops howled with joy when orders came to join the invasion army for Cuba. They won their first victories in Florida, fighting off other regiments to capture a train to take them to the wharf and then seizing the only available troopship to Cuba. The Rough Riders set sail on June 14, 1898, and Lieutenant Colonel Roosevelt, who had performed a war dance for the troops the night before, caught their mood: "We knew not whither we were bound, nor what we were to do; but we believed that the nearing future held for us many chances of death and hardship, of honor and renown. If we failed, we would share the fate of all who fail; but we were sure that we would win, that we should score the first great triumph in a mighty world-movement."

America Looks Outward

The overseas expansion of the 1890s differed in several important respects from earlier expansionist moves of the United States. The American Republic had expanded from its beginnings. After the first landings in Jamestown and Plymouth, settlers pushed westward: into the trans-Appalachian region, the Louisiana Territory, Florida, Texas, California, Arizona, and New Mexico. Most of these lands were contiguous with existing territories of the United States, and most were intended for settlement, usually agricultural.

The expansion of the 1890s moved into island possessions, the bulk of them already thickly populated. The new territories were held less for settlement than as naval bases, trading outposts, or commercial centers on major trade routes. More often than not, they were viewed as colonies, not as states-in-the-making.

Historian Samuel F. Bemis described the overseas expansion of the 1890s as "the great aberration," a time when the country adopted expansionist policies that did not fit with prior experience. Other historians, pointing to expansionist tendencies in thought and foreign policy that surfaced during the last half of the nineteenth century, have found a developing pattern that led naturally to the overseas adventures of the 1890s. In this view, "the United States did not set out on an expansionist path in the late 1890's in a sudden, spur-of-the-moment fashion. The overseas empire that Americans controlled in 1900 was not a break in their history, but a natural culmination."

Catching the Spirit of Empire

Most people in most times in history tend to look inward, and Americans in these years following the Civil War were no exception. Among other things, they focused on Reconstruction, the movement westward, and the growing industrial system. They took seriously the well-remembered advice of George Washington's Farewell Address to "steer clear" of foreign entanglements. Throughout the nineteenth century Americans enjoyed "free security" without fully appreciating it. Sheltered by two oceans and the British navy, they could enunciate bold policies like the Monroe Doctrine while remaining virtually impregnable to foreign attack.

Some people urged abolition of the foreign service, considering it an unnecessary expenditure, a dangerous profession that might lead to entanglement in the struggles of the world's great powers. A New York newspaper called it a "relic of medieval, monarchical trumpery," and if not that, it certainly became at times a dumping ground of the spoils system. Presidents named ambassadors from lists of politicians, journalists, and business leaders who, though successful in their own fields, had no training in languages or diplomatic relations.

In the 1870s and after, several developments combined to shift attention outward across the seas. The end of the frontier, announced officially in the census report of 1890, sparked fears about diminishing opportunities at home. Further growth, it seemed, must take place abroad, as John A. Kasson, an able and experienced diplomat, said in the *North American Review*: "We are rapidly utilizing the whole of our continental territory. We must turn our eyes abroad, or they will soon look inward upon discontent."

Factories and farms multiplied, producing more goods than the domestic market could consume. Both farmers and industrialists looked for new overseas markets, and the growing volume of exports—including more and more manufactured goods—changed the nature of American trade relations. American exports of merchandise amounted to $393 million in 1870, $858 million in 1890, and $1.4 billion in 1900. In 1898 the United States exported more than it imported, beginning a trend that lasted through the 1960s.

Political leaders—James G. Blaine was one—began to argue for the vital importance of foreign markets to continued economic growth. Blaine, secretary of state under Garfield and again under Harrison, aggressively sought a new empire of markets in Latin America and Asia. To some extent, he and others were also caught up in a worldwide scramble for empire. In the last third of the century Great Britain, France, and Germany divided up Africa and looked covetously at Asia. The idea of imperialistic expansion was in the air, and the great powers measured their greatness by the colonies they acquired. Inevitably, some Americans—certain business interests

■ Entitled "The World Is My Market, My Customers Are All Mankind," this cartoon of the 1870s reflects America's growing interest in foreign markets.

and foreign-policy strategists, for example—caught the spirit and wanted to enter the international hunt for territory (see p. 610).

Intellectual currents that supported expansion drew on Charles Darwin's theories of evolution. Adherents pointed, for example, to *The Origin of Species*, which mentioned in its subtitle *The Preservation of Favored Races in the Struggle for Life*. Applied to human and social development, biological concepts seemed to call for the triumph of the fit and the elimination of the unfit. "In this world," said Theodore Roosevelt, who thought of himself as one of the fit, "the nation that has trained itself to a career of unwarlike and isolated ease is bound, in the end, to go down before other nations which have not lost the manly and adventurous qualities."

Haeckel's Biogenetic Law, then a popular theory, suggested that the development of the individual repeated the development of the race. Primitive peoples thus were in the arrested stages of childhood or adolescence; they needed supervision and protective treatment. In a similar vein,

John Fiske, a popular writer and lecturer, argued for Anglo-Saxon racial superiority, a result of the process of natural selection. The English and Americans, Fiske said, would occupy every land on the globe that was not already "civilized," bringing the advances of commerce and democratic institutions.

Such views were widespread among the lettered and unlettered alike. In Cuba, one of the Rough Riders ushered a visiting Russian prince around the trenches, informing him with ill-considered enthusiasm: "You see, Prince, the great result of this war is that it has united the two branches of Anglo-Saxon people; and now that they are together they can whip the world, Prince! they can whip the world!" Eminent scholars like John W. Burgess, a professor of political science at Columbia University, argued in similar though more dignified fashion that people of English origin were destined to impose their political institutions on the world.

The career of Josiah Strong, a Congregational minister and fervent expansionist, suggested the strength of the developing ideas. A champion of overseas missionary work, Strong traveled extensively through the West for the Home Missionary Society, and in 1885, drawing on his experiences, he published a book entitled *Our Country: Its Possible Future and Its Present Crisis*. An immediate best-seller, the book called upon foreign missions to civilize the world under the Anglo-Saxon races. Strong became a national celebrity.

Our Country argued for expanding American trade and dominion. "The world is to be Christianized and civilized. And what is the process of civilizing but the creating of more and higher wants. Commerce follows the missionary." A special people, the bearers of civil liberty and Christianity, Americans were members of a God-favored race destined to lead the world. Anglo-Saxons already owned one third of the earth, Strong said, and in a famous passage he concluded that they must take more.

Then will the world enter upon a new stage of its history—the final competition of races for which the Anglo-Saxon is being schooled. If I do not read amiss, this powerful race will move down upon Mexico, down upon Central and South America, out upon the islands of the sea, over upon Africa and beyond. And can anyone doubt that the result of this competition of races will be the "survival of the fittest"?

Taken together, these developments in social, political, and economic thought prepared Americans for a larger role in the world. The change was gradual, and there was never a day when people awoke with a sudden realization of their interests overseas. But change there was, and by the 1890s Americans were ready to reach out into the world in a more determined and deliberate fashion than ever before. For almost the first time, they felt the need for a foreign "policy."

Foreign Policy Approaches: 1867–1900

Rarely consistent, American foreign policy in the last half of the nineteenth century took different approaches to different areas of the world. In relation to Europe, where the dominant world powers were, policymakers promoted trade and tried to avoid diplomatic entanglements. In North and South America, they based policy on the Monroe Doctrine, a recurrent dream of annexing Canada or Mexico, a hope for extensive trade, and Pan-American unity against the nations of the Old World. In Asia, they coveted Hawaii and other outposts on the sea lanes to China.

Secretary of State William Henry Seward, who served from 1861 to 1869, aggressively pushed an expansive foreign policy. "Give me . . . fifty, forty, thirty more years of life," he told a Boston audience in 1867, "and I will give you possession of the American continent and control of the world." Seward, it turned out, had only five more years of life, but he developed a vision of an American empire stretching south in Latin America and west to the shores of Asia. He wanted Canada and Mexico, islands in the Caribbean as strategic bases to protect a canal across the isthmus, and Hawaii and other islands as stepping-stones to Asia.

Seward tried unsuccessfully to negotiate a commercial treaty with Hawaii in 1867, and the same year he annexed the Midway Islands, a small atoll group twelve hundred miles west of Hawaii. In 1867 he concluded a treaty with Russia for the purchase of Alaska (which was promptly labeled "Seward's Folly") partly to sandwich western Canada between American territory and lead to its annexation. In all this, Seward's target remained the Asian market, which he and many others considered a virtually bottomless outlet for farm and manufactured goods. As the American empire spread, he thought, Mexico City would become its capital.

Mexico itself presented a difficult problem, for the French had taken advantage of the Civil War to create there a puppet state under Archduke Maximilian, the younger brother of Austria's Hapsburg emperor. Popular sentiment in the United States opposed the French adventure, and once the Civil War ended Seward's tone became firmer. By 1867 Napoleon III of France tired of the expense, and he withdrew his troops. Refusing to leave, Maximilian was captured and executed by the Mexicans. For the American public, the affair symbolized a victory for the Monroe Doctrine and growing American power in the hemisphere.

Secretary of State Hamilton Fish, an urbane New Yorker, followed Seward in 1869, serving under President Ulysses S. Grant. An avid expan-

■ *Cartoonists had a field day when Seward purchased Alaska. Here, he invites the Alaskan representative to "bring Mr. McSeal along with you to Washington."*

sionist, Grant wanted to extend American influence in the Caribbean and Pacific, though Fish, more conservative, often restrained him. They moved first to repair relations with Great Britain. The first business was settlement of the *Alabama* claims—demands that Britain pay the United States for damages caused by Confederate vessels which, like the *Alabama*, had been built and outfitted in British shipyards (see chapter 15). Negotiating patiently, Fish signed the Treaty of Washington in 1871, providing for arbitration of the *Alabama* issue and other nettlesome controversies. The treaty, one of the landmarks in the peaceful settlement of international disputes, marked a significant step in cementing Anglo-American relations.

Grant and Fish looked most eagerly to Latin America. In 1870 Grant became the first president to proclaim the nontransfer principle—"hereafter no territory on this continent shall be regarded as subject to transfer to a European power." Fish also promoted the independence of Cuba, restive under Spanish rule, while holding off the annexation desired by the more eager Grant. Influenced by speculators, Grant tried to annex Santo Domingo in 1869 but was thwarted by powerful Republicans in the Senate who disliked foreign involvement and feared a subsequent attempt to annex Haiti.

James G. Blaine served as secretary of state only six months, until Garfield's assassination, but laid extensive plans to establish closer commercial relations with Latin America. His successor, Frederick T. Frelinghuysen, changed Blaine's approach but not his strategy. Like Blaine, Frelinghuysen wanted to find Caribbean markets for American goods; he negotiated separate reciprocity treaties with Mexico, Cuba and Puerto Rico, the British West Indies, Santo Domingo, and Colombia. Using these treaties, Frelinghuysen hoped not only to obtain markets for American goods but to bind these countries to American interests.

When Blaine returned to the State Department in 1889 under President Benjamin Harrison, he moved again to expand markets in Latin America. Drawing on earlier ideas, he envisaged a hemispheric system of peaceful intercourse, arbitration of disputes, and expanded trade. He also wanted to annex Hawaii. "I think there are only three places that are of value and not already

taken, that are not continental," he wrote Harrison in 1891. "One is Hawaii and the others are Cuba and Puerto Rico." The last two might take a generation to acquire, but "Hawaii may come up for decision at any unexpected hour and I hope we shall be prepared to decide it in the affirmative."

Harrison and Blaine toyed with naval acquisitions in the Danish West Indies, Santo Domingo, Haiti, and Peru, but in general they focused on Pan-Americanism and tariff reciprocity. Blaine presided over the first Inter-American Conference in Washington on October 2, 1889. Delegates from nineteen American nations were present, and Blaine urged them to unite Latin America and the United States in a customs union and create a way to settle conflicts. The delegates rejected both proposals but did create the International Bureau of the American Republics, later renamed the Pan-American Union, for the exchange of general information including political, scientific, and cultural knowledge. The conference, a major step in hemispheric relations, led to later meetings promoting trade and other agreements.

Reciprocity, Harrison and Blaine hoped, would divert Latin American trade from Europe to the United States. Working hard to sell the idea in Congress, Blaine lobbied for a reciprocity provision in the McKinley Tariff Act of 1890 (see chapter 20), and once that was enacted he negotiated important reciprocity treaties with most Latin American nations. The treaties suffered from the depression of the 1890s; nevertheless, they resulted in greater American exports of flour, grain, meat, iron, and machinery. Exports to Cuba jumped by a third between 1891 and 1893, then dropped precipitously when the 1894 Wilson-Gorman Tariff Act ended reciprocity.

Grover Cleveland, Harrison's successor, also pursued an aggressive policy toward Latin America. In 1895 he brought the United States precariously close to war with Great Britain over a boundary dispute between Venezuela and British Guiana. Cleveland sympathized with Venezuela, and he and Secretary of State Richard Olney urged Britain to arbitrate the dispute. When Britain failed to act, Olney drafted a stiff diplomatic note affirming the Monroe Doctrine and denying European nations the right to meddle in Western Hemisphere affairs.

Four months passed before Lord Salisbury,

A SIMPLE DEFINITION.

Master Johnny Bull. "MONROE DOCTRINE! WHAT *IS* THE 'MONROE DOCTRINE'?"
Master Jonathan. "WA-AL—GUESS IT'S THAT EVERYTHING EVERYWHERE BE-LONGS TO *US!*"

■ *John Tenniel's scathing definition of the Monroe doctrine in this cartoon from* Punch *reflects the British view that the U.S. reserved exclusive rights to act like a colonial power in the Western Hemisphere.*

the British foreign secretary, replied. Rejecting Olney's arguments, he sent two letters, the first bluntly repudiating the Monroe Doctrine as international law. The second letter, carefully reasoned and sometimes sarcastic, rejected Olney's arguments for the Venezuelan boundary. Enraged, Cleveland defended the Monroe Doctrine, and he asked Congress for authority to appoint a commission to decide the boundary and enforce its decision. "I am fully alive to the responsibility incurred and keenly realize all the consequences that may follow," he told Congress, plainly implying war.

Preoccupied with larger diplomatic problems in Africa and Europe, Britain changed its position. In November 1896 the two countries signed a treaty of arbitration, under which Great Britain received much of the disputed territory and Venezuela retained control of the vital Orinoco River. Though the Cleveland-Olney approach was clumsy, the Venezuelan incident demonstrated growing American power of persuasion in the Western

Hemisphere. Cleveland and Olney persuaded Great Britain to recognize United States dominance, and they sharpened American influence in Latin America. The Monroe Doctrine assumed new importance. In averting war, an era of Anglo-American friendship was begun.

The Lure of Hawaii and Samoa

The islands of Hawaii offered a tempting way station to Asian markets. In the early 1800s they were already called the "Crossroads of the Pacific," and trading ships of many nations stopped there. In 1820 the first American missionaries arrived to convert the islanders to Christianity. Like missionaries elsewhere, they advertised Hawaii's economic and other benefits and attracted new settlers. Their children later came to dominate Hawaiian political life and played an important role in annexation.

After the Civil War the United States tightened its connections with the islands. The reciprocity treaty of 1875 allowed Hawaiian sugar to enter the United States free of duty and bound the Hawaiian monarchy to make no territorial or economic concessions to other powers. The treaty increased Hawaiian economic dependence on the United States; its political clauses effectively made Hawaii an American protectorate. In 1887 a new treaty reaffirmed these arrangements and granted the United States exclusive use of Pearl Harbor, a magnificent harbor that had early caught the eye of naval strategists.

Following the 1875 treaty, white Hawaiians became more and more influential in the islands' political life. The McKinley Tariff Act of 1890 ended the special status given Hawaiian sugar and in addition awarded American producers a bounty of two cents a pound. Hawaiian sugar production dropped dramatically, unemployment rose, and property values fell. The following year the weak King Kalakaua died, bringing to power a strong-willed nationalist, Queen Liliuokalani. Resentful of white minority rule, she decreed a new constitution that gave greater power to native Hawaiians.

Unhappy, the American residents revolted in early 1893 and called on the United States for help. John L. Stevens, the American minister in Honolulu, sent 150 marines ashore from the

Windjammers, loaded with a sugar cargo, shown in Honolulu Harbor in 1882.

Queen Liluokalani, a fierce nationalist, composed the lovely Hawaiian song "Aloha Oe." Her stubborn resistance to annexation could only postpone, not prevent, it.

cruiser *Boston*, and within three days the bloodless revolution was over. Queen Liliuokalani surrendered "to the superior force of the United States," and the victorious rebels set up a provisional government. On February 14, 1893, Harrison's Secretary of State John W. Foster and delegates of the new government signed a treaty annexing Hawaii to the United States.

But only two weeks remained in Harrison's term, and the Senate refused to ratify the agreement. Five days after taking office, Cleveland withdrew the treaty; he then sent a representative to investigate the cause of the rebellion. The investigation revealed the American role in it, and Cleveland decided to restore the queen to her throne. He made that demand, but the provisional government in Hawaii politely refused and instead established the Republic of Hawaii, which the embarrassed Cleveland, unable to do otherwise, recognized.

The debate over Hawaiian annexation, continuing through the 1890s, foreshadowed the later debate over the treaty to end the Spanish-American War. People in favor of annexation pointed to Hawaii's strategic location, argued that Japan or other powers might seize the islands if the United States did not, and suggested that Americans had a responsibility to civilize and Christianize the native Hawaiians. Opponents warned that annexation might lead to a colonial army and colonial problems, the inclusion of a "mongrel" population in the United States, and rule over an area not destined for statehood.

Annexation came swiftly in July 1898 in the midst of excitement over victories in the Spanish-American War. The year before, President William McKinley had sent a treaty of annexation to the Senate. "We need Hawaii just as much and a good deal more than we did California," he said privately. "It is Manifest Destiny." But opposition quickly arose, and the treaty stalled. Japan protested against it, pointing out that Japanese made up a quarter of the Hawaiian population. Japan dispatched a cruiser to Honolulu; the Navy Department sent the battleship *Oregon* and ordered naval forces to take Hawaii if the Japanese made threatening moves.

Hawaii and Samoa

The location of the Hawaiian Islands and Samoa in the Pacific Ocean is shown in the small-scale map at the top.

In 1898 annexationists redoubled arguments about Hawaii's commercial and military importance. McKinley and congressional leaders switched strategies to seek a joint resolution, rather than a treaty, for annexation. A joint resolution required only a majority of both houses, while a treaty needed a two-thirds vote in the Senate. Bolstered by the new strategy, the annexation measure moved quickly through Congress, and McKinley signed it on July 7, 1898. His signature, giving the United States a naval and commercial base in the mid-Pacific, realized a goal of policymakers since the 1860s.

While Hawaii represented a step toward China,

the Samoan Islands, three thousand miles to the south, sat astride the sea lanes of the South Pacific. Americans showed early interest in Samoa, and in 1872 a naval officer negotiated a treaty granting the United States the use of Pago Pago, a harbor on the island of Tuitula. The Senate rejected it but six years later approved a similar agreement providing for a naval station there. The agreement bound the United States to use its good offices to adjust any disputes between the Samoan chiefs and foreign governments. Great Britain and Germany also secured treaty rights in Samoa, and thereafter the three nations jockeyed for position.

The situation grew tense in 1889 when warships from all three countries gathered in a Samoan harbor. But a sudden hurricane destroyed the fleets, and tensions eased. A month later delegates from Britain, Germany, and the United States met in Berlin to negotiate the problem. Britain and Germany wanted to divide up the islands; Secretary of State Blaine held out for some degree of authority by the indigenous population, with American control over Pago Pago.

The agreement, an uneasy one, ended in 1899 when the United States and Germany divided Samoa and compensated Britain with lands elsewhere in the Pacific. Germany claimed the two larger islands in the chain; the United States kept Tuitula and the harbor at Pago Pago.

The New Navy

Large navies were vital in the scramble for colonies, and in the 1870s the United States had almost no navy. One of the most powerful fleets in the world during the Civil War, the American navy had fallen into rapid decline. By 1880 there were fewer than two thousand vessels, only forty-eight of which could fire a gun. Ships rotted, and many officers left the service. "It was easy then," said George Dewey, later a hero of the war with Spain, "for an officer to drift along in his grade, losing interest and remaining in the navy only because he was too old to change his occupation."

Conditions changed during the 1880s. A group of rising young officers, steeped in a new naval philosophy, argued for an expanded navy equipped with fast, aggressive fleets capable of fighting battles across the seas. This group had its

greatest influence in a special Naval Advisory Board, formed by the secretary of the navy in 1881. Big-navy proponents pointed to the growing fleets of Great Britain, France, and Germany, arguing that the United States needed greater fleet strength to protect its interests in the Caribbean and Pacific.

In 1883 Congress authorized construction of four steel ships, marking the beginning of the new navy. Experts also worked to improve naval management and the quality of fleet personnel, and between 1885 and 1889 Congress budgeted funds for thirty additional ships. The initial building program focused on lightly armored, fast cruisers for raiding enemy merchant ships and protecting American shores, but after 1890 the program shifted to the construction of a seagoing, offensive battleship navy capable of challenging the strongest fleets of Europe.

Alfred Thayer Mahan and Benjamin F. Tracy were two of the main forces behind the new navy. Austere and scholarly, Mahan was the era's most influential naval strategist. After graduating from the Naval Academy in 1859, he devoted a lifetime to studying the influence of sea power in history;

for over two decades he headed the Newport Naval War College, where officers imbibed the latest in strategic thinking. A clear, logical writer, Mahan summarized his beliefs in three major books: *The Influence of Sea Power Upon History, 1660–1783* (1890), *The Influence of Sea Power Upon the French Revolution and Empire, 1793–1812* (1892), and *The Interest of America in Sea Power* (1897).

Mahan's reasoning was simple and persuasive. Industrialism, he argued, produced vast surpluses of agricultural and manufactured goods, for which markets must be found. Markets involved distant ports; reaching them required a large merchant marine and a powerful navy to protect it. Navies, in turn, needed coaling stations and repair yards. Coaling stations meant colonies, and colonies became strategic bases, the foundation of a nation's wealth and power. The bases might serve as markets themselves, but they were more important as stepping-stones to other objectives, the markets of Latin America and Asia.

Mahan called attention to the worldwide race for power, a race, he warned, the United States could not afford to lose. "All around us now is strife; 'the struggle of life,' 'the race of life' are phrases so familiar that we do not feel their significance till we stop to think about them. Everywhere nation is arrayed against nation; our own no less than others." To compete in the struggle the United States must expand. It needed strategic bases, a powerful, oceangoing navy, a canal across the isthmus to link the East coast with the Pacific, and Hawaii as a way station on the route to Asia.

Mahan influenced a generation of policymakers in the United States and Europe; one of them, Benjamin F. Tracy, became Harrison's secretary of the navy in 1889. Between then and 1893 Tracy organized the Bureau of Construction and Repair to design and build new ships, established the Naval Reserve in 1891, saved from a budget cut the Naval War College where Mahan lectured, and ordered construction of the first American submarine in 1893. He also started the first heavy rapid-fire guns, smokeless powder, torpedoes, and heavy armor. Above all, Tracy joined with big-navy advocates in Congress to push for a far-ranging battleship fleet capable of attacking distant enemies. He wanted two fleets of battleships, eight in the Pacific and twelve in the Atlantic. He got four first-class battleships.

In 1889, when Tracy entered office, the United States ranked twelfth among world navies; in 1893, when he left, it ranked seventh and was climbing rapidly. "The sea," he predicted in 1891, "will be the future seat of empires. And we shall rule it as certainly as the sun doth rise." By the end of the decade the navy had seventeen steel battleships, six armored cruisers, and many smaller craft. It ranked third in the world.

■ *Mr. Dooley, the irreverent Irish-American saloon keeper created by Finley Peter Dunne, often aimed his sardonic humor at the "Establishment."*

eth century. It brought colonies and millions of colonial subjects; it brought imperial dreams and responsibilities. The war strengthened the office of the presidency, swept the nation together in a tide of emotion, and confirmed the long-standing belief in the superiority of the New World over the Old. Afterward, Americans looked outward as never before, touched, they were sure, with a special destiny.

They seemed a chosen people, as Mr. Dooley pointed out to his friend Hennessy over the Archey Road bar. "We're a gr-reat people" said Hennessy, in his rolling Irish brogue. "We ar-re that," replied Mr. Dooley. "We ar-re that. An th' best iv it is we know we ar-re."

War with Spain

The war with Spain in 1898 built a mood of national confidence, altered older, more insular patterns of thought, and reshaped the way Americans saw themselves and the world. When the war ended, American possessions stretched into the Caribbean and deep into the Pacific. American influence went further still, and the United States was recognized as a "world power."

The Spanish-American War established the United States as a dominant force for the twenti-

A War for Principle

By the 1890s Cuba and the nearby island of Puerto Rico comprised nearly all that remained of Spain's once vast empire in the New World. Several times Cuban insurgents had rebelled against Spanish rule, including a decade-long rebellion from 1868 to 1878 (the Ten Years' War) that failed to settle the conflict. The depression of 1893 damaged the Cuban economy, and the Wilson-Gorman Tariff of 1894 prostrated it. Duties on sugar, Cuba's lifeblood, were raised 40 percent. With the island's sugar market in ruins, discent with Spanish rule heightened, and in late February 1895 revolt again broke out.

Recognizing the importance of the nearby United States, Cuban insurgents established a junta in New York City to raise money, purchase weapons, and wage a propaganda war to sway American public opinion. Conditions in Cuba were grim. The insurgents pursued a hit-and-run, scorched-earth policy to force the Spanish to leave. Spain committed more than two hundred thousand soldiers; the Spanish commander, who had won with similar tactics in 1878, tried to pin the insurgents in the eastern part of the island where they could be cornered and destroyed.

When this strategy failed, Spain in January 1896 sent a new commander, General Valeriano Weyler y Nicolau. Relentless and brutal, Weyler gave the rebels ten days to lay down their arms. He then put into effect a "reconcentration" policy designed to move the native population into camps and destroy the rebellion's popular base. Herded into fortified areas, Cubans died by the thousands, victims of unsanitary conditions, overcrowding, and disease.

There was a wave of sympathy for the insurgents stimulated by the newspapers (see the special feature on pp. 614–15). But "yellow" journalism did not cause the war. It stemmed from larger conflicts in policies and perceptions between Spain and the United States. Grover Cleveland, under whose administration the rebellion began, preferred Spanish rule to the kind of turmoil that might invite foreign intervention. Opposed to the annexation of Cuba, he issued a proclamation of neutrality and tried to restrain public opinion. In 1896 Congress passed a resolution favoring recognition of Cuban belligerency, but Cleveland ignored it. Instead, he offered to mediate the struggle, an offer Spain declined.

Taking office in March 1897, President McKinley also urged neutrality but tilted more toward the insurgents. He immediately sent a trusted aide on a fact-finding mission to Cuba; the aide reported in mid-1897 that Weyler's policy had wrapped Cuba "in the stillness of death and the silence of desolation." The report in hand, McKinley offered to mediate the struggle, but concerned over the suffering, he protested against

■ *The illustration below appeared in* Harper's Weekly. *Entitled "Starvation by Proclamation," it shows Cubans being marched into one of General Weyler's "reconcentration" camps. Frederic Remington's article (right) in the* New York Journal *describes the cruel manner in which the "guerillas"—irregular troops employed by the Spanish—treated the Cubans ("Pacificos").*

SPANISH GUERILLAS BRINGING "PACIFICOS" INTO CAMP

GUINES, CUBA, *January 15, 1897.* The acts of the terrible savages, or irregular troops called "guerillas," employed by the Spaniards, pass all understanding by civilized man. The American Indian was never guilty of the monstrous crimes that they commit.

Their treatment of women is unspeakable, and as for the men captured by them alive, the blood curdles in my veins as I think of the atrocity, of the cruelty, practiced on these helpless victims.

My picture illustrates one case where the guerillas saw fit to bring their captives into the lines, trussed up at the elbows, after their fashion. *The New York* Journal, *January 24, 1897.*

Spain's "uncivilized and inhuman" conduct. The United States, he made clear, did not contest Spain's right to fight the rebellion but insisted it be done within humane limits.

Late in 1897 a change in government in Madrid brought a temporary lull in the crisis. The new government recalled Weyler and agreed to offer the Cubans some form of autonomy. It also declared an amnesty for political prisoners and released Americans in Cuban jails. The new initiatives pleased McKinley, though he again warned Spain that it must find a humane end to the rebellion. Then, in January 1898 Spanish army officers led riots in Havana against the new autonomy policy and shook his confidence in Madrid's control over conditions in Cuba.

McKinley ordered the battleship *Maine* to Havana as a gesture of strength and goodwill. On February 9, 1898, the *New York Journal*, a leader of the "yellow press," published a letter stolen from Enrique Dupuy de Lôme, the Spanish ambassador in Washington. The letter was a private letter to a friend, and in it de Lôme called McKinley "weak," "a would-be politician," and "a bidder for the admiration of the crowd." Many Americans were angered by the insult; McKinley himself was more worried about other sections of the letter which revealed Spanish insincerity in the negotiations. De Lôme immediately resigned and went home, but the damage was done.

A few days later, at 9:40 in the evening of February 15, an explosion tore through the hull of the *Maine*, riding at anchor in Havana harbor. The ship, a trim symbol of the new steel navy, sank quickly; 266 lives were lost. McKinley cautioned patience and promised an immediate investigation. Crowds gathered quietly on Capitol Hill and outside the White House, mourning the lost men. Soon there was a new slogan, "Remember the *Maine* and to Hell with Spain!"

The most recent study of the *Maine* incident blames the sinking on an accidental internal explosion, caused perhaps by spontaneous combustion in poorly ventilated coal bunkers. In 1898 Americans blamed it on Spain. Spaniards were hanged in effigy in many communities. Roosevelt, William Jennings Bryan, and others urged war, but McKinley delayed, hopeful that Spain might yet agree to an armistice and perhaps Cuban independence. "I have been through one war; I have seen the dead piled up; and I do not want to see another," he told a White House visitor.

In early March 1898, wanting to be ready for war if it came, McKinley asked Congress for $50 million in emergency defense appropriations, a request Congress promptly approved. The vote stunned Spain: it was unanimous, and allowing the President unusual latitude, it appropriated the money "for the National defense and for each and every purpose connected therewith to be expended at the discretion of the President." In late March the report of the investigating board blamed the sinking of the *Maine* on an external (and thus presumably Spanish) explosion. Pressures for war increased.

On March 27 McKinley cabled Spain his final terms. He asked Spain to declare an armistice, end the reconcentration policy, and—implicitly—move toward Cuban independence. When the Spanish answer came, it conceded some things, but not, in McKinley's judgment, the important ones. Spain offered a suspension of hostilities, not an armistice, and it left it to the Spanish commander in Cuba to set the length and terms of the

■ *Headlines like these in William Randolph Hearst's* New York Journal *left little doubt among his readers that Spain had sunk the* Maine.

Reporting the Spanish–American War

The force of the newspaper is the greatest force in civilization.
Under republican government, newspapers form and express public opinion.
They suggest and control legislation.
They declare wars.
They punish criminals, especially the powerful.
They reward with approving publicity the good deeds of citizens everywhere.
The newspapers control the nation because THEY REPRESENT THE PEOPLE.

So proclaimed William Randolph Hearst, owner of the *New York Journal* in the paper's September 25, 1898, issue. Proud of the power of the press, Hearst and a handful of other publishers built newspaper empires that not only reported events but also influenced their outcome.

Several of these empires took shape during the 1890s. The American population was growing rapidly, and so there were more people to read newspapers. In addition, more and more Americans were literate. Publishers did not hesitate to take advantage of the growing urban market. Technological improvements helped the spread of information: new machines made newspapers faster to print; larger type, a new half-tone engraving process for clearer pictures, and color cartoon supplements made them more appealing.

In 1865 there were about five hundred daily newspapers in the country with a total circulation of about two million. By 1900 there were over two thousand dailies with a circulation of over fifteen million. Papers sold for only one or two cents a copy. At that price publishers could not make money on the paper itself, so they recouped their losses on advertising. Advertisers wanted readers, and to attract more and more of them, publishers used new methods. They lured buyers with banner headlines and front-page photographs. Stories stressed sex and scandals, and more cartoons and comic strips appeared.

One of the first publishing magnates, Joseph Pulitzer bought the *New York World* in 1883 and within a year increased its sales from fifteen thousand a day to one hundred thousand. Pulitzer had little competition until 1895 when William Randolph Hearst, an aggressive publisher from San Francisco, bought the *New York Journal*. Hearst was thirty-two. The son of a multimillionaire, he had been expelled from Harvard, had traveled widely, and discovered a love for power and attention. Although he was shy and relatively inexperienced, money from his father and a desire to enter the world of newspaper publishing helped launch his career.

Fiercely competitive for "scoops" and circulation, Hearst and Pulitzer experimented with several new features: headlines that ran across the front page, profuse illustrations, a large Sunday paper with a comic section printed in color, and special sports' and women's sections. A cartoon character, "The Yellow Kid," appeared daily in both the *Journal* and the *World*, and they became known as "yellow journals." Stressing the sensational, "yellow journals" aimed to make news as well as report it. Hearst told his reporters: "Don't wait for things to turn up. Turn them up!"

The new journalism reached a peak in the crisis in Cuba between 1895 and 1898. When the short-lived rebellion of 1895 broke out, correspondents flocked to Cuba to cover it. Pulitzer sent the novelist Stephen Crane and printed reports from a young Englishman named Winston Churchill. Hearst sent the star *Journal* reporter Richard Harding Davis and the famous Western artist Frederic Remington to sketch scenes of Spanish cruelty. Both Hearst and Pulitzer sided with the rebels. Denouncing Spanish policy, they attacked General Valeriano Weyler—"Butcher," the *Journal* nicknamed him—and other Spanish generals.

SPANIARDS SEARCH WOMEN ON AMERICAN STEAMERS

Hearst was particularly proud of the story of Evangelina Cisneros, the seventeen-year-old niece of the rebellion's president. In August 1897, Evangelina was sentenced to twenty years in prison for aiding the rebels. Sensing the story's potential, Hearst started a letter-writing campaign to the queen of Spain to win her release. Soon he decided on a more direct method. He sent reporter Karl Decker to Havana to rescue Evangelina. Renting the house next door to the prison, Decker broke into the prison, freed Evangelina, and, disguising her as a boy, smuggled her out of Havana. On October 10, 1897, the *Journal* broke the news with the headline: "An American Newspaper Accomplishes at a Single Stroke What the Best Efforts of Diplomacy Failed Utterly to Bring About in Many Months."

Once war erupted between the United States and Spain, Hearst and his rivals stepped up their efforts. They employed hundreds of correspondents and hired a fleet of swift boats to carry stories to Florida for transmission back to New York. The correspondents both reported and fought in the war. At one point, Hearst considered sinking a ship in the Suez Canal to keep the Spanish fleet from reaching the Philippines, and from aboard a chartered steamer, he personally watched the destruction of Cervera's fleet off Santiago. Waving a revolver, he waded ashore to capture a handful of Spanish sailors who survived the battle. The efforts paid off in newspaper sales. When Hearst bought the *Journal*, it was selling 77,000 copies a day. At the war's height, its sales had increased to over 1.5 million daily.

After the war, Hearst cartoonists like Homer Davenport turned their skillful attention to the trusts and other issues. Showing the lack of restraint that characterized "yellow journalism," the *Journal*, a Democratic newspaper, again and again criticized President McKinley, even suggesting that assassination might be in order. In September 1901, McKinley was shot, and when reports circulated that the assassin had a copy of the *Journal* in his pocket, the public turned on Hearst. The *Journal*'s circulation dropped sharply. The new journalism continued into the twentieth century—Hearst himself went on to establish a famous publishing empire—but "yellow journalism" itself was never the same again.

suspension. It also revoked the reconcentration policy. But the Spanish response made no mention of a true armistice, McKinley's offer to mediate, or Cuba's independence.

Reluctantly McKinley prepared his war message. It was long and temperate—at seven thousand words even deliberately boring; it suggested the possibility of further negotiations. Congress heard it on April 11, 1898. On April 19 Congress passed a joint resolution declaring Cuba independent and authorizing the President to use the army and navy to expel the Spanish from Cuba. An amendment by Colorado Senator Henry M. Teller pledged that the United States had no intention of annexing the island.

On April 21, Spain severed diplomatic relations. The following day McKinley proclaimed a blockade of Cuba and called for 125,000 volunteers. On Monday, April 25, Congress passed a declaration of war. Late that afternoon McKinley signed it.

Some historians have suggested that in leading the country toward war McKinley was weak and indecisive, a victim of war hysteria in the Congress and country; others have called him a wily manipulator for war and imperial gains. In truth he was neither. Throughout the Spanish crisis McKinley pursued a moderate middle course that sought to protect American interests, promote Cuba's independence, and allow Spain time to adjust to the loss of the remnant of empire. He also wanted peace, but in the end the conflicting national interests of the two countries brought them to war.

"A Splendid Little War"

Ten weeks after the declaration of war the fighting was over. For Americans they were ten glorious, dizzying weeks, with victories to fill every headline and slogans to suit every taste. No war can be a happy occasion for those who fight it, but the Spanish-American War came closer than most. Declared in April, it ended in August. Relatively few Americans died, and the quick victory seemed to verify burgeoning American power. John Hay, soon to be McKinley's secretary of state, called it "a splendid little war."

At the outset the United States was militarily unprepared. Like the navy, the army had shrunk drastically since the day twenty-three years before when Grant's great Civil War army marched sixty abreast, 200,000-strong, down Washington's Pennsylvania Avenue. In 1898 the regular army consisted of only 28,000 officers and men, most of them more experienced in quelling Indian uprisings than fighting large-scale battles. The Indian wars did produce effective, small-scale forces, well-trained and tightly disciplined, but the army was unquestionably too small for war against Spain.

When McKinley called for 125,000 volunteers, as many as 1 million young Americans responded. Ohio alone had 100,000 volunteers. Keeping the regular army units intact, War Department officials enlisted the volunteers in National Guard units that were then integrated into the national army. Men clamored to join. William Jennings Bryan, a pacifist by temperament, took command of a regiment of Nebraska volunteers; Roosevelt chafed to get to the front; and young Cordell Hull, who became secretary of state in the 1930s, was "wildly eager to leave at once." The secretary of war feared "there is going to be more trouble to satisfy those who are not going than to find those who are willing to go."

In an army inundated with men, problems of equipment and supply quickly appeared. The regulars had the new .30 caliber Krag-Jorgensen rifles, but National Guard units carried Civil War Springfield rifles that used old, black powder cartridges. The cartridges gave off a puff of smoke when fired, neatly marking the troops' position. Spanish troops were better equipped; they had modern Mausers with smokeless powder, which they used to devastating effect. Food was also a problem, as was sickness. The War Department fell behind in supplies and received many complaints about the canned beef it offered the men. Tropical disease felled many soldiers. Scores took ill after landing in Cuba and the Philippines, and it was not uncommon for half a regiment to be unable to answer the bugle call.

Americans then believed that "a foreign war should be fought by the hometown military unit acting as an extension of their community." Soldiers identified with their hometowns, dressed in the local fashion, and thought of themselves as members of a town unit in a national army. The poet Carl Sandburg, twenty years old in 1898, rushed to join the army and called his unit a "living part" of his hometown of Galesburg, Illinois. And the citizens of Galesburg, for their part, took a special interest in Sandburg's unit, in a fashion repeated in countless towns across the country.

Not surprisingly, then, National Guard units mirrored the social patterns of their communities. Since everyone knew each other, there was an easygoing familiarity, tempered by the deference that went with hometown wealth, occupation, education, and length of residence. Enlisted men resented officers who grabbed too much authority, and they expected officers and men to call each other by their first names. Sandburg knew most of the privates in his unit, had worked for his corporal, and had gone to school with the first lieutenant. "Officers and men of the Guard mingle on a plane of beautiful equality," said a visitor to one volunteer camp. "Privates invade the tents of their officers at will, and yell at them half the length of the street."

Each community thought of the hometown unit as *its* unit, an extension of itself. In later wars the government censored news and dominated press relations; there was little censorship in the war with Spain, and the freshest news arrived in the latest letter home. Small-town newspapers printed news of the men; townswomen knit special red or white bellybands of stitched flannel, thought to ward off tropical fevers; towns sent food, clothing, and occasionally even local doctors to the front. At the close of the war the Clyde (Ohio) Ladies Society collected funds to provide each member of the town's company a medal struck on behalf of the town.

"Smoked Yankees"

When the invasion force sailed for Cuba, nearly one fourth of it was black. In 1898 the regular army included four regiments of black soldiers, the Twenty-fourth and Twenty-fifth Infantry and the Ninth and Tenth Cavalry. Black regiments had served with distinction in campaigns against the Indians in the West. Most black troops in fact were posted in the West; no eastern community would accept them. A troop of the Ninth Cavalry was stationed in Virginia in 1891, but whites protested and the troop was ordered back to the West.

When the war broke out, the War Department called for five black volunteer regiments. The army needed men, and military authorities were sure that black men had a natural immunity to the climate and diseases of the tropics. But most state governors refused to accept black volunteers. Only Alabama, Ohio, and Massachusetts mustered in black units in response to McKinley's first call for volunteers. Company L of the Sixth Massachusetts Regiment took part in the invasion of Puerto Rico in July 1898, the only one of the black volunteer units to see action in the Caribbean. Black leaders, among them P. B. S. Pinchback, former acting governor of Louisiana, and George White of North Carolina, the lone black member of Congress, protested the discrimination. The McKinley administration intervened, and in the end the volunteer army included over ten thousand black troops.

Orders quickly went out to the four black regular-army regiments in the West to move to camps in the South to prepare for the invasion of Cuba. Crowds and cheers followed the troop trains across the Plains, but as they crossed into Kentucky and Tennessee, the cheering stopped. Welcoming crowds were kept away from the trains, and the troops were hustled onward. Station restaurants refused to serve them; all waiting rooms were segregated. "It mattered not if we were soldiers of the United States, and going to fight for the honor of our country," Sergeant Frank W. Pullen of the Twenty-fourth Infantry wrote; "we were 'niggers' as they called us and treated us with contempt."

Many soldiers were not prepared to put up with the treatment. Those stationed near Chickamauga Park, Tennessee, shot "at some whites who insulted them" and desegregated the railroad cars on the line into Chattanooga. Troops training near Macon, Georgia, refused to ride in the segregated "trailers" attached to the trolleys, and fights broke out. Discovering a Macon park with a sign saying "Dogs and niggers not allowed," they invaded it and removed the sign.

More than four thousand black troops trained near Tampa and Lakeland, Florida, where they found segregated saloons, cafes, and drugstores. "Here the Negro is not allowed to purchase over the same counter in some stores as the white man purchases over . . . ," George W. Prioleau, a chaplain, charged. "Why sir, the Negro of this country

The 24th and 25th Negro Infantry Divisions served with exceptional gallantry on San Juan Hill (left). Charles Young (below), an 1889 graduate of West Point, was the only black officer in the army, except for a few chaplains.

is a freeman and yet a slave. Talk about fighting and freeing poor Cuba and of Spain's brutality; of Cuba's murdered thousands, and starving reconcentradoes. Is America any better than Spain?"

Near Lakeland, units of the Tenth Cavalry pistol-whipped a drugstore owner who refused to serve a black soldier at the soda fountain. Just before the army's departure for Cuba, the tensions in Tampa erupted in a night of rioting. Drunken white soldiers from an Ohio regiment shot at a black child, black soldiers retaliated, and when the night ended, three white and twenty-seven black soldiers were wounded.

When the invasion force sailed a few days later, segregation continued on some of the troop ships. Blacks were assigned to the lowest decks, or whites and blacks were placed on different sides of the ship. But the confusion of war often ended the problem, if only temporarily. Blacks took command as white officers died, and Spanish troops soon came to fear the "smoked Yankees," as they called them. Black soldiers played a major role in the Cuban campaign and probably staved off defeat for the Rough Riders at San Juan Hill. In Cuba they won twenty-six Certificates of Merit and five Congressional Medals of Honor.

The Course of the War

Mahan's Naval War College had begun studying strategy for a war with Spain in 1895. By 1898 it had a detailed plan for operations in the Caribbean and Pacific. Naval strategy was simple: destroy the Spanish fleet, damage Spain's merchant marine, and harry the colonies or the coast of Spain. Planners were excited; two steam-powered armored fleets had yet to meet in battle anywhere in the world. The army's task was more difficult. It must defend the United States, invade Cuba and probably Puerto Rico, and undertake possible action in far-flung places like the Philippines or Spain.

Even before war was declared, the secretary of war arranged joint planning between the army and navy. Military intelligence was plentiful, and planners knew the numbers and location of the Spanish troops. Earlier they had rejected a proposal to send an officer in disguise to map Cuban harbors; such things, they said, were simply not done in peacetime. Still, the War Department's new Military Information Division, a sign of the increasing professionalization of the army, had detailed diagrams of Spanish fortifications in Havana and other points. On the afternoon of April 20, 1898, McKinley summoned the strategists to the White House, and to the dismay of those who wanted a more aggressive policy, they decided on the limited strategy of blockading Cuba, sending arms to the insurgents, and annoying the Spanish with small thrusts by the army.

Victories soon changed the strategy. In the case of war, long-standing naval plans had called for a holding action against the Spanish base in the Philippines. On May 1, 1898, with the war barely a week old, Commodore George Dewey, commander of the Asiatic Squadron located at Hong Kong, crushed the Spanish fleet in Manila Bay. Suddenly, Manila and the Philippines lay within American grasp. At home, Dewey portraits, songs, and poems blossomed everywhere, and his calm order to the flagship's captain—"You may fire when ready, Gridley"—hung on every tongue. Dewey had two modern cruisers, a gunboat, and a Civil War paddle steamer. He sank eight Spanish warships; one American sailor died —of heat stroke. Dewey had no troops to attack the Spanish army in Manila, but the War Department, stunned by the speed and size of the victory, quickly raised an expeditionary force. On August 13, 1898, the troops accepted the surrender of Manila, and with it, the Philippines.

McKinley and his aides were worried about Admiral Pascual Cervera's main Spanish fleet, thought to be headed across the Atlantic for an attack on Florida. On May 13 the navy found Cervera's ships near Martinique in the Caribbean but then lost them again. A few days later Cervera slipped secretly into the harbor of Santiago de Cuba, a city on the island's southern coast. But a spy in the Havana telegraph office alerted the Americans, and on May 28, a superior American force under Admiral William T. Sampson bottled Cervera up.

On June 14 an invasion force of about seventeen thousand men set sail from Tampa. Seven days later they landed at Daiquiri on Cuba's southeastern coast. All was confusion, but the Spanish offered no resistance. Immediately the Americans pushed west toward Santiago, which they hoped to surround and capture. At first the advance was peaceful, through the lush tropical countryside.

The first battle broke out at Las Guasimas, a

Spanish-American War: Pacific Theater

Commodore Dewey, promoted to admiral immediately after the naval victory at Manila Bay, was the first hero of the war.

crossroads on the Santiago road. After a sharp fight, the Spanish fell back. On July 1 the Rough Riders, troops from the four black regiments, and the other regulars reached the strong fortifications at El Caney and San Juan Hill. Black soldiers of the Twenty-fifth Infantry charged the El Caney blockhouses, surprising the Spanish defenders with Comanche yells. For the better part of a day the defenders fought stubbornly and held back the army's elite corps. In the confusion of battle, Roosevelt rallied an assortment of infantry and cavalry to take Kettle Hill, adjacent to San Juan Hill.

They charged directly into the Spanish guns, Roosevelt at their head, mounted on a horse, a blue polka-dot handkerchief floating from the brim of his sombrero. "I waved my hat and we went up the hill with a rush," he recalled in his autobiography. It was not quite so easy. Losses were heavy; eighty-nine Rough Riders were killed or wounded in the attack. Dense foliage concealed the enemy; smokeless powder gave no clue to their position. At nightfall the surviving Spanish defenders withdrew, and the Americans

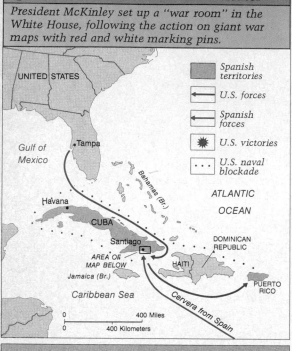

Spanish American War: Cuban Theater

President McKinley set up a "war room" in the White House, following the action on giant war maps with red and white marking pins.

Spanish territories

U.S. forces

Spanish forces

U.S. victories

U.S. naval blockade

UNITED STATES

Gulf of Mexico

Tampa

Havana

CUBA

Santiago

AREA OF MAP BELOW

Jamaica (Br.)

Caribbean Sea

Bahamas (Br.)

ATLANTIC OCEAN

DOMINICAN REPUBLIC

HAITI

PUERTO RICO

Cervera from Spain

0   400 Miles
0   400 Kilometers

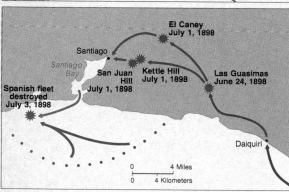

El Caney
July 1, 1898

Santiago

Santiago Bay

San Juan Hill
July 1, 1898

Kettle Hill
July 1, 1898

Las Guasimas
June 24, 1898

Spanish fleet destroyed
July 3, 1898

Daiquiri

0   4 Miles
0   4 Kilometers

prepared for the counterattack. "We have won so far at a heavy cost," Roosevelt wrote home, "but the Spaniards fight very hard and charging these entrenchments against modern rifles is terrible. We are within measurable distance of a terrible military disaster."

American troops now occupied the ridges overlooking Santiago. They were weakened by sickness, but the Spanish, not knowing that, decided the city was lost. The Spanish command in Havana ordered Cervera to run for the open sea, although he knew the attempt was hopeless. On the morning of July 3 his squadron steamed down the bay and out through the harbor's narrow channel, but the waiting American fleet closed

in, and in a few hours every Spanish vessel was destroyed. Two weeks later Santiago surrendered.

Soon thereafter army troops, meeting little resistance, occupied Puerto Rico. Cervera had commanded Spain's only battle fleet, and when it sank, Spain was helpless against attacks on the colonies or even its own shores. The war was over. Lasting 113 days, it took relatively few lives, most of them the result of accident, yellow fever, malaria, and typhoid in Cuba. Of the 5500 Americans who died in the war, only 379 were killed in battle. The navy lost one man in the battle at Santiago Bay, and none at all in the stunning victory in Manila Bay.

Debate over Empire

Late in the afternoon of August 12, 1898, representatives of Spain and the United States met in McKinley's White House office to sign the preliminary instrument of peace. Secretary of State William R. Day beckoned a presidential aide over to a large globe, remarking: "Let's see what we get by this."

What the United States got was an expansion of its territory and an even larger expansion of its responsibilities. According to the preliminary agreement, Spain granted independence to Cuba, ceded Puerto Rico and the Pacific island of Guam to the United States, and allowed Americans to occupy Manila until the two countries reached final agreement on the Philippines. To McKinley, the Philippines were the problem. Puerto Rico was close to the mainland, and it appealed even to many of the opponents of expansion. Guam was small and unknown; it escaped attention. The Philippines, on the other hand, were huge, sprawling, and thousands of miles from America.

McKinley weighed a number of alternatives for the Philippines, but he liked none of them. He felt he could not give the islands back to Spain; public opinion would not allow it. He might turn them over to another nation, but then they would fall, as he later said, "a golden apple of discord, among the rival powers." Germany, Japan, Great Britain, and Russia had all expressed interest in acquiring them. Germany even sent a large fleet to Manila and laid plans to take the Philippines if the United States let them go.

Rejecting those alternatives, McKinley considered independence for the islands but was soon talked out of it. Nearly everyone who had been there believed the people were not ready for independence. He thought of establishing an American protectorate but discarded the idea, convinced it would bring American responsibilities without full American control. Sifting the alternatives, McKinley decided there was only one practical policy: annex the Philippines, with an eye to future independence after a period of tutelage.

At first hesitant, American opinion was swinging to the same conclusion. Religious and missionary organizations appealed to McKinley to hold on to the Philippines in order to Christianize them. Some merchants and industrialists saw them as the key to the China market and the wealth of Asia. Many Americans simply regarded them as the legitimate fruits of war. In October 1898, representatives of the United States and Spain met in Paris to discuss a peace treaty. Spain agreed to recognize Cuba's independence, assume the Cuban debt, and cede Puerto Rico and Guam to the United States.

Acting on instructions from McKinley, the American representatives demanded the cession of the Philippines. "Grave as are the responsibilities and unforeseen as are the difficulties which are before us, the President can see but one plain path of duty—the acceptance of the archipelago," the instructions said. In return, the United States offered a payment of $20 million. Spain resisted but had little choice, and on December 10, 1898, the American and Spanish representatives signed the Treaty of Paris.

Submitted to the Senate for ratification, the treaty set off a storm of debate throughout the country. Industrialist Andrew Carnegie, reformer Jane Addams, labor leader Samuel Gompers, prominent Republicans like Thomas B. Reed and John Sherman, Mark Twain, William Dean Howells, and a host of others argued forcefully against annexing the Phillipines. Carnegie felt so strongly he offered to buy Filipino independence with a personal check for $20 million. Annexation of the Philippines, the anti-imperialists protested over and over again, violated the very principles of independence and self-determination on which the country was founded.

Some labor leaders feared the importation of cheap labor from new Pacific colonies. Other anti-imperialists argued against assimilation of different races, "Spanish-Americans," as one said, 'with all the mixture of Indian and negro blood, and Malays and other unspeakable Asiatics, by the tens of millions!" Such racial views were at least as common among those favoring expansion, and in any event the anti-imperialists usually focused on different arguments. The exercise of tyranny abroad, they were sure, would result in tyranny at home. "This nation," declared William Jennings Bryan, "cannot endure half republic and half colony—half free and half vassal."

In November 1898, opponents of expansion formed the Anti-Imperialist League to fight against the peace treaty. Local leagues sprang up in Boston, New York, Philadelphia, and many other cities; the parent league claimed thirty thousand members and over half a million "contributors." Membership centered in New England; the cause was less popular in the West and South. It enlisted more Democrats than Republicans, though never a majority of either. The anti-imperialists lacked a coherent program. Some favored keeping naval bases in the conquered areas. Some wanted Hawaii and Puerto Rico but not the Philippines. Others wanted nothing to do with any colonies. Most simply

■ *A* Puck *cartoon entitled "School Begins" satirizes Uncle Sam's course in civilization, in which he assures his new class they will soon be glad they learned it.*

■ *During the bitterly fought Philippine war, Americans shelled and then burned Manila (below).*

■ *Aguinaldo's guerrilla fighters at an outpost (above). The Filipinos battled for three years before surrendering.*

wished that Dewey had sailed away after beating the Spanish at Manila Bay.

The debate in the Senate lasted a month. Pressing hard for ratification, McKinley earlier toured the South to rally support and consulted closely with senators. Though opposed to taking the Philippines, Bryan supported ratification in order to end the war; his support influenced some Democratic votes. Still, on the final weekend before the vote, the treaty was two votes short. That Saturday night, news reached Washington that fighting had broken out between American troops and Filipino insurgents who demanded immediate independence. The news increased pressure to ratify the treaty, which the Senate did on February 6, 1899, with two votes to spare. The United States had a colonial empire.

Guerrilla Warfare in the Philippines

Historians rarely write of the Philippine-American War, but it was an important event in American history. The war with Spain was over in a few months; war with the Filipinos lasted more than three years. Four times as many American soldiers fought in the Philippines as in Cuba. For the first time Americans fought men of a different color in an Asian guerrilla war. The Philippine-American War of 1898–1902 took a heavy toll: 4300 American lives and perhaps as many as 57,000 Filipino lives.

Emilio Aguinaldo, the Filipino leader, was twenty-nine years old in 1898. An early organizer of the anti-Spanish resistance, he had gone into exile in Hong Kong, from where he welcomed the outbreak of the Spanish-American War. Certain the United States would grant independence, he worked for an American victory. Filipino insurgents helped guide Dewey into Manila Bay, and Dewey himself sent a ship to Hong Kong to bring back Aguinaldo to lead a native uprising against the Spanish. On June 12, 1898, the insurgents proclaimed their independence.

Cooperating with the Americans, they drove the Spanish out of many areas of the islands. In the liberated regions Aguinaldo established local governments with appointed provincial governors. He waited impatiently for American recognition, but McKinley and others doubted the Filipinos were ready. Shortly thereafter fighting broke out between the Filipinos and Americans.

By late 1899 the American army had defeated and dispersed the organized Filipino army, but claims of victory proved premature. Aguinaldo and his advisers shifted to guerrilla tactics, striking suddenly and then melting into the jungle or friendly native villages. In many areas the Americans ruled the day, the guerrillas the night. The Americans found themselves using Weyler-like tactics. After any attack on an American patrol, they burned all the houses in the nearest district. They established protected "zones" and herded Filipinos into them. Seizing or destroying all food outside the zones, they starved many guerrillas into submission.

In 1900 McKinley sent a special Philippine Commission under William Howard Taft, a prominent Ohio judge. Directed to establish a civil government, the commission organized municipal administrations and in stages created a government for the Philippines. In March 1901 five American soldiers tricked their way into Aguinaldo's camp deep in the mountains and took him prisoner. Back in Manila, he signed a proclamation urging his people to end the fighting. Some guerrillas held out for another year but to no avail. On July 4, 1901, authority was transferred from the army to Taft, who was named civilian governor of the islands, and his civilian commission. McKinley reaffirmed his purpose to grant the Filipinos self-government as soon as they were ready for it.

Given broad powers, the Taft Commission introduced many changes. New schools provided education and vocational training for Filipinos of all social classes. The Americans built roads and bridges, reformed the judiciary, restructured the tax system, and introduced sanitation and vaccination programs. They established local governments built on Filipino traditions and hierarchies. Taft encouraged Filipino participation in government. During the following decades other measures broadened Filipino rights; independence came on July 4, 1946, nearly fifty years after Aguinaldo proclaimed it.

Governing the Empire

Ruling the colonies raised new and perplexing questions. How could—and how should—the distant dependencies be governed? Did their inhabitants have the rights of American citizens? Some people contended that acquisition did not automatically incorporate the new possessions into the United States and endow them with constitutional privileges. Others argued that "the Consti-

Chronology

1867	United States purchases Alaska from Russia Midway Islands are annexed
1871	Treaty of Washington between United States and Great Britain sets precedent for peaceful settlement of international disputes
1875	Reciprocity treaty with Hawaii binds Hawaii economically and politically to United States
1878	United States acquires naval base in Samoa
1883	Congress approves funds for construction of first modern steel ships; beginning of modern navy
1887	New treaty with Hawaii gives United States exclusive use of Pearl Harbor
1889	First Inter-American Conference meets in Washington, D.C.
1893	American settlers in Hawaii overthrow Queen Liliuokalani; provisional government established
1895	Cuban insurgents rebel against Spanish rule
1898	Battleship *Maine* explodes in Havana harbor (February) Congress declares war against Spain (April) Commodore Dewey defeats Spanish fleet at Manila Bay (May) United States annexes Hawaii (July) Americans defeat Spanish at El Caney, San Juan Hill (actually Kettle Hill), and Santiago (July) Spain sues for peace (August) Treaty of Paris ends Spanish-American War (December)
1899	Congress ratifies Treaty of Paris United States sends "open-door" notes to Britain, Germany, France, Russia, Japan, and Italy Philippine-American War erupts
1900	Foraker Act establishes civil government in Puerto Rico
1901	Platt Amendment authorizes American intervention in Cuba
1902	Philippine-American War ends with American victory

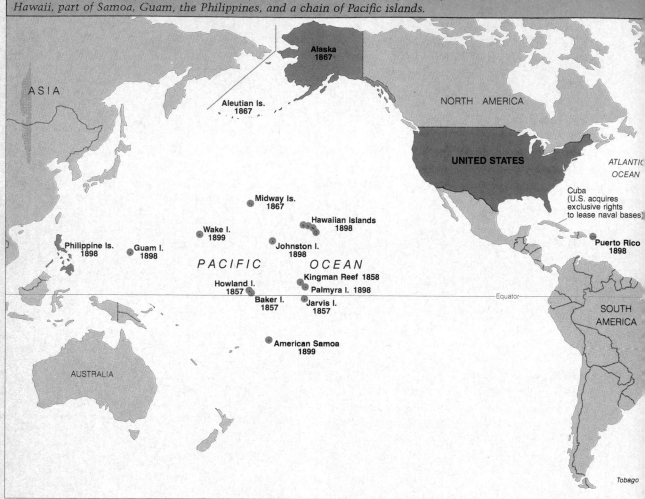

American Empire, 1900

With the Treaty of Paris, the United States gained an expanded colonial empire stretching from the Caribbean to the far Pacific. It embraced Puerto Rico, Alaska, Hawaii, part of Samoa, Guam, the Philippines, and a chain of Pacific islands.

tution followed the flag," meaning that acquisition made the possessions part of the nation and thus entitled to all constitutional guarantees. A third group suggested that only "fundamental" constitutional guarantees—citizenship, the right to vote, and the right to trial by jury—not "formal" privileges—the right to use American currency, the right to be taxed, and the right to run for the presidency—were applicable to the new empire.

In a series of cases between 1901 and 1904 (*De Lima* v. *Bidwell*, *Dooley* v. *U.S.*, and *Downes* v. *Bidwell*), the Supreme Court asserted the principle that the Constitution did not automatically and immediately apply to the people of an annexed territory and did not confer upon them all

the privileges of United States citizenship. Instead, Congress could specifically extend such constitutional provisions as it saw fit.

Four dependencies—Hawaii, Alaska, Guam, and Puerto Rico—were organized quickly. In 1900 Congress granted territorial status to Hawaii, gave American citizenship to all citizens of the Hawaiian republic, authorized an elective legislature, and provided for a governor appointed from Washington. A similar measure made Alaska a territory in 1912. Guam and the island of Tutuila were simply placed under the control of naval officers.

Unlike the Filipinos, Puerto Ricans readily accepted the war's outcome, and McKinley early withdrew troops from the island. The Foraker Act

Toward Empire

of 1900 established civil government in Puerto Rico. It organized the island as a territory, made its residents citizens of Puerto Rico (United States citizenship was extended to them in 1917), and empowered the president to appoint a governor general and a council to serve as the upper house of the legislature. A lower house of delegates was to be elected.

Cuba proved a trickier matter. McKinley asserted the authority of the United States over conquered territory and promised to govern the island until the Cubans had established a firm and stable government of their own. "I want you to go down there to get the people ready for a republican form of government," he instructed General Leonard Wood, commander of the army in Cuba until 1902. "I leave the details of procedure to you. Give them a good school system, try to straighten out their ports, and put them on their feet as best you can. We want to do all we can for them and to get out of the island as soon as we safely can."

Wood moved quickly to implement the instructions. Early in 1900 he completed a census of the Cuban population, conducted municipal elections, and arranged the election of delegates to a constitutional convention. The convention adopted a constitution modeled on the U.S. Constitution and, at Wood's prodding, included provisions for future relations with the United States. Known as the Platt Amendment, the provisions stipulated that Cuba should make no treaties with other powers that might impair its independence, acquire no debts it could not pay, and lease naval bases to the United States. Most important, the amendment empowered the United States to intervene in Cuba to maintain orderly government.

Between 1898 and 1902 the American military government worked hard for the economic and political revival of the island. It repaired the damage of the civil war, built roads and schools, and established order in rural areas. A public health campaign headed by Dr. Walter Reed, an army surgeon, wiped out yellow fever. Most troops withdrew at the end of 1899, but a small American occupation force remained until May 1902. When it sailed for home, the Cubans at last had their independence, although they were under the clear domination of their neighbor to the north.

The Open Door

Poised in the Philippines, the United States had become an Asian power on the doorsteps of China. Weakened by years of warfare, China in 1898 and 1899 was unable to resist foreign influence. Japan, England, France, Germany, and Russia eyed it covetously, dividing the country into "spheres of influence." They forced China to grant "concessions" that allowed them exclusive rights to develop particular areas and threatened American hopes for extensive trade with the country.

McKinley first outlined a new China policy in September 1898 when he said that Americans sought more trade, "but we seek no advantages in the Orient which are not common to all. Asking only the open door for ourselves, we are ready to accord the open door to others." In September 1899 Secretary of State John Hay addressed identical diplomatic notes to England, Germany, and Russia, and later to France, Japan, and Italy, asking them to join the United States in establishing the "Open Door." The policy urged three

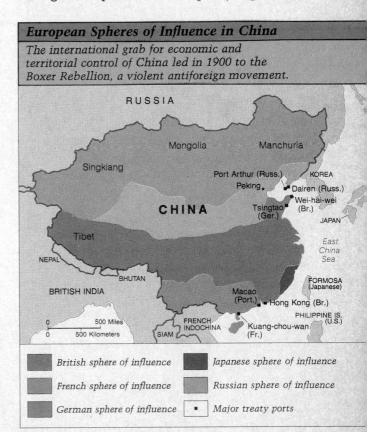

European Spheres of Influence in China

The international grab for economic and territorial control of China led in 1900 to the Boxer Rebellion, a violent antiforeign movement.

British sphere of influence

French sphere of influence

German sphere of influence

Japanese sphere of influence

Russian sphere of influence

■ Major treaty ports

The United States broadened its Open Door policy in 1900 with a second round of notes that included all China, not just the areas under European spheres of influence.

agreements: nations possessing a sphere of influence would respect the rights and privileges of other nations in that sphere; the Chinese government would continue to collect tariff duties in all spheres; and nations would not discriminate against other nations in levying port dues and railroad rates within their respective spheres of influence.

Under the Open Door policy, the United States would retain many commercial advantages that were endangered by the partition of China into spheres of influence. McKinley and Hay also attempted to preserve for the Chinese some semblance of national authority. Great Britain most nearly accepted the principle of the Open Door. Russia declined to approve it, and the other powers, sending evasive replies, stated they would only agree if all the other nations did. Hay turned the situation to American advantage by boldly announcing in March 1900 that all the powers had accepted the Open Door policy.

The war over, Roosevelt and the Rough Riders sailed for home in mid-August 1898. They sauntered through the streets of New York, the heroes of the city. A few weeks later Roosevelt bade them farewell. They presented him with a reproduction of Frederick Remington's famed bronze, *The Bronco-Buster*, and close to tears, he told them: "I am proud of this regiment beyond measure." Roosevelt later wrote an account of the war in which he played so central a role that Mr. Dooley suggested "If I was him, I'd call th' book 'Alone in Cubia.'" By then Roosevelt was already

governor of New York and on his way to the White House.

Other soldiers were also glad to be home, although sometimes resentful of the reception they found. "The war is over now," said Winslow Hobson, a black trooper from the Ninth Ohio, "and Roosevelt . . . and others (white of course) have all there is to be gotten out of it." Bravery in Cuba and the Philippines won some recognition for black soldiers, but the war itself set back the cause of civil rights. It spurred talk about "inferior" races, at home and abroad, and united whites in the North and South. "The Negro might as well know it now as later," a black editor said, "the closer the North and South get together by this war, the harder he will have to fight to maintain a footing." A fresh outburst of segregation and lynching occurred during the decade after the war.

McKinley and the Republican party soared to new heights of popularity. Firmly established, the Republican majority dominated politics until the 1930s. Scandals arose about the canned beef and the conduct of the War Department, but there was none of the sharp sense of deception and betrayal that was to mark the years after World War I. In a little more than a century the United States had grown from thirteen states stretched along a thin Atlantic coastline into a world power that reached from the Caribbean to the Pacific. As Seward and others had hoped, the nation now dominated its own hemisphere, dealt with European powers on more equal terms, and was a major power in Asia.

Recommended Reading

The best general account of the development of American foreign policy during the last part of the nineteenth century is Walter LaFeber, *The New Empire: An Interpretation of American Expansion, 1860–1898* (1963). Robert L. Beisner, *From the Old Diplomacy to the New, 1865–1900* (1975), and Charles S. Campbell, Jr., *Transformation of American Foreign Relations, 1865–1900* (1976), give useful overviews that suggest important changes that took place in the 1890s. J. A. S. Grenville and George Berkeley Young present a series of significant essays in *Politics, Strategy and American Diplomacy: Studies in Foreign Policy, 1873–1917* (1966).

Ernest R. May analyzes the causes of the Spanish-American War in *Imperial Democracy: The Emergence of America as a Great Power* (1961); for a briefer treatment, see H. Wayne Morgan, *America's Road to Empire: The War with Spain and Overseas Expansion* (1965). Lewis L. Gould persuasively reassesses McKinley's diplomacy and wartime leadership in *The Presidency of William McKinley* (1980).

Graham A. Cosmas presents a detailed account of military organization and strategy in *An Army for Empire: The United States Army in the Spanish-American War* (1971), while Willard B. Gatewood, Jr., *"Smoked Yankees" and the Struggle for Empire: Letters from Negro Soldiers, 1898–1902* (1971), offers a fascinating glimpse of the thoughts of some black soldiers in the war. Gerald F. Linderman relates the war to the home front in *The Mirror of War: American Society and the Spanish-American War* (1974).

Additional Bibliography

On American foreign policy during this period, see David M. Pletcher, *The Awkward Years: American Foreign Relations under Garfield and Arthur* (1962); David F. Healy, *U.S. Expansionism: The Imperialist Urge in the 1890's* (1970); Milton Plesur, *America's Outward Thrust: Approaches to Foreign Affairs, 1865–1890* (1971); Richard W. Leopold, *The Growth of American Foreign Policy* (1962); and Tom E. Terrill, *The Tariff, Politics, and American Foreign Policy, 1874–1901* (1973).

For policies toward specific areas, see R. P. Gilson, *Samoa 1830 to 1900: The Politics of a Multi-Cultural Community* (1970); Charles S. Campbell, Jr., *Anglo-American Understanding, 1898–1903* (1957); Thomas J. McCormick, *China Market: America's Quest for Informal Empire, 1893–1901* (1967); Marilyn B. Young, *Rhetoric of Empire: American China Policy, 1895–1901* (1968); Merze Tate, *The United States and the Hawaiian Kingdom: A Political History* (1965); and William A. Russ, Jr., *The Hawaiian Republic, 1894–98 and Its Struggle to Win Annexation* (1961).

Books on naval and military developments during these years include J. D. Hittle, *The Military Staff* (1949); Walter R. Herrick, *The American Naval Revolution* (1966); William R. Braisted, *The United States Navy in the Pacific, 1897–1909* (1958); Peter Karsten, *The Naval Aristocracy* (1972); Benjamin J. Cooling, *Gray Steel and Blue Water Navy* (1979); and Kenneth J. Hagan, *American Gunboat Diplomacy and the Old Navy, 1877–1889* (1973).

For the background of the war with Spain, see Julius W. Pratt, *Expansionists of 1898: The Acquisition of Hawaii and the Spanish Islands* (1936); Walter Millis, *The Martial Spirit: A Study of Our War with Spain* (1931); Philip S. Foner, *The Spanish-Cuban-American War and the Birth of American Imperialism, 1895–1902*, 2 vols. (1972); J. E. Wisan, *The Cuban Crisis as Reflected in the New York Press, 1895–1898* (1934); and Hyman G. Rickover, *How the Battleship Maine Was Destroyed* (1976).

Biographies of the period's leading personalities include H. Wayne Morgan, *William McKinley and His America* (1963); Margaret Leech, *In the Days of McKinley* (1959); Robert Seager, II, *Alfred Thayer Mahan* (1977); and Ronald Spector, *Admiral of the New Empire: The Life and Career of George Dewey* (1974). See also Theodore Roosevelt, *The Rough Riders* (1899); Russell A. Alger, *The Spanish-American War* (1901); John D. Long, *The New American Navy*, 2 vols. (1903); and H. Wayne Morgan, ed., *Making Peace with Spain: The Diary of Whitelaw Reid, September-December 1898* (1965).

The course of the war itself can be followed in Frank Freidel, *The Splendid Little War* (1958); Orestes Femara, *The Last Spanish War* (1937); Frederick Funston, *Memories of Two Wars: Cuba and Philippine Experiences* (1914); Charles H. Brown, *The Correspondents' War: Journalists in the Spanish-American War* (1967); David A. Gerber, *Black Ohio and the Color Line, 1860–1915* (1976); and Herschel V. Cashin et al., *Under Fire with the Tenth U.S. Cavalry* (1899).

For the debate over expansion and the treaty with Spain, consult Richard E. Welch, Jr., *George Frisbie Hoar and the Half-Breed Republicans* (1971); E. Berkeley Tompkins, *Anti-Imperialism in the United States: The Great Debate, 1890–1920* (1970); Daniel B. Schirmer, *Republic or Empire: American Resistance to the Philippine War* (1972); Thomas J. Osborne, *"Empire Can Wait": American Opposition to Hawaiian Annexation, 1893–1898* (1981); and Göran Rystad, *Ambiguous Imperialism: American Foreign Policy and Domestic Politics at the Turn of the Century* (1975).

Policy toward Cuba and the Philippines is covered in Richard E. Welch, Jr., *Response to Imperialism: The United States and the Philippine-American War, 1899–1902* (1979); David F. Healy, *The United States in Cuba, 1898–1902* (1963); James H. Hitchman, *Leonard Wood and Cuban Independence, 1898–1902* (1971); John Morgan Gates, *Schoolbooks and Krags: The United States Army in the Philippines, 1898–1902* (1973); Glenn A. May, *Social Engineering in the Philippines* (1980); and Peter W. Stanley, *A Nation in the Making: The Philippines and the United States, 1899–1921* (1974). Willard B. Gatewood, Jr., *Black Americans and the White Man's Burden, 1898–1903* (1975) is a thorough and thought-provoking study.

chapter 22

THE PROGRESSIVE ERA

In 1902 Samuel S. McClure, the shrewd owner of *McClure's Magazine*, sensed something astir in the country that his reporters were not covering. Like *Life*, *Munsey's*, the *Ladies' Home Journal*, and *Cosmopolitan*, *McClure's* was reaching more and more people—more than a quarter of a million readers a month. Americans were snapping up the new popular magazines filled with eye-catching illustrations and up-to-date fiction. Advances in photoengraving during the 1890s dramatically reduced the cost of illustrations; at the same time income from advertisements rose sharply. By the turn of the century some magazines earned as much as $60,000 an issue from advertising alone, and publishers could price them as low as $.10 a copy.

McClure was always chasing new ideas and readers, and in 1902, certain that something was happening in the public mood, he told one of his editors, thirty-six-year-old Lincoln Steffens, a former Wall Street reporter, to find out what it was. "Get out of here, travel, go—somewhere . . . ," he said to Steffens. "Buy a railroad ticket, get on a train, and there, where it lands you, there you will learn to edit a magazine."

McClure's, it turned out, had an unpaid bill from the Lackawanna Railroad, and Steffens traveled west. In Saint Louis he came across a young district attorney named Joseph W. Folk who had found a trail of corruption linking politics and some of the city's respected business leaders. Eager for help, Folk did not mind naming names to the visiting editor from New York. "It is good business men that are corrupting our bad politicians . . . ," he stressed again and again. "It is the leading citizens that are battening on our city." Steffens' story, "Tweed Days in St. Louis," appeared in the October 1902 issue of *McClure's*.

The November *McClure's* carried the first installment of Ida Tarbell's scathing "History of the Standard Oil Company," and in January 1903 Steffens was back with "The Shame of Minneapolis," another tale of corrupt partnership between business and politics. McClure had what he' wanted, and in the January issue he printed an editorial, "Concerning Three Articles in this Number of *McClure's*, and a Coincidence that May Set Us Thinking." Steffens on Minneapolis, Tarbell on Standard Oil, and an article on abuses in labor unions—all, McClure said, on different topics but actually on the same theme: corruption in American life. "Capitalists, workingmen, politicians, citizens—all breaking the law, or letting it be broken."

Readers were enthralled, and articles and books by other muckrakers—Theodore Roosevelt coined the unflattering term in 1906 to describe the practice of exposing the corruption of public and prominent figures—spread swiftly. *Collier's* had articles on questionable stock-market practices, patent medicines, and the beef trust. Novelist Upton Sinclair tackled the meat packers in *The Jungle* (1906). In 1904 Steffens collected his *McClure's* articles in *The Shame of the Cities*, with an introduction expressing confidence that reform was possible, "that our shamelessness is superficial, that beneath it lies a pride which, being real, may save us yet."

Muckraking flourished from 1903 to 1909, and while it did, good writers and bad investigated almost every corner of American life: government, labor unions, big business, Wall Street, health care, the food industry, child labor, women's rights, prostitution, ghetto living, and life insurance. "Time was," Mr. Dooley, the fictional character of humorist Finley Peter Dunne, said to Mr. Hennessy, when magazines

was very ca'ming to the mind. Angabel an' Alfonso dashin' f'r a marriage license. Prom'nent lady authoresses makin' pomes at the moon. . . . Th' idee ye got fr'm these here publications was that life was wan glad sweet song. . . .

But now whin I pick me fav-rite magazine off th' flure, what do I find? Ivrything has gone wrong. . . . All th' pomes by th' lady authoresses that used to begin: "Oh, moon, how fair!" now begin: "Oh, Ogden Armour, how awful!" . . . Graft ivrywhere. "Graft in th' Insurance Companies," "Graft in Congress," "Graft be an Old Grafter," "Graft in Its Relations to th' Higher Life". . . .

During the progressive era, McClure's magazine was at the front of the journalistic crusade for reform, which took the form of muckraking articles by such writers as Ida Tarbell (right). Her exposé of the Standard Oil Company ran side by side with Lincoln Steffens' article on the alliances between business and corrupt political machines in several cities.

An' so it goes, Hinnissy . . . till I don't thrust anny man anny more. . . . I used to be nervous about burglars, but now I'm afraid iv a night call fr'm th' prisidint iv th' First National Bank.

The muckrakers were a journalistic voice of a larger movement in American society. Called *progressivism*, it lasted from the mid-1890s through World War I. Like muckraking itself, it reflected concern with the state of society and a conviction that human compassion and scientific investigation could bring problems to light and solve them. Progressivism took on the character of Theodore Roosevelt and Woodrow Wilson, two important national spokesmen, but it affected large numbers of people and expressed at many levels the excitement of progress and change.

The Spirit of Progressivism

In one way or another, progressivism touched all aspects of society. Politically, it fostered a reform movement that sought cures for the problems of city, state, and nation. Intellectually, it drew on the expertise of the new social sciences and reflected a shift from older absolutes of class and religion to newer schools of thought that emphasized physiological explanations for behavior, the role of the environment in human development, and the relative nature of truth. Culturally, it inspired fresh modes of expression in dance, film, painting, literature, and architecture. Touching individuals in different ways, progressivism became a set of attitudes as well as a definable movement.

Unlike Populism, which grew mostly in the rural South and West, progressivism drew support across society. "The thing that constantly amazed me," said William Allen White, a leading progressive journalist, "was how many people were with us." Progressivism appealed to the expanding middle class, prosperous farmers, and skilled laborers; it also attracted significant support in the business community.

Leadership came mainly from young, educated men and women. Many of them belonged to the professions—law, medicine, religion, business, teaching, and social work—and they thought they could use their expertise to improve society. They believed in progress and disliked waste. No single issue or concern united them all. Some progressives wanted to clean up city governments, others to clean up city streets. Some wanted to purify politics or control corporate abuses, others to eradicate poverty or prostitution. Some demanded social justice in the form of woman's rights, child labor laws, temperance, and factory safety. They were Democrats, Republicans, Socialists, and independents.

Progressives believed in a better world and in the ability of people to achieve it. They paid to people, as a friend said of social reformer Florence Kelley, "the high compliment of believing that, once they knew the truth, they would act upon it." Progress depended on knowledge. The progressives stressed individual morality and collective action, the scientific method, and the value of expert opinon. Like contemporary business leaders, they valued system, planning, management, and predictability. They wanted not only reform but efficiency. In the introduction to *The Shame of the Cities*, Steffens said the cure for American ills lay in "good conduct in the individual, simple honesty, courage, and efficiency."

Progressivism also fed on an organizational impulse that encouraged people to join forces, share information, and solve problems. Between 1890 and 1920, a host of national societies and associations took shape—nearly four hundred of them in just three decades. Many new associations such as the American Medical Association (reorganized in 1901) and the U.S. Chamber of Commerce (1912) reflected the increasingly authoritative voice of the professions. Other groups such as the National Child Labor Committee, which lobbied for legislation to regulate the employment and working conditions of children, were formed to attack specific issues.

Believing in government as an agent of change, the progressives wanted to curb the influence of "special interests" and make government follow the public will. Once it did, they welcomed government action at whatever level was appropriate. The use of federal power increased, along with the power and prestige of the presidency. Most important, the progressives believed in the ability of experts to solve problems. At every level—local, state, and federal—thousands of commissions and agencies took form. Staffed by trained experts, they oversaw a multitude of matters ranging from railroad rates to public health.

Historians once viewed progressivism as the triumph of one group in society over another. In this view, farmers took on the hated and powerful railroads; upstart reformers challenged the city bosses; business interests fought for favorable legislation; youthful professionals carved out their place in society. Now historians stress the way progressivism brought people together rather than driving them apart. Disparate groups united in an effort to improve the well-being of many groups in society.

Reform in the Cities and States

Progressivism began in the cities during the 1890s. It first took form around settlement workers and others interested in freeing individuals from the crushing impact of cities and factories. Ministers, intellectuals, social workers, and lawyers joined in a social-justice movement that focused national attention on the need for tenement house laws, more stringent child labor legislation, and better working conditions for women. They brought pressure on municipal agencies for more and better parks, playgrounds, day nurseries, schools, and community services. Blending private and public action, settlement leaders turned increasingly to government aid. "Private beneficence," Jane Addams said, "is totally inadequate to deal with the vast numbers of the city's disinherited."

The Social-Justice Movement

Social-justice reformers were more interested in social cures than individual charity. They saw problems as endless and interrelated; individuals became part of a city's larger patterns. With that insight, social-service casework shifted from a focus on an individual's well-being to a scientific analysis of neighborhoods, occupations, and classes.

In the spring of 1900 the Charity Organization Society of New York held a tenement-house exhibition that graphically presented the new kind of sociological data. Put together by Lawrence Veiller, a young social worker, the exhibition included over a thousand photographs, detailed maps of slum districts, statistical tables and charts, and graphic cardboard depictions of tenement blocks. Never before had so much information been pulled together in one place. Veiller correlated data on poverty and disease with housing conditions, and he pointed out that new slums were springing up in more areas of the city.

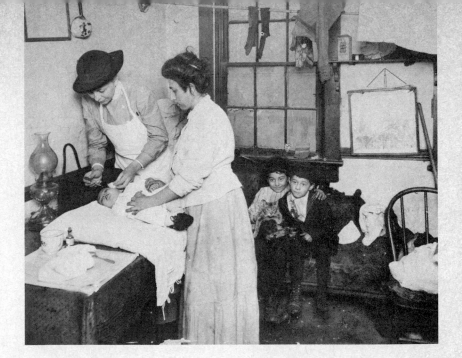

An Infant Welfare Society nurse treats the baby of an immigrant family in Chicago. A host of medical discoveries and the growth of the quality medical education fostered an interest in public health work among the social-justice reformers.

Stirred by the public outcry, Governor Theodore Roosevelt appointed the New York State Tenement House Commission to do something about the problem.

With Veiller's success as a model, study after study analyzed the condition of the poor. Books and pamphlets like *The Standard of Living Among Working Men's Families in New York City* (1909) contained pages of data on family budgets, women's wages and working conditions, child labor, and other matters. Between 1910 and 1913 the U.S. Commissioner of Labor issued a massive nineteen-volume report on *Conditions of Women and Children Wage-Earners in the United States.*

Banding together to work for change, social-justice reformers formed the National Conference of Charities and Corrections, which in 1915 became the National Conference of Social Work. Controlled by social workers, the conference reflected the growing professionalization of reform. Through it, social workers discovered each other's efforts, shared methodology, and tried to establish themselves as a separate field within the social sciences. Once content with informal training sessions in a settlement-house living room, they now formed complete professional schools at Chicago, Harvard, and other universities. After 1909 they had their own professional magazine, the *Survey,* and instead of piecemeal reforms they aimed at a comprehensive program of minimum wages, maximum hours, workers' compensation, and widows' pensions.

Women played a very large role in the social-justice movement. Feminists were particularly active, especially in the political sphere, between 1890 and 1914—feminists were more active then, in fact, than at any time until the 1960s. Some working-class women pushed for higher wages and better working conditions. College-educated women—five thousand a year graduated after 1900—took up careers in the professions, from which some of them supported reform. From 1890 to 1910 the work of a number of national women's organizations, including the National Council of Jewish Women, National Congress of Mothers, and the Women's Trade Union League, furthered the aims of the progressive movement.

The National Association of Colored Women was founded in 1895, fifteen years before the better known, male-oriented National Association for the Advancement of Colored People (NAACP). Aimed at social welfare, the women's organization was the first black social-service agency in the country. At the local level, black women's clubs established kindergartens, day nurseries, playgrounds, and retirement homes.

From two hundred thousand members in 1900, the General Federation of Women's Clubs grew to over one million by 1912. The clubs met, as they had before, for coffee and literary conversation, but they also began to look closely at conditions around them. In 1904 Mrs. Sarah P. Decker, the federation's new president, told the national convention: "Ladies, you have chosen me your leader. Well, I have an important piece of news to give you. Dante is dead. He has been dead for several centuries, and I think it is time that we dropped the study of his *Inferno* and turned our attention to our own."

Forming an Industrial Section and a Committee on Legislation for Women and Children, the federation supported reforms to safeguard child and women workers, improve schools, ensure pure food, and beautify the community. Reluctant at first, it finally lent support in 1914 to woman suffrage, a cause that dated back to the first woman's rights convention in Seneca Falls, New York, in 1848. Divided over tactics, the suffrage movement suffered from disunity, male opposition, indecision over whether to seek action at the state or at the national level, resistance from the Catholic Church, and opposition from liquor interests, who linked the cause to prohibition.

In 1900 Carrie Chapman Catt, a superb organizer, became president of the National American Woman Suffrage Association, which by 1920 had nearly two million members. Catt and Anna Howard Shaw, who became the association's head in 1904, believed in organization and peaceful lobbying to win the vote. Alice Paul and Lucy Burns, founders of the Congressional Union, were more militant; they interrupted public meetings, focused on Congress rather than the states, and in 1917 picketed the White House. The issue attracted many progressives who believed woman's suffrage would purify politics. In 1918 the House passed a constitutional amendment stating simply that the right to vote shall not be denied "on account of sex." The Senate and enough states followed, and the Nineteenth Amendment took effect in 1920.

The social-justice movement had most success in passing state laws limiting the working hours of women. By 1913 thirty-nine states set maximum working hours for women or banned the employment of women at night. Illinois had a ten-hour law; California and Washington, eight-hours. Wisconsin, Oregon, and Kansas allowed expert commissions to set different hours depending on the degree of strain in various occupations. As early as 1900, thanks to groups such as the National Child Labor Committee, twenty-eight

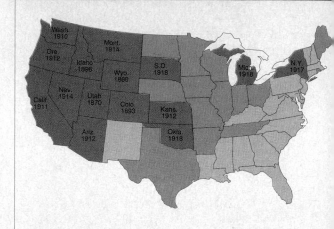

Woman Suffrage Before 1920

State by state gains in woman suffrage were limited to the Far West and were agonizingly slow in the early years of the twentieth century.

Equal suffrage with effective date

Partial woman suffrage

No woman suffrage

■ *A woman suffrage parade, New York, October 23, 1915. Women finally won the right to vote in 1920, seventy-two years after the idea was proposed at Seneca Falls.*

states had laws regulating child labor. But the courts often ruled against such laws, and families —needing extra income—sometimes ignored them. Parents sent children off to jobs with orders to lie about their age.

In 1916 President Woodrow Wilson backed a law to limit child labor, the Keating-Owen Act, but in *Hammer* v. *Dagenhart* (1918) the Supreme Court overturned it as an improper regulation of local labor conditions. In 1919 Congress tried again in the Second Child Labor Act, also struck down by the Court in *Bailey* v. *Drexel Furniture Company* (1922). Not until the 1930s did Congress succeed in passing a Court-supported national child labor law.

A Ferment of Ideas

A dramatic shift in ideas became one of the most important forces behind progressive reform. Building on the developments of the 1890s (see chapter 19), writers in law, economics, history, sociology, psychology, and a host of other fields advanced ideas that together challenged the status quo and called for change.

A new doctrine, called pragmatism, emerged in this ferment of ideas. A famous Harvard psychologist, William James, popularized the pragmatic approach to knowledge. Pragmatists posited that the human mind is not a fixed structure but is constantly changing. Moreover, its thoughts have meaning only in relation to their consequences— the actions they inspire. James' question was "what is the 'cash value' of a thought, idea or belief?" Does it work? Does it make a difference to the individual who experiences it? "The ultimate test for us of what a truth means," said James, "is the conduct it dictates."

The most influential educator of the Progressive era, John Dewey, applied pragmatism to educational reform. He argued that thought evolves in relation to the environment and that education is directly related to experience. In 1896 he and his wife founded a separate School of Pedagogy at the University of Chicago, with a laboratory where educational theory based on the newer philosophical and psychological studies could be tested and practiced.

Dewey introduced an educational revolution that stressed children's needs and capabilities. He described his beliefs and methods in a number of books, notably *School and Society* (1899) and *Democracy and Education* (1916). New ideas in education, he said, are "as much a product of the changed social situation, and as much an effort to meet the needs of the society that is forming, as are changes in modes of industry and commerce." He opposed memorization and dogmatic, authoritarian teaching methods; he emphasized personal growth, free inquiry, and creativity.

Providing an overarching framework within which others could fit, William James and Dewey had a great effect on other thinkers. Edward A. Ross, a reform sociologist, called in *Sin and Society* (1907) for "pure environmentalism" and a new standard of morality. Economist Richard T. Ely (see chapter 19) rejected the conservative "laws" of classical economics and developed theories that placed economics in a changing environment. In *The Theory of the Leisure Class* (1899) and *The Instinct of Workmanship* (1914) Thorstein Veblen argued that everything was flux, the only law was the lack of laws, and modern business was an anarchic struggle for profit. Reform was not only permissible; it could provide order and efficiency in an industrial and entrepreneurial system characterized by disorder.

Rejecting the older view of the law as universal and unchanging, lawyers and legal theorists instead viewed it as a reflection of the environment —an instrument for social change. Law reflected the environment that shaped it. A movement grew among judges for "sociological jurisprudence" that related the law to social reform.

In Denver, Colorado, after Judge Ben Lindsey sentenced a boy to reform school for stealing coal, the boy's mother rushed forward and, in grief, beat her head against the wall. Lindsey investigated the case; he found that the father was a smelting worker dying of lead poisoning; the family needed coal for heat. Children, he concluded, were not born with a genetic tendency to crime; they were made good or bad by the environment in which they grew. Lindsey "sentenced" youthful offenders to education and good care. He worked for playgrounds, slum clearance, public baths, and technical schools. Known as the "Kids' Judge," he attracted visitors from as far away as Japan.

Louis D. Brandeis graduated from Harvard Law School in 1878 and became a corporation lawyer

■ *Laundry owner Curt Muller (above, arms folded) challenged an Oregon law limiting the length of the working day for women to ten hours. Lawyer Louis D. Brandeis (right, top), using a mass of statistics, sociological data, and expert testimony compiled with the help of Lillian Wald (right, bottom), defended the law before the Supreme Court.*

and near-millionaire. But like many others, he changed his mind about social issues during the depression of the 1890s, and as the "People's Attorney," he fought corporate abuses and political corruption. In 1908 he accepted an invitation from the National Consumers' League to defend an Oregon law limiting working hours for women to ten hours a day.

Brandeis decided on a new kind of argument. With the help of Lillian Wald, he compiled masses of medical and sociological data, and when he submitted to the Court a 104-page brief, only 2 pages examined traditional legal precedents. The rest included reports from factory inspectors, health and hygiene commissioners, and expert commissions—all showing that the ten-hour law was necessary to protect the health, safety, and morals of women in Oregon.

Agreeing, the Supreme Court in *Muller* v. *Oregon* (1908) upheld the Oregon statute, and the famous "Brandeis Brief," based on environmental data rather than legal precedent, influenced law-

yers and courts across the country. Like so many other reform efforts during these years, it focused on the effects of the environment, suggesting that changes in the way in which people lived and worked—through social and political reforms—could improve their condition.

Socialism, a reformist political philosophy, grew dramatically before the First World War. Organized in 1901, the Socialist party of America doubled in membership between 1904 and 1908, then tripled in the four years after that. Torn by factions, it enlisted some intellectuals, factory workers, disillusioned Populists, miners, and lumberjacks. By 1911 there were socialist mayors in thirty-two cities, including Berkeley, California; Butte, Montana; and Flint, Michigan. Although its doctrines were aimed at an urban proletariat, the Socialisty party drew support in rural Texas, Missouri, Arkansas, Idaho, and Washington. In Oklahoma it attracted as much as a third of the vote.

Eugene V. Debs, five times the party's presidential candidate, offset the popular image of the wild-eyed radical. Gentle and reflective, he was thrust into prominence by the Pullman strike (see chapter 20). Like the party he led, Debs never developed a cohesive platform, nor was he an effective organizer. But he was eloquent, passionate, and visionary. An excellent speaker, he captivated audiences, attacking the injustices of capitalism and urging a workers' republic. Running for president, he gained 100,000 votes in 1900; 400,000 in 1904; and 900,000 in 1912, the party's peak year.

Reform in the Cities

In the early years of the twentieth century, urban reform movements, many of them born in the 1890s, spread across the nation. In 1894 the National Municipal League was organized, and it became the forum for debate over civic reform, changes in the tax laws, and municipal ownership of public utilities. Within a few years nearly every city had a variety of clubs and organizations directed at improving the quality of city life.

"For two generations," Frederic C. Howe said in 1905, "we have wrought out the most admirable laws and then left the government to run itself. This has been our greatest fault." In the 1880s reformers like Howe would call an evening conference, pass resolutions, and then go home; after 1900 they formed associations, adopted long-range policies, and hired employees to achieve them. In the mid-1890s only Chicago had an urban reform league with a full-time paid executive; within a decade there were such leagues in every major city.

In city after city reformers reordered municipal government. Tightening controls on corporate activities, they broadened the scope of utility regulation and restricted city franchises. They updated tax assessments, often skewed in favor of corporations, and tried to clean up the electoral machinery. Devoted to efficiency, they developed a trained civil service to oversee planning and operations. The generation of the 1880s also believed in civil service, but the goal then was mostly negative: to get spoilsmen out and "good" people in. Now the goal was efficiency and above all, results.

In constructing their model governments,

urban reformers often turned to recent advances in business management and organization. They stressed continuity and expertise, a system in which professional experts staffed a government overseen by elective officials. At the top the elected leader surveyed the breadth of city, state, or national affairs and defined directions. Below, a corps of experts—trained in the various disciplines of the new society—funneled the definition into specific, scientifically based policies.

Reformers thus created a growing number of regulatory commissions and municipal departments. They hired engineers to oversee utility and water systems, physicians and nurses to improve municipal health, and city planners to oversee park and highway development. They created specialized "academies" to train police and firefighters. Imitated by the state and federal governments, the proliferation of experts and commissions widened the gap between voters and decision makers but dramatically improved the efficiency of government.

As cities exploded in size, they freed themselves from the tight controls of state legislatures and began to experiment with their governments. Struggling to recover from a devastating hurricane in 1900, Galveston, Texas, pioneered the commission form of government: a form of municipal government in which commissions of appointed experts, rather than elected officials, ran the city. Wanting nonpartisan expertise, Staunton, Virginia, was the first city to hire a city manager. Other cities followed, and by 1910 over a hundred cities were using either the commission or manager type of government.

In the race for reform, a number of city mayors won national reputations—among them Seth Low in New York City and Hazen S. Pingree in Detroit—working to modernize taxes, clean up politics, lower utility rates, and control the awarding of valuable city franchises. In Toledo, Ohio, Mayor Samuel M. ("Golden Rule") Jones, a wealthy manufacturer, took billy clubs away from the police, established free kindergartens, playgrounds, and night schools, and improved wages for city workers.

In Cleveland, Ohio, Tom L. Johnson showed an innovative approach to city government. A millionaire who had made his fortune manipulating city franchises, Johnson one day read Henry George's *Progress and Poverty* (see chapter 19) and turned to reform. Elected mayor of Cleveland, he served from 1901 to 1909 and collected a group of aggressive and talented young advisers. Frederic C. Howe, Newton D. Baker, and Edward Bemis—all of whom later won national reputations—shaped Johnson's ideas on taxes, prison reform, utility regulation, and other issues facing the city.

Johnson combined shrewdness and showmanship. Believing in an informed citizenry, he held outdoor meetings in huge tents. He used colorful charts to give Cleveland residents a course in utilities and taxation. He cut down on corruption, cut off special privilege, updated taxes, and gave Cleveland a reputation as the country's best-governed city.

Finding it difficult to regulate powerful city utilities and keep their costs down, Johnson and mayors in other cities turned more and more to public ownership of gas, electricity, water, and transportation. Called "gas and water socialism," the idea spread swiftly. In 1896 fewer than half of American cities owned their own waterworks; by 1915 almost two thirds did.

Action in the States

Reformers soon discovered, however, that many problems lay beyond a city's boundaries, and they turned for action to the state and federal governments. From the 1890s to 1920 they worked to stiffen state laws regulating the labor of women and children, create and strengthen commissions to regulate railroads and utilities, impose corporate and inheritance taxes, improve mental and penal institutions, and allocate more funds for state universities, the training ground for the experts and educated citizenry needed for the new society.

Maryland passed the first workers' compensation law in 1902; soon most industrial states had such legislation. After 1900 many states adopted factory inspection laws, and by 1916 almost two thirds of the states mandated insurance for the victims of factory accidents. By 1914, twenty-five states had enacted employers' liability laws.

To regulate business, virtually every state created regulatory commissions, empowered to examine corporate books and hold public hearings. Building on earlier experience, after 1900 they were given new power to initiate actions, rather than await complaints, and in some cases to set maximum prices and rates. Dictating company practices, they pioneered regulatory methods later adopted in federal legislation of 1906 and 1910. Some business leaders supported the federal laws in order to get rid of "the intolerable supervision" of dozens of separate state commissions.

Historians have long praised the regulation movement, but the commissions did not always act wisely or even in the public interest. Elective commissions often produced commissioners who had little knowledge of corporate affairs. To win election, some promised specific rates or reforms, a violation of the commission's investigative functions. Appointive commissions sometimes fared better, but they too had to oversee extraordinarily complex businesses like the railroads. Shaping everything from wages to train schedules, the commissions affected railroad profits and growth. In the end, the regulatory commissions damaged the railroad industry.

Emphasizing people's involvement in politics, progressives backed three measures to make officeholders responsive to popular will: the initiative, which allowed voters to propose new laws; the referendum, which allowed them to accept or reject a law at the ballot box; and the recall, which gave them a way to remove an elected official from office. Oregon adopted the initiative and referendum in 1902; by 1912 twelve states had them. That year Congress added the Seventeenth Amendment to the Constitution to provide for the direct election of U.S. senators. By 1916 all but three states had direct primaries, which allowed the people, rather than nominating conventions, to choose candidates for office.

As attention shifted from the cities to the states, reform governors throughout the country won growing reputations. Joseph Folk, Steffens' hero in Saint Louis, became the governor of Missouri in 1904. Hiram Johnson won fame in California for his shrewd and forceful campaign against the Southern Pacific Railroad. In the East were Charles Evans Hughes in New York and Woodrow Wilson, the former president of Princeton University, in New Jersey.

Robert M. La Follette became the most famous reform governor. A graduate of the University of Wisconsin, La Follette served three terms in Congress during the late 1880s. A staunch Republican, he supported the tariff and other Republican doctrines but the Democratic landslide of 1890 turned him out of office. Moving to state politics, he became interested in reform, and in 1901 he became governor of Wisconsin. Then forty-five years old, La Follette was talented, aggressive, and a superb stump speaker.

In the following six years, he put together the "Wisconsin Idea," one of the most important reform programs in the history of state government. He established an industrial commission, the first in the country, to regulate factory safety and sanitation. He improved education, workers' compensation, public utility controls, and resource conservation. He lowered railroad rates and raised railroad taxes. Under La Follette's prodding, Wisconsin became the first state to adopt a direct primary for all political nominations. It also became the first to adopt a state income tax.

Like other progressives, La Follette drew on expert advice and relied on academic figures like Richard Ely and Edward Ross at the University of Wisconsin. La Follette supporters established the first Legislative Reference Bureau in the university's library; the bureau stocked the governor and his allies with facts and figures to support the measures they wanted. Theodore Roosevelt called La Follette's Wisconsin "the laboratory of democracy," and the "Wisconsin Idea" soon spread to many other states, including New York, California, Michigan, Iowa, and Texas.

■ *The most famous of the reform leaders in the states was Wisconsin's Robert M. "Fighting Bob" La Follette.*

The Mass Society

"Life in the States," an English visitor said in 1900, "is one perpetual whirl of telephones, telegrams, phonographs, electric bells, motors, lifts, and automatic instruments." If not quite that, conditions were better than just a few years before. Farms and factories were once again prosperous; in 1901, for the first time in years, the economy reached full capacity. Farm prices rose almost 50 percent between 1900 and 1910. Unemployment dropped. "In the United States of today," a Boston newspaper said in 1904, "everyone is middle class. The resort to force, the wild talk of the nineties are over. Everyone is busily, happily getting ahead."

The start of a new century influenced people's outlook. Excited about beginning the twentieth century, people believed that technology and enterprise would shape a better life. Savoring the word "new," they talked of the new poetry, new cinema, new history, new democracy, new woman, new art, new immigration, new morality, and new city. Magazines picked up the word; there were the *New Republic* and the *New Statesman.* Presidents Roosevelt and Wilson called their political programs the New Nationalism and the New Freedom.

The word "mass" also cropped up frequently. Victors in the recent war with Spain, Americans took pride in teeming cities, burgeoning corporations, and other marks of the mass society. They flocked more and more to mass entertainment, enjoyed the fruits of mass production, read mass-circulation newspapers and magazines, and took mass transit from the growing spiral of suburbs into the central cities.

An Urban Nation

In 1920 the median age of the population was only twenty-five. (It is now thirty.) Immigration accounted for part of the youthfulness, since most immigrants were young, and so did death rates. Thanks to medical advances and better living conditions, death rates dropped in the early years of the century; the average life span in-

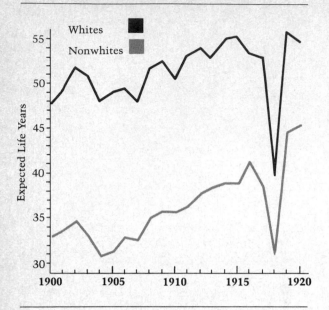

Life Expectancy, 1900–1920

Whites
Nonwhites

Expected Life Years

55

50

45

40

35

30

1900   1905   1910   1915   1920

creased. Between 1900 and 1920, life expectancy rose from forty-nine to fifty-six years for white women and from forty-seven to fifty-four years for white men. It rose from thirty-three to forty-five years for blacks and other racial minorities.

Infant mortality remained high; nearly 10 percent of white babies and 20 percent of minority babies died in their first year of life. In comparison to today, fewer babies on average survived to adolescence, and fewer people survived beyond middle age. In 1900 the death rate among people between forty-five and sixty-five was more than twice the modern rate. As a result, there were relatively fewer older people—in 1900 only 4 percent of the population was older than sixty-five compared to nearly 12 percent today. Fewer children than today knew their grandparents. Still, improvements in health care helped people live longer, and as a result, the incidence of cancer and heart disease increased.

In 1900 six of every ten Americans lived on farms or in towns of fewer than twenty-five hundred people. But the flight from the farms continued, and a decade later only five in ten still lived there. By 1920 fewer than a third of all Americans lived on farms; fewer than half lived in rural areas.

Cities grew, and by any earlier standards, they grew on a colossal scale. Downtowns became a central hive of skyscrapers, department stores, warehouses, and hotels. Strips of factories radiated from the center. As street railways spread, cities took on a systematic pattern of socioeconomic segregation, usually in rings. The innermost ring filled with immigrants, circled by a belt of working-class housing. The remaining rings marked areas of rising affluence outward toward wealthy suburbs, which themselves formed around shopping strips and grid patterns of streets that restricted social interaction.

The giants were New York, Chicago, and Philadelphia, industrial cities that turned out every kind of product from textiles to structural steel. Smaller cities like Rochester, New York, or Cleveland, Ohio, specialized in manufacturing a specific line of goods or processing regional products for the national market. Railroads instead of highways tied things together; in 1916 the rail network, the leading one in the world, reached its peak—254,000 miles of track that carried over three fourths of intercity freight tonnage.

Step by step cities adopted their twentieth-century forms. Between 1909 and 1915 Los Ange-

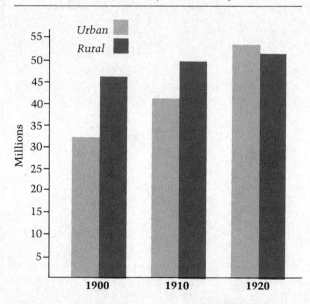

Urban and Rural Population, 1900–1920 (in millions)

Urban
Rural

Millions

55
50
45
40
35
30
25
20
15
10
5

1900   1910   1920

Source: U.S. Bureau of the Census, Historical Statistics of the United States, Colonial Times to 1970, Bicentennial Edition, Washington, D.C., 1975.

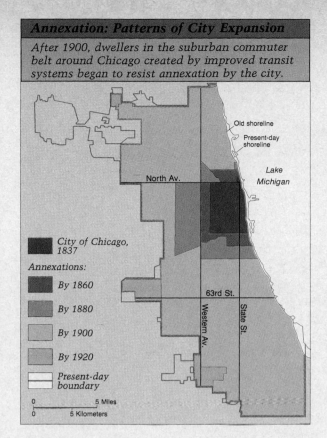

Annexation: Patterns of City Expansion

After 1900, dwellers in the suburban commuter belt around Chicago created by improved transit systems began to resist annexation by the city.

Old shoreline
Present-day shoreline
North Av.
Lake Michigan

City of Chicago, 1837

Annexations:
By 1860
By 1880
By 1900
By 1920
Present-day boundary

63rd St.
Western Av.
State St.

0 5 Miles
0 5 Kilometers

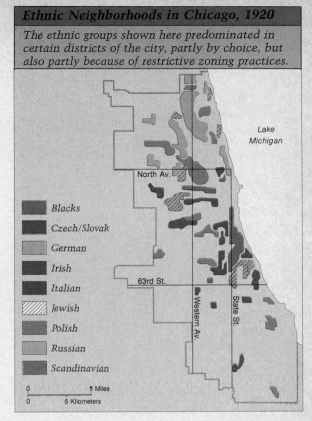

Ethnic Neighborhoods in Chicago, 1920

The ethnic groups shown here predominated in certain districts of the city, partly by choice, but also partly because of restrictive zoning practices.

Lake Michigan
North Av.

Blacks
Czech/Slovak
German
Irish
Italian
Jewish
Polish
Russian
Scandinavian

63rd St.
Western Av.
State St.

0 5 Miles
0 5 Kilometers

les, a city of three hundred thousand people, passed a series of ordinances that gave rise to modern urban zoning. For the first time the ordinances divided a city into three districts of specified use: a residential area, an industrial area, and an area open to residence and a limited list of industries. Other cities followed. Combining several features, the New York Zoning Law of 1916 became the model for the nation; within a decade 591 cities copied it.

Zoning ordered city development, keeping skyscrapers out of factory districts, factories out of the suburbs. It also had powerful social repercussions. In the South zoning became a tool to extend racial segregation; in northern cities it acted against ethnic minorities. Jews in New York, Italians in Boston, Poles in Detroit, blacks in Chicago—zoning laws held them all at arm's length. Like other migrants, blacks often preferred to settle together, but zoning also helped put them there. By 1920 ten districts in Chicago were more than three-quarters black. In Los An-

geles, Cleveland, Detroit, and Washington, D.C., most blacks lived in only two or three wards.

While many people fled the farm, farmers themselves prospered, the beneficiaries of greater production and expanding urban markets. Rural Free Delivery, begun in 1893, helped diminish the farmers' sense of isolation. In ways since forgotten, it changed farm life. The delivery of mail to the farm door opened that door to a wider world; it exposed farmers to urban thinking, national advertising, and political events. In 1911 over a billion newspapers and magazines were delivered over RFD routes.

Parcel post (1913) permitted the sending of packages through the U.S. mail. Mail-order houses flourished; rural merchants suffered. Packages went both ways—President Woodrow Wilson's first parcel-post delivery had eight pounds of New Jersey apples—and within a year 300 million packages were being mailed annually. While telephones and electricity did not reach most rural areas for decades, better roads, mail-order cata-

■ *With rural free delivery people in even the most remote areas had access to the world of goods described in the catalogues of the large mail-order houses.*

logs, and other innovations knit farmers into the larger society. Early in the new century Mary E. Lease—who in her Populist days had urged Kansas farmers to raise less corn and more Hell—moved to Brooklyn.

Life on the farm was tiring and often difficult. Land prices rose with crop prices, and farm tenancy increased, especially in the South. Tenancy grew from one quarter of all farms in 1880 to more than one third in 1910. In South Carolina, Georgia, Alabama, and Mississippi, it amounted to nearly two thirds. Many southern tenant farmers were black, and they suffered from farm-bred diseases. In 1909 the Rockefeller Sanitary Commission, acting on recent scientific discoveries, began a sanitation campaign that eventually wiped out the hookworm disease, and in 1912 the U.S. Public Health Service began work on rural malaria.

Improvements in telescopes and microscopes allowed scientists to look farther out and closer up than ever before. Using the new 100-inch telescope on Mount Wilson in California, Edwin P. Hubble showed that galaxies existed beyond the Milky Way. Other astronomers proved empirically what Copernicus had claimed centuries before: the earth revolves around the sun. Biologists concentrated upon the cell; they studied the protoplasm that formed the basis of life, and terms like chromosome, gene, and hormone became household words. "A few years ago the possibility of investigating by direct experiment the internal structure of atoms, or the topographical grouping of heredity units in the germ cells would have seemed a wild dream," Edmund B. Wilson, a Columbia University scientist, said in 1915. "Today these questions stand among the substantial realities of scientific inquiry."

Toward a Consumer Society

As factories produced more, people bought more. In 1900 business firms spent about $95 million on advertising; twenty years later they spent over $500 million. Ads and billboards touted cigarettes, cars, perfumes, and cosmetics. Advertising agencies boomed, and using new sampling techniques, they developed modern concepts of market testing and research. In an important side effect, sampling customer preferences also made business more responsive to public opinion on social and political issues.

Mass production swept the clothing industry and dressed more Americans better than any people ever before. Using lessons learned in making uniforms during the Civil War, manufacturers for the first time developed standard clothing and shoe sizes that fit most bodies. Clothing prices dropped; the availability of inexpensive, "off-the-rack" clothes lessened distinctions between rich and poor. By 1900 nine of every ten men and boys wore the new "ready-to-wear" clothes.

In 1900 people employed in manufacturing earned on average $418 a year. Two decades later they earned $1342 a year, though inflation took much of the increase. While the middle class expanded, the rich also grew richer. In 1920 the new income tax showed the first accurate tabulation of income, and it confirmed what many had suspected all along. Five percent of the population received almost one fourth of all income.

Kuppenheimer Clothes

SOLD BY

■ *A 1910 advertisement for men's ready-to-wear clothing features two collegians sporting the latest styles.*

Society's Masses

National networks of products and consumers helped fuel the mass society. But it also depended on an enormous increase in the labor force to work in the factories, mines, and forests. Women and blacks played larger roles. Immigration soared. Between 1901 and 1910 nearly 8.8 million immigrants entered the United States; between 1911 and 1920 another 5.7 million came.

Women worked in larger and larger numbers. In 1900 more than 5 million worked—one fifth of all adult women—and among those aged fourteen to twenty-four, the work rate was almost one third. Of those employed, single women outnumbered married women by seven to one; yet more than a third of married women worked. Most women held service jobs. Only a small number held higher paying jobs as professionals or managers.

In the 1890s women made up over a quarter of medical school graduates. Adopting rigid standards, men gradually squeezed them out, and by the 1920s only about 5 percent of the graduates were women. Few women taught in colleges and universities, and those that did were expected to resign if they married. In 1906 Harriet Brooks, a promising physicist at Barnard College in New York, became engaged and refused to resign; the dean told her icily that Barnard expected a married woman to "dignify her home-making into a profession, and not assume that she can carry on two full professions at a time."

More women than men graduated from high school, and with professions like medicine and science largely closed to them, they often turned to the new "business schools" that offered training in stenography, typing, and bookkeeping. In 1920 over a quarter of all employed women held clerical jobs. Many others taught school.

In 1907 and 1908 investigators studied 22,000 women workers in Pittsburgh; 60 percent of them earned less than $7 a week, a minimum for "decent living." Fewer than 1 percent held skilled jobs; most tended machines, wrapped and labeled, or did handwork that required no particular skill. In New York, many women toiled as garment workers from eight in the morning to six in the evening, with an hour off on Saturdays. They earned $7 to $12 a week, nothing at all during slack season. They had to buy their own needles and thread and pay for electricity and chairs to sit on.

Critics charged that women's employment endangered the home, threatened their reproductive functions, and even, as one man said, stripped them of "that modest demeanor that lends a charm to their kind." Adding to the fears, the birth rate continued to drop between 1900 and 1920, and the divorce rate soared, in part because working-class men took advantage of the newer moral freedom and deserted their families in growing numbers. By 1916 there was one divorce for every nine marriages as compared to one for twenty-one in 1880.

David Graham Phillips, a novelist troubled by the woman's problem, depicted a husband's oppression of his wife in *The Hungry Heart*, published in 1909. "He kissed her, patted her cheek, went back to his work." When the wife grew restless, the husband knew why: "A few more years'll wash away the smatter she got at college, and this restlessness of hers will yield to nature, and she'll be content and happy in her womanhood. . . . As grandfather often said, it's a dreadful mistake, educating women beyond their sphere." Such views, mild as they were, got Phillips assassinated by a lunatic who claimed the novelist was "trying to destroy the whole ideal of womanhood."

Many children worked. In 1900 about three million children—nearly 20 percent of those between the ages of five and fifteen—held full- or almost full-time jobs. Twenty-five thousand boys under sixteen worked in mining; twenty thousand children under twelve, mainly girls, worked in southern cotton mills. Gradually the use of child labor shrank, reflecting in part the growing recognition of the importance of childhood. Families focused greater and greater attention on the children, and child-rearing became a central—perhaps *the* central—concern of family life.

As the middle-class family changed from an economic to an emotional unit, middle-class women claimed increasing pride in homemaking and motherhood. Mother's Day, the national holiday, was formally established in 1913. With families preferring smaller numbers of children, birth control became a more acceptable practice. Margaret Sanger, a nurse and social reformer, led a campaign to give physicians broad discretion in prescribing contraceptives. When Sanger became involved in the birth-control movement, the federal Comstock Law banned the interstate transport of contraceptive devices and information (see the special feature on pp. 646–47).

Blacks and Mexican-Americans

At the turn of the century eight of every ten blacks lived in rural areas, mainly in the South. Most were poor sharecroppers. "Jim Crow" laws segregated many schools, railroad cars, hotels, and hospitals. Poll taxes and other devices disfranchised blacks and many poor whites. Violence was common; between 1900 and 1914, white mobs murdered over a thousand black people.

Two murders occurred near Vicksburg, Mississippi, in 1904. Looking for the killer of a white planter, a mob captured a black man and woman, their guilt or innocence unknown. They were tied to trees, and their fingers and ears were cut off as souvenirs. "The most excruciating form of punishment consisted in the use of a large corkscrew in the hands of some of the mob. This instrument was bored into the flesh of the man and the woman, in the arms, legs and body, and then pulled out, the spirals tearing out big pieces of raw, quivering flesh every time it was withdrawn." Finally, both people were thrown on a fire and burned to death, "a relief," a witness said, "to the maimed and suffering victims."

Many blacks labored in the cotton farms, railroad camps, sawmills, and mines of the South

PICKING SLATE

LAD FELL TO DEATH IN BIG COAL CHUTE

Dennis McKee Dead and Arthur Allbecker Had Leg Burned In the Lee Mines.

Falling into a chute at the Chauncey colliery of the George S. Lee Coal Company at Avondale, this afternoon, Dennis McKee, aged ██ of West Nanticoke, was smothered to death and

He was removed to his home at Avondale.

Both boys were employed as breaker boys, and going too close to the chutes fell in. Fellow workmen rushed to their assistance and soon

Breaker boys, who picked out pieces of slate from the coal as it rushed past, often became bent-backed after years of working fourteen hours a day in the coal mines. Accidents—and death—were common.

under conditions of peonage. Peons traded their lives and labor for food and shelter. Often illiterate, they were forced to sign contracts allowing planters "to use such force as he or his agents may deem necessary to require me to remain on his farm and perform good and satisfactory services." Armed guards patrolled the camps and whipped those trying to escape. "In the woods," a peon said, "they can do anything they please, and no one can see them but God."

Few blacks belonged to labor unions, and almost always blacks earned less than whites in the same job. In Atlanta white electricians earned $5.00 a day, blacks $3.50. Black songs like "I've Got a White Man Workin' for Me" (1901) voiced more hope than reality. The illiteracy rate among blacks dropped from 45 percent in 1900 to 30 percent in 1910, but nowhere were they given equal school facilities, teachers' salaries, or educational materials. In 1910 scarcely eight thousand black youths were attending high schools in all the states of the Southeast. South Carolina spent $13.98 annually for the education of each white child, $1.13 for each black child.

In 1905 a group of black leaders met near Niagara Falls, New York, and pledged action on behalf of voting, equal access to economic opportunity, integration, and equality before the law. At their head was sociologist W. E. B. Du Bois, now a professor of history and economics at Atlanta University. The Niagara movement rejected Booker T. Washington's gradualist approach, which, Du Bois said, would produce "a voteless herd to run the machines and wash the dishes for the new aristocracy. Negroes would be educated enough to be useful but not enough, or not in the right way, to be able to assert self-respect." In *The Souls of Black Folk* (1903) and other works, Du Bois eloquently called for justice and equality. "By every civilized and peaceful method," he said, "we must strive for the right which the world accords to man."

Race riots broke out in Atlanta, Georgia, in 1906 and Springfield, Illinois, in 1908, the latter the home of Abraham Lincoln. Unlike the riots of the 1960s, white mobs invaded black neighborhoods, burning, looting, and killing. They lynched two blacks—one eighty-four years old—in Springfield. Mary Ovington, a white anthropology student, was outraged, and along with other reformers, white and black, issued a call for

■ The wish to have "our children . . . enjoy fairer conditions than have fallen to our lot" was the impetus behind both the Niagara movement (top) and the NAACP, which sponsored the 1917 parade in New York City, pictured at bottom.

Margaret Sanger and the Birth Control Movement

At the start of the twentieth century, birth control was an issue fraught with social and religious controversy. Devout Christians—Protestants and Catholics—opposed it as a violation of God's law; the overseers of society's moral behavior feared it might foster, if not promiscuity, an overindulgence in sexual activity. Theodore Roosevelt said it meant "race death: a sin for which there is no atonement." The Comstock Act of 1873 banned from the U.S. mails all information on contraceptives and birth control, and by 1914 twenty-two states had enacted laws that prohibited outright or greatly inhibited the dissemination of such information. That year Margaret Sanger formally launched her campaign for birth control.

Born in 1883, Sanger grew up in Corning, New York, an upstate factory town. Her father, an Irish-born stonecutter, encouraged his children to think for themselves. "Leave the world better because you, my child, have dwelt in it," he told Margaret. One of eleven children, Margaret from an early age linked poverty to large families. "Our childhood," she said, "was one of longing for things that were always denied."

Sanger became a nurse; eager for excitement and romance, she settled in New York City, married, and had three children. Restless, and finding her marriage confining, she discovered Greenwich Village, a favorite haunt of the period's intense young radicals. On McDougal Street in the Village, Sanger met Socialist leader Eugene V. Debs; young reporter and revolutionary, John Reed, later to be honored by the Bolsheviks and buried in the Kremlin; William D. "Big Bill" Haywood of the radical Industrial Workers of the World (IWW); and feminist and socialist agitator, Emma Goldman.

The Village was filled with vibrant people determined to improve the world. Stimulated by the exciting talk, Sanger joined the Socialist party and worked to organize women for socialism in New York City. In 1912 she marched in the IWW picket lines in the great strike at the textile mills in Paterson, New Jersey. Pursuing her nursing career, Sanger worked on the lower East Side of New York where thousands upon thousands of people were crowded into tenement houses. Struck by the ignorance of tenement women about their own bodies, she wrote in 1912 a series of newspaper articles about venereal disease and personal hygiene, entitled "What Every Girl Should Know"; the Post Office Department banned it from the mails.

That same year Sanger watched at the bedside of Sadie Sachs, a poor working woman dying from a self-induced abortion. Warned that she might not survive another pregnancy, Sachs had asked for contraceptive advice, but the doctor had suggested only that she make her husband sleep on the roof. After Sachs died, Sanger spent hours walking the streets and thinking about birth and children and poverty. She resolved that night, she later said, "to seek out the root of the evil, to do something to change the destiny of mothers whose miseries were as vast as the sky."

The answer was birth control—a term she and several friends coined in 1914. Sanger spent a year absorbing medical opinion and learning about contraceptives, and then began publishing the journal *Woman Rebel.* Aimed at the working class, the journal touched on birth control, but its chief focus was on social revolution, particularly on raising the social consciousness of working women, encouraging them "to think for themselves" and "to have an ideal." It ran for only seven issues before it was banned by the post office. Sanger, indicted under the Comstock Act, fled to Europe.

There, after considerable reflection, she decided that birth control was a medical matter, not a social or revolutionary one. It belonged in the hands of physicians and their patients, with physicians free to prescribe contraception and other measures when appropriate. Women should "decide for themselves whether they shall become mothers, under what conditions, and when." Working through the National Birth Control League and other groups, Sanger broadened the movement's base beyond the socialists and feminists who had originally backed it. Settlement-house workers had been cool to birth control at first, but soon they too lent support.

Sanger returned to the United States, and the government, preoccupied with other issues, dropped the indictment against her. In October 1916, again defying the law, she opened the nation's first birth-control clinic in the teeming Brownsville section of Brooklyn, New York. Police soon raided the clinic, and Sanger was sentenced to thirty days in jail. On appeal, the New York State Court of Appeals upheld the sentence, but in an important victory for Sanger, it ruled that physicians should have greater discretion in prescribing birth control.

Late in 1916 Sanger formed the New York Birth Control League to push for legislation to give physicians even broader discretion. The league's argument that birth control would be an effective means of promoting the social welfare was a persuasive idea that convinced a wide variety of groups. Some reformers thought that smaller families would raise the standard of living of the poor. Other people thought birth control might limit the number of "undesirables" in the population. Eugenicists who wanted to improve the human species through genetic control saw it as a way to reduce the proportion of the unwanted and unfit in the society. Gradually Sanger herself reflected such arguments. "More children from the fit, less from the unfit—that is the chief issue," she said in 1919.

In 1921 Sanger organized a nationwide movement through the American Birth Control League; it held clinics and conferences to educate the public. In the photo above, volunteers are selling the "Birth Control Review." Although the Catholic Church remained opposed, the movement spread among Protestants, Jews, and those who did not attend church. In 1940 Eleanor Roosevelt, the popular First Lady, came out in support of family planning, and by the 1940s every state except Massachusetts and Connecticut had legalized the distribution of birth-control information.

When Margaret Sanger died in 1966, the birth-control pill had the approval of the Federal Drug Administration, and its use was widespread. The cause she had championed—once so shocking and radical—was won in American society.

the conference that organized the National Association for the Advancement of Colored People. Created in 1910, within four years the NAACP grew to fifty branches and over six thousand members. The eight top officers included one black—Director of Publicity and Research W. E. B. Du Bois.

At the beginning of the twentieth century, Mexicans for the first time immigrated in large numbers, especially after a revolution in 1909 forced many to flee across the northern border into Texas, New Mexico, Arizona, and California. Their exact numbers were unknown. American officials did not count border crossings until 1907, and even then, many migrants avoided the official immigration stations. Almost all came from the Mexican lower class, eager to escape peonage and violence in their native land. Labor agents—called *coyotes*—usually in the employ of large corporations or working for ranchers, recruited Mexican workers. After the turn of the century, almost 10 percent of the total population of Mexico moved to the American Southwest.

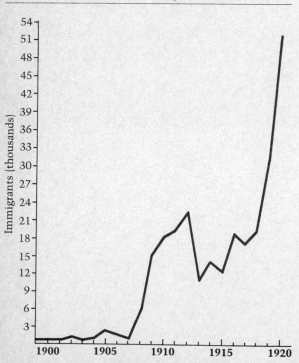

Mexican Immigration to the United States, 1900–1920

The "New" Immigration

Between 1901 and 1920 the extraordinarily high total of 14.5 million immigrants entered the country, more than in any previous twenty-year period. Continuing the recent trend (see chapter 19), many came from southern and eastern Europe. Still called the "new" immigrants, they met hostility from "older" immigrants of northern European stock who questioned their values and appearance.

From 1901 to 1914, some 3 million Italians and 1.5 million Jews and 4 million Slavs from central and eastern Europe entered the country. In 1907, the year of greatest influx, 1.3 million immigrants entered; about half of them came from Italy, Austria-Hungary, Poland, and Russia. Most were Catholic or Jewish in religion. More than a third were illiterate, and most, coming from peasant backgrounds, were unskilled. Over two thirds were males.

Labor agents—called *padroni* among the Italians, Greeks, and Syrians—recruited immigrant workers, found them jobs, and deducted a fee from their wages. Headquartered in Salt Lake City, Leonidas G. Skliris, the "Czar of the Greeks," provided workers for the Utah Copper Company and the Western Pacific Railroad. In Chicago at the turn of the century *padroni* employed more than one fifth of all Italians; in New York City they controlled two thirds of the entire labor force.

Immigrant patterns often departed from traditional stereotypes. Immigrants, for example, moved both ways. Fifty percent or more of some groups returned home, although the numbers varied among groups. Jews and Czechs often brought their families to resettle in America; Serbs and Poles tended to come singly, intent on earning enough money to make a fresh start at home. Many Italian men virtually commuted, "birds of passage" who returned home every slack season. However, the outbreak of World War I interrupted the practice and trapped hundreds of thousands of Italians and others who had planned to return to Europe.

Older residents lumped the newcomers together, ignoring geographic, religious, and other differences. Preserving important regional distinctions, Italians tended to settle as Calabreses, Venetians, Abruzzis, and Sicilians. Native Americans viewed them all simply as Italians. Henry Ford and other employers tried to erase the differences through English classes and deliberate "Americanization" programs. The Ford Motor Company ran a school where immigrant employees were first taught to say: "I am a good American." At the graduation ceremony, the pupils acted out a gigantic pantomime in which, clad in their old-country dress, they filed into a

■ *The Pledge of Allegiance, adopted in 1882, was part of the Americanization process for millions of immigrant children.*

Immigration to the United States, 1900–1920 (by area of origin)

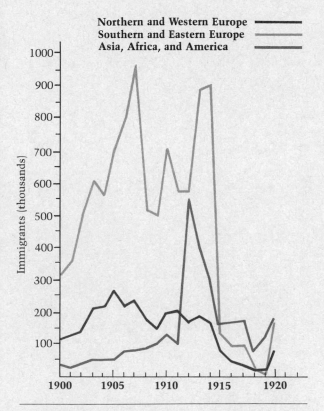

Northern and Western Europe ━━━
Southern and Eastern Europe ━━━
Asia, Africa, and America ━━━

Note: For purposes of classification, Northern and Western Europe includes Great Britain, Ireland, Scandinavia, the Netherlands, Belgium, Luxembourg, Switzerland, France and Germany. Southern and Eastern Europe includes Poland, Austria-Hungary, Russia and the Baltic States, Rumania, Bulgaria, European Turkey, Italy, Spain, Portugal, and Greece. Asia, Africa, and America includes Asian Turkey, China, Japan, India, Canada, the Caribbean, Latin America, and all of Africa.

Source: U.S. Bureau of the Census, Historical Statistics of the United States, Colonial Times to 1970, Bicentennial Edition, Washington, D.C., 1975.

large "melting pot." When they emerged, they were wearing identical American-made clothes, and each was waving a little American flag.

In similar fashion, the International Harvester Corporation taught Polish laborers to speak English, but it had other lessons in view as well. According to "Lesson One," drilled into the Polish "pupils":

I hear the whistle. I must hurry.
I hear the five minute whistle.
It is time to go into the shop.
I take my check from the gate board and hang it on the department board.
I change my clothes and get ready to work.
The starting whistle blows.
I eat my lunch.
It is forbidden to eat until then.
The whistle blows at five minutes of starting time.
I get ready to go to work.
I work until the whistle blows to quit.
I leave my place nice and clean.
I put all my clothes in the locker.
I must go home.

Nativist sentiment, which had accompanied earlier waves of immigrants, intensified. Old-stock Americans sneered at the newcomers' dress and language. Racial theories emphasized the superiority of northern Europeans (see chapter 21) and the new "science" of eugenics suggested controls over the population growth of "inferior" peoples. Hostility against Catholics and Jews was common but touched other groups as well.

Congress passed statutes requiring literacy tests designed to curtail immigration from southern and eastern Europe, but they were vetoed by William Howard Taft in 1913, and Woodrow Wilson in 1915 and 1917. In 1917 Congress passed such a measure over Wilson's veto. Other measures tried to limit immigration from Mexico and Japan, and in 1902 a law passed that prohibited immigration from China.

Entertainment for the Masses

Thanks to changing work rules and mechanization, many Americans benefited from more leisure time. The average work week for manufacturing laborers fell from sixty hours in 1890 to fifty-one in 1920. By the early 1900s white-collar workers might spend only eight to ten hours a day at work and a half-day on weekends. The new leisure time gave more people more opportunity to play.

Baseball entrenched itself as the national pastime. Automobiles and streetcars carried growing numbers of fans to ballparks; attendance at major-league games doubled between 1903 and 1920. Football also drew fans, although critics attacked the sport's violence and the use of "tramp athletes," nonstudents whom colleges paid to play. In 1905, the worst year, 18 players were killed and 150 seriously injured.

Alarmed, President Theodore Roosevelt—who had once said, "I am the father of three boys [and] if I thought any one of them would weigh a possible broken bone against the glory of being chosen to play on Harvard's football team I would disinherit him"—called a White House conference to clean up college sports. The conference founded the Intercollegiate Athletic Association, which in 1910 became the National Collegiate Athletic Association.

Movie theatres opened everywhere. By 1910 there were ten thousand of them, drawing a weekly audience of ten million people. Admis-

■ *The movies became the nation's mass entertainment. Here, an audience enjoys a Keystone Comedy while a piano player accompanies the silent action with appropriate sound effects.*

sion was usually five cents, and movies stressing laughter and pathos appealed to a mass market. In 1915 D. W. Griffith, a talented and creative director, produced the first movie spectacular, *The Birth of a Nation*. Griffith adopted new film techniques, including close-ups, fade-outs, artistic camera angles, and dramatic battle scenes.

Before 1910 band concerts were the country's most popular entertainment. As many as twenty thousand amateur bands played in parks on summer Sunday afternoons. John Philip Sousa, the famous "March King," led a touring band that profited from the self-confident nationalism that followed the Spanish-American War. "A march," Sousa said, "should make a man with a wooden leg step out," and robust, patriotic marches like "The Stars and Stripes Forever" (1896) earned him wealth and popularity.

Soon, automobiles, phonographs, and radios began to lure audiences away from the concerts. By 1901 phonograph and record companies included the Victor Talking Machine Company, the Edison Speaking Machine Company, and Columbia Records. Ornate mahogany Victrolas became standard fixtures in middle-class parlors. Early records were usually of vaudeville skits; orchestral recordings began in 1906. In 1919 2.25 million phonographs were produced; two years later more than 100 million records were sold.

As record sales grew, families sang less and listened more. Music became a business. In 1909 Congress enacted a copyright law that provided a two-cent royalty on each piece of music on phonograph records or piano rolls. The royalty, small as it was, offered welcome income to composers and publishers, and in 1914 composer Victor Herbert and others formed the American Society of Composers, Authors and Publishers (ASCAP) to protect musical rights and royalties.

The faster rhythms of syncopated ragtime became the rage, especially after 1911 when Irving Berlin, a Russian immigrant, wrote "Alexander's Ragtime Band." Ragtime set off a nationwide dance craze. Secretaries danced on their lunch hour, the first night clubs opened, and restaurants and hotels introduced dance floors. Waltzes and polkas gave way to a host of new dances, many with animal names: the Fox Trot, Bunny Hop, Turkey Trot, Snake, and Kangaroo Dip. Partners were not permitted to dance too close; bouncers tapped them on the shoulder if they got closer than nine inches. The aging John D. Rockefeller hired a private instructor to teach him the tango,

■ *Although they were denounced as indecent and disgusting, the turkey trot and other "animal" dances were extremely popular. A young woman in New Jersey was jailed for fifty days for doing the turkey trot.*

although Yale University banned that dance at its 1914 Junior Prom.

Vaudeville, increasingly popular after 1900, reached maturity around 1915. Drawing on the immigrant experience, it voiced the variety of city life and included skits, songs, comics, acrobats, and magicians. Dances and jokes showed an earthiness new to mass audiences. By 1914 stage runways extended into the crowd; performers had bared their legs and were beginning to show signs of the midriff. Fanny Brice, Ann Pennington, the "shimmy" queen, and Eva Tanguay—who sang "It's All Been Done Before but Not the Way I Do It"—starred in Florenz Ziegfeld's *Follies*, the peak of vaudeville.

In songs like "St. Louis Blues" (1914), W. C. Handy took the black southern folk music of the blues to northern cities. Gertrude "Ma" Rainey, the daughter of minstrels, sang in black vaudeville for nearly thirty-five years. Performing in Chattanooga, Tennessee, about 1910, she came across a twelve-year-old orphan, Bessie Smith, who became the "Empress of the Blues." Smith's voice was huge and sweeping. Recording for the "Race" division of Columbia Records, she made over eighty records that together sold nearly ten million copies.

Another musical innovation came north from New Orleans. Charles (Buddy) Bolden, a cornetist, Ferdinand "Jelly Roll" Morton, a pianist, and a youngster named Louis Armstrong played an improvisational music that had no formal name. Reaching Chicago, it became "jas," then "jass," and finally, "jazz." Jazz jumped, and jazz musicians relied on feeling and mood. A restaurant owner once asked "Jelly Roll" Morton to play a waltz. "*Waltz*?" Morton exclaimed. "Man, these people want to *dance*! And you talking about waltz. This is the *Roll* you're talking to."

Popular fiction reflected changing interests. Kate Douglas Wiggins' *Rebecca of Sunnybrook Farm* (1903) and Lucy M. Montgomery's *Anne of Green Gables* (1908) showed the continuing popularity of rural themes. Westerns also sold well, but readers turned more and more to detective thrillers with hard-bitten city detectives and science fiction tales featuring the latest dream in technology. The Tom Swift series, begun in 1910, looked ahead to spaceships, ray guns, and gravity nullifiers.

Edward L. Stratemeyer, the mind behind Tom

Swift, brought the techniques of mass production to book writing. In 1906 he formed the Stratemeyer Literary Syndicate that employed a stable of writers to turn out hundreds of Tom Swift, Rover Boys, and Bobbsey Twins stories for young readers. Burt Standish, another prolific author, took the pen name of Gilbert Patten and created the character of Frank Merriwell, wholesome college athlete. As Patten said: "I took the three qualities I most wanted him to represent—frank and merry in nature, well in body and mind—and made the name Frank Merriwell." The Merriwell books sold twenty-five million copies.

The Fine Arts

"There is a state of unrest all over the world in art as in all other things," the director of New York's Metropolitan Museum said in 1908. "It is the same in literature, as in music, in painting, and in sculpture."

Isadora Duncan and Ruth St. Denis transformed the dance. Departing from traditional ballet steps, both women stressed improvisation, emotion, and the human form. "Listen to the music with your soul . . .," Duncan told her students. "Unless your dancing springs from an inner emotion and expresses an idea, it will be meaningless." Draped in flowing robes, she revealed more of her legs than some thought tasteful, while she proclaimed the "noblest art is the nude." After a triumphant performance with the New York Symphony in 1908, her ideas and techniques swept the country. Duncan died tragically in 1927; her neck broken when her long red scarf caught in the wheel of a racing car.

The lofts and apartments of New York's Greenwich Village attracted artists, writers, and poets interested in experimentation and change. To these artists, the city was the focus of national life and the sign of a new culture. Robert Henri and the realist painters—known to their critics as the Ashcan School—relished the city's excitement. They wanted, a friend said, "to paint truth and to paint it with strength and fearlessness and individuality."

To the realists, a painting carried into the future the look of life as it happened. With the same feel for the environment that Brandeis and other reformers had shown, their paintings de-

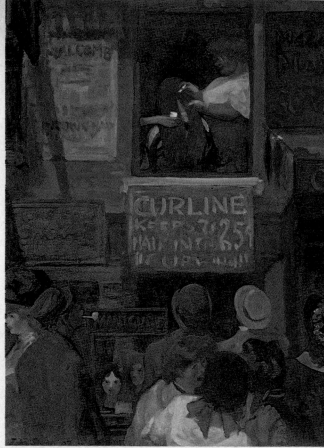

■ Hairdresser's Window *by John Sloan. One of the Ashcan realists, Sloan found his subject matter in the tenements, cafes, and barrooms of the modern city.*

picted street scenes, colorful crowds, and slum children swimming in the river. In paintings like the "Cliff Dwellers," George W. Bellows captured the color and excitment of the tenements; John Sloan, one of Henri's most talented students, painted the vitality of ordinary people and familiar scenes.

In 1913 a show at the New York Armory presented sixteen hundred modernist paintings, prints, and sculptures. The work of Picasso, Cézanne, Matisse, Brancusi, Van Gogh, and Gauguin dazed and dazzled American observers. Critics attacked the show as worthless and depraved; a Chicago official wanted it banned from the city because the "idea that people can gaze at this sort of thing without [it] hurting them is all bosh."

The Post-Impressionists changed the direction of twentieth-century art and influenced adventuresome American painters. John Marin, Max Weber, Georgia O'Keeffe, Arthur Dove, and other modernists experimented in ways foreign to Henri's realists. Defiantly avant garde, they shook off convention and experimented with new forms. Using bold colors and abstract patterns, they worked to capture the energy of urban life. "I see great forces at work, great movements," Marin said, "the large buildings and the small buildings, the warring of the great and the small. . . . I can hear the sound of their strife, and there is a great music being played."

There was an extraordinary outburst of poetry. In 1912 Harriet Monroe started the magazine *Poetry* in Chicago, the hotbed of the new poetry; Ezra Pound and Vachel Lindsay, both daring experimenters with ideas and verse, published in the first issue. T. S. Eliot published the classic "Love Song of J. Alfred Prufrock" in *Poetry* in 1915. Attacked bitterly by conservative critics, the poem established Eliot's leadership among a group of poets, many of them living and writing in London, who rejected traditional meter and rhyme as artificial constraints. Eliot, Pound, and Amy Lowell, among others, believed that the poet's task was to capture fleeting images in verse.

Others experimenting with new techniques in poetry included Robert Frost (*North of Boston*, 1915), Edgar Lee Masters (*Spoon River Anthology*, 1915), and Carl Sandburg (*Chicago Poems*, 1916). Sandburg's poem "Chicago" celebrated the vitality of the city:

Come and show me another city with lifted
head singing so proud to be alive and coarse
and strong and cunning.
Fierce as a dog with tongue lapping for action,
cunning as a savage pitted against the wilderness,

. . . .
Bareheaded,
Shoveling,
Wrecking,
Planning,
Building, breaking, rebuilding,
. . . .

Bragging and laughing that under his wrist is
the pulse, and under his ribs the heart of the
people,

■ Brooklyn Bridge *by Joseph Stella. Stella used fragments of color and dynamic patterns to capture the movement and intensity of a big city.*

Laughing!
Laughing the stormy, husky, brawling laughter
of Youth, half-naked, sweating, proud to be
Hog Butcher, Tool Maker, Stacker of Wheat,
Player with Railroads and Freight Handler to
the Nation.

Manners and morals change slowly, and many Americans overlooked the importance of the first two decades of this century. Yet sweeping change was underway; anyone who doubted it could visit a gallery, see a film, listen to music, or read one of the new literary magazines. Garrets and galleries were filled with a breathtaking sense of change. "There was life in all these new things," Marsden Hartley, a modernist painter, recalled. "There was excitement, there was healthy revolt, investigation, discovery, and an utterly new world out of it all."

The ferment of progressivism in city, state, and nation reshaped the country. In a burst of reform, people built playgrounds, restructured taxes, regulated business, won the vote for women, shortened working hours, altered political systems, opened kindergartens, and improved factory safety. They tried to fulfill the national promise of dignity and liberty.

At most, the years of progressive reform lasted from the 1890s to 1921, and in large measure they were compressed into a single decade between 1906 and American entry into World War I. Many problems the progressives addressed, they did not solve; and some important ones, like race, they did not even tackle. Yet their regulatory commissions, direct primaries, city improvements, and child-labor laws marked an era of important, gradual, and measured reform.

After 1905 the progressives looked more and more to Washington. For one thing, Teddy Roosevelt was there, with his zest for publicity and alluring grin. But progressives also had a growing sense that many concerns—corporations and conservation, factory safety and child labor—crossed state lines. Federal action seemed desirable; specific reforms fit into a larger plan perhaps best seen from the nation's center. Within a few years La Follette and Hiram Johnson became senators, and while reform went on back home, the focus of progressivism shifted to Washington.

Recommended Reading

There are several important analyses of the progressive era, including Robert H. Wiebe, *The Search for Order, 1877–1920* (1967); Richard Hofstadter, *The Age of Reform* (1955); Samuel P. Hays, *The Response to Industrialism* (1957); and Gabriel Kolko, *The Triumph of Conservatism* (1963). C. Vann Woodward, *Origins of the New South, 1877–1913* (1951) is a superb account of developments in the South. Lewis L. Gould, ed., *The Progressive Era* (1974), covers the period from varying perspectives; William L. O'Neill, *The Progressive Years* (1975) is a useful overview. C. Vann Woodward, *The Strange Career of Jim Crow* (1955), traces the civil-rights setbacks of the Progressive years.

Samuel P. Hays offers an influential interpretation of progressivism in *Conservation and the Gospel of Efficiency* (1959). Albro Martin, *Enterprise Denied: Origins of the Decline of American Railroads, 1897–1917* (1971), argues persuasively that reformers damaged as well as regulated. Intellectual currents are traced in Charles Forcey, *The Crossroads of Liberalism* (1961); social justice reforms in Harold U. Faulkner, *The Quest for Social Justice, 1898–1914* (1931); and the important tax issue in Clifton K. Yearley, *The Money Machines: The Breakdown and Reform of Governmental and Party Finance in the North, 1860–1920* (1970).

Additional Bibliography

Studies of the muckrakers include David M. Chalmers, *The Social and Political Ideas of the Muckrackers* (1964) and Harold S. Wilson, *McClure's Magazine and the Muckrakers* (1970). Lincoln Steffens, *The Shame of the Cities* (1904) and *Autobiography of Lincoln Steffens* (1931) and Upton Sinclair, *The Jungle* (1906), give contemporary flavor.

Sam Bass Warner, Jr., *Streetcar Suburbs* (1962) and *The Urban Wilderness* (1972) are excellent on urban developments, including zoning and industrial growth. On urban reform, see John D. Buenker, *Urban Liberalism and Progressive Reform* (1973); Roy M. Lubove, *The Progressive and the Slums* (1962); and Martin J. Schiesl, *The Politics of Efficiency: Municipal Administration and Reform in America, 1880–1920* (1977). Bradley R. Rice, *Progressive Cities: The Commission Government Movement in America, 1901–1920* (1977) is recent and helpful.

Books on specific cities include Melvin Holli, *Reform in Detroit: Hazen S. Pingree and Urban Politics* (1969); James B. Crooks, *Politics and Progress: The Rise of Urban Progressivism in Baltimore, 1895 to 1911* (1968); Zane L. Miller, *Boss Cox's Cincinnati* (1968); and Jack Tager, *The Intellectual as Urban Reformer: Brand Whitlock and the Progressive Movement* (1968).

Statewide movements are covered in George E. Mowry's influential study, *The California Progressives* (1951); Spencer C. Olin, Jr., *California's Prodigal Sons: Hiram Johnson and the Progressives, 1911–1917* (1968); David P. Thelen, *The New Citizenship: Origins of Progressivism in Wisconsin, 1885–1900* (1972); Herbert Margulies, *The Decline of the Progressive Movement in Wisconsin, 1890–1920* (1968); Ransom E. Noble, Jr., *New Jersey Progressivism Before Wilson* (1946); Sheldon Hackney, *Populism to Progressivism in Alabama* (1969); Richard M. Abrams, *Conservatism in a Progressive Era: Massachusetts Politics, 1900–1912* (1964); and H. L. Warner, *Progressivism in Ohio, 1897–1917* (1964).

Studies of youth, age, and family life include Joseph Kett, *Rites of Passage: Adolescence in America* (1977); W. Andrew Achenbaum, *Old Age in the New Land* (1978); William L. O'Neill, *Divorce in the Progressive Era* (1967); Carl N. Degler, *At Odds: Women and the Family in America* (1980); Michael Gordon, ed., *The American Family in Social-Historical Perspective* (1973); Tamara K. Hareven, ed., *Anonymous Americans* (1971) and *Transitions: The Family and Life Course in Historical Perspective* (1978). For birth control, see Linda Gordon, *Woman's Body, Woman's Right: A Social History of Birth Control in America* (1976) and David M. Kennedy, *Birth Control in America: The Career of Margaret Sanger* (1970).

See also Eleanor Flexner, *Century of Struggle: The Women's Rights Movement in the United States* (1959); William L. O'Neill, *Everyone Was Brave: The Rise and Fall of Feminism in America* (1969); Leslie Woodcock Tentler, *Wage-Earning Women: Industrial Work and Family Life in the United States, 1900–1930* (1979); Sheila M. Rothman, *Woman's Proper Place* (1978); and Ellen Condliffe Lagemann, *A Generation of Women: Education in the Lives of the Progressive Reformers* (1979).

On Du Bois, see Elliot M. Rudwick, *W. E. B. Du Bois* (1968). Other useful books include George M. Frederickson, *The Black Image in the White Mind* (1971); Charles F. Kellogg, *NAACP: A History of the National Association for the Advancement of Colored People, 1909–1920* (1967); Louis R. Harlan, *Separate and Unequal: Public School Campaigns and Racism in the Southern Seaboard States, 1900–1915* (1968); Allen H. Spear, *Black Chicago* (1967); and Idus A. Newby, *Jim Crow's Defense: Anti-Negro Thought in America, 1900–1930* (1965).

Leonard Dinnerstein, Roger L. Nichols, and David M. Reimers, *Natives and Strangers: Ethnic Groups and the Building of America* (1979), offer a useful overview of Mexican-Americans and the "new" immigrants. See also Oscar Handlin, *The Uprooted* (1951); John Higham, *Strangers in the Land: Patterns of American Nativism* (1955); Josef J. Barton, *Peasants and Strangers* (1975); Donald B. Cole, *Immigrant City: Lawrence, Massachusetts, 1845–1921* (1963); and John E. Bodnar, *Immigration and Industrialization* (1977). Thomas Kessner, *The Golden Door, Italian and Jewish Immigrant Mobility in New York City, 1880–1915* (1977), is excellent.

For the ways in which Americans entertained themselves, see Gunther Barth, *City People* (1980); Allison Danzig, *History of American Football* (1956); Russel B. Nye, *The Unembarrassed Muse: The Popular Arts in America* (1970); John E. DiMeglio, *Vaudeville U.S.A.* (1973); Ronald L. Davis, *A History of Music in American Life, Volume II: The Gilded Years, 1865–1920* (1980); and Robert Sklar, *Movie-Made America: A Social History of the American Movies* (1975).

chapter 23

FROM ROOSEVELT TO WILSON: NATIONAL POLITICS IN THE AGE OF PROGRESSIVISM

On a sunny spring morning in 1909 Theodore Roosevelt, wearing the greatcoat of a colonel of the Rough Riders, left New York for a safari in Africa. An ex-president at the age of fifty, he had turned over the White House to his chosen successor, William Howard Taft (see page 656), and was now off for "the joy of wandering through lonely lands, the joy of hunting the mighty and terrible lords" of Africa, "where death broods in the dark and silent depths."

Some hoped he would not return. "I trust some lion will do its duty," Wall Street magnate J. P. Morgan said. Always prepared, Roosevelt took nine extra pairs of eyeglasses, and just in case, several expert hunters accompanied him. When the nearsighted Roosevelt took aim, three others aimed at the same moment. "Mr. Roosevelt had a fairly good idea of the general direction," the safari leader said, "but we couldn't take chances with the life of a former president." Though he had built a reputation as an ardent conservationist, Roosevelt shot nine lions, five elephants, thirteen rhinoceroses, seven hippopotamuses, and assorted other game—acquiring nearly three hundred trophies in all.

It was good fun, and afterward Roosevelt set off on a tour of Europe. He argued with the pope, dined with the king and queen of Italy—an experience he likened to "a Jewish wedding on the East Side of New York"—and happily spent five hours reviewing troops of the German empire. Less happily, he followed events back home where, in the judgment of many friends, Taft was not working out as president. Gifford Pinchot, Roosevelt's close companion in the conservation movement, came to Italy to complain personally about Taft, and at almost every stop there were letters from other disappointed Republicans.

Taft was puzzled by it all. Honest and warm-hearted, he had intended to continue Roosevelt's policies, even writing Roosevelt that he would "see to it that your judgment in selecting me as your successor and bringing about that succession shall be vindicated . . ." But events turned out differently. The conservative and progressive wings of the Republican party split, and Taft often sided with the conservatives. Among progressive Republicans, Taft's troubles stirred talk of a Roosevelt "Back from Elba" movement, akin to Napoleon's return from exile.

Thousands gathered to greet Roosevelt on his return from Europe. He sailed into New York harbor on June 18, 1910, to the sound of naval guns and loud cheers. In characteristic fashion, he had helped make the arrangements: "If there is to be a great crowd, do arrange it so that the whole crowd has a chance to see me and that there is as little disappointment as possible." Greeting Pinchot, one of Taft's leading opponents, with a hearty "Hello, Gifford," Roosevelt slipped away

Former President Theodore Roosevelt (center) was welcomed as a conquering hero and hailed as "the world's first citizen" on his return from his tour abroad. Young Franklin and Eleanor Roosevelt are at far right.

to his home in Oyster Bay, New York, where other friends awaited him.

He carried with him a touching letter from Taft, received just before he left Europe. "I have had a hard time—I do not know that I have had harder luck than other Presidents, but I do know that thus far I have succeeded far less than have others. I have been conscientiously trying to carry out your policies but my method of doing so has not worked smoothly." Taft invited Teddy to spend a night or two at the White House, but Roosevelt declined—saying that ex-presidents should not visit Washington. Relations between the two friends cooled. "It is hard, very hard," Taft said in 1911, "to see a devoted friendship going to pieces like a rope of sand."

A year later there was no longer thought of friendship, only a desperate fight between Taft and Roosevelt for the Republican presidential nomination. Taft chided Roosevelt for saying in his speeches nothing but "I, I, I" and called him a demagogue. Roosevelt in turn labeled Taft a puzzlewit and fathead. The name-calling was "pleasant and homelike," Mr. Dooley said. "Ivrybody callin' each other liars and crooks not like pollyytical inimies, d'ye mind, but like old frinds that has been up late dhrinkin' together."

The Changing Face of Industrialism

Businesses were large in the three decades after the Civil War, but in the years between 1895 and 1915 they became mammoth, employing thousands of workers and equipped with assembly lines to turn out huge numbers of the company's product. Inevitably, management attitudes changed, as did business organization and worker roles.

The Innovative Model T

Mass production of automobiles began in the first years of the century. Using an assembly-line system that foreshadowed later techniques, Ransom E. Olds turned out five thousand Olds runabouts in 1904. But Olds' days of leadership were numbered. In 1903 Henry Ford and a small group of associates formed the Ford Motor Company, the firm that transformed the business.

Ford was forty years old. He had tried farming and hated it; during the 1890s he worked as an engineer for Detroit's Edison Company but spent his spare time designing internal combustion engines and automobiles. At first, like many others in the industry, he concentrated on luxury and racing cars. Racing his own cars, Ford became the "speed demon" of Detroit; in 1904 he set the world's land speed record—over ninety miles per hour—in the 999, a large red racer that shot flames from the motor.

In 1903 Ford sold the first Ford car. The price was high, and in 1905 Ford raised prices still higher. Sales plummeted. In 1907 he lowered the price; sales and revenues rose. Ford learned an important lesson of the modern economy: a smaller unit profit on a large number of sales meant enormous revenues. Early in 1908 he introduced the Model T, a four-cylinder, twenty-horsepower "Tin Lizzie," costing $850, and available only in black. Eleven thousand were sold the first year.

"I am going to democratize the automobile," Ford proclaimed. "When I'm through everybody will be able to afford one, and about everyone will have one." The key was mass production, and after many experiments, Ford copied the techniques of meat packers who moved animal carcasses along overhead trolleys from station to station. Adapting the process to automobile assembly, Ford in 1913 set up moving assembly lines in his plant in Highland Park, Michigan, that dramatically reduced the time and cost of producing cars. Emphasizing continuous movement, he strove for a nonstop flow from raw material to finished product. In 1914 he sold 248,000 Model T's.

That year Ford workers assembled a car in ninety-three minutes, one tenth the time it had taken just eight months before. By 1925 the Ford plant turned out 9109 Model T's, a new car for every ten seconds of the working day.

While Ford was putting more and more cars on the road, the 1916 Federal Aid Roads Act, a little-noticed measure, set the framework for road building in the twentieth century. Removing control from county governments, it required every state desiring federal funds to establish a highway department to plan routes, oversee con-

struction, and maintain roads. In states that had such departments, the federal government paid half the cost of building the roads. Providing for a planned highway system, the act produced a national network of two-lane, all-weather intercity roads.

The Burgeoning Trusts

As businesses like Ford's grew, capital and organization became increasingly important, and the result was the formation of a growing number of trusts. Standard Oil started the trend in 1882 (see chapter 18), but the greatest momentum came two decades later. Between 1898 and 1903 a series of mergers and consolidations swept the economy. Many smaller firms disappeared, swallowed up in giant corporations. By 1904 large-scale combinations of one form or another controlled nearly two fifths of the capital in manufacturing in the country.

The result was not monopoly, but oligopoly—control of a commodity or service by a small

■ (Top) Assembling magnetos on the Ford line. One worker could do it in twenty minutes; twenty-nine workers, properly arranged, could do it in five minutes. (Bottom) One day's output of car chassis at the Ford Highland Park plant in 1913.

■ (Right) As early as 1886 cartoonist Thomas Nast attacked trusts. Here the people's welfare is sinking as the Statue of Liberty is defaced.

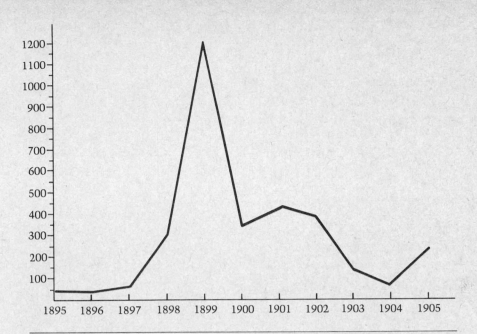

number of large, powerful companies. Six great financial groups dominated the railroad industry; a handful of holding companies controlled utilities and steel. Rockefeller's Standard Oil owned about 85 percent of the oil business. Large companies like Standard Oil and American Tobacco weathered the depression of the 1890s, and after 1898, financiers and industrialists followed their example and formed the Amalgamated Copper Company, Consolidated Tobacco, U.S. Rubber, and a host of others.

By 1909 just 1 percent of the industrial firms were producing nearly half the manufactured goods. Giant businesses reached abroad for raw materials and new markets. United Fruit, an empire of plantations and steamships in the Caribbean, exploited opportunities created by victory in the war with Spain. U.S. Steel worked with overseas companies to fix the price of steel rails, an unattainable dream just a few years before. For decades competition had sent rail prices up and down; now they stayed at $28 a ton, and through the famous "Gary dinners" in which Elbert H. Gary of U.S. Steel brought steel executives together, market conditions were fixed over wide areas of the industry.

Though the trend has been overstated, finance capitalists like J. P. Morgan tended to replace the industrial capitalists of an earlier era. Able to finance the mergers and reorganizations, investment bankers played a greater and greater role in the economy. A multibillion-dollar financial house, J. P. Morgan and Company operated a network of control that ran from New York to every industrial and financial center in the nation. Like other investment firms, it held directorships in many corporations, creating "interlocking directorates" that allowed it to control many businesses. In 1913 two banking groups—Morgan's and Rockefeller's—held 341 directorships in 112 corporations with an aggregate capital of more than $22 billion.

Massive business growth set off a decade-long debate over what government should do about the trusts. Some critics who believed that the giant companies were responsible for stifling individual opportunity and raising prices wanted to break them up into small competitive units. Others argued that large-scale business was a mark of the times; it produced more goods and better lives. The debate over the trusts influenced politics throughout the Progressive era.

Managing the Machines

Mass production changed the direction of American industry. Size, system, organization, and marketing became increasingly important. Management focused on speed and product, not on workers. Assembly-line technology changed tasks and, to some extent, values. The goal was no longer to make a unique product that would be better than the one before. "The way to make automobiles," Ford said as early as 1903, "is to make one automobile like another automobile, to make them all alike, to make them come through the factory just alike."

In a development that rivaled assembly lines in importance, businesses established industrial research laboratories where scientists and engineers developed new products. General Electric founded the first one in 1900 in a barn. It soon attracted experts who designed improvements in light bulbs, invented the cathode tube, worked on early radio, and even tinkered with atomic theory. Du Pont opened its labs in 1911, Eastman Kodak in 1912, and Standard Oil in 1919. As the source of new ideas and technology, the labs altered life in the twentieth century.

Through all this, business became large-scale, mechanized, and managed. While many shops still employed fewer than a dozen workers, the proportion of such shops shrank. By 1920 close to one half of all industrial workers worked in factories employing more than 250 people. More than a third worked in factories that were part of multiplant companies.

Industries that processed materials—iron and steel, paper, cement, and chemicals—were increasingly continuous and automatic. In the glass industry, machines ended the domination of highly skilled and well-paid craft workers. In 1908 Irving W. Colburn invented a machine to manufacture plate glass; the Libbey-Owens-Ford Company bought the patent; and Ford soon had a glassmaking machine from which emerged every day for two years a 3½-mile ribbon of automobile window glass, eventually reaching a length of almost 2000 miles.

Workers tending such ribbons could not fall behind. Foremen still managed the laborers on the factory floor, but more and more the rules came down from a central office where trained, professional managers supervised production flow. Systematic record keeping, cost accounting, and inventory and production controls became widespread. Workers lost control of the work pace. "If you need to turn out a little more," a manager at Swift and Company said, "you speed up the conveyor a little and the men speed up to keep pace." It worked. In the automobile industry, output per manhour multiplied an extraordinary four times between 1909 and 1919.

Folkways of the work place—workers passing job-related knowledge to each other, performing their tasks with little supervision, setting their own pace, and in effect running the shop—gave way to "scientific" labor management. More than anyone else, Frederick Winslow Taylor, an inventive mechanical engineer, strove to extract maximum efficiency from each worker. Taylor proposed two major reforms. First, management must take responsibility for job-related knowledge and classify it into "rules, laws, and formulae." Second, management should control the work place "through *enforced* standardization of methods, *enforced* adoption of the best implements and working conditions, and *enforced* cooperation."

Taylor's methods included time-and-motion studies, training workers for particular tasks, and differential pay rates that rewarded those who worked fastest. "In the past," he stated in *The Principles of Scientific Management* (1911), "the man has been first; in the future the system must be first." Armed with stopwatches, his disciples reduced a factory's operations to the simplest tasks, then devised the most efficient way to perform them. Although few factories wholly adopted Taylor's principles, he had great influence, and the doctrines of scientific management spread through American industry.

Workers caught up in the changing industrial system experienced the benefits of efficiency and productivity; in some industries they earned more. But they suffered important losses as well. Performing repetitive tasks, they seemed part of the machinery, to whose pace and needs they moved. Bored, they might easily lose pride of workmanship, though many workers, it is clear, did not. Efficiency engineers experimented with tools and methods, a process many workers found unsettling. Yet the goal was to establish routine—to work out, as someone said of a garment worker, "one single precise motion each second, 3600 in one hour, and all exactly the same." Praising that worker, the manager said: "She is a sure machine."

Jobs became not only monotonous but dangerous. Under the pressure of speed, boredom or miscalculation could bring disaster. Meat cutters sliced fingers and hands. Illinois steel mills, a magazine said, were "Making Steel and Killing Men"; one mill had forty-six deaths in 1906 alone. Injuries were part of many jobs. "The machines go like mad all day," a garment worker said, "because the faster you work the more money you get. Sometimes in my haste I get my finger caught and the needle goes right through it . . . I bind the finger up with a piece of cotton and go on working."

In March 1911 a fire at the Triangle Shirtwaist Company in New York focused attention on unsafe working conditions. When the fire started, five hundred men and women—mostly Italians, and Jews from eastern Europe—were just finishing their workday. Firefighters arrived within minutes, but they were already too late. Terrified seamstresses raced to the exits to try to escape the flames; most exit doors were closed, locked by the company to prevent theft and shut out union organizers. Many died in the stampede down the narrow stairways or the single fire escape. Still others, trapped on the building's top stories far above the reach of the fire department's ladders, jumped to their death on the street below. One hundred forty-six people died.

A few days later eighty thousand people marched silently in the rain in a funeral procession up Fifth Avenue. A quarter million people watched. New York's governor appointed a State Factory Investigating Commission that recommended laws to shorten the workweek and improve safety conditions in factories and stores.

■ *Fire nets were of no avail to the Triangle garment workers who jumped from the upper stories to escape the flames.*

Conflict and Conciliation

Strikes and absenteeism increased after 1910; labor productivity dropped 10 percent between 1915 and 1918, the first such decline in memory. In many industries labor turnover became a serious problem; workers changed jobs in droves. Union membership grew. In 1900 only about 1 million workers belonged to unions—less than 4 percent of the work force. By 1920 5 million belonged, about 13 percent of the work force. There were 8 million female workers in 1910, but only 125,000 belonged to unions. Most unions did not want them, and through outright prohibition or other techniques, they discouraged female applicants.

Samuel Gompers' American Federation of Labor increased from 250,000 members in 1897 to 1.7 million in 1904. By far the largest union organization, it remained devoted to the interests of skilled craftsmen. While it aimed partly at better wages and working conditions, it also sought to limit entry into the craft and protect worker prerogatives. Within limits, the AFL found acceptance among giant business corporations eager for conservative policies and labor stability.

Unlike the AFL, the Industrial Workers of the World (IWW) tried to organize the unskilled and foreign-born laborers working in the mass-production industries. Founded in Chicago in 1905, it aimed to unite the American working class into a mammoth union to promote labor's interests. Its motto—"an injury to one is an injury to all"—stressed labor solidarity as had the earlier Knights of Labor. But unlike the Knights, the IWW, or Wobblies as they were often known, urged social revolution.

Labor Union Membership, 1897–1920

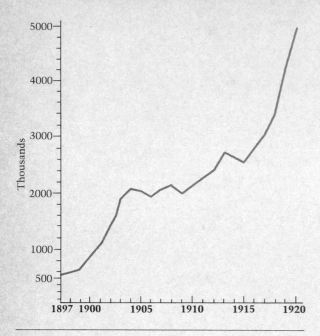

As Joe Hill, the IWW's legendary folk poet, wrote:

If the workers took a notion
  They could stop all speeding trains;
Every ship upon the ocean
  They can tie with mighty chains.

Every wheel in the creation
  Every mine and every mill;
Fleets and armies of the nation,
  Will at their command stand still.

IWW leaders included "Mother" Jones, a famous veteran of battles in the Illinois coalfields; Elizabeth Gurley Flynn, a fiery young radical who joined as a teen-ager; and William D. (Big Bill) Haywood, the strapping, one-eyed founder of the Western Federation of Miners.

The IWW led a number of major strikes. The Lawrence, Massachusetts (1912), and Paterson, New Jersey (1912), strikes attracted national attention: Lawrence when the strikers sent their children, ill-clad and hungry, out of the city to stay with sympathetic families; Paterson when they rented New York's Madison Square Garden

for a massive labor pageant. IWW leaders welcomed the revolutionary tumult sweeping Russia and other countries. In the United States, they thought, a series of local strikes would bring about capitalist repression, then a general strike, and eventually a workers' commonwealth.

The IWW fell short of these objectives, but during its lifetime—from 1905 to the mid-1920s—it made major gains among immigrant workers in the Northeast, migrant farm labor on the Plains, and loggers and miners in the South and Far West. In factories like Ford's, it recruited workers resentful of the speed-ups on the assembly lines. Although IWW membership probably amounted to no more than one hundred thousand at any one time, workers came and left so often that its total membership may have reached as high as one million.

Concerned about labor unrest, business leaders turned to the new fields of applied psychology and personnel management. A school of industrial psychology emerged. As Taylor had, industrial psychologists studied workers' routines, but they showed that output was also affected by job satisfaction. While most businesses pushed ahead

■ *Elizabeth Gurley Flynn, labor's "Joan of Arc," addresses textile workers on strike at Paterson, New Jersey.*

with efficiency campaigns, a few established industrial-relations departments, hired public relations firms to improve their corporate image, and linked productivity to job safety and happiness.

Ivy L. Lee, a pioneer in the field of corporate public relations, advised clients like the Pennsylvania Railroad and Standard Oil on how to improve relations with labor and the public. Calling himself, a "physician to corporate bodies," Lee urged complete openness on the company's part. To please employees, companies printed newsletters and organized softball teams; they awarded prizes and celebrated retirements. Ford created a "Sociology Department" staffed by 150 experts who showed workers how to budget their incomes and care for their health. They even taught them how to shop for meat.

On January 5, 1914, Ford took another significant step. He announced the Five-Dollar Day, "the greatest revolution," he said, "in the matter of rewards for workers ever known to the industrial world." With a stroke, he doubled the wage rate for common labor, reduced the working day from nine hours to eight, and established a personnel department to place workers in appropriate jobs. The next day, ten thousand applicants stood outside the gates.

As a result, Ford had the pick of the labor force. Turnover declined; absenteeism, previously as much as a tenth of all Ford workers every day, fell to .3 percent. Output increased; the IWW at Ford collapsed. At first scornful of the "utopian" plan, business leaders across the country soon copied it, and on January 2, 1919, Ford announced the Six-Dollar Day.

■ *State troopers confront millhands on strike at Lawrence, Massachusetts, in 1912. The IWW reached its peak membership of 250,000 during the Lawrence strike.*

The Changing Face of Industrialism

Amoskeag

In size, system, and worker relations, the record of the Amoskeag Company textile mills was revealing. Located beside the Merrimack River in Manchester, New Hampshire, the mills—an enormous complex of factories, warehouses, canals, and machinery—had been built in the 1830s. By the turn of the century they were producing nearly fifty miles of cloth an hour, more cloth each day than any other mills in the world. Amoskeag Manufacturing Company was the area's largest employer.

The face of the mills, an almost solid wall of red brick, stretched nearly a mile in length. Archways and bridges pierced the façade. Amoskeag resembled a walled, medieval city within which workers found "a total institution, a closed and almost self-contained world." At first the mills employed young women, but by 1900 more and more immigrant males staffed the machines. French Canadians, Irish, Poles, and Greeks—seventeen thousand in all—worked there, and their experiences revealed a great deal about factory work and life at the turn of the century.

The company hired and fired at will, and it demanded relentless output from the spindles and spinning frames. Yet it also viewed employees as its "children" and looked for total loyalty in return, an expectation often realized. Workers identified with Amoskeag and, decades later, still called themselves Amoskeag men and women. "We were all like a family," one said.

Most Amoskeag workers preferred the industrial world of the mills to the farms they had left behind. They did not feel displaced; they knew the pains of industrial life; and they adapted in ways that fit their own needs and traditions. Families played a large role. They neither disintegrated nor lost their relationships. French Canadians and others often came in family units. One or two family members left the farm for the mills, maintained close ties with those back home, and then sent for others in a form of "chain migration."

Once in Manchester, families often worked in the same workrooms. Looking after each other, they asked foremen for transfers and promotions for relatives; they taught their children technical skills and how to get along with bosses and fellow workers. Although low-paid, Amoskeag employees took pride in their work, and for many of them, a well-turned out product provided dignity and self-esteem.

The company long showed a paternal interest in employee welfare, and in 1910 it inaugurated a deliberate welfare and efficiency program. The program aimed to increase productivity, accustom immigrants to industrial work, instill company loyalty, and curb labor unrest. Playgrounds and visiting nurses, home-buying plans, a cooking school, and dental service were part of the plan.

Amoskeag workers' fair. Employees exhibited craft items and baked goods at an annual company event. Many firms between 1910 and 1917 adopted employee programs similar to those introduced at Amoskeag.

The Amoskeag Textile Club held employee dinners and picnics, organized shooting clubs and a baseball team, sponsored Christmas parties for the children, and put out the *Amoskeag Bulletin*, a monthly magazine of employee news and achievements.

From 1885 to 1919 no strike touched the mills. Therafter, however, labor unrest increased. Overproduction and foreign competition took their toll, and Amoskeag closed in 1935.

The Republican Roosevelt

In September 1901 President William McKinley died of gunshot wounds (see chapter 20); Vice-President Theodore Roosevelt succeeded him in the White House. McKinley and Roosevelt had moved in similar directions, and the new President initially vowed to carry on McKinley's policies. He continued some, developed others of his own, and in the end brought to them all the particular exuberance of his own personality.

At age forty-three, Roosevelt was then the youngest president in American history. In contrast to the dignified McKinley, he was open, aggressive, and high-spirited. At his desk by 8:30 every morning, he worked through the day, and there were usually visitors for breakfast, lunch, and dinner. Politicians, labor leaders, industrialists, poets, artists, and writers paraded through the White House.

In personal conversation Roosevelt was persuasive and charming. He read widely and he held opinions on every issue—literature, art, marriage, divorce, conservation, business, football, and even spelling. An advocate of simplified spelling, he once instructed government printers to use "thru" for "through" and "dropt" for "dropped." Public opposition forced him to withdraw the order, and shortly afterward, as he was watching a naval review in Long Island Sound, a launch marked "Pres Bot" steamed by. Roosevelt laughed with delight.

If McKinley cut down on presidential isolation, Roosevelt virtually ended it. The presidency, he thought, was "the bully pulpit," a forum of ideas and leadership for the nation. The president was "a steward of the people bound actively and affirmatively to do all he could for the people." Self-confident, Roosevelt enlisted talented associates, including Elihu Root, secretary of war and later secretary of state; William Howard Taft, secretary of war; Gifford Pinchot, the nation's chief forester and leading conservationist; and Oliver Wendell Holmes, Jr., whom he named to the Supreme Court.

In 1901 Roosevelt invited Booker T. Washington, the prominent black educator, to lunch at the White House. Many Southerners protested— "a crime equal to treason," a newspaper said—

Theodore Roosevelt is shown here addressing a group of black businessmen in 1910. Booker T. Washington is seated next to Roosevelt.

and they protested again when Roosevelt appointed several blacks to important federal offices in South Carolina and Mississippi. At first Roosevelt tried to build a biracial, "black-and-tan" southern Republican party, hoping it would foster racial progress and his own renomination in 1904. He also denounced lynching and ordered the Justice Department to act against peonage.

But Roosevelt soon retreated. In some areas of the South he supported "lily-white" Republican organizations, and his policies often reflected his own belief in black inferiority. He said nothing when a race riot broke out in Atlanta in 1906, although twelve persons died. He joined others in blaming black soldiers stationed near Brownsville, Texas, after a night of violence there in August 1906. Acting quickly and on little evidence, he discharged "without honor" three companies of black troops. Six of the soldiers who were discharged held the Congressional Medal of Honor.

Busting the Trusts

"There is a widespread conviction in the minds of the American people that the great corporations known as trusts are in certain of their features and tendencies hurtful to the general welfare," Roosevelt reported to Congress in 1901. Like most people, however, the President wavered on the trusts. Large-scale production and industrial growth, he believed, were natural and beneficial; they needed only to be controlled. Still he distrusted the trusts' impact on local enterprise and individual opportunity. Distinguishing between "good" and "bad" trusts, he pledged to protect the former while controlling the latter.

At first Roosevelt hoped the glare of publicity would be enough to uncover and correct business evils, and in public he both praised and attacked the trusts. Mr. Dooley poked fun at his wavering: "'Th' trusts,' says he, 'are heejous monsthers built up be th' enlightened intherprise iv th' men that have done so much to advance progress in our beloved country,' he says. 'On wan hand I wud stamp thim undher fut; on th' other hand not so fast.'"

In 1903 Roosevelt asked Congress to create a Department of Commerce and Labor, with a Bureau of Corporations empowered to investigate corporations engaged in interstate commerce. Congress balked; Roosevelt called in reporters, and in an off-the-record interview, charged that John D. Rockefeller had organized the opposition to the measure. After that accusation, editorials and many public figures clamored for action, and the proposal passed easily in a matter of weeks.

Roosevelt also undertook more direct legal action. On February 14, 1902, he instructed the Justice Department to bring suit against the Northern Securities Company for violation of the Sherman Antitrust Act. It was a shrewd move. A mammoth holding company, Northern Securities controlled the massive rail networks of the Northern Pacific, Great Northern, and Chicago, Burlington & Quincy railroads. Some of the most prominent names in business were behind the giant company—J. P. Morgan and Company, the Rockefeller interests, Kuhn, Loeb and Company, and railroad operators James J. Hill and Edward H. Harriman.

Shocked by Roosevelt's action, Morgan charged that the President had not acted like a "gentleman," and Hill talked glumly of having "to fight for our lives against the political adventurers who have never done anything but pose and draw a salary." Morgan rushed to Washington to complain and to ask whether there were plans to "attack my other interests," notably U.S. Steel. "No," Roosevelt replied, "unless we find out they have done something that we regard as wrong."

In 1904 the Supreme Court, in a five to four decision, upheld the suit against Northern Securities and ordered the company dissolved. Roosevelt was jubilant, and he followed up the victory with several other antitrust suits. In 1902 he had moved against the beef trust, an action applauded by western farmers and urban consumers alike. After a lull, he initiated suits in 1906 and 1907 against the American Tobacco Company, the Du Pont Corporation, the New Haven Railroad, and Standard Oil.

But Roosevelt's policies were not always clear, nor his actions always consistent. He invited Morgan to the White House to confer with him and allowed the president of National City Bank to preview a draft of his third annual message to Congress. Roosevelt also asked for (and received) business support in his bid for reelection in 1904. Large donations came in from industrial leaders, and Morgan himself later testifed that he gave

■ *A 1904 cartoon depicts TR as "Jack the Giant-Killer" battling the Wall Street titans. Actually Roosevelt dissolved relatively few trusts.*

$150,000 to Roosevelt's campaign. In 1907 the President permitted Morgan's U.S. Steel to absorb the Tennessee Coal and Iron Company, an important competitor.

Roosevelt, in truth, was not a "trust-buster," although he was frequently called that. William Howard Taft, his successor in the White House, initiated forty-three antitrust indictments in four years—nearly twice as many as the twenty-five Roosevelt initiated in the seven years of his presidency.

"Square Deal" in the Coalfields

A few months after announcing the Northern Securities suit, Roosevelt intervened in a major labor dispute involving the anthracite coal miners of northeastern Pennsylvania. Led by John Mitchell, a moderate labor leader, the United Mine Workers demanded wage increases, an eight-hour workday, and company recognition of the union. The coal companies refused, and in May 1902, 140,000 miners walked off the job. The mines closed.

As the months passed and the strike continued, coal prices rose. With winter coming on, schools, hospitals, and factories ran short of coal. Public opinion turned against the companies. Morgan and other industrial leaders privately urged them to settle, but George F. Baer, head of one of the largest companies, refused: "The rights and interests of the laboring man," Baer said, "will be protected and cared for—not by the labor agitators, but by the Christian men to whom God in his infinite wisdom has given the control of the property interests of this country."

Roosevelt was furious. Complaining of the companies' arrogance, he invited both sides in the dispute to an October 1902 conference at the White House. There, Mitchell took a moderate tone and offered to submit the issues to arbitration, but the companies again refused to budge. Roosevelt ordered the army to prepare to seize the mines and then leaked word of his intent to Wall Street leaders.

Alarmed, Morgan and others again urged settlement of the dispute, and at last the companies retreated. They agreed to accept the recommendations of an independent commission the President would appoint. In late October the strikers returned to work, and in March 1903 the commission awarded them a 10-percent wage increase and a cut in working hours. It recommended, however, against union recognition. The coal companies, in turn, were encouraged to raise prices to offset the wage increase.

More and more Roosevelt saw the federal government as an honest and impartial "broker" between powerful elements in society. Rather than leaning toward labor, he pursued a middle way to curb corporate or labor abuses, abolish privilege, and enlarge individual opportunity. Often he backed reforms in part to head off more radical measures.

During the 1904 campaign Roosevelt called his actions in the coal miners' strike a "square deal" for both labor and capital, a term that stuck to his administration. His actions stood in powerful contrast to Grover Cleveland's in the 1894 Pullman strike (see chapter 20). Roosevelt was not the first president to take a stand for labor, but he was

President Roosevelt with mine workers after the settlement of the 1902 strike in the coalfields. His conciliatory position improved his standing with the working classes.

the first to bring opposing sides in a labor dispute to the White House to settle it. He was the first to threaten to seize a major industry, and he was the first to appoint a commission whose decision both sides agreed to accept.

Another Term

In the election of 1904, the popular Roosevelt soundly drubbed his Democratic opponent, Alton B. Parker of New York, and the Socialist party candidate, Eugene V. Debs of Indiana. Roosevelt attracted a large campaign chest, campaigned strenuously, and won votes everywhere. In a landslide victory he received 57 percent of the vote to Parker's 38 percent, and on election night

The Election of 1904

Candidate	Party	Popular Vote	Electoral Vote
T. Roosevelt	Republican	7,626,593	336
Parker	Democrat	5,082,898	140
Debs	Socialist	402,489	0
Swallow	Prohibition	258,596	0

he savored the public's confidence. Overjoyed, he pledged that "under no circumstances will I be a candidate for or accept another nomination," a statement he later regretted.

Following his election, Roosevelt in late 1904 laid out a reform program that included railroad regulation, employers' liability for federal employees, greater federal control over corporations, and laws regulating child labor, factory inspection, and slum clearance in the District of Columbia. He turned first to railroad regulation. In 1903 he had worked with Congress to pass the Elkins Act to prohibit railroad rebates and increase the powers of the Interstate Commerce Commission (ICC). The Elkins Act, a moderate law, was framed with the consent of railroad leaders. In 1904 and 1905 the President wanted much more, and he urged Congress to empower the ICC to set reasonable and nondiscriminatory rates and prevent inequitable practices.

Widespread demand for railroad regulation strengthened Roosevelt's hand. In the Midwest and Far West the issue was a popular one, and reform Governors La Follette in Wisconsin, Albert C. Cummins in Iowa, and Hiram Johnson in California (see chapter 22) urged federal action. Roosevelt maneuvered cannily. As the legislative battle opened, he released figures showing that Standard Oil had reaped $750,000 a year from rebates. He also skillfully traded congressional support for a strong railroad measure in return for his promise to postpone a reduction of the tariff, a stratagem that came back to plague President Taft.

Triumph came with passage of the Hepburn Act of 1906. A significant achievement, the act strengthened the rate-making power of the Interstate Commerce Commission. It increased membership on the ICC from five to seven, empowered it to fix reasonable maximum railroad rates, and broadened its jurisdiction to include oil-pipeline, express, and sleeping-car companies. ICC orders were binding, pending any court appeals, thus placing the burden of proof upon the companies. Delighted, Roosevelt viewed the Hepburn Act as a major step in his plan for continuous, expert federal control over industry.

President Roosevelt signed two important laws to regulate the food and drug industries. Both laws reflected public outcry over adulterated and poisonous food and drugs. Muckraking articles had touched frequently on filthy conditions in meat-packing houses, and Upton Sinclair's *The Jungle* (1906) described them in terms graphic enough to send people reeling from the dinner table:

> There would be meat stored in great piles in rooms; and the water from leaky roofs would drip over it, and thousands of rats would race about on it. It was too dark in these storage places to see well, but a man could run his hand over these piles of meat and sweep off handfuls of the dried dung of rats. These rats were nuisances, and the packers would put poisoned bread out for them; they would die, and then rats, bread, and meat would go into the hoppers together.

After reading *The Jungle*, Roosevelt ordered an investigation. The result, he said, was "hideous," and he threatened to publish the entire "sickening report" if Congress did not act. Meat sales plummeted in the United States and Europe. Demand for reform grew. Alarmed, the meat packers themselves supported a reform law, which they hoped would be just strong enough to still the clamor. The Meat Inspection Act of 1906, stronger than the packers wanted, set rules for sanitary meat packing and government inspection of meat products.

A second measure, the Pure Food and Drug Act, passed more easily on June 30, 1906 (see the special feature in this chapter).

An expert on birds, Roosevelt loved nature and the wilderness, and some of his most enduring accomplishments came in the field of conservation. Working closely with Pinchot, Chief of the Forest Service, he established the first comprehensive national conservation policy. He undertook a major reclamation program, created the federal Reclamation Service, and strengthened the forest preserve program in the Department of Agriculture. Broadening the concept of conservation, he placed power sites, coal lands, and oil reserves as well as national forests in the public domain.

When Roosevelt took office in 1901 there were 45 million acres in government preserves. In 1908 there were almost 195 million. That year he called a National Conservation Congress attended by forty-four governors and hundreds of experts. Roosevelt formed the National Commis-

■ *Early twentieth-century meat-processing scenes like this are idyllic compared to those described in Upton Sinclair's* The Jungle, *which became the most successful of the muckraking books.*

sion on the Conservation of Natural Resources to look after waters, forests, lands, and minerals. With Pinchot as head, it drew up an inventory of the nation's natural resources.

As 1908 approached, Roosevelt became increasingly strident in his demand for sweeping reforms. He attacked "malefactors of great wealth," urged greater federal regulatory powers, criticized the conservatism of the federal courts, and called for laws protecting factory workers. Many business leaders blamed him for a severe financial panic in the autumn of 1907, and conservatives in Congress stiffened their opposition. Divisions between Republican conservatives and progressives grew.

The Election of 1908

Candidate	Party	Popular Vote	Electoral Vote
Taft	Republican	7,676,258	321
Bryan	Democrat	6,406,801	162
Debs	Socialist	420,380	0
Chafin	Prohibition	252,821	0

Immensely popular, Roosevelt prepared in 1908 to turn over the White House to William Howard Taft, his close friend and colleague. "The Roosevelt policies will not go out with the Roosevelt administration," a party leader said. "If Taft weakens, he will annihilate himself." As expected, Taft soundly defeated the Democratic standard-bearer William Jennings Bryan, who was making his third try for the presidency. The Republicans retained control of Congress. Taft prepared to move into the White House, ready and willing to carry on the Roosevelt legacy.

The Ordeal of William Howard Taft

The Republican national convention that nominated Taft had not satisfied either Roosevelt or Taft. True, Taft won the presidential nomination as planned, but conservative Republicans beat back the attempts of progressive Republicans to influence the convention. They named a conservative for vice-president, and the platform reflected conservative views on labor, the courts, and other issues. Taft wanted a pledge to lower the tariff but got only a promise of revision, which might lower—or raise—it. La Follette, Cummins, and other progressive Republicans were openly disappointed.

Taking office in 1909, Taft felt "just a bit like a fish out of water." The son of a distinguished Ohio family, and a graduate of Yale Law School, he became an Ohio judge, solicitor general of the United States, and a judge of the federal circuit court. In 1900 McKinley asked him to head the Philippine Commission, charged with the difficult and challenging task of forming a civil government in the Philippines. Later Taft was named the first governor general of the Philippines. In 1904 Roosevelt appointed him secretary of war.

In all these positions Taft made his mark as a skillful administrator. He worked quietly behind the scenes, avoided controversy, and shared none of Roosevelt's zest for politics. A good-natured man, Taft had personal charm and infectious humor. He fled from fights rather than seeking them out and disliked political maneuvering, preferring instead quiet solitude. "I don't like politics," he said. "I don't like the limelight."

■ *Taft played golf with gusto, despite his inability to place the ball on a tee and his habit of losing all the balls before the end of the match.*

Weighing close to three hundred pounds, Taft enjoyed conversation, golf and bridge, good food, and plenty of rest. Compared to Roosevelt and Wilson, he was lazy. He was also honest, kindly, and amiable, and in his own way he knew how to get things done. Reflective, he preferred the life of a judge, but his wife, Helen H. Taft, who enjoyed politics, prodded him toward the White House. When a Supreme Court appointment opened in 1906, Taft reluctantly turned it down. "Ma wants him to wait and be president," his youngest son said.

Taft's years as president were not happy. Mrs. Taft's health soon collapsed, and as it turned out, Taft presided over a Republican party torn with tensions that Roosevelt had either brushed aside or concealed. The tariff, business regulation, and other issues split conservatives and progressives and Taft often wavered or sided with the conservatives. Taft revered the past and distrusted change . Although an ardent supporter of Roosevelt, he never had Roosevelt's faith in the ability of government to impose reform and alter individual behavior. He named five corporation attorneys to his cabinet, leaned more to business than to labor, and spoke of a desire to "clean out the unions."

At the time and later, Taft's reputation suffered in contrast to the flair of Roosevelt and the moral majesty of Woodrow Wilson. He deserved better. Taft was an honest and sincere president, who—sometimes firm, sometimes befuddled—faced a series of important and troublesome problems during his term of office.

Party Insurgency

Taft started his term with an attempt to curb the powerful Republican Speaker of the House, Joseph "Uncle Joe" Cannon of Illinois. Using the powers of his position, Cannon set House procedures, appointed committees, and virtually dictated legislation. Straightforward and crusty, he often opposed reform. In March 1909 thirty Republican congressmen joined Taft's effort to curb Cannon's power, and the President sensed success. But Cannon retaliated and, threatening to block all tariff bills, forced a compromise. Taft stopped the anti-Cannon campaign in return for Cannon's pledge to help with tariff cuts.

Republicans were divided over the tariff, and there was a growing party insurgency against high rates. The House quickly passed a bill providing for lower rates, but in the Senate, protectionists raised them. Senate leader Nelson A. Aldrich of Rhode Island introduced a revised bill that added over eight hundred amendments to the House rates. It placed no duties on curling stones, false teeth, canary-bird seed, and hog bristles, which brought a chuckle from Mr. Dooley. "Th' new Tariff Bill," he said, "put these familyar commodyties within th' reach iv all."

Angry, La Follette and other Republicans attacked the bill as the child of special interests. In speeches on the Senate floor they called themselves "progressives," invoked Roosevelt's name,

and urged Taft to defeat the high-tariff proposal. Caught between protectionists and progressives, Taft wavered, then tried to compromise. In the end he backed Aldrich. The Payne-Aldrich Act, passed in November 1909, called for higher rates than the original House bill, though it lowered them from the Dingley Tariff of 1897 (see chapter 20). An unpopular law, it helped discredit Taft and revealed the tensions in the Republican party.

Republican progressives and conservatives drifted apart. Taft tried to find middle ground but leaned more and more toward the conservatives. During a nationwide speaking tour in the autumn of 1909 he praised Aldrich, scolded the low-tariff insurgents, and called the Payne-Aldrich Act "the best bill that the Republican party ever passed." Traveling through the Midwest, he pointedly ignored La Follette, Cummins, and other progressive Republicans.

When Congress met in 1910, progressive Republicans no longer looked to Taft for leadership. As before, they challenged Cannon's power, and again Taft wavered. In an outcome embarrassing to the President, the progressives won, managing to curtail Cannon's authority to dictate committee assignments and schedule debate. In progressive circles there was growing talk of a Roosevelt return to the White House.

■ *A 1910 cartoon shows Taft snarled in the intracacies of office as his disapproving mentor looks on.*

Patent Medicines and the Pure Food and Drug Act

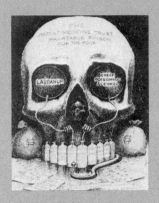

Around 1900, at the same time the science of medicine was making enormous strides, patent medicines were selling in record volume. Everybody was curing everything with Mrs. Winslow's Soothing Syrup, Perkins' Infallible Aromatic and Disinfectory Pastile, and of course Lydia E. Pinkham's famous Vegetable Compound for women. Often suspicious of doctors, and eager for quick, inexpensive cures, Americans in 1904 spent almost $100 million on patent medicines. About 50,000 such medicines were sold in the United States.

By the beginning of the twentieth century, the germ theory of disease was several decades old, and it was known that different germs cause different diseases. But no one seemed surprised that each patent medicine—according to the ads, at least—could cure almost everything. Ads for Helmbold's Buchu, one of the period's popular remedies, claimed it cured "General Debility, Mental and Physical Depression, Imbecility, Determination of Blood to the Head, Confused Ideas, Hysteria, General Irritability, . . . Dyspepsia, Emaciation, Low Spirits, Disorganization or Paralysis of the Organs of Generation," and several other ills.

Some patent medicine makers quickly recognized the marketing potential of the germ theory. Germ-killing medicines, including William

Radam's hot-selling Microbe Killer, soon appeared. A gardener in Austin, Texas, Radam decided that all diseases had a single, germ-related cause—and thus a single cure. He mixed water with hydrochloric and sulphuric acid taken from his gardening shed, added a dash of red wine, and produced the Microbe Killer. Patented as a gardening aid, Radam sold the concoction as a medicine. By the early 1890s seventeen factories were producing gallon jugs of the mixture. Radam left Austin for a mansion on Fifth Avenue in New York City.

Other patent medicines contained cocoa, axle grease, beet sugar, glue, or castor oil. Some contained cocaine or morphine; many had large amounts of alcohol. Hostetter's Bitters was a popular medicine, and no wonder: nearly a third of each dose was alcohol. "You could get drunk on one bottle," the poet Carl Sandburg said. Hostetter's sold nearly a million bottles a year. In some towns, saloons served it at the bar.

Before long people began questioning the effectiveness of such medicines. Temperance groups were among the first to raise questions, sure that the medicines were little more than hard liquor in disguise. (Indeed, patent medicine sales had a way of booming wherever prohibition was adopted.) In 1905 the American Medical Association (AMA), a group that reflected the growing professionalization of medicine, created a special council of chemists and pharmacists to analyze patent medicine ingredients. The American Pharmaceutical Association also urged a listing of ingredients on the label of each bottle.

Involving greedy entrepreneurs who fed on the fears of gullible consumers, the patent medicines were a target tailor-made for the muckrakers. Samuel Hopkins Adams, a reporter for *Collier's*, had once considered a career in medicine; he resented the way in which patent medicine makers misled people who needed proper medical treatment. Like other muckrakers, he combined a zeal for facts with a desire to improve the lot of mankind. During 1904 and 1905 he studied ads, interviewed manufacturers, and sent samples of medicines to scientists for analysis.

On October 7, 1905, Adams broke the story in *Collier's* under the title "The Great American Fraud." "Gullible America," he began, "will spend this year some seventy-five millions of dollars in the purchase of patent medicines. In consideration of this sum it will swallow huge quantities of alcohol, an appalling amount of opiates and narcotics . . . and, far in excess of all other ingredients, undiluted fraud." Running until February 1906, the story included ten articles, in which Adams named 264 medicines, doctors, and companies. Newspapers summarized the findings; editorials demanded action. The AMA printed Adams' articles in a booklet that sold half a million copies.

While researching the story, Adams had sent medicine samples to Dr. Harvey W. Wiley, the chief chemist of the Department of Agriculture. A physician as well as a chemist, Wiley was energetic and innovative, with a flair for the dramatic—he was the third person in Washington to drive a car and the first to have a collision. He and his twelve young assistants became known as the "Poison Squad" in 1902, when they tested various food preservatives, determined to put an end to adulterated foods.

Wiley and the Poison Squad then began testing patent medicines. Wiley published the results of those tests, lectured on the issue to women's clubs and other groups, and urged Congress and President Theodore Roosevelt to curb the industry. In his 1905 message to Congress—issued in the midst of Adams' stories in *Collier's*— Roosevelt recommended federal regulation of "misbranded and adulterated foods, drinks, and drugs."

In February 1906 the Senate quickly passed a pure food and drug bill, amid indications that opponents planned to kill it in the House. If that was their plan, Upton Sinclair's *The Jungle*, which appeared in late February, created a sensation that aroused the public. Far from killing the bill, the House strengthened it, and on June 30, 1906, Roosevelt signed the new law. It required manufacturers to list the amount of alcohol, cocaine, morphine, and certain other ingredients on the label.

The law did not ban patent medicines. Instead, it relied on an assumption underlying much of the legislation of the progressive era—once people knew the facts, they would safely choose the right course. The assumption was not always correct, and patent medicines continued to sell after 1906. Kickapoo Cough *Cure*—one of the first medicines seized under the new law— simply changed its name to Kickapoo Cough *Syrup* and went on selling. Even today Americans spend almost $1 billion a year on products similar to those Adams and Wiley questioned in 1906.

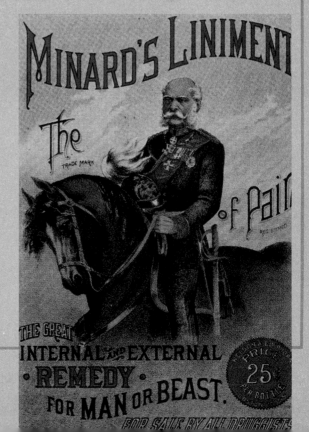

The Ballinger-Pinchot Affair

The conservation issue dealt another blow to relations between Roosevelt and President Taft. In 1909 Richard A. Ballinger, Taft's secretary of the interior, offered for sale a million acres of public land that Pinchot, who had stayed on as Taft's chief forester, had withdrawn from sale. Pinchot protested and, seizing on a report that Ballinger had helped sell valuable Alaskan coal lands to a syndicate that included J. P. Morgan, asked Taft to intervene. After investigating, Taft supported Ballinger on every count, although he asked Pinchot to remain in office.

Pinchot refused to drop the matter. Behind the scenes he provided material for two anti-Ballinger magazine articles, and he wrote a critical public letter that Senator Dolliver of Iowa read to the Senate. Taft had had enough He fired the insubordinate Pinchot, an appropriate action, but again lost in the process. Although a conservationist himself, the President had fired one of the nation's leading conservationists. Newspapers followed the controversy for months, and muckrakers assailed the administration's "surrender" to Morgan and other "despoilers of the national heritage."

The Ballinger-Pinchot controversy obscured Taft's important contributions to conservation. He won from Congress the power to remove lands from sale, and he used it to conserve more land than Roosevelt did. Still, the controversy tarred Taft, and it upset his old friend Roosevelt. Pinchot hurried to Italy where Roosevelt was on tour; he talked again with Roosevelt within days of TR's arrival home in June 1910.

Taft's Final Years

Interested in railroad regulation, Taft backed a bill in 1910 to empower the ICC to fix maximum railroad rates. Progressive Republicans favored that plan but attacked Taft's suggestion of a special Commerce Court to hear appeals from ICC decisions because most judges were traditionally conservative in outlook and usually rejected attempts to regulate railroad rates. Democratic and Republican progressives tried to amend the bill to strengthen it; Taft made support of it a test of party loyalty.

The Mann-Elkins Act of 1910 gave something to everyone. It gave the ICC power to set rates, stiffened long- and short-haul regulations, and placed telephone and telegraph companies under ICC jurisdiction. These provisions delighted progressives. The act also created a Commerce Court, pleasing conservatives. In a trade-off, conservative Republican Senate leaders pledged their support for a statehood bill for Arizona and New Mexico, which were both predicted to be Democratic. In return, enough Democratic senators promised to vote for the Commerce Court provision to pass the bill. While pleased with the act, Taft and the Republican party lost further ground. In votes on its key provisions, Taft raised the issue of party regularity, and progressive Republicans defied him.

Withholding patronage, Taft attempted to defeat the progressive Republicans in the 1910 elections. He helped form antiprogressive organizations, and he campaigned against progressive Republican candidates for the Senate. In California he opposed Hiram Johnson, the progressive Republican champion; in Wisconsin, the home of La Follette, he sent Vice-President James S. Sherman to take control of the state convention. Progressive Republicans retaliated by organizing a nationwide network of anti-Taft Progressive Republican Clubs.

The 1910 election results were a major setback for Taft and the Republicans—both conservatives and progressives. In party primaries, progressive Republicans overwhelmed most Taft candidates, and in November, the Democrats beat virtually everyone. They swept the urban-industrial states from New York to Illinois. New York, New Jersey, Indiana, and even Taft's Ohio elected Democratic governors. For the first time since 1894, Republicans lost control of both the House and the Senate. In all, they lost fifty-eight seats in the House and ten in the Senate. Disappointed, Taft called it "not only a landslide, but a tidal wave and holocaust all rolled into one general cataclysm."

Despite the defeat, Taft pushed through several important measures before his term ended. With the help of the new Democratic House, he backed laws to regulate safety in mines and on railroads, create a Children's Bureau in the federal government, establish employers' liability for all work done on government contracts, and mandate an eight-hour workday for government workers. In 1909 Congress initiated a constitutional amendment authorizing an income tax, perhaps the most significant legislative measure of the twentieth century. The Sixteenth Amendment took effect early in 1913.

An ardent supporter of competition, Taft relentlessly pressed a campaign against trusts. The Sherman Antitrust Act, he said in 1911, "is a good law that ought to be enforced, and I propose to enforce it." That year the Supreme Court in cases against Standard Oil and American Tobacco established the "rule of reason," which allowed the Court to determine whether a business was a "reasonable" restraint on trade. Taft thought the decisions gave the Court too much discretion, and he pushed ahead with the antitrust effort.

In October 1911, he sued U.S. Steel for its acquisition of the Tennessee Coal and Iron Company in 1907. Roosevelt had approved the acquisition (see p. 669), and the suit seemed designed to impugn his action. Enraged, he attacked Taft, and Taft, for once, fought back. He accused Roosevelt of undermining the conservative tradition in the country and began working to undercut the influence of the progressive Republicans. Increasingly now, Roosevelt listened to anti-Taft Republicans who urged him to run for president in 1912. In the following months he sounded Republican sentiment for a presidential bid. In February 1912 he announced: "My hat is in the ring."

Differing Philosophies in the Election of 1912

Delighted Democrats looked on as Taft and Roosevelt fought for the Republican nomination. As the incumbent president, Taft controlled the party machinery, and when the Republican convention met in June 1912, he took the nomination. In early July the Democrats met in Baltimore and, confident of victory for the first time in two decades, struggled through forty-six ballots before finally nominating Woodrow Wilson, the reform-minded governor of New Jersey.

A month later the anti-Taft and progressive Republicans—now calling themselves the Progressive Party—whooped it up in Chicago. Roosevelt himself was there to give a stirring "Confession of Faith" and listen to the delegates sing:

Thou wilt not cower in the dust,
  Roosevelt, O Roosevelt!
Thy gleaming sword shall never rust,
  Roosevelt, O Roosevelt!

Naming Roosevelt for president, the Progressive —soon known as the "Bull Moose"—party convention set the stage for the first important three-cornered presidential contest since 1860.

Saddened, Taft was out of the running before the campaign even began. "I think I might as well give up so far as being a candidate is concerned," he said in July. "There are so many people in the country who don't like me." Taft stayed at home and made no speeches before the election. Roosevelt campaigned strenuously, even completing one speech after being shot in the chest. "I have a message to deliver," he said, "and will deliver it as long as there is life in my body."

Roosevelt's message involved a program he called the New Nationalism. An important phase in the shaping of twentieth-century American political thought, it demanded a national approach to the country's affairs and a strong president to deal with them. The New Nationalism called for efficiency in government and society. It exalted the executive and the expert, urged social-justice reforms to protect workers, women, and

■ *The Bull Moose party's highly recognizable candidate is characterized in this cartoon as "the latest arrival at the political zoo."*

■ *To overcome the impression of him as an austere scholar, Wilson campaigned vigorously in 1912, stumping the country from the rear of a train.*

election of 1912 offered competing philosophies of government. Both Roosevelt and Wilson saw the central problem of the American nation as economic growth and its effect on individuals and society. Both focused on the government's relation to business; both believed in bureaucratic reform; and both wanted to use government to protect the ordinary citizen. But Roosevelt welcomed federal power, national planning, and business growth; Wilson distrusted them all.

On election day Wilson won 6.3 million votes to 4.1 million for Roosevelt and 900,000 for Eugene V. Debs, the Socialist party candidate. Taft, the incumbent president, finished third with 3.5 million votes; he carried only Vermont and Utah for 8 electoral votes. The Democrats also won outright control of both houses.

Woodrow Wilson's New Freedom

children, and accepted "good" trusts. The New Nationalism encouraged large concentrations of labor and capital, serving the nation's interests under a forceful federal executive.

For the first time in the history of a major political party, the Progressive campaign enlisted women in its organization. Some labor leaders, who saw potential for union growth, and some business leaders, who saw relief from destructive competition and labor strife, supported the new party.

Wilson, in contrast, set forth a program called the New Freedom that emphasized business competition and small government. A states' rights Democrat, he wanted to rein in federal authority, using it only to sweep away special privilege, release individual energies, and restore competition. Drawing on the thinking of Louis D. Brandeis, the brilliant shaper of reform-minded law, he echoed the Progressive party's social-justice objectives, while continuing to attack Roosevelt's planned state. For Wilson the vital issue was not a planned economy but a free one. "The history of liberty is the history of the limitation of governmental power . . .," he said in October 1912. "If America is not to have free enterprise, then she can have freedom of no sort whatever."

In the New Nationalism and New Freedom, the

If under Roosevelt social reform took on the excitement of a circus, "under Wilson," one historian said, "it acquired the dedication of a sunrise service." Born in Virginia in 1856, Wilson was the son of a Presbyterian minister. As a young man he wanted a career in public service, and he trained himself carefully in history and oratory. At age sixteen he became fascinated with the English parliamentary system, a fascination that shaped his scholarly career and perhaps his diplomacy in the First World War (see chapter 24). A moralist, he reached judgments easily, and once reached, almost nothing shook them. Opponents called him stubborn and smug. "He gives me the creeps," a Maryland ward boss said. "The time I met him, he said something to me, and I didn't know whether God or him was talking."

After graduating from Princeton University and the University of Virginia Law School, Wilson found that practicing law bored him. Shifting to history, from 1890 to 1902 he served as professor of jurisprudence and political economy at Princeton. In 1902 he became president of the university. Eight years later he was governor of New Jersey, where he led a campaign to reform election procedures, abolish corrupt practices, and strengthen railroad regulation.

Wilson's rise was rapid, and he knew relatively

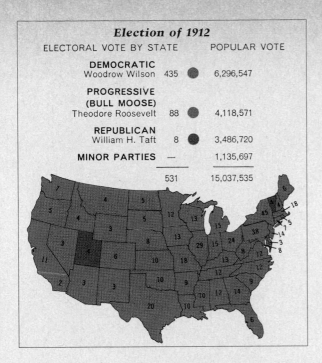

Election of 1912

ELECTORAL VOTE BY STATE		POPULAR VOTE
DEMOCRATIC Woodrow Wilson	435	6,296,547
PROGRESSIVE (BULL MOOSE) Theodore Roosevelt	88	4,118,571
REPUBLICAN William H. Taft	8	3,486,720
MINOR PARTIES	—	1,135,697
	531	15,037,535

On the day of his inauguration, Wilson called Congress into special session to lower the tariff. When the session opened on April 8, 1913, Wilson himself was there, the first president since John Adams in 1801 to appear personally before Congress. In forceful language, he urged Congress to reduce tariff rates.

As the bill moved through Congress, Wilson showed exceptional skill. He worked closely with congressional leaders, and when lobbyists threatened the bill in the Senate, he appealed for popular support. The result was a triumph for Wilson and the Democratic party. The Underwood Tariff Act passed in 1913. The first tariff cut in nineteen years, it lowered rates about 15 percent and removed duties from sugar, wool, and several other consumer goods.

To make up for lost revenue, the act also levied a modest, graduated income tax, authorized under the just-ratified Sixteenth Amendment. Marking a significant shift in the American tax structure, it imposed a 1 percent tax on individuals and corporations earning more than $4000 annually and an additional 1 percent tax on incomes over $20,000. Above all, the act reflected a new unity within the Democratic party which, unlike its experience under Grover Cleveland, had worked together to pass a difficult tariff law.

Wilson himself emerged as an able leader. "At a single stage," a foreign editor said, "[he went] from the man of promise to the man of achievement." Encouraged by his success, Wilson decided to keep Congress in session through the hot Washington summer. Now he focused on banking reform, and the result in December 1913 was the Federal Reserve Act, the most important domestic law of his administration.

Meant to provide the United States with a sound yet flexible currency, the act established the country's first efficient banking system since Andrew Jackson killed the Second Bank of the United States in 1832 (see chapter 10). It created twelve regional banks, each to serve the banks of its district. The regional banks, in turn, answered to a Federal Reserve Board, appointed by the president, which governed the nationwide system.

A compromise law, the act blended public and private control of the banking system. Private

little about national issues and personalities. But he learned fast, and in some ways the lack of experience served him well. He had few political debts to repay, and he brought fresh perspectives to older issues. Ideas intrigued Wilson; details bored him. Although he was outgoing at times, he could also be cold and aloof, and aides soon learned that he preferred loyalty and flattery to candid criticism.

Prone to self-righteousness, Wilson often turned differences of opinion into bitter personal quarrels. Like Roosevelt, he believed in strong presidential leadership. A scholar of the party system, he cooperated closely with Democrats in Congress, and his legislative record placed him among the most effective presidents. Forbidding in individual conversation, Wilson could move crowds with graceful oratory. Unlike Taft, and even more than Roosevelt, he could inspire.

His inaugural address was eloquent. "The Nation," he said, "has been deeply stirred, stirred by a solemn passion, stirred by the knowledge of wrong, of ideals lost, of government too often debauched and made an instrument of evil. The feelings with which we face this new age of right and opportunity sweep across our heartstrings like some air out of God's own presence."

bankers owned the federal reserve banks but answered to the presidentially appointed Federal Reserve Board. The reserve banks were authorized to issue currency and through the discount rate—the interest rate at which they loaned money to member banks—could raise or lower the amount of money in circulation. Monetary affairs no longer depended solely on the price of gold. Within a year nearly half the nation's banking resources were in the Federal Reserve System.

The Clayton Antitrust Act (1914) completed Wilson's initial legislative program. Like previous antitrust measures, it reflected confusion over how to discipline a growing economy without putting a brake on output. In part it was a response to the revelations of the Pujo Committee of the House, a congressional committee investigating Wall Street. Publicized by Brandeis in a disquieting series of articles, "Other People's Money," the committee discovered a pyramid of money and power capped by the Morgan-Rockefeller empire that, through "interlocking directorates," controlled companies worth $22 billion, over one tenth of the national wealth.

The Clayton Act outlawed such directorates and prohibited unfair trade practices. It forbade pricing policies that created monopoly, and it made corporate officers personally responsible for antitrust violations. Delighting Samuel Gompers and the labor movement, the act declared that unions were not conspiracies in restraint of trade, outlawed the use of injunctions in labor disputes unless necessary to protect property, and approved lawful strikes and picketing. To Gompers' dismay, the courts continued to rule against union activity.

A related law established a powerful Federal Trade Commission to oversee business methods. Composed of five members, the commission could demand special and annual reports, investigate complaints, and order corporate compliance, subject to court review. At first Wilson opposed the commission concept, which was an approach more suitable to Roosevelt's New Nationalism, but he changed his mind and, along with Brandeis, called it the cornerstone of his antitrust plan. To reassure business leaders, he appointed a number of conservatives to the new commission and to the Federal Reserve Board.

In November 1914 Wilson proudly announced the completion of his New Freedom program.

Tariff, banking, and antitrust laws promised a brighter future, he said, and it was now "a time of healing because a time of just dealing." Many Progressives were aghast. To think society's ills were so easily cured, the *New Republic* said, "casts suspicion either upon his own sincerity or upon his grasp of the realities of modern social and industrial life."

Retreat and Advance

Distracted by the start of war in Europe, Wilson gave less attention to domestic issues for over a year. When he returned to concern with reform, he adopted more and more of Roosevelt's New Nationalism and blended it with the New Freedom in ways that set it off from his earlier policies.

One of Wilson's problems was the Congress. To his dismay, the Republicans gained substantially in the 1914 elections. Reducing the Democratic majority in the House, they swept key industrial and farm states. At the same time a recession struck the economy, which had been hurt by the outbreak of the European war in August 1914. Some business leaders blamed the tariff and other New Freedom laws. On the defensive, Wilson soothed business sentiment and invited bankers and industrialists to the White House. He allowed companies fearful of antitrust actions to seek advice from the Justice Department.

Preoccupied with such problems, Wilson blocked significant action in Congress through most of 1915. He refused to support a bill providing minimum wages for women workers, sidetracked a child-labor bill on the ground that it was unconstitutional, and opposed a bill to establish long-term credits for farmers. He also refused to endorse woman suffrage, arguing that the right to vote was a state, not a federal matter.

Wilson's record on race disappointed blacks and many progressives. He had appealed to black voters during the 1912 election, and a number of black leaders campaigned for him. Soon after the inauguration, Oswald Garrison Villard, a leader of the NAACP, proposed a National Race Commission to study the problem of race relations. Initially sympathetic, Wilson rejected the idea because he feared he might lose southern Democratic votes in Congress. A Virginian himself, he appointed many Southerners to high office, and for the first time since the Civil War, southern views on race dominated the nation's capital.

At one of Wilson's first cabinet meetings the postmaster general proposed the segregation of all blacks in the federal service. No one dissented, including Wilson. Several government bureaus promptly began to segregate workers in offices, shops, restrooms, and restaurants. Employees who objected were fired. Black leaders protested, and they were joined by progressive leaders and clergymen. Surprised at the protest, Wilson backed quietly away from the policy, although he continued to insist that segregation benefited blacks.

As the year 1916 began, Wilson again pushed for reform, and the result—a virtual river of reform laws—began the second, national-minded phase of the New Freedom. In part Wilson was motivated by the approaching presidential election. A minority president, he owed his victory in 1912 to the split in the Republican party, now almost healed. Roosevelt was moving back into Republican ranks, and there were issues connected with the war in Europe that he might use against Wilson (see the next chapter). Moreover, many progressives were voicing disappointment with Wilson's limited reforms and his failure to support more advanced reform legislation such as farm credits, child labor, and women's suffrage.

Moving quickly to patch up the problem, Wilson named Brandeis to the Supreme Court in January 1916. Popular among progressives, Brandeis was also the first person of Jewish faith to serve on the Court. When conservatives in the Senate tried to defeat the nomination, Wilson stood firm and won, earning further praise from progressives, Jews, and others. In May he reversed his stand on farm loans and accepted a rural credits bill to establish farm-loan banks backed by federal funds. The Federal Farm Loan Act of 1916 created a Federal Farm Loan Board to give farmers credit similar to the Federal Reserve's benefits for trade and industry.

Wilson was already popular within the labor movement. Going beyond Roosevelt's policies, which had sought a balance between business and labor, he defended union recognition and collective bargaining. In 1913 he appointed William B. Wilson, a respected leader of the United Mine

Chronology

1900	General Electric founds the first industrial research laboratory
1901	Theodore Roosevelt becomes president
1902	Roosevelt sues the Northern Securities Company for violation of antitrust act Coal miners in northeastern Pennsylvania strike for wage increases, eight-hour day, and union recognition
1903	Department of Commerce and Labor created Ford Motor Company formed
1904	Roosevelt elected president
1905	Industrial Workers of the World (IWW) established
1906	Hepburn Act strengthens power and authority of ICC Congress passes Meat Inspection Act and Pure Food and Drug Act
1908	Taft elected president
1909	Payne-Aldrich Tariff Act divides Republican party
1910	Mann-Elkins Act passed to regulate railroads Taft fires Gifford Pinchot, head of U.S. Forest Service Democrats sweep midterm elections
1911	Frederick Winslow Taylor publishes *The Principles of Scientific Management* Fire at the Triangle Shirtwaist Company kills 146 people
1912	Progressive party formed; nominates Roosevelt for president Woodrow Wilson elected president IWW leads strikes in Massachusetts and New Jersey
1913	Underwood Tariff Act lowers rates Federal Reserve Act reforms U.S. banking system Ford introduces the moving assembly line in Highland Park plant Sixteenth Amendment authorizes Congress to collect taxes on incomes
1914	Clayton Act strengthens antitrust legislation Ford workers assemble an automobile in 93 minutes
1916	Wilson wins reelection Federal Aid Roads Act creates national road network

■ *(Top) Strikers' tent colony at Ludlow before the militia and mine guards charged it on April 20, 1914. (Bottom) The ruins of Ludlow after the fourteen-hour attack that killed twenty-six people.*

Workers, as the first head of the Labor Department, and he strengthened the department's Division of Conciliation. In 1914 in Ludlow, Colorado, state militia and mine guards fired machine guns into a tent colony of coal strikers, killing twenty-six men, women, and children. Outraged, Wilson stepped in and used federal troops to end the violence while negotiations to end the strike went on.

In August 1916 a threatened railroad strike again revealed Wilson's sympathies with labor. Like Roosevelt, he invited the two sides to the White House where he urged the railroad companies to grant an eight-hour day and labor leaders to abandon the demand for overtime pay. Labor leaders accepted the proposal; railroad leaders did not. "I pray God to forgive you, I never can," Wilson said as he left the room. Soon he signed the Adamson Act (1916) that imposed the eight-hour day on interstate railways and established a federal commission to study the railroad problem. Ending the threat of a strike, the act marked a milestone in the expansion of the federal government's authority to regulate industry.

With Wilson leading the way, the flow of reform legislation continued until the election. The Federal Workmen's Compensation Act established workers' compensation for government employees. The Keating-Owen Act, the first federal child-labor law, prohibited the shipment in interstate commerce of products manufactured by children under the age of fourteen. It too expanded the authority of the federal government. The Warehouse Act, similar to the subtreasury proposal the Populists urged in the 1890s (see chapter 20), authorized licensed warehouses to issue negotiable receipts for farm products deposited with them.

In September Wilson signed the Tariff Commission Act creating an expert commission to recommend tariff rates. The same month, the Revenue Act of 1916 boosted income taxes and furthered tax reform. Four thousand members of the National American Woman Suffrage Association cheered when Wilson finally came out in support of woman suffrage. "You touched our hearts and won our fealty," Carrie Chapman Catt, the association's president, told him. Two weeks later he endorsed the eight-hour day for all the nation's workers.

The 1916 presidential election was close, but Wilson won it on the issues of peace and progressivism (see chapter 24). By the end of 1916 he and the Democratic party had enacted most of the important parts of Roosevelt's Progressive party platform of 1912. To do it, Wilson abandoned portions of the New Freedom and accepted much of the New Nationalism, including greater federal power and commissions governing trade and tariffs. In mixing the two programs, he blended some of the competing doctrines of the progressive era, established the primacy of the federal government, and foreshadowed the pragmatic outlook of Franklin D. Roosevelt's New Deal.

In 1909 Taft rode to his inauguration in a horse and carriage; in 1913 Wilson rode in an automobile. In May 1918, the post office began airmail service between New York City and Washington, D.C. Change was evident throughout the country, as Americans and their institutions continued to adjust to a life of cities and suburbs, factories and mass production.

The institution of the presidency expanded. The president replaced Congress and the states as the center of national authority. From the White House radiated executive departments that guided a host of activities. Independent commissions, operating within flexible laws, supplemented executive authority.

Government at all levels accepted responsibility for the welfare of various elements in the social order. A reform-minded and bureaucratic society took shape, in which men and women, labor and capital, political parties and social classes competed for shares in the expansive framework of twentieth-century life.

After Napoleon's defeat in 1815, a century of peace began in western Europe, and as the decades passed, war seemed a dying institution. "It looks as though this were going to be the age of treaties rather than the age of wars," an American said in 1912, "the century of reason rather than the century of force." It was not to be. Two years later the most devastating of wars broke out in Europe, and in 1917 Americans were fighting on the battlefields of France.

Recommended Reading

George Mowry, *The Era of Theodore Roosevelt* (1958), and Arthur S. Link, *Woodrow Wilson and the Progressive Era* (1954), trace the social and economic conditions of the period. See also Henry F. Pringle's biography, *Theodore Roosevelt* (1931), John M. Blum's perceptive and brief *The Republican Roosevelt* (1954), and William H. Harbaugh's thoughtful *The Life and Times of Theodore Roosevelt*, rev. ed. (1975). Donald E. Anderson, *William Howard Taft* (1973), and Paolo E. Coletta, *The Presidency of William Howard Taft* (1973), study Taft. The definitive biography of Wilson is Arthur S. Link, *Wilson*, 5 vols. (1947–1965).

Work, workers, and the industrial society are perceptively treated in Herbert G. Gutman, *Work, Culture and Society in Industrializing America* (1977); David Montgomery, *Workers' Control in America: Studies in the History of Work, Technology, and Labor Struggles* (1979); and David Brody, *Workers in Industrial America: Essays on the Twentieth Century Struggle* (1980). Stephan Thernstrom, *The Other Bostonians* (1973), is the best study of social and economic mobility.

Additional Bibliography

Roger Burlingame, *Henry Ford* (1954) and Allan Nevins and Frank E. Hill, *Ford*, 3 vols. (1954–1963) cover Ford's career, while Alfred D. Chandler, *Strategy and Structure: Chapters in the History of American Industrial Enterprise* (1962); Samuel Haber, *Efficiency and Uplift: Scientific Management in the Progressive Era* (1964); and Frederick A. White, *American Industrial Research Laboratories* (1961), provide useful overviews. See also Tamara K. Hareven and Randolph Langenbach, *Amoskeag: Life and Work in an American Factory-City* (1978).

The labor movement is covered in Harold Livesay, *Samuel Gompers and Organized Labor in America* (1978); Melvyn Dubofsky, *We Shall Be All: A History of the Industrial Workers of the World* (1969); Susan Estabrook Kennedy, *If All We Did Was To Weep At Home: A History of White Working Class Women in America* (1979); and Barbara Mayer Wertheimer, *We Were There: The Story of Working Women in America* (1977).

On specific issues, see O. E. Anderson, *The Health of a Nation: Harvey W. Wiley and the Fight for Pure Food* (1958); Craig West, *Banking Reform and the Federal Reserve, 1863–1923* (1977); Aileen Kraditor, *The Ideas of the Woman Suffrage Movement, 1890–1920* (1981); David W. Southern, *The Malignant Heritage: Yankee Progressives and the Negro Question, 1901–1914* (1968); James H. Timberlake, *Prohibition and the Progressive Crusade* (1963); and Walter I. Trattner, *Crusade for the Children* (1970).

On politics, see George E. Mowry, *Theodore Roosevelt and the Progressive Movement* (1946); Kenneth W. Hechler, *Insurgency: Personalities and Politics of the Taft Era* (1940); Norman M. Wilensky, *Conservatives in the Progressive Era: The Taft Republicans of 1912* (1965); and L. J. Holt, *Congressional Insurgents and the Party System, 1909–1916* (1967).

Helpful biographies include David P. Thelen, *Robert M. La Follette and the Insurgent Spirit* (1976); R. S. Maxwell, *La Follette and the Rise of the Progressives in Wisconsin* (1956); G. Wallace Chessman, *Theodore Roosevelt and the Politics of Power* (1969); Edmund Wilson, *The Rise of Theodore Roosevelt* (1979); William Manners, *TR and Will* (1969); John M. Blum, *Woodrow Wilson and the Politics of Morality* (1962); John M. Mulder, *Woodrow Wilson: The Years of Preparation* (1978); and Henry F. Pringle, *Life and Times of William Howard Taft*, 2 vols. (1939).

Alpheus Thomas Mason, *Brandeis: A Free Man's Life* (1946); Harold W. Currie, *Eugene V. Debs* (1976); and Dewey W. Grantham, Jr., *Hoke Smith and the Politics of the New South* (1958) are valuable studies.

Contemporary accounts include Herbert Croly, *The Promise of American Life* (1909); Walter Lippmann, *Drift and Mastery* (1914); William Allen White, *The Old Order Changeth* (1910) and *The Autobiography of William Allen White* (1946); and Charles Seymour, ed., *The Intimate Papers of Colonel House*, 4 vols. (1926–1928).

chapter 24

THE
NATION
AT WAR

On the morning of May 1, 1915, the German government printed an important advertisement in the *New York World:*

NOTICE—
Travellers intending to embark on the Atlantic voyage are reminded that a state of war exists between Germany and her allies and Great Britain and her allies; that the zone of war includes the waters adjacent to the British Isles; that, in accordance with formal notice given by the Imperial German Government, vessels flying the flag of Great Britain, or of any of her allies, are liable to destruction in those waters and that travellers sailing in the war zone on ships of Great Britain or her allies do so at their own risk.

At 12:30 that afternoon, the British steamship *Lusitania* set sail from New York to Liverpool.

The steamer was two hours late, but it held several speed records and could easily make up the time. The passenger list of 1257 was the largest since the outbreak of war in Europe. Alfred G. Vanderbilt, the millionaire sportsman, was aboard; so were Charles Frohman, a famous New York theatrical producer, and Elbert Hubbard, a popular writer who jested that a submarine attack might help sell his new book. While some passengers chose the *Lusitania* for speed, others liked the modern staterooms, more comfortable than the older ships of the competing American Line.

Six days later, the *Lusitania*, on schedule, reached the coast of Ireland. German U-boats patrolled these dangerous waters. When the war began in 1914, Great Britain imposed a naval blockade of Germany. In return, Germany in February 1915 declared the area around the British Isles a war zone; all enemy vessels, armed or unarmed, were at risk. Germany had only a handful of U-boats, but submarine warfare was new and frightening. On behalf of the United States President Woodrow Wilson protested the German action, and on February 10 he warned Germany of its "strict accountability" for any American losses resulting from U-boat attacks.

Off Ireland, the passengers lounged on the deck of the *Lusitania.* As in peacetime, the ship sailed straight ahead, with no zigzag maneuvers to throw off pursuit. But the submarine U-20 was there, and the commander, seeing a large ship, fired a single torpedo. Seconds after it hit, a boiler exploded and blew a hole in the *Lusitania's* side. The ship listed immediately, hindering the launching of lifeboats, and in eighteen minutes it sank. Nearly 1200 people died, including 128 Americans. As the ship's bow lifted and went under, the U-20 commander for the first time read the name: *Lusitania.*

The sinking, the worst since the *Titanic* went down with 1500 people in 1912, horrified Americans. Theodore Roosevelt called it "an act of piracy" and demanded war. On the French front the Germans had just introduced poison gas, another alarming new weapon, and there were reports of German atrocities in Belgium. Still, most Americans wanted to stay out of war; like Wilson, they hoped negotiations could solve the problem. "There is such a thing," Wilson said a few days after the sinking, "as a man being too proud to fight. There is such a thing as a nation being so right that it does not need to convince others by force."

In a series of diplomatic notes Wilson demanded a change in German policy. The first *Lusitania* note (May 13, 1915) called on Germany to abandon unrestricted submarine warfare, disavow the sinking, and compensate for lost American lives. Germany sent an evasive reply, and Wilson drafted a second *Lusitania* note (June 9) insisting on specific pledges. Fearful that the demand would lead to war, Secretary of State William Jennings Bryan resigned rather than sign the note. Wilson sent it anyway and followed with a third note (July 21)—almost an ultimatum—warning Germany that the United States would view similar sinkings as "deliberately unfriendly."

Unbeknown to Wilson, Germany had already ordered U-boat commanders not to sink passenger liners without warning. In August 1915 a U-boat mistakenly torpedoed the British liner *Arabic*, killing two Americans. Wilson protested,

With the sinking of the Lusitania, the American people learned first-hand of the horrors of total war. President Wilson's decision to protest the incident through diplomacy kept the United States out of the war—but only temporarily.

New York Tribune

First to Last—the Truth: News · Editorials · Advertisements

SATURDAY, MAY 8, 1915.   PRICE ONE CENT

900 Die as Lusitania Goes to Bottom; 400 Americans on Board Torpedoed Ship; Washington Stirred as When Maine Sank

CAPITAL AROUSED, SITUATION GRAVEST YET FACED IN WAR

Washington Determined That Germany Shall Not Be Allowed to Shirk Responsibility for Deaths.

GREATLY FEARS LOSS OF AMERICANS

President Shows Nervousness as Bulletins of Disaster Come In—Strongest Protest Yet Made—Planned Even if No U.S. Citizens Were Lost

THE LUSITANIA, SUNK BY GERMAN TORPEDO, WITH HEAVY LOSS OF LIFE.

Dying and Injured Brought in with Other Survivors to Queenstown—Some Landed at Kinsale and Clonakilty.

TWO TORPEDOES FIRED, SAYS STEWARD

Attack Made About Eight Miles from Irish Coast in Broad Daylight and in Fine Weather—Survivor Tells of Bravery of Cunard Officers.

---

and Germany, eager to keep the United States out of the war, backed down. The *Arabic* pledge (September 1) promised to stop and warn liners, unless they tried to resist or escape. Germany also apologized for American deaths on the *Arabic*, and for the rest of 1915 U-boats hunted freighters, not passenger liners.

Although Wilson's diplomacy had achieved his immediate goal, the *Lusitania* and *Arabic* crises contained the elements that led to war. Trade and travel tied the world together, and Americans no longer hid behind safe ocean barriers. New weapons, such as the submarine, strained old rules of international law. But while Americans sifted the conflicting claims of Great Britain and Germany, they hoped for peace. A generation of progressives, inspired with confidence in human progress, did not easily accept war.

Wilson also hated war, but he found himself caught up in a worldwide crisis that demanded the best in American will and diplomacy. In the end diplomacy failed, and in April 1917 the United States entered a war that changed the nation's history.

A New World Power

American foreign policy from 1901 to 1920 was aggressive and nationalistic. During these years the United States intervened in Europe, the Far East, and Latin America. It dominated the Caribbean.

In 1898 the United States left the peace table possessing the Philippines, Puerto Rico, and Guam. Holding distant possessions required a colonial policy; it also required a change in foreign policy, reflecting an outward approach. From the Caribbean to the Pacific, policymakers paid attention to issues and countries they had earlier ignored. Like other nations in these years, the United States built a large navy, protected its colonial empire, and became increasingly involved in international affairs.

The nation also became more and more involved in economic ventures abroad. Turning out goods from textiles to steel, mass-production industries sold products overseas, and financiers invested in Asia, Africa, Latin America, and Europe. During the years between the Spanish-American War and World War I, investments abroad rose from $445 million to $2.5 billion. While investments and trade never wholly dictated American foreign policy, they fostered greater involvement in foreign lands.

"I Took the Canal Zone"

Convinced the United States should take a more active international role, Theodore Roosevelt spent his presidency preparing the nation for world power. Along with Secretary of War Elihu Root, he modernized the army, using lessons from the war with Spain. Roosevelt and Root established the Army War College, imposed stiff tests for the promotion of officers, and in 1903 created a general staff to oversee military planning and mobilization. Determined to end dependence on the British fleet, Roosevelt doubled the navy's strength during his term in office.

Stretching his authority to the limits, Roosevelt took steps to consolidate the country's new position in the Caribbean and Central America. European powers, which had long resisted American initiatives there, now accepted American supremacy. Preoccupied with problems in Europe and Africa, Great Britain agreed to United States plans for an isthmian canal in Central America and withdrew much of its military force from the area.

Roosevelt wanted a canal to link the Atlantic and Pacific oceans across the isthmus connecting North and South America. When the war with Spain started in 1898, it took the battleship *Oregon* seventy-one days to sail from San Francisco around Cape Horn to its battle station in the Atlantic; years later naval experts still shuddered at the thought. Secretary of State John Hay negotiated with Britain the Hay-Pauncefote Treaty of 1901 that permitted the United States to construct and control an isthmian canal, providing it would be free and open to ships of all nations.

Delighted, Roosevelt began selecting the route. One route, fifty miles long, wandered through the rough, swampy terrain of the Panama region of Colombia. A French company had recently tried and failed to dig a canal there. Northwest of Panama, another route ran through mountainous Nicaragua. Although two hundred miles in length, it followed natural waterways, a factor that would make construction easier.

An Isthmian Canal Commission investigated both routes in 1899 and recommended the shorter route through Panama. Roosevelt backed the idea, and he authorized Hay to negotiate an agreement with the Colombian chargé d'affaires, Tomas Herrán. The Hay-Herrán Convention (1903) gave the United States a ninety-nine-year lease, with option for renewal, on a canal zone six miles in width. In exchange, the United States agreed to pay Colombia a one-time fee of $10 million and an annual rental of $250,000.

To Roosevelt's dismay, the Colombian Senate rejected the treaty, in part because it infringed upon Colombian sovereignty. The Colombians also wanted more money. Calling them "jack rabbits" and "contemptible little creatures," Roosevelt considered seizing Panama, then hinted he would welcome a Panamanian revolt from Colombia. In November 1903 the Panamanians took the hint, and Roosevelt moved quickly to support them. Sending the cruiser *Nashville* to prevent Colombian troops from putting down the revolt, he promptly recognized the new Republic of Panama.

Two weeks later the Hay–Bunau-Varilla Treaty with Panama granted the United States control of a canal zone ten miles wide across the Isthmus of Panama. In return, the United States guaranteed the independence of Panama and agreed to pay the same fees offered Colombia. Using giant steam shovels and thousands of black laborers from Jamaica, engineers cut their way across the isthmus. On August 15, 1914, the first ocean steamer sailed through the completed canal, which cost $275 million to build.

The Panama Canal Zone

Construction of the canal began in 1904, and despite landslides, steamy weather, and yellow fever, work was completed in 1914.

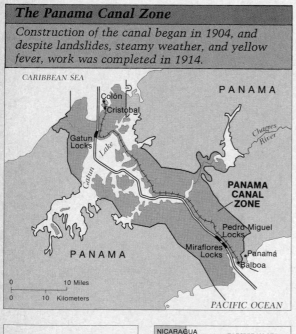

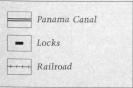

■ *The battleship* Ohio *sailing in the Panama Canal in 1915.*

Roosevelt's actions angered many Latin Americans. Trying to soothe feelings, Wilson agreed in 1914 to pay Colombia $25 million in cash, give it preferential treatment in using the canal, and express "sincere regret" over American actions. Roosevelt was furious, and his friends in the Senate blocked the agreement. Colombian-American relations remained strained until 1921, when the two countries signed a treaty that included Wilson's first two provisions but omitted the apology.

For his part, Roosevelt took great pride in the canal, calling it "by far the most important action in foreign affairs." Defending his methods, he said in 1911: "If I had followed traditional conservative methods, I would have submitted a dignified state paper of 200 pages to Congress and the debate on it would have been going on yet; but I took the Canal Zone and let Congress debate; and while the debate goes on the Canal does also."

The Roosevelt Corollary

With interests in Puerto Rico, Cuba, and the canal, the United States developed a Caribbean policy to ensure its dominance in the region. It established protectorates over some countries and subsidized others to keep them dependent. When necessary, it purchased islands to keep them out of the hands of other powers, as in the

case of the Danish West Indies (now the Virgin Islands), bought in 1917 to prevent the Germans from acquiring them.

From 1903 to 1920 the United States intervened often in Latin America to protect the canal, promote regional stability, and exclude foreign influence. One problem worrying American policymakers was the scale of Latin American debts to European powers. Many countries in the Western Hemisphere owed money to European governments and banks, but often these nations were poor, prone to revolution, and unable to pay. The situation invited European intervention. In 1902 Venezuela defaulted on debts; England, Germany, and Italy sent Venezuela an ultimatum and blockaded its ports. American pressure forced a settlement of the issue, but the general problem remained.

Roosevelt was concerned about it, and in 1904, when the Dominican Republic defaulted on its debts, he was ready with a major announcement. Known as the Roosevelt Corollary of the Monroe Doctrine, the policy warned Latin American nations to keep their affairs in order or face American intervention.

Applying the new policy immediately, Roosevelt in 1905 took charge of the Dominican Republic's revenue system. American officials collected customs and saw to the payment of debt. Within two years Roosevelt also established protectorates in Cuba and Panama. In 1912 the United States Senate added the Lodge Corollary, which warned foreign corporations not to purchase harbors and other sites of military significance in Latin America. Continued by Taft, Wilson, and other presidents, the Roosevelt Corollary guided American policy in Latin America until the 1930s, when Franklin D. Roosevelt's Good Neighbor policy replaced it.

Ventures in the Far East

The Open Door policy toward China (see chapter 21) and possession of the Philippine Islands shaped American actions in the Far East. Congress refused to arm the Philippines, and the islands were vulnerable to the growing power of Japan. Roosevelt wanted to balance Russian and Japanese power, and he was not unhappy at first when war broke out between them in 1904. As

■ *A cartoon from* Judge *entitled "The World's Constable." The Roosevelt Corollary claimed the right of the U.S. to exercise "an international police power."*

Japan won victory after victory, however, Roosevelt grew worried. He offered to mediate the conflict, and both Russia and Japan accepted: Russia because it was losing, and Japan because it was financially drained.

In August 1905 Roosevelt convened a peace conference at Portsmouth, New Hampshire. The conference ended the war, but Japan emerged as the dominant force in the Far East. Adjusting policy, Roosevelt sent Secretary of War Taft to Tokyo to negotiate the Taft-Katsura Agreement (1905), which recognized Japan's dominance over Korea in return for its promise not to invade the Philippines. Giving Japan a free hand in Korea violated the Open Door policy, but Roosevelt argued that he had little choice.

In a show of strength, he sent the American fleet around the world, including a stop in Tokyo in October 1908. Critics at home predicted dire consequences, and European naval experts felt certain Japan would attack the fleet. Instead, the Japanese welcomed it, even posting ads to sell the sailors Mitsukoshi washing powder to "rid yourselves of the seven blemishes on the way home." For the moment Japanese-American relations improved. In 1908 the two nations signed the comprehensive Root-Takahira Agreement in which they promised to maintain the status quo in the Pacific, uphold the Open Door, and support Chinese independence.

In later years tensions grew in the Far East. The segregation of Japanese children in San Francisco schools in 1906 aroused Japan's resentment; anger mounted in 1913 when the California legislature prohibited Japanese residents from owning property in the state. At the start of the First World War, Japan seized some German colonies, and in 1915 it issued the Twenty-One Demands insisting on authority over China. Coveting an Asian empire, Japan eyed American possessions in the Pacific.

Taft and Dollar Diplomacy

In foreign as well as domestic affairs, President Taft tried to continue Roosevelt's policies. For secretary of state he chose Philander C. Knox, Roosevelt's attorney general, and together they pursued a policy of "dollar diplomacy" to promote American financial and business interests abroad. The policy had profit-seeking motives, but it also aimed to substitute economic ties for military alliances and bring lasting peace.

Intent, like Roosevelt, on supremacy in the Caribbean, Taft worked to replace European loans with American ones, thereby reducing the danger of outside meddling. In 1909 he asked American bankers to assume the Honduran debt in order to fend off English bondholders. A year later he persuaded them to take over the assets of the National Bank of Haiti, and in 1911 he helped Nicaragua secure a large loan in return for American control of Nicaragua's National Bank. When Nicaraguans revolted against the agreement, Taft sent marines to put them down. A marine detachment remained in the country intermittently until the 1930s.

In the Far East, Knox worked closely with Willard Straight, an agent of American bankers, who argued that dollar diplomacy was the financial arm of the Open Door. Straight had close ties to Edward H. Harriman, the railroad magnate, who wanted to build railroads in Manchuria. Roosevelt had tacitly promised Japan he would keep American investors out of the area, and Knox's plan reversed the policy. Trying to organize an international syndicate to loan China money to purchase the Manchurian railroads,

Knox approached England, Japan, and Russia. In January 1910 all three turned him down.

The outcome was a blow to American policy and prestige in Asia. Russia and Japan found reasons to cooperate with each other, and they staked out spheres of influence in violation of the Open Door. Japan resented Taft's initiatives in Manchuria, and China's distrust of the United States deepened. Instead of cultivating friendship, as Roosevelt had envisioned, Taft started an intense rivalry with Japan for commercial advantage in China.

Foreign Policy Under Wilson

When he took office in 1913, Woodrow Wilson knew little about foreign policy. As a Princeton professor, he had studied Congress and the presidency, but his books made only passing reference to foreign issues, and during the 1912 campaign he mentioned foreign policy only when it affected domestic concerns. "It would be the irony of fate if my administration had to deal chiefly with foreign affairs," he said to a friend just before becoming president. And so it was. During his two terms Wilson faced crisis after crisis in foreign affairs, including the outbreak of World War I.

A supremely self-confident man, Wilson conducted his own diplomacy. He composed important diplomatic notes on his own typewriter, sent personal emissaries abroad, and carried on major negotiations without the knowledge of his secretaries of state. Failing to find the right persons for key diplomatic posts, he filled these positions with party regulars like James W. Gerard, his ambassador to Germany, for whom he had contempt. On Gerard's dispatches, Wilson penciled notes: "Ordinarily our Ambassador ought to be backed up as [a matter] of course, but—this ass? It is hard to take it seriously." Or, the next day: "Who can fathom this? I wish they would hand this idiot his passports!"

The idealistic Wilson believed in a principled, ethical world in which militarism, colonialism, and war were brought under control. He stressed moral purposes over material interests and said during one crisis: "The force of America is the force of moral principle." Rejecting the policy of dollar diplomacy, Wilson initially chose a course of moral diplomacy, designed to bring right to the world, preserve peace, and extend to other peoples the blessings of democracy.

Conducting Moral Diplomacy

William Jennings Bryan, whom Wilson appointed as secretary of state, was also an amateur in foreign relations. Trusting in the common people, he was skeptical of experts in the State Department. To key posts abroad he appointed "deserving Democrats," believing they could do the job as well as career diplomats. Bryan was a fervent pacifist, and like Wilson, he believed in the American duty to "help" less-favored nations.

In 1913 and 1914 he embarked on an idealistic campaign to negotiate treaties of arbitration throughout the world. Known as "cooling-off" treaties, they provided for submitting all international disputes to permanent commissions of investigation. Neither party could declare war or increase armaments until the investigation ended, usually within one year. The idea drew on the era's confidence in commissions and the sense that human reason, given time for emotions to fade, could settle problems without war. Bryan negotiated cooling-off treaties with thirty nations, including Great Britain, France, and Italy. Germany refused to sign one. Based on a generous idea, the treaties were naive, and they did not work.

Wilson and Bryan promised a dramatic new approach in Latin America, concerned not with the "pursuit of material interest" but with "human rights" and "national integrity." Signaling the change, in 1913 they negotiated the treaty with Colombia apologizing for Roosevelt's Panamanian policy. Yet in the end Wilson, distracted by other problems and impatient with the results of his idealistic approach, continued the Roosevelt-Taft policies. He defended the Monroe Doctrine, gave unspoken support to the Roosevelt Corollary, and intervened in Latin America more than had either Roosevelt or Taft.

In 1914 Wilson negotiated a treaty with Nicaragua to grant the United States exclusive rights to build a canal and lease sites for naval bases. This treaty made Nicaragua an American satellite. In 1915 he sent marines into Haiti to quell a revolution; they stayed until 1934. In 1916 he occupied

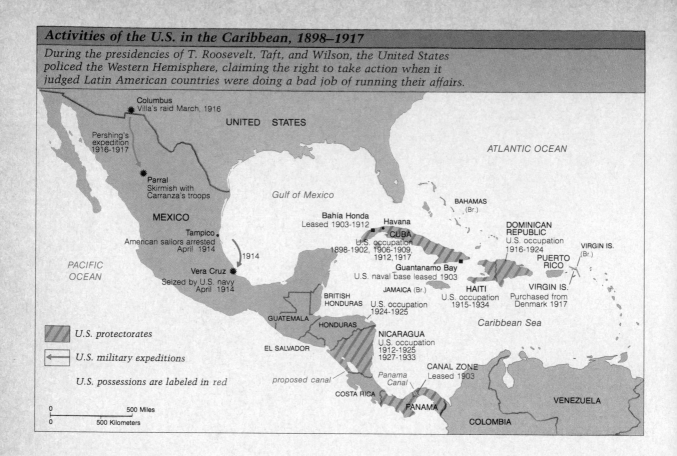

Activities of the U.S. in the Caribbean, 1898–1917

During the presidencies of T. Roosevelt, Taft, and Wilson, the United States policed the Western Hemisphere, claiming the right to take action when it judged Latin American countries were doing a bad job of running their affairs.

Columbus
Villa's raid March, 1916

UNITED STATES

Pershing's expedition 1916-1917

Parral
Skirmish with Carranza's troops

Gulf of Mexico

ATLANTIC OCEAN

BAHAMAS (Br.)

MEXICO

Bahia Honda
Leased 1903-1912

Havana

DOMINICAN REPUBLIC
U.S. occupation 1916-1924

Tampico
American sailors arrested April 1914

CUBA
U.S. occupation 1898-1902, 1906-1909, 1912,1917

VIRGIN IS. (Br.)

PUERTO RICO

PACIFIC OCEAN

1914

Vera Cruz
Seized by U.S. navy April 1914

Guantanamo Bay
U.S. naval base leased 1903

HAITI
U.S. occupation 1915-1934

VIRGIN IS.
Purchased from Denmark 1917

JAMAICA (Br.)

BRITISH HONDURAS
U.S. occupation 1924-1925

Caribbean Sea

GUATEMALA

HONDURAS

U.S. protectorates

NICARAGUA
U.S. occupation 1912-1925 1927-1933

EL SALVADOR

U.S. military expeditions

U.S. possessions are labeled in red

proposed canal

Panama Canal

CANAL ZONE
Leased 1903

VENEZUELA

COSTA RICA

PANAMA

0   500 Miles
0   500 Kilometers

COLOMBIA

the Dominican Republic, establishing a protectorate that lasted until 1924. By 1917 American troops "protected" Nicaragua, Haiti, the Dominican Republic, and Cuba—four nations that were U.S. dependencies in all but name.

Troubles Across the Border

Porfirio Díaz, president of Mexico for thirty-seven years, was overthrown in 1911. Díaz had encouraged foreign investments in Mexican mines, railroads, oil, and land; by 1913 Americans had invested over $1 billion. Most Mexicans remained poor and uneducated, however; his overthrow led to a decade of violence that tested Wilson's policies and brought the United States close to war with Mexico.

A liberal reformer, Francisco I. Madero, followed Díaz as president in 1911. But Madero could not keep order in the troubled country, and opponents of his reforms undermined him. With support from wealthy landowners, the army, and

the Catholic Church, General Victoriano Huerta ousted Madero in 1913, threw him in jail, and murdered him. Most European nations immediately recognized Huerta, but Wilson, calling him a "butcher," refused to do so. Instead, he announced a new policy toward revolutionary regimes in Latin America. To win American recognition, they must not only exercise power but reflect "a just government based upon law, not upon arbitrary or irregular force."

On that basis Wilson withheld recognition from Huerta and maneuvered to oust him. Early in 1914 he stationed naval units off Mexico's ports to cut off arms shipments to the Huerta regime, but the action produced trouble. On April 9, 1914, several American sailors, ashore in Tampico to purchase supplies, were arrested. They were promptly released, but the American admiral demanded an apology and a twenty-one-gun salute to the American flag. Huerta agreed—if the Americans also saluted the Mexican flag.

Wilson asked Congress for authority to use military force if needed; then just as Congress

■ *The goal of his policy in Latin America, Wilson once said, was "to teach the South American republics to elect good men." In the cartoon, Wilson shakes his finger at Mexico in obvious disapproval of the Mexican Revolution and Huerta's government. The President fared little better with Carranza, Huerta's successor. The troops that Wilson ordered into México to seize Pancho Villa clashed twice with Carranza's army.*

acted, he learned that a German ship was landing arms at Vera Cruz on Mexico's eastern coast. With Wilson's approval, American warships shelled the harbor, and marines went ashore. Against heavy resistance, they took the city. Outraged, Mexicans of all factions denounced the invasion, and for a time the two countries hovered on the edge of war.

Retreating hastily, Wilson explained that he desired only to help Mexico. Argentina, Brazil, and Chile came to his aid with an offer to mediate the dispute, and tensions eased. In July 1914, cut off from funds, Huerta resigned. Wilson recognized the new government, headed by Venustiano Carranza, an associate of Madero. Early in 1916, Francisco ("Pancho") Villa, one of Carranza's generals, revolted. Hoping to goad the United States into an action that would help him seize power, he raided border towns, injuring American civilians. In January, he removed seventeen Americans from a train in Mexico and murdered them. Two months later he invaded Columbus, New Mexico, killing sixteen Americans and burning the town. (See the picture essay on the Mexican-American experience following p. 704.)

Stationing militia along the border, Wilson ordered General John J. Pershing on a punitive expedition to seize Villa in Mexico. Pershing led six thousand troops deep into Mexican territory. At first, Carranza agreed to the drive, but as the Americans pushed farther and farther into his country he changed his mind. As the wily Villa eluded Pershing, Carranza protested bitterly, and Wilson, worried about events in Europe, ordered Pershing home.

Wilson's policy had laudable goals; he wanted to help the Mexicans achieve political and agrarian reform, but his motives and methods were condescending. Wilson tried to impose gradual, progressive reform on a society sharply divided along class and other lines. With little forethought, he interfered in the affairs of another country, and in doing so he revealed the themes—moralism, combined with pragmatic self-interest and a desire for peace—that also shaped his policies in Europe.

Toward War

In May 1914, Colonel Edward M. House, Wilson's close friend and personal adviser, sailed to Europe on a fact-finding mission. Tensions there were rising. "The situation is extraordinary," he reported to Wilson. "It is jingoism [extreme nationalism] run stark mad. . . . There is too much hatred, too many jealousies."

Large armies dominated the European continent. A web of alliances entangled nations, maximizing the risk that a local conflict could produce a wider war. In Germany the ambitious Kaiser Wilhelm II coveted a world empire to match those of Britain and France. Germany had military treaties with Turkey and Austria-Hungary, a sprawling Central European country of many nationalities. Linked in another alliance, England, France, and Russia agreed to aid each other in case of attack.

On June 28, 1914, a Balkan assassin in the service of Serbia murdered Archduke Franz Ferdinand, heir to the Austro-Hungarian throne. With-

in weeks Germany, Turkey, and Austria-Hungary (the Central Powers) were at war with England, France, and Russia (the Allied Powers). Americans were shocked at the events. "I had a feeling that the end of things had come . . . ," one of Wilson's cabinet members said. "I stopped in my tracks, dazed and horror-stricken." Wilson immediately proclaimed neutrality and asked Americans to remain "impartial in thought as well as in action."

The war, he said, was one "with which we have nothing to do, whose causes cannot touch us." In private, Wilson was stunned. A man who loved peace, he had long admired the British parliamentary system, and he respected the leaders of the British Liberal party, who supported social programs akin to his own. "Everything I love most in the world," he said, "is at stake."

The Neutrality Policy

In general Americans accepted neutrality. They saw no need to enter the conflict, especially after

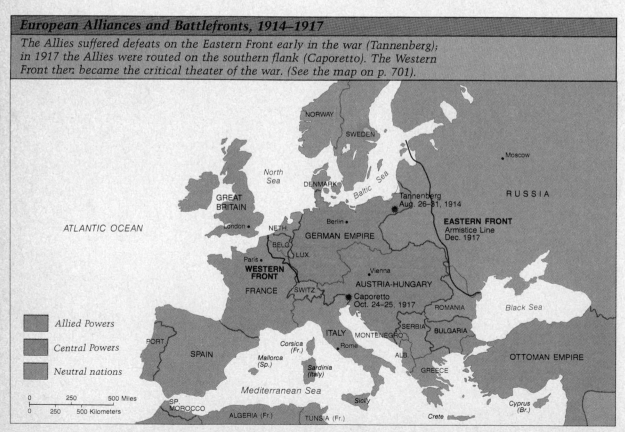

European Alliances and Battlefronts, 1914–1917

The Allies suffered defeats on the Eastern Front early in the war (Tannenberg); in 1917 the Allies were routed on the southern flank (Caporetto). The Western Front then became the critical theater of the war. (See the map on p. 701).

the Allies in September 1914 halted the first German drive toward Paris. They resisted involvement in other countries' problems and had a tradition of freedom from foreign entanglements. Among progressives, there was added reason to resist. War violated the very spirit of progressive reform. Why demand safer factories and then kill men by the millions in war?

To many progressives, England represented international finance, an institution they detested. Germany, on the other hand, had pioneered some of their favorite social reforms. Furthermore, progressives and others tended to put the blame for war on the greed of "munition manufacturers, stockbrokers, and bond dealers" eager for wartime profits. "Do you want to know the cause of the war?" Henry Ford, who was no progressive, asked. "It is capitalism, greed, the dirty hunger for dollars." Above all, progressives were sure that war would end reform. It consumed money and attention; it inflamed emotions.

As a result, Jane Addams, Florence Kelley, Frederic C. Howe, Lillian Wald, and other progressives fought to keep the United States out of war. In late 1915 they formed the American Union Against Militarism, to throw, they said, "a monkey wrench into the machinery" of war. Throughout 1915 and 1916 *La Follette's Magazine*, the voice of the progressive leader, railed against the Morgans, Rockefellers, Du Ponts, and "the thirty-eight corporations most benefited by war orders." In 1915 Addams and Wald helped organize the League to Limit Armament, and shortly thereafter, Addams and Carrie Chapman Catt formed the Woman's Peace Party to organize women against the war.

The war's outbreak also tugged at the emotions of millions of immigrant Americans. Those who came from the British Isles tended to support the Allies; those from Ireland tended to support Germany, hoping that Britain's wartime troubles might free their homeland from British domination. The large population of German-Americans often sympathized with the Central Powers. But many people thought that, in a nation of immigrants, a policy of neutrality offered benefits from a domestic point of view as well as from the viewpoint of foreign policy.

At the deepest level, a majority in the country, bound by common language and institutions, sympathized with the Allies and blamed Germa-

Although Germany's invasion of Belgium and reports of German atrocities shocked Americans, most still adhered to the attitude expressed in the cartoon above: "Don't mix in a family quarrel."

REMEMBER BELGIUM

Buy Bonds Fourth Liberty Loan

ny for the war. Like Wilson, many Americans admired English literature, customs, and law; they remembered Lafayette and the times when France had helped the United States in its early years. Germany, on the other hand, seemed arrogant and militaristic. When the war began, it invaded Belgium to strike at France and violated a treaty which the German chancellor called "just a scrap of paper." Many Americans resented the violation, and they liked it even less when German troops executed Belgian civilians who resisted.

Both sides sought to sway American opinion, and fierce propaganda campaigns flourished. The German Literary Defense Committee distributed over a million pamphlets during the first year of the war. German propaganda tended to stress strength and will; Allied propaganda called on historical ties and took advantage of German atrocities, both real and alleged. In the end, the propaganda probably made little difference. Ties of heritage and the course of the war, not propaganda, decided the American position. At the outset, whichever side they cheered for, Americans of all persuasions preferred simply to remain at peace.

Freedom of the Seas

The demands of trade tested American neutrality and confronted Wilson with difficult choices. Under international law, neutral countries were permitted to trade in nonmilitary goods with all belligerent countries. But Great Britain controlled the seas, and it intended to cut off shipments of war materials to the Central Powers.

As soon as war broke out, Britain blockaded German ports and limited the goods Americans could sell to Germany. American ships had to carry cargoes to neutral ports from which, after examination, they could be carried to Germany. As time passed, Britain stepped up the economic sanctions by forbidding the shipment to Germany of all foodstuffs and most raw materials, seizing and censoring mail, and "blacklisting" American firms that dealt directly with the Central Powers. British ships often stopped American ships and confiscated cargoes.

Again and again Wilson protested against such infringements on neutral rights. Sometimes Britain complied, sometimes not, and Wilson often grew angry. But needing American support and supplies, Britain pursued a careful strategy to disrupt German-American trade without disrupting Anglo-American relations. After forbidding cotton shipments to Germany in 1915, it agreed to buy enough cotton to make up for the losses. When necessary it also promised to reimburse American businesses after war's end.

Other than the German U-boats, there were no constraints on trade with the Allies, and a flood of Allied war orders fueled the American economy. England and France bought huge amounts of arms, grain, cotton, and clothing. To finance the purchases, the Allies turned to American bankers for loans. By 1917 loans to Allied governments

exceeded $2 billion, while loans to Germany came to only $27 million.

Loans and trade drew the United States ever closer to the Allied cause. And even though Wilson often protested English maritime policy, the protests involved American goods and money whereas Germany's submarine policy threatened American lives.

The U-Boat Threat

A relatively new weapon, the *Unterseeboot*, or submarine, strained the guidelines of international law. Traditional law required a submarine to surface, warn the target to stop, send a boarding party to check papers and cargo, then allow time for passengers and crew to board lifeboats before sinking the vessel. Flimsy and slow, submarines could ill-afford to surface while the prey radioed for help. If they did surface, they might be rammed or blown up by deck guns.

When Germany announced the submarine campaign in February 1915, Wilson protested sharply, calling the sinking of merchant ships without checking cargo "a wanton act." The Germans promised not to sink American ships—an agreement that lasted until 1917—and thereafter the issue became the right of Americans to sail on the ships of belligerent nations. In March an American citizen aboard the British liner *Falaba* perished when the ship was torpedoed off the Irish coast. Bryan urged Wilson to forbid Americans to travel in the war zones, but the President, determined to stand by the principles of international law, refused.

Wilson reacted more harshly in May and August of 1915 when U-boats sank the *Lusitania* and *Arabic*. He demanded that the Germans protect passenger vessels and pay for American losses. Fearing war, Bryan resigned as secretary of state and was replaced by Robert Lansing, a lawyer and counselor in the State Department. Lansing favored the Allies and believed that democracy was threatened in a world dominated by Germany. He urged strong stands against German violations of American neutrality.

In February 1916 Germany declared unrestricted submarine warfare against all *armed* ships. Lansing protested and told Germany it would be held strictly accountable for American losses. A month later, a U-boat torpedoed the unarmed French channel steamer, *Sussex*, without warning, injuring several Americans. Arguing that the sinking violated the *Arabic* pledge, Lansing urged Wilson to break relations with Germany. Wilson rejected the advice, but on April 18 sent an ultimatum to Germany that unless it immediately called off attacks on cargo and passenger ships, the United States would sever relations.

The kaiser, convinced he did not yet have enough submarines to risk war, yielded. In the *Sussex* pledge of May 4, 1916, he agreed to Wilson's demands and promised to shoot on sight only ships of the enemy's navy. But he attached the condition that the United States compel the Allies to end their blockade and comply with international law. Wilson accepted the pledge but turned down the condition.

The *Sussex* pledge marked the beginning of a short period of friendly relations between Germany and the United States. The agreement applied not only to passenger liners, but to *all* merchant ships, belligerent or not. There was one problem: Wilson had taken such a strong position that if Germany renewed submarine warfare on merchant shipping, war was likely. But most Americans viewed the agreement as a diplomatic stroke for peace by Wilson, and the issues of peace and preparedness dominated the presidential election of 1916.

"He Kept Us Out of War"

The "preparedness" issue pitted antiwar groups against those who wanted to prepare for war. The American Rights Committee, the National Security League, and other groups urged stepped-up military measures in case of war. In the summer of 1915 they persuaded the War Department to hold a training camp in Plattsburg, New York, in which regular army officers trained twelve hundred civilian volunteers in modern warfare. The following summer sixteen thousand volunteers participated in such training camps.

Bellicose as always, Teddy Roosevelt led the preparedness campaign. He called Wilson "yellow" for not pressing Germany harder and scoffed at the popular song "I Didn't Raise My Boy to Be a Soldier," which he compared to singing "I Didn't Raise My Girl to Be a Mother." Defending the

■ *Roosevelt's campaign for preparedness became a personal attack on Wilson, whom he called a "coward" and "weakling."*

military's state of readiness, Wilson refused to be stampeded just because "some amongst us are nervous and excited." In fact, when government revenue dropped in 1915, he cut military appropriations.

Wilson's position was attacked from both sides as preparedness advocates charged cowardice, while pacifists denounced any attempt at military readiness. The difficulty of his situation, plus the growing U-boat crisis, soon changed Wilson's mind. In mid-1915 he asked the War Department to increase military planning, and he quietly notified congressional leaders of a switch in policy. Later that year Wilson approved large increases in the army and navy, a move that upset many peace-minded progressives. In January 1916 he toured the country to promote preparedness, and in June, with an American flag draped over his shoulder, he marched in a giant preparedness parade in Washington.

For their standard-bearer in the presidential election of 1916, the Republicans nominated Charles Evans Hughes, a moderate justice of the Supreme Court. Hughes seemed to have all the qualifications for victory. A former reform governor of New York, he could lure back the Roosevelt Progressives, while at the same time appealing to the Republican conservatives. To woo the Roosevelt wing, Hughes called for a tougher line against Germany, thus allowing the Democrats to label him the "war" candidate. Even so, Roosevelt and others considered Hughes a "bearded iceberg," a dull campaigner who wavered on important issues.

The Democrats renominated Wilson in a convention marked by spontaneous demonstrations for peace. Determined to outdo Republican patriotism, Wilson himself had ordered the convention's theme to be "Americanism." The delegates were to sing "America" and "The Star-Spangled Banner," and to cheer any mention of America and the flag. They did it all dutifully but then broke into spontaneous applause at the mention of Wilson's careful diplomatic moves. As the keynote speaker reviewed them, the delegates shouted: "What did we do? What did we do?" The speaker shouted back: "We didn't go to war! We didn't go to war!"

Picking up the theme, perhaps with reservation, Wilson said in October: "I am not expecting this country to get into war." The campaign slogan, "He kept us out of war" was repeated again and again, and just before the election, the Democrats took full-page ads in leading newspapers:

You Are Working—Not Fighting!
Alive and Happy;—Not Cannon Fodder!
Wilson and Peace with Honor?
            or
Hughes with Roosevelt and War?

On election night, Hughes had swept most of the East, and Wilson retired at 10 P.M., thinking he had lost. During the night the results came in from California, New Mexico, and North Dakota; all supported Wilson—California by a mere 3773 votes. Wilson won with 9.1 million votes against 8.5 million for Hughes. Holding the Democratic South, he carried key states in the Midwest and West and took large portions of the labor and progressive vote. Women—who were then allowed to vote in presidential elections in twelve states—also voted heavily for Wilson.

The Final Months of Peace

Just before election day Great Britain further limited neutral trade, and there were reports from Germany of a renewal of unrestricted submarine

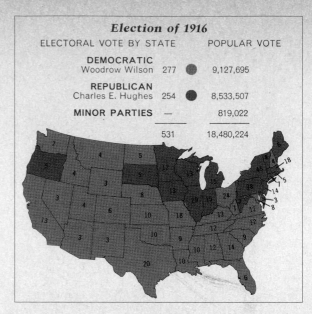

Election of 1916

	ELECTORAL VOTE BY STATE	POPULAR VOTE
DEMOCRATIC Woodrow Wilson	277	9,127,695
REPUBLICAN Charles E. Hughes	254	8,533,507
MINOR PARTIES	—	819,022
	531	18,480,224

warfare. Fresh from his election victory, Wilson redoubled his efforts for peace. Aware that time was running out, he hoped to start negotiations to end the bloodshed and create a peaceful postwar world.

In December 1916, he sent messages to both sides asking them to state their war aims. Should they do so, he pledged the "whole force" of the United States to end the war. The Allies refused, although they promised privately to negotiate if the German terms were reasonable. The Germans replied evasively and in January 1917 revealed their real objectives. Close to forcing Russia out of the war, Germany sensed victory and wanted teritory in eastern Europe, Africa, Belgium, and France.

On January 22, in an eloquent speech before the Senate, Wilson called for a "peace without victory." Outlining his own aims, he urged respect for all nations, freedom of the seas, arms limitations, and a league of nations to keep the peace. "Only a peace between equals can last, only a peace the very principle of which is equality and a common participation in a common benefit." The speech made a great impression on many Europeans, but it was too late. The Germans had decided a few weeks before to unleash the submarines and gamble on a quick end to the war. Even as Wilson spoke, U-boats were in the Atlantic west of Ireland, preparing to attack.

On January 31, the German ambassador in Washington informed Lansing that beginning Feb-

A new and terrifying weapon of the war was the German U-boat, which attacked silently and without warning. Germany's decision to wage unrestricted submarine warfare provoked Wilson into asking for a declaration of war.

ruary 1, U-boats would sink on sight all ships—passenger or merchant, neutral or belligerent, armed or unarmed—in the waters around England and France. Staking everything on a last effort, the Germans calculated that if they could sink six hundred thousand tons of shipping a month, they could defeat England in six months. As he had pledged in 1916, Wilson broke off relations with Germany, although he still hoped for peace.

On February 25 the British government privately gave Wilson a telegram intercepted from Arthur Zimmermann, the German foreign minister, to the German ambassador in Mexico. A day later, Wilson asked Congress for authority to arm merchant ships to deter U-boat attacks. When La Follette and a handful of others threatened to filibuster, Wilson divulged the contents of the Zimmermann telegram. It proposed an alliance with Mexico in case of war with the United States, offering financial support and recovery of Mexico's "lost territory" in New Mexico, Texas, and Arizona.

Spurred by a wave of public indignation, the House passed Wilson's measure, but La Follette and others still blocked action in the Senate. On March 9, 1917, Wilson ordered merchant ships armed on his own authority. Three days later he announced the arming, and on March 13 the navy instructed all vessels to fire on submarines. Between March 12 and March 21, U-boats sank five American ships, and Wilson decided to wait no longer.

He called Congress into special session and at 8:30 in the evening on April 2, 1917, asked for a declaration of war. "It is a fearful thing to lead this great peaceful people into war, into the most terrible and disastrous of all wars, civilization itself seeming to be in the balance. But the right is more precious than peace, and we shall fight for the things which we have always carried nearest our hearts,—for democracy, . . . for the rights and liberties of small nations, for a universal dominion of right by such a concert of free peoples as shall bring peace and safety to all nations and make the world itself at last free."

Congressmen broke into applause and crowded the aisles to congratulate Wilson. "My message today was a message of death for our young men," he said afterward. "How strange it seems to applaud that."

Over There

With a burst of patriotism, the United States entered a war its new allies were in danger of losing. That same month, the Germans sank 881,000 tons of Allied shipping, the highest amount of the war. There were mutinies in the French army; a costly British drive in Flanders stalled. In November the Bolsheviks seized power in Russia and soon signed a separate peace treaty with Germany (see the map on p. 694), freeing German troops to fight in

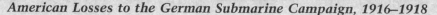

American Losses to the German Submarine Campaign, 1916–1918

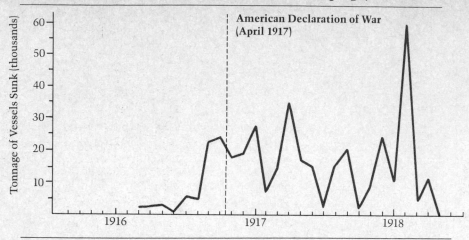

American Declaration of War
(April 1917)

Source: U.S. Department of the Navy, American Ship Casualties of the World War (1923).

the West. German and Austrian forces routed the Italian army on the southern flank and the Allies braced for a spring 1918 offensive.

Mobilization

The United States was not prepared for war. Some Americans hoped the declaration of war itself might daunt the Germans; others hoped money and arms, not troops, would be sufficient to produce victory. "Good Lord!" one senator exclaimed just after war was declared. "You're not going to send soldiers over there, are you?"

Bypassing older generals, Wilson named "Black Jack" Pershing, leader of the Mexican campaign, to head the American Expeditionary Force (AEF). Pershing inherited an army unready for war. In April 1917 it had 200,000 officers and men, equipped with 300,000 old rifles, 1500 machine guns, 55 out-of-date airplanes, and 2 field radio sets. Its most recent battle experience had been chasing Pancho Villa around northern Mexico. It had not caught him.

The armed forces had two war plans: War Plan Orange that provided for a defensive war against Japan in the Pacific, and War Plan Black that countered a possible German attack in the Caribbean. Wilson had ordered military commanders not to plan because it violated neutrality. "When

the Acting Chief of Staff went to look at the secret files where the plans to meet the situation that confronted us should have been found," Pershing later said, "the pigeonhole was empty."

Although some in Congress preferred a voluntary army of the kind that had fought in the Spanish-American War, Wilson turned to conscription, which he felt was both efficient and democratic. In May 1917 Congress passed the Selective Service Act, providing for the registration of all men between the ages of twenty-one and thirty. Early in June 9.5 million men registered. The act ultimately registered 24.2 million men, about 2 million of whom were inducted into the army. Defending the draft, Wilson said it was not really a draft at all, but a "selection from a nation which has volunteered in mass."

War in the Trenches

World War I may have been the most terrible war of all time, more terrible even than the vast devastation of World War II. After the early offensives, the European armies dug themselves into trenches, in places only hundreds of yards apart. Artillery, poison gas, hand grenades, and a new weapon—rapid-fire machine guns—kept them pinned down.

Even in moments of respite, the mud, rats, cold, fear, and disease took a heavy toll. Deafening bombardments shook the earth, and there was a high incidence of shell shock. From time to time troops went "over the top" in an effort to break through, but the costs were enormous. The German offensive at Verdun in 1916 killed 600,000 men; the British lost 20,000 dead on the first day of an offensive on the Somme.

The first American soldiers reached France in June 1917. By March of the following year, 300,000 Americans were there, and by war's end, 2 million men had crossed the Atlantic. No troop ships were sunk, a credit to the British and American navies. In the summer of 1917 Admiral William S. Sims, a brilliant strategist, pushed through a convoy plan that used Allied destroyers to escort merchant vessels across the ocean. At first resisted by English captains who liked to sail alone, the plan soon cut shipping losses in half.

As expected, on March 21, 1918, the Germans launched a massive assault in western Europe. Troops from the Russian front added to the force, and by May they had driven Allied forces back to the Marne River, just fifty miles from Paris. More than 27,000 Americans, including four black regiments, saw their first action. They blocked the Germans at the town of Château-Thierry, and four weeks later forced them out of Belleau Wood, a crucial strongpoint. On July 15 the Germans threw everything into a last drive for Paris, but in three days they were finished. "On the 18th," the German chancellor said, "even the most optimistic among us knew that all was lost. The history of the world was played out in three days."

With the German drive stalled, the Allies counterattacked along the entire front. On September 12, 1918, half a million Americans and a smaller contingent of French drove the Germans from the St. Mihiel salient, twelve miles south of Verdun. Two weeks later, 896,000 Americans attacked between the Meuse River and the Argonne Forest. Focusing on a main railroad supply line for the German army in the West, they broke through in early November, cut the line, and drove the Germans back along the whole front.

The Western Front: U.S. Participation, 1918

The turning point of the war came in July, when the German advance was halted at the Marne. The "Yanks," now a fighting force, were thrown into the breach. They played a dramatic role in stemming the tide and mounting the counteroffensives that ended the war.

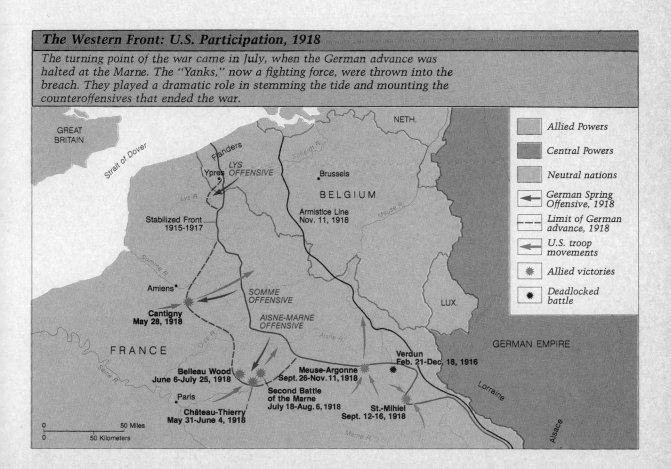

■ *Soldiers in the front-line trenches at the Meuse, October 1918. A scant 1200 yards separated the Allied and the German lines.*

■ *German prisoners and American wounded returning from the front lines of the Meuse-Argonne. More Americans died in that campaign than in the rest of the war.*

The German high command knew that the war was lost. On October 6, 1918, Germany appealed to Wilson for an armistice, and by the end of the month, Turkey, Bulgaria, and Austria-Hungary were out of the war. At 4 A.M. on November 11, Germany signed the armistice. The AEF lost 48,909 dead and 230,000 wounded; losses to disease brought the total of dead to over 112,000.

The American contribution, although small in comparison to the enormous costs to European nations, was vital. Fresh, enthusiastic American troops raised Allied morale; they helped turn the tide at a crucial point in the war. American troops marched down the boulevards of Paris in the parade celebrating victory, but no black soldiers were allowed to march. They were also left out of a French mural depicting the different races in the war, even though black servicemen from the English and French colonies were represented.

Over Here

Victory at the front depended on economic and emotional mobilization at home. Consolidating federal authority, Wilson moved quickly in 1917 and 1918 to organize war production and distribution. An idealist who knew how to sway public opinion, he also recognized the need to enlist American emotions. To him, the war for people's minds, the "conquest of their convictions," was as vital as events on the battlefield.

The Conquest of Convictions

A week after war was declared, Wilson formed the Committee on Public Information (CPI) and asked George Creel, an outspoken progressive journalist, to head it. Creel hired other progressives like Ida Tarbell and Ray Stannard Baker and recruited thousands of people in the arts, advertising, and film industries to publicize the war. He worked out a system of voluntary censorship with the press, plastered walls with colorful posters, and issued more than 75 million pamphlets.

Creel also enlisted 75,000 "four-minute men" to give quick speeches at public gatherings and places of entertainment on "Why We Are Fighting" and "The Meaning of America." At first they were instructed to stress facts and stay away from hate, but by the beginning of 1918 the instructions shifted to portray the Germans as blood-

■ *Film actor Douglas Fairbanks calls for the purchase of war bonds at a rally on Wall Street.*

thirsty Huns bent on world conquest. Exploiting a new medium, the CPI promoted films like *The Prussian Cur* and *The Kaiser, the Beast of Berlin*. Creel secretly subsidized several prowar groups and formed the CPI's Division of Industrial Relations to rally labor to the war.

Helped along by the propaganda campaign, anti-German sentiment spread rapidly. Many schools stopped offering instruction in the German language, California's state education board calling it a language "of autocracy, brutality, and hatred." Sauerkraut became "liberty cabbage"; saloon-keepers removed pretzels from the bar. Orchestral works by Bach, Beethoven, and Brahms vanished from some symphonic programs, and the New York Philharmonic agreed not to perform the music of living German composers. Government agents harassed Karl Muck, the conductor of the Boston Symphony, imprisoned him for over a year, and then after the war ended, deported him. German-Americans and antiwar figures were badgered, beaten, and in some cases killed.

Vigilantism, sparked often by superpatriotism of a ruthless sort, flourished. Frequently if focused on radical antiwar figures like Frank Little, an IWW official in Butte, Montana, who was taken from his boardinghouse in August 1917, tied to the rear of an automobile, and dragged through the streets until his kneecaps were scraped off. Little was then hanged from a railroad trestle. In April 1918 a Missouri mob seized Robert Prager, a young man whose sole crime was being born in Germany. They bound him with an American flag, paraded him through town, and then lynched him. A jury acquitted the mob's members—who wore red, white, and blue ribbons to court—as one juror shouted: "Well, I guess nobody can say we aren't loyal now."

Rather than curbing the repression, Wilson encouraged it. "Woe be to the man or group of men that seeks to stand in our way," he told peace advocates soon after the war began. At his request, Congress passed the Espionage Act of 1917, which imposed sentences of up to twenty years in prison for persons found guilty of aiding the enemy, obstructing recruitment of soldiers, or encouraging disloyalty. It allowed the postmaster general to remove from the mails materials that incited treason or insurrection. The Trading-with-the-Enemy Act of 1917 authorized the government to censor the foreign-language press.

In 1918 Congress passed the Sedition Act, imposing harsh penalties on anyone using "disloyal,

■ *"The return of the Goth," an illustration by Boardman Robinson, expresses what many Americans really thought of Germany.*

profane, scurrilous, or abusive language" about the government, flag, or uniform. In all, over fifteen hundred persons were arrested under the new laws. People indicted or imprisoned included a Californian who laughed at rookies drilling at an army camp, a woman who greeted a Red Cross solicitor in a "hostile" way, and an editor who printed the sentence: "We must make the world safe for democracy even if we have to 'bean' the Goddess of Liberty to do it."

The sedition laws clearly went beyond any clear or present danger. There were, to be sure, German spies in the country, and the Germans wanted to encourage strikes in American arms factories. But the danger did not warrant a nationwide program of repression. Conservatives seized on the laws to stamp out socialists. Wilson's postmaster general banned from the mails more than a dozen socialist publications, including the *Appeal to Reason* which went to over half a million people weekly. In 1918 Eugene V. Debs, the Socialist party leader, delivered a speech denouncing capitalism and the war. He was convicted for violation of the Espionage Act and spent the war in a penitentiary in Atlanta. Nominated as the Socialist party candidate in the presidential election of 1920, Debs—prisoner

9653—won nearly a million votes, but the Socialist movement never fully recovered from the repression of the war.

A Bureaucratic War

Quick, effective action was needed to win the war, and to meet the need, Wilson and Congress set up an array of new federal agencies, nearly five thousand in all. Staffed largely by businessmen, the agencies drew on funds and powers of a hitherto unknown scope. At night the secretary of the treasury sat in bed, a yellow pad on his knees, adding up the money needed to finance the war. "The noughts attached to the many millions were so boisterous and prolific," he later said, "that, at times, they would run clear over the edge of the paper."

The War Industries Board, one of the most powerful of the agencies, oversaw the production of all American factories. Headed by millionaire Bernard M. Baruch, a Wall Street broker and speculator, it determined priorities, allocated raw materials, and fixed prices. It told manufacturers what they could and could not make. The WIB set the output of steel and regulated the number of stops on elevators. Working closely with business, Baruch for a time acted as the dictator of the American economy.

Herbert Hoover, the hero of a campaign to feed starving Belgians, headed a new Food Administration, and he set out with customary energy to supply food to the armies overseas. Appealing to the "spirit of self-sacrifice," Hoover convinced people to save food by observing "meatless" and "wheatless" days. He fixed prices to boost production, bought and distributed wheat, and encouraged people to plant "victory gardens" behind homes, churches, and schools. He sent half a million persons door-to-door to get housewives to sign cards pledging their cooperation. One householder—Wilson—set an example by grazing sheep on the White House lawn.

At another new agency, the Fuel Administration, Harry A. Garfield, the president of Williams College, introduced daylight saving time, rationed coal and oil, and imposed gasless days when motorists could not drive. To save coal, he shut down nonessential factories one day a week, and in January 1918, he closed all factories east of

MEXICAN-AMERICAN EXPERIENCE IN THE SOUTHWEST

From California to Texas in the early 1820s, one could enter the northern fringes of a rich civilization born out of three centuries of contacts between the Spanish and the Indians. Already a distinctly Mexican culture was emerging from the blend of European and native societies. Spaniards, with little concept of race, had mated and married Indian girls much more frequently than had Englishmen. They had fathered children (called Mestizos) who grew up knowing two worlds and who had developed a culture that reflected both. Missionaries had carried Spanish language, customs, manners, and morals to Apaches, Tejones, and other Indian tribes. Because the lower clergy had often championed the freedom of Indians from the tyranny of Spanish landlords, many natives had flocked to the church. Indians had blended Catholic beliefs with their own, while teaching Spaniards about both foods and farming methods.

By the early 1830s this borderlands Hispanic society flourished among thirty thousand people thinly spread from the Rio Grande Valley in Texas to northern California. Most of these people lived on *ranchos* (several hundred thousand others still lived as Indians) where cattle and horses produced colorful traditions. Here the American cowboy, or *vaquero* as the Mexicans called him, was born. His hat, his fine leather tooling of saddles, boots, and belts reflected the ornate artistry of Spanish culture. To fight boredom on these sprawling and lonely spreads, *vaqueros* made sport of roping and branding, the stuff of later rodeos. Both men and women became expert equestrians and, especially in California, took to the ancient Spanish sport of bull-baiting.

Americans who visited the West in the period often painted a romantic picture of a life both lavish and violent among colorful people. On wealthy *ranchos* it could be all that. On other

One of the last of the Spanish viceroys in Mexico, Don Jose de Iturrigara shown here with his family, about 1805.

Widespread and well-accepted, intermarriage between Spaniards and Indians in the early colonial period produced an interesting blend of racial types. Here an anonymous artist depicts a mestizo father, Spanish mother, and their child.

vast tracts of sun-baked land, especially in south Texas, *ranchero* families and the *vaqueros* lived among mesquites and cacti. Houses were made of mud bricks. Luxuries were few.

Life usually revolved around an extended family of several generations residing together. Children and young adults, even after marriage, accepted leadership and discipline from parents. They respected elders and valued family solidarity. Fathers headed these clans, but women enjoyed a status their English-American counterparts at the time never had. Wives held half-title to all property in a marriage (producing community property laws in many southwestern states). Women often ran business affairs on the *ranchos*.

When the United States conquered this civilization in the 1840s, there were immense differences between rich and poor. But soon wealthy landowners, middle-class farmers, and poverty-stricken peasants all shared the common fate of conquered people. Over the next half-century, Americans stripped the Mexicans of their land. They passed laws barring Chinese and Mexicans from working in the California mines. Squatters carved up ranches and then established English-speaking courts and boards to approve their thefts. Armed mobs sometimes lynched Mexican gold miners or burned crops and slaughtered cattle. In Texas, racist white settlers believed Mexicans were too inferior to deserve the land. So they taxed the *rancheros* out of business or used Texas Rangers to scare them away.

The mounted herdsmen (vaquero) tended the great cattle herds of the California (ranchero) landowners.

Early nineteenth-century drawing of a monk giving alms to an Indian child.

This intrepid Californio horsewoman is hoping to ground the bull by twisting his tail.

Such violence produced Mexican folk heroes who fought back. In California in the 1850s Joaquin Murieta killed Anglos suspected of mistreating Mexicans while Juan Cortina did the same in south Texas. To white authorities these men were bandits. To Mexican-Americans they were gallant heroes, defenders of home and hearth, inspirations for folk songs and legends.

Conquest disrupted families, drove most Mexican-Americans into poverty, and even undermined many extended families. Yet Mexican-Americans clung to their traditional culture: religious ceremonies for the living and the dead, unique foods and festivals, respect for tradition and authority, and a brightly hued palette of artistic expression.

At the turn of the century, fewer than three hundred thousand Mexican-Americans lived in the United States. In the next thirty years more than a million newcomers joined their ranks, fleeing the poverty of Mexico or the revolution that erupted there in 1910 and produced bloodshed for a decade. Between 1900 and 1910 the Mexican population of Texas and New Mexico nearly doubled; in Arizona it more than doubled; in California it quadrupled. In all four states it doubled again between 1910 and 1920. In time, this fresh class of Mexican-Americans and their children transformed the Southwest. They built most of the early highways in Texas, New Mexico, and Arizona; dug the irrigation ditches that produced an agricultural miracle in the Lower Rio

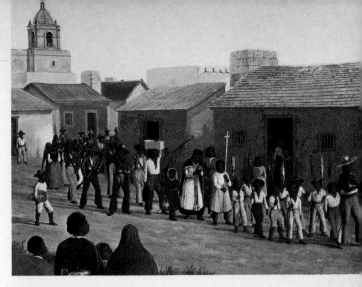

San Antonio was a Mexican city of lime-washed adobe houses in 1843 when Jean Louis Gentilz painted these scenes: a religious procession at the funeral of an infant; a busy market street and a festival featuring the rousing fandango dance.

Grande Valley of Texas; laid railroad track; and picked the cotton and vegetables that clothed and fed millions of other Americans. Many lived in shacks and shanties along the railroad tracks, isolated in a separate Spanish-speaking world.

Yet American society imposed harsh rules on these people. Segregation laws and practices often kept them out of hotels and other public accommodations. Schools either barred them or, ironically, tried to anglicize them in segregated facilities. Teachers changed Juan to Johnny, Araceli to Sally, and permitted no Spanish to be spoken on the playground. Yet again, Mexican-Americans clung to their culture. Their overcrowded *barrios* (neighborhoods) were both pockets of poverty and cultural islands of emotional comforts—family life, foods, and festivals remained familiar. During World War I many Mexican-Americans carried their culture into northern cities—Saint Louis, Chicago, Detroit, and Pittsburgh—as jobs opened there. Barrios developed in all these cities and elsewhere.

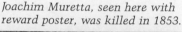

Joachim Muretta, seen here with reward poster, was killed in 1853.

New Mexico, 1897. No costly machinery, but goats, thresh the crop.

The Lugo family, Mexican-Americans of Southern California, 1888.

the Mississippi for four days to divert coal to munitions ships stranded in New York harbor. A fourth agency, the Railroad Administration, dictated rail traffic over nearly four hundred thousand miles of track—standardizing rates, limiting passenger travel, and speeding arms shipments. The War Shipping Board coordinated shipping, the Emergency Fleet Corporation supervised shipbuilding, and the War Trade Board oversaw foreign trade.

As never before, the government intervened in American life. When strikes threatened the telephone and telegraph companies, it simply seized and ran them. Businessmen, paid a nominal dollar a year, flocked to Washington to run the new agencies, and the partnership between government and business grew closer. As government expanded, business expanded as well, responding to wartime contracts. Industries like steel, aluminum, and cigarettes boomed in a war that displayed the triumph of large-scale industrial organization.

Labor in the War

The war also brought organized labor into the partnership with government, although the results were more limited than in the business-government alliance. Samuel Gompers, president of the AFL, served on Wilson's Council of National Defense, an advisory group formed to unify business, labor, and government. Gompers hoped to trade labor peace for labor advances, and he formed a War Committee on Labor to enlist workers' support for the war. With the blessing of the Wilson administration, membership in the AFL and other unions grew from about 2.7 million in 1916 to more than 4 million in 1919.

Hoping to encourage production and avoid strikes, Wilson adopted many of the objectives of the social-justice reformers. He supported an eight-hour day in war-related industries and improved wages and working conditions. In May 1918, he named Felix Frankfurter, a brilliant young law professor, to head a new War Labor Board. The agency standardized wages and hours, and at Wilson's direction, it protected the right of labor to organize and bargain collectively. Although it did not forbid strikes, it used various tactics to discourage them. It enforced decisions

■ War brought the mobilization of American railroads, farms, and factories. (Top) Brass shell casings fabricated at a plant in Toledo, Ohio, are readied for shipment to the Western Front. (Bottom) A woman worker in a defense plant welding with an acetylene torch.

Measuring the Mind

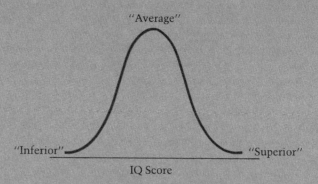

"Average"

"Inferior"   "Superior"

IQ Score

From 1870 to 1920 scientists and physicians explored new ideas about the mind. In Europe the Viennese psychiatrist Sigmund Freud studied the unconscious, which, he thought, shaped human behavior. Russia's Ivan Pavlov tested the conditioned reflex in mental activity (Pavlov's dogs), and in the United States William James, the psychologist and philosopher, examined emotions and linked psychology to everyday problems.

As one way of understanding *the mind*, psychologists studied the mental processes of a great many minds, a task to which the relatively new science of statistics lent a hand. Testing large samples of subjects, they developed the concept of the "normal" and "average," helpful boundaries used to determine an individual's place in the population. In 1890 the psychologist James McKeen Cattell tested one hundred freshmen at the University of Pennsylvania for vision and hearing, sensitivity to pain, reaction time, and memory. He called these examinations by a new name—"mental tests"—and the idea spread. In 1895 the American Psychological Association (APA) set up a special committee to promote the nationwide collection of mental statistics.

Work was underway on both sides of the ocean,

and in 1905 Alfred Binet and Théodore Simon, two French psychologists, devised a metric intelligence scale. Seizing on the idea that until maturity, intelligence increases with age, they tested children of various ages to find an average level of performance for each age. Once they had determined the average, they could compare any child's test performance with it and thus distinguish between the child's "mental age" and chronological age. In 1912 William Stein, a German psychologist, introduced the "Intelligence Quotient," found by dividing a person's mental age by the chronological age. In 1916 Lewis M. Terman of Stanford University improved Binet's test, and the term *I.Q.* became part of the American vocabulary.

Employers and educators, however, remained skeptical of measuring intelligence. Thus, when the United States entered World War I, psychologists at once saw the opportunity to overcome the doubts and prove their theories. Huge numbers of men needed to be recruited, classified, and assigned to units quickly. Why not use the new mental tests? APA leaders formed twelve committees, including one on the Psychological Examination of Recruits, to explore the military uses of psychology.

Preferring to issue promotions on the basis of seniority, the army resisted the "mental meddlers," but the APA persuaded the War Department to make use of the tests. In early 1918 psychological examiners were posted at all training camps to administer the Alpha Test to literates and the Beta Test (with instructions given in pantomime) to illiterates and those who did not understand English. At the start of each Alpha Test, the examiners put the men at ease by explaining that the army was "not looking for crazy people. The aim is to help find out what we are best fitted to do." On the Beta Test, which was made up largely of pictures, the examiners were reminded that Beta men "sometimes sulk and refuse to work."

On the basis of the tests, the examiners classified recruits as "superior," "average," or "inferior." From the "superior" category, they selected men for officer training, a helpful winnowing process in an army that expanded quickly from 9000 officers to 200,000. That task done, they distributed the remaining "superior," "average," and "inferior" men among each military unit. In all, the examiners tested 1.7 million men—by far the largest testing program in human history to that time. To some degree the tests served their purpose, but they also seemed to raise questions about the education and mental ability of many American men.

For one thing, there was the extent of illiteracy —nearly a quarter of the draft-age men in 1918 could neither read nor write. (A third, incidentally, were physically unfit for service.) There was also the limited schooling of the recruits, most of whom had left school between the fifth and seventh grades. More alarming, according to the test results, 47 percent of the white draftees and 89 percent of the black draftees had a "mental age" of twelve years or under, which classified them as "feeble-minded." Did that mean half or more of the American population was feeble-minded?

The tests also turned up racial and national distinctions—or so some of the examiners concluded. Men of "native" backgrounds and "old" immigrant stock (from Northern Europe and the British Isles) tended to score well and fall in the "superior" category; "new" immigrants (from central and southern Europe) tended to score less well and rank as "inferior." Among Russian, Polish, and Italian draftees, more than half were classified as "inferior." Such results came as no surprise to those who had long doubted the intelligence of the "new" immigrants, nor did the fact that 80 percent of the blacks taking the Alpha Test scored in the inferior range.

Some observers, however, wondered what the tests really measured. The APA examiners claimed they measured "native intelligence," but questions about Edgar Allan Poe's poem "The Raven" or the paintings of Rosa Bonheur required answers that native intelligence alone could not supply. When blacks and whites scored comparably on the early Beta Test, the examiners decided that something must be wrong with the test, so they changed the questions until the scores showed the expected racial differences. Most of those taking the Beta Test had never taken a written test before; many had probably never held a pencil.

Still skeptical, the army discontinued the tests the moment the war ended, but what the army rejected, the nation adopted. Businesses, government, and above all, educational institutions found greater and greater uses for intelligence testing. In 1926 the College Entrance Examination Board (CEEB) administered the first Scholastic Aptitude Test (SAT), designed to test "intelligence" and predict performance in college. In 1935 it established scoring ranges from 200 to 800, with the average score set at 500. During World War II SAT tests were widely used. In 1947 the CEEB became part of a new Educational Testing Service that spurred an educational revolution by making intelligence instead of social or economic standing the main criterion of college admissions.

Before long, intelligence testing—the measuring of minds—touched every aspect of American life. Shaping lives and careers, it pushed some people forward and held others back, in the military, industry, the civil service, and higher education. "Intelligence tests . . . " an expert said in 1971, "have more and more become society's instrument for the selection of human resources."

in well-publicized cases; when the Smith and Wesson arms factory in Massachusetts and the Western Union telegraph company disobeyed the WLB's union rules, it took them over.

The WLB also ordered that women be paid equal wages for equal work in war industries. In 1914 the flow of European immigrants suddenly stopped because of the war, and in 1917 the draft began to take large numbers of American men. The result was a labor shortage, filled by women, blacks, and Mexican-Americans. A million women worked in war industries. Some of them took jobs previously held by men, but for the most part, they moved from one set of "women's jobs" into another. From the beginning of the war to the end, the number of women in the work force held steady at about eight million, and unlike the experience in World War II, large numbers of housewives did not leave the home for machine shops and arms plants.

Still, there were some new opportunities and in some cases higher pay. In food, airplane, and electrical plants, women made up a fifth or more of the work force. As their wages increased, they also increased their expectations; some became more militant, and there was growing conflict with male co-workers. To set standards for female employment, a Women's Bureau was established in the Department of Labor, but the government's influence varied. In the federally run railroad industry, women often made wages equal to those of men; in the federally run telephone industry, they did not.

Looking for more people to fill wartime jobs, corporations found another major source among southern blacks. Beginning in 1916, northern labor agents travelled across the South, promising jobs, high wages, and free transportation. Soon the word flashed from town to town, and the movement northward became a flood. Between 1916 and 1918 over 450,000 blacks left the Old South for the booming industrial cities of Saint Louis, Chicago, Detroit, and Cleveland. In the decade before 1920, Detroit's black population grew by over 600 percent, Cleveland's by over 300 percent, and Chicago's by 150 percent.

Most of the newcomers were young, unmarried, and skilled or semiskilled. The men found jobs in factories, railroad yards, steel mills, packing houses, and coal mines; black women worked in textile factories, department stores, and restaurants. In their new homes, blacks found greater racial freedom but also different living conditions. If the South was often hostile, the North could be impersonal and lonely. Accustomed to the pace of the farm—ruled by the seasons and the sun—those blacks who were able to enter the industrial sector now worked for hourly wages in mass-production industries, where time clocks and foremen dictated the daily routine.

Racial tensions increased, resulting in part from growing competition for housing and jobs. In mid-1917 a race war in East Saint Louis, Illinois, killed nine whites and about forty blacks. In July 1919, the month President Wilson returned from the peace conference in Paris, a race riot in Washington, D.C., killed six people. Riots in Chicago that month killed thirty-eight—fifteen whites and twenty-three blacks—and there were later outbreaks in New York City and Omaha. Lynch mobs killed forty-eight blacks in 1917, sixty-three in 1918, and seventy-eight in 1919. Ten of the victims in 1919 were war veterans, several still in uniform.

Blacks were more and more inclined to fight back. Two hundred thousand blacks served in France—42,000 as combat troops. Returning home, they expected better treatment. "I'm glad I went," a black veteran said. "I done my part and I'm going to fight right here till Uncle Sam does his." Roscoe Jameson, Claude McKay, and other black poets wrote biting poetry, some of it—like Fenton Johnson's "The New Day"—drawn from the war experience:

For we have been with thee in No Man's Land,
Through lake of fire and down to Hell itself;
And now we ask of thee our liberty,
Our freedom in the land of Stars and Stripes.

"Lift Ev'ry Voice and Sing," composed in 1900, became known as the "Negro National Anthem." Parents bought black dolls for their children, and W. E. B. Du Bois spoke of a "New Negro," proud and more militant: "We return. We return from fighting. We return fighting."

Eager for cheap labor, farmers and ranchers in the Southwest persuaded the federal government to relax immigration restrictions, and between 1917 and 1920 over 100,000 Mexicans migrated into Texas, Arizona, New Mexico, and California. The Mexican-American population grew from

■ *A wounded doughboy is welcomed home, New York City, March 1919. Most of the black combat troops in the war served with units assigned to the French command.*

385,000 in 1910 to 740,000 in 1920. Tens of thousands of Mexican-Americans moved to Chicago, Saint Louis, Omaha, and other northern cities to take wartime jobs. Often scorned and insecure, they created urban *barrios,* similar to the Chinatowns and Little Italys around them.

Like most wars, World War I affected patterns at home as much as abroad. Business profits grew, factories expanded, and industries turned out huge amounts of war goods. Government authority swelled, and people came to expect different things of their government. Labor made some gains, as did women and blacks. Society assimilated some of the shifts, but social and economic tensions grew, and when the war ended, they spilled over in the strikes and violence of the "Red Scare" of 1919 (see chapter 25).

The United States emerged from the war the strongest economic power in the world. In 1914 it was a debtor nation, and American citizens owed foreign investors about $3 billion. Five years later the United States had become a creditor nation. Foreign governments owed over $10 billion, and foreign citizens owed American investors nearly $3 billion. The war marked a shift in economic power rarely equalled in history.

The Treaty of Versailles

Long before the fighting ended, Wilson began to formulate plans for the peace. On January 8, 1918, appearing before Congress to rebut Bolshevik arguments that the war was merely a struggle among imperialists, the President outlined terms for a far-reaching, nonpunitive settlement. Wilson's Fourteen Points (see p. 710) were generous and farsighted, but they failed to satisfy wartime emotions.

England and France distrusted Wilsonian idealism as the basis for peace. They wanted Germany disarmed and crippled; they wanted its colonies; and they were skeptical of the principle of self-determination. As the end of the war neared, the Allies, who had made secret commitments with one another, balked at making the Fourteen Points the basis of peace. When Wilson threatened to negotiate a separate treaty with Germany, however, they accepted.

Wilson had won an important victory, but difficulties lay ahead. As Georges Clemenceau, the seventy-eight-year-old French premier, said: "God gave us the Ten Commandments, and we broke them. Wilson gives us the Fourteen Points. We shall see."

A Peace at Paris

Just before the peace conference began, Wilson appealed to voters to elect a Democratic Congress in the 1918 elections—"if you have approved of my leadership and wish me to continue to be your unembarrassed spokesman in affairs at home and abroad . . ." The Democrats lost both the House and Senate, enabling Wilson's opponents to announce that voters had rejected his policies. In fact, the Democratic losses stemmed largely from domestic problems, such as the price of wheat and cotton. But they hurt Wilson, who soon would be negotiating with European leaders buoyed by rousing victories at their own polls.

Two weeks after the elections, Wilson announced that he would attend the peace conference. This was a dramatic break from tradition, and his personal involvement drew attacks from Republicans. They renewed the criticism when he named the rest of the delegation: Secretary of State Lansing, Colonel House, General Tasker H.

Woodrow Wilson's Fourteen Points, 1918: Success and Failure in Implementation

1. Open covenants of peace openly arrived at	Not fulfilled
2. Absolute freedom of navigation upon the seas in peace and war	Not fulfilled
3. Removal of all economic barriers to the equality of trade among nations	Not fulfilled
4. Reduction of armaments to the level needed only for domestic safety	Not fulfilled
5. Impartial adjustment of colonial claims	Not fulfilled
6. Evacuation of all Russian territory; Russia to be welcomed into the society of free nations	Not fulfilled
7. Evacuation and restoration of Belgium	**Fulfilled**
8. Evacuation and restoration of all French lands; return of Alsace-Lorraine to France	**Fulfilled**
9. Readjustment of Italy's frontiers along lines of Italian nationality	Compromised
10. Self-determination for the former subjects of the Austro-Hungarian Empire	Compromised
11. Evacuation of Rumania, Serbia, and Montenegro; free access to the sea for Serbia	Compromised
12. Self-determination for the former subjects of the Ottoman Empire; secure sovereignty for Turkish portion	Compromised
13. Establishment of an independent Poland, with free and secure access to the sea	**Fulfilled**
14. Establishment of a League of Nations affording mutual guarantees of independence and territorial integrity	Not fulfilled

Source: Data from G. M. Gathorne-Hardy, The Fourteen Points and the Treaty of Versailles (Oxford Pamphlets on World Affairs, no. 6, 1939), pp. 8–34; Thomas G. Paterson et al., American Foreign Policy, A History Since 1900, 2d ed., Vol. 2, pp. 282–93.

Bliss, a military expert, and Henry White, a career diplomat. Wilson named no member of the Senate, and the only Republican in the group was White.

In selecting the delegation, Wilson passed over Henry Cabot Lodge, the powerful Republican senator from Massachusetts who opposed the Fourteen Points and would soon head the Senate Foreign Relations Committee. He also decided not to appoint Elihu Root or ex-President Taft, both of them enthusiastic internationalists. Never good at accepting criticism or delegating authority, Wilson wanted a delegation he could control—an advantage at the peace table but not in any battle over the treaty at home.

Upon his arrival in Europe, Wilson received a tumultuous welcome in England, France, and Italy. Never before had such crowds acclaimed a democratic political figure. In Paris two million people lined the Champs-Elysées, threw flowers at him, and shouted "Wilson *le Juste* [the just]" as his carriage drove by. Overwhelmed, Wilson was sure that people shared his goals, but he was wrong: like their leaders, they hated Germany and wanted victory unmistakably reflected in the peace.

Opening in January 1919, the Peace Conference at Paris continued until May. Although twenty-seven nations were represented, the "Big Four" dominated it: Wilson; Clemenceau of France, tired and stubborn, determined to end the German threat forever; David Lloyd George, the crafty British prime minister who had pledged to squeeze Germany "until the pips squeak"; and the Italian prime minister, Vittorio Orlando. A clever negotiator, Wilson traded various "small" concessions for his major goals—national self-determination, a reduction in tensions, and a League of Nations to enforce the peace.

Wilson had to surrender some important prin-

When Wilson arrived in Europe in December 1918, cheering crowds in England, France, and Italy hailed him as the "peacemaker from America." The painting (right) by Sir William Orpen recreates the signing of the treaty in the Hall of Mirrors at the palace of Versailles. The German delegates, Dr. Johannes Bell (seated, back to artist) and Herman Müller (next to Bell), sign under the watchful eyes of the Allied delegates. At the left are the five American delegates: General Tasker Bliss, Colonel House, Henry White, Secretary of State Lansing, and President Wilson.

ciples. Departing from the Fourteen Points, the treaty created two new independent nations—Poland and Czechoslovakia—with large German-speaking populations, a violation of self-determination. It divided up the German colonies in Asia and Africa. Instead of a peace without victory, it made Germany accept responsibility for the war and demanded enormous reparations —which eventually totaled $33 billion. It made no mention of disarmament, free trade, or freedom of the seas. Instead of an open covenant openly arrived at, the treaty was drafted behind closed doors.

But Wilson deflected some of the most extreme Allied demands, and he won his coveted Point 14, a League of Nations, designed, "to achieve international peace and security." The League included a general Assembly; a smaller Council composed of the United States, Great Britain, France, Italy, Japan, and four nations to be elected by the

Europe After the Treaty of Versailles, 1919

The treaty changed the map of Europe, creating a number of new and reconstituted nations. (Note boundary changes from prewar map on p. 694.)

Assembly; and a court of international justice. League members pledged to submit to arbitration every dispute threatening peace and to enjoin military and economic sanctions against nations resorting to war. Article X, for Wilson the heart of the League, obligated members to protect each other's independence and territorial integrity.

The draft treaty in hand, Wilson returned home in February 1919 to discuss it with Congress and the people. Most Americans, the polls showed, favored the League; thirty-three governors endorsed it. But over dinner with the Senate and House Foreign Relations Committees, Wilson learned of the strength of congressional opposition to it. On March 5, Senator Lodge produced a "round robin" signed by thirty-seven senators declaring they would not vote for the treaty without amendment. Should those numbers hold up, Lodge had enough votes to defeat it.

Returning to Paris, Wilson attacked his critics, while privately he worked for changes to improve the chances of Senate approval. The Allies won major concessions in return, but they amended the League draft treaty, agreeing that domestic affairs remained outside League jurisdiction, exempting the Monroe Doctrine, and allowing nations to withdraw after two years' notice. On June 28, 1919, they signed the treaty in the Hall of Mirrors at Versailles, and Wilson started home for his most difficult fight.

Rejection in the Senate

There were ninety-six senators in 1919, forty-nine of them Republicans. Fourteen Republicans, led by William E. Borah of Idaho, were the "irreconcilables" who opposed the League on any grounds. "If the Savior of man," Borah said, "would revisit the earth and declare for a League of Nations, I would be opposed to it." Frank B. Kellogg of Minnesota led a group of twelve "mild reservationists" who accepted the treaty but wanted to insert several reservations that would not greatly weaken it. Finally, there were the Lodge-led "strong reservationists," twenty-three of them in all, who wanted major changes that the Allies would have to approve.

With only four Democratic senators opposed to the treaty, the Democrats and compromise-minded Republicans had enough votes to ratify it,

once a few reservations were inserted. Biding for time to allow public opposition to grow, Lodge scheduled lengthy hearings and spent two weeks reading the 268-page treaty aloud. Democratic leaders urged Wilson to appeal to the Republican "mild reservationists," but he angrily refused. "Anyone who opposes me in that I'll crush!"

Fed up with Lodge's tactics, Wilson set out in early September to take the case directly to the people. Crossing the Midwest, his speeches aroused little emotion, but on the Pacific Coast he won ovations, which heartened him. On his way back to Washington, he stopped in Pueblo, Colorado, where he delivered one of the most eloquent speeches of his career. People wept as he talked of Americans who died in battle and the hope that they would never fight again in foreign lands. That night Wilson felt ill. He returned to Washington, and on October 2, Mrs. Wilson found him lying unconscious on the floor of the White House, the victim of a stroke that paralyzed his left side.

After the stroke, Wilson could not work more than an hour or two at a time. No one was allowed to see him except family members, his secretary, and his physician. For over seven months he did not meet with the cabinet. Secretary of State Lansing convened cabinet meetings, but when Wilson learned of them, he ordered Lansing to stop and then cruelly forced him to resign. Focusing his remaining energy on the fight over the treaty, Wilson lost touch with other issues, and critics charged that his wife, Edith Bolling Wilson, ran the government.

On November 6, 1919, while Wilson convalesced, Lodge finally reported the treaty out of committee, along with "Fourteen Reservations," one for each of Wilson's points. The most important reservation stipulated that implementation of Article X, Wilson's key article, required the action of Congress in each case.

That day the President's floor leader in the Senate told him that the Democrats could not pass the treaty without reservations. "Is it possible?" Wilson asked sadly. "It might be wise to compromise," the senator said. "Let Lodge compromise!" Wilson replied. When Mrs. Wilson urged her husband to accept the Lodge reservations, he said: "Better a thousand times to go down fighting than to dip your colors to dishonorable compromise."

■ In this cartoon, Humanity points the finger of blame at the U.S. Senate, the ogre responsible for killing the peace treaty.

aside. The Democrats nominated Governor James M. Cox of Ohio, along with the young and popular Franklin D. Roosevelt, assistant secretary of the navy, for vice-president. Wilson called for "a great and solemn referendum" on the treaty. The Democratic platform endorsed the treaty but agreed to accept reservations to clarify the American role in the League.

On the Republican side, Senator Warren G. Harding of Ohio, who had nominated Taft in 1912, won the presidential nomination. Harding waffled on the treaty, but it made little difference. Voters wanted a change. Harding won in a landslide, taking 61 percent of the vote and beating Cox by 7 million votes. Without a peace treaty, the United States remained technically at war, and it was not until July 1921, almost three years after the last shot was fired, that Congress passed a joint resolution ending the war.

On November 19, the treaty—with the Lodge reservations—failed, 39 to 55. Following Wilson's instructions, the Democrats voted against it. A motion to approve without the reservations lost 38 to 53, with only one Republican voting in favor. The defeat brought pleas for compromise, but neither Wilson nor Lodge would back down. When the treaty with reservations again came up for vote on March 19, 1920, Wilson ordered the Democrats to hold firm against it. Although twenty-one of them defied him, enough obeyed his orders to defeat it, 49 to 35, seven votes short of the necessary two-thirds majority.

To Wilson, walking now with the help of a cane, one chance remained: the presidential election of 1920. For a time he thought of running for a third term himself, but his party shunted him

■ A hearty, down-to-earth handshaker, Warren G. Harding loved meeting and greeting people. An althorn player, the President poses here with a tuba.

The Election of 1920

Candidate	Party	Popular Vote	Electoral Vote
Harding	Republican	16,133,314	404
Cox	Democrat	9,140,884	127
Debs	Socialist	913,664	0

After 1919 there was disillusionment. World War I was feared before it started, popular while it lasted, and hated when it ended. To a whole generation that followed, it appeared futile, killing without cause, sacrifice without benefit. Books, plays, and movies—Hemingway's *A Farewell to Arms*, John Dos Passos' *Three Soldiers* (1921), Laurence Stallings and Maxwell Anderson's *What Price Glory?* (1924) among others—showed it as waste, horror, and death.

The war and its aftermath damaged the humanitarian, progressive spirit of the early years of the century. It killed "something precious and perhaps irretrievable in the hearts of thinking men and women." Progressivism survived well into the 1920s and the New Deal, but it no longer had the old conviction and broad popular support. Bruising fights over the war and the League drained people's energy and enthusiasm.

Confined to bed, Woodrow Wilson died in Washington in 1924, three years after Harding, the new president, promised "not heroics but healing; not nostrums but normalcy; not revolution but restoration." Nonetheless, the "war to end all wars," and the spirit of Woodrow Wilson left an indelible imprint on the country.

Recommended Reading

American foreign policy between 1901 and 1921 has been the subject of considerable study. Richard W. Leopold, *The Growth of American Foreign Policy* (1962) is balanced and informed. Howard K. Beale, *Theodore Roosevelt and the Rise of America to World Power* (1956), traces foreign policy during the early years; Robert E. Osgood, *Ideals and Self-Interest in America's Foreign Relations* (1953), and William Appleman Williams, *Roots of the Modern American Empire* (1969), explore the forces underlying American foreign policy.

David McCullough gives a lively account of the building of the Panama Canal in *The Path Between the Seas* (1977). For American policy toward Latin America, see Dana G. Munro's detailed account, *Intervention and Dollar Diplomacy in the Caribbean, 1900–1920* (1964). Arthur S. Link examines Wilson's foreign policy in his exceptional five-volume biography, *Wilson* (1947–1965) and in *Woodrow Wilson: Revolution, War, and Peace* (1979). N. Gordon Levin, Jr., *Woodrow Wilson and World Politics: America's Response to War and Revolution* (1968), places Wilson in the larger context of world events.

Ernest R. May studies American policy before the war in *The World War and American Isolation, 1914–*

1917 (1959). Bradford Perkins, *The Great Rapprochement: England and the United States, 1895–1914* (1968), examines the growing friendship between the two countries. Studies of events at home during the war include David M. Kennedy, *Over Here* (1980); Robert D. Cuff, *The War Industries Board* (1973); and Maurine W. Greenwald, *Women, War, and Work* (1980).

Woodrow Wilson and the Lost Peace (1944) and *Woodrow Wilson and the Great Betrayal* (1945) by Thomas A. Bailey are dated but thorough on Wilson's efforts at Versailles. Arthur Walworth, *America's Moment, 1918: American Diplomacy at the End of World War I* (1977), also examines Wilson's attempt to create a peaceful world order.

Additional Bibliography

For background to American policy in these years, see Richard D. Challener, *Admirals, Generals, and American Foreign Policy, 1898–1914* (1973) and Paul P. Abrahams, *The Foreign Expansion of American Finance and Its Relationship to the Foreign Economic Policies of the United States, 1907–1921* (1976). David H. Burton, *Theodore Roosevelt, Confident Imperialist* (1968); Frederick Marks III, *Velvet on Iron: The Diplomacy of Theodore Roosevelt* (1979); and C. E. Neu, *An Uncertain Friendship: Theodore Roosevelt and Japan, 1906–1909* (1967), trace Roosevelt's policies.

On Taft and Wilson, see Ralph E. Minger, *William Howard Taft and United States Foreign Policy* (1975); Walter V. Scholes and Marie V. Scholes, *The Foreign Policies of the Taft Administration* (1970); and John Morton Blum, *Woodrow Wilson and the Politics of Morality* (1956). For relations with Latin America, see Dexter R. Perkins, *The United States and the Caribbean*, rev. ed. (1966) and two books by Lester D. Langley: *Struggle for the American Mediterranean* (1975) and *The United States and the Caribbean, 1900–1970* (1980).

On Mexico, see Peter Calvert, *The Mexican Revolution, 1910–1914* (1968); Lloyd Gardner, *Wilson and Revolutions, 1913–1921* (1976); and Robert E. Quirk, *An Affair of Honor: Woodrow Wilson and the Occupation of Veracruz* (1962). Several books deal with policies in the Far East, including Charles Vevier, *United States and China, 1906–1913* (1955); Charles S. Campbell, *Special Business Interests and the Open Door Policy* (1951); Warren I. Cohen, *America's Response to China*, 2d ed. (1980); Raymond A. Esthus, *Theodore Roosevelt and Japan* (1966); and Jerry Israel, *Progressivism and the Open Door: America and China, 1905–1921* (1971).

Historians have long debated the reasons for America's entry into the war; see, for example, Charles Seymour, *American Diplomacy During the World War* (1934) and *American Neutrality, 1914–1917* (1935); Patrick Devlin, *Too Proud to Fight: Woodrow Wilson's Neutrality* (1974); David M. Smith, *Robert Lansing and American Neutrality* (1958); Ross Gregory, *The Origins of American Intervention in the First World War* (1971); and Jeffrey J. Safford, *Wilsonian Maritime Diplomacy* (1978).

The war at home is followed in John G. Clifford, *The Citizen Soldiers* (1972); William Preston, Jr., *Aliens and Dissenters: Federal Suppression of Radicals, 1903–1933* (1963); H. C. Peterson and Gilbert C. Fite, *Opponents of War, 1917–1918* (1957); Carol S. Gruber, *Mars and Minerva: World War I and the Uses of Higher Learning in America* (1975); and Stephen Vaughn, *Holding Fast the Inner Lines: Democracy, Nationalism, and the Committee on Public Information* (1980).

On military intervention, see Harvey DeWeerd, *President Wilson Fights His War* (1968); E. M. Coftman, *The War to End All Wars* (1968); Frank E. Vandiver, *Black Jack: The Life and Times of John J. Pershing*, 2 vols. (1977); Russell F. Weigley, *The American Way of War* (1973); Laurence Stallings, *The Doughboys* (1963); and Arthur E. Barbeau and Henri Florette, *The Unknown Soldiers: Black American Troops in World War I* (1974).

The Treaty of Versailles and the struggle for ratification are covered in Arno J. Mayer, *Politics and Diplomacy of Peacemaking* (1967); Charles L. Mee, Jr., *The End of Order, Versailles, 1919* (1980); Warren F. Kuehl, *Seeking World Order* (1969); L. W. Martin, *Peace Without Victory* (1958); and Ralph A. Stone, *The Irreconcilables* (1970).

Wesley M. Bagby, *The Road to Normalcy* (1962); Seward W. Livermore, *Politics Is Adjourned: Woodrow Wilson and the War Congress, 1916–1918* (1966); and David Burner, *The Politics of Provincialism: The Democratic Party in Transition, 1918–1932* (1967) are excellent studies of domestic politics of the era.

chapter 25

TRANSITION TO MODERN AMERICA

The moving assembly line that Henry Ford perfected in 1914 for manufacture of the Model T marked only the first step toward full mass production and the beginning of America's worldwide industrial supremacy. A year later, Ford began buying large plots of land along the Rouge River southeast of Detroit, Michigan. He already had a vision of a vast industrial tract where machines, moving through a sequence of carefully arranged manufacturing operations, would transform raw materials into finished cars, trucks, and tractors. The key would be control over the flow of goods at each step along the way, from lake steamers and railroad cars bringing in the coal and iron ore, to overhead conveyor belts and huge turning tables carrying the moving parts past the stationary workers on the assembly line. "Everything must move," Ford commanded, and by the mid-1920s at River Rouge, as the plant became known, it did.

Ford began fulfilling his industrial dream in 1919 when he built a blast furnace and foundry to make engine blocks for both the Model T and his tractors. By 1924, more than forty thousand workers were turning out nearly all the metal parts used in making Ford vehicles. A tractor factory was so efficient that it took just over twenty-eight hours to convert raw ore into a new farm implement.

Visitors from all over the world came to marvel at River Rouge. Some were disturbed by the jumble of machines (by 1926, there were forty-three thousand in operation) and the apparent congestion on the plant floor, but industrial experts recognized that the arrangement led to incredible productivity because "the work moves and the men stand still." A trained engineer summed it up best when he wrote that a visitor "sees each unit as a carefully designed gear which meshes with other gears and operates in synchronism with them, the whole forming one huge, perfectly-timed, smoothly-operating industrial machine of almost unbelieveable efficiency."

In May 1927, after producing over fifteen million Model Ts, Ford closed the assembly line at Highland Park. For the next six months, his engineers worked on designing a more compact and efficient assembly line at River Rouge for the Model A, which went into production in November. By then River Rouge had more than justified Ford's vision. "Ford had brought together everything at a single site and on a scale no one else

The tall smokestacks of the River Rouge plant rose more than three hundred feet into the sky, and the sprawling series of buildings eventually covered nearly two thousand acres of land. Every day ships, trains, and trucks brought to the plant a steady stream of raw materials for transformation into cars, trucks, and tractors going out to consumers all over the world.

had ever attempted," concluded historian Geoffrey Perrett. "The Rouge plant became to a generation of engineers far more than a factory. It was a monument."

Mass production, born in Highland Park in 1914 and perfected at River Rouge in the 1920s, became the hallmark of American industry. Other car makers copied Ford's methods and soon his emphasis on the flow of parts moving past stationary workers became the standard in nearly every American factory. The moving assembly line—with its emphasis on uniformity, speed, precision, and coordination—took away the last vestiges of craftsmanship and turned workers into near robots. It led to amazing efficiency that produced both high profits for manufacturers and low prices for buyers. By the mid-1920s, the cost of the Model T had dropped from $950 to only $290.

Most important, mass production led to a consumer-goods revolution. American factories turned out a flood of automobiles and electric appliances that made life easier and more pleasant for the vast majority of the American people. The result was the creation of a new America, one in which individualism was sacrificed to conformity as part of the price to be paid for a new era of abundance.

The twenties, often seen as a time of escape and frivolity before the onset of the Depression, actually marked a beginning, a time when the American people learned to adapt to life in the city, when they decided (wisely or not) to center their existence upon the automobile, and when they rejected their rural past while still longing for the old values it had created. It is in the 1920s that we can find the roots of modern America—the America we know today.

The Second Industrial Revolution

The first Industrial Revolution in the late nineteenth century had catapulted the United States into the forefront of the world's richest and most highly developed nations. With the advent of the new consumer-goods industries, the American people by the 1920s enjoyed the highest standard of living of any nation on earth. After a brief postwar depression, 1922 saw the beginning of a great boom that peaked in 1927 and lasted until 1929. In this brief period, American industrial output nearly doubled, and the gross national product rose by 40 percent. Most of this explosive growth took place in industries producing goods for consumers—automobiles, appliances, furniture, clothing. Equally important, the national per-capita income increased by 30 percent to $681 in 1929. American workers became the highest paid in history and thus were able to buy the

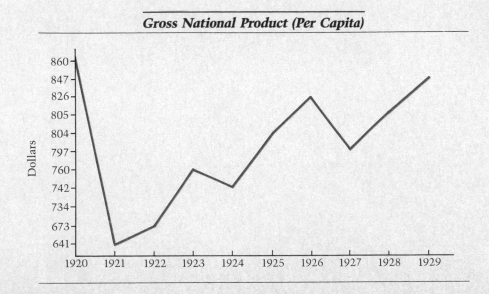

Gross National Product (Per Capita)

flood of new goods they were turning out on the assembly lines.

The key to the new affluence lay in technology. The moving assembly line pioneered by Ford became the standard feature in nearly all American plants. Electric motors replaced steam engines as the basic source of energy in factories; by 1929, 70 percent of all industrial power came from electricity. Efficiency experts broke down the industrial process into minute parts in time and motion studies and then showed managers and workers how to maximize the output of their labor. Production per man-hour increased an amazing 75 percent over the decade; in 1929, a work force no larger than that of 1919 was producing almost twice as many goods.

Patterns of Economic Growth

Automobiles were the most conspicuous of the consumer products that flourished in the 1920s but certainly not the only ones. The electrical industry grew nearly as quickly. Central power stations, where massive steam generators converted coal into electricity, brought current into the homes of city and town dwellers. Two thirds of all American families enjoyed electricity by the end of the decade, and they spent vast sums on washing machines, vacuum cleaners, refrigerators, and ranges. The new appliances eased the burdens of the housewife and ushered in an age of leisure.

Radio broadcasting and motion-picture production also boomed in the 1920s. The early success of KDKA in Pittsburgh stimulated the growth of more than eight hundred independent radio stations, and by 1929 NBC had formed the first successful radio network. Five nights a week "Amos 'n Andy," a comic serial featuring two "blackface" vaudevillians, held the attention of millions of Americans. The film industry thrived in Hollywood, reaching its maturity in the mid-1920s when in every large city there were huge theaters seating as many as four thousand people. With the advent of the "talkies" in 1929, average weekly movie attendance climbed to nearly one hundred million.

Other industries prospered as well. Production of light metals such as aluminum and magnesium grew into a major business. Chemicals came

■ For "a dollar down and a dollar a week" Americans of the 1920s could purchase the latest household electrical appliance—a washing machine, for example, or a fan or an iron or a refrigerator.

of age with the invention of synthetics, ranging from rayon for clothing to cellophane for packaging. Americans found a whole new spectrum of products to buy—cigarette lighters, wristwatches, heat-resistant glass cooking dishes, and rayon stockings to name just a few.

The corporation continued to be the dominant economic unit in the 1920s. Growing corporations now had hundreds of thousands of stockholders, and one individual or family rarely held more than 5 percent of the stock. The enormous profits generated by these corporations enabled their managers to finance growth and expansion internally, thus freeing companies from their earlier dependence on investment bankers like J. P. Morgan. Voicing a belief in social responsibility and enlightened capitalism, the new professional class operated independently of outside restraint. In the last analysis, the corporate managers were accountable only to other managers.

Another wave of mergers accompanied the

growth of corporations during the 1920s. From 1920 to 1928, some eight thousand mergers took place as more and more small firms proved unable to compete effectively with the new giants. By the end of the decade, the two hundred largest nonfinancial corporations owned almost half of the country's corporate wealth. The oligopoly in the automobile industry set the example for other areas. The greatest abuses took place in public utilities where promoters like Samuel Insull built vast paper empires by gaining control of operating power companies and then draining them of their assets.

The most distinctive feature of the new consumer-oriented economy was the stress on marketing. Advertising earnings rose from $1.3 billion in 1915 to $3.4 billion in 1926. Skillful practitioners like Edward Bernays and Bruce Barton sought to control public taste and consumer spending by identifying the good life with the possession of the latest product of American industry, whether a car, a refrigerator, or a cigarette. Chain stores advanced rapidly at the expense of small retail shops. A&P dominated the retail food industry, growing from 400 stores in 1912 to 15,500 by 1932. Woolworth's "five and tens" spread almost as rapidly, while such drugstore chains as Rexall and Liggetts—both owned by one huge holding company—opened outlets in nearly every town and city in the land.

Uniformity and standardization, the characteristics of mass production, now prevailed. The farmer in Kansas bought the same kind of car, the same groceries, and the same pills as the factory worker in Pennsylvania. Sectional differences in dress, food, and furniture began to disappear. Even the regional accents that distinguished Americans in different parts of the country were threatened with extinction by the advent of radio and films which promoted a standard national dialect devoid of any local flavor.

Economic Weaknesses

The New Era, as businessmen labeled the decade, was not as prosperous as it first appeared. The revolution in consumer goods disguised the decline of many traditional industries in the 1920s. Railroads, overcapitalized and poorly managed, suffered from internal woes and from the compe-

tition of the growing trucking industry. Coal was another troubled industry, with petroleum and natural gas beginning to replace it as a fuel. Cotton textiles declined with the development of rayon and other synthetic fibers. The New England mills moved south in search of cheap labor, leaving behind thousands of unemployed workers and virtual ghost towns in the nation's oldest industrial center.

Hardest hit of all was agriculture. American farmers had expanded production to meet the demands of World War I, when they fed a nation at war and most of Europe as well. A sharp cutback in exports in 1919 caused a rapid decline in prices. By 1921, farm exports had fallen by more than $2 billion. Throughout the 1920s, the farmers' share of the national income dropped until by 1929 the per-capita farm income was only $273, compared to the national average of $681.

Workers were better off in the 1920s, but they did not share fully in the decade's affluence. The industrial labor force remained remarkably steady for a period of economic growth; the technical innovations meant that the same number of workers could produce far more than before. Most of the new jobs came in the lower-paying service industry. During the decade, factory wage rates rose only a modest 11 percent; by 1929 nearly half of all American families had an income of less than $1500. At the same time, however, conditions of life improved. Prices remained stable, even dropping somewhat in the early twenties, so that workers enjoyed a gain in real wages.

Organized labor proved unable to advance the interests of workers in the 1920s. Conservative leadership in the AFL neglected the task of organizing the vast number of unskilled laborers in the mass-production industries. Aggressive management weakened the appeal of unions by portraying them as radical after a series of strikes in 1919. Many businessmen used the injunction and "yellow-dog" contracts, which forbade employees from joining unions, to establish open shops and deny workers the benefits of collective bargaining. Other employers wooed their workers away from unions using techniques of welfare capitalism, spending money to improve plant conditions and winning employee loyalty with pensions, paid vacations, and company cafeterias. The net result was a decline in union membership from a postwar high of five million to less than three million by 1929.

Black workers remained on the bottom, both economically and socially. Nearly half a million blacks had migrated northward from the rural South during World War I. Some found jobs in northern industries, but many more worked in menial service areas, collecting garbage, washing dishes, and sweeping floors. Yet even these jobs offered them a better life than they found on the depressed southern farms, where millions of blacks still lived in poverty, and so the migration continued. The black ghettos in northern cities grew rapidly in the 1920s; Chicago's black population doubled during the decade, while New York's rose from 152,467 to 327,706, with most blacks living in Harlem.

Middle- and upper-class Americans were the groups who thrived in the 1920s. The rewards of the second Industrial Revolution went to the managers—the engineers, bankers, and executives who directed the new industrial economy. Corporate profits nearly doubled in ten years, and income from dividends rose 65 percent, nearly six times the rate of workers' wages. Bank accounts, reflecting the accumulated savings of the upper-middle and wealthy classes, rose from $41.1 billion to $57.9 billion. These were the people who bought the fine new houses in the suburbs and who could afford more than one car. Their conspicuous consumption helped fuel the prosperity of the 1920s, but their disposable income eventually became greater than their material wants. The result was speculation, as those with idle money began to invest heavily in the stock market to reap gains from the industrial growth.

The economic trends of the decade had both positive and negative implications for the future. On the one hand, there was the solid growth of new consumer-based industries. Automobiles and appliances were not passing fancies; their production and use became a part of the modern American way of life, creating a high standard of living that evoked the envy of the rest of the world. The future pattern of American culture—cars and suburbs, shopping centers and skyscrapers—was determined by the end of the 1920s.

But at the same time there were ominous signs of danger. The unequal distribution of wealth, the saturation of the market for consumer goods, and the growing speculation all created economic instability. The boom of the twenties would end in a great crash; yet the achievements of the decade would survive even that dire experience to shape the future of American life.

The New Urban Culture

The city replaced the countryside as the focal point of American life in the 1920s. The 1920 census revealed that for the first time slightly more than half of the population lived in cities, defined broadly to include all places of more than 2500 people. During the decade, the metropolitan areas grew rapidly as both whites and blacks from rural areas came seeking jobs in the new consumer industries. Between 1920 and 1930 cities with populations of 250,000 or more had added some 8 million people to their ranks. New York alone grew by nearly 25 percent, while Detroit more than doubled its population during the decade.

The skyscraper soon became the most visible feature of the city. Faced with inflated land prices, builders turned upward—developing a distinctively American architectural style in the process. New York led the way with the ornate Woolworth Building in 1913. The sleek 102-story Empire State Building, completed in 1930, was for years the tallest building in the world. Other cities erected their own jagged skylines. By 1929, there were 377 buildings over 20 stories tall across the nation. Most significantly, the skyscraper came to symbolize the new mass culture. "The New York skyscrapers are the most striking manifestation of the triumph of numbers," wrote one French observer. "One cannot understand or like them without first having tasted and enjoyed the thrill of counting or adding up enormous totals and of living in a gigantic, compact and brilliant world."

In the metropolis, life was different. The old community ties of home, church, and school were loosening, but there were important gains—new ideas, new creativity, new perspectives. Some city dwellers became lost and lonely without the old institutions; others thrived in the urban environment.

■ Its 102 stories rising 1250 feet into the sky (222 feet were added in 1950), the Empire State Building had space for 25,000 tenants.

creased, and even though women earned nearly one third of all graduate degrees, only 4 percent of the full professors were female. For the most part, the professions were reserved for men, with women relegated to such stereotypical fields as teaching and nursing.

To be sure, women had won the right to vote in 1919, but the Nineteenth Amendment proved to have less impact than its proponents had hoped. Once achieved, it robbed women of a unifying cause, and the suffrage itself did little to change the prevailing sex roles in society. Men remained the principal breadwinners in the family; women cooked, cleaned, and reared the children. "The creation and fulfillment of a successful home," a *Ladies Home Journal* writer advised women, "is a bit of craftsmanship that compares favorably with building a beautiful cathedral."

■

One of the hard-won rights that women finally realized in 1920 was the right to vote, celebrated here in a cover from Leslie's Illustrated Weekly Newspaper.

Family Life in the 1920s

The urban culture of the 1920s witnessed important changes in the American family. This vital institution began to break down under the impact of economic and social change. A new freedom for women and children seemed to be emerging in its wake.

Women had already begun to leave the home in the early twentieth century as the second Industrial Revolution opened up new jobs for them. World War I speeded up the process, but in the 1920s there was no great permanent gain in the number of working women. Although two million more women were employed in 1930 than in 1920, this represented an increase of only 1 percent. Most women workers, moreover, had lower-paying jobs, ranging from stenographers to maids. The number of women doctors actually de-

The feminist movement, however, still showed signs of vitality in the 1920s. One group, led by Alice Paul's National Woman's Party (NWP), lobbied for full equality for women under the law. In 1923, the NWP succeeded in having an Equal Rights Amendment introduced in Congress. The amendment stated: "Men and women shall have equal rights throughout the United States and every place subject to its jurisdiction." Other women's organizations, notably the League of

Women Voters, opposed the amendment on the grounds that women needed legal protection, especially laws guaranteeing them at least a minimum wage and limiting the maximum length of the workday.

The drive for the ERA failed in the twenties, but social feminists were more successful in pushing for humanitarian reform, notably the Sheppard-Towner Act of 1921 which provided for federal aid to establish state programs for maternal and infant health care. Although the failure to enact the child-labor amendment in 1925 marked the beginning of a decline in humanitarian reform, for the rest of the decade women's groups continued to work for good-government measures, for the inclusion of women on juries, and for consumer legislation.

A generational change had a profound impact on feminism in the 1920s. Instead of crusading for social progress, young women concentrated on individual self-expression by rebelling against Victorian restraints. Some quickly adopted what critic H. L. Mencken called the flapper image, portrayed most strikingly by artist John Held, Jr. Cutting their hair short, raising their skirts above the knee, and binding their breasts, "flappers" set out to compete on equal terms with men on the golf course and in the speakeasy. Young women delighted in shocking their elders—they rouged their cheeks and danced the Charleston. For the first time, women smoked cigarettes and drank alcohol in public. The flappers assaulted the traditional double standard in sex, demanding that equality with men should include sexual fulfillment before and during marriage. The new permissiveness led to a sharp rise in the divorce rate; by 1928, there were 166 divorces for every 1000 marriages, compared to only 81 in 1900.

The sense of woman's emancipation was heightened by a drop in the birthrate and the abundance of consumer goods. With fewer children to care for and with washing machines and vacuum cleaners to ease their household labor, women of the 1920s seemed to have more leisure time. Yet appearances were deceptive. Advertisers eagerly sought out women as buyers of consumer products, but wives exercised purchasing power only as delegated by their husbands. Many women could not enjoy the new labor-saving devices—one fourth of the homes in Cleveland lacked running water in the twenties, and three

■ John Held, Jr.'s Sweet Girl Graduate combined the innocence of ruffled skirts with the sophistication of rouged cheeks, bobbed hair, and long cigarette.

quarters of the nation's families did not have washing machines. The typical childless woman spent between forty-three and fifty hours a week on household duties; for mothers, the average work week was fifty-six hours, far longer than that of their husbands. And despite the talk of the "new woman," the flappers fell victim to the sex-role conditioning of their parents. Boys continued to play with guns and grew up to head their families; girls played with dolls and looked forward to careers as wives and mothers. "In the 1920s, as in the 1790s," concluded historian June Sochen, "marriage was the only approved state for women."

The family, however, did change. It became smaller as new techniques of birth control enabled couples to limit their offspring. More and more married women took jobs outside the home, bringing in an income and gaining a measure of independence (although their rate of pay was always lower than that for men). Young people, who had once joined the labor force when they entered their teens, now discovered adolescence as a stage of life. A high-school education was no longer uncommon, and college attendance increased.

This prolonged adolescence led to new strains on the family in the form of youthful revolt. Freed of the traditional burden of earning a living at an early age, youth in the 1920s went on a great spree. Heavy drinking, casual sex encounters, and a constant search for excitement became the hallmarks of the upper-class youth immortalized by F. Scott Fitzgerald. "I have been kissed by dozens of men," one of his characters commented. "I suppose I'll kiss dozens more." The theme of rebellion against parental authority, which runs through all aspects of the 1920s, was at the heart of the youth movement.

■ Mother: "It's broccoli, dear." Child: "I say it's spinach, and I say the hell with it."

■ In the George Bellows painting (right), Argentina's Luis Firpo knocks Jack Dempsey out of the ring. Dempsey came back to win the fight in the second round.

The Roaring Twenties

Frivolity and excitement ran high in the cities as crime waves and highly publicized sports events flourished. Prohibition ushered in such distinctive features of the decade as speakeasies, bootleggers, and bathtub gin. Crime rose sharply as middle- and upper-class Americans willingly broke the law to gain access to alcoholic beverages. City streets became the scene of violent shootouts between rival bootleggers; by 1929, Chicago had witnessed over five hundred gangland murders. Underworld czars like Al Capone controlled illicit empires; Capone's produced revenue of $60 million a year.

Sports became a national mania in the 1920s as people found more leisure time. Golf boomed, with some two million men and women playing on nearly five thousand courses across the country. Spectator sports attracted even more attention. Boxing drew huge crowds to see fighters like Jack Dempsey and Gene Tunney. Baseball attendance soared. More than twenty million fans attended games in 1927, the year Babe Ruth became a national idol by hitting sixty home runs. On college campuses, football became more popular than ever. Universities vied with each other in building massive stadiums, seating upward of seventy thousand people.

In what Frederick Lewis Allen called "the ballyhoo years," the popular yearning for excitement led people to seek vicarious thrills in all kinds of ways—applauding Charles Lindbergh's solo flight

Lindbergh Flies the Atlantic

At 7:52 A.M., Friday, May 20, 1927, Charles A. Lindbergh took off in the *Spirit of St. Louis*, a small single-engine airplane, from Roosevelt Field on Long Island. It was the first break in the weather after a long week of waiting in New York. Thirty-three hours and thirty minutes later, he landed at Le Bourget Aerodrome just outside Paris, completing the first solo Atlantic crossing in a heavier-than-air craft and winning the $25,000 Orteig Prize for the first nonstop flight between New York and Paris.

Lindbergh had been the dark horse in the transatlantic race. His career as a barnstormer, army air corps reserve officer, and air mail pilot could not compare to the reputations of the famous explorers and war aces planning to make the flight, and his late arrival among the ranks of the competitors relegated him to the back pages of newspapers. But a series of disasters befell the larger, more expensive multiengined aircraft flown by his better-known rivals, opening the way for this latecomer. Reporters, impressed by a pilot flying solo in a comparatively inexpensive single-engine plane, nicknamed Lindbergh "the Flyin' Fool."

More than a hundred thousand people awaited his landing at Le Bourget. Lindbergh was carried off on the shoulders of the crowd before his feet touched French soil. He was feted by the French people, decorated by their government and, when he flew on to Belgium and England, received similar laurels. Upon returning to the United States, Lindbergh led a parade through Washington, D. C.; at its end, he joined President and Mrs. Coolidge on a large reviewing stand at the base of the Washington Monument. Cheering crowds filled the Capitol Mall. In an uncharacteristically long and glowing speech, Coolidge described the young pilot's achievement as another chapter in "the same story of valor and victory by a son of the people that shines through every page of American history." At the conclusion of his address, Coolidge presented Lindbergh with the Distinguished Flying Cross, the first of such medals to be bestowed upon an American aviator. Two days later, in New York, there was another parade; police estimated the crowd to be in excess of 3 million, and Lindbergh received similar if somewhat smaller receptions throughout the country on his forty-eight-state tour. Lindbergh's flight had captured the imagination of the American people.

But the public fascination with Lindbergh and his flight represented more than the preoccupation with adventure and excitement so common in the 1920s. It was not just hero worship. To Europeans, Lindbergh was an unofficial goodwill ambassador whose bravery enhanced the American image in Europe. To his fellow citizens, he personified traditional American virtues in the modern industrial world.

Lindbergh's flight, as the President noted, *was* a shining example of the American tradition of individual initiative and self-reliance. The press reveled in Lindbergh's "conquest," describing him in terms reminiscent of those used in the winning of the West: as a "pioneer" of aviation opening a new "frontier." The theme was heroic individualism. Such references to America's hallowed past demonstrated a continuity between the values that had made America great and Lindbergh's successful Atlantic crossing. Industrialization and urbanization in the twentieth century had not sapped the American spirit, as many had feared. The nation could rejoice in the vitality of traditional American virtues.

But that was only half the story. While the pilot may have embodied what many Americans considered best in the past, his plane was a product of the technological and industrial progress that was their future. Lindbergh did not attribute his success merely to individual effort; the plane that carried him to France was, in his own words, "the culmination of twenty years of aeronautical research." Giving the *Spirit of St. Louis* its due, he entitled his autobiographical account *We*, referring to his plane and himself as partners in an epochal achievement. In his Washington address, Coolidge praised "American genius and industry" as the "silent partner" in Lindbergh's flight.

The significance of Charles Lindbergh's flight lay in harmonizing America's past with its future —the integration of a tradition of individual initiative with progress, technology, and industry. Lindbergh and the *Spirit of St. Louis* represented the best of both worlds. The days of the self-sufficient individual as an American norm may have ended, but modern America now at least had a symbolic manifestation that the cherished ideal still lived. Lindbergh's flight, moreover, provided an exciting look into the ever greater human command of the machine. (The picture below is of the enthusiastic reception Lindbergh received at Croydon, England.)

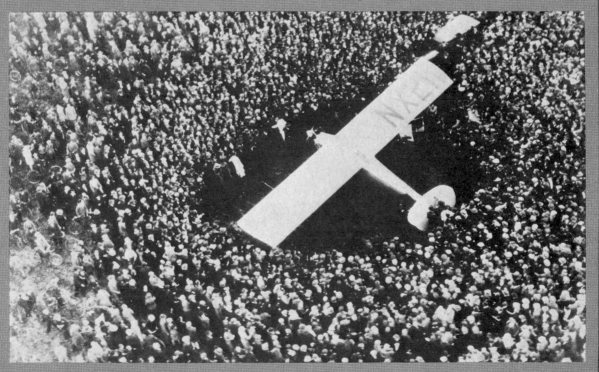

across the Atlantic, cheering Gertrude Ederle's swim across the English Channel, and flocking to such bizarre events as six-day bicycle races, dance marathons, and flagpole-sittings. It was a time of pure pleasure-seeking, when people sought to escape from the increasingly drab world of the assembly line by worshiping heroic individuals.

Sex became another focal point in the 1920s as Victorian standards began to crumble. Sophisticated city dwellers seemed to be intent on exploring a new freedom in sexual expression. Plays and novels focused on adultery, and the new urban tabloids—led by the *New York Daily News*—delighted in telling their readers about love nests and kept women. The popular songs of the decade, like "Hot Lips" and "Burning Kisses," were less romantic and more explicit. Hollywood exploited the obsession with sex by producing movies with such provocative titles as *Up in Mable's Room*, *A Shocking Night*, and *Women and Lovers*. Theda Bara and Clara Bow, the "vamp" and the "it" girl, set the model for feminine seductiveness while Rudolph Valentino became the heartthrob of millions of American women. Young people embraced the new permissiveness joyfully, with the automobile giving couples an easy way to escape parental supervision.

There is considerable debate, however, over the extent of the sexual revolution in the '20s. Later studies by Dr. Alfred C. Kinsey (see the special feature in chapter 29) showed that premarital intercourse was twice as common among women born after 1900 than for those born before the turn of the century. But a contemporary survey of over two thousand middle-class women by Katherine B. Davis found that only 7 percent of those who were married had had sexual relations before marriage and that only 14 percent of the single women had engaged in intercourse. Actual changes in sexual behavior are beyond the historian's reach, hidden in the privacy of the bedroom, but the old Victorian prudery was a clear casualty of the 1920s. Sex was no longer a taboo subject; men and women now could and did discuss it openly.

The Literary Flowering

The greatest cultural advance of the 1920s was the outpouring of literature. The city gave rise to a new class of intellectuals—writers who commented on the new industrial society. Many had been uprooted by World War I. They were bewildered by the rapidly changing social patterns of the 1920s and appalled by the materialism of American culture. Some fled to Europe to live as expatriates, congregating in Paris cafes to bemoan the loss of American innocence and purity. Others stayed at home, observing and condemning the excesses of a business civilization. All shared a sense of disillusionment and wrote pessimistically of the flawed promise of American life. Yet, ironically, their body of writing revealed a profound creativity that suggested that America was coming of age intellectually.

The exiles included the poets Ezra Pound and T. S. Eliot and the novelist Ernest Hemingway. Pound discarded rhyme and meter in a search for clear, cold images that conveyed reality. Like many of the writers of the 1920s, he reacted against World War I, expressing a deep regret for the tragic waste of a whole generation in defense of a "botched civilization."

Eliot, who was born in Missouri but became a British citizen, displayed even more profound despair. In *The Waste Land*, which appeared in 1922, he evoked images of fragmentation and sterility that had a powerful impact on the other disillusioned writers of the decade. He reached

■ *Clara Bow was selected by author Elinor Glyn as the girl with "It"—a quality defined as "that strange magnetism which attracts both sexes."*

the depths in *The Hollow Men* (1925), a biting description of the emptiness of modern man.

Ernest Hemingway sought redemption from the modern plight in the romantic individualism of his heroes. Preoccupied with violence, he wrote of men alienated from society who found a sense of identity in their own courage and quest for personal honor. His own experiences, ranging from driving an ambulance in the war to stalking lions in Africa, made him a legendary figure; his greatest impact on other writers, however, came from his sparse, direct, and clean prose style.

The writers who stayed home were equally disdainful of contemporary American life. F. Scott Fitzgerald chronicled American youth in *This Side of Paradise* (1920) and *The Great Gatsby* (1925), writing in bittersweet prose about "the beautiful and the damned." Amid the glitter of life among the wealthy on Long Island's North Shore came the haunting realization of emptiness and lack of human concern.

Sinclair Lewis became the most popular of the critical novelists. *Main Street*, published in 1920, satirized the values of small-town America as dull, complacent, and narrow-minded; *Babbitt*, which appeared two years later, poked fun at the commercialism of the 1920s, portraying George Babbitt as the stereotype of the energetic, go-getting businessman who hailed the decade as a New Era.

Most savage of all was H. L. Mencken, the Baltimore newspaperman and literary critic who founded the *American Mercury* in 1923. Declaring war on the "homo boobiens," Mencken mocked everything he found distasteful in America from the Rotary Club to the Ku Klux Klan. "From Boy Scouts, and from Home Cooking, from Odd Fellows' funerals, from Socialists, from Christians—Good Lord, deliver us," he pleaded. It was not difficult to discover what Mencken disliked; the hard part was finding out what he affirmed, other than wit and a clever turn of phrase. A born cynic, he served as a zealous guardian of public integrity in an era of excessive boosterism.

The cultural explosion of the 1920s was surprisingly broad. It included novelists like Sherwood Anderson and John Dos Passos—who described the way the new machine age undermined such traditional American values as craftsmanship and a sense of community—and

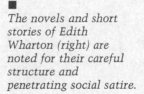

Chronicler of the Jazz Age, F. Scott Fitzgerald, shown here (above) with his wife Zelda and daughter Scottie, became a living symbol of the era.

The novels and short stories of Edith Wharton (right) are noted for their careful structure and penetrating social satire.

playwrights such as Eugene O'Neill, Maxwell Anderson, and Elmer Rice who added greatly to the stature of American theater. Women writers were particularly effective in dealing with regional themes. Edith Wharton continued to write penetratingly about eastern aristocrats in books like *The Age of Innocence* (1921), while Willa Cather and Ellen Glasgow focused on the plight of women in the Midwest and the South respectively in their short stories and novels. These writers portrayed their heroines in the traditional roles of wives and mothers, but playwright Zona Gale (who won the Pulitzer Prize for drama in 1920 for *Miss Lulu Bett*) used her title character

The loneliness of life in the city is the theme suggested by Edward Hopper's Automat (left).

In his poetry, fiction, and nonfiction Langston Hughes (below) described to the world the black experience in the United States.

to depict the dilemmas facing an unmarried woman in American society.

Art and music lagged behind literature but still made significant advances. Edward Hopper and Charles Burchfield captured the ugliness of city life and the loneliness of its inhabitants in their realistic paintings. Aaron Copland and George Gershwin added a new vitality to American music, but the greatest contribution came from the spread of jazz as blacks migrated northward—first to Saint Louis, Kansas City, and Chicago, and finally to New York. The form of jazz known as the blues, so expressive of the suffering of American blacks, became an authentic national folk music, and performers like Louis Armstrong enjoyed worldwide popularity.

The cultural growth of the 1920s was the work of blacks as well as whites. W. E. B. Du Bois, the editor of *Crisis*, became the intellectual voice of the black community developing in New York City's Harlem. In 1917, James Weldon Johnson, who had been a professor of literature at Fisk University, published *Fifty Years and Other Poems* in which the title poem commented on the half-century of suffering that had followed the Emancipation Proclamation. As other black writers gathered around them, Du Bois and Johnson became the leaders of the Harlem Renaissance. The NAACP moved its headquarters to Harlem, and in 1923 the Urban League began publishing *Opportunity*, a magazine devoted to scholarly studies of racial issues.

A black literary flowering quickly developed. In 1922, critics hailed the appearance of Claude McKay's book of verses, *White Shadows*. In stark images, McKay expressed both his resentment against racial injustice and his pride in blackness. Countee Cullen and Langston Hughes won critical acclaim for the beauty of their poems and the eloquence of their portrayal of the black tragedy.

Art and music also flourished during Harlem's golden age. Plays and concerts at the 135th Street YMCA; floor shows at Happy Rhone's nightclub (attended by many white celebrities); rent parties where jazz musicians played to raise money for writers, artists, and neighbors to help them pay their bills—all were part of the ferment that made Harlem "the Negro Capital of the World" in the 1920s. "Almost everything seemed possible above 125th Street in the early twenties for these Americans who were determined to thrive separately to better proclaim the ideals of integration," comments historian David Lewis. "You could be black and proud, politically assertive and economically independent, creative and disciplined—or so it seemed."

Although its most famous writers were identified with New York's Harlem, the new black cultural awareness spread to other cities in the form of poetry circles and theater groups. The number of black college graduates rose from 391 in 1920 to 1903 by 1929. Although blacks were still an oppressed minority in American life, a few were beginning in the 1920s to take the first steps toward achieving cultural and intellectual fulfillment.

In retrospect, there is a striking paradox about the literary flowering of the twenties. Nearly all the writers, black as well as white, cried out against the conformity and materialism of the contemporary scene. They were critical of mass production and reliance on the machine; they wrote wistfully of the disappearance of the artisan and of a more relaxed way of life. Few took any interest in politics or in social reform. They retreated instead into individualism, seeking an escape from the prevailing business civilization in their art. Whether they went abroad or stayed home, the writers of the '20s turned inward to avoid being swept up in the consumer-goods revolution. Yet despite their withdrawal, and indeed perhaps because of it, they produced an astonishingly rich and varied body of work. American writing had a greater intensity and depth than in the past; American writers, despite their alienation, had placed their country in the forefront of world literature.

The Rural Counterattack

Dominance by the urban centers led to a response that produced an ugly side of the twenties—a side where prejudice and bigotry, hate and intolerance flourished. For millions of Americans who lived in the countryside, either on farms or in small towns, the city came to represent all that was evil in contemporary life. Largely Anglo-Saxon and steeped in traditional Protestantism, these rural folk condemned the urban-centered crime, radicalism, and modernism which they felt were threatening their own way of life. Saloons, whorehouses, little Italys and little Polands, Communist cells, free love, and atheism—all were identified with the city. As the urban areas grew in population and influence, the countryside struck back in a deliberate if doomed attempt to restore a lost purity to American life.

Other factors contributed to the intensity of rural counterattack. The war had unleashed a nationalistic spirit that craved unity and conformity. In a nation where one third of the people were foreign-born, the attack on immigrants and the call for 100 percent Americanism took on a frightening zeal. When the war was over, groups like the American Legion tried to root out "un-American" behavior and insisted on cultural as well as political conformity. And the prewar progressive reform spirit added to the social tension. Stripped of much of its former idealism, progressivism focused on such social problems as drinking and illiteracy to justify repressive measures like Prohibition and immigration restriction. The result was tragic. Amid the emergence of a new urban culture, a wave of rural-inspired movements sought to preserve the values of an earlier America. They succeeded only in complicating life in an already difficult period of cultural transition.

The "Red Scare"

The first and most intense outbreak of national alarm came in 1919. The heightened nationalism of World War I, aimed at achieving unity at the expense of ethnic diversity, found a new target in bolshevism. The Russian Revolution and the triumph of Marxism frightened many Americans. A growing turn to communism among American radicals (especially the foreign-born) accelerated the fears, although the numbers involved were tiny—at most there were sixty thousand Communists in the United States in 1919. But they were located in the cities, and their influence appeared to be magnified with the outbreak of widespread labor unrest.

A general strike in Seattle, a police strike in Boston, and a violent strike in the iron and steel industry thoroughly alarmed the American people in the spring and summer of 1919. A series of bombings led to panic. First the mayor of strike-bound Seattle received a small brown package containing a homemade bomb; then an alert New York postal employee detected sixteen bombs addressed to a variety of famous citizens (includ-

"UNGRATEFUL SCUM!"

THE LAND OF OPPORTUNITY

VICIOUS ALIENS

DEPORTATION

■ With flagrant disregard for due process of law and basic civil liberties, Attorney General A. Mitchell Palmer ordered raids on "dangerous aliens" and "foreign subversives."

ing John D. Rockefeller); and finally, on June 2, a bomb shattered the front of Attorney General A. Mitchell Palmer's home. Although the man who delivered it was blown to pieces, authorities quickly identified him as an Italian anarchist from Philadelphia.

In the ensuing public outcry, Attorney General Palmer led the attack on the alien threat. A Quaker and progressive, Palmer abandoned his earlier liberalism to launch a massive roundup of foreign-born radicals. In a series of raids that began on November 7, federal agents seized suspected anarchists and Communists and held them for deportation with no regard for due process of law. In December, 249 aliens—including such well-known radical leaders as Emma Goldman and Alexander Berkman—were sent to Russia aboard the *Buford*, dubbed the "Soviet Ark" by the press. Nearly all were innocent of the charges against them. A month later, Palmer rounded up nearly four thousand suspected Communists in a single evening. Federal

agents broke into homes, meeting halls, and union offices without search warrants. Many native-born Americans were caught in the dragnet and spent several days in jail before being released; aliens rounded up were deported without hearings or trials.

For a time, it seemed that this Red Scare reflected the prevailing views of the American people. Instead of condemning their government's action, citizens voiced their approval and even urged more drastic steps. One patriot said his solution to the alien problem was simple: "S.O.S.—ship or shoot." General Leonard Wood, the army chief of staff, favored placing Bolsheviks on "ships of stone with sails of lead," while evangelist Billy Sunday preferred to take "these ornery, wild-eyed Socialists" and "stand them up before a firing squad and save space on our ships." Inflamed by public statements like these, a group of legionnaires in Centralia, Washington, dragged a radical from the town jail, castrated him, and hanged him from a railway bridge. The coroner's report blandly stated that the victim "jumped off with a rope around his neck and then shot himself full of holes."

The very extremism of the Red Scare led to its rapid demise. Courageous government officials in the Department of Labor insisted on due process and full hearings before anyone else was deported. Prominent public leaders began to speak out against the acts of terror. Charles Evans Hughes, the defeated GOP candidate in 1916, offered to defend six Socialists expelled from the New York legislature; Ohio Senator Warren G. Harding, the embodiment of middle-class values, expressed his opinion that "too much has been said about bolshevism in America." Finally, Palmer himself, with evident presidential ambition, went too far. In April 1920, he warned of a vast revolution to occur on May 1; the entire New York City police force, some eleven thousand strong, was placed on duty. When no bombings or violence took place on May Day, the public began to react against Palmer's hysteria. Despite a violent explosion on Wall Street in September that killed thirty-three people, the Red Scare died out by the end of 1920. Palmer passed into obscurity, the tiny Communist party became torn with factionalism, and the American people tried hard to forget their momentary loss of balance.

Yet the Red Scare exerted a continuing influence on American society in the 1920s. The foreign-born lived in the uneasy realization that they were viewed with hostility and suspicion. Two Italian aliens in Massachusetts, Nicola Sacco and Bartolomeo Vanzetti, were arrested in May 1920 for a payroll robbery and murder. They faced a prosecutor and jury who condemned them more for their ideas than for any evidence of criminal conduct and a judge who referred to them as "those anarchist bastards." Despite a worldwide effort that became the chief liberal cause of the 1920s, the courts rejected all appeals. Sacco and Vanzetti, a shoemaker and a fish peddler, died in the electric chair on August 23, 1927. Their fate symbolized the bigotry and intolerance that lasted through the '20s and made this decade one of the least attractive in American history.

■ *Ben Shahn's* The Passion of Sacco and Vanzetti *(1931–1932) depicts the members of the committee who investigated the trial and confirmed its fairness.*

Prohibition

In December 1917, Congress adopted the Eighteenth Amendment, prohibiting the manufacture and sale of alcoholic beverages. A little over a year later, Nebraska became the necessary thirty-sixth state to ratify, and Prohibition became the law of the land.

As implemented under the Volstead Act, beginning January 16, 1920, it was illegal for anyone to make, sell, or transport any drink that contained more than half of 1 percent alcohol by volume. Prohibition was the result of both a rural effort of the Anti-Saloon League, backed by Methodist and Baptist clergymen, and the urban Progressive concern over the social disease of drunkenness, especially among industrial workers. The moral issue had already led to the enactment of Prohibition laws in twenty-six states by 1920; the real tragedy would occur in the effort to extend this "noble experiment" to the growing cities, where it was deeply resented by ethnic groups like the Germans and the Irish and nearly totally disregarded by the well-to-do and the sophisticated.

Prohibition did in fact lead to a decline in drinking. Americans consumed much less alcohol in the twenties than in the prewar years. Rural areas became totally dry, and in the cities the consumption of alcoholic beverages dropped sharply among the lower classes, who could not afford the high prices for bootleg liquor. Among the middle class and the wealthy, however, drinking became fashionable. Bootleggers supplied whiskey, which quickly replaced lighter spirits like wine and beer. The alcohol was either smuggled from abroad (a $40-million business by 1924) or illicitly manufactured in America. Such exotic products as Jackass Brandy, Soda Pop Moon, and Yack Yack Bourbon were common—and all could be fatal. Despite the risk of illness or death, Americans consumed some 150 million quarts of liquor a year in the twenties as bootleggers took in nearly $2 billion annually, about 2 percent of the gross national product.

Urban resistance to Prohibition finally led to its repeal in 1933. But in the intervening years, it damaged American society by breeding a profound disrespect for the law. The flamboyant excesses of bootleggers were only the more obvious evils spawned by Prohibition. In city after city, police openly tolerated the traffic in liquor,

and judges and prosecutors agreed to let bootleggers pay merely token fines, creating almost a system of licenses. The countryside felt vindicated, yet rural and urban America alike suffered from this overzealous attempt to legislate morals.

The Ku Klux Klan

The most ominous expression of rural protest against the city was the rebirth of the Ku Klux Klan. On Thanksgiving night in 1915, on Stone Mountain in Georgia, Colonel William J. Simmons and thirty-four followers founded the modern Klan. Only "native born, white, gentile Americans" were permitted to join "the Invisible Empire, Knights of the Ku Klux Klan." Membership grew slowly during World War I, but after 1920, fueled by postwar fears and shrewd promotional techniques, the Klan mushroomed. In villages, towns, and small cities across the South and West, Anglo-Saxon Protestant men flocked into the newly formed chapters, seeking to relieve their anxiety over a changing society by embracing the weird rituals and by demonstrating their hatred against blacks, aliens, Jews, and Catholics.

The Klan of the 1920s, unlike the night riders of the post-Civil War era, was not just antiblack;

the threat to American culture, as Klansmen perceived it, came from aliens—Italians and Russians, Jews and Catholics. They attributed much of the tension and conflict in society to the prewar flood of immigrants, foreigners who spoke different languages, worshiped in strange churches, and lived in distant, threatening cities. The Klansmen struck back by coming together and enforcing their own values. They punished blacks who did not know their place, women who practiced the new morality, and aliens who refused to conform. Beating, flogging, burning with acid—even murder—were condoned. But they also tried more peaceful methods of coercion, formulating codes of behavior and seeking communitywide support.

The Klan entered politics, at first hesitantly, then with growing confidence. The KKK gained control of the legislatures in Texas, Oklahoma, Oregon, and Indiana; in 1924, it blocked a resolution of censure at the Democratic National Convention. With nearly five million members by the mid-1920s, the Klan seemed to be fully established.

Its appeal lay in the sanctuary it offered to insecure and anxious people. Protestant to the core, the members found in the local Klavern a reassurance missing in their churches. The poor and ignorant became enchanted with the titles, ranging from Imperial Wizard to Grand Dragon, and gloried in the ritual that centered around the letter "K." Thus each Klan had its own Klalendar, held its weekly Klonklave in the local Klavern, and followed the rules set forth in the Kloran. Members found a sense of identity in the group activities, whether they were peaceful picnics, ominous parades in white robes, or fiery cross-burnings at night.

Although it was a male organization, the Klan did not neglect the family. There was a Women's Order, a Junior Order for boys, and a Tri-K Klub for girls. Members had to be born in America, but foreign-born Protestants were allowed to join a special Krusaders affiliate. Only blacks, Catholics, Jews, and prostitutes were beyond redemption to these lonely and anxious men who came together to chant:

> United we stick
> Divided we're stuck.
> The better we stick
> The better we Klux!

The Klan fell even more quickly than it rose. Its more violent activities—which included kidnap-

■ *A KKK initiation ceremony. Only native-born white Americans "who believe in the tenets of the Christian religion" were admitted into the Klan.*

ing, lynching, setting fire to synagogues and Catholic churches, and in one case, the murder of a priest—began to offend the nation's conscience. Misuse of funds and sexual scandals among Klan leaders, notably in Indiana, repelled many of the rank and file; effective counterattacks by traditional politicians ousted the KKK from control in Texas and Oklahoma. Membership declined sharply after 1925; by the end of the decade, the Klan had virtually disappeared. But its spirit lived on, testimony to the recurring demons of nativism and hatred that have surfaced periodically throughout the American experience.

Immigration Restriction

The nativism that permeated the Klan found its most successful outlet in the immigration legislation of the 1920s. The sharp increase in immigration in the late nineteenth century had led to a broad-based movement, spearheaded by organized labor and by New England aristocrats like Henry Cabot Lodge, to restrict the flow of people from Europe. In 1917, over Wilson's veto, Congress enacted a literacy test which reduced the number of immigrants. The war caused a much more drastic decline—from an average of 1 million a year between 1900 and 1914 to only 110,000 in 1918.

After the armistice, however, rumors began to spread of an impending flood of people seeking to escape war-ravaged Europe. Kenneth Roberts, a popular historical novelist, warned that all Europe was on the move, with only the limits of available steamship space likely to stem the flow. Worried congressmen spoke of a "barbarian horde" and a "foreign tide" that would inundate the United States with "dangerous and deadly enemies of the country." Even though the actual number of immigrants, 810,000 in 1920 (less than the prewar yearly average), did not match these projections, Congress responded in 1921 by passing an emergency immigration act. The new quota system restricted immigration from Europe to 3 percent of the number of nationals from each country living in the United States in 1910.

The 1921 act failed to satisfy the nativists. The quotas still permitted more than 500,000 Europeans to come to the United States in 1923, nearly half of them from southern and eastern Europe. The declining percentage of Nordic immigrants alarmed writers like Madison Grant, who warned the American people that the Anglo-Saxon stock that had founded the nation was about to be overwhelmed by lesser breeds with inferior genes. "These immigrants adopt the language of the native American, they wear his clothes and are beginning to take his women, but they seldom adopt his religion or understand his ideals," Grant wrote.

Psychologists, relying on primitive IQ' tests used by the army in World War I, confirmed this judgment (see the special feature on "Measuring the Mind" in chapter 24). One senator claimed that all the nation's ills were due to an "intermingled and mongrelized people" as he demanded that racial purity replace the older reliance on the melting pot. In 1924, Congress adopted the National Origins Quota Act, which limited immigration from Europe to 150,000 a year; allocated most of the places to immigrants from Great Britain, Ireland, Germany, and Scandinavia; and banned all Oriental immigrants. The measure passed Congress with overwhelming rural support; not a single congressman south of the Mason-Dixon line or west of the Mississippi River voted against it.

The new restrictive legislation marked the most enduring achievement of the rural counterattack. Unlike the Red Scare, Prohibition, and the Klan, the quota system would survive until the 1960s, enforcing a racist bias that excluded Asians and limited the immigration of Italians, Greeks, and Poles to a few thousand a year while permitting a steady stream of Irish, English, and Scandinavian immigrants. The large corporations, no longer dependent on armies of unskilled immigrant workers, did not object to the 1924 law; the machine had replaced the immigrant on the assembly line. Yet even here the rural victory was not complete. A growing tide of Mexican laborers, exempt from the quota act, flowed northward across the Rio Grande to fill the continuing need for unskilled workers on the farms and in the service trades. The Mexican immigrants, as many as 100,000 a year, marked the strengthening of an element in our national ethnic mosaic that would grow in size and influence until it became a major force in modern American society.

The Fundamentalist Controversy

The most famous of all the rural attacks on the new urban culture was the Scopes trial held in Dayton, Tennessee. There in 1925, William Jennings Bryan, who had unsuccessfully run for president several times in previous decades, engaged in a crusade against the theory of evolution, appearing as a chief witness against John Scopes, a high-school biology teacher who had initiated the case by deliberately violating a new Tennessee law that forbade the teaching of Darwin's theory.

In the trial, Bryan testified under oath that he believed Jonah had been swallowed by a big fish and declared, "It is better to trust in the Rock of Ages than in the age of rocks." Chicago defense attorney Clarence Darrow succeeded in making Bryan look ridiculous. The court found Scopes guilty but let him off with a token fine; Bryan, exhausted by his efforts, died a few days later. H. L. Mencken, who covered the trail in person, rejoiced in the belief that fundamentalism was dead.

GATHERING DATA FOR THE TENNESSEE TRIAL

■ *Religious fundamentalism, which experienced a rebirth of popularity after World War I, clashed with current scientific theory in the Scopes trial.*

In reality, however, the traditional rural religious beliefs were stronger than ever. As middle- and upper-class Americans drifted into a genteel Christianity which stressed good works and respectability, the Baptist and Methodist churches continued to hold on to the old faith. In addition, aggressive fundamentalist sects such as the Churches of Christ, the Pentecostals, and Jehovah's Witnesses grew rapidly. The number of churches actually declined during the decade but church membership increased from 41.9 million in 1916 to 54.5 million in 1926. More and more rural dwellers drove their cars into town instead of going to the local crossroads chapel.

Many of those who came to the city in the twenties brought their religious beliefs with them and found new outlets for their traditional ideas. Thus evangelist Aimee Semple McPherson enjoyed amazing success in Los Angeles with her "Four-Square Gospel," building the Angelus Temple to seat over five thousand worshipers. And in Fort Worth, the Reverend J. Frank Norris erected a six-thousand-seat sanctuary for the First Baptist Church, bathing it in spotlights so that it could be seen for thirty miles across the north Texas prairie.

Far from dying out, as divinity professor Thomas G. Oden noted, biblical fundamentalism retained "remarkable grass-roots strength among the organization men and the industrialized mass society of the 20th century." The rural counterattack, while challenged by the city, did enable some older American values to survive in the midst of the new mass-production culture.

Politics of the Twenties

The tensions between the city and the countryside also shaped the course of politics in the 1920s. On the surface, it was a Republican decade. The GOP controlled the White House from 1921 to 1933 and had majorities in both houses of Congress from 1918 to 1930. The Republicans used their return to power after World War I to halt further reform legislation and to establish a friendly relationship betwen government and business. Important shifts were taking place, however, in the American electorate. The Democrats, although divided into competing urban and rural wings, were laying the groundwork for the future by winning over millions of new voters, especially among the ethnic groups in the cities. The rising tide of urban voters indicated a fundamental shift away from the Republicans toward a new Democratic majority.

Harding, Coolidge, and Hoover

The Republicans regained the White House in 1920 with the election of Warren G. Harding of Ohio. A dark-horse contender, Harding won the GOP nomination when the convention deadlocked and he became the compromise choice. Handsome and dignified, Harding reflected both the virtues and blemishes of small-town America. Originally a newspaper publisher in Marion, he had made many friends and few enemies throughout his career as a legislator, lieutenant governor, and finally, after 1914, a United States senator. Conventional in outlook, Harding was a genial man who lacked the capacity to govern and who delegated power broadly as president.

He made some good cabinet choices, notably Charles Evans Hughes as secretary of state and Herbert C. Hoover as secretary of commerce, but two corrupt offficials—Attorney General Harry Daugherty and Secretary of the Interior Albert Fall—sabotaged his administration. Daugherty became involved in a series of questionable deals that led ultimately to his forced resignation; Fall was the chief figure in the Teapot Dome scandal. Two oil promoters gave Fall nearly $400,000 in loans and bribes; in return, he helped them secure leases on naval oil reserves in Elk Hills, California, and Teapot Dome, Wyoming. The scandal came to light after Harding's death from a heart attack in 1923. Fall eventually served a year in jail, and the reputation of the Harding administration never recovered.

Vice-President Calvin Coolidge assumed the presidency upon Harding's death, and his honesty and integrity quickly reassured the nation. Coolidge, born in Vermont of old Yankee stock, had first gained national attention in 1919 as governor of Massachusetts when he had dealt firmly with a Boston police strike by declaring, "There is no right to strike against the public safety by anybody, anywhere, any time." A reserved, reticent man, Coolidge became famous for his epigrams,

In this cartoon, Attorney General Daugherty struggles to keep the skeletons of corruption—the scandals of the Harding administration—hidden in the closet.

gent, and immensely hard-working, Hoover embodied the nation's faith in individualism and free enterprise.

As secretary of commerce under Harding and Coolidge, he had sought cooperation between government and business. He used his office to assist American manufacturers and exporters in expanding their overseas trade, and he strongly supported a trade association movement to encourage cooperation rather than cutthroat competition among smaller American companies. He did not view business and government as antagonists. Instead, he saw them as partners, working together to achieve efficiency and affluence for all Americans. His optimistic view of the future led him to declare in his speech accepting the Republican presidential nomination in 1928 that "we in America today are nearer to the final triumph over poverty than ever before in the history of any land."

Republican Policies

During the 1920 campaign, Warren Harding urged a return to "not heroism, but healing, not nostrums, but normalcy." Misreading his speechwriter's "normality," he coined a new word that became the theme for the Republican administrations of the '20s. Aware that the public was tired of zealous reform-minded presidents like Teddy Roosevelt and Woodrow Wilson, Harding and his successors sought a return to traditional Republican policies. In some areas they were successful, but in others they were forced to adjust to the new realities of a mass-production society. The result was a mixture of traditional and innovative measures that was neither wholly reactionary nor entirely progressive.

The most obvious attempt to go back to the Republicanism of William McKinley came in tariff and tax policy. Fearful of a flood of postwar European imports, Congress passed an emergency tariff act in 1921 and followed it a year later with the protectionist Fordney-McCumber Tariff Act. The net effect was to raise the basic rates substantially over the moderate Underwood Tariff schedules of the Wilson period.

Secretary of the Treasury Andrew Mellon, a wealthy Pittsburgh banker and industrialist, worked hard to achieve a similar return to

which contemporaries mistook for wisdom. "The business of America is business," he proclaimed. "The man who builds a factory builds a temple; the man who works there worships there." Consistent with this philosophy, he believed his duty was simply to preside benignly, not govern the nation. Calvin Coolidge, one observer noted, "aspired to become the least President the country ever had; he attained his desire." Satisfied with the prosperity of the mid-twenties, the people responded favorably. Coolidge was elected to a full term by a wide margin in 1924.

When Coolidge announced in 1927 that he did not "choose to run," Herbert Hoover became the Republican choice to succeed him. By far the ablest GOP leader of the decade, Hoover epitomized the American myth of the self-made man. Orphaned as a boy, he had worked his way through Stanford University and had gained both wealth and fame as a mining engineer. During World War I, he had displayed admirable administrative skills in directing Wilson's food program at home and relief activities abroad. Sober, intelli-

■ *Calvin Coolidge hosts an informal press conference on the porch of his Vermont home. Reserved and aloof—a complete contrast to the affable Harding—Coolidge believed in silence and inactivity. "Four fifths of all our troubles in this life would disappear," he said, "if we would just sit down and be still."*

"normalcy" in taxation. Condemning the high wartime tax rates on businesses and wealthy individuals, Mellon pressed for repealing an excess-profits tax on corporations and slashing personal rates on the very rich. Using the new budget system adopted by Congress in 1921, he reduced government spending from its World War I peak of $18 billion to just over $3 billion by 1925, thereby creating a slight surplus. Congress responded in 1926 by cutting the highest income-tax bracket to a modest 20 percent.

The revenue acts of the 1920s greatly reduced the burden of taxation; by the end of the decade, the government was collecting a third less than it had in 1921, and the number of people paying income taxes dropped from over 6.5 million to 4 million. Yet the greatest relief went to the wealthy. The public was shocked to learn in the 1930s that J. P. Morgan and his nineteen partners had paid no income tax at all during the depths of the Depression.

The growing crisis in American farming during the decade forced the Republican administrations to seek new solutions. The end of the European war led to a sharp decline in farm prices and a return to the problem of overproduction. South-ern and western lawmakers formed a farm bloc in Congress to press for special legislation for American agriculture. The farm bloc supported the higher tariffs, which included protection for constituents' crops, and helped secure passage of legislation to create federal supervision over stockyards, packinghouses, and grain trading.

This special-interest legislation failed to get at the root of overproduction, however. Farmers then supported more controversial measures designed to raise domestic crop prices by having the government sell the surplus overseas at low world prices. Coolidge vetoed the legislation on grounds that it involved unwarranted government interference in the economy.

Yet the government's role in the economy increased rather than lessened in the 1920s. Republicans widened the scope of federal activity and nearly doubled the ranks of government employees. Herbert Hoover led the way in the Commerce Department, establishing new bureaus to help make American industry more efficient in housing, transportation, and mining. Under his leadership, the government encouraged corporations to develop welfare programs that undercut trade unions, and he tried to minimize labor disturbances by devising new federal machinery to mediate disputes. Instead of going back to the laissez-faire tradition of the nineteenth century, the Republican administrations of the twenties were pioneering a close relationship betwen government and private business.

The Divided Democrats

While the Republicans ruled in the 1920s, the Democrats seemed bent on self-destruction. The Wilson coalition fell apart in 1920 as pent-up dissatisfaction stemming from the war enabled Harding to win by a landslide. The pace of the second Industrial Revolution and the growing urbanization in the twenties split the party in two. One faction centered in the rural South and West. Traditional Democrats who had supported Wilson stood for Prohibition, fundamentalism, the Klan, and other facets of the rural counterattack against the city. In contrast, a new breed of Democrat was emerging in the metropolitan areas of the North and Midwest. Immigrants and their descendants began to become active in the Democratic party. Catholic or Jewish in religion and strongly opposed to Prohibition, they had little in common with their rural counterparts.

The split within the party surfaced dramatically at the national convention in New York in 1924. Held in Madison Square Garden, a hall built in the 1890s and too small and cramped for the more than one thousand delegates, the convention soon degenerated into what one observer described as a "snarling, cursing, tenuous, suicidal, homicidal roughhouse." City slickers mocked the "rubes and hicks" from the "sticks"; populist orators struck back by denouncing the city as "wanting in national ideals, devoid of conscience . . . rooted in corruption, directed by greed and dominated by selfishness." An urban resolution to condemn the Ku Klux Klan led to a spirited response from the rural faction and its defeat by a single vote. Then for nine days, in the midst of a stifling heat wave, the delegates divided between Alfred E. Smith, the governor of New York, and William G. McAdoo of California, Wilson's secretary of the treasury. When it became clear that neither the city nor the rural candidate could win a majority, both men withdrew; on the 103rd ballot, the weary Demo-

crats finally chose John W. Davis, a former West Virginia congressman and New York corporation lawyer, as their compromise nominee.

In the ensuing election, the conservative Davis had difficulty in distinguishing his views from those of Republican President Calvin Coolidge. For the discontented, Senator Robert LaFollette offered an alternative by running on an independent Progressive party ticket. Coolidge won the election easily, receiving fifteen million votes to eight million for Davis and nearly five million for LaFollette. Davis had made the poorest showing of any Democratic candidate in the twentieth century.

The Election of 1924

Candidate	Party	Popular Vote	Electoral Vote
Coolidge	Republican	15,717,553	382
Davis	Democrat	8,386,169	136
LaFollette	Progressive	4,814,050	13

Yet the Democrats were in far better shape than this setback indicated. Beginning in 1922, the party had made heavy inroads into the GOP majority in Congress. The Democrats took seventy-eight seats away from Republicans in that election, many of them in the cities of the East and Midwest. In New York alone, they gained thirteen new congressmen, all but one in districts with heavy immigrant populations. Even in 1924, the Republican vote in the nation's largest cities declined as many urban voters chose LaFollette in the absence of an attractive Democratic candidate. By 1926, the Democrats were within one vote of controlling the Senate and had picked up nine more seats in the House in metropolitan areas. The large cities were swinging clearly into the Democratic column; all the party needed was a charismatic leader who could fuse the older rural elements with the new urban voters.

The Election of 1928

The selection of Al Smith as the Democratic candidate in 1928 indicated the growing power of the city. Born on the lower east side of Manhattan of mixed Irish-German ancestry, Smith was the prototype of the urban Democrat. He was Catholic; he was associated with a big-city machine; he was a wet who wanted to end Prohibition. Starting out in the Fulton Fish Market as a boy, he had joined Tammany Hall and gradually climbed the political ladder, rising from subpoena server to state legislator to governor, a post he held with distinction for nearly a decade. Rejected by rural Democrats in 1924, he still had to prove that he could unite the South and West behind his leadership. His lack of education, poor grammar, and distinctive New York accent all hurt him, as did his eastern provincialism. When reporters asked him about his appeal in the states west of the Mississippi, he replied, "What states *are* west of the Mississippi?"

The choice facing the American voter in 1928 seemed unusually clear-cut. Herbert Hoover was a Protestant, a dry, and an old-stock American who stood for efficiency and individualism; Smith was a Catholic, a wet, and a descendant of immigrants who was closely associated with big-city politics. Just as Smith appealed to new voters in the cities, so Hoover won the support of many old-line Democrats who feared the city, Tammany Hall, and the pope.

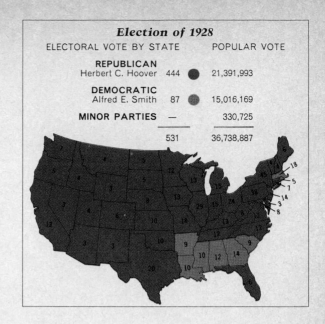

Election of 1928

ELECTORAL VOTE BY STATE		POPULAR VOTE
REPUBLICAN		
Herbert C. Hoover	444	21,391,993
DEMOCRATIC		
Alfred E. Smith	87	15,016,169
MINOR PARTIES	—	330,725
	531	36,738,887

■ *The happy warrior, Al Smith, in his familiar brown derby, campaigning from a train platform in 1928.*

■ *Republican candidate Herbert Hoover (below) campaigned on a platform that stressed continued economic prosperity.*

by more than six million votes and carrying such traditionally Democratic states as Oklahoma, Texas, and Florida. But Smith succeeded for the first time in winning a majority of votes for the Democrats in the nation's twelve largest cities. A new Democratic electorate was emerging, consisting of Catholics and Jews, Irish and Italians, Poles and Greeks. Now the task was to unite the traditional Democrats of the South and West with the urban voters of the Northeast and Midwest.

The 1920s marked a major transition in American politics as well as in social and economic development. The moving assembly line, the consumer-goods revolution, and the urban-centered culture all became permanent hallmarks of modern American life. Yet despite the very real economic progress achieved in the '20s, the decade ended in a grave depression that lasted all through the '30s. Only after World War II would the American people enjoy an abundance and prosperity rooted in the industrial transformation that began in the 1920s.

Yet beneath the surface, as Allan J. Lichtman points out, there were "striking similarities between Smith and Hoover." Both were self-made men who embodied the American belief in freedom of opportunity and upward mobility. Neither advocated any significant degree of economic change nor any redistribution of national wealth or power. Though religion proved to be the most important issue in the minds of the voters, hurting Smith far more than Prohibition or his identification with the city, the Democratic candidate's failure to spotlight the growing cracks in prosperity and offer alternative economic policies ensured his defeat.

The 1928 election was a dubious victory for the Republicans. Hoover won easily, defeating Smith

Recommended Reading

William Leuchtenburg provides the best overview of the 1920s in *The Perils of Prosperity, 1914–1932* (1958). He stresses the theme of rural-urban conflict and claims that the achievements of the decade were more significant than its failures. The essays in John Braeman, Robert H. Bremner, and David Brody, eds., *Change and Continuity in Twentieth Century America: The 1920s* (1968) illuminate important aspects of the period.

A fully detailed account of economic developments in the decade is George Soule, *Prosperity Decade* (1947). Two classic studies, Frederick Lewis Allen, *Only Yesterday* (1931) and Helen Lynd and Robert Lynd, *Middletown* (1929), offer valuable insights into social and cultural trends. The most recent overview of the decade is Geoffrey Perrett, *America in the Twenties* (1982).

The spirit of rural discontent with the new urban society is captured best in Lawrence Levine, *Defender of the Faith* (1965), an account of the last ten years of William Jennings Bryan's life. For changing political alignments of the 1920s, see David Burner, *The Politics of Provincialism* (1968).

Additional Bibliography

General surveys of the 1920s include Ellis W. Hawley, *The Great War and the Search for a Modern Order* (1979) and Donald McCoy, *Coming of Age* (1973). Books on economic themes are John B. Rae, *The American Automobile* (1965); James J. Flink, *The Car Culture* (1975); Allen Nevins and Frank E. Hill, *Ford: Expansion and Challenge, 1915–1933* (1957); James Prothro, *The Dollar Decade* (1954); Otis A. Pease, *The Responsibilities of American Advertising* (1959); and Alfred D. Chandler, Jr., *Strategy and Structure* (1962). The best books on labor are Irving Bernstein, *The Lean Years* (1960) and Robert H. Zieger, *Republicans and Labor, 1919–1929* (1969). James Shideler discusses the postwar agricultural depression in *Farm Crisis* (1957).

Social history is covered in Preston Slosson, *The Great Crusade and After* (1930); Paul Carter, *Another Part of the Twenties* (1976); and Elizabeth Stevenson, *Babbitts and Bohemians* (1967). For family life, see John Sirjamaki, *The American Family in the 20th Century* (1953) and Paula S. Fass, *The Damned and the Beautiful* (1977).

The role of women in the 1920s is examined in William Chafe, *The American Woman* (1972); J. Stanley Lemons, *The Woman Citizen* (1973); Susan D. Becker, *The Origins of the Equal Rights Amendment* (1981); and Winifred D. Wandersee, *Women's Work and Family Values, 1920–1940* (1981). For blacks in the 1920s, see Nathan Huggins, *Harlem Renaissance* (1971); Gilbert Osofsky, *Harlem* (1966); and David Levering Lewis, *When Harlem Was in Vogue* (1981), a lively account of black culture.

Frederick Hoffman, *The Twenties* (1955) and Alfred Kazin, *On Native Grounds* (1942) survey the literary trends during the decade. Other studies of this subject are Roderick Nash, *The Nervous Generation* (1969); Robert Crunden, *From Self to Society* (1972); Malcolm Cowley, *Exile's Return* (1934); and Edmund Wilson, *Shores of Light* (1952). Biographies of major literary figures of the period include William Manchester, *Disturber of the Peace* (1951) on H. L. Mencken; Arthur Mizener, *The Far Side of Paradise* (1951) on F. Scott Fitzgerald; Mark Shorer, *Sinclair Lewis* (1961); and Carlos Baker, *Hemingway* (1956).

Studies of political fundamentalism include Robert K. Murray, *Red Scare* (1955) and Stanley Coben, *A. Mitchell Palmer* (1963) on the postwar panic over radicalism; Andrew Sinclair, *Prohibition* (1962) and Herbert Asbury, *The Great Illusion* (1950) on the noble experiment; David Chalmers, *Hooded Americans* (1965), Arnold S. Rice, *The Ku Klux Klan in American Politics* (1962), and Kenneth T. Jackson, *The Ku Klux Klan in the City* (1967) on the KKK; Robert A. Divine, *American Immigration Policy* (1957) and John Higham, *Strangers in the Land* (1955) on nativism and immigration restriction; and Norman Furniss, *The Fundamentalist Controversy* (1954) and Ray Ginger, *Six Days or Forever?* (1956) on the attack on Darwinism and the Scopes trial.

For political developments during the 1920s, see Robert Murray, *The Harding Era* (1969) and *The Politics of Normalcy* (1973); Burl Noggle, *Teapot Dome* (1962); Francis Russell, *The Shadow of Blooming Grove: Warren G. Harding and His Times* (1968); Joan H. Wilson, *Herbert Hoover* (1975); and David Burner, *Herbert Hoover: A Public Life* (1979). Allan Lichtman, *Prejudice and the Old Politics* (1979) and Kristi Andersen, *The Creation of a Democratic Majority, 1928–1936* (1979) offer contrasting interpretations of the election of 1928.

chapter 26

FRANKLIN D. ROOSEVELT AND THE NEW DEAL

The prosperity of the twenties came to an abrupt halt in October 1929. The stock market, which had boomed during the decade, suddenly faltered. Investors who had borrowed heavily to take part in the speculative mania which swept Wall Street suddenly were forced to sell their securities to cover their loans. The wave of selling triggered an avalanche. On October 24, later known as Black Thursday, nearly thirteen million shares were traded as highfliers like RCA and Westinghouse lost nearly half their value. Bankers had only brief success in trying to stem the decline; panic overcame their feeble efforts on October 29, the worst day in stock-exchange history, when sellers dumped over sixteen million shares and the industrial average fell by forty-three points. The panic ended in November, with stocks at 1927 levels. For the next four years, there was a steady drift downward, until by 1932 prices were 80 percent below their 1929 highs.

The Great Depression which followed the crash of 1929 was the most devastating economic blow that the nation ever suffered. It lasted for ten years, dominating every aspect of American life during the thirties. Unemployment rose to twelve million by 1932, and though it dipped midway through the decade, it still stood at ten million by 1939. Children grew up thinking that economic deprivation was the norm rather than the exception in America. Year after year, people kept looking for a return to prosperity, but the outlook remained bleak and dismal. Intractable and all-encompassing, the Depression loosened its grip on the nation only after the outbreak of World War II. And even then, it left enduring psychological scars—never again would the Americans who lived though it be quite so optimistic about their economic future.

The Depression led to a profound shift in American political loyalties. The Republicans, dominant since the 1890s, gave way to a new Democratic majority. The millions of immigrants who had come to the United States before World War I became more active politically, as did their children when they reached voting age. The result was the election of Franklin D. Roosevelt to the presidency and the development of the New Deal, a broad program of relief, recovery, and reform that greatly increased the role of government in American life.

The Great Depression

The economic collapse altered American attitudes. In the twenties, optimism had prevailed as people looked forward to an ever increasing flow of consumer goods and a better way of life. But after 1929, bleak despair set in. Factories closed, machines fell silent, and millions upon millions of people walked the streets, looking for jobs that did not exist.

The Great Bull Market

The consumer-goods revolution contained the seeds of its own collapse. The steady expansion of the automobile and appliance industries led gradually to a saturation of the market. Each year after 1924, the rate of increase in the sale of cars and refrigerators and ranges slowed, a natural consequence of more and more people already owning these durable goods. Production began to falter, and in 1927, the nation underwent a mild recession. The sale of durable goods declined, and construction of houses and buildings fell slightly. If corporate leaders had heeded these warning signs, they might have responded by raising wages or lowering prices, both effective ways to stimulate purchasing power and sustain the consumer-goods revolution. Or if government officials had recognized the danger signals and forced a halt in installment-buying and slowed bank loans, the nation might have experienced a sharp but brief depression.

Neither government nor business leaders were so farsighted. The Federal Reserve Board lowered the discount rate, charging banks less for loans in an attempt to stimulate the economy. Much of this additional credit, however, went not into solid investment in factories and machinery but instead into the stock market, touching off a new wave of speculation that obscured the growing economic slowdown and ensured a far greater crash to come.

Individuals with excess cash began to invest heavily in the stock market, betting that the already impressive rise in security prices would bring them even greater windfall profits. The market had advanced in spurts during the decade; the value of all stocks listed on the New York Stock Exchange rose from $27 billion in 1925 to $67 billion in early 1929. The strongest surge began in the spring of 1928, when investors ignored the declining production figures in the belief that they could make a killing in the market. People took their savings and bet on speculative stocks. Corporations used their large cash reserves to supply money to brokers who in turn loaned it to investors on margin; in 1929, for example, the Standard Oil Company of New Jersey loaned out $69 million a day in this fashion.

Investors could now play the market on credit, buying stock listed at $100 a share with $10 down and $90 on margin, the broker's loan for the balance. If the stock advanced to $150, the investor could sell and reap a gain of 500 percent on the $10 investment. And in the bull-market climate of the twenties, everyone was sure that the market would go up.

By 1929, it seemed that the whole nation was engaged in speculation. In city after city, brokers opened branch offices, each complete with a stock ticker and a huge board covered with the latest Wall Street quotations. People crowded into the customers' rooms, filling the seats and greeting the latest advances of their favorite stocks with shouts of approval. So great was the public's interest in the stockmarket that newspapers carried the stock averages on their front pages.

In reality, though, more people were spectators than speculators; fewer than three million Americans owned stocks in 1919, and only about five hundred thousand were active buyers and sellers. But the bull market became a national obsession, assuring everyone that the economy was healthy and preventing any serious analysis of its underlying flaws. When the market soared to over $80 billion in total value by mid-summer, the *Wall Street Journal* discounted any possibility of a

At their height, the 1920s were a zany, get-rich-quick era in which millions of Americans either played or watched the stock market.

decline, proclaiming, "The outlook for the fall months seems brighter than at any time."

The great crash in October 1929 put a sudden and tragic end to the speculative mania. The false confidence that had kept the economy from collapsing in 1927 evaporated overnight. Suddenly, corporations and financial institutions were no longer willing to provide capital for stock-market purchases. More important, investors and bankers cut off consumer credit as well, drying up buying power and leading to a sharp decline in the sales of consumer goods. Factories began to cut back production, laying off some workers and reducing hours for others. The layoffs and cutbacks lowered purchasing power even further, so fewer people bought cars and appliances. More factory layoffs resulted, and some plants closed entirely, leading to even less money for the purchase of consumer goods.

This downward economic spiral continued for four years. By 1932, unemployment had swelled to 25 percent of the work force. Steel production was down to 12 percent of capacity, and the vast assembly lines in Detroit produced only a trickle of cars each day. The Gross National Product fell to 67 percent of the 1929 level. The bright promise of mass production had ended in a nightmare.

The basic explanation for the Great Depression lies in the fact that U.S. factories produced more goods than the American people could consume. There were other contributing causes—unstable economic conditions in Europe, the agricultural decline since 1919, corporate mismanagement, and excessive speculation—but at bottom people simply did not have enough money to buy the consumer products coming off the assembly lines. The market for such products was not fully saturated. In 1929, there were still millions of Americans who did not own a car or radio or a refrigerator. But they lacked the money to buy any of these creature comforts. Installment sales had helped bridge the gap, but by 1929 the burden of debt was just too great.

The failure of the new economic system to distribute wealth more broadly was the chief difficulty. Too much money had gone into profits, dividends, and industrial expansion, and not enough into the hands of the workers, who were also consumers. Factory productivity had increased 43 percent during the decade, but the wages of industrial workers had only gone up 11 percent (See chapter 25). If the billions that went into stock-market speculation had been used instead to increase wages—which would then have increased consumer purchasing power—production and consumption could have been brought into balance. Yet it is too much to expect that the prophets of the New Era could have foreseen this flaw and corrected it. They were pioneering a new industrial system, and only out of the bitter experience of the Depression would they discover the full dynamics of the consumer-goods economy.

Effect of the Depression

It is difficult to measure the human cost of the Great Depression. The material hardships were bad enough. Men and women lived in lean-tos made of scrap wood and metal, and families went without meat and fresh vegetables for months, existing on a diet of soup and beans. The psychological burden was even greater: Americans suffered through year after year of grinding poverty with no letup in sight. The unemployed stood in line for hours waiting for a relief check; veterans sold apples or pencils on street corners, their manhood—once prized so highly by the nation—now in question. People left the city for the countryside, but they found no salvation on the farm. Crops rotted in the fields because prices were too low to make harvesting worthwhile; sheriffs fended off angry crowds as banks foreclosed long-overdue mortgages on once-prosperous farms.

Few escaped the suffering. Blacks who had left the poverty of the rural South for factory jobs in the North were among the first to be laid off. Mexican-Americans, who had flowed in to replace European immigrants, met with competition from angry citizens, now willing to do stoop labor in the fields and work as track layers on the

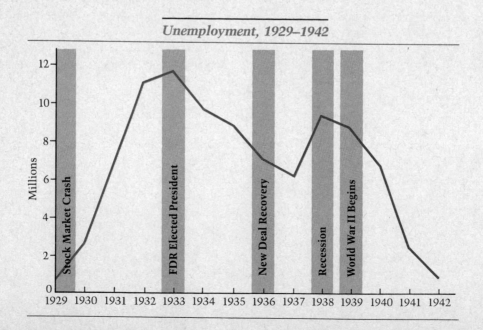

Unemployment, 1929–1942

■ Unemployment devastated thousands, who attempted to redeem their honor by selling apples or advertising their labor. The suddenly homeless gathered in hobo camps, like the New York City "Hooverville" above, while others crowded together on The Park Bench, as shown in the painting by Reginald Marsh (left).

railroads. Immigration officials used technicalities to halt the flow across the Rio Grande and even to reverse it; nearly a half million Mexicans were deported in the 1930s, including families with children born in the United States.

The poor—black, brown, and white—survived because they knew better than most Americans how to exist in poverty. They stayed in bed in cold weather, both to keep warm and to avoid unnecessary burning up of calories; they patched their shoes with pieces of rubber from discarded tires, heated only the kitchens of their homes, and ate scraps of food that others would reject.

The middle class, which had always lived with high expectations, was hit hard. Professionals and white-collar workers refused to ask for charity even while their families went without food; one New York dentist and his wife turned on the gas and left a note saying, "We want to get out of the way before we are forced to accept relief money." People who fell behind in their mortgage payments lost their homes and then faced eviction when they could not pay the rent. Health care declined. Middle-class people stopped going to doctors and dentists regularly, unable to make the required cash payment in advance for services.

Even the well-to-do were affected, giving up many of their former luxuries and weighed down with guilt as they watched former friends and business associates join the ranks of the impoverished. "My father lost everything in the Depression" became an all-too-familiar refrain among young people who dropped out of college.

Many Americans sought escape in movement. Men and boys, and even women, rode the rails in search of jobs, hopping freights to move south in the winter or west in the summer. On the Missouri Pacific alone, the number of vagrants increased from just over thirteen thousand in 1929 to nearly two hundred thousand in 1931. One town in the Southwest hired special policemen to keep vagrants from leaving the boxcars. Those who became tramps had to keep on the move, but they did find a sense of community in the hobo jungles that sprang up along the major railroad routes. Here a man could find a place to eat and sleep and people with whom to share his misery. Louis Banks, a black veteran, told interviewer Studs Terkel what these informal camps were like:

Black and white, it didn't make any difference who you were, 'cause everybody was poor. All friendly, sleep in a jungle. We used to take a big pot and cook food, cabbage, meat and beans all together. We all set together, we made a tent. Twenty-five or thirty would be out on the side of the rail, white and colored. They didn't have no mothers or sisters, they didn't have no home, they were dirty, they had overalls on, they didn't have no food, they didn't have anything.

Fighting the Depression

The Great Depression presented an enormous challenge for American political leadership. The inability of the Republicans to overcome the economic catastrophe provided the Democrats with the chance to regain power. Although they failed to achieve full recovery before the outbreak of World War II, the Democrats did succeed in alleviating the suffering and establishing their political dominance.

Hoover and Voluntarism

Herbert Hoover was the Depression's most prominent victim. When the downturn began in late 1929, he tried to rally the nation with bold forecasts of better days ahead. His repeated assertion that prosperity was just around the corner bred cynicism and mistrust. Expressing complete faith in the American economic system, Hoover relied primarily on voluntary cooperation with business to halt the slide. He called the leaders of industry to the White House and secured their agreement to maintain prices and wages at high levels. Yet within a few months, employers were reducing wages and cutting prices in a desperate effort to survive.

Hoover also believed in voluntary efforts to relieve the human suffering brought about by the Depression. He called on private charities and local governments to help feed and clothe those in need. But when these sources were exhausted, he rejected all requests for direct federal relief, asserting that such handouts would undermine the character of proud American citizens.

As the Depression deepened, Hoover reluctantly began to move beyond voluntarism to undertake more sweeping governmental measures. A new Federal Farm Board loaned money to aid cooperatives and bought up surplus crops in the open market in a vain effort to raise farm prices. At Hoover's request, Congress cut taxes in an attempt to restore public confidence and adopted a few federal public-works projects, such as Boulder Dam, to provide jobs for idle men.

To help imperiled banks and insurance companies, Hoover proposed and Congress established the Reconstruction Finance Corporation established in early 1932. The RFC loaned government money to financial institutions to save them from bankruptcy. Hoover's critics, however, pointed out that while he favored aid to business, he still opposed measures such as direct relief and massive public works that would help the millions of unemployed.

By 1932, Hoover's efforts to overcome the Depression had clearly failed. The Democrats had gained control of the House of Representatives in the 1930 elections and were pressing the President to take bolder action, but Hoover stubbornly resisted. His public image suffered its sharpest blow in the summer of 1932 when he ordered General Douglas MacArthur to clear out a group of ragged World War I veterans who had marched on Washington in a vain effort to get a bonus bill passed in Congress. Mounted troops drove the bonus marchers out of their shanties in Anacostia Flats along the Potomac, blinding the veterans with tear gas and burning their shacks.

Meanwhile, the nation's banking structure approached collapse. Bank failures rose steadily in 1931 and 1932 as customers responded to rumors of bankruptcy by rushing in to withdraw their deposits, thereby causing a bank's failure. The banking crisis completed the nation's disenchantment with Hoover; the people were ready for a new leader in the White House.

The Emergence of Roosevelt

The man who stepped forward to meet this national need was Franklin D. Roosevelt. Born into the old Dutch colonial aristocracy of New York, FDR was a distant cousin of the Republican Teddy. He grew up with all the advantages of wealth—private tutors, his own sailboat and pony, frequent trips to Europe, and education at Groton and Harvard. His strong-willed mother smoothed all the obstacles in the path of her only child and gave him a priceless sense of inner security. After graduation from Harvard, he briefly attended law school but left to plunge into politics. He served in the New York legislature and then went to Washington as assistant secretary of the navy under Wilson, a post he filled

Bank Failures, 1929–1933

Year	Failures
1933	5190
1932	2294
1931	1456
1930	1352
1929	659

Source: Data compiled from C. D. Bremer, American Bank Failures *(New York: Columbia University Press, 1935), p. 42.*

capably during World War I. He met with defeat in 1920 as the Democratic vice-presidential candidate and had begun a banking career when an attack of polio crippled him in the summer of 1921. Refusing to give in, he fought back bravely, and though he never again walked unaided, he reentered politics in the mid-twenties and was elected governor of New York in 1928.

Roosevelt's dominant trait was his ability to persuade and convince other people. He possessed a marvelous voice, deep and rich, a winning smile, and a bouyant confidence that he could easily transmit to others. Some felt he was too vain and superficial as a young man, but his bout with polio gave him both an understanding of human suffering and a broad political appeal as a man who had faced heavy odds and overcome them. He understood the give-and-take of politics, knew how to use flattery to win over doubters, and was especially effective in exploiting the media, whether in bantering with newspaper reporters or reaching out to the American people on the radio. Although his mind was quick and agile, he had little patience with philosophical nuances; he dealt with the appearance of issues, not their deeper substance, and he displayed a flexibility toward political principles that often dismayed even his warmest admirers.

Roosevelt took advantage of the opportunity offered by the Depression. With the Republicans discredited, he cultivated the two wings of the divided Democrats, appealing to both the traditionalists from the South and West and the new urban elements in the North. After winning the party's nomination in 1932, he broke with tradition by flying to Chicago and accepting in person, telling the cheering delegates, "I pledge you—I pledge myself to a new deal for the American people."

In the fall, he defeated Herbert Hoover in a near landslide for the Democrats. Roosevelt tallied 472 electoral votes as he swept the South and West and carried nearly all the large industrial states as well. Farmers and workers, Protestants and Catholics, immigrants and native-born rallied behind the new leader who promised to restore prosperity. Roosevelt not only met the challenge of the Depression but also solidified the shift to the Democratic party and created an enduring coalition that would dominate American politics for a half-century.

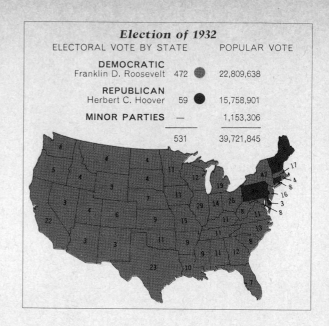

The Hundred Days

When Franklin Roosevelt took the oath of office on March 4, 1933, the nation's economy was on the brink of collapse. Unemployment stood at nearly thirteen million, one fourth of the labor force; banks were closed in thirty-eight states. On inauguration morning, the governors of New York and Illinois closed the banks in the nation's two largest cities, thus bringing the country's financial transactions to a halt. Speaking from the steps of the Capitol, FDR declared boldly, "First of all, let me assert my firm belief that the only thing we have to fear is fear itself—nameless, unreasoning, unjustified terror." Then he announced that he would call Congress into special session and request "broad executive power to wage a war against the emergency, as great as the power that would be given to me if we were in fact invaded by a foreign foe."

Within the next ten days, Roosevelt won his first great New Deal victory by saving the nation's banks. On March 5, he issued a decree closing the banks and called Congress back into session. His aides drafted new banking legislation and presented it to Congress on March 9; a few hours later, both houses passed it, and FDR signed the new legislation that evening. The measure provided for government supervision

■ *Through his fireside chats, FDR became the first president to use the immediacy of the national media to reach and reassure the American public.*

of nationalizing the banks, he had simply thrown the government's resources behind them and preserved private ownership. Though some other New Deal measures would be more radical, Roosevelt set the tone in the banking crisis. He was out to reform and restore the American economic system, not change it drastically.

For the next three months, until it adjourned in June, Congress responded to a series of presidential initiatives. During these "Hundred Days," Roosevelt sent fifteen major requests to Congress and received back fifteen pieces of legislation. A few created permanent agencies that have become a part of American life: the Federal Deposit Insurance Corporation (FDIC) to protect bank deposits and the Tennessee Valley Authority (TVA) to build dams that would both control floods and provide electricity to modernize a poverty-stricken area of the upper South. Other New Deal agencies were temporary in nature, designed to meet the specific economic problems of the Depression. None were completely successful; the Depression would continue for another six years, immune even to Roosevelt's magic. But psychologically the nation turned the corner in the spring of 1933. Under FDR, the government seemed to be responding to the economic crisis, enabling people for the first time since 1929 to look to the future with hope.

and aid to the banks. Strong ones would be reopened with federal support, weak ones closed, and those in difficulty bolstered by government loans.

On March 12, FDR addressed the nation by radio in the first of his fireside chats. In conversational tones, he told the public what he had done. Banks would begin to reopen the next day, with the government standing behind them. Other banks, once they became solvent, would open later, and the American people could safely put their money back into these institutions. The next day, March 13, the nation's largest and strongest banks opened their doors; at the end of the day, customers had deposited more cash than they withdrew. The crisis was over; gradually other banks opened, and the runs and failures ceased.

"Capitalism was saved in eight days," boasted one of Roosevelt's advisers. Most surprising was the conservative nature of FDR's action. Instead

---

Legislation Enacted During the Hundred Days (March 9–June 16, 1933)

Emergency Banking Relief Act	March 9
Beer-Wine Revenue Act	March 22
Unemployment Relief Act	March 31
Agricultural Adjustment Act	May 12
Federal Emergency Relief Act	May 12
Tennessee Valley Authority Act	May 18
Securities Act of 1933	May 27
Gold Repeal Joint Resolution	June 5
Home Owners' Refinancing Act	June 13
Farm Credit Act	June 16
Banking Act of 1933	June 16
Emergency Railroad Transportation Act	June 16
National Industrial Recovery Act	June 16

Roosevelt and Recovery

Two major New Deal programs launched during the Hundred Days were aimed at industrial and agricultural recovery. The first was the National Recovery Administration (NRA), FDR's attempt to achieve economic advance through planning and cooperation between government, business, and labor. In the midst of the Depression, businessmen were intent on stabilizing production and raising prices for their goods. Spokesmen for labor were equally determined to spread work through maximum hours and to put a floor under workers' income with minimum wages. The NRA hoped to achieve both goals by permitting companies in each major industry to cooperate in writing codes of fair competition which would set realistic limits on production, allocate percentages to individual producers, and set firm guidelines on prices. Section 7a of the enabling act mandated protection for labor in all the codes by establishing maximum hours, minimum wages, and the guarantee of collective bargaining by unions. No company could be compelled to join, but the New Deal sought complete participation by appealing to patriotism. Each firm that took part could display a blue eagle and stamp this symbol on its products. With energetic Hugh Johnson in charge, the NRA quickly enrolled the nation's leading companies and unions. By the summer of 1933, more than 500 industries had adopted codes that covered 2.5 million workers.

■ *Although the NRA quickly bogged down in a bureaucratic morass, the NRA blue eagle became a widely respected symbol of a business' patriotism.*

The NRA quickly bogged down in a huge bureaucratic morass. The codes proved to be too detailed to enforce easily. Written by the largest companies, these rules favored big business at the expense of smaller competitors. Labor quickly became disenchanted with Section 7a. The minimum wages were often near the starvation level, while business got around the requirement for collective bargaining by creating company unions that did not represent the real needs of workers. After a brief upsurge in the spring of 1933, industrial production began to sag as disillusionment with the NRA grew. By 1934, more and more businessmen were complaining about the new agency, calling it the "National Run Around." When the Supreme Court finally invalidated the NRA in 1935 on constitutional grounds, few mourned its demise. The idea of trying to overcome the Depression by relying on voluntary cooperation between competing businessmen and labor leaders had collapsed in the face of individual self-interest and greed.

The New Deal's attempt at farm recovery fared a little better. Henry A. Wallace, FDR's secretary of agriculture, came up with an answer to the farmers' old dilemma of overproduction. The government would act as a clearinghouse for producers of major crops, arranging for them to set production limits for wheat, cotton, corn, and other leading crops. Under the Agricultural Adjustment Act (AAA) passed by Congress in May 1933, the government would allocate acreage among individual farmers, encouraging them to take land out of production by paying them subsidies (raised by a tax on food processors). Unfortunately, Wallace preferred not to wait until the 1934 planting season to implement this program, and so farmers were paid in 1933 to plow under crops they had already planted and to kill livestock they were raising. Faced with the problem of hunger in the midst of plenty, the New Deal seemed to respond by destroying the plenty.

The AAA program worked better in 1934 and 1935 as land removed from production led to smaller harvests and rising farm prices. Farm income rose for the first time since World War I, increasing from $2 billion in 1933 to $5 billion by 1935. Severe weather, especially dust-bowl conditions in the Great Plains, contributed to the crop-limitation program, but most of the gain in farm income came from the subsidy payments themselves rather than from higher market prices.

On the whole, large farmers benefited most from the program. Possessing the capital to buy machinery and fertilizer, they were able to farm more efficiently than before on fewer acres of land. Small farmers, tenants, and sharecroppers did not fare as well, receiving very little of the government payments and often being driven off the land as owners took the acreage previously cultivated by tenants and sharecroppers out of production. Some three million people left the land in the thirties, crowding into the cities where they swelled the relief rolls. In the long run, the New Deal reforms improved the efficiency of American agriculture, but at a real human cost.

The Supreme Court eventually found the AAA unconstitutional in 1936, but Congress reenacted it in modified form that year and again in 1938. The system of allotments, now financed directly by the government, became a standard feature of the farm economy. Other New Deal efforts to assist the rural poor, notably the Farm Security Administration (FSA), sought to loan tenants and sharecroppers money to acquire land of their own, but the sums appropriated by Congress were too modest. The FSA was able to extend loans to fewer than 2 percent of the nation's tenant farmers. "Obviously," the FSA director informed Roosevelt, "this . . . program can be regarded as only an experimental approach to the farm tenancy problem." The result of the New Deal for American farming was to hasten its transformation into a business in which only the efficient and well-capitalized would thrive.

Roosevelt and Relief

The New Deal was far more successful in meeting the most immediate problem of the 1930s— relief for the millions of unemployed and destitute citizens. Roosevelt never shared Hoover's distaste for direct federal support; on May 12, 1933, in response to FDR's March request, Congress authorized the RFC to distribute $500 million to the states to help individuals and families in need.

Roosevelt brought in Harry Hopkins to direct the relief program. A former social worker who

■ *"Hunger is not debatable," said Harry Hopkins, the brash but selfless New Dealer who distributed $5 million of relief in his first two hours in office.*

seemed to live on black coffee and çigarettes, Hopkins set up a desk in the hallway of the RFC building and proceeded to spend over $5 million in less than two hours. By the end of 1933, Hopkins had cut through red tape to distribute money to nearly one sixth of the American people. The relief payments were modest in size, but they enabled millions to avoid starvation and stay out of humiliating breadlines.

Another, more imaginative early effort was the Civilian Conservation Corps (CCC), which was Roosevelt's own idea. The CCC enrolled youth from city families on relief and sent them to the nation's parks and recreational areas to build trails and improve public facilities. Ultimately, more than two million young men served in the CCC, contributing both to their families' incomes and to the nation's welfare.

Hopkins realized the need to do more than just keep people alive, and he soon became an advocate of work relief. Hopkins argued that the government should put the jobless to work, not just to encourage self-respect, but also to enable them to earn enough to purchase consumer goods and thus stimulate the entire economy. A Public Works Administration (PWA) headed by Secretary of the Interior Harold Ickes had been authorized

Federal work relief programs helped millions maintain their self-respect. Workers in the CCC (left) received $30 a month for planting trees and digging drainage ditches, while the WPA provided work for artists and writers.

in 1933, but Ickes, intent on the quality of the projects rather than human needs, failed to put many people to work. In the fall of 1933, Roosevelt created the Civil Works Administration (CWA) and charged Hopkins with getting people off the unemployment lines and relief rolls and back to work. Hopkins had over four million men and women at work by January 1934, building roads, schools, playgrounds, and athletic fields. Many of the workers were unskilled, and some of the projects were shoddy, but at least the CWA enabled people to work and earn enough money to survive the winter. Roosevelt, appalled at the huge expenditures involved, ended the CWA in 1934 and forced Hopkins to return to federal relief payments as the only source of aid to the jobless.

The final commitment to the idea of work relief came in 1935 when Roosevelt established the Works Progress Administration (WPA) to spend nearly $5 billion authorized by Congress for emergency relief. The WPA, under Hopkins, put the unemployed on the federal payroll so that they could earn enough to meet their basic needs and help stimulate the stagnant economy. Conservatives complained that the WPA amounted to nothing more than hiring the jobless to do make-work tasks with no real value. But Hopkins cared less about what was accomplished than about helping those who had been unemployed for years

to get off the dole and gain self-respect by working again.

In addition to the usual construction and conservation projects, the WPA tried to preserve the skills of American artists, actors, and writers. The Federal Theatre Project produced plays, circuses, and puppet shows that enabled entertainers to practice their crafts and to perform before people who often had never seen a professional production before. Similar projects for writers and artists led to a series of valuable state guidebooks and to murals that adorned public buildings across the land. A separate National Youth Administration (NYA) found part-time jobs for young people still in school and developed projects—ranging from automobile repairing in New York City to erecting tuberculosis isolation units in Arizona—for 2.5 million young adults.

The WPA helped ease the burden for the unemployed, but it failed to overcome the Depression. Rather than spending too much, as his critics charged, Roosevelt's greatest failure was not spending enough. The WPA never employed at any one time more than three million of the ten million jobless. The wages, although larger than relief payments, were still pitifully low, averaging only $52 a month. Thus the WPA failed to prime the American economy by increasing consumer purchasing power. Factories remained closed and machinery idle because the American people did not have the money, either from relief or the WPA, to buy cars, radios, appliances, and the other consumer goods that had been the basis for the prosperity of the 1920s. By responding to basic human needs, Roosevelt had made the Depression bearable. The New Deal's failure, however, to go beyond relief to achieve prosperity led to a growing frustration and the appearance of more radical alternatives that challenged the conservative nature of the New Deal and forced FDR to shift to the left.

As the Depression continued, it became apparent that the stopgap measures of the New Deal would have to be replaced by more sweeping reforms.

Democratic victory in the 1934 congressional elections, FDR responded by embracing a reform program that marked the climax of the New Deal.

Roosevelt and Reform

In 1935 the focus of the New Deal shifted from relief and recovery to reform. During his first two years in office, FDR had concentrated on fighting the Depression by shoring up the sagging American economy. Only a few new agencies, notably TVA, sought to make permanent changes in national life. Roosevelt was developing a "broker-state" concept of government, responding to pressures from organized elements such as corporations, labor unions, and farm groups while ignoring the needs and wants of the dispossessed who had no clear political voice. The early New Deal tried to assist bankers and industrialists, large farmers, and members of the labor unions, but it did little to help unskilled workers and sharecroppers.

The continuing depression and the high unemployment began to build pressures for more sweeping changes. Roosevelt faced the choice of either providing more radical programs, ones designed to end historical inequities in American life, or deferring to others who put forth solutions to the nation's ills. Bolstered by an impressive

Angry Voices

The signs of discontent were visible everywhere by 1935. In the upper Midwest, progressives and agrarian radicals, led by Minnesota Governor Floyd Olson, were calling for government action to raise farm and labor income. "I am a radical in the sense that I want a definite change in the system," Olson declared. "I am not satisfied with patching." Upton Sinclair, the muckraking novelist, nearly won the governorship of California in 1934 running on the slogan "End Poverty in California," while in the East a violent strike in the textile industry shut down plants in twenty states. The most serious challenge to Roosevelt's leadership, however, came from three demagogues who captured national attention in the mid-thirties.

The first was Father Charles Coughlin, a Roman Catholic priest from Detroit, who had originally supported FDR. Speaking to a rapt nationwide radio audience in his rich, melodious voice, Coughlin appealed to the discontented with a strange mixture of crank monetary schemes and anti-Semitism. He broke with the

New Deal in late 1934, denouncing it as the "Pagan Deal," and founded his own National Union for Social Justice. Increasingly vitriolic, he called for monetary inflation and the nationalization of the banking system in his weekly radio sermons to an audience of more than thirty million.

A more benign but equally threatening figure appeared in California. Dr. Francis Townsend, a sixty-seven-year-old physician, came forward in 1934 with a scheme to assist the elderly, who were suffering greatly during the Depression. The Townsend Plan proposed giving everyone over the age of sixty a monthly pension of $200 with the proviso that it must be spent within thirty days. Although designed less as an old-age pension plan than as a way to stimulate the economy, the proposal understandably had its greatest appeal among the elderly. They embraced it as a holy cause, joining Townsend Clubs across the country. Despite the criticism from economists that the plan would transfer over half the national income to less than 10 percent of the population, more than ten million people signed petitions endorsing the Townsend Plan, and few politicians dared oppose it.

The third new voice of protest was that of Huey Long, the flamboyant senator from Louisiana. Like Coughlin an original supporter of the New Deal, Long turned against FDR and by 1935 had become a major political threat to the President. A shrewd, ruthless, yet witty man, Long had a remarkable ability to mock those in power. The Kingfish (a nickname he borrowed from "Amos 'n Andy") announced a nationwide "Share the Wealth" movement in 1934. He spoke grandly of taking from the rich to make "Every Man a King," guaranteeing each American a home worth $5000 and an annual income of $2500. To finance the plan, Long advocated seizing all fortunes of more than $5 million and levying a tax of 100 percent on incomes over $1 million. By 1935, Long claimed to have founded twenty-seven thousand Share the Wealth Clubs and had a mailing list of over seven million people, including workers, farmers, college professors, and even bank presidents. Threatening to run as a third-party candidate in 1936, Long generated fear among Democratic leaders that he might attract three or four million votes, possibly enough to swing the election to the Republicans.

Social Security

When the new Congress met in January 1935, Roosevelt was ready to support a series of reform measures designed to take the edge off national dissent. The recent elections had increased Democratic congressional strength significantly, with the Republicans losing thirteen seats in the House and retaining less than one third of the Senate. Many of the Democrats were to the left of Roosevelt, favoring increased spending and more sweeping federal programs. "Boys—this is our hour," exulted Harry Hopkins. "We've got to get everything we want . . . now or never." Congress quickly appropriated $4.8 billion for the WPA and was prepared to enact virtually any proposal that Roosevelt offered.

The most significant reform enacted in 1935 was the Social Security Act. The Townsend movement had reminded Americans that the United States, alone among modern industrial nations, had never developed a welfare system to aid the aged, the disabled, and the unemployed. A cabinet committee began studying the problem in 1934, and President Roosevelt sent its recommendations to Congress the following January.

The proposed legislation had three major parts. First, it provided for old-age pensions financed equally by a tax on employers and workers, with no government contributions. Second, it set up a system of unemployment compensation on a federal-state basis, with employers paying a payroll tax and with each state setting the benefit levels and administering the program locally. Finally, it provided for direct federal grants to the states, on a matching basis, for welfare payments to the blind, handicapped, needy elderly, and dependent children.

Although there was criticism from conservatives who mourned the passing of traditional American reliance on self-help and individualism, the chief objections came from those who argued that the administration's measure did not go far enough. Democratic leaders, however, defeated efforts to incorporate Townsend's proposal for $200-a-month pensions and increases in unemployment benefits. Congress then passed the Social Security Act by overwhelming margins.

Ever since, critics have pointed out its shortcomings. The old-age pensions were paltry. Designed to begin in 1942, they ranged from $10 to

Despite the administration's boosterism, many felt that Social Security could not fulfill its promises.

realized that establishing a system of federal welfare went against deeply rooted American convictions. He insisted on a tax on participants to give those involved in the pension plan a vested interest in Social Security. He wanted them to feel that they had earned their pensions and that in the future no one would dare take them away. "With those taxes in there," he explained privately, "no damned politician can ever scrap my social security program." Above all, FDR had succeeded in establishing the principle of governmental responsibility for the aged, the handicapped, and the unemployed. Whatever the defects of the legislation, Social Security stood as a landmark of the New Deal, creating a system to provide for the welfare of individuals in a complex industrial society.

Labor Legislation

The other major reform achievement in 1935 was passage of the National Labor Relations Act. Senator Robert Wagner of New York introduced legislation in 1934 to outlaw company unions and other unfair labor practices in order to ensure collective bargaining for unions. FDR, who had little knowledge of labor-management relations and apparently little interest in them, opposed the bill. In 1935, however, Wagner began to gather broad support for his measure, which passed the Senate in May with only twelve opposing votes, and the President, seeing passage as likely, gave it his approval. The bill moved quickly through the House, and Roosevelt signed it into law in July.

$85 a month. Nor was everyone covered; those who most needed protection in their old age, such as farmers and domestic servants, were not included. The regressive feature of the act was even worse. All participants, regardless of income or economic status, paid in at the same rate, with no supplement from the general revenue. The trust fund also took out of circulation money that was desperately needed to stimulate the economy in the 1930s.

Other portions of the act were equally open to question. The cumbersome unemployment system offered no aid to those currently out of work, only to people who would lose their jobs in the future, and the benefits (depending on the state) ranged from barely adequate to substandard. The outright grants to the handicapped and dependent children were minute in terms of the need; in New York City, for example, a blind person received only $5 a week in 1937.

The conservative nature of the legislation reflected Roosevelt's own fiscal orthodoxy, but even more it was a product of his political realism. Despite the severity of the Depression, he

The Wagner Act, as it became known, created a National Labor Relations Board to preside over labor-management relations and enable unions to engage in collective bargaining with federal support. The act outlawed a variety of union-busting tactics and in its key provision decreed that whenever the majority of a company's workers voted for a union to represent them, management would be compelled to negotiate with the union on all matters of wages, hours, and working conditions. With this unprecedented government sanction, labor unions could now proceed to recruit the large number of unorganized workers throughout the country. The Wagner Act, the most far-reaching of all New Deal measures, led to the revitalization of the American labor movement and a permanent change in labor-management relations.

Three years later, Congress passed a second law which had a lasting impact on American workers —the Fair Labor Standards Act. A long-sought goal of the New Deal, this measure aimed to establish both minimum wages and maximum hours of work per week. Since labor unions usually were able to negotiate adequate levels of pay and work for their members, the act was aimed at unorganized workers and met with only grudging support from unions. Southern conservatives opposed it strongly, both on ideological grounds (it meant still greater government involvement in private enterprise) and because it threatened the very low wages in the South which had attracted northern industry since Reconstruction.

Roosevelt finally succeeded in winning passage of the Fair Labor Standards Act in 1938, but only at the cost of exempting many key industries from its coverage. The act provided for a minimum wage of forty cents an hour by 1940 and a standard work week of forty hours, with time and a half for overtime. Despite its loopholes, the legislation did lead to pay raises for the twelve million workers earning less than forty cents an hour. More important, like Social Security it set up a system—however inadequate—which Congress could build upon in the future to reach more generous and humane levels.

Other New Deal reform measures met with a mixed reception in Congress. Proposals to break up the huge public-utility holding companies created by promoters in the 1920s and to levy a "soak-the-rich" tax on the wealthy stirred up bitter debate, and these bills were passed only in greatly weakened form. Roosevelt was more successful in passing a banking act that made important reforms in the Federal Reserve System. He also gained congressional approval of the Rural Electrification Administration (REA), which helped to bring electricity to the 90 percent of American farms without it in the 1930s.

All in all, Roosevelt's record in reform was similar to that in relief and recovery—modest success but no sweeping victory. A cautious and pragmatic leader, FDR moved far enough to the left to overcome the challenges of Coughlin, Townsend, and Long without venturing too far from the mainstream. His reforms improved the quality of life in America significantly, but he made no effort to correct all the nation's social and economic wrongs.

Impact of the New Deal

The New Deal had a broad influence on the quality of life in the United States in the 1930s. Government programs reached into areas hitherto untouched. Many of them brought about long overdue improvements, but others failed to make any significant dent in historic inequities. The most important advances came with the dramatic growth of labor unions; failure to help women and minorities was the most disappointing result.

Rise of Organized Labor

Trade unions were weak at the onset of the Depression, with a membership of fewer than three million workers. Most were in the American Federation of Labor (AFL), composed of craft unions which served the needs of skilled workers. The nation's basic industries like steel and automobiles were unorganized; the great mass of unskilled workers thus fared poorly in terms of

---

Later New Deal Legislation

1934 Farm Mortgage Refinancing Act
Gold Reserve Act
Civil-Works Emergency Relief Act
Home Owners' Loan Act
Farm Mortgage Foreclosure Act
Bank Deposit Insurance Act
Silver Purchase Act
Securities Exchange Act
Labor Dispute Joint Resolution
Railway Pension Act
Communication Act

1935 Emergency Relief Appropriation Act
Wagner-Connery Labor Relations Act
Social Security Act
Public Utility Holding Company Act
Work Relief Act

1937 National Housing Act
Bankhead-Jones Farm Tenancy Act

1938 Fair Labor Standards Act

wages and working conditions. Section 7a of the NRA had led to some growth in AFL ranks, but the Federation's conservative leaders, eager to cooperate with business, failed to take full advantage of the opportunity to organize the mass-production industries.

John L. Lewis, head of the United Mine Workers, took the lead in forming the Committee on Industrial Organization (CIO) in 1935. The son of a Welsh coal miner, Lewis was a dynamic and ruthless man. He had led the mine workers since 1919 and was determined to spread the benefits of unions throughout industry. Lewis first battled with the leadership of the AFL, and then—after being expelled—he renamed his group the Congress of Industrial Organizations and announced in 1936 that he would use the Wagner Act to extend collective bargaining to the nation's auto and steel industries.

Within five years, Lewis had scored a remarkable series of victories. Some came easily. The big steel companies, led by U.S. Steel, surrendered without a fight in 1937; management realized that with federal support the unions were in a strong position. There was greater resistance in the automobile industry. When General Motors, the first target, resisted, the newly created United Automobile Workers (UAW) developed an effective strike technique. In January 1937, GM workers in Flint, Michigan, simply sat down in the factory, refusing to leave until the company rec-

■

A dynamic and ruthless labor organizer, John L. Lewis (top) resolved to use the Wagner Act to unionize unskilled workers in the steel and auto industries. The first opponent, General Motors, succumbed peaceably to a sit-down strike, but other employers used police to forcibly remove unarmed pickets. Philip Evergood's 1937 painting, The American Tragedy *(left), depicts the violence of the Republic Steel strike.*

ognized their union and threatening to destroy the valuable tools and machines if they were removed forcibly. When the Michigan governor refused to call out the National Guard, General Motors conceded defeat in the sit-down strike and signed a contract with the UAW. Chrysler quickly followed suit, but Henry Ford refused to give in and fought the UAW, hiring strikebreakers and beating up organizers. In 1941, however, Ford finally recognized the UAW. Smaller steel companies, led by Republic Steel, engaged in even more violent resistance; in one incident in 1938 police shot ten strikers. The companies eventually reached a settlement with the steelworkers' union in 1941.

By the end of the 1930s, the CIO had some five million members, slightly more than the AFL. The successes were remarkable—in addition to the auto-making and steel, organizers for the CIO and the AFL had been successful in the textile, rubber, electrical, and metal industries. For the first time, unskilled as well as skilled were unionized. Women and blacks benefited from the creation of the CIO, not because the union followed enlightened policies, but simply because they made up a substantial proportion of the unskilled work force.

Yet despite these impressive gains, only 28 percent of all Americans (excluding farm workers) belonged to unions by 1940. Millions in the restaurant, retail, and service trades remained unorganized, working long hours for very low wages. Employer resistance and traditional hostility to unions blocked further progress, as did the aloof attitude of President Roosevelt, who commented, "A plague on both your houses" during the steel strike. The Wagner Act had helped open the way, but labor leaders like Lewis, Philip Murray of the Steel Workers Organizing Committee, and Walter Reuther of the United Automobile Workers deserved most of the credit for the gains that were achieved.

The New Deal and Minorities

The Roosevelt adminstration's attempts to aid the downtrodden were least effective with blacks and other racial minorities. The Depression had hit blacks with special force. Sharecroppers and tenant farmers had seen the price of cotton drop from eighteen to six cents a pound, far below the level to sustain a family on the land. In the cities, the saying "First Fired, Last Hired" proved all too true; by 1933, over 50 percent of urban blacks were unemployed. Hard times sharpened racial prejudice. "No Jobs for Niggers Until Every White Man Has a Job" became a rallying cry for whites in Atlanta.

The New Deal helped blacks survive the Depression, but it never tried to confront squarely the racial injustice built into the federal relief programs. Although the programs served blacks as well as whites, in the South the weekly payments blacks received were much smaller. In the early days, NRA codes permitted lower wage scales for blacks, while the AAA led to the eviction of thousands of Negro tenants and sharecroppers. Black leaders referred to the NRA as standing for "Negro Robbed Again" and dismissed the AAA as "a continuation of the same old raw deal." Nor did later reform measures help very much. Neither the minimum wage nor Social Security covered those working as farmers or domestic servants, categories that comprised 65 percent of all black workers. Thus an NAACP official commented that Social Security "looks like a sieve with the holes just large enough for the majority of Negroes to fall through."

Despite this bleak record, blacks rallied behind Roosevelt's leadership, abandoning their historic ties to the Republican party. In 1936, over 75 percent of those blacks who voted supported FDR. In part, this switch came in response to Roosevelt's appointment of a number of prominent blacks to high-ranking government positions, such as William H. Hastie in the Interior Department and Mary McLeod Bethune (founder and president of Bethune-Cookman College) in the National Youth Administration. Eleanor Roosevelt spoke out eloquently throughout the decade against racial discrimination, most notably in 1939 when the Daughters of the American Revolution refused to let black contralto Marian Anderson sing in Constitution Hall. The First Lady and Interior Secretary Harold Ickes arranged for the singer to perform at the Lincoln Memorial, where seventy-five thousand gathered to hear her on Easter Sunday.

Perhaps the most influential factor in the blacks' political switch was the color-blind policy of Harry Hopkins. He had over one million blacks

■ *With the statue of Abraham Lincoln as a backdrop, black contralto Marian Anderson sings on the steps of the Lincoln Memorial in a concert given April 9, 1939.*

The New Deal relief program, however, did aid many thousands of Mexican-Americans in the Southwest in the 1930s, although migrant workers had difficulty meeting state requirements. The WPA hired Mexican-Americans for a variety of construction and cultural programs, but after 1937 such employment was denied to aliens. Overall, the pattern was one of very great economic hardship and relatively little federal assistance for Mexican-Americans.

The American Indian, after decades of neglect, fared slightly better under the New Deal. Roosevelt appointed John Collier, a social worker who championed Indian rights, to serve as commissioner of Indian affairs. In 1934, Congress passed the Indian Reorganization Act, a reform measure designed to stress tribal unity and autonomy instead of attempting (as previous policy had done) to transform Indians into self-sufficient farmers by granting them small plots of land (see chapter 17). Collier employed more Native Americans in the Indian Bureau, supported educational programs on the reservations, and encouraged tribes to produce native handiwork such as blankets and jewelry. Modest gains occurred, but the one third of a million Indians remained the nation's most impoverished citizens.

Women in the Thirties

The decade witnessed a continued decline in the status of American women. In the midst of the Depression, there was little concern expressed for protecting or extending their rights. The popular idea that women worked for "pin money" while men were the breadwinners for their families led employers to discriminate in favor of men when cutting the work force. Working women "are holding jobs that rightfully belong to the God-intended providers of the household," declared a Chicago civic group. More than three fourths of the nation's school boards refused to hire wives, and more than half of them fired women teachers who married. Federal regulations prohibited more than one member of a family from working in the civil service, and almost always it was the wife who had to defer to her husband. A Gallup poll revealed that 82 percent of the people disapproved of working wives, with 75 percent of the women polled agreeing.

working for the WPA by 1939, many of them in teaching and artistic positions as well as in construction jobs. Overall, the New Deal provided assistance to 40 percent of the nation's blacks during the Depression. Uneven as his record was, Roosevelt had still done more to aid this oppressed minority than any previous president since Lincoln. One black newspaper commented that while "relief and WPA are not ideal, they are better than the Hoover bread lines and they'll have to do until the real thing comes along."

The New Deal did far less for Mexican-Americans. Engaged primarily in agricultural labor, these people found their wages in California fields dropping from thirty-five to fourteen cents an hour by 1933. The pool of migrant labor expanded rapidly with dust-bowl conditions in the Great Plains and the subsequent flight of "Okies" and "Arkies" to the cotton fields of Arizona and the truck farms of California. The Roosevelt administration cut off any further influx from Mexico by barring entry of any immigrant "likely to become a public charge"; local authorities rounded up migrants and shipped them back to Mexico to relieve their welfare rolls.

Many of the working women in the 1930s were either single or the sole support of an entire family. Yet their wages remained lower than those for men, and their unemployment rate ran higher than 20 percent throughout the decade. Women over thirty-five found it particularly hard to find or retain jobs during the Depression. The New Deal offered little encouragement. NRA codes sanctioned lower wages for women, permitting laundries, for example, to pay them as little as fourteen cents an hour. The minimum wage did help those women employed in industry, but too many worked as maids and waitresses, jobs not covered by the law. By 1940, the percentage of women in the work force was no higher than it had been in 1910, and the traditional sexual inequities in the marketplace were as great as ever.

The one area of advance in the 1930s came in government. Eleanor Roosevelt set an example which encouraged millions of American women. Instead of presiding sedately over the White House, she traveled continually around the country, always eager to uncover wrongs and bring them to the President's attention (see the special feature in this chapter). Frances Perkins, the secretary of labor, became the first woman cabinet member, and FDR appointed women as ambassadors and federal judges for the first time.

Women also were elected to office in larger numbers in the thirties. Hattie W. Carraway of Arkansas succeeded her husband in the Senate, winning a full term in 1934. That same year voters elected six women to the House of Representatives. Public service, however, was one of the few professions open to women. The nation's leading medical and law schools discouraged women from applying, and the percentage of female faculty members in colleges and universities continued to decline in the 1930s. In sum, the decade was a grim one for American women.

End of the New Deal

The New Deal reached its high point in 1936, when Roosevelt was overwhelmingly reelected and the Democratic party strengthened its hold on Congress. But this political triumph was deceptive. In the next two years, Roosevelt met with a series of defeats in Congress. Yet despite

■ *The few advances made by working women in the 1930s came in government, as personified by Secretary of Labor Frances Perkins, the first woman cabinet member, shown here greeting steelworkers in Pittsburgh.*

these setbacks, he remained a popular political leader who had restored American self-confidence as he attempted to meet the challenges of the Depression.

The Election of 1936

Franklin Roosevelt enjoyed his finest political hour in 1936. A man who loved the give-and-take of politics, FDR faced challenges from both the left and the right as he sought reelection. Father Coughlin and Gerald L. K. Smith, who inherited Huey Long's following after the senator's assassination in 1935, organized a Union party, with North Dakota Progressive Congressman William Lemke heading the ticket. At the other extreme, a group of wealthy industrialists formed the Liberty League to fight what they saw as the New Deal's assault on property rights. The Liberty League attracted prominent Democrats, including Al Smith, but in 1936 it endorsed the Republican presidential candidate, Governor Alfred M. Landon of Kansas. A moderate, colorless figure, Landon disappointed his backers by refusing to campaign for repeal of the popular New Deal reforms.

Roosevelt ignored Lemke and the Union party, focusing attention instead on the assault from the right. Democratic spokesmen condemned the Liberty League as a "millionaire's union" and reminded the American people of how much Roosevelt had done for them in fighting unemployment and providing relief. In his speeches, FDR condemned the "economic royalists" who were "unanimous in their hatred for me." "I welcome their hatred," he declared, and promised that in his second term these forces would meet "their master."

This frank appeal to class sympathies proved enormously successful. Roosevelt won easily, receiving five million more votes than he had gotten in 1932 and outscoring Landon in the electoral college by 523 to 8. The Democrats did almost as well in Congress, piling up margins of 331 to 89 in the House and 76 to 16 in the Senate (with 4 not aligned with either major party).

Equally important, the election marked the creation of a new political coalition that would dominate American politics for the next three decades. FDR, building on the inroads into the Republican majority that Al Smith had begun in 1928, carried urban areas by impressive margins, winning 3.6 million more votes than his opponents in the nation's twelve largest cities. He held on to the traditional Democratic votes in the

Presidential Voting in Chicago by Ethnic Groups, 1924–1932 (Percent Democratic)

	1924	1928	1932
Czechoslovakians	40	73	83
Poles	35	71	80
Lithuanians	48	77	84
Yugoslavs	20	54	67
Italians	31	63	64
Germans	14	58	69
Jews	19	60	77

Source: John M. Allswang, A House for All Peoples: Ethnic Politics in Chicago, 1890–1936 (Lexington: University Press of Kentucky, 1971).

South and West and added to them by appealing strongly to the diverse religious and ethnic groups in the northern cities—Catholics and Jews, Italians and Poles, Irish and Slavs. The strong support of labor, together with three quarters of the black vote, indicated that the nation's new alignment followed economic as well as cultural lines. The poor and the oppressed, who in the Depression years included many middle-class Americans, became attached to the Democratic party, leaving the GOP in a minority position, limited to the well-to-do and to rural and small-town Americans of native stock.

The Supreme Court Fight

FDR proved to be far more adept at winning electoral victories than in achieving his goals in Congress. In 1937, he attempted to use his recent success to overcome the one obstacle remaining in his path—the Supreme Court. During his first term, the Court had ruled several New Deal programs unconstitutional, most notably the NRA and the AAA. Only three of the nine justices were sympathetic to the need for emergency measures in the midst of the Depression. Two others were unpredictable, sometimes approving New Deal measures and sometimes opposing them. Four justices were bent on using the Constitution to block Roosevelt's proposals. All were elderly men, and one, Willis Van Devanter, had planned to retire in 1932 but remained on the Court because he believed Roosevelt to be "unfitted and unsafe for the Presidency."

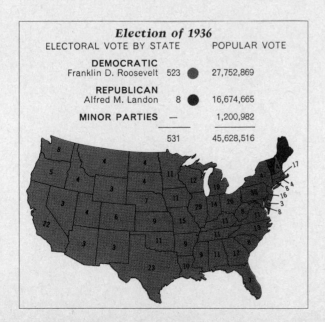

Election of 1936

ELECTORAL VOTE BY STATE		POPULAR VOTE
DEMOCRATIC Franklin D. Roosevelt	523	27,752,869
REPUBLICAN Alfred M. Landon	8	16,674,665
MINOR PARTIES	—	1,200,982
	531	45,628,516

Eleanor Roosevelt and the Quest for Social Justice

Eleanor Roosevelt entered public life as a reformer long before she became the First Lady. Although she loved and admired her uncle Theodore, her side of the Roosevelt family was more active in New York society than politics. In a family environment where the social graces were highly prized, Eleanor grew up shy and insecure. She turned to voluntary social work for fulfillment, where her relationships were based on common interests and ideals rather than social standing. Before her marriage to Franklin Roosevelt in 1905, she had been active in the New York settlement-house movement and the Consumers' League. Like many reformers of her day, she found her sense of social justice upset by the existence of poverty and inequality. Avoiding politics, which she then considered a "sinister affair," she limited her activities to nonpartisan reform and relief organizations.

After her marriage, she curtailed her social work, placing her responsibilities as a wife and mother first, as she believed a woman should. Though always a supportive partner, Mrs. Roosevelt did not develop a taste for politics despite her husband's tenure in the New York State Senate and later as assistant secretary of the navy during World War I. But when FDR was stricken with polio in 1921, she was determined that he return to political life as soon as possible; such a goal, she thought, was the best antidote to his pain and depression. While she worked tirelessly to speed his physical recovery, she also struck out on her own to keep the Roosevelt name alive in New York politics. In the newly formed League of Women Voters, the Women's City Club, the Non-Partisan Legislative Committee, and the New York State Democratic party, Eleanor Roosevelt brought her reformer's impulse to politics. In these organizations she formed the nucleus of an "old-girls' network" that she would employ entensively during the New Deal years. Her newly acquired political and organizational skills as well as her knowledge and speeches served her husband well in his gubernatorial and presidential campaigns.

In a speech delivered in 1928, Mrs. Roosevelt commented on the need to "bring government closer to the people" and to "develop the human side of government." Focusing on those whose needs were greatest, Eleanor Roosevelt was an advocate for the dispossessed. She advanced their interests within the administration, working hardest for women and blacks, whose voices were least often heard.

FDR appealed to the "forgotten man"; his wife concerned herself with the "forgotten woman." She worked with Harry Hopkins to achieve equity for women on relief and to create more jobs for women under the auspices of the CWA and the WPA. With Frances Perkins, she arranged to establish camps for unemployed girls patterned after the CCC while she continued to work with the Women's Trade Union League to guarantee women equal pay for equal work on federal projects. In her syndicated newspaper column "My Day," she often dealt with the problems faced by women during the Depression. She even held press conferences to which only women reporters were invited to ensure employment for at least a handful of female journalists.

The First Lady's office became, in effect, a clearing house for federally sponsored programs for women, and her endorsement often meant the difference between success or failure. She took advantage of her position to expedite the programs she thought most important. She saw to it that whenever possible women administrators were hired to supervise projects for women, but there were precious few programs for women to be administered. Although Mrs. Roosevelt was instrumental in the few gains made by women through the New Deal, her advocacy could not overcome the sexual stereotypes that continued to limit the role of women in the work force.

She worked equally hard for blacks, but with little more to show for her efforts. "We can have no group beaten down, underprivileged," said the First Lady in a radio address in 1934, "without reaction on the rest." In one sentence, she captured the essence of her appeal for justice and equality for blacks. Social justice was not merely desirable for blacks; it was necessary to ensure the vitality of American democracy. She spoke eloquently in favor of equal opportunity for blacks and sought their inclusion in New Deal programs. She worked with Hopkins to include more blacks in federal projects and lobbied within the administration for the appointment of black men and women to administer the programs designed specifically for them. Publicly, she endeavored to set an example for all Americans by addressing black audiences throughout the country, presiding over a more egalitarian

White House, and resigning her membership in the DAR over the Marian Anderson incident (see p. 762).

In her struggle against racial discrimination, Mrs. Roosevelt sometimes found her desires in conflict with her husband's attempts to keep the coalition of Democratic voters intact. His fear of alienating southern supporters caused him to temporize on the antilynching bill and abolition of the poll tax, both of which he considered desirable but not "must" legislation. Mrs. Roosevelt's support of these measures, however, put the Roosevelt name behind them. In her efforts to secure passage of the legislation, she arranged for meetings between FDR and Walter White of the NAACP. She briefed White to prepare him for FDR's objections in his conference with the President. When she asked FDR if he minded her public support of the antilynching bill, he replied, "Certainly not. . . . I can always say, 'Well, that is my wife; I can't do anything about her.'" Thus it appears that the President and Mrs. Roosevelt were of one mind, but she was able to support a cause that he felt it impolitic to advocate himself.

This distinction between the First Lady's activities as a representative of the Roosevelt administration and her actions as a private citizen was often a difficult one to establish. It is even harder to assess accurately her impact on the policies of the New Deal. Eleanor Roosevelt was revered by millions of Americans who saw in her the very essence of American ideals. Her support of women and blacks was instrumental in swaying their support to the Roosevelt coalition. Still, the telling fact remains that the plight of the two groups to which she devoted the lion's share of her attention during the Depression—women and blacks—was only slightly relieved. This is not to minimize her achievements. As the self-appointed conscience of the Roosevelt administration, she exposed the areas where the New Deal had not been realized. Her accessibility to the public and her willingness to serve its interests gave encouragement to those who had lost all hope. Her courage and vitality in the pursuit of human rights and equality made her the embodiment of reform and social justice in the New Deal.

FDR's battle with the Supreme Court provoked both sympathy and contempt among political cartoonists of the day. In the cartoon on the left, the NRA blue eagle lies dead, nailed to the wall by the Supreme Court. The cartoon on the right, entitled "That's the kind of sailor he is," satirizes FDR's Court-packing scheme.

When Congress convened in 1937, the President offered a startling proposal to overcome the Court's threat to the New Deal. Instead of seeking a constitutional amendment either to limit the Court's power or to clarify the constitutional issues, FDR chose an oblique attack. Declaring that the Court was falling behind schedule because of the age of its members, he asked Congress to appoint a new justice for each member of the Court over the age of seventy, up to a maximum of six.

Although this "court-packing" scheme, as critics quickly dubbed it, was perfectly legal, it outraged not only conservatives but liberals as well, who realized it could set a dangerous precedent for the future. Republicans wisely kept silent, letting prominent Democrats such as Senator Burton Wheeler of Montana lead the fight against Roosevelt's plan. Despite all-out pressure from the White House, resistance in the Senate blocked early action on the proposal.

The Court defended itself well. Chief Justice Charles Evans Hughes testified tellingly to the Senate Judiciary Committee, pointing out that in fact the Court was up-to-date and not behind schedule as Roosevelt charged. The Court then surprised observers with a series of rulings approving such controversial New Deal measures as

the Wagner Act and Social Security. In the midst of the struggle, Justice Van Devanter resigned, enabling FDR to make his first appointment to the Court since taking office in 1933. Feeling that he had proved his point, the President allowed his court-packing plan to die in the Senate.

During the next few years, four more vacancies occurred, and Roosevelt was able to appoint such distinguished jurists as Hugo Black, William O. Douglas, and Felix Frankfurter to the Supreme Court. Yet the price was high. The Court fight had badly weakened the President's relations with Congress, opening up deep rifts with members of his own party. Many senators and representatives who had voted reluctantly for Roosevelt's measures during the depths of the Depression new felt free to oppose any further New Deal reforms.

The New Deal in Decline

The legislative record during Roosevelt's second term was meager. Aside from the minimum wage and a maximum-hour law passed in 1938, Congress did not extend the New Deal into any new areas. Attempts to institute national health insurance met with stubborn resistance, as did

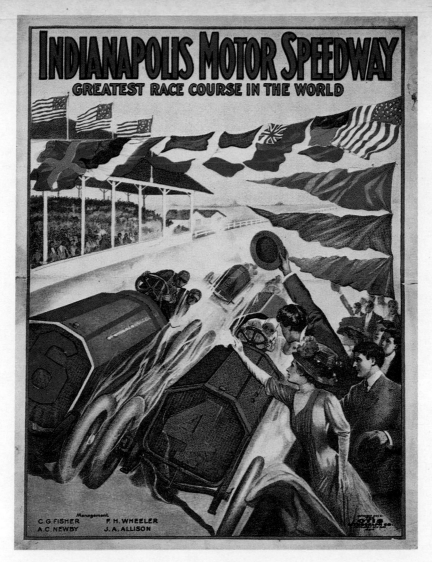

CULTURE OF THE AUTOMOBILE

The nature of the consumer-goods revolution in the transition to modern America is epitomized in the "car culture." In 1920, there were ten million cars in the nation; by the end of the decade, twenty-six million autos were on the road. Production jumped from less than two million a year to over five million by 1929.

The automobile boom, at its peak from 1922 to 1927, depended on the apparently insatiable appetite of the American people for cars. But as the decade continued, the market became saturated as more and more of those who could afford the novel luxury had become car owners. Marketing became as crucial as production. Automobile makers began to rely heavily on advertising and annual model changes, seeking to make customers dissatisfied with their old vehicles and eager to order new ones. Installment buying helped prolong the boom. By 1925,

The first Indy 500-mile auto race at the speedway was held in 1911. Ray Harroun won, driving a Marmon Wasp that averaged 74.59 miles per hour.

The auto is an indispensable part of the public service message in this 1937 highway billboard.

During the Depression years most Americans could not heed the message of this poster; they had to hang on to their old cars.

Their vintage car piled high, migrant farm workers in California travel from one job to another.

The end of the road. Early auto graveyard on Lincoln Highway near Lancaster, Pennsylvania.

Not even the Great Depression could shake the grip of the car culture on American life, even though sales of new cars dropped by 75 percent between 1929 and 1932. Instead of buying new automobiles, owners nursed along their old ones so that by 1939 there were nearly thirty million vehicles on the road, three million more than in 1929. It is no accident that the word "jalopy" was coined in the 1930s to describe the decrepit Dodges and battered Model T Fords that still chugged down American streets and highways. Even the Okies went West on wheels, riding in old flivvers piled high with mattresses and household goods, children, and pets.

Despite economic near-paralysis, there were innovations. Manufacturers began to soften their boxlike designs with curved, "streamlined" styling. Each fall millions of Americans waited for next year's models to appear, eager to see what fresh wonders Detroit had created. A nation that had always revered symbols of movement, from the *Mayflower* to the covered wagon, now had a new icon to worship.

efforts by civil-rights advocates to pass antilynching legislation. Disturbed by this growing congressional resistance, Roosevelt set out in the spring of 1938 to defeat a number of conservative Democratic congressmen and senators. His targets gleefully charged the President with interference in local politics; only one of the men he sought to defeat lost in the primaries. The failure of this attempted purge further undermined Roosevelt's strained relations with Congress.

The worst blow came in the economic sector. The slow but steady improvement in the economy suddenly gave way to a sharp recession in the late summer of 1937. In the next ten months, industrial production fell by one third, and nearly four million workers lost their jobs. Critics of the New Deal quickly labeled the downturn "the Roosevelt recession," and businessmen claimed it reflected a lack of confidence in FDR's leadership.

Actually, Roosevelt was at fault. In an effort to reduce expanding budget deficits, he had cut back sharply on WPA and other government programs after the election. Federal contributions to consumer purchasing power fell from $4.1 billion in 1936 to less than $1 billion in 1937. For several months, Roosevelt refused to heed calls from economists to renew heavy government spending. Finally, in April 1938, Roosevelt asked Congress for a $3.75-billion relief appropriation, and the economy began to revive. But FDR's premature attempt to balance the budget had meant two more years of hard times and had marred his reputation as the energetic foe of the Depression.

The political result of the attempted purge and the recession was a strong Republican upsurge in 1938. The GOP won an impressive 81 seats in the House and 8 more in the Senate, as well as 13 governorships. The party many thought dead suddenly had new life. The Democrats still held a sizable majority in Congress, but their margin in the House was particularly deceptive. There were 262 Democratic representatives to 169 Republicans, but 93 southern Democrats held the balance of power. After 1938, more and more often anti-New Deal Southerners voted with Republican conservatives to block social and economic reform measures. Thus not only was the New Deal over by the end of 1938, but a new bipartisan conservative coalition that would prevail for a quarter century had formed in Congress.

Chronology

1932	Franklin D. Roosevelt elected president
1933	Emergency Banking Relief Act passed in one day (March) Twenty-first Amendment repeals Prohibition (December)
1934	Securities and Exchange Commission authorized (June)
1935	Works Progress Administration (WPA) hires unemployed (April) Wagner Act grants workers collective bargaining (July) Congress passes Social Security Act (August)
1936	FDR wins second term as president
1937	Auto Workers' sit-down strike forces General Motors contract (February) FDR loses Court-packing battle (July) Roosevelt recession begins (August)
1938	Congress sets minimum wage at forty cents an hour (June)

Evaluation of the New Deal

The New Deal lasted a brief five years, and most of its measures came in two legislative bursts in the spring of 1933 and the summer of 1935. Yet its impact on American life was enduring. Nearly every aspect of economic, social, and political development in the decades that followed bore the imprint of Roosevelt's leadership.

The least impressive achievement of the New Deal came in the economic realm. Whatever credit Roosevelt is given for relieving human suffering in the depths of the Depression must be balanced against his failure to achieve recovery in the 1930s. The moderate nature of his programs, especially the unwieldy NRA, led to only slow and halting industrial recovery. Although much of the advance came as a result of government spending, FDR never embraced the concept of planned deficits, striving instead for a balanced budget. As a result, the nation had barely reached the 1929 level of production a decade later, and there were still nearly ten million men and women unemployed.

Equally important, Roosevelt refused to make any sweeping changes in the American economic system. Aside from the TVA, there were no broad experiments in nationalization and no attempt to alter free enterprise beyond imposing some limited forms of governmental regulation. The New Deal did nothing to alter the basic distribution of wealth and power in the nation. The outcome was the preservation of the traditional capitalist system with a thin overlay of federal control.

More significant change occurred in American society. With the adoption of Social Security, the government acknowledged for the first time its responsibility to provide for the welfare of those unable to care for themselves in an industrial society. The Wagner Act helped stimulate the growth of labor unions to balance corporate power, and the minimum-wage law provided a much-needed floor for many workers.

Yet the New Deal tended to help only the more vocal and organized groups, such as union members and commercial farmers. Those without effective voices or political clout—blacks and Mexican-Americans, women, sharecroppers, restaurant and laundry workers—received little help from the New Deal. For all the appealing rhetoric about the "forgotten man," Roosevelt did little more than Hoover in responding to the long-term needs of the dispossessed.

The most lasting impact of the Roosevelt leadership came in politics. Taking advantage of emerging ethnic voters and capitalizing on the frustration growing out of the Depression, FDR proved to be a genius at forging a new coalition. He overcame the friction between rural and urban Democrats that had prolonged Republican supremacy in the 1920s and attracted new groups to the Democratic party, principally blacks and organized labor. His political success led to a major realignment that lasted long after he left the scene.

His political achievement also reveals the true nature of Roosevelt's success. He was a brilliant politician who recognized the essence of leadership in a democracy—appealing directly to the people and infusing them with a sense of purpose. Thus despite his limitations as a reformer, Roosevelt proved to be the man the American people needed in the 1930s—the leader who helped them endure and survive the Great Depression.

Recommended Reading

The best overall account of political developments in the 1930s is William Leuchtenburg, *Franklin D. Roosevelt and the New Deal* (1963). Leuchtenburg offers a balanced treatment but concludes by defending Roosevelt's record. For a more critical view, see James MacGregor Burns, *Roosevelt: The Lion and the Fox* (1956), which portrays FDR as an overly cautious political leader. An exhaustive study of the New Deal through 1936 is Arthur M. Schlesinger, Jr., *The Age of Roosevelt*, 3 vols. (1957–1960), written from a sympathetic point of view. The best critique of Roosevelt's policies is the brief but perceptive book by Paul Conkin, *The New Deal* (1967).

Additional Bibliography

General accounts of the 1930s include Broadus Mitchell, *Depression Decade* (1947) on economic developments; Dixon Wecter, *The Age of the Great Depression* (1948) on social themes; John Braeman, Robert H. Bremner, and David Brody, eds., *The New Deal*, 2 vols. (1975), a collection of essays on both national and state trends; and John Allswang, *The New Deal and American Politics* (1978), a political survey.

Books on the Great Depression include John Kenneth Galbraith, *The Great Crash* (1955); Robert Sobel, *The Great Bull Market* (1968); Caroline Bird, *The Invisible Scar* (1963); and Studs Terkel, *Hard Times* (1970). Harris Warren, *Herbert Hoover and the Great Depression* (1959); Jordan Schwartz, *Interregnum of Despair* (1970); and Albert Romasco, *The Poverty of Abundance* (1965) all deal with Hoover's failure to stem the Depression.

Frank Freidel, *Franklin D. Roosevelt*, 4 vols. (1952–1976) is the most comprehensive biography of FDR, but the most recent volume only covers through mid-1933. Other biographical accounts of value are Rexford G. Tugwell, *The Democratic Roosevelt* (1957) and Alfred B. Rollins, *Roosevelt and Howe* (1962). The rich memoir literature for the New Deal includes Frances Perkins, *The Roosevelt I Knew* (1946); Raymond Moley, *The First New Deal* (1966); and Samuel I. Rosenman, *Working with Roosevelt* (1952). For biographies of Eleanor Roosevelt, see Joseph Lash, *Eleanor and Franklin* (1971) and Tamara K. Hareven, *Eleanor Roosevelt* (1968). Susan Ware traces the role of women in the New Deal in *Beyond Suffrage* (1981). J. Joseph Huthmacher has written a fine biography of a major New Deal figure, *Senator Robert Wagner and the Rise of Urban Liberalism* (1968).

The transition from Hoover and the beginning of the New Deal is traced in Elliot Rosen, *Hoover, Roosevelt and the Brains Trust* (1977). The best of many books dealing with farm problems in the 1930s are Richard Kirkendall, *Social Scientists and Farm Politics in the Age of Roosevelt* (1966); Paul Conkin, *Tomorrow a New*

World (1959); Van Perkins, *Crisis in Agriculture (1969)*; Sidney Baldwin, *Poverty and Politics* (1968); and Donald Worster, *Dust Bowl* (1979). Searle F. Charles traces Harry Hopkins' role in the New Deal in *Minister of Relief* (1963), while William McDonald describes the WPA's cultural activities in detail in *Federal Relief Administration and the Arts* (1969). For labor developments, see Sidney Fine, *Sit Down: The General Motors Strike of 1936-37* (1969) and two books by Irving Bernstein: *The New Deal's Collective Bargaining Policy* (1950) and *The Turbulent Years* (1970).

Among the many books surveying the various New Deal programs, the most useful are John Salmond, *The Civilian Conservation Corps, 1933–1942* (1967); Thomas K. McCraw, *TVA and the Power Fight, 1933–1939* (1971); and Jane D. Mathews, *The Federal Theatre, 1935–1939* (1967). Two other important books on the New Deal are Otis L. Graham, Jr., *An Encore for Reform* (1967) and Ellis Hawley, *The New Deal and the Problem of Monopoly, 1933–1939* (1965).

Studies by critics of the New Deal include George Wolfskill, *Revolt of the Conservatives* (1962); T. Harry Williams, *Huey Long* (1969); Abraham Holtzman, *The Townsend Movement* (1963); Charles Tull, *Father Coughlin and the New Deal* (1965); Sheldon Marcus, *Father Coughlin* (1973); and Alan Brinkley, *Voices of Protest: Huey Long, Father Coughlin, and the Great Depression* (1982). For intellectual radicalism in the 1930s, see Daniel Aaron, *Writers on the Left* (1960) and Richard Pells, *Radical Visions and American Dreams* (1973).

Raymond Wolters offers a critical view of Roosevelt's policies toward blacks in *Negroes and the Great Depression* (1970); Harvard Sitkoff is more positive in *A New Deal for Blacks* (1978). Abraham Hoffman deals with the repatriation issue in *Unwanted Mexican-Americans in the Great Depression* (1974). For the impact of the Depression on women, see William H. Chafe, *The American Woman* (1972); Winifred Wandersee, *Women's Work and Family Values, 1920–1940* (1981); and Lois Sharf, *To Work and to Wed* (1980).

Leonard Baker describes Roosevelt's attempt to pack the Supreme Court in *Back to Back* (1967). The best account of the waning of the reform impulse in Congress is James T. Patterson, *Congressional Conservatism and the New Deal* (1967).

UNITED
we are strong

UNITED we will win

chapter 27

AMERICA
AND THE WORLD,
1921–1945

On August 27, 1928, U.S. Secretary of State Frank B. Kellogg, French Foreign Minister Aristide Briand, and representatives of twelve other nations met in Paris to sign a treaty outlawing war. Several hundred spectators crowded into the ornate clock room of the Quai d'Orsay to watch the historic ceremony. Six huge kleig lights illuminated the scene so that photographers could record the moment for a world eager for peace. Briand opened the ceremony with a speech in which he declared, "Peace is proclaimed," and then Kellogg signed the document with a foot-long gold pen given to him by the citizens of Le Havre as a token of Franco-American friendship. In the United States, a senator called the Kellogg-Briand Treaty "the most telling action ever taken in human history to abolish war."

In reality, the Pact of Paris was the result of a determined American effort to avoid involvement in the European alliance system. In June 1927, Briand had sent a message to the American people inviting the United States to join with France in signing a treaty to outlaw war between the two nations. The invitation struck a sympathetic response, especially among pacifists who had advocated the outlawing of war throughout the 1920s, but the State Department feared correctly that Briand's true intention was to establish a close tie between France and the United States. The French had already created a network of alliances with the smaller countries of Eastern Europe; an antiwar treaty with the United States would at least ensure American sympathy, if not involvement, in case of another European war. Kellogg delayed several months and then outmaneuvered Briand by proposing that the pledge against war not be confined just to France and the United States, but instead be extended to all nations. An unhappy Briand, who had wanted a bilateral treaty with the United States, had no choice but to agree, and so the diplomatic charade finally culminated in the elaborate signing ceremony in Paris.

Eventually the signers of the Kellogg-Briand Treaty included nearly every nation in the world, but the effect was negligible. All promised to renounce war as an instrument of national policy, except of course, as the British made clear in a reservation, in matters of self-defense. The treaty relied solely on the moral force of world opinion. The Pact of Paris was, as one senator shrewdly commented, only "an international kiss."

Unfortunately, the Kellogg-Briand Pact was symbolic of American foreign policy in the years after World War I. Instead of asserting the role of leadership its resources and power commanded, the United States kept aloof from other nations. America went its own way, extending trade and economic dominance but refusing to take the lead in maintaining world order. This retreat from responsibility seemed unimportant in the 1920s when the very exhaustion from World War I ensured relative peace and tranquillity. But in the '30s, when threats to world order arose in Europe and Asia, the American people retreated even deeper, searching for an isolationist policy that would spare them the agony of another great war.

■ "Married Again" is the caption of this 1928 cartoon depicting the hopeful promise of the Kellogg-Briand Treaty. This wicked world is once again pledging fidelity to peace "forever and ever and ever."

There was no place to hide in the modern world. The Nazi onslaught in Europe and the Japanese expansion in Asia finally led to American entry into World War II in late 1941, at a time when the chances for an Allied victory seemed most remote. With incredible swiftness, the nation mobilized its military and industrial strength. American armies were soon fighting on three continents, the U.S. Navy controlled the world's oceans, and the nation's factories were sending a vast stream of war supplies to more than twenty Allied countries.

When victory came in 1945, the United States was by far the most powerful nation in the world. But instead of the enduring peace that might have permitted a return to a less active foreign policy, the onset of the Cold War with the Soviet Union brought on a new era of tension and conflict. This time the United States could not retreat from responsibility. World War II was a coming of age for American foreign policy.

Retreat, Reversal, and Rivalry

"The day of the armistice America stood on the hilltops of glory, proud in her strength, invincible in her ideals, acclaimed and loved by a world free of an ancient fear at last," wrote journalist George Creel in 1920. "Today we writhe in a pit of our own digging, despising ourselves and despised by the betrayed peoples of earth." The bitter disillusionment Creel described ran through every aspect of American foreign policy in the 1920s. In contrast to Wilsonian idealism, American diplomats made loans, negotiated treaties and agreements, and pledged the nation's good faith, but they were careful not to make any binding commitments on behalf of world order. The result was neither isolation nor involvement but rather a cautious middle course that managed to alienate friends and encourage foes.

Retreat in Europe

The United States emerged from World War I as the richest nation on earth, displacing England from its prewar position of economic primacy.

The Allied governments owed the United States a staggering $10 billion in war debts, money they had borrowed during and right after the conflict. Each year of the 1920s saw the nation increase its economic lead as the balance of trade tipped heavily in America's favor. The war-ravaged countries of Europe borrowed enormous amounts from American bankers to rebuild their economies; Germany alone absorbed over $3 billion in American investments during the decade. By 1929, American exports totaled more than $7 billion a year, three times the prewar level, and American overseas investment had risen to $17.2 billion.

The European nations could no longer compete on equal terms. The high American tariff, first imposed in 1922 and then raised again in 1930, frustrated attempts by England, France, and a defeated Germany to earn the dollars necessary to meet their American financial obligations. The Allied partners in World War I asked Washington to cancel the $10 billion in war debts, particularly after they were forced to scale down their demands for German reparations payments. American leaders from Wilson to Hoover indignantly refused this request, claiming that the ungrateful Allies were trying to repudiate their sacred obligations.

Only a continuing flow of private American capital to Germany allowed the payment of reparations to the Allies and the partial repayment of the war debts in the 1920s. The financial crash of 1929 halted the flow of American dollars across the Atlantic and led to subsequent default on the debt payments, with accompanying bitterness on both sides of the ocean.

Political relations fared little better. The United States never joined the League of Nations, nor did it take part in the attempts by England and France to negotiate European security treaties. American observers attended League sessions and occasionally took part in economic and cultural missions in Geneva. But the Republican administrations of the twenties refused to compromise American freedom of action by embracing collective security, the principle on which the League was founded. And FDR, always realistic, made no effort to renew Wilson's futile quest. Thus the United States remained aloof from the European balance of power and refused to stand behind the increasingly shaky Versailles settlement.

The United States ignored the Soviet Union throughout the 1920s. American businessmen, however, wanted to sell their machinery and tools to Russia for that country's rapid industrialization. They began to press for diplomatic recognition of the Bolshevik regime which had come to power in the Russian Revolution of 1917. In 1933, Franklin Roosevelt finally ended the long estrangement by signing an agreement opening up diplomatic relations between the two countries. The Soviets soon went back on promises to stop all subversive activity in the United States and to settle prerevolutionary debts, but at least the two nations had opened a channel of communication, even if they rarely understood one another.

Reversal in Latin America

United States policy in the Western Hemisphere was both more active and more enlightened than in Europe. The State Department sought new ways in the 1920s to pursue traditional goals of political dominance and economic advantage in Latin America. The outcome of World War I lessened any fears of European threats to the area and thus enabled the United States to dismantle the interventions in the Caribbean carried out by Roosevelt, Taft, and Wilson (see chapter 24). At the same time, both Republican and Democratic administrations worked hard to extend American trade and investment in the nations to the south.

Under Harding, Coolidge, and Hoover, American marines were withdrawn from Haiti and the Dominican Republic, and in 1924 the last detachment left Nicaragua, ending a twelve-year occupation. Renewed unrest there the next year, however, led to a second intervention in Nicaragua, which did not end until the early 1930s.

Showing a new sensitivity, the State Department released the Clark Memorandum in 1930, a policy statement repudiating the controversial Roosevelt Corollary to the Monroe Doctrine. Under the Monroe Doctrine, the United States had no right to intervene in neighboring states, declared Undersecretary of State J. Reuben Clark, although he asserted a traditional claim to protect American lives and property under international law.

When FDR took office in 1933, relations with Latin America were far better than they had been

On his South American tour to promote the *Good Neighbor policy*, FDR greets the president of Uruguay.

under Wilson, but American trade in the hemisphere had fallen drastically as the Depression worsened. Roosevelt moved quickly to solidify the improved relations and gain economic benefits. With his usual flair for the dramatic, he proclaimed a policy of the "good neighbor" and then proceeded to win goodwill by renouncing the imperialism of the past.

In 1933, Secretary of State Cordell Hull signed a conditional pledge of nonintervention at a Pan-American conference in Montevideo, Uruguay. A year later, the United States renounced its right to intervene in Cuban affairs (the Platt Amendment) and loosened its grip on Panama. By 1936, American troops were no longer occupying any Latin American nation. FDR personally cemented the new policy by traveling to Buenos Aires to sign an agreement that forbade intervention "directly or indirectly, and for whatever reason" in the internal affairs of an American state.

The United States had not changed its basic goal of political and economic dominance in the hemisphere; rather, the new policy of benevolence reflected Roosevelt's belief that cooperation and friendship were more effective tactics than threats and armed intervention. Mexico tried his patience in 1938 by nationalizing its oil resources; with admirable restraint, the President finally negotiated a settlement in 1941 on terms favorable to Mexico. Yet this economic loss was more than offset by the new trade opportunities opened up by the Good Neighbor policy. American commerce with Latin America increased fourfold in the 1930s, and investment rose substantially from its Depression low. Most important, FDR succeeded in forging a new policy of regional collective security. As the ominous events leading to World War II unfolded in Europe and Asia, the nations of the Western Hemisphere looked to the United States for protection against external danger.

Rivalry in Asia

In the years following World War I, the United States and Japan were on a collision course in the Pacific. The Japanese, lacking the raw materials to sustain their developing industrial economy, were determined to expand onto the Asian mainland. They had taken Korea by 1905 and during World War I had extended their control over the mines, harbors, and railroads of Manchuria, the industrial region of northeast China. The American Open Door policy remained the primary obstacle to complete Japanese dominion over China. The United States thus faced the clear-cut choice of either abandoning China or forcefully opposing Japan's expansion. American efforts to avoid making this painful decision postponed the eventual showdown but not the growing rivalry.

The first attempt at a solution came in 1921 when the United States convened the Washington Conference. The major objective was a political settlement of the tense Asian situation, but the most pressing issue was a dangerous naval race between Japan and the United States. Both nations were engaged in extensive shipbuilding programs begun during the war. Great Britain was forced to compete in order to preserve its traditional control of the sea; even so, projected construction indicated that both the United States and Japan would overtake the British navy by the end of the decade. Japan, spending nearly one third of its budget on naval construction, was eager for an agreement; in the United States, growing congressional concern over appropriations suggested the need for slowing the naval buildup.

In his welcoming address at the Washington Conference, Secretary of State Charles Evans Hughes outlined a specific plan for naval disarmament, calling for the scrapping of sixty-six battleships—thirty American, nineteen British, and seventeen Japanese. Three months later, delegates signed a Five Power Treaty embodying the main elements of Hughes' proposal: limitation of capital ships (battleships and aircraft carriers) in a ratio of 5–5–3 for the United States, Britain, and Japan respectively and 1.75–1.75 for France and Italy. England reluctantly accepted equality with the United States, while Japan agreed to the lower ratio only in return for an American pledge not to fortify Pacific bases such as the Philippines and Guam. The treaty cooled off the naval race even though it did not include cruisers, destroyers, or submarines.

The Washington Conference produced two other major agreements, the Nine Power Treaty and the Four Power Treaty. The first simply pledged everyone to uphold the Open Door policy, while the other compact replaced the old Anglo-Japanese alliance with a new Pacific security pact signed by the United States, Great Britain, Japan, and France. Neither document contained any enforcement provision beyond a promise to consult in case of a violation. In essence, the Washington treaties formed a parchment peace, a pious set of pledges that attempted to freeze the status quo in the Pacific.

This compromise lasted less than a decade. In September 1931, Japanese forces overran Manchuria, violating the Nine Power Treaty and the Kellogg-Briand Pact in a brutal act of aggression. The United States, paralyzed by the Depression, responded feebly. Secretary of State Henry L. Stimson sent an observer to Geneva to assure cooperation with the League of Nations, which was content to investigate the "incident." In January 1932, Stimson fell back on moral force, issuing notes vowing that the United States would not recognize the legality of the Japanese seizure of Manchuria. Despite ultimate concurrence by the League on nonrecognition, the Japanese ignored the American moral sanction and incorporated the former Chinese province, now renamed Manchukuo, into their expanding empire.

Aside from the good-neighbor approach in the Western Hemisphere, American foreign policy faithfully reflected the prevailing disillusionment with world power that gripped the country after World War I. The United States avoided taking any constructive steps toward preserving world order, preferring instead the empty symbolism of the Washington treaties and the Kellogg-Briand Pact.

Isolationism

The retreat from an active world policy in the 1920s turned into a headlong flight back to isolationism in the '30s. Two factors were responsible. First, the Depression made foreign policy seem remote and unimportant to most Americans. As unemployment increased and the economic crisis intensified after 1929, many people grew apathetic about events abroad. Second, the danger of war abroad, when it did finally penetrate the American consciousness, served only to strengthen the desire to escape involvement.

Three powerful and discontented nations were on the march in the 1930s—Germany, Italy, and Japan. In Germany, Adolf Hitler came to power in 1933 as the head of a National Socialist, or Nazi, movement. A shrewd, charismatic, and eloquent leader, Hitler capitalized on both domestic discontent and bitterness over World War I. Blaming the Jews for all of Germany's ills, he quickly imposed a totalitarian dictatorship in which the Nazi party ruled and the führer was supreme. At first, his foreign policy seemed harmless, but as he consolidated his power, the ultimate threat to world peace became clearer. Hitler took Germany out of the League of Nations, reoccupied the Rhineland, and formally denounced the Treaty of Versailles. His boasts of uniting all Germans into a Greater Third Reich that would last a thousand years filled his European opponents with terror, blocking any effective challenge to his regime.

In Italy, another dictator, Benito Mussolini, had come to power in 1922. Emboldened by Hitler's success, he embarked on an aggressive foreign policy in 1935. His invasion of the independent African nation of Ethiopia led its emperor, Haile Selassie, to call upon the League of Nations for support. With England and France far more concerned about Hitler, the League's halfway measures utterly failed to halt Mussolini's conquest. "Fifty-two nations had combined to resist aggres-

Captured German painting. Millions of Germans idolized Adolph Hitler, portrayed here as a white knight. After the painting came into American hands, a GI slashed Hitler's face to indicate his displeasure with the mystique of the Fuhrer.

sion," commented historian A. J. P. Taylor; "all they accomplished was that Haile Selassie lost all his country instead of only half." Collective security had failed its most important test.

Japan formed the third element in the threat to world peace. Militarists began to dominate the government in Tokyo by the mid-1930s, using tactics of fear and even assassination against their liberal opponents. By 1936, Japan had left the League of Nations and had repudiated the Washington treaties. A year later, its armies began an invasion of China that marked the beginning of the Pacific phase of World War II.

The resurgence of militarism in Germany, Italy, and Japan undermined the Versailles settlement and threatened to destroy the existing balance of power. England and France in Europe proved as powerless as China in Asia to stop the tide of aggression. In 1937, the three totalitarian nations signed an anti-Comintern pact completing a Berlin-Rome-Tokyo axis. Their alliance ostensibly was aimed at the Soviet Union, but in fact it threatened the entire world. Only a determined American response could unite the other nations against this Axis threat. Unfortunately,

■ *Benito Mussolini, dictator of Italy, shown conferring with his partner in the Rome-Berlin axis. Mussolini, sometimes called the "sawdust Caesar," was clearly subordinate to Hitler, who dominated the partnership.*

the United States deliberately abstained from assuming this role of leadership until it was nearly too late.

The Lure of Pacifism and Neutrality

The growing danger of war abroad led to a rising American desire for peace and noninvolvement. Memories of World War I contributed heavily. The novel *All Quiet on the Western Front,* as well as the movie based on it, reminded people of the brutal trench warfare. Historians began to treat the Great War as a mistake, criticizing Wilson for failing to preserve American neutrality and claiming that the clever British had duped the United States into entering the war. Walter Millis advanced this thesis in a popular book, *America's Road to War, 1914–1917,* published in 1935. It was hailed as a vivid description of the process by which "a peace-loving democracy, muddled but excited, misinformed and whipped to a frenzy, embarked upon its greatest foreign war."

American youth made clear their determina-

tion not to repeat the mistakes of their elders. Pacifism swept across college campuses. A Brown University poll indicated 72 percent of the students opposed military service in wartime. At Princeton, undergraduates formed the Veterans of Future Wars, a parody on veterans' groups, to demand a bonus of $1000 apiece before they marched off to a foreign war! In April 1934, students and professors alike walked out of class to attend massive antiwar rallies, which became an annual rite of spring in the 1930s. Amid demonstrators carrying signs reading "Abolish the R.O.T.C." and "Build Schools—Not Battleships," pacifist orators urged students to sign a pledge not to support their country "in any war it might conduct."

The pacifist surge found a scapegoat in the munitions industry. The publication of several books exposing the unsavory business tactics of large arms dealers such as Krupps in Germany and Vickers in Britain led to a demand to curb these "merchants of death." Senator Gerald Nye of North Dakota headed a special Senate committee which spent two years investigating American munitions dealers. The committee revealed the enormous profits such firms as Du Pont reaped from World War I, but Nye went further, charging that bankers and munitions makers were responsible for American intervention in 1917. No proof was forthcoming, but the public— prepared to believe the worst of businessmen during the Depression—accepted the "merchants-of-death" thesis.

The Nye Committee's revelations culminated in neutrality legislation. In 1935, Senator Nye and another Senate colleague introduced measures to ban arms sales and loans to belligerents and to prevent Americans from traveling on belligerent ships. By outlawing the activities that led to World War I, they hoped the United States could avoid involvement in the new conflict. This "never-again" philosophy proved irresistible. In August 1935, Congress passed the first of three neutrality acts. The 1935 law banned the sale of arms to nations at war and warned American citizens not to sail on belligerent ships. In 1936, a second act added a ban on loans, and in 1937, a third neutrality act made these prohibitions permanent and required, on a two-year trial basis, that all trade other than munitions be conducted on a cash-and-carry basis.

779

Isolationism

President Roosevelt played a passive role in the adoption of the neutrality legislation. At first opposed to the arms embargo, he finally approved it for six months in 1935 in a compromise designed to save important New Deal legislation in Congress. Yet he also appeared to share the isolationist assumption that a European war would have no impact on vital national interests. He termed the first neutrality act "entirely satisfactory" when he signed it. Others in the administration criticized the mandatory nature of the new law, pointing out that it prevented the United States from distinguishing between aggressors and their victims. Privately, Roosevelt expressed some of the same reservations, but publicly he bowed to the prevailing isolationism. He signed the subsequent neutrality acts without protest, and during the 1936 election he delivered an impassioned denunciation of war. "I hate war," he told an audience in Chautauqua, New York. "I have passed unnumbered hours, I shall pass unnumbered hours, thinking and planning how war may be kept from this nation."

Yet FDR did take a few steps to try to limit the nation's retreat into isolationism. His failure to invoke the neutrality act after the Japanese invasion of China in 1937 enabled the hard-pressed Chinese to continue buying arms from the United States. A year later, he used his influence to block a proposal by Indiana Congressman Louis Ludlow to require a nationwide referendum before Congress could declare war. FDR's strongest public statement came in Chicago in October 1937 when he denounced "the epidemic of world lawlessness" and called for an international effort to "quarantine" this disease. When reporters asked him if his call for "positive efforts to preserve peace" signaled a repeal of the neutrality acts, however, Roosevelt quickly reaffirmed this isolationist legislation. Whatever his private yearning for cooperation against aggressors, the President had no intention of challenging the prevailing public mood of the 1930s.

War in Europe

The neutrality legislation played directly into the hands of Adolf Hitler. Bent on the conquest of Europe, he could now proceed without worrying about American interference. In March 1938, he seized Austria in a bloodless coup. Six months later, he was demanding the Sudetenland, a province of Czechoslovakia with a large German population. When the British and French leaders agreed to meet with Hitler at Munich, FDR voiced his approval. Roosevelt carefully kept the United States aloof from the subsequent surrender of the Sudetenland. At the same time, he gave his tacit approval of the Munich agreement by telling the British prime minister that he shared his "hope and belief that there exists today the greatest opportunity in years for the establishment of a new order based on justice and on law."

Six months after the meeting at Munich, Hitler violated his promises by seizing nearly all of Czechoslovakia. In the United States, Roosevelt permitted the State Department to press for neutrality revision. An administration proposal to repeal the arms embargo and place *all* trade with belligerents, including munitions, on a cash-and-carry basis soon met stubborn resistance from isolationists. They argued that cash-and-carry would favor England and France, who controlled the sea. The House rejected the measure by a narrow margin, and the Senate's Foreign Relations Committee voted 12 to 11 to postpone any action on neutrality revision.

In July 1939, Roosevelt finally abandoned his aloof position and held a meeting with Senate leaders to plead for reconsideration. Warnings of the imminence of war in Europe by both the President and the secretary of state failed to impress the isolationists. Senator William Borah, who had led the fight against the League of Nations in 1919, responded that he felt the chances for war in Europe were remote. After canvassing the senators present, Vice-President John Nance Garner bluntly told FDR that neutrality revision was dead. "You haven't got the votes," Garner commented, "and that's all there is to it."

On September 1, 1939, Hitler began World War II by invading Poland. England and France responded two days later by declaring war, although there was no way they could prevent the German conquest of Poland. Russia had played a key role, refusing Western overtures for a common front against Germany and finally signing a nonaggression treaty with Hitler in late August. The Nazi-Soviet Pact enabled Germany to avoid a two-front war; the Russians were rewarded with a generous slice of eastern Poland.

Hitler sent his armies into Poland with tremendous force and firepower, devastating the country. Below, a motorized division drives through a town battered by repeated bombings. When Jews, such as these residents of the Warsaw Ghetto (right), fell into the hands of the Nazi occupiers, they were deported to slave labor camps that soon turned into mass extermination camps.

President Roosevelt reacted to the outbreak of war by proclaiming American neutrality, but the successful aggression by Nazi Germany brought into question the isolationist assumption that American well-being did not depend upon the European balance of power. Strategic as well as ideological considerations began to undermine the earlier belief that the United States could safely pursue a policy of neutrality and noninvolvement. The long retreat from responsibility was about to end as Americans came to realize that their own democracy and security were at stake in the European war.

The Road to War

For two years the United States tried to remain at peace while war raged in Europe and Asia. In contrast to Wilson's attempt to be impartial during most of World War I, however, the American people displayed an overwhelming sympathy for the Allies and total distaste for Germany and Japan. Roosevelt made no secret of his preference for an Allied victory, but a fear of isolationist criticism compelled him to move slowly, and often deviously, in adopting a policy of aid for England and France—short of actually entering the war.

From Neutrality to Undeclared War

Two weeks after the outbreak of war in Europe, Roosevelt called Congress into special session to revise the neutrality legislation. He wanted to repeal the arms embargo in order to supply weapons to England and France, but he refused to state this aim openly. Instead he asked Congress to replace the arms embargo with cash-and-carry regulations. Belligerents would be able to purchase war supplies in the United States, but they would have to pay cash and transport the goods in their own ships. Public opinion strongly supported the President, and Congress passed the revised neutrality policy by heavy margins in early November 1939.

A series of dramatic German victories had a profound impact on American opinion. Quiet during the winter of 1939–1940, the Germans struck with lightning speed and devastating effect in the spring. In April, they seized Denmark and Norway, and on May 10, 1940, they unleashed the *blitzkreig* (lightning war) on the western front. Using tanks, armored columns, and dive bombers in close coordination, the Germany army cut deep into the Allied lines, dividing the British and French forces. Within three weeks, the British were driven off the continent. In another three weeks, France fell to Hitler's victorious armies.

Americans were stunned. Hitler had taken only six weeks to achieve what Germany had failed to do in four years of fighting in World War I. Suddenly they realized that they did have a stake in the outcome; if England fell, Hitler might well gain control of the British navy. The Atlantic would no longer be a barrier; instead, it would be a highway for German penetration of the New World.

Roosevelt responded by invoking a policy of all-out aid to the Allies short of war. In a speech at Charlottesville, Virginia, in June (just after Italy entered the war by invading France), he denounced Germany and Italy as representing "the gods of force and hate" and vowed that "the whole of our sympathies lies with those nations that are giving their life blood in combat against these forces." It was too late to help France, but in early September, FDR announced the transfer of fifty old destroyers to England in exchange for rights to build air and naval bases on eight British possessions in the Western Hemisphere. Giving warships to a belligerent nation was clearly a

A hastily organized flotilla of privately owned small boats chugged across the Channel from England at the end of May 1940 and performed the miracle of Dunkirk—rescuing a third of a million British troops trapped on the beach at the French Channel port, under heavy bombardment from German planes. A supreme effort by the Royal Air Force won superiority in the sky over the evacuation area.

breach of neutrality, but Roosevelt stressed the importance of guarding the Atlantic approaches, calling the destroyers-for-bases deal "the most important action in the reinforcement of our national defense that has been taken since the Louisiana Purchase."

Isolationists cried out against this departure from neutrality. A headline in the *Saint Louis Post-Dispatch* read, "Dictator Roosevelt Commits Act of War." A group of Roosevelt's opponents in the Midwest formed the America First Committee to protest the drift toward war. Such diverse individuals as aviator-hero Charles Lindbergh, conservative Senator Robert A. Taft of Ohio, socialist leader Norman Thomas, and liberal educator Robert M. Hutchins condemned FDR for involving the United States in a foreign conflict. Voicing belief in a "Fortress America," they denied that Hitler threatened American security and claimed that the nation had the strength to defend itself regardless of what happened in Europe.

To support the administration's policies, opponents of the isolationists organized the Committee to Defend America by Aiding the Allies. Eastern Anglophiles, moderate New Dealers, and liberal Republicans made up the bulk of the membership, with Kansas newspaper editor William Allen White serving as chairman. The White Committee, as it became known, advocated unlimited assistance to England short of war, although some of its members privately favored entry into the conflict. Above all, the interventionists challenged the isolationist premise that events in Europe did not affect American security. "The future of western civilization is being decided upon the battlefield of Europe," White declared.

In the ensuing debate, the American people gradually came to agree with the interventionists. The battle of Britain helped. "Every time Hitler bombed London, we got a couple of votes," noted one interventionist. Frightened by the events in Europe, Congress approved large sums for preparedness, increasing the defense budget from $2 billion to $10 billion during 1940. Roosevelt courageously asked for a peacetime draft, the first in American history, to build up the army; in September, Congress agreed.

The sense of crisis affected domestic politics. Roosevelt ran for an unprecedented third term in

The Election of 1940			
Candidate	Party	Popular Vote	Electorial Vote
Roosevelt	Democrat	27,263,448	449
Willkie	Republican	22,336,260	82

1940 because of the European war; the Republicans nominated Wendell Willkie, a former Democratic businessman who shared FDR's commitment to aid for England. Both candidates made appeals to peace sentiment during the campaign, but Roosevelt's decisive victory made it clear that the nation supported his increasing departure from neutrality.

After the election, FDR took his boldest step. Responding to British Prime Minister Winston Churchill's warning that England was running out of money, the President asked Congress to approve a new program to lend and lease goods and weapons to countries fighting against aggressors. Roosevelt's call for America to become "the great arsenal of democracy" seemed straightforward enough, but he acted somewhat deviously by naming the program Lend-Lease and by comparing it to loaning a neighbor a garden hose to put out a fire.

Isolationists angrily denounced Lend-Lease as both unnecessary and untruthful. "Lending war equipment is a good deal like lending chewing gum," commented Senator Taft. "You don't want it back." In March 1941, however, Congress voted by substantial margins to authorize the President to "sell, transfer title to, exchange, lease, lend, or otherwise dispose of" war supplies to "any country the President deems vital to the defense of the United States." The accompanying $7-billion appropriation ended the "cash" part of cash-and-carry and ensured Britain full access to American war supplies.

The "carry" problem still remained. German submarines were sinking over five hundred thousand tons of shipping a month. England desperately needed the help of the American navy in escorting convoys across the U-boat-infested waters of the North Atlantic. Roosevelt, fearful of

■ *Kneeling at the Capitol Plaza in Washington, women from various mothers' groups conduct a pray-in to protest the passage of the lend-lease bill.*

In Euro from tior dea Ge th A t ... the nation to the brink of war in ...evelt opened himself to criticism ...s in the domestic debate. Interven-...at he had been too cautious in ...e danger to the nation from Nazi ...ionists were equally critical of ...aiming that he had misled the ...le by professing peace while plot-...Roosevelt was certainly less than ...executive discretion to engage ...ive acts in the North Atlantic. ...e interventionists that in the ...security would be threatened ...ry in Europe. But he also was ...en in September 1941 showed ...cent of the American people ...of World War II. Realizing that ...tion into war would be disas-...or time, inching the country ...aiting for the Axis nations to ...nove. Japan finally obliged at

isolationist reaction, responded with naval patrols in the eastern half of the ocean. Hitler placed his submarine commanders under strict restraints to avoid drawing America into the European war. Nevertheless, incidents were bound to occur. In September 1941, after a U-boat narrowly missed torpedoing an American destroyer pursuing it, Roosevelt denounced the German submarines as the "rattlesnakes of the Atlantic" and issued orders for the navy to convey British ships halfway across the ocean.

Undeclared naval war quickly followed. On October 17, 1941, a German submarine damaged the U.S. destroyer *Kearney;* ten days later, another U-boat sank the *Reuben James,* killing over one hundred American sailors. FDR issued orders for the destroyers to shoot U-boats on sight. He also asked Congress to repeal the "carry" section of the neutrality laws and permit American ships to deliver supplies to England. In mid-November, Congress approved these moves by slim margins. Now American merchant ships as well as destroyers would become targets for German attacks. By December, it seemed only a matter of weeks—or months at most—until repeated sinkings would lead to a formal declaration of war against Germany.

Showdown in the Pacific

Japan had taken advantage of the war in Europe to expand forces in Asia. Although successful after ...in conquering the populous coastal areas of China, the Japanese had been unable to defeat Chiang Kai-shek, whose forces retreated into the vast interior of the country. The German defeat of France and the Netherlands in 1940, however, left their colonial possessions in the East Indies and Indochina vulnerable and defenseless. Japan now set out to incorporate these territories—rich in oil, tin, and rubber—into a Greater East Asia Co-Prosperity Sphere.

The Roosevelt administration countered with economic pressure. Japan was heavily dependent upon the United States for shipments of petroleum and scrap iron and steel. In July 1940, President Roosevelt signed an order setting up a licensing and quota system for the export of these crucial materials to Japan and banned the sale of aviation gasoline altogether. With Britain fighting for survival and France and the Netherlands occupied by Germany, the United States was now employing economic sanctions to defend Southeast Asia against Japanese expansion.

Tokyo appeared not to be impressed. In early

September, Japanese troops occupied strategic bases in the northern part of French Indochina. Later in the month, Japan signed the Tripartite Pact with Germany and Italy, a defensive treaty that confronted the United States with a possible two-ocean war. The new Axis alignment confirmed American suspicions that Japan was part of a worldwide totalitarian threat. Roosevelt and his advisers, however, saw Germany as the primary danger; thus they pursued a policy of all-out aid to England while hoping that economic measures alone would deter Japan.

The embargo on aviation gasoline, extended to include scrap iron and steel in late September 1940, was a burden Japan could bear, but a possible ban on all oil shipments was a different matter. Japan lacked petroleum reserves of its own and was entirely dependent on imports from the United States and the Dutch East Indies. In an attempt to ease the economic pressure through negotiation, Japan sent a new envoy to Washington in the spring of 1941. But these talks quickly broke down. Tokyo wanted nothing less than a free hand in China and an end to American sanctions, while the United States insisted on an eventual Japanese evacuation of all China.

In July 1941, Japan invaded southern Indochina, beginning the chain of events that led to war. Washington knew of this aggression before it occurred. Naval intelligence experts had broken the Japanese diplomatic code and were intercepting and reading all messages between Tokyo and the Japanese embassy in Washington. President Roosevelt responded on July 25, 1941, with an order freezing all Japanese assets in the United States. This step, initially intended only as a temporary warning to Japan, soon became a permanent embargo due to positive public reaction and State Department zeal. Trade with Japan, including the vital oil shipments, came to a complete halt. When the Dutch government-in-exile took similar action, Japan faced a dilemma: in order to have oil shipments resumed, Tokyo would have to end its aggression; the alternative would be to seize the needed petroleum supplies in the Dutch East Indies, an action that would mean war.

After one final diplomatic effort failed, General Hideki Tojo, an army militant, became the new premier of Japan. To mask its war preparations, Tokyo sent yet another envoy to Washington with new peace proposals. Code-breaking enabled American diplomats to learn that the Japanese terms were unacceptable even before they were formally presented. Army and navy leaders urged President Roosevelt to seek at least a temporary settlement with Japan to give them time to prepare American defenses in the Pacific. Secretary of State Cordell Hull, however, refused to allow any concession; on November 20, he sent a stiff ten-point reply to Tokyo that included a demand for Japanese withdrawal from China.

The Japanese response came two weeks later. On the evening of December 6, 1941, the first thirteen parts of the reply to Hull's note arrived in Washington, with the fourteenth part to follow the next morning. Naval intelligence actually decoded the message faster than the Japanese embassy clerks. A messenger delivered the text to President Roosevelt late that night; after glancing at it, he commented, "This means war." The next day, December 7, the fourteenth part arrived, revealing that Japan totally rejected the American position.

Officials in Washington immediately sent warning messages to American bases in the Pacific, but they failed to arrive in time. At 7:55 in the morning, just before 1 P.M. in Washington, squadrons of Japanese carrier-based planes caught the American fleet at Pearl Harbor totally by surprise. In little more than an hour, they crippled the American Pacific fleet and its major base, sinking eight battleships and killing more than twenty-four hundred American sailors.

In Washington, the Japanese envoys had requested a meeting with Secretary Hull at 1 P.M.. Just before the meeting news arrived of the attack on Pearl Harbor. An irate Cordell Hull read the note the Japanese handed him and then, unable to restrain himself any longer, burst out, "In all my fifty years of public service, I have never seen a document that was more crowded with infamous falsehoods and distortions—on a scale so huge that I never imagined until today that any government was capable of uttering them."

The next day, President Roosevelt termed December 7 "a date which will live in infamy" and asked Congress to declare war against Japan. With only one dissenting vote, both houses did so. On December 11, Germany and Italy declared war against the United States; the nation was now fully involved in World War II.

■ Naval air installation at Pearl Harbor, December 7, 1941, during the surprise attack. Stunned servicemen watch the raging fires.

■ War headline in extra editions, December 8 (top). Congress declared was on Japan that afternoon after FDR addressed the nation (bottom).

The whole country united behind Roosevelt's leadership to seek revenge for Pearl Harbor and to defeat the Axis threat to American security. After the war, however, critics charged that FDR had entered the conflict by a back door, claiming that the President had deliberately exposed the Pacific fleet to attack. Subsequent investigations uncovered negligence in both Hawaii and Washington but no evidence to support the conspiracy charge. Commanders in Hawaii, like most military experts, believed that the Japanese would not launch an attack on a base four thousand miles away from Japan. FDR, like too many Americans, had badly underestimated the daring and skill of the Japanese; he and the nation alike paid a heavy price for this cultural and racial prejudice. But there was no plot. Roosevelt could not have known that Hitler, so restrained in the Atlantic, would reverse his policy and declare war against the United States after Pearl Harbor. Perhaps the most frightening aspect of the whole episode is that it took the shock of the Japanese sneak attack to make the American people aware of the full extent of the Axis threat to their well-being and lead them to end the long retreat from responsibility.

Turning the Tide Against the Axis

In the first few months after the United States entered the war, the outlook for victory was bleak. In Europe, Hitler's armies controlled virtually the entire continent, from Norway in the north to Greece in the south. Despite the non-aggression pact, German armies had penetrated deep into Russia after an initial invasion in June 1941. Although they had failed to capture either Moscow or Leningrad, the Nazi forces had conquered the Ukraine and by the spring of 1942 were threatening to sweep across the Volga and seize the oil fields in the Caucasus. In North Africa, General Erwin Rommel's Afrika Korps had pushed the British back into Egypt and threatened the Suez Canal (see the map on p. 788).

The situation was no better in Asia. The Pearl Harbor attack had enabled the Japanese to move unopposed across Southeast Asia. Within three months they had conquered Malaya and the Dutch East Indies, with its valuable oil fields, and were pressing the British back both in Burma and New Guinea. American forces under General Douglas MacArthur had tried vainly to block the Japanese conquest of the Philippines. MacArthur finally escaped by torpedo boat to Australia; the American garrison at Corregidor surrendered after a long seige, the survivors then enduring the cruel death march across the Bataan peninsula. With the American navy still recovering from the devastation at Pearl Harbor, Japan controlled the western half of the Pacific (see the map on p. 790).

Over the next two years, the United States and its allies would finally halt the German and Japanese offensives in Europe and Asia. But then they faced the difficult process of driving back the enemy, freeing the vast conquered areas, and finally defeating the Axis powers on their home territory. It would be a difficult and costly struggle that would require great sacrifice and heavy losses; World War II would test American will and resourcefulness to the hilt.

Wartime Partnerships

The greatest single advantage that the United States and its partners possessed was their willingness to form a genuine coalition to bring about the defeat of the Axis powers. Although there were many strains within the wartime alliance, it did permit a high degree of coordination. In striking contrast was the behavior of Germany and Japan, each fighting a separate war without any attempt at cooperation.

The United States and Britain achieved a complete wartime partnership. Prewar military talks led to the formation of a Combined Chiefs of Staff, headquartered in Washington, which directed Anglo-American military operations. The close cooperation between President Roosevelt and Prime Minister Churchill ensured a common strategy. The leaders decided at the outset that a Germany victory posed the greater danger and thus gave priority to the European theater in the conduct of the war. In a series of meetings in December 1941, Roosevelt and Churchill signed a Declaration of the United Nations, eventually subscribed to by twenty-six countries, that pledged them to fight together until the Axis powers were defeated.

Relations with the other members of the United Nations coalition in World War II were not quite so harmonious. The decision to defeat Germany first displeased the Chinese, who had been at war with Japan since 1937. Roosevelt tried to appease Chiang Kai-shek with a trickle of supplies, flown in at great risk by American airmen over the Himalayas from India. France posed a more delicate problem. FDR virtually ignored the Free French government in exile under General Charles de Gaulle. Roosevelt preferred to deal with the Vichy regime, despite its collaboration with Germany, because it still controlled the French fleet and retained France's overseas territories.

The greatest strain of all within the wartime coalition was with the Soviet Union. Although Roosevelt had ended the long period of nonrecognition in 1933, close ties had failed to develop. The Russian refusal to pay prerevolutionary debts, together with continued Soviet support of domestic Communist activity in the United States in the 1930s, intensified American distaste for Stalin's regime. The great Russian purge trials and the temporary Nazi-Soviet alliance from 1939 to 1941, along with deep-seated cultural and ideological differences, made wartime cooperation difficult.

World War II in Europe and North Africa

The tide of battle shifted in this theater during the winter of 1942–1943. The massive German assault on the eastern front was turned back by the Russians at Stalingrad, and the Allied forces recaptured North Africa.

Legend:
- Axis Powers before World War
- Extent of Axis co... early Nov. 1942
- Allies
- Neutral nations
- Allied troop movements
- Major battles

ICELAND

Leningrad besieged Sept. 1941– Jan. 19, 1944

Moscow

SOVIET UNION

FINLAND

NORWAY

SWEDEN

EST.

LAT. Sept. 1944

Stalingrad Aug. 21, 1942– Jan. 31, 1943

Volga

Northern Ireland

North Sea

DEN.

LITH.

July 1944

Aug. 1943

GREAT BRITAIN

IRELAND

Berlin surrendered May 2, 1945

East Prussia (Ger.)

Warsaw

POLAND

March 1944

Ukraine

Aug. 1944

Caucas...

London

ATLANTIC OCEAN

NETH.

BELG.

Apr. 1945

GERMANY

Czechoslovakia

D-Day June 6, 1944

FRANCE

Normandy

Battle of the Bulge Dec. 16, 1944– Jan. 31, 1945

Austria

HUNG.

Dec. 1944

ROM.

Aug. 1944

Black Sea

Paris liberated Aug. 1944

SWITZ.

YUGO.

Danube R.

VICHY FRANCE occupied Nov. 1942

Aug. 1944

BULG.

TURKEY

ITALY

Rome liberated June 4, 1944

ALB. (It.)

GREECE

PORT.

SPAIN

SYRIA

Sicily

July 1943

Crete (Greece)

Rhodes (It.)

Cyprus (Br.)

LEB.

Nov. 1942

Sp. Morocco

ALGERIA

Kasserine Pass Feb. 14–22, 1943

Mediterranean Sea

PALESTINE (Br.)

TRANSJORD.

Suez Canal

MOROCCO

FRENCH NORTH AFRICA (Vichy France)

Joined Allies Nov. 1942

TUNISIA

Nov. 1942

El Alamein Oct. 23–Nov. 5, 1942

Nile R.

LIBYA (It.)

EGYPT

0   200   400 Miles
0   200   400 Kilometers

Ever the pragmatist, Roosevelt tried hard to break down the old hostility and establish a more cordial relationship with Russia during the war. Even before Pearl Harbor, he extended Lend-Lease aid, and after American entry into the war, this economic assistance grew rapidly, limited only by the difficulty in delivering the supplies. Eager to keep Russia in the war, the President promised a visiting Russian diplomat in May 1942 that the United States would create a second front in Europe by the end of that year, a pledge he could not fulfill. In January 1943, Roosevelt joined with

Churchill at the Casablanca conference to declare a policy of unconditional surrender, vowing that the Western Allies would fight on until the Axis nations were completedly defeated.

Despite these promises, the Soviet Union bore the brunt of battle against Hitler in the early years of the war, fighting alone against more than two hundred German divisions. The United States and England, grateful for the respite to build up their forces, could do little more than offer promises of future help and send Lend-Lease supplies. The result was a rift that never fully healed—one that did not prevent the defeat of Germany but did ensure future tensions and uncertainties between the Soviet Union and the Western nations.

Halting the German Blitz

From the outset, the United States favored an invasion across the English Channel as the key to victory in Europe. Army planners, led by Chief of Staff George C. Marshall and his protégé, Dwight D. Eisenhower, were convinced that such a frontal assault would be the quickest way to win the war. Roosevelt concurred, in part because it fulfilled his second-front commitment to the Soviets.

The initial plan, drawn up by Eisenhower, called for a full-scale invasion of Europe in the spring of 1943, with provision for a temporary beachhead in France in the fall of 1942 if necessary to keep Russia in the war. Marshall surprised everyone by placing Eisenhower, until then a relatively junior general, in charge of implementing the plan.

But the British, remembering the heavy casualties of trench warfare in World War I, preferred a perimeter approach, with air and naval attacks around the edge of the continent, until Germany was properly softened up for the final invasion. Their strategists assented to the basic plan but strongly urged that a preliminary invasion of North Africa be launched in the fall of 1942. Roosevelt, too, wanted American troops engaged in combat against Germany before the end of 1942 to offset growing pressure at home to concentrate on the Pacific; hence, after he overruled objections from his military advisers, American and British troops landed on the Atlantic and Mediterranean coasts of Morocco and Algeria in November 1942.

The British launched an attack against Rommel at El Alamein in Egypt and soon forced the Afrika Korps to retreat across Libya to Tunisia. Eisenhower, delayed by poor roads and bad weather, was slow in bringing up his forces, and in their first encounter with Rommel at the Kasserine Pass in the desert south of Tunis, inexperienced American troops suffered a humiliating defeat. General George Patton quickly rallied the demoralized soldiers, and by May 1943, Germany had been driven from Africa, leaving behind nearly three hundred thousand troops.

During these same months, the Red Army had broken the back of German military power in the battle of Stalingrad. Turned back at the critical bend in the Volga, Hitler had poured in division after division in what was ultimately a losing cause; never again would Germany be able to take the offensive in Europe.

At Churchill's insistence, FDR agreed to follow up the North African victory with the invasion first of Sicily and then Italy in the summer of 1943. Italy dropped out of the war when Mussolini fled to Germany, but the Italian campaign

■ *American troops entering Palermo, Sicily, on July 23, 1943. Italy soon capitulated, but the Italian campaign bogged down under fierce German resistance.*

proved to be a strategic dead end. Germany sent in enough divisions to establish a strong defensive line in the mountains south of Rome; American and British troops were forced to fight their way slowly up the peninsula, suffering heavy casualties.

More important, these Mediterranean operations delayed the second front, postponing it eventually to the spring of 1944. Meanwhile, the Soviets began to push the Germans out of Russia and looked forward to the liberation of Poland, Hungary, and Romania, where they could establish "friendly" Communist regimes. Having borne the brunt of the fighting against Nazi Germany, Russia was ready to claim its reward—the postwar domination of Eastern Europe.

Checking Japan in the Pacific

The decision to defeat Germany first and the vast expanses of the Pacific dictated the nature of the war against Japan—amphibious, island-hopping campaigns rather than any attempt to reconquer the Dutch East Indies, Southeast Asia, and China. There would be two separate American operations. One, led by Douglas MacArthur based in Australia, would move from New Guinea back to the Philippines, while the other, commanded by Admiral Chester Nimitz from Hawaii, was directed at key Japanese islands in the Central Pacific. The original plan called for the two offensives to come together for the final invasion of the Japanese home islands.

World War II in the Pacific

The tide of battle turned in the Pacific the same year as in Europe. The balance of sea power shifted back to the United States from Japan after the naval victories of 1942.

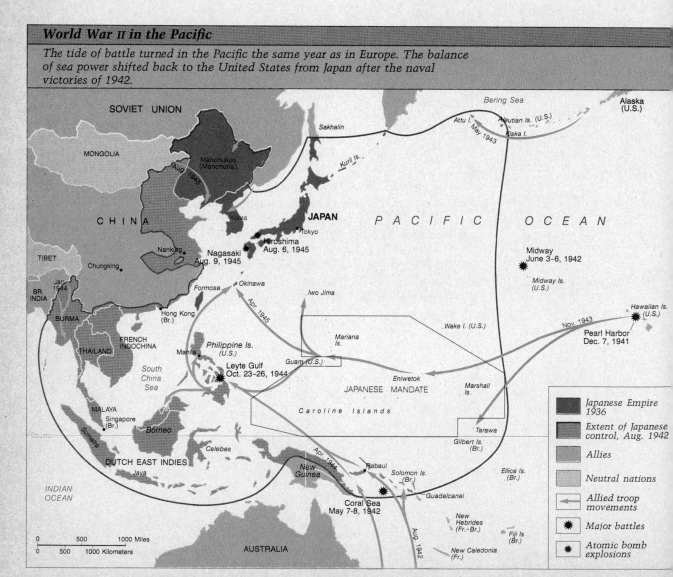

Success in the Pacific depended above all else on control of the sea. The devastation at Pearl Harbor gave Japan the initial edge, but fortunately the United States had not lost any of its four aircraft carriers. In the battle of the Coral Sea in May 1942, American naval forces blocked a Japanese thrust to outflank Australia. The turning point came one month later at Midway. A powerful Japanese task force threatened to seize this remote American outpost, over a thousand miles west of Pearl Harbor; Japan's real objective was the destruction of what remained of the American Pacific fleet. Superior American air power enabled Nimitz's forces to engage the enemy at long range. Japanese fighters shot down thirty-five of forty-one attacking torpedo bombers, but a second wave of dive bombers scored hits on three Japanese carriers. The battle of Midway ended with the loss of four Japanese aircraft carriers compared to just one American. It was the first defeat the modern Japanese navy had ever suffered, and it left the United States in control of the Central Pacific.

Encouraged by this victory, American forces launched their first Pacific offensive in the Solomon Islands, east of New Guinea, in August 1942. Both sides suffered heavy losses, but six months later the last Japanese were driven from the key island of Guadalcanal. At the same time, MacArthur began the long, slow, and bloody job of driving the Japanese back along the north coast of New Guinea.

By early 1943, the defensive phase of the war with Japan was over. The enemy surge had been halted in both the Central and the Southwest Pacific, and the United States was preparing to penetrate the Gilbert, Marshall, and Caroline islands and recapture the Philippines. Just as Russia had broken German power in Europe, so the United States, fighting alone except for Australia and New Zealand, had halted the Japanese. And, like the Soviet plans for Eastern Europe, America expected to reap the rewards of victory by dominating the Pacific in the future.

The Home Front

World War II had a greater impact than the Depression on the future of American life. While American soldiers and sailors fought abroad, the nation

American war production was twice that of all Axis countries. Here, Boeing aircraft workers celebrate the completion of their five-thousandth bomber.

underwent sweeping social and economic changes at home.

American industry made the nation's single most important contribution to victory. Even though over fifteen million Americans served in the armed forces, it was the nearly sixty million who worked on farms and factories who achieved the miracle of production that ensured the defeat of Germany and Japan. The manufacturing plants that had run at half-capacity through the 1930s now hummed with activity. In Detroit, automobile assembly lines were converted to produce tanks and airplanes; Henry Ford built the giant Willow Run factory, covering sixty-seven acres, where forty-two thousand workers turned out a B-24 bomber every hour. Henry J. Kaiser, a California industrialist who constructed huge West Coast shipyards to meet the demand for cargo vessels and landing craft, operated on an equally large scale. His Richmond, California, plant lowered the time to build a merchant ship from 105 to 14 days. In part, America won the battle of the Atlantic by building ships faster than German U-boats could sink them.

This vast industrial expansion, however, created many problems. In 1942, President Roosevelt appointed Donald Nelson, a Sears, Roebuck executive, to head a War Production Board (WPB). A jovial, easy-going man, Nelson soon was outmaneuvered by the army and the navy, which preferred to negotiate directly with large corporations. The WPB allowed business rapid depreciation, and thus huge tax credits, for new plants and awarded lucrative cost-plus contracts for urgently needed goods. Shortages of such critical materials as steel, aluminum, and copper led to an allocation system based on military priorities. Rubber, cut off by the Japanese conquest of Southeast Asia, was particularly scarce; the administration finally began gasoline-rationing in 1943 to curb pleasure-driving and prolong tire life. The government itself built fifty-one synthetic rubber plants which by 1944 were producing nearly one million tons for the tires of American airplanes and military vehicles. All in all, the nation's factories turned out twice as many goods as did German and Japanese industry combined.

Roosevelt revealed the same tendency toward compromise in directing the economic mobilization as he did in shaping the New Deal. When the Office of Price Administration—which tried to curb inflation by controlling prices and rationing scarce goods like sugar, canned food, and shoes— clashed with the WPB, FDR appointed James Byrnes to head an Office of Economic Stabilization. Byrnes, a former South Carolina senator and Supreme Court justice, used political judgment to settle disputes between agencies and keep all groups happy. The President was also forced to compromise with Congress, which pared down the administration's requests for large tax increases. Half the cost of the war was financed by borrowing; the other half came from revenues. A $7-billion revenue increase in 1942 included so many first-time taxpayers that in the following year the Treasury Department instituted a new practice—withholding income taxes from workers' wages.

The result of this wartime economic explosion was a growing affluence. Despite the federal incentives to business, heavy excess-profit taxes and a 94 percent tax rate for the very rich kept the wealthy from benefiting unduly. The huge increase in federal spending, from $9 billion in 1940 to $98 billion in 1944, spread through American society. A government agreement with labor unions in 1943 held wage rates to a 15 percent increase, but the long hours of overtime resulted in doubling and sometimes tripling the weekly paychecks of factory workers. Farmers shared in the new prosperity as their incomes quadrupled

During and immediately after the war, ration stamps were issued for scarce food items, shoes, tires and gasoline.

between 1940 and 1945. For the first time in the twentieth century, the lowest fifth of wage earners increased their share of the national income in relation to the more affluent; their income rose by 68 percent between 1941 and 1945, compared to a 20 percent increase for the well-to-do. Most important, this rising income ensured postwar prosperity. Workers and farmers saved their money, channeling much of it into government war bonds, waiting for the day when they could buy the cars and home appliances they had done without during the long years of depression and war.

A Nation on the Move

The war led to a vast migration of the American population. Young men left their homes for training camps and then for service overseas. Defense workers and their families, some nine million people in all, moved to the new booming shipyards, munitions factories, and aircraft plants. Norfolk, Virginia; San Diego, California; Mobile, Alabama, and other centers of defense production grew by more than 50 percent in just a year or two. Rural areas lost population while coastal regions, especially along the Pacific and Gulf of Mexico, drew millions of people. The location of army camps in the South and West created boom conditions in the future Sunbelt, as did the concentration of aircraft factories and shipyards in this region. California had the greatest gains, adding nearly two million to its population in less than five years.

This movement of people caused severe social problems. Housing was in short supply. Migrating workers crowded into house trailers and boardinghouses, bringing unexpected windfalls to landlords. In one boom town, a reporter described an old Victorian house that had five bedrooms on the second floor. "Three of them," he wrote, "held two cots apiece, the two others held three cots." But the owner revealed that "the third floor is where we pick up the velvet. . . . We rent to workers in different shifts . . . three shifts a day . . . seven bucks a week apiece."

Family life suffered under these crowded living conditions. An increase in the number of marriages, as young people searched for something to hang on to in the midst of wartime turmoil, was offset by a rising divorce rate. The baby boom that would peak in the 1950s began during the war, but children suffered. There were few day-care centers for working women to use; "latch-key children" and "eight-hour orphans" were all too common. Schools in the boom areas were unable to cope with the influx of new students; a teacher shortage, intensified by the lure of higher wages in war industries, compounded the educational crisis.

Despite these problems, women found the war a time of economic opportunity. The demand for workers led to a dramatic rise in female employment, from fourteen million working women in 1940 to nineteen million by 1945. Women entered industries once viewed as exclusively male; by the end of the war, they worked alongside men tending blast furnaces in steel mills and welding hulls in shipyards. Few challenged the traditional view of sex roles, yet the wartime experience helped undermine the concept that woman's only proper place was in the home. Women enjoyed the hefty weekly paychecks, which rose by 50 percent from 1941 to 1943, and they took pride in their contributions to the war effort. "To hell with the life I have had," commented a former fashion designer. "This war is too damn serious, and it is too damn important to win it."

Blacks shared in the wartime migration, but their social and economic gains were limited by

■ *"Rosie the Riveter," a song extolling women workers, was very popular during the war. This photograph from* Life *is by Margaret Bourke-White.*

persistent racial prejudice. Nearly one million served in the armed forces, but few saw combat. The army placed blacks in segregated units, usually led by white officers, and used them for service and construction tasks. The navy was even worse, relegating them to menial jobs until late in the war. Blacks were denied the chance to become petty officers, Secretary of the Navy Frank Knox explained, because experience had shown that "men of the colored race . . . cannot maintain discipline among men of the white race."

Black civilians fared a little better. In 1941, black labor leader A. Philip Randolph threatened a massive march on Washington to force President Roosevelt to end racial discrimination in defense industries and government employment and to integrate the armed forces. FDR compromised, persuading Randolph to call off the march and drop his integration demand in return for an executive order creating a Fair Employment Practices Committee (FEPC) to ban racial discrimination in war industries. As a result, black employment by the federal government rose from sixty thousand in 1941 to two hundred thousand by the end of the war, but the FEPC proved less successful in the private sector. Weak in funding and staff, the FEPC was able to act on only one third of the eight thousand complaints it received. The nationwide shortage of labor was more influential than the FEPC in accounting for the rise in black employment during wartime. Blacks moved from the rural South to northern and western cities, finding jobs in the automobile, aircraft, and shipbuilding industries.

This movement of an estimated seven hundred thousand people helped transform the race problem from a regional issue into a national concern that could no longer be ignored. The limited housing and recreational facilities for both black and white war workers created tensions that led to urban race riots. On a hot Sunday evening in June 1943, blacks and whites began exchanging insults and then blows near Belle Island recreation park in Detroit. The next day, a full-scale riot broke out in which twenty-three blacks and nine whites died. The fighting raged for twenty-four hours until National Guard troops were

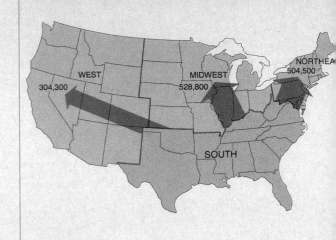

Black Migration from the South, 1940–1950

Movement was from the Southeast to the Mid-Atlantic and New England states and from the south central states to the Midwest and Far West.

The migration of blacks from the South to northern cities was recorded in a series of sixty tempora panels by Jacob Lawrence, a black artist. The paintings are done in sharp primary colors and a forceful but simple design. They form a continuous narrative of visual history and black experience.

brought in to restore order. Later that summer, only personal intervention by New York Mayor Fiorello LaGuardia quelled a Harlem riot that took the lives of six blacks.

These outbursts of racial violence fueled the resentments that would grow into the postwar civil-rights movement. For most blacks, despite the economic gain, World War II was a reminder of the inequality of American life. "Just carve on my tombstone," remarked one black soldier in the Pacific, "here lies a black man killed fighting a yellow man for the protection of a white man."

One third of a million Mexican-Americans served in the armed forces and shared some of the same experiences as blacks. Although they were not as completely segregated, many served in the Eighty-eighth Division, made up largely of Mexican-American officers and troops, which earned the nickname "Blue Devils" in the Italian campaign. At home, Spanish-speaking people left the rural areas of Texas, New Mexico, and California for jobs in the cities, especially in aircraft plants and petroleum refineries. Despite low wages and union resistance, they improved their economic position substantially. But they still faced discrimination based both on skin color and language, most notably in the Los Angeles "zoot-suit" riots in 1943 when white sailors attacked Mexican-American youths dressed in their distinctive long jackets and flared pants tightly pegged at the ankles. The racial prejudice heightened feelings of ethnic identity and led returning Mexican-American veterans to form organizations such as the American G.I. Forum to press for equal rights in the future.

A tragic counterpoint to the voluntary movement of American workers in search of jobs was the forced relocation of 112,000 Japanese-Americans from the West Coast. Responding to racial fears in California after Pearl Harbor, President Roosevelt approved an army order in February 1942 to move both the Issei (Japanese-Americans who had emigrated from Japan) and the Nisei (people of Japanese ancestry born in the United States and therefore American citizens) to concentration camps in the interior. Forced to sell their farms and businesses at distress prices, the Japanese-Americans lost not only their liberty but also most of their worldly goods. Herded into ten hastily built detention centers in seven western states, they lived as prisoners in tar-papered

■ *A bewildered Nisei toddler, tagged like a piece of luggage and guarded by a GI, waits to be taken to a detention camp.*

barracks behind barbed wire, guarded by armed troops.

Appeals to the Supreme Court proved fruitless; in 1944, six justices upheld relocation on grounds of national security in wartime. Beginning in 1943, individual Japanese-Americans could win release by pledging their loyalty and finding a job away from the West Coast; some thirty-five thousand left the camps during the next two years. The government finally closed the detention centers in January 1945, but nearly five thousand former prisoners chose to return to Japan at the war's end. The Japanese-Americans never experienced the torture and mass death of the German concentration camps, but their treatment was a disgrace to a nation fighting for freedom and democracy.

Win-the-War Politics

Franklin Roosevelt used World War II to strengthen his leadership and maintain Democratic political dominance. As war brought about prosperity and removed the economic discontent that had sustained the New Deal, FDR announced that "Dr. New Deal" had given way to "Dr. Win-the-War." Congress, already controlled by a conservative coalition of southern Democrats and northern Republicans, had almost slipped into GOP hands in 1942. With a very low voter turnout, due in part to the large numbers of men in service and uprooted workers who failed to establish residency requirements for voting, the Republicans won forty-four new seats in the House and nine in the Senate and elected governors in New York and California as well.

In 1944, Roosevelt responded to the Democratic slippage by dropping Henry Wallace, his liberal and visionary vice-president, for Harry Truman, a moderate and down-to-earth Missouri senator who was acceptable to all factions of the Democratic party. Equally important, FDR received increased political support from organized labor, which had grown in membership during the war from ten to fifteen million. The newly organized Political Action Committee (PAC) of the CIO, headed by Sidney Hillman, conducted massive door-to-door drives to register millions of workers and their families.

The Republicans nominated Thomas E. Dewey, who had been elected governor of New York after gaining fame as a prosecutor of organized crime. Dewey, moderate in his views, played down opposition to the New Deal and instead tried to make Roosevelt's age and health the primary issues, along with the charge that the Democrats were soft on communism. Referring to Hillman's role in the campaign and Communist leader Earl Browder's endorsement of FDR, a GOP poster proclaimed, "YOU don't have to 'clear everything with Sidney.' Vote Republican and keep the Communists, Hillman and Browder from running your country and your life."

Despite his abrasive campaign style, Dewey did not advocate a return to isolationism. The Republican party was trying hard to shake the obstructionist image it had gained during the League of Nations fight in 1919; it went on record in 1943 as favoring American postwar cooperation for world peace. Indeed, Dewey pioneered a bipartisan approach to foreign policy. He accepted wartime planning for the future United Nations and kept the issue of an international organization out of the campaign.

Reacting to the issues of his age and health, especially after a long bout with influenza in the spring, FDR disregarded the advice of his doctors and took a five-hour, rain-soaked drive through

■ The most controversial of the Big Three wartime conferences was the February 1945 meeting at the Russian Black Sea resort of Yalta.

the streets of New York City in an open car just before the election. His vitality impressed the voters, and in November 1944 he swept back into office for a fourth term, although the margin of 3.6 million votes was his smallest yet. But the vigorous campaign had taken its toll. Suffering from high blood pressure and congestive heart disease, the President was thin and pale, tiring easily after only a few hours of work. He rallied his waning energy to attend the Yalta Conference in Russia with Churchill and Stalin, but his health continued to fail after his return in mid-February.

The Election of 1944			
Candidate	Party	Popular Vote	Electoral Vote
Roosevelt	Democrat	25,611,936	432
Dewey	Republican	22,013,372	99

In early April, FDR left Washington for Warm Springs, Georgia, where he had always been able to relax. He was sitting for his portrait at midday on April 12, 1945, when he suddenly complained of a "terrific headache," then slumped forward and died. The nation mourned a man who had gallantly met the challenges of depression and global war. Many grieved that FDR did not live to see the final triumph over the Axis powers, but he must have known that victory was at hand. Unfortunately, he had taken no steps to prepare his successor, the inexperienced Harry Truman, for the difficult problems that lay ahead.

Victory

World War II ended with surprising swiftness. Once the Axis tide had been turned by 1943 in Europe and Asia, it did not take long for Russia, the United States, and England to mount the offensives that drove Germany and Japan back across the vast areas they had conquered and set the stage for their final defeat.

The long-awaited second front finally came on June 6, 1944. For two years, the United States and England concentrated on building up an invasion force of nearly three million troops and a vast armada of ships and landing craft to carry them across the English Channel. In hopes of catching Hitler by surprise, Eisenhower chose the Normandy peninsula, where the absence of good harbors had led to lighter German fortifications. Allied aircraft bombed the roads, bridges, and rail lines of northern France for six weeks preceding the assault in order to block the movement of German reinforcements once the invasion began.

D-day was originally set for June 5, but bad weather forced a delay. Relying on a forecast of a break in the storm, Eisenhower gambled on going ahead on June 6. During the night, three divisions parachuted down behind the German defenses; at dawn, the British and American troops fought their way ashore along a forty-mile stretch of beach, encountering stiff German resistance at several points. By the end of the day, however, Eisenhower had won his beachhead; a week later, more than a third of a million men were slowly pushing back the German forces through the hedgerows of Normandy. The breakthrough came

■ The nation's grief at FDR's death is mirrored in the face of this serviceman as the President's funeral cortege passes.

■ Before the D-Day takeoff, General Eisenhower, the Supreme Allied Commander offers a last word to paratroopers who will be dropped behind German lines.

on July 25 when General Omar Bradley decimated the enemy with a massive artillery and aerial bombardment at Saint-Lô, opening a gap for General George Patton's Third Army. American tanks raced across the French countryside, trapping thousands of Germans and liberating Paris by August 25. Allied troops reached the Rhine River by September, but a shortage of supplies, especially gasoline, forced a three-month halt.

Hitler took advantage of this breathing spell to deliver a daring counterattack. In mid-December, the remaining German armored divisions burst through a weak point in the Allied lines in the Ardennes Forest, planning a breakout to the coast that would have cut off nearly one third of Eisenhower's forces. A combination of tactical surprise and bad weather, which prevented Allied air support, led to a huge bulge in the American lines. But an airborne division dug in at the key crossroads of Bastogne, in Belgium, and held off a much larger German force. Allied reinforcements and clearing weather then combined to end the attack. By committing nearly all his reserves to the Battle of the Bulge, Hitler delayed Eisenhower's advance into Germany, but he had fatally weakened German resistance in the West.

The end came quickly. A massive Russian offensive began in mid-January and swept across the Oder River toward Berlin. General Bradley's troops, finding a bridge left virtually intact by the retreating Germans, crossed the Rhine on March 7. Eisenhower overruled the British, who favored one concentrated drive on Berlin. Instead the Allied forces advanced on a broad front, capturing the industrial Ruhr basin and meeting the Russians at the Elbe by the last week in April. With the Red Army already in the suburbs of Berlin, Adolf Hitler committed suicide on April 30. A week later, on May 7, 1945, Eisenhower accepted the unconditional surrender of all German forces. Just eleven months and a day after the landings in Normandy, the Allied forces had brought the war in Europe to a successful end.

War Aims and Wartime Diplomacy

The American contribution to Hitler's defeat was relatively minor compared to the damage inflicted by the Soviet Union. At the height of the German invasion of Russia, more than 300 Soviet divisions had been locked in battle with 250 German ones, a striking contrast to the 58 divisions the United States and Britain used in the Normandy invasion. As his armies overran Poland and the Balkan countries, Joseph Stalin was determined to retain control over this region, which had been the historic pathway for Western invasion into Russia. Delay in opening the second front and an innate distrust of the West convinced the Soviets that they should maximize their territorial gains by imposing Communist regimes on Eastern Europe.

American postwar goals were quite different. Now believing that the failure to join the League of Nations in 1919 had led to the coming of World War II, the American people and their leaders vowed to put their faith in a new attempt at collective security. At Moscow in 1943, Secretary of State Cordell Hull won Russian agreement to participate in a future world organization at the war's end. In the first wartime Big Three conference, held at Teheran, Iran, in late 1943, Stalin reaffirmed this commitment and also indicated to President Roosevelt that Russia would enter the war against Japan once Germany was defeated.

By the time the Big Three met again at Yalta, in February 1945, the military situation favored the Russians. While British and American forces were still recovering from the Battle of the Bulge, the Red Army was advancing to within fifty miles of Berlin. Stalin drove a series of hard bargains. He refused to give up his plans for Communist domination of Poland and the Balkans, although he did agree to Roosevelt's request for a Declaration of Liberated Europe, which called for free elections without providing for any method of enforcement or supervision. More important for the United States, Stalin promised to enter the Pacific war three months after Germany surrendered. In return, Roosevelt offered extensive concessions in Asia, including Russian control over Manchuria. While neither a sellout nor a betrayal, as some critics have charged, Yalta was a diplomatic victory for the Soviets—one that reflected Russia's major contribution to a victory in Europe.

The defeat of Nazi Germany dissolved the bond between the United States and the Soviet Union in World War II. With very different histories, cultures, and ideologies, the two nations had little in common beyond their enmity toward

Hitler. At the Potsdam Conference in July 1945, the growing rift between the former allies became apparent. The United States condemned the Soviet insistence on control of Poland and the Balkans; the Russians were equally adamant in their demands for German reparations. The seeds of the future cold war were beginning to sprout even before the Second World War had ended.

Triumph and Tragedy in the Pacific

The total defeat of Germany in May 1945 turned all eyes toward Japan. Although the Combined Chiefs of Staff had originally estimated that it would take eighteen months after Germany's surrender to conquer Japan, American forces moved with surprising speed. Admiral Nimitz swept through the Gilbert, Caroline, and Marshall islands in 1944, securing bases for further advances and building airfields for American B-29s to begin a deadly bombardment of the Japanese home islands. General MacArthur cleared New Guinea of the last Japanese defender in early 1944 and began planning his long-heralded return to the Philippines. American troops landed on the island of Leyte on October 20, 1944, and Manila fell by the end of the year. The Japanese navy, in a Pacific version of the Battle of the Bulge, launched a daring three-pronged attack on the American invasion fleet in Leyte Gulf. The U.S. Navy rallied to blunt all three Japanese thrusts, sinking four carriers and ending any further Japanese naval threat.

The defeat of Japan was now only a matter of time. The United States had three possible ways to proceed. The military favored a full-scale invasion, beginning on the southernmost island of Kyushu in November 1945 and culminating with an assault on Honshu (the main island of Japan) and a climactic battle for Tokyo in 1946, with casualties expected to run into the hundreds of thousands. Diplomats suggested a negotiated peace, urging that the United States modify the unconditional-surrender formula to permit Japan to retain the institution of the emperor. At Potsdam, Churchill and Truman did issue a call for surrender, warning Japan it faced utter destruction, but they made no mention of the emperor.

The third possibility involved the highly secret

Chronology	
1922	Washington Naval Conference limits tonnage
1926	World Court rejects qualified U.S. entry
1928	Kellogg-Briand Pact outlaws war (August) Clark Memorandum repudiates Roosevelt Corollary (December)
1931	Japan occupies China's Manchurian province
1933	FDR extends diplomatic recognition to USSR
1936	Hitler's troops reoccupy Rhineland
1937	FDR signs permanent Neutrality Act (May) FDR urges quarantine of aggressor nations (October) Japanese planes sink U.S.S. *Panay* in China (December)
1938	Ludlow war referendum buried in Congress (January) Munich Conference appeases Hitler (September)
1939	Germany invades Poland; World War II begins
1941	Japanese attack Pearl Harbor; United States enters World War II
1942	U.S. defeats Japanese at battle of Midway (June) Allies land in North Africa (November)
1943	Soviets smash Nazis at Stalingrad
1944	Allies land on Normandy beachheads
1945	Big Three met at Yalta (February) FDR dies; Harry Truman becomes president (April) Germany surrenders unconditionally (May) U.S. drops atomic bombs on Hiroshima and Nagasaki; Japan surrenders (August)

Manhattan Project. Since 1939, the United States had spent $2 billion to develop an atomic bomb based on the fission of radioactive uranium and plutonium. On July 16, 1945, they successfully tested their handiwork at Alamogordo, New Mexico (see the special feature in this chapter).

Scientists and the Atomic Bomb

The years between World Wars I and II saw great progress in the study of atomic physics as scientists throughout Europe and America sought to unlock the secrets of the atom. These scientists considered themselves to be members of an international community of scholars, sharing their discoveries irrespective of nationality. But the rise of Nazi Germany threatened this free exchange of ideas, leading many of the great physicists from Europe to seek refuge in England and the United States.

Many physicists thought atomic energy had little application, but others feared even the slightest possibility of such awesome power in the hands of Hitler. The best safeguard, they reasoned, would be to keep secret all progress in atomic research. Leo Szilard, for example, a Hungarian-born physicist who had studied with Albert Einstein at the University of Berlin and emigrated to the United States in 1933, even tried to prevail upon his colleagues not to publish their findings. When Szilard's plan for self-censorship failed, he and several of his fellow émigrés decided to warn the American government of the possible military uses of atomic fission.

After an unsuccessful attempt to interest the Department of the Navy in atomic energy, Szilard decided to appeal directly to President Roosevelt. First he went to Einstein (pictured in photo above) for assistance, and his old mentor lent his name and prestige to Szilard's endeavor. Szilard probably penned the "Einstein Letter"; nonetheless, it represented Einstein's deep concern about the state of atomic research and the growing German threat. Upon reading the letter, FDR turned to his attache', General Edwin "Pa" Watson, and said, "Pa, this requires action."

The President soon assembled an advisory group known as the Uranium Committee to determine the feasibility of atomic weapons. Although it had been émigré scientists who brought the possibility of an atomic bomb to the attention of the American government, they were excluded from the deliberations of the Uranium Committee. Foreign-born scientists were not considered a good security risk.

Ironically, these security measures contributed to the ultimate benefit of Allied atomic research. In America and Britain, foreign scientists—barred from participating in high-priority military projects such as the development of radar—devoted themselves single-mindedly to atomic energy. When Otto Frisch and Rudolph Pierels, two German refugees who fled to England, developed a theoretical design for an atomic bomb, the British government decided to pursue further research. Upon reading the British report, Vannevar Bush, chairman of the newly created National Defense Research Committee, recommended that the U.S. government take steps to ascertain the possible applications of atomic energy. Though still cautious in his projection of its military potential, he suggested that "if such an explosive were made, it would be thousands of times more powerful than existing explosives and its use might be determining."

In 1942, after the limited States had joined the war against the Axis powers, research on atomic energy entered a new phase. Roosevelt and Churchill agreed to a joint atomic research program, based in America where it could be insulated from the European war. Control of the project was transferred from civilian committees to the War Department. By the fall of 1942, the atomic bomb project, code-named the Manhattan Engineering District, was under way, and General Leslie R. Groves of the Army Corps of Engineers was in command.

The scientists on the Manhattan Project feared that they were lagging behind Germany in the race to harness atomic power. Everyone on the project felt that speed was of the utmost importance. But the desire to proceed quickly brought the scientists into conflict with their military partners. The Manhattan Project was compartmentalized. Communication between labs as well as individuals was limited to designated channels. Mail was scrutinized by military censors. Knowledge of the overall progress of the project was kept on a "need-to-know" basis. The military considered such security measures necessary to prevent information leaks; the scientists objected to their isolation within the project. Most of the researchers who joined the operation did so for the intellectual challenge as well as for patriotic reasons. In recruiting personnel for the Los Alamos lab, Robert Oppenheimer found that the greatest attraction was the opportunity to participate in the world's most advanced atomic physics program. Once in the project, however, scientists found themselves cut off from their colleagues working in other areas and unable to ascertain where their work fit in the larger design. The Manhattan Project was not the intellectually free atmosphere that many of the scientists desired; neither was it the all-military operation preferred by General Groves.

But security regulations and academic freedom were not the only issues creating tensions within the project. Enrico Fermi and his team of theoretical physicists at the Chicago Metallurgical Laboratory overcame the first and greatest obstacle in December 1942, creating a self-sustaining chain reaction. The most important activities then shifted to the other labs. As one scientist observed, it became "a question of development and the solving of a multitude of mechanical problems."

These physicists now had time to reflect on the actual use of the atomic bomb and its postwar implications. As the German collapse drew ever nearer and military intelligence discovered that the Nazis were in fact years behind the Allies in atomic research, the Chicago scientists began to raise questions: when and how the atomic bomb should be deployed; the likelihood of a postwar arms race; and the possibilities for international control of atomic energy. Recognizing clearly that the atomic bomb could not long remain a secret, members of the Manhattan Project appealed to Roosevelt, and later to President Truman, to take steps to ensure a peaceful postwar world. But after several years of work and the signs of expenditure of $2 billion, the atomic bomb had developed its own momentum. Few outside the project's labs considered forswearing its use, and the signs of deterioration in the wartime alliance with the Soviet Union did not bode well for international control.

Those working at the Los Alamos lab had the least time to ruminate about their work, for theirs was the final step in the development of the atomic bomb. Throughout 1944 and early 1945, they worked feverishly to complete their task before the war's end. On July 16, 1945, after several delays, the first atomic bomb was tested in a remote section of desert near Alamogordo, New Mexico. The blast created a fireball brighter than several suns; a mushroom cloud rose 40,000 feet into the sky; windows were broken 125 miles away; a blind woman saw the light. In General Groves' assessment, "The test was successful beyond the most optimistic expectations." From the control bunker in the New Mexico desert, Oppenheimer was reminded of a passage from the Hindu *Bhagavad-Gita* as he witnessed the explosion. "I am become death, destroyer of worlds."

■ *These traumatized victims of the first A-bomb blast August 6, 1945, over Hiroshima are seeking first aid a few hours after the explosion.*

Informed of this achievement upon his arrival at Potsdam, President Truman authorized the army air force to use the atomic bomb against Japan. Truman had been unaware of the existence of the Manhattan Project before he became president on April 12. Now he simply followed the recommendation of a committee headed by Secretary of War Henry L. Stimson to drop the bomb on a Japanese city without any prior warning. Neither Truman nor Stimson had any qualms about this momentous decision. They viewed it as a legitimate wartime measure, one designed to save the lives of hundreds of thousands of Americans and Japanese that would be lost in a full-scale invasion.

Weather conditions on the morning of August 6 dictated the choice of Hiroshima as the bomb's target. The explosion incinerated four square miles of the city, instantly killing more than sixty thousand. Two days later, Russia entered the war against Japan, and the next day, August 9, the United States dropped a second bomb on Nagasaki. There were no more atomic bombs available, but no more were needed. The emperor personally broke a deadlock in the Japanese cabinet and persuaded his ministers to surrender unconditionally on August 14, 1945. Three weeks later, Japan signed a formal capitulation agreement on the decks of the battleship *Missouri* in Tokyo Bay to bring World War II to its official close.

The second great war of the twentieth century has had a lasting impact on American life. For the first time, the nation's military potential had been reached. In 1945, the United States was unquestionably the strongest country on the earth, with eleven million men and women in uniform, a vast array of shipyards, aircraft plants, and munitions factories in full production, and a monopoly over the atomic bomb. For better or worse, the nation was now launched on a global career. In the future, the United States would be involved in all parts of the world, from Western Europe to remote jungles in Asia, from the nearby Caribbean to the distant Persian Gulf. And despite its enormous strength in 1945, the nation's new world role would encompass failure and frustration as well as power and dominion.

The legacy of war was equally strong at home. Four years of fighting brought about industrial recovery and unparalleled prosperity. The old pattern of unregulated free enterprise was as much a victim of the war as of the New Deal; big government and huge deficits had now become the norm as economic control passed from New York and Wall Street to Washington and Pennsylvania Avenue. The war led to far-reaching changes in American society that would only become apparent decades later. Such distinctive patterns of recent American life as the baby boom and the growth of the Sun belt can be traced back to wartime origins. The Second World War was a watershed in twentieth-century America, ushering in a new age of global concerns and domestic upheaval.

Recommended Reading

The best general account of American attitudes toward the world in the 1920s can be found in Selig Adler, *The Isolationist Impulse* (1957). Robert Dallek provides a thorough account of FDR's diplomacy in *Franklin D. Roosevelt and American Foreign Policy, 1932–1934* (1979). For a more critical view, see Robert A. Divine, *Roosevelt and World War II* (1969).

Two good books on the continuing controversy over Pearl Harbor are Roberta Wohlstetter, *Pearl Harbor: Warning and Decision* (1962), and Gordon W. Prange, *At Dawn We Slept* (1981). Both authors deny the charge that Roosevelt deliberately exposed the naval base to attack.

In his brief overview of wartime diplomacy, *American Diplomacy During the Second World War* (1964), Gaddis Smith stresses the tensions within the victorious coalition. The two best accounts of the home front are Richard Polenberg, *War and Society* (1972) and John W. Blum, *V Was for Victory* (1976).

Additional Bibliography

On American foreign policy in the period between the wars, see Selig Adler, *The Uncertain Giant, 1921–1941* (1965); Arnold A. Offner, *The Origins of the Second World War* (1975); L. Ethan Ellis, *Republican Foreign Policy, 1921–1933* (1971); Robert H. Ferrell, *Peace in Their Time* (1952); Charles Chatfield, *For Peace and Justice* (1971); Charles DeBenedetti, *Origins of the Modern American Peace Movement, 1915–1929* (1978); Michael J. Hogan, *Informal Entente* (1977); Melvin P. Leffler, *The Elusive Quest* (1978); Akira Iriye, *After Imperialism* (1965); Roger Dingman, *Power in the Pacific* (1976); Thomas H. Buckley, *The United States and the Washington Conference, 1921–1922* (1970); Dorothy Borg, *The United States and the Far Eastern Crisis of 1933–38* (1964); and Robert F. Smith, *The United States and Revolutionary Nationalism in Mexico, 1916–1932* (1972).

For foreign policy during the Hoover years, see Robert H. Ferrell, *American Diplomacy in the Great Depression* (1957); Alexander DeConde, *Herbert Hoover's Latin American Policy* (1951); and Armin Rappaport, *Henry L. Stimson and Japan* (1963). Diplomatic developments in the 1930s under FDR are covered in Dorothy Borg, *The United States and the Far Eastern Crisis of 1933–1938* (1964); Stephen E. Pelz, *Race to Pearl Harbor* (1974); Bryce Wood, *The Making of the Good Neighbor Policy* (1961); Irwin F. Gellman, *Good Neighbor Diplomacy* (1979); Dick Steward, *Trade and Hemisphere* (1979); Manfred Jonas, *Isolationism in America, 1935–1941* (1966); Robert A. Divine, *The Illusion of Neutrality* (1962); and Wayne A. Cole, *Senator Gerald Nye and American Foreign Relations* (1963).

Examinations of Roosevelt's policies during World War II include Robert Sherwood, *Roosevelt and Hopkins* (1948); James M. Burns, *Roosevelt: Soldier of Freedom* (1970); and Lloyd Gardner, *Economic Aspects of New Deal Diplomacy* (1964). For details of the American entry into the war, see William L. Langer and S. Everett Gleason, *The Challenge to Isolation* (1950) and *The Undeclared War* (1953); Robert A. Divine, *The Reluctant Belligerent*, 2d ed. (1979); Bruce Russett, *No Clear and Present Danger* (1972); Wayne S. Cole, *America First* (1953); Warren F. Kimball, *The Most Unsordid Act: Lend-Lease, 1939–1941* (1969); David Reynolds, *The Creation of the Anglo-American Alliance, 1937–1941* (1982); Saul Friedlander, *Prelude to Downfall: Hitler and the United States* (1967); Herbert Feis, *The Road to Pearl Harbor* (1950); Paul W. Schroeder, *The Axis Alliance and Japanese-American Relations: 1941* (1958); Dorothy Borg and Shumpei Okamoto, eds., *Pearl Harbor as History* (1973); and Harry Elmer Barnes, ed., *Perpetual War for Perpetual Peace* (1953).

Military and strategic aspects of World War II are covered in A. Russell Buchanan, *The United States and World War II*, 2 vols. (1964); Chester Wilmot, *The Struggle for Europe* (1952); Kent Roberts Greenfield, *American Strategy in World War II* (1963); and Mark A. Stoller, *The Politics at the Second Front, 1941–1943* (1977). For wartime diplomacy, see Herbert Feis, *Churchill, Roosevelt and Stalin* (1957); William H. McNeill, *America, Britain, and Russia, 1941–1946* (1953); Tang Tsou, *America's Failure in China* (1963); Michael Schaller, *The U.S. Crusade in China, 1936–1945* (1979); Akira Iriye, *Power and Culture* (1981); Diane Clemens, *Yalta* (1970); and Ralph B. Levering, *American Opinion and the Russian Alliance, 1939–1945* (1976).

On the atomic bomb, see Richard G. Hewlett and Oscar E. Anderson, *The New World, 1939–1946* (1962); Gar Alperovitz, *Atomic Diplomacy* (1965); Martin Sherwin, *A World Destroyed* (1975); Herbert Feis, *The Atomic Bomb and the End of World War II* (1966); and Robert J. C. Butow, *Japan's Decision to Surrender* (1954). Social developments during World War II are examined in Roger Daniels, *Concentration Camps, USA* (1971); Karen Anderson, *Wartime Women* (1981); Neil A. Wynn, *The Afro-Americans and the Second World War* (1976); and A. Russell Buchanan, *Black Americans in World War II* (1977).

THE
ONSET OF
THE COLD WAR

"I am getting ready to go see Stalin and Church-ill," President Truman wrote to his mother in July 1945, "and it is a chore." On board the cruiser *Augusta*, the new President continued to complain about the upcoming Potsdam Conference in his diary. "How I hate this trip!" he confided. "But I have to make it—win, lose or draw—and we must win. . . . I [am] giving nothing away except to save starving people and even then I hope we can only help them to help themselves."

Halfway around the world, Joseph Stalin left Moscow a day late because of a slight heart attack. The Russian leader hated to fly, so he traveled by rail. He ordered the heavily guarded train to detour around Poland for fear of an ambush, further delaying his arrival. When he made his entrance into Potsdam, a suburb of Berlin miraculously spared the total destruction that his forces had created in the German capital, he was ready to claim the spoils of war.

These two men, one the veteran revolutionary who had been in power for two decades, the other an untested leader in office for barely three months, symbolized the enormous differences that now separated the wartime allies. Stalin was above all the realist. Brutal in securing total control at home, he was more flexible in his foreign policy, bent on exploiting Russia's victory in World War II rather than aiming at world domination. Cunning and caution were the hallmarks of his diplomatic style. Small in stature, ungainly in build, he radiated a catlike quality as he waited behind his unassuming façade, ready to dazzle an opponent with his "brilliant, terrifying tactical mastery." Truman, in contrast, personified traditional Wilsonian idealism. Lacking Roosevelt's guile, the new President placed his faith in international cooperation. Like many Americans, he believed implicitly in his country's innate goodness. Self-assured to the point of cockiness, he came to Potsdam clothed in the armor of self-righteousness.

The two men met for the first time on July 17, 1945. "I told Stalin that I am no diplomat," the President recorded in his diary, "but usually said yes and no to questions after hearing all the argument." The Russian dictator's reaction remains a mystery, but Truman felt that the first encounter went well. "I can deal with Stalin," he wrote. "He is honest—but smart as hell."

Together with Winston Churchill and his replacement, Clement Attlee, whose Labour party had just triumphed in British elections, Truman and Stalin clashed for the next ten days over such difficult issues as reparations, the Polish border, and the fate of Eastern Europe. Truman presented the ideas and proposals formulated by his advisers; he saw his task as essentially procedural, and when he presided, he moved the agenda along in brisk fashion. After he had "banged through" three items one day, he commented, "I am not going to stay around this terrible place all summer, just to listen to speeches. I'll go home to the Senate for that." In an indirect, roundabout way, he informed Stalin of the existence of the atomic bomb, tested successfully in the New Mexico desert just before the conference began. Truman offered no details, and the impassive Stalin asked for none, commenting only that he hoped the United States would make "good use of it against the Japanese."

Reparations proved to be the crucial issue at Potsdam. The Russians wanted to rebuild their war-ravaged economy with German industry; the United States feared it would be saddled with the entire cost of caring for the defeated Germans. A compromise was finally reached. Each side would take reparations primarily from its own occupation zone, a solution that foreshadowed the future division of Germany. "Because they could not agree on 'how to govern Europe,'" wrote historian Daniel Yergin, Truman and Stalin "began to divide it." The other issues were referred to the newly created Council of Foreign Ministers, which would meet in the fall in London.

The conference thus ended on an apparent note of harmony; beneath the surface, however, the bitter antagonism of the Cold War was festering. America and Russia, each distrustful of the other, were preparing for a long and bitter confrontation.

President Truman, Churchill, and Stalin relax in the palace garden before the meeting at Potsdam, July 25, 1945. The conference dealt with the division of Germany into four occupation zones and recognized Soviet occupation of German territory east of the Oder River, but the mutual suspicion apparent at Potsday soon crystallized as the Cold War.

A dozen years later, Truman reminisced to an old associate about Potsdam. "What a show that was!" Describing himself as "an innocent idealist" surrounded by wolves, he claimed that all the agreements reached there were "broken as soon as the unconscionable Russian Dictator returned to Mosow!" And then he added ruefully, "And I liked the little son of a bitch. . . ."

The Cold War Begins

The conflict between the United States and the Soviet Union began gradually. For two years, the nations tried to adjust their differences, primarily over three crucial issues, through discussion and negotiation. The Council of Foreign Ministers provided the forum. Beginning in London during the fall of 1945 and meeting with their Russian counterparts in Paris, New York, and Moscow, American diplomats searched for a way to live in peace with a suspicious Soviet Union.

The Division of Europe

The fundamental disagreement was over who would control postwar Europe. In the east, the Red Army had swept over Poland and the Bal-

kans, laying the basis for Soviet domination there. American and British forces had liberated Western Europe from Scandinavia to Italy. The Russians, mindful of past invasions from the west across the plains of Poland, were intent on imposing Communist governments loyal to Moscow in the Soviet sphere. The United States, on the other hand, upheld the principle of national self-determination, insisting that the people in each country should freely choose their postwar rulers. The Soviets saw this demand for free elections as subversive, since they knew that popularly chosen regimes would be unfriendly to Russia. Suspecting American duplicity, Stalin brought down an "Iron Curtain" (Churchill's phrase) from the Baltic to the Adriatic as he created a series of satellite governments.

Germany was the key. The temporary zones of occupation gradually hardened into permanent lines of division. Ignoring the Potsdam Conference agreement that the country be treated as an economic unit, the United States and Great Britain were by 1946 refusing to permit the Russians to take reparations from the industrial Western zones. The initial harsh occupation policy gave way to more humane treatment of the German people and a slow but steady economic recovery. The United States and England merged their zones and championed the idea of the unification of all Germany. Russia, fearing a resurgence of

German military power, responded by intensifying the communization of its zone, which included the jointly occupied city of Berlin. By 1947, England, France, and the United States were laying plans to transfer their authority to an independent West Germany.

The Soviet Union consolidated its grip on Eastern Europe in 1946 and 1947. One by one, Communist regimes replaced coalition governments in Poland, Hungary, Rumania, and Bulgaria. Moving cautiously to avoid provoking the West, Stalin used communism as a means to dominate half of Europe, both to protect the security of the Soviet state and to advance its international power. The climax came in March 1948 when a coup in Czechoslovakia overthrew a democratic government and gave the Soviets a strategic foothold in Central Europe.

The division of Europe was an inevitable outgrowth of World War II. Both sides were intent on imposing their values in the areas liberated by their troops. The Russians were no more likely to withdraw from Eastern Europe than the United States and Britain were from Germany, France, and Italy. A frank recognition of competing spheres of influence might have avoided further escalation of tension. But the Western nations, remembering Hitler's aggression in the 1930s, began to see Stalin as an equally dangerous threat to their well-being. Instead of accepting him as a

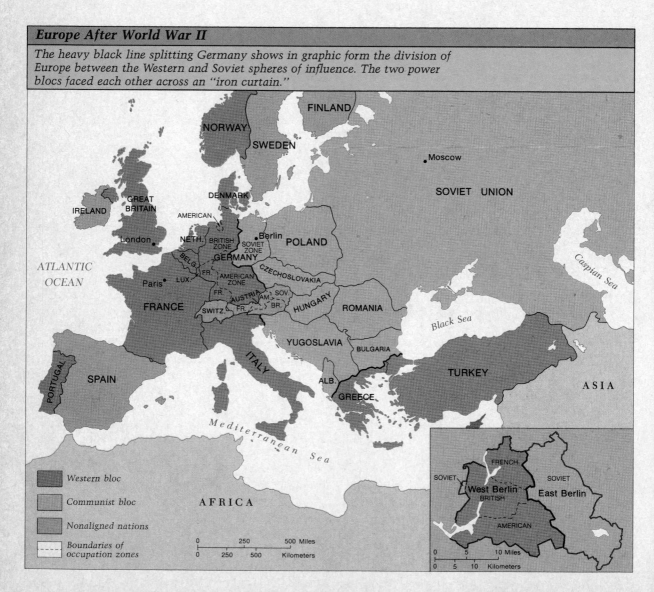

Europe After World War II

The heavy black line splitting Germany shows in graphic form the division of Europe between the Western and Soviet spheres of influence. The two power blocs faced each other across an "iron curtain."

Western bloc

Communist bloc

Nonaligned nations

Boundaries of occupation zones

cautious leader bent on protecting Russian security, they perceived him as an aggressive dictator leading a Communist drive for world domination.

Withholding Economic Aid

The Second World War had inflicted enormous damage on Russia. The brutal fighting had taken between fifteen and twenty million Russian lives, destroyed over thirty thousand factories, and torn up forty thousand miles of railroad track. The industrialization that Stalin had achieved at such great sacrifice in the 1930s had been badly set back; even agricultural production had fallen by half during the war. Outside aid and assistance were vital for the reconstruction of the Soviet Union.

American leaders knew of Russia's plight and hoped to use it to good advantage. Wartime ambassador Averell Harriman wrote in 1944 that economic aid was "one of the most effective weapons at our disposal" in dealing with Russia. President Truman was convinced that economically "we held all the cards and the Russians had to come to us."

There were two possible forms of postwar assistance—loans and Lend-Lease. In January 1945, the Soviets requested a $6-billion loan to finance postwar reconstruction. Despite initial American encouragement, President Roosevelt deferred action on this request; as relations with Russia cooled, the chances for action dimmed. "Our experience," commented Harriman in April 1945, had "incontrovertibly proved it was not possible to bank goodwill in Moscow." By the war's end, the loan request, though never formally turned down, was dead.

Lend-Lease proved no more successful. In the spring of 1945, Congress instructed the administration not to use Lend-Lease for postwar reconstruction. President Truman went further, however, by signing an order on May 11, 1945, terminating all shipments to Russia, including those already at sea. The State Department saw the action as applying "leverage against the Soviet Union"; Stalin termed it "brutal." Heeding Russian protests, Truman resumed Lend-Lease shipments, but only until the war was over in August. After that, all Lend-Lease ended.

Deprived of American assistance, the Russians were forced to rebuild their economy through reparations. American and British resistance prevented them taking reparations in Western Germany, but the Soviets systematically removed factories and plants from other areas they controlled, including their zone of Germany, Eastern Europe, and Manchuria. Slowly the Russian economy recovered from the war, but the bitterness over the American refusal to extend aid convinced Stalin of Western hostility and thus deepened the growing antagonism.

The Atomic Dilemma

Overshadowing all else was the atomic bomb. Used by the United States with deadly success at Hiroshima and Nagasaki, the new weapon raised problems that would have been difficult for friendly nations to resolve. Given the uneasy state of Russian-American relations, the effect was disastrous.

The wartime policy followed by Roosevelt and Churchill ensured a postwar nuclear arms race. Instead of informing their major ally of the developing atomic bomb, they kept it a closely guarded secret. Stalin learned of the Manhattan Project through espionage and responded by starting a Soviet atomic program in 1943. By the time Truman informed Stalin of the weapon's existence at Potsdam, the Russians were well on the way to making their own bomb.

After the war, the United States developed a disarmament plan based on turning control of fissionable material, then the processing plants, and ultimately its stockpile of bombs over to an international agency. When President Truman appointed financier Bernard Baruch to present this proposal to the United Nations, Baruch insisted on changing it in several important ways, adding sanctions against violators and exempting the international agency from the UN veto. Ignoring scientists who pleaded for a more cooperative position, Baruch followed instead the advice of Army Chief of Staff Dwight D. Eisenhower, who cited the rapid demobilization of American armed forces (from nearly twelve million in 1945 to less than two million in 1947) to argue that "we cannot at this time limit our capability to produce or use this weapon." In effect, the Baruch Plan, with its multiple stages and emphasis on inspection, would preserve the American atomic monopoly for the indefinite future.

The Soviets responded predictably. Diplomat Andrei Gromyko presented a simple plan calling for a total ban on the production and use of the new weapon as well as the destruction of all existing bombs. The Russian proposal was founded on the same perception of national self-interest as the Baruch Plan. Though Russia had also demobilized rapidly, it still had nearly three million men under arms in 1947 and wished to use its conventional strength to the utmost by outlawing the atomic bomb.

No agreement was possible. Neither the United States nor the Soviet Union could abandon its position without surrendering a vital national interest. Wanting to preserve its monopoly, America stressed inspection and control; hoping to neutralize the U.S. advantage, Russia advocated immediate disarmament. The nuclear dilemma, inherent in the Soviet-American rivalry, blocked any national settlement. Instead, the two superpowers agreed to disagree. Trusting neither each other nor any form of international cooperation, each concentrated on taking maximum advantage of its wartime gains. Thus the Russians exploited the territory they had conquered in Europe while the United States retained its economic and strategic advantages over the Soviet Union. The result was the Cold War.

Containment

A major departure in American foreign policy occurred in January 1947 when General George C. Marshall, the wartime army chief of staff, became secretary of state. Calm, mature, and orderly of mind, Marshall had the ability—honed in World War II—to think in broad, strategic terms. An extraordinarily good judge of ability, he relied on gifted subordinates to handle the day-by-day implementation of his policies. In the months after taking office, he came to rely on two men in particular: Dean Acheson and George Kennan.

Acheson, an experienced Washington lawyer and bureaucrat, was appointed undersecretary of state and given free rein by Marshall to conduct American diplomacy. In appearance, he seemed

■ Dean Acheson helped formulate the Truman doctrine for aid to Greece and Turkey and was one of the principal architects of the Marshall Plan for assistance to wartorn Europe.

more British than American, with his impeccable Ivy League clothes and bushy mustache. A man of keen intelligence, he had a carefully cultivated reputation for arrogance and a low tolerance for mediocrity. As an ardent Anglophile, he wanted to see the United States take over a faltering Britain's role as the supreme arbiter of world affairs. Recalling the lesson taught by the Munich Conference of September 1938, he opposed appeasement and advocated a policy of negotiating only from strength.

Marshall's other mainstay was George Kennan, who headed the newly created Policy Planning Staff. A career foreign-service officer, Kennan had become a Soviet expert, mastering Russian history and culture as well as speaking the language fluently. He served in Moscow after U.S. recognition in 1933 and again during World War II, developing there a profound distrust for the Soviet regime. In a crucial telegram in 1946, he warned that the Kremlin believed "that there can be no compromise with rival power" and advocated a policy of containment, arguing that only strong and sustained resistance could halt the outward flow of Russian power. As self-assured as Acheson, Kennan believed that neither Congress nor public opinion should interfere with the conduct of foreign policy by the experts.

In the spring of 1947, a sense of crisis impelled Marshall, Acheson, and Kennan to set out on a new course in American diplomacy. Dubbed "containment," after an article by Kennan in *Foreign Affairs*, the new policy both consolidated the evolving postwar anticommunism and established guidelines that would shape America's role in the world for the next two decades.

The Truman Doctrine

The initial step came in response to an urgent British request. Since March 1946, England had been supporting the Greek government in a bitter civil war against Communist guerrillas. On February 21, 1947, the British informed the United States that they could no longer afford to aid Greece or Turkey, the latter under heavy pressure from the Soviets for access to the Mediterranean. Believing that the Russians were responsible for the strife in Greece (in fact, they were not), Marshall, Acheson, and Kennan quickly decided that the United States would have to take over Britain's role in the eastern Mediterranean.

Worried about congressional support, especially since the Republicans had gained control of Congress in 1946, Marshall called a meeting with the legislative leadership in late February. He outlined the problem, and then Acheson took over to describe "a highly possible Soviet breakthrough" that "might open three continents to Soviet penetration." Comparing the situation in Greece to one rotten apple spoiling an entire barrel, Acheson warned that "the corruption of Greece would infect Iran and all to the East . . . Africa . . . Italy and France." Claiming that the Soviets were "playing one of the greatest gambles in history," Acheson concluded that "we and we alone were in a position to break up the play."

The awed congressional leaders were deeply impressed. Finally, Republican Senator Arthur M. Vandenberg spoke up, saying he would support the President, but adding that to ensure public backing, Truman would have to "scare hell" out of the American people.

The President followed the senator's advice. On March 12, 1947, he asked Congress for $400 million for military and economic assistance to

■ *Critics expressed doubts about the Truman Doctrine, as in this cartoon, but the national mood was shifting toward approval of the containment policy.*

Greece and Turkey. He made clear that more was involved than just these two countries—the stakes in fact were far higher. "It must be the policy of the United States," Truman told the Congress, "to support free peoples who are resisting attempted subjugation by armed minorities or by outside pressure." After a brief debate, both the House and the Senate approved the program by margins of better than three to one.

The Truman Doctrine marked a formal declaration of cold war against the Soviet Union. Truman used the crisis in Greece to secure congressional approval and build a national consensus for the policy of containment. In less than two years, the civil war in Greece ended, but the American commitment to oppose Communist expansion, whether by internal subversion or external aggression, placed the United States on a collision course with the Soviet Union around the globe.

The Marshall Plan

Western Europe was far more vital to U.S interests than was the eastern Mediterranean, yet by 1947 many Americans felt the area was open to

ΘΑ ΤΟΥ ΑΜΕΡΙΚΑΝΙΚΟΥ ΣΧΕΔΙΟΥ ΜΑΡΣΑΛΛ
ΔΙΑ ΤΗΝ ΕΛΛΑΔΑ
ΔΟΠΤΙΟΝ ΑΥΤΟ ΜΕΤΑΦΕΡΕΤΑΙ ΔΙΑ ΤΗΣ ΣΙΔΗΡΟΔΡΟΜΙΚΗΣ
ΜΗΣ ΑΘΗΝΩΝ - ΘΕΣΣΑΛΟΝΙΚΗΣ ΤΩΝ ΣΕΚ ΜΗΚΟΥΣ
ΧΙΛΙΟΜΕΤΡΩΝ. ΤΩΡΑ ΑΙ ΔΥΟ ΜΕΓΑΛΕΙΤΕΡΑΙ ΠΟΛΕΙΣ ΤΗΣ
ΔΟΣ ΣΥΝΔΕΟΝΤΑΙ ΚΑΙ ΠΑΛΙΝ ΣΙΔΗΡΟΔΡΟΜΙΚΩΣ ΔΙΑ
ΤΗΝ ΦΟΡΑΝ ΑΠΟ ΤΟ 1944

AMERICAN MARSHALL PLAN GOODS
FOR GREECE
S FREIGHT IS BEING TRANSPORTED OVER THE
-MILE ATHENS-SALONIKA RAILROAD LINE OF
K-RR. GREECE'S TWO LARGEST CITIES ARE NOW
ED BY RAIL FOR THE FIRST TIME SINCE
1944

■ *The European Recovery Program (Marshall Plan) created for the United States an enormous reservoir of good will in Europe.*

Soviet penetration. The problem was economic in nature. Despite $9 billion in piecemeal American loans, England, France, Italy, and the other European countries had great difficulty in recovering from World War II. Food was scarce, with millions existing on less than fifteen hundred calories a day; industrial machinery was broken down and obsolete; and workers were demoralized by years of depression and war. The cruel winter of 1947, the worst in fifty years, compounded the problem. Resentment and discontent led to growing Communist voting strength, especially in Italy and France. Unless the United States could do something to reverse the process, it seemed as though all Europe might drift into the Communist orbit.

In the weeks following proclamation of the Truman Doctrine, American officials dealt with this problem. Secretary of State Marshall, returning from a frustrating Council of Foreign Ministers meeting in Moscow, warned that "the patient is sinking while the doctors deliberate." Acheson believed that it was time to extend American "economic power" in Europe both "to call an

effective halt to the Soviet Union's expansionism" and "to create a basis for political stability and economic well-being." The experts drew up a plan for the massive infusion of American capital to finance the economic recovery of Europe. Speaking at a Harvard commencement on June 5, 1947, Marshall presented the broad outline. He offered extensive economic aid to all the nations of Europe if they could reach agreement on ways to achieve "the revival of a working economy in the world so as to permit the emergence of political and social conditions in which free institutions can exist."

The fate of the Marshall Plan depended on the reaction of the Soviet Union and the U.S. Congress. Marshall had taken, in the words of one American diplomat, "a hell of a gamble" by including Russia in his offer of aid. At a meeting of the European nations in Paris in July 1947, the Soviet foreign minister ended the suspense by abruptly withdrawing. Neither Russia nor its satellites would take part, apparently because Moscow saw the Marshall Plan as an American attempt to weaken Soviet control over Eastern Europe. The other European countries then made a formal request for $17 billion over the next four years.

Congress responded cautiously to this proposal, appointing a special joint committee to investigate. The administration lobbied vigorously, pointing out that the Marshall Plan would help the United States by stimulating trade with Europe as well as checking Soviet expansion. It was the latter argument, however, that proved decisive. When the Czech coup touched off a war scare in March 1948, Congress quickly approved the Marshall Plan by heavy majorities. Over the next four years, the huge American investment paid rich dividends, generating a broad industrial revival in Western Europe that became self-sustaining by the 1950s. The threat of Communist domination faded, and a prosperous Europe proved to be a bonanza for American farmers, miners, and manufacturers.

The Western Military Alliance

The third and final phase of containment came in 1949 with the establishment of the North Atlantic Treaty Organization (NATO). NATO grew out of European fears of Russian military aggression. Recalling Hitler's tactics in the 1930s, the people of Western Europe wanted assurance that the United States would protect them from attack as they began to achieve economic recovery. American diplomats were sympathetic. "People could not go ahead and make investments for the future," commented Averell Harriman, "without some sense of security."

England, France, and the Low Countries (Belgium, the Netherlands, and Luxembourg) began the process in March 1948 when they signed the Brussels Treaty, providing for collective self-defense. In January 1949, President Truman called for a broader defense pact including the United States; ten European nations, from Norway in the North to Italy in the south, joined the United States and Canada in signing the North Atlantic Treaty in Washington on April 4, 1949. This historic departure from the traditional policy of isolation—the United States had not signed such a treaty since the French alliance in the eighteenth century—caused extensive debate, but the Senate ratified it in July by a vote of 82 to 13.

There were two main features of NATO. First, the United States committed itself to the defense of Europe in the key clause which stated that "an armed attack against one or more . . . shall be considered an attack against them all." In effect, the United States was extending its atomic shield over Europe. The second feature was designed to reassure worried Europeans that the United States would honor this commitment. In late 1950, President Truman appointed General Dwight D. Eisenhower to the post of NATO supreme commander and authorized the stationing of four American divisions in Europe to serve as the nucleus of the NATO army. Now any Russian assault would automatically involve American troops and thus deter the Soviet Union.

The Western military alliance escalated the developing Cold War. Whatever its advantage in building a sense of security among worried Europeans, it represented an overreaction to the Soviet danger. Americans and Europeans alike were attempting to apply the lesson of Munich to the Cold War. But Stalin was not Hitler, and the Soviets were not the Nazis. There was no evidence of any Russian plan to invade Western Europe, and in the face of the American atomic bomb, none was likely. All NATO did was to intensify Russian fears of the West and thus increase the level of international tension.

The Berlin Blockade

The main Russian response to containment came in 1948 at the West's most vulnerable point. American, British, French, and Soviet troops each occupied a sector of Berlin, but the city was located over one hundred miles within the Russian zone of Germany (see the map of postwar Europe on p. 808). Stalin decided to test his opponents' resolve by cutting off all rail and highway traffic to Berlin on June 20, 1948.

The timing was very awkward for Harry Truman. He had his hands full resisting efforts to force him off the Democratic ticket, and he faced a difficult reelection effort against a strong Republican candidate, Governor Thomas E. Dewey of New York. Immersed in election-year politics, Truman was caught unprepared by the Berlin blockade. The alternatives were not very appealing. The United States could withdraw its forces and lose not just a city, but the confidence of all Europe; it could try to send in reinforcements and fight for Berlin; or it could sit tight and attempt to find a diplomatic solution. Truman made the basic decision in characteristic fashion, telling the military that there would be no thought of pulling out. "We were going to stay, period," an aide reported Truman as saying.

In the next few weeks, the President and his advisers developed ways to implement this decision. Rejecting proposals for provoking a showdown by sending an armored column down the main highway, the administration adopted a two-phase policy. The first part was a massive airlift of food, fuel, and supplies for both the ten thousand troops and the two million civilians in Berlin. A fleet of fifty-two C-54s and eighty C-47s began making two daily round-trip flights to Berlin, carrying 2500 tons every twenty-four hours. Then, to guard against Soviet interruption of the airlift, Truman transferred sixty American B-29s, planes capable of delivering atomic bombs, to bases in England. The President was bluffing; the B-29s were not equipped with atomic bombs, but at the time the threat was effective.

For a few weeks, the world teetered on the edge

of war. Stalin did not attempt to disrupt the flights to Berlin, but he rejected all American diplomatic initiatives. The airlift gradually increased to more than four thousand tons a day, but at any time the Russians could have halted it by jamming radar or shooting down the defenseless cargo planes. Governor Dewey patriotically supported the President's policy, thus removing foreign policy from the presidential campaign. Yet for Truman the tension was fierce. In early September he asked his advisers to brief him "on bases, bombs, Moscow, Leningrad, etc." "I have a terrible feeling afterward that we are very close to war," he confided in his diary. "I hope not."

Slowly the tension eased. The Russians did not shoot down any planes, and the daily airlift climbed to nearly seven thousand tons. Truman, a decided underdog, won a surprising second term in November over a complacent Dewey (see the map of the 1948 election on p. 839), in part because the Berlin crisis had rallied the nation behind his leadership. In early 1949, the Soviets gave in, ending the blockade in return for another meeting of the Council of Foreign Ministers on Germany—a conclave that proved as unproductive as all the earlier ones.

The Berlin crisis marked the end of the initial phase of the Cold War. The airlift had given the United States a striking political victory, showing the world the triumph of American ingenuity over Russian stubbornness. Yet it could not disguise the fact that the Cold War had cut Europe in two. Behind the Iron Curtain, the Russians had consolidated control over the areas won by their troops in the war. The United States had used the Marshall Plan to revitalize Western Europe, but a divided continent was a far cry from the wartime hopes for a peaceful world. And the rivalry that began in Europe would soon spread into a worldwide contest between the superpowers. Such was the bitter legacy of World War II.

The Cold War Expands

The rivalry between the United States and the Soviet Union grew in the late 1940s and early 1950s. Both sides ended the postwar demobilization and began to rebuild their military forces with new methods and new weapons. Equally significant, the diplomatic competition spread from Europe to Asia as each of the superpowers sought to enhance its influence in the Orient. By the time Truman left office in early 1953, the Cold War had taken on global proportions.

The Military Dimension

After World War II, American leaders were intent on reforming the nation's military system in light of the wartime experience. Two goals were uppermost. First, nearly everyone agreed in the aftermath of Pearl Harbor that the armed services should be unified into an integrated military system. The developing Cold War reinforced this decision. Without unification, declared George Marshall in 1945, "there can be little hope that we will be able to maintain through the years a military posture that will secure for us a lasting peace." Equally important, planners realized the need for new institutions to coordinate military and diplomatic strategy so that the nation could cope effectively with threats to its security.

In 1947, Congress responded by passing the National Security Act. It established a Department of Defense, headed by a civilian secretary of cabinet rank presiding over three separate services—the army, the navy, and the new air force. In addition, the act created the Central Intelligence Agency (CIA) to coordinate the intelligence-gathering activities of various government agencies. Finally, the act provided for a National Security Council (NSC)—composed of the service secretaries, the secretary of defense, and the secretary of state—to advise the president on all matters regarding the nation's security.

Despite the appearance of equality among the services, the air force quickly emerged as the dominant power in the atomic age, both to deter an enemy from attacking the nation's vital interests and to wage war if deterrence failed. President Truman, intent on cutting back defense expenditures, favored the air force in his 1949 military budget, allotting this branch over one half the total sum. After the Czech coup and the resulting war scare, Congress granted an additional $3 billion, much of it earmarked for the air force. The appropriation included funds for a new B-36 to replace the B-29 as the nation's primary strategic bomber.

American military planners received an even greater boost in the fall of 1949 when the Soviet Union exploded its first atomic bomb. President Truman appointed a high-level committee to explore mounting an all-out effort to build a hydrogen bomb to maintain American nuclear supremacy.

Some scientists had technical objections to the H-bomb, which was still far from being perfected, while others opposed the new weapon on moral grounds, claiming that its enormous destructive power (intended to be one thousand times greater than the atomic bomb) made it unthinkable. George Kennan suggested a new effort at international arms control with the Soviets, but Dean Acheson—who succeeded Marshall as secretary of state in early 1949—felt it was imperative that the United States develop the hydrogen bomb before the Soviet Union. When Acheson presented the committee's favorable report to the President in January 1950, Truman took only seven minutes to decide to go ahead with the awesome new weapon.

At the same time, Acheson ordered the Policy Planning Staff, now headed by Paul Nitze after Kennan resigned in protest, to draw up a new statement of national defense policy. NSC-68, as the document eventually became known, was based on the premise that the Soviet Union sought "to impose its absolute authority over the rest of the world" and thus "mortally challenged" the United States. Rejecting such options as appeasement or a return to isolation, Nitze advocated a massive expansion of American military power so that the United States could halt and overcome the Soviet threat. Contending that the nation could afford to spend "upward of 50 percent of its gross national product" for security, NSC-68 proposed increasing defense spending from $13 to $45 billion annually. Approved in principle by the National Security Council in April 1950, NSC-68 stood as a symbol of the Truman administration's determination to win the Cold War regardless of cost.

The Cold War in Asia

The Soviet-American conflict developed more slowly in Asia. At Yalta, the two superpowers had agreed to a Far Eastern balance of power, with the Russians dominating Northeast Asia and the Americans in control of the Pacific, including both Japan and its former island empire.

The United States moved quickly to consolidate its sphere of influence. General Douglas MacArthur, in charge of Japanese occupation, denied the Soviet Union any role in the recon-

Views of the Cold War: The Debate Among Historians

The outbreak of the Cold War between the United States and the Soviet Union led to an intense and bitter controversy among American historians. One group blamed the conflict solely on the Soviet Union, claiming that the Russians were bent on world domination; opponents argued that the United States had provoked the Cold War through attempts to establish a Pax Americana after World War II.

The scholarly debate followed the course of the Cold War itself. When the diplomatic contest between the United States and Russia was at its height in the 1950s, American historians maintained that the Cold War was clearly the result of Soviet aggression. This orthodox view stemmed from an attempt to absorb the lessons of the 1930s, when the Western democracies had failed to halt the aggression of Germany and Japan until it was almost too late. Citing Munich and the folly of appeasement, historians asserted that Stalin and the Soviet Union were pursuing the same kind of expansionist policies in Europe that Hitler and Nazi Germany had been guilty of in the 1930s. Some saw the Russians as aiming at dominance in Europe; others believed the Soviets desired world domination. The most influential of these writers, former State Department official Herbert Feis, found the origin of the Cold War in the failure of Franklin D. Roosevelt to prepare the American people for the postwar expansion of the Soviet Union.

According to this orthodox view, the Russians nearly achieved their aggressive plan. Weak American diplomacy enabled Stalin to establish an Iron Curtain over Eastern Europe, and by 1947 there was a growing danger of Communist penetration into such Western European countries as Italy and France. Then in the spring of 1947, American policy suddenly met the challenge. According to Joseph Jones in *The Fifteen Weeks*, the President and the secretary of state reversed American policy at the last minute with the Truman Doctrine and the Marshall Plan. These two measures, along with NATO in 1949, formed the essence of containment, the American determination to preserve a favorable balance of power in Europe to check the Russian drive for world control.

This highly nationalistic view of how the Cold War began prevailed through the early 1960s. It justified heavy American military expenditures by portraying the United States as the protector of the free world. The belated and defensive American response to Soviet aggression also fitted neatly into a familiar pattern. Three times in the twentieth century—in 1917, in 1941, and again in 1947—the United States had reluctantly acted to preserve a decent and civilized world.

In the next decade, however, two developments undermined this complacent explanation. First, the escalation of the Vietnam War in 1965 led to a new mood of doubt and dissent over American foreign policy. As the wisdom of U.S. intervention in Vietnam came into question, historians began to probe the roots of the Cold War to find out why Americans had ended up fighting an unpopular war in Southeast Asia. Second, the State Department archives and the private papers of American diplomats were opened for historical research in the 1960s, providing scholars with a behind-the-scenes view of policymaking that often contradicted the accepted version.

The early revisionists, notably Denna F. Fleming and Gar Alperovitz, tended to blame the Cold War on the transfer of power from Roosevelt to Truman and particularly on the decision to drop the atomic bomb. According to this view, Roosevelt tried hard to cooperate with the Soviets, relying on his personal ties with Stalin to ensure postwar cooperation. FDR understood the historic Russian concern over security, which led to an insistence on friendly regimes in Eastern Europe. Truman, however, lacking Roosevelt's experience in foreign policy, immediately antagonized the Russians by challenging their control over Poland and the Balkans. According to Alperovitz, Truman even tried to use the atomic bomb to force a Russian retreat in Eastern Europe, and his decision to use this dread weapon was based as much on a desire to overwhelm the Soviets as to defeat Japan.

Later revisionists gave greater weight to economic factors in accusing the United States of starting the Cold War. Writers such as Gabriel Kolko argued that it was an American need to dominate world markets that lay behind the refusal to accept Soviet control of Eastern Europe. A capitalist system that needed to expand overseas to overcome its own inherent weaknesses prevented the United States from reaching a territorial settlement with Russia that could have led to a peaceful world. Thus a powerful and expansionist United States, not an insecure Soviet Union, was responsible for the Cold War.

In the 1970s, as détente mellowed Soviet-American relations, a more balanced view of the origins of the diplomatic conflict emerged. Writers like John Lewis Gaddis and Daniel Yergin, who became known as postrevisionists, began to treat the Cold War as a historical event that transcended simple accusations of national guilt. Rather than challenging the revisionists completely, they tried to incorporate their views into a broader explanation that stressed the inevitability of the Cold War.

The postrevisionists based their explanation on the confusion and misunderstanding prevalent at the end of World War II. The United States, misled by the experience with Hitler in the 1930s, mistook Stalin's attempt to bolster Russian security in Eastern Europe for a design for world conquest. When Truman responded with containment, which was essentially an effort to preserve the balance of power in postwar Europe, the Russians thought that America and its allies were bent on encircling and eventually destroying the Soviet Union. A vicious cycle then began, with each nation perceiving every step taken by the other as a threat to its existence. Neither the United States nor the Soviet Union alone was guilty of beginning the Cold War; both must share responsibility for this tragedy.

The postrevisionist explanation is very close to an early explanation for the Cold War advanced by historian William H. McNeill. Writing in 1950, McNeill pointed out that throughout history victorious coalitions had split apart as soon as the common enemy was overcome. The defeat of the Axis had created a vacuum of power in which the United States and the Soviet Union were bound to clash to determine who would control the future of Europe.

Yet even this view does not explain why the competition between the two nations became so intense. Other wartime alliances have dissolved without creating such a fierce rivalry. Here is where the atomic bomb played a key role. The existence of a new weapon of vast destructive power added an unknown element to the international arena, one that was beyond all previous experience. The very survival of the two antagonists became a genuine matter of concern in the nuclear age. Thus Hiroshima not only ended the Second World War; it also created the unstable diplomatic climate that gave rise to the Cold War.

struction of Japan. Instead he supervised the transition of the Japanese government into a constitutional democracy, shaped along Western lines, in which Communists were barred from all government posts. The Japanese willingly renounced war in their new constitution, relying instead on American forces to protect their security. American policy was equally nationalistic in the Pacific. A trusteeship arrangement with the United Nations merely disguised the fact that the United States held full control over the Marshall, Mariana, and Caroline islands. American scientists conducted atomic bomb tests at Bikini atoll in 1946, and by 1949, MacArthur was declaring that the entire Pacific "had become an Anglo-Saxon lake and our line of defense runs through the chain of islands fringing the coast of Asia."

As defined at Yalta, China lay between the Soviet and American spheres. When World War II ended, the country was torn between Chiang Kai-shek's Nationalists in the South and Mao Tse-tung's Communists in the North. Chiang had many advantages, including American political and economic backing and official Soviet recognition. But corruption was widespread among the Nationalist leaders, and a raging inflation that soon reached 100 percent a year devastated the Chinese middle classes and thus eroded Chiang's base of power. Mao used tight discipline and patriotic appeals to strengthen his hold on the peasantry and extend his influence. When the Soviets abruptly vacated Manchuria in 1946, after stripping it of virtually all the industrial machinery Japan had installed, Mao inherited control of this rich northern province. Ignoring American advice, Chiang rushed north to occupy Manchurian cities, overextending his supply lines and exposing his forces to Communist counterattack.

American policy aimed at averting a Chinese civil war. Before he became secretary of state, George Marshall undertook the difficult task of forming a coalition government between Chiang and Mao. For a few months in early 1946, Marshall appeared to have succeeded, but Chiang's attempts to gain control of Manchuria doomed the agreement. In reality, there was no basis for compromise. Chiang insisted he "was going to liquidate Communists," while Mao was trying to play off the United States against Russia in his bid for power. By 1947, as China plunged into full-scale civil war, the Truman administration had

During World War II Mao Tse-tung, leader of the Communist forces in China, fought the Japanese, sometimes alongside American GIs. Later, Mao triumphed over the Nationalists and created a Marxist China.

given up any meaningful effort to influence the outcome. Political mediation had failed, military intervention was out of the question, and a policy of continued American economic aid served only to appease domestic supporters of Chiang Kai-shek; 80 percent of the military supplies ended up in Communist hands.

The climax came at the end of the decade. Mao's forces drove the Nationalists out of Manchuria in late 1948 and advanced across the Yangtze by mid-1949. Acheson released a lengthy White Paper justifying American policy in China on the grounds that the civil war there "was beyond the control of the government of the United States." An American military adviser concurred, telling Congress that the Nationalist defeat was due to "the world's worst leadership" and "a complete loss of will to fight." Republican senators, however, disagreed, blaming American diplomats for sabotaging the Nationalists and terming the White Paper "a 1054-page whitewash of a wishful, do-nothing policy." While the domestic debate raged over responsibility for the loss of China, Chiang's forces fled the mainland for sanctuary on Formosa (Taiwan) in December 1949. Two months later, Mao and Stalin signed a Sino-Soviet treaty of mutual assistance that clearly placed China in the Russian orbit.

The American response to the Communist triumph in China was twofold. First, the State Department refused to recognize the legitimacy of the new regime in Peking, maintaining instead formal diplomatic relations with the Nationalists on Formosa. Citing the Sino-Soviet alliance, Assistant Secretary of State Dean Rusk called the Peking regime "a colonial Russian government" and declared, "It is not the Government of China. It does not pass the first test. It is not Chinese." Then, to compensate for the loss of China, the United States focused on Japan as its main ally in Asia. The State Department encouraged the buildup of Japanese industry, and the Pentagon expanded American bases on the Japanese home islands and Okinawa. A Japanese-American security pact led to the end of American occupation by 1952. The Cold War had now split Asia in two.

The Korean War

The showdown between the United States and the Soviet Union in Asia came in Korea. Traditionally the cockpit of international rivalry in Northeast Asia, Korea had been divided at the thirty-eighth parallel in 1945. The Russians occupied the industrial North, installing a Communist government under the leadership of Kim Il-Sung. In the agrarian South, Syngman Rhee, a conservative nationalist, emerged as the American-sponsored ruler. Neither regime heeded a UN call for elections to unify the country. The two superpowers pulled out most of their occupation forces by 1949. The Russians, however, helped train a well-equipped army in the North, while the United States—fearful that Rhee would seek unification through armed conquest—gave much more limited military assistance to South Korea.

On June 25, 1950, the North Korean army suddenly crossed the thirty-eighth parallel in great strength. The Soviet role in this act of aggression is shrouded in mystery. Presumably Stalin ordered the attack in an attempt to expand the Soviet sphere in Asia and to counter the

American buildup of Japan. Yet there is also evidence to suggest that Kim Il-Sung acted on his own, confident that the Russians would have no choice but to back his move.

There was nothing ambiguous about the American response. President Truman saw the invasion as a clear-cut case of Soviet aggression reminiscent of the 1930s. "Communism was acting in Korea just as Hitler, Mussolini, and the Japanese had acted ten, fifteen, and twenty years earlier," he commented in his memoirs. Following the advice of Acheson, the President convened the UN Security Council and, taking advantage of a temporary Soviet boycott, secured a resolution condemning North Korea as an aggressor and

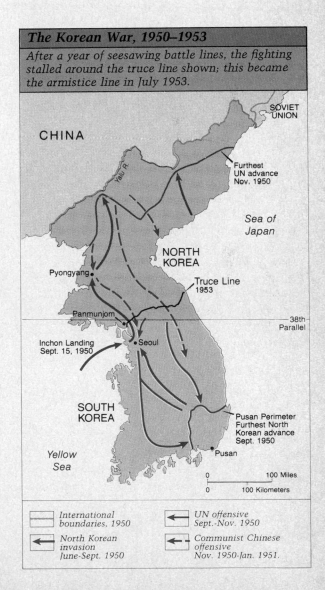

The Korean War, 1950–1953

After a year of seesawing battle lines, the fighting stalled around the truce line shown; this became the armistice line in July 1953.

SOVIET UNION

CHINA

Yalu R.

Furthest UN advance Nov. 1950

Sea of Japan

NORTH KOREA

Pyongyang

Truce Line 1953

Panmunjom

38th Parallel

Inchon Landing Sept. 15, 1950

Seoul

SOUTH KOREA

Pusan Perimeter Furthest North Korean advance Sept. 1950

Yellow Sea

Pusan

0   100 Miles
0   100 Kilometers

International boundaries, 1950

North Korean invasion June–Sept. 1950

UN offensive Sept.–Nov. 1950

Communist Chinese offensive Nov. 1950–Jan. 1951.

calling on the member nations to engage in a collective-security action. Within a few days, American troops from Japan were in combat in South Korea. The conflict, which would last for more than three years, was technically a police action fought under UN auspices; in reality, the United States was at war with a Soviet satellite in Asia.

In the beginning, the fighting went badly as the North Koreans continued to drive down the peninsula. But by August, American forces had halted the Communist advance near Pusan. In September, General MacArthur changed the whole complexion of the war by carrying out a brilliant amphibious assault at Inchon, on the waist of Korea, cutting off and destroying most of the North Korean army in the South. Encouraged by this victory, Truman began to shift from his original goal of restoring the thirty-eighth parallel to a new one, the unification of Korea by military force.

The administration ignored warnings from Peking, sent by way of India, against an American invasion of North Korea; "I should think it would be sheer madness for the Chinese to intervene," commented Dean Acheson. MacArthur was even more confident. "We are no longer fearful of their intervention," he told Truman at a Wake Island conference in mid-October. Noting that the Chinese had no air force, the general prophesied that

if they crossed the Yalu River into Korea, "there would be the greatest slaughter."

Rarely has an American president received worse advice than Truman did from Acheson and MacArthur. The UN forces crossed the thirty-eighth parallel in October, advanced confidently to the Yalu in November, and then were completely routed by a massive Chinese counterattack that drove them out of all North Korea by December. MacArthur finally stabilized the fighting near the thirty-eighth parallel, but when Truman decided to give up his attempt to unify Korea, the general protested to Congress, calling for a renewed offensive and proclaiming, "There is no substitute for victory."

Truman courageously relieved the popular hero of the Pacific of his command on April 11, 1951. At first, MacArthur seemed likely to force the President to back down. Huge crowds came forward to welcome him home and hear him call for victory over the Communists in Asia. At a special congressional hearing, the administration struck back effectively by warning that MacArthur's strategy would expose all Europe to Soviet attack. General Omar Bradley, Truman's chief military adviser, succinctly pointed out that a "showdown" with communism in Asia would be "the wrong war, at the wrong place, at the wrong time, and with the wrong enemy."

Congress and the American people came to accept MacArthur's recall. The Korean War settled into a stalemate near the thirty-eighth parallel as truce talks with the Communists bogged down for the rest of Truman's term in office. The President could take heart from the fact that he had achieved his primary goal, defense of South Korea and the principle of collective security. Yet by taking the gamble to unify Korea by force, he had confused the American people and humiliated the United States in the eyes of the world.

In the last analysis, the most significant result of the Korean conflict was the massive American rearmament it brought about. The war led to the implementation of NSC-68—the army expanded to 3.5 million troops, the defense budget increased to $50 billion a year by 1952, and the United States acquired military bases in distant quarters of the world, ranging from Saudi Arabia to Morocco. America was now committed to waging a global contest against the Soviet Union with arms as well as words.

■ *President Truman and General MacArthur at Wake Island in October 1950 when hopes were high for total victory in Korea.*

After the Chinese onslaught of November 1950, U.S. Marines retreated to the sea along icy roads in near-zero weather. They faced three Chinese divisions in the bloody struggle but managed to bring out their wounded and their equipment.

Eisenhower and the Cold War

Significant changes took place in American foreign policy with the election of Dwight D. Eisenhower in 1952. Unlike 1948, when bipartisan agreement over containment and the Berlin blockade prevailed, in 1952 the Cold War was a primary issue in the presidential campaign. After defeating Ohio Senator Robert A. Taft for the GOP nomination, General Eisenhower ran against Democratic candidate Adlai E. Stevenson, the governor of Illinois, on a platform condemning containment as "futile" and "immoral." Instead of abandoning the captive peoples of Eastern Europe to Communist enslavement, the Republicans promised their liberation. Eisenhower backed away from these vague words during the campaign, however, preferring to focus on the stalemated Korean War. Criticizing the Truman administration for failing either to win a victory or negotiate a truce, Eisenhower promised that if elected, he would go to Korea personally to work out a solution. A grateful nation responded by choosing him over Stevenson by a margin of 55 to 45 percent.

Despite his lack of experience in American domestic politics, Eisenhower was unusually well prepared to lead the nation at the height of the Cold War. His long years of military service had exposed him to a wide variety of international issues, both in Asia and in Europe, and to an even broader array of world leaders, such as Douglas MacArthur, Winston Churchill, and Charles de Gaulle. His gifts were primarily political and diplomatic rather than strictly military. He was blessed with a sharp, pragmatic mind and organizational genius that enabled him to plan and carry out large enterprises, grasping the precise relationship between the parts and the whole. Above all, he had a serene confidence in his own ability. At the end of his first day in the White House, he confided in his diary: "Plenty of worries and difficult problems. But such has been my portion for a long time—the result is that this just seems like a continuation of all I've been doing since July 1941. . . . "

Eisenhower chose John Foster Dulles as his secretary of state. The myth soon developed that Ike gave Dulles free rein to conduct American diplomacy. Appearances were deceptive. Eisenhower preferred to work behind the scenes. He let Dulles make the public speeches and appearances before congressional committees, where his hard-line views placated GOP extremists. But Dulles carefully consulted with the President before every appearance, meeting frequently with Eisen-

(Above) Secretary of State John Foster Dulles shown reporting to President Eisenhower and the nation after a European tour in 1955. (Right) Cartoonist Herblock, a sharp critic of Dulles' hard line, depicts him in a Superman suit pushing Uncle Sam to the brink of nuclear war.

hower at the White House and telephoning him several times a day. Ike respected his secretary of state's broad knowledge of foreign policy and his skill in conducting American diplomacy, but he made all the major decisions himself. "There's only one man I know who has seen *more* of the world and talked with more people and *knows* more than he does," Ike said of Dulles, "and that's me."

From the outset, Eisenhower was determined to bring the Cold War under control. Ideally, he wanted to end it, but as a realist, he would settle for a relaxation of tensions with the Soviet Union. In part, he was motivated by a deeply held budgetary concern. Defense spending had increased from $15 billion to $50 billion under Truman; Ike was convinced that the nation was in danger of going bankrupt unless military spending was reduced. As president, he inaugurated a "new look" for American defense, cutting back on the army and navy and relying even more heavily than Truman had on the air force and its nuclear striking power. As a result, the defense budget dropped to $40 billion annually. In 1954, Dulles announced reliance on massive retaliation —in fact a continuance of Truman's policy of deterrence. Rather than becoming involved in limited wars such as Korea, the United States

would consider the possibility of using nuclear weapons to halt any Communist aggression which threatened vital U.S. interests anywhere in the world.

While he permitted Dulles to make his veiled nuclear threats, Eisenhower's fondest dream was to end the arms race. Sobered by the development of the hydrogen bomb, successfully tested by the United States in November 1952 and by the Soviet Union in August 1953, the President began a new effort at disarmament with the Russians. Yet before this initiative could take effect, Ike had to weather a series of crises around the world that tested his skill and patience to the utmost.

Confrontations in Asia

The first task facing the new president was to end the Korean War. Before taking office, Eisenhower fulfilled his campaign promise to travel to Korea. Once there, he quickly ruled out a military offensive as too costly in lives and money. Despite objections from Dulles, who wanted to give "the Chinese one hell of a licking," Ike preferred the path of diplomacy. In the spring of 1953, he had Dulles deliver a secret warning to China by way of India: Unless the Chinese agreed to a truce, the

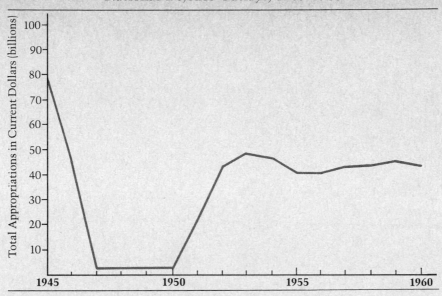

National Defense Outlays, 1945–1960

Source: Compiled from U.S. Bureau of the Census, Historical Statistics of the United States, Colonial Times to 1970, *Bicentennial Edition, Washington, D.C., 1975.*

United States would use its nuclear weapons to break the stalemate. Mao, impressed by Ike's threat and shaken by the death of Stalin in March, agreed to negotiate. American and Communist diplomats signed a truce agreement on July 2, 1953, which ended the fighting but left Korea divided—as it had been before the war—near the thirty-eighth parallel.

The President was not as successful in dealing with Indochina, another trouble spot he inherited from Truman. Since 1950 the United States had been giving the French economic and military aid in their civil war against Communist guerrillas led by Ho Chi Minh. The Chinese increased their support to Ho's forces after the Korean War ended, until by the spring of 1954 the French were on the brink of defeat. The Viet Minh had trapped nearly ten thousand French troops at Dien Bien Phu deep in the interior of northern Indochina; in desperation France turned to the United States for help. Admiral Arthur Radford, chairman of the Joint Chiefs of Staff, proposed an American air strike to lift the siege. Although the other Joint Chiefs had doubts about this plan, hawkish Republican senators were clamoring for action.

Eisenhower decided against Radford's proposal, but he killed it in his typically indirect fashion. Fearful that an air attack would lead to an inter-

vention by ground forces, Ike insisted that both Congress and American allies in Europe approve the policy in advance. Congressional leaders, recalling the recent Korean debacle, were reluctant; the British were appalled and ruled out any joint action. The President used these objections to turn down intervention in Indochina in 1954. Much later, just before the American involvement in the Vietnam War in the 1960s, he stated his reasons more candidly. "The jungles of Indochina would have swallowed up division after division of United States troops," he explained. Equally important, he believed that U.S. involvement in France's war would have compromised the American "tradition of anti-colonialism." "The standing of the United States as the most powerful of the anti-colonial powers is an asset of incalculable value to the Free World," he concluded.

Dien Bien Phu fell to the Communists in May 1954. At an international conference held in Geneva during the following summer, Indochina was divided at the seventeenth parallel. Ho gained control of North Vietnam, while the French continued to rule in the South, with provision for a general election within two years to unify the country. The election was never held, largely because the United States feared it

Ho Chi Minh, a dedicated Vietnamese nationalist and founder of that country's Communist party, led the movement that drove the French from Indochina in 1954.

would result in an overwhelming mandate for Ho Chi Minh. In the fall of 1954, the United States replaced France as the major supporter of the new government of South Vietnam led by Ngo Dinh Diem. Vietnam, like Korea, was split in two, but unfortunately this solution was only temporary.

Communist China posed an even graver problem for the Eisenhower administration. In the fall of 1954, the mainland government threatened to seize islands off the coast of China, notably Quemoy and Matsu, occupied by the Nationalists. Fearful that this would be the first step toward an invasion of Formosa, Eisenhower permitted Dulles to sign a security treaty with Chiang Kai-shek committing the United States to defend Formosa. When the Communists began shelling the offshore islands, Eisenhower persuaded Congress to pass a resolution authorizing him to use force to defend Formosa and "closely related localities."

Despite repeated requests, however, the President refused to say whether he would use force to repel a Chinese attack on Quemoy or Matsu. Instead he and Dulles hinted at the use of nuclear weapons, but they carefully stated that their action would depend on whether they considered an attack on the offshore islands part of a larger offensive aimed at Formosa. The Chinese leaders, unsure whether Eisenhower was bluffing, decided not to test American resolve. The shelling stopped in 1955, and though the Communists resumed it again in 1958, another firm but equally ambiguous American response forced them to desist. In his memoirs, Eisenhower took pride that he had threaded his way "with watchfulness and determination, through narrow and dangerous waters between appeasement and global war."

Turmoil in the Middle East

The gravest crisis came in the Middle East when Egyptian leader Gamal Nasser seized the Suez Canal in July 1956. England and France were ready to use force immediately; their citizens owned the canal company, and their economies were dependent on the canal for the flow of oil from the Persian Gulf. President Eisenhower, however, was staunchly opposed to intervention, preferring to seek a diplomatic solution with Nasser, who kept the canal running smoothly. For three months, Dulles did everything possible to restrain the European allies, but finally they decided to take a desperate gamble—invade Egypt and seize the canal while relying on the United States to prevent any Russian interference.

Eisenhower was furious when England and France launched their attack in early November. Campaigning for reelection against Adlai Stevenson on the slogan of keeping the peace, Ike had to abandon domestic politics to deal with the threat of war. "The White House crackled with barracks-room language," reported one observer; the President told an aide that the Western allies had made "a complete *mess* and *botch* of things." Unhesitatingly, he instructed Dulles to sponsor a UN resolution calling for British and French withdrawal from Egypt. Yet when the Russians supported the American proposal and went further, threatening rocket attacks on British and French cities and even offering to send "volunteers" to fight in Egypt, Eisenhower made it clear that he would not tolerate Soviet interference. He put the Strategic Air Command on alert and said of the Russians, "If those fellows start something, we may have to hit 'em—and, if necessary, with everything in the bucket."

Just after noon on election day, November 6, 1956, British Prime Minister Anthony Eden

■ *The first wave of U.S. Marines splashed ashore on the beach near Beirut, Lebanon, in July 1958. Sent to avert a Christian-Moslem civil war, they stayed only one hundred days.*

some fourteen thousand troops airlifted from bases in Germany. The military wanted to occupy the entire country, but Eisenhower insisted on limiting American forces to the area of Beirut. The mission of the troops, he argued, was "not primarily to fight," but simply to show the flag. Lebanese political leaders quickly agreed on a successor to Chamoun, and American soldiers left the country before the end of October. This restrained use of force achieved Eisenhower's primary goal of quieting the explosive Middle East. It also served, as Secretary of State Dulles pointed out, "to reassure many small nations that they could call on us in a time of crisis."

Covert Actions

In addition to keeping the peace amid these dangerous crises, the Eisenhower administration worked behind the scenes in the 1950s to expand the nation's global influence. In 1953, the CIA was instrumental in overthrowing a popularly elected government in Iran and placing the Shah in full control of that country. American oil companies were rewarded with lucrative concessions, and Eisenhower felt that he had gained a valuable ally on the Russian border. But these short-run gains created a deep-seated animosity among Iranians that would haunt the United States in the future.

Closer to home, in Latin America, Eisenhower once again relied on covert action. In 1954, the CIA masterminded the overthrow of a leftist regime in Guatemala. The immediate advantage was in denying the Soviets a possible foothold in the Western Hemisphere, but Latin Americans resented the thinly disguised interference of the United States in their internal affairs. More important, when Fidel Castro came to power in Cuba in 1959, the Eisenhower administration—after a brief effort at conciliation—adopted a hard line that helped drive Cuba into the Soviet orbit and led to new attempts at covert action.

Eisenhower's record as a Cold Warrior was thus mixed. His successful ending of the Korean War and his peacekeeping efforts in Indochina and Formosa and in the Suez crisis are all to his credit. Yet his reliance on coups and subversion directed by the CIA in Iran and Guatemala reveal Ike's corrupting belief that the ends justified the

called the President to inform him that England and France were ending their invasion. Eisenhower breathed a sigh of relief. American voters rallied behind Ike, electing him to a second term by a near landslide. As a result of the Suez crisis, the United States replaced England and France as the main Western influence in the Middle East. With Russia strongly backing Egypt and Syria, the Cold War had found yet another battleground.

Two years later, Eisenhower found it necessary to intervene in the strategic Middle Eastern country of Lebanon. Political power in this neutral nation was divided between Christian and Moslem elements. When the outgoing Christian president, Camille Chamoun, broke with tradition by seeking a second term, Moslem groups (aided by Egypt and Syria) threatened to launch a rebellion. At first, Eisenhower turned down Chamoun's request for American intervention to avert a civil war, but after an unexpected nationalist coup overthrew the pro-Western government of Iraq, Ike decided to act in order to uphold the U.S. commitment to political stability in the Middle East.

American marines from the Sixth Fleet moved swiftly ashore on July 15, 1958, securing the Beirut airport and preparing the way for a force of

means. Nevertheless, Eisenhower did display an admirable ability to stay calm and unruffled in moments of great tension, reassuring the nation and the world. And above all, he could boast, as he did in 1962, of his ability to keep the peace. "In those eight years," he reminded the nation, "we lost no inch of ground to tyranny . . . . One war was ended and incipient wars were blocked."

Waging Peace

Eisenhower hoped to ease Cold War tensions by ending the nuclear arms race. The advent of the hydrogen bomb intensified his concern over nuclear warfare; by 1955, both the United States and the Soviet Union had added this dread new weapon to their arsenals. With new long-range ballistic missiles being perfected, it was only a matter of time before Russia and the United States would be capable of destroying each other completely. Peace, as Winston Churchill noted, now depended on a balance of terror.

Throughout the fifties, Eisenhower sought a way out of the nuclear dilemma. In April 1953, shortly after Stalin's death, he gave a speech in which he called on the Russians to join him in a new effort at disarmament, pointing out that "every warship launched, every rocket fired signifies, in the final sense, a theft from those who hunger and are not fed, those who are cold and are not clothed." When the Soviets ignored this appeal, the President tried again in December 1953. Addressing the UN General Assembly, he outlined an "atoms-for-peace" plan whereby the United States and the Soviet Union would donate fissionable material to a new UN agency to be used for peaceful purposes. Despite Ike's appeal "to serve the needs rather than the fears of mankind," the Russians again rebuffed him. Undaunted, Eisenhower tried once more. At the Geneva summit conference in 1955, Ike proposed to Nikita Khrushchev, just emerging as Stalin's successor after a two-year struggle for power, a way to break the disarmament deadlock. "Open skies," as reporters dubbed the plan, would overcome the traditional Russian objection to on-site inspection by having both superpowers open their territory to mutual aerial surveillance. Unfortunately, Khrushchev dismissed open skies as "a very transparent espionage device," and the Geneva Conference ended without any significant breakthrough in the Cold War.

After his reelection in 1956, the President made a new effort to initiate nuclear-arms control. Concern over atmospheric fallout from nuclear testing had led presidential candidate Adlai Stevenson to propose a mutual ban on such experiments. At first Eisenhower rejected the test-ban idea, arguing it could be effective only as part of a comprehensive disarmament agreement, but the Russians supported it. Finally, in 1958, the President changed his mind after American and Soviet scientists developed a system to detect nuclear testing in the atmosphere without on-site inspection. In October 1958, Eisenhower and Khrushchev each voluntarily suspended further weapons tests pending the outcome of a conference held at Geneva to work out a test-ban treaty. Although the Geneva Conference failed to make progress, neither the United States nor the Soviet Union resumed testing for the remainder of Ike's term in office.

The suspension of testing halted the pollution of the world's atmosphere, but it did not lead to the improvement in Russian-American relations that Eisenhower sought. In the late 1950s, Khrushchev took advantage of the Soviet feat in

■ *Eisenhower talking to Soviet leader Khrushchev during Khrushchev's American tour in 1959.*

■ Cartoonist Herblock's view of the Khrushchev-Eisenhower meetings.

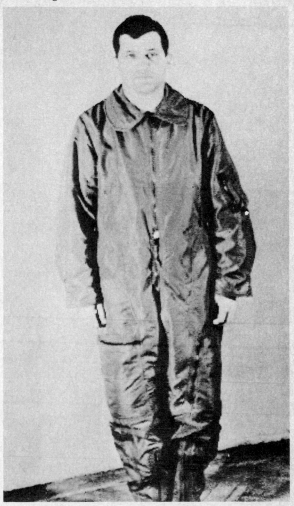

■ The capture of U-2 pilot Gary Powers, shot down over Russia, put an end to Soviet-American plans for a Moscow summit meeting in 1960.

launching Sputnik, the first artificial satellite to orbit the earth, to intensify the Cold War. Playing on Western fears that the Soviets had made a breakthrough in missile technology, the Russian leader began to issue threats, proclaiming, "We will bury capitalism," and telling Americans, "Your grandchildren will live under Communism." The most serious threat of all came in November 1958 when Khrushchev declared that within six months he would sign a separate peace treaty with East Germany, thereby ending American, British, and French occupation rights in Berlin.

Eisenhower met the second Berlin crisis as firmly as Truman had the first. He refused to abandon the city, but he also tried to avoid a military showdown. Prudent diplomacy forced Khrushchev to extend his ultimatum indefinitely. After a trip to the United States, culminating in a personal meeting with Eisenhower at Camp David, the Russian leader agreed to attend a summit conference in Paris in May 1960.

This much-heralded meeting never took place. On May 1, two weeks before the leaders were to convene in Paris, the Soviets shot down an American U-2 plane piloted by Francis Gary Powers. The United States had been overflying Russia since 1956 in these high-altitude spy planes,

gaining vital information about the Soviet missile program. When Eisenhower belatedly took full responsibility for the Powers' overflight, Khrushchev responded with a scathing personal denunciation and a refusal to meet with the American president.

Eisenhower deeply regretted the breakup of the Paris summit, telling an aide that "the stupid U-2 mess" had destroyed all his efforts for peace. Sadly he concluded that "he saw nothing worthwhile left for him to do now until the end of his presidency." Khrushchev marked time for the next nine months, waiting for the American people to choose a new president. Eisenhower did make a final effort at peace, however. Three days

Chronology

1945	Truman meets Stalin at Potsdam Conference (July) World War II ends with Japanese surrender (August)
1946	Winston Churchill gives "Iron Curtain" speech
1947	Truman Doctrine announced to Congress (March) George Marshall outlines Marshall Plan (June)
1948	Soviets begin blockade of Berlin (June); U.S. begins airlift of supplies to Berlin civilians
1949	NATO treaty signed in Washington (April) Soviet Union tests its first atomic bomb (August)
1950	Truman authorizes building of hydrogen bomb (January) North Korea invades South Korea (June)
1951	Truman recalls MacArthur from Korea
1952	Dwight D. Eisenhower elected president
1953	Stalin dies (March) Korean War truce signed at Panmunjon (July)
1954	Fall of Dien Bien Phu to Viet Minh ends French control of Indochina
1955	Eisenhower meets Krushchev at Geneva summit
1956	England and France touch off Suez crisis
1957	Russia launches Sputnik satellite
1958	United States and Russia halt nuclear testing
1959	Fidel Castro takes power in Cuba
1960	American U-2 plane shot down over Russia

prophetic. In the next few years, the level of defense spending would skyrocket as the Cold War escalated under his successors in the White House. The military-industrial complex reached its acme of power in the 1960s when the United States realized the full implications of Truman's doctrine of containment. Eisenhower had succeeded in keeping the peace for eight years, but he had failed to halt the momentum of the Cold War he had inherited from Harry Truman. Ike's efforts to ease tension with the Soviet Union were dashed by his own distrust of communism and by Khrushchev's belligerent rhetoric and behavior. Still, he had begun the process of relaxing tensions that would survive the troubled sixties, flourish briefly under the name of détente in the next decade, and then become yet another casualty of the continuing Cold War.

Recommended Reading

The Cold War has spawned a vast array of books, some enduring in nature and many that are already outdated. The best general guide to American diplomacy since World War II is Walter LaFeber, *America, Russia and the Cold War, 1945–1980*, 4th ed. (1980). LaFeber, who writes from a moderately revisionist perspective, is more concerned with explaining the course of American foreign policy than in criticizing it. On the much-debated question of the origins of the Cold War, the best balanced account is Daniel Yergin, *Shattered Peace* (1977), a book which characterizes American policy as flawed by misunderstanding rather than by ill will.

The classic account of containment is still the lucid recollection of its chief architect, George Kennan, *Memoirs, 1925–1950* (1967). John L. Gaddis uses Kennan's ideas as a point of departure for his account of the changing nature of American Cold War policy in *Strategies of Containment* (1982). For developments in the Far East, consult the perceptive book by Akira Iriye, *The Cold War in Asia* (1974).

The groundwork for the recent reevaluation of Dwight D. Eisenhower as an effective leader in foreign policy was laid by Emmet J. Hughes in his memoir *The Ordeal of Power* (1962). Hughes, a speechwriter for Eisenhower, was the first to play down the influence of John Foster Dulles. For a more recent examination of Ike's achievements in foreign policy, see Robert A. Divine, *Eisenhower and the Cold War* (1981).

Additional Bibliography

Surveys of American foreign policy since 1945 include Stephen Ambrose, *Rise to Globalism*, 2d ed. (1980); John Spanier, *American Foreign Policy Since World War II*, 8th ed. (1980); Ralph Levering, *The Cold War, 1945–*

before leaving office, he delivered a farewell address in which he gave a somber warning about the danger of massive military spending. "In the councils of government, we must guard against the acquisition of unwarranted influence, whether sought or unsought, by the military-industrial complex," he declared. "The potential for the disastrous rise of misplaced power exists and will persist."

Rarely has an American president been more

1972 (1982); and James A. Nathan and James K. Oliver, *United States Foreign Policy and World Order*, 2d ed. (1981). Adam B. Ulam provides a perceptive summary of Soviet-American relations for this period in *The Rivals* (1971). For a good critique, see John C. Donovan, *The Cold Warriors* (1974).

Gar Alperovitz began the revisionist controversy over the origins of the Cold War in *Atomic Diplomacy* (1965), which focuses on Truman's use of the atomic bomb as a veiled diplomatic weapon. Other revisionist accounts include Lloyd Gardner, *Architects of Illusion* (1970); Joyce Kolko and Gabriel Kolko, *The Limits of Power* (1972); Thomas G. Paterson, *Soviet-American Confrontation* (1973); and Lawrence Wittner, *American Intervention in Greece, 1943–1949* (1982). For a brief, moderate revisionist view, see Thomas G. Paterson, *On Every Front* (1979). Robert Tucker offers a shrewd assessment of revisionism in *The Radical Left and American Foreign Policy* (1971). Post revisionist studies include John L. Gaddis, *The United States and the Origins of the Cold War* (1972); Vojtech Mastny, *Russia's Road to the Cold War* (1979); and Robert L. Messer, *The End of an Alliance* (1982). For a lively account of the Potsdam Conference, see Charles L. Mee, *Meeting at Potsdam* (1975).

The foreign policy of the Truman administration is covered in Harry S. Truman, *Memoirs*, 2 vols. (1955, 1956) and two works by Robert J. Donovan: *Conflict and Crisis* (1977) and *Tumultuous Years* (1982). See also Robert H. Ferrell, *George C. Marshall* (1966); Gaddis Smith, *Dean Acheson* (1972); David S. McLellan, *Dean Acheson* (1976); and Dean Acheson, *Present at the Creation* (1969). For military policy, see Walter Millis, ed., *The Forrestal Diaries* (1951); Richard F. Haynes, *The Awesome Power* (1973); Warner R. Schilling et al., *Strategy, Politics and Defense Budgets* (1962); and Thomas H. Etzold and John L. Gaddis, eds., *Containment* (1976). Studies of special interest include Gregg Herken, *The Winning Weapon* (1980) on atomic diplomacy under Truman; Joseph Jones, *The Fifteen Weeks* (1955), a classic Cold Warrior account of the Truman Doctrine; and Jean Edward Smith, *The Defense of Berlin* (1964) on the two Berlin crises.

For the Cold War in the Far East, consult Tang Tsou, *America's Failure in China, 1941–1950* (1963); Herbert Feis, *Contest Over Japan* (1968); Dorothy Borg and Waldo Heinrichs, eds., *The Uncertain Years: Chinese-American Relations, 1947–1950* (1980); Russell D. Buhite, *Soviet-American Relations in Asia, 1945–1954* (1982); William W. Strueck, *The Road to Confrontation* (1981); and Robert M. Blum, *Drawing the Line* (1982). Books on the Korean War include David Rees, *Korea: The Limited War and American Politics* (1968); Charles W. Dobbs, *The Unwanted Symbol* (1981); Bruce Cumings, *The Origins of the Korean War* (1981); and John W. Spanier, *The Truman-MacArthur Controversy and the Korean War* (1959). For Indochina, see Ellen J. Hammer, *The Struggle for Indochina, 1940–1955* (1966) and Melvin Gurtov, *The First Vietnamese Crisis* (1967).

The most fully detailed biography of Eisenhower is the critical one by Peter Lyon, *Eisenhower: Portrait of the Hero* (1974). For a more sympathetic yet fragmentary account, see William B. Ewald, *Eisenhower the President* (1981). Blanche W. Cook uses recently available materials to offer a critique of Ike's diplomacy in *The Declassified Eisenhower* (1981). Eisenhower's two volumes of memoirs, *Mandate for Change* (1963) and *Waging Peace* (1966), are full and revealing accounts. For information on specific topics, see Richard Immerman, *The CIA in Guatemala* (1982); Chester Cooper, *The Lion's Last Roar* (1978) on the Suez crisis; Robert W. Stookey, *America and the Arab States* (1975) on the Middle East; Robert A. Divine, *Blowing on the Wind* (1978) on the nuclear test-ban issue; and Burton Kaufman, *Trade and Aid* (1982) on foreign economic policy.

chapter 29

AFFLUENCE
AND ANXIETY

On May 7, 1947, William Levitt announced plans to build two thousand rental houses in a former potato field on Long Island, thirty miles from midtown Manhattan. Using mass production techniques he had learned while erecting navy housing during the war, Levitt quickly built four thousand homes and rented them to young veterans. A change in government financing regulations led him to begin offering his houses for sale in 1948 for a small amount down and a low monthly payment. Young couples, crowded in city apartments or still living with their parents, rushed out to buy Levitt's houses. By 1949, he had sold the four thousand, and by the time Levittown—as he called the new community—was completed in 1951, it contained over seventeen thousand homes.

Levitt eventually built two more Levittowns, one in Pennsylvania and one in New Jersey; each contained the same curving streets, neighborhood parks and playgrounds, and community swimming pools as did the first development. Some observers denounced Levittown, seeing it as the symbol of conformity and materialism, but William Levitt had tapped the postwar desire of young Americans to move to the suburbs and raise their children outside the central city.

The secret of Levittown's appeal was the basic house, a 720-square-foot Cape Cod design built on a concrete slab. It had a kitchen, two bedrooms and bath, a living room complete with a fireplace and sixteen-foot picture window, and an expansion attic with room for two more bedrooms. Levitt built only one interior, but there were four different facades to break the monotony. The original house sold for $6990 in 1948; even the improved model, a ranch-style house, sold for less than $10,000 in 1951.

Levitt's houses were ideal for young people just starting out in life. They were cheap, comfortable, and efficient, and each home came with a refrigerator, cooking range, and washing machine. Despite the conformity of the houses, the three Levittowns were surprisingly diverse communities; residents had a wide variety of religious, ethnic, and occupational backgrounds. Blacks,

however, were rigidly excluded. In time, as the more successful families moved on to larger homes in more expensive neighborhoods, the Levittowns became enclaves for lower-middle-class families.

Levittown symbolized the most significant social trend of the postwar era in the United States—the flight to the suburbs. The residential areas surrounding cities like New York and Chicago nearly doubled in the 1950s. While central cities remained relatively stagnant during the decade, suburbs grew by 46 percent; by 1960 some sixty million people, one third of the nation, lived in suburban rings around the cities. This massive shift in population from the central city was accompanied by a baby boom that started during World War II. Young married couples began to have three, four, or even five children (compared with only one or two children in American families during the 1930s). These larger families led to a 19 percent growth in the nation's population

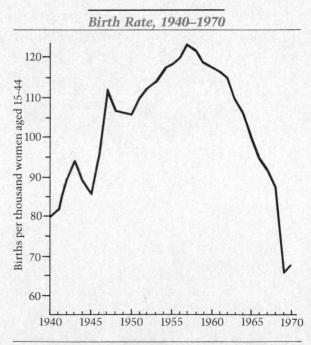

Birth Rate, 1940–1970

Births per thousand women aged 15–44

Source: *U.S. Bureau of the Census*, Historical Statistics of the United States, Colonial Times to 1970, *Bicentennial Edition, Washington, D.C., 1975.*

Shoppers in a New York City department store in 1951 besiege the salesclerks at the electric mixer counter. Consumers were starved for home appliances, which had been unaffordable before the war and unavailable during the war.

between 1950 and 1960, the greatest increase in growth rate since 1910.

The economy boomed as residential construction soared. By 1960, one fourth of all existing homes were less than ten years old and factories were turning out large quantities of appliances and television sets for the new households. A multitude of new consumer products—ranging from frozen foods to filter cigarettes, from high fidelity phonographs to cars equipped with automatic transmissions and tubeless tires—appeared in stores and showrooms. In the suburbs, the supermarket replaced the corner grocer, carrying a vast array of items that enabled homemakers to provide their families with a more varied diet.

A new affluence replaced the poverty and hunger of the Great Depression, but many Americans could not forget the haunting memories of the thirties. The absorption with material goods took on an almost desperate quality, as if a profusion of houses, cars, and home appliances could guarantee that the nightmare of depression would never return. Critics were quick to disparage the quality of life in suburban society. They condemned the conformity, charging the newly affluent with forsaking traditional American individualism to live in identical houses, drive look-alike cars, and accumulate the same material possessions. Folk-

A Sunday outing in the 1950s. The family car was embellished with much shiny chrome and elongated tailfins.

singer Malvina Reynolds caught the essence of postwar suburbia in her 1963 song:

Little boxes on the hillside,
Little boxes made of ticky tacky
Little boxes on the hillside,
Little boxes all the same.
There's a green one and a pink one
And a blue one and a yellow one
And they're all made out of ticky tacky
And they all look just the same.

("Little Boxes," words and music by Malvina Reynolds. Copyright © 1962 Schroder Music Co. (ASCAP) Used by permission. All rights reserved.)

Events abroad added to the feeling of anxiety in the postwar years. Nuclear war became a frighteningly real possibility. The rivalry with the Soviet Union led to a new red scare, resulting in charges of treason and betrayal being leveled at loyal Americans. Frustrated by the stalemate with

■ *A suburban development in the Bay area of California, perceived as a study in patterned uniformity. It features upgraded "ticky-tacky" houses.*

Russia, many Americans cheered demagogues like Senator Joseph McCarthy, who looked for the Communist enemy at home rather than abroad. Loyalty oaths and book-burning revealed how insecure Americans had become in the era of the Cold War. Thus beneath the bland surface of suburban affluence, a dark current of distrust and insecurity marred the picture of a nation fulfilling its economic destiny.

The Postwar Boom

For fifteen years following World War II, the nation witnessed a period of unparalleled economic growth. A pent-up demand for consumer goods fueled a steady industrial expansion. And heavy government spending during the Cold War added an extra stimulus to the economy, offsetting brief recessions in 1949 and 1953 and moderating a steeper one in 1957–1958. By the end of the decade, the American people had achieved an affluence that finally erased the lingering memories of the Great Depression.

The Stress of Reconversion

The task of reconverting American industry from its wartime production of guns, tanks, and bombers back to the creation of consumer goods led to considerable stress and tension. Prices and wages caused most of the concern. Congress, responding to the public's distaste for continuing wartime regulations, voted in 1946 to weaken price controls. With returning servicemen and affluent civilians vying for scarce goods, prices rose 25 percent in less than two years. Workers, accustomed to wartime paychecks heavy with overtime, began to demand higher wages and shorter hours. A wave of labor unrest swept over the country in the spring of 1946, culminating in two critical strikes: a walkout by coal miners that threatened to close down much of American industry and a paralyzing strike by railroad workers.

President Truman was caught in the middle. Sensitive to union demands, he permitted businessmen to negotiate large pay increases and then pass on the cost to consumers in the form of higher prices. He criticized Congress for weakening wartime price controls, but he failed to insist that the controls be retained, and he offered nothing else to curb inflation. Housewives blamed him for the rising price of food, while organized labor condemned Truman as the country's "No. 1 Strikebreaker" when he asked Congress for power to draft striking railway workers into the army.

The Republicans seized on the nation's economic woes to attack the Democrats, declaring "To err is Truman" and adopting a very effective slogan in the 1946 congressional elections: "Had enough?" The American people, weary of inflation and labor unrest, responded by electing a majority of Republicans to both the House and the Senate for the first time since 1930.

Postwar Prosperity

Although the GOP-dominated Eightieth Congress had little to do with it, the economy began to move forward as the result of two long-term factors. First, American consumers—after being held in check by depression and then by wartime scarcities—finally had a chance to indulge their suppressed appetites for material goods. At the war's end, personal savings stood at more than $37 billion, providing a powerful stimulus to consumption. Initially, American factories could not turn out enough automobiles and appliances to satisfy the horde of buyers. By 1950, however, production lines had finally caught up with the demand. In that year, Americans bought more than six million cars, and the gross national product (GNP) reached $318 billion (50 percent higher than in 1940).

The Cold War provided the additional stimulus the economy needed when postwar expansion slowed. The Marshall Plan and other foreign-aid programs financed a heavy export trade. Then the outbreak of the Korean War helped overcome a brief recession and ensure continued prosperity as the government spent massive amounts on guns, planes, and munitions. In 1952, the nation spent $44 billion, two thirds of the federal budget, on national defense. Although Eisenhower managed to bring about some modest reductions, defense spending continued at a level of $40 billion throughout the decade.

■ *The deluge of advertising images of the 1950s was transformed into the "pop" art of the 1960s, using such popular and commonplace objects as these Coke bottles, painted by Andy Warhol.*

It was in the 1950s that the nation achieved a level of affluence that erased the persisting fear of another Great Depression. The baby boom and the spectacular growth of suburbia served as great stimulants to the consumer-goods industries. Manufacturers turned out an ever increasing number of refrigerators, washing machines, and dishwashers to equip the kitchens of Levittown and its many imitators across the country. The automobile industry thrived with suburban expansion as two-car families became more and more common. In 1955, in an era when oil was abundant and gasoline sold for less than 30¢ a gallon, Detroit sold a record 8 million cars. The electronics industry boomed. Consumers were eager to acquire the latest marvel of home entertainment—the television set.

In addition, commercial enterprises snapped up office machines and the first generation of computers; industry installed electronic sensors and processors as it underwent extensive automation, and the military displayed an insatiable appetite for electronic devices for its planes and ships. As a result, American industry averaged more than $10 billion a year in capital investment, and employment rose above the long-sought goal of sixty million.

Yet the economic abundance of the 1950s was not without its problems. While some sections of the nation (notably the emerging Sunbelt areas of the South and West) benefited enormously from the growth of the aircraft and electronics industries, older manufacturing regions, such as New England, did not fare as well. The steel industry increased its capacity during the decade, but it began to fall behind the rate of national growth. Agriculture continued to experience bumper crops and low prices so that rural regions, like the vast areas of the Plains States, failed to share in the general affluence. Unemployment persisted despite the boom, rising to over 7 percent in a sharp recession that hit the country in the fall of 1957 and lasted through the summer of 1958. The rate of economic growth slowed in the second half of the decade, causing concern about the continuing vitality of the American economy.

None of these flaws, however, could disguise the fact that the nation was prospering to an extent no one dreamed possible in the 1930s. The GNP grew to $440 billion by 1960, more than double the 1940 level. More important, workers now labored fewer than forty hours a week; they rarely worked on Saturdays, and nearly all enjoyed a two-week paid vacation each year. By the mid-1950s, the average American family had twice as much real income to spend as its counterpart had possessed in the boom years of the 1920s. From 1945 to 1960, per-capita disposable income rose by $500—to $1845—for every man, woman, and child in the country. The American people, in one generation, had moved from poverty and depression to the highest standard of living the world had ever known.

Life in the Suburbs

Sociologists had difficulty describing the nature of suburban society in the fifties. Some saw it as classless, while others noted the absence of both the very rich and the very poor and consequently labeled it "middle class." Rather than forming a homogenous social group, though, the suburbs contained a surprising variety of people, whether classified as "upper lower," "lower middle," and "upper middle" or simply as blue collar, white collar, and professional. Doctors and lawyers often lived in the same developments as shoe salesmen and master plumbers. The traditional

In the early 1950s television viewing at home became a significant leisure-time pursuit. It was a group activity that involved the whole family. Evenings out at the movies became less and less frequent.

distinctions of ancestry, education, and size of residence no longer differentiated people so easily.

Yet suburbs could vary widely, from working-class communities clustered near factories built in the countryside to old, elitist areas like Scarsdale, New York, and Shaker Heights, Ohio. Most were almost exclusively white and Christian, but suburbs like Great Neck on Long Island and Richmond Heights outside Miami enabled Jews and blacks to take part in the flight from the inner city.

Life in all these suburban communities depended on the automobile. Highways and expressways allowed husbands to commute to jobs in the cities, often an hour or more away. The car was equally essential for wives. They shopped at the stores that first grew up in "miracle miles" along the highways and later at the shopping centers that began to dot the countryside by the mid-1950s. Children rode buses to school, then were driven to piano lessons and Little League ball games. Two cars became a necessity for almost every suburban family, thus helping to spur the boom in automobile production.

The home became the focus for activities and aspirations. The postwar shortage of housing which often forced young couples to live with their parents or in-laws created an intense de-mand for new homes in the suburbs. When questioned, prospective buyers expressed a desire for "more space," for "comfort and roominess," and for "privacy and freedom of action" in their new residences. Men and women who moved to the suburbs prized the new kitchens with their built-in dishwashers, electric ovens, and gleaming counters; the extra bedrooms that ensured privacy from and for the children; the large garages that could be converted into recreation rooms; and the small, neat lawns that gave them an area for outdoor activities as well as a new way to compete with their neighbors. "Togetherness" became the code word of the fifties. Families did things together, whether gathering around the TV sets that dominated living rooms, attending community activities, or taking vacations in the huge station-wagons of the era.

The emphasis on family life did not encourage the development of feminism. The end of the war saw many women who had entered the work force return to the home, where the role of wife and mother continued to be viewed as the ideal one for women in the 1950s. Trends toward getting married earlier and having larger families reinforced the tendency of women to devote all their efforts to housework and childraising rather than acquiring professional skills and pursuing careers outside the home. Adlai Stevenson, ex-

Percentage of Wives in the Labor Force	
Year	Percentage
1950	24.8
1951	26.7
1952	26.8
1953	27.7
1954	28.1
1955	29.4
1956	30.2
1957	30.8
1958	31.4
1959	32.3
1960	31.7

Source: Compiled from U.S. Bureau of the Census, Historical Statistics of the United States, Colonial Times to 1970, Bicentennial Edition, Washington, D.C., 1975.

tolling "the humble role of housewife," told Smith College graduates that there was much they could do "in the living room with a baby in your lap or in the kitchen with a can opener in your hand." Dr. Benjamin Spock's 1946 bestseller, *Baby and Child Care*, became a fixture in millions of homes, while the traditional women's magazines like *McCall's* and *Good Housekeeping* thrived by featuring articles on natural childbirth and inspirational pieces such as "Homemaking Is My Vocation."

Nonetheless, the number of working wives doubled between 1940 and 1960. By the end of the fifties, 40 percent of American women had jobs outside the home. The heavy expenses involved in rearing and educating children led wives and mothers to seek ways to augment the family income, inadvertently preparing the way for a new demand for equality in the 1960s.

Farewell to Reform

It is not surprising that the spirit of reform underlying the New Deal failed to flourish in the postwar years. Growing affluence took away the sense of grievance and the cry for change that was so strong in the thirties. Eager to enjoy the new prosperity after years of want and sacrifice, the American people turned away from federal regulation and welfare programs.

Truman and the Fair Deal

Harry S. Truman attempted to carry on the New Deal tradition of Franklin D. Roosevelt. For ten years, he had been a loyal Democratic senator, faithfully supporting Roosevelt's recovery and reform measures in Congress. He was a respected legislator, with a reputation for being hard-working, reliable, and intensely partisan. But he was relatively unknown to the public, and his background as a Missouri county judge associated with Kansas City machine politics did little to inspire confidence in his ability to lead the nation. Surprisingly well read—especially in history and biography—Truman possessed sound judgment, the ability to reach decisions quickly, and a fierce and uncompromising sense of right and wrong.

Two weaknesses marred his performance in the White House. One was a fondness for old friends, which resulted in the appointment of many Missouri and Senate cronies to high office. Men like Attorney General Tom Clark, Secretary of the Treasury Charles Snyder and White House military aide Harry Vaughn brought little credit to the Truman administration, while the loss of such effective public servants as Secretary of the Interior Harold Ickes and Labor Secretary Frances Perkins hurt. Truman's other serious limitation was his lack of political vision. He tried to perpetuate FDR's New Deal, but he engaged in a running battle with Congress rather than pursuing a coherent legislative program.

The fact that the postwar mood was not conducive to a new outburst of reform, of course, handicapped Truman's performance. Not only were the American people enjoying material prosperity, but also the Cold War diverted attention from domestic problems. In September 1945, the President outlined a broad program designed to ensure economic security, but his proposal soon dropped out of sight as the nation became distracted by labor unrest and inflation. Congress did pass the Employment Act of 1946, which asserted the principle that the government was responsible for the state of the economy. One of the provisions of the act was the creation of a Council of Economic Advisers to guide the president, but the original goal of mandatory federal planning to achieve full employment failed to survive the legislative process.

After the Republican victory in 1946, relations between the President and Congress became increasingly stormy. Truman successfully vetoed two GOP measures to give large tax cuts to the wealthy, but Congress overrode his veto of the Taft-Hartley Act in 1947. Designed to redress the imbalance in labor-management relations created by the Wagner Act, the Taft-Hartley Act outlawed specific unfair labor union practices—including the closed shop and secondary boycotts—and it permitted the president to invoke an eighty-day cooling-off period to delay strikes that might endanger national health or safety. Despite Truman's claim that it was a "slave-labor" bill, American unions were able to survive its provisions.

President Truman's political fortunes reached their lowest ebb in early 1948. Former Vice-President Henry A. Wallace, claiming to represent the New Deal, announced his third-party (Progressive) candidacy in the presidential contest that year. Worried Democratic party leaders sought to persuade Truman to step aside and allow General Dwight D. Eisenhower to become the Democratic candidate. When Eisenhower turned down bids from both parties, the Democrats reluctantly renominated Truman. The prospects for victory in the fall, however, looked very dim—especially after disgruntled Southerners bolted the Democratic party to nominate Strom Thurmond, the governor of South Carolina, on a States' Rights party ticket.

The defection of the Dixiecrats in the South and Wallace's liberal followers in the North led political experts to predict an almost certain Republican victory. Governor Thomas E. Dewey of New York, the GOP candidate, was so certain of winning that he waged a cautious and bland campaign designed to give him a free hand once he was in the White House. With nothing to lose, Truman barnstormed around the country denouncing the "do-nothing" Republican Eightieth Congress. The President's "give-'em-hell" tactics reminded voters of how much they owed the Democrats for helping them survive the Depression. To the amazement of the pollsters, Truman won a narrow but decisive victory in November. The old Roosevelt coalition—farmers, organized labor, urban ethnic groups, and blacks—had held together, enabling Truman to remain in the White House and the Democrats to gain control of Congress.

A triumphant Truman announced his legislative program on January 5, 1949. Venturing beyond an extension of FDR's proposals to increase the minimum wage and broaden Social Security

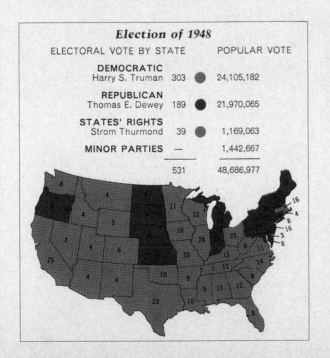

Election of 1948

ELECTORAL VOTE BY STATE			POPULAR VOTE
DEMOCRATIC Harry S. Truman	303	●	24,105,182
REPUBLICAN Thomas E. Dewey	189	●	21,970,065
STATES' RIGHTS Strom Thurmond	39	●	1,169,063
MINOR PARTIES	—		1,442,667
	531		48,686,977

■ *A jubilant Harry Truman, on the morning after his 1948 election win, displays the headline blazoned on the front page of the* Chicago Tribune—*a newspaper that believed the pollsters.*

coverage, he called for a "Fair Deal," a reform package that comprised a new program of national medical insurance, federal aid to education, enactment of a Fair Employment Practices Commission (FEPC) to prevent economic discrimination against blacks, and an overhaul of the farm subsidy program.

The Fair Deal was never enacted. Except for raising the minimum wage to seventy-five cents an hour and broadening Social Security to cover ten million more Americans, Congress refused to pass any of Truman's health, education, or civil-rights measures. The nation's doctors waged an effective campaign against the President's health-insurance plan, and southern senators blocked any action of FEPC. Aid to education, repeal of Taft-Hartley, and the new farm program all failed to win congressional approval. In part, Truman was to blame for trying to secure too much too soon; if he had selected one or two measures and given them priority, he might have been more successful. More important, however, was the fact that despite the Democratic victory in 1948, Congress remained under the control of a bipartisan conservative coalition of northern Republicans and southern Democrats, the same alignment that had halted Roosevelt's reforms after 1938.

Although his legislative failure became certain in 1950 when war once again subordinated domestic issues to foreign policy, President Truman deserves credit for maintaining and consolidating the New Deal. His spirited leadership prevented any Republican effort to repeal the gains of the 1930s. Moreover, even though he failed to get any new measures enacted, he broadened the reform agenda and laid the groundwork for future advances in health care, aid to education, and civil rights.

■ *Eisenhower accepting the Republican nomination in 1952. Ike possessed a forceful personality and had the knack of dealing successfully with difficult people.*

Eisenhower's Modern Republicanism

In 1952, the American people turned to Dwight D. Eisenhower, the hero of World War II, to restore their sense of national self-confidence. Truman's second term had witnessed increasing bitterness and frustration. Senator Joseph McCarthy had exploited a developing red scare (see pp. 842–45), the Korean War had settled into a bloody stalemate, and several of Truman's aides had been caught in scandals involving personal gifts.

Eisenhower seemed to be the perfect man to clean up "the mess in Washington." Immensely popular because of his amiable manner, winning smile, and heroic stature, he alone appeared to have the ability to unite a divided nation. In the 1952 campaign, Ike displayed hidden gifts as a politician in running against Adlai Stevenson, the eloquent Illinois governor whose appeal was limited to diehard Democrats and liberal intellectuals. Despite the embarrassment caused by the disclosure of a secret fund benefiting his running mate, Richard Nixon of California, Eisenhower won easily. He carried thirty-nine states, including four in the formerly solid Democratic South. The Republican party, however, did not fare as well; it gained just a slight edge in the House and controlled the Senate by only one seat.

Moderation was the keynote of the Eisenhower presidency. His major goal from the outset was to restore calm and tranquillity to a badly divided nation. Unlike FDR and Truman, he had no commitment to social change or economic reform. Ike was a fiscal conservative who was intent on balancing the budget. Yet unlike some Republicans of the extreme right wing, he had no

The Election of 1952			
Candidate	Party	Popular Vote	Electoral Vote
Eisenhower	Republican	33,936,137	442
Stevenson	Democrat	27,314,649	89

plans to dismantle the social programs of the New Deal. He sought instead to keep military spending in check, to encourage as much private initiative as possible, and to reduce federal activities to the bare minimum. Defining his position as "Modern Republicanism," he claimed that he was "conservative when it comes to money and liberal when it comes to human beings."

On domestic issues, Eisenhower elected to delegate authority and to play a passive role. He concentrated his own efforts on the Cold War abroad. The men he chose to run the nation reflected his preference for successful corporation executives. Thus George Humphrey, an Ohio industrialist, carried out a policy of fiscal stringency as secretary of the treasury, while Charles E. Wilson (the former head of General Motors) sought to keep the Pentagon budget under control as secretary of defense. Neither man was wholly successful, and both were guilty of tactless public statements. Humphrey warned that unless Congress showed budgetary restraint "we're gonna have a depression which will curl your hair," and Wilson gained notoriety by proclaiming "what was good for our country was good for General Motors, and vice versa."

Eisenhower was equally reluctant to play an active role in dealing with Congress. A fervent believer in the separation of powers, Ike did not wish to engage in intensive lobbying. He left congressional relations to aides such as Sherman Adams, a former New Hampshire governor who served as White House chief of staff. Adams' skill at resolving problems at lower levels insulated Eisenhower from many of the nation's pressing domestic problems.

The Election of 1956			
Candidate	Party	Popular Vote	Electoral Vote
Eisenhower	Republican	35,585,245	457
Stevenson	Democrat	26,030,172	73

Relations with Congress were weakened further by Republican losses in the midterm election of 1954. The Democrats regained control of both houses and kept it throughout the 1950s. The President had to rely on two Texas Democrats, Senate Majority Leader Lyndon B. Johnson and House Speaker Sam Rayburn, for legislative action; at best, it was an awkward and uneasy relationship.

The result was a very modest legislative record. Eisenhower did continue the basic social measures of the New Deal. In 1954, he signed bills extending Social Security benefits to more than seven million Americans, raising the minimum wage to $1 an hour, and adding four million workers to those eligible for unemployment benefits. He consolidated the administration of welfare programs by creating the Department of Health, Education and Welfare in 1953. Oveta Culp Hobby, the first woman to hold a cabinet post in a Republican administration, headed the new department. But Ike steadfastly opposed Democratic plans for compulsory health insurance—which he condemned as the "socialization of medicine"—and comprehensive federal aid to education, preferring to leave everything except school construction in the hands of local and state authorities. This lack of presidential support and the continuing grip of the conservative coalition in Congress blocked any further reform in the 1950s.

The one significant legislative achievement of the Eisenhower years came with the passage of the Highway Act of 1956. After a twelve-year delay, Congress appropriated funds for a 41,000-mile interstate highway system consisting of multilane divided expressways that would connect all the nation's major cities. Justified on grounds of national defense, the 1956 act pleased a variety of highway users: the trucking industry, automobile clubs, organized labor (eager for construction jobs), farmers (needing to speed their crops to market), and state highway officials (anxious for the 90 percent of the funding contributed by the federal government). Eisenhower's insistence that general revenue funds not be used to provide the federal share—estimated at $25 billion—of the total cost led to the creation of a highway trust fund raised by taxes on fuel, tires, and new cars and trucks. Built over the next twenty years, the interstate highway system had a profound influence on American life. It stimulated the economy and shortened travel time dramatically, while intensifying the nation's dependence on the automobile and distorting metropolitan growth patterns into long strips paralleling the new expressways.

The Interstate Highway System

The Interstate Highway System

Overall, the Eisenhower years marked an era of political moderation. The American people, enjoying the abundance of the 1950s, seemed quite content with legislative inaction. The President was sensitive to the nation's economic health; when recessions developed in 1953 and again in 1957 after his landslide reelection victory, he quickly abandoned his goal of a balanced budget in favor of a policy advocating government spending to restore prosperity. These steps, along with modest increases in New Deal welfare programs, led to a steady growth in the federal budget from $29.5 billion in 1950 to $76.5 in 1960. Eisenhower was able to balance the budget in only three of his eight years in office, and the $12-billion deficit in 1959 was larger than any ever before recorded in peacetime. Thus Eisenhower maintained the New Deal legacy of federal responsibility for social welfare and the state of the economy while successfully resisting demands for more extensive government involvement in American life.

The Second Red Scare

In the midst of the affluence and apathy of postwar American life, one issue stirred up deep passion—a blind, unreasoning fear of communism. Locked in the Cold War with the Soviet Union, the American people began to look for the enemy at home as well as abroad. The result was a prolonged emotional outburst that led to an oppressive conformity in thought and belief.

The Loyalty Issue

Fear of radicalism had been a recurrent feature of American life since the early days of the Republic. Federalists had tried to suppress dissent with the Alien and Sedition Acts in the 1790s; the Know Nothings had campaigned against foreigners and Catholics in the 1850s, and the first red scare after World War I had been directed against both aliens and radicals. The Cold War heightened the traditional belief that subversion from abroad endangered the Republic. Bold rhetoric from members of the Truman administration, portraying the men in the Kremlin as inspired revolutionaries bent on world conquest, frightened the American people. They viewed the Soviet Union as a successor to Nazi Germany—a totalitarian police state that threatened the basic liberties of a free people.

A series of revelations of Communist espionage activities reinforced these fears. Canadian officials uncovered a Soviet spy ring in 1946, and the House Un-American Activities Committee held hearings indicating that Communist agents had flourished in the Agriculture and Treasury departments in the 1930s.

The most famous disclosure came in August 1948, however, when Whittaker Chambers, a repentant Communist, accused Alger Hiss of having been a Soviet spy in the 1930s. When Hiss, who had been a prominent State Department official, denied the charges, Chambers led investigators to a hollowed-out pumpkin on his Maryland farm. Inside the pumpkin were microfilms of confidential government documents. Chambers claimed that Hiss had passed these State Department materials to him in the late 1930s. Although the statute of limitations prevented a

■ *The conviction of Alger Hiss, shown here on his way to prison, convinced many Americans that internal subversion threatened the nation's survival.*

charge of treason against Hiss, he was convicted of perjury in January 1950 and sentenced to a five-year prison term.

Although Truman tried to dismiss the loyalty issue as a "red herring," he felt compelled to take protective measures, thus lending substance to the charges of subversion. In March 1947, he began a loyalty program, instituting security checks of government employees in order to root out Communists. Originally intended to remove subversives for whom "reasonable grounds exist for belief that the person involved is disloyal," within four years the Loyalty Review Board was dismissing workers as security risks if there was "reasonable doubt" of their loyalty. Thousands of government workers lost their jobs, charged with guilt by association with radicals or with membership in left-wing organizations. Often those charged had no chance to face their accusers.

In 1948, the Justice Department further heightened fears of subversion. It charged eleven officials of the Communist party with advocating the violent overthrow of the government. After a long trial, the jury found them guilty, and the party officials received prison sentences and heavy fines; in 1951, the Supreme Court upheld these convictions as constitutional.

Such repressive measures failed, however, to reassure the nation. Events abroad intensified the sense of danger. The Communist triumph in China in the fall of 1949 came as a shock; soon there were charges that "fellow travelers" in the State Department were responsible for "the loss of China." In September 1949, when the Truman administration announced that the Russians had detonated their first atomic bomb, the ending of America's nuclear monopoly was blamed on Soviet espionage. In early 1950, Klaus Fuchs—a British scientist who had worked on the wartime Manhattan Project—admitted giving the Russians vital information about the A-bomb.

A few months later, the government charged American Communists Ethel and Julius Rosenberg with conspiracy to transmit atomic secrets to the Soviet Union. In 1951, a jury found the Rosenbergs guilty of treason, and Judge Irving Kaufman sentenced them to die for what he termed their "loathsome offense." Despite their insistent claims of innocence and worldwide appeals on their behalf, the Rosenbergs were electrocuted on June 19, 1953. Thus by the early 1950s, nearly all the ingredients were at hand for

■ *Three days before Julius and Ethel Rosenberg were executed for treason, their two young sons, ten and six years old, marched to the White House to plead executive clemency for their parents.*

a new outburst of hysteria—fear of Russia, evidence of espionage, and a belief in a vast unseen conspiracy. The only element missing was a leader to release this new outburst of intolerance.

McCarthyism in Action

On February 12, 1950, Senator Joseph R. McCarthy of Wisconsin delivered a routine Lincoln's Birthday speech in Wheeling, West Virginia. This little known Republican suddenly attracted national attention when he declared, "I have here in my hand a list of 205—a list of names that were made known to the Secretary of State as being members of the Communist Party and who nevertheless are still working and shaping policy in the State Department." The charge that there were Communists in the State Department—repeated in different places with the number changed to 57, then 81—was never substantiated. But McCarthy's Wheeling speech triggered a four-and-a-half-year crusade to hunt down alleged Communists in government. The stridency and sensationalism of the senator's accusations soon won the name "McCarthyism."

McCarthy's basic technique was the multiple untruth. He leveled a bevy of charges of treasonable activities in government. While officials were refuting his initial accusations, he brought forth a steady stream of new ones, so that the corrections never caught up with the latest blast. He failed to unearth a single confirmed Communist in government, but he kept the Truman administration in turmoil. Drawing on an army of informers, primarily disgruntled federal workers with grievances against their colleagues and superiors, he charged government agencies with harboring and protecting Communist agents, and he accused the State Department of deliberately losing the Cold War. His briefcase bulged with documents, but he did very little actual research, relying instead on reports (often outdated) from earlier congressional investigations. He exploited the press with great skill, combining current accusations with promises of future disclosures to guarantee headlines.

The secret of McCarthy's power was the fear he engendered among his Senate colleagues. In 1950, Maryland Senator Millard Tydings, who headed a committee critical of McCarthy's activities, failed to win reelection when McCarthy opposed him; after that, other senators ran scared. McCarthy delighted in making sweeping, startling charges of Communist sympathies against prominent public figures. A favorite target was aristocratic Secretary of State Dean Acheson, whom he ridiculed as the "Red Dean," with his "cane, spats and tea-sipping little finger"; he even went after General George Marshall, claiming that the wartime army chief of staff was an agent of the Communist conspiracy. Nor were fellow Republicans immune. One GOP senator was described as "a living miracle in that he is without question the only man who has lived so long with neither brains nor guts."

These attacks on the wealthy, famous, and privileged won McCarthy a devoted national following. Even though at the height of his influence in early 1954 he gained the approval of only 50 percent of the respondents in a Gallup poll. McCarthy drew a disproportionate backing from working-class Catholics and ethnic groups, especially the Irish, Poles, and Italians, who normally voted Democratic. He offered a simple solution to the complicated Cold War: defeat the enemy at home rather than continue to engage in costly foreign-aid programs and entangling alliances abroad. Above all, McCarthy appealed to conservative Republicans in the Midwest who shared his right-wing views and felt cheated by Truman's upset victory in 1948. Even GOP leaders who viewed McCarthy's tactics with distaste, such as Robert A. Taft of Ohio, quietly encouraged him to attack the vulnerable Democrats.

The Legacy of McCarthyism

McCarthy did not end his crusade with the Republican victory in 1952. Instead, he used his new position as chairman of the Senate Committee on Government Operations as a base for ferreting out Communists on the federal payroll. He made a series of charges against the foreign-affairs agencies and demanded that certain books be purged from American information libraries overseas. Eisenhower's advisors urged the President to use his own great prestige to stop McCarthy. But Ike refused such a confrontation, saying, "I will not get into a pissing contest with that skunk."

The Wisconsin senator finally overreached

Senator Joseph McCarthy's unsubstantiated charges of Communist infiltration of the army led to his downfall. Army counsel Joseph Welch (left) listens wearily to McCarthy's rambling diatribe.

himself. In early 1954, he uncovered a suspected Communist dentist in the military and proceeded to attack the upper echelons of the United States Army, telling one much-decorated general that he was "not fit to wear the uniform." The controversy culminated in the televised Army-McCarthy hearings. For six weeks, the senator revealed his crude, bullying behavior to the American people. Viewers were repelled by his frequent outbursts that began with the insistent cry, "Point of order, Mr. Chairman, point of order," and by his attempt to slur the reputation of a young lawyer associated with army counsel Joseph Welch. This last maneuver led Welch to condemn McCarthy for his "reckless cruelty" and ask rhetorically, as millions watched on television, "Have you no sense of decency, sir . . . ?"

Courageous Republicans, led by George Aiken of Vermont and Margaret Chase Smith of Maine, joined with Democrats to bring about the Senate's censure of McCarthy in December 1954, by a vote of 67 to 22. Once rebuked, McCarthy fell quickly from prominence. He died three years later virtually unnoticed and unmourned.

Yet his influence was profound. Not only did he paralyze national life with what a Senate subcommittee described as "the most nefarious campaign of half-truth and untruth in the history of the Republic," but he also helped impose a political and cultural conformity that froze dissent for the rest of the 1950s. Long after McCarthy's passing, the nation tolerated loyalty oaths for teachers, the banning of left-wing books in public libraries, and the blacklisting of entertainers in radio, television, and films. Freedom of expression was inhibited, and the opportunity to try out new ideas and approaches was lost as the United States settled into a sterile Cold War consensus.

The Struggle over Civil Rights

Although the Cold War gave birth to the ugly loyalty issue, it had a more positive effect on another social problem—the denial of civil rights to black Americans. The contradiction between the denunciation of the Soviet Union for its human-rights violations and the second-class status of Afro-Americans began to arouse the national conscience. Fighting for freedom against Communist tyranny abroad, Americans had to face the reality of the continued denial of freedom to a submerged minority at home.

Blacks had benefited economically from World War II, but they were still a seriously disadvantaged group. Those who had left the South for better opportunities in northern and western cities were concentrated in blighted and segregated neighborhoods, working at low-paying jobs, suffering economic and social discrimination, and failing to share fully in the postwar prosperity.

In the South, conditions were much worse. State laws forced blacks to live almost totally segregated from white society. Not only did blacks attend separate (and almost always inferior) schools, but they also were rigidly excluded from all public facilities. They were forced to use separate waiting rooms in train stations, separate seats on all forms of transportation, separate drinking fountains, and even separate telephone booths. "Segregation was enforced at all places of public entertainment, including libraries, auditoriums, and circuses," Chief Justice Earl Warren noted. "There was segregation in the hospitals, prisons, mental institutions, and nursing homes. Even ambulance service was segregated."

■ *Train station in Atlanta, 1956. By this time the armed forces were desegregated, but this black airman was required by Georgia law to sit in a "Colored Waiting Room."*

Civil Rights as a Political Issue

Truman was the first president to attempt to alter the historic pattern of racial discrimination in the United States. In 1946 he appointed a presidential commission on civil rights. A year later, in a sweeping report entitled "To Secure These Rights" the commission recommended the reinstatement of the wartime Fair Employment Practices Committee (FEPC), the establishment of a permanent civil-rights commission, and the denial of federal aid to any state that condoned segregation in schools and public facilities. The President's ten-point legislative program in 1948 included some of these measures, notably a new FEPC and a civil-rights commission. But southern resistance blocked any action by Congress, and the inclusion of a strong civil-rights plank in the 1948 Democratic platform led to the walkout of some southern delegations and a separate States'-Rights (Dixiecrat) ticket in several states of the South that fall.

Black voters in the North responded by backing Truman overwhelmingly over Dewey in the 1948 election. In key states—California, Ohio, and Illinois—it was the black voters in Los Angeles, Cleveland, and Chicago that ensured the Democratic victory. Truman responded by including civil-rights legislation in his Fair Deal program in 1949. Once again, however, determined southern opposition blocked congressional action on a permanent FEPC and an antilynching measure.

Even though President Truman had been unable to secure any significant legislation, he had succeeded in adding civil rights to the liberal agenda. From this time forward, it would be an integral part of the Democratic reform program. And Truman was able to use his executive power to assist blacks. He strengthened the civil-rights division of the Justice Department, which aided black groups in their efforts to challenge school segregation and restrictive housing covenants in the courts. Most important, in 1948 Truman issued an order calling for the desegregation of the armed forces. The navy and the air force quickly complied, but the army resisted until the manpower needs of the Korean War finally overcame the military's objections. By the end of the 1950s, the armed forces had become far more integrated than American society at large.

Desegregating the Schools

The nation's schools soon became the primary target of civil-rights advocates. The NAACP concentrated first on universities, successfully waging an intensive legal battle to win admission for qualified blacks to graduate and professional schools. Led by Thurgood Marshall, NAACP lawyers then took on the broader issue of segregation in the country's public schools. Challenging the 1896 Supreme Court decision (*Plessy* v. *Ferguson*) which upheld the constitutionality of separate but equal public facilities, Marshall argued that even substantially equal but separate schools did profound psychological damage to black children and thus violated the Fourteenth Amendment.

A unanimous Supreme Court agreed in its 1954 decision in the case of *Brown* v. *Board of Education of Topeka*. Chief Justice Earl Warren, recently appointed by President Eisenhower, wrote the landmark opinion which flatly declared that "separate educational facilities are inherently un-equal." To divide grade-school children "solely because of their race," Warren argued, "generates a feeling of inferiority as to their status in the community that may affect their hearts and minds in a way unlikely ever to be undone." Despite this sweeping language, Warren realized that it would be difficult to change historic patterns of segregation quickly. Accordingly, in 1955 the Court ruled that implementation should proceed "with all deliberate speed" and left the details to the lower federal courts.

The process of desegregating the schools proved to be agonizingly slow. Officials in the border states quickly complied with the Court's ruling, but states deeper in the South responded with a policy of massive resistance. Local White Citizens' Councils organized to fight for retention of racial separation; 101 congressmen and senators signed a Southern Manifesto in 1956 which denounced the *Brown* decision as "a clear abuse of judicial power." School boards, encouraged by this show of defiance, found a variety of ways to evade the Court's ruling. The most successful

■ *Linda Brown (left). Her parents were the plaintiffs in the* Brown v. Board of Education of Topeka *landmark Supreme Court case. Thurgood Marshall (right), a leading black activist, was chief counsel for the Browns.*

was the passage of pupil-placement laws. These laws enabled local officials to assign individual students to schools on the basis of scholastic aptitude, ability to adjust, and "morals, conduct, health and personal standards." These stalling tactics led to long disputes in the federal courts; by the end of the decade, less than 1 percent of the black children in the Deep South attended school with whites.

A conspicuous lack of presidential support further weakened the desegregation effort. Dwight Eisenhower was not a racist, but he believed that people's attitudes could not be changed by "cold lawmaking"—only "by appealing to reason, by prayer, and by constantly working at it through our own efforts." Quietly and unobtrusively, he worked to achieve desegregation in federal facilities, particularly in veterans' hospitals, navy yards, and the District of Columbia school system. Yet he refrained from endorsing the *Brown* decision, which he told an aide he believed had "*set back* progress in the South *at least fifteen years.*"

Southern leaders mistook Ike's silence for tacit support of segregation. In 1957, Governor Orville Faubus of Arkansas called out the national guard to prevent the integration of Little Rock's Central High School on grounds of a threat to public order. After 270 armed troops turned back 9 young black students, a federal judge ordered the guardsmen removed; but when the blacks entered the school, a mob of 500 jeering whites surrounded the building. Eisenhower, who had told Faubus that "the Federal Constitution will be upheld by me by every legal means at my command," sent in 1000 paratroopers to ensure the rights of the 9 blacks to attend Central High. The children finished the school year under armed guard. Then Little Rock authorities closed Central High School for the next two years; when it reopened, there were only 3 blacks in attendance.

Despite the snail's pace of school desegregation, the *Brown* decision led to other advances. In 1957, the Eisenhower administration proposed the first general civil-rights legislation since Reconstruction. Strong southern resistance and compromise by both the administration and Senate Democratic leader Lyndon B. Johnson of Texas weakened the bill considerably. The final act, however, did create a permanent Commission for Civil Rights, one of Truman's original

Angry whites taunt one of the black students trying to pass through the lines of Arkansas National Guardsmen to enroll in Little Rock's Central High School in 1957.

goals. It also provided for federal efforts aimed at "securing and protecting the right to vote." A second civil-rights act in 1960 slightly strengthened the voting-rights section.

Like the desegregation effort, the attempt to ensure black voting rights in the South was still largely symbolic. Southern registrars used a variety of devices, ranging from intimidation to unfair tests, to deny blacks the suffrage. Yet the actions of Congress and the Supreme Court marked a vital turning point in national policy toward racial justice.

The Beginnings of Black Activism

The most dynamic force for change came from blacks themselves. The shift from legal struggles in the courts to black protest in the streets began with an incident in Montgomery, Alabama. On December 1, 1955, Rosa Parks—a black seamstress who had been active in the local NAACP chapter—violated a city ordinance by refusing to give up her seat to a white person on a local bus.

■ *Rosa Parks' refusal to move to the back of the bus in Montgomery led to a citywide bus boycott in 1955 organized by Rev. Martin Luther King, Jr., who soon came to the attention of the police (bottom left). Lunch counter sit-ins were another effective protest tactic (top right).*

After her arrest, blacks gathered to protest and found a young, eloquent leader in Martin Luther King, Jr. The son of a successful Atlanta preacher, King had studied theology at Boston University and only recently had taken his first church in Montgomery. He agreed to lead a massive boycott of the city's bus system, which depended heavily on black patronage.

The Montgomery bus boycott started out with a modest goal. Instead of challenging the legality of segregated seating, King simply asked that seats be taken on a first-come, first-served basis, with blacks being seated from the back and the whites from the front of each bus. As the protest continued, however, and as they endured both legal harassment and sporadic acts of violence, the blacks began to be more assertive. An effective system of car pools enabled the protesters to avoid using the city buses. Soon they were insisting on a complete end to segregated seating as they sang their new song of protest:

Ain't gonna ride them buses no more
Ain't gonna ride no more
Why in the hell don't the white folk know
That I ain't gonna ride no more.

The boycott ended in victory a year later when the Supreme Court ruled the Alabama segregated-seating law unconstitutional. King had won far more than this limited dent in the wall of segregation, however. He had provided blacks with a new weapon to fight racial oppression. Drawing on his study of Mahatma Gandhi's techniques of peaceful opposition to imperial authority in India, King worked out a philosophy of passive resistance that stressed nonviolence and love. "Blood may flow in the streets. of Montgomery, before we receive our freedom," he told his followers at the height of the boycott, "but it must be our blood and not that of the white man. We must not harm a single hair on the head of our white brothers." The ultimate goal for King was to reunite the broken community through bonds of Christian love. The result, he prophesied, would be to enable future historians to say of the effort, "There lived a great people—a black people—who injected new meaning and dignity into the veins of civilization."

A year after the successful bus boycott, King founded the Southern Christian Leadership Conference (SCLC) to direct the crusade against segregation. Then in February 1960 another spontaneous event sparked a further advance for passive resistance. Four black students from North Carolina Agricultural and Technical College sat down at a dime-store lunch counter in Greensboro, North Carolina, and refused to move after being denied service. Other students, both whites and blacks, joined in similar "sit-ins" across the South, as well as "kneel-ins" at churches and "wade-ins" at swimming pools. By the end of the year, some fifty thousand young people had succeeded in desegregating public facilities in over a hundred southern cities. Several thousand of the demonstrators were arrested and put in jail, but the movement gained strength, leading to the formation of the Student Nonviolent Coordinating Committee (SNCC) in April 1960. From this time on, SCLC and SNCC, with their tactic of direct, though peaceful, confrontation, would replace the NAACP and its reliance on court action in the forefront of the civil-rights movement. The change would eventually lead to dramatic success, but it also ushered in a period of heightened tension and social turmoil in the 1960s.

The Good Life?

Despite the second red scare and the civil-rights movement, the consumer culture remained the dominant social theme of the 1950s. Yet even with an abundance of creature comforts and added hours of leisure time, the quality of life left many Americans anxious and dissatisfied.

Areas of Greatest Growth

Organized religion flourished in the climate of the 1950s. Ministers, priests, and rabbis all commented on the rise in church and synagogue attendance in the new communities. Will Herberg claimed that religious affiliation had become the primary identifying feature of modern American life, dividing the nation into three separate segments—Protestant, Catholic, and Jewish.

Some observers condemned the bland, secular nature of suburban churches, which seemed to be an integral part of the consumer society. "On weekdays one shops for food," wrote one critic, "on Saturdays one shops for recreation, and on Sundays one shops for the Holy Ghost." But the popularity of religious writer Norman Vincent Peale, with his positive gospel that urged people to "start thinking faith, enthusiasm and joy," suggested that the new churches filled a genuine if shallow human need. At the same time, the emergence of neo-orthodoxy in Protestant seminaries (notably through the ideas of Reinhold Niebuhr) and the rapid spread of radical forms of fundamentalism (such as the Assemblies of God) indicated that millions of Americans still were searching for a more personal religious faith.

Schools provided an immediate growth problem for the new suburban communities. The unprecedented increase in the number of school-age children, from twenty to thirty million in the first eight grades, overwhelmed the resources of many local districts, leading to demands for federal aid. Congress granted limited help for areas affected by defense plants and military bases, but Eisenhower's reluctance to unbalance the budget —along with traditional adherence to state control over public education—blocked further federal assistance.

Equally important, a controversy arose over the nature of education in the 1950s. Critics of "progressive" education called for sweeping educational reforms and a new stress on traditional academic subjects. Suburban communities often had bitter fights; affluent parents demanded kindergarten enrichment programs and grade-school foreign-language instruction while working-class people resisted such costly innovations. The one thing all seemed to agree on was the desirability of a college education. The number of young people attending colleges increased from 1.5 million in 1940 to 3.6 million by 1960, leading to a rapid expansion of universities.

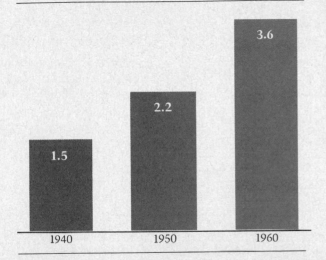

College Student Enrollment, 1940–1960 (in millions)

Year	Enrollment
1940	1.5
1950	2.2
1960	3.6

■ *In this scene from Marty, a memorable TV play performed live in 1953, Marty (Rod Steiger) and his newfound friend (Nancy Marchand) try to break through the barriers of shyness.*

The largest growth area was the exciting new medium of television. From a shaky start just after the war, TV boomed in the fifties, pushing radio aside and even undermining many of the nation's mass-circulation magazines. By 1957, the three networks controlled the airwaves, reaching forty million sets over nearly five hundred stations. Advertisers soon took charge of the new medium, using many of the techniques first pioneered in radio—including pretaped commercials, quiz shows, and soap operas.

At first, the insatiable demand for programs encouraged a burst of creativity. Playwrights such as Reginald Rose, Rod Serling, and Paddy Chayefsky wrote a series of notable dramas for *Play-house 90, Studio One,* and the *Goodyear Television Playhouse.* Broadcast live from cramped studios, these productions thrived on tight dramatic structures, movable scenery, and frequent close-ups of the actors. *Marty,* Paddy Chayefsky's deceptively simple story of a Bronx butcher's decision to marry, epitomized the golden age of television. Later made into a successful movie, *Marty* reflected its author's belief that "there is far more exciting drama in the reasons why a man gets married than in why he murders someone."

Advertisers, however, quickly became disillusioned with the live anthology programs, which usually dealt with controversial subjects or focused on ordinary people and events. In contrast, sponsors wanted shows that stressed excitement, glamour, and instant success. Westerns and situation comedies soon prevailed after a fling with quiz shows ended in scandal.

The Kinsey Reports:
Exploring Human Sexual Behavior

"Kinsey brought sex out of the bedroom and into the world's parlor." So said a colleague of Alfred Kinsey (see photo above), a scholar who achieved national prominence as an expert on sex. Kinsey was thrust into the public eye by the publication of his two studies: *Sexual Behavior in the Human Male* (1948) and its sequel *Sexual Behavior in the Human Female* (1953). When he died in 1956, he was one of the best-known research scientists in the United States.

Kinsey's road to fame as an authority on human sexual behavior was not a straight path. He was the eldest child of uneducated parents. His father, a self-taught engineer, was determined that his son would follow in his footsteps. But at the end of his sophomore year in college, Kinsey decided to study biology instead; his angry father then cut off his financial support. Undeterred, he pursued his interest in biology and zoology, completed his doctorate at Harvard in 1920, and received an assistant professorship in zoology at Indiana University.

Kinsey's early years in Bloomington were productive. He married and raised a family, published a biology textbook, and wrote two major studies of the gall wasp—an insect on which he was an international authority. In 1938, when a new course on marriage was offered at the University, Kinsey turned his attention to human sexual behavior. Taking an interdisciplinary approach, the new class drew lecturers from biology, medicine, sociology, law, economics, and ethics. Kinsey was chosen to chair the faculty committee in charge of the curriculum.

The course was a great success, but Kinsey was distressed by the lack of scientific literature on human sexual behavior. He found that there was no reliable body of statistics describing sexual activity among humans. To provide such information, Kinsey began interviewing his students, recording their sexual histories much as he would thousands of others later in his large-scale studies.

Over the next sixteen years, Kinsey and his colleagues conducted over 18,000 interviews while compiling data for his studies. In 1947, he founded the Institute for Sex Research at Indiana University. A total of 5300 males were interviewed for *Sexual Behavior in the Human Male*; the responses of 5940 women were used in *Sexual Behavior in the Human Female*. Though some racial minorities were interviewed, only whites were used in the publications. Even among whites, the sample was haphazard but not random, a fact that the statisticians among his critics were quick to point out.

While some social scientists found Kinsey's sampling techniques questionable, his interviewing techniques were highly regarded. Kinsey created an immediate rapport with his subjects and treated all reports with matter-of-fact detachment. Questions were phrased to encourage honesty and openness. Reports of married couples were checked against one another to ensure honesty, and selected respondents were reinterviewed to verify the accuracy of their recollections. All responses were anonymous; they were recorded on IBM cards according to a secret numerical code. Kinsey even had plans for the destruction of the data in case law-enforcement officials demanded access to the records.

Kinsey tried to present his findings on human sexual behavior with the same empirical objectivity that he used in his zoological studies. He considered himself a scientist, not a moralist. But amid the charts, graphs, and statistics, there was a message in Kinsey's reports: toleration. He wrote in the introduction to his volume on men, "This is first of all a report on what people do which raises no question of what they should do." Sex was "a normal biologic function, acceptable in whatever form it is manifested."

In 1948, after the publication of *Sexual Behavior in the Human Male*, George Gallup asked Americans, "Do you think it is a good thing or a bad thing to have this information on sex available?" Of those polled, 57 percent thought it was a good thing, 11 percent thought it was bad, 4 percent thought it acceptable "if properly presented" and kept from children, and 28 percent had no opinion. When Gallup asked the same question about Kinsey's study of women in 1953, 49 percent favored it, 19 percent opposed it, 4 percent gave it qualified approval, and 28 percent still had no opinion. Part of the decline in Kinsey's positive rating can be attributed to his assault on sexual stereotypes. Challenging popular belief, Kinsey showed that women possessed the same sexual needs and desires as men and were not motivated solely by any maternal instinct. But the lower rating also represented the growing force of a vocal minority opposed to Kinsey's research.

Despite the general interest in Kinsey's studies and the popularity of his books, many segments of American society attacked his work. His fellow academics criticized him for engaging in research which was beyond his competence as a zoologist. Statisticians, psychologists, and sociologists reacted against his invasion of their academic domains. Freudian psychiatrists criticized his departure from psychoanalytical orthodoxy, while humanists objected to the impersonalization and quantification of this most intimate aspect of human behavior. But the most vociferous attacks came from the Christian clergy.

Spanning the spectrum from Reinhold Niebuhr to Billy Graham, they denounced Kinsey for his biological approach to sex and his failure to address its moral and religious aspects. Graham went so far as to suggest that "it is impossible to estimate the damage this book will do to the already deteriorating morals of America." And in Kinsey's home state, the Indiana chapter of the National Council of Catholic Women demanded "some reassurance that Indiana University is still a place fit for the educating of youth of our state." A Presbyterian minister in Indianapolis even saw "a kinship" between the Kinsey Reports and communism.

Indiana University remained staunch in its support of Kinsey. The Rockefeller Foundation, however—the source of a large percentage of Kinsey's funds—was not so steadfast. At the urging of Representative B. C. Reece, a conservative Tennessee Republican, Congress formed a committee to investigate tax-exempt foundations. Reece admitted to the press that the real reason for the committee was to investigate the financial backing of the Kinsey Reports. The Rockefeller Foundation, worried about a congressional investigation and the bad publicity it might create, turned down the Kinsey Institute's request for continued support in 1954. Two years later Alfred Kinsey died, his work, in his own opinion, still largely incomplete.

In retrospect, the objections to the Kinsey Reports do not seem credible. Kinsey did not advocate premarital or extramarital sex, homosexuality, promiscuity, or communism. He merely showed America its sexual habits, in all their infinite variety. Although many of his critics accused him of trivializing sex, reducing it to bar graphs and statistics, he can be more accurately credited with demystifying human sexual behavior.

Aware that audiences were fascinated by contestants with unusual expertise (a shoemaker answering tough questions on operas, a grandmother stumping experts on baseball), producers began giving away huge cash prizes on *The $64,000 Question* and *Twenty-one*. In 1959, the nation was shocked when Charles Van Doren, a Columbia University professor, confessed that he had been given the answers in advance to win $129,000 on *Twenty-one*. The three networks quickly dropped all the big-prize quiz programs, replacing them with comedy, action, and adventure shows such as *The Untouchables* and *Bonanza*. Despite its early promise of artistic innovation, television had become a technologically sophisticated but safe conveyor of the consumer culture.

Critics of the Consumer Society

One striking feature of the 1950s was the abundance of self-criticism. A number of widely read books explored the flaws in the new suburbia. John Keats' *The Crack in the Picture Window* described the endless rows of tract houses "vomited up" by developers as "identical boxes spreading like gangrene." Their occupants—whom he dubbed the Drones, the Amiables, and the Fecunds—lost any sense of individuality in their obsession with material goods.

Richard and Katherine Gordon were more concerned about the psychological toll of suburban life in their 1960 book *The Split Level Trap*. They labeled the new life-style "Disturbia" and bemoaned the "haggard" men, "tense and anxious" women, and the "gimme" kids it produced. The most sweeping indictment came in William H. Whyte's *The Organization Man* (1956), based on a study of the Chicago suburb of Park Forest. Whyte perceived a change from the old Protestant ethic, with its emphasis on hard work and personal responsibility, to a new social ethic, where everything centered on "the team" and the ultimate goal was "belongingness." The result was a stifling conformity and the loss of personal identity.

The most influential social critic of the fifties was Harvard sociologist David Riesman. His book *The Lonely Crowd* appeared in 1950 and set the tone for intellectual commentary about suburbia for the rest of the decade. Riesman described the shift from the "inner-directed" American of the past who had relied on such traditional values as self-denial and frugality to the "other-directed" American of the consumer society who constantly adapted his behavior to conform to social pressures. The consequence—a decline in individualism and a tendency for people to become acutely sensitive to the expectations of others—produced a bland and tolerant society of consumers lacking creative and adventurous people.

C. Wright Mills was a far more caustic, though less popular, commentator on American society in the 1950s. Anticipating government statistics that revealed that white-collar workers (sales clerks, office workers, bank tellers) now outnumbered blue-collar workers (miners, factory workers, millhands), Mills described the new middle class in ominous terms in his books *White Collar* (1951) and *Power Elite* (1956). The corporation was the villain for Mills, depriving office workers of their own identities and imposing an impersonal discipline through manipulation and propaganda. The industrial assembly line had given way to an even more dehumanizing workplace, the modern office. "At rows of blank-looking counters sat rows of blank-looking girls with blank, white folders in their blank hands, all blankly folding blank papers."

This disenchantment with the consumer culture reached its most eloquent expression with the "beats," a literary group that rebelled against the materialistic society of the 1950s. Jack Kerouac's novel *On the Road*, published in 1957, set the tone for the new movement. The name came from the quest for beatitude, a state of inner grace that is sought in Zen Buddhism. Flouting the respectability of suburbia, the "beatniks"—as middle-class America termed them—were easily identified by their long hair, bizarre clothing, and penchant for sexual promiscuity and drug experimentation. They were conspicuous dropouts from a society they found senseless. Poet Lawrence Ferlinghetti, who held forth in the City Lights Bookshop in San Francisco (a favorite resort of the beats), summed it up this way: "I was a wind-up toy someone had dropped wound up into a world already running down."

Despite the disapproval they evoked from mainstream Americans, the beat generation had only compassion for their detractors. "We love everything," Kerouac proclaimed, "—Bill Gra-

■ *"Beat" writers like Jack Kerouac bemoaned the conformity and staleness of the 1950s. Kerouac's cross-country wanderings provided the material for his novel,* On the Road, *written in 1957.*

ham, the Big Ten, Rock and Roll, Zen, apple pie, Eisenhower—we dig it all." Yet as highly visible nonconformists in an era of stifling conformity, the beats demonstrated a style of social protest that would flower into the counterculture of the sixties.

The Reaction to Sputnik

The profound insecurity that underlay American life throughout the fifties burst into view in October 1957, when the Soviets sent the satellite Sputnik into orbit around the earth. The public's reaction to this impressive scientific feat was panic. The declining rate of economic growth; the recession of 1957–1958; the growing concern that American schools, with their frills and frivolities and their emphasis on social adjustment, were lagging behind their Russian counterparts—all contributed to a conviction that the nation had

somehow lost its previously unquestioned primacy in the eyes of the world.

In the late 1950s, the President and Congress moved to restore national confidence. Eisenhower appointed James R. Killian, president of the Massachusetts Institute of Technology, as his special assistant for science and technology and to oversee a crash program in missile development. The House and Senate followed by creating the National Aeronautics and Space Administration (NASA) in 1958. Congress appropriated vast sums to allow the agency to compete with the Russians in the space race. Soon a new group of heroes, the astronauts, began the training that led to suborbital flights and eventually to John Glenn's five-hour flight around the globe in 1962. (See the picture essay on the space program following p.864.)

Congress also sought to match the Soviet educational advances by passing the National Defense Education Act (NDEA). This legislation authorized federal financing of scientific and foreign-language programs in the nation's schools and colleges. Soon American students were hard at work mastering the "new physics" and the "new math."

The belief persisted, however, that the faults lay deeper, that in the midst of affluence and abundance Americans had lost their competitive edge. Economists pointed to the higher rate of Soviet economic growth, and social critics bemoaned a supermarket culture that stressed consumption over production, comfort over hard work. Disturbed by the charge that the nation had lost its sense of purpose, President Eisenhower finally appointed a Commission on National Goals "to develop a broad outline of national objectives for the next decade and longer." Ten prominent citizens from all walks of life, led by Henry W. Wriston of Brown University, issued a report which called for increased military spending abroad, greater economic growth at home, broader educational opportunities, and more government support for both scientific research and the advancement of the arts. The consensus seemed to be that rather than a change of direction, all the United States needed was a renewed commitment to the pursuit of excellence.

The fifties ended on a mixed note. The temporary despair engendered by Sputnik had led to a healthy, if excessive, national self-assessment.

ment, the sense of stagnation, even decline, lingered on through Eisenhower's second term, offering the Democrats a tempting issue to exploit in the 1960 election.

Recommended Reading

Two excellent books survey the social, cultural, and political trends in the United States during the postwar period. In *One Nation Divisible* (1980), Richard Polenberg analyzes class, ethnic, and racial changes, while William Leuchtenburg offers a fine overview of American life since 1945 in *A Troubled Feast*, updated ed. (1983).

The best book on the Truman period is Alonzo L. Hamby, *Beyond the New Deal* (1973), which focuses on Truman's attempts to preserve and extend the liberal reform tradition. Charles Alexander provides a balanced view of the Eisenhower years in *Holding the Line* (1975), portraying the Republican president as an able chief executive who was well suited to the times.

Of the many books on the postwar red scare, Earl Latham's *The Communist Controversy in Washington* (1966) is the most thorough and reliable. There is no single volume that deals with all aspects of the civil-rights movement, but two fine biographies—David L. Lewis' *King* (1970) and Stephen B. Oates' *Let the Trumpet Sound* (1982)—present perceptive portraits of Martin Luther King, Jr., the movement's most influential leader.

Douglas Miller and Marian Novak offer a comprehensive catalogue of social and cultural developments in *The Fifties: The Way We Really Were* (1977). The most incisive account of suburban life is Scott Donaldson's *The Suburban Myth* (1969), which rebuts many of the contemporary critiques.

Additional Bibliography

Biographies of Truman include Merle Miller, *Plain Speaking* (1973); Margaret Truman, *Harry S. Truman* (1973); Robert H. Ferrell, *Harry S. Truman and the Modern American Presidency* (1982); and two volumes by Robert J. Donovan: *Conflict and Crisis* (1977) and *Tumultuous Years* (1982). Studies of specific policies include Barton J. Bernstein, ed., *Politics and Policies of the Truman Administration* (1970); R. Alton Lee, *Truman and Taft-Hartley* (1966); Susan M. Hartmann, *Truman and the 80th Congress* (1971); Allen J. Matusow, *Farm Policies and Politics in the Truman Administration* (1966); and Monte M. Poen, *Harry S. Truman and the Medical Lobby* (1979).

Three studies of the 1948 election are Irwin Ross, *The Loneliest Campaign* (1968); Norman D. Markowitz, *The Rise and Fall of the People's Century: Henry A. Wallace and American Liberalism, 1941–1948* (1973); and Allen Yarnell, *Democrats and Progressives* (1973). John Blum offers an interesting selection from

Amid the self-criticism, there was much that Americans of the fifties could point to with pride. They had created a booming consumer society which provided the great majority with an opportunity for a rich and full life and banished fears of another Great Depression. The standard of living Americans achieved in the 1950s would become the aspiration of most of the world's population in the decades to come. Yet despite this achieve-

Henry Wallace's diary in *The Price of Vision* (1973), while James T. Patterson gives an excellent portrait of Senator Robert A. Taft in *Mr. Republican* (1968).

Herbert Parmet began the scholarly reappraisal of Dwight Eisenhower in *Eisenhower and the American Crusades* (1973). Other useful books on the Eisenhower years include Fred Greenstein, *The Hidden Hand Presidency* (1982); Elmo Richardson, *The Presidency of Dwight D. Eisenhower* (1979); Samuel Lubell, *The Future of American Politics* (1952); Garry Wills, *Nixon Agonistes* (1971); John Bartlow Martin, *Adlai Stevenson and the World* (1977); James L. Sundquist, *Politics and Policy: The Eisenhower, Kennedy and Johnson Years* (1968); Gary W. Reichard, *The Reaffirmation of Republicanism: Eisenhower and the 83rd Congress* (1975); and Mark Rose, *Interstate* (1979). For economic developments during the 1950s, consult Edward S. Flash, *Economic Advice and Presidential Leadership* (1965); Harold G. Vatter, *The U.S. Economy in the 1950's* (1962); and two books by John Kenneth Galbraith: *American Capitalism* (1952) and *The Affluent Society* (1958).

The relationship of the Truman administration to the Communist issue is covered in Allan D. Harper, *The Politics of Loyalty* (1970); Athan G. Theoharis, *Seeds of Repression* (1971); and Richard Freeland, *The Truman Doctrine and the Origins of McCarthyism* (1972). Other works on the second red scare are Walter Goodman, *The Committee* (1968); Victor Navasky, *Naming Names* (1980); Allen Weinstein, *Perjury: The Hiss-Chambers Case* (1978); and William L. O'Neill, *A Better World* (1982), which examines its impact on American intellectuals. Among the many books on McCarthyism, the best are Thomas C. Reeves, *The Life and Times of Joe McCarthy* (1982); Richard H. Rovere, *Senator Joe McCarthy* (1959); Michael P. Rogin, *The Intellectuals and McCarthy* (1967); Robert Griffith, *The Politics of Fear* (1970); Richard M. Fried, *Men Against McCarthy* (1976); Edwin R. Bagley, *Joe McCarthy and the Press* (1981); and David Oshinski, *A Conspiracy So Immense: The World of Joe McCarthy* (1983).

Truman's contributions to the civil-rights movement are surveyed critically in Harry C. Berman, *The Politics of Civil Rights in the Truman Administration* (1970) and more sympathetically in Donald R. McCoy and Richard T. Ruetten, *Quest and Response* (1973). Other important books on civil rights are Richard Dalfiume, *Desegregation of the U.S. Armed Forces* (1969); Richard Kluger, *Simple Justice* (1975) on the *Brown* decision; Benjamin Muse, *Ten Years of Prelude* (1964); Steven Lawson, *Black Ballots* (1977) on the voting rights issue; and Numan V. Bartley, *The Rise of Massive Resistance* (1969) on the southern reaction.

Bernard Rosenberg and D. M. White, eds., *Mass Culture* (1957) is a useful anthology of cultural trends. Other significant books on social and intellectual themes in the 1950s include David Potter, *People of Plenty* (1954), a perceptive analysis of abundance; William Dobriner, ed., *The Suburban Community* (1958), a helpful collection of scholarly essays; Herbert Gans, *The Levittowners* (1967); Will Herberg, *Protestant, Catholic, Jew* (1955); Lawrence Lipton, *The Holy Barbarians* (1959) on the "beat generation"; Eric Barnouw, *The Image Empire* (1970), a critical view of television; Kent Anderson, *Television Fraud* (1978) on the rigged TV quiz shows; Lloyd Swenson et al., *This New Ocean* (1966) on the early space program; and Barbara B. Clowse, *Brainpower and the Cold War* (1981) about the impact of Sputnik on the educational controversy.

chapter 30

THE CLIMAX
OF LIBERALISM

On Monday evening, September 26, 1960, John F. Kennedy and Richard M. Nixon faced each other in the nation's first televised debate between two presidential candidates. Kennedy, as the relatively unknown Democratic challenger, had proposed the debates; Nixon, confident of his mastery of television, had accepted even though as Eisenhower's vice-president and the early front-runner in the election he had more to lose and less to gain. In the Chicago studios of CBS, technicians worked all day adjusting the lights, arranging the cameras, and making technical changes to satisfy the two candidates' media advisers.

Richard Nixon arrived an hour early, looking tired and ill at ease. He was still recuperating from a knee injury which had slowed his campaign and left him pale and weak as he pursued a hectic catch-up schedule. Makeup experts offered to hide Nixon's heavy beard and soften his prominent jowls, but the GOP candidate declined, preferring to let an aide apply a light coat of Max Factor's "Lazy Shave," a pancake cosmetic. John Kennedy, tanned from open-air campaigning in California and rested by a day spent nearly free of distracting activity, refused to wear any makeup. He did, however, change from a gray to a dark blue suit better adapted to the intense lighting on the set.

At 8:30 P.M. central time, moderator Howard K. Smith welcomed an audience estimated at seventy-seven million to this historic event. Kennedy led off, echoing Abraham Lincoln by saying that the nation faced the question of "whether the world will exist half-slave and half-free." Although the ground rules limited the first debate to domestic issues, Kennedy argued that foreign and domestic policy were inseparable. He accused the Republicans of letting the country drift at home and abroad. "I think it's time America started moving again," he concluded. Nixon, caught off-guard, seemed to agree with Kennedy's assessment of the nation's problems, but he contended that he had better solutions. "Our disagreement," the vice-president pointed out, "is not about the goals for America but only about the means to reach those goals."

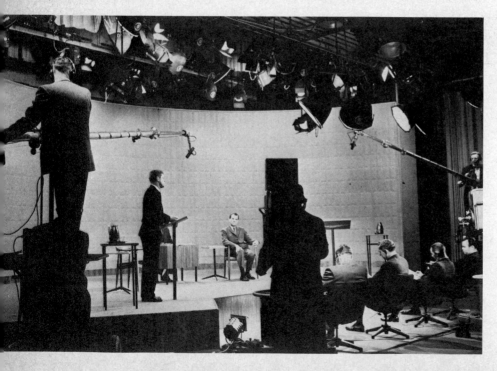

Nearly 110 million viewers watched the four televised debates between presidential candidates John F. Kennedy and Richard Nixon. Kennedy's polished performance helped dispel fears that he was too young and inexperienced for the job.

For the rest of the hour, the two candidates answered questions from a panel of journalists. Radiating confidence and self-assurance, Kennedy used a flow of statistics and details to create the image of a man deeply knowledgeable about all aspects of government. Nixon fought back with a defense of the Eisenhower record, but he seemed nervous and unsure of himself. The reaction shots of each candidate listening to the other's remarks showed Kennedy calm and serene, Nixon tense and uncomfortable.

Polls taken over the next few weeks revealed a sharp swing to Kennedy. Many Democrats and independents who had thought him too young or too inexperienced were impressed by his performance. Nixon suffered more from his unattractive image than from what he said; those who heard the debate on radio thought that the Republican candidate more than held his own. In the three additional debates held during the campaign, Nixon improved his performance notably by wearing makeup to soften his appearance and by taking the offensive from Kennedy on the issues. But the damage had been done. A postelection poll revealed that of four million voters who were influenced by the debates, three million voted for Kennedy.

The televised debates were only one of many factors influencing the outcome of the 1960 election. In essence, Kennedy won because he took full advantage of all his opportunities. Lightly regarded by Democratic leaders, he won the nomination by appealing to the rank-and-file in the primaries, but then astutely chose Lyndon Johnson of Texas as his running mate to blunt Nixon's southern strategy.

During the fall campaign, Kennedy exploited the national mood of frustration that had followed Sputnik. At home, he promised to stimulate the lagging economy and carry forward long-overdue reforms in education, health care, and civil rights under the banner of the "New Frontier." Abroad, he pledged a renewed commitment to the Cold War, vowing that he would lead the nation to victory over the Soviet Union. He met the issue of his Catholicism head on, telling a group of Protestant ministers in Houston that as president he would always place country above religion. In the shrewdest move of all, he won over black voters by helping to secure the release of Martin Luther King, Jr., from a Georgia jail

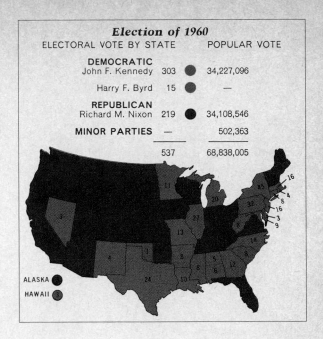

Election of 1960

ELECTORAL VOTE BY STATE		POPULAR VOTE
DEMOCRATIC		
John F. Kennedy	303	34,227,096
Harry F. Byrd	15	—
REPUBLICAN		
Richard M. Nixon	219	34,108,546
MINOR PARTIES	—	502,363
	537	68,838,005

where the civil-rights leader was being held on a trumped-up charge.

The Democratic victory in 1960 was paper-thin. Kennedy's edge in the popular vote was only two tenths of 1 percent, and his wide margin in the electoral college (303 to 219) was tainted by voting irregularities in several states—notably Illinois and Texas—which went Democratic by very slender majorities. Yet even though he had no mandate, Kennedy's triumph did mark a sharp political shift. In contrast to the aging Eisenhower, Kennedy symbolized youth, energy, and ambition. His mastery of the new medium of television reflected his sensitivity to the changes taking place in American life in the sixties. He came to office promising reform at home and advance abroad. Over the next five years, he and Lyndon Johnson achieved many of their goals only to find the nation caught up in new and even greater dilemmas.

Waging the Cold War

From the day he took office, John F. Kennedy gave foreign policy top priority. In part, this decision reflected the perilous world situation, the immediate dangers ranging from a developing civil war in Vietnam to the emergence of Fidel Castro as a Soviet ally in Cuba. But it also corresponded to Kennedy's personal priorities. As a congressman and senator, he had been an intense Cold Warrior, supporting containment after World War II, lamenting the loss of China, and accusing the Eisenhower administration of allowing the Russians to open up a dangerous missile gap. Bored by committee work and legislative details, he had focused on foreign policy in the Senate, gaining a seat on the Foreign Relations Committee and publishing a book of speeches, *The Strategy of Peace*, in early 1960.

In his inaugural address, Kennedy indicated an intense concern with the Cold War. Ignoring the domestic issues aired during the campaign, he dealt exclusively with the world. "Let every nation know, whether it wishes us well or ill, that we shall pay any price, bear any burden, meet any hardship, support any friend, oppose any foe," the new President declared, "to assure the survival and success of liberty. We will do all this and more."

His appointments reflected his determination to win the Cold War. His choice of Dean Rusk, an experienced but unassertive diplomat, to head the State Department indicated that Kennedy planned to be his own secretary of state. He surrounded himself with young, pragmatic advisers who prided themselves on toughness: McGeorge Bundy, dean of Harvard College, became national security adviser; Walt W. Rostow, an MIT economist, was Bundy's deputy; and Robert McNamara, the youthful president of the Ford Motor Company, took over as secretary of defense.

These New Frontiersmen, later dubbed "the best and the brightest" by journalist David Halberstam, all shared a hard-line view of the Soviet Union and the belief that American security depended upon superior force and the willingness to use it. Walt Rostow summed up their view of the contest with Russia best when he wrote, "The cold war comes down to this test of whether we and the democratic world are fundamentally tougher and more purposeful in the defense of our vital interests than they are in the pursuit of their global ambitions."

Flexible Response

The first goal of the Kennedy administration was to build up the nation's armed forces. During the 1960 campaign, Kennedy had warned that the Soviets were opening a missile gap. In fact, the United States had a significant lead in nuclear striking power by early 1961, with a fleet of over 600 B-52 bombers, 2 Polaris submarines, and 16 Atlas ICBMs capable of delivering more than 2000 warheads against Russian targets. Nevertheless, the new administration, intent on putting the Soviets on the defensive, authorized the construction of an awesome nuclear arsenal that included 1000 Minuteman solid-fuel ICBMs (five times the number Eisenhower had felt necessary) and 32 Polaris submarines carrying 656 missiles. The United States thus opened a missile gap in reverse, creating the possibility of a successful American first strike.

■ *In his inaugural address, Kennedy challenged young people to ask "what can you do for your country?"*

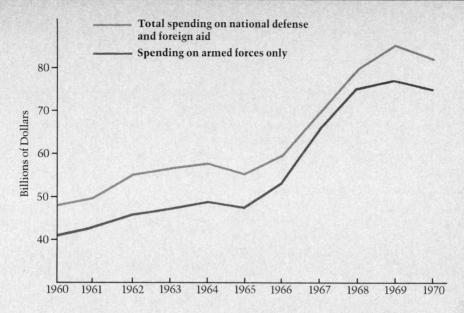

U.S. Government Spending on National Defense and Foreign Aid, 1960–1970

Total spending on national defense and foreign aid

Spending on armed forces only

Billions of Dollars

1960 1961 1962 1963 1964 1965 1966 1967 1968 1969 1970

Source: Compiled from U.S. Bureau of the Census, Historical Statistics of the United States, Colonial Times to 1970, *Bicentennial Edition, Washington, D.C., 1975.*

At the same time, the Kennedy administration augmented conventional military strength. Secretary of Defense McNamara developed plans to add five combat-ready army divisions, three tactical air wings and a ten-division strategic reserve. These vast increases led to a $6-billion jump in the defense budget in 1961 alone. The President took a personal interest in counterinsurgency. He expanded the Special Forces unit at Fort Bragg, North Carolina, and insisted, over army objections, that it adopt a distinctive green beret as a symbol of its elite status.

The purpose of this buildup was to create an alternative to Eisenhower's policy of massive retaliation. Instead of responding to Communist moves with nuclear threats, the United States could now call on a wide spectrum of force—ranging from ICBMs to Green Berets. Thus, as Robert McNamara explained, the new strategy of flexible response meant that the United States could "choose among several operational plans. . . . We shall be committed only to a system that gives us the ability to use our forces in a controlled and deliberate way." The danger, how-

ever, was that the existence of such a powerful arsenal would tempt the new administration to test its strength against the Soviet Union.

Crisis over Berlin

The first confrontation came in Germany. Since 1958, Soviet Premier Khrushchev had been threatening to sign a peace treaty that would put access to the isolated western zones of Berlin under the control of East Germany. The steady flight of skilled workers to the West through the Berlin escape route weakened the East German regime dangerously, and the Soviets felt they had to resolve this issue quickly.

At a summit meeting in Vienna in June 1961, Kennedy and Khrushchev focused on Berlin as the key issue. Pointing out that sixteen years had passed since the end of World War II, the Russian leader called the current situation "intolerable" and announced that the Soviet Union would proceed with an East German peace treaty. Kennedy was equally adamant, defending the American presence in Berlin and refusing to give up occupation rights which he considered crucial to the defense of Western Europe. In their last session, the failure to reach agreement took on an ominous tone. "I want peace," Khrushchev declared, "but, if you want war, that is your problem." "It is you, not I," the young President replied, "who wants to force a change." When the Soviet leader said he would sign a German peace treaty by December, Kennedy added, "It will be a cold winter."

The climax came sooner than either man expected. On July 25, Kennedy delivered an impassioned televised address to the American people in which he called the defense of Berlin "essential" to "the entire Free World." Announcing a series of arms increases, including $3 billion more in defense spending and a nationwide program of fallout shelters, the President took the unprecedented step of calling more than 150,000 reservists and National Guardsmen to active duty. Above all, he sought to convince Khrushchev of his determination and resolve. "I hear it said that West Berlin is militarily untenable," he commented. "And so was Bastogne. And so, in fact, was Stalingrad. Any dangerous spot is tenable if men—brave men—will make it so."

Aware of superior American nuclear striking power, Khrushchev settled for a stalemate. On August 13, the Soviets sealed off their zone of the city. They began the construction of the Berlin Wall to stop the flow of brains and talent to the West. For a brief time, Russian and American tanks maneuvered within sight of each other at Checkpoint Charlie, but by fall the tension gradually eased. The Soviets signed the separate peace treaty; Berlin—like Germany and, indeed, all Europe—remained divided between the East and the West. Neither side could claim a victory, but Kennedy felt that at least he had proved America's willingness to honor its commitments.

Containment in Southeast Asia

Two weeks before Kennedy's inaugural, Nikita Khrushchev gave a speech in Moscow in which he declared Soviet support for "wars of national liberation." The Russian leader's words were actually aimed more at China than the United

A grim symbol of the Cold War, the brick and barbed-wire Berlin Wall forms a solid barrier in front of the Brandenburg Gate, a historic Prussian war monument.

THE SPACE PROGRAM
COMMITMENT TO THE FUTURE

"These are extraordinary times," said President John F. Kennedy in a special message to Congress on May 25, 1961, "and we face an extraordinary challenge." The contest was with the Soviet Union, and outer space was the field of honor. Russia had stolen a march on the United States, sending a man into orbit before an American had even reached outer space. "Now is the time," Kennedy observed, "time for this nation to take a clearly leading role in space achievements." Project Apollo, a manned lunar landing within the decade, was our answer to the challenge.

Man had always looked to the heavens with awe and wonder, but the American space program was not the product of romantic or scientific curiosity. Clearly, there was a race, a "space race," and America's preeminence in world affairs was at stake.

Russia and the United States had been competing in rocket technology since World War II. As the disaffected allies marched into Germany, each sought to gain the secrets of the German V-2, the first supersonic ballistic missile. Although the Soviet Zone of occupation contained the primary V-2 plant, the U.S. Army's *Operation Paperclip* brought to the United States most of the top personnel of the German Rocket program. Werner Von Braun and more than one hundred other German scientists and engineers were recruited for the army missile program. American military rocketry continued to receive priority over civilian space projects. President Eisenhower's fiscal conservatism and his low estimate of the significance of space exploration prevailed until the successful launch of the Soviet satellite *Sputnik I* on October 4, 1957.

The flag of the United States on lunar soil, amid the footprints of Neil Armstrong and Edwin Aldrin, astronauts on the Apollo 11 *moon trip.*

While Eisenhower publicly dismissed *Sputnik* as an event of only "scientific interest" and denied the existence of a "space race," American confidence was shaken. Both houses of Congress established Space Committees; Eisenhower created the National Aeronautics and Space Administration (NASA); and the satellite program planned new *Explorers*, *Pioneers*, and other unmanned experiments. In the fall of 1958, Project Mercury, the United States' first manned space program, was announced.

Meanwhile, the Soviets pursued a variety of outer space objectives. Soviet spacecraft hit the moon and photographed its dark side. *Sputnik V* launched two dogs into orbit and returned them safely to earth. But despite these Soviet successes, Eisenhower rejected NASA's proposed lunar mission, judging its benefits too narrowly scientific and its cost far too high. He continued to advocate a slow and steady program, with little sense of urgency.

John Kennedy pointed to Eisenhower's lack of initiative in space programs in his 1960 presidential campaign. "We are in a strategic space race with the Russians," he said in a campaign statement, "and we are losing." Referring to space as America's New Frontier, Kennedy created a slogan for his administration. But it took two unsettling events in April 1961 to gain his endorsement of Project Apollo.

Sputnik I on its support stand before launching. The first news of Sputnik was not carried in Soviet newspapers until two days after the launch.

The Mercury-Redstone rocket fails its first test, November 21, 1960. It later successfully carried astronauts Alan B. Shepard, Jr., and Virgil I. (Gus) Grissom into space.

On April 12, Soviet Cosmonaut Yuri Gagarin's first successful manned orbit of the earth put America even further behind in the space race. Despite the Kennedy rhetoric about closing the gap, the Soviet lead seemed greater than ever. Then, less than one week after the Gagarin flight, the American-sponsored invasion of Cuba at the Bay of Pigs collapsed in humiliating failure. Just as the Soviets gained worldwide acclaim in space, the United States was humiliated in Cuba, and—as Kennedy well knew—prestige is not merely a matter of public relations but a real factor in world affairs. The combination of these events led the President, already predisposed toward space exploration, to look to NASA for a way to redeem America's tarnished image. Kennedy had three criteria in mind: the project would have to be spectacular, achievable within the decade, and a guaranteed American "first." Project Apollo fit the bill. "If we can get to the moon before the Russians," said Kennedy, "then we should." Eight years and nearly $24 billion later, on July 20, 1969, the Kennedy program came to fruition. Astronaut Neil Armstrong stepped out onto the surface of the moon and uttered the first words ever spoken on earth's natural satellite. "That's one small step for a man," he said, "one giant leap for mankind."

Twenty-three days before astronaut Alan B. Shepard, Jr., rode into space on the Mercury-Redstone rocket, Soviet cosmonaut Yuri A. Gagarin orbited the earth once.

Tethered to a twenty-five-foot umbilical cord, astronaut Edward H. White II "walks" in space on June 3, 1965. By the end of 1966 the United States had flown ten manned missions; the Soviets had flown none.

The historic first walk by Apollo 11 astronauts Neil A. Armstrong and Edwin E. Aldrin, Jr., on July 20, 1969. Shown here is the Lunar Landing Module and Roving Vehicle (moon buggy) at Hadley Base.

Although the American space program was active before 1961, the Kennedy decision to send men to the moon marked the beginning of its heyday. Gemini, Apollo, Skylab, and the Space Shuttle are all products of the space race. Tremendously successful, American space projects have nonetheless had their detractors. Even at the time, many questioned the wisdom of spending billions on space when millions of Americans were ill-fed, ill-housed, and under-educated. While more time must pass before an even-handed assessment of the American space program is possible, it is evident today that there was not much of a contest; the United States won handily. Whether those feats of technological prowess enhanced American prestige and strengthened the United States international position is more problematic. The space program did, however, provide Americans with a renewed sense of pride and accomplishment.

President John F. Kennedy and Dr. Wernher von Braun. After World War II, German engineer von Braun was instrumental in developing the rocketry that launched the space and moon missions.

Despite the controversy over the billions of dollars spent on the race to the moon, Americans have always gathered to watch rocket launchings. Through television coverage, millions of other people worldwide have followed the American space program.

On March 1, 1962, New York City sponsored a traditional ticker-tape parade for astronaut John H. Glenn, Jr., the first American to orbit the earth. After leaving the space program, Glenn was elected to the U.S. Senate.

States; the two powerful Communist nations were now rivals for influence in the Third World. But the new American President, ignoring the growing Sino-Soviet split, concluded that the United States and Russia were locked in struggle for the hearts and minds of the uncommitted in Asia, Africa, and Latin America.

Calling for a new policy of nation-building, Kennedy advocated financial and technical assistance designed to help Third World nations achieve economic modernization and stable, pro-Western governments. Measures ranging from the formation of the idealistic Peace Corps to the creation of the ambitious Alliance for Progress—a massive economic aid program for Latin America—were part of this effort. Unfortunately, Kennedy relied even more on counterinsurgency and the Green Berets to beat back the Communist challenge.

Southeast Asia offered the gravest test. In land-locked Laos, the Pathet Lao, a pro-Communist rebel group, overthrew an American-backed government in early 1961. In response, the President sent a regiment of marines to nearby Thailand and beefed up the team of 500 military advisers in Laos. But when the Joint Chiefs of Staff warned that American intervention might require as many as 250,000 troops and that they could guarantee victory only "if we are given the right to use nuclear weapons," Kennedy decided to accept a Soviet offer to negotiate. A year later, Russian and American diplomats in Geneva signed an agreement to neutralize Laos.

In nearby South Vietnam, however, Kennedy became involved in a deepening civil conflict. The insurgency began as a spontaneous protest against the repressive policies of Premier Ngo Dinh Diem, who had come to power in 1955 in Saigon with American support. In March 1960, the Communist government of North Vietnam, led by the venerable Ho Chi Minh, began directing efforts of the Viet Cong rebels in the South. As the guerrilla war intensified in the fall of 1961, the President sent two trusted advisers, Walt Rostow and General Maxwell Taylor, to South Vietnam. They returned favoring the dispatch of eight thousand American combat troops. "As an area for the operation of U.S. troops," reported General Taylor, "SVN [South Vietnam] is not an excessively difficult or unpleasant place to operate. . . . The risks of backing into a major

■ *Protesting the policies of the Diem government, a Buddhist monk sets himself aflame in a ritual suicide.*

Asian war by way of SVN," he concluded, "are present but are not impressive."

The President decided against sending in combat troops in 1961, but he authorized substantial increases in economic aid to Diem and in the size of the military mission in Saigon. The number of American advisers grew from fewer than a thousand in 1961 to over sixteen thousand by late 1963. The flow of supplies and the creation of "strategic hamlets," fortified villages designed to protect the peasantry from the Viet Cong, slowed the Communist momentum. American helicopters gave government forces mobility against the Viet Cong for the first time, but by 1963 the situation had again become critical. Diem had failed to win the support of his own people; Buddhist monks set themselves aflame in public protests; and even Diem's own generals plotted his overthrow.

President Kennedy was in a quandary. He realized that the fate of South Vietnam would be determined not by America but by the Vietnamese. "In the final analysis," he said in September 1963, "it is their war. They are the ones who have to win it or lose it." But at the same time,

Kennedy was not prepared to accept the possible loss of all Southeast Asia. Saying it would be "a great mistake" to withdraw from South Vietnam, he told reporters, "Strongly on our mind is what happened in the case of China at the end of World War II, where China was lost. . . . We don't want that." Although aides later claimed he planned to pull out after the 1964 election, Kennedy raised the stakes by tacitly approving a coup that led to Diem's overthrow and death on November 1, 1963. The resulting power vacuum in Saigon made further American involvement in Vietnam almost certain.

Containing Fidel Castro

Kennedy's determination to check global Communist expansion reached a peak of intensity in Cuba. In the 1960 campaign, pointing to the growing ties between the Soviet Union and Fidel Castro's regime, he had accused the Republicans of permitting a "Communist satellite" to arise on "our very doorstep." Kennedy had even issued a statement backing "anti-Castro forces in exile," calling them "fighters for freedom" who held out hope for "overthrowing Castro."

In reality, the Eisenhower administration had been training a group of Cuban exiles in Guatemala since March 1960 as part of a CIA plan to topple the Castro regime. Many of the new President's advisers had doubts about the proposed invasion. Some saw little chance for success because the operation depended heavily on a broad uprising of the Cuban people. Others—notably Senator William Fulbright of Arkansas, chairman of the Foreign Relations Committee—viewed it as an immoral act that would discredit the United States. "The Castro regime is a thorn in the flesh," Fulbright argued, "but it is not a dagger in the heart." The President, however, committed by his own campaign rhetoric and assured of success by the military, decided to go ahead.

On April 17, 1961, fourteen hundred Cuban exiles moved ashore at the Bay of Pigs on the southern coast of Cuba. Even though the United States had masterminded the entire operation, Kennedy insisted on covert action, even canceling at the last minute a planned American air strike on the beachhead. With air superiority, Castro's well-trained forces had no difficulty in quashing the invasion. They killed nearly five hundred exiles and forced the rest to surrender within forty-eight hours.

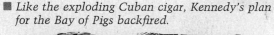
■ Like the exploding Cuban cigar, Kennedy's plan for the Bay of Pigs backfired.

■ Cold War allies: Cuban premier Fidel Castro (right) and Soviet premier Nikita Khrushchev (left).

Aghast at the swiftness of the defeat, President Kennedy took personal responsibility for the failure. In his address to the American people, however, he showed no remorse for arranging the violation of a neighboring country's sovereignty, only regret at the outcome. Above all, he expressed renewed defiance, warning the Soviets that "our restraint is not inexhaustible." He went on to assert that the United States would resist "Communist penetration" in the Western Hemisphere, terming it part of the "primary obligations . . . to the security of our nation." For the remainder of his presidency, Kennedy continued to harass the Castro regime, imposing an economic blockade on Cuba, supporting a continuing series of raids by exile groups operating out of Florida, and failing to stop the CIA from experimenting with bizarre plots to assassinate Fidel Castro.

At the Brink

The climax of Kennedy's crusade came in October 1962 with the Cuban missile crisis. Throughout the summer and early fall, the Soviets engaged in a massive arms buildup in Cuba, ostensibly to protect Castro from an American invasion. In the United States, Republican candidates in the 1962 congressional elections called for a firm American response; Kennedy contented himself with a stern warning against the introduction of any offensive weapons, which he believed would directly threaten American security. Khrushchev publicly denied any such intent, but secretly he took a daring gamble, building twenty-four medium-range (one thousand mile) and eighteen intermediate-range (two thousand mile) missile sites in Cuba. Later he claimed his purpose was purely defensive, but most likely he was responding to the pressures from his own military to close the enormous strategic gap in nuclear striking power that Kennedy had opened.

On October 14, 1962, American U-2 planes finally discovered the missile sites that were nearing completion. As soon as he learned of the Russian action, Kennedy decided to seek a showdown with Khrushchev. Insisting on absolute secrecy, he convened a special group of advisers to consider how to respond.

An initial preference for an immediate air strike gradually gave way to discussion of either a full-scale invasion or a naval blockade. The President and his advisers ruled out diplomacy, rejecting a proposal to offer the withdrawal of obsolete American missiles from Turkey in return for a similar Russian pullout in Cuba. Kennedy finally agreed to a two-step procedure. He would proclaim a quarantine of Cuba to prevent the arrival of new missiles and threaten a nuclear strike to force the removal of those already there. If the Russians did not cooperate, then the United States would invade Cuba and dismantle the missiles by force.

On the evening of October 22, the President informed the nation of the existence of the Soviet missiles and his plans to remove them. He spared no words in blaming Khrushchev for "this clandestine, reckless and provocative threat to world peace," and he made it clear that any missile attack from Cuba would lead to "a full retaliatory response upon the Soviet Union."

For the next six days, the world hovered on the brink of nuclear catastrophe. Khrushchev replied defiantly, accusing Kennedy of pushing mankind "to the abyss of a world nuclear-missile war." In the Atlantic, some sixteen Soviet ships continued on course toward Cuba, while the American navy was deployed to intercept them five hundred miles from the island. In Florida, nearly a quarter of a million men were being concentrated in the largest invasion force ever assembled in the continental United States.

The first break came at midweek when the Soviet ships suddenly halted to avert a confrontation at sea. "We're eyeball to eyeball," commented Secretary of State Dean Rusk, "and I think the other fellow just blinked." Kennedy felt better on Friday when Khrushchev sent him a long, rambling letter offering a face-saving way out— Russia would remove the missiles in return for an American promise never to invade Cuba. The President was ready to accept when a second Russian message raised the stakes by insisting that the American missiles be withdrawn from Turkey. Kennedy refused to bargain; Khrushchev had endangered world peace by putting the missiles in Cuba secretly, and he must take them out immediately. Nevertheless, while the military went ahead with plans for the invasion of Cuba, the President, heeding his brother's advice, decided to make one last appeal for peace. Ignoring the second Russian message, he sent a cable to Khrushchev accepting his original offer.

On Saturday night, October 27, Robert Kennedy—the President's brother and most trusted adviser—met with Soviet ambassador Anatoly Dobrynin to make it clear that this was the last chance to avert nuclear confrontation. "We had to have a commitment by tomorrow that those bases would be removed," Robert Kennedy recalled telling him. "He should understand that if they did not remove those bases, we would remove them." Then the President's brother calmly remarked that if Khrushchev did not back down, "there would be not only dead Americans but dead Russians as well."

At nine the next morning, Khrushchev agreed to remove the missiles in return for Kennedy's promise not to invade Cuba. The crisis was over.

On the surface, Kennedy appeared to have won a striking personal and political victory. His party successfully overcame the Republican challenge in the November elections and his own popularity reached new heights in the Gallup poll. The American people, on the defensive since Sputnik, suddenly felt that they had proved their superiority over the Russians; they were bursting with national pride. Arthur Schlesinger, Kennedy's confidant and later his biographer, claimed that the Cuban crisis showed the "whole world . . . the ripening of an American leadership unsurpassed in the responsible management of power. . . . It was this combination of toughness and restraint, of will, nerve and wisdom, so brilliantly controlled, so matchlessly calibrated, that dazzled the world."

The Cuban missile crisis had more substantial results as well. Shaken by their close call, Kennedy and Khrushchev agreed to install a "hot line" to speed direct communication between Washington and Moscow in an emergency. Long-stalled negotiations over the reduction of nuclear testing suddenly resumed, leading to the limited test ban treaty of 1963, which outlawed tests in the atmosphere while still permitting them underground. Above all, Kennedy displayed a new maturity as a result of the crisis. In a speech at American University in June 1963, he shifted from the rhetoric of confrontation to that of conciliation. Speaking of the Russians, he said, "Our most basic common link is the fact that we all inhabit this planet. We all breathe the same air. We all cherish our children's future. And we are all mortal."

Despite these hopeful words, the missile crisis also had an unfortunate consequence. Those who believed that the Russians understood only the language of force were confirmed in their penchant for a hard line. Hawks who had backed Kennedy's military buildup felt that events had justified a policy of nuclear superiority. The Russian leaders drew similar conclusions. Aware that the United States had a four-to-one advantage in nuclear striking power during the Cuban crisis, one Soviet official told his American counterpart, "Never will we be caught like this again." After 1962, the Soviets embarked on a crash program to build up their navy and to overtake the American lead in nuclear missiles. Within five years, they had the nucleus of a modern fleet and had surpassed the United States in ICBMs. Kennedy's fleeting moment of triumph thus ensured the escalation of the arms race. His legacy was a bittersweet one of short-term success and long-term anxiety.

The New Frontier at Home

Kennedy hoped to change the course of history at home as well as abroad. In the 1960 campaign, he had accused the Republicans of letting the nation drift, pointing to high unemployment, the low rate of economic growth, and the failure to act on such serious national problems as health care and education. His call to get the nation moving again promised a bold new effort at economic stimulation and legislative reform. This appeal was particularly attractive to young people, who had shunned political involvement during the Eisenhower years.

The new administration reflected Kennedy's aura of youth and energy. Major cabinet appointments went to activists—notably Connecticut Governor Abraham Ribicoff as secretary of health, education and welfare; labor lawyer Arthur J. Goldberg as secretary of labor; and Arizona Congressman Stuart Udall as secretary of the interior. The most controversial choice was Robert F. Kennedy, the President's brother, as attorney general. Critics scoffed at his lack of legal experience, leading JFK to note jokingly that he wanted to give Bobby "a little experience before he goes out to practice law." In fact, the President prized his brother's loyalty and shrewd political advice.

Equally important were the members of the White House staff who handled domestic affairs. Like their counterparts in foreign policy, these New Frontiersmen—Kenneth O'Donnell, Theodore Sorenson, Richard Goodwin, and Walter Heller—prided themselves on being tough-minded and pragmatic. In contrast to Eisenhower, Kennedy relied heavily on academics and intellectuals to help him infuse the nation with energy and a new sense of direction.

Kennedy's greatest asset was his own personality. A cool, attractive, and intelligent man, he possessed a sense of style that endeared him to the American public. He invited artists and musicians as well as corporate executives to White House entertainments; and his speeches were filled with references to Emerson and Shakespeare. He seemed to be a new Lancelot, bent on calling forth the best in national life; admirers likened his inner circle to King Arthur's court at Camelot. Reporters loved him, both for his fact-filled and candid press conferences and for his witty comments. Thus, after the Bay of Pigs fiasco, when his standing in the polls actually went up, he remarked, "It's just like Eisenhower. The worse I do, the more popular I get."

The Congressional Obstacle

Neither Kennedy's wit nor charm proved strong enough to break the logjam in Congress. Since the late 1940s, a series of reform bills ranging from health care to federal aid to education had been stalled on Capitol Hill. Kennedy had embraced these traditional Democratic measures in his campaign, labeling them the New Frontier and promising their adoption. Despite his triumph in 1960, however, the election complicated his task. The Democrats lost twenty seats in the House and two in the Senate; even though they retained majorities in both branches, a conservative coalition of northern Republicans and southern Democrats opposed all efforts at reform.

The situation was especially critical in the House, where 101 southern representatives held the balance of power between 160 northern Dem-

With their gala dinners and balls, the Kennedys brought a glamorous tone to the White House. Here, at an April 1962 party for Nobel Prize laureates, poet Robert Frost greets the couple.

ocrats and 174 Republicans. Aided by Speaker Sam Rayburn, Kennedy was able to enlarge the Rules Committee and overcome a traditional conservative roadblock, but the narrowness of the vote, 217 to 212, revealed how difficult it would be to enact reform measures. "There is no sense in raising hell and then not being successful," JFK noted ruefully after Catholic objections to his aid to education bill—which excluded federal money for church schools—led to its defeat in the House. Discouraged, the President gave up the fight for health care in the Senate; he settled instead for a modest increase in the minimum wage and the passage of manpower training and area-redevelopment legislation.

Kennedy had no more success in enacting his program in 1962 and 1963. The conservative coalition stood firmly against education and health-care proposals. Shifting ground, the President did win approval for a trade-expansion act in 1962 designed to lower tariff barriers, but no significant reform legislation was passed. Although the composition of Congress was the main obstacle, Kennedy's greater interest in foreign policy and his distaste for legislative infighting contributed to the outcome. JFK did not enjoy "blarneying with pompous congressmen and simply would not take the time to do it," one observer noted. As a result, the New Frontier languished in Congress.

Economic Advance

Kennedy gave a higher priority to the sluggish American economy. During the last years of Eisenhower's administration, the rate of growth had slowed to just over 2 percent annually, while unemployment rose to new heights with each recession. JFK was determined to recover quickly from the recession he had inherited and to stimulate the economy to achieve a much higher rate of long-term growth. In part, he wanted to redeem his campaign pledge to get the nation moving again; he also felt that the United States had to surpass the Soviet Union in economic vitality.

Kennedy received conflicting advice from the experts. Those who claimed the problem was essentially technological urged manpower-training and area-redevelopment programs to modernize American industry. Others called for long-overdue federal spending to rebuild the nation's public facilities—from parks and playgrounds to decaying bridges and courthouses in the cities. Kennedy sided with the first group, largely because Congress was opposed to massive spending on public works.

The actual stimulation of the economy, however, came not from social programs but from greatly increased appropriations for defense and space. The $6-billion increase in the arms budget in 1961 gave the economy a great lift, and Kennedy's decision to send a man to the moon (a decision made only a week after the Bay of Pigs debacle) eventually cost $25 billion. By 1962, over half the federal budget was devoted to space and defense; aircraft and computer companies in the South and West benefited, but unemployment remained uncomfortably high in the older industrial areas of the Northeast and Midwest.

The administration's desire to keep the inflation rate low led to a serious confrontation with the business community. Kennedy relied on informal wage and price guidelines to hold down the cost of living. But in April 1962, just after the President had persuaded the steelworkers' union to accept a new contract with no wage increases and only a few additional benefits, U.S. Steel head

Roger Blough informed Kennedy that his company was raising steel prices by $6 a ton. Outraged, the President publicly called the increase "a wholly unjustifiable and irresponsible defiance of the public interest" and accused Blough of displaying "contempt for the interests of 185 million Americans." Privately, Kennedy was even blunter. He confided to aides, "My father always told me that all businessmen were sons-of-bitches, but I never believed it till now."

Roger Blough soon gave way. The President's tongue-lashing, along with a cutoff in Pentagon steel orders and the threat of an antitrust suit, forced him to reconsider. When several smaller steel companies refused to raise their prices in hopes of expanding their share of the market, U.S. Steel rolled back its prices. The business community deeply resented the President's action, and when the stock market, which had been rising steadily since 1960, suddenly fell sharply in late May 1962, analysts were quick to label the decline "the Kennedy market."

Troubled by his strained relations with business and by the continued lag in economic growth, the President decided to adopt a more unorthodox approach in 1963. Walter Heller, chairman of the Council of Economic Advisers, had been arguing for a major cut in taxes since 1961 in the belief that it would stimulate consumer spending and give the economy the jolt it needed. The idea of a tax cut and resulting deficits

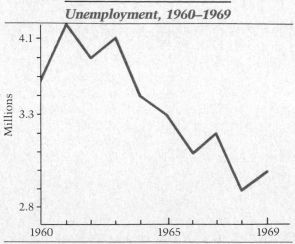

Source: Compiled from U.S. Bureau of the Census, Historical Statistics of the United States, Colonial Times to 1970, *Bicentennial Edition*, Washington, D.C., 1975.

during a period of prosperity went against economic orthodoxy, but Kennedy finally gave his approval. In January 1963, the President proposed a tax reduction of $13.5 billion, asserting that "the unrealistically heavy drag of Federal income taxes on private purchasing power" was the "largest single barrier to full employment." When finally enacted by Congress in 1964, the massive tax cut led to the longest sustained economic advance in American history.

Kennedy's economic policy was far more successful than his legislative efforts. Although the rate of economic growth doubled to 4.5 percent by the end of 1963 and unemployment was reduced substantially, the cost of living rose only 1.3 percent a year. Personal income went up 13 percent in the early 1960s, but the greatest gains came in corporate profits—up 67 percent in this period. Yet critics pointed out that the Kennedy administration failed to close the glaring loopholes in the tax laws that benefited the rich and that it did not make any effort to help those at the bottom by forcing a redistribution of national wealth. And despite the overall economic growth, the public sector continued to be neglected. "I am not sure what the advantage is," complained economist John Kenneth Galbraith, "in having a few more dollars to spend if the air is too dirty to breathe, the water too polluted to drink, the commuters are losing out in the struggle to get in and out of the cities, the streets are filthy, and the schools so bad that the young, perhaps wisely, stay away."

Moving Slowly on Civil Rights

Kennedy faced a genuine dilemma over the issue of civil rights. Despite his own lack of a strong record while in the Senate, he had portrayed himself during the 1960 campaign as a crusader for black rights. He had promised to launch an attack on segregation in the Deep South and had endeared himself to blacks across the nation when he helped win Martin Luther King's release from a Georgia jail. Fear of alienating the large bloc of southern Democrats, however, forced him to play down civil-rights legislation.

The President's solution was to defer congressional action in favor of executive leadership in this area. He directed his brother, Attorney General Robert Kennedy, to continue and expand the Eisenhower administration's efforts to achieve voting rights for southern blacks. To register previously disfranchised blacks, the Justice Department worked with the civil-rights movement —notably the Student Non-Violent Coordinating Committee (SNCC)—in the Deep South. In two years, the Kennedy administration increased the number of voting-rights suits fivefold, but the attorney general could not force the FBI to provide protection for the civil-rights volunteers who risked their lives by encouraging blacks to register. "SNCC's only contact with federal authority," noted one observer, "consisted of the FBI agents who stood by taking notes while local policemen beat up SNCC members."

Other efforts had equally mixed results. Vice-President Lyndon Johnson headed a presidential Commission on Equal Employment Opportunities that worked with defense industries and other government contractors to increase jobs for blacks. But a limited budget and a reliance on voluntary cooperation prevented any dramatic gains; black employment improved only in direct proportion to economic growth in the early 1960s.

Kennedy did succeed in appointing a number of blacks to high government positions: Robert Weaver became chief of the federal housing agency, and Thurgood Marshall, who pleaded the *Brown* v. *Topeka* school desegregation case before the Supreme Court, was named to the United States Circuit Court. On the other hand, among his judicial appointments, Kennedy included one Mississippi jurist who referred to blacks in court as "niggers" and once compared them to "a bunch of chimpanzees."

The civil-rights movement refused to accept Kennedy's indirect approach. In May 1961, the Congress of Racial Equality (CORE) sponsored a "freedom ride" in which a biracial group attempted to test a 1960 Supreme Court decision outlawing segregation in all bus and train stations used in interstate commerce. When they arrived in Birmingham, Alabama, the freedom riders were attacked by a mob of angry whites. "It's the most horrible thing I've ever seen," a Justice Department official reported. "It's terrible, terrible." The attorney general quickly dispatched several hundred federal marshals to protect the freedom riders, but the President was more upset at the

■ *With his diploma in hand, James Meredith leaves the podium after receiving his degree in graduation exercises at the University of Mississippi, September 18, 1963.*

distraction the protestors created. Deeply involved in the Berlin crisis, Kennedy directed one of his aides to get in touch with the leaders of CORE. "Tell them to call it off," he demanded. "Stop them."

In September, after the attorney general finally convinced the Interstate Commerce Commission to issue an order banning segregation in interstate terminals and buses, the freedom rides ended. The Kennedy administration then sought to prevent further confrontations by involving civil-rights activists in its voting drive.

A pattern of belated reaction to southern racism marked the basic approach of the Kennedys. When James Meredith courageously sought admission to the all-white University of Mississippi in 1962, the President and the attorney general worked closely with Mississippi Governor Ross Barnett to avoid violence. A transcript of Robert Kennedy's conversation with Governor Barnett

on September 25 indicates the attorney general's concern for the legal, rather than the moral issues involved:

RFK: *I think the problem is that the federal courts have acted and when there is a conflict between your state and the federal courts under arrangements made some years ago—*

BARNETT: *The institution is supported by the taxpayers of this state and controlled by the Trustees.*

RFK: *Governor, you are a part of the United States.*

BARNETT: *... I am going to treat you with every courtesy, but I won't agree to let that boy get to Ole Miss. I will never agree to that. I would rather spend my whole life in a penitentiary than do that.*

RFK: *I have a responsibility to enforce the laws of the United States.*

BARNETT: *I appreciate that. You have a responsibility. Why don't you let the NAACP run their own affairs and quit cooperating with that crowd? ...*

Despite Barnett's later promise of cooperation, the night before Meredith enrolled at the University of Mississippi, a mob attacked the federal marshals and National Guard troops sent to protect him. The violence left 2 dead and 375 injured, including 166 marshals and 12 guardsmen, but Meredith attended the university and eventually graduated.

In 1963, Kennedy sent the deputy attorney general to face down Governor George C. Wallace, an avowed racist who had promised "to stand in the schoolhouse door" to prevent the integration of the University of Alabama. After a brief confrontation, Wallace yielded to federal authority, and two black students peacefully desegregated the state university.

"I Have a Dream"

Martin Luther King, Jr., finally forced Kennedy to abandon his cautious tactics and come out openly in behalf of racial justice. In the spring of 1963, King began a massive protest in Birmingham, one of the South's most segregated cities. Public marches and demonstrations aimed at integrating public facilities and opening up jobs for blacks quickly led to police harassment and many arrests, including that of King himself. Police Commissioner Eugene "Bull" Connor was determined to crush the civil-rights movement; King was equally determined to prevail. Writing from his cell in Birmingham, he vowed an active campaign to bring the issue of racial injustice to national attention (see the special feature in this chapter).

Bull Connor played directly into King's hands. On May 3, as six thousand children marched in place of the jailed protesters, authorities broke up a demonstration with clubs, snarling police dogs, and high-pressure water hoses strong enough to take the bark off a tree. With a horrified nation watching scene after scene of this brutality on television, the Kennedy administration quickly intevened to arrange a settlement with the Birmingham civic leaders that ended the violence and granted the blacks most of their demands.

More important, Kennedy finally ended his long hesitation and sounded the call for action. "We are confronted primarily with a moral issue," he told the nation on June 11. "It is as old as the Scriptures and is as clear as the American Constitution. . . ." Eight days later, the administration sponsored civil-rights legislation providing equal access to all public accommodations as well as an extension of voting rights for blacks.

Despite pleas from the government for an end to demonstrations and protests, the movement's leaders decided to keep pressure on the administration. They scheduled a massive march on Washington for August 1963. The President and the attorney general persuaded the sponsors to tone down their rhetoric—notably one speech by a SNCC leader which termed the Kennedy legislation "too little, too late." On August 28, more than two hundred thousand marchers gathered for a day-long rally in front of the Lincoln Memorial where they listened to hymns, speeches, and prayers for racial justice (see the chapter opening photo on p. 858). The climax of the event was Martin Luther King's eloquent description of his dream for America. It concluded:

When we let freedom ring, when we let it ring from every village and every hamlet, from every state and every city, we will be able to speed up that day when all God's children, black men and white men, Jews and Gentiles, Protestants and Catholics, will be able to join hands and sing, in the words of that old Negro spiritual. "Free at last! Free at last! Thank God almighty, we are free at last!"

The attempts of blacks to end discrimination and secure their civil rights met violent resistance in Birmingham, Alabama, where police used snarling dogs, fire hoses, clubs, and electric cattle prods to turn back the unarmed demonstrators.

By the time of Kennedy's death in November 1963, his civil-rights legislation was well on its way to passage in Congress. Yet even this achievement did not fully satisfy his critics. For two years, they had waited for him to deliver on his campaign promise to wipe out housing discrimination "with a stroke of the pen." When the executive order on housing was finally issued in November 1962, it proved disappointing; it ignored all past discrimination and applied only to homes and apartments financed by the federal government. For many, Kennedy had raised hopes for racial equality that he never fulfilled.

But unlike Eisenhower, he had provided presidential leadership for the civil-rights movement. His emphasis on executive action gradually paid off, especially in extending voting rights. By early 1964, 40 percent of southern blacks had the franchise, compared to only 28 percent in 1960. Moreover, Kennedy's sense of caution and restraint, painful and frustrating as it was to black activists, had proved well founded. Avoiding an early, and possibly fatal, defeat in Congress, he had waited until a national consensus emerged and then had carefully channeled it behind effective legislation. Behaving very much the way Franklin Roosevelt did in guiding the nation into World War II, Kennedy chose to be a fox rather than a lion on civil rights.

The Supreme Court and Reform

The most active impulse for social change in the early 1960s came from a surprising source: the usually staid and conservative Supreme Court. Under the leadership of Earl Warren, a pragmatic jurist more noted for his political astuteness than his legal scholarship, the Court ventured into new areas. A group of liberal judges—especially William O. Douglas, Hugo Black, and William J. Brennan, Jr.—argued for social reform, while advocates of judicial restraint (such as John Marshall Harlan and Felix Frankfurter) fought stubbornly against the new activism.

In addition to ruling against segregation, the Warren Court in the Eisenhower years had angered conservatives by protecting the constitutional rights of victims of McCarthyism. In *Yates* v. *U.S.* (1956), the judges reversed the conviction of fourteen Communist leaders, claiming that government prosecutors had failed to prove that the accused had actually organized a plot to overthrow the government. Mere advocacy of

Black Voter Registration Before and After the Voting Rights Act of 1965

State	1960	1966	Increase	Percentage of Increase over 1960
Alabama	66,000	250,000	184,000	278.8
Arkansas	73,000	115,000	42,000	57.5
Florida	183,000	303,000	120,000	65.6
Georgia	180,000	300,000	120,000	66.7
Louisiana	159,000	243,000	84,000	52.8
Mississippi	22,000	175,000	153,000	695.4
North Carolina	210,000	282,000	72,000	34.3
South Carolina	58,000	191,000	133,000	229.3
Tennessee	185,000	225,000	40,000	21.6
Texas	227,000	400,000	173,000	76.2
Virginia	100,000	205,000	105,000	105.0

Source: Compiled from U.S. Bureau of the Census, Statistical Abstract of the United States: 1982–83 (103d edition) Washington, D.C., 1982.

The liberal political activism of the Supreme Court during the 1960s drew sharp criticism and led to demands for the impeachment of Chief Justice Earl Warren. This billboard was erected on a highway near Decatur, Illinois, in 1963.

revolution, the Court said, did not justify conviction. In 1957, the Court issued a series of rulings that led dissenting Justice Tom Clark to protest what he saw as giving defendants "a Roman holiday for rummaging through confidential information as well as vital national secrets."

The resignation of Felix Frankfurter in 1962 enabled President Kennedy to appoint Secretary of Labor Arthur Goldberg, a committed liberal, to the Supreme Court. With a clear majority now favoring judicial intervention, the Warren Court issued a series of landmark decisions designed to extend to state and local jurisdictions the traditional rights afforded the accused in federal courts. Thus, in *Gideon* v. *Wainwright* (1963), *Escobedo* v. *Illinois* (1964), and *Miranda* v. *Arizona* (1966), the majority decreed that defendants had to be provided lawyers, had to be informed of their constitutional rights, and could not be interrogated or induced to confess to a crime without defense counsel being present. In effect, the Court extended to the poor and the ignorant those constitutional guarantees that had always been available to the rich and to persons aware of their rights—notably hardened criminals.

The most far-reaching Warren Court decisions came in the area of legislative reapportionment—a "political thicket" that Justice Frankfurter had always refused to enter. In 1962, the Court ruled in *Baker* v. *Carr* that Tennessee had to redistribute its legislative seats to give citizens in Mem-

phis equal representation. Subsequent decisions reinforced the ban on rural overrepresentation as the Court proclaimed that places in all legislative bodies, including the House of Representatives, be allocated on the basis of "people, not land or trees or pastures." The principle of "one man, one vote" greatly increased the political power of cities at the expense of rural areas; it also involved the Court directly in the reapportionment process, frequently forcing judges to draw up new legislative and congressional districts.

The activism of the Supreme Court stirred up a storm of criticism. The rulings that extended protection to criminals and those accused of subversive activity led some Americans to charge that the court was encouraging crime and weakening national security. The John Birch Society, an extreme anti-Communist group, demanded the impeachment of Earl Warren. Decisions banning school prayers and permitting pornography incensed many conservative Americans, who saw the Court as undermining moral values. "They've put the Negroes in the schools," complained one southern congressman, "and now they've driven God out." Legal scholars worried more about the weakening of the Court's prestige as it became more directly involved in the political process. On balance, however, the Warren Court helped achieve greater social justice by protecting the rights of the underprivileged and by permitting dissent and free expression to flourish.

Letter from Birmingham Jail

April 16, 1963

On Good Friday in the spring of 1963, the Reverend Dr. Martin Luther King, Jr., was arrested during a civil-rights parade in Birmingham, Alabama. King, in Birmingham at the request of the local chapter of his Southern Christian Leadership Conference, was held incommunicado for twenty-four hours in solitary confinement and barred from seeing even his lawyer. During his eight days in jail, several Alabama priests, rabbis, and ministers wrote to the local newspaper, asking blacks not to support King's civil-rights efforts. In reply, Dr. King wrote a nine-thousand-word statement, "begun on the margins of the newspaper [and] continued on scraps of writing paper supplied by a friendly Negro trusty, and concluded on a pad my attorneys were eventually permitted to leave me."

My Dear Fellow Clergymen:

While confined here in the Birmingham city jail, I came across your recent statement calling my present activities "unwise and untimely."

. . . I am cognizant of the interrelatedness of all communities and states. I cannot sit idly by in Atlanta and not be concerned about what happens in Birmingham. Injustice anywhere is a threat to justice everywhere. We are caught in an inescapable network of mutuality, tied in a sin-gle garment of destiny. Whatever affects one directly, affects all indirectly.

. . . There can be no gainsaying the fact that racial injustice engulfs this community. Birmingham is probably the most thoroughly segregated city in the United States. Its ugly record of brutality is widely known. Negroes have experienced grossly unjust treatment in the courts. There have been more unsolved bombings of Negro homes and churches in Birmingham than in any other city in the nation. . . .

You may well ask "Why direct action? Why sit-ins, marches and so forth? Isn't negotiation a better path?" You are quite right in calling for negotiation. Indeed, this is the very purpose of direct action. Nonviolent direct action seeks to create such a crisis and foster such a tension that a community which has constantly refused to negotiate is forced to confront the issue. It seeks so to dramatize the issue that it can no longer be ignored. . . .

For years now I have heard the word "Wait!" It rings in the ear of every Negro with piercing familiarity. . . .

We have waited for more than 340 years for our constitutional and God-given rights . . . . But when you have seen vicious mobs lynch your mothers and fathers at will and drown your sisters and brothers at whim; when you have seen hate-filled policemen curse, kick and even kill your black brothers and sisters; when you see the vast majority of your twenty million Negro brothers smothering in an airtight cage of poverty in the midst of an affluent society; when you suddenly find your tongue twisted and your speech stammering as you seek to explain to your six-year-old daughter why she can't go to the public amusement park that has just been advertised on television, and see tears welling up in her eyes when she is told that Funtown is closed to colored children; . . . when you have to concoct an answer for a five-year-old son who is asking "Daddy, why do white people treat colored people so mean?"; when you take a cross-country drive and find it necessary to sleep night after night in the uncomfortable corners of your automobile because no motel will accept you; when you are humiliated day in and day out by nagging signs reading "white" and "colored"; when your first name becomes "nigger," and your middle name becomes "boy" (however old you are) and your last name becomes "John," and your wife and mother are never given the respected title "Mrs."; . . . when you are forever fighting a degenerating sense of "nobodiness"— then you will understand why we find it difficult to wait. . . .

I must make two honest confessions to you, my Christian and Jewish brothers. First, I must confess that over the past few years I have been gravely disappointed with the white moderate. I have almost reached the regrettable conclusion that the Negro's great stumbling block in his stride toward freedom is not the White Citizen's Counciler or the Ku Klux Klanner, but the white moderate, who is more devoted to "order" than to justice; who prefers a negative peace which is the absence of tension to a positive peace which is the presence of justice; who constantly says: "I agree with you in the goal you seek, but I cannot agree with your methods of direct action"; who paternalistically believes he can set the timetable for another man's freedom; who lives by a mythical concept of time and who constantly advises the Negro to wait for a "more convenient season." Shallow understanding from people of good will is more frustrating than absolute misunderstanding from people of ill will. Lukewarm acceptance is much more bewildering than out-

right rejection . . . .

Let me take note of my other major disappointment. I have been so greatly disappointed with the white church and its leadership. Of course, there are some notable exceptions. . . .

. . . But even if the church does not come to the aid of justice, I have no despair about the future. . . . We will reach the goal of freedom in Birmingham and all over the nation, because the goal of America is freedom. Abused and scorned though we may be, our destiny is tied up with America's destiny. Before the pilgrims landed at Plymouth, we were here. Before the pen of Jefferson etched the majestic words of the Declaration of Independence across the pages of History, we were here. For more than two centuries our forebears labored in this country without wages; they made cotton king. . . . If the inexpressible cruelties of slavery could not stop us, the opposition we now face will surely fail. . . .

One day the South will recognize its real heroes. They will be the James Merediths. . . . They will be old, oppressed, battered Negro women, symbolized in a seventy-two-year-old woman in Montgomery, Alabama, who rose up with a sense of dignity and with her people decided not to ride segregated buses, and who responded with ungrammatical profundity to one who inquired about her weariness "My feets is tired, but my soul is at rest." They will be the young high school and college students, the young ministers of the gospel and a host of their elders, courageously and nonviolently sitting in at lunch counters and willingly going to jail for conscience' sake. One day the South will know that when these disinherited children of God sat down at lunch counters, they were in reality standing up for what is best in the American dream and for the most sacred values in our Judeo-Christian heritage. . . .

. . . Let us all hope that the dark clouds of racial prejudice will soon pass away and the deep fog of misunderstanding will be lifted from our fear-drenched communities, and in some not too distant tomorrow the radiant stars of love and brotherhood will shine over our great nation with all their scintillating beauty.

Yours for the cause of Peace and Brotherhood,
Martin Luther King, Jr.

"Let Us Continue"

The New Frontier came to a sudden and violent end on November 22, 1963, when Lee Harvey Oswald assassinated John F. Kennedy during a motorcade in downtown Dallas. The shock of losing the young President, who had become a symbol of hope and promise for a whole generation, stunned the entire world. The American people were bewildered by the rapid sequence of events: the brutal killing of their beloved President; the televised slaying of Oswald by Jack Ruby in the basement of the Dallas police station; the heroic behavior of Kennedy's widow, Jacqueline, at the ensuing state funeral; and the hurried Warren Commission report, which identified Oswald as the lone assassin. Afterward critics would charge that Oswald had been part of a vast conspiracy, but at the time the prevailing national reaction was a numbing sense of loss.

Vice-President Lyndon B. Johnson moved quickly to fill the vacuum left by Kennedy's death. Sworn in on board Air Force One as he returned to Washington, he soon met with a stream of world leaders to reassure them of American political stability. Five days after the tragedy in Dallas, Johnson spoke eloquently to a special joint session of Congress. Recalling JFK's summons in his inaugural address, "Let us begin," the new President declared. "Today in the moment of new resolve, I would say to all my fellow Americans, 'let us continue.'" Asking Congress to enact Kennedy's tax and civil-rights bills as a tribute to the fallen leader, LBJ concluded, "Let us here highly resolve that John Fitzgerald Kennedy did not live or die in vain."

Johnson in Action

Lyndon Johnson suffered from the inevitable comparison with his young and stylish predecessor. LBJ was acutely aware of his own lack of education and polish; he sought to surround himself with Kennedy advisers and insiders, hoping that their learning and sophistication would rub off on him. Johnson's assets were very real—an intimate knowledge of Congress, an incredible energy and determination to succeed, and a fierce ego. When a young marine officer tried to direct him to the proper helicopter, saying, "This one is

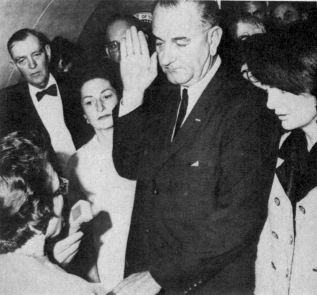

■ *Aboard Air Force One on the return from Dallas to Washington, D.C., Judge Sarah Hughes administers the presidential oath of office to Lyndon Johnson. His wife and JFK's widow look on.*

■ *Moments after this photograph was taken in the Dallas police headquarters, accused presidential assassin Lee Harvey Oswald was fatally shot.*

yours," Johnson replied, "Son, they are all my helicopters."

LBJ's height and intensity gave him a powerful presence; he dominated any room he entered, and he delighted in using his physical power of persuasion. One Texas politician explained why he had given in to Johnson: "Lyndon got me by the lapels and put his face on top of mine and he talked and talked and talked. I figured it was either getting drowned or joining."

Yet LBJ found it impossible to project his intelligence and vitality to large audiences. Unlike Kennedy, he wilted before the camera, turning his televised speeches into stilted and awkward performances. Trying to belie his reputation as a riverboat gambler, he came across like a foxy grandpa, clever and calculating and not to be trusted. He lacked Kennedy's wit and charm, and reporters delighted in describing the way he berated his aides or shocked the nation by baring his belly to show the scar from a recent operation.

Whatever his shortcomings in style, however, Johnson possessed far greater ability than Kennedy in dealing with Congress. He entered the White House with more than thirty years experience in Washington as legislative aide, congressman, and senator. His encyclopedic knowledge of the legislative process and his shrewd manipulation of individual senators had enabled him to become the most influential Senate majority leader in history. Famed for "the Johnson treatment," a legendary ability to use personal persuasion to gain his goals, Johnson in fact relied more on his close ties with the Senate's power brokers —or "whales," as he called them—than on his exploitation of the "minnows."

Above all, Johnson sought consensus. Indifferent to ideology, he had moved easily from New Deal liberalism to oil-and-gas conservatism as his career advanced. He had carefully cultivated Richard Russell of Georgia, leader of the Dixie bloc, but he also had taken Hubert Humphrey, a Minnesota liberal, under his wing. He had performed a balancing act on civil rights, working with the Eisenhower administration on behalf of the 1957 Voting Rights Act, yet carefully weakening it to avoid alienating southern Democrats. When Kennedy dashed Johnson's own intense presidential ambitions in 1960, LBJ had gracefully agreed to be his running mate and had endured the humiliation of the vice-presidency loyally

■ *LBJ was very successful at persuading Congress to enact the legislation he favored. Here he holds the signed bill authorizing his "war on poverty."*

and silently. Suddenly thrust into power, Johnson used his gifts wisely. Citing his favorite scriptural passage from Isaiah, "Come now, and let us reason together, saith the Lord," he concentrated on securing passage of Kennedy's tax and civil-rights bills in 1964.

The tax cut came first. Aware of the power wielded by Senate Finance Committee Chairman Harry Byrd, a Virginia conservative, Johnson astutely lowered Kennedy's projected $101.5-billion budget for 1965 to $97.9 billion. Although Byrd voted against the tax cut, he let the measure out of his committee, telling Johnson, "I'll be working for you behind the scenes." In February, Congress reduced personal income taxes by more than $10 billion, touching off a sustained economic boom. Consumer spending increased by an impressive $43 billion in the next eighteen months, and new jobs opened up at the rate of one million a year.

Johnson was even more influential in passing the Kennedy civil-rights measure. Staying in the background, he encouraged liberal amendments that strengthened the bill in the House. With Hubert Humphrey leading the floor fight in the Senate, Johnson refused all efforts at compromise, counting on growing public pressure to force northern Republicans to abandon their traditional alliance with southern Democrats. Everett M. Dirksen of Illinois, the GOP leader in the Senate, met repeatedly with Johnson at the White House. When LBJ refused to yield, Dirksen finally announced, "The time has come for equality of opportunity in sharing in government, in education, and in employment," and led a Republican vote to end a fifty-seven-day filibuster.

The 1964 Civil Rights Act, signed on July 2, made illegal the segregation of blacks in public facilities, established a Fair Employment Practices Committee to lessen racial discrimination in employment, and protected the voting rights of blacks. An amendment sponsored by segregationists in an effort to weaken the bill added sex to the prohibition of discrimination in Title VII of the act; in the future, women's groups would use this clause to secure government support for greater equality in employment and education.

The Election of 1964

Passage of two key Kennedy measures within six months did not satisfy Johnson. Having established the theme of continuity, he now set out to win the presidency in his own right. Eager to surpass Kennedy's narrow victory in 1960, he hoped to win by a great landslide.

Searching for a cause of his own, LBJ found one in the issue of poverty. Beginning in the late 1950s, economists had warned that the prevailing affluence only disguised a persistent and deep-seated problem of poverty. John Kenneth Galbraith had urged a policy of increased public spending to help the poor, but Kennedy ignored Galbraith's advice. In 1962, however, Michael Harrington's book *The Other America* attracted national attention. Writing with passion and eloquence, Harrington claimed that nearly one fifth of the nation, some thirty-five million Americans, lived in poverty.

Three groups predominated among the poor—blacks, the aged, and households headed by women. The problem, Harrington contended, was that the poor were invisible, living in slums or depressed areas like Appalachia and cut off from the educational facilities, medical care, and employment opportunities afforded more affluent Americans. Moreover, poverty was a vicious cycle. The children of the poor were trapped in the same culture of poverty as their parents, living without hope or knowledge of how to enter the mainstream of American life.

Johnson quickly took over proposals that Kennedy had been developing and made them his own. In his State of the Union address in January 1964, LBJ announced, "This administration, today, here and now, declares unconditional war on poverty in America." Over the next eight months, Johnson fashioned a comprehensive poverty program under the direction of R. Sargent Shriver, Kennedy's brother-in-law. The President added $500 million to existing programs to come up with a $1-billion effort which Congress passed in August 1964.

The new Office of Economic Opportunity (OEO) set up a wide variety of programs, ranging from Head Start for preschoolers to the Job Corps for high-school dropouts in need of vocational training. The emphasis was on self-help, with the government providing money and know-how so that the poor could reap the benefits of neighborhood day-care centers, consumer-education classes, legal-aid services, and adult remedial-reading programs. The level of funding was never high enough to meet the OEO's ambitious goals, and a controversial attempt to include representatives of the poor in the Community Action Program led to bitter political feuding with city and state officials. Nonetheless, the war on poverty, along with the economic growth provided by the tax cut, helped reduce the ranks of the poor by nearly ten million between 1964 and 1967.

For Johnson, the new program established his reputation as a reformer in an election year. He still faced two obstacles. The first was Robert F. Kennedy, the late president's brother who continued as attorney general but who wanted to become vice-president and Johnson's eventual successor in the White House. Desperate to prove his ability to succeed without Kennedy help, LBJ commented, "I don't need that little runt to win," and chose Hubert Humphrey as his running mate.

The other hurdle was the Republican candidate, Senator Barry Goldwater, an outspoken con-

Among those whom LBJ hoped would benefit from the war on poverty were people like Tom Fletcher, an unemployed sawmill worker, and his eight children, shown here (left) greeting the President and Lady Bird. LBJ's declaration of war on poverty soon turned into a blueprint for the "Great Society," an ambitious plan for social improvement that included such projects as the Head Start program (bottom left) and the Job Corps (below).

servative from Arizona. An attractive and articulate man, Goldwater openly advocated a rejection of the welfare state and a return to unregulated free enterprise. To Johnson's delight, Goldwater chose to place ideology ahead of political expediency. The senator spoke out boldly against the Tennessee Valley Authority, denounced Social Security, and advocated a hawkish foreign policy. "In Your Heart, You Know He's Right," read the Republican slogan, leading the Democrats to reply, "Yes, Far Right," and in reference to a careless Goldwater comment about using nuclear weapons, Johnson backers punned, "In Your Heart, You Know He Might."

Johnson stuck carefully to the middle of the road, embracing the liberal reform program—which he now called "The Great Society"—while stressing his concern for balanced budgets and fiscal orthodoxy. The more Goldwater sagged in the polls, the harder Johnson campaigned, determined to achieve his treasured landslide. On election day, LBJ did even better than FDR had in 1936, taking 61.1 percent of the popular vote and sweeping the electoral college; Goldwater carried only Arizona and five states of the Deep South.

The Election of 1964

Candidate	Party	Popular Vote	Electoral Vote
Johnson	Democrat	43,126,584	486
Goldwater	Republican	27,177,838	52

Equally important, the Democrats achieved huge gains in Congress, controlling the House by a margin of 295 to 140 and the Senate by 68 to 32. Kennedy's legacy and Goldwater's candor had enabled Johnson to break the conservative grip on Congress for the first time in a quarter of a century.

The Triumph of Reform

LBJ moved quickly to secure his legislative goals. Despite solid majorities in both Houses, including seventy freshman Democrats who had ridden into office on his coattails, Johnson knew he would have to enact the Great Society as swiftly as possible. "You've got to give it all you can, that first year," he told an aide. "Doesn't matter what kind of majority you come in with. You've got just one year when they treat you right, and before they start worrying about themselves."

Johnson gave two traditional Democratic reforms—health care and education—top priority. Aware of strong opposition to a comprehensive medical program, LBJ settled for Medicare, which mandated health insurance under the Social Security program for Americans over age sixty-five, with a supplementary Medicaid program for the indigent. To symbolize the end of a long struggle, Johnson flew to Independence, Missouri, so that Truman could witness the ceremonial signing of the Medicare law.

LBJ overcame the religious hurdle on education by supporting a child-benefit approach, allocating federal money to advance the education of students in parochial as well as public schools. The Elementary and Secondary Education Act of 1965 provided over $1 billion in federal aid, with the largest share going to school districts with the highest percentage of impoverished pupils. During his administration, federal aid to education increased sharply.

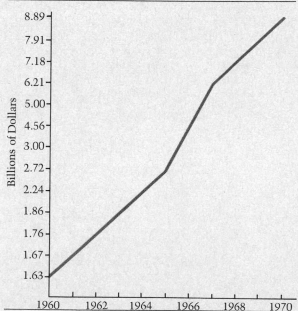

Federal Aid to Education, 1960–1970

Source: Compiled from U.S. Bureau of the Census, Historical Statistics of the United States, Colonial Times to 1970, Bicentennial Edition, Washington, D.C., 1975.

Civil rights proved to be the most difficult test of Johnson's leadership. Martin Luther King, concerned that three million southern blacks were still denied the right to vote, in early 1965 chose Selma, Alabama, as a test case. The white authorities in Selma, led by Sheriff James Clark, used cattle prods and bullwhips to break up the demonstrations and jailed over two thousand blacks. Johnson intervened in March, after TV cameras showed Sheriff Clark's deputies brutally halting a march from Selma to Montgomery. The President ordered the Alabama National Guard to federal duty to protect the demonstrators, had the Justice Department draw up a new voting-rights bill, and personally addressed the Congress on civil rights. "I speak tonight for the dignity of man and the destiny of democracy," he began. Calling the denial of the right to vote "deadly wrong," LBJ issued a compelling call to action. "Their cause must be our cause too. Because it is not just Negroes, but really it is all of us who must overcome the crippling legacy of bigotry and injustice."

Five months later, Congress passed the Voting Rights Act of 1965. Once again Johnson had worked with Senate Republican leader Dirksen to break a southern filibuster and assure passage of a measure. The act banned literacy tests in states and counties in which less than half the population had voted in 1964 and provided for federal registrars in these areas to assure blacks the franchise.

The results were dramatic. In less than a year, 166,000 blacks were added to the voting rolls in Alabama, while black registration went up 400 percent in Mississippi. By the end of the decade, the percentage of eligible black voters who had registered had risen from 40 to 65 percent. For the first time since Reconstruction, blacks were playing an active and effective role in southern politics.

Before the Eighty-ninth Congress ended its first session in the fall of 1965, it had passed eighty-nine bills. These included measures to create two new cabinet departments (Transportation, and Housing and Urban Affairs); acts to provide for highway safety and to ensure clean air and water; and large appropriations for higher education, public housing, and the continuing war on poverty. In nine months, Johnson had enacted the entire Democratic reform agenda, moving the nation beyond the New Deal by mandating federal concern for health, education, and the quality of life in both city and countryside.

The man responsible for this great leap forward, however, had failed to win the public adulation he so deeply desired. His legislative skills had made the most of the opportunities offered by the 1964 Democratic landslide, but the people did not respond to Johnson's leadership with the warmth and praise they had showered on Kennedy. Reporters continued to portray him as a crude wheeler-dealer; as a maniac who drove around Texas back roads at ninety miles an hour, one hand on the wheel and the other holding a glass of beer; or as a bully who picked up his dog by the ears. No one was more aware of this lack of affection than LBJ himself. His public support, he told an aide, is "like a Western river, broad but not deep." Tragically, Johnson was right. When foreign-policy problems soon eroded his popularity, few remembered his remarkable legislative achievements. Yet in one brief outburst of reform, he had accomplished more than any president since FDR.

All the Way with LBJ

Lyndon Johnson's strengths as a legislative leader were offset by his liabilities in foreign policy. LBJ had no background or feeling for international affairs. Even more than in domestic policy, he relied heavily on Kennedy's advisers—notably Secretary of State Rusk, Secretary of Defense McNamara, and McGeorge Bundy (the national security adviser until he was replaced in 1966 by the even more hawkish Walt Rostow).

Despite his lack of experience in world affairs, Johnson brought deeply held beliefs to bear on diplomatic problems. "What I learned as a boy in my teens and in college about World War I was that it was our lack of strength and failure to show stamina," he told biographer Doris Kearns, "that got us into that war." Watching the failure of isolation and appeasement in the 1930s only reinforced his conviction—shared by his generation—that war came from weakness, not from strength. He had also seen the devastating political impact of the Communist triumph in China on the Democratic party in the 1940s. "I am not going to lose Vietnam," he told the American ambassador to Saigon just after taking office in 1963. "I am not going to be the President who saw Southeast Asia go the way China went."

Aware of the problem Castro had caused John Kennedy, LBJ moved firmly to contain communism in the Western Hemisphere. When a military junta overthrew a leftist regime in Brazil, Johnson offered covert aid and open encouragement. He was equally forceful in compelling Panama to restrain rioting aimed at the continued American presence in the Canal Zone.

In 1965, to block the possible emergence of a Castro-type government, LBJ sent twenty thousand American troops to the Dominican Republic. Johnson's flimsy justification—ranging from the need to protect American tourists to a dubious list of suspected Communists among the rebel leaders—served only to alienate liberal critics in the United States, particularly Senate Foreign Relations Committee Chairman William Fulbright, a former Johnson favorite. The intervention ended in 1966 with the election of a conservative government. Senator Fulbright, however, continued his criticism of Johnson's foreign policy by publishing *The Arrogance of Power*, a biting analysis of the fallacies of containment. Fulbright's defection symbolized a growing gap between the President and liberal intellectuals; the more LBJ struggled to uphold the traditional Cold War policies he had inherited from Kennedy, the more he found himself under attack from Congress, the media, and the universities.

The Vietnam Dilemma

The situation in Vietnam plagued Johnson from the outset. He took office only three weeks after the coup that had removed Diem and left a vacuum of power. In 1964, seven different governments ruled South Vietnam; there were three governments within one month. According to an American officer, the atmosphere in Saigon "fairly smelled of discontent," with "workers on strike, students demonstrating, [and] the local press pursuing a persistent campaign of criticism of the new government." Resisting pressure from the Joint Chiefs of Staff for direct American military involvement, LBJ simply continued Kennedy's policy of economic and technical assistance. He sent in seven thousand more military

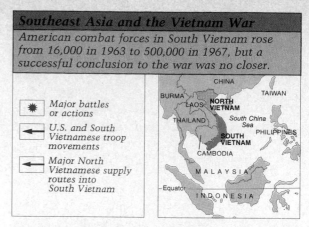

Southeast Asia and the Vietnam War

American combat forces in South Vietnam rose from 16,000 in 1963 to 500,000 in 1967, but a successful conclusion to the war was no closer.

- Major battles or actions
- U.S. and South Vietnamese troop movements
- Major North Vietnamese supply routes into South Vietnam

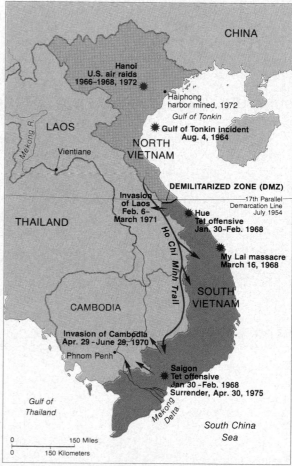

advisers and an additional $50 million in aid, but he insisted it was still up to the Vietnamese themselves to win the war. At the same time, he expanded American support for covert operations, including amphibious raids on the North.

These undercover activities led directly to the

Gulf of Tonkin affair. On August 2, 1964, North Vietnamese torpedo boats attacked the *Maddox*, an American destroyer engaged in electronic intelligence-gathering in the Gulf of Tonkin, in the mistaken belief that the American ship had been involved in a South Vietnamese raid nearby. The *Maddox* escaped unscathed, but to show American resolve, the navy sent in another destroyer, the *C. Turner Joy*. On the evening of August 4, the two destroyers, responding to sonar and radar contacts, opened fire on North Vietnamese gunboats in the area. Later investigation suggested that the North Vietnamese gunboats had not attacked the American ships, but Johnson ordered retaliatory air strikes on North Vietnamese naval bases.

The next day the President asked Congress to pass a resolution authorizing him to take "all necessary measures to repel any armed attack against the forces of the United States and to prevent further aggression." He did not in fact need this authority; he had already ordered the retaliatory air strike without it. Later, critics charged that LBJ wanted a blank check from Congress to carry out the future escalation of the Vietnam War, but such a motive is unlikely. He had already rejected immediate military intervention. In part, he wanted the Gulf of Tonkin Resolution to demonstrate to North Vietnam the American determination to defend South Vietnam at any cost. "The challenge we face in Southeast Asia today," he told Congress, "is the same challenge that we have faced with courage and that we have met with strength in Greece and Turkey, in Berlin and Korea . . . ." He also wanted to preempt the Vietnam issue from his Republican opponent, Barry Goldwater, who had been advocating a tougher policy. By taking a firm stand on the Gulf of Tonkin incident, Johnson could both impress the North Vietnamese and outmaneuver a political rival at home.

Congress responded with alacrity. The House acted unanimously, while only two senators (Wayne Morse of Oregon and Ernest Gruening of Alaska) voted against the Gulf of Tonkin Resolution. Johnson appeared to have won a spectacular victory. His standing in the Gallup poll shot up from 42 to 72 percent, and he had effectively blocked Goldwater from exploiting Vietnam as a campaign issue.

In the long run, however, this easy victory

"Only Thing We're Sure Of—There Is a Tonkin Gulf!"

■ *Although the Gulf of Tonkin Resolution won the nearly unanimous approval of Congress, Johnson's action drew harsh criticism later.*

proved very costly. Once having used force against North Vietnam, LBJ was more likely to do so in the future. And although he apparently had no intention of widening the conflict in August 1964, the congressional resolution was phrased broadly enough to enable him to use whatever level of force he wished—including unlimited military intervention. Above all, when he did wage war in Vietnam, he left himself open to the charge of deliberately misleading Congress. Presidential credibility proved to be Johnson's ultimate Achilles' heel; in that sense, his political downfall began with the Gulf of Tonkin Resolution.

Escalation

The full-scale American involvement in Vietnam began in 1965 in a series of steps designed primarily to prevent a North Vietnamese victory. With the political situation in Saigon growing more hopeless every day, the President's advisers urged

Although the United States conducted thousands of air strikes over North Vietnam and committed half a million troops to the South, it failed to win the advantage. North Vietnamese and Viet Cong continued to disappear silently into the dense foliage of the jungle after surprise attacks. Bill Mauldin depicts Johnson's two options—all-out war or complete pullout—as equally precarious.

the bombing of the North as the only conceivable solution. American air attacks would serve several purposes: they would block North Vietnamese infiltration routes, make Hanoi pay a heavy price for its role, and lift the sagging morale of the South Vietnamese. But most important, as McGeorge Bundy reported after a visit to Pleiku (site of a Viet Cong attack on an American base which took nine lives), "Without new U.S. action defeat appears inevitable—probably not in a matter of weeks or perhaps even months, but within the next year or so." Johnson responded in February 1965 by ordering a long-planned aerial bombardment of selected North Vietnamese targets.

The air strikes, aimed at impeding the Communist supply line and damaging Hanoi's economy, proved ineffective. In April, Johnson authorized the use of American ground forces in South Vietnam, but he restricted them to defensive operations intended to protect American air bases. The Joint Chiefs, as well as civilian advisers like Walt Rostow, then pressed the President for both unlimited bombing and an invasion of the North. Rejecting the clear-cut alternatives of withdrawal or the massive use of force, LBJ settled for a steady military escalation designed to compel Hanoi to accept a diplomatic solution. In July, the President permitted a gradual increase in

The Strategists

the bombing of North Vietnam and allowed American ground commanders to conduct combat operations in the South. Most ominously, he approved the immediate dispatch of fifty thousand troops to Vietnam and the future commitment of fifty thousand more.

These July decisions formed "an open-ended commitment to employ American military forces as the situation demanded," writes historian George Herring, and they were "the closest thing to a formal decision for war in Vietnam." Convinced that withdrawal would destroy American credibility before the world and that an invasion of the North would lead to World War III, Johnson opted for large-scale but limited military intervention. Moreover, LBJ feared the domestic consequences of either extreme. A pullout could cause a massive political backlash at home, as conservatives condemned him for betraying South Vietnam to communism. All-out war, however, would mean the end of his social programs. Once Congress focused on the conflict, he explained to biographer Doris Kearns, "that bitch of a war" would destroy "the woman I really loved—the Great Society." So he settled for a limited war, committing a half-million American troops to battle in Southeast Asia, all the while pretending it was a minor engagement and refusing to ask the American people for the support and sacrifice required for victory.

Lyndon Johnson was not solely responsible for the Vietnam War. He inherited both a policy that assumed that Vietnam was a vital national interest and a deteriorating situation in Saigon that demanded a more active American role. Truman, Eisenhower, and Kennedy had taken the United States deep into the Vietnam maze; it was Johnson's fate to have to find a way out. But LBJ must bear full responsibility for the way he tried to resolve his dilemma. The failure to confront the people with the stark choices they faced, the insistence on secrecy and deceit, the refusal to acknowledge that he had committed the nation to a dangerous military involvement—these were Johnson's sins in Vietnam. His own lack of self-confidence in foreign policy and his fear of domestic reaction led directly to his undoing.

In retrospect, 1965 marks a watershed in recent American history. It was the year that saw the culmination of the reform impulse with the

	Chronology
1960	John F. Kennedy narrowly wins presidential election
1961	JFK establishes Peace Corps (March) U.S.-backed Bay of Pigs invasion crushed by Cubans (April) JFK commits U.S. to landing a man on the moon by 1969 (May)
1962	James Meredith is first black to enroll at University of Mississippi (September) Cuban missile crisis takes world to brink of nuclear war (October)
1963	United States, Great Britain, and USSR sign Limited Nuclear Test Ban Treaty (August) JFK assassinated; Lyndon B. Johnson sworn in as president (November)
1964	President Johnson declares war on poverty (January) Congress passes Civil Rights Act (July) Congress overwhelmingly passes Gulf of Tonkin Resolution (August) Johnson wins presidency in landslide victory (November)
1965	Martin Luther King, Jr., leads Selma-Montgomery march (March) Medicare legislation provides aged with medical care (July) LBJ commits 50,000 American troops to combat in Vietnam (July) Johnson signs Voting Rights Act (August) 184,300 U.S. troops fighting in Vietnam (December)

greatest outpouring of welfare legislation since the New Deal. But it was also the year which saw the policy of global containment reach its fullest expression in the jungles of Southeast Asia. Lyndon Johnson set out to fulfill the mandate he had inherited from John Kennedy—to enact a stalled reform program and halt any Communist advance abroad. The tragedy of Lyndon Johnson was not that he ignored his obligations, but that he attempted to carry them out, only to find that his efforts did not bring him the acclaim and stature that he so desperately wanted.

For the American people, 1965 ushered in a new era of turmoil and unrest. The traditional reliance on government action to achieve greater affluence and wider opportunities for all Americans gave way to a rejection of liberalism by both the left and the right. The search for order abroad provoked an even angrier reaction, and Vietnam became a symbol of national humiliation and shame. The years after 1965 would find the nation seeking new political values to replace those shattered under Kennedy and Johnson. It would prove to be a long and difficult quest.

Recommended Reading

The best general treatment of the political and diplomatic trends of the 1960s is Jim F. Heath, *Decade of Disillusionment* (1975), which stresses the continuity in policy between the Kennedy and Johnson administrations. The debate over the merits of Kennedy's performance in the White House is reflected in Arthur M. Schlesinger, Jr., *A Thousand Days* (1965), a highly laudatory view by a JFK partisan, and in Bruce Miroff, *Pragmatic Illusions* (1976), which offers a radical critique of both foreign and domestic aspects of the New Frontier. By far the most complete and analytical study of Kennedy's foreign policy is Roger Hilsman, *To Move a Nation* (1967), which is particularly strong on Vietnam and the Cuban missile crisis.

Eric Goldman has provided the most comprehensive account of the Johnson administration in *The Tragedy of Lyndon Johnson* (1969). Like Schlesinger, Goldman writes both as historian and White House insider, but he balances his sympathetic treatment of the Great Society with a critical view of LBJ's foreign policy. Another insider, Harry McPherson, offers a candid portrait of Johnson both as Senate majority leader and president in *A Political Education* (1972). For the Vietnam War, the most balanced and reliable survey is George Herring, *America's Longest War* (1979).

Additional Bibliography

Kennedy's career before he became president is discussed in James MacGregor Burns, *John Kennedy*, 2d ed. (1961); Joan Blair and Clay Blair, Jr., *The Search for JFK* (1976); and Herbert Parmet, *Jack* (1980). Favorable evaluations of the Kennedy presidency include Theodore Sorenson, *Kennedy* (1965); Benjamin Bradlee, *Conversations with Kennedy* (1975); and Lewis J. Paper, *The Promise and the Performance* (1975). For a more critical view, see Henry Fairlie, *The Kennedy Promise* (1973) and Garry Wills, *The Kennedy Imprisonment* (1981), the latter dealing with Robert and Edward Kennedy as well. The best-balanced account is Herbert Parmet, *JFK: The Presidency of John F. Kennedy* (1983). William Manchester, *Death of a President* (1967), gives the standard view of JFK's assassination; the best of the many dissenting accounts is Edward J. Epstein, *Inquest* (1966).

British journalist Louis Heren offers an objective and lucid survey of the Johnson presidency in *No Hail, No Farewell* (1970). Other books on LBJ include the President's memoirs, *The Vantage Point* (1971); Robert Novak and Rowland Evans, *Lyndon B. Johnson* (1966); Doris Kearns, *Lyndon Johnson and the American Dream* (1976); Merle Miller, *Lyndon* (1980); and two books that focus on his Texas background, Alfred Steinberg, *Sam Johnson's Boy* (1965) and Ronnie Dugger, *The Politician* (1982). The most detailed account of Johnson's early career is Robert Caro's critical volume *The Path to Power* (1982); for a briefer but more astute assessment of Johnson's complex character, see George Reedy, *Lyndon Johnson: A Memoir* (1982). Robert A. Divine, ed., *Exploring the Johnson Years* (1981) contains seven essays surveying major themes of the Johnson administration.

For political developments in the first half of the sixties, see Theodore White, *The Making of the President* (1961), the first in a series of election books; Sidney Kraus, *The Great Debates* (1962) on the Nixon-Kennedy TV debates; and two memoirs by prominent Democrats, Larry O'Brien, *No Final Victories* (1974) and Hubert H. Humphrey, *The Education of a Public Man* (1976).

Books on economic developments include Seymour Harris, *Economics of the Kennedy Years* (1964); Hobart Rowen, *The Free Enterprisers* (1964); and Jim F. Heath, *John F. Kennedy and the Business Community* (1969). Among studies of the Supreme Court are Alexander Bickel, *Politics and the Warren Court* (1965); Richard C. Cortner, *The Apportionment Cases* (1970); Anthony Lewis, *Gideon's Trumpet* (1965); and G. Edward White, *Earl Warren* (1982).

Victor S. Navasky's account of Robert Kennedy as attorney general, *Kennedy Justice* (1971) is quite critical. More sympathetic books on the same topic are Arthur Schlesinger, Jr., *Robert Kennedy and His Times* (1976); Carl Brauer, *John F. Kennedy and the Second Reconstruction* (1977); and Harris Wofford, *Of Kennedys and Kings* (1980). For civil-rights developments under Johnson, consult Benjamin Muse, *The American Negro Revolution* (1969) and David Garrow, *Protest at Selma* (1976).

The Great Society, particularly in regard to welfare and the war on poverty, can be traced in John C. Donovan, *The Politics of Poverty* (1973); Gilbert Steiner, *The State of Welfare* (1971); Sar Levitan, *The Great Society's Poor Law* (1969); James T. Patterson, *America's Struggle Against Poverty* (1982); and Julie Roy Jeffrey, *Education for the Children of the Poor* (1976).

Kennedy's foreign policy is subjected to critical scrutiny in Richard J. Walton, *Cold War and Counterrevolution* (1972) and Louise FitzSimmons, *The Kennedy Doctrine* (1972). Philip Geyelin analyzes LBJ's foreign-policy weaknesses in *Lyndon B. Johnson and the World* (1966), while Walt W. Rostow defends both the Kennedy and Johnson records in *The Diffusion of Power* (1972). Concerning nuclear weapons in the 1960s, consult Michael Mandelbaum, *The Nuclear*

Question (1979); Desmond Ball, *Politics and Force Levels* (1981); and Harland B. Moulton, *Nuclear Superiority and Parity* (1972).

On Latin America, Theodore Draper, *Castro's Revolution* (1962); Peter Wyden, *The Bay of Pigs* (1979); Elie Abel, *The Missile Crisis* (1966); Robert F. Kennedy, *Thirteen Days* (1968); Graham Allison, *The Essence of Decision* (1971); and Herbert Dinerstein, *The Making of the Missile Crisis* (1976) all deal with aspects of the Cuban problem. Books on Johnson's intervention in the Dominican Republic include John B. Martin, *Overtaken by Events* (1966); Jerome Slater, *Intervention and Negotiation* (1970); Abraham Lowenthal, *The Dominican Intervention* (1972); and Piero Gleijeses, *The Dominican Crisis* (1976).

David Halberstam, *The Best and the Brightest* (1972) focuses on decision-making in Washington in regard to the Vietnam War. Other books on Vietnam are Neil Sheehan, ed., *The Pentagon Papers* (1971); Chester Cooper, *The Lost Crusade* (1970); Robert Shaplen, *The Lost Revolution* (1965); Leslie H. Gelb and Richard K. Betts, *The Irony of Vietnam* (1979); and two works on the Gulf of Tonkin incident, Joseph C. Goulden, *Truth Is the First Casualty* (1969) and Anthony Austin, *The President's War* (1971).

Biographies and memoirs relating to foreign policy include Warren Cohen, *Dean Rusk* (1980); Chester Bowles, *Promises to Keep* (1971); Glen T. Seaborg, *Kennedy, Khrushchev and the Test Ban* (1982); and Thomas Powers, *The Man Who Kept the Secrets* (1979), which uses the career of Richard Helms to illuminate the history of the CIA.

chapter 31

PROTEST AND REACTION: FROM VIETNAM TO WATERGATE

"We are the people of this generation, bred in at least modest comfort, housed now in universities, looking uncomfortably to the world we inherit." So began the preamble to the Port Huron Statement, a manifesto of the newly reorganized Students for a Democratic Society (SDS) that became the call to arms for an entire generation. Like most revolutions, this one began small. Only fifty-nine delegates attended the convention held at a union summer camp in Port Huron, Michigan, in June 1962. The two main organizers, Al Haber and Tom Hayden, recent graduates of the University of Michigan, hoped to transform their small student-protest group into the vehicle that would rid American society of poverty, racism, and violence.

Their timing was perfect. College enrollments were climbing rapidly as a result of the post-World War II baby boom and growing affluence. There were twenty-seven million young people between the ages of fourteen and twenty-four in 1960; before the end of the decade, more than half the American population would be under age thirty. And many, repelled by the crass materialism of American life—with its endless suburbs and shopping centers—were ready to embrace a new life-style based on the belief that "man is sensitive, searching, poetic, and capable of love." They were ready to create what Jack Newfield called "a new adversary culture based on community and psychic liberation. Drugs, rock music, underground papers, long hair, colorful dress and liberated sex," he explained, "are all part of it."

In some ways, the sixty-six-page proposal adopted at Port Huron was prosaic, repeating many conventional liberal reforms, such as expanded public housing and broader health-insurance programs. But it offered a startling new approach by advocating "participatory democracy" as its main tactic for social change. "We seek the establishment of a democracy of individual participation" in order to achieve two goals: "that the individual share in those social decisions determining the quality and direction of his life" and "that society be organized to encourage independence in men." In contrast to both traditional liberalism and old-fashioned socialism, the SDS sought salvation through the individual rather than the group. Personal control of one's life and destiny, not simply the creation of new bureaucracies, became the hallmark of the New Left.

In the next few years, the SDS grew phenomenally. The 10 original campus chapters swelled to 151 by 1966; the Port Huron Statement, despite its length, was distributed across the nation—20,000 copies by 1964; 40,000 two years later. Spurred on by the Vietnam War and massive campus unrest, the SDS could count more than 100,000 followers and was responsible for disruptions at nearly 1000 colleges in 1968. Yet its very emphasis on the individual and its fear of bureaucracy left it leaderless and subject to division and disunity. By 1970 a split between factions, some of which were given to violence, led to its complete demise.

The meteoric career of the SDS symbolized the turbulence of the 1960s. For a brief time, it seemed as though the nation's youth had gone berserk, indulging in a wave of experimentation with drugs, sex, and rock music. Older Americans felt that all the nation's traditional values, from the Puritan work ethic to the family, were under attack. In fact, only a minority of American youth joined in the cultural insurgency.

In small towns and among blue-collar workers in the cities, young people went to Friday-night high-school football games, cheered John Wayne as he wiped out the Viet Cong in the movie, *The Green Berets*, and attended church with their parents on Sunday. The rebellion was generally limited to children of the upper middle class, products of "economic surplus and spiritual starvation." But like the flappers of the 1920s, they set the tone for an entire era and left a lasting impression on American society.

Years of Turmoil

The agitation of the 1960s was at its height from 1965 to 1968, the years that marked the escalation of the Vietnam War. Disturbances that began on college campuses quickly spread to infect the entire society, from the ghettos of the cities to the lettuce fields of the Southwest. All who felt disadvantaged—students, blacks, browns, women, hippies—took to the streets to give vent to their feelings.

The Student Revolt

The first sign of student rebellion came in the fall of 1964 at the prestigious University of California at Berkeley. A small group of radical students resisted university efforts to deny them a place to solicit volunteers and funds for off-campus causes. Forming the Free Speech Movement (FSM), they struck back by occupying administration buildings and blocking the arrest of a nonstudent protester. For the next two months, the campus was in turmoil. The administration overreacted, calling in the police; the faculty, predictably, condemned the radicals' tactics but supported their goals; the rest of the student body, distraught at the size, complexity, and impersonality of the university, rallied behind the FSM.

In the end, the protesters won the rights of free speech and association that they championed, and youth everywhere had a new model for effective direct action. The hero was Mario Savio, a student who had eloquently summed up the cause by likening the university to a great machine and telling others "you've got to put your bodies upon the gears, and upon the wheels, upon the levers, upon all the apparatus, and you've got to make it stop."

The Free Speech Movement at Berkeley offered many insights into the causes of campus unrest. It was fueled in part by student suspicion of an older, Depression-born generation that viewed affluence as the answer to all problems. The catchword of the movement was coined by activist Jack Weinberg in the midst of the turmoil: "Don't trust anyone over thirty." Unable to exert much influence on the power structure that directed the consumer society, the students turned on the university, which they viewed as the faithful servant of the corporate and political elite as it trained hordes of technicians to operate the new computers, harbored the research laboratories that perfected dreadful weapons, and regimented its students with IBM punch cards. The feeling of powerlessness that underlay the Berkeley riots were best revealed by the protester carrying the sign that read, "I am a UC student. Please don't bend, fold, spindle or mutilate me."

War, racism, and poverty were the three great evils that student radicals addressed. Many were involved first in the civil-rights cause, but after

Powerless but determined to gain the "Establishment's" attention, the children of the upper middle class began their crusade against poverty, racism, and war by "taking it to the streets."

As outrage about Vietnam grew, the SDS was able to enlist the support of prominent entertainers like Joan Baez, shown here at a protest rally in Texas.

In a scene that was to be repeated countless times across the nation, unarmed protestors faced a cordon of army troops. This confrontation took place at the Pentagon in October 1967.

blacks began to take over the leadership in this area by 1965, white militants found a new issue—the Vietnam War. The first student teach-ins began at the University of Michigan in March 1965; soon they spread to campuses across the nation. More than twenty thousand protesters, under SDS auspices, gathered in Washington in April to listen to entertainers Joan Baez and Judy Collins sing antiwar songs and hear journalist I. F. Stone and Senator Ernest Gruening of Alaska, who voted against the Gulf of Tonkin Resolution, denounce Johnson's war. "End the War in Vietnam Now, Stop the Killing," read the signs.

As the fighting in Southeast Asia intensified in 1966 and 1967, the protests grew larger and the slogans more extreme. "Hey, Hey, LBJ, How Many Kids Have You Killed Today?" chanted students as they proclaimed, "Hell, No, We Won't Go!" At the Pentagon in October 1967, over one hundred thousand demonstrators—mainly students, but housewives, teachers, and young professionals as well—confronted a cordon of military policemen guarding the heart of the nation's war machine. From the windows above, Secretary of Defense McNamara and his generals looked down on the protesters. "The troops you employ belong to us and not to you," an SDS leader shouted up to them through his bullhorn. "They don't belong to the generals."

The climax came in the spring of 1968. Driven both by opposition to the war and concern for social justice, the SDS and black radicals at Columbia University joined forces in April. They seized five buildings, effectively paralyzing one of the country's leading colleges. After eight days of tension, the New York City police regained control. In the melee more than two hundred students were injured and seven hundred were arrested. The brutal repression quickened the pace of protest elsewhere. Students held sit-ins at more than forty colleges, ranging from Cheyney State in Pennsylvania to Northwestern in Illinois. Violent marches and arrests took place at sixty others.

The students failed to stop the war, but they did succeed in gaining a voice in their education. University administrations allowed undergraduates to sit on faculty committees to plan the curriculum and gave up their once rigid control of dormitory and social life. But the students' greatest impact lay outside politics and the campus.

They spawned a cultural uprising that transformed the manners and morals of America.

The Cultural Revolution

In contrast to the political revolt of the elitist SDS, the cultural rebellion by youth in the sixties was pervasive. Led by college students, young people challenged the prevailing adult values, in clothing, hairstyles, sexual conduct, work habits, and music. Blue jeans and love beads took the place of business suits and wristwatches; long hair and unkempt beards for men, bare feet and bralessness for women became the new uniform of protest. Families gave way to communes; once quiet and conservative neighborhoods like San Francisco's Haight-Ashbury district became havens for runaways and drug users, the "flower children" of the sixties.

Theorists quickly emerged to extol the new way of life. Theodore Roszak gloried in the rejection of modern science and technology in his influential book, *The Making of a Counter Culture* (1969). "In its place," he wrote, "there must be a new culture in which the non-intellective capacities of personality . . . become the arbiters of the true, the good and the beautiful." Yale law school professor Charles Reich portrayed the emergence of a new world of love, beauty, and racial harmony in his rhapsodic work, *The Greening of America* (1970). He dubbed the new society "Consciousness III." Herbert Marcuse, the visionary Marxist who became the guru of the new culture, called for people to overcome capitalist repression and live by an "aesthetic ethos."

Music became the touchstone of the new departure. Folk singers like Joan Baez and Bob Dylan, popular for their songs of social protest in the mid-sixties, gave way to rock groups such as the Beatles, whose lyrics were often suggestive of drug use, and finally to "acid rock" as symbolized by the Grateful Dead. The climactic event of the decade came at the Woodstock concert at Bethel in upstate New York when four hundred thousand young people indulged in a three-day orgy of rock music, drug experimentation, and public sexual activity.

Former Harvard psychology professor Timothy Leary encouraged youth to join him in trying out the drug scene. Millions accepted his invitation, "Tune in, turn on, drop out," literally, as they

The cultural revolution—and the challenge to adult values, life-styles, and standards of living—climaxed in August 1969 at the Woodstock music festival, billed as "Three Days of Peace and Music." Despite rainy weather, extreme shortages of food and water, and massive traffic jams, the three-day happening inspired idealistic visions of a "Woodstock nation."

experimented with marijuana and with LSD—a new and dangerous chemical hallucinogen. Yippie leader Jerry Rubin praised drugs for leading to "the total end of the Protestant ethic: screw work, we want to know ourselves."

The Yippies, led by Rubin and Abbie Hoffman, represented the ultimate expression of cultural insurgency. Shrewd buffoons who mocked the consumer culture, they delighted in capitalizing on the mood of social protest to win attention. Once, when testifying before a congressional committee investigating internal subversion, Rubin dressed as a revolutionary war soldier; Hoffman appeared in the gallery of the New York Stock Exchange in 1967, raining money down on the cheering brokers below. The Yippies succeeded in revealing the hypocrisy of American society, but in the process they fragmented the protest movement; serious radicals dismissed these so-called flower children as parasites.

Black Power

The civil-rights movement, which had spawned the mood of protest in the sixties, fell on hard times. The legislative triumphs of 1964 and 1965 were relatively easy victories over southern bigotry; now the movement faced the far more complex problem of achieving economic equality in the cities of the North, where more than half of the nation's blacks lived. Mired in poverty, crowded into ghettos from Harlem in New York City to Watts in Los Angeles, blacks had actually fallen further behind whites in disposable income since the beginning of the integration effort. The civil-rights movement had raised the expectations of urban blacks for improvement; frustration mounted as they failed to experience any significant economic gain.

The first sign of trouble came in the summer of 1964, when black teen-agers in Harlem and Rochester, New York, rioted. The next summer, a massive outburst of rage and destruction swept over Watts as the inhabitants burned buildings and looted stores. Riots in the summer of 1966 were less destructive, but in 1967 the worst ones yet took place in Newark and Detroit, where forty-three were killed and hundreds injured. The mobs attacked the shops and stores, expressing a burning grievance against a consumer society from which they were excluded by their poverty. One participant in the Detroit mayhem likened it to "an outing," with the whole family taking part. "The rebellion—it was caused by the commercials," he explained. "I mean you saw all those things you'd never been able to get—go out and get 'em. Men's clothing, furniture, appliances, color TV. All that crummy TV glamour just hanging out there."

The civil-rights coalition fell apart, a victim of both its legislative success and economic failure. Black militants took over the leadership of SNCC; they disdained white help and even reversed Martin Luther King's insistence on nonviolence. The split over tactics became public during a Mississippi Freedom March in 1966 in which King pleaded for a continuation of peaceful protest. SNCC's new leader, Stokely Carmichael, disagreed, telling blacks that they should seize power in those parts of the South where they outnumbered whites. "I am not going to beg the white man for anything I deserve," he said, "I'm going to take it." A few days later, in Greenwood, Mississippi, Carmichael raised the cry of "black power" to the cheers of six hundred marchers.

The slogan, which marked a radical change from King's call for peaceful integration of the races, caught on quickly. SNCC spoke of the need for blacks to form "our own institutions, credit unions, co-ops, political parties" and even write "our own history." Others went further than calls for ethnic separation. H. Rap Brown, who replaced Carmichael as the leader of SNCC in 1967, told a black crowd in Cambridge, Maryland, to "get your guns" and "burn this town down," while Huey Newton, one of the founders of the militant Black Panther party, proclaimed, "We make the statement, quoting from Chairman Mao, that Political Power comes through the Barrel of a Gun."

King suffered the most from this extremism. He tried to keep control of the civil-rights movement by leading a campaign for better housing for blacks in Chicago, only to meet with indifference from the ghetto-dwellers and bitter hostility from the city's political machine and working-class whites. His denunciation of the Vietnam War cost him the support of the Johnson administration and alienated him from the more conservative civil-rights groups like the NAACP and the Urban League. He finally seized on poverty as the proper

Summer in Detroit in 1967 was marred by violent riots, as black frustration peaked and looters grabbed the consumer goods they could not afford to buy.

enemy for attack, but before he could lead his Poor People's March on Washington in 1968, he was assassinated in Memphis in early April.

Both blacks and whites realized that the nation had lost its most eloquent spokesman for racial harmony. His tragic death elevated King to the status of a martyr, but it also led to one last outbreak of urban violence, as blacks exploded in Washington, D.C., burning buildings within a few blocks of the White House. "It was as if the city were being abandoned to an invading army," wrote a British journalist. "Clouds of smoke hung over the Potomac, evoking memories of the London blitz. . . ."

Yet there was a positive side to the emotions engendered by black nationalism. Spokesmen began to urge blacks to take pride in their ethnic heritage, to embrace their blackness as a positive value. Sales of hair-straighteners, long a staple in black barber and beauty shops, plummeted; blacks began to wear Afro hairstyles and dress in dashikis, stressing their African roots. Students began to demand new black-studies programs in the colleges; the word Negro—identified with white supremacy of the past—virtually disappeared from usage overnight, replaced by the favored Afro-American" or "black." Singer James Brown best expressed the sense of racial identity: "Say It Loud—I'm Black and I'm Proud."

■ *The world witnessed both pride and protest when 1968 Olympic medalists Tommie Smith (center) and John Carlos raised the black power salute during the national anthem.*

Ethnic Nationalism

Other groups quickly emulated the black phenomenon. American Indians decried the callous use of their identity as football mascots; in response, universities such as Stanford changed their symbols. Puerto Ricans demanded that their history be included in school and college texts. Polish, Italian, and Czech groups insisted on respect for their nationalities. Congress acknowledged these demands with passage of the Ethnic Heritage Studies Act of 1972. Instead of trying to melt all groups down into a standard American type, Congress now gave what one sponsor of the measure called "official recognition to ethnicity as a positive constructive force in our society today." Some $15 million was appropriated to subsidize ethnic-studies courses in schools and colleges across the nation.

Mexican-Americans were in the forefront of the ethnic groups that became active in the 1970s. The primary impulse came from the efforts of César Chávez to organize the poorly paid grape pickers and lettuce workers in California into the National Farm Workers Association (NFWA). Building on the earlier efforts of Filipinos, who had organized some field workers,

Chávez appealed to ethnic nationalism in mobilizing Mexican-American field hands to strike against grape growers in the San Joaquin Valley in 1965. The NFWA's main demand, a wage of $1.40 an hour, was relatively modest, but Chávez's techniques were more radical. Rallying Mexican farm workers with a red flag featuring a bold thunderbird (a cultural symbol), he soon won the attention of the media. A national boycott of grapes by Mexican-Americans and their sympathizers among the young people of the counter-culture led to a series of hard-fought victories over the growers. The five-year struggle resulted in a union victory in 1970, but at an enormous cost—95 percent of the farm workers involved had lost their homes and their cars. Undaunted, Chávez turned next to the lettuce fields, and although he met with resistance from both the growers and the Teamster's Union, he succeeded in raising the hourly wage of farm workers in California to $3.53 by 1977 (it had been $1.20 in 1965).

Chávez's efforts helped spark an outburst of ethnic consciousness among Mexican-Americans that swept through the urban barrios of the Southwest. Aware that a majority of their compatriots were functionally illiterate as a result of language difficulties and inferior schools, Mexi-

Ethnic Identities

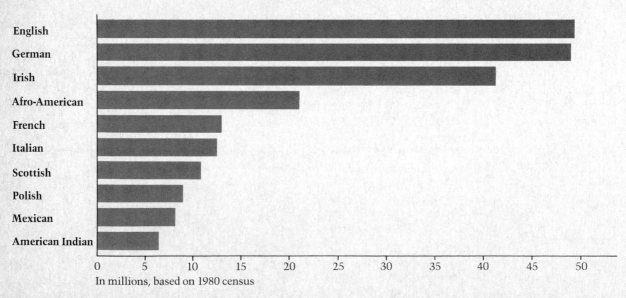

In millions, based on 1980 census

Source: U.S. Bureau of the Census

The Chicano movement had a broad cultural impact. In California and Texas, Mexican-Americans began forming paramilitary organizations known as the Brown Berets. This militancy led inevitably to suspicion and hostility on the part of whites as well as to police harassment, which served only to intensify the Brown Berets' radical stance. At the same time, other Chicanos succeeded in compelling the Frito-Lay Company to replace their Frito Bandito, a threatening cartoon character who stole corn chips, with Frito Amigo, who gave them away to children. A more significant cultural milestone came in 1967 with the founding of *El Grito: A Journal of Contemporary Mexican-American Thought* which published scholarly articles on Chicano history and culture.

Women's Liberation

Active as they were in the civil-rights and anti-war movements, women soon learned that the male leaders of protest causes were little different from corporate executives—they expected women to fix the food and type the communiqués while the men made the decisions. Or as Stokely Carmichael once said in jest, "The position of women in our movement should be prone." Understandably, women soon realized that they could only achieve respect and equality by mounting their own protest.

In some ways, the position of women in American society was worse in the 1960s than it had been in the '20s. After forty years, there was a lower percentage of women enrolled in the nation's colleges and professional schools. There had been a great upsurge in female employment (nearly two thirds of all new jobs in the sixties went to women), but women with college degrees earned only half as much as similarly trained men. Women were still relegated to stereotyped occupations like nursing and teaching; there were few female lawyers and even fewer women doctors. And sex roles, as portrayed on television commercials, continued to call for the husband to be the breadwinner and the wife to be the homemaker.

Betty Friedan was the first to seize upon the sense of grievance and discrimination that developed among women in the 1960s. The beginning

■ *By organizing successful strikes among the poorly paid grape and lettuce pickers in California, César Chávez sparked pride among Mexican-Americans.*

can-American leaders campaigned for bilingual programs and improved educational opportunities. Young activists began to call themselves Chicanos, which had previously been a derogatory term, and to take pride in their cultural heritage; in 1968, they succeeded in establishing the first Mexican-American studies program at California State College at Los Angeles. Campus leaders called for reform, urging high-school students to insist on improvements. "If you are a student at Lincoln [high school] you should be angry!" declared activist Raúl Ruiz in 1967. "You should demand! You should protest! You should organize for better education! This is your right! This is your life!" Heeding such appeals, nearly ten thousand students at East Los Angeles high schools walked out of class in March 1968. These walkouts sparked similar movements in San Antonio, Texas, and Phoenix, Arizona, and led to significant reforms, such as the introduction of bilingual programs in grade schools and the hiring of more Chicano teachers at all levels.

of the effort to raise women's consciousness was her 1963 book, *The Feminine Mystique*. Calling the American home "a comfortable concentration camp," she attacked the prevailing view that women were completely contented with their housekeeping and child-rearing tasks, claiming that housewives had no self-esteem and no sense of identity. "I'm a server of food and putter on of pants and a bedmaker," a mother of four told Friedan, "somebody who can be called on when you want something. But who am I?"

Working Wives, 1960–1969

Year	Percent (as percentage of all married women)
1960	31.7
1961	34.0
1962	33.7
1963	34.6
1964	35.3
1965	35.7
1966	36.5
1967	37.8
1968	39.1
1969	40.4

Source: Compiled from U.S. Bureau of the Census, Historical Statistics of the United States, Colonial Times to 1970, *Bicentennial Edition, Washington, D.C., 1975.*

The 1964 Civil Rights Act helped women attack economic inequality head-on by making it illegal to discriminate in employment on the basis of sex. Women filed suit for equal wages, demanded that companies provide day care for their infants and preschool children, and entered politics to lobby against laws which—in the guise of protection of a weaker sex—were unfair to women. As the women's liberation movement grew, its advocates began to attack laws banning abortion and waged a campaign to toughen the enforcement of rape laws. They even attacked the hallowed Miss America contest for its sexist tone.

The women's movement met with many of the same obstacles as other protest groups in the '60s. The moderate leadership of the National Organization of Women (NOW), founded by Betty Friedan in 1966, soon was challenged by those with more extreme views. Ti-Grace Atkinson and Susan Brownmiller attacked revered institutions

■ *In addition to real concerns about unequal wages and opportunities, many women felt suffocated and unfulfilled by their traditional roles in society.*

—the family and the home—and even denounced sexual intercourse with men because it is a method of male domination. Many women were repelled by the bra-burning and harsh rhetoric of the extremists and expressed satisfaction with their lives. "Where do they get the lunatic idea that women had rather work for a boss than stay home and run their own domain?" asked one female critic. But despite these disagreements, most women supported the effort to achieve equal status with men, and in 1972 Congress responded by approving the Equal Rights Amendment to the Constitution. This measure, first introduced in Congress in 1923, now could be voted on by state legislatures, the final step in the ratification process.

The Election of 1968

The turmoil of the sixties reached a crescendo in 1968 as the American people responded to the two dominant events of the decade—the war in Vietnam and the cultural insurgency at home. To add to the chaos, this election year witnessed a series of bizarre events, including two assassinations, the withdrawal from the race of an incumbent president, and the emergence of the most effective third-party candidate in fifty years.

Stalemate in Vietnam

The war in Southeast Asia cast a long shadow over the election of 1968. The escalation begun in 1965 had failed to produce the expected American victory. Bombing of the North proved ineffective, failing either to damage an essentially agrarian economy or to block the flow of supplies southward through Laos and Cambodia. In fact, the American air attacks, with their inadvertent civilian casualties, gave North Vietnam a powerful propaganda weapon which it used to sway world opinion against the United States.

The war in the South went no better. Despite the steady increase in American ground forces, from 184,000 in late 1965 to more than 500,000 by early 1968, the Viet Cong still controlled much of the countryside. The search-and-destroy tactics employed by the American commander, General William Westmoreland, proved ill-suited. The Viet Cong, aided by North Vietnamese regulars, were waging a war of insurgency, avoiding fixed positions and striking from ambush. In a vain effort to destroy the enemy, Westmoreland used superior American firepower wantonly, devastating the countryside, causing many civilian casualties, and driving the peasantry into the arms of the guerrillas.

The climax came in late January 1968 when the Viet Cong launched the Tet offensive. To mark the lunar New Year, the VC recklessly attacked the South Vietnamese cities and provincial capitals. American and government troops quickly beat back this bold assault, but at home television viewers were shocked by scenes of Viet Cong guerrillas fighting within the walls of the American embassy compound in Saigon. The outcome

■ *Despite LBJ's optimistic predictions that victory was at hand, by early 1968 it became apparent that American troops were trapped in a bloody stalemate.*

was a tactical defeat for the Communists but a decided political setback for the United States. President Johnson had been hammering away at the idea that the war was almost over; suddenly it appeared to be nearly lost. CBS-TV newscaster Walter Cronkite took a quick trip to Saigon to find out what had happened. Horrified at what he saw, he exclaimed to his guides, "What the hell is going on? I thought we were winning the war." He returned home to tell his audience, "It seems now more certain than ever that the bloody experience of Vietnam is to end in a stalemate."

President Johnson reluctantly came to the same conclusion after the Joint Chiefs of Staff requested an additional 205,000 men to achieve victory in Vietnam following the Tet offensive. He began to listen to his new secretary of defense, Clark Clifford, who replaced Robert McNamara in January 1968. In mid-March, after receiving advice from a group of experienced Cold Warriors, including such illustrious figures as Dean Acheson and McGeorge Bundy, the President decided to limit the bombing of North Vietnam in an effort to open up peace negotiations with Hanoi. In a speech to the nation on Sunday evening,

■ In 1967 British cartoonist Leslie Illingworth showed LBJ caught in "The Time Machine," in which LBJ was fated to be ground down, despite his panic-striken and exhausting scramble.

March 31, 1968, Johnson outlined his plans for a new effort at ending the war peacefully, and then concluded by saying, as proof of his sincerity, "I shall not seek, and I will not accept, the nomination of my party for another term as your President." Thus a stunned nation learned that Lyndon Johnson had become the first major political casualty of the Vietnam War.

The Democrats Divide

Johnson's withdrawal had come in response to political as well as military realities. By 1966, the antiwar movement had spread from the college campuses to Capitol Hill. Former supporters such as Senator William Fulbright now began to question the conflict. Housewives and middle-class professionals began attending the antiwar rallies; respected commentators such as Walter Lippmann and Professor Hans Morgenthau came out against the Vietnam War as foolish and unproductive. Johnson began to feel like a prisoner in the White House, since in his infrequent public appearances he was hounded by larger and larger groups of antiwar demonstrators, whose taunts and jeers wounded him deeply.

The essentially leaderless protest against the war took on a new quality on January 3, 1968, when Senator Eugene McCarthy, a Democrat from Minnesota, announced that he was challenging LBJ for the party's presidential nomination. McCarthy at first seemed an unlikely candidate. A cool, aloof, almost arrogant intellectual, he was motivated primarily by a belief that Kennedy and Johnson had abused the power of the presidency. A devout Catholic, he raised the banner of idealism, telling audiences, "Whatever is morally necessary must be made politically possible."

Protest and Reaction: From Vietnam to Watergate

It was his stance against the war, however, that attracted the support of American youth. College students flocked to his support, shaving their beards and cutting their hair to be "clean for Gene." In the New Hampshire primary in early March, the nation's earliest political test, McCarthy shocked the political experts by coming within a few thousand votes of defeating President Johnson.

McCarthy's strong showing in New Hampshire led Robert Kennedy, who had been weighing the risks in challenging Johnson, to enter the presidential race. Despite the obvious charge of opportunism he faced, Kennedy had a much better chance than did McCarthy to defeat LBJ and win in the fall. Elected senator from New York in 1964, Bobby Kennedy had become an effective spokesman for the disadvantaged, as well as an increasingly severe critic of the Vietnam War. Unlike McCarthy, whose appeal was largely limited to upper-middle-class whites and college students, Kennedy attracted strong support among blue-collar workers, blacks, Chicanos and other minorities who formed the nucleus of the continuing New Deal coalition. Moreover, in contrast to McCarthy, whose cool wit and lack of

passion bothered even his staunchest admirers, Kennedy provoked an intense emotional loyalty among his followers.

Lyndon Johnson's dramatic withdrawal caused an uproar in the Democratic party. With Johnson's tacit backing and strong support from party regulars and organized labor, Vice-President Hubert H. Humphrey immediately declared his candidacy. Humphrey, a classic Cold War liberal who had worked equally hard for social reform at home and American expansion abroad, was totally unacceptable to the antiwar movement. Accordingly, he decided to avoid the primaries and work for the nomination within the framework of the party.

Kennedy and McCarthy, the two antiwar candidates, were thus left to contest the spring primaries, causing agonizing choices among those who stood for change. Kennedy won everywhere except in Oregon, but his narrow victory in California ended in tragedy when a Palestinian immigrant, Sirhan Sirhan, assassinated him in a Los Angeles hotel.

With his strongest opponent struck down, Hubert Humphrey had little difficulty turning back the challenges from Eugene McCarthy and

■ *Alarmed by the militant antiwar demonstrators drawn to the Democratic convention, Chicago Mayor Daley erected barbed wire fences around the convention hall.*

■ *McCarthy's antiwar stance won the support of thousands of college students who went "clean for Gene."*

■ *Frustrated by the outcome of the Democratic convention, thousands of unarmed, middle-class antiwar college students gathered for an evening rally in Chicago's Grant Park. Within hours, thousands would be gassed and clubbed in what was later termed a "police riot."*

George McGovern, a last-minute replacement for Kennedy, at the Chicago convention. Backed by that city's political boss, Mayor Richard Daley, the vice-president relied on party leaders to defeat an antiwar resolution and win the nomination on the first ballot by a margin of more than two to one. Those hoping for change had to be content with one small victory—the abolition of the unit rule among state delegations, which would make open conventions possible in the future.

Humphrey's triumph was marred by violence outside the heavily guarded convention hall. Radical groups had urged their members to come to Chicago to agitate; the turnout was relatively small but included many who were ready to provoke the authorities in their despair over the convention's outcome. Epithets and cries of "pigs" brought about a savage response from Daley's police, who shared their mayor's contempt for the protesters. "The cops had one thing on their mind," commented journalist Jimmy Breslin. "Club and then gas, club and then gas, club and then gas."

The bitter fumes of tear gas hung in the streets for days afterward; the battered heads and bodies

of demonstrators and innocent bystanders alike flooded the city's hospital emergency rooms. What an official investigation later termed a "police riot" marred Humphrey's nomination and made a sad mockery out of his call for "the politics of joy." The Democratic party itself had become the next victim of the Vietnam War.

The Republican Resurgence

The primary beneficiary of the Democratic debacle was Richard Nixon. Written off as politically dead after his unsuccessful race for governor of California in 1962, Nixon had slowly rebuilt his place within the party by working loyally for Barry Goldwater in 1964 and for GOP congressional candidates two years later. Positioning himself squarely in the middle, with Governor Nelson Rockefeller of New York to his left and Governor Ronald Reagan, who had inherited Goldwater's following, to his right, he quickly became the front-runner for the Republican nomination. At the GOP convention in Miami Beach —blissfully tranquil compared to the Democrats'

dicapped by LBJ's stubborn refusal to speed up the diplomatic preliminaries to full-scale peace talks and to end all bombing of North Vietnam. His campaign gradually gained momentum, however, as he picked up support from union leaders and from blacks who remembered his strong stand on civil rights. When he broke with Johnson in late September by announcing in Salt Lake City that if elected he would "stop the bombing of North Vietnam as an acceptable risk for peace," he began to overtake Nixon.

Unfortunately for Humphrey, a third-party candidate cut deeply into the normal Democratic majority. George Wallace had first gained national attention as the racist governor of Alabama whose motto was, "Segregation now . . . segregation tomorrow . . . segregation forever." In 1964, he had shown surprising strength in Democratic primaries in northern states. His appeal was to blue-collar workers and white ethnics—Poles, Italians, Greeks—who believed that many of the gains made by blacks during the 1960s had come at their expense.

experience in Chicago—Nixon won an easy first-ballot nomination and chose Maryland Governor Spiro Agnew as his running mate. Agnew, little-known on the national scene, was a former Rockefeller backer who had won the support of conservatives by taking a strong stand against black rioters.

In the fall campaign, Nixon opened up a wide lead by avoiding controversy and reaping the benefit of discontent with the Vietnam War. He exploited television skillfully, appearing before carefully arranged panels to answer friendly questions. He played the peace issue shrewdly, appearing to advocate an end to the conflict without ever taking a definite stand. The United States should "end the war and win the peace," he declared, hinting that he had a secret formula for peace but never revealing what it was. Above all, he chose the role of reconciler for a nation torn by emotion, a leader who promised to bring a divided country together again.

Humphrey, in contrast, found himself hounded by antiwar demonstrators who heckled him constantly. He walked a tightwire, desperate for the continued support of President Johnson but han-

■ By appealing to the urban working classes who felt threatened by black gains, third-party candidate George Wallace cut deeply into the Democratic majority that might have supported Humphrey.

By attacking both black spokesmen and their liberal white allies, Wallace appealed to the sense of powerlessness among the urban working classes. "Liberals, intellectuals and long hairs have run the country for too long," Wallace told his followers. "When I get to Washington," he promised, "I'll throw all these phonies and their briefcases into the Potomac."

Running on the ticket of the American Independence Party with General Curtis LeMay—whose solution to the Vietnam War was to "nuke 'em back to the Stone Age"—as his running mate, Wallace was a close third in the September polls, gaining support from more than 20 percent of the electorate. But as the election neared, his following declined. Humphrey continued to gain, especially after Johnson agreed in late October to end all bombing of North Vietnam. By the first week in November, the outcome was too close for the experts to call.

Nixon won the election with the smallest share of the popular vote of any winning candidate since 1916. But he swept a broad band of states from Virginia and the Carolinas through the Midwest to the Pacific for a clear-cut victory in the electoral college. Humphrey held on to the urban Northeast, scoring well only among blacks and manual laborers. Wallace took just five states in the Deep South, but his heavy inroads into blue-collar districts in the North shattered the New Deal coalition.

The election marked a repudiation of the politics of protest and the cultural insurgency of the mid-sixties. The combined popular vote for Nixon and Wallace, 56.5 percent of the electorate, signified that there was a silent majority that was fed up with violence and confrontation. The "social issue"—a growing concern over psychedelic drugs, rock music, lack of decorum in dress and behavior, and sexual permissiveness—had replaced the traditional economic issue to erode the normal Democratic majority and elect a Republican president. Or as Richard Scammon put it, most of the voters were made up of "the unyoung, the unblack, and the unpoor." By voting for Nixon and Wallace, the American people were sending out a message: they wanted a return to traditional values and an end to the war in Vietnam.

Nixon in Power

The man who took office as the thirty-sixth president of the United States on January 20, 1969, seemed to be a new Nixon. Gone was the fiery rhetoric and the penchant for making enemies. In their place, observers found an air of moderation and restraint. He appeared to have his emotions under firm control. The scars of too many political battles had given him a veneer of toughness, even of indifference. But beneath the surface, he remained bitter, hurt, and sensitive to criticism.

An innately shy man, Nixon hoped to enjoy the power of the presidency in splendid solitude. Described by Barry Goldwater as "the most complete loner I've ever known," Nixon assembled a powerful White House staff whose main task was to isolate him from Congress, the press, and even his own cabinet. Loyal subordinates like H. R. Haldeman and John Ehrlichman took charge of domestic issues, often making decisions without even consulting Nixon, who once said that "the country could run itself domestically without a President." Foreign policy was Nixon's great passion, and here he relied heavily on Henry Kissinger, his national security adviser, to formulate

Election of 1968

ELECTORAL VOTE BY STATE		POPULAR VOTE
REPUBLICAN Richard M. Nixon	301	31,770,237
DEMOCRATIC Hubert H. Humphrey	191	31,270,533
AMERICAN INDEPENDENT George C. Wallace	46	9,906,141
MINOR PARTIES	—	239,908
	538	73,186,819

ALASKA 3
HAWAII 4
WASH., D.C. 3

For their roles in the Watergate cover-up, Nixon aides Jeb Stuart Magruder, H. R. Haldeman, and John Ehrlichman served time in federal prison. Nixon was granted a "full, free, and absolute pardon" by his successor, Gerald Ford.

policy, leaving Secretary of State William Rogers to keep the State Department bureaucrats busy with minor details.

The Nixon White House soon could be likened to a fortress under siege. Distrusting everyone, from the media to members of his own party, the President sought to rule the nation without help from either Congress or his cabinet. An almost paranoid belief that he was surrounded by enemies led Nixon to authorize wiretapping and covert surveillance to plug news leaks to the press and to preserve secrecy. In his quest for privacy, the President cut himself off from the nation and thus sowed the seeds of his downfall.

Reshaping the Great Society

Nixon began his first term on a hopeful note, promising the nation peace and respite from the chaos of the sixties. Rejecting the divisions that had split Americans apart, he promised in his inaugural address to "bring us together." "We cannot learn from one another until we stop shouting at one another—until we speak quietly enough so that our words can be heard as well as our voices."

Nixon's moderation promised a return to the politics of accommodation that had characterized the Eisenhower era. Faced with a Democratic Congress, Nixon, like Ike, appeared ready to accept the main outlines of the welfare state. Instead of any massive overthrow of the Great Society, he focused on making the federal bureaucracy function more efficiently.

Daniel Patrick Moynihan, a Democrat who had helped LBJ design his reforms, joined the White House staff as urban affairs adviser and came up with the Family Assistance Plan as a way to overhaul the clumsy welfare system. Instead of piecemeal handouts, each poor family would receive an annual payment of $1600, a variation of a guaranteed annual wage, which had long been a goal of liberals. Democrats, however, quickly criticized Moynihan's plan for the low level of payments and a provision requiring heads of poor households to register for employment as a condition for receiving the annual payment. Despite its many attractive features, including substantial aid to the working poor, the Family Assistance Plan failed to win congressional approval.

Nixon was more successful with his effort to shift responsibility for social problems from Washington to state and local authorities. He developed the concept of revenue sharing, by which federal funds would be dispersed to state, county, and city agencies to meet local needs. Conservatives, who objected to separating the pain of collecting public funds from the pleasure of disbursing them, opposed the plan, but in 1972 Congress finally approved a measure to share $30.1 billion with local governments over a five-year period. An accompanying ceiling of $2.5 billion a year on federal welfare payments, however, meant that much of the revenue-sharing payments had to be allocated by cities and states to programs previously paid for by the federal government.

In the area of civil rights Nixon made a shrewd political move. Action by Congress and the outgoing Johnson administration had ensured that massive desegregation of southern schools, delayed for over a decade by legal action, would finally begin just as Nixon took office. Nixon and his attorney general, John Mitchell, decided to shift the responsibility for this process to the courts. In the summer of 1969, the Justice Department asked a federal judge to delay the integration of thirty-three school districts in Mississippi. The Supreme Court quickly ruled against the Justice Department, declaring that "the obligation of every school district is to terminate dual school systems at once." Thus, in the minds of southern white voters, it was the hated Supreme Court, not Richard Nixon, who had forced them to integrate their schools.

Nixon used similar tactics in his attempt to reshape the Supreme Court along more conservative lines. His appointment of Warren Burger, an experienced federal judge with moderate views to replace the retiring Earl Warren as Chief Justice, met with little objection. But when the President nominated Clement Haynesworth of South Carolina to fill another vacancy on the Court, liberal Democrats led an all-out attack. The Senate, troubled by conflict-of-interest charges against Haynesworth, who in fact had a sound record as a federal judge, rejected the appointment. Seventeen Republicans voted with the majority.

Nixon then responded by offering the name of G. Harrold Carswell, a Florida jurist whose legal record was so bad that one senator finally defended him on the dubious grounds that "there are lots of mediocre judges." When the senators rejected Carswell by a narrow margin, Nixon de-

nounced them for insulting "millions of Americans who live in the South." Once again, the President had used the Supreme Court to enhance his political appeal to Southerners.

Nixon finally filled the Court position with Harry Blackmun, a reputable conservative from Minnesota, who easily won confirmation. Subsequently, the President appointed Lewis Powell, a distinguished Virginia lawyer, and William Rehnquist, a rigidly conservative Justice Department attorney from Arizona, to the Supreme Court. Surprisingly, the Burger Court, despite its more conservative make-up, did not engage in any massive overturn of the Warren Court's decisions. It continued to uphold the legality of desegregation, ruling in 1971 that busing was a necessary and proper way of achieving integrated schools. In other rulings, it restricted the government's right to wiretap suspected subversives, overturned state laws prohibiting abortion, and insisted that the death penalty only be invoked under very limited and precise circumstances.

The moderation of the Supreme Court and the legislative record of the Nixon administration indicated that the nation was not yet ready to abandon the reforms adopted in the 1960s. The pace of change slowed down in areas such as civil rights and welfare, but the commitment to social justice was still clear.

Nixonomics

The economy posed a more severe test for Richard Nixon. He inherited a growing inflation that accompanied the Vietnam War, the product of Lyndon Johnson's unsuccessful attempt to wage the war without raising taxes. The budget deficit was a staggering $25 billion in 1968 and the inflation rate had risen to 5 percent. Strongly opposed to the idea of federal controls, Nixon rejected suggestions of national guideposts to hold down wages and prices. Instead, he opted for a reduction in government spending while encouraging the Federal Reserve Board to curtail the money supply, forcing up interest rates and slowing the rate of business expansion.

The result was disastrous. Inflation continued, reaching nearly 6 percent by the end of 1970, the highest rate since the Korean War. At the same time the economy underwent its first major recession since 1958. The stock market tumbled; the Dow-Jones average fell from over 900 to just above 600, the sharpest drop in thirty years. Unemployment rose to 6 percent by the end of 1970, and business failures jumped alarmingly.

The collapse of the Penn Central Railroad was the most spectacular bankruptcy in the nation's history. Democrats quickly coined a new word, "Nixonomics," to describe the disaster. According to Democratic Chairman Larry O'Brien, it meant that "all the things that should go up—the stock market, corporate profits, real spendable income, productivity—go down, and all the things that should go down—unemployment, prices, interest rates—go up."

Conditions seemed to worsen in 1971. Inflation continued unabated, and the nation's balance of trade became negative as imports exceeded exports by a substantial margin, leading to a weakening of the dollar abroad.

In mid-August, Nixon acted suddenly and boldly to halt the economic decline. Abandoning his earlier resistance to controls, he announced a ninety-day freeze on wages and prices to be followed by federally imposed guidelines in both areas. The new secretary of the treasury, Democrat John Connally, carried out a devaluation of the dollar which, along with a 10 percent surtax on all imports, led to a greatly improved balance of trade. The sudden Nixon economic reversal quickly ended the recession. Industrial production increased by over 5 percent in the first quarter of 1972 and the Dow-Jones average broke the 1000 barrier for the first time.

Building a Republican Majority

"The Great Nixon Turnaround," as historian Lloyd Gardner termed it, came too late to help the Republicans in the 1970 congressional elections. From the time he took office in 1969, the President was obsessed with the fact that he had received only 43 percent of the popular vote in 1968. He owed his election to the third-party candidacy of George Wallace. The Republicans were still a minority party, and to be reelected in 1972, Nixon would need to win over southern whites and blue-collar workers who had followed Wallace out of the Democratic Party.

Attorney General John Mitchell, who had been

Nixon's campaign manager in 1968, had devised a southern strategy to help achieve a Republican majority by 1972. The administration's well-publicized objection to school desegregation in the South and the attempt to put Haynesworth and Carswell on the Court were part of this design. Kevin Phillips, one of Mitchell's aides, urged the Nixon administration to direct its appeal to "middle Americans"—southern whites, Catholic ethnic groups, blue-collar workers, and, above all, the new suburbanites of the South and West. In his 1969 book, *The Emerging Republican Majority*, Phillips argued that the GOP's future lay in the Sunbelt. "From space-center Florida across the booming Texas plains to the Los Angeles-San Diego suburban corridor," he contended, "the nation's fastest-growing areas are strongly Republican and conservative."

Nixon unleashed his vice-president, Spiro Agnew, the former governor of Maryland, in an attempt to exploit the social issue in the 1970 election. Blaming all national problems—from drug abuse and sexual permissiveness to crime in the streets—on Democratic liberals and their allies in the media, Agnew delivered a series of scathing speeches. He denounced intellectuals as "an effete corps of impudent snobs," branded television commentators as "a tiny and closed fraternity of privileged men," and damned the press in general as "nattering nabobs of negativism." Despite howls of protest, Agnew proved to be an effective political weapon, as blue-collar workers began displaying on their cars bumper stickers with the proud assertion, "Spiro Is My Hero."

The Democrats struck back by changing their tactics. Warned by Richard Scammon and Ben Wattenberg in *The Real Majority* (1970) that most voters were not young, black, or poor, Democratic candidates were careful to stress economic issues, blaming the Republicans for both inflation and recession. On the social issue, they joined in the chorus against crime, pornography, and drugs. Running for the Senate in Minnesota, Hubert Humphrey reversed his previous stand and came out against gun control; in Illinois, Adlai Stevenson, III, campaigned for reelection wearing an American flag in his lapel.

The outcome was a standoff. Agnew's attacks helped the GOP to limit the usual off-year losses in the House to nine seats, while the Republicans actually gained two votes in the Senate. But the Democrats did well in state elections and proved once again that economic issues were crucial in American politics. Nixon and the Republicans still did not command a national majority.

In Search of Détente

Richard Nixon gave foreign policy top priority, and he proved surprisingly adept at it. In Kissinger, he had a White House specialist who had devoted his life to the study of diplomacy. A refugee from Nazi Germany, Kissinger had become a professor of government at Harvard, the author of several influential books, and an acknowledged authority on international affairs. Nixon and Kissinger approached foreign policy from a similar realistic perspective. "They recognized a cold and logical world without fated allies or enemies—only interested parties," comment-

ed one close observer. Instead of viewing the Cold War as an ideological struggle for survival with communism, they saw it as a traditional great-power rivalry, one to be managed and controlled rather than to be won.

Kissinger had a grand design. Realizing that recent events, especially the Vietnam War and the rapid Soviet arms buildup of the 1960s, had eroded America's position of primacy in the world, he planned a strategic retreat. There were five major centers of power by the 1970s—the United States, Russia, China, Japan, and the NATO countries of Western Europe. Russia had great military strength, but its economy was weak and it had a dangerous rival in China. Kissinger planned to use American trade—notably grain and high technology—to induce Soviet cooperation, while at the same time improving U.S. relations with China. With Russia neutralized, the United States would then focus on its economic rivalry with Japan and the countries of Western Europe.

■ Kissinger's search for détente began with a calculated decision to improve relations with China, the USSR's next-door rival. In a highly publicized state visit, Nixon and Chinese leaders were seen sharing banquets and touring the Great Wall of China.

Nixon and Kissinger shrewdly played the China card as their first step toward achieving détente—that is, a relaxation of tension—with the Soviet Union. In the summer of 1971, the administration revealed that Kissinger had secretly gone to China and had made the arrangements for a state visit by President Nixon. The following February, accompanied by a planeload of reporters and television camera crews, Nixon made a triumphal tour of China, meeting with the Communist leaders and ending more than two decades of Sino-American hostility. The problem of Taiwan prevented full-scale diplomatic relations, but Nixon agreed to establish an American liaison mission in Peking as a first step toward ultimate recognition.

The Soviets, who viewed China as a dangerous adversary along a two-thousand-mile frontier in Asia, responded by agreeing to reach an arms-control pact with the United States. The Strategic Arms Limitation Talks (SALT) had been underway since 1969. During a visit to Moscow in May 1972, President Nixon signed two vital documents with Soviet leader Leonid Brezhnev. The first limited the two superpowers to two hundred antiballistic missiles (ABMs) apiece; the second froze the number of offensive ballistic missiles for a five-year period. SALT I recognized the existing Soviet lead in missiles, but the American deployment of multiple warheads that could each be individually targeted (MIRV), ensured a continuing American strategic advantage.

The SALT I agreements were most important as a symbolic first step toward control of the nuclear-arms race. They signified that the United States and Russia were trying to achieve a settlement of their differences by peaceful means. The sale of American grain to Russia, along with proposed trade agreements to share more advanced American computer technology with the Soviets, seemed to promise a genuine relaxation of the dangerous tensions of the Cold War.

A triumphant Kissinger (left) and Nixon (right) clink glasses to celebrate the signing of two vital arms agreements with Soviet leader Leonid Breshnev (center) in Moscow on May 26, 1972.

SALT I achieved what this 1970 cartoon had portrayed as a staggering if not impossible task.

"Do Me A Favor—Help Me Drop It!"

RUSSIAN MISSILE SYSTEMS

U.S. MISSILE SYSTEMS

Ending the Vietnam War

Vietnam remained the one foreign-policy challenge that Nixon could not overcome. He had a three-part plan to end the conflict—renewed bombing, a hard line in negotiations with Hanoi, and the gradual withdrawal of American troops. The last tactic, known as Vietnamization, proved the most successful. The plan involved training the troops of South Vietnam to take over the American combat role. The number of American soldiers in Vietnam dropped from 543,000 in 1968 to 39,000 by 1972; domestic opposition to the war declined sharply with the accompanying drop in casualties and reductions in the draft call.

" I NEVER DID SAY HOW, BUT I TOLD YOU I'D GET YOU OUT OF VIETNAM "

■ Trying to "get out" of Vietnam by expanding the war into neutral Cambodia incensed both political cartoonists and antiwar demonstrators.

U.S. Troop Levels in Vietnam
(as of Dec. 31 of each year)

Year	Number of Troops (in thousands)
1960	900
1961	3,200
1962	11,300
1963	16,300
1964	23,300
1965	184,300
1966	385,300
1967	485,600
1968	536,100
1969	475,200
1970	334,600
1971	156,800
1972	24,200

Source: U.S. Department of Defense.

The call for renewed bombing proved the most controversial part of the plan. As early as the spring of 1969, Nixon secretly ordered raids on Communist supply lines in neutral Cambodia. Then in April 1970, he ordered both air and ground strikes into Cambodia. These relieved pressure on hard-pressed South Vietnamese forces but caused a massive outburst of antiwar protests at home. Students demonstrated against the invasion of Cambodia on campuses across the nation. Tragedy struck at Kent State University in Ohio in early May. After rioters had fire-bombed an ROTC building, the governor sent in national guard troops who were taunted and harassed by irate students. The guardsmen then opened fire, killing four students and wounding eleven more. The victims were innocent bystanders; two were young women caught in the fusillade on their way between classes. A week later two black students were killed at Jackson State College in Mississippi; soon there were riots and protests on nearly every campus in the country in what one educator called "the most disastrous month of May in the history of American higher education."

Nixon had little sympathy for the demonstrators, telling aides that they were "bums" who were intent on "blowing up the campuses." The "silent majority" to whom he appealed seemed to agree; one poll showed that most Americans blamed the students, not the national guard, for the deaths at Kent State. Construction workers showed their support for the President by attacking student protesters in New York City and then marching on City Hall shouting, "All the way, U.S.A." An "Honor America Day" program, held in Washington, D.C., on July 4 attracted 250,000 people who heard Billy Graham and Bob Hope endorse the President's policies. Nixon's Cambodian invasion did little to shorten the Vietnam War, but the public reaction reinforced the President's resolve not to surrender.

The third tactic, negotiation with Hanoi, finally proved successful. Beginning in the summer

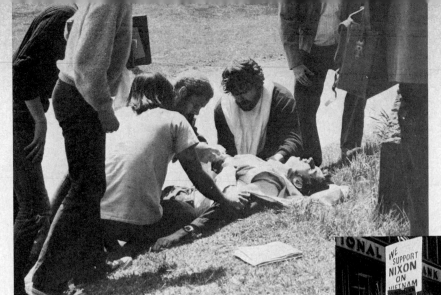

By May of 1970, the antiwar movement threatened to divide the nation. At Kent State, unarmed and innocent bystanders were shot. Members of the "silent majority" (below) took to the streets in anti-antiwar protests.

of 1969, Kissinger held a series of secret meetings with North Vietnam's foreign minister, Le Duc Tho. In the summer and fall of 1972, after heavy American B-52 raids on North Vietnam had halted a Communist thrust into the South, the two sides were near agreement. South Vietnamese objections blocked a settlement before the 1972 election. When Hanoi tried to make last-minute changes, Nixon ordered a series of savage B-52 raids on Hanoi that finally led to the signing of a truce on January 27, 1973. In return for the release of all American prisoners of war, the United States agreed to remove its troops from South Vietnam within sixty days. The political clauses allowed the North Vietnamese to keep their troops in the South, thus virtually guaranteeing future control of all Vietnam by the Communists.

The agreement was, in fact, a disguised surrender, but finally the American combat role in the Vietnam War was over. After eight years of fighting, the loss of more than fifty-six thousand American lives, and the expenditure of over $100 billion, the United States had emerged from the quagmire in Southeast Asia. Yet known only to a few insiders around the President, the nation was already deeply enmeshed in another dilemma—what Gerald R. Ford termed "the long national nightmare" of Watergate.

■ Through four years of secret meetings, Kissinger and Hanoi's Le Duc Tho finally negotiated an end to the American combat role in Vietnam.

Surviving in Vietnam

Vietnam ranks after World War II as America's second most expensive war. Between 1950 and 1975, the United States spent $123 billion on combat in Southeast Asia. More importantly, Vietnam ranks—after our Civil War and World Wars I and II—as the nation's fourth deadliest war, with 57,661 Americans killed in action.

Yet, when the last U.S. helicopter left Saigon, Americans suffered what historian George Herring terms "collective amnesia." Everyone, even those who had fought in 'Nam,' seemed to want to forget Southeast Asia. It took nearly ten years for the government to erect a national monument to honor those who served in Vietnam. The Vietnam Veterans Memorial in Washington, D.C., (see photo above) was dedicated in November 1982; on its polished black granite walls are carved the names of the dead and missing in action. And only in 1981 did collections of oral histories of some of those who served in Vietnam appear: Al Santoli's well-documented *Everything We Had: An Oral History of the Vietnam War by Thirty-three American Soldiers Who Fought It*, and Mark Baker's *Nam: The Vietnam War in the Words of the Men and Women Who Fought There*. Both books demonstrate that in the steaming jungles of Vietnam one thing mattered most: survival.

One Vietnam veteran expressed the general feeling of men in combat: "War is not killing. Killing is the easiest part. . . . Sweating twenty-four hours a day, seeing guys drop all around you from heatstroke, not having food, not having water, sleeping only three hours a night for weeks at a time, that's what war is. Survival."

During his term President Kennedy ordered a more than tenfold increase in the number of U.S. advisers in Vietnam. Yet, for the ten to twelve thousand predominantly career soldiers there by December of 1962, Vietnam seemed a nice little nine-to-five war. Recalls radio technician Jan Barry of the army's 18th Aviation Company, "If we wanted to go out and chase people around and shoot at them . . . we had a war going. If we didn't . . . they left us alone." In those early days, even the Special Forces Green Berets "used to stop at four-thirty and have a happy hour and get drunk," says Barry, adding that "there was no war after four-thirty. On Saturdays, no war. On Sundays, no war. On holidays, no war. That's right, a nine-to-five war."

Within two years, however, the Joint Chiefs of Staff and President Johnson committed fifty thousand American troops to combat in Vietnam, and the nice little war turned grim. By mid-1967, in fact, more than four hundred thousand Americans were fighting in Vietnam. As many as three hundred died each week. Combat, recalls 26th

Marine Division scout-sniper James Hebron, turned out "totally different" from what he had expected when he had joined the corps at age seventeen early in 1967. "There was no romance at all," says Hebron. During one combat period, Hebron's Bravo Company went without a hot meal for seven months. During that same operation, he notes, "I didn't brush my teeth for two months," explaining that "they sent toothbrushes . . . we had to use them to clean our rifles."

The Screaming Eagles of the elite 101st Airborne Division arrived in Vietnam shortly before the Tet offensive of January 1968. Lieutenant Robert Santos, destined to become one of the division's most decorated men, told his platoon, "two things can happen to you. You can get wounded and go home early. Or you can die." He added that the "best way to go home is whole. If you stick with me . . . and learn from the [more experienced men] you won't get wounded. You won't die." Santos and his men earned a basketful of medals for valor in combat. Lieutenant Santos explains those medals in grim terms: "My responsibility was to kill and in the process of killing to be so good at it that I indirectly saved my men's lives." So, notes Santos, "You come home with the high body count, high kill ratio," but, he concludes, "there's nothing, nothing, that's very satisfying about that."

Few who served in Vietnam survived unscathed, whether psychologically or physically. One of the 303,600 Americans wounded during the long war was 101st Airborne platoon leader James Bombard, first shot and then blown up by a mortar round during the bitter Tet fighting at Hue in February 1968. He describes his traumatic experience as

feeling the bullet rip into your flesh, the shrapnel tear the flesh from your bones and the blood run down your leg. . . . To put your hand on your chest and to come away with your hand red with your own blood, and to feel it running out of your eyes and out of your mouth, and seeing it spurt out of your guts, realizing you were dying. . . . I was ripped open from the top of my head to the tip of my toes. I had forty-five holes in me.

Somehow Bombard survived Vietnam.

The fighting continued for four years after President Nixon took office. Robert Rawls served as a rifleman with the 1st Cavalry Division from early 1969 to early 1970. He recalls:

We got fire fights after fire fights. My first taste of death. After fire fights you could smell it. They brought the [dead men] back wrapped in ponchos. . . . they just threw them up on the helicopter and [piled empty, reusable supply cases] on top of them. You could see the guys' feet hanging out. . . . I had nightmares. . . . I can still see those guys.

As the war dragged on, pacifist frustration at home paralleled the bitterness of those who had fought in Vietnam. John Muir's experience is typical. Early in the war, Muir had served as a rifleman with the 1st Marine Division during the battle of Dong Ha. Muir's single company fought continuously for four days and four nights, frequently in hand-to-hand combat, against two divisions of the North Vietnamese Army. When the marines were relieved, only ninety-one men —all wounded—were still able to fight at all. Muir's squad, however, had been wiped out: he had ended up throwing rocks at his attackers.

"It was a major battle," recalls Muir. "We did a fine job there. If it had happened in World War II, they still would be telling stories about it. But it happened in Vietnam, so nobody knows about it."

Withdrawing U.S. forces from Vietnam ended only the combat. Returning veterans fought government disclaimers concerning the toxicity of the defoliant Agent Orange. VA hospitals across the nation still contain thousands of para- and quadriplegic Vietnam veterans, as well as the maimed from earlier wars. Throughout America the "walking wounded" find themselves still embroiled in the psychological aftermath of Vietnam. To this day, says former 1st Infantry Division combat medic David Ross, "If I'm walking someplace and there's grass, I find myself sometimes doing a shuffle and looking down at the ground. . . . I'm looking for a wire or a piece of vine that looks too straight, might be a [land mine] trip wire. Some of the survival habits you pick up stay residual for a long time."

The Crisis of Democracy

"The illegal we do immediately; the unconstitutional takes a little longer," Henry Kissinger once said jokingly of the Nixon administration. Unfortunately, he was far closer to the truth than anyone realized.

The Politics of Deceit

Richard Nixon's consuming distrust of even his own associates quickly led to a series of underhanded and illegal activities. In the spring of 1969, he ordered the bombing of Cambodia without informing Congress. When details began to leak to the press, the President ordered wiretaps on the telephones of both reporters and members of Kissinger's National Security Council staff. A year later, White House aide Tom Charles Huston drew up a proposal for a new secret committee of FBI and CIA officials to coordinate undercover federal operations. The Huston plan contemplated—in the name of national security—wiretapping, electronic eavesdropping, and "surreptitious entries"—a bureaucratic euphemism for burglaries and break-ins. Only the opposition of FBI director J. Edgar Hoover, who feared a threat to his own agency's independence, blocked implementation of this illegal scheme.

When the *New York Times* and the *Washington Post* began publishing the Pentagon Papers, a classified Defense Department study of the Vietnam War, Nixon decided to take drastic measures to plug any further leaks of secret documents. His aides created a self-styled "plumbers" unit within the White House directed by G. Gordon Liddy, a former FBI agent, and E. Howard Hunt, a veteran of the CIA. Charged with preserving secrecy and discrediting those who kept the press informed, Hunt and Liddy set out to embarrass Daniel Ellsberg, the Defense Department official who had leaked the Pentagon Papers. In a vain effort to find damaging information, they went so far as to break into the office of Ellsberg's psychiatrist in Los Angeles.

Elsewhere in the White House, aides John Dean and Charles Colson were busy preparing an enemies list, which contained the names of several hundred prominent Americans, ranging from movie stars like Jane Fonda and Paul Newman to journalists and educators such as columnist James Reston and Kingman Brewster, president of Yale University. The White House labored under a siege mentality that seemed to justify any and all measures necessary to defeat its opponents, who were thought to include the media, the intellectual community, and virtually all minority groups.

Nixon went to great lengths to guarantee his reelection in 1972. A Committee to Re-elect the President (CREEP) was formed, headed by Attorney General John Mitchell. Specialists in dirty tricks, notably Donald Segretti, harassed Democratic contenders, while G. Gordon Liddy, of the White House "plumbers," developed an elaborate plan to spy on the opposition. Liddy's scheme included bugging the Democratic national headquarters in the Watergate complex in Washington. In the early morning hours of June 17, James McCord and four other men working under the direction of Hunt and Liddy were caught by police during a break-in at Watergate. The continuing abuse of power had finally culminated in an illegal act which soon threatened to bring down the entire Nixon administration.

The Election of 1972

The irony of the Watergate break-in was that by the time it occurred, Nixon's election was assured. Aided by Segretti's dirty tricks, which included issuing phony press releases and campaign documents to embarrass such prominent contenders as Edmund Muskie and Hubert Humphrey, the Democrats destroyed themselves. First Muskie, the front-runner, replying in the New Hampshire primary to a Segretti-inspired letter accusing him of prejudice against French Canadians, lost his composure. Then a lone assassin, Arthur Bremer, shot and seriously wounded George Wallace, who was succeeding in his promise to "rattle the eye teeth of the Democratic party" in the spring primaries. Paralyzed, Wallace was forced to drop out of the race, leaving Nixon with a complete monopoly over the political right.

Senator George McGovern of South Dakota then became the leading Democratic candidate. Aided by rules that he had helped write

■ *The unceremonious dumping of vice-presidential nominee Thomas Eagleton (left) tarnished McGovern's image and cost him critical support.*

which opened up the party convention to women, youth, and minorities, McGovern emerged as the Democratic nominee. He ran on a platform that advocated a negotiated settlement in Vietnam, the right to abortion, and tolerance of diverse life-styles. The South Dakota senator hoped to unite the New Left with traditional Democratic voters, but his strong stand against the Vietnam War and in favor of social reform was perceived as "anti-establishment" by middle-class America and greatly strengthened Nixon's appeal.

McGovern quickly lost what little strength he had by his inept handling of the vice-presidential nomination. Originally selecting Missouri Senator Thomas Eagleton, McGovern dumped him for R. Sargent Shriver of Maryland when it was disclosed that Eagleton had undergone psychiatric treatment for depression. Integrity had been McGovern's strongest point; when he dropped Eagleton from the ticket despite a promise to stand behind him "1000 percent," that quality was called into question. Under the slogan, "Come Home, America," McGovern attempted to wage a crusade against the war and on behalf of reform, but his stiff speaking style (which one commentator said sounded like a minister saying grace at a Rotary lunch) and his self-righteous

manner appealed only to those already committed to his cause.

Richard Nixon shrewdly let McGovern's apparent extremism and New Left support become the main issue in the campaign, rather than the President's own record in office. Staying carefully aloof from partisanship, Nixon let others campaign for him, relying heavily on the recent improvement in the economy and his foreign-policy triumphs with China and Russia to sway the nation's voters.

The result was a stunning victory. Nixon won a popular landslide with 60.8 percent of the vote—second only to Lyndon Johnson's record in 1964—and an even more decisive sweep of the electoral college, taking every state but Massachusetts. The very low turnout and Democratic control of both Houses of Congress suggests that the election was primarily a repudiation of McGovern and the radicalism he appeared to stand for, rather than an endorsement of Richard Nixon. The voting patterns did suggest, however, the beginning of a major political realignment, as only blacks, Jews, and low-income voters continued to vote overwhelmingly Democratic. The GOP made significant gains in the South and West, thus giving substance to Kevin Phillips' prediction of an emerging Republican majority based in the Sunbelt.

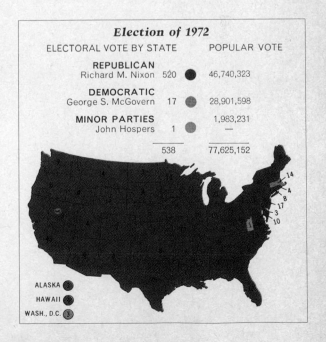

Election of 1972

ELECTORAL VOTE BY STATE		POPULAR VOTE
REPUBLICAN Richard M. Nixon	520	46,740,323
DEMOCRATIC George S. McGovern	17	28,901,598
MINOR PARTIES John Hospers	1	1,983,231 —
	538	77,625,152

ALASKA

HAWAII

WASH., D.C. 3

The Watergate Scandal

Only Richard Nixon knew how fragile his victory was in 1972. The President apparently had no foreknowledge of the Watergate break-in, but he was deeply implicated in the attempt to cover up the involvement of White House aides in the original burglary. On June 23, only six days after the crime, he ordered the CIA to keep the FBI off the case, on the specious grounds that it involved national security. The President even urged his aides to lie under oath, if necessary. "I don't give a [expletive deleted] what happens," Nixon said to John Mitchell. "I want you all to stonewall it, let them plead the Fifth Amendment, cover-up, or anything else. . . ."

In the short run, the cover-up, directed by White House counsel John Dean, worked. Hunt and Liddy were convicted for their roles in the Watergate break-in, but they carefully avoided implicating either CREEP or Nixon's inner circle of advisers. Despite some very revealing stories by reporters Bob Woodward and Carl Bernstein in the *Washington Post*, the public was kept ignorant of the true dimensions of the Watergate affair.

The first thread unraveled when federal judge John Sirica, known for his firmness toward criminals, sentenced the burglars to long jail terms. James McCord was the first to crack, informing Sirica that he had received money from the White House and had been promised a future pardon in return for his silence. By April 1973, Nixon was forced to fire John Dean, who refused to become the scapegoat for the cover-up, and to allow Haldeman and Ehrlichman, who were deeply implicated, to resign. The Senate then appointed a special committee to investigate the Watergate episode, with North Carolina Democrat Sam Ervin as chairman. In a week of dramatic testimony, John Dean revealed the President's personal involvement in the cover-up. Still Nixon hoped to weather the storm, since it was basically a matter of whose word was to be believed, that of the President or of a discredited aide.

The existence of tapes of conversations in the Oval Office, recorded regularly since 1970, finally brought Nixon down. At first the President tried to invoke executive privilege to withhold the tapes. When Archibald Cox, appointed as Watergate special prosecutor, demanded the release of the tapes, Nixon responded by firing Cox. When Attorney General Eliot Richardson refused to remove Cox, Nixon fired him too. But the new Watergate prosecutor, Leon Jaworski, continued

The faces of Senators Howard Baker (left) and Sam Ervin (center) became familiar to a large television audience, who daily watched them uncover new and alarming dimensions of the Watergate scandal.

Threatened by the release of his secret tapes and facing three articles of impeachment, an embattled Richard Nixon resigned the presidency on August 9, 1974, as his loyal family watched.

to press for the tapes. Nixon tried to release only a few of the less damaging ones, but the Supreme Court ruled unanimously in June 1974 that the tapes had to be turned over to Judge Sirica.

By that time the House Judiciary Committee, acting on evidence compiled by the staff of the Ervin committee, voted three articles of impeachment, charging Nixon with obstruction of justice, abuse of power, and contempt of Congress. Faced with the release of tapes which directly implicated him in the cover-up, the President finally chose to resign on August 9, 1974.

Nixon's resignation proved to be the culmination of the Watergate scandal. The entire episode revealed both the weaknesses and strengths of the American political system. Most regrettable was the abuse of presidential authority—a reflection both of the growing power of the modern presidency and of the fatal flaws in Richard Nixon's character. Unlike such previous executive-branch scandals as the Whiskey Ring and Teapot Dome, Watergate involved a lust for power rather than for money. Realizing that he had reached the White House almost by accident, Nixon did everything possible to retain his hold on his office. He used the "plumbers" to maintain executive secrecy, he directed the Internal Revenue Service and the Justice Department to punish his enemies and reward his friends, and he created CREEP to free himself from dependency on the Republican Party in his quest for reelection.

But Watergate also demonstrated the vitality of a democratic society. The press, particularly Woodward and Bernstein, showed how investigative reporting could unlock even the most closely guarded executive secrets. Judge Sirica proved that an independent judiciary was still the best bulwark for individual freedom. And Congress rose to the occasion, both by carrying out a successful investigation of executive misconduct and by following a scrupulous and nonpartisan impeachment process that left Nixon with no chance to escape his ultimate fate.

The nation survived the shock of Watergate with its institutions intact. The presidency was shorn of its excessive power. Attorney General John Mitchell and twenty-five presidential aides were sentenced to jail terms. Future occupants of the White House would never again feel that they were above the law. Congress, in decline since Lyndon Johnson's exercise of executive dominance, was rejuvenated, with its members now intent on extending congressional authority into all areas of American life.

Chronology

1963 Betty Friedan publishes *The Feminine Mystique*

1966 National Organization for Women (NOW) formed

1967 Riots in Detroit kill 43, injure 2000, leave 5000 homeless

1968 Viet Cong launch Tet offensive (January)
Johnson announces he will not seek reelection (March)
Martin Luther King, Jr., assassinated in Memphis, Tennessee (April)
Robert F. Kennedy assassinated in Los Angeles, California (June)

1970 U.S. forces invade Cambodia (April)
Ohio National Guardsmen kill four students at Kent State University (May)

1971 *New York Times* publishes the Pentagon Papers (June)
Nixon announces wage-and-price freeze (August)

1972 President Nixon visits China (February)
U.S. and USSR sign SALT I accords in Moscow (May)
White House "Plumbers" unit breaks into Democratic headquarters in Watergate complex (June)
Richard Nixon wins reelection in landslide victory over McGovern

1973 U.S. and North Vietnam sign truce ending Vietnam War (January)

1974 Supreme Court orders Nixon to surrender White House tapes (June)
Richard M. Nixon resigns presidency (August)

There was, however, one lasting casualty. The people's faith in politicians was severely shaken. The events of the 1960s and the early '70s, ranging from the Vietnam War to Watergate, from ghetto riots to violent antiwar demonstrations, had left the American people in a mood of cynicism and despair. Nixon had broken the slender bond of trust between those who govern and those who are governed. After the Watergate experience, the ultimate challenge facing presidential aspirants was to offer the kind of inspired leadership that would rekindle the flagging democratic spirit.

Recommended Reading

The most penetrating analysis of the youthful protesters of the 1960s is Kenneth Keniston, *Young Radicals* (1968). Keniston, a social psychologist, interviewed a group of antiwar activists in 1967 to arrive at a detailed assessment of their motives and aspirations. For a broader picture of the New Left and the SDS in particular, see Irwin Unger, *The Movement* (1974).

Garry Wills provides the most revealing portrait of the career and character of Richard Nixon in *Nixon Agonistes* (1970). Wills concentrates on the prepresidential years; for Nixon in office, the best accounts are two memoirs: William Safire, *Before the Fall* (1975), a speechwriter's account that focuses on domestic policy; and Henry Kissinger, *The White House Years* (1979), the national security adviser's view of Nixon's foreign policy.

The best books on Watergate are still the two contemporary accounts by Bob Woodward and Carl Bernstein. *All the President's Men* (1974) tells how these two reporters penetrated the cover-up; in *The Final Days* (1976), they detail Nixon's fall from power.

Additional Bibliography

Books on the New Left include S. Kirkpatrick Sale, *SDS* (1973); Jack Newfield, *A Prophetic Minority* (1966); Christopher Lasch, *The Agony of the American Left* (1969); Edward J. Bacciocco, *The New Left in America* (1974); and Todd Gitlin, *The Whole World Is Watching* (1981), a scholary account by a former SDS leader that blames the media for the New Left's downfall. For other aspects of the youth rebellion, see Paul Goodman, *Growing Up Absurd* (1960) and Lewis Feuer, *The Conflict of Generations* (1972). Representative books reflecting the views of the counterculture are Charles Reich, *The Greening of America* (1970); Herbert Marcuse, *An Essay on Liberation* (1969); and Theodore Roszak, *The Making of a Counter Culture* (1969).

The transition from the quest for integration to the assertion of black power is traced in James C. Harvey, *Black Civil Rights During the Johnson Administration* (1973); Clayborne Carson, *In Struggle* (1981); and Stokely Carmichael and C. V. Hamilton, *Black Power* (1967). For the urban riots of the sixties, see Robert Conot, *Rivers of Blood, Years of Darkness* (1967) on Watts; John Hersey, *The Algiers Hotel Incident* (1968) on Detroit; and James W. Button, *Black Violence* (1978), which shows the impact of the riots on federal policy. The growing self-consciousness of other minorities is described in Michael Novak, *The Rise of the Unmeltable Ethnics* (1973); Matt Meier and Feliciano Rivera, *The Chicanos* (1972); and Rodolfo Acuña, *Occupied America: A History of Chicanos*, 2d ed. (1981). For the emerging feminist movement, see two books by William Chafe, *The American Woman* (1972) and *Women and Equality* (1977); and Sara Evans, *Personal Politics* (1979).

The tumultuous election of 1968 is described in Theodore White, *The Making of the President, 1968* (1969) and Lewis Chester, Godfrey Hodgson, and Bruce Page, *American Melodrama* (1969). For Wallace's role, see Jody Carlson, *George C. Wallace and the Politics of Powerlessness, 1964–1976* (1981). Fawn Brodie traces Nixon's prepresidential career critically in *Richard Nixon* (1981); Earl Mazo and Stephen Hess are more sympathetic in *Nixon* (1968). Other important books on Nixon include Jules Witcover, *The Resurrection of Richard Nixon* (1970); Rowland Evans and Robert Novak, *Nixon in the White House* (1971); and the President's own memoir, *RN* (1978). For Nixon's domestic policies, see Leonard Silk, *Nixonomics* (1972); Daniel Moynihan, *Politics of a Guaranteed National Income* (1973); and two books on the Supreme Court nomination controversies by Richard Harris, *Justice* (1970) and *Decision* (1971).

The major shifts in American politics in the late 1960s are described in Richard N. Scammon and Ben J. Wattenberg, *The Real Majority* (1970); S. Kirkpatrick Sale, *Power Shift* (1975); David L. Broder, *The Party's Over* (1971); Samuel Lubell, *The Hidden Crisis in American Politics* (1970); and Frederick G. Dutton, *The Changing Sources of Power* (1971).

Henry Brandon, *The Retreat of American Power* (1973); Tad Szulc, *The Illusion of Peace* (1978); and Stanley Hoffman, *Primacy or World Order* (1978) all describe Nixon's foreign policy and the search for détente. Books that focus on Kissinger's role include Marvin Kalb and Bernard Kalb, *Kissinger* (1974), a sympathetic view; Roger Morris, *Uncertain Greatness* (1977), a critical analysis; and Seyom Brown, *The Crisis of Power* (1979), a balanced account. For SALT, see John Newhouse, *Cold Dawn* (1973). William Shawcross, a British journalist, blames Kissinger for the secret bombing of Cambodia in *Sideshow* (1979).

Books on the antiwar movement and the violent protests in 1970 include Alexander Kendrick, *The Wound Within* (1974); Thomas Powers, *The War at Home* (1973); John Mueller, *War, Presidents and Public Opinion* (1973); I. F. Stone, *The Killings at Kent State* (1971); Noam Chomsky, *American Power and the New Mandarins* (1977); and Lawrence M. Baskir and William A. Strauss, *Chance and Circumstance* (1978), a study of the impact of the draft on American youth. The different lessons drawn from the Vietnam experience are expounded in Earl C. Ravenal, *Never Again* (1978), a plea for nonintervention, and Norman Podhoretz, *Why We Were in Vietnam* (1982), a defense of the war.

The election of 1972 is dealt with uncritically by Theodore White in *The Making of the President, 1972* (1973) and entertainingly by Hunter S. Thompson in *Fear and Loathing: On the Campaign Trail '72* (1973).

General accounts of Watergate include Theodore White, *Breach of Faith* (1975); Jonathan Schell, *Time of Illusion* (1976); and J. Anthony Lukas, *Nightmare* (1976). For the abuse of power that reached its culmination in the Watergate affair, see Arthur M. Schlesinger, Jr., *The Imperial Presidency* (1973); David Wise, *The American Police State* (1976); and Athan Theoharis, *Spying on Americans* (1978). Among the many memoirs by Watergate participants, the most revealing is John Dean, *Blind Ambition* (1976).

chapter 32

THE
AGE OF
SCARCITY

On October 6, 1973, Egypt and Syria launched a surprise attack on Israel. The invasion, which came while the Israelis were observing the Jewish holy day of atonement, Yom Kippur, caught American leaders completely off-guard. After recovering from the initial shock, President Nixon and Henry Kissinger, who had become secretary of state in September, expected Israel to repel the Arab invaders and display the same military dominance it had used to win the Six Day War in 1967. In that conflict, Israel had devastated its Arab neighbors, taking possession of the Golan Heights from Syria, the Sinai peninsula from Egypt, and Jerusalem and the West Bank from Jordan. Instead of increasing Israeli security, however, these conquests had only added to Middle East tensions. They unified the Arab countries, who now called for the return of their lands, and increased Egyptian and Syrian dependence on the Soviet Union for arms and political support.

Henry Kissinger saw the outbreak of the Yom Kippur War as an opportunity to shift American policy from its traditional pro-Israeli position to a more neutral stance. The secretary of state wanted the United States to play the role of honest broker between Israel and its Arab neighbors. To achieve that position, he was hoping that the Yom Kippur War would end without a clear-cut victory for either side, permitting the United States to step in and arrange a diplomatic settlement.

Events nearly betrayed Kissinger's strategy. The initial Egyptian and Syrian attacks proved surprisingly successful, finally leading Nixon and Kissinger to approve a massive resupply of Israel in mid-October. But when the Israeli counterattack drove the Syrians back toward Damascus and trapped an entire Egyptian army near the Suez Canal, the secretary intervened diplomatically to prevent a victory for Israel that would preclude American mediation. Joint Soviet-American efforts to arrange a cease-fire nearly broke down in the face of Israeli militancy. Kissinger then ordered a worldwide nuclear alert that persuaded both the Soviets and the Israelis that the United States was intent on imposing a political settlement. Finally, the fighting ended in late October.

Kissinger's apparent diplomatic triumph, however, was offset by an unforeseen consequence of

■ *Egyptian and Israeli tanks fight it out on the sands of the Sinai peninsula during the Yom Kippur War of 1973. With the help of Henry Kissinger's shuttle diplomacy the combatants disengaged and an uneasy truce was established.*

the Yom Kippur War. On October 17, the Arab members of the Organization of Petroleum Exporting Countries (OPEC) announced a 5 percent cut in oil production, with additional cuts of 5 percent each month until Israel gave up the lands it had seized in 1967. President Nixon announced a $2.2 billion aid package for Israel on October 19, and the next day Saudi Arabia cut off oil shipments to the United States and to the Netherlands, the European nation that had most strongly supported American policy in the Middle East.

The Arab oil embargo had a disastrous impact on the American economy. First, it produced a worldwide shortage of oil. Arab producers cut production by 25 percent from the September 1973 level, leading to a curtailment of 10 percent in the world supply. For the United States, which imported one third of its daily consumption, it meant a loss of nearly two million barrels a day. Increased imports from Iran, Libya, and Nigeria helped offset the Arab embargo, but American consumers began to panic. Long lines formed at automobile service stations as motorists kept filling their tanks in fear of running out of gas.

A dramatic increase in oil prices proved to be a far more significant result of the embargo. The relatively low price of oil had been creeping upward in the early 1970s as demand began to match supply; after the Arab embargo began, OPEC, led by the Shah of Iran, raised crude oil prices fourfold. In the United States, gasoline prices at the pumps nearly doubled in a few weeks time, while the cost of home heating fuel rose even more sharply.

President Nixon responded with a series of temporary measures, including pleas to turn down thermostats in homes and offices, close service stations on weekends to curb pleasure driving, and reduce automobile speed limits to fifty miles per hour. He also outlined a plan for American energy independence. Designed to end reliance on imported oil, the plan encouraged conservation and the use of alternative sources of energy, such as coal and nuclear power. When the Arab oil embargo ended in March, after Kissinger negotiated an Israeli pullback in the Sinai, the American public relaxed. Gasoline once again became plentiful, thermostats were raised, and people rekindled their love affair with the automobile.

But the energy crisis did not end with the

■ "Hat in Hand" shows a new and unaccustomed posture for Uncle Sam following the Arab oil embargo.

lifting of the embargo. The Arab action marked the beginning of a new era in American history. The United States, with only 6 percent of the world's population, had been using nearly 40 percent of the earth's energy supplies. The vast reserves of petroleum and natural gas had fueled American economic expansion down through World War II, and then oil imports had sustained postwar growth with artificially low energy costs. In 1970, domestic oil production began to decline; the embargo served only to highlight the fact that the nation was now dependent on other countries, notably those in the Persian Gulf, for its economic well-being.

The consequences soon became clear. The growing shortage of oil and natural gas led to a steady increase in energy costs which contributed heavily to inflation. The revenues sent to OPEC members further weakened the American economy, leading to periodic recessions, higher interest rates, and the slowing of economic growth. A nation that based its way of life on abundance and expansion suddenly was faced with the reality of limited resources and economic stagnation. A land of plenty now had to face the challenge of scarcity.

Energy and the Economy

The energy crisis that began with the Arab oil embargo in 1973 had a profound impact. The price American consumers paid for oil went up sixfold during the 1970s. The result was rampant inflation, rising unemployment, and an end to the postwar era of rapid economic growth.

The Oil Shocks

Cheap energy had been the underlying force behind the amazing expansion of the American economy after World War II. The world price of oil had actually declined in the 1950s and '60s as huge new fields in the Middle East and North Africa came into production. The GNP had more than doubled between 1950 and 1973; the American people had come to base their way of life on gasoline prices that averaged about $.35 a gallon. The huge gas-guzzling cars, the flight to the suburbs, the long drive to work each day, the detached houses heated by fuel oil and natural gas and cooled by central air conditioning represented a dependence on inexpensive energy that everyone took for granted.

The first great oil shock of the '70s came with the Yom Kippur War and the resulting Arab oil embargo. Few had noticed a gradual increase in OPEC prices in the early 1970s; the world level had risen from $1.80 a barrel to $3.07 by mid-1973, but the regulated domestic price had remained stable at the $3.00 mark. Global demand for oil, intensified by the explosive economic development of Western Europe and Japan as well as the United States, had now caught up with oil production. In the ensuing shortfall, the OPEC nations quickly raised prices, first to over $5.00 a barrel, then to $11.65.

The effect on the American economy was devastating. In 1979, consumers had to pay an additional $16.4 billion to cover the cost of imported oil. Gasoline prices jumped from $.35 to $.65 a gallon; the cost of manufacturing went up proportionately, while utility rates rose sharply as a result of the higher cost of fuel oil and natural gas. Suddenly the American people faced drastic and unexpected increases in such everyday expenses as driving to work and heating their homes.

The result was a sharp decline in consumer spending and the worst recession since World War II. The GNP dropped by 6 percent in 1974 and unemployment rose to over 9 percent, the highest level since the Great Depression of the 1930s. Detroit was hit the hardest. Buyers shied away from big cars with their low gas mileage, but many were skeptical of the first generation of American-made small cars, notably the Ford Pinto and the Chevrolet Vega. Sales declined by 20 percent, and by the fall of 1974, Detroit's big three automakers had laid off more than 225,000 workers.

President Gerald R. Ford, who followed Richard Nixon into the White House, was concerned at first with inflation; he responded belatedly to the economic crisis by proposing a tax cut to stimulate consumer spending. Congress passed a $22.8 billion reduction in taxes in early 1975 which included rebates averaging $130 for each individual taxpayer, an across-the-board cut in personal income tax rates, and an increase in investment tax credits for business. With this stimulus, the economy gradually recovered by 1976, but the resulting budget deficits helped keep inflation above 5 percent and prevented a return to full economic health.

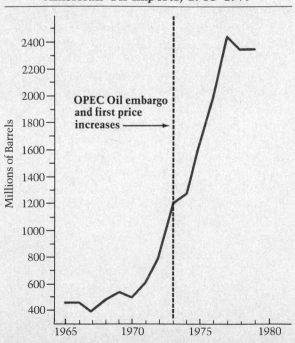

American Oil Imports, 1966–1979

OPEC Oil embargo and first price increases ⟶

Millions of Barrels

The next administration, headed by Jimmy Carter of Georgia, had little more success in achieving a rapid rate of economic growth. Continued federal deficits and relatively high interest rates kept the economy sluggish throughout 1977 and '78. Then in 1979 the outbreak of the Iranian Revolution and the overthrow of the shah touched off another oil shock. Although the cutoff of Iranian oil led to a shortfall of only 3 percent of the world's oil supply, the members of the OPEC cartel took advantage of the situation to raise prices by a staggering $21 a barrel over the next eighteen months. The price of oil, which had actually declined in relation to industrial prices in the mid-1970s, now shot up to over $30 a barrel. Gasoline prices climbed to more than $1 a gallon at American service stations, and an even greater wave of inflation than the 1973 increase occurred.

The American people panicked. When lines began to form at gas stations in California and Florida in early May 1979, drivers started filling their tanks every day or two. Soon stations were jammed and supplies ran short as the nation's normal inventory shifted from underground storage reservoirs to motorists' gas tanks. Service stations began closing on weekends, and in state after state governors experimented with plans regulating gasoline purchases. The long lines frustrated American drivers; incidents of violence began to mount and the public took out its fury on the Carter administration. In June, the President's staff warned him of the danger in the "worsening short-term energy crisis." "Nothing else has so frustrated, confused, angered the American people," Carter was told, "or so targeted their distress at you personally."

By the fall of 1979, world supply had caught up with demand, and the oil scare ended. But the price of gasoline remained at over a dollar a gallon, and the inflation rate began to reach double-digit levels again. The twin oil shocks of the seventies had left the economy battered and had undermined the average American's faith in the future.

The Search for an Energy Policy

The oil shocks of 1973 and 1979 were but two symptoms of a much deeper energy crisis. Put

■ *The age of cheap and abundant oil was ending. As prices climbed and supplies dwindled, Americans found themselves waiting in long gas lines.*

simply, the United States was running out of the fossil fuels on which it had relied for its economic growth in the past. Domestic oil production peaked in 1970 and declined every year thereafter; there were more ample reserves of natural gas, but both fuels were nonrenewable sources of energy that would eventually be exhausted. American political leaders had to devise a national policy to meet not only the temporary shortfalls of the seventies but also the long-term energy problem inherent in past reliance on fossil fuels.

The success of the environmental movement in the late 1960s and early '70s compounded the problem. Efforts to protect the environment and curtail pollution of the nation's air and water had led to significant legislative restrictions on American industry. Congress created the Environmental Protection Agency in 1970 to monitor industry and passed a Clean Air Act that encouraged public utilities to shift from using coal, which polluted the atmosphere, to clean-burning fuel oil and natural gas to generate electricity. The observance of Earth Day in April 1970, complete with a

■ *(Top) Earth Day protestors dramatize the dangers of environmental pollution. (Bottom) Santa Barbara sea birds trapped in oil slicks.*

the end of the decade, groups such as the Sierra Club and Friends of the Earth had failed in their efforts to halt the gradual relaxation of environmental regulations to permit strip-mining of coal and offshore drilling for oil.

The nation's leaders had an even more difficult time devising a coherent and workable long-term national energy policy. Gerald Ford placed a high premium on expanding production as a means of overcoming the shortage. The Republicans advocated removing price controls on oil and natural gas to give wildcatters the incentive to bring in new supplies of these fuels. Greater production of coal, expanded nuclear power plants, and new technology to explore the possibilities of synthetic fuels and solar energy were all parts of the Republican approach to the energy problem.

The Democrats, in contrast, stressed price controls and conservation. In Congress, Democratic leaders were intent on shielding American consumers from the full brunt of the world price increase. They wanted to continue an elaborate system of price controls instituted by Nixon in 1973, and they favored stand-by plans for gas rationing as a better way to allocate scarce supplies than relying on the marketplace. Democratic conservation measures included plans for tax breaks for those who insulated their homes, pressure on automakers to improve gas mileage for cars, and large appropriations for mass-transit systems for American cities.

The nation failed to adopt either the Republican or the Democratic energy plans; instead, Congress tried to muddle through with elements of both approaches. Thus, on the production front, Ford was able to win approval for building the Alaskan pipeline, which made an additional 1.5 million barrels of oil a day available to American consumers. Carter placed a strong emphasis on reviving the lagging American coal industry. Congress continued the price controls on domestic oil for another forty months in late 1975, and in its most significant step toward conservation, mandated annual increases in gasoline mileage that forced Detroit to produce more fuel-efficient cars. Since nearly 10 percent of the world's oil production was burned up every day on American highways, this one congressional act would result eventually in substantial gasoline savings.

The overall outcome, however, was a patchwork that fell far short of a coherent national

massive parade up New York City's Fifth Avenue, and outrage over an oil spill in the Santa Barbara channel, reflected the national consensus behind the environmental movement.

The energy crunch pitted the environmentalists and advocates of economic growth in direct confrontation. Those who put ecology first lost out. In the mid-1970s, Congress authorized construction of the Alaskan pipeline over environmentalists' objections and ordered public utilities to resume burning coal to produce electricity. By

strategy for solving the energy problem. Neither Ford's appeal for decontrol nor Carter's call for a national conservation effort that would be "the moral equivalent of war" worked. Oil imports actually increased by 50 percent between 1973 and 1979, rising from 6 million to 9 million barrels a day, nearly half of the nation's daily petroleum usage. When the oil shock of 1979–1980 revealed how vulnerable the American economy was to OPEC, Carter reversed his policy and asked Congress to decontrol the price of domestic oil.

The Great Inflation

The gravest consequence of the oil shocks was inflation. The startling increase in price levels in the 1970s stemmed from many causes. The Vietnam War, particularly Johnson's early attempts to avoid a tax increase to pay for the fighting, created budget deficits that grew from $63 billion for the entire decade of the sixties to a total of $420 billion in the seventies. A worldwide shortage of food, resulting from both rapid population increases and poor harvests around the globe in the mid-1970s, triggered a 20 percent rise in American food prices in 1973 alone. But above all else, it was the sixfold increase in petroleum prices that raised the cost of every economic

activity, from transportation to farming, from manufacturing to mining, that was the primary source of the great inflation of the 1970s.

The impact on consumers was staggering. The price of an automobile jumped 72 percent between 1973 and 1978, while the cost of new homes went up 67 percent in the same period. During the decade, the price of a hamburger doubled, milk went from $.28 to $.59 a quart, and the cost of a loaf of bread—the proverbial staff of life—rose from $.24 to $.89. Corresponding wage increases failed to do more than keep most Americans even; for the first time since World War II, real wages did not increase in the 1970s, and in 1980 the real income of the average American family fell by 5.5 percent.

Curbing inflation proved to be beyond the power of the federal government. President Ford's early efforts to roll back prices by rhetoric—including the WIN (Whip Inflation Now) buttons—were a casualty of the 1974 recession. President Carter proved equally powerless. His attempts to cut back on government spending in order to balance the budget were more than offset by the price rises of 1979 and 1980 that followed the second oil shock. Finally, in October 1979, the Federal Reserve Board, led by Carter appointee Paul Volcker, began a sustained effort to halt inflation by mandating increased bank reserves to curtail the supply of money in circulation. The

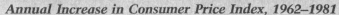

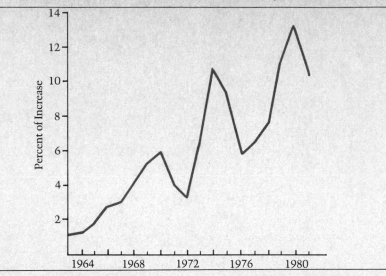

Source: U.S. Bureau of the Census, Statistical Abstract of the United States: 1982–83 (103d edition) Washington, D.C., 1982.

new tight money policy served only to heighten inflation in the short run by driving interest rates up to record levels. By the spring of 1980, the prime interest rate reached 20 percent.

The Shifting American Economy

Inflation and the oil shocks helped bring about significant changes in American business and industry in the 1970s. The most obvious result was the slowing of the rate of economic growth, with the GNP advancing only 3.2 percent for the decade, compared to 3.7 percent in the 1960s. More important, American industry began to lose its position of primacy in world markets. In 1959, U.S. firms had been the leaders in eleven of thirteen major industrial sectors, ranging from manufacturing to banking. By 1976, American companies led in only seven areas, and in all but one category—aerospace—U.S. corporations had declined in relation to Japanese and Western European competitors.

The most serious losses came in the heavy industries where the United States had once led the world. In 1946, American firms had produced 60 percent of the world's iron and steel; by 1978, they accounted for only 16 percent. New steel producers in Western Europe, Japan, and the Third World, using more advanced technology

and aided by government subsidies, were producing steel far more efficiently than their American counterparts. As a result, by the end of the 1970s, fully 20 percent of all iron and steel used in the United States was imported, and American firms were closing down their obsolete mills in the East and Midwest, idling thousands of workers.

Foreign competition did even more damage in the automobile industry. The oil shocks led to a consumer demand for small, efficient cars. German and Japanese automakers seized the opportunity to expand their once small volume of sales in the United States. By 1977, imported cars had captured 18.3 percent of the American market, with Japan leading the way with its well-built and fuel-saving Toyotas, Datsuns, and Hondas. In response, Detroit spent $70 billion retooling to produce a new fleet of smaller, lighter, front-wheel-drive cars, but American manufacturers barely survived the foreign invasion. Only government-backed loans helped the Chrysler Corporation stave off bankruptcy.

In other areas, American corporations fared much better. The multinationals that had emerged in the boom years of the 1960s continued to thrive. IBM sold computers all over the globe, while Pepsi-Cola outmaneuvered its traditional rival to penetrate the Iron Curtain. The growth of conglomerates—huge corporations that combined many dissimilar industrial concerns—

accelerated as companies like Gulf & Western and the Transamerica Corporation diversified by buying up Hollywood studios, insurance companies, and recreational-equipment manufacturers. The growth of high-technology industries proved to be the most profitable new trend of the 1970s. Computer companies and electronics firms grew at a rapid rate, especially after the development of the silicon chip, a small, wafer-thin microprocessor that can perform complex calculations almost instantly. Video games, automated cash registers, and home computers were but a few of the new products made possible by the technological revolution.

■ Electronics firms clustered around California's San Jose area, nicknamed the "silicon valley," like microchips in a computer.

The result was a geographic shift of American industry from the East and Midwest to the Sunbelt. Electronics manufacturers flourished in California, Texas, and North Carolina, where they grew up around major universities. The absence of well-entrenched labor unions, the availability of skilled labor, and the warm, attractive climate of the southern and western states lured many new concerns to the Sunbelt. At the same time, the decline of the steel and auto industries was leading to massive unemployment and economic stagnation in the northern industrial heartland. The one exception was New England, where the rise of new scientific companies around Boston helped offset the earlier decline of the textile industry.

The overall pattern was one of an economy in transition. The oil shocks had caused serious problems of inflation, slower economic growth, and rising unemployment rates. But American business still displayed the enterprise and the ability to develop new technologies that gave promise of continued economic vitality in the 1980s.

Politics After Watergate

The energy crisis and the economic dislocations of the mid-1970s could not have come at a worse time. Watergate had a paralyzing impact on the American political system. An awareness that the Cold War had led to an imperial presidency created a growing demand to weaken the power of the president and strengthen congressional authority. The result was an increasing tension between the White House and Capitol Hill which prevented the kind of strong, effective leadership needed to meet the unprecedented problems of the 1970s.

The Ford Administration

Gerald R. Ford had the distinction of being the first president who had not been elected to national office. Richard Nixon had appointed him to the vice-presidency to succeed Spiro Agnew, who had been forced to resign in order to avoid prosecution for accepting bribes while he was governor of Maryland. Ford, a longtime Michigan congressman who had risen to the post of House minority leader, was a popular choice. Amiable and unpre-

■ *The transfer of presidential power from Richard Nixon to Gerald Ford took place on August 9, 1974, shortly after this photo was taken.*

tentious, he seemed ready to restore public confidence in the presidency when he replaced Nixon in August 1974.

Ford's honeymoon lasted only a month. On September 8, 1974, he shocked the nation by announcing that he had granted Richard Nixon a full and unconditional pardon for all federal crimes he "committed or may have committed or taken part in" during his presidency. Some critics charged darkly that Nixon and Ford had made a secret bargain; others pointed out how unfair it was for Nixon's aides to serve their prison terms while the chief criminal went free. Ford apparently acted in an effort to end the bitterness over Watergate, but his attempt backfired, eroding public confidence in his leadership and linking him indelibly with the scandal.

Ford proved equally inept in his relations with Congress. Though he prided himself on his good relations with members of both houses, he opposed such Democratic measures as federal aid to education and control over strip-mining. In a little more than a year, he vetoed thirty-nine separate bills. In fact, Ford, who as a congressman had opposed virtually every Great Society measure, proved far more conservative than Nixon in the White House. He urged federal agencies to do nothing to disturb "maximum freedom for private enterprise," and he openly opposed school busing, to the dismay of civil-rights advocates.

The 1976 Campaign

Ford's weak record and the legacy of Watergate made the Democratic nomination a prize worth fighting for in 1976. A large field of candidates entered the contest, but a virtual unknown, former Georgia Governor Jimmy Carter, quickly became the front-runner. Aware of the voters' disgust with politicans of both parties, Carter ran as an outsider, portraying himself as a Southerner who had no experience in Washington and one who could thus give the nation fresh and untainted leadership. As one astonished Democrat, Averell Harriman, exclaimed, "Carter? How can Carter be nominated? I don't know him and don't know anyone who does."

Appearing refreshingly candid, Carter claimed to be an honest man, ready to deal fairly with the American people. On television the basic Carter commercial showed him sitting on a rail at his Georgia peanut farm, dressed in blue jeans, looking directly into the camera and saying, "I'll never tell a lie."

Carter swept through the primaries and won the Democratic nomination easily, naming Senator Walter Mondale of Minnesota as his running mate. Victory in November seemed assured. Ford had barely beaten back a determined challenge from former California Governor Ronald Reagan, who was the idol of the right wing. The polls gave Carter a thirty-three-point lead when the campaign began, but he quickly lost ground as he began to hedge on the issues. President Ford counterattacked, saying of his Democratic opponent, "he wavers, he wanders, he wiggles and he waffles." But Ford, who had developed a reputation as a bumbler from both his uninspired leadership and occasional physical stumbles on golf courses and airport ramps, reinforced his own image of ineptitude. In a televised debate, responding to a question about Iron Curtain countries, he declared that "there is no Soviet domination of Eastern Europe."

Carter won an extremely narrow victory in 1976. Despite Watergate and Ford's weak record, the Democratic candidate took only 49.98 percent of the popular vote. Ford swept nearly the entire West, but Carter carried the South and key northern industrial states like New York and Ohio. Far more than most recent elections, the

The Election of 1976

Candidate	Party	Popular Vote	Electoral Vote
Carter	Democrat	40,830,763	297
Ford	Republican	39,147,793	240
McCarthy	Independent	756,631	

outcome turned on class and racial factors. "The affluent, the well-educated, the suburbanites largely went for Ford," commented one observer, "the socially and economically disadvantaged for Carter." The black vote clinched the victory for the Democrats. Carter received over 90 percent of the votes of blacks, and their ballots provided the margin of victory in Ohio, Pennsylvania, and seven southern states.

Disenchantment with Carter

The new President, described by an associate as "superficially self-effacing but intensely shrewd," was an ambitious and intelligent politician. He had a rare gift for sensing what people wanted and appearing to give it to them. Liberals thought he clearly stood with them; conservatives were equally convinced that he was on their side. He was especially adept at utilizing symbols. He emerged from airplanes carrying his own garment bag; after his inauguration he walked up Pennsylvania Avenue hand-in-hand with his wife Rosalynn and daughter Amy. "Look," he seemed to be saying, "I am just an ordinary citizen who happens to be in the White House."

The substance, however, failed to match the style. He had no discernible political philosophy, no clear sense of direction. He sought the White House convinced that he was brighter and better than his competitors, but once there he had no cause or mission to fulfill. He called himself a populist, but that label meant little more than an appeal to the common man, a somewhat ironic appeal, given Carter's personal wealth.

■ *Despite his intelligence and hard work, Jimmy Carter's policies seemed to lack vision, and the public began to question his ability to lead.*

"The idea of a millionaire populist has always amused me," commented his attorney general, fellow Georgian Griffin Bell, "since the two persuasions seem contradictory."

The makeup of his administration reflected the conflicting tendencies that would eventually destroy the Carter administration. In the White House, he surrounded himself with close associates from Georgia, fellow outsiders like presidential adviser Hamilton Jordan and press secretary Jody Powell. Yet he picked established Democrats for key cabinet positions; Cyrus Vance, a New York lawyer, as secretary of state; Joseph Califano, a former aide to Lyndon Johnson, to head HEW; and Michael Blumenthal, the president of the Bendix Corporation, as secretary of the treasury. In the lower ranks, however, he selected liberal activists, followers of George McGovern, Ted Kennedy, and Ralph Nader, people who were intent on regulating business and preserving the environment. The result was bound to be tension and conflict, as the White House staff and the federal bureaucracy worked at cross purposes, one group seeking change while the other attempted to protect the President.

Lacking both a clear set of priorities and a coherent political philosophy, the Carter administration was doomed to fail. The President strove hard for a balanced budget but was forced to accept mounting deficits. Federal agencies fought to save the environment and help consumers but served only to anger industry. For example, head of the highway safety program Joan Claybrook, a former associate of Ralph Nader, recalled 12.9 million automobiles in 1977. Her predecessor in 1976 had recalled only 3.4 million.

In the crucial area of social services, Joseph Califano failed repeatedly in his efforts to carry out long-overdue reforms. His attempt to overhaul the nation's welfare program, which had become a $30-billion annual operation serving some thirty million Americans, won little support from the White House. Carter's unwillingness to take the political risks involved in revamping the overburdened Social Security system by reducing benefits and raising the retirement age blocked Califano's efforts. And the HEW secretary finally gave up his attempt to draw up a workable National Health Insurance plan when he was caught in the crossfire between President Carter and Senator Kennedy.

Informed by his pollsters in 1979 that he was losing the nation's confidence, Carter sought desperately to redeem himself. After a series of meetings at Camp David with a wide variety of advisers, he gave a speech in which he attributed the blame for his failure to the American people, accusing them of creating "a crisis of confidence . . . that strikes at the very heart and soul and spirit of our national will." Then a week after what his critics termed the "national malaise" speech, he requested the resignation of Califano and Treasury Secretary Blumenthal. But neither the attempt to pin responsibility on the American people nor the firing of cabinet members could hide the fact that Carter, despite his good intentions and hard work, had failed to provide the bold leadership the nation needed.

From Détente to Renewed Cold War

America's position in the world declined sharply in the 1970s. In part, the fault was internal. The Vietnam War left the American people convinced that the nation should never again intervene abroad and Watergate discredited strong presidential leadership, shifting power over foreign policy to Congress. The new national consensus was symbolized by the War Powers Act, passed in 1973, which required the President to consult with Congress before sending American troops into action overseas. At the same time, external events and developments, notably the control over oil exercised by OPEC and the threats posed by revolutionary nationalism in the Middle East and Latin America, further weakened American foreign policy. No longer able to dominate the international scene, the United States began to play the role of spectator, and at times even of victim.

American diplomats tried three different strategies in the '70s in an effort to adjust to the new realities of power. During the Ford presidency, Secretary of State Kissinger continued the policy of détente. Aware that the Soviet Union had neutralized America's traditional nuclear advantage, Kissinger sought to use both economic incentives and Russian fear of China to moderate Soviet policy. In the Carter administration,

Estimated Total Costs of U.S. Wars, 1775–1980
(in millions of dollars)

	Wartime Costs	Veterans' Benefit Costs	Interest Payments on War Loans	Estimated Long-term Costs
American Revolution	100	28	20	148
War of 1812	93	20	14	127
Mexican War	73	26	10	109
Civil War (Union side only)*	3,200	3,289	1,200	7,689
Spanish-American War	400	2,096	60	2,556
World War I	26,000	13,383	11,100	50,383
World War II	288,000	57,565	200,000	545,565
Korean Conflict	54,000	9,564	7,500	71,064
Vietnam Conflict	111,000	9,330	3,000	123,330

*Costs to the Confederate side are estimated at $1 billion.
Source: U.S. Bureau of the Census, Statistical Abstract of the United States: 1982–83 (103d edition) Washington, D.C., 1982.

American foreign policy oscillated between two poles. Although Secretary of State Cyrus Vance tried to maintain elements of détente, President Carter called for an American crusade on behalf of human rights in the world. At the same time, National Security Adviser Zbigniew Brzezinski advocated more hawkish policies which stressed the Soviet arms buildup and the need for confrontation. By the late 1970s, Brzezinski's hard line had triumphed over both Vance's version of détente and Carter's concern for human rights.

Retreat in Asia and Africa

It was Gerald Ford's fate to reap where Nixon had sown. In 1974, Congress cut in half the administration's request for $1.4 billion in military aid to South Vietnam. A year later, when a North Vietnamese offensive proved surprisingly successful, Ford was unable to get Congress to grant any additional aid. Bereft of American assistance and weakened by internal corruption, the South Vietnamese government was unable to stop the advance on Saigon in April 1975. American forces concentrated on evacuating 150,000 loyal South Vietnamese, but many more were left behind when the last helicopter left the roof of the embassy in Saigon. Bitter and humiliated, the American people dejectedly watched the televised scene as the North Vietnamese celebrated their conquest of the South.

■ *Through television, millions of Americans watched the fall of Saigon. Thousands of South Vietnamese sought refuge in the U.S. embassy compound.*

Less than a month later, Ford had a chance to remind the world of American power. The Khmer Rouge government of Cambodia seized an American freighter, the *Mayaguez*, and imprisoned its crew. When the Communists ignored the initial American protest, Ford authorized an armed attack on Cambodia by two thousand marines from bases in Thailand. By the time the American forces landed on a small offshore island, Cambodia had freed the crewmen. The nation took pride in the President's resort to force, but forty Americans paid for his decision with their lives.

Events in Africa, however, proved that caution and restraint were still the hallmark of American foreign policy in the 1970s. The new nation of Angola had won its independence from Portugal in 1974, only to be caught up in a civil war between rival forces. The United States and China backed one group in this small country, but the Soviet Union, using several thousand Cuban troops, helped put a rival faction in power.

Despite repeated pleas from Ford and Kissinger, Congress refused to sanction American interven-tion. Covert action by the CIA proved ineffective, but the government of Angola turned out to be neutral, relying on technical assistance from the United States to offset military aid from Russia. Most Americans were relieved by the outcome in Angola, not sharing Kissinger's belief that the nation had been "traumatized by Vietnam as we were by Munich."

Accommodation in Latin America

President Carter was more successful than Ford in adjusting to the growing nationalism in the world, particularly in Central America, where the United States had imposed order for most of the twentieth century by backing reactionary regimes.

The first test came in Panama. Resentment over American ownership of the Panama Canal had led Lyndon Johnson to enter into negotiations aimed at the eventual return of the waterway to Panama. Carter completed the long diplo-

Central America and the Caribbean

United States involvement in Central American trouble spots intensified in the 1980s.

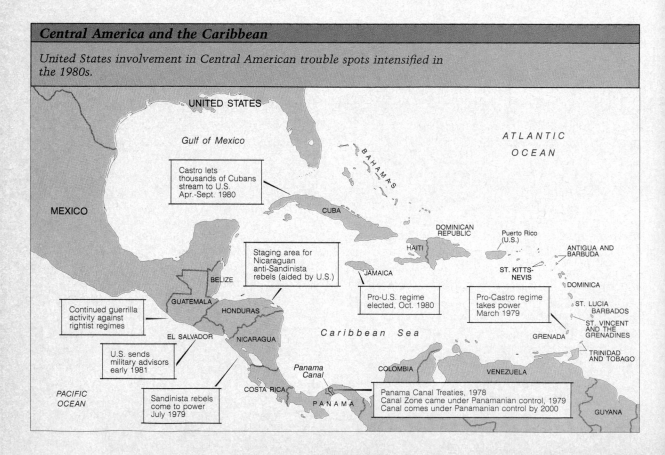

■ *An eighteen-year-old guerrilla fighter at a rebel camp in El Salvador. Known as "Claudia," which is not her real name, she is part of a rebel group battling the Salvadoran military forces.*

encouraged left-wing guerrillas to step up attacks on the governments of Guatemala and El Salvador. Carter hoped to find responsible democratic leaders to support in these countries, but both situations quickly deteriorated into classic struggles between the conservative elite, who controlled the land and the army, and radicals who rallied the peasantry to their side. The situation was most critical in El Salvador, where Carter decided to back the government against the rebels, authorizing increased American military aid just before he left office in January 1981. Carter was unable to find a workable alternative between the extremes of reactionary dictatorship and radical revolution in Central America. His successor in the White House faced a dangerous situation in the hemisphere.

The Quest for Peace in the Middle East

The inconclusive results of the Yom Kippur War gave Henry Kissinger the opportunity to play the role of peacemaker in the troubled Middle East. Shuttling back and forth between Cairo and Jerusalem, and then to Damascus, the secretary of state finally succeeded in arranging a pullback of Israeli forces in both the Sinai and the Golan Heights. Although he failed to achieve his goal of an Arab-Israeli settlement, Kissinger had succeeded in demonstrating that the United States could play the role of neutral mediator between the Israelis and Arabs. And equally important, he had detached Egypt from dependence on the Soviet Union, thereby weakening Russian influence in the Middle East.

Jimmy Carter tried at first to bring the Soviets back into the Middle Eastern peacemaking process by proposing a big power settlement. In November 1977, however, Egyptian President Anwar Sadat stunned the world by traveling to Jerusalem in an effort to reach agreement directly with Israel. The next year, Carter abandoned his efforts to work with the Russians and instead invited both Sadat and Israeli Prime Minister Menachem Begin to negotiate under his guidance at Camp David. For thirteen days, President Carter met with Sadat and Begin, finally emerging with the ambiguous Camp David accords. A framework for negotiations, rather than an actual

matic process in 1977 by signing two treaties. One restored sovereignty in the 500-square-mile canal zone to Panama, while the other provided for gradual Panamanian responsibility for operating the canal, with appropriate safeguards for its use and defense by the United States. Despite the intense opposition of right-wing Republicans, who charged Carter with "giving away" the Panama Canal, the Senate ratified the treaties in 1978, and thus paved the way for the return of the canal to Panama by the year 2000.

Carter tried to be equally understanding when a group of Nicaraguan leftists known as the Sandinistas began a revolt against dictator Anastasio Somoza, who fell from power in 1979. The United States had withheld support from Somoza and worked with several Latin American nations, notably Venezuela and Mexico, to establish a new Nicaraguan government that included both rebel and business leaders. Congressional reluctance to extend economic aid, however, and the regime's gradual shift to the left, including closer ties with Castro's Cuba, created a widening rift between the United States and Nicaragua by the end of the 1970s.

The success of the Sandinistas in Nicaragua

peace settlement, the Camp David agreements dealt gingerly with the problem of Palestinian autonomy in the West Bank and Gaza Strip areas.

In 1979, Israel and Egypt signed a peace treaty which provided for the gradual return of the entire Sinai to Egypt but left the fate of the Palestine Arabs vague and unsettled. By excluding both the Palestine Liberation Organization (PLO) and the Soviet Union from the negotiations, the United States alienated Egypt from the other Arab nations and drove the more radical states closer to the Soviet Union.

Any sense of progress in the Middle East as a result of Camp David was quickly offset in 1979 with the outbreak of the Iranian Revolution. Under Nixon and Kissinger, the United States had come to depend heavily on the shah and his powerful army for defense of the vital Persian Gulf. Carter continued the close relationship with the shah, despite growing signs of domestic discontent with his leadership. In a visit to Teheran in late 1977, the President praised the shah for making Iran "an island of stability" and for per-

■ *The Camp David accords in 1978 set the stage for a peace treaty between Egypt and Israel. Here a beaming Jimmy Carter watches as Prime Minister Begin embraces President Sadat. But this personal triumph for Carter was short-lived.*

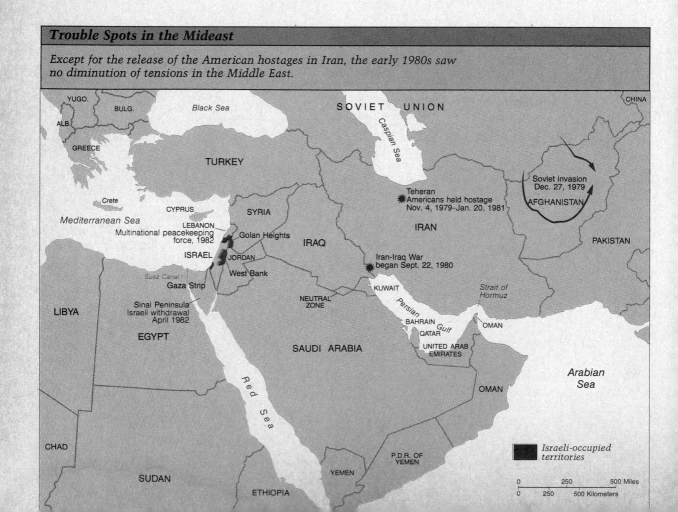

Trouble Spots in the Mideast

Except for the release of the American hostages in Iran, the early 1980s saw no diminution of tensions in the Middle East.

sonally deserving "the respect and the admiration and love which your people give to you." Yet little more than a year later Iran was in chaos as the exiled Ayatollah Ruhollah Khomeini led a fundamentalist Moslem revolt against the shah.

Unaware of the deep resentment most Iranians felt toward the shah—a resentment based both on dislike of sweeping modernization programs and police-state rule—the Carter administration misjudged the nature of the Iranian Revolution. At first the United States encouraged the shah to remain in Iran, but when he decided to leave the country in January 1979, Carter tried to work with a moderate regime rather than encourage an army coup. With Khomeini's return from exile, Moslem militants quickly came to power in Teheran. In October 1979, Carter permitted the exiled shah to enter the United States for medical treatment. Irate mobs in Iran denounced the United States and on November 4, militant students seized the U.S. embassy in Teheran and took fifty-eight Americans prisoner.

The prolonged hostage crisis revealed the extent to which American power had declined in the 1970s. Carter relied first on diplomacy and economic reprisals in a vain attempt to free the hostages. American allies in Western Europe and Japan, dependent on Middle Eastern oil, quickly disassociated themselves from the United States, while Khomeini offset the American economic embargo by signing trade agreements with the Soviet Union. In an attempt to impress the Iranians, the United States concentrated its naval forces in the Indian Ocean. In his State of the Union message in January 1980, the president enunciated a new Carter Doctrine, telling the world that the United States would fight to protect the vital oil supplies of the Persian Gulf. "Twin threats to the flow of oil—from regional instability and now potentially from the Soviet Union—require that we firmly defend our vital interest when threatened."

Carter was unable to back up these brave words with meaningful action. Plans for a rapid deployment force were prepared, but it would be several years before these mobile troops could be deployed. In April 1980, the President authorized a desperate rescue mission that ended in failure when several helicopters broke down in the Iranian desert. The mission was aborted, an accident cost the lives of eight crewmen, and Secretary of

■ *Americans were shocked by the deep anger Iranian mobs directed toward the Americans staffing the U.S. embassy in Teheran.*

■ *The burnt helicopters in the Iranian desert emphasized America's frustration and its inability to rescue the hostages.*

From Détente to Renewed Cold War

State Cyrus Vance—who had opposed the rescue attempt—resigned in protest. The hostage crisis dragged on through the summer and fall of 1980, a symbol of American weakness that proved to be a powerful political handicap to Carter in the upcoming presidential election.

The End of Détente

The policy of détente was already in trouble when Carter took office in 1977. Congressional refusal to relax trade restrictions on the Soviet Union had doomed Kissinger's attempts to win political concessions from the Soviets through economic incentives. The Kremlin's repression of the growing dissident movement, led by nuclear physicist Andrei Sakharov, and its harsh policy restricting the emigration of Soviet Jews had caused many Americans to doubt the wisdom of seeking accommodation with the Soviet Union.

President Carter's emphasis on human rights appeared to the Russians to be a direct repudiation of détente. In his inaugural address, Carter reaffirmed his concern over the mistreatment of human beings anywhere in the world, declaring "our commitment to human rights must be absolute." It was easier said than done. Carter did withhold aid from authoritarian governments in Chile and Argentina, but equally repressive regimes in South Korea and the Philippines continued to receive generous American support. Human rights proved, in the words of one presidential aide, "absolute in principle but flexible in application." The Soviets, however, were disturbed by the principle, particularly after Carter received Soviet exiles in the White House.

Secretary of State Vance concentrated on continuing the main pillar of détente, the strategic arms limitation talks (SALT). In 1974, President Ford had met with Brezhnev in Vladivostok and reached tentative agreement on the outline of SALT II. The chief provision was for a ceiling of 2400 nuclear launchers by each side, a level which would not require either Russia or the United States to give up any existing delivery vehicles. In March 1977, Vance went to Moscow to propose a drastic reduction in this level; the Soviets, already angry over human rights, rejected the American proposal as an attempt to overcome the Russian lead in land-based ICBMs.

Zbigniew Brzezinski, Carter's national security adviser, worked from the outset to reverse the policy of détente. Commenting that he was "the first Pole in 300 years in a position to really stick it to the Russians," he favored confrontation with the Kremlin. Although Carter signed a SALT II treaty with Russia in 1978 which lowered the ceiling on nuclear delivery systems to 2250, growing opposition in the Senate played directly into Brzezinski's hand. He prevailed on the President to advocate adoption of a new MX missile to replace the existing Minuteman ICBMs, which some experts thought were now vulnerable to a Soviet first strike. This new weapons system, together with the planned Trident submarine, ensured that regardless of SALT, the nuclear arms race would be speeded up in the 1980s.

Brzezinski also was successful in persuading the President to use China to outmaneuver the Soviets. After a trip to China in 1978, Brzezinski arranged for the sale of advanced technology to China (including items denied the Russians), and the possibility of resuming full diplomatic relations was explored. Finally, on January 1, 1979, the United States and China exchanged ambassa-

■ Soviet tanks rolled into Afghanistan in December 1979, dealing a near-mortal blow to East-West détente.

Military Power: United States vs. USSR, 1980–1981

	United States	Soviet Union
Intercontinental Ballistic Missiles (ICBMs)	1,052[a]	1,398
Submarine-launched Ballistic Missiles (SLBMs)	576[b]	950
Long-Range Strategic Bombers	348[c]	156
Total Delivery Vehicles (ICBMs, SLBMs, Bombers)	1,976	2,504
Nuclear Warheads	9,200	6,000
European Nuclear Forces[d]	924	2,537
Anti-Ballistic Missile Launchers (ABM)	·0	32
Aircraft Carriers	12	1
Armed Forces Personnel	3,050,000 (plus 2,768,000 NATO forces)	4,822,000 (plus 1,122,000 Warsaw Pact forces)

Although the United States lagged behind the Soviet Union in certain categories, the U.S. Department of Defense and other government sources explained that the figures revealed a basic equivalence in strategic nuclear power. Moreover, in measuring the fighting abilities of both sides, technological skills, qualities of leadership, and economic strength must be considered. Also, some of the Soviet military power was deployed, not against Western Europe or the United States, but against China.

[a]*Fifty-two single-warhead Titan-IIs (two others were out of commission and not counted); 450 single-warhead Minuteman IIs; and 550 MIRVed Minuteman IIIs.*

[b]*80 Polaris; 304 Poseidon; 192 Trident.*

[c]*B-52s*

[d]*Total launchers for Western allies (NATO and France) and Warsaw Pact. Figures represent bombers and missiles. The Soviets disputed the figures (disagreeing on which weapons should be counted) and offered instead: 1,031 for the Western allies and 1.055 for the Warsaw Pact. Under NATO auspices, the United States set 1983 for deployment of 108 Pershing missiles and 464 ground-launched cruise missiles in Europe.*

Source: Thomas G. Paterson and J. G. Clifford, American Foreign Policy: A History (Lexington, Mass.: D. C. Heath, 1983).

dors, thereby completing the reconciliation that Nixon had begun in 1971. The new relationship between China and the United States presented the Soviet Union with the problem of defending itself against two distinct enemies.

The Cold War, in abeyance for nearly a decade, resumed with full fury in December 1979 when the Soviet Union invaded Afghanistan. Although this move was apparently defensive in nature, designed to ensure a regime friendly to the Soviet Union, it appeared to many as the beginning of a Soviet thrust toward the Indian Ocean and the Persian Gulf. Carter responded to this aggression with a series of stern acts: the United States banned the sale of high technology to Russia, embargoed the export of grain, resumed draft registration, and even boycotted the 1980 Mos-

cow Olympics. These American moves did not halt the invasion of Afghanistan; instead, they put the United States and Russia back on a collision course.

The results doomed détente. Aware that he could not get a two-thirds vote in the Senate, Carter withdrew the SALT II treaty. Right-wing groups in the United States began to warn of Soviet military superiority and call for a massive American arms build-up. The hopeful phrases of détente gave way to belligerent rhetoric as groups like the Committee on the Present Danger called for an all-out effort against the Soviet Union. Jimmy Carter, who had come into office hoping to advance human rights and control the nuclear arms race, now found himself a victim of the renewed Cold War.

Cycles in History

Most historians believe that the events and trends they describe are unique, reflecting a variety of individual characteristics that make each war, each election, and each era different. Yet some scholars have noticed that certain trends tend to recur over long periods of time; others go even further, suggesting that there are cyclical rhythms in American history that make it possible to predict the future.

The two most plausible cycles relate to political behavior and to foreign policy. In 1949, Arthur M. Schlesinger, Sr., a noted cultural historian, described an oscillation between liberalism and conservatism in American politics from the Revolution through World War II (see Table 1). Periods of liberal reform alternated with eras of

1. Schlesinger's Political Periods

Liberal	Conservative
1765–1787	1787–1801
1801–1816	1816–1829
1829–1841	1841–1861
1861–1869	1869–1901
1901–1919	1919–1931
1931–1947	(1947–1962)*
(1962–1978)*	(1978–1993)*

*Arthur M. Schlesinger, Paths to the Present, p. 81. Copyright 1949, by the Macmillan Company. *projected*

conservatism in approximately sixteen-year cycles. Presenting his findings at the end of a liberal era, Schlesinger prophesied that the conservative swing would last until 1962, and then would give way to a new surge of liberalism, that would continue until about 1978. The election of John F. Kennedy and the adoption of Lyndon Johnson's Great Society program in the mid-1960s fits in neatly with Schlesinger's prediction, as does Ronald Reagan's conservative triumph in 1980, which was foreshadowed by Republican gains in the 1978 congressional elections.

Political scientist Frank L. Klingberg, writing in 1952, offered an equally persuasive explanation of the fluctuation between isolation and internationalism in American foreign policy. Periods of introversion, Klingberg argued, alternated about every twenty-five years with eras of an active world policy throughout American history (see Table 2). Klingberg's forecast for the future proved nearly as accurate as Schlesinger's. The shift to an active world policy which began in 1940, would continue until the late 1960s, he claimed, and then would give way to a period of relative withdrawal through the early 1990s. The Vietnam War triggered a strong protest movement which forced Lyndon Johnson to begin winding down the conflict in 1968, and led to a policy of détente in the 1970s under Nixon and Ford.

2. Klingberg's Foreign Policy Moods

Isolation	Participation
1776–1798	1798–1824
1824–1844	1844–1871
1871–1891	1891–1919
1919–1940	(1940–1967)*
(1967–1988)*	(1988–2015)*

Frank L. Klingberg, "The Historical Alternation of Moods in American Foreign Policy," *World Politics* (1952): 250.
*projected

Both scholars see the cycles as reflecting a deep-seated and natural rhythm comparable to the tides that ebb and flow in the world's oceans. Neither war nor depression seems to alter the pattern, and even strong leaders such as Abraham Lincoln and Franklin Roosevelt had to adapt themselves to this basic law of American life. Both authors see the pendulum-like swing between opposite poles as a healthy mechanism, which enables the nation to adapt to change while holding on to inherited values. Schlesinger calls it a "balance wheel of orderly evolution," which ensures "a fair field" for both liberals and conservatives over time. Klingberg is slightly less enthusiastic, but he still feels that the alternating pattern holds promise of continued American leadership in world affairs.

In addition to predicting future trends, the Schlesinger and Klingberg cycles reveal a significant correlation between domestic politics and foreign policy. During periods of conservative control, the nation has tended toward isolation, while during liberal eras, a more active foreign policy has prevailed. From 1776 to 1947, the span covered by both authors, liberalism was in vogue eighty years and conservatism ninety-one. For forty-eight of the eighty liberal years, the nation pursued an active world policy. The link between isolationism and conservatism is not quite as strong; for fifty-one of the ninety-one years of conservative dominance, the United States was in a stage of withdrawal from world affairs (see Table 3).

What do these cycles tell us of the future? Schlesinger's pattern suggests that we can expect the current era of Reaganism to persist through the decade of the 1980s, with a shift back to liberalism likely around 1993. Klingberg's analysis forecasts a continued passive world role until about 1988, when we can expect a return to a more active foreign policy. And in keeping with the nation's historic tendencies, the liberal administrations of the final decade of the twentieth century and the early years of the twenty-first will be extending American power and influence once again on a global basis.

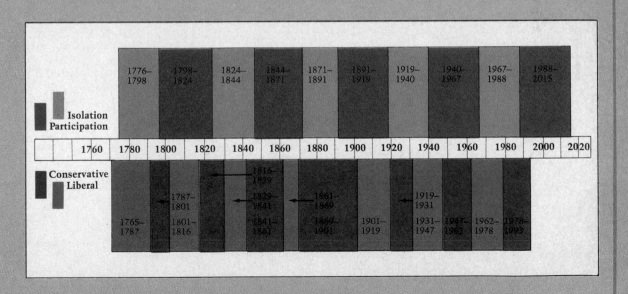

A Decade of Social Change

The 1970s witnessed a series of significant shifts in American society that paralleled the economic changes brought about by inflation and the oil shocks. The nation's population in 1980 stood at just over 226 million, a gain of 11.4 percent from 1970, the smallest rate of increase since the census of 1940. The vast majority—nearly 186 million—were white, while blacks still formed the largest ethnic minority—26.5 million.

A People on the Move

The most striking finding of the 1980 census was that for the first time in American history more than half of the population lived in the South and West. The states of the Northeast and Midwest had virtually stood still (New York had actually lost population in the 1970s), while the Sunbelt, notably Florida, California, and Texas, had boomed. This population shift reflected the changing economic realities of the decade. College-educated men and women, especially young professionals, and blue-collar workers with skills in demand gravitated to the Sunbelt, where more and more American corporations were moving their offices and factories.

The cities of the North suffered the most from this mass exodus. New York City, which almost went bankrupt midway through the decade, lost nearly a million people between 1970 and 1980. Midwestern cities like Cleveland and Saint Louis were equally hard hit, each losing a quarter of its population in just ten years as whites led the move either to the Sunbelt or to nearby suburbs. The central cities of the North and West lost many of their best-educated and most affluent citizens, leaving them with large low-income populations—mainly minority groups—with very expensive social needs.

Another striking population trend was the nationwide rise in the number of the elderly. At the beginning of the century, only 4.1 percent of the

Migration to the Sunbelt, 1970–1981

The growing electoral power of the Sunbelt helped Ronald Reagan win the 1980 presidential election.

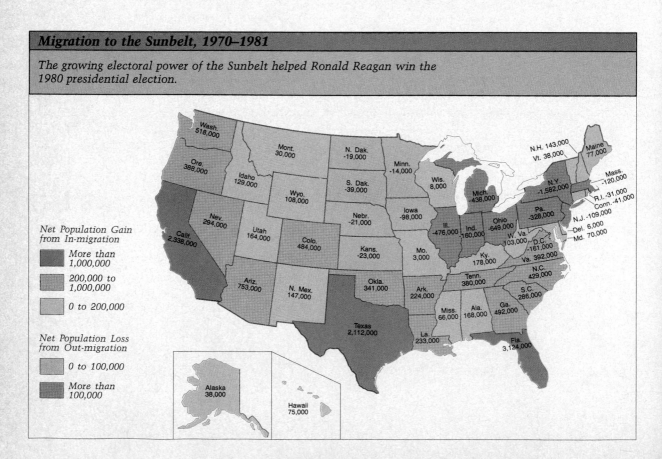

Net Population Gain from In-migration

- More than 1,000,000
- 200,000 to 1,000,000
- 0 to 200,000

Net Population Loss from Out-migration

- 0 to 100,000
- More than 100,000

■ *Houston skyline. The growth and prosperity of the Sunbelt is reflected in the gleaming new skyscrapers erected in cities like Houston, Texas, during the 1970s and early '80s.*

population was age sixty-five or older; by 1980, those over sixty-five made up 11.3 percent, and people over seventy-five were the single fastest growing group of all. Major advances in medicine had increased life expectancy from sixty-three in the 1930s to seventy-two by the mid-1970s. By 1980 American women could expect to live to age seventy-seven. There were a huge number of widows, many lonely and insecure, living on the edge of poverty. Yet thanks to the indexing of Social Security payments to inflation, the elderly fared relatively well economically during the decade.

A more traditional American process, that of immigration, underwent a surprising shift in the 1970s. A nation that had been built on a predominantly European influx suddenly found itself adding millions of Asians and Latin Americans to its population, with very few newcomers arriving from Europe. More than 5 million immigrants entered the United States in the 1970s, with the annual rate rising to over 700,000 by the end of the decade. In 1978, Mexico provided the most, 92,000 legal entrants and probably as many more illegal ones, with Vietnam close behind at 88,000 followed by the Philippines with 37,000 and Cuba with 30,000. In contrast, only 14,200 came from England, 7400 from Italy and a mere 982 from Ireland. The newcomers from Asia and Latin America filled the traditional economic role of

the immigrant, working at the dirty and difficult jobs that most Americans shunned, often for low wages and without receiving any government assistance. Their cultural, linguistic, and ethnic differences, however, created an assimilation problem at least as great as that of the "new" immigrants from southern and eastern Europe in the late nineteenth century.

Although the 1980 census revealed many departures from past experience, it also reaffirmed some traditional American patterns. In the face of inflation and unemployment, the American people continued to be prosperous. The median family income rose to $21,023, with just 11 percent of the population living below the government's official poverty line. Not only were Americans living longer, but thanks to Medicare, Medicaid, and private health plans, they were receiving better medical care than ever before, with health expenditures rising to $476 per person. A declining birthrate lowered enrollments in elementary and secondary schools, leading to better teacher-student ratios, while college attendance continued to climb. By 1981, there were nearly 12 million college students, compared to only a million and a half in 1941. Now more than 20 percent of the nation's young people received a college degree, compared to 12 percent of their parents' generation.

The overall picture was of a society in transition. The rising figures of crime, teen-age pregnancy, and drug use were balanced by better health and educational opportunities than any previous generation had enjoyed. Pockets of poverty, notably in the older industrial states, were matched by boom areas. America was still the land of opportunity for immigrants, even if they came now from Mexico and Vietnam, rather than Poland and Italy. And despite the ravages of inflation and the shock of the energy crunch, people continued to look to the future, aware of the new age of limitations in which they lived, but confident that they could still achieve the American dream.

■ *Naval cadets at Annapolis. Some women won admission to service academies during the 1970s, but most working women continued to face job discrimination.*

*Drawing by H. Martin: © 1980
The New Yorker Magazine, Inc.*

The Changing Role of Women

The entry of women into the work force accelerated in the 1970s, climbing to a new high. Some 10 million women took jobs in the period from 1965 to 1975, compared to 7 million men. By the end of the decade, 52 percent of all adult women were working, and their ranks included 6 million more working wives than in 1970.

Women scored some impressive breakthroughs. They began to enter corporation boardrooms, became presidents of major universities, and were admitted to West Point and Annapolis. The appointment of Sandra Day O'Connor to the Supreme Court in 1981 marked a historic first. Yet despite the growing number of female elected officials, doctors, and lawyers, the vast majority of

working women still suffered from economic discrimination. The Equal Pay Act, passed by Congress in 1972, and a number of lawsuits which forced corporations to pay women equal wages for equal work, helped close the gap, but the sex differential still remained. As late as 1980, the median pay for working women was only 60 percent of that for men.

Women had fewer children in the 1970s than in earlier decades. The birthrate, which had peaked at over 3.5 births for every woman of childbearing age in the late 1950s, dropped to less than 2 by the mid-1970s. This trend toward smaller families was related to the great increase in working wives, an increase that was intensified by the economic pressures caused by inflation in the 1970s. Many women who pursued careers put off childbearing, waiting until they had established themselves professionally, while others simply decided to forgo children entirely. The drop in the birthrate also reflected the later age of marriage in the seventies, as well as the ever larger number of single women.

The postwar increase in the divorce rate continued unabated. Where marriages once outnumbered divorces by five to one in the 1950s, by 1980 the ratio was down to two to one. Marital breakup lost its stigma; for many, marriage ceased to be a sacred institution. The rise in the divorce rate resulted in a tremendous increase in what the census dubbed "one-parent households," reflecting a sharp decline in traditional family units. The number of one-parent families—nearly always a case of the mother rearing the children alone, rose by 79 percent during the decade. By the end of the 1970s, 22 percent of all American children were reared in homes with only one parent; in the case of blacks, the figure was 56 percent.

The women's movement sought two different but related objectives in the 1970s. The first was ratification of the Equal Rights Amendment. Approved by Congress in 1972, the amendment stated simply, "Equality of rights under the law shall not be denied or abridged by the United States or any state on account of sex." Within a year, twenty-two states had approved the amendment, but the efforts gradually faltered and finally stalled just three states short of ratification. The opposition came in part from working-class women who feared, as one union leader explained, that those employed as "maids, laundry workers, hospital cleaners, or dishwashers" would lose the protection of state laws that regulated wages and hours of work for women. Right-wing activist Phyllis Schlafly led an organized effort to defeat ERA, claiming that the amendment would lead to unisex toilets, homosexual marriages, and the drafting of women. The National Organization for Women (NOW) fought back, persuading Congress to extend the time for ratification by three years and waging intense campaigns for approval in Florida and Illinois. But the deadline for ratification finally passed on June 30, 1982, with the ERA forces still three states short. NOW leader Eleanor Smeal vowed a continuing struggle, declaring, "The crusade is not over. We know that we are the wave of the future."

The women's movement was more successful in its fight for reproductive rights. Heartened by the 1973 Supreme Court decision, *Roe* v. *Wade*, which struck down state laws banning abortions, feminists worked hard to extend the right of women to choose whether to have children. Right-to-life groups, backed by the Catholic

■ *Many women reasoned that rights granted by statute could easily be repealed in the future, therefore they embarked on a crusade to pass an equal rights amendment to the Constitution.*

church, fundamentalist Protestants, and extreme conservatives, sought to deny the use of public funds to pay for abortions, thereby limiting the exercise of this right to those women who could afford it. With the strong support of President Carter, Congress passed the Hyde amendment which forbade the use of federal money to pay for abortions, and in 1981 the Supreme Court upheld this legislation. Despite this setback, pro-choice groups organized privately funded family-planning agencies and abortion clinics to give poor women the opportunity to exercise control over their reproductive function.

Advance and Retreat for Blacks

For middle-class blacks, the 1970s were a decade of progress; they began to reap the gains of the affirmative-action programs spawned by LBJ's Great Society. By 1976, one third of all black workers held white-collar jobs, double the rate in 1960, and nearly 30 percent earned more than $12,000 a year. Education proved the key to black advances. With more than one million blacks enrolled in college by 1980, the opportunities for a middle-class style of life were greatly increased.

Many well-educated and affluent blacks tended to behave like whites in similar circumstances. Some joined the flight to the suburbs, leaving the central city in even larger proportions than whites. Others flocked to the Sunbelt, reversing the historic movement of rural blacks from the South to the North. In the 1970s, many young blacks, trained as doctors, lawyers, or business executives, returned to the cities of the South to pursue their careers. A 1978 survey by *Ebony* magazine identified Atlanta, Dallas, and Houston among the ten most attractive American cities for blacks. Atlanta and New Orleans both had black mayors by the end of the decade and, in fact, the South had become the most thoroughly integrated of all the nation's regions.

Occupations by Sex and Race, 1972 and 1980

Title of Occupation	Total Employed (millions) 1972	Total Employed (millions) 1980	1972 Percentage Female	1972 Percentage Nonwhite	1980 Percentage Female	1980 Percentage Nonwhite
Professional/Technical	11.4	15.6	39.3	7.2	44.3	8.9
Accountants	0.7	1.0	21.7	4.3	36.2	8.2
Computer specialists	0.2	0.5	16.8	5.5	25.7	8.0
Engineers	1.1	1.4	0.8	3.4	4.0	5.9
Lawyers and Judges	0.3	0.5	3.8	1.9	12.8	4.2
Life/Physical Scientists	0.2	0.3	10.0	7.8	20.3	9.6
Physicians/Dentists and related	0.6	0.7	9.3	6.3	12.9	8.2
Professors	0.4	0.5	28.0	7.2	33.9	7.1
Engineering/Science technicians	0.8	1.0	9.1	5.2	17.8	8.8
Writers/Artists/Entertainers	0.8	1.2	31.7	4.8	39.3	5.9
Sales	5.3	6.1	41.6	3.6	45.3	5.1
Real estate Agents/Brokers	0.3	0.5	36.7	2.6	50.7	2.1
Clerks-retail	2.3	2.3	68.9	5.0	71.1	7.2
Clerical	14.2	18.1	75.6	8.7	80.1	11.1
Bookkeepers	1.5	1.9	97.9	3.6	90.5	5.5
Clerical supervisors	0.1	0.2	57.8	10.1	70.5	12.0
Office machine operators	0.6	0.9	71.4	13.1	72.6	17.5
Secretaries	2.9	3.8	99.1	5.2	99.1	6.7
Crafts Workers	10.8	12.5	3.6	6.9	6.0	8.3
Blue-collar supervisors	1.4	1.7	6.9	6.0	10.8	7.8
Machinists and Jobsetters	0.4	0.6	0.6	6.2	4.0	8.7
Tool and die makers	0.1	0.1	0.5	2.2	2.8	2.3
Mechanics (except automobile)	1.7	2.1	1.0	5.3	2.6	7.5
Transport equipment operators	3.2	3.4	4.2	14.8	8.0	15.3
Laborers (nonfarm)	4.2	4.4	6.3	20.2	11.6	16.9
Farmers and Farm Managers	1.6	1.4	5.9	3.3	10.6	2.6
Farm Laborers/Supervisors	1.3	1.2	32.1	15.1	27.0	13.3
Service (non-private household)	9.5	11.9	57.0	10.5	58.9	18.2
Service (private household)	1.4	1.0	97.6	40.6	97.5	33.2

Source: U.S. Bureau of the Census, Statistical Abstract of the United States: 1982–83 (103d edition) Washington, D.C., 1982.

The Age of Scarcity

Yet despite these gains, there were also setbacks for blacks in the 1970s. The whole affirmative-action process was brought into question by the case of Allen Bakke, a white applicant to the medical school of the University of California at Davis. Bakke claimed that his rights had been violated when his application was rejected, because his credentials were better than those of several minority applicants who were awarded some of the 16 places reserved for "disadvantaged students" in the class of 100. When the highest state court in California ruled in favor of Bakke in 1976, the university appealed the verdict to the Supreme Court.

The Court issued its long-awaited ruling on June 28, 1978. By a five-to-four margin, the justices ruled in favor of Bakke, asserting that the use of "explicit racial classification" had denied him equal protection under the Fourteenth Amendment. At the same time, however, by a similar five-to-four vote, the Court upheld the principle of affirmative action, claiming that universities could make race "simply one element" in their effort to select a diverse student body.

In subsequent decisions, the Court upheld an affirmative-action program designed by Kaiser Aluminum to help advance minority workers and ordered American Telephone and Telegraph to hire more blacks and women to make up for past discrimination. It was Justice Harry A. Blackmun, a Nixon appointee, who explained the Court's position best by declaring, "in order to get beyond racism, we must first take account of race."

The plight of lower-class blacks, however, revealed that affirmative action had only a limited impact on their economic status. By the end of the seventies, fully one third of the nation's blacks lived below the poverty line, earning less than $8000 a year. In 1981, the median income for a black family was only $12,674, just over half of that of whites. Poor blacks, lacking education and job skills, could not join the migration to the Sunbelt and were stuck instead in the decaying central cities of the East and Midwest. Unemployment rates for blacks ran about 14 percent, twice that for whites, and among black teen-agers the level was a staggering 40 percent. As a result, most blacks did not share in the general affluence of the seventies.

■ *To minorities, the affirmative action guidelines set by the Supreme Court in the Alan Bakke case were too restrictive.*

The Emerging Hispanics and Other Minorities

People with Spanish surnames, labeled Hispanics in the census, were the fastest growing of all ethnic groups in the United States in the 1970s. By 1980, there were over 14 million Hispanics in the country, an increase of more than 50 percent in ten years. The official statistics broke them down into four major categories: nearly 9 million Mexican-Americans, 2 million Puerto Ricans, 800,000 Cubans, and nearly 3 million more from other Latin countries.

Mexican-Americans, the largest group, were concentrated in the Southwest—3.6 million in California and 2.8 million in Texas. Cubans predominated in Florida, especially around Miami, and Puerto Ricans were centered in the North-

During the 1970s, Mexicans crossed the border in great numbers, hoping to better their lives. Many came without proper documentation. Here, border guards use a helicopter to spot people making an illegal entry.

east, particularly in New York City. These varied Hispanic groups had several features in common. All were relatively youthful, with a median age of twenty-two; most were relatively poor, with one fourth falling below the poverty line; and the great majority worked in either blue-collar or menial service jobs.

In the 1970s Chicanos, as Mexican-American activists preferred to call themselves, became vocal in expressing their grievances. They succeeded in winning a federal mandate for bilingual education, compelling elementary schools in states like Texas and California to teach Chicano schoolchildren in Spanish as well as in English. Mexican-American political leaders became active in local politics, leading the Democratic and Republican parties to bid for their votes. In Texas, José Angel Gutiérrez founded a third party, La Raza Unida. Although La Raza failed to win statewide influence, Gutiérrez succeeded in the early 1970s in gaining control of first the school board and then the city government of Crystal City, a South Texas community with a heavy Mexican population.

The entry of several million illegal immigrants from Mexico, once derisively called "wetbacks" and now known as "undocumented aliens," created a substantial social problem for the nation and especially for the Southwest. Critics charged that the flagrant violation of the nation's border with Mexico had led to an "invisible subculture outside the boundaries of law and legitimate institutions." They argued that these aliens took jobs away from American citizens, kept wages artificially low, and received extensive welfare benefits for which they were ineligible.

Defenders of the "illegals" contended that the nation gained from the abundant supply of workers who were willing to do the back-breaking jobs in fields and factories shunned by most Americans. Moreover, these illegal aliens usually paid sales and withholding taxes but rarely used government services for fear of being deported. Whichever view is correct, the fact remains that by 1980 there was an exploited class of illegal aliens living on the edge of poverty. The *Wall Street Journal* summed it up best by observing, "The people who benefit the most from this situation are certainly the employers, who have access to an underground market of cheap, productive labor, unencumbered by minimum wage laws, union restrictions or pension requirements."

The existence of several million illegal aliens from Mexico, along with the more than 14 million people with Spanish surnames counted in the 1980 census, meant that Hispanics were second only to the nation's 26.5 million blacks as a minority group. Other substantial ethnic groups included Chinese, bolstered by a steady flow of immigrants from Taiwan, who achieved higher educational levels and greater affluence than other minorities, and South Vietnamese, mainly refugees who came to the United States after the North Vietnamese conquest in 1975. Concentrated in coastal states, especially California and Texas, the Vietnamese immigrants gravitated toward commercial fishing and retail trade, sometimes coming into conflict with native-born Americans who resented the newcomers' competition. Like the blacks and Hispanics, the Asian immigrants—despite their educational advances—tended to form an underclass that did not share fully in the benefits of the American way of life. In the late twentieth century, as in the nineteenth, the "melting pot" was inadequate as a description of the nation's ethnic mosaic.

The Conservative Resurgence

The liberal Democratic political coalition first put together by Franklin D. Roosevelt in the early 1930s finally broke apart in the late 1970s. The Watergate scandal gave the Democrats a brief reprieve, but by the end of the decade the Republican party was taking advantage of a new conservative mood to make inroads into such traditionally Democratic voting groups as union members, Jews, and Southerners.

Thunder on the Right

During the 1970s, many signs pointed to growing public disenchantment both with liberal reliance on government to solve all the nation's problems and with increasing permissiveness in American society. In California, realtor Howard Jarvis led a popular rebellion against escalating property taxes; in 1978, the state's voters passed Proposition 13, which called for a 57 percent cut in taxes and resulted in a gradual reduction in social services. Concern over greater social acceptance of homosexuality and rising abortion and divorce rates impelled religious groups to engage in political activity to defend traditional family values. Jerry Falwell, a successful Virginia radio and television evangelist, founded the Moral Majority, a fundamentalist group dedicated to preserv-

■ *The growing political activity of religious conservatives, such as the Moral Majority led by Rev. Jerry Falwell, has been marked by successful campaigning for favored candidates.*

ing the American way of life. The Moral Majority held workshops and seminars to teach its followers how to become active in local politics, and it also issued "morality ratings" for congressmen and senators.

Conservatives proved far more skillful than liberals in mastering new political techniques. They developed direct-mail lists to elicit campaign contributions from millions of small givers; they used polls to single out the most effective issues to exploit; they perfected the system of telephone banks to get out the vote on behalf of conservative candidates on election day. Watergate induced reforms in campaign financing helped the right far more than they did liberals. Republicans especially benefited from a provision permitting PACs (political action committees) to raise and spend unlimited sums on behalf of favored candidates.

Conservatives also succeeded, for the first time since World War II, in making their cause intellectually respectable. Scholars and academics on the right flourished in new "think tanks," such as the American Enterprise Institute in Washington. William Buckley and Milton Friedman proved to be effective advocates of conservative causes in print and on television. Neo-conservatism, led by Norman Podheretz' *Commentary*, became fashionable among intellectuals, who denounced liberals for being too soft on the Communist threat abroad and too willing to compromise high standards at home in the face of demands for equality from blacks, women, and the disadvantaged. Scholars and political leaders—including such former liberal stalwarts as Daniel Patrick Moynihan, Nathan Glazer, and Daniel Bell—called for a reaffirmation of capitalism and a new emphasis on what was right about America rather than an obsessive concern with social ills.

By the end of the decade, Ronald Reagan had emerged as the most effective political spokesman for the conservative resurgence. A former movie actor and liberal Democrat, Reagan had embraced conservatism in the 1950s after a bitter fight against Communist influence in the Screen Actors Guild. As host of "General Electric Theater," a weekly television program, and then as a traveling lecturer for his sponsor, Reagan began to speak out in favor of business and against government regulation. In 1964, he scored a smashing success with a televised appeal for Barry Goldwater. Two years later, he easily won election as governor of California, terming himself a "citizen politician" to explain his qualifications and charming the voters with his magnetic smile.

■ *Ronald Reagan swept to victory in 1980. His great skill as a communicator was born of years as a sportscaster and movie actor.*

Reagan served two terms as governor of California. He delegated authority broadly to a small group of aides, preferring to play the role of "chairman of the board." Despite some initial difficulties, he proved to be an able administrator and effective political leader. But his sights were already set on Washington. As a selfmade man who had risen from humble origins, he believed in the traditional values of hard work and individualism and he felt it was his duty to "take government off the backs of the people." The man who had once called those on welfare "a faceless mass waiting for handouts" wanted to dismantle the elaborate Washington bureaucracy and return all social programs to the states. In 1976, he had barely lost out to Gerald Ford; he was now determined to win the presidency in 1980 and end the long period of rule by a liberal elite. "Are we going to have an elitist government that makes the decisions for people's lives," he asked, "or are we going to believe, as we had for so many decades, that the people can make decisions for themselves?"

The Reagan Victory

Jimmy Carter, the politician who had so skillfully used the Watergate trauma to win the presidency, now found himself on the defensive. Inflation, touched off by the second oil shock of the 1970s, reached double-digit figures—13.3 percent in 1979 and 12.4 percent in 1980. The Federal Reserve Board's effort to shrink the money supply had led to a recession, with unemployment reaching 7.8 percent by July 1980. What Ronald Reagan dubbed the "misery index," the combined rate of inflation and unemployment, hit 28 percent early in 1980 and stayed higher than 20 percent throughout the year.

Foreign policy proved almost as damaging to Carter. The Soviet invasion of Afghanistan eroded hopes for continued détente; the hostage crisis in Iran highlighted the nation's sense of helplessness in the face of flagrant violations of its sovereignty. In the short run, Carter used that crisis to beat back the challenge to his renomination by fellow Democrat Edward Kennedy. The President stayed in the White House during the spring primaries, reminding the voters of his devotion to duty, while the Massachusetts senator campaigned amid continuing questions about his behavior a decade earlier at Chappaquiddick, where a young woman had drowned in the car he drove off a bridge. His explanations failed to allay suspicions about the incident. The Democrats rallied behind Carter, although the convention delegates displayed a notable lack of enthusiasm in renominating him.

Ronald Reagan, meanwhile, recovered from a brief stumble to sweep aside his Republican challengers and win the nomination easily, naming George Bush as his running mate. In the fall campaign, Reagan hammered away at the state of the economy and of the world. He blamed Carter for inflation, which robbed workers of any gain in real wages, and scored heavily among traditionally Democratic blue-collar groups. Reagan also accused Carter of allowing the Soviets to outstrip the United States militarily and promised a massive buildup of American forces if he were elected. Although Republican strategists thought that Carter might attempt an "October surprise"—a negotiated release of the American hostages at the height of the campaign—the Iranian situation actually helped Reagan by accentuating U.S. weakness in the world.

Carter struck back by claiming that Reagan was too reckless to conduct American foreign policy in the nuclear age. Charging that this election would decide "whether we have peace or war," the President tried to portray his Republican challenger as a warmonger. The attack backfired. In a televised debate arranged late in the campaign, Reagan reassured the American people of his devotion to peace, leaving Carter with the onus of trying to land a low blow. At the end of the confrontation, Reagan scored impressively when he ended a summation of the country's dire economic condition by suggesting voters ask themselves simply, "Are you better off now than you were four years ago? Is it easier for you to go and buy things in the stores than it was four years ago?"

On election day, the American people answered with a resounding no. Reagan carried forty-four states and gained 51 percent of the popular vote. Carter won only six states and 41 percent of the popular vote, while liberal John Anderson, running as an independent candidate, received the remaining 8 percent but failed to carry a single state. Reagan clearly benefited from

Election of 1980

ELECTORAL VOTE BY STATE		POPULAR VOTE
REPUBLICAN		
Ronald W. Reagan	489	43,899,248
DEMOCRATIC		
Jimmy Carter	49	35,481,435
INDEPENDENT		
John B. Anderson	—	5,719,437
MINOR PARTIES	—	1,395,558
	538	86,495,678

ALASKA
HAWAII 4
WASH., D.C. 3

the growing political power of the Sunbelt; he carried every state west of the Mississippi and in the South lost only Georgia, Carter's home state. Even more impressive were his inroads into the old New Deal coalition. Reagan received 50.5 percent of the blue-collar vote and 46 percent of the Jewish vote, the best showing by a Republican since 1928. Only one group remained loyal to Carter, blacks, who gave him 85 percent of their ballots.

Even more surprising was the sweeping nature of the Republican victory. For the first time since 1954, the GOP gained control of the Senate, 53 to 46, and the party picked up 33 seats in the House to narrow the Democratic margin from 114 to 50. Liberals were the chief losers in Congress, many of them victims of a vendetta waged by the Moral Majority.

The meaning of the election was less clear than the outcome. Nearly all observers agreed that the voters had rendered a judgment on the Carter administration. "The most important issue of this campaign," commented pollster Robert Teeter, "was Jimmy Carter's record." But most experts did not feel that the outcome reflected a major realignment in American politics equivalent to the Democratic victory of FDR in 1932. Voters were expressing a distaste for current economic conditions, not a strongly held ideological preference. Political scientist Walter Dean Burnham termed the result "a conservative revitalization," but one which stopped short of making the Republicans the dominant party.

Journalist Theodore White disagreed, calling the outcome "a rejection of an entire system of ideas, those framed by the Great Society, perhaps even those rooted in the New Deal." White may well be right. In the eight presidential elections since 1952, Republican candidates have received 52.3 percent of the popular vote, compared to 47.7 percent for the Democrats; they won four elections (1952, 1956, 1972, and 1980) by landslides, one (1968) narrowly, and lost two close ones (1960 and 1976). Only in 1964 did the Republicans lose by a wide margin. The movement of the population from the Northeast and Midwest to the South and West, along with the flight from the city, helped the Republicans far more than the Democrats. Thus Reagan's victory in 1980 could signal a momentous shift in American party fortunes, marking the beginning of GOP dominance to rival the Democratic control of the previous half century.

Reaganomics

Reagan viewed his election as a mandate to achieve two goals: end inflation and regain American military parity with Russia. He hoped to conquer inflation by cutting back on government spending, especially on social programs. At the same time he would continue to support the Federal Reserve's policy, begun by Chairman Paul Volcker in 1979, of slowing the growth of the money supply. His determination to increase defense spending sharply in order to catch up with the Soviets, however, ran directly counter to his budget-cutting proposals. Moreover, Reagan's commitment to supply-side economics—the idea that lowering taxes would stimulate private investment and increase productivity—was bound to lead to large federal deficits, which in turn would fuel inflation and high interest rates.

Undaunted, Reagan unveiled his plans for economic revitalization in two televised speeches in February 1981. "I regret to say that we are in the worst economic mess since the Great Depres-

sion," he informed the nation. The President's solution was to depart from the conventional economic wisdom and enact deep cuts in spending and in taxes simultaneously. He called upon Congress to reduce income taxes by 10 percent a year for three years and then proposed a cut of $41.4 billion in the 1982 federal budget. Sparing only the military and what Reagan called the "truly deserving needy," the spending reductions cut heavily into social programs such as food stamps and Medicaid, with the main burden falling on lower-income groups.

Despite nominal Democratic control of the House, Congress quickly approved the new program, dubbed "Reaganomics" by the press. A group of conservative Democrats led by Congressman Phil Gramm of Texas, mainly from the South and hence dubbed "boll weevils," joined with Republicans in passing a budget resolution in May 1981 that cut $35 billion from 175 domestic programs. Two months later Congress enacted the largest tax cut in American history. Reagan accepted a change which limited the reduction in the first year to 5 percent, but full 10 percent cuts in 1982 and 1983 meant that personal income taxes would be reduced by 25 percent, a change that greatly benefited those with high incomes. At the same time, military spending increased from $165 billion to nearly $200 billion.

■ *After 444 days in captivity, the Americans held hostage in Iran were released on January 20, 1981, the day of Ronald Reagan's inauguration as president.*

■ *Reagonomics did succeed in bringing down inflation to less than 7 percent by mid-1982, but at a heavy social cost. Tax cuts and higher military spending led to a major recession in which 10 percent of the work force stood in lines for unemployment compensation over many months. Even so-called recession-proof jobs were adversely affected.*

Financial experts who warned that the large deficits caused by the combination of tax cuts and heavy military spending would lead to recession proved correct. The huge government borrowing forced the interest rate to rise in financial markets; the prime climbed back to over 18 percent by the end of the year, and mortgage rates reached 17 percent. The result was a drastic slowdown in business expansion and a sharp decline in sales of cars and houses. By 1982, the nation was in the throes of a major recession, with unemployment reaching a postwar high of 10 percent in October.

The voters finally had a chance to express their disenchantment with Reaganomics in the 1982 congressional elections. The Republicans lost twenty-six seats in the House, ending conservative control of that body, and barely held on to a four-seat majority in the Senate. Democrats gained seven governorships, five in the Midwest, traditionally a Republican stronghold. The largest

voter turnout in an off-year election since 1962, and a particularly heavy black vote, helped the Democrats, who won back many of the blue-collar workers who had been wooed by Reagan in 1980.

The 1982 elections revealed the contradictory nature of the national mood. Apparently, the voters were displeased with the massive unemployment and deepening recession, which they attributed to Reaganomics. "To put it bluntly," commented pollster Louis Harris, "people have had the daylights scared out of them in terms of the economy." But still they expressed considerable doubt that the Democrats, who failed to offer an alternative remedy, could do better in restoring economic health. In fact, Reagan had accomplished his major campaign promise of stemming inflation; the rate dropped to just over 10 percent in 1981 and down to less than 7 percent in 1982. Yet the cost the nation had to pay for price stability—10 percent unemployment and one third of factory capacity idle—proved politically damaging to the Republicans.

Unfortunately, the economic future of the United States in the 1980s lay beyond the simple slogans of partisan political debate. The era of abundance touched off by World War II had come to an end in the 1970s. The period of rapid industrial growth and consumer prosperity, made possible by artificially low energy costs and the absence of foreign competition, had become a victim of the energy crisis and the industrial advances in Western Europe and Japan. The easy solutions of the past, notably a reliance on government spending made possible by a steadily expanding economy, would no longer be possible. The true test facing the American democratic system was to produce leaders and programs that could reconcile the people to the new age of scarcity in which they now lived.

Recommended Reading

The best account of the impact of the Yom Kippur War on American foreign policy is the second volume of Henry Kissinger's memoirs, *Years of Upheaval* (1982). The secretary of state describes the course of American foreign policy during Nixon's abbreviated second term.

Richard Barnet gives a thorough description of the impact of the energy crisis and foreign industrial competition on the American economy in the 1970s in *The Lean Years* (1980). Two superior collections of essays on the impact of the oil shocks are Robert Stobaugh and Daniel Yergin, eds., *Energy Future* (1980) and Daniel Yergin and Martin Hillenbrand, eds., *Global Insecurity* (1982).

The most satisfactory account of political developments in the 1970s, culminating in the election of Ronald Reagan, is the last of Theodore White's chronicles of presidential politics, *America in Search of Itself* (1982).

Additional Bibliography

For the Ford administration, the most useful books are Richard Reeves, *A Ford, Not a Lincoln* (1975); Clark Mollenhoff, *The Man Who Pardoned Nixon* (1976); Robert Hartmann, *Palace Politics* (1980), an insider's account by a disgruntled aide; and the President's own memoir, Gerald R. Ford, *A Time to Heal* (1979). On the election of 1976, see Jules Witcover, *Marathon* (1977) and Elizabeth Drew, *American Journal* (1977).

Books on the Carter administration include James Wooten, *Dasher* (1978) and Betty Glad, *Jimmy Carter* (1980), which focus on Carter's political career; Haynes Johnson, *In the Absence of Power* (1980), a journalist's view of the Carter presidency; and five memoirs: Joseph Califano, *On Governing America* (1981), which is critical of the President; Griffin Bell, *Taking Care of the Law* (1982), a defensive view by the attorney general; Jimmy Carter, *Keeping Faith* (1982), a sketchy and disappointing account; Zbigniew Brzezinski, *Power and Principle* (1983), a candid critique of Carter's foreign policy; and Cyrus Vance, *Hard Choices* (1983), which defends his record as secretary of state.

The major developments in the Middle East are traced in Edward R. F. Sheehan, *The Arabs, Israelis and Kissinger* (1976) and William B. Quandt, *Decade of*

Decisions (1977). Other books on foreign-policy issues of the 1970s are Strobe Talbot, *Endgame* (1979), on the negotiation of SALT II; Roy Rowan, *The Four Days of the Mayaguez* (1975); John Stockwell, *In Search of Enemies* (1976), an exposé of CIA activities in Angola; Barry Rubin, *Paved with Good Intentions* (1980), on U.S. policy in Iran; and Michael Ledeen and William Lewis, *Debacle* (1981), on the Iranian hostage crisis. Jonathan Schell, *The Fate of the Earth* (1982) is a frightening description of the danger of nuclear war.

For additional information on economic themes, see John Blair, *The Control of Oil* (1976); Peter R. Odell, *Oil and World Power*, 5th ed. (1979); and Richard Barnet and Ronald Muller, *Global Reach* (1974), on the rise of the multinationals. The fate of affirmative action in the 1970s is traced in Allan P. Sindler, *Bakke, DeFunis, and Minority Admissions* (1978) and J. Harvie Wilkinson, III, *From Brown to Bakke* (1979). Arthur Corwin examines problems of Mexican immigration critically in *Immigrants—and Immigrants* (1978). For the women's movement in the seventies, see Jo Freeman, *The Politics of Women's Liberation* (1979).

Good accounts of the resurgence of conservative thought are Peter Steinfels, *The Neo-Conservatives* (1979) and Norman Podheretz, *Breaking Ranks* (1979). On Reagan's political career, see Lou Cannon, *Reagan* (1982); Bill Boyarsky, *Ronald Reagan* (1981); and Rowland Evans and Robert Novak, *The Reagan Revolution* (1981). The election of 1980 is dealt with in Thomas Ferguson and Joel Rogers, eds., *The Hidden Election of 1980* (1981); Jack W. Germond and Jules Witcover, *Blue Smoke and Mirrors* (1981); Elizabeth Drew, *Portrait of an Election* (1981); and John F. Stacks, *Watershed* (1982).

The Declaration of Independence

In Congress, July 4, 1776

The Unanimous Declaration
of the thirteen United States of America,

When in the Course of human events, it becomes necessary for one people to dissolve the political bands which have connected them with another, and to assume among the Powers of the earth, the separate and equal station to which the Laws of Nature and of Nature's God entitle them, a decent respect to the opinions of mankind requires that they should declare the causes which impel them to the separation.

We hold these truths to be self-evident, that all men are created equal, that they are endowed by their Creator with certain unalienable Rights, that among these are Life, Liberty and the pursuit of Happiness. That to secure these rights, Governments are instituted among Men, deriving their just powers from the consent of the governed, That whenever any Form of Government becomes destructive of these ends, it is the Right of the People to alter or to abolish it, and to institute new Government, laying its foundation on such principles and organizing its powers in such form, as to them shall seem most likely to effect their Safety and Happiness. Prudence, indeed, will dictate that Governments long established should not be changed for light and transient causes; and accordingly all experience hath shown, that mankind are more disposed to suffer, while evils are sufferable, than to right themselves by abolishing the forms to which they are accustomed. But when a long train of abuses and usurpations, pursuing invariably the same Object evinces a design to reduce them under absolute Despotism, it is their right, it is their duty, to throw off such Government, and to provide new Guards for their future security.—Such has been the patient sufferance of these Colonies; and such is now the necessity which constrains them to alter their former Systems of Government. The history of the present King of Great Britain is a history of repeated injuries and usurpations, all having in direct object the establishment of an absolute Tyranny over these States. To prove this, let Facts be submitted to a candid world.

He has refused his Assent to Laws, the most wholesome and necessary for the public good.

He has forbidden his Governors to pass Laws of immediate and pressing importance, unless suspended in their operation till his Assent should be obtained; and when so suspended, he has utterly neglected to attend to them.

He has refused to pass other Laws for the accommodation of large districts of people, unless those people would relinquish the right of Representation in the Legislature, a right inestimable to them and formidable to tyrants only.

He has called together legislative bodies at places unusual, uncomfortable, and distant from the depository of their Public Records, for the sole purpose of fatiguing them into compliance with his measures.

He has dissolved Representative Houses repeatedly, for opposing with manly firmness his invasions on the rights of the people.

He has refused for a long time, after such dissolutions, to cause others to be elected; whereby the Legislative Powers, incapable of Annihilation, have returned to the People at large for their exercise; the State remaining in the mean time exposed to all the dangers of invasion from without, and convulsions within.

He has endeavoured to prevent the population of these States; for that purpose obstructing the Laws for Naturalization of Foreigners; refusing to pass others to encourage their migrations hither, and raising the conditions of new Appropriations of Lands.

He has obstructed the Administration of Justice, by refusing his Assent to Laws for establishing Judiciary Powers.

He has made Judges dependent on his Will alone, for the tenure of their offices, and the amount and payment of their salaries.

He has erected a multitude of New Offices, and sent hither swarms of Officers to harass our people, and eat out their substance.

He has kept among us, in times of peace, Standing Armies without the Consent of our legislatures.

He has affected to render the Military independent of and superior to the Civil Power.

He has combined with others to subject us to a jurisdiction foreign to our constitution, and unacknowledged by our laws; giving his Assent to their acts of pretended Legislation:

For quartering large bodies of armed troops among us:

For protecting them, by a mock Trial, from Punishment for any Murders which they should commit on the Inhabitants of these States:

For cutting off our Trade with all parts of the world:

For imposing taxes on us without our Consent:

For depriving us in many cases, of the benefits of Trial by Jury:

For transporting us beyond Seas to be tried for pretended offences:

For abolishing the free System of English Laws in a neighbouring Province, establishing therein an Arbitrary government, and enlarging its Boundaries so as to render it at once an example and fit instrument for introducing the same absolute rule into these Colonies:

For taking away our Charters, abolishing our most valuable Laws, and altering fundamentally the Forms of our Governments:

For suspending our own Legislatures, and declaring themselves invested with Power to legislate for us in all cases whatsoever.

He has abdicated Government here, by declaring us out of his Protection and waging War against us.

He has plundered our seas, ravaged our Coasts, burnt our towns, and destroyed the lives of our people.

He is at this time transporting large armies of foreign mercenaries to compleat the works of death, desolation and tyranny, already begun with circumstances of Cruelty & perfidy scarcely paralleled in the most barbarous ages, and totally unworthy the Head of a civilized nation.

He has constrained our fellow Citizens taken Captive on the high Seas to bear Arms against their Country, to become the executioners of their friends and Brethren, or to fall themselves by their Hands.

He has excited domestic insurrections amongst us, and has endeavoured to bring on the inhabitants of our frontiers, the merciless Indian Savages, whose known rule of warfare, is an undistinguished destruction of all ages, sexes and conditions.

In every stage of these Oppressions We have Petitioned for Redress in the most humble terms: Our repeated Petitions have been answered only by repeated injury. A Prince, whose character is thus marked by every act which may define a Tyrant, is unfit to be the ruler of a free people.

Nor have We been wanting in attentions to our British brethren. We have warned them from time to time of attempts by their legislature to extend an unwarrantable jurisdiction over us. We have reminded them of the circumstances of our emigration and settlement here. We have appealed to their native justice and magnanimity, and we have conjured them by the ties of our common kindred to disavow these usurpations, which would inevitably interrupt our connections and correspondence. They too have been deaf to the voice of justice and of consanguinity. We must, therefore, acquiesce in the necessity, which denounces our Separation, and hold them, as we hold the rest of mankind, Enemies in War, in Peace Friends.

We, therefore, the Representatives of the united States of America, in General Congress, Assembled, appealing to the Supreme Judge of the world for the rectitude of our intentions, do, in the Name, and by authority of the good People of these Colonies, solemnly publish and declare, That these United Colonies are, and of Right ought to be Free and Independent States; that they are Absolved from all Allegiance to the British Crown, and that all political connection between them and the State of Great Britain, is and ought to be totally dissolved; and that as Free and Independent States, they have full power to levy War, conclude Peace, contract Alliances, establish Commerce, and to do all other Acts and Things which Independent States may of right do. And for the support of this Declaration, with a firm reliance on the Protection of Divine Providence, we mutually pledge to each other our Lives, our Fortunes and our sacred Honor.

JOHN HANCOCK

BUTTON GWINNETT	THOS. NELSON, JR.	RICHD. STOCKTON
LYMAN HALL	FRANCIS LIGHTFOOT LEE	JNO. WITHERSPOON
GEO. WALTON	CARTER BRAXTON	FRAS. HOPKINSON
WM. HOOPER	ROBT. MORRIS	JOHN HART
JOSEPH HEWES	BENJAMIN RUSH	ABRA. CLARK
JOHN PENN	BENJA. FRANKLIN	JOSIAH BARTLETT
EDWARD RUTLEDGE	JOHN MORTON	WM. WHIPPLE
THOS. HEYWARD, JUNR.	GEO. CLYMER	SAML. ADAMS
THOMAS LYNCH, JUNR.	JAS. SMITH	JOHN ADAMS
ARTHUR MIDDLETON	GEO. TAYLOR	ROBT. TREAT PAINE
SAMUEL CHASE	JAMES WILSON	ELBRIDGE GERRY
WM. PACA	GEO. ROSS	STEP. HOPKINS
THOS. STONE	CAESAR RODNEY	WILLIAM ELLERY
CHARLES CARROLL OF CARROLLTON	GEO. READ	ROGER SHERMAN
GEORGE WYTHE	THO. M'KEAN	SAM'EL. HUNTINGTON
RICHARD HENRY LEE	WM. FLOYD	WM. WILLIAMS
TH. JEFFERSON	PHIL. LIVINGSTON	OLIVER WOLCOTT
BENJ. HARRISON	FRANS. LEWIS	MATTHEW THORNTON
	LEWIS MORRIS	

We the People of the United States, in Order to form a more perfect Union, establish Justice, insure domestic Tranquility, provide for the common defence, promote the general Welfare, and secure the Blessings of Liberty to ourselves and our Posterity, do ordain and establish this Constitution for the United States of America.

Article I.

Section 1

All legislative Powers herein granted shall be vested in a Congress of the United States, which shall consist of a Senate and House of Representatives.

Section 2

The House of Representatives shall be composed of Members chosen every second Year by the People of the several States, and the Electors in each State shall have the Qualifications requisite for Electors of the most numerous Branch of the State Legislature.

No Person shall be a Representative who shall not have attained to the Age of twenty five Years, and been seven Years a Citizen of the United States, and who shall not, when elected, be an Inhabitant of that State in which he shall be chosen.

Representatives and direct Taxes shall be apportioned among the several States which may be included within this Union, according to their respective Numbers, which shall be determined by adding to the whole Number of free Persons, including those bound to Service for a Term of Years, and excluding Indians not taxed, three fifths of all other Persons.[1] The actual Enumeration shall be made within three Years after the first Meeting of the Congress of the United States, and within every subsequent Term of ten Years, in such Manner as they shall by Law direct. The Number of Representatives shall not exceed one for every thirty Thousand, but each State shall have at Least one Representative; and until such enumeration shall be made, the State of New Hampshire shall be entitled to chuse three, Massachusetts eight, Rhode-Island and Providence Plantations one, Connecticut five, New-York six, New Jersey four, Pennsylvania eight, Delaware one, Maryland six, Virginia ten, North Carolina five, South Carolina five, and Georgia three.

When vacancies happen in the Representation from any State, the Executive Authority thereof shall issue Writs of Election to fill such Vacancies.

The House of Representatives shall chuse their Speaker and other Officers; and shall have the sole Power of Impeachment.

Section 3

The Senate of the United States shall be composed of two Senators from each State, chosen by the Legislature thereof, for six Years; and each Senator shall have one Vote.

Immediately after they shall be assembled in Consequence of the first Election, they shall be divided as equally as may be into three Classes. The Seats of the Senators of the first Class shall be vacated at the Expiration of the second Year, of the second Class at the Expiration of the fourth Year, and of the third Class at the Expiration of the sixth Year, so that one third may be chosen every second Year; and if Vacancies happen by Resignation, or otherwise, during the Recess of the Legislature of any state, the Executive thereof may make temporary Appointments until the next Meeting of the Legislature, which shall then fill such Vacancies.[2]

No Person shall be a Senator who shall not have attained to the Age of thirty Years, and been nine Years a Citizen of the United States, and who shall not, when elected, be an Inhabitant of that State for which he shall be chosen.

The Vice President of the United States shall be President of the Senate, but shall have no Vote, unless they be equally divided.

The Senate shall chuse their other Officers, and also a President pro tempore, in the Absence of the Vice President, or when he shall exercise the Office of President of the United States.

The Senate shall have the sole Power to try all Impeachments. When sitting for that Purpose, they shall be on Oath or Affirmation. When the President of the United States is tried the Chief Justice shall preside: And no Person shall be convicted whithout the Concurrence of two thirds of the Members present.

Judgment in Cases of Impeachment shall not extend further than to removal from Office, and disqualification to hold and enjoy any Office of honor, Trust or

---

[1] "Other Persons" being black slaves. Modified by Amendment XIV, Section 2.

[2] Provisions changed by Amendment XVII.

Profit under the United States: but the Party convicted shall nevertheless be liable and subject to Indictment, Trial, Judgment and Punishment, according to Law.

Section 4

The Times, Places and Manner of holding Elections for Senators and Representatives, shall be prescribed in each State by the Legislature thereof; but the Congress may at any time by Law make or alter such Regulations, except as to the Places of chusing Senators.

The Congress shall assemble at least once in every Year, and such Meeting shall be on the first Monday in December, unless they shall by Law appoint a different Day.[3]

Section 5

Each House shall be the Judge of the Elections, Returns and Qualifications of its own Members, and a Majority of each shall constitute a Quorum to do Business; but a smaller Number may adjourn from day to day, and may be authorized to compel the Attendance of absent Members, in such Manner, and under such Penalties as each House may provide.

Each House may determine the Rules of its Proceedings, punish its Members for disorderly Behaviour, and, with the Concurrence of two thirds, expel a Member.

Each House shall keep a Journal of its Proceedings, and from time to time publish the same, excepting such Parts as may in their Judgment require Secrecy; and the Yeas and Nays of the Members of either House on any question shall, at the Desire of one fifth of those Present, be entered on the Journal.

Neither House, during the Session of Congress, shall, without the Consent of the other, adjourn for more than three days, nor to any other Place than that in which the two Houses shall be sitting.

Section 6

The Senators and Representatives shall receive a Compensation for their Services, to be ascertained by Law, and paid out of the Treasury of the United States. They shall in all Cases, except Treason, Felony and Breach of the Peace, be privileged from Arrest during their Attendance at the Session of their respective Houses, and in going to and returning from the same; and for any Speech or Debate in either House, they shall not be questioned in any other Place.

No Senator or Representative shall, during the Time for which he was elected, be appointed to any civil Office under the Authority of the United States, which shall have been created, or the Emoluments whereof shall have been encreased during such time; and no Person holding any Office under the United States, shall be a Member of either House during his Continuance in Office.

[3]Provision changed by Amendment XX, Section 2.

Section 7

All Bills for raising Revenue shall originate in the House of Representatives; but the Senate may propose or concur with Amendments as on other Bills.

Every Bill which shall have passed the House of Representatives and the Senate, shall, before it become a Law, be presented to the President of the United States; If he approve he shall sign it, but if not he shall return it, with his Objections to that House in which it shall have originated, who shall enter the Objections at large on their Journal, and proceed to reconsider it. If after such Reconsideration two thirds of that House shall agree to pass the Bill, it shall be sent, together with the Objections, to the other House, by which it shall likewise be reconsidered, and if approved by two thirds of that House, it shall become a Law. But in all such Cases the Votes of both Houses shall be determined by yeas and Nays, and the Names of the Persons voting for and against the Bill shall be entered on the Journal of each House respectively. If any Bill shall not be returned by the President within ten Days (Sundays excepted) after it shall have been presented to him, the Same shall be a Law, in like Manner as if he had signed it, unless the Congress by their Adjournment prevent its Return, in which Case it shall not be a Law.

Every Order, Resolution, or Vote to which the Concurrence of the Senate and House of Representatives may be necessary (except on a question of Adjournment) shall be presented to the President of the United States; and before the Same shall take Effect, shall be approved by him, or being disapproved by him, shall be repassed by two thirds of the Senate and House of Representatives, according to the Rules and Limitations prescribed in the Case of a Bill.

Section 8

The Congress shall have Power To lay and collect Taxes, Duties, Imposts and Excises, to pay the Debts and provide for the common Defence and general Welfare of the United States; but all Duties, Imposts and Excises shall be uniform throughout the United States;

To borrow Money on the credit of the United States;

To regulate Commerce with foreign Nations, and among the several States, and with the Indian Tribes;

To establish an uniform Rule of Naturalization, and uniform Laws on the subject of Bankruptcies throughout the United States;

To coin Money, regulate the Value thereof, and of foreign Coin, and fix the Standard of Weights and Measures;

To provide for the Punishment of counterfeiting the Securities and current Coin of the United States;

To establish Post Offices and post Roads;

To promote the Progress of Science and useful Arts, by securing for limited Times to Authors and Inventors the exclusive Right to their respective Writings and Discoveries;

To constitute Tribunals inferior to the supreme Court;

To define and punish Piracies and Felonies committed on the high Seas, and Offences against the Law of Nations;

To declare War, grant Letters of Marque and Reprisal, and make Rules concerning Captures on Land and Water;

To raise and support Armies, but no Appropriation of Money to that Use shall be for a longer Term than two Years;

To provide and maintain a Navy;

To make Rules for the Government and Regulation of the land and naval Forces;

To provide for calling forth the Militia to execute the Laws of the Union, suppress Insurrections and repel Invasions;

To provide for organizing, arming, and disciplining, the Militia, and for governing such Part of them as may be employed in the Service of the United States, reserving to the States respectively, the Appointment of the Officers, and the Authority of training the Militia according to the discipline prescribed by Congress;

To exercise exclusive Legislation in all Cases whatsoever, over such District (not exceeding ten Miles square) as may, by Cession of particular States, and the Acceptance of Congress, become the Seat of the Government of the United States, and to exercise like Authority over all Places purchased by the Consent of the Legislature of the State in which the Same shall be, for the Erection of Forts, Magazines, Arsenals, dock-Yards, and other needful Buildings;—And

To make all Laws which shall be necessary and proper for carrying into Execution the foregoing Powers, and all other Powers vested by this Constitution in the Government of the United States, or in any Department or Officer thereof.

Section 9

The Migration or Importation of such Persons as any of the States now existing shall think proper to admit, shall not be prohibited by the Congress prior to the Year one thousand eight hundred and eight, but a Tax or duty may be imposed on such Importation, not exceeding ten dollars for each Person.

The Privilege of the Writ of Habeas Corpus shall not be suspended, unless when in Cases of Rebellion or Invasion the public Safety may require it.

No Bill of Attainder or ex post facto Law shall be passed.

No Capitation, or other direct, Tax shall be laid, unless in Proportion to the Census or Enumeration herein before directed to be taken.

No Tax or Duty shall be laid on Articles exported from any State.

No Preference shall be given by any Regulation of Commerce or Revenue to the Ports of one State over those of another: nor shall Vessels bound to, or from, one State, be obliged to enter, clear, or pay Duties in another.

No Money shall be drawn from the Treasury, but in Consequence of Appropriations made by Law; and a

regular Statement and Account of the Receipts and Expenditures of all public Money shall be published from time to time.

No Title of Nobility shall be granted by the United States: And no Person holding any Office of Profit or Trust under them, shall, without the Consent of the Congress, accept of any present, Emolument, Office, or Title, of any kind whatever, from any King, Prince, or foreign State.

Section 10

No State shall enter into any Treaty, Alliance, or Confederation; grant Letters of Marque and Reprisal; coin Money; emit Bills of Credit; make any Thing but gold and silver Coin a Tender in Payment of Debts; pass any Bill of Attainder, ex post facto Law, or Law impairing the obligation of Contracts, or grant any Title of Nobility.

No State shall, without the Consent of the Congress, lay any Imposts or Duties on Imports or Exports, except what may be absolutely necessary for executing its inspection Laws: and the net Produce of all Duties and Imposts, laid by any State on Imports or Exports, shall be for the Use of the Treasury of the United States; and all such Laws shall be subject to the Revision and Controul of the Congress.

No State shall, without the Consent of Congress, lay any Duty of Tonnage, keep Troops, or Ships of War in time of Peace, enter into any Agreement or Compact with another State, or with a foreign Power, or engage in War, unless actually invaded, or in such imminent Danger as will not admit of delay.

Article II.

Section 1

The executive Power shall be vested in a President of the United States of America. He shall hold his Office during the Term of four Years, and, together with the Vice President, chosen for the same Term, be elected, as follows:

Each State shall appoint, in such Manner as the Legislature thereof may direct, a Number of Electors, equal to the whole Number of Senators and Representatives to which the State may be entitled in the Congress: but no Senator or Representative, or Person holding an Office of Trust or Profit under the United States, shall be appointed an Elector.

The Electors shall meet in their respective States, and vote by Ballot for two Persons, of whom one at least shall not be an Inhabitant of the same State with themselves. And they shall make a List of all the Persons voted for, and of the Number of Votes for each; which List they shall sign and certify, and transmit sealed to the Seat of the Government of the United States, directed to the President of the Senate. The President of the Senate shall, in the Presence of the Senate and House of Representatives, open all the

Certificates, and the Votes shall then be counted. The Person having the greatest Number of Votes shall be the President, if such Number be a Majority of the whole Number of Electors appointed; and if there be more than one who have such Majority, and have an equal Number of Votes, then the House of Representatives shall immediately chuse by Ballot one of them for President; and if no Person have a Majority, then from the five highest on the List the said House shall in like Manner chuse the President. But in chusing the President, the Votes shall be taken by States, the Representation from each State having one Vote; A quorum for this Purpose shall consist of a Member or Members from two thirds of the States, and a Majority of all the States shall be necessary to a Choice. In every Case, after the Choice of the President, the Person having the greatest Number of Votes of the Electors shall be the Vice President. But if there should remain two or more who have equal Votes, the Senate shall chuse from them by Ballot the Vice President.[4]

The Congress may determine the Time of chusing the Electors, and the Day on which they shall give their Votes; which Day shall be the same throughout the United States.

No person except a natural born Citizen, or a Citizen of the United States, at the time of the Adoption of this Constitution, shall be eligible to the Office of President; neither shall any Person be eligible to that Office who shall not have attained to the Age of thirty five Years, and been fourteen Years a Resident within the United States.

In Case of the Removal of the President from Office, or of his Death, Resignation, or Inability to discharge the Powers and Duties of the said Office, the Same shall devolve on the Vice President, and the Congress may by Law provide for the Case of Removal, Death, Resignation or Inability, both of the President and Vice President, declaring what Officer shall then act as President, and such Officer shall act accordingly, until the Disability be removed, or a President shall be elected.

The President shall, at stated Times, receive for his Services, a Compensation, which shall neither be encreased nor diminished during the Period for which he shall have been elected, and he shall not receive within that Period any other Emolument from the United States, or any of them.

Before he enter on the Execution of his Office, he shall take the following Oath or Affirmation:—"I do solemnly swear (or affirm) that I will faithfully execute the Office of President of the United States, and will to the best of my Ability, preserve, protect and defend the Constitution of the United States."

Section 2

The President shall be Commander in Chief of the Army and Navy of the United States, and of the Militia of the several States, when called into the actual

[4]Provisions superseded by Amendment XII.

Service of the United States; he may require the Opinion, in writing, of the principal Officer in each of the executive Departments, upon any Subject relating to the Duties of their respective Offices, and he shall have Power to grant Reprieves and Pardons for Offences against the United States, except in Cases of Impeachment.

He shall have Power, by and with the Advice and Consent of the Senate, to make Treaties, provided two thirds of the Senators present concur; and he shall nominate, and by and with the Advice and Consent of the Senate, shall apppoint Ambassadors, other public Ministers and Consuls, Judges of the supreme Court, and all other Officers of the United States, whose Appointments are not herein otherwise provided for, and which shall be established by Law: but the Congress may by Law vest the Appointment of such inferior Officers, as they think proper in the President alone, in the Courts of Law, or in the Heads of Departments.

The President shall have Power to fill up all Vacancies that may happen during the Recess of the Senate, by granting Commissions which shall expire at the End of their next Session.

Section 3

He shall from time to time give to the Congress Information of the State of the Union, and recommend to their Consideration such Measures as he shall judge necessary and expedient; he may, on extraordinary Occasions, convene both Houses, or either of them, and in Case of Disagreement between them, with Respect to the Time of Adjournment, he may adjourn them to such Time as he shall think proper; he shall receive Ambassadors and other public Ministers; he shall take Care that the Laws be faithfully executed, and shall Commission all the Officers of the United States.

Section 4

The President, Vice President and all civil Officers of the United States, shall be removed from Office on Impeachment for, and Conviction of, Treason, Bribery, or other high Crimes and Misdemeanors.

Article III.

Section 1

The judicial Power of the United States, shall be vested in one supreme Court, and in such inferior Courts as the Congress may from time to time ordain and establish. The Judges, both of the supreme and inferior Courts, shall hold their offices during good Behaviour, and shall, at stated Times, receive for their Services, a Compensation, which shall not be diminished during their Continuance in Office.

Section 2

The judicial Power shall extend to all Cases, in Law

and Equity, arising under this Constitution, the Laws of the United States, and Treaties made, or which shall be made, under their Authority;—to all Cases affecting Ambassadors, other public Ministers and Consuls;—to all Cases of admiralty and maritime Jurisdiction;—to Controversies to which the United States shall be a Party;—to Controversies between two or more States;—between a State and Citizens of another State;—between Citizens of different States,—between Citizens of the same State claiming Lands under Grants of different States, and between a State, or the Citizens thereof, and foreign States, Citizens or Subjects.[5]

In all Cases affecting Ambassadors, other public Ministers and Consuls, and those in which a State shall be Party, the supreme Court shall have original Jurisdiction. In all the other Cases before mentioned, the supreme Court shall have appellate Jurisdiction, both as to Law and Fact, with such Exceptions, and under such Regulations as the Congress shall make.

The Trial of all Crimes, except in Cases of Impeachment, shall be by Jury; and such Trial shall be held in the State where the said Crimes shall have been committed, but when not committed within any State, the Trial shall be at such Place or Places as the Congress may by Law have directed.

Section 3

Treason against the United States, shall consist only in levying War against them, or in adhering to their Enemies, giving them Aid and Comfort. No person shall be convicted of Treason unless on the Testimony of two Witnesses to the same overt Act, or on Confession in open Court.

The Congress shall have Power to declare the Punishment of Treason, but no Attainder of Treason shall work Corruption of Blood, or Forfeiture except during the Life of the Person attainted.

Article IV.

Section 1

Full Faith and Credit shall be given in each State to the public Acts, Records, and judicial Proceedings of every other State. And the Congress may by general Laws prescribe the Manner in which such Acts, Records and Proceedings shall be proved, and the Effect thereof.

Section 2

The Citizens of each State shall be entitled to all Privileges and Immunities of Citizens in the several States.

A Person charged in any State with Treason, Felony, or other Crime, who shall flee from Justice, and be found in another State, shall on Demand of the executive Authority of the State from which he fled, be

[5]Clause changed by Amendment XI.

delivered up, to be removed to the State having Jurisdiction of the Crime.

No Person held to Service or Labour in one State, under the Laws thereof, escaping into another, shall, in Consequence of any Law or Regulation therein, be discharged from such Service or Labour, but shall be delivered up on Claim of the Party to whom such Service or Labour may be due.

Section 3

New States may be admitted by the Congress into this Union; but no new State shall be formed or erected within the Jurisdiction of any other State; nor any State be formed by the Junction of two or more States, or Parts of States, without the Consent of the Legislatures of the States concerned as well as of the Congress.

The Congress shall have Power to dispose of and make all needful Rules and Regulations respecting the Territory or other Property belonging to the United States; and nothing in this Constitution shall be so construed as to Prejudice any Claims of the United States, or of any particular States.

Section 4

The United States shall guarantee to every State in this Union a Republican Form of Government, and shall protect each of them against Invasion; and on Application of the Legislature, or of the Executive (when the Legislature cannot be convened) against domestic violence.

Article V.

The Congress, whenever two thirds of both Houses shall deem it necessary, shall propose Amendments to this Constitution, or, on the Application of the Legislatures of two thirds of the several States, shall call a Convention for proposing Amendments, which, in either Case, shall be valid to all Intents and Purposes, as Part of this Constitution, when ratified by the Legislatures of three fourths of the several States, or by Conventions in three fourths thereof, as the one or the other Mode of Ratification may be proposed by the Congress; Provided that no Amendment which may be made prior to the Year One thousand eight hundred and eight shall in any Manner affect the first and fourth Clauses in the Ninth Section of the first Article; and that no State without its Consent, shall be deprived of its equal Suffrage in the Senate.

Article VI.

All Debts contracted and Engagements entered into, before the Adoption of this Constitution, shall be as valid against the United States under this Constitution, as under the Confederation.

This Constitution, and the Laws of the United States which shall be made in Pursuance thereof; and all Treaties made, or which shall be made, under the Authority of the United States, shall be the supreme Law of the Land; and the Judges in every State shall be bound thereby, any Thing in the Constitution or Laws of any State to the Contrary notwithstanding.

The Senators and Representatives before mentioned, and the Members of the several State Legislatures, and all executive and Judicial Officers, both of the United States and of the several States, shall be bound by Oath or Affirmation, to support this Constitution; but no religious Test shall ever be required as a Qualification to any Office of public Trust under the United States.

Article VII.

The Ratification of the Conventions of nine States, shall be sufficient for the Establishment of this Constitution between the States so ratifying the Same.

done in Convention by the Unanimous Consent of the States present the Seventeenth Day of September in the Year of our Lord one thousand seven hundred and Eighty seven and of the Independence of the United states of America the Twelfth[6] IN WITNESS whereof We have hereunto subscribed our Names,

[6]The Constitution was submitted on September 17, 1787, by the Constitutional Convention, was ratified by the conventions of several states at various dates up to May 29, 1790, and became effective on March 4, 1789.

GEORGE WASHINGTON,
President and Deputy from Virginia

New Hampshire
JOHN LANGDON
NICHOLAS GILMAN

Massachusetts
NATHANIEL GORHAM
RUFUS KING

Connecticut
WILLIAM S. JOHNSON
ROGER SHERMAN

New York
ALEXANDER HAMILTON

New Jersey
WILLIAM LIVINGSTON
DAVID BREARLEY
WILLIAM PATERSON
JONATHAN DAYTON

Pennsylvania
BENJAMIN FRANKLIN
THOMAS MIFFLIN
ROBERT MORRIS
GEORGE CLYMER
THOMAS FITZSIMONS
JARED INGERSOLL
JAMES WILSON
GOUVERNEUR MORRIS

Delaware
GEORGE READ
GUNNING BEDFORD, JR.
JOHN DICKINSON
RICHARD BASSETT
JACOB BROOM

Maryland
JAMES McHENRY
DANIEL OF ST. THOMAS JENIFER
DANIEL CARROLL

Virginia
JOHN BLAIR
JAMES MADISON, JR.

North Carolina
WILLIAM BLOUNT
RICHARD DOBBS SPRAIGHT
HU WILLIAMSON

South Carolina
J. RUTLEDGE
CHARLES C. PINCKNEY
PIERCE BUTLER

Georgia
WILLIAM FEW
ABRAHAM BALDWIN

Amendments to the Constitution

Amendment I

Congress shall make no law respecting an establishment of religion, or prohibiting the free exercise thereof; or abridging the freedom of speech, or of the press; or the right of the people peaceably to assemble, and to petition the Government for a redress of grievances.

Amendment II

A well regulated Militia being necessary to the security of a free State, the right of the people to keep and bear Arms, shall not be infringed.

Amendment III

No Soldier shall, in time of peace be quartered in any house, without the consent of the Owner, nor in time of war, but in a manner to be prescribed by law.

Amendment IV

The right of the people to be secure in their persons, houses, papers, and effects, against unreasonable searches and seizures, shall not be violated, and no Warrants shall issue, but upon probable cause, supported by Oath or affirmation, and particularly describing the place to be searched, and the persons or things to be seized.

Amendment V

No person shall be held to answer for a capital, or otherwise infamous crime, unless on a presentment or indictment of a Grand Jury, except in cases arising in the land or naval forces, or in the Militia, when in actual service in time of War or public danger; nor shall any person be subject for the same offense to be twice put in jeopardy of life or limb; nor shall be compelled in any criminal case to be a witness against himself, nor be deprived of life, liberty, or property, without due process of law; nor shall private property be taken for public use, without just compensation.

Amendment VI

In all criminal prosecutions, the accused shall enjoy the right to a speedy and public trial, by an impartial jury of the State and district wherein the crime shall have been committed, which district shall have been previously ascertained by law, and to be informed of the nature and cause of the accusation; to be confronted with the witnesses against him; to have compulsory process for obtaining witnesses in his favor, and to have the Assistance of Counsel for his defence.

Amendment VII

In Suits at common law, where the value in controversy shall exceed twenty dollars, the right of trial by jury shall be preserved, and no fact tried by a jury, shall be otherwise re-examined in any Court of the United States, than according to the rules of the common law.

Amendment VIII

Excessive bail shall not be required, nor excessive fines imposed, nor cruel and unusual punishments inflicted.

Amendment IX

The enumeration in the Constitution, of certain rights, shall not be construed to deny or disparage others retained by the people.

Amendment X

The powers not delegated to the United States by the Constitution, nor prohibited by it to the States, are reserved to the States respectively, or the people.[7]

Amendment XI

The Judicial power of the United States shall not be construed to extend to any suit in law or equity, commenced or prosecuted against one of the United States by Citizens of another State, or by Citizens or Subjects of any Foreign State.[8]

---

[7]The first ten amendments were all proposed by Congress on September 25, 1789, and were ratified and adoption certified on December 15, 1791.
[8]Proposed by Congress on March 4, 1794, and declared ratified on January 8, 1798.

Amendment XII

The Electors shall meet in their respective states, and vote by ballot for President and Vice-President, one of whom, at least, shall not be an inhabitant of the same state with themselves; they shall name in their ballots the person voted for as President, and in distinct ballots the person voted for as Vice-President, and they shall make distinct lists of all persons voted for as President, and of all persons voted for as Vice-President, and of the number of votes for each, which lists they shall sign and certify, and transmit sealed to the seat of the government of the United States, directed to the President of the Senate;—The President of the Senate shall, in the presence of the Senate and House of Representatives, open all the certificates and the votes shall then be counted;—The person having the greatest number of votes for President, shall be the President, if such number be a majority of the whole number of Electors appointed; and if no person have such majority, then from the persons having the highest numbers not exceeding three on the list of those voted for as President, the House of Representatives shall choose immediately, by ballot, the President. But in choosing the President, the votes shall be taken by states, the representation from each state having one vote; a quorum for this purpose shall consist of a member or members from two-thirds of the states, and a majority of all the states shall be necessary to a choice. And if the House of Representatives shall not choose a President whenever the right of choice shall devolve upon them, before the fourth day of March next following, then the Vice-President shall act as President, as in the case of the death or other constitutional disability of the President.—The person having the greatest number of votes as Vice-President, shall be the Vice-President, if such number be a majority of the whole number of Electors appointed, and if no person have a majority, then from the two highest numbers on the list, the Senate shall choose the Vice-President; a quorum for the purpose shall consist of two-thirds of the whole number of Senators, and a majority of the whole number shall be necessary to a choice. But no person constitutionally ineligible to the office of President shall be eligible to that of Vice President of the United States.[9]

Amendment XIII

Section 1
Neither slavery nor involuntary servitude, except as a punishment for crime whereof the party shall have been duly convicted, shall exist within the United States, or any place subject to their jurisdiction.

Section 2
Congress shall have power to enforce this article by appropriate legislation.[10]

[9]Proposed by Congress on December 9, 1803; declared ratified on September 25, 1804; supplemented by Amendments XX and XXIII.
[10]Proposed by Congress on January 31, 1865; declared ratified on December 18, 1865.

Amendment XIV

Section 1
All persons born or naturalized in the United States, and subject to the jurisdiction thereof, are citizens of the United States and of the State wherein they reside. No State shall make or enforce any law which shall abridge the privileges or immunities of citizens of the United States; nor shall any State deprive any person of life, liberty, or property, without due process of law; nor deny to any person within its jurisdiction the equal protection of the laws.

Section 2
Representatives shall be apportioned among the several States according to their respective numbers, counting the whole number of persons in each State, excluding Indians not taxed. But when the right to vote at any election for the choice of electors for President and Vice-President of the United States, Representatives in Congress, the Executive and Judicial officers of a State, or the members of the Legislature thereof, is denied to any of the male inhabitants of such State, being twenty-one years of age, and citizens of the United States, or in any way abridged, except for participation in rebellion, or other crime, the basis of representation therein shall be reduced in the proportion which the number of such male citizens shall bear to the whole number of male citizens twenty-one years of age in such State.

Section 3
No person shall be a Senator or Representative in Congress, or elector of President and Vice President, or hold any office, civil or military, under the United States, or under any State, who, having previously taken an oath, as a member of Congress, or as an officer of the United States, or as a member of any State legislature, or as an executive or judicial officer of any State, to support the Constitution of the United States, shall have engaged in insurrection or rebellion against the same, or given aid or comfort to the enemies thereof. But Congress may by a vote of two-thirds of each House, remove such disability.

Section 4
The validity of the public debt of the United States, authorized by law, including debts incurred for payment of pensions and bounties for services in suppressing insurrection or rebellion, shall not be questioned. But neither the United States nor any State shall assume or pay any debt or obligation incurred in aid of insurrection or rebellion against the United States, or any claim for the loss or emancipation of any slave; but all such debts, obligations and claims shall be held illegal and void.

Section 5
The Congress shall have power to enforce, by appropriate legislation, the provisions of this article.[11]

[11]Proposed by Congress on June 13, 1866; declared ratified on July 28, 1868.

Amendment XVI

Section 1
The right of citizens of the United States to vote shall not be denied or abridged by the United States or by any State on account of race, color, or previous condition of servitude.

Section 2
The Congress shall have power to enforce this article by appropriate legislation.[12]

Amendment XVI

The Congress shall have power to lay and collect taxes on incomes, from whatever source derived, without apportionment among the several States, and without regard to any census or enumeration.[13]

Amendment XVII

The Senate of the United States shall be composed of two Senators from each State, elected by the people thereof, for six years; and each Senator shall have one vote. The electors in each State shall have the qualifications requisite for electors of the most numerous branch of the State legislatures.

When vacancies happen in the representation of any State in the Senate, the executive authority of such State shall issue writs of election to fill such vacancies: *Provided*, That the legislature of any State may empower the executive thereof to make temporary appointments until the people fill the vacancies by election as the legislature may direct.

This amendment shall not be so construed as to affect the election or term of any Senator chosen before it becomes valid as part of the Constitution.[14]

Amendment XVIII

Section 1
After one year from the ratification of this article the manufacturer, sale, or transportation of intoxicating liquors within, the importation thereof into, or the exportation thereof from the United States and all territory subject to the jurisdiction thereof for beverage purposes is hereby prohibited.

Section 2
The Congress and the several States shall have concurrent power to enforce this article by appropriate legislation.

[12]Proposed by Congress on February 26, 1869; declared ratified on March 30, 1870.
[13]Proposed by Congress on July 12, 1909; declared ratified on February 25, 1913.
[14]Proposed by Congress on May 13, 1912; declared ratified on May 31, 1913.

Section 3
This article shall be inoperative unless it shall have been ratified as an amendment to the Constitution by the legislatures of the several States, as provided in the Constitution, within seven years from the date of the submission hereof to the States by the Congress.[15]

Amendment XIX

The right of citizens of the United States to vote shall not be denied or abridged by the United States or by any State on account of sex.

Congress shall have power to enforce this article by appropriate legislation.[16]

Amendment XX

Section 1
The terms of the President and Vice President shall end at noon on the 20th day of January, and the terms of Senators and Representatives at noon on the 3d day of January, of the years in which such terms would have ended if this article had not been ratified; and the terms of their successors shall then begin.

Section 2
The Congress shall assemble at least once in every year, and such meeting shall begin at noon on the 3d day of January, unless they shall by law appoint a different day.

Section 3
If, at the time fixed for the beginning of the term of the President, the President elect shall have died, the Vice President elect shall become President. If a President shall not have been chosen before the time fixed for the beginning of his term, or if the President elect shall have failed to qualify, then the Vice President elect shall act as President until a President shall have qualified; and the Congress may by law provide for the case wherein neither a President elect nor a Vice President elect shall have qualified, declaring who shall then act as President, or the manner in which one who is to act shall be selected, and such person shall act accordingly until a President or Vice President shall have qualified.

Section 4
The Congress may by law provide for the case of the death of any of the persons from whom the House of Representatives may choose a President whenever the right of choice shall have devolved upon them, and for the case of the death of any of the persons from whom the Senate may choose a Vice President whenever the right of choice shall have devolved upon them.

[15]Proposed by Congress on December 18, 1917; declared ratified on January 29, 1919; repealed by Amendment XXI.
[16]Proposed by Congress on June 4, 1919; declared ratified on August 26, 1920.

Section 5

Sections 1 and 2 shall take effect on the 15th day of October following the ratification of this article.

Section 6

This article shall be inoperative unless it shall have been ratified as an amendment to the Constitution by the legislatures of three-fourths of the several States within seven years from the date of its submission.[17]

Amendment XXI

Section 1

The eighteenth article of amendment to the Constitution of the United States is hereby repealed.

Section 2

The transportation or importation into any States, Territory, or possession of the United States for delivery or use therein of intoxicating liquors, in violation of the laws thereof, is hereby prohibited.

Section 3

This article shall be inoperative unless it shall have been ratified as an amendment to the Constitution by conventions in the several States, as provided in the Constitution, within seven years from the date of the submission hereof to the States by the Congress.[18]

Amendment XXII

Section 1

No person shall be elected to the office of the President more than twice, and no person who has held the office of President, or acted as President, for more than two years of a term to which some other person was elected President shall be elected to the office of the President more than once. But this Article shall not apply to any person holding the office of President when this Article was proposed by the Congress, and shall not prevent any person who may be holding the office of President, or acting as President, during the term within which this Article becomes operative from holding the office of President or acting as President during the remainder of such term.

Section 2

This article shall be inoperative unless it shall have been ratified as an amendment to the Constitution by the legislatures of three-fourths of the several States within seven years from the date of its submission to the States by the Congress.[19]

Amendment XXIII

Section 1

The District constituting the seat of Government of the United States shall appoint in such manner as the Congress shall direct:

A number of electors of President and Vice President equal to the whole number of Senators and Representatives in Congress to which the District would be entitled if it were a State, but in no event more than the least populous State; they shall be in addition to those appointed by the States, but they shall be considered, for the purposes of the election of President and Vice President, to be electors appointed by a State; and they shall meet in the District and perform such duties as provided by the twelfth article of amendment.

Section 2

The Congress shall have power to enforce this article by appropriate legislation.[20]

Amendment XXIV

Section 1

The right of citizens of the United States to vote in any primary or other election for President or Vice President, for electors for President or Vice President, or for Senator or Representative in Congress, shall not be denied or abridged by the United States or any state by reason of failure to pay any poll tax or other tax.

Section 2

The Congress shall have the power to enforce this article by appropriate legislation.[21]

Amendment XXV

Section 1

In case of the removal of the President from office or his death or resignation, the Vice President shall become President.

Section 2

Whenever there is a vacancy in the office of the Vice President, the President shall nominate a Vice President who shall take the office upon confirmation by a majority vote of both houses of Congress.

Section 3

Whenever the President transmits to the President pro tempore of the Senate and the Speaker of the House of Representatives his written declaration that he is unable to discharge the powers and duties of his office,

---

[17]Proposed by Congress on March 2, 1932; declared ratified on February 6, 1933.
[18]Proposed by Congress on February 20, 1933; declared ratified on December 5, 1933.
[19]Proposed by Congress on March 24, 1947; declared ratified on March 1, 1951.

[20]Proposed by Congress on June 16, 1960; declared ratified on April 3, 1961.
[21]Proposed by Congress on August 27, 1962; declared ratified on January 23, 1963.

and until he transmits to them a written declaration to the contrary, such powers and duties shall be discharged by the Vice President as Acting President.

Section 4

Whenever the Vice President and a majority of either the principal officers of the executive departments or of such other body as Congress may by law provide, transmit to the President pro tempore of the Senate and the Speaker of the House of Representatives their written declaration that the President is unable to discharge the powers and duties of his office, the Vice President shall immediately assume the powers and duties of the office as Acting President.

Thereafter, when the President transmits to the President pro tempore of the Senate and the Speaker of the House of Representatives his written declaration that no inability exists, he shall resume the powers and duties of his office unless the Vice President and a majority of either the principal officers of the executive department or of such other body as Congress may by law provide, transmit within four days to the President pro tempore of the Senate and the Speaker of the House of Representatives their written declaration that the President is unable to discharge the powers and duties of his office. Thereupon Congress shall decide the issue, assembling within 48 hours for that purpose if not in session. If the Congress, within 21 days after receipt of the latter written declaration, or, if Congress is not in session, within 21 days after Congress is required to assemble, determines by two-thirds vote of both houses that the President is unable to discharge the powers and duties of his office, the Vice President shall continue to discharge the same as Acting President; otherwise, the President shall resume the powers and duties of his office.[22]

Amendment XXVI

Section 1

The right of citizens of the United States, who are 18 years of age or older, to vote shall not be denied or abridged by the United States or any state on account of age.

Section 2

The Congress shall have the power to enforce this article by appropriate legislation.[23]

---

[22]Proposed by Congress on July 6, 1965; declared ratified on February 10, 1967.
[23]Proposed by Congress on March 23, 1971; declared ratified on June 30, 1971.

Choosing the President

Presidential Election Year	Elected to Office			
	President	Party	Vice President	Party
1789	George Washington		John Adams	Parties not yet established
1792	George Washington		John Adams	Federalist
1796	John Adams	Federalist	Thomas Jefferson	Democratic-Republican
1800	Thomas Jefferson	Democratic-Republican	Aaron Burr	Democratic-Republican
1804	Thomas Jefferson	Democratic-Republican	George Clinton	Democratic-Republican
1808	James Madison	Democratic-Republican	George Clinton	Democratic-Republican
1812	James Madison	Democratic-Republican	Elbridge Gerry	Democratic-Republican
1816	James Monroe	Democratic-Republican	Daniel D. Tompkins	Democratic-Republican
1820	James Monroe	Democratic-Republican	Daniel D. Tompkins	Democratic-Republican
1824	John Quincy Adams	National Republican	John C. Calhoun Withdrew from the Presidential race to run for Vice President on both the Adams and the Jackson tickets.	Democratic
1828	Andrew Jackson	Democratic	John C. Calhoun	Democratic
1832	Andrew Jackson	Democratic	Martin Van Buren	Democratic
1836	Martin Van Buren	Democratic	Richard M. Johnson First and only Vice President elected by the Senate (1837), having failed to receive a majority of electoral votes.	Democratic
1840	William Henry Harrison	Whig	John Tyler	Whig

Major Opponents and Notable Contenders				Selection of Electors
For President	Party	For Vice President	Party	
				By state legislature
George Clinton	Democratic-Republican			By state legislature
Thomas Pinckney	Federalist			By state legislature
Aaron Burr	Democratic-Republican			
John Adams	Federalist			By state legislature
Charles Cotesworth Pinckney	Federalist			
Charles Cotesworth Pinckney	Federalist	Rufus King	Federalist	By state legislature
Charles Cotesworth Pinckney	Federalist	Rufus King	Federalist	By state legislature
George Clinton	Eastern Republican			
De Witt Clinton	Democratic-Republican/Federalist	Charles Jared Ingersoll	Democratic-Republican/Federalist	By state legislature
Rufus King	Federalist	John Eager Howard	Federalist	By state legislature
				By state legislature
Andrew Jackson	Democratic	Nathan Sanford	Democratic-Republican	By popular vote in 18 states
Henry Clay	Democratic-Republican	Nathaniel Macon	Democratic-Republican	
William H. Crawford	Democratic-Republican			
John Quincy Adams	National Republican	Richard Rush	National Republican	By popular vote
Henry Clay	National Republican	John Sergeant	National Republican	By popular vote
William Wirt	Anti-Masonic	Amos Ellmaker	Anti-Masonic	
Daniel Webster	Whig	John Tyler	Whig	By popular vote
Hugh L. White	Whig	Francis Granger	Anti-Masonic	
William Henry Harrison	Anti-Masonic			
Martin Van Buren	Democratic	Richard M. Johnson	Democratic	By popular vote
James G. Birney	Liberty	Thomas Earle	Liberty	

Presidential Election Year	Elected to Office			
	President	Party	Vice President	Party
1844	James K. Polk	Democratic	George M. Dallas	Democratic
1848	Zachary Taylor	Whig	Millard Fillmore	Whig
1852	Franklin Pierce	Democratic	William R. King	Democratic
1856	James Buchanan	Democratic	John C. Breckinridge	Democratic
1860	Abraham Lincoln	Republican	Hannibal Hamlin	Republican
1864	Abraham Lincoln	National Union/ Republican	Andrew Johnson	National Union/ Democratic
1868	Ulysses S. Grant	Republican	Schuyler Colfax	Republican
1872	Ulysses S. Grant	Republican	Henry Wilson	Republican
1876	Rutherford B. Hayes	Republican	William A. Wheeler	Republican
1880	James A. Garfield	Republican	Chester A. Arthur	Republican
1884	Grover Cleveland	Democratic	Thomas A. Hendricks	Democratic
1888	Benjamin Harrison	Republican	Levi P. Morton	Republican
1892	Grover Cleveland	Democratic	Adlai E. Stevenson	Democratic
1896	William McKinley	Republican	Garret A. Hobart	Republican
1900	William McKinley	Republican	Theodore Roosevelt	Republican
1904	Theodore Roosevelt	Republican	Charles W. Fairbanks	Republican

Major Opponents and Notable Contenders				Selection of Electors
For President	Party	For Vice President	Party	
Henry Clay	Whig	Theodore Frelinghuysen	Whig	By popular vote
James G. Birney	Liberty	Thomas Morris	Liberty	
Lewis Cass	Democratic	William O. Butler	Democratic	By popular vote
Martin Van Buren	Free-Soil	Charles F. Adams	Free-Soil	
Winfield Scott	Whig	William A. Graham	Whig	By popular vote
John P. Hale	Free-Soil	George W. Julian	Free-Soil	
John C. Frémont	Republican	William L. Dayton	Republican	By popular vote
Millard Fillmore	American	Andrew J. Donelson	American	
John Bell	Constitutional Union	Edward Everett	Constitutional Union	By popular vote
Stephen A. Douglas	Democratic	Herschel V. Johnson	Democratic	
John C. Breckinridge	Democratic	Joseph Lane	Democratic	
George B. McClennan	Democratic	George H. Pendleton	Democratic	By popular vote
Horatio Seymour	Democratic	Francis P. Blair	Democratic	By popular vote
Horace Greeley	Democratic and Liberal Republican	B. Gratz Brown	Democratic and Liberal Republican	By popular vote
Charles O'Conor	Democratic	John Quincy Adams II	Democratic	
James Black	Temperance	John Russell	Temperance	
Samuel J. Tilden	Democratic	Thomas A. Hendricks	Democratic	By popular vote
Peter Cooper	Greenback	Samuel F. Cary	Greenback	
Green Clay Smith	Prohibition	Gideon T. Stewart	Prohibition	
Winfield S. Hancock	Democratic	William H. English	Democratic	By popular vote
James B. Weaver	Greenback	B. J. Chambers	Greenback	
Neal Dow	Prohibition	H. A. Thompson	Prohibition	
James G. Blaine	Republican	John A. Logan	Republican	By popular vote
John P. St. John	Prohibition	William Daniel	Prohibition	
Benjamin F. Butler	Greenback	A. M. West	Greenback	
Grover Cleveland	Democratic	Allen G. Thurman	Democratic	By popular vote
Clinton B. Fisk	Prohibition	John A. Brooks	Prohibition	
Alson J. Streeter	Union Labor	C. E. Cunningham	Union Labor	
Benjamin Harrison	Republican	Whitelaw Reid	Republican	By popular vote
James B. Weaver	Populist	James G. Field	Populist	
John Bidwell	Prohibition	James B. Cranfill	Prohibition	
William Jennings Bryan	Democratic, Populist, and National Silver Republican	Arthur Sewall	Democratic and National Silver Republican	By popular vote
		Thomas E. Watson	Populist	
Joshua Levering	Prohibition	Hale Johnson	Prohibition	
John M. Palmer	National Democratic	Simon B. Buckner	National Democratic	
William Jennings Bryan	Democratic and Fusion Populist	Adlai E. Stevenson	Democratic and Fusion Populist	By popular vote
Wharton Barker	Anti-Fusion Populist	Ignatius Donnelly	Anti-Fusion Populist	
Eugene V. Debs	Social Democratic	Job Harriman	Social Democratic	
John G. Woolley	Prohibition	Henry B. Metcalf	Prohibition	
Alton B. Parker	Democratic	Henry G. Davis	Democratic	By popular vote
Eugene V. Debs	Socialist	Benjamin Hanford	Socialist	
Silas C. Swallow	Prohibition	George W. Carroll	Prohibition	

Presidential Election Year	Elected to Office			
	President	Party	Vice President	Party
1908	William Howard Taft	Republican	James S. Sherman	Republican
1912	Woodrow Wilson	Democratic	Thomas R. Marshall	Democratic
1916	Woodrow Wilson	Democratic	Thomas R. Marshall	Democratic
1920	Warren G. Harding	Republican	Calvin Coolidge	Republican
1924	Calvin Coolidge	Republican	Charles G. Dawes	Republican
1928	Herbert C. Hoover	Republican	Charles Curtis	Republican
1932	Franklin D. Roosevelt	Democratic	John N. Garner	Democratic
1936	Franklin D. Roosevelt	Democratic	John N. Garner	Democratic
1940	Franklin D. Roosevelt	Democratic	Henry A. Wallace	Democratic
1944	Franklin D. Roosevelt	Democratic	Harry S Truman	Democratic
1948	Harry S Truman	Democratic	Alben W. Barkley	Democratic
1952	Dwight D. Eisenhower	Republican	Richard M. Nixon	Republican
1956	Dwight D. Eisenhower	Republican	Richard M. Nixon	Republican
1960	John F. Kennedy	Democratic	Lyndon B. Johnson	Democratic
1964	Lyndon B. Johnson	Democratic	Hubert H. Humphrey	Democratic
1968	Richard M. Nixon	Republican	Spiro T. Agnew	Republican
1972	Richard M. Nixon	Republican	Spiro T. Agnew	Republican
1976	Jimmy Carter	Democratic	Walter Mondale	Democratic
1980	Ronald Reagan	Republican	George Bush	Republican

For President	Party	For Vice President	Party	
William Jennings Bryan	Democratic	John W. Kern Benjamin Hanford	Democratic	By popular vote
Eugene V. Debs	Socialist	Aaron S. Watkins	Socialist	
Eugene W. Chafin	Prohibition		Prohibition	
William Howard Taft	Republican	James S. Sherman	Republican	By popular vote
Theodore Roosevelt	Progressive	Hiram W. Johnson	Progressive	
Eugene V. Debs	Socialist	Emil Seidel	Socialist	
Eugene W. Chafin	Prohibition	Aaron S. Watkins	Prohibition	
Charles E. Hughes	Republican	George R. Kirkpatrick	Socialist	By popular vote
Allen L. Benson	Socialist			
J. Frank Hanly	Prohibition	Ira D. Landrith	Prohibition	
Charles W. Fairbanks	Republican			
James M. Cox	Democratic	Franklin D. Roosevelt	Democratic	By popular vote
Eugene V. Debs	Socialist	Seymour Stedman	Socialist	
John W. Davis	Democratic	Charles W. Bryan	Democratic	By popular vote
Robert M. LaFollette	Progressive	Burton K. Wheeler	Progressive	
Alfred E. Smith	Democratic	Joseph T. Robinson	Democratic	By popular vote
Norman Thomas	Socialist	James H. Maurer	Socialist	
Herbert C. Hoover	Republican	Charles Curtis	Republican	By popular vote
Norman Thomas	Socialist	James H. Maurer	Socialist	
Alfred M. Landon	Republican	Frank Knox	Republican	By popular vote
William Lemke	Union	Thomas C. O'Brien	Union	
Wendell L. Willkie	Republican	Charles L. McNary	Republican	By popular vote
Thomas E. Dewey	Republican	John W. Bricker	Republican	By popular vote
Thomas E. Dewey	Republican	Earl Warren	Republican	By popular vote
J. Strom Thurmond	States' Rights Democratic	Fielding L. Wright	States' Rights Democratic	
Henry A. Wallace	Progressive	Glen H. Taylor	Progressive	
Adlai E. Stevenson	Democratic	John J. Sparkman	Democratic	By popular vote
Adlai E. Stevenson	Democratic	Estes Kefauver	Democratic	By popular vote
Richard M. Nixon	Republican	Henry Cabot Lodge	Republican	By popular vote
Barry M. Goldwater	Republican	William E. Miller	Republican	By popular vote
Hubert H. Humphrey	Democratic	Edmund S. Muskie	Democratic	By popular vote
George C. Wallace	American Independent	Curtis E. LeMay	American Independent	
George S. McGovern	Democratic	R. Sargent Shriver	Democratic	By popular vote
Gerald R. Ford	Republican	Robert J. Dole	Republican	By popular vote
Jimmy Carter	Democratic	Walter Mondale	Democratic	
John B. Anderson	Independent			
Ed Clark	Libertarian			

Cabinet Members for Each Administration

The Washington Administration

Secretary of State	Thomas Jefferson	1789–1793
	Edmund Randolph	1794–1795
	Timothy Pickering	1795–1797
Secretary of Treasury	Alexander Hamilton	1789–1795
	Oliver Wolcott	1795–1797
Secretary of War	Henry Knox	1789–1794
	Timothy Pickering	1795–1796
	James McHenry	1796–1797
Attorney General	Edmund Randolph	1789–1793
	William Bradford	1794–1795
	Charles Lee	1795–1797
Postmaster General	Samuel Osgood	1789–1791
	Timothy Pickering	1791–1794
	Joseph Habersham	1795–1797

The John Adams Administration

Secretary of State	Timothy Pickering	1797–1800
	John Marshall	1800–1801
Secretary of Treasury	Oliver Wolcott	1797–1800
	Samuel Dexter	1800–1801
Secretary of War	James McHenry	1797–1800
	Samuel Dexter	1800–1801
Attorney General	Charles Lee	1797–1801
Postmaster General	Joseph Habersham	1797–1801
Secretary of Navy	Benjamin Stoddert	1798–1801

The Jefferson Administration

Secretary of State	James Madison	1801–1809
Secretary of Treasury	Samuel Dexter	1801
	Albert Gallatin	1801–1809
Secretary of War	Henry Dearborn	1801–1809
Attorney General	Levi Lincoln	1801–1805
	Robert Smith	1805
	John Breckinridge	1805–1806
	Caesar Rodney	1807–1809
Postmaster General	Joseph Habersham	1801
	Gideon Granger	1801–1809
Secretary of Navy	Robert Smith	1801–1809

The Madison Administration

Secretary of State	Robert Smith	1809–1811
	James Monroe	1811–1817
Secretary of Treasury	Albert Gallatin	1809–1813
	George Campbell	1814
	Alexander Dallas	1814–1816
	William Crawford	1816–1817
Secretary of War	William Eustis	1809–1812
	John Armstrong	1813–1814
	James Monroe	1814–1815
	William Crawford	1815–1817
Attorney General	Caesar Rodney	1809–1811
	William Pinkney	1811–1814
	Richard Rush	1814–1817
Postmaster General	Gideon Granger	1809–1814
	Return Meigs	1814–1817
Secretary of Navy	Paul Hamilton	1809–1813
	William Jones	1813–1814
	Benjamin Crowninshield	1814–1817

The Monroe Administration

Secretary of State	John Quincy Adams	1817–1825
Secretary of Treasury	William Crawford	1817–1825
Secretary of War	George Graham	1817
	John C. Calhoun	1817–1825
Attorney General	Richard Rush	1817
	William Wirt	1817–1825
Postmaster General	Return Meigs	1817–1823
	John McLean	1823–1825
Secretary of Navy	Benjamin Crowninshield	1817–1818
	Smith Thompson	1818–1823
	Samuel Southard	1823–1825

The John Quincy Adams Administration

Secretary of State	Henry Clay	1825–1829
Secretary of Treasury	Richard Rush	1825–1829
Secretary of War	James Barbour	1825–1828
	Peter Porter	1828–1829
Attorney General	William Wirt	1825–1829
Postmaster General	John McLean	1825–1829
Secretary of Navy	Samuel Southard	1825–1829

The Jackson Administration

Secretary of State	Martin Van Buren	1829–1831
	Edward Livingston	1831–1833
	Louis McLane	1833–1834
	John Forsyth	1834–1837
Secretary of Treasury	Samuel Ingham	1829–1831
	Louis McLane	1831–1833
	William Duane	1833
	Roger B. Taney	1833–1834
	Levi Woodbury	1834–1837
Secretary of War	John H. Eaton	1829–1831
	Lewis Cass	1831–1837
	Benjamin Butler	1837
Attorney General	John M. Berrien	1829–1831
	Roger B. Taney	1831–1833
	Benjamin Butler	1833–1837
Postmaster General	William Barry	1829–1835
	Amos Kendall	1835–1837
Secretary of Navy	John Branch	1829–1831
	Levi Woodbury	1831–1834
	Mahlon Dickerson	1834–1837

The Van Buren Administration

Secretary of State	John Forsyth	1837–1841
Secretary of Treasury	Levi Woodbury	1837–1841
Secretary of War	Joel Poinsett	1837–1841
Attorney General	Benjamin Butler	1837–1838
	Felix Grundy	1838–1840
	Henry D. Gilpin	1840–1841
Postmaster General	Amos Kendall	1837–1840
	John M. Niles	1840–1841
Secretary of Navy	Mahlon Dickerson	1837–1838
	James Paulding	1838–1841

The William Harrison Administration

Secretary of State	Daniel Webster	1841
Secretary of Treasury	Thomas Ewing	1841
Secretary of War	John Bell	1841
Attorney General	John J. Crittenden	1841
Postmaster General	Francis Granger	1841
Secretary of Navy	George Badger	1841

The Tyler Administration

Secretary of State	Daniel Webster	1841–1843
	Hugh S. Legaré	1843
	Abel P. Upshur	1843–1844
	John C. Calhoun	1844–1845
Secretary of Treasury	Thomas Ewing	1841
	Walter Forward	1841–1843
	John C. Spencer	1843–1844
	George Bibb	1844–1845
Secretary of War	John Bell	1841
	John C. Spencer	1841–1843
	James M. Porter	1843–1844
	William Wilkins	1844–1845
Attorney General	John J. Crittenden	1841
	Hugh S. Legaré	1841–1843
	John Nelson	1843–1845
Postmaster General	Francis Granger	1841
	Charles Wickliffe	1841
Secretary of Navy	George Badger	1841
	Abel P. Upshur	1841
	David Henshaw	1843–1844
	Thomas Gilmer	1844
	John Y. Mason	1844–1845

The Polk Administration

Secretary of State	James Buchanan	1845–1849
Secretary of Treasury	Robert J. Walker	1845–1849
Secretary of War	William L. Marcy	1845–1849
Attorney General	John Y. Mason	1845–1846
	Nathan Clifford	1846–1848
	Isaac Toucey	1848–1849
Postmaster General	Cave Johnson	1845–1849
Secretary of Navy	George Bancroft	1845–1846
	John Y. Mason	1846–1849

The Taylor Administration

Secretary of State	John M. Clayton	1849–1850
Secretary of Treasury	William Meredith	1849–1850
Secretary of War	George Crawford	1849–1850
Attorney General	Reverdy Johnson	1849–1850
Postmaster General	Jacob Collamer	1849–1850
Secretary of Navy	William Preston	1849–1850
Secretary of Interior	Thomas Ewing	1849–1850

The Fillmore Administration

Secretary of State	Daniel Webster	1850–1852
	Edward Everett	1852–1853
Secretary of Treasury	Thomas Corwin	1850–1853
Secretary of War	Charles Conrad	1850–1853
Attorney General	John J. Crittenden	1850–1853
Postmaster General	Nathan Hall	1850–1852
	Sam D. Hubbard	1852–1853
Secretary of Navy	William A. Graham	1850–1852
	John P. Kennedy	1852–1853
Secretary of Interior	Thomas McKennan	1850
	Alexander Stuart	1850–1853

The Pierce Administration

Secretary of State	William L. Marcy	1853–1857
Secretary of Treasury	James Guthrie	1853–1857
Secretary of War	Jefferson Davis	1853–1857
Attorney General	Caleb Cushing	1853–1857
Postmaster General	James Campbell	1853–1857
Secretary of Navy	James C. Dobbin	1853–1857
Secretary of Interior	Robert McClelland	1853–1857

The Buchanan Administration

Secretary of State	Lewis Cass	1857–1860
	Jeremiah S. Black	1860–1861
Secretary of Treasury	Howell Cobb	1857–1860
	Philip Thomas	1860–1861
	John A. Dix	1861
Secretary of War	John B. Floyd	1857–1861
	Joseph Holt	1861
Attorney General	Jeremiah S. Black	1857–1860
	Edwin M. Stanton	1860–1861
Postmaster General	Aaron V. Brown	1857–1859
	Joseph Holt	1859–1861
	Horatio King	1861
Secretary of Navy	Isaac Toucey	1857–1861
Secretary of Interior	Jacob Thompson	1857–1861

The Lincoln Administration

Secretary of State	William H. Seward	1861–1865
Secretary of Treasury	Samuel P. Chase	1861–1864
	William P. Fessenden	1864–1865
	Hugh McCulloch	1865
Secretary of War	Simon Cameron	1861–1862
	Edwin M. Stanton	1862–1865
Attorney General	Edward Bates	1861–1864
	James Speed	1864–1865
Postmaster General	Horatio King	1861
	Montgomery Blair	1861–1864
	William Dennison	1864–1865
Secretary of Navy	Gideon Welles	1861–1865
Secretary of Interior	Caleb B. Smith	1861–1863
	John P. Usher	1863–1865

The Andrew Johnson Administration

Secretary of State	William H. Seward	1865–1869
Secretary of Treasury	Hugh McCulloch	1865–1869
Secretary of War	Edwin M. Stanton	1865–1867
	Ulysses S. Grant	1867–1868
	Lorenzo Thomas	1868
	John M. Schofield	1868–1869
Attorney General	James Speed	1865–1866
	Henry Stanbery	1866–1868
	William M. Evarts	1868–1869

Postmaster General	William Dennison	1865–1866
	Alexander Randall	1866–1869
Secretary of Navy	Gideon Welles	1865–1869
Secretary of Interior	John P. Usher	1865
	James Harlan	1865–1866
	Orville H. Browning	1866–1869

The Grant Administration

Secretary of State	Elihu B. Washburne	1869
	Hamilton Fish	1869–1877
Secretary of Treasury	George S. Boutwell	1869–1873
	William Richardson	1873–1874
	Benjamin Bristow	1874–1876
	Lot M. Morrill	1876–1877
Secretary of War	John A. Rawlins	1869
	William T. Sherman	1869
	William W. Belknap	1869–1876
	Alphonso Taft	1876
	James D. Cameron	1876–1877
Attorney General	Ebenezer Hoar	1869–1870
	Amos T. Ackerman	1870–1871
	G. H. Williams	1871–1875
	Edwards Pierrepont	1875–1876
	Alphonso Taft	1876–1877
Postmaster General	John A. J. Creswell	1869–1874
	James W. Marshall	1874
	Marshall Jewell	1874–1876
	James N. Tyner	1876–1877
Secretary of Navy	Adolph E. Borie	1869
	George M. Robeson	1869–1877
Secretary of Interior	Jacob D. Cox	1869–1870
	Columbus Delano	1870–1875
	Zachariah Chandler	1875–1877

The Hayes Administration

Secretary of State	William B. Evarts	1877–1881
Secretary of Treasury	John Sherman	1877–1881
Secretary of War	George W. McCrary	1877–1879
	Alex Ramsey	1879–1881
Attorney General	Charles Devens	1877–1881
Postmaster General	David M. Key	1877–1880
	Horace Maynard	1880–1881
Secretary of Navy	Richard W. Thompson	1877–1880
	Nathan Goff, Jr.	1881
Secretary of Interior	Carl Schurz	1877–1881

The Garfield Administration

Secretary of State	James G. Blaine	1881
Secretary of Treasury	William Windom	1881
Secretary of War	Robert T. Lincoln	1881
Attorney General	Wayne MacVeagh	1881
Postmaster General	Thomas L. James	1881
Secretary of Navy	William H. Hunt	1881
Secretary of Interior	Samuel J. Kirkwood	1881

The Arthur Administration

Secretary of State	F. T. Frelinghuysen	1881–1885
Secretary of Treasury	Charles J. Folger	1881–1884
	Walter Q. Gresham	1884
	Hugh McCulloch	1884–1885
Secretary of War	Robert T. Lincoln	1881–1885
Attorney General	Benjamin H. Brewster	1881–1885
Postmaster General	Timothy O. Howe	1881–1883
	Walter Q. Gresham	1883–1884
	Frank Hatton	1884–1885
Secretary of Navy	William H. Hunt	1881–1882
	William E. Chandler	1882–1885
Secretary of Interior	Samuel J. Kirkwood	1881–1882
	Henry M. Teller	1882–1885

The First Cleveland Administration

Secretary of State	Thomas F. Bayard	1885–1889
Secretary of Treasury	Daniel Manning	1885–1887
	Charles S. Fairchild	1887–1889
Secretary of War	William C. Endicott	1885–1889
Attorney General	Augustus H. Garland	1885–1889
Postmaster General	William F. Vilas	1885–1888
	Don M. Dickinson	1888–1889
Secretary of Navy	William C. Whitney	1885–1889
Secretary of Interior	Lucius Q. C. Lamar	1885–1888
	William F. Vilas	1888–1889
Secretary of Agriculture	Norman J. Colman	1889

The Benjamin Harrison Administration

Secretary of State	James G. Blaine	1889–1892
	John W. Foster	1892–1893
Secretary of Treasury	William Windom	1889–1891
	Charles Foster	1891–1893
Secretary of War	Redfield Proctor	1889–1891
	Stephen B. Elkins	1891–1893
Attorney General	William H. H. Miller	1889–1891
Postmaster General	John Wanamaker	1889–1893
Secretary of Navy	Benjamin F. Tracy	1889–1893
Secretary of Interior	John W. Noble	1889–1893
Secretary of Agriculture	Jeremiah M. Rusk	1889–1893

The Second Cleveland Administration

Secretary of State	Walter Q. Gresham	1893–1895
	Richard Olney	1895–1897
Secretary of Treasury	John G. Carlisle	1893–1897
Secretary of War	Daniel S. Lamont	1893–1897
Attorney General	Richard Olney	1893–1895
	James Harmon	1895–1897
Postmaster General	Wilson S. Bissell	1893–1895
	William L. Wilson	1895–1897
Secretary of Navy	Hilary A. Herbert	1893–1897
Secretary of Interior	Hoke Smith	1893–1896
	David R. Francis	1896–1897
Secretary of Agriculture	Julius S. Morton	1893–1897

The McKinley Administration

Secretary of State	John Sherman	1897–1898
	William R. Day	1898
	John Hay	1898–1901
Secretary of Treasury	Lyman J. Gage	1897–1901
Secretary of War	Russell A. Alger	1897–1899
	Elihu Root	1899–1901
Attorney General	Joseph McKenna	1897–1898
	John W. Griggs	1898–1901
	Philander C. Knox	1901
Postmaster General	James A. Gary	1897–1898
	Charles E. Smith	1898–1901
Secretary of Navy	John D. Long	1897–1901
Secretary of Interior	Cornelius N. Bliss	1897–1899
	Ethan A. Hitchcock	1899–1901
Secretary of Agriculture	James Wilson	1897–1901

The Theodore Roosevelt Administration

Secretary of State	John Hay	1901–1905
	Elihu Root	1905–1909
	Robert Bacon	1909
Secretary of Treasury	Lyman J. Gage	1901–1902
	Leslie M. Shaw	1902–1907
	George B. Cortelyou	1907–1909
Secretary of War	Elihu Root	1901–1904
	William H. Taft	1904–1908
	Luke E. Wright	1908–1909
Attorney General	Philander C. Knox	1901–1904
	William H. Moody	1904–1906
	Charles J. Bonaparte	1906–1909
Postmaster General	Charles E. Smith	1901–1902
	Henry C. Payne	1902–1904
	Robert J. Wynne	1904–1905
	George B. Cortelyou	1905–1907
	George von L. Meyer	1907–1909
Secretary of Navy	John D. Long	1901–1902
	William H. Moody	1902–1904
	Paul Morton	1904–1905
	Charles J. Bonaparte	1905–1906
	Victor H. Metcalf	1906–1908
	Truman H. Newberry	1908–1909
Secretary of Interior	Ethan A. Hitchcock	1901–1907
	James R. Garfield	1907–1909
Secretary of Agriculture	James Wilson	1901–1909
Secretary of Labor and Commerce	George B. Cortelyou	1903–1904
	Victor H. Metcalf	1904–1906
	Oscar S. Straus	1906–1909
	Charles Nagel	1909

The Taft Administration

Secretary of State	Philander C. Knox	1909–1913
Secretary of Treasury	Franklin MacVeagh	1909–1913
Secretary of War	Jacob M. Dickinson	1909–1911
	Henry L. Stimson	1911–1913
Attorney General	George W. Wickersham	1909–1913
Postmaster General	Frank H. Hitchcock	1909–1913

Secretary of Navy	George von L. Meyer	1909–1913
Secretary of Interior	Richard A. Ballinger	1909–1911
	Walter L. Fisher	1911–1913
Secretary of Agriculture	James Wilson	1909–1913
Secretary of Labor and Commerce	Charles Nagel	1909–1913

The Wilson Administration

Secretary of State	William J. Bryan	1913–1915
	Robert Lansing	1915–1920
	Bainbridge Colby	1920–1921
Secretary of Treasury	William G. McAdoo	1913–1918
	Carter Glass	1918–1920
	David F. Houston	1920–1921
Secretary of War	Lindley M. Garrison	1913–1916
	Newton D. Baker	1916–1921
Attorney General	James C. McReynolds	1913–1914
	Thomas W. Gregory	1914–1919
	A. Mitchell Palmer	1919–1921
Postmaster General	Albert S. Burleson	1913–1921
Secretary of Navy	Josephus Daniels	1913–1921
Secretary of Interior	Franklin K. Lane	1913–1920
	John B. Payne	1920–1921
Secretary of Agriculture	David F. Houston	1913–1920
	Edwin T. Meredith	1920–1921
Secretary of Commerce	William C. Redfield	1913–1919
	Joshua W. Alexander	1919–1921
Secretary of Labor	William B. Wilson	1913–1921

The Harding Administration

Secretary of State	Charles E. Hughes	1921–1923
Secretary of Treasury	Andrew Mellon	1921–1923
Secretary of War	John W. Weeks	1921–1923
Attorney General	Harry M. Daugherty	1921–1923
Postmaster General	Will H. Hays	1921–1922
	Hubert Work	1922–1923
	Harry S. New	1923
Secretary of Navy	Edwin Denby	1921–1923
Secretary of Interior	Albert B. Fall	1921–1923
	Hubert Work	1923

Secretary of Agriculture	Henry C. Wallace	1921–1923
Secretary of Commerce	Herbert C. Hoover	1921–1923
Secretary of Labor	James J. Davis	1921–1923

The Coolidge Administration

Secretary of State	Charles E. Hughes	1923–1925
	Frank B. Kellogg	1925–1929
Secretary of Treasury	Andrew Mellon	1923–1929
Secretary of War	John W. Weeks	1923–1925
	Dwight F. Davis	1925–1929
Attorney General	Henry M. Daugherty	1923–1924
	Harlan F. Stone	1924–1925
	John G. Sargent	1925–1929
Postmaster General	Harry S. New	1923–1929
Secretary of Navy	Edwin Denby	1923–1924
	Curtis D. Wilbur	1924–1929
Secretary of Interior	Hubert Work	1923–1928
	Roy O. West	1928–1929
Secretary of Agriculture	Henry C. Wallace	1923–1924
	Howard M. Gore	1924–1925
	William M. Jardine	1925–1929
Secretary of Commerce	Herbert C. Hoover	1923–1928
	William F. Whiting	1928–1929
Secretary of Labor	James J. Davis	1923–1929

The Hoover Administration

Secretary of State	Henry L. Stimson	1929–1933
Secretary of Treasury	Andrew Mellon	1929–1932
	Ogden L. Mills	1932–1933
Secretary of War	James W. Good	1929
	Patrick J. Hurley	1929–1933
Attorney General	William D. Mitchell	1929–1933
Postmaster General	Walter F. Brown	1929–1933
Secretary of Navy	Charles F. Adams	1929–1933
Secretary of Interior	Ray L. Wilbur	1929–1933
Secretary of Agriculture	Arthur M. Hyde	1929–1933

Secretary of Commerce	Robert P. Lamont	1929–1932
	Roy D. Chapin	1932–1933
Secretary of Labor	James J. Davis	1929–1930
	William N. Doak	1930–1933

The Franklin D. Roosevelt Administration

Secretary of State	Cordell Hull	1933–1944
	E. R. Stettinius, Jr.	1944–1945
Secretary of Treasury	William H. Woodin	1933–1934
	Henry Morgenthau, Jr.	1934–1945
Secretary of War	George H. Dern	1933–1936
	Henry A. Woodring	1936–1940
	Henry L. Stimson	1940–1945
Attorney General	Homer S. Cummings	1933–1939
	Frank Murphy	1939–1940
	Robert H. Jackson	1940–1941
	Francis Biddle	1941–1945
Postmaster General	James A. Farley	1933–1940
	Frank C. Walker	1940–1945
Secretary of Navy	Claude A. Swanson	1933–1940
	Charles Edison	1940
	Frank Knox	1940–1944
	James V. Forrestal	1944–1945
Secretary of Interior	Harold L. Ickes	1933–1945
Secretary of Agriculture	Henry A. Wallace	1933–1940
	Claude R. Wickard	1940–1945
Secretary of Commerce	Daniel C. Roper	1933–1939
	Harry L. Hopkins	1939–1940
	Jesse Jones	1940–1945
	Henry A. Wallace	1945
Secretary of Labor	Frances Perkins	1933–1945

The Truman Administration

Secretary of State	James F. Byrnes	1945–1947
	George C. Marshall	1947–1949
	Dean G. Acheson	1949–1953
Secretary of Treasury	Fred M. Vinson	1945–1946
	John W. Snyder	1946–1953
Secretary of War	Robert P. Patterson	1945–1947
	Kenneth C. Royall	1947
Attorney General	Tom C. Clark	1945–1949
	J. Howard McGrath	1949–1952
	James P. McGranery	1952–1953
Postmaster General	Frank C. Walker	1945
	Robert E. Hannegan	1945–1947
	Jesse M. Donaldson	1947–1953
Secretary of Navy	James V. Forrestal	1945–1947
Secretary of Interior	Harold L. Ickes	1945–1946
	Julius A. Krug	1946–1949
	Oscar L. Chapman	1949–1953
Secretary of Agriculture	Clinton P. Anderson	1945–1948
	Charles F. Brannan	1948–1953
Secretary of Commerce	Henry A. Wallace	1945–1946
	W. Averell Harriman	1946–1948
	Charles W. Sawyer	1948–1953
Secretary of Labor	Lewis B. Schwellenbach	1945–1948
	Maurice J. Tobin	1948–1953
Secretary of Defense	James V. Forrestal	1947–1949
	Louis A. Johnson	1949–1950
	George C. Marshall	1950–1951
	Robert A. Lovett	1951–1953

The Eisenhower Administration

Secretary of State	John Foster Dulles	1953–1959
	Christian A. Herter	1959–1961
Secretary of Treasury	George M. Humphrey	1953–1957
	Robert B. Anderson	1957–1961
Attorney General	Herbert Brownell, Jr.	1953–1958
	William P. Rogers	1958–1961
Postmaster General	Arthur E. Summerfield	1953–1961
Secretary of Interior	Douglas McKay	1953–1956
	Fred A. Seaton	1956–1961
Secretary of Agriculture	Ezra T. Benson	1953–1961
Secretary of Commerce	Sinclair Weeks	1953–1958
	Lewis L. Strauss	1958–1959
	Frederick H. Mueller	1959–1961
Secretary of Labor	Martin P. Durkin	1953
	James P. Mitchell	1953–1961
Secretary of Defense	Charles E. Wilson	1953–1957
	Neil H. McElroy	1957–1959
	Thomas S. Gates, Jr.	1959–1961
Secretary of Health, Education and Welfare	Oveta Culp Hobby	1953–1955
	Marion B. Folsom	1955–1958
	Arthur S. Flemming	1958–1961

The Kennedy Administration

Secretary of State	Dean Rusk	1961–1963
Secretary of Treasury	C. Douglas Dillon	1961–1963
Attorney General	Robert F. Kennedy	1961–1963
Postmaster General	J. Edward Day	1961–1963
	John A. Gronouski	1963

Secretary of Interior	Stewart L. Udall	1961–1963
Secretary of Agriculture	Orville L. Freeman	1961–1963
Secretary of Commerce	Luther H. Hodges	1961–1963
Secretary of Labor	Arthur J. Goldberg W. Willard Wirtz	1961–1962 1962–1963
Secretary of Defense	Robert S. McNamara	1961–1963
Secretary of Health, Education and Welfare	Abraham A. Ribicoff Anthony J. Celebrezze	1961–1962 1962–1963

The Lyndon Johnson Administration

Secretary of State	Dean Rusk	1963–1969
Secretary of Treasury	C. Douglas Dillon Henry H. Fowler	1963–1965 1965–1969
Attorney General	Robert F. Kennedy Nicholas Katzenbach Ramsey Clark	1963–1964 1965–1966 1967–1969
Postmaster General	John A. Gronouski Lawrence F. O'Brien Marvin Watson	1963–1965 1965–1968 1968–1969
Secretary of Interior	Stewart L. Udall	1963–1969
Secretary of Agriculture	Orville L. Freeman	1963–1969
Secretary of Commerce	Luther H. Hodges John T. Connor Alexander B. Trowbridge Cyrus R. Smith	1963–1964 1964–1967 1967–1968 1968–1969
Secretary of Labor	W. Willard Wirtz	1963–1969
Secretary of Defense	Robert F. McNamara Clark Clifford	1963–1968 1968–1969
Secretary of Health, Education and Welfare	Anthony J. Celebrezze John W. Gardner Wilbur J. Cohen	1963–1965 1965–1968 1968–1969
Secretary of Housing and Urban Development	Robert C. Weaver Robert C. Wood	1966–1969 1969
Secretary of Transportation	Alan S. Boyd	1967–1969

The Nixon Administration

Secretary of State	William P. Rogers Henry A. Kissinger	1969–1973 1973–1974
Secretary of Treasury	David M. Kennedy John B. Connally George P. Shultz William E. Simon	1969–1970 1971–1972 1972–1974 1974
Attorney General	John N. Mitchell Richard G. Kleindienst Elliot L. Richardson William B. Saxbe	1969–1972 1972–1973 1973 1973–1974
Postmaster General	Winton M. Blount	1969–1971
Secretary of Interior	Walter J. Hickel Rogers Morton	1969–1970 1971–1974
Secretary of Agriculture	Clifford M. Hardin Earl L. Butz	1969–1971 1971–1974
Secretary of Commerce	Maurice H. Stans Peter G. Peterson Frederick B. Dent	1969–1972 1972–1973 1973–1974
Secretary of Labor	George P. Shultz James D. Hodgson Peter J. Brennan	1969–1970 1970–1973 1973–1974
Secretary of Defense	Melvin R. Laird Elliot L. Richardson James R. Schlesinger	1969–1973 1973 1973–1974
Secretary of Health, Education and Welfare	Robert H. Finch Elliot L. Richardson Casper W. Weinberger	1969–1970 1970–1973 1973–1974
Secretary of Housing and Urban Development	George Romney James T. Lynn	1969–1973 1973–1974
Secretary of Transportation	John A. Volpe Claude S. Brinegar	1969–1973 1973–1974

The Ford Administration

Secretary of State	Henry A. Kissinger	1974–1977
Secretary of Treasury	William E. Simon	1974–1977
Attorney General	William Saxbe Edward Levi	1974–1975 1975–1977
Secretary of Interior	Rogers Morton Stanley K. Hathaway Thomas Kleppe	1974–1975 1975 1975–1977
Secretary of Agriculture	Earl L. Butz John A. Knebel	1974–1976 1976–1977
Secretary of Commerce	Frederick B. Dent Rogers Morton Elliot L. Richardson	1974–1975 1975–1976 1976–1977
Secretary of Labor	Peter J. Brennan John T. Dunlop W. J. Usery	1974–1975 1975–1976 1976–1977

Secretary of Defense	James R. Schlesinger	1974–1975
	Donald Rumsfeld	1975–1977
Secretary of Health, Education and Welfare	Casper Weinberger	1974–1975
	Forrest D. Mathews	1975–1977
Secretary of Housing and Urban Development	James T. Lynn	1974–1975
	Carla A. Hills	1975–1977
Secretary of Transportation	Claude Brinegar	1974–1975
	William T. Coleman	1975–1977

The Carter Administration

Secretary of State	Cyrus R. Vance	1977–1980
	Edmund Muskie	1980–1981
Secretary of Treasury	W. Michael Blumenthal	1977–1979
	G. William Miller	1979–1981
Attorney General	Griffin Bell	1977–1979
	Benjamin R. Civiletti	1979–1981
Secretary of Interior	Cecil D. Andrus	1977–1981
Secretary of Agriculture	Robert Bergland	1977–1981
Secretary of Commerce	Juanita M. Kreps	1977–1979
	Philip M. Klutznick	1979–1981
Secretary of Labor	F. Ray Marshall	1977–1981
Secretary of Defense	Harold Brown	1977–1981
Secretary of Health, Education and Welfare	Joseph A. Califano	1977–1979
	Patricia R. Harris	1979
Secretary of Health and Human Services	Patricia R. Harris	1979–1981
Secretary of of Education	Shirley M. Hufstedler	1979–1981
Secretary of Housing and Urban Development	Patricia R. Harris	1977–1979
	Moon Landrieu	1979–1981
Secretary of Transportation	Brock Adams	1977–1979
	Neil E. Goldschmidt	1979–1981
Secretary of Energy	James R. Schlesinger	1977–1979
	Charles W. Duncan	1979–1981

The Reagan Administration

Secretary of State	Alexander M. Haig	1981–1982
	George Shultz	1982–
Secretary of Treasury	Donald Regan	1981–
Attorney General	William French Smith	1981–
Secretary of Interior	James Watt	1981–
Secretary of Agriculture	John Block	1981–
Secretary of Commerce	Malcolm Baldrige	1981–
Secretary of Labor	Raymond Donovan	1981–
Secretary of Defense	Casper Weinberger	1981–
Secretary of Health and Human Services	Richard Schweiker	1981–1983
	Margaret Heckler	1983–
Secretary of Education	Terrel Bell	1981–
Secretary of Housing and Urban Development	Samuel Pierce	1981–
Secretary of Transportation	Drew Lewis	1981–1983
	Elizabeth Dole	1983–
Secretary of Energy	James Edwards	1981–1982
	Donald Hodel	1982–

Supreme Court Justices

Name	Terms of Service[1]	Appointed by	Name	Terms of Service[1]	Appointed by
John Jay, N.Y.	1789–1795	Washington	George Shiras, Jr., Pa.	1892–1903	B. Harrison
James Wilson, Pa.	1789–1798	Washington	Howell E. Jackson, Tenn.	1893–1895	B. Harrison
John Rutledge, S.C.	1790–1791	Washington	Edward D. White, La.	1894–1910	Cleveland
William Cushing, Mass.	1790–1810	Washington	Rufus W. Peckham, N.Y.	1896–1909	Cleveland
John Blair, Va.	1790–1796	Washington	Joseph McKenna, Cal.	1898–1925	McKinley
James Iredell, N.C.	1790–1799	Washington	Oliver W. Holmes, Mass.	1902–1932	T. Roosevelt
Thomas Johnson, Md.	1792–1793	Washington	William R. Day, Ohio	1903–1922	T. Roosevelt
William Paterson, N.J.	1793–1806	Washington	William H. Moody, Mass.	1906–1910	T. Roosevelt
John Rutledge, S.C.[2]	1795	Washington	Horace H. Lurton, Tenn.	1910–1914	Taft
Samuel Chase, Md.	1796–1811	Washington	Charles E. Hughes, N.Y.	1910–1916	Taft
Oliver Ellsworth, Conn.	1796–1800	Washington	Willis Van Devanter, Wy.	1911–1937	Taft
Bushrod Washington, Va.	1799–1829	J. Adams	Joseph R. Lamar, Ga.	1911–1916	Taft
Alfred Moore, N.C.	1800–1804	J. Adams	**Edward D. White,** La.	1910–1921	Taft
John Marshall, Va.	1801–1835	J. Adams	Mahlon Pitney, N.J.	1912–1922	Taft
William Johnson, S.C.	1804–1834	Jefferson	James C. McReynolds, Tenn.	1914–1941	Wilson
Brockholst Livingston, N.Y.	1807–1823	Jefferson	Louis D. Brandeis, Mass.	1916–1939	Wilson
Thomas Todd, Ky.	1807–1826	Jefferson	John H. Clarke, Ohio	1916–1922	Wilson
Gabriel Duvall, Md.	1811–1835	Madison	**William H. Taft,** Conn.	1921–1930	Harding
Joseph Story, Mass.	1812–1845	Madison	George Sutherland, Utah	1922–1938	Harding
Smith Thompson, N.Y.	1823–1843	Monroe	Pierce Butler, Minn.	1923–1939	Harding
Robert Trimble, Ky.	1826–1828	J. Q. Adams	Edward T. Sanford, Tenn.	1923–1930	Harding
John McLean, Ohio	1830–1861	Jackson	Harlan F. Stone, N.Y.	1925–1941	Coolidge
Henry Baldwin, Pa.	1830–1844	Jackson	**Charles E. Hughes,** N.Y.	1930–1941	Hoover
James M. Wayne, Ga.	1835–1867	Jackson	Owen J. Roberts, Penn.	1930–1945	Hoover
Roger B. Taney, Md.	1836–1864	Jackson	Benjamin N. Cardozo, N.Y.	1932–1938	Hoover
Philip P. Barbour, Va.	1836–1841	Jackson	Hugo L. Black, Ala.	1937–1971	F. Roosevelt
John Cartron, Tenn.	1837–1865	Van Buren	Stanley F. Reed, Ky.	1938–1957	F. Roosevelt
John McKinley, Ala.	1838–1852	Van Buren	Felix Frankfurter, Mass.	1939–1962	F. Roosevelt
Peter V. Daniel, Va.	1842–1860	Van Buren	William O. Douglas, Conn.	1939–1975	F. Roosevelt
Samuel Nelson, N.Y.	1845–1872	Tyler	Frank Murphy, Mich.	1940–1949	F. Roosevelt
Levi Woodbury, N.H.	1845–1851	Polk	**Harlan F. Stone,** N.Y.	1941–1946	F. Roosevelt
Robert C. Grier, Pa.	1846–1870	Polk	James F. Byrnes, S.C.	1941–1942	F. Roosevelt
Benjamin R. Curtis, Mass.	1851–1857	Fillmore	Robert H. Jackson, N.Y.	1941–1954	F. Roosevelt
John A. Campbell, Ala.	1853–1861	Pierce	Wiley B. Rutledge, Iowa	1943–1949	F. Roosevelt
Nathan Clifford, Me.	1858–1881	Buchanan	Harold H. Burton, Ohio	1945–1958	Truman
Noah H. Swayne, Ohio	1862–1881	Lincoln	**Frederick M. Vinson,** Ky.	1946–1953	Truman
Samuel F. Miller, Iowa	1862–1890	Lincoln	Tom C. Clark, Texas	1949–1967	Truman
David Davis, Ill.	1862–1877	Lincoln	Sherman Minton, Ind.	1949–1956	Truman
Stephen J. Field, Cal.	1863–1897	Lincoln	**Earl Warren,** Cal.	1953–1969	Eisenhower
Salmon P. Chase, Ohio	1864–1873	Lincoln	John Marshall Harlan, N.Y.	1955–1971	Eisenhower
William Strong, Pa.	1870–1880	Grant	William J. Brennan, Jr., N.J.	1956–	Eisenhower
Joseph P. Bradley, N.J.	1870–1892	Grant	Charles E. Whittaker, Mo.	1957–1962	Eisenhower
Ward Hunt, N.Y.	1873–1882	Grant	Potter Stewart, Ohio	1958–1981	Eisenhower
Morrison R. Waite, Ohio	1874–1888	Grant	Byron R. White, Colo.	1962–	Kennedy
John M. Harlan, Ky.	1877–1911	Hayes	Arthur J. Goldberg, Ill.	1962–1965	Kennedy
William B. Woods, Ga.	1881–1887	Hayes	Abe Fortas, Tenn.	1965–1970	Johnson
Stanley Matthews, Ohio	1881–1889	Garfield	Thurgood Marshall, Md.	1967–	Johnson
Horace Gray, Mass.	1882–1902	Arthur	**Warren E. Burger,** Va.	1969–	Nixon
Samuel Blatchford, N.Y.	1882–1893	Arthur	Harry A. Blackmun, Minn.	1970–	Nixon
Lucius Q. C. Lamar, Miss.	1888–1893	Cleveland	Lewis F. Powell, Jr., Va.	1971–	Nixon
Melville W. Fuller, Ill.	1888–1910	Cleveland	William H. Rehnquist, Ariz.	1971–	Nixon
David J. Brewer, Kan.	1890–1910	B. Harrison	John Paul Stevens, Ill.	1975–	Ford
Henry B. Brown, Mich.	1891–1906	B. Harrison	Sandra Day O'Connor, Ariz.	1981–	Reagan

Chief Justices in bold type
[1] The date on which the justice took his judicial oath is here used as the date of the beginning of his service, for until that oath is taken he is not vested with the prerogatives of his office. Justices, however, receive their commissions ("letters patent") before taking their oath—in some instances, in the preceding year.
[2] Acting Chief Justice; Senate refused to confirm appointment.

Credits

Positions of the photographs are indicated in abbreviated form as follows: top (t), bottom (b), center (c), left (l), right (r). All photographs not credited are the property of Scott, Foresman.

Chapter Openers

Chapter 1

525 Library of Congress   526 Culver Pictures   527 Culver Pictures   528 *Puck*, March 6, 1901   530 (t) Brown Brothers 530 (b) Thomas Alva Edison Foundation, Detroit   532 Courtesy The Great Atlantic & Pacific Tea Co.   534 (t) Library of Congress 534 (b) The Byron Collection, Museum of the City of New York 535 Courtesy The Bancroft Library   537 Library of Congress 539 (b) *Harper's Weekly*, July 16, 1892   540 *Harper's Weekly*, 1877 541 Stefan Lorant Collection.

Chapter 19

547 The Huntington Library, San Marino, California   548 Missouri Historical Society   550 (l) Culver Pictures   550 (r) Bettmann Archive   551 Museum of the City of New York   552 American Telephone & Telegraph Company   553 Brown Brothers   555 (tl) The College Archive, Smith College, Northampton, MA   555 (tr) Brown Brothers   555 (b) Bettmann Archive   558 Prints Division, New York Public Library, Astor, Lenox and Tilden Foundations 560 Chicago Historical Society   562 (l) Brown Brothers   562 (tr) Library of Congress   562 (br) *Harper's Weekly*   564 From Roger Butterfield, *The American Past*, Simon & Schuster   567 (l) Museum of the City of New York   567 (r) Photograph by Jessie Tarbox Beals, Jacob A. Riis Collection, Museum of the City of New York   569 Jane Addams Memorial Collection, The Library, University of Illinois at Chicago

Chapter 20

574 (l) Culver Pictures   574 (r) Library of Congress   577 *Judge*, The New-York Historical Society   582 Culver Pictures 583 Kansas State Historical Society, Topeka   585 Library of Congress   586 (t) Free Library of Philadelphia   586 (b) Bettmann Archive   589 (l) International Museum of Photography at George Eastman House   589 (r) Valentine Museum, Richmond, Virginia 590 (t) By permission of the Trustees of the Estate of Samuel L. Clemens (Mark Twain) deceased   590 (b) Illustration "The Whitewash Scene" by Worth Brehm from *The Adventures of Tom Sawyer* by Mark Twain, Illustrations copyright 1910 by Worth Brehm, Renewed 1937 by Mrs. Worth Brehm, Reprinted by permission of Harper & Row, Publishers, Inc.   591 (t) Culver Pictures   591 (b) Bettmann Archive   593 J. Doyle DeWitt Collection   594 From L. Frank Baum, *The Wizard of Oz*, Reilly & Lee Co.   596 Courtesy of The Bancroft Library, University of California, Berkeley   599 *Puck*, March 14, 1900

Chapter 21

604 The New-York Historical Society   605 Granger Collection 607 *Punch*, November 2, 1895   608 (t) Hawaii State Archives 608 (b) Culver Pictures   610 (l) *Puck*, March 2, 1881   610 (r) Library of Congress   611 Bettman Archive   612 (l) Granger Collection   612 (r) *New York Journal*, January 15, 1897   613 *New York Journal*, February 17, 1898   614 *New York Journal*, January 17, 1897   615 Culver Pictures   618 (l) Chicago Historical Society 618 (r) Courtesy of USMA Archives, West Point, N.Y.   621 New York Public Library, Astor, Lenox and Tilden Foundations   622 (both) Library of Congress   626 Culver Pictures

Chapter 22

631 (l) The Lawrence Lee Pelletier Library, Allegheny College   631 (r) Culver Pictures   633 Chicago Historical Society   634 Culver Pictures   636 (l) Courtesy Mrs. Neill Whisnant, Portland, Oregon 636 (tr) Brown Brothers   636 (br) Brown Brothers   639 Brown Brothers   642 Sears, Roebuck and Co.   643 Warshaw Collection

of Business Americana, Smithsonian Institution   644 (l) U.S. Department of Labor   644 (r) International Museum of Photography at George Eastman House   645 (t) Schomberg Collection, New York Public Library, Astor, Lenox and Tilden Foundations   645 (b) Bettmann Archive   646 The Sophia Smith Collection (Women's History Archive), Smith College, Northampton, MA   647 The Sophia Smith Collection (Women's History Archive), Smith College, Northampton, MA   649 The Jacob A. Riis Collection, Museum of the City of New York   650 Bettmann Archive   651 A.B. Walker in LIFE 652 Wadsworth Atheneum, Hartford, Connecticut, Ella Gallup Sumner and Mary Catlin Sumner Collection   653 Yale University Art Gallery, Gift of Collection Société Anonyme

Chapter 23

658 Brown Brothers   660 (t) Courtesy, Ford Archives, Henry Ford Museum, Dearborn, Michigan   660 (c) Courtesy, Ford Archives, Henry Ford Museum, Dearborn, Michigan   660 (r) The New York Public Library   663 Brown Brothers   665 (both) Brown Brothers 666 Manchester (N.H.) Historic Association   667 Culver Pictures 669 *Puck*, Jan. 13, 1904   670 National Park Service   671 Brown Brothers   672 Library of Congress   673 *Puck*, June 22, 1910 674 *Colliers*, 1905   675 Warshaw Collection of Business Americana, Smithsonian Institution   677 *New York Herald*, July 1912 679 Brown Brothers   682 National Archives

Chapter 24

689 Library of Congress   690 *Puck*, 1901   693 (l) Library of Congress   693 (r) Brown Brothers   695 (t) *Puck*, Oct. 16, 1915 695 (b) West Point Museum   697 *Des Moines Register and Leader*, July, 1915   699 (l) UPI   702 National Archives   703 National Archives   702–03 Smithsonian Institution   704 New York Public Library, Picture Collection   705 (both) National Archives 708 UPI   711 (tl) National Archives   711 (tr) Imperial War Museum   713 (t) Kirby in the *World Journal Tribune*, 1920   713 (b) The Ohio Historical Society, Inc.

Chapter 25

718 Brown Brothers   720 *Vanity Fair* April, 1929   723 (l) Brown Brothers   723 (r) *Frank Leslie's Illustrated Newspaper*, September 11, 1920   724 LIFE, June 3, 1926   725 (l) Drawing by Carl Rose; © 1928, 1956. The New Yorker Magazine, Inc.   725 (r) *Dempsey and Firpo*, 1924 by George Bellows. Oil on canvas. 51 × 63¼ inches. Collection of Whitney Museum of American Art. Acq. # 31.95 726 Brown Brothers   727 Brown Brothers   728 UPI   729 (t) Brown Brothers   729 (b) Collection of American Literature, the Beinecke Rare Book and Manuscript Library, Yale University   730 (l) Des Moines Art Center, James D. Edmundson Fund, 1958   730 (r) UPI   732 Chicago Historical Society   733 *The Passion of Sacco and Vanzetti*, 1931–32 by Ben Shahn. From the Sacco and Vanzetti Series of 23 paintings. Tempera. 84½ × 48 inches. Collection of Whitney Museum of American Art. Gift of Edith and Milton Lowenthal in memory of Juliana Force. Acq. # 49.22.   734 Smithers Collection. Humanities Research Center. The University of Texas at Austin 735 Culver Pictures   736 Rollin Kirby, 1925   738 LIFE, 1922 739 From Stefan Lorant's *The Glorious Burden*. Authors Edition, Inc., Lenox, MA   741 Museum of the City of New York   741 (r) UPI

Chapter 26

747 Library of Congress   749 (tl) Wide World   749 (tr) *The Detroit News*   749 (bl) Collection of Nebraska Art Association, Courtesy of Sheldon Memorial Art Gallery, University of Nebraska, Lincoln

749 (br) UPI   751 Brown Brothers   753 Franklin D. Roosevelt Library, National Archives and Records Service   754 Culver Pictures   755 Franklin D. Roosevelt Library, National Archives and Records Service   756 (l) Wide World   756 (r) Library of Congress   757 Library of Congress   759 Social Security Administration   761 (t) UPI   761 (c) Library of Congress   ' 761 (b) Courtesy Mrs. Philip Evergood   763 UPI   764 Brown Brothers   766 Franklin D. Roosevelt Library, National Archives and Records Service   768 (l) Daniel Robert Fitzpatrick, St. Louis *Post-Dispatch*   768 (r) Historical Pictures Service, Chicago

Chapter 27

774 William A. Ireland *The Columbus Dispatch*, 1928   776 Wide World   778 U.S. Army/Center of Military History   779 National Archives   781 (t) UPI   781 (b) H. Roger-Viollet   782 National Maritime Museum, London   784 Wide World   786 (l) Navy Department/National Archives   786 (r) Wide World   786 (b) *San Francisco Chronicle*, December 8, 1941   789 U.S. Army   791 Vernon T. Manion. Courtesy Boeing Aircraft Corporation, Seattle   793 Margaret Bourke-White, LIFE Magazine © Time, Inc.   794 Jacob Lawrence. "The migrants arrive in great numbers." No. 40 in the series *The Migration of the Negro*. (1940–41) Tempera on composition board, 18 × 21". Collection, The Museum of Modern Art, New York. Gift of Mrs. David M. Levy.   795 Library of Congress   796 Franklin D. Roosevelt Library, National Archives and Records Service   797 (t) Edward Clark, LIFE Magazine © 1945 Time, Inc.   797 (b) U. S. Army   800 Culver Pictures   802 Wide World

Chapter 28

807 Bettmann Archive   810 UPI   811 Courtesy of Richmond *Times-Dispatch*.   812 UPI   814 Bettmann Archive   818 © Bruce Barbey/Magnum Photos, Inc.   820 UPI   821 Bettmann Archive   822 (l) UPI   822 (r) from Herblock's *Special for Today* (Simon & Schuster, 1958)   824 UPI   825 UPI   826 UPI   827 (l) Herbert L. Block, *The Washington Post*, 1959. From *Straight Herblock* (Simon & Schuster, 1964)   827 (r) UPI

Chapter 29

833 (t, b) Bettmann Archive   834 Robert Isaacs   835 Green Coca-Cola Bottles, 1962. Oil on canvas. 82¼ × 57 inches. Collection of the Whitney Museum of American Art.   836 Bettmann Archive   837 Bettmann Archive   839 UPI   840 Bob Henriques/Magnum Photos, Inc.   843 (t, b) UPI   845 UPI   846 UPI   847 (l) Carl Iwasaki, Life Magazine, Inc.   847 (r) Eve Arnold/Magnum Photos, Inc.   848 UPI   849 (tl) UPI   849 (tr) © Bruce Roberts/Photo Researchers, Inc.   849 (b) Charles Moore/Black Star   851 Culver Pictures   852 Bettmann Archive   855 Culver Pictures

Chapter 30

860 UPI   862 Black Star   864 UPI   865 UPI   866 (l) UPI   866 (r) Leslie Illingworth. Apr. 21, 1961. Scratchboard. 11 3/16 × 8 13/16 in. Courtesy The National Library of Wales.   869 UPI   872 Wide World   873 Charles Moore/Black Star   875 Wide World   876 Charles Moore/Black Star   878 (l) Jim Murray/Black Star   878 (r) UPI   879 UPI   881 (t) UPI   881 (bl) Michael D. Sullivan   881 (br) Paul Conklin   885 Courtesy Bill Canfield—*Star-Ledger* (Newark) 1968   886 (t) © Philip Jones Griffiths/Magnum Photos, Inc.   886 (b) Bill Mauldin, *The Sun-Times* (Chicago), 1966. Copyright 1966—Chicago Sun Times. Reproduced by courtesy of Wil-Jo Associates, Inc., and Bill Mauldin.

Chapter 31

893 Wayne Miller/Magnum Photos, Inc.   894 (t) UPI   894 (b) Peter A. Lake/Black Star   895 Burk Uzzle/Woodfin Camp and Associates   897 (t) Detroit Free Press/Black Star   897 (b) UPI   899 © Paul Fusco/Magnum Photos, Inc.   900 © Betty Lane/Photo Researchers, Inc.   901 Robert Ellison/Empire News/Black Star   902 (t) Courtesy The Lyndon Baines Johnson Library   902 (b) *The Time Machine*. Leslie Illingworth. Sept. 13, 1967, in *Punch*. Scratchboard. 15¼ × 12½ in. Courtesy The Lyndon Baines Johnson Library Collection, Austin, Tex.   903 (l) Charles Harbutt/Archive Pictures, Inc.   903 (r) UPI   904 Roger Malloch/Magnum Photos, Inc.   905 (t) Elliott Erwitt/Magnum Photos, Inc.   905 (b) UPI   907 Courtesy The White House   910 (l) Zoom/Magnum Distribution   910 (r) Distributed by Magnum Photos, Inc.   911 (bl) UPI   911 (br) Pat Oliphant. The Denver Post, 1970   912 By John Fischetti, Chicago Daily News, 1970, Courtesy of Field Newspaper Syndicate   913 (t) © Howard E. Ruffner/Black Star   913 (c) © Paul Fusco/Magnum Photos, Inc.   913 (b) UPI   914 Susan Meiselas/Magnum Photos, Inc.   917 Leonard Freed/Magnum Photos, Inc.   918 Mark Godfrey/Archive Pictures, Inc.   919 Mark Godfrey/Archive Pictures, Inc.

Chapter 32

924 Peter Arnold, Inc.   925 "Hat in Hand." (Editorial cartoon by Lou Grant of the Oakland *Tribune*. Copyright, Los Angeles *Times* Syndicate. Reprinted with permission.)   927 Tony Korody/Sygma   928 (t) UPI   928 (b) Peter Arnold, Inc.   929 © 1979 David Moore/Black Star   931 (t) Chuck O'Rear/West Light   931 (b) Jim Balog/Black Star   932 Wide World   933 Arthur Grace/Sygma   935 Nik Wheeler/Black Star   937 UPI   938 D. B. Owen/Black Star © 1983   939 (t) P. Chauvel/Sygma   939 (b) J. L. Atlan/Sygma   940 SIPA/Black Star   945 Dan Connolly/Liaison Agency   946 (r) Paul Conklin   947 Paul Conklin   949 Martin A. Levick/Black Star   950 Alex Webb/Magnum Photos, Inc.   951 Dennis Brack/Black Star   952 UPI   954 Mark Sherman/Bruce Coleman   955 Alex Webb/Magnum Photos, Inc.

Picture Essay 7
The Automobile Culture: 1920–1939
following p. 768

1 Bettmann Archive

2 (tl, r) Culver Pictures (bl) Brown Brothers

3 (tl) Security Pacific National Bank Photograph Collection/Los Angeles Public Library (tr) Culver Pictures (bl) Minnesota Historical Society (br) Library of Congress

4 (tl) Library of Congress (bl) UPI (br) Culver Pictures

Picture Essay 8
The Space Race:
Commitment to the Future
following p. 864

1 NASA

2 (t) SOVFOTO (bl) © 1957 by The New York Times Company. Reprinted by permission (r) NASA

3 (l) NASA (tr) TASS from SOVFOTO (br) NASA

4 (l) Ralph Morse, LIFE Magazine © 1962, Time, Inc. (tr) Wide World (br) M. Naythons/Gamma-Liaison

In addition, the authors and publisher acknowledge with gratitude permission to reprint, quote from, or adapt the following materials. (The numbers shown below refer to pages of this text.)

509 Hamlin Garland, *A Son of the Middle Border*. P. F. Collier & Son, 1914.   **533** Excerpt from *The Price* by Arthur Miller. Copyright © 1968, 1969 by Arthur Miller and Ingeborg M. Miller, Trustee. All rights reserved. Reprinted by permission of Viking Penguin Inc. and International Creative Management, Inc.   **559** (Map) Adapted from *Historic City: The Settlement of Chicago*, City of Chicago, Department of Planning.   **641** (Map) Adapted from *Historic City: The Settlement of Chicago*, City of Chicago, Department of Planning.   **653** From "Chicago" in *Chicago Poems* by Carl Sandburg, copyright 1916 by Holt, Rinehart and Winston, Inc.; renewed 1944 by Carl Sandburg. Reprinted by permission of Harcourt Brace Jovanovich, Inc.   **664** Joe Hill, "Workers of the World, Awaken!" cited in *American Folksongs of Protest* by John Greenway. University of Pennsylvania Press, 1953. **673** Upton Sinclair, *The Jungle*, 1906.   **709** "The New Day" by Fenton Johnson cited in *The Book of American Negro Poetry*, ed. by James Weldon Johnson. New York: Harcourt, Brace and Company, 1931. **750** Studs Terkel, *Hard Times*. New York: Pantheon Books, 1970, p. 41. **876–77** From "Letter from Birmingham Jail—April 16, 1963" from *Why We Can't Wait* by Martin Luther King, Jr. Copyright © 1963 by Martin Luther King, Jr. Reprinted by permission of Harper & Row, Publishers, Inc. and Joan Daves.

Index

The letter *m* preceding a page number indicates that there is a map on that page.

Dickinson, John, 115–117, 158–159, 169
Diem, Ngo Dinh, 865, 866, 884
Dingley Tariff of 1897, 597, 673
Diplomacy. See Foreign Policy
Dirksen, Everett M., 880, 883
Disappearing quorum rule in Congress, 579
Diseases: from Americas to Europe, 8; from Europe to Americas, 7, 8, 10
District of Columbia. See Washington, D.C.
Divorce: in postrevolutionary America, 155; in late 1800s and early 1900s, 502; 1900–1920, 643; in 1920s, 724; during World War II, 793; in 1970s, 946–947
Dix, Dorothea, 312
Dobrynin, Anatoly, 868
Dodd, Samuel T. C., 528
Dodge, Grenville M., 522–523
Dollar diplomacy in foreign policy, 690–691
Dolliver, Jonathan P., 672
Domesticity ideology, 305–306
Domestic policies, foreign policy related to, 943
Dominican Republic, troops to, 884
Dooley v. U.S. case, 624
Door, Rheta Childe, 552
Dos Passos, John, 714, 729
Douglas, Stephen A.: anti-Lecompton stand of, 401; in Compromise of 1850, 387; in election of 1856, 397; in election of 1858, 401–403, 414; in election of 1860, 405–406; and Kansas-Nebraska Act, 391–393; against secession, 419; as senator, 387, 391–393
Douglas, William O., 768, 875
Douglass, Frederick, 314, 344
Dove, Arthur, 653
Downes v. Bidwell case, 624
Draft: during Civil War, 422, 425, 436; in World War I, 700; before World War II (in peacetime), 783
Drake, Edwin L., 258, 527
Drake, Sir Francis, 24, 28
Dred Scott v. Sanford (1859) case, 399–401
Dreiser, Theodore, 592
Driggus, Emanuel, 73
Drug industries, regulation of, 670–671, 675
Drugs: in early 1900s (patent medicines), 674–675; in 1960s, 895–896
Du Bois, W. E. B., 450, 555, 556, 645, 648, 709, 730
Dueling in Old South, 334–336
Duke, James B., 531
Dulles, John Foster, 821–822, 824, 825
Duncan, Isadora, 652
Duncan, Stephen, 333
Dunmore, Lord John Murray, 135
Dunn, Richard, 58
Dunne, Finley Peter, 531–532, 630–631
Durand, Asher, 279
Dutch, the, Navigation Acts used against, 78–79
Dutch West Indies Company colony, 51–52
Dwight, Rev. Timothy, 300
Dylan, Bob, 895

■

Eagleton, Thomas, 917
Early, Peter, 226
Earp, Wyatt, 505
Earth Day in 1970, 927–928
Eastman, George, 529
Eaton, John, 284

Eaton, Peggy O'Neale, 284, 286
Eaton, Theophilus, 50
Eaton, William, 215
Economic interests and party choice in 1840s, 294
Economic mobility in industry, 1800s, 536
Economic thought in late 1800s, 567
Economy: of American colonies, 94–96; during Carter administration, 927–929; energy problems affecting, 926–931; during Ford administration, 926; Hamilton's program for, 186–187, 190–191; instability of, after American Revolution, 164–166; during Kennedy administration, 870–871; market, of early 1800s, 254–256; during Nixon administration, 908–909; of North, during Civil War, 422, 437; and politics of 1820s and 1830s, 273; during Reagan administration, 954–956; shifts in, 1970s, 930–931; of South, 255, 324–331, 420–421, 460–462; time periods for: 1700s, 94–96; early 1800s, 254–256, 273; Civil War, 422–423, 436, 437; Reconstruction, 460–462; 1920s, 719–722; 1930s (see Great Depression); after World War II, 833–838; 1970s, 923–957; of West, cycles in, 499–506. See also Depressions; Inflation; Panics; Recessions
Eden, Anthony, 824–825
Ederle, Gertrude, 725, 728
Edison, Thomas A., 516, 528, 530–531, 574–575
Education: in American colonies, 65, 70; bilingual, 1970s, 950; of black Americans, 462, 554–556, 645, 731, 846–848, 948; college (see College education); controversy over, 1950s, 851; Dewey revolution in, 635; federal aid to, 850, 882; of immigrants, 560, 898–899; integration of, 847–848, 872–873, 908, 909; during Johnson administration, 882; of Mexican-Americans, 1960s, 898–899; of Native Americans, 490–491; public, 307, 310–311, 553–554; in reaction to Sputnik, 855; segregation of, 1870s–1900, 553–554; student voice in, 894; women in, 1800s, 306; during World War II, 793. See also Schools
Edward VI (king of England), 22
Edwards, Jonathan, 99, 101
Ehrlichman, John, 906, 918
Einstein, Albert, 800
Eisenhower, Dwight D., 861, 879; and Cold War, 821–828; and Cuba, 866; defense spending by, 835; on desegregation, 848; disarmament efforts of, 809, 822, 826–828; in election of 1948 (refusal to run), 839; in election of 1952, 821, 840; in election of 1956, 824–825; and federal aid to schools, 850; and McCarthyism, 844–845; as NATO supreme commander, 813, 816; on nuclear weapons, 822–824; as president, 821–828, 835, 844–845, 850, 861, 866, 879, 887; and Vietnam, 887; in World War II, 789, 797–798
Elderly, rising numbers of, 1970s, 944–945
Elections. See Congressional elections; Presidential elections
Electoral college in late 1700s, 199, 206
Electrical industry, growth of, 720
Electric lights, invention of, 531
Elementary and Secondary Education Act of 1965, 882
Eliot, Charles W., 554
Eliot, T. S., 653, 728–729
Elizabeth I (queen of England), 21–27
Elkins Act of 1903, 670

Elliott, Robert Brown, 464
Elliott, Bishop Stephen, 398
Ellsberg, Daniel, 916
Ellsworth, Oliver, 184, 205
El Salvador, military aid to, 937
Ely, Richard T., 567, 635, 639
Emancipation of slaves, 433–435, 451–452. See also Abolitionist movement; Slavery
Embargo, early 1800s, 228–229
Embargo Act of 1807, 228, 230
Emerson, Ralph Waldo, 279, 311, 319, 398, 404
Employment: of black Americans, 535, 644–645, 722, 948; by sex and race, 1972 and 1980, 948; of women (see Working women). See also Labor; Unemployment
Employment Act of 1946, 838
Encomienda system, 16–18
Energy crisis of 1970s, 925–931
Energy policy of 1970s, 927–929
Engerman, Stanley, 329, 330
England. See Great Britain
Enlightenment in American colonies, 1700s, 97–98
Enrollment Act of 1863, 437
Entertainment: 1860–1880s, 549–551; 1890–1920, 650–653; 1920s, 720, 725, 728
Environmental movement of late 1960s and early 1970s, 927–928. See also Conservation policy
Environmental Protection Agency, 927
Equality: as goal after American Revolution, 155, 156; meaning of, in mid-1800s, 274–275, 278
Equal Pay Act of 1972, 946
Equal rights, arguments about, 1820s and 1830s, 273–274
Equal Rights Amendment (proposed), 723–724, 900, 947
Equal Rights party, 291
Equiano, Olaudah, 76
Ericsson, Leif, 10
Eric the Red, 10
Erie Canal, building of, 251
Erskine, David M., 230
Ervin, Sam, 918
Escobedo v. Illinois (1964) case, 875
Espionage Act of 1917, 703, 704
Ethiopia invaded by Mussolini, 778
Ethnic Heritage Studies Act of 1972, 898
Ethnic nationalism of 1960s, 898–899. See also Black Americans, nationalism of, 1960s
Ethnic theaters, 559–560
Europe: Catholicism in, 21–22; division of, after World War II, m808, 807–809; in exploration of Americas, 10–12; nation-states of, rise of, 10–11; New Monarchs in, 11, 14; and Native Americans, 6–8; after Treaty of Versailles, m711; U.S. retreat from, 1920s, 775–776; World War I in, m694; World War II in, 780–781, m788, 789–790
Evangelicalism in 1800s, 298–304
Evans, Augusta Jane, 278
Evans, Oliver, 258
Evolution theories of Darwin, 566, 567, 604
Expansionism: of Japan, time periods for: following World War I, 777–778; in 1930s, 778; during World War II, 784–785, 787, 790–791; of U.S., time periods for: early 1800s, 241–248; mid-1800s, 351–379; 1890s, 603–611, 621–626 (see also Spanish-American War); 1901–1920, 687–691
Explorations of Americas, m14–15, 10–20

Fuller, Margaret, 319
Fulton, Robert, 216, 249
Fundamentalist controversy of 1920s, 736–737.
  See also Religion
Fur trade, 19, 242–243, 353

■

Gaddis, John Lewis, 817
Gadsden, Christopher, 132
Gage, Thomas, 132–134, 136
Galbraith, John Kenneth, 871, 880
Gale, Zona, 729
Gallatin, Albert, 217, 228, 235, 236
Galloway, Joseph, 133
Gallup, George, 853
Gama, Vasco da, 13
Gandhi, Mohandas K., 850
Gardner, Lloyd, 909
Gardoqui, Don Diego de, 166
Garfield, Harry A., 704
Garfield, James A., 564–565, 577–578
Garland, Hamlin, 509, 549–550, 581, 590
Garland, Judy, 595
Garner, John Nance, 780
Garrett, Pat, 499
Garrison, William Lloyd, 314–317, 324, 383, 471
Garvey, Andrew, 563
Gary, Elbert H., 661
Gatell, Frank Otto, 258, 421
Gates, Horatio, 140, 143
Gates, Sir Thomas, 36
Gauguin, Paul, 652
General Trades' Union of the City and County of Philadelphia, 277
Genêt, Edmond, 193
Geneva Conference of 1955, 826–827
George, David Lloyd, 710
George, Henry, 546, 566, 583, 637–638
George, Milton, 582
George I (king of England), 109
George II (king of England), 113, 121
George III (king of England), 115, 121, 127, 130, 132, 133, 135, 136
Georgia colony, 109–111
Georgia invaded during Civil War, 440, 441
Gerard, James W., 691
Germain, Lord George, 140, 142
Germany: Berlin blockade in, 813–814; Berlin crisis of 1961 in, 863–864; immigration to America from, 92, 375–376, 393; time periods for: World War I, 686–687, 694–702; 1930s, 778; World War II, 780–784, 786, 787, 789–790, 796–798; after World War II, 807–809
Geronimo (Apache chief), 493
Gerry, Elbridge, 200
Gershwin, George, 730
Gettysburg, battle of, 438–439
Gettysburg Address, 415
Ghent, Treaty of (1814), 235–236
Ghost Dances of Teton Sioux, 490
Gibbons v. *Ogden* (1824) case, 264
Gibbs, James, 93
Gideon v. *Wainwright* (1963) case, 875
Gilbert, Sir Humphrey, 25–26
Gillette, William, 463
Gilman, Charlotte Perkins, 552
Gilman, Daniel Coit, 554
Gladden, Washington, 568

Glasgow, Ellen, 729
Glazer, Nathan, 952
Glenn, John, 855
Glidden, Joseph F., 508
Glorious Revolution: in Great Britain, 33; in Massachusetts Bay Colony, 82–84; in New York colony, 85–86
Godkin, E. L., 549
Goldberg, Arthur J., 868, 875
Gold bond sales during Cleveland administration, 588
Goldman, Emma, 646, 732
Gold rushes in 1800s, 370, 488, m503, 500–503
Gold standard: versus free coinage of silver, 592–593, 596; triumph of, 598, 599
Gold Standard Act of 1900, 598
Goldwater, Barry: in 1964 election, 885, 904, 952; on Nixon, 906; as senator, 880, 882
Goliad massacre, 356
Gompers, Samuel, 537–538, 621, 663, 680, 705
Good Neighbor policy of Franklin Roosevelt, 689, 776, 777
Goodnight, Charles, 494, 505
Goodwin, Richard, 869
Goodyear, Charles, 258, 372
Gordon, Katherine, 854
Gordon, Richard, 854
Gordon, Thomas, 102, 122
Gorgas, Josiah, 423
Gorras Blancas, Las (The White Caps), 499
Gould, Jay, 464, 469, 523, 537
Government: of American colonies, assemblies in, 106–107 (*see also specific colonies*); of Great Britain, 39, 121–122; Spanish, in Americas, 16–18; U.S. (*see entries beginning with* Federal)
Governors, power of, reduced by state constitutions, 157
Graebner, Norman, 370
Graham, Billy, 853, 912
Graham, Sylvester, 320
Gramm, Phil, 954
Grand Alliance of European monarchs, 265–266
Granges, 509, 581, 582
Grant, Madison, 735–736
Grant, Ulysses S.: corruption under, 469, 520, 577–578; in election of 1872, 469, 472; expansionist policy of, 605–606; as general, 425, 428, 437–442; as president, 464–469, 472, 577–578, 605–606; War Department leadership turned down by, 458
Grasse, François Joseph Paul, Comte de, 146
Grateful Dead, 895
Gray, John P., 565
Great Awakening, 97–101
  Second, 299–302, 315
Great Britain: and American Revolution, 121–122, 125–132, 136–143, 146; arbitration treaty of 1896 with, 607; Confederacy efforts to involve in Civil War, 431–433; constitution of, 101–102; France at war with, 107–115, 192–193, 227–236; Glorious Revolution in, 33; House of Burgesses in, 39; Ireland colonized by, 25–26; nationalism in, 23–24; in North America, with troops, 107–115, 123, 125, 129, 136–143, 146, m195; North American colonization by, 26–29, 31–59 (*see also* American colonies); North American explorations by, 20; Orders in Council of, 227, 231; Oregon treaty with, 365–366; Parliament of, 121–122; politics in, 1700s, 102;

Protestantism of, 21–23, 44–47; Reformation in, 21–23; religion in, 21–24, 44–47; Stuart monarchs of, 33; trade with, after American Revolution, 164; Tudor monarchs of, 21–22; U.S. relations with: in late 1700s, 192–196, 200; in 1870s, 606; U.S. at war with, in early 1800s, 227–236; wars in and with (not including World Wars I and II), 23–24, 107–115, 121–122, 125–132, 136–143, 146, 192–193, 227–236; Whigs versus George III in, 121; in World War I, 686, 687, 694, 696, 698–702; in World War II, 782–784 (see also World War II, Allies in)
Great Depression of 1930s, 845–771; causes of, 746–748; effects of, 748–750; fighting, 750–770 (*see also* New Deal); unemployment during, 746–749
Great Society of Lyndon Johnson, 882–883, 907–908, 942, 948, 949
Great Wagon Road, m96
Greece, civil war in, 811
Greeley, Horace, 318, 469, 472, 482, 484
Green, Duff, 362
Greenback Labor party, 466
Greenback party, 466
Greenbacks after Civil War, 465–466
Greene, Nathanael, 146
Greenough, Horatio, 279
Greenville, Treaty of (1795), 196
Gregg, William, 328
Grenville, George, 125–127
Grenville, Sir Richard, 26, 27
Grierson, Benjamin H., 493
Griffith, D. W., 450, 650
Grimké, Angelina, 317, 471
Grimké, Sarah, 317
Gromyko, Andrei, 810
Groves, Leslie R., 801
Gruening, Ernest, 885, 894
Guadalcanal, occupation of, 791
Guadalupe Hidalgo, Treaty of (1848), 369
Guam: acquisition of, 620; as dependency, 624
Guiteau, Charles J., 564–565, 578
Gulf of Tonkin affair, 885
Gutiérrez, José Angel, 950
Gutman, Herbert G., 348, 535
Guy Fawkes Day, 144

■

Haber, Al, 892
Haeckel's Biogenetic Law, 604
Hakluyt, Richard, 28–29, 33, 37
Halberstam, David, 862
Haldeman, H. R., 906, 918
Haley, Jack, 595
Hall v. *DeCuir* (1878) case, 477
Halleck, Henry W., 430
Hamilton, Alexander, 152, 177; as abolitionist, 154; Adams (John) opposed by, 201–206; at Constitutional Convention, 169; constitutional reforms of, 165; death of, 225; and election of 1796, 199; and federalism, 175; and foreign affairs, 192–195, 200–201; on human nature, 185; Jefferson opposing, 182, 184–187, 190–195; and political party birth, 182, 195–197, 199–201; as provisional army officer, 201–202, 205; as secretary of treasury, 183–187, 190–195
Hamilton, Dr. Alice, 533
Hammer v. *Dagenhart* (1918) case, 635

I–8

McCoy, Joseph G., 504
McCulloch, Hugh, 465
McCulloch v. *Maryland* (1819) case, 264
Macdonough, Thomas, 234
McDowell, Irvin, 428
McGovern, George, 904, 916–917, 934
McGuffey, William Holmes, 553
McGuffey's Readers, 310–311, 553
McHenry, James, 199, 202, 205
McJunkin, George, 4
McKay, Claude, 709, 730
Mackay, John W., 501
McKinley, William, 738; assassination of, 598, 615, 667; and Cuba, 612–613, 625; in election of 1896, 593, 596; in election of 1900, 598; Hawaii annexation by, 608–609; newspaper criticism of, 615; Open Door policy of, 625–626, 689–690, 777; and Philippines, 620–625; as president, 577, 597–598, 608–626; and Spanish-American War, 613, 616, 617, 619, 626
McKinley Tariff Act of 1890, 579, 588, 606, 607
Maclay, William, 187
McManes, James, 563
M'Naghten Rule, 565
McNamara, Robert, 862, 863, 883, 894, 901
McNeill, William H., 817
Macon, Nathaniel, 223–224, 230
Macon's Bill Number Two, 230
McPherson, Aimee Semple, 737
McPherson, James, 404
Macune, Dr. Charles W., 582
Macy, R. H., 532
Madero, Francisco I., 692
Madison, James, 152, 166, 171, 198; as abolitionist, 154; and Bill of Rights, 175–178; constitutional reforms of, 165; and election of 1796, 199; on European titles, 182; and *Federalist* papers, 168, 175; Hamilton's policies opposed by, 187, 190, 191, 203, 204; in *Marbury* v. *Madison*, 222–223; and nation-building, 259; political ideology of, 167–169; on presidency power, 183; after presidency, 266; as president, 217, 229–236; on transportation, 248, 260
Magazines in early 1900s, 630–631. *See also* Newspapers
Mahan, Alfred Thayer, 610–611
Mail-order companies, 532
Maine battleship, sinking of, 613
Manhattan Project, 799–802, 809
Manifest Destiny doctrine, 363–370
Mann, Horace, 310
Mann-Elkins Act of 1910, 676
Mansfield, Arabella, 534
Manufacturing. *See* Industrialization; Industry(ies); *entries beginning with* Industrial
Mao Tse-tung, 818, 819, 823
Marbury, William, 222–223
Marbury v. *Madison* (1803) case, 222–223
Marches on Washington: black Americans in 1963, 874; of World War I veterans, 751
Marcuse, Herbert, 895
Marcy, William, 393
Marin, John, 653
Market economy of early 1800s, 254–256
Marquette, Père Jacques, 19
Marriages: in 1800s, 304–306; interracial, in early Mexico, 18; of slaves, 347–348; during World War II, 793. *See also* Divorce; Families
Marshall, Alfred, 533
Marshall, George C., 789, 810–812, 815, 818, 844

Marshall, John: in Burr trial, 226; as Chief Justice of Supreme Court, 206, 222–224, 263–264; as midnight judge, 206; in negotiations with France, 200, 201; on states' rights, 204
Marshall, Thurgood, 847, 871
Marshall Plan, 811–812, 814, 816, 835
Mary I (queen of England), 22
Mary II (queen of England), 83–85
Maryland colony, 42–43, 86
Mason, George, 127, 157, 169, 174, 175, 177
Mason, James M., 432
Massachusetts, state constitution of, 157–158
Massachusetts Bay colony, 46–50, 82–85
Massachusetts Bay Company, 83, 84
Mass entertainment, 1890–1920, 650–652. *See also* Entertainment
Mass production: of automobiles, 659–660, 662, 718–719 (*See also* Ford, Henry, as automaker); of clothing, 642; in industry, 372, 662–663, 718–721
Mass society: education of, 1870–1900, 553–554; 1890s–1920, 639–645, 648–654
Masters, Edgar Lee, 653
Masterson, William B. (Bat), 505
Mather, Cotton, 84, 86
Mather, Increase, 84
Matisse, Henri, 652
Maximilian (emperor of Mexico), 605
Mayaguez incident, 936
Mayflower Compact, 44
Meade, George, 438–439
Meat Inspection Act of 1906, 671
Mechanics' Union of Trade Associations, 277
Medical care: in 1800s, 547–548; in 1960s, 882; in 1980, 945
Medicare and Medicaid programs, 882
Mellon, Andrew, 738–739
Melville, Herman, 279, 352–353
Mencken, H. L., 561, 724, 729, 736
Mercantilism in 1600s, 77–78
Merchant marine in early 1800s, 213, 216
Meredith, James, 872–873
Mergers in 1920s, 721
Merk, Frederick, 369–370
Merrimack, 428, 429
Metacomet (King Phillip), 82–83
Mexican-Americans: in army, 795; as cowboys, 504–505; education of, 898–899; immigration of, 648, 736, 750, 950; nationalism of, 898–899; under New Deal, 763; time periods for: 1800s, 499, 504–505; 1900–1920, 648; 1930s, 763; World War II, 795; 1960s, 898–899; 1970s, 949–950
Mexican War (1846), m367, 366–370
Mexico: borderlands of, in mid-1800s, 353–356; borderlands of, Spanish exploration of, 18–19; cession of, slavery problem in, 383–387; interracial marriages in, 18; relations with, under Wilson, 692–693; Spanish conquest of, 16–18
Middle class in 1920s, 722. *See also* Society, American, classes and ranking in
Middle colonies, m53, 50–56, 85–86, 91–92
Middle East: in 1950s, 824–825; in 1970s and early 1980s, m938, 937–940. *See also* Arab oil embargo; Iran; Israel, wars in
Midnight appointees (judges) of Adams, 206, 217–218, 222–223
Midway, battle of, 791
Migration: of black Americans, 708–709, m794, 948; in early 1800s, 241–248; of Native Americans, 6 (*see also* Native Americans, forced relocations of); to Oregon, 1840s

and 1850s, 358–360; to Texas, mid-1800s, 354–357; to West, 244–248, 494–499; during World War II, 792–795. *See also* Immigration; Population
Milbourne, Jacob, 86
Military alliance, Western, after World War II, 813
Military-industrial complex in 1960s, 828
Military power: of Soviet Union, 941; of U.S., 611–613, 616–620, 934. *See also specific wars*
Military spending, 835, 862–863, 870, 954–955
Military system. *See* Armed forces; Army, U.S.; Navy, U.S.
Miller, Arthur, 533
Millis, Walter, 777
Mills, C. Wright, 854
Mills, Clark, 279
Mills, Rev. Samuel John, 302
Minimum wage: under Eisenhower, 841; under Truman, 840
Mining: coal (*see entries beginning with* Coal); gold, 370, 388, m503, 500–503; safety laws for, 676
Minorities under New Deal, 762–763. *See also specific entries, for example*: Black Americans; Mexican-Americans
Minor v. *Happersett* (1875) case, 575
Minutemen, 133–134
Miranda v. *Arizona* (1966) case, 875
Missionaries to civilize non–Anglo-Saxons, 604–605. *See also* Religion
Mississippi, settlement to, 244–246
Missouri Compromise, m262, 261–263, 392, 399, 400, 417, 418
Missouri crisis of 1819–1820, 383
Mitchell, John (attorney general), 908, 909, 916, 918, 919
Mitchell, John (labor leader), 669
Modernity, 1920s roots of, 717–723
Modern Republicanism of Eisenhower, 840–842
Molasses Act of 1733, 95, 125
Mondale, Walter, 933
Money: in early 1800s, growth of, 255–256; issued during Civil War, 465–466
Monitor, 428
Monopolies, 528
Monroe, James: and commercial treaty with Great Britain, 228; and election of 1808, 229; on expansion of U.S. territory, 241; Latin American recognition by, 265; and Louisiana Purchase, 218, 219; as president, 240, 260–261, 265; on transportation projects, 260
Monroe Doctrine, 266–267, 605–607, 712; Lodge Corollary to, 689; Roosevelt Corollary to, 689, 776
Montcalm, Louis Joseph de, 114–115
Montesquieu, Baron de, 167, 175
Montezuma, 16
Montgomery, Lucy M., 651
Montgomery bus boycott, 849–850
Moody, Dwight L., 548–549
Moore, Harriet, 653
Moral diplomacy of Woodrow Wilson, 691–692
Morality and manners, 1877–1890, 548–549
Moral Majority, 951
Moral reform societies, 302
Moral revivalism in 1800s, 297–321
Morgan, Daniel, 146
Morgan, Edmund S., 38, 82
Morgan, Frank, 595
Morgan, J. Pierpont, 527, 658, 668–669, 739; as financier, 524, 526, 531, 588, 661, 676, 720

America and the World: The United States and Its Possessions

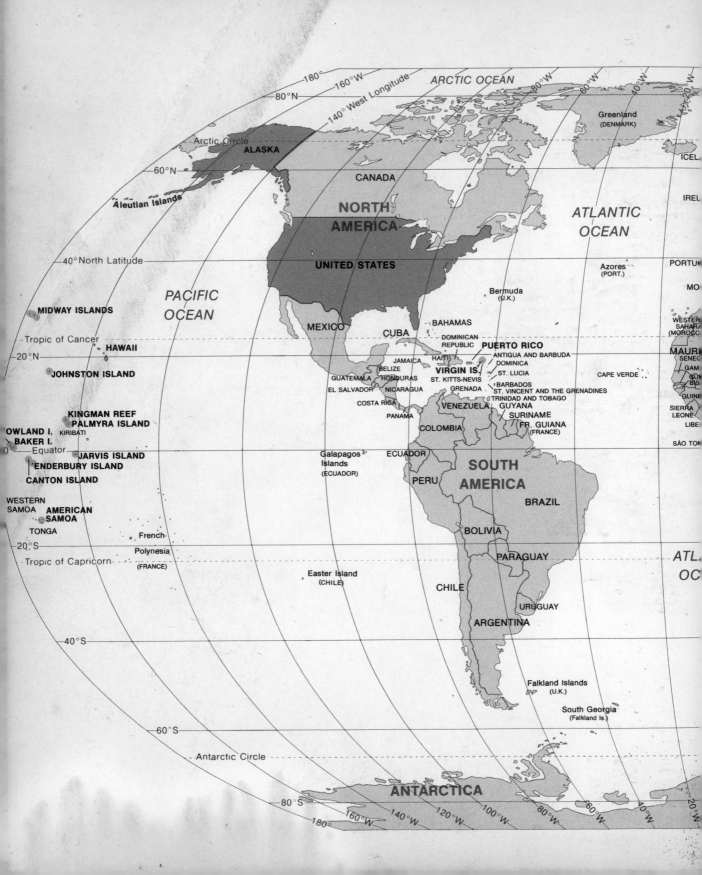

ARCTIC OCEAN

180°
160°W
140° West Longitude
80°N
80°W
60°W
40°W
20°W

Greenland
(DENMARK)

Arctic Circle
ALASKA
60°N
CANADA
ICEL.
Aleutian Islands
NORTH
AMERICA
ATLANTIC
OCEAN
IREL.
40° North Latitude
UNITED STATES
Azores
(PORT.)
PORTU.
PACIFIC
OCEAN
Bermuda
(U.K.)
MO
MIDWAY ISLANDS
MEXICO
BAHAMAS
CUBA
DOMINICAN
REPUBLIC
PUERTO RICO
WESTER
SAHAR
(MOROCC
Tropic of Cancer
HAWAII
JAMAICA
HAITI
ANTIGUA AND BARBUDA
DOMINICA
MAURI
20°N
BELIZE
VIRGIN IS.
ST. LUCIA
CAPE VERDE
SENEC
JOHNSTON ISLAND
GUATEMALA
HONDURAS
ST. KITTS-NEVIS
BARBADOS
GAM
BIS
EL SALVADOR
NICARAGUA
GRENADA
ST. VINCENT AND THE GRENADINES
TRINIDAD AND TOBAGO
GUINE
COSTA RICA
VENEZUELA
GUYANA
KINGMAN REEF
PALMYRA ISLAND
PANAMA
SURINAME
FR. GUIANA
(FRANCE)
SIERRA
LEONE
LIBE
OWLAND I.
KIRIBATI
COLOMBIA
SÃO TOM
BAKER I.
Equator
JARVIS ISLAND
Galapagos
Islands
(ECUADOR)
ECUADOR
SOUTH
AMERICA
ENDERBURY ISLAND
PERU
CANTON ISLAND
BRAZIL
WESTERN
SAMOA
AMERICAN
SAMOA
BOLIVIA
TONGA
French
PARAGUAY
20°S
Polynesia
(FRANCE)
ATL
Tropic of Capricorn
Easter Island
(CHILE)
CHILE
OC
URUGUAY
ARGENTINA
40°S
Falkland Islands
(U.K.)
South Georgia
(Falkland Is.)
60°S
Antarctic Circle
ANTARCTICA
80°S
160°W
140°W
120°W
100°W
80°W
60°W
40°W
20°
180°